D1495396

An *Index to*

WOMEN'S STUDIES ANTHOLOGIES

Research Across the Disciplines, 1980-1984

An Index to
WOMEN'S STUDIES ANTHOLOGIES
Research Across the Disciplines, 1980-1984

Sara Brownmiller

Ruth Dickstein

G.K. HALL & CO.
An Imprint of Macmillan Publishing Company
NEW YORK

Maxwell Macmillan Canada
TORONTO

Maxwell Macmillan International
NEW YORK OXFORD SINGAPORE SYDNEY

The paper used in this publication meets the minimum requirements of American National
Standard for Information Sciences—Permanence of Paper for Printed Library Materials.
ANSI Z39.48–1984. ⊗™
MANUFACTURED IN THE UNITED STATES OF AMERICA

Contents

Introduction

Women's studies scholars and librarians have long been keenly aware that much original writing and research about women is published in anthologies and collections, as well as in scholarly journals. From the beginning of women's studies, anthologies have provided a critical vehicle for the publication of significant and original work in the field. Michelle Zimbalist Rosaldo and Louise Lamphere, editors of *Woman, Culture, and Society*[1], published an anthology of the most significant articles and arguments in feminist theory and anthropology for the 1970s. This groundbreaking book is but one example of many anthologies in the broad preview of women's studies.

Traditionally, articles relating to women appearing in the journal literature have been indexed in mainstream indexes or in specialized women's studies indexes. However, the wealth of research on women published in anthologies is virtually inaccessible in periodical indexes or in library catalogs. Periodical indexes do not index anthologies, while library catalogs are unable to provide the level of cataloging which would allow access to individual articles within collections.

In addition to collections of essays, published proceedings is another area of original works that remain inaccessible to the researcher. This index has been compiled in order to provide a convenient method of locating scholarly writings in these types of publications. The goal is to enhance subject and author access to resources about women.

Indexes to anthologies are extremely rare. Only four indexes of this type were identified. The first, a two volume *Index to Sociology Readers*[2] covering the period from 1960-1965, was compiled in 1973. This was followed by Richard Quay's *Index to Anthologies on Postsecondary Education, 1964-1978*[3] which focused on higher education. Susan Cardinale published *Anthologies By and About Women: An Analytical Index* in 1982,[4] which indexed collections published primarily in the late 1960s and 1970s. Finally, the *Chicano Anthology Index: A Comprehensive Author, Title, and Subject Index to Chicano Anthologies, 1965-1987* was published in 1990[5].

This work is a continuation of the Cardinale publication. It is an index to almost 500 anthologies in all disciplines published between 1980 and 1984. A subsequent volume will index collections published between 1985 and 1989. Cardinale's monumental index provides access to the contents of 375 anthologies published in the late 1960s and the 1970s. The tremendous growth in published works about women's studies in the 1980s dictates that this work appear in two volumes.

A measure of this growth is exemplified by the numbers of titles appearing in the subject volume of Books in Print[6] (SBIP) under the heading "WOMEN" and its subdivisions. The 1970 subject volume contained 5 1/2 pages of books under the headings and subheadings for WOMAN/WOMEN. This grew to 29 pages in the 1980 guide, and by 1989 the number of pages of women's books had reached 58. While the total size of the SBIP has little more than doubled in the last twenty years, the number of books listed under WOMEN (including subdivisions and phrases) grew by more than ten fold.

Identification of Titles

Because of the large number of anthologies relating to women's studies, several strategies were used to identify those edited works which were candidates for indexing. The initial list was compiled from *New Books on Women and Feminism*[7] (NBWF). The authors read through each bibliographic citation, selecting those which listed an editor. In addition, the appropriate volumes of the *Essay and General Literature Index*[8] were reviewed for titles which related to women and women's issues, but this proved to be a meager source for locating women's anthologies not already listed in NBWF.

To insure comprehensiveness, searches were performed in two online catalogs: Janus, the online catalog at the University of Oregon, and Melvyl, the online catalog for the University of California system. A surprisingly large number of titles were identified in this way which had not appeared in either NBWF or *Essay and General Literature Index*. In Janus, a search strategy was constructed which looked for a variety of terms relating to women.[9] The search was limited by date, one year at a time, to make the retrieval more manageable. The Janus search relied solely on words in the titles, since keyword searching of subject headings is not available. The Melvyl search followed a similar technique except that keyword

in subject headings was selected, as well as searching a single year at a time. Because of the inability of online catalogs to allow searching for edited works as a condition of the search, extremely large sets were retrieved. Each of these sets had to be reviewed title by title to identify those which were edited. Titles identified from Janus and Melvyl were then merged to create a single list and remove duplicates.

Criteria for Selection

Works selected for this index focused on women and women's issues. No attempt was made to identify individual articles on women and women's issues which were included in anthologies focusing on specific subject disciplines. Anthologies composed primarily of creative works such as fiction, poetry or photographs; reprints of special journal issues; edited collections of personal memoirs or biographical sketches; and self-help information were not selected for inclusion.

Excluding these exceptions, this work includes edited works of collected essays, proceedings, and primary research across all subject disciplines, whose primary focus is on women or feminist issues. The only exception was collections covering clinical medicine.

Software

The key to producing this work required the identification of software that had the capability of producing a variety of indexes from a single record. Discussions were held with several computer software specialists to try to identify a commercial software which would meet the needs of the index. Although Procite had many valuable features, the version available at the beginning of this project could not provide a system for linking keywords with specific chapters. It was finally determined that a relational database software was required. Paradox allowed the greatest flexibility. However, software modifications had to be made to accommodate the unique features in bibliographic citations. The authors are most appreciative of the programming skills of Graig Roylance who was able to take descriptions of what was needed and turn them into a workable program.

Organization

This index is organized into five parts. The first part, Anthologies and Tables of Contents, contains complete bibliographic information about each analyzed volume, including a listing of each chapter title, author(s) of chapters, and pagination. The anthology titles are listed in alphabetical order by title. Each book is numbered and each chapter is lettered. The subsequent indexes refer back to the appropriate book number and chapter letter for complete bibliographic information. In the Anthologies section, the editors of each work are listed as they appear on the title page. The authors of chapter entries are listed in alphabetical order. A problem with the indexing software did not allow chapter authors to be listed in the order in which they appeared in the original Table of Contents.

The second section, Subject Index, groups the books into 36 broad categories. For researchers trying to identify books covering a broad subject discipline, this grouping will prove helpful. Books covering more than one subject are listed in all appropriate categories. The 36 subject categories combine Cardinale's subjects with the subject groupings used in NBWF, supplemented by a few the authors felt were lacking in these two lists such as Children and Older Women. The subject categories used are listed at the beginning of the Subject Index.

The third part, Editor Index, is an alphabetical list of each editor listed in the Anthology section. Following the editor's name is the title of the edited volume and its entry number in the Anthology section.

This section is followed by the Author Index, an alphabetical listing of chapter authors. Under each author's name is the book entry number and chapter letter, as well as the full title of the authored chapter. This index enables one to easily identify chapters written by a single author that are published in different collections. Forms of author names may vary in the Anthology & Table of Contents section, as they were transcribed as they appeared in each anthology. However, attempts were made to verify correct forms with Library of Congress cataloging to bring all titles written by the same person under one form of entry. Some names could not be verified and thus the different versions of the name were kept in tact as they were listed in the Tables of Contents.

The fifth and largest section is the Keyword Index. For those conducting subject searching it should be used in conjunction with the Subject Index which identifies the broad subject of an entire volume. Thus, a book about crime may include individual chapters about subjects in other categories, with the keyword index providing access to more precise subjects. As a rule, all important words in the chapter titles are indexed.

The singular form was used for all permutations of a particular word (Socialize for Socialized, Socialization, etc.). American English spelling is the preferred keyword

spelling (Labor for Labour, Organization for Organisation).

Cross references are provided for many terms to assist users in locating alternate forms of a term or related terms, (Literature see also Fiction, Short Story, Drama, Science Fiction). In a few cases an attempt to relieve a researcher from looking up many entries under a variety of keywords resulted in one particular form being selected as the preferred term. An appropriate "see" reference from all unused forms is made. For example, Adolescent was preferred over Teen, Teenage, or Adolescence; African American Woman was the preferred term with see references from Negro and Black. Black was used for black women outside of the United States.

For some keywords, a long list of related terms are appropriate. Rather than provide the entire list under each term, 13 Keywords were designated as umbrella terms and show the complete list. The individual terms have a single "see also" reference back to the umbrella term. For example, the Keyword "Family" has 15 see also references, while the Keyword "Parent" has a single "see also" reference to "Family". The list of these umbrella terms is provided at the beginning of the Keyword Index.

Because of the recurrent use of the terms "Woman", "Women" and "Female", none of these words were used as Keywords except when they were a part of a bound concept, such as, Woman's Suffrage or Women's Studies, or descriptive of a group of women, Older Woman or Asian Woman, for example.

In several instances keywords were added to clarify and augment titles. Where cities are named in a title, the country, or state in the case of the United States, was added to the keyword city and a separate entry was made for the country or state. Complete author's names were added to the keyword list when only an author's last name or the title of a book was referred to in the chapter title. Rather than list all of the dates that appear in a chapter title individually, dates were grouped under keywords for the relevant century. When dates covered more than one century, the chapter was indexed under all relevant centuries.

While books that were solely compilations of creative works were not included, on occasion, a volume of essays included some creative pieces, interviews or transcripts of speeches. The authors of these pieces were listed in the author index, and a keyword for the type of material was used in the keyword listing. These creative works were listed under: Poem, Interview, Short Story and Speech respectively.

Women native to a particular country were listed under the name of the country. However, women of one nationality living in another country were indexed by the name of the nationality. For example Turkish women living in Turkey were entered under "Turkey", but Turkish women living in Great Britain were listed under "Turkish Woman".

All chapters were indexed except those with nondescript titles, such as Introduction or Conclusion. If one of these chapters included in its title keywords of note, the chapter was indexed.

Acknowledgements

This project has been a challenge and a learning experience. We were fortunate to have had the support and encouragement of our colleagues and institutions from the University of Oregon and the University of Arizona. The Center for the Study of Women in Society at the University of Oregon was especially important for awarding Sara Brownmiller a Faculty Research Grant for the software development and to cover other project expenses. The sabbatical leave granted to Ruth Dickstein by the University of Arizona was crucial to her completing the project. Atifa Rawan and Maria Hoopes, valued colleagues for both authors at the University of Arizona Library, gave needed advice on the correct form of author names.

It goes without saying that any errors or inconsistencies in indexing are solely the responsibility of the authors, who are still amazed that they completed this project in only one year.

Jed and Tristan Mecham, the sons of Sara Brownmiller, willingly and cheerfully gave up game time on the computer so that Mom could work on "the book". And finally much valuable emotional support was given by Steve Dickstein and Milo Mecham, both of whom lost a wife to the computer.

References

1. Rosaldo, Michelle Zimbalist and Louise Lamphere, eds. 1974. *Woman, Culture, and Society*. Stanford, CA: Stanford University Press.

2. Abramson, Harold J. and Nicholas Sofios, eds. 1973. *Index to Sociology Readers*. Metuchen, NJ: Scarecrow Press.

3. Quay, Richard H., ed. 1980. *Index to Anthologies on Postsecondary Education, 1960-1978*. Westport, CT: Greenwood Press.

4. Cardinale, Susan, comp. 1982. *Anthologies By and About Women: An Analytical Index*. Westport, CT: Greenwood Press.

5. Garcia-Ayvens, Francisco, ed. 1990. *Chicano Anthology Index: A Comprehensive Author, Title, and Subject Index to Chicano Anthologies, 1965-1987.* Berkeley: Chicano Studies Library Publications Unit, University of California at Berkeley.

6. *Books in Print.* New York: Bowker, 1957-.

7. *New Books on Women & Feminism.* Madison, WI: Women's Studies Librarian-at-Large, University of Wisconsin System, 1979-.

8. *Essay and General Literature Index.* New York: H. W. Wilson, 1933-.

9. In Janus the keyword option was searched with the words "women* or woman* or femin* or gender* or lesbian*". The resulting list was then limited by year. In Melvyl the search used the subject heading option with the following strategy: sw women* or sw woman* or sw feminis* or sw lesbian or sw lesbianism or sw sex* and date.

ANTHOLOGIES
AND
TABLES OF CONTENTS

1. 10 Women of Mystery. Bargainnier, Earl F., ed. Bowling Green, OH: Bowling Green University Press, 1981. a) Dorothy Sayers. Klein, Kathleen Gregory, p.8-39; b) Josephine Tey. Talburt, Nancy Ellen, p.40-76; c) Ngaio Marsh. Bargainnier, Earl F., p.78-105; d) P. D. James. Joyner, Nancy C., p.109-123; e) Ruth Rendell. Bakerman, Jane S., p.127-149; f) Anna Katharine Green. Hayne, Barrie, p.153-178; g) Mary Roberts Rinehart. Cohn, Jan, p.183-220; h) Margaret Millar. Reilly, John M., p.224-246; i) Emma Lathen. Bedell, Jeanne F., p.249-267; j) Amanda Cross. Carter, Steven F., p.270-296.

2. Abortion: Moral and Legal Perspectives. Garfield, Jay L. and Hennessey, Patricia, eds. Amherst, MA: The University of Massachusetts Press, 1984. a) *Roe v Wade*: Majority opinion and Rehnquist dissent. p.11-34; b) The legacy of *Roe v Wade*. Benshoof, Janet, p.35-44; c) *Roe v Wade*: A study in male ideology. MacKinnon, Catharine, p.45-54; d) The juridical status of the fetus: A proposal for legal protection of the unborn. King, Patricia A., p.57-80; e) Personhood and the abortion debate. Macklin, Ruth, p.81-102; f) Understanding Blackmun's argument: The reasoning of *Roe v Wade*. Wertheimer, Roger, p.105-122; g) A human life statute. Galebach, Stephen H., p.123-147; h) Constitutional privacy, religious disestablishment, and the abortion decisions. Richards, David A.J., p.148-174; i) Killing and letting die. Foot, Philippa, p.177-185; j) Abortion and self-defense. Davis, Nancy, p.186-210; k) Abortion and the claims of samaritanism. Michaels, Meredith W., p.213-226; l) Abortion, slavery, and the law: A study in moral character. Thomas, Laurence, p.227-237; m) Abortion, privacy, and personhood: From *Roe v Wade* to the human life statute. Wikler, Daniel, p.238-259.

3. Abortion: Understanding Differences. Callahan, Daniel and Callahan, Sidney, eds. New York: Plenum Press, 1984. a) Social science and ethical issues: The policy implications of poll data on abortion. Lamanna, Mary Ann, p.1-23; b) Abortion and the meaning of life. Luker, Kristin, p.25-45; c) Reflections on abortion, values, and the family. Elshtain, Jean Bethke, p.47-72; d) Commentary to chapter 3 (chapter c). Harding, Sandra, p.73-80; e) A family perspective on abortion. Ooms, Theodora, p.81-107; f) Commentary to chapter 4 (chapter e). Mahowald, Mary B., p.109-115; g) Children, personhood, and a pluralistic society. Abernethy, Virginia, p.117-135; h) Commentary to chapter 5 (chapter g). Elshtain, Jean Bethke, p.137-143; i) More trouble than they're worth? Children and abortion. Meehan, Mary, p.145-170; j) Commentary to chapter 6 (chapter i). Ooms, Theodora, p.171-175; k) Abortion and equality. Mahowald, Mary B., p.177-196; l) Commentary to chapter 7 (chapter k). Segers, Mary C., p.197-201; m) Beneath the surface of the abortion dispute: Are women fully human? Harding, Sandra, p.203-224; n) Commentary to chapter 8 (chapter m). Cahill, Lisa Sowle, p.225-228; o) Abortion and the culture: Toward a feminist perspective. Segers, Mary C., p.229-252; p) Commentary to chapter 9 (chapter o).

Meehan, Mary, p.253-259; q) Abortion, autonomy, and community. Cahill, Lisa Sowle, p.261-276; r) Commentary to chapter 10 (chapater q). Abernethy, Virginia, p.277-283; s) Value choices in abortion. Callahan, Sidney, p.285-301; t) Commentary to chapter 11 (chapter s). Callahan, Daniel, p.303-307; u) The abortion debate: Is progress possible? Callahan, Daniel, p.309-324; v) Commentary to chapter 12 (chapter u). Callahan, Sidney, p.325-330.

4. Adolescent Pregnancy: Perspectives for the Health Professional. Smith, Peggy B. and Mumford, David M., eds. Boston, MA: G. K. Hall, 1980. a) Adolescent psychosexual development. Lipsitz, Joan Scheff, p.1-13; b) Administrative concerns. Ingersoll, Ralph W., p.14-22; c) Psychiatric aspects of adolescent pregnancy. Youngs, David D., p.23-31; d) Adolescent sexuality, pregnancy, and childbearing. Safro, Ivor L., p.32-47; e) Social implications of teenage childbearing. Crawford, Albert G. and Furstenberg Jr., Frank F., p.48-76; f) Programs for sexually active teens. Smith, Peggy B., p.77-97; g) Venereal disease and the adolescent. McCormick, Nancy and Mumford, David M., p.98-141; h) Issues surrounding adolescent pregnancy terminations. Kaufman, Raymond H. and Poindexter, Alfred N., p.142-154; i) Parenting education. Smith, Peggy B., p.155-172; j) Legal aspects of adolescent pregnancy. Bunch, Peggy L. and Dowben, Carla W., p.173-197; k) Ethical issues of adolescent pregnancy. Kolenda, Konstantin, p.198-214; l) Sex education. Smith, Peggy B., p.215-239; m) Sexual counseling for adolescents. Schiller, Patricia, p.240-249.

5. African Women in the Development Process. Nelson, Nici, ed. London: Frank Cass, 1981. a) Conceptualizing the labor force: The underestimation of women's economic activities. Benería, Lourdes, p.10-28; b) Women and agriculture in sub-Saharan Africa: Implications for development. Bryson, Judy C., p.29-46; c) Mobilizing village women: Some organizational and management considerations. Nelson, Nici, p.47-58; d) An analysis of the impact of labour migration on the lives of women in Lesotho. Gordon, Elizabeth, p.59-76; e) Perspectives in development: The problem of nurses and nursing in Zambia. Schuster, Ilsa, p.77-97; f) Development policies in Tanzania - some implications for women. Caplan, Pat, p.98-108; g) Gambian women: Unequal partners in rice development projects? Dey, Jennie, p.109-122; h) Developing women's cooperatives: An experiment in rural Nigeria. Ladipo, Patricia, p.123-136.

6. African Women South of the Sahara. Hay, Margaret Jean and Stichter, Sharon, eds. London: Longman, 1984. a) Women in the rural economy: Past, present and future. Henn, Jeanne K., p.1-18; b) Women in the rural economy: Contemporary variations. Guyer, Jane I., p.19-32; c) Women in the urban economy. Robertson, Claire C., p.33-50; d) Women in the changing African family. White, Luise, p.53-68; e) Women's voluntary associations. Wipper, Audrey, p.69-86; f) Women in religion and in secular ideology. Strobel, Margaret, p.87-101; g) Women in

African literature. LaPin, Deirdre, p.102-118; h) Women in the arts. Aronson, Lisa, p.119-138; i) African women in politics. O'Barr, Jean, p.140-155; j) Women in contemporary national liberation movements. Urdang, Stephanie, p.156-169; k) The impact of development policies on women. Lewis, Barbara, p.170-187; l) Appendix: Some selected statistics on African women. Stichter, Sharon, p.188-194.

7. Against Sadomasochism: A Radical Feminist Analysis. Linden, Robin Ruth, et al., eds. East Palo Alto, CA: Frog in the Well, 1982.
a) Introduction: Against sadomasochism. Linden, Robin Ruth, p.1-15; b) Letter from a former masochist. Jonel, Marissa, p.16-22; c) Pornography and the sexual revolution: The backlash of sadomasochism. Wagner, Sally Roesch, p.23-44; d) Sadomasochism and the social construction of desire. Rian, Karen, p.45-50; e) On the history of cultural sadism. Barry, Kathleen, p.51-65; f) Interview with Audre Lorde. Lorde, Audre and Star, Susan Leigh, p.66-71; g) Feminism and sadomasochism: Self-critical notes. Bar On, Bat-Ami, p.72-82; h) Sadomasochism and the liberal tradition. Hein, Hilde, p.83-89; i) Why I'm against S/M liberation. Atkinson, Ti-Grace, p.90-92; j) Sadomasochism: A personal experience. Harris, Elizabeth, p.93-95; k) A response to Samois. Meredith, Jesse, p.96-98; l) Racism and sadomasochism: A conversation with two black lesbians. Mason, Rose, Pagano, Darlene and Sims, Karen, p.99-105; m) An opinionated piece on sadomasochism. Norris, Maryel, p.106-108; n) The politics of sado-masochistic fantasies. Morgan, Robin, p.109-123; o) Sadomasochism: Eroticized violence, eroticized powerlessness. Stoltenberg, John, p.124-130; p) Swastikas: The street and the university. Star, Susan Leigh, p.131-136; q) Is sadomasochism feminist? A critique of the Samois position. Nichols, Jeanette, Pagano, Darlene and Rossoff, Margaret, p.137-146; r) The saga of Sadie O. Massey. Walker-Crawford, Vivienne, p.147-152; s) Sadism, masochism, and lesbian-feminism. Hoagland, Sarah Lucia, p.153-163; t) Smokers protest healthism. Tiklicorect, Paula, p.164-165; u) New expanded-type version lesbian handkerchief code. Mathis, Melissa Bay, p.166-167; v) Lesbian S & M: The politics of dis-illusion. Butler, Judy, p.168-175; w) Sadomasochism: A contra-feminist activity. Russell, Diana E. H., p.176-183; x) Sadomasochism and the erosion of self: A critical reading of *Story of O*. Griffin, Susan, p.184-204; y) Hunger and thirst in the house of distorted mirrors. Lesh, Cheri, p.202-204; z) A letter of the times, or should this sado-masochism be saved? Walker, Alice, p.205-208.

8. Aggression, Adaptations, and Psychotherapy. Notman, Malkah T. and Nadelson, Carol C., eds. New York: Plenum Press, 1982.
a) Social change and psychotherapeutic implications. Nadelson, Carol C. and Notman, Malkah T., p.3-16; b) Aggression in women: Conceptual issues and clinical implications. Miller, Jean Baker, et al., p.17-28; c) Women and violence. Benedek, E.P. and Farley, G.A., p.29-46; d) Wife abuse: Culture as destiny. Carmen, Elaine (Hilberman), p.47-64; e) Incest. Tisza, Veronica, p.65-82; f) The adolescent girl in a group home. Mathe, Mirjam and Rudes, Nancy, p.83-94; g) Juvenile delinquency in girls. Fisher, Susan M. and Hurwitz, Irving, p.95-114; h) Childhood and adolescent suicidal behavior, with an emphasis on girls. Pfeffer, Cynthia R., p.115-130; i) The organic-functional controversy. Nadelson, Theodore, p.133-146; j) The painful woman: Complaints, symptoms, and illness. Lipsitt, Don R., p.147-171; k) Emotional reactions to miscarriage. Cohen, Karen A. and Friedman, Rochelle, p.173-187; l) Depression in women: Epidemiology, explanations, and impact on the family. Klerman, Gerald L. and Weissman, Myrna M., p.189-200; m) The myofascial pain dysfunction syndrome: An unheeded neuromuscular disorder. Heiberg, Astrid Nøklebye and Helöe, Berit, p.201-216; n) Women and alcohol abuse. McCrady, Barbara S., p.217-244; o) The therapeutic alliance in psychoanalytic treatment. Silber, Earle, p.247-262; p) Research on gender and psychotherapy. Genack, Abraham, Hauser, Stuart T. and Kirshner, Lewis A., p.263-272; q) Special issues for women in psychotherapy. Lerner, Harriet E., p.273-286; r) Conflict and psychological development: Women in the family. Miller, Jean Baker, p.287-299.

9. Alcohol and Drug Problems in Women. Kalant, Oriana Josseau, ed. New York: Plenum Press, 1980.
a) Sex differences in alcohol and drug problems - some highlights. Kalant, Oriana Josseau, p.1-24; b) Temperance and women in 19th-century United States. Levine, Harry Gene, p.25-67; c) Sex differences in the prevalence of problem drinking. Ferrence, Roberta G., p.69-124; d) Sex differences in psychoactive drug use: Recent epidemiology. Ferrence, Roberta G. and Whitehead, Paul C., p.125-201; e) Longitudinal studies of alcohol and drug problems: Sex differences. Robins, Lee N. and Smith, Elizabeth M., p.203-232; f) Sex differences in the inheritance of alcoholism. Swinson, Richard P., p.233-262; g) Some behavioral and biological aspects of alcohol problems in women. Mello, Nancy K., p.263-298; h) Nature and development of alcoholism in women. Boothroyd, Wilfred E., p.299-329; i) Sex differences in morbidity of alcoholics. Wilkinson, Patricia, p.331-364; j) Sex differences in mortality: A comparison of male and female alcoholics. Popham, Robert E. and Schmidt, Wolfgang, p.365-384; k) Alcoholism in women: Treatment modalities and outcomes. Annis, Helen M. and Liban, Carolyn B., p.385-422; l) Dependence on psychotropic drugs and analgesics in men and women. Bell, David S., p.423-463; m) Opiate dependence in women. Martin, Catherine A. and Martin, William R., p.465-485; n) Problems related to the use of tobacco by women. Gritz, Ellen R., p.487-543; o) Sex differences in the effects of alcohol and other psychoactive drugs on endocrine function: Clinical and experimental evidence. Cicero, Theodore J., p.545-593; p) The effects of alcohol on the fetus and offspring. Rosett, Henry L., p.595-652; q) The effects of opiates, sedative-hypnotics, amphetamines, cannabis, and other psychoactive drugs on the fetus and newborn. Fehr, Kevin O'Brien and Finnegan, Loretta P., p.653-723.

10. Alcohol Problems in Women: Antecedents, Consequences, and Intervention. Wilsnack, Sharon C. and Beckman, Linda J., eds. New York: Guilford Press,1984.
a) "When angels fall": Women's drinking as cultural preoccupation and as reality. Fillmore, Kaye Middleton, p.7-36; b) Drinking and drinking problems among female adolescents: Patterns and influences. Thompson, Kevin M. and Wilsnack, Richard W., p.37-65; c) Alcohol use and abuse in ethnic minority women. Leland, Joy, p.66-96; d) Multiple substance abuse among women with alcohol-related problems. Celentano, David D. and McQueen, David V., p.97-116; e) Vulnerability to the biomedical consequences of alcoholism and alcohol-related problems among women. Hill, Shirley Y., p.121-154; f) Alcohol use and reproduction. Ervin, Cynthia H. and Little, Ruth E., p.155-188; g) Drinking, sexuality, and sexual dysfunction in women. Wilsnack, Sharon C., p.189-227; h) Antecedents of alcohol problems in women. Gomberg, Edith S. Lisansky and Lisansky, Judith M., p.233-259; i) Alcohol use and marital violence: Female and male differences in reactions to alcohol. Frieze, Irene Hanson and Schafer, Patricia Cooney, p.260-279; j) Female alcohol abuse: Its effects on the family. Klerman, Lorraine V. and Willams, Carol N., p.280-312; k) Patterns of women's use of alcohol treatment agencies. Amaro, Hortensia and Beckman, Linda J., p.319-348; l) Therapeutic issues in the treatment of alcoholic women. Braiker, Harriet B., p.349-368; m) Treatment outcome of alcoholic women: The state of the art in relation to sex bias and expectancy effects. Vannicelli, Marsha, p.369-412; n) Prevention of alcohol problems in women. Ferrence, Roberta G., p.413-442.

11. Alcoholism in Women. Eddy, Cristen C. and Ford, John L., eds. Dubuque, IA: Kendall/Hunt Publishing Co., 1980.
a) Sex-role adjustment in women alcoholics. Parker, Frederick B., p.6-15; b) Femininity by the bottle. Wilsnack, Sharon C., p.16-24; c) Women and men problem drinkers: Sex differences in patients served by Iowa's community alcoholism centers. Mulford, Harold A., p.25-39; d) The effects of alcohol on anxiety in problem and nonproblem drinking women. Eddy, Cristen C., p.40-54; e) Prevention of alcohol problems in women: Current status. Wilsnack, Sharon C., p.58-73; f) Women employees and job-based alcoholism programs. Beyer, Janice M. and Trice, Harrison M., p.74-92; g) Women on skid row. Bahr, Howard M. and Garrett, Gerald A., p.93-108; h) Fetal alcohol syndrome and drinking during pregnancy. Eddy, Cristen C. and Olson, Christine M., p.109-116; i) Diagnosis, casefinding, and treatment of alcohol problems in women. Blume, Sheila B., p.122-141; j) Alcoholism and the lesbian community. Weathers, Brenda, p.142-149; k) Marital therapy of women alcoholics. Dinaburg, Daniel, Feigenbaum, Elliot and Glick, Ira D., p.150-160; l) Women helping women: Opening the door to treatment. Sandmaier, Marian, p.161-170; m) Women and alcohol. Kirkpatrick, Jean, p.171-181.

12. Alice Through the Microscope: The Power of Science Over Women's Lives. Birke, Lynda, et al., eds. London: Virago, 1980.
a) Science education: Did she drop out or was she pushed? Curran, Libby, p.22-41; b) Psychological sex differences. Sayers, Janet, p.42-61; c) Sociobiology: So what? Janson-Smith, Deirdre, p.62-86; d) The tyrannical womb: Menstruation and menopause. Best, Sandy and Birke, Lynda, p.89-107; e) From zero to infinity: Scientific views of lesbians. Birke, Lynda, p.108-123; f) 'Sickness is a woman's business?': Reflections on the attribution of illness. Standing, Hilary, p.124-138; g) The obsessive orgasm: Science, sex and female sexuality. Faulkner, Wendy, p.139-162; h) Technology in the lying-in room. Brighton Women and Science Group, p.165-181; i) Contraception: The growth of a technology. Walsh, Vivien, p.182-207; j) Reproductive engineering: The final solution? Allen, Pat and Hanmer, Jalna, p.208-227; k) The masculine face of science. Wallsgrove, Ruth, p.228-240.

13. All Her Labours. Women and Labour Publications Collective, ed. Sydney, Australia: Hale & Iremonger, 1984.
a) Deconstructing the masculine universe: The case of women's work. Matthews, Jill Julius, p.11-23; b) Capitalism, gender and the labour process: Two case studies. Pringle, Rosemary, p.24-40; c) Photo essay: Women and work. Haselgrove, Margaret, p.41-57; d) Besides our size it's because we are women: The strike by the laundry workers union 15 January - 5 February 1982. Greenwood, Janet, p.58-69; e) Bearers of burdens: Occupational safety without discrimination. Refshauge, Chloe, p.70-83; f) Queensland public service women. Thomas, Kath, p.85-92; g) Tribute to Joan Curlewis. Lowenstein, Wendy, p.93-95; h) Women working in heavy industry in World War II. Curlewis, Joan, p.97-108; i) Women and unions in Australia. White, Kate, p.109-120; j) Some problems and developments in Marxist feminist theory. Johnson, Carol, p.121-132; k) Conditions of entry: Women and politics in Australia. Sawer, Marian, p.133-147; l) Feminism: An early tradition amongst western Australian labor women. Joyce, Robin R., p.148-169.

14. All the Women Are White, All the Blacks are Men, but Some of Us Are Brave: Black Women's Studies. Hull, Gloria T., Scott, Patricia Bell and Smith, Barbara, eds. Old Westbury, NY: The Feminist Press, 1982.
a) Introduction: The politics of black women's studies. Hull, Gloria T. and Smith, Barbara, p.xvii-xxxii; b) A black feminist's search for sisterhood. Wallace, Michele, p.5-12; c) A black feminist statement. Combahee River Collective, p.13-22; d) Selected bibliography on black feminism. Scott, Patricia Bell, p.23-33; e) One child of one's own: A meaningful digression within the work(s) - an excerpt. Walker, Alice, p.37-44; f) Racism - a white issue. Pence, Ellen, p.45-47; g) Racism and women's studies. Smith, Barbara, p.48-51; h) Face-to-face, day-to-day - racism CR. Cross, Tia, et al., p.52-56; i) Studying slavery: Some literary and pedagogical considerations on the black female slave. Stetson, Erlene, p.61-84; j) Debunking Sapphire: Toward a non-racist and non-sexist social sci-

ence. Scott, Patricia Bell, p.85-92; k) Two representative issues in contemporary sociological work on black women. Higginbotham, Elizabeth, p.93-98; l) Black women's health: Notes for a course. Smith, Beverly, p.103-114; m) Three's a crowd: The dilemma of the black woman in higher education. Carroll, Constance M., p.115-128; n) Slave codes and liner notes. Russell, Michelle, p.129-140; o) Black women and the church. Grant, Jacquelyn, p.141-152; p) Toward a black feminist criticism. Smith, Barbara, p.157-175; q) "This infinity of conscious pain": Zora Neale Hurston and the black female literary tradition. Bethel, Lorraine, p.176-188; r) Researching Alice Dunbar-Nelson: A personal and literary perspective. Hull, Gloria T., p.189-195; s) Black-eyed blues connections: Teaching black women. Russell, Michelle, p.196-207; t) Teaching *Black-eyed Susans*: An approach to the study of black women writers. Washington, Mary Helen, p.208-217; u) Afro-American women 1800-1910: A selected bibliography. Yellin, Jean Fagan, p.221-244; v) Afro-American women poets of the nineteenth century: A guide to research and bio-bibliographies of the poets. Sherman, Joan R., p.245-260; w) On the novels written by selected black women: A bibliographical essay. Dandridge, Rita B., p.261-279; x) Black women playwrights from Grimké to Shange: Selected synopses of their works. Miller, Jeanne-Marie A., p.280-296; y) American black women composers: A selected annotated bibliography. Williams, Ora, et al., p.297-306; z) A listing of non-print materials on black women. Brown, Martha H., p.307-326.

15. Alternative Materials in Libraries. Danky, James P. and Shore, Elliott, eds. Metuchen, NJ: Scarecrow Press, 1982. a) Libraries and alternatives. Schuman, Patricia Glass, p.1-5; b) The alternative press and the mass media: Two case studies. Kettering, Terri A., p.6-11; c) The acquisition of alternative materials. Danky, James P., p.12-30; d) Access to alternatives: New approaches in cataloging. Berman, Sanford, p.31-66; e) Reference service for alternative publications. Shore, Elliott and Tsang, Daniel, p.67-83; f) Alternative roads to alternative media. Roberts, Don, p.84-94; g) Publishers on libraries: Walking through walls. Kruchkow, Diane, p.95-100; h) Publishers on libraries: Stake your claim. Peattie, Noel, p.100-104; i) Publishers on libraries: Small presses and the library. Hogan, Judy, p.104-107; j) Publishers on libraries: The library as motherlode: A feminist view. West, Celeste, p.107-110; k) Alternative and small publishers view libraries: An empirical study. Tsang, Daniel, p.111-121; l) Collections of contemporary alternative materials in libraries: A directory. Case, Patricia J., p.122-149.

16. Alternative Social Services for Women. Gottlieb, Naomi, ed. New York: Columbia University Press, 1980. a) Women and mental health: The problem of depression. Gottlieb, Naomi, p.3-22; b) Cognitive-behavioral strategies for the treatment of depression in women. Richey, Cheryl A., p.22-42; c) Issues in feminist therapy: The work of a woman's study group. Hauser, Barbara B., Masnick, Barbara R. and Radov, Carol G., p.42-49; d) Therapeutic aspects of consciousness-raising groups.

Brodsky, Annette M., p.49-60; e) Women and health care. Gottlieb, Naomi, p.61-81; f) The feminist Women's Health Center. p.81-97; g) The Gynecorps Project. p.97-102; h) A pelvic teaching program. Women's Community Health Center, p.101-110; i) Women and chemical dependency. Gottlieb, Naomi, p.111-131; j) The first two years: A profile of women entering Women, Inc. Martin-Shelton, Darla, Schwingl, Pamela J. and Sperazi, Laura, p.131-158; k) Alcoholism and the lesbian community. Weathers, Brenda, p.158-169; l) CASPAR: A women's alcoholism program. p.169-176; m) Battered women. Baxter, Vee and Hutchins, Trova, p.179-211; n) Counselor's roles. Resnik, Mindy, p.212-234; o) Rape victims. Stevens, Doris A., p.235-251; p) Women as single parents: Alternative services for a neglected population. Burden, Dianne, p.255-279; q) The older woman. Gottlieb, Naomi, p.280-309; r) Women in midstream. Campbell, Julie, Levine, Irma and Page, Jane, p.310-319; s) The displaced homemaker. Bracht, Dona Lansing, p.320-331; t) The ethnic minority woman. p.332; u) Alternative social services and the black woman. Solomon, Barbara, p.333-340; v) Social services and the Hispanic woman. Cepeda, Rita, p.340-345.

17. American Novelists Revisited: Essays in Feminist Criticism. Fleischmann, Fritz, ed. Boston, MA: G.K. Hall, 1982. a) Charles Brockden Brown: Feminism in fiction. Fleischmann, Fritz, p.6-41; b) Fenimore Cooper's heroines. Belfiglio, Genevieve and House, Kay, p.42-57; c) Thwarted nature: Nathaniel Hawthorne as feminist. Baym, Nina, p.58-77; d) Four novels of Harriet Beecher Stowe: A study in nineteenth-century androgyny. Crumpacker, Laurie, p.78-106; e) On Herman Melville. Patterson-Black, Gene, p.107-142; f) Mark Twain's capers: A chameleon in King Carnival's court. Ballorain, Rolande, p.143-170; g) W.D. Howells: The ever-womanly. Crowley, John W., p.171-188; h) *The Bostonians*: Feminists and the new world. Auerbach, Nina, p.189-208; i) Cool Diana and the Blood-red muse: Edith Wharton on innocence and art. Ammons, Elizabeth, p.209-224; j) Stephen Crane and the fallen women. Green, Carol Hurd, p.225-242; k) Brother Theodore, hell on women. Wolstenholme, Susan, p.243-264; l) Mothers, daughters, and the "art necessity": Willa Cather and the creative process. O'Brien, Sharon, p.265-298; m) The question of Gertrude Stein. Secor, Cynthia, p.299-310; n) Fitzgerald's women: Beyond winter dreams. McCay, Mary A., p.311-324; o) William Faulkner: A feminist consideratión. Wittenberg, Judith Bryant, p.325-338; p) Hemingway and Fauntleroy: An androgynous pursuit. Spilka, Mark, p.339-370; q) Zora Neale Hurston: Changing her own words. Wall, Cheryl A., p.371-393; r) Papa Dick and Sister-Woman: Reflections on women in the fiction of Richard Wright. Williams, Sherley Anne, p.394-415.

18. And the Poor Get Children: Radical Perspectives on Population Dynamics. Michaelson, Karen L., ed. New York: Monthly Review Press, 1981. a) Introduction: Population theory and the political econ-

omy of population processes. Michaelson, Karen L., p.11-35; b) The ideology of population control. Mamdani, Mahmood, p.39-49; c) "Reproductive choice" in the contemporary United States: A social analysis of female sterilization. Petchesky, Rosalind Pollack, p.50-88; d) Rural family size and economic change: A Middle Eastern case. Aswad, Barbara C., p.89-105; e) Population policy, family size, and the reproduction of the labor force in India: The case of Bombay. Michaelson, Karen L., p.106-127; f) Cross-national labor migrants: Actors in the international division of labor. Petras, Elizabeth McLean, p.131-153; g) Population dynamics and migrant labor in South Africa. Edmunds, Marianna, p.154-179; h) The effects of plantation economy on a Polynesian population. Larson, Eric H., p.180-193; i) Neo-Malthusian ideology and colonial capitalism: Population dynamics in southwestern Puerto Rico. Wessman, James W., p.194-220; j) Country roads take me home: The political economy of wage-labor migration in an eastern Kentucky community. Tudiver, Sari, p.221-245.

19. Anne Hutchinson: Troubler of the Puritan Zion. Bremer, Francis J., ed. Huntington, NY: Robert E. Krieger, 1981.
a) Thine eyes shall see thy teachers. Battis, Emery, p.11-15; b) Mrs. Hutchinson's behavior in terms of menopausal symptoms. Battis, Emery, p.16-17; c) The Antinomian controversy. Hall, David, p.21-27; d) The theological dimension. Stoever, William K.B., p.28-37; e) The image of Adam and the image of Christ. Rosenmeier, Jesper, p.38-47; f) The case against Anne Hutchinson. Morgan, Edmund S., p.51-57; g) Jezebel before the judges. Morris, Richard B., p.58-64; h) The political trial. Schwartz, Jack and Withington, Anne F., p.65-72; i) Wayward Puritans. Erikson, Kai T., p.75-84; j) The Antinomian language controversy. Caldwell, Patricia, p.85-95; k) Anne Hutchinson and the Puritan attitude toward women. Barker-Benfield, Ben, p.99-111; l) The case of the American Jezebels. Koehler, Lyle, p.112-123; m) Footsteps of Anne Hutchinson. Colacurcio, Michael, p.124-139; n) Saints and sisters. Dunn, Mary Maples, p.140-149.

20. The Art of Margaret Atwood: Essays in Criticism. Davidson, Arnold E. and Davidson, Cathy N., eds. Toronto, Canada: Anansi Press, 1981.
a) The where of here: Margaret Atwood and a Canadian tradition. Djwa, Sandra, p.15-34; b) Atwood's haunted sequences: *The Circle Game, The Journals of Susanna Moodie*, and *Power Politics*. McCombs, Judith, p.35-54; c) Margaret Atwood and the poetics of duplicity. Grace, Sherrill E., p.55-68; d) Meridians of perception: A reading of *The Journals of Susanna Moodie*. Weir, Lorraine, p.69-79; e) The making of *Selected Poems*, the process of surfacing. Wagner, Linda W., p.81-94; f) One woman leads to another. Irvine, Lorna, p.95-106; g) Minuets and madness: Margaret Atwood's *Dancing Girls*. Thompson, Lee Briscoe, p.107-122; h) The dark voyage: *The Edible Woman* as romance. McLay, Catherine, p.123-138; i) *Surfacing* and the rebirth journey. Pratt, Annis, p.139-157; j) *Lady Oracle*: The narrative of a fool-heroine. Thomas,

Clara, p.159-175; k) Janus through the looking glass: Atwood's first three novels. Lecker, Robert, p.177-203; l) Prospects and retrospects in *Life Before Man*. Davidson, Arnold E. and Davidson, Cathy N., p.205-221; m) Bashful but bold: Notes on Margaret Atwood as critic. Woodcock, George, p.223-241; n) A checklist of writings by and about Margaret Atwood. Horne, Alan J., p.243-285.

21. Asian Women in Transition. Chipp, Sylvia A. and Green, Justin J., eds. University Park, PA: Pennsylvania State University Press, 1980.
a) Women in Asian cities, their political and economic roles: Research problems and strategies. Kallgren, Joyce K., p.16-35; b) The Japanese woman: Evolving views of life and role. Pharr, Susan J., p.36-61; c) Women in the People's Republic of China. Johnson, Kay Ann, p.62-103; d) Female elite goals and national development: Some data from the Philippines. Green, Justin J., p.108-122; e) Some changing socioeconomic roles of village women in Malaysia. Strange, Heather, p.123-151; f) Women in Indonesian politics: The myth of functional interest. Douglas, Stephen A., p.152-181; g) Expanding women's horizons in Indonesia: Toward maximum equality with minimum conflict. Willner, Ann Ruth, p.182-190; h) Political change: Muslim women in conflict with Parda: Their role in the Indian Nationalist Movement. Minault, Gail, p.194-203; i) The modern Pakistani woman in a Muslim society. Chipp, Sylvia A., p.204-226; j) Women in politics: A case study of Bangladesh. Jahan, Rounaq, p.227-250; k) Indira Gandhi as head of government. Koshal, Manjulika, p.251-262.

22. Aspects of Female Existence: Proceedings from the St. Gertrud Symposium "Women in the Middle Ages". Carlé, Birte, et al., eds. Copenhagen: Gyldendal, 1980.
a) "Glory is like a circle in the water"...Thoughts and suggestions towards a definition of feminine historical research. Rudhart, Blanca-Maria, p.15-27; b) Wills, deeds, and charters as sources for the history of medieval women. Jexlev, Thelma, p.28-40; c) Iconography as a means of research on the history of the status of women. Morris, Joan, p.41-49; d) Le rôle et la place de la femme provenant de la classe sociale inférieure dans la vie quotidienne du Moyen-Age. Dembinska, Maria, p.50-57; e) Women in Latin Medieval literature in Denmark e.g. annals and chronicles. Damsholt, Nanna, p.58-68; f) Une contribution au débat concernant le status de la femme dans les villes du Danemark au Moyen-Age. Nielsen, Eva Trein, p.69-78; g) Structural patterns in the legends of the holy women of Christianity. Carlé, Birte, p.79-86; h) La lyrique portugaise primitive de "Cantigas de Amigo". Lemaire, Ria, p.87-114; i) Un écrit militant de Christine de Pizan: *Le Ditié de Jehanne d'Arc*. Dulac, Liliane, p.115-134; j) New trends in the Danish women's movement, 1970-1978. Gerlach-Nielsen, Merete, p.135-142.

23. Australian Women and the Political System. Simms, Marian, ed. Melbourne, Australia: Longman Cheshire, 1984.
a) Political science, women and feminism. Simms,

Marian, p.1-19; b) Black sisterhood: The situation of urban aboriginal women and their relationship to the white women's movement. Burgmann, Meredith, p.20-47; c) Losing the numbers game: Women, tokenism and power. Clarke, Jocelyn, p.48-58; d) Women, feminism and the political process. Walmsley, Robyn, p.59-65; e) Labor women: Political housekeepers or politicians? Joyce, Robin, p.66-76; f) The Parliamentary wife: Participant in the 'two-person single career'. Whip, Rosemary, p.77-88; g) 'Women candidates speak'. Sawer, Marian, p.89-93; h) Women and women's issues in the 1980 federal elections. Sawer, Marian, p.94-108; i) 'A woman's place is in the House and in the Senate': Women and the 1983 elections. Simms, Marian, p.109-120; j) The politics of the National Women's Advisory Council. Connors, Lyndsay, p.121-131; k) The employment of women in the commonwealth public service: The creation and reproduction of a dual labour market. Deacon, Desley, p.132-150; l) Psychoanalysis and feminist social theory of gender. Thornton, Merle, p.151-175; m) 'Law reform and human reproduction': Implications for women. Albury, Rebecca, p.176-190; n) *A Theory of Justice* and love: Rawls on the family. Kearns, Deborah, p.191-203.

24. The Bases of Human Sexual Attraction. Cook, Mark, ed. London: Academic Press, 1981.
a) Physical attractiveness, sex roles and heterosexual attraction. Dion, Karen, p.3-22; b) Social background, attitudes and sexual attraction. Byrne, Donn and Fisher, William, p.23-63; c) The influence of special sexual desires. Gosselin, Chris, p.65-89; d) Perceptual and cognitive mechanisms in human sexual attraction. Reardon, Richard and Tesser, Abraham, p.93-144; e) Social skill and human sexual attraction. Cook, Mark, p.145-177; f) Process, filter and stage theories of attraction. Murstein, Bernard, p.179-211; g) Human sexuality in cross-cultural perspective. Anderson, Roxanne and Rosenblatt, Paul, p.215-250; h) The dramaturgy of sexual relations. Harré, Rom, p.251-274; i) Sexual attraction in animals. Manning, Aubrey, p.275-291.

26. Battered Women and Their Families: Intervention Strategies and Treatment Programs. Roberts, Albert R., ed. New York: Springer Publishing, 1984.
a) Emergency room intervention: Detection, assessment, and treatment. Boyd, Vicki D. and Klingbeil, Karil S., p.7-32; b) Conjoint therapy for the treatment of domestic violence. Geller, Janet A. and Wasserstrom, Janice, p.33-48; c) Group treatment of children in shelters for battered women. Alessi, Joseph J. and Hearn, Kristin, p.49-61; d) Crisis intervention with battered women. Roberts, Albert R., p.65-83; e) Intervention with the abusive partner. Roberts, Albert R., p.84-115; f) Police intervention. Roberts, Albert R., p.116-128; g) Family trouble clinic: Family service of Detroit and Wayne County. Cantomi, Lucile, p.129-143; h) Children's observations of interparental violence. Carlson, Bonnie E., p.147-167; i) Coping with wife abuse: Personal and social networks. Bowker, Lee H., p.168-191.

27. Be Good, Sweet Maid: An Anthology of Women & Literature. Todd, Janet, ed. New York: Holmes & Meier, 1981.
a) Artists and mothers: A false alliance. Auerbach, Nina, p.9-19; b) The art of *Mansfield Park*. Uffen, Ellen Serlen, p.21-30; c) Frankenstein's daughter: Mary Shelley and Mary Wollstonecraft. Todd, Janet, p.31-39; d) Ambivalence in the Gynogram: Sade's utopian woman. Fink, Beatrice, p.41-51; e) George Sand and the myth of femininity. Rabine, Leslie, p.55-68; f) *Sonnets from the Portuguese*: A negative and a positive context. Zimmerman, Susan, p.69-81; g) "Old maids have friends": The unmarried heroine of Trollope's Barsetshire novels. Weissman, Judith, p.83-92; h) Beauty in distress: *Daniel Deronda* and *The House of Mirth*. Rooke, Constance, p.93-102; i) Rebellions of good women. Spacks, Patricia Meyer, p.103-112; j) Virginia Woolf's Miss Latrobe: The artist's last struggle against masculine values. Gillespie, Diane Filby, p.115-122; k) *A Passage to India* as "marriage fiction": Forster's sexual politics. Showalter, Elaine, p.123-134; l) Violet Hunt's *Tales of the Uneasy*: Ghost stories of a worldly woman. Secor, Marie and Secor, Robert, p.135-145; m) Women and madness in the fiction of Joyce Carol Oates. Goodman, Charlotte, p.149-158; n) A conversation with May Sarton. Shelley, Dolores, p.159-166; o) Quebec women writers. Makward, Christiane, p.167-174.

28. Behavior and the Menstrual Cycle. Friedman, Richard C., ed. New York: Marcel Dekker, 1982.
a) The physiology of the menstrual cycle. Linkie, Daniel M., p.1-21; b) The neuroendocrinologic control of the menstrual cycle. Ferin, Michel, p.23-42; c) Neuroendocrine regulation of sexual behavior. Davis, Paula G. and McEwen, Bruce S., p.43-64; d) Hypothalamic peptides and sexual behavior. Dudley, Carol A. and Moss, Robert L., p.65-76; e) The psychology of the menstrual cycle: Biological and physiological perspectives. Parlee, Mary Brown, p.77-99; f) Cognitive behavior and the menstrual cycle. Sommer, Barbara, p.101-127; g) Epidemiological patterns of sexual behavior in the menstrual cycle. Morris, Naomi M. and Udry, J. Richard, p.129-153; h) Sexual behavior and the menstrual cycle. Williams, Ann Marie and Williams, Gregory D., p.155-176; i) A developmental analysis of menstrual distress in adolescence. Brooks-Gunn, Jeanne and Ruble, Diane N., p.177-197; j) Dysmenorrhea and dyspareunia. Fuchs, Fritz, p.199-216; k) Premenstrual tension: An overview. Dalton, Katharina, p.217-242; l) Classification of premenstrual syndromes. Endicott, Jean and Halbreich, Uriel, p.243-265; m) Estrogens and central nervous system function: Electroencephalography, cognition, and depression. Klaiber, Edward L., et al., p.267-289; n) The menstrual cycle in anorexia nervosa. Halmi, Katherine A., p.291-297; o) Psychopathology and the menstrual cycle. Hurt, Stephen W., et al., p.299-316; p) Premenstrual tension in borderline and related disorders. Stone, Michael H., p.317-344; q) Oral contraceptives and the menstrual cycle. Bennett, Susan E. and Glick, Ira, p.345-365; r) Recent trends in the treatment of premen-

strual syndrome: A critical review. Green, Judith, p.367-395; s) Premenstrual tension: Etiology. Janowsky, David S. and Rausch, Jeffrey L., p.397-427.

29. Behavior Modification with Women. Blechman, Elaine A., ed. New York: Guilford Press, 1984.
a) Women's behavior in a man's world: Sex differences in competence. Blechman, Elaine A., p.3-33; b) Unraveling the nature of sex roles. Barlow, David H. and Beck, J. Gayle, p.34-59; c) Behavioral assessment of women clients. MacDonald, Marian L., p.60-93; d) Dissemination of behavioral interventions with women: Needed - a technology. Stolz, Stephanie B., p.94-108; e) Sexuality. Hoon, Emily Franck, Krop, Harry D. and Wincze, John P., p.113-142; f) Interpersonal effectiveness in assertive situations. Linehan, Marsha M., p.143-169; g) Marriage and the family: An unconscious male bias in behavioral treatment? Gurman, Alan S. and Klein, Marjorie H., p.170-189; h) Parenting: Training mothers as behavior therapists for their children. Atkeson, Beverly M. and Strauss, Cyd C., p.190-220; i) Health maintenance: Exercise and nutrition. Foreyt, John P. and Goodrick, G. Ken, p.221-244; j) Physical aggression: Treating the victims. Frank, Ellen and Stewart, Barbara Duffy, p.245-274; k) Depression: A behavioral-cognitive approach. Johnson, Belinda A., Miller III, Ivan W. and Norman, William H., p.275-307; l) Physiological and reproductive disorders. Calhoun, Karen S. and Sturgis, Ellie T., p.308-340; m) Anxiety-related disorders, fears, and phobias. Goldfried, Marvin R. and Padawer, Wendy J., p.341-372; n) Weight disorders: Overweight and anorexia. Fodor, Iris Goldstein and Thal, Jodi, p.373-398; o) Female delinquents. Alexander, James F. and Warburton, Janet R., p.401-427; p) Women and alcoholism. McCrady, Barbara S., p.428-449; q) Aging women. Wisocki, Patricia A., p.450-476; r) Mentally retarded mothers. Budd, Karen S. and Greenspan, Stephen, p.477-506.

30. Between Women: Biographers, Novelists, Critics, Teachers and Artists Write about Their Work on Women. Ascher, Carol, DeSalvo, Louise and Ruddick, Sara, eds. Boston, MA: Beacon Press, 1984.
a) Living our life. Shulman, Alix Kates, p.1-13; b) In quest of Ding Ling (In quest of myself). Feuerwerker, Yi-Tsi Mei, p.15-33; c) A portrait of the *Puttana* as a middle-aged Woolf scholar. DeSalvo, Louise, p.35-53; d) Trying to make things real. Vaught, Bonny, p.55-69; e) Music into words. Wood, Elizabeth, p.71-83; f) On "Clearing the Air": My letter to Simone de Beauvoir. Ascher, Carol, p.85-103; g) Alice Dunbar-Nelson: A personal and literary perspective. Hull, Gloria T., p.105-111; h) This is who she is to me: On photographing women. Koolish, Lynda, p.113-135; i) New combinations: Learning from Virginia Woolf. Ruddick, Sara, p.137-159; j) Exiles. Chabran, Myrtha, p.161-169; k) Hannah Arendt: Thinking as we are. Minnich, Elizabeth Kamarck, p.171-185; l) "She is the one you call sister": Discovering Mary Wilkins Freeman. Glasser, Leah Blatt, p.187-211; m) Farewell to the farm. Sternburg, Janet, p.213-218; n) "Charlotte's Web": Reading *Jane Eyre* over time. Lazarre, Jane, p.221-

235; o) Silence: Access and aspiration. Stetson, Erlene, p.237-251; p) Anna O./Bertha Pappenheim and me. Jackowitz, Ann, p.253-273; q) Ordinary. Extraordinary. Stevens, May, p.275-309; r) Sister/outsider: Some thoughts on Simone Weil. Cliff, Michelle, p.311-325; s) Carrington revisited. Wilson, J.J., p.327-341; t) I had been hungry all the years. Tax, Meredith, p.343-355; u) Daughters writing: Toward a theory of women's biography. Chevigny, Bell Gale, p.357-379; v) Invisible mending. Marcus, Jane, p.381-395; w) Biographer and subject: A critical connection. Cook, Blanche Wiesen, p.397-411; x) May Sarton: A metaphor for my life, my work, and my art. Wheelock, Martha, p.413-429; y) Looking for Zora. Walker, Alice, p.431-447.

31. Beyond Domination: New Perspectives on Women and Philosophy. Gould, Carol C., ed. Totowa, NJ: Rowman & Allanheld, c1983, 1984.
a) Private rights and public virtues: Women, the family, and democracy. Gould, Carol C., p.3-18; b) Human biology in feminist theory: Sexual equality reconsidered. Jaggar, Alison, p.21-42; c) Is gender a variable in conceptions of rationality? A survey of issues. Harding, Sandra, p.43-63; d) A different reality: Feminist ontology. Whitbeck, Caroline, p.64-88; e) Concepts of woman in psychoanalytic theory: The nature-nurture controversy revisited. Donchin, Anne, p.89-103; f) Sexism, religion, and the social and spiritual liberation of women today. Ruether, Rosemary Radford, p.107-122; g) Liberating philosophy: An end to the dichotomy of matter and spirit. Hein, Hilde, p.123-144; h) Pornography and the erotics of domination. Kittay, Eva Feder, p.145-174; i) From domination to recognition. Aboulafia, Mitchell, p.175-185; j) Women's work and sex roles. Moulton, Janice and Rainone, Francine, p.189-203; k) The political nature of relations between the sexes. Rothenberg, Paula, p.204-220; l) Feminist theory: The private and the public. Nicholson, Linda, p.221-230; m) Women and their privacy: What is at stake? Allen, Anita L., p.233-249; n) A feminist analysis of the Universal Declaration of Human Rights. Holmes, Helen Bequaert, p.250-264; o) Rights-conflict, pregnancy, and abortion. Smith, Janet Farrell, p.265-273; p) Sex preselection: From here to fraternity. Steinbacher, Roberta, p.274-282; q) Contemporary feminist perspectives on women and higher education. Perreault, Geraldine, p.283-309.

32. Beyond the Eternal Feminine: Critical Essays on Women and German Literature. Cocalis, Susan L. and Goodman, Kay, eds. Stuttgart, Germany: Akademischer Verlag Hans-Dieter Heinz, 1982.
a) The eternal feminine is leading us on. Cocalis, Susan L. and Goodman, Kay, p.1-45; b) A critical appraisal of Goethe's *Iphigenie*. Horsley, Ritta Jo, p.47-74; c) *Faust*: The tragedy reexamined. Guenther, Margaret B., p.75-98; d) Kleist's nation of Amazons. Angress, Ruth, p.99-134; e) *Wally, die Zweiflerin* and *Madonna*: A discussion of sex-socialization in the nineteenth century. Meyer, Marsha, p.135-158; f) A German writer and feminist in nineteenth century America: An archival study of Mathilde Franziska

Anneke. Wagner, Maria M., p.159-175; g) German women writers in the nineteenth century: Where are they? Frederiksen, Elke, p.177-201; h) Laura Marholm and the question of female nature. Scott-Jones, Marilyn, p.203-223; i) Gabriele Reuter: Romantic and realist. Johnson, Richard L., p.225-244; j) Ricarda Huch: Myth and reality. Frank, Miriam, p.245-260; k) "Eine frau, aber mehr als das, eine Persönlichkeit, aber mehr als das: eine frau": The structural analysis of the female characters in the novels of Max Frisch. Knapp, Mona, p.261-289; l) Sociological implications of Gabriele Wohmann's critical reception. Morris-Farber, Nina, p.291-309; m) The left-handed compliment: Perspectives and stereotypes in criticism. Frieden, Sandra, p.311-333; n) The question of a feminist aesthetic and Karin Struck's *Klassenliebe*. Adelson, Leslie, p.335-349; o) Verena Stefan's *Häutungen*: Homoeroticism and feminism. Tubach, Sally Patterson, p.351-380; p) Our language, our selves: Verena Stefan's critique of patriarchal language. Clausen, Jeanette, p.381-400; q) Literary emasculation: Household imagery in Christa Reinig's *Entmannung*. McAlister-Hermann, Judith, p.401-419; r) Irmtraud Morgner's *Leben und Abenteuer der Trobadora Beatriz*. Martin, Biddy, p.421-439.

33. Beyond Their Sex: Learned Women of the European Past. Labalme, Patricia H., ed. New York: New York University Press, 1980.
a) The education of women in the Middle Ages in theory, fact, and fantasy. Ferrante, Joan M., p.9-42; b) Women, learning, and power: Eleonora of Aragon and the Court of Ferrara. Gundersheimer, Werner L., p.43-65; c) Book-lined cells: Women and humanism in the early Italian Renaissance. King, Margaret L., p.66-90; d) Learned women of early modern Italy: Humanists and university scholars. Kristeller, Paul Oskar, p.91-116; e) Learned women in the Europe of the sixteenth century. Bainton, Roland H., p.117-128; f) Women's roles in early modern Venice: An exceptional case. Labalme, Patricia H., p.129-152; g) Gender and genre: Women as historical writers, 1400-1820. Davis, Natalie Zemon, p.153-182.

34. Biological Woman - The Convenient Myth: A Collection of Feminist Essays and a Comprehensive Bibliography. Hubbard, Ruth, Henifin, Mary Sue and Fried, Barbara, eds. Cambridge, MA: Schenkman Publishing, 1982.
a) Have only men evolved? Hubbard, Ruth, p.17-46; b) Boys will be boys will be boys: The language of sex and gender. Fried, Barbara, p.47-69; c) From sin to sickness: Hormonal theories of lesbianism. Birke, Lynda I. A., p.71-90; d) Social bodies: The interaction of culture and women's biology. Lowe, Marian, p.91-116; e) No fertile women need apply: Employment discrimination and reproductive hazards in the workplace. Henifin, Mary Sue and Stellman, Jeanne M., p.117-145; f) Sterilization abuse. Rodriguez-Trias, Helen, p.147-160; g) Changing minds: Women, biology, and the menstrual cycle. Best, Sandy and Birke, Lynda I. A., p.161-184; h) Taking the men out of menopause. Bart, Pauline and Grossman, Marlyn, p.185-206; i) Displaced - the midwife by the male

physician. Brack, Datha Clapper, p.207-226; j) Black women's health: Notes for a course. Smith, Beverly, p.227-239; k) The quirks of a woman's brain. Walsh, Mary Roth, p.241-263; l) Adventures of a woman in science. Weisstein, Naomi, p.265-281; m) Bibliography: Women, science, and health. Amatniek, Joan Cindy and Henifin, Mary Sue, p.289-376.

35. Biopolitics and Gender. Watts, Meredith W., ed. New York: The Haworth Press, 1984.
a) Introduction: Biopolitics and gender. Watts, Meredith W., p.1-27; b) Biology, gender, and politics: An assessment and critique. Baer, Denise L. and Bositis, David A., p.29-66; c) Political ideology, sociobiology, and the U.S. women's rights movement. Kay, Susan Ann and Meikle, Douglas B., p.67-95; d) The biopolitics of sex: Gender, genetics, and epigenetics. Schubert, Glendon, p.97-128; e) Sex, endocrines, and political behavior. Jaros, Dean and White, Elizabeth S., p.129-145; f) Power structures and perceptions of power holders in same-sex groups of young children. Jones, Diane Carlson, p.147-164; g) Explaining "male chauvinism" and "feminism": Cultural differences in male and female reproductive strategies. Masters, Roger D., p.165-210.

36. Birth Control and Controlling Birth: Women-Centered Perspectives. Holmes, Helen B., Hoskins, Betty B. and Gross, Michael, eds. Clifton, NJ: Humana Press, 1980.
a) Reproductive technologies: The birth of a women-centered analysis. Holmes, Helen B., p.3-20; b) Historical styles of contraceptive advocacy. Berkman, Joyce Avrech, p.27-36; c) Ethical problems in government-funded contraceptive research. Cowan, Belita, p.37-46; d) Value conflicts in biomedical research into future contraceptives. Korenbrot, Carol, p.47-53; e) Status of contraceptive technology development. Ans, Jacki and Atkinson, Linda E., p.55-59; f) Women-controlled research. Punnett, Laura, p.61-69; g) Woman-controlled birth control: A feminist analysis of natural birth control. Women's Community Health Center, p.71-78; h) Depo-provera and sterilization abuse overview. Cassidy, Marie M., p.97-99; i) Depo-provera: Some ethical questions about a controversial contraceptive. Levine, Carol, p.101-105; j) The depo-provera weapon. Corea, Gena, p.107-116; k) Sterilization abuse and Hispanic women. Sewell, Sandra Serrano, p.121-123; l) Depo-provera and sterilization abuse discussion. p.129-139; m) Man-midwifery and the rise of technology: The problem and proposals for resolution. Wertz, Dorothy C., p.147-166; n) The electronic fetal monitor in perinatology. Klapholz, Henry, p.167-173; o) Drugs, birth, and ethics. Brackbill, Yvonne, p.175-182; p) Benefits and risks of electronic fetal monitoring. Banta, David, p.183-191; q) Ethical issues in childbirth technology. Ruzek, Sheryl Burt, p.197-202; r) A report on birth in three cultures. Ekstrom, Susan Cope, p.213-221; s) Community alternatives to high technology birth. Gaskin, Ina May, p.223-229; t) Contrasts in the birthing place: Hospital and birth center. Avery, Byllye Y. and Levy, Judith M., p.231-238; u) Ethical issues relating to childbirth as experienced by the birthing woman and midwife.

Luce, Judith Dickson, p.239-244; v) Midwives in many settings. Swallow, Helen, p.245-250; w) A Native American response. Cook, Katsi, p.251-258; x) An obstetrician's perspective. Gray, Mary Jane, p.259-260; y) Policymaking and projections overview. Holmes, Helen B., p.267-268; z) Forces impacting on the policymaker. Lashof, Joyce, p.269-274; aa) C/SEC: A special-interest interpersonal group brings about change. Shearer, Beth, p.277-282; bb) The ethicist in policymaking. Lebacqz, Karen, p.283-287.

37. Black Families. McAdoo, Harriette Pipes, ed. Beverly Hills, CA: Sage, 1981.
a) Conceptualizations of black families. Dodson, Jualynne, p.23-37; b) Interpreting the African heritage in Afro-American family organization. Sudarkasa, Niara, p.37-54; c) Old-time religion: Benches can't say "Amen". Pipes, William Harrison, p.54-76; d) African-American family life: An instrument of culture. Nobles, Wade W., p.77-86; e) Perspectives on black family empirical research: 1965-1978. Johnson, Leanor Boulin, p.87-102; f) A demographic picture of black families. Glick, Paul C., p.106-126; g) Economics and mobility: A theoretical rationale for urban black family well-being. Davis, Frank G., p.127-138; h) Black education: A cultural-ecological perspective. Ogbu, John U., p.139-154; i) Patterns of upward mobility in black families. McAdoo, Harriette Pipes, p.155-170; j) Race and marital status: An overview. Staples, Robert, p.173-175; k) Black men in America: The quest for "manhood". Cazenave, Noel A., p.176-185; l) Women's values regarding marriage and the family. Heiss, Jerold, p.186-198; m) Attitudes toward procreation among black adults. Harrison, Algea, p.199-208; n) Parenting in black families with young children: A historical perspective. Peters, Marie F., p.211-224; o) Involvement of fathers in the socialization of black children. McAdoo, John L., p.225-237; p) Support systems of significant others in black families. Manns, Wilhelmina, p.238-251; q) Group identity development within black families. Gurin, Gerald, Jackson, James S. and McCullough, Wayne R., p.252-263; r) Multiple public benefits and poor black families. Hill, Robert B., p.266-277; s) Policies affecting the status of black children and families. Moore, Evelyn K., p.278-290; t) An advocacy agenda for black families and children. Edelman, Marian Wright, p.291-300.

38. The Black Woman. Rodgers-Rose, La Frances, ed. Beverly Hill, CA: Sage, 1980.
a) The black woman: A historical overview. Rodgers-Rose, La Frances, p.15-28; b) Some demographic characteristics of the black woman: 1940 to 1975. Rodgers-Rose, La Frances, p.29-41; c) Black fertility: Recent demographic and sociological influences. Brinkley-Carter, Christina, p.43-61; d) The black woman and family roles. McCray, Carrie Allen, p.67-78; e) The black woman and child rearing. Hale, Janice, p.79-87; f) She who is black and mother: In sociology and fiction, 1940-1970. Wade-Gayles, Gloria, p.89-106; g) "The means to put my children through": Child-rearing goals and strategies among

black female domestic servants. Dill, Bonnie Thornton, p.107-123; h) Black mothers and the extended family support network. McAdoo, Harriet Pipes, p.125-144; i) Marital interaction goals of black women: Strengths and effects. Rutledge, Essie Manuel, p.145-159; j) On marital relations: Perceptions of black women. Myers, Lena Wright, p.161-172; k) Role transition in early adulthood: Orientations of young black women. Engram, Eleanor, p.175-187; l) Black female professionals: Dilemmas and contradictions of status. Leggon, Cheryl Bernadette, p.189-202; m) Dilemmas of black females in leadership. Dumas, Rhetaugh Graves, p.203-215; n) "Holding back the ocean with a broom": Black women and community work. Gilkes, Cheryl Townsend, p.217-231; o) Political behavior of American black women: An overview. Prestage, Jewel L., p.233-245; p) Dialectics of black male-female relationships. Rodgers-Rose, La Frances, p.251-263; q) Depression in black women: A theoretical appraisal. Carrington, Christine H., p.265-271; r) Black female suicides: Is the excitement justified? Aldridge, Delores P., p.273-284; s) The women's liberation movement: Understanding black women's attitudes. Hemmons, Willa Mae, p.285-299; t) The self/group actualization of black women. Wilson, Geraldine L., p.301-314.

39. The Black Woman Cross-Culturally. Steady, Filomina Chioma, ed. Cambridge, MA: Schenkman Publishing Co., 1981.
a) The black woman cross-culturally: An overview. Steady, Filomina Chioma, p.7-41; b) Female employment and family organization in West Africa. Sudarkasa, Niara, p.49-63; c) Asante queen mothers in government and politics in the nineteenth century. Aidoo, Agnes Akosua, p.65-77; d) Women's political participation Nigeria. Okonjo, Kamene, p.79-106; e) Tanzanian women in nation building. Ladner, Joyce, p.107-117; f) The role of women in the revolution in Guinea-Bissau. Urdang, Stephanie, p.119-139; g) The African woman as entrepreneur: Problem and perspectives on their roles. Simms, Ruth, p.141-168; h) The second sex in town. Gugler, Josef, p.169-184; i) Women in indigenous African cults and churches. Jules-Rosette, Benetta, p.185-207; j) Definitions of women and development: An African perspective. Pala, Achola O., p.209-214; k) The black woman in South Africa: An Azanian profile. Rivkin, Elizabeth Thaele, p.215-229; l) The role of women in the struggle against *apartheid* in South Africa. Lapchik, Richard E., p.231-261; m) Racism and tradition: Black womanhood in historical perspective. Ladner, Joyce A., p.269-288; n) Female slave resistance: The economics of sex. Hine, Darlene Clark and Wittenstein, Kate, p.289-299; o) Discrimination against Afro-American women in the woman's movement, 1830-1920. Terborg-Penn, Rosalyn, p.301-315; p) Black women and racial "uplift" prior to emancipation. Perkins, Linda, p.317-334; q) The myth of the black matriarchy. Staples, Robert, p.335-348; r) Sex roles and survival strategies in the urban black community. Stack, Carol B., p.349-367; s) The incarcerated black female: The case of social double jeopardy. French,

Laurence, p.369-381; t) Black women and music: A survey from Africa to the new world. Jackson-Brown, Irene V., p.383-401; u) Images of black women in Afro-American poetry. Rushing, Andrea Benton, p.403-416; v) Household and family in the Caribbean: Some definitions and concepts. Gonzalez, Nancie Solien, p.421-429; w) Women's role in West Indian society. Justus, Joyce Bennett, p.431-450; x) Black women and survival: A Maroon case. Bilby, Kenneth and Steady, Filomina Chioma, p.451-467; y) Social inequality and sexual status in Barbados. Makiesky-Barrow, Susan and Sutton, Constance, p.469-498; z) Female status, the family and male dominance in a West Indian community. Moses, Yolanda T., p.499-513; aa) Economic role and cultural tradition. Mintz, Sidney W., p.515-534; bb) The black woman in Haitian society and literature. Latortue, Regine, p.535-560; cc) West Indian characteristics of the black Carib. Gonzalez, Nancie Solien, p.565-574; dd) The spread of capitalism in rural Colombia: Effects on poor women. Rubbo, Ann, p.575-594; ee) Images of the woman of color in Brazilian literature: O Cortico, Clara Dos Anjos, Gabriela Cravo E Canela, and O Quinze. Nunes, Maria Luisa, p.595-614.

40. Black Women Writers (1950-1980): A Critical Evaluation. Evans, Mari, ed. Garden City, NY: Anchor Books, 1984.
a) Shades and slashes of light. Angelou, Maya, p.3-5; b) Maya Angelou and the autobiographical statement. Cudjoe, Selwyn R., p.6-24; c) Reconstruction of the composite self: New images of black women in Maya Angelou's continuing autobiography. O'Neale, Sondra, p.25-36; d) Salvation is the issue. Bambara, Toni Cade, p.41-47; e) From baptism to resurrection: Toni Cade Bambara and the incongruity of language. Burks, Ruth Elizabeth, p.48-57; f) Music as theme: The jazz mode in the works of Toni Cade Bambara. Traylor, Eleanor W., p.58-70; g) The field of the fever, the time of the tall-walkers. Brooks, Gwendolyn, p.75-78; h) Gwendolyn Brooks: Poet of the whirlwind. Gayle Jr., Addison, p.79-87; i) Gwendolyn Brooks' poetic realism: A developmental survey. Kent, George, p.88-105; j) A candle in a gale wind. Childress, Alice, p.111-116; k) Alice Childress's dramatic structure. Hay, Samuel A., p.117-128; l) The literary genius of Alice Childress. Killens, John O., p.129-133; m) A simple language. Clifton, Lucille, p.137-138; n) Tell the good news: A view of the works of Lucille Clifton. McCluskey, Audrey T., p.139-149; o) Lucille Clifton: Warm water, greased legs, and dangerous poetry. Madhubuti, Haki, p.150-160; p) My father's passage. Evans, Mari, p.165-169; q) The art of Mari Evans. Dorsey, David, p.170-189; r) Affirmation in the works of Mari Evans. Edwards, Solomon, p.190-200; s) An answer to some questions on how I write: In three parts. Giovanni, Nikki, p.205-210; t) Nikki Giovanni: Taking a chance on feeling. Giddings, Paula, p.211-217; u) Sweet soft essence of possibility: The poetry of Nikki Giovanni. Harris, William J., p.218-228; v) About my work. Jones, Gayl, p.233-235; w) Singing a deep song: Language as evidence in the novels of Gayl Jones. Dixon, Melvin, p.236-248; x) Escape from Trublem: The fiction of Gayl Jones.

Ward Jr., Jerry W., p.249-257; y) My words will be there. Lorde, Audre, p.261-268; z) In the name of the father: The poetry of Audre Lord. Brooks, Jerome, p.269-276; aa) The unicorn is black: Audre Lorde in retrospect. Martin, Joan, p.277-291; bb) The closing of the circle: Movement from division to wholeness in Paule Marshall's fiction. Collier, Eugenia, p.295-315; cc) And called every generation blessed: Theme, setting, and ritual in the works of Paule Marshall. McCluskey Jr., John, p.316-334; dd) Rootedness: The ancestor as foundation. Morrison, Toni, p.339-345; ee) The quest for self: Triumph and failure in the works of Toni Morrison. Lee, Dorothy H., p.346-360; ff) Theme, characterization, and style in the works of Toni Morrison. Turner, Darwin T., p.361-369; gg) An amen arena. Rodgers, Carolyn, p.373-376; hh) Imagery in the women poems: The art of Carolyn Rodgers. Jamison, Angelene, p.377-392; ii) Running wild in her soul: The poetry of Carolyn Rodgers. Parker-Smith, Bettye J., p.393-410; jj) Ruminations/Reflections. Sanchez, Sonia, p.415-418; kk) Sonia Sanchez: The bringer of memories. Madhubuti, Haki, p.419-432; ll) The poetry of Sonia Sanchez. Williams, David, p.433-448; mm) Writing *The Color Purple*. Walker, Alice, p.453-456; nn) Alice Walker: The black woman artist as wayward. Christian, Barbara, p.457-477; oo) Alice Walker's women: In search of some peace of mind. Parker-Smith, Bettye J., p.478-493; pp) Fields watered with blood: Myth and ritual in the poetry of Margaret Walker. Collier, Eugenia, p.499-510; qq) Music as theme: The blues mode in the works of Margaret Walker. Traylor, Eleanor, p.511-525.

41. Black Working Women Debunking the Myths: A Multidisciplinary Approach. Berkeley, CA: Center for the Study, Education and Advancement of Women, University of California, 1982(?).
a) Working women in the United States: A look at the facts. Wilkerson, Margaret B., p.3-6; b) The concept of class in the novels of black women. Christian, Barbara, p.87-91; c) Sources of life satisfaction: The different worlds of black women and white women. Almquist, Elizabeth and Freudiger, Patricia, p.93-118; d) Black women and the political process in the United States. Hernandez, Aileen, p.119-131; e) Shifts in the occupational and employment status of black women: Current trends and future implications. Malveaux, Julianne, p.133-168; f) Stress and support networks of working single black mothers. McAdoo, Harriette, p.169-196; g) Invited presentation: The black professional woman — career success and interpersonal failure. Staples, Robert, p.197-209.

42. Blueprint for Living: Perspectives for Latter-Day Saint Women. Mouritsen, Maren M., ed. Provo, UT: Brigham Young University, 1980.
a) Our sisters in the church. Kimball, Spencer W., p.1-4; b) The American Woman's Movement. Spafford, Belle S., p.6-16; c) Keys for a woman's progression. Kimball, Camilla E., p.17-25; d) Our heritage. Jacobsen, Florence S., p.26-31; e) Blueprints for living. Smith, Barbara B., p.32-43; f) Patriarchy and matriarchy. Nibley, Hugh W.,

p.44-61; g) Except you become as little children.
Shumway, Naomi M., p.62-68; h) Daughters of God.
Cannon, Elaine A., p.69-76; i) Drifting, dreaming, direct-
ing. Kapp, Ardeth Greene, p.77-88; j) Happily ever after.
Taylor, Jean, p.94-97; k) A woman's role and destiny.
Smith, Ida, p.98-102; l) Gospel principles and women.
Ford, Kimberly, p.103-106; m) A response, and more
questions. Barlow, Sally, p.107-111; n) The traditional
role of the Mormon woman. Maxwell, Colleen, p.112-115;
o) The stewardship of talents. Eldredge, Yoshie Akimoto,
p.116-120; p) Women in the light of the Gospel. Rasmus,
Carolyn J., p.121-125.

43. Building Feminist Theory: Essays from Quest. New York:
Longman, 1981.
a) Political change: Two perspectives on power. Hartsock,
Nancy, p.3-19; b) The future of female separatism.
Valeska, Lucia, p.20-31; c) Fundamental feminism:
Process and perspective. Hartsock, Nancy, p.32-43; d)
Beyond either/or: Feminist options. Bunch, Charlotte,
p.44-56; e) The illusion of androgyny. Raymond, Janice,
p.59-66; f) Not for lesbians only. Bunch, Charlotte, p.67-
73; g) If all else fails, I'm still a mother. Valeska, Lucia,
p.74-83; h) Sexual harassment, working women's dilemma. Silverman, Deirdre, p.84-93; i) Who wants a piece of
the pie? Frye, Marilyn, p.94-100; j) An open letter to the
academy. Russell, Michelle, p.101-110; k) Staying alive.
Hartsock, Nancy, p.111-122; l) Class realities: Create a
new power base. Kollias, Karen, p.125-138; m) Class attitudes and professionalism. McKenney, Mary, p.139-148;
n) Race and class: Beyond personal politics. Fisher-
Manick, Beverly, p.149-160; o) Patriarchy and capitalism.
Phelps, Linda, p.161-173; p) Do feminists need Marxism?
Flax, Jane, p.174-185; q) The reform tool kit. Bunch,
Charlotte, p.189-201; r) Put your money where your
movement is. Fisher-Manick, Beverly, p.202-211; s)
Confrontation: Black/white. Apuzzo, Ginny and Powell,
Betty, p.212-222; t) Female leaders: Who was
Rembrandt's mother? St. Joan, Jackie, p.223-235; u) The
Beguines: A medieval women's community. Clark,
Garcia, p.236-242; v) Reflections on science fiction. Russ,
Joanna, p.243-250; w) The feminist workplace.
MacDonald, Nancy, p.251-259; x) Building feminist orga-
nizations. Freeman, Alexa and MacMillan, Jackie, p.260-
267.

44. Careers of Professional Women. Silverstone, Rosalie and
Ward, Audrey, eds. London: Croom Helm, 1980.
a) The bimodal career. Ward, Audrey and Silverstone,
Rosalie, p.10-18; b) Accountancy. Silverstone, Rosalie,
p.19-50; c) Architecture. Wigfall, Valerie, p.51-82; d)
Dentistry. Fox, Brenda and Seward, Margaret, p.83-98; e)
Medicine. Elston, Mary Ann, p.99-139; f) Nursing.
MacGuire, Jillian, p.140-164; g) Physiotherapy. Ward,
Audrey, p.165-184; h) Teaching. Kelsall, R. Keith, p.185-
206; i) Summing Up. Silverstone, Rosalie and Ward,
Audrey, p.207-220.

45. The Challenge of Change: Perspectives on Family, Work,
and Education. Horner, Matina, Nadelson, Carol C. and

Notman, Malkah T., eds. New York: Plenum Press, 1983.
a) American demographic directions. Keyfitz, Nathan,
p.5-22; b) The challenge of sex equality: Old values revisited or a new culture? Chafe, William H., p.23-37; c) Do
changes in women's rights change women's moral judgements? Gilligan, Carol, p.39-60; d) Emerging patterns of
female leadership in formal organizations, or must the
female leader go formal? Lipman-Blumen, Jean, p.61-91;
e) Ground rules for marriage: Perspectives on the pattern
of an era. Bernard, Jessie, p.97-121; f) Psychological orientations to the work role: 1957-1976. Veroff, Joseph,
p.123-180; g) The American divorce rate: What does it
mean? What should we worry about? Bane, Mary Jo,
p.181-198; h) Family roles in a twenty-year perspective.
Douvan, Elizabeth, p.199-217; i) Assessing personal and
social change in two generations. Block, Jeanne H. and
Mitchell, Valory, p.223-262; j) The past and future of the
undergraduate woman. Katz, Joseph, p.263-273; k)
Changing sex roles: College graduates of the 1960's and
1970's. Salt, Patricia and Stewart, Abigail, p.275-296; l)
Sex differences in the educational and occupational goals
of black college students: Continued inquiry into the
black matriarchy theory. Fleming, Jacqueline, p.297-316;
m) Change and constancy: A hundred years' tale.
Rapoport, Rhona and Rapoport, Robert, p.317-323.

46. A Challenge to Social Security: The Changing Roles of
Women and Men in American Society. Burkhauser,
Richard V. and Holden, Karen C., eds. New York:
Academic Press, 1982.
a) Concepts underlying the current controversy about
women's social security benefits. Lampman, Robert J.
and MacDonald, Maurice, p.21-39; b) Supplemental
OASI benefits to homemakers through current spouse
benefits, a homemaker credit, and child-care drop-out
years. Holden, Karen C., p.41-72; c) Earnings sharing:
Incremental and fundamental reform. Burkhauser,
Richard V., p.73-99; d) Women and a two-tier social security system. Munnel, Alicia H. and Stiglin, Laura E.,
p.101-130; e) The double-decker alternative for eliminating dependency under social security. Berry, David E.,
Garfinkel, Irwin and Warlick, Jennifer L., p.131-167; f)
Disability insurance under proposed reforms. Burfield,
William B. and Johnson, William G., p.169-199; g)
Occupational pension plans and spouse benefits. King,
Francis P., p.201-228; h) The housewife and social security
reform: A feminist perspective. Bergmann, Barbara R.,
p.229-233; i) Incremental change in social security needed
to result in equal and fair treatment of men and women.
Myers, Robert J., p.235-245; j) The changing nature of
social security. Ross, Stanford G., p.247-252.

47. Change and Choice: Women and Middle Age. Menell,
Zoë and Musgrave, Beatrice, eds. London: Peter Owen,
1980.
a) A time of change. Dally, Ann, p.10-23; b) The
menopause: Physiological, pathological, and psychological aspects. Morris, Norman, p.25-34; c) Questions
women want to ask about the menopause. Hailes, Jean,
p.35-53; d) Sex. Koadlow, Elsie and Tunnadine, Prudence,

p.54-65; e) Married life. Dominian, Jack, p.66-84; f) The family. Coghlan, Mary, p.85-102; g) Work. Wheeler-Bennett, Joan, p.103-114; h) Moral choice. Oppenheimer, Helen, p.115-126; i) Middle age: Loss or gain? (interview). p.127-170; j) Conclusion: Living through the middle years, p.171-179.

48. Changing Boundaries: Gender Roles and Sexual Behavior. Allgeier, Elizabeth Rice and McCormick, Naomi B., eds. Palo Alto, CA: Mayfield Publishing, 1983. a) The intimate relationship between gender roles and sexuality. Allgeier, Elizabeth Rice and McCormick, Naomi B., p.1-14; b) Sexual socialization and gender roles in childhood. Parsons, Jacquelynne Eccles, p.19-48; c) Becoming sexual in adolescence. Goodchilds, Jacqueline D. and Zellman, Gail L., p.49-63; d) The courtship game: Power in the sexual encounter. Jesser, Clinton J. and McCormick, Naomi B., p.64-86; e) Sexual response and gender roles. Radlove, Shirley, p.87-105; f) What do women and men want from love and sex? Hatfield, Elaine, p.106-134; g) Sexuality and gender roles in the second half of life. Allgeier, A. R., p.135-157; h) Reproduction, roles, and responsibilities. Allgeier, Elizabeth Rice, p.163-181; i) Gender roles and sexuality in the world of work. Gutek, Barbara A. and Nakamura, Charles Y., p.182-201; j) Sink or swing? The lifestyles of single adults. Phillis, Diane E. and Stein, Peter J., p.202-225; k) The intimate relationships of lesbians and gay men. Gordon, Steven L. and Peplau, Letitia Anne, p.226-244; l) Gender roles and sexual violence. Cherry, Frances, p.245-260; m) Gender, gender-role identification, and response to erotica. Fisher, William A., p.261-284; n) Future influences on the interaction of gender and human sexual expression. Allgeier, Elizabeth Rice and McCormick, Naomi B., p.285-299.

49. The Changing Composition of the Workforce: Implications for Future Research and Its Application. Glickman, Albert S., ed. New York: Plenum Press, 1982. a) Charting a course. Glickman, Albert S., p.3-12; b) When is old? Sheppard, H. L., p.15-18; c) The age mix of the labor force in 1990: Implications for labor market research. Andrisani, P. J. and Daymont, T. N., p.19-45; d) Postscripts and prospects. Stagner, R., p.47-66; e) Implications of the increasing participation of women in the work force in the 1990's. Tenopyr, M. L., p.69-76; f) The feminization of the labor force: Research for industrial/organizational psychology. Nieva, V. F., p.77-103; g) Commentary on studies of gender-mix in labor market research. Korman, A. K., p.105-109; h) Human resource planning and the intuitive manager: Models for the 1990's. Reynierse, J. H., p.113-123; i) The setting and the reality for labor relations in the 90's. Kuhns, E. D., p.125-134; j) Leadership and management in the 1990's. Bass, B. M., p.135-143; k) Reflections on polarities and bias. Alderfer, C. P., p.145-151; l) We can influence the future! Allen, D. W., p.155-160; m) College student values and the world of work. Astin, H. S., p.161-171; n) Whom should the schools serve, When...? Moore, J. W., p.173-178.

50. The Changing Experience of Women. Whitelegg, Elizabeth, et al., eds. Oxford: Martin Robertson, 1982. a) The butcher, the baker, the candlestickmaker: The shop and the family in the Industrial Revolution. Hall, Catherine, p.2-16; b) The home turned upside down? The working-class family in cotton textiles 1780-1850. Hall, Catherine, p.17-29; c) Women's work in nineteenth-century London: A study of the years 1820-1850. Alexander, Sally, p.30-44; d) Women's work and the family in nineteenth-century Europe. Scott, Joan and Tilly, Louise, p.45-70; e) The 'family wage'. Barrett, Michèle and McIntosh, Mary, p.71-87; f) The need for women's labour in the First World War. Braybon, Gail, p.90-104; g) Women as a reserve army of labour: A note on recent British experience. Bruegel, Irene, p.105-120; h) Typing our way to freedom: Is it true that new office technology can liberate women? Morgall, Janine, p.121-135; i) Feminism and science. Arditti, Rita, p.136-146; j) The state and training programmes for women. Wickham, Ann, p.147-163; k) The unnatural family. Edholm, Felicity, p.166-177; l) Monogamy, marriage and economic dependence. Comer, Lee, p.178-189; m) The violent event. Dobash, Rebecca and Dobash, Russell, p.190-206; n) From disregard to disrepute: The position of women in family law. Brophy, Julia and Smart, Carol, p.207-225; o) Technology and changes in the division of labour in the American home. Bose, Christine, p.226-238; p) Anger and tenderness: The experience of motherhood. Rich, Adrienne, p.239-251; q) Biological sex differences and sex stereotyping. Bartels, Else, p.254-266; r) Developmental aspects of gender. Kessler, Suzanne and McKenna, Wendy, p.267-285; s) Female sexuality. Freud, Sigmund, p.286-294; t) Alleged psychogenic disorders in women - a possible manifestation of sexual prejudice. Lennane, Jean and Lennane, John, p.297-308; u) Competing ideologies of reproduction: Medical and maternal perspectives on pregnancy. Graham, Hilary and Oakley, Ann, p.309-326; v) Rape and the masculine mystique. Russell, Diana, p.327-336; w) Women in official statistics. Allin, Paul and Hunt, Audrey, p.337-351; x) Making science feminist. Rose, Hilary, p.352-372; y) 'Guardians of the race' or 'vampires upon the nation's health'? Female sexuality and its regulation in early twentieth-century Britain. Bland, Lucy, p.373-388; z) Oppressive dichotomies: The nature/culture debate. Brown, Penelope and Jordanova, L., p.389-399.

51. Changing Perspectives on Menopause. Voda, Ann M., Dinnerstein, Myra and O'Donnell, Sheryl R., eds. Austin, TX: University of Texas Press, 1982. a) Toward a biosocial paradigm for menopause research: Lessons and contributions from the behavioral sciences. Koeske, Randi Daimon, p.3-23; b) Bad maps for an unknown region: Menopause from a literary perspective. Kincaid-Ehlers, Elizabeth, p.24-38; c) Biochemical findings and medical management of the menopause. Archer, David F., p.39-48; d) A cross-cultural exploration of the end of the childbearing years. Brown, Judith K., p.51-59; e) Attitudes of families toward menopause. Dege, Kristi and Gretzinger, Jacqueline, p.60-69; f) Perceptions of

menopause by Papago women. Kearns, Bessie Jean Ruley, p.70-83; g) Variation in Navajo menopause: Toward an explanation. Wright, Ann L., p.84-99; h) Neuroendocrine mechanisms of reproductive aging in women and female rats. Henrik, Elizabeth, p.100-123; i) Potential role of the pineal gland in the human menstrual cycle. Blask, David E., p.124-135; j) Menopausal hot flash. Voda, Ann M., p.136-159; k) Smoking, alcohol, and body mass relationships to early menopause: Implications for risk of cardiovascular disease. Hill, Judith, p.160-169; l) Erik Erikson and Doris Lessing: Psychological theory and the female novel of development. Reuter, Jeanette and Zak, Michele W., p.170-186; m) Changing views of "the change": A critical review and suggestions for an attributional approach. Bart, Pauline B. and Perlmutter, Ellen, p.187-199; n) A sociocultural approach. Brooks-Gunn, Jeanne, p.203-208; o) Expectations regarding menstrual symptoms: Effects on evaluation and behavior of women. Brooks-Gunn, Jeanne and Ruble, Diane N., p.209-219; p) Menopausal distress: A model for epidemiologic investigation. Woods, Nancy Fugate, p.220-238; q) Psychosocial aspects of the menopause. Severne, Liesbeth, p.239-247; r) Cultural models for coping with menopause. Griffen, Joyce, p.248-262; s) The fallacy of bodily reductionism. Stimpson, Catharine R., p.265-272; t) A critique of menopause research. Goodman, Madeleine J., p.273-288; u) Predicting the close of menstrual life. Treloar, Alan E., p.289-304; v) Endocrine functions in the woman's second half of life. Dyrenfurth, Inge, p.307-334; w) Aging, menopause, and estrogens: The clinician's dilemma. Friederich, Mary Anna, p.335-345; x) Sociological observations on ethical issues implicated in estrogen replacement therapy at menopause. Olesen, Virginia, p.346-360; y) Male and female menopause: A cultural put-on. Flint, Marcha, p.363-375; z) The Interdisciplinary Society for Menstrual Cycle Research: Creating knowledge from our experience. Dan, Alice J., p.379-384; aa) Beyond oppositional analysis: Concluding remarks. Koeske, Randi Daimon, p.385-387.

52. The Changing Position of Women in Family and Society: A Cross-National Comparison. Lupri, Eugen, ed. Leiden: E. J. Brill, 1983.
a) The changing positions of women and men in comparative perspective. Lupri, Eugen, p.3-42; b) The changing roles of Canadian women in family and work: An overview. Lupri, Eugen and Mills, Donald L., p.43-77; c) A comparative view on the changing position of women in the United States. Tomeh, Aida K., p.78-119; d) The position of women in the Netherlands: Marginal change. Schoonenboom, I.J., Veld, L. in't and Veld-Langeveld, H.M. in't, p.120-135; e) Female marital behaviour in French society. Michel, Andrée, p.136-147; f) The position of Austrian women in the family: Some data, many questions, and a few interpretations. Köckeis-Stangl, Eva, p.148-178; g) The changing role of women: The case of Italy. Cavalli, Alessandro, p.179-189; h) Changing sex roles in the Greek family and society. Dijkers, Marcellinus and Safilios-Rothschild, Constantina, p.190-206; i) The changing status and role of women in Japan.

Meguro, Yoriko and Morioka, Kiyomi, p.207-224; j) The changing role of Swedish women in family and society. Trost, Jan, p.225-242; k) Economic and family roles of men and women in Northern Europe: A historical cross-national comparison. Haavio-Mannila, Elina, p.243-260; l) Soviet women in family and society. Slesarev, G.A. and Yankova, Z.A., p.261-275; m) Women and the family in Poland. Siemienska, Renata, p.276-295; n) Women in Czechoslovakia. Wagnerová, Alena K., p.296-310; o) Change in the system of social power: Conditions for the social equality of women in Yugoslavia. Buric, Olivera, p.311-330; p) Women's roles and conjugal family systems in Ghana. Oppong, Christine, p.331-343; q) The changing position of black women in South Africa. Steyn, Anna F. and Uys, J.M., p.344-372; r) Economic recession and Swiss women's attitudes towards marital role segregation. Held, Thomas and Levy, René, p.373-395; s) Egalitarianism in marriage? Graduate education and the sexual division of labour in the Canadian family. Symons, Gladys L., p.396-417; t) Wife and/or worker: Sex role concepts of Canadian female students. Denis, Ann B., p.418-429; u) The industrialization of housework. Eichler, Margrit, p.430-443.

53. The Changing Risk of Disease in Women: An Epidemiologic Approach. Gold, Ellen B., ed. Boston, MA: D. C. Heath, 1984.
a) Sex differences in disease risk. Rice, Dorothy P., et al., p.1-24; b) The relationship of the sex hormone/prostaglandin interaction to female and male longevity. Ramey, Estelle R. and Ramwell, Peter, p.25-36; c) The effect of employment, family and job stress on coronary heart disease patterns in women. Eaker, Elaine D. and Haynes, Suzanne G., p.37-48; d) Health effects of becoming widowed. Goldberg, Evelyn L., p.49-63; e) Changing patterns of smoking and risk of disease. Higgins, Millicent W., p.65-79; f) Women as victims of crime. Alexander, Cheryl S., p.81-87; g) Women, alcohol, and the risk of disease. Ashley, Mary Jane, p.89-105; h) Health hazards associated with oral contraceptives. Berendes, Heinz W., p.107-115; i) Pelvic inflammatory disease: Causes and consequences. Gray, Ronald H. and Silkey, Beryl, p.117-125; j) Environmental exposures and spontaneous abortion. Kline, Jennie, p.127-138; k) An epidemiologic perspective of mental illness and childbirth. Paffenbarger Jr., Ralph S., p.139-152; l) Epidemiology of pituitary adenomas. Gold, Ellen B., p.153-167; m) Time trends of cancer incidence and mortality among women. Devesa, Susan S., p.169-183; n) Risk factors for benign and malignant breast disease. Ernster, Virginia L., p.185-198; o) Etiologic factors for invasive and noninvasive cervical abnormalities. Brinton, Louise A., p.199-210; p) Estrogens and endometrial cancer. Hulka, Barbara S., p.211-220; q) Risk factors for ovarian cancer. Hernandez, Enrique, Rosenblatt, Karin and Rosenshein, Neil B., p.221-231; r) Epidemiology of coronary heart disease in women. Szklo, Moyses, p.233-241; s) Hypertension in women - a review. Detre, Katherine M., p.243-255; t) Sex differences in diabetes mellitus. Barrett-Connor, Elizabeth and Wingard, Deborah L., p.257-286;

u) Epidemiology of osteoporosis. Kelsey, Jennifer L., p.287-298; v) Implications of epidemiologic data for developing health policy for women. Gordis, Leon, p.299-315.

54. Chicanas and Alcoholism: A Socio-Cultural Perspective of Women. Arevalo, Rodolfo and Minor, Marianne, eds. San Jose, CA: School of Social Work, San Jose State University, 1981.
a) A systems model for planning culturally specific programs. Minor, Marianne, p.1-4; b) The unidentified problem of alcoholism among Hispanic women. Steinhart, Clara, p.5-9; c) New approaches for prevention and education of alcoholism among Hispanic women. Regalado, Rose, p.11-14; d) Program planning for Hispanic women: One ideal model. Castro, Laura, p.15-18; e) Commonalities among female alcoholics. Hudson, Ann and Lovinfosse, Lee, p.21-27; f) Feminist therapy with female alcoholics. Valverde, Lucia, p.29-44; g) Structural family therapy: The Sanchez family. Taylor, Nancy, p.45-55.

55. Child Pornography and Sex Rings. Burgess, Ann Wolbert and Clark, Marieanne Lindeqvist, ed. Lexington, MA: LexingtonBooks, 1984.
a) Child pornography in the 1970s. Beranbaum, Tina M., et al., p.7-23; b) Scope of the problem: Investigation and prosecution. Belanger, Albert J., et al., p.25-50; c) Typology of sex rings exploiting children. Belanger, Albert J., et al., p.51-81; d) Collectors. Lanning, Kenneth V., p.83-92; e) Typology of collectors. Burgess, Ann W., Hartman, Carol R. and Lanning, Kenneth V., p.93-109; f) Impact of child pornography and sex rings on child victims and their families. Burgess, Ann W., et al., p.111-126; g) Youth prostitution. Janus, Mark-David, Price, Virginia and Scanlon, Barbara, p.127-146; h) The role of community health centers. Knuckman, Paul, p.149-161; i) Victim advocacy as therapy. Dill, David L., p.163-176; j) Treatment issues with children involved in pornography and sex rings. Burgess, Ann W., Hartman, Carol R. and Powers, Patricia, p.177-185; k) Combating child pornography and prostitution: One county's approach. Rabun Jr., John B., p.187-200; l) Appendix A: Legal resources on sexual exploitation of children. Davidson, Howard A., p.201-204; m) Appendix B: Review of legal cases regarding US Code, Section 1461 (mailing obscene or crime-inciting matter). Similes, Kurt, p.205-212; n) Appendix C: Cases related to obscenity issues. Davidson, Howard A., p.213-214; o) Appendix D: Fighting adult entertainment centers at the grassroots level. Hawkins, Patricia A., p.215.

56. Childbirth: Alternatives to Medical Control. Romalis, Shelly, ed. Austin, TX: University of Texas Press, 1981.
a) Having a baby: A story essay. Bromberg, Joann, p.33-62; b) Natural childbirth and the reluctant physician. Romalis, Shelly, p.63-91; c) Taking care of the little woman: Father-physician relations during pregnancy and childbirth. Romalis, Coleman, p.92-121; d) The deliverers: A woman doctor's reflections on medical socialization. Carver, Cynthia, p.122-144; e) Awake and aware, or

false consciousness: The cooption of childbirth reform in America. Rothman, Barbara Katz, p.150-180; f) Studying childbirth: The experience and methods of a woman anthropologist. Jordan, Brigitte, p.181-216; g) Alternative maternity care: Resistance and change. Lubic, Ruth Watson, p.217-249.

57. Childhood Sexual Learning: The Unwritten Curriculum. Roberts, Elizabeth J., ed. Cambridge, MA: Ballinger Publishing Co., 1980.
a) Dimensions of sexual learning in childhood. Roberts, Elizabeth J., p.1-15; b) Toward an understanding of sexual learning and communication: An examination of social learning theory and nonschool learning environments. Kahn, Janet and Kline, David, p.17-66; c) Work, the family, and children's sexual learning. Greenblat, Cathy Stein, p.67-112; d) Television as a sphere of influence on the child's learning about sexuality. Bell, Norma and Himmelweit, Hilde T., p.113-137; e) Sexual learning in the elementary school. Carrera, Michael, p.139-159; f) Peer communication and sexuality. Rogers, Everett M. and Strover, Sharon L., p.161-183; g) Social services and sexual learning. Bane, Mary Jo and Holt, Steven A., p.185-212; h) Religion and sexual learning of children. Collins, Sheila, p.213-242; i) Human sexuality: Messages in public environments. Ladd, Florence C., p.243-257; j) Sexuality and social policy: The unwritten curriculum. Roberts, Elizabeth J., p.259-278.

58. Chinese Women in Southeast Asia. Lebra, Joyce and Paulson, Joy, eds. Singapore: Times Books International, 1980.
a) Immigration to Southeast Asia. Lebra, Joyce, p.1-31; b) Prostitution. Jackson, Laura, p.32-65; c) Bazaar and service occupations. Lebra, Joyce, p.66-96; d) Housewives. Kail, Andreé, p.97-131; e) Women in education. Ward, Shirley, p.132-154; f) Women in modern occupations. Paulson, Joy, p.155-184; g) Women in medicine. Dilatush, Lois, p.185-212; h) Family planning and population policies. Dilatush, Lois, p.213-230.

59. Christian Feminism: Visions of a New Humanity. Weidman, Judith L., ed. San Francisco: Harper & Row, 1984.
a) Feminist theology and spirituality. Ruether, Rosemary Radford, p.9-32; b) Emerging issues in feminist biblical interpretation. Fiorenza, Elisabeth Schüssler, p.33-54; c) The feminist redemption of Christ. Brock, Rita Nakashima, p.55-74; d) Women and ministry: Problem or possibility? Russell, Letty M., p.75-92; e) American women and life-style change. Roberts, Nanette M., p.95-116; f) Liberating work. Fischer, Clare B., p.117-140; g) Human sexuality and mutuality. Harrison, Beverly Wildung, p.141-157; h) Re-membering: A global perspective on women. Parvey, Constance F., p.158-179.

60. Class, Race, and Sex: The Dynamics of Control. Swerdlow, Amy and Lessinger, Hanna, eds. Boston, MA: G. K. Hall, 1983.
a) Notes toward a feminist dialectic. Bridenthal, Renate,

p.3-9; b) Male vice and female virtue: Feminism and the politics of prostitution in nineteenth-century Britain. Walkowitz, Judith R., p.10-30; c) The feminist theology of the black Baptist church, 1880-1900. Brooks, Evelyn, p.31-59; d) Crisis, reaction, and resistance: Women in Germany in the 1920's and 1930's. Grossmann, Atina, p.60-74; e) The social enforcement of heterosexuality and lesbian resistance in the 1920's. Duggan, Lisa, p.75-92; f) The twenties' backlash: Compulsory heterosexuality, the consumer family, and the waning of feminism. Rapp, Rayna and Ross, Ellen, p.93-110; g) Antifeminism and the New Right. Eisenstein, Zillah, p.111-125; h) Feminism, the family, and the New Right. Rosenberg, Jan, p.126-137; i) The New Right and the abortion issue. Desposito, Lisa, p.138-153; j) Difference and domination in the women's movement: The dialectic of theory and practice. Hartsock, Nancy, p.157-172; k) "On the hem of life": Race, class, and the prospects for sisterhood. Dill, Bonnie Thornton, p.173-188; l) Black family life-styles: A lesson in survival. Boyd-Franklin, Nancy, p.189-199; m) Laid bare by the system: Work and survival for black and Hispanic women. Higginbotham, Elizabeth, p.200-215; n) Issues of race and class in women's studies: A Puerto Rican woman's thoughts. Jorge, Angela, p.216-220; o) Reproduction and class divisions among women. Petchesky, Rosalind Pollack, p.221-242; p) Women's role in economic development: Practical and theoretical implications of class and gender inequalities. Beneria, Lourdes and Sen, Gita, p.243-259; q) Defining and combating sexual harassment. Taub, Nadine, p.263-275; r) Women on welfare: Public policy and institutional racism. Valentine, Bettylou, p.276-287; s) From slavery to social welfare: Racism and the control of black women. Gilkes, Cheryl Townsend, p.288-300; t) Religion as an instrument of social control. Quaglio, Francine, p.301-307; u) Women, media, and the dialectics of resistance. Robinson, Lillian S., p.308-324; v) The challenge of profamily politics: A feminist defense of sexual freedom. Willis, Ellen, p.325-338.

61. Clio Was a Woman: Studies in the History of American Women. Deutrich, Mabel E. and Purdy, Virginia C., eds. Washington, D.C.: Howard University Press, 1980. a) What we wish we knew about women: A dialog. Chafe, William H. and Scott, Anne F., p.3-14; b) An abundance of riches: The women's history sources survey. Hinding, Andrea, p.23-29; c) National Archives resources for research in the history of American women. Purdy, Virginia C., p.31-44; d) Black women in pre-federal America. Gregory, Chester W., p.53-70; e) Women in the American revolution: Vignettes or profiles? Chalou, George C., p.73-90; f) Women, civilization, and the Indian question. Young, Mary E., p.98-110; g) Women and radical reform in antebellum upstate New York: A profile of grassroots female abolitionists. Wellman, Judith, p.113-127; h) The Woman's Land Army, World War I. Martelet, Penny, p.136-146; i) Mary McLeod Bethune and the National Youth Administration. Smith, Elaine M., p.149-177; j) Darkness before the dawn: The status of women in the Depression years. Hargreaves,

Mary W. M., p.178-188; k) Women in the military service. Hartmann, Susan M., p.195-205; l) Women in the civilian labor force. Straub, Eleanor F., p.206-226; m) Edith Bolling Wilson: A documentary view. James, Edith, p.234-240; n) Eleanor Roosevelt's role in women's history. Lash, Joseph P., p.243-253; o) Photographs as historical documents (American women through the camera's eye). Malan, Nancy E., p.260-304; p) Retrospect and prospect. Ryan, Mary P., p.307-319.

62. Co-education Reconsidered. Deem, Rosemary, ed. Milton Keynes, England: Open University Press, 1984. a) Introduction: Co-education reconsidered - reviving the debate. Deem, Rosemary, p.xi-xx; b) Co-education: Perspectives and debates in the early twentieth century. Brehony, Kevin, p.1-20; c) The politics of single-sex schools. Shaw, Jennifer, p.21-36; d) How shall we educate our sons? Arnot, Madeleine, p.37-55; e) The realities of mixed schooling. Stantonbury Campus Sexism in Education Group, Bridgewater Hall School, p.57-73; f) Single-sex setting. Smith, Stuart, p.75-88; g) Conclusion: Co-education, equal educational opportunity and change. Deem, Rosemary, p.89-94.

63. Coed Prison. Smykla, John Ortiz, ed. New York: Human Sciences Press, 1980. a) The sexually integrated prison: A legal and policy evaluation. Ruback, Barry, p.33-60; b) Characteristics of co-correctional institutions. Ross, James, et al., p.61-82; c) Co-corrections - FCI Forth Worth after three years. Campbell, Charles F., p.83-109; d) A coed prison. Heffernan, Esther and Krippel, Elizabeth, p.110-119; e) A study of a coeducational correctional facility. Almy, Linda, et al., p.120-149; f) Styles of doing time in a coed prison: Masculine and feminine alternatives. Wilson, Nanci Koser, p.150-171; g) Problems with research in co-corrections. Smykla, John Ortiz, p.172-180; h) The development of a scale to assess inmate and staff attitudes toward co-corrections. Cavior, Helene Enid and Cohen, Stanley H., p.181-202; i) Co-correctional models. Ross, James, et al., p.203-220; j) Sex-role differentiation in a co-correctional setting. Lambiotte, Joellen, p.221-247; k) Women in a coed joint. Heffernan, Esther and Ross, James G., p.248-261; l) Two losers don't make a winner: The case against the co-correctional institution. Crawford, Jacqueline K., p.262-268; m) The ERA and coed prisons. Arditi, Ralph R., et al., p.269-272.

64. Colette: The Woman, the Writer. Eisinger, Erica Mendelson and McCarty, Mari Ward, eds. University Park, PA: Pennsylvania State University Press, 1981. a) A womanly vocation. Mallet-Joris, Françoise (author), Gibbard, Eleanor Reid (translator), p.7-15; b) The first steps in a writer's career. Sarde, Michèle Blin, p.16-21; c) Colette and the enterprise of writing: A reappraisal. Ketchum, Anne Duhamel, p.22-31; d) Colette and the art of survival. Whatley, Janet, p.32-39; e) Colette and the epistolary novel. Stewart, Joan Hinde, p.43-53; f) The relationship between meaning and structure in Colette's *Rain-moon*. Norell, Donna, p.54-66; g) A typology of

women in Colette's novels. Romanowski, Sylvie, p.66-74; h) The test of love and nature: Colette and lesbians. Stockinger, Jacob, p.75-94; i) *The Vagabond*: A vision of androgyny. Eisinger, Erica, p.95-103; j) Colette and art nouveau. Dehon, Claire, p.104-115; k) Colette and Ravel: The enchantress and the illusionist. Crosland, Margaret, p.116-124; l) The theatre as literary model: Role-playing in *Chéri* and *The Last of Chéri*. McCarty, Mari, p.125-134; m) Writing, language, and the body. Resch, Yannick, p.137-149; n) Polymorphemic perversity: Colette's illusory "real". Relyea, Suzanne, p.150-163; o) The anamnesis of a female "I": In the margins of self-portrayal. Miller, Nancy K., p.164-175; p) Image structure, codes, and recoding in *The Pure and the Impure*. Cothran, Ann and Crowder, Diane, p.176-184; q) Colette and signs: A partial reading of a writer "born *not* to write". Makward, Christiane, p.185-192.

65. Comparable Worth and Wage Discrimination: Technical Possibilities and Political Realities. Remick, Helen, ed. Philadelphia, PA: Temple University Press, 1984.
a) "A want of harmony": Perspectives on wage discrimination and comparable worth. Steinberg, Ronnie J., p.3-27; b) Socioeconomic explanations of job segregation. England, Paula, p.28-46; c) Some psychological factors affecting job segregation and wages. Shepela, Sharon Toffey and Viviano, Ann T., p.47-58; d) Some problems with contemporary job evaluation systems. Beatty, James R. and Beatty, Richard W., p.59-78; e) Effect of choice of factors and factor weights in job evaluation. Treiman, Donald J., p.79-89; f) Dilemmas of implementation: The case of nursing. Remick, Helen, p.90-98; g) Major issues in *a priori* applications. Remick, Helen, p.99-117; h) A policy-capturing application in a union setting. Johannesson, Russell, Koziara, Karen Shallcross and Pierson, David, p.118-137; i) Assessing pay discrimination using national data. Hartmann, Heidi I., Roos, Patricia A. and Treiman, Donald J., p.137-154; j) Economic models as a means of calculating legal compensation claims. Bergmann, Barbara R. and Gray, Mary W., p.155-172; k) Canada's equal pay for work of equal value law. Cadieux, Rita, p.173-196; l) A review of federal court decisions under Title VII of the Civil Rights Act of 1964. Heen, Mary, p.197-219; m) The role of labor. Grune, Joy Ann, Johnson, Eve and Portman, Lisa, p.219-237; n) Comparable worth under various federal and state laws. Boone, Carroll, Dean, Virginia and Roberts, Patti, p.238-266; o) Developments in selected states. Cook, Alice H., p.267-283; p) Technical possibilities and political realities: Concluding remarks. Remick, Helen and Steinberg, Ronnie J., p.285-302.

66. Comparable Worth: Issues and Alternatives. Livernash, E. Robert, ed. Washington, DC: Equal Employment Adivsory Council, 1980.
a) The emerging debate. Milkovich, George T., p.23-47; b) Job evaluation and pay setting: Concepts and practices. Schwab, Donald P., p.49-77; c) The market system. Hildebrand, George, p.79-106; d) Wage setting and collective bargaining. Northrup, Herbert R., p.107-136; e) A

foreign perspective. Bellace, Janice R., p.137-173; f) Statistical biases in the measurement of employment discrimination. Roberts, Harry V., p.173-195; g) The legal framework. McDowell, Douglas S. and Williams, Robert E., p.197-249.

67. Comparable Worth: Issues and Alternatives (2nd edition). Livernash, E. Robert, ed. Washington, D.C.: Equal Employment Advisory Council, 1984.
a) The emerging debate. Milkovich, George T., p.23-47; b) Job evaluation and pay setting: Concepts and practices. Schwab, Donald P., p.49-77; c) The market system. Hildebrand, George, p.79-106; d) Wage setting and collective bargaining. Northrup, Herbert R., p.107-136; e) A foreign perspective. Bellace, Janice R., p.137-172; f) Statistical biases in the measurement of employment discrimination. Roberts, Harry V., p.173-195; g) The legal framework. Bagby, Thomas R. and Williams, Robert E., p.197-266; h) An analysis of the National Academy of Sciences' comparable worth study. McDowell, Douglas S., p.267-288.

68. Comparative Perspectives of Third World Women: The Impact of Race, Sex, and Class. Lindsay, Beverly, ed. New York: Praeger, 1980.
a) Perspectives of third world women: An introduction. Lindsay, Beverly, p.1-22; b) Introduction: Women in developing countries. Lindsay, Beverly, p.25-30; c) African women and national development. Lewis, Shelby, p.31-54; d) Women in Zaire: Disparate status and roles. Adams, Lois, p.55-77; e) Issues confronting professional African women: Illustrations from Kenya. Lindsay, Beverly, p.78-95; f) Chinese women: The relative influences of ideological revolution, economic growth, and cultural change. Wang, Bee-Lan Chan, p.96-122; g) Up from the harem? The effects of class and sex on political life in northern India. Devon, Tonia K., p.123-142; h) Caribbean women: The impact of race, sex, and class. Joseph, Gloria I., p.143-161; i) Women in Cuba: The revolution within the revolution. Cole, Johnnetta B., p.162-178; j) Ancient song, new melody in Latin America: Women and film. Wieser, Nora Jasquez, p.179-199; k) Introduction: Minority women in the United States. Lindsay, Beverly, p.203-205; l) Native American women: Twilight of a long maidenhood. Wittstock, Laura Waterman, p.207-228; m) La chicana: Guadalupe or malinche. Gonzales, Sylvia A., p.229-250; n) The black woman: Liberated or oppressed? Puryear, Gwendolyn Randall, p.251-275; o) The schooling of Vietnamese immigrants: Internal colonialism and its impact on women. Kelly, Gail P., p.276-296; p) Third world women and social reality: A conclusion. Lindsay, Beverly, p.297-310.

69. Concepts of Femininity and the Life Cycle. Nadelson, Carol C. and Notman, Malkah T., eds. New York: Plenum Press, 1982.
a) Feminine development: Changes in psychoanalytic theory. Notman, Malkah, p.3-29; b) Changing views of the relationship between femininity and reproduction.

Nadelson, Carol and Notman, Malkah, p.31-42; c) Changing sex stereotypes. Zinberg, Norman E., p.43-75; d) The black woman growing up. Zimmerman, Veva H., p.77-92; e) The early mother-child relationship: A developmental view of woman as mother. Brazelton, T. Berry and Keefer, Constance H., p.95-109; f) To marry or not to marry. Nadelson, Carol and Notman, Malkah, p.111-120; g) Maternal work and children. Nadelson, Carol and Notman, Malkah, p.121-133; h) Midlife concerns of women: Implications of menopause. Notman, Malkah, p.135-144; i) Marriage and midlife: The impact of social change. Mathews, Mary Alice, Nadelson, Carol and Polonsky, Derek C., p.145-158; j) Separation: A family developmental process of midlife. Zilbach, Joan J., p.159-167; k) Women and aging. Edinburg, Golda M., p.169-194.

70. Conference on the Educational and Occupational Needs of American Indian Women. (Wu, Rosalind), ed. Washington, DC: National Institute of Education, 1980.
a) Insignificance of humanity, "Man is tampering with the moon and the stars": The employment status of American Indian women. Whiteman, Henrietta V., p.37-61; b) Current educational status of American Indian girls. Scheirbeck, Helen Maynor, p.63-81; c) The status of American Indian women in higher education. Kidwell, Clara Sue, p.83-121; d) Organizing American Indian women. Blanchard, Evelyn Lance, p.123-140; e) The interaction of culture and sex roles in the schools. Medicine, Beatrice, p.141-158; f) Health problems facing American Indian women. Wood, Rosemary, p.159-183; g) American Indian children: Foster care and adoptions. Walker, Tillie, p.185-209; h) Indian boarding schools and Indian women: Blessing or curse? Attneave, Carolyn L. and Dill, Agnes, p.211-230; i) Relevancy of tribal interests and tribal diversity in determining the educational needs of American Indians. Keshena, Rita, p.231-250; j) Transition from the reservation to an urban setting and the changing roles of American Indian women. Williams, Agnes F., p.251-284; k) American Indian women: Their relationship to the federal government. Hunt, JoJo, p.293-312.

71. Conference on the Educational and Occupational Needs of Asian-Pacific-American Women. (Wu, Rosalind), ed. Washington, DC: National Institute of Education, 1980.
a) Keynote address. Lott, Juanita Tamayo, p.7-16; b) Some effects of childrearing practices on the value systems of Asian-American women. Nievera, Fe C., p.39-64; c) Mental health issues among Asian-American women. Homma-True, Reiko, p.65-87; d) Impediments to Asian-Pacific-American women organizing. Wong, Germaine Q., p.89-103; e) Asian women in professional health schools, with emphasis on nursing. Loo, Fe V., p.105-133; f) Educational alternatives for Asian-Pacific women. Cordova, Dorothy L., p.135-156; g) Chairperson's report. Nishi, Setsuko Matsunaga, p.160-180; h) Immigration of Asian women and the status of recent Asian women immigrants. Pian, Canta, p.181-209; i) The effects of Asian-American kinship systems on women's educational

and occupational attainment. Osako, Masako Murakami, p.211-236; j) The early socialization of Asian-American female children. Cheong, Jacqueline Leong and Fillmore, Lily Wong, p.237-253; k) Economic and employment status of Asian-Pacific women. Cabezas, Amado Y. and Fong, Pauline L., p.255-321; l) Social mobility of Asian women in America: A critical review. Hirata, Lucie Cheng, p.323-341; m) Elderly Pacific Island and Asian-American women: A framework for understanding. Fujii, Sharon M., p.343-357; n) Asian wives of U.S. servicemen: Women in triple jeopardy. Kim, Bok-Lim C., p.359-379.

72. Conference on the Educational and Occupational Needs of Hispanic Women. (Wu, Rosalind), ed. Washington, DC: National Institute of Education, 1980.
a) The lack of political involvement of Hispanic women as it relates to their educational background and occupational opportunities. Barragán, Polly Baca, p.39-45; b) Puerto Rican women in education and potential impact on occupational patterns. Correa, Gladys, p.47-63; c) The cult of virginity. García, Frieda, p.65-73; d) Latinas in educational leadership: Chicago, Illinois. Mulcahy, Elena Berezaluce, p.75-86; e) Puerto Rican women in higher education in the United States. Martínez, Margaret and Nieves, Josephine, p.87-115; f) Impediments to Hispanic women organizing. Shepro, Theresa Aragón, p.117-137; g) Guidance and counseling of Spanish-background girls. Ayala-Vázquez, Nancy, p.155-174; h) Hispanic women move forward - Out of a marginal status. Bithorn, María Angélica, p.167-178; i) Chicana evolution (poem). Gonzales, Sylvia, p.179-185; j) La Chicana: An overview. Gonzales, Sylvia, p.186-212; k) Social issues confronting Hispanic-American women. Jiménez-Vázquez, Rosa, p.213-249; l) Chicana identity: Interaction of culture and sex roles. Nieto, Consuelo, p.251-276; m) The need for an anthropological and cognitive approach to the education of Hispanic women. Viera, Silvia, p.277-289.

73. Conference on the Educational and Occupational Needs of White Ethnic Women. (Wu, Rosalind), ed. Washington, DC: National Institute of Education, 1980.
a) Ethnic women and the media. Noschese, Christine, p.41-51; b) Organizing neighborhood women for political and social action. Lowry, I. Elaine, p.55-62; c) Developing a neighborhood-based health facility. Wilson, Elaine, p.63-67; d) The Museo Italo Americano: My involvement with the Italian American community in San Francisco. Nardelli-Haight, Giuliana and Scherini, Rose, p.68-75; e) The status of East European women in the family: Tradition and change. Krickus, Mary Ann, p.76-100; f) The role of learning in the lives of Finnish and other ethnic women and a proposal for self-education. Lee, Sirkka Tuomi, p.101-114; g) Changing needs of ethnic women in higher education. Scanlon, Laura Polla, p.115-128; h) The economic struggles of female factory workers: A comparison of French, Polish, and Portuguese immigrants. Lamphere, Louise, et al., p.129-152; i) Irish, Italian, and Jewish women at the grassroots level: A historical and sociological perspective. McCourt, Kathleen, p.153-179; j) Family roles and identities of Scandinavian and German

women. Woehrer, Carol, p.180-209; k) Achieving the dreams beyond tradition: Counseling white ethnic American girls. Verheyden-Hilliard, Mary Ellen, p.210-231.

74. Contemporary Women Authors of Latin America: Introductory Essays. Meyer, Doris and Fernández Olmos, Margarite, eds. Brooklyn, NY: Brooklyn College Press, 1983.
a) "Feminine" testimony in the works of Teresa de la Parra, María Luisa Bombal, and Victoria Ocampo. Meyer, Doris, p.3-15; b) Success and the Latin American writer. Dauster, Frank, p.16-21; c) Rosario Castellanos and the structures of power. Anderson, Helene M., p.22-32; d) Affirmation and resistance: Women poets from the Caribbean. Waldman, Gloria Feiman, p.33-57; e) The paradoxes of Silvina Bullrich. Frouman-Smith, Erica, p.58-71; f) Elena Poniatowska: Witness for the people. Starcevic, Elizabeth, p.72-77; g) From a woman's perspective: The short stories of Rosario Ferré and Ana Lydia Vega. Fernández Olmos, Margarite, p.78-90; h) A woman and her poems (essay). Cuza Malé, Belkis, p.93-95; i) The word, that milk cow (essay). Valenzuela, Luisa, p.96-97; j) The arc of paradox (essay). Pizarro, Agueda, p.98-101.

75. Country Papers on Career Services for Women in Asia. Shipstone, Norah, ed. Lucknow, India: Asian Women's Institute, 1980.
a) Women's employment in Japan. Muramatsu, Yasuko and Oda, Yukiko, p.1-26; b) Employment of Korean women. Chung, Jinyoung, p.27-36; c) Working women in Korea. Cho, Hyoung and Kim, Yung-Chung, p.37-54; d) Career counselling for poor rural and urban women of South India. Phanuel, Mirabai, p.55-65; e) Working women in India. Dass, Tehrim and Wallace, Irene, p.66-82; f) Career and employment of women in Pakistan. Singha, Santosh, p.83-106; g) Current status of employment of women in Lebanon. Richards, Evelyn L., p.107-121.

76. A Creative Tension: Key Issues of Socialist-Feminism. Meulenbelt, Anja, et al. eds. Boston, MA: South End Press, 1984.
a) The women's movement and motherhood. Sevenhuijsen, Selma and Vries, Petra de, p.9-25; b) Domestic and public. Mossink, Marijke, p.26-42; c) The dual heritage. Outshoorn, Joyce, p.43-59; d) Feminism and psychoanalysis. Komter, Aafke, p.60-84; e) 'The policing of families'. Sevenhuijsen, Selma and Withuis, Jolande, p.85-102; f) Women's struggles in the third world. Hoogenboom, Annemiek and Voets, Annemieke, p.103-129.

77. Creative Women in Changing Societies: A Quest for Alternatives. Stokland, Torill, Vajrathon, Mallica and Nicol, Davidson, eds. Dobbs Ferry, NY: Transnational Publishers, 1982.
a) Creative women in political change. Mutukwa, Gladys, p.21-29; b) Creative women in economic and social change. Vajrathon, Mallica, p.31-37; c) Creative women in

scientific-technological and medical change. Pfafflin, Sheila M., p.39-49; d) Creative women in artistic and literary change. Boone, Sylvia Ardyn, p.51-55; e) An eclectic workshop. Konie, Gwendoline, p.57-65.

78. The Criminal Justice System and Women: Women Offenders, Victims, Workers. Price, Barbara Raffel and Sokoloff, Natalie J., eds. New York: Clark Boardman Co., 1982.
a) The criminal law and women. Price, Barbara Raffel and Sokoloff, Natalie J., p.9-33; b) The etiology of female crime: A review of the literature. Klein, Dorie p.35-60; c) Females under the law: 'Protected' but unequal. Armstrong, Gail, p.61-75; d) Guilty by reason of sex: Young women and the juvenile justice system. Chesney-Lind, Meda, p.77-103; e) The new female offender: Reality or myth? Smart, Carol, p.105-116; f) Trends in female crime: It's still a man's world. Steffensmeier, Darrell J., p.117-129; g) Sex role stereotypes and justice for women. Feinman, Clarice, p.131-139; h) National study of women's correctional programs. Glick, Ruth M. and Neto, Virginia V., p.141-154; i) You can't be a mother and be in prison...can you? Impacts of the mother-child separation. Baunach, Phyllis Jo, p.155-169; j) Women prisoners and the law: Which way will the pendulum swing? Alpert, Geoffrey P., p.171-182; k) Violence against women: Some considerations regarding its causes and eliminations. Klein, Dorie, p.203-221; l) Rape: The all-American crime. Griffin, Susan, p.223-239; m) Forcible rape: Institutionalized sexism in the criminal justice system. Robin, Gerald D., p.241-261; n) Battered women: Society's problem. Martin, Del, p.263-290; o) The prostitute as victim. James, Jennifer, p.291-315; p) Concurrent and consecutive abuse: The juvenile prostitute. Bracey, Dorothy H., p.317-322; q) Incest: Whose reality, whose theory?. Butler, Sandra, p.323-333; r) Pornography and repression: A reconsideration. Diamond, Irene, p.335-351; s) Sexual harassment: The experience. MacKinnon, Catharine A., p.353-367; t) A sexist selection process keeps qualified women off the bench. Ness, Susan, p.379-383; u) Women in a male-dominated profession: The women lawyers. Engelberg, Laurie and Patterson, Michelle, p.385-397; v) A century of women in policing. Gavin, Susan and Price, Barbara Raffel, p.399-412; w) Female patrol officers: A review of the physical capability issue. Townsey, Roi D., p.413-425; x) Why two women cops were convicted of cowardice. Dreifus, Claudia, p.427-435; y) Doing time with the boys: An analysis of women correctional officers in all-male facilities. Petersen, Cheryl Bowser, p.437-460; z) Marxist feminism: Implications for criminal justice. Natalizia, Elena M. and Rafter, Nicole Hahn, p.465-483; aa) Postscript: The future of women and the criminal law. Price, Barbara Raffel and Sokoloff, Natalie J., p.485-490.

79. The Custom-Made Child?: Women-Centered Perspectives. Gross, Michael, Holmes, Helen B. and Hoskins, Betty B., eds. Clifton, NJ: Humana Press, 1981.
a) Reproductive technologies: The birth of a women-centered analysis. Holmes, Helen B., p.1-18; b) The

DES controversy: Discovery, distribution and regulation. Bell, Susan E., p.23-28; c) Assessment of risks from DES: An analysis of research on those exposed during pregnancy or in utero. Tilley, Barbara C., p.29-38; d) The legal aspects of the DES case: What can be done. Rozovsky, Fay A., p.39-46; e) DES and drugs in pregnancy: A consumer reaction. Erhart, Robin, p.47-50; f) DES: Ten points of controversy. Holtzman, Joan Hirsch, p.51-55; g) DES discussion. Davis, Anne J. (moderator), p.57-61; h) A look at prenatal diagnosis within the context of changing parental and reproductive norms. Kenen, Regina H., p.67-73; i) Prenatal diagnosis. Ampola, Mary G., p.75-80; j) Antenatal diagnosis: The physician-patient relationship. Locke, Elaine, p.81-87; k) Policy decisions in prenatal diagnosis: The example of fetal alcoholism syndrome. Abramson, Fredric D., p.89-93; l) The politics of prenatal diagnosis: A feminist ethical analysis. Peterson, Susan Rae, p.95-104; m) Prenatal diagnosis discussion. Major, Gerene D. (moderator), p.105-115; n) Neonatology: Directions and goals. Edwards, Maureen, p.123-127; o) Perfectibility and the neonate: The burden of expectations on mothers and their health providers. Carlton, Wendy, p.129-133; p) Decisions about handicapped newborns: Values and procedures. Axelsen, Diana E., p.135-144; q) Response. Whitbeck, Caroline, p.145-146; r) Rights of a handicapped neonate: What every parent and professional should know. Bendix, Helga M., p.147-154; s) Living with an impaired neonate and child: A feminist issue. Lapham, E. Virginia Sheppard, p.155-164; t) Neonate discussion. Musemeche, Catherine A. (moderator), p.165-174; u) Technical aspects of sex preselection. Nentwig, M. Ruth, p.181-186; v) Futuristic implications of sex preselection. Steinbacher, Roberta, p.187-191; w) Unnatural selection: On choosing children's sex. Powledge, Tabitha M., p.193-199; x) Response. Mathis, Martha, p.201-203; y) Response. Connors, Denise, p.205-207; z) Sex preselection: A response. Raymond, Janice G., p.209-212; aa) Sex preselection: Discussion moderator's remarks. Culpepper, Emily Erwin (moderator), p.213-214; bb) Sex preselection discussion. Culpepper, Emily Erwin (moderator); p.215-224; cc) Biological manipulations for producing and nurturing mammalian embryos. Herlands, Rosalind L., p.231-240; dd) Ethics and reproductive technology. Salladay, Susan Anthony, p.241-248; ee) Response. Mayrand, Theresa, p.249-251; ff) Manipulative reproductive technologies discussion: Part I. Hoskins, Betty B. (moderator), p.253-257; gg) The case against in vitro fertilization and implantation. Hubbard, Ruth, p.259-262; hh) In defense of in vitro fertilization. Menning, Barbara, p.263-267; ii) In vitro fertilization and embryo transfer: The process of making public policy. Murray, Robert F., p.269-274; jj) Manipulative reproductive technologies discussion: Part II. Hoskins, Betty B. (moderator), p.275-280; kk) The biology of utopia: Science fiction perspectives on ectogenesis. Livingston, Dennis, p.281-289; ll) Ectogenesis and ideology. Logan, Rebecca L., p.291-293; mm) Manipulative reproductive technologies discussion: Part III. Hoskins, Betty B. (moderator), p.295-300; nn)

Reflections: Uncovering patriarchal agendas and exploring woman-oriented values. Culpepper, Emily Erwin, p.301-310.

80. Day Care: Scientific and Social Policy Issues. Zigler, Edward F. and Gordon, Edmund W., eds. Boston, MA: Auburn House, 1982.
a) Social-emotional consequences of day care for preschool children. Rutter, Michael, p.3-32; b) Infant day care: Relationships between theory and practice. Provence, Sally, p.33-55; c) Changing aspects of the family: A psychoanalytic perspective on early intervention. Siegler, Ava L., p.56-71; d) Janus faces day care: Perspectives on quality and cost. Ruopp, Richard R. and Travers, Jeffrey, p.72-101; e) Developmental consequences of out-of-home care for infants in a low-income population. Byron, Egeland and Farber, Ellen A., p.102-125; f) Environmental differences among day care centers and their effects on children's development. McCartney, Kathleen, et al., p.126-151; g) Day care and children's responsiveness to adults. Robertson, Anne, p.152-173; h) Parents and day care workers: A failed partnership? Turner, Pauline and Zigler, Edward F., p.174-182; i) The Yale Child Welfare Research Program: Description and results. Naylor, Audrey, Provence, Sally and Rescorla, Leslie A., p.183-199; j) A five-year follow-up of participants in the Yale Child Welfare Research Program. Trickett, Penelope K., et al., p.200-222; k) The problem of infant day care. Frye, Douglas, p.223-242; l) A methodological comment on "The problem of infant day care". Seitz, Victoria, p.243-251; m) Families, children, and child care. Hatch, Orrin G., p.255-259; n) Child care - A commitment to be honored. Kennedy, Edward M., p.260-263; o) The politics of federal day care regulation. Nelson, John R., p.267-306; p) Beyond the stalemate in child care public policy. Beck, Rochelle, p.307-337; q) The battle for day care in America: A view from the trenches. Goodman, Jody and Zigler, Edward F., p.338-350; r) The dilemma of affordable child care. Winget, W. Gary, p.351-377; s) The prospects and dilemmas of child care information and referral. Levine, James A., p.378-401; t) Considering proprietary child care. Glennon, Theresa and Kagan, Sharon L., p.402-412; u) Day care: A black perspective. Moore, Evelyn, p.413-444; v) Health care services for children in day care programs. Janis, Juel M. and Richmond, Julius B., p.445-456; w) School-age child care. School-Age Child Care Project, p.457-475; x) Day care and early childhood education. Almy, Millie, p.476-496.

81. Decades of Discontent: The Women's Movement, 1920-1940. Scharf, Lois and Jensen, Joan M., eds. Westport, CT: Greenwood, 1983.
a) The new woman: Changing views of women in the 1920s. Freedman, Estelle B., p.21-42; b) The economics of middle-income family life: Working women during the Great Depression. Wandersee, Winifred D., p.45-58; c) Chicanas and Mexican immigrant families 1920-1940: Women's subordination and family exploitation. González, Rosalinda M., p.59-84; d) Flawed victories: The experiences of black and white women workers in

Durham during the 1930s. Janiewski, Dolores, p.85-109;
e) The projection of a new womanhood: The movie moderns in the 1920's. Ryan, Mary P., p.113-130; f) Culture
and radical politics: Yiddish women writers in America,
1890-1940. Pratt, Norma Fain, p.131-152; g)
Photographing women: The Farm Security
Administration work of Marion Post Wolcott. Boddy,
Julie, p.153-176; h) Two washes in the morning and a
bridge party at night: The American housewife between
the wars. Cowan, Ruth Schwartz, p.177-196; i) All pink
sisters: The War Department and the feminist movement
in the 1920s. Jensen, Joan M., p.199-221; j) International
feminism between the wars: The National Woman's Party
versus the League of Women Voters. Becker, Susan,
p.223-242; k) "The forgotten woman": Working women,
the New Deal, and women's organizations. Scharf, Lois,
p.243-259; l) Discontented black feminists: Prelude and
postscript to the passage of the nineteenth amendment.
Terborg-Penn, Rosalyn, p.261-279; m) Socialist feminism
between the two World Wars: Insights from oral history.
Gluck, Sherna, p.279-297.

82. Developing Nations: Challenges Involving Women.
Stoecker, Barbara J., Montgomery, Evelyn I. and Gott, S.
Edna, eds. Lubbock, TX: International Center for Arid
and Semi-Arid Land Studies, Texas Tech University, 1982.
a) Critical issues in women in development. Youssef,
Nadia, p.5-14; b) AID and women in development.
Cloud, Kathleen, p.15-22; c) Participation through Title
XII, consortia, and the project process in AID. Matlock,
Gerald and Staudt, Kathleen, p.23-36; d) AID: Promise
and performance. Staudt, Kathleen, p.37-47; e) The
development process: A holistic approach. Thomas,
Gerald W., p.51-66; f) Appropriate technology. Anson,
Cynthia and Hill, Frances, p.67-80; g) Nutrition and
health. Lamb, Neven P. and Smith, Betty Jo, p.81-94; h)
Income-generating projects. Urdaneta, Maria-Luisa,
p.95-100; i) Agriculture, forestry, conservation and
women. Hoskins, Marilyn W., p.101-104; j) Livestock and
range management. Albin, Robert C., Bryant, Fred C.
and Henderson, Helen K., p.105-115; k) Land tenure and
cooperatives: Origin, development and persistence of
Navajo matrifocality in subsistence, production, exchange
and tenure. Campbell, Robert G., p.117-121; l) Tenure
and the role of the female. Mathia, Gene A., p.121-126;
m) Participation by women in Guatemalan cooperatives.
Elbow, Gary S., p.126-133; n) Dynamics of social and cultural change. Schoepf, Brooke, p.137-153; o) Women's
roles and culturally sensitive programs. Morrissey,
Marietta (moderator), et al., p.155-169; p) Views of
women in international development. Cloud, Kathleen,
p.171-173; q) Issues and alternatives in planning projects
for women. Hoskins, Marilyn W., p.177-181; r)
Curriculum: Preparation for involvement. Bennett,
William F., Vengroff, Linda and Vengroff, Richard, p.183-
200; s) Household structure in Africa. Staudt, Kathleen,
p.201-204; t) The female family business: A Guatemalan
example. Ehlers, Tracy Bachrach, p.205-209; u) NEMOW:
A project that stumbled and why. Dennis, Philip A. and
Montgomery, Evelyn I., p.211-226; v) How your organiza-

tion can participate. Preisinger, Arthur A., p.227-236; w)
Practicalities of participation. Clements, Helen, Dooley,
Fred and Mack, Delores, p.237-248.

83. A Dialogue on Third World Women: Learning through
the Humanities. Washington, D.C.: D.C. Community
Humanities Council, 1984.
a) Science and the status quo. Sacks, Karen Brodkin, p.7-
16; b) Women, art and community in Papua New Guinea.
Foerstel, Lenora, p.17-29; c) Gender, race and class in the
United States: Lessons from third world women.
Mullings, Leith, p.30-47; d) Woman and the international
division of labor. Safa, Helen, p.48-62; e) Working class
Jamaican women: Trade unions and political activity.
Bolles, Lynn, p.63-81; f) Working women in Latin
America. Bunster, Ximena, p.82-92; g) Class conscious-
ness and world view of a Bolivian mining woman. Nash,
June, p.93-104; h) The church, the unions, women and
the opposition in Brazil. Alves, Maria Helena, p.105-121;
i) Racism and sexism: They ain't genetic you know! Cole,
Johnetta, p.122-140.

84. Discovering Reality: Feminist Perspectives on
Epistemology, Metaphysics, Methodology, and
Philosophy of Science. Harding, Sandra and Hintikka,
Merrill B., eds. Dordrecht, Holland: D. Reidel Pub. Co.,
1983.
a) Woman is not a rational animal: On Aristotle's biology
of reproduction. Lange, Lynda, p.1-15; b) Aristotle and
the politicization of the soul. Spelman, Elizabeth V., p.17-
30; c) The unit of political analysis: Our Aristotelian
hangover. Stiehm, Judith Hicks, p.31-43; d) Have only
men evolved? Hubbard, Ruth, p.45-69; e) Evolution and
patriarchal myths of scarcity and competition. Averill,
Mary Beth and Gross, Michael, p.71-95; f) Charlotte
Perkins Gilman: Forerunner of a feminist social science.
Palmeri, Ann, p.97-119; g) The trivialization of the notion
of equality. Marcil-Lacoste, Louise, p.121-137; h) How
can language be sexist? Hintikka, Jaakko and Hintikka,
Merrill B., p.139-148; i) A paradigm of philosophy: The
adversary method. Moulton, Janice, p.149-164; j) The
man of professional wisdom. Addelson, Kathryn Pyne,
p.165-186; k) Gender and science. Keller, Evelyn Fox,
p.187-205; l) The mind's eye. Grontkowski, Christine R.
and Keller, Evelyn Fox, p.207-224; m) Individualism and
the objects of psychology. Scheman, Naomi, p.225-244; n)
Political philosophy and the patriarchal unconscious: A
psychoanalytic perspective on epistemology and metaphysics. Flax, Jane, p.245-281; o) The feminist standpoint:
Developing the ground for a specifically feminist historical materialism. Hartsock, Nancy C. M., p.283-310; p)
Why has the sex/gender system become visible only now?
Harding, Sandra, p.311-324.

85. Doing Feminist Research. Roberts, Helen, ed. London:
Routledge & Kegan Paul, 1981.
a) Women and their doctors: Power and powerlessness in
the research process. Roberts, Helen, p.7-29; b)
Interviewing women: A contradiction in terms. Oakley,
Ann, p.30-61; c) Reminiscences of fieldwork among the

Sikhs. Pettigrew, Joyce, p.62-82; d) Men, masculinity and the process of sociological enquiry. Morgan, David, p.83-113; e) Women in stratification studies. Delphy, Christine, p.114-128; f) Occupational mobility and the use of the comparative method. Llewellyn, Catriona, p.129-158; g) The expert's view? The sociological analysis of graduates' occupational and domestic roles. Chisholm, Lynne and Woodward, Diana, p.159-185; h) The gatekeepers: A feminist critique of academic publishing. Spender, Dale, p.186-202.

86. Double Exposure: Women's Health Hazards on the Job and at Home. Chavkin, Wendy, ed. New York: Monthly Review Press, 1984.
a) The clean, light image of the electronics industry: Miracle or mirage? Baker, Robin and Woodrow, Sharon, p.21-36; b) The risks of healing: The hazards of the nursing profession. Coleman, Linda and Dickinson, Cindy, p.37-56; c) The health hazards of office work. Fleishman, Jane, p.57-69; d) The particular problems of video display terminals. Henifin, Mary Sue, p.69-80; e) Closed office-building syndrome. Chavkin, Wendy, p.81-85; f) Following the harvest: The health hazards of migrant and seasonal farmworking women. Jasso, Sonia and Mazorra, Maria, p.86-99; g) Sexual harassment and women's health. Crull, Peggy, p.100-120; h) Minority women, work, and health. Mullings, Leith, p.121-138; i) Protection for women: Trade unions and labor laws. Kessler-Harris, Alice, p.139-154; j) Mother, father, worker: Men and women and the reproduction risks of work. Hatch, Maureen, p.161-179; k) Keeping women in their place: Exclusionary policies and reproduction. Scott, Judith A., p.180-195; l) Walking a tightrope: Pregnancy, parenting, and work. Chavkin, Wendy, p.196-213; m) The home is the workplace: Hazards, stress, and pollutants in the household. Rosenberg, Harriet G., p.219-245; n) From grassroots activism to political power: Women organizing against environmental hazards. Freudenberg, Nicholas and Zaltzberg, Ellen, p.246-272.

87. Dual-Career Couples. Pepitone-Rockwell, Fran, ed. Beverly Hills, CA: Sage, 1980.
a) Three generations of dual-career family research. Rapoport, Rhona and Rapoport, Robert N., p.23-48; b) Catalytic movements: Civil rights and women. Pepitone-Rockwell, Fran, p.49-53; c) Intellectual development of women. Lynn, David B., p.55-71; d) Young marrieds: Wives' employment and family role structure. Fish, Margaret, Hawkes, Glenn R. and Nicola, JoAnn, p.75-89; e) Dual-career marriages: Benefits and costs. Nadelson, Carol C. and Nadelson, Theodore, p.91-109; f) Spouses' contributions to each other's roles. Barnewolt, Debra, Lopata, Helena Z. and Norr, Kathleen, p.111-141; g) Parenthood, marriage, and careers: Situational constraints and role strain. Johnson, Colleen Leahy and Johnson, Frank A., p.143-161; h) Time management and the dual-career couple. Seiden, Anne E., p.163-189; i) The balancing act: Coping strategies for emerging family lifestyles. Lawe, Barbara and Lawe, Charles, p.191-203; j) Coordinated-career couples: Convergence and diver-

gence. Butler, Matilda and Paisley, William, p.207-228; k) Equal opportunity laws and dual-career couples. Moore, Donna M., p.229-240; l) Salary and job performance differences in dual-career couples. Bryson, Jeff B. and Bryson, Rebecca, p.241-259; m) Going shopping: The professional couple in the job market. Matthews, Janet R. and Matthews, Lee H., p.261-281.

88. Early Female Development: Current Psychoanalytic Views. Mendell, Dale, ed. New York: SP Medical & Scientific Books, 1982.
a) On the origins of gender identity. Formanek, Ruth, p.1-24; b) The anal phase. Oliner, Marion Michel, p.25-60; c) Considerations about the development of the girl during the separation-individuation process. Bergman, Anni, p.61-80; d) The inner-genital phase-prephallic and preoedipal. Kestenberg, Judith S., p.81-125; e) A suggested developmental sequence for a preoedipal genital phase. Glover, Laurice and Mendell, Dale, p.127-174; f) The female oedipus complex: Its antecedents and evolution. Bergmann, Maria V., p.175-201; g) The latency period. Silverman, Martin A., p.203-226; h) Narcissistic development. Lachmann, Frank M., p.227-248.

89. The Economics of Women and Work. Amsden, Alice H., ed. New York: St. Martin's Press, 1980.
a) Labor force participation of married women: A study of labor supply. Mincer, Jacob, p.41-51; b) A theory of the allocation of time. Becker, Gary, p.52-81; c) Time spent in housework. Vanek, Joann, p.82-90; d) Women's work and the family in nineteenth-century Europe. Scott, Joan W. and Tilly, Louise A., p.91-124; e) Economic perspectives on the family. Sawhill, Isabel V., p.125-139; f) Class struggle and the persistence of the working-class family. Humphries, Jane, p.140-165; g) Family investments in human capital: Earnings of women. Mincer, Jacob and Polachek, Solomon, p.169-205; h) The statistical theory of racism and sexism. Phelps, Edmund S., p.206-210; i) Determinants of the structure of industrial type labor markets. Doeringer, Peter B., p.211-231; j) A theory of labor market segmentation. Edwards, Richard C., Gordon, David M. and Reich, Michael, p.232-241; k) Structured labour markets, worker organization and low pay. Rubery, Jill, p.242-270; l) Occupational segregation, wages and profits when employers discriminate by race and sex. Bergmann, Barbara R., p.271-282; m) Sexual discrimination in the labour market. Chiplin, Brian and Sloane, Peter J., p.283-321; n) The female-male differential in unemployment rates. Niemi, Beth, p.325-349; o) Curing high unemployment rates among blacks and women. Bergmann, Barbara R., p.350-358; p) The 1974-1975 recession and the employment of women. Organisation for Economic Co-operation and Development, p.359-385; q) Wives' labor force behavior and family consumption patterns. Strober, Myra H., p.386-399; r) The employment of wives and the inequality of family income. Sweet, James A., p.400-409.

90. Educational Policy and Management: Sex Differentials. Schmuck, Patricia A., Charters, W. W. and Carlson,

Richard O., eds. New York: Academic Press, 1981.
a) The sex dimension - An overview. Charters, W. W. and Schmuck, Patricia A., p.1-7; b) Women in educational administration: A descriptive analysis of dissertation research and paradigm for future research. Shakeshaft, Charol, p.9-31; c) Sex equity in educational policies and practices. Charters, W. W., p.35-53; d) The concept of sex equity in jurisprudence. Jacklin, Pamela, p.55-72; e) Clues to sex bias in the selection of school administrators: A report from the Oregon network. Schmuck, Patricia A. and Wyant, Spencer H., p.73-97; f) The problem of sex bias in curriculum materials. Hutchison, Barbara, p.99-114; g) The sex dimension of careers in educational management: Overview and synthesis. Carlson, Richard O. and Schmuck, Patricia A., p.117-130; h) Jobs and gender: A history of the structuring of educational employment by sex. Strober, Myra H. and Tyack, David B., p.131-152; i) Ambitions and the opportunity for professionals in the elementary school. Jovick, Thomas D., p.153-168; j) "If they can, I can": Women aspirants to administrative positions in public schools. Edson, Sakre K., p.169-185; k) Male and female career paths in school administration. Paddock, Susan C., p.187-199; l) Administrative careers in public school organizations. Gaertner, Karen N., p.199-217; m) The sex dimension of school organization: Overview and synthesis. Schmuck, Patricia A., p.221-234; n) The sources and dynamics of sexual inequality in the profession of education. Johnson, Miriam and Stockard, Jean, p.235-254; o) The impact of organizational structures on issues of sex equity. Wheatley, Margaret, p.255-271; p) Hormones and harems: Are the activities of superintending different for a woman? Pitner, Nancy J., p.273-295; q) The influence of gender on the verbal interactions among principals and staff members: An exploratory study. Gilbertson, Marilyn, p.297-306; r) The gender of principals and principal/teacher relations in elementary schools. Charters, W. W. and Jovick, Thomas D., p.307-331.

91. The Emerging Christian Woman: Church and Society Perspectives. Alexander, Anna Vareed, Faria, Stella and Tellis-Nayak, Jessie B., eds. Indore, India: Satprakashan Sanchar Kendra, 1984.
a) A new outlook on women: Psychological and biological. Monteiro, Rita, p.3-11; b) Religion and menstruation. Park, Sun Ai, p.12-18; c) Feminist liberation theology: Its past and future. Coll, Regina, p.19-33; d) The feminist viewpoint. Drego, Pearl, p.34-47; e) Theological issues raised by feminism. Hug, Jim, p.48-54; f) The role of the church in the oppression of women. Fernando, Chitra, p.55-62; g) Challenge of feminism to the church: A Bishop's perspective. Dingman, Maurice, p.63-68; h) Woman's image of herself. Katoppo, Marianne, p.69-75; i) Through the feminist looking glass: Images of women. Alexander, Anna Vareed, p.76-89; j) From chauvinism and clericalism to priesthood: The long march. Groome, Thomas H., p.90-104; k) Women in ministries. Leeuwen, Gerwin van, p.105-113; l) Preacher and priest: Typologies of ministry and ordination of women. Ruether, Rosemary Radford, p.114-120; m) Moral theology from a feminist

perspective. Helen and Josantony, p.121-132; n) Is partnership possible? Ordained men and unordained women in ministry. Durka, Gloria, p.133-148; o) Bondage: Denial or fundamental rights to women. Kishwar, Madhu, p.149-163; p) Sex roles defined: As others see us. Tellis, Bernie, p.164-168; q) Women... Where are you? Women in the Protestant churches. Gnanadason, Aruna, p.169-180; r) New wine in new skins: Women in secular institutes. Crescy, John, p.181-188; s) Religious women in North India. Velamkunnel, Joseph, p.189-202; t) Women religious and the new society. Carol, M., p.203-212; u) Women community workers. Tellis-Nayak, Jessie B., p.213-225; v) Sammelan of the spirit. Grant, Sara, p.226-232; w) Church and women: A course. Webster, Ellen Low and Webster, John C.B., p.235-266.

92. The Endless Day: Some Case Material on Asian Rural Women. Epstein, T. Scarlett and Watts, Rosemary A., eds. Oxford: Pergamon, 1981.
a) An action-oriented study of the role of women in rural development. Epstein, T. Scarlett, p.3-9; b) Bangladesh: Beliefs and customs observed by Muslim rural women during their life cycle. Nath, Jharna, p.13-28; c) Pakistan: *Mor* and *Tor*: Binary and opposing models of Pukhtun womanhood. Ahmed, Zeenat and Akbar, S., p.31-46; d) Pakistan: The role of women in reciprocal relationships in a Punjab village. Naveed-I-Rahat, p.47-81; e) Indonesia: Married women's work pattern in rural Java. Mangkuprawira, Sjafri, p.85-106; f) Indonesia: Socio-economic aspects of food consumption in rural Java. Sjafri, Aida, p.107-127; g) The advantages of functional education and credit facilities for Javanese rural women. Bangun, Masliana, p.128-154; h) Rural women and their multiple roles. Epstein, T. Scarlett, p.157-167.

93. Equal Employment Policy for Women: Strategies for Implementation in the United States, Canada, and Western Europe. Ratner, Ronnie Steinberg, ed. Philadelphia, PA: Temple University Press, 1980.
a) The policy and problem: Overview of seven countries. Ratner, Ronnie Steinberg, p.1-52; b) Collective bargaining as a strategy for achieving equal opportunity and equal pay: Sweden and West Germany. Cook, Alice H., p.53-78; c) Equal pay and equal opportunity law in France. Loree, Marguerite J., p.79-107; d) The effectiveness of federal laws prohibiting sex discrimination in employment in the United States. Greenberger, Marcia, p.108-128; e) Strategies for improving the economic situation of women in the United States: Systemic thinking, systemic discrimination, and systemic enforcement. Robertson, Peter C., p.128-142; f) Administering anti-discrimination legislation in Great Britain. Nandy, Dipak, p.142-159; g) The enforcement of laws against sex discrimination in England: Problems of institutional design. Jowell, Jeffrey, p.159-175; h) Equality between men and women in the labor market: The Swedish National Labor Market Board. Rollen, Berit, p.179-198; i) Vocational training, the labor market, and the unions. Cook, Alice H., p.199-226; j) Leadership training for union women in the United States: Route to equal opportunity.

Wertheimer, Barbara M., p.226-241; k) The role of the National Action Committee on the Status of Women in facilitating equal pay policy in Canada. Marsden, Lorna R., p.242-260; l) Implementing equal pay and equal opportunity legislation in Great Britain. Seear, Nancy, p.261-277; m) Improving job opportunities for women from a U.S. corporate perspective. Shaeffer, Ruth Gilbert, p.277-310; n) The impact of organizational structure: Models and methods for change. Kanter, Rosabeth Moss, p.311-327; o) Equal employment opportunity for women in West Germany today. Daubler-Gmelin, Herta, p.329-349; p) Women's stake in a high-growth economy in the United States. Smith, Ralph E., p.350-365; q) Social policies and the family: Their effect on women's paid employment in Great Britain. Land, Hilary, p.366-388; r) Integration of family policy and labor market policy in Sweden. Liljestrom, Rita, p.388-404; s) Beyond equal pay for equal work: Comparable worth in the state of Washington. Remick, Helen, p.405-419; t) Equal employment policy for women: Summary of themes and issues. Ratner, Ronnie Steinberg, p.419-440; u) The contribution of labor market data in combating employment discrimination. Bergmann, Barbara R., p.443-457; v) Work analysis as a means to achieve equal pay for working women: The Federal Republic of Germany. Helberger, Christof, p.458-483.

94. Ethnicity, Class and Gender in Australia. Bottomley, Gill and Lepervanche, Marie M. de, eds. Sydney, Australia: George Allen & Unwin, 1984.
a) Immigration and class: The Australian experience. Collins, Jock, p.1-27; b) Ethnicity, multiculturalism and neo-conservatism. Jakubowicz, Andrew, p.28-48; c) The 'naturalness' of inequality. Lepervanche, Marie de, p.49-71; d) Migrantness, culture and ideology. Morrissey, Michael, p.72-81; e) Multiculturalism and education policy. Cope, Bill and Kalantzis, Mary, p.82-97; f) Women on the move: Migration and feminism. Bottomley, Gill, p.98-108; g) Non English-speaking women: Production and social reproduction. Martin, Jeannie, p.109-122; h) A new Australian working class leadership: The case of Ford Broadmeadows. Tracy, Constance Lever, p.123-143; i) Migrant communities and class politics: The Greek community in Australia. Kakakios, Michael and Van Der Velden, John, p.144-164; j) Generations and class: Sicilian-Australians in Melbourne. Hampel, Bill, p.165-182; k) Religion, law and family disputes in a Lebanese Muslim community in Sydney. Humphrey, Michael, p.183-198.

95. European Women on the Left: Socialism, Feminism, and the Problems Faced by Political Women, 1880 to the Present. Slaughter, Jane and Kern, Robert, eds. Westport, CT: Greenwood, 1981.
a) Anna Kuliscioff: Russian revolutionist, Italian feminist. Springer, Beverly Tanner, p.13-27; b) Clara Zetkin: A Socialist approach to the problem of women's oppression. Honeycut, Karen, p.29-49; c) When radical and socialist feminism were joined: The extraordinary failure of Madeleine Pelletier. Boxer, Marilyn J., p.51-73; d) Sylvia

Pankhurst: Suffragist, feminist, or socialist? Edmondson, Linda, p.75-100; e) Alexandra Kollontai and the Russian Revolution. Stites, Richard, p.101-123; f) Feminism: The essential ingredient in Federica Montseny's anarchist theory. Fredricks, Shirley, p.125-145; g) Margarita Nelken: Women and the crisis of Spanish politics. Kern, Robert, p.147-162; h) Communist women and the fascist experience. Cammett, John M., p.163-177; i) Humanism versus feminism in the socialist movement: The life of Angelica Balabanoff. Slaughter, Jane, p.179-194; j) Ulrike Meinhof: An emancipated terrorist? Kramer, David, p.195-219.

96. The Evolving Female: Women in Psychosocial Context. Heckerman, Carol Landau, ed. New York: Human Sciences Press, 1980.
a) Introduction: An historical view of psychotherapy and women's rights. p.13-29; b) The mental health problems of women: Social roles and the individual. p.31-44; c) Passion as a mental health hazard. Loewenstein, Sophie Freud, p.45-73; d) Mothers and their children: A study of low-income families. Belle, Deborah, p.74-91; e) The experience of abortion. Belovitch, Tamara E., p.92-106; f) Women and employment: Some emotional hazards. Lemkau, Jeanne Parr, p.107-137; g) From renunciation to rebellion: The female in literature. Shuey, William A., p.138-159; h) Toward choice and differentiation in the midlife crises of women. Loewenstein, Sophie Freud, p.158-188; i) From traditional psychoanalysis to alternatives to psychotherapy. p.189-206; j) A new look at the psychoanalytic view of the female. Salzman, Leon, p.207-221; k) Assertion training for women. Gambrill, Eileen D. and Richey, Cheryl A., p.222-267; l) The role and function of women's consciousness raising: Self-help, psychotherapy, or political activation? Bond, Gary R. and Lieberman, Morton A., p.268-306; m) The treatment of depressed women: The efficacy of psychotherapy. Weissman, Myrna M., p.307-324; n) Math anxiety and female mental health: Some unexpected links. Donady, Bonnie, Kogelman, Stanley and Tobias, Sheila, p.325-345.

97. Excellence, Reform and Equity in Education: An International Perspective. Kelly, Gail P., ed. Buffalo, NY: Comparative Education Center, State University of New York, 1984.
a) Women, educational reform and the process of change. Deem, Rosemary, p.1-30; b) In/Forming schooling: Space/time/textuality in compulsory state provided "mass" schooling systems. Corrigan, Philip, p.31-68; c) The political economy of text publishing. Apple, Michael W., p.69-102; d) Parents, children and the state. David, Miriam E., p.103-134; e) Public education and the discourse of crisis, power and vision. Giroux, Henry, p.135-174.

98. Exploring the Other Half: Field Research with Rural Women in Bangladesh. Islam, Shamima, ed. Dacca, Bangladesh: Women for Women, 1982.
a) Getting to know a rural community in Bangladesh. Rizvi, Najma, p.21-39; b) Research on women in

Bangladesh: Notes on experiences from the field. Westergaard, Kirsten, p.40-55; c) Access to village women: Experiences in breaking barriers. Islam, Shamima, p.56-74; d) Becoming an 'insider': Women's privileges in village field work. Blanchet, Therese, p.75-90; e) Learning from poor women: A method of village study. Arens, Jenneke, p.91-105; f) Anthropological approach to study of rural women in Bangladesh: Experience of a female researcher. Islam, Mahmuda, p.106-116; g) Field research on women in the Comilla District, Bangladesh. Von-Harder, Gudrun Martius, p.117-124; h) Personal account of the role of a supervisor in the Bangladesh fertility survey. Begum, Saleha, p.127-135; i) Working through local female investigators: Experiences in a broad survey. Hasan, Yousuf, p.136-145; j) Survey research with rural women in Bangladesh. Hasna, Mahbuba Kaneez and Marum, M. Elizabeth, p.146-161; k) Action research with rural women in Bangladesh: Some observations and experiences. Abdullah, Tahrunnessa, p.165-171; l) Towards the making of a documentary film on rural women in Bangladesh. Lawhead, Helen D., p.172-187; m) Methodological issues in longitudinal and comparative research in Bangladesh. McCarthy, Florence E., p.191-205; n) Methodological interventions in programme assessment and evaluation research. Feldman, Shelley, p.206-222.

99. Exploring Women's Past: Essays in Social History. Crawford, Patricia, ed. Sydney, Australia: George Allen & Unwin, 1984.
a) Brides of Christ and poor mortals: Women in medieval society. Ker, Margaret, p.7-47; b) From the woman's view: Pre-industrial England, 1500-1750. Crawford, Patricia, p.49-85; c) 'Helpmeet for man': Women in mid-nineteenth century western Australia. Anderson, Margaret, p.87-127; d) Victorian spinsters: Dutiful daughters, desperate rebels and the transition to the new women. Jalland, Patricia, p.129-170; e) 'As good a bloody woman as any other woman...': Prostitutes in western Australia, 1895-1939. Davidson, Raelene, p.171-206.

100. Expressions of Power in Education: Studies of Class, Gender and Race. Gumbert, Edgar B., ed. Atlanta, GA: Georgia State University, 1984.
a) The dialectic of education: An alternative approach to education and social change in developing countries. Carnoy, Martin, p.9-27; b) Teaching and 'women's work': A comparative historical and ideological analysis. Apple, Michael W., p.29-49; c) The Indian and African presence in the Americas: Some aspects of historical distortion. Carew, Jan R., p.51-67.

101. The Extended Family: Women and Political Participation in India and Pakistan. Minault, Gail, ed. Delhi, India: Chanakya Publications, 1981.
a) Introduction: The extended family as metaphor and the expansion of women's realm. Minault, Gail, p.3-18; b) Social reform and women's participation in political culture: Andhra and Madras. Leonard, John G. and Leonard, Karen I., p.19-43; c) The Indian women's move-

ment: A struggle for women's rights or national liberation? Forbes, Geraldine, p.49-82; d) Sisterhood or separation? The All-India Muslim Ladies' Conference and the Nationalist Movement. Minault, Gail, p.83-108; e) Catalysts or helpers? British feminists, Indian women's rights, and Indian independence. Ramusack, Barbara N., p.109-150; f) Kinship, women, and politics in twentieth-century Punjab. Gilmartin, David, p.151-173; g) Nationalism, universalization, and the extended female space in Bombay City. Pearson, Gail, p.174-191; h) The Indian women's movement and national development: An overview. Lateef, Shahida, p.195-216; i) Two faces of protest: Alternative forms of women's mobilization in West Bengal and Maharashtra. Basu, Amrita, p.217-262; j) The All-Pakistan Women's Association and the 1961 Muslim family laws ordinance. Chipp-Kraushaar, Sylvia, p.263-287; k) Towards equality? Cause and consequence of the political prominence of women in India. Katzenstein, Mary Fainsod, p.286-303.

102. Face to Face: Fathers, Mothers, Masters, Monsters - Essays for a Nonsexist Future. Murray, Meg McGavran, ed. Westport, CT: Greenwood, 1983.
a) A society without fathers: Cooperative commonwealth or harmonious ant-heap? Lasch, Christopher, p.3-19; b) Breaking free of symbolic bondage: From feminine submission to a vision of equality. Murray, Meg McGavran, p.21-43; c) Tiamat and her children: An inquiry into the persistence of mythic archetypes of woman as monster/villainess/victim. Robbins, Kittye Delle, p.47-69; d) Religion and the fearful father: Vision of liberation or American-style fascism? Collins, Sheila, p.71-87; e) Toward psychoanalytic feminism: The mother in dream-stealing, the father in dreams. George, Diana Hume and Luce, Nancy A., p.89-128; f) Why the fathers cannot solve the problems: Some possible clues. Miller, Jean Baker, p.129-141; g) The good-provider role: Its rise and fall. Bernard, Jessie, p.145-167; h) A primer on women and the democratization of the workplace. Parry, Susan M., p.169-180; i) Beyond consciousness raising: Changing sexist institutions. Lauter, Paul, p.181-190; j) Women at the top. Doudna, Christine, p.191-200; k) The work got done: An interview with Clara Mortenson Beyer. Murray, Meg McGavran, p.203-232; l) A political diary of an assertive woman. Chambers, Marjorie Bell, p.233-241; m) Women in the U.S. Foreign Service: A quiet revolution. Good, Barbara J., p.243-253; n) "No more squeezing into one". Ferguson, Mary Anne, p.257-271; o) Public nurturance and the man on horseback. Boulding, Elise, p.273-291; p) Afterword: Toward the mobilization of Eros. Dinnerstein, Dorothy, p.293-309.

103. Families, Politics, and Public Policy: A Feminist Dialogue on Women and the State. Diamond, Irene, ed. New York: Longman, 1983.
a) Contemporary American families: Decline or transformation? Flax, Jane, p.21-40; b) The state, the patriarchal family, and working mothers. Eisenstein, Zillah, p.41-58; c) Battered women's shelters and the political economy of sexual violence. Grossholtz, Jean, p.59-69; d) The trans-

formation of patriarchy: The historic role of the state. Bardaglio, Peter and Boris, Eileen, p.70-93; e) Women and the Reagan revolution: Thermidor for the social welfare economy. Erie, Steven P., Rein, Martin and Wiget, Barbara, p.94-119; f) Women and housing: The impact of government housing policy. Simms, Margaret C., p.123-138; g) Fiscal policy and family structure. Leader, Shelah Gilbert, p.139-147; h) Housework: Rethinking the costs and benefits. Ferree, Myra Marx, p.148-167; i) Why the United States has no child-care policy. Joffe, Carole, p.168-182; j) Gender and child-custody determinations: Exploding the myths. Polikoff, Nancy D. p.183-202; k) Women and child support. Hunter, Nan D., p.203-219; l) Teenage sexuality and public policy: An agenda for gender education. Harper, Anne L., p.220-235; m) Daddy's right: Incestuous assault. Armstrong, Pamela and Begus, Sarah, p.236-249; n) The politics of wife abuse. Gelb, Joyce, p.250-262; o) Work, gender, and technological innovation. Boneparth, Ellen and Stoper, Emily, p.265-278; p) Women in a revolutionary society: The state and family policy in China. Robinson, Jean C., p.279-294; q) Family responsibilities as a labor market issue: A Scandinavian perspective. Nielsen, Ruth, p.295-299; r) Antigone's daughters: Reflections on female identity and the state. Elshtain, Jean Bethke, p.300-311; s) The family impact statement: Ideology and feasibility. Boles, Janet K., p.312-321; t) Reproductive freedom and the right to privacy: A paradox for feminists. Brown, Wendy, p.322-338; u) "Sisters" or "comrades"? The politics of friends and families. Ackelsberg, Martha A., p.339-356; v) Afterword: Feminism and families in a liberal policy. Shanley, Mary Lyndon, p.357-361.

104. Family and Work in Rural Societies: Perspectives on Non-Wage Labour. Long, Norman, ed. London: Tavistock Publications, 1984.
a) Aspects of non-capitalist social relations in rural Egypt: The small peasant household in an Egyptian delta village. Glavanis, Kathy R.G., p.30-60; b) Cash crop production and family labour: Tobacco growers in Corrientes, Argentina. Melhuus, Marit, p.61-82; c) Interhousehold co-operation in Peru's southern Andes: A case of multiple sibling-group marriage. Skar, Sarah Lund, p.83-98; d) Co-operation on and between eastern Finnish family farms. Abrahams, Ray G., p.99-115; e) The estimation of work in a northern Finnish farming community. Ingold, Tim, p.116-134; f) A note on the custom of 'paying off' on family farms in Poland. Kocik, Lucjan, p.135-141; g) Women's work in rural south-west England. Bouquet, Mary, p.142-159; h) Domestic work in rural Iceland: An historical overview. Johnson, Marie, p.160-174; i) The organization of labour in an Israeli kibbutz. Bowes, Alison M., p.175-198.

105. The Family in Change. Trost, Jan, ed. Västerås, Sweden: International Library, 1980.
a) Changing family and changing society. Trost, Jan, p.7-22; b) Modern and traditional elements in the expectations of young married couples regarding their marital life. Cseh-Szombathy, László, p.23-30; c) Marital expecta-

tions of wives in contemporary Poland. Mogey, John and Piotrowski, Jerzy, p.31-39; d) Recent data reflecting upon the sexual revolution in America. Christensen, Harold T., p.41-51; e) Toward a theory of extramarital sexual relationships. Reiss, Ira L., p.53-60; f) The family, the child, and social change. Martinson, Floyd, p.61-73; g) Social structure, family socialization, and children's achievement goals: A comparative analysis. Tallman, Irving, p.75-87; h) Developing family invulnerability to stress: Coping patterns and strategies wives employ in managing family separations. McCubbin, Hamilton I., et al., p.89-103; i) Towards a new definition of divorce. Commaille, Jacques, p.105-112; j) Some correlates of marital trust. Larzelere, Robert E. and Lewis, Robert A., p.113-119; k) Marriage, estrangement, sobriety and recidivism: Some crucial process variables in the case of alcoholic men and their wives. Wiseman, Jacqueline P., p.121-147; l) Physical violence in a nationally representative sample of American families. Gelles, Richard J., Steinmetz, Suzanne K. and Straus, Murray A., p.149-165.

106. The Family in Political Thought. Elshtain, Jean Bethke, ed. Amherst, MA: University of Massachusetts Press, 1982.
a) Introduction: Toward a theory of the family and politics. Elshtain, Jean Bethke, p.7-30; b) Philosopher queens and private wives: Plato on women and the family. Okin, Susan Moller, p.31-50; c) Aristotle, the public-private split, and the case of the suffragists. Elshtain, Jean Bethke, p.51-65; d) Political and marital despotism: Montesquieu's *Persian Letters*. Shanley, Mary Lyndon and Stillman Peter G., p.66-79; e) Marriage contract and social contract in seventeenth-century English political thought. Shanley, Mary Lyndon, p.80-95; f) Julie and "La Maison Paternelle": Another look at Rousseau's *La Nouvelle Héloïse*. Tanner, Tony, p.96-124; g) Hegel's conception of the family. Landes, Joan B., p.125-144; h) Patriarchal liberalism and beyond: From John Stuart Mill to Harriet Taylor. Krouse, Richard W., p.145-172; i) Oedipus as hero: Family and family metaphors in Nietzsche. Strong, Tracy B., p.173-196; j) The working-class family: A Marxist perspective. Humphries, Jane, p.197-222; k) The family in contemporary feminist thought: A critical review. Flax, Jane, p.223-253; l) Contemporary critical theory and the family: Private world and public crisis. Norton, Theodore Mills, p.254-268; m) Kafka and Laing on the trapped consciousness: The family as political life. Glass, James, p.269-287; n) "Thank heaven for little girls": The dialectics of development. Elshtain, Jean Bethke, p.288-302.

107. The Female Athlete: A Socio-Psychological and Kinanthropometric Approach. Borms, J., Hebbelinck, M. and Venerando, A., eds. Basel, Germany: S. Karger, 1981.
a) Women's sports - the unlikely myth of equality. Cheska, A. T., p.1-11; b) Attitudes to women in sport: Preface towards a sociological theory. Ferris, E. A. E., p.12-29; c) Women and sport: A leisure studies perspective. Talbot, M. J., p.30-40; d) The influence of the traditional sex roles on women's participation and engagement in sport.

Fasting, K. and Tangen, J. O., p.41-48; e) Personality research: Implications for women in sport. Harris, D. V., p.49-57; f) Sugar and spice and everything nice: Is that what female athletes behave like? Salmela, J. H., p.58-62; g) Differences in athletic aggression among Egyptian female athletes. Allawy, M. H., p.63-66; h) Machover test applied to 130 Italian female top athletes. Rota, S., et al., p.67-73; i) Proportionality and body composition in male and female Olympic athletes: A kinanthropometric overview. Ross, W. D. et al., p.74-84; j) Somatotypes of female athletes. Carter, J. E. L., p.85-116; k) Influence of athletic training on the maturity process of girls. Märker, K., p.117-126; l) Physique of female athletes - anthropological and proportional analysis. Eiben, O. G., p.127-141; m) Asymmetry of limb circumferences in female athletes. Zaharieva, E., p.142-149; n) Some differences between men and women in various factors which determine swimming performance. Persyn, U. and Vervaecke, H., p.150-156; o) Body composition and somatotype characteristics of sportswomen. Bale, P., p.157-167; p) Differences in males and females in joint movement range during growth. Merni, F., et al., p.168-175; q) Somatic and motor characteristics of female gymnasts. Beunen, G., Claessens, A. and van Esser, M., p.176-185; r) Physique of college women athletes in five sports. Slaughter, M. H., et al., p.186-191; s) Measures of body size and form of elite female basketball players. Giese, W. K., Spurgeon, J. H. and Spurgeon, N. L., p.192-200; t) Body build of female Olympic rowers. Hebbelinck, M., et al., p.201-205; u) Body segment contributions of female athletes to translational and rotational requirements of non-twisting springboard dive takeoffs. Miller, D. I., p.206-215.

108. The Female Autograph. Stanton, Domna C. and Plottel, Jeanine Parisier, eds. New York: New York Literary Forum, 1984.
a) Autogynography: Is the subject different? Stanton, Domna C., p.5-22; b) Ceremonies of the alphabet: Female grandmatologies and the female autograph. Gilbert, Sandra Caruso Mortola and Gubar, Susan Dreyfuss David, p.23-52; c) The female hand in Heian Japan: A first reading. Bowring, Richard, p.55-62; d) Autobiography of a new 'creatur': Female spirituality, selfhood, and authorship in *The Book of Margery Kempe*. Mueller, Janel M., p.63-75; e) To restore honor and fortune: *The Autobiography of Lenor López de Córdoba*. Johnson, Elaine Dorough and Kaminsky, Amy Katz, p.77-88; f) Artemisia Gentileschi: The artist's autograph in letters and paintings. Garrard, Mary D., p.91-105; g) Giving weight to words: Madame de Sévigné's letters to her daughter. Goldsmith, Elizabeth C., p.107-115; h) *My Childhood Years*: A memoir by the czarist cavalry officer, Nadezhda Durova. Zirin, Mary Fleming, p.119-141; i) Neither auction block nor pedestal: *The Life and Religious Experience of Jaren Lee, A Coloured Lady*. Foster, Frances Smith, p.143-169; j) Fanny Mendelssohn Hensel: Musician in her brother's shadow. Citron, Marcia J., p.171-179; k) Women as law clerks: Catherine G. Waugh. Cott, Nancy F., p.181-190; l) The female sociograph: The theater of Viriginia Woolf's letters. Stimpson, Catharine

R., p.193-203; m) Of sparrows and condors: The autobiography of Eva Perón. Navarro, Marysa, p.205-211; n) *Difficult Journey - Mountainous Journey*, the memoirs of Fadwa Tuqan. Divine, Donna Robinson, p.213-233; o) *My Life...This Curious Object*: Simone de Beauvoir on autobiography. Bair, Deirdre, p.237-245; p) Women and autobiography at author's expense. Lejeune, Philippe, p.247-260; q) My memory's hyperbole. Kristeva, Julia, p.261-276.

109. The Female Gothic. Fleenor, Juliann E., ed. Montreal, Quebec: Eden Press, 1983.
a) Somebody's trying to kill me and I think it's my husband: The modern gothic. Russ, Joanna, p.31-56; b) "But why do they read those things?" The female audience and the gothic novel. Mussell, Kay J., p.57-68; c) Victoria Holt's gothic romances: A structuralist inquiry. Bowman, Barbara, p.69-81; d) Had-I-but-known: The marriage of gothic terror and detection. Maio, Kathleen L., p.82-90; e) The reconstruction of the gothic feminine ideal in Emily Brontë's *Wuthering Heights*. Conger, Syndy McMillen, p.91-106; f) Domestic gothic: The imagery of anger in Christina Stead's *The Man Who Loved Children*. Lidoff, Joan, p.109-122; g) Monsters and madwomen: Changing female gothic. Stein, Karen F., p.123-137; h) Gothic transformations: Isak Dinesen and the gothic. James, Sibyl, p.138-152; i) The mirror and the cameo: Margaret Atwood's comic/gothic novel, *Lady Oracle*. Vincent, Sybil Korff, p.153-163; j) "A forced solitude": Mary Shelley and the creation of Frankenstein's monster. Tillotson, Marcia, p.167-175; k) Terror-gothic: Nightmare and dream in Ann Radcliffe and Charlotte Brontë. Ronald, Ann, p.176-186; l) Place and eros in Radcliffe, Lewis, and Brontë. Nichols, Nina da Vinci, p.187-206; m) The Radcliffean gothic model: A form for feminine sexuality. Wolff, Cynthia Griffin, p.207-223; n) The gothic prism: Charlotte Perkins Gilman's gothic stories and her autobiography. Fleenor, Juliann E., p.227-241; o) The maternal legacy: The grotesque tradition in Flannery O'Connor's female gothic. Kahane, Claire, p.242-256; p) Dreaming of children: Literalization in *Jane Eyre* and *Wuthering Heights*. Homans, Margaret, p.257-279.

110. Female Labor Supply: Theory and Estimation. Smith, James P., ed. Princeton, NJ: Princeton University Press, 1980.
a) Estimating labor supply functions for married women. Schultz, T. Paul, p.25-89; b) Married women's labor supply: A comparison of alternative estimation procedures. Cogan, John, p.90-118; c) Hours and weeks in the theory of labor supply. Hanoch, Giora, p.119-165; d) Assets and labor supply. Smith, James P., p.166-205; e) Sample selection bias as a specification error. Heckman, James, p.206-248; f) A multivariate model of labor supply: Methodology and estimation. Hanoch, Giora, p.249-326; g) Labor supply with costs of labor market entry. Cogan, John, p.327-364.

111. The Female Offender. Griffiths, Curt Taylor and Nance, Margit, eds. Vancouver, B.C.: Simon Fraser University,

1980.
a) Re-discovering Lilith: Misogyny and the "new" female criminal. Lind, Meda Chesney, p.1-35; b) Female terrorists: Competing perspectives. Corrado, Raymond R. p.37-50; c) Women's criminality in Poland. Plenska, Danuta, p.51-67; d) Family violence: Women as offenders or victims. Harris, Holly, p.69-80; e) Social-psychological research and relevant speculation on the issue of domestic violence. Dutton, Donald G., p.81-91; f) The female juvenile offender. Brager, Marilyn, p.93-97; g) Juvenile prostitution. Boyer, Debra and James, Jennifer, p.99-118; h) Contingency management in a juvenile treatment setting. Olson, Robert C., p.119-141; i) The Hillcrest School of Oregon: Guided group interaction in a juvenile institution. Gould, David, Hanneman, Kathleen and Robinson, Marcelle, p.143-162; j) Prison homosexuality: Re-examining conventional wisdom. Propper, Alice M., p.163-194; k) The treatment of convicted female offenders in the criminal justice system. Chapman, Jane Roberts, p.195-200; l) Women in court: Assisting the female offender. MacMillan, Margaret, p.201-212; m) Beyond incarceration: A women's alternative. Johnson, Sharon M., p.213-220; n) Managing the female offender: Some observations. Chinnery, Doug, p.221-227; o) Managing the female offender: Crisis and change in the California Institution for Women. Anderson, Kathleen M., p.229-240; p) Prison treatment of female offenders in Mexico. Galindo, Antonio Sanchez, p.241-255; q) Sex-role concepts among federal female offenders. Conroy, Mary Alice, p.257-269; r) Drug abuse and criminality among women in detention. Miller, Brenda A., p.271-288; s) Issues in the application of parole guidelines to females. Alder, Christine and Bazemore, Gordon, p.289-307; t) Recent development in probation and parole in British Columbia. Harrison, Ted, p.309-317; u) Problems of policy development in criminal justice. Krasnick, Mark, p.319-325.

112. Female Scholars: A Tradition of Learned Women Before 1800. Brink, J. R., ed. Montreal, Quebec: Eden Press Women's Publications, 1980.
a) Christine de Pisan: First professional woman of letters (French, 1364-1430?). Altman, Leslie, p.7-23; b) Caterina Corner, Queen of Cyprus (Venetian, 1454?-1510). Robbert, Louise Buenger, p.24-35; c) Marguerite de Navarre and her circle (French, 1492-1549). Blaisdell, C. J., p.36-53; d) María de Zayas y Sotomayor: Sibyl of Madrid (Spanish, 1590?-1661?). Foa, Sandra M., p.54-67; e) Anna Maria van Schurman: The star of Utrecht (Dutch, 1607-1678). Irwin, Joyce L., p.68-85; f) Bathsua Makin: Educator and linguist (English, 1608?-1675?). Brink, J. R., p.86-100; g) Madame de Sévigné: Chronicler of an age (French, 1626-1696). Ojala, Jeanne A., p.101-118; h) Sor Juana Inés de la Cruz: Mexico's tenth muse (Mexican, 1651-1695). Flynn, Gerard, p.119-136; i) Elizabeth Elstob: The Saxon nymph (English, 1683-1765). Green, Mary Elizabeth, p.137-160; j) Mercy Otis Warren: Playwright, poet, and historian of the American revolution (American, 1728-1814). Bollinger, Sharon L. and Wilson, Joan Hoff, p.161-182.

113. Female Soldiers - Combatants or Noncombatants? Historical and Contemporary Perspectives. Goldman, Nancy Loring, ed. Westport, CT: Greenwood Press, 1982.
a) Great Britain and the World Wars. Goldman, Nancy Loring and Stites, Richard, p.21-45; b) Germany and the World Wars. Tuten, Jeff M., p.47-60; c) Russia: Revolution and war. Griesse, Anne Eliot and Stites, Richard, p.61-84; d) Yugoslavia: War of resistance. Jancar, Barbara, p.85-105; e) Vietnam: War of insurgency. Duiker, William J., p.107-122; f) Algeria: Anticolonial war. Amrane, Djamila, p.123-135; g) Israel: The longest war. Bloom, Anne R., p.137-162; h) Greece: Reluctant presence. Brown, James and Safilios-Rothschild, Constantina, p.165-177; i) Japan: Cautious utilization. Wiegand, Karl L., p.179-188; j) Denmark: The small NATO nation. Sorensen, Henning, p.189-201; k) Sweden: The neutral nation. Törnqvist, Kurt, p.203-214; l) The problem. Quester, George H., p.217-235; m) The argument against female combatants. Tuten, Jeff M., p.237-265; n) The argument for female combatants. Segal, Mady Wechsler, p.267-290.

114. The Feminine Eye: Science Fiction and the Women Who Write It. Staicar, Tom, ed. New York: Frederick Ungar, 1982.
a) Leigh Brackett: No "long goodbye" is good enough. Arbur, Rosemarie, p.1-13; b) C. L. Moore's classic science fiction. Mathews, Patricia, p.14-24; c) Andre Norton: Humanity amid the hardware. Schlobin, Roger C., p.25-31; d) C. J. Cherryh and tomorrow's new sex roles. Brizzi, Mary T., p.32-47; e) Toward new sexual identities: James Tiptree, Jr.. Frisch, Adam J., p.48-60; f) Holding fast to feminism and moving beyond: Suzy McKee Charnas's *The Vampire Tapestry*. Barr, Marleen, p.60-72; g) Marion Zimmer Bradley's ethic of freedom. Shwartz, Susan M., p.73-88; h) Sex, satire, and feminism in the science fiction of Suzette Haden Elgin. Chapman, Edgar L., p.89-103; i) From alienation to personal triumph: The science fiction of Joan D. Vinge. Yoke, Carl, p.103-130.

115. Feminine in the Church. Furlong, Monica, ed. London: SPCK, 1984.
a) Women and the ministry: A case for theological seriousness. Williams, Rowan, p.11-27; b) The ordination of women in the Roman Catholic Church. Doyle, Eric, p.28-43; c) Women and authority in the scriptures. Carey, George, p.44-55; d) 'The faltering words of men': Exclusive language in the liturgy. Morley, Janet, p.56-70; e) The ordination of women and the 'maleness' of the Christ. Norris, R.A., p.71-85; f) Jesus the Jew and women. Williams, Jane, p.86-99; g) Crumbs from the table: Towards a whole priesthood. Hoad, Anne, p.100-118; h) Mary: My sister. Robson, Jill, p.119-138; i) Stereotyping the sexes in society and in the Church. Santer, Henriette, p.139-149; j) Called to priesthood: Interpreting women's experience. Tanner, Mary, p.150-162; k) The right time. Baker, John Austin, p.163-177; l) Snakes and ladders:

Reflections on hierarchy and the fall. Clark, Peter, p.178-194.

116. "Femininity", "Masculinity", and "Androgyny": A Modern Philosophical Discussion. Vetterling-Braggin, Mary, ed. Totowa, N.J.: Rowman & Allanheld, 1982.
a) The feminine as a universal. Dickason, Anne, p.10-30; b) Sex roles: The argument from nature. Trebilcot, Joyce, p.40-48; c) Nurture theories: A critique. Duran, Jane, p.49-59; d) Freud: Masculinity, femininity, and the philosophy of mind. Flanagan, Owen J., p.60-76; e) "Femininity," resistance and sabotage. Hoagland, Sarah Lucia, p.85-98; f) The political epistemology of "masculine" and "feminine". Soble, Alan, p.99-127; g) Sex and social roles: How to deal with the data. Grim, Patrick, p.128-147; h) Two forms of androgynism. Trebilcot, Joyce, p.161-169; i) Is androgyny the answer to sexual stereotyping? Warren, Mary Anne, p.170-186; j) Are androgyny and sexuality compatible? Pielke, Robert G., p.187-196; k) On curing conceptual confusion: Response to Mary Anne Warren. Beardsley, Elizabeth Lane, p.197-200; l) Women's work: Views from the history of philosophy. Nicholson, Linda, p.203-221; m) Sex roles and the sexual division of labor. Moulton, Janice and Rainone, Francine, p.222-241; n) The obligations of mothers and fathers. Held, Virginia, p.242-258; o) Sex equality in sports. English, Jane, p.259-267; p) Women and "masculine" sports: Androgyny qualified. Postow, B.C., p.268-278; q) Sex equality and education in Plato's Just State. Martin, Jane, p.279-300.

117. Feminism and Art History: Questioning the Litany. Broude, Norma and Garrard, Mary D., eds. New York: Harper & Row, 1982.
a) Introduction: Feminism and art history. Broude, Norma and Garrard, Mary D., p.1-17; b) Matrilineal reinterpretation of some Egyptian sacred cows. Luomala, Nancy, p.19-31; c) The great goddess and the palace architecture of Crete. Scully, Vincent, p.33-43; d) Mourners on Greek vases: Remarks on the social history of women. Havelock, Christine Mitchell, p.45-61; e) Social status and gender in Roman art: The case of the saleswoman. Kampen, Natalie Boymel, p.63-77; f) Eve and Mary: Conflicting images of medieval woman. Kraus, Henry, p.79-99; g) Taking a second look: Observations on the iconography of a French queen, Jeanne de Bourbon (1338-1378). Sherman, Claire Richter, p.101-117; h) Delilah. Kahr, Madlyn Millner, p.119-145; i) Artemisia and Susanna. Garrard, Mary D., p.147-171; j) Judith Leyster's *Proposition* - Between virtue and vice. Hofrichter, Frima Fox, p.173-181; k) Art history and its exclusions: The example of Dutch art. Alpers, Svetlana, p.183-199; l) Happy mothers and other new ideas in eighteenth-century French art. Duncan, Carol, p.210-219; m) Lost and *Found*: Once more the fallen woman. Nochlin, Linda, p.221-245; n) Degas's "Misogyny". Broude, Norma, p.247-269; o) Gender or genius? The women artists of German expressionism. Comini, Alessandra, p.271-293; p) Virility and domination in early twentieth-century vanguard painting.

Duncan, Carol, p.293-313; q) Miriam Schapiro and "femmage": Reflections on the conflict between decoration and abstraction in twentieth-century art. Broude, Norma, p.315-329; r) Quilts: The great American art. Mainardi, Patricia, p.331-346.

118. Feminism and Process Thought: The Harvard Divinity School/Claremont Center for Process Studies Symposium Papers. Davaney, Sheila Greeve, ed. New York: Edwin Mellen Press, 1981.
a) Androgynous life: A feminist appropriation of process thought. Saiving, Valerie C., p.11-31; b) Feminism and process thought: A two-way relationship. Cobb, John B., p.32-61; c) Openness and mutuality in process thought and feminist action. Suchocki, Marjorie, p.62-82; d) The dynamics of female experience: Process models and human values. Washbourn, Penelope, p.83-105; e) Becoming human: A contextual approach to decisions about pregnancy and abortion. Lambert, Jean, p.106-138.

119. Feminism, Culture and Politics. Brunt, Rosalind and Rowan, Caroline, eds. London: Lawrence and Wishart, 1982.
a) Inverts and experts: Radclyffe Hall and the lesbian identity. Ruehl, Sonja, p.15-36; b) Feminism and the definition of cultural politics. Barrett, Michèle, p.37-58; c) 'Mothers, vote labour!' The state, the labour movement and working-class mothers, 1900-1918. Rowan, Caroline, p.59-84; d) 'What kind of woman is she?' Women and Communist Party politics, 1941-1955. Davis, Tricia, p.85-107; e) The family in socialist-feminist politics. McIntosh, Mary, p.109-129; f) Invisible struggles: The politics of ageing. Keyworth, Florence, p.131-142; g) 'An immense verbosity': Permissive sexual advice in the 1970s. Brunt, Rosalind, p.143-170; h) Sexual politics and psychoanalysis: Some notes on their relation. Coward, Rosalind, p.171-187.

120. Feminism in Canada: From Pressure to Politics. Finn, Geraldine and Miles, Angela R., eds. Montreal: Black Rose Books, 1982.
a) Memoirs of an ontological exile: The methodological rebellions of feminist research. Vickers, Jill McCalla, p.27-46; b) Feminism and the critique of scientific method. Benston, Margaret, p.47-66; c) Gynocentric values and feminist psychology. Wine, Jeri Dawn, p.67-87; d) The problem of studying "economic man". Cohen, Marjorie, p.89-101; e) Feminism and the writing and teaching of history. Pierson, Ruth and Prentice, Alison, p.103-118; f) To grow a daughter: Cultural liberation and the dynamics of oppression in Jamaica. Yawney, Carole, p.119-144; g) On the oppression of women in philosophy — or, Whatever happened to objectivity? Finn, Geraldine, p.145-173; h) The personal is political: Feminism and the helping professions. Levine, Helen, p.175-209. i) Ideological hegemony in political discourse: Women's specificity and equality. Miles, Angela R., p.213-227; j) Thoughts on women and power. Cohen, Yolande, p.229-250; k) Feminist praxis. O'Brien, Mary, p.251-268; l) My body in writing. Gagnon, Madeleine,

p.269-282; m) Fighting the good fight: Separation or integration? Hughes, Patricia, p.283-297.

121. Feminist Critics Read Emily Dickinson. Juhasz, Suzanne, ed. Bloomington, IN: Indiana University Press, 1983.
a) Introduction: Feminist critics read Emily Dickinson. Juhasz, Suzanne, p.1-21; b) The wayward nun beneath the hill: Emily Dickinson and the mysteries of womanhood. Gilbert, Sandra M., p.22-44; c) Emily Dickinson's nursery rhymes. Mossberg, Barbara Antonina Clarke, p.45-66; d) Notes on sleeping with Emily Dickinson. Keller, Karl, p.67-79; e) "Oh, Susie, it is dangerous": Emily Dickinson and the archetype of the masculine. Dobson, Joanne A., p.80-97; f) "The love of thee-a prism be": Men and women in the love poetry of Emily Dickinson. Morris, Adalaide, p.98-113; g) "Oh, vision of language!": Dickinson's poems of love and death. Homans, Margaret, p.114-133; h) How "low feet" stagger: Disruptions of language in Dickinson's poetry. Miller, Cristanne, p.134-157; i) "Ransom in a voice": Language as defense in Dickinson's poetry. Diehl, Joanne Feit, p.156-176.

122. Feminist Pedagogy and the Learning Climate. Loring, Katherine, ed. Ann Arbor, MI: Great Lakes Colleges Association, 1984.
a) Rethinking the ways we teach. Thorne, Barrie, p.1-10; b) Black studies/women's studies: Points of convergence. Butler, Johnnella, p.11-17; c) Seeking feminist transformation of the sciences and the teaching of science. Edwards, Kathryn, p.18-28; d) The learning climate and the non-traditional student. Gordon-McCord, Sue, p.29-33; e) The best feminist criticism is a new criticism. Ruthchild, Geraldine, p.34-40; f) The social determination of science: Some implications for women's studies. Bernstein, Stanley, p.41-45; g) Bem's gender schema theory. Hyde, Janet, p.46-53; h) In search of excellence in academic libraries, or, challenging the henhouse model. Saunders, Laverna, p.54-60; i) Levels of female criminal activity as a correlate of female societal power. Williams, Yvonne, p.61-70; j) A comparison of the movements toward equality in Yugoslavia and England. Weisman, Ellen, p.71-77; k) How women and men write about themselves (less differently than you might expect). Lamb, Catherine, p.78-84; l) Finding one's way through the labyrinth: A symposium on women's lives: Introduction. Jameson, Penny, p.85; m) Finding one's way through the labyrinth: A symposium on women's lives: Methodology. Jameson, Penny, p.86-88; n) Finding one's way through the labyrinth: A symposium on women's lives: Life stories. Vacca, Linnea Brandwein, p.89-92; o) Finding one's way through the labyrinth: A symposium on women's lives: Meals — chaos or community. Loux, Ann Kimble, p.93-96; p) Ibsen's *A Doll's House*: A directorial perspective on performing Nora. Watson, Dwight, p.97-104; q) Marital metaphors in the Judeo-Christian tradition: A feminist critique. Dickie, Jane R. and Ludwig, Thomas E., p.109-116.

123. A Feminist Perspective in the Academy: The Difference It Makes. Langland, Elizabeth and Gove, Walter, eds.

Chicago: University of Chicago Press, 1981.
a) The difference it makes. Spacks, Patricia Meyer, p.7-24; b) New directions for feminist criticism in theatre and the related arts. Reinhardt, Nancy S., p.25-51; c) The feminist critique in religious studies. Ruether, Rosemary Radford, p.52-66; d) What the women's movement has done to American history. Degler, Carl N., p.67-85; e) Speaking from silence: Women and the science of politics. Keohane, Nannerl O., p.86-100; f) How the study of women has restructured the discipline of economics. Barrett, Nancy S., p.101-109; g) Anthropology and the study of gender. Shapiro, Judith, p.110-129; h) Changing conceptions of men and women: A psychologist's perspective. Spence, Janet T., p.130-148; i) Women in sociological analysis: New scholarship versus old paradigms. Epstein, Cynthia Fuchs, p.149-162.

124. Feminist Re-visions: What Has Been and Might Be. Patraka, Vivian and Tilly, Louise A., eds. Ann Arbor, MI: Women's Studies Program, University of Michigan, 1983.
a) Rediscovering the "New Woman" of the 1890's: The stories of "George Egerton". Vicinus, Martha, p.12-25; b) Naming, magic and documentary: The subversion of the narrative in *Song of Solomon*, *Ceremony*, and *China Men*. Rabinowitz, Paula, p.26-42; c) Notes on technique in feminist drama: *Apple Pie* and *Signs of Life*. Patraka, Vivian, p.43-63; d) Widening the dialogue on feminist science fiction. Howard, June, p.64-96; e) The founding of the first Sherpa nunnery, and the problem of "women" as an analytic category. Ortner, Sherry B., p.98-134; f) Transvestitism and the ideology of gender: Southeast Asia and beyond. Yengoyan, Aram, p.135-148; g) Psychology views mothers and mothering: 1897-1980. Contratto, Susan, p.149-178; h) How psychology constructed masculinity: The theory of male sex role identity. Pleck, Joseph H., p.179-196; i) Feminist research methodology groups: Origins, forms, functions. Reinharz, Shulamit, p.197-229; j) The Women's Trade Union League school for women organizers. Jacoby, Robin Miller, p.230-256; k) Split brain research and its implications for feminist education. Wahlstrom, Billie J., p.257-282; l) Women and peace. Douvan, Elizabeth and Kaboolian, Linda, p.283-307; m) The defeat of the Equal Rights Amendment. Pleck, Elizabeth, p.308-322; n) The ERA campaign: Reflections on interpretation and practice. Duley-Morrow, Margot, p.323-332.

125. Feminist Theorists: Three Centuries of Women's Intellectual Traditions. Spender, Dale, ed. London: The Women's Press, 1983.
a) Aphra Behn: A scandal to modesty. Goreau, Angeline, p.8-27; b) Mary Astell: Inspired by ideas. Kinnaird, Joan K., p.28-39; c) Mary Wollstonecraft: Sexuality and women's rights. Brody, Miriam, p.40-59; d) Harriet Martineau: A reassessment. Weiner, Gaby, p.60-74; e) Margaret Fuller: Feminist writer and revolutionary. Urbanski, Marie Mitchell Olesen, p.75-89; f) Barbara Bodichon: Integrity in diversity. Matthews, Jacquie, p.90-123; g) Lucy Stone: Radical beginnings. Wheeler, Leslie, p.124-136; h) Matilda Joslyn Gage: Active intellectual.

Spender, Lynne, p.137-145; i) Josephine Butler: From sympathy to theory. Uglow, Jenny, p.146-164; j) Hedwig Dohm: Passionate theorist. Duelli-Klein, Renate, p.165-183; k) Millicent Garrett Fawcett: Duty and determination. Oakley, Ann, p.184-202; l) Charlotte Perkins Gilman: The personal is political. Lane, Ann J., p.203-217; m) Emma Goldman: Anarchist Queen. Shulman, Alix Kates, p.218-228; n) Olive Schreiner: New women, free women, all women. Stanley, Liz, p.229-243; o) Vida Goldstein: The women's candidate. Weiner, Gaby, p.244-255; p) Christabel Pankhurst: Reclaiming her power. Sarah, Elizabeth, p.256-284; q) Alice Paul: The quintessential feminist. Willis, Jean L., p.285-295; r) Virginia Woolf: The life of natural happiness. Black, Naomi, p.296-313; s) Vera Brittain: Feminist in a new age. Mellown, Muriel, p.314-334; t) Mary Ritter Beard: Women as force. Lane, Ann J., p.335-347; u) Simone de Beauvoir: Dilemmas of a feminist radical. Evans, Mary, p.348-365; v) Modern feminist theorists: Reinventing rebellion. Spender, Dale, p.366-380.

126. Feminist Visions: Toward a Transformation of the Liberal Arts Curriculum. Fowlkes, Diane L. and McClure, Charlotte S., eds. University, AL: The University of Alabama Press, 1984.
a) The genesis of feminist visions for transforming the liberal arts curriculum. Fowlkes, Diane L. and McClure, Charlotte S., p.3-11; b) Women as knowers. Stimpson, Catharine R., p.15-24; c) Women knowing: Feminist theory and perspectives on pedagogy. Fowlkes, Diane L. and McClure, Charlotte S., p.27-30; d) Research on women's communication: Critical assessment and recommendations. McMahan, Eva M., Stacks, Don W. and Wood, Julia T., p.31-41; e) Darwin and sexism: Victorian causes, contemporary effects. Hogsett, A. Charlotte and Rosser, Sue V., p.42-52; f) A feminist challenge to Darwinism: Antoinette L. B. Blackwell on the relations of the sexes in nature and society. Tedesco, Marie, p.53-65; g) The contest between androgyny and patriarchy in early western tradition. Ochshorn, Judith, p.66-83; h) Against the grain: A working feminist art criticism. Langer, Sandra L., p.84-96; i) The fallen woman in fiction. Flanders, Jane, p.97-109; j) Redefining the family and women's status within the family: The case of southern Appalachia. Anglin, Mary, p.110-118; k) Sexism and racism: Obstacles to the development of black women in South Africa. Locke, Mamie, p.119-129; l) Of paradigm and paradox: The case of Mary Boykin Chesnut. Muhlenfeld, Elisabeth S., p.130-138; m) Careers in landscape architecture: Recovering for women what the "ladies" won and lost. Howett, Catherine M., p.139-148; n) Does equality mean sameness? A historical perspective on the college curriculum for women with reflections on the current situation. Herman, Debra, p.149-157; o) Sex differences in the brain: Implications for curriculum change. Wundram, Ina Jane, p.158-169; p) Human sexuality: New insights from women's history. Harper, Anne L., p.170-183.

127. Fiction by American Women: Recent Views. Bevilacqua, Winifred Farrant, ed. Port Washington, NY: Associated Faculty Press, 1983.
a) The sentimentalists: Promise and betrayal in the home. Kelley, Mary, p.11-19; b) Thanatos and Eros: Kate Chopin's *The Awakening.* Wolff, Cynthia Griffin, p.21-39; c) "The temptation to be a beautiful object": Double standard and double bind in *The House of Mirth.* Fetterley, Judith, p.41-50; d) The forgotten reaping-hook: Sex in *My Antonia.* Gelfant, Blanche H., p.51-66; e) *Ida,* A great American novel. Secor, Cynthia, p.67-76; f) Winning: Katherine Anne Porter's women. Carson, Barbara Harrell, p.77-89; g) The visionary art of Flannery O'Connor. Oates, Joyce Carol, p.91-99; h) "A ritual for being born twice": Sylvia Plath's *The Bell Jar.* Perloff, Marjorie G., p.101-112; i) Eruptions of funk: Historicizing Toni Morrison. Willis, Susan, p.113-129; j) *Fear of Flying:* Developing the feminist novel. Reardon, Joan, p.131-143.

128. Flawed Liberation: Socialism and Feminism. Miller, Sally M., ed. Westport, CT: Greenwood Press, 1981.
a) Daniel DeLeon and the woman question. Seretan, L. Glen, p.3-12; b) Women in the party bureaucracy: Subservient functionaries. Miller, Sally M., p.13-35; c) May Wood Simons: Party theorist. Kreuter, Gretchen and Kreuter, Kent, p.37-60; d) Lena Morrow Lewis: Her rise and fall. Buhle, Mari Jo, p.61-86; e) The "Jennie Higginses" of the "New South in the West": A regional survey of socialist activists, agitators, and organizers, 1901-1917. Basen, Neil K., p.87-111; f) The politics of mutual frustration: Socialists and suffragists in New York and Wisconsin. Buenker, John D., p.113-144; g) Women socialists and their male comrades: The Reading experience, 1927-1936. Pratt, William C., p.145-178; h) Commentary. Miller, Sally M., p.179-184; i) Appendix: Woman and the social problem. Simons, May Wood, p.185-196.

129. Freedom, Feminism, and the State: An Overview of Individualist Feminism. McElroy, Wendy, ed. Washington, D.C.: Cato Institute, 1982.
a) The roots of individualist feminism in 19th-century America. McElroy, Wendy, p.3-26; b) Human rights not founded on sex. Grimké, Angelina, p.29-33; c) Anarchism and American traditions. Cleyre, Voltairine de, p.35-47; d) Give me liberty. Lane, Rose Wilder, p.49-59; e) Antigone's daughters. Elshtain, Jean Bethke, p.61-75; f) Government is women's enemy. Kinksy, Lynn and Presley, Sharon, p.77-83; g) An "age of consent" symposium. Harman, Lillian, p.87-100; h) Irrelevancies. Marvin, Bertha, p.101-109; i) Prostitution. "Danielle", p.111-115; j) Marriage contract. Blackwell, Henry and Stone, Lucy, p.119-120; k) Legal disabilities of women. Grimké, Sarah, p.121-127; l) Cupid's yokes. Heywood, Ezra H., p.129-142; m) Love, marriage and divorce. Andrews, Stephen Pearl, p.143-151; n) Body housekeeping. Heywood, Angela, p.155-157; o) The persecution of Moses Harman. Day, Stanley, p.159-168; p) If you liked gun control, you'll love the antiabortion amendment. Combs, Beverly J., p.169-175; q) Relations between parents and children. Davidson, Clara Dixon, p.179-187; r) The Speech of Polly

Baker. p.189-191; s) Some problems of social freedom. Harman, Lillian, p.193-201; t) Are feminist businesses capitalistic? Nichols, Rosalie, p.207-212; u) The economic position of women. La Follette, Suzanne, p.213-235; v) Trade unionism and women's work. Anthony, Susan, p.237-265; w) Protective labor legislation. Taylor, Joan Kennedy, p.267-270; x) State aid to science. Kelly, Gertrude, p.275-284; y) Women and the rise of the American medical profession. Ehrenreich, Barbara and English, Deirdre, p.285-300; z) Cardinal Gibbons's ignorance. Dietrick, Ellen Battelle, p.305-309; aa) The economic tendency of freethought. Cleyre, Voltairine de, p.311-322; bb) A right to make laws? Spooner, Lysander, p.327-330; cc) Perpetual vassalage. Heywood, Ezra H., p.331-333; dd) Patriotism: A menace to liberty. Goldman, Emma, p.337-348.

130. French Women and the Age of Enlightenment. Spencer, Samia I., ed. Bloomington, IN: Indiana University Press, 1984.
a) Women and the law. Rogers, Adrienne, p.33-48; b) Women and politics. Conner, Susan P., p.49-63; c) Women, democracy, and revolution in Paris, 1789-1794. Applewhite, Harriet B. and Levy, Darline Gay, p.64-79; d) Women and education. Spencer, Samia I., p.83-96; e) Women and family. Fairchilds, Cissie, p.97-110; f) Women and work. Fox-Genovese, Elizabeth, p.111-127; g) Women versus clergy, women pro clergy. Graham, Ruth, p.128-140; h) Women as muse. Runte, Roseann, p.143-154; i) Women and the theatre arts. Mittman, Barbara G., p.155-169; j) Women and music: Ornament of the profession? Rempel, Ursula M., p.170-180; k) Women in science. Gardiner, Linda, p.181-193; l) The novelists and their fictions. Stewart, Joan Hinde, p.197-211; m) The memorialists. Kinsey, Susan R., p.212-225; n) The epistolières. Curtis, Judith, p.226-241; o) Women and the visual arts. Rice, Danielle, p.242-255; p) Women and the Encyclopédie. Malueg, Sara Ellen Procious, p.259-271; q) Montesquieu and women. Kra, Pauline, p.272-284; r) Voltaire and women. Russo, Gloria M., p.285-295; s) Diderot and women. McLaughlin, Blandine L., p.296-308; t) Rousseau's "antifeminism" reconsidered. May, Gita, p.309-317; u) The death of an ideal: Female suicides in the eighteenth-century French novel. Thomas, Ruth P., p.321-331; v) The problem of sexual equality in Sadean prose. Laborde, Alice M., p.332-344; w) The edifying examples. Lee, Vera G., p.345-354; x) The view from England. Rogers, Katharine M., p.357-368; y) The view from Germany. Prather, Charlotte C., p.369-379; z) The view from Russia. Wilberger, Carolyn Hope, p.380-394; aa) The view from Spain: Rocco *finesse* and *espirit* versus plebian manners. Rudat, Eva M. Kahiluoto, p.395-406; bb) Conclusion: The legacy of the eighteenth century: A look at the future. Moses, Claire G., p.407-415.

131. Future Females: A Critical Anthology. Barr, Marleen S., ed. Bowling Green, OH: Bowling Green State University Popular Press, 1981.
a) Science fiction women before liberation. Rabkin, Eric S., p.9-25; b) Alexei Panshin's almost non-sexist *Rite of Passage*. Jones, Anne Hudson, p.26-36; c) "She pluck'd, she eat". Merritt, James D., p.37-41; d) Woman as nature in science fiction. Sanders, Scott, p.42-59; e) Coming Home: Four feminist utopias and patriarchal experience. Pearson, Carol, p.63-70; f) Recent feminist utopias. Russ, Joanna, p.71-85; g) A footnote to Russ's "Recent feminist utopias". Scholes, Robert, p.86-87; h) An ambiguous legacy: The role and position of women in the English Eutopia. Sargent, Lyman Tower, p.88-99; i) A woman appeared. Charnas, Suzy McKee, p.103-108; j) In and out of time: The form of Marge Piercy's novels. Kress, Susan, p.109-122; k) You, U.K. Le Guin. Holland, Norman N., p.125-137; l) Charles Bronson, Samurai, and other feminine images: A transactive response to *The Left Hand of Darkness*. Barr, Marleen S., p.138-154; m) A female captain's enterprise: The implications of *Star Trek's* "Turnabout Intruder". Whetmore, Edward, p.157-161; n) A personal response to Whetmore's "A female captain's enterprise". Berger, Arthur Asa, p.162-163; o) Where's all the fiction in science fiction? Berman, Jeffrey, p.164-176; p) The future females: A selected checklist through 1979. Schlobin, Roger C., p.179-189.

132. The Future of Difference. Eisenstein, Hester and Jardine, Alice, eds. Boston, MA: G. K. Hall, 1980.
a) Prelude: The future of difference. Jardine, Alice, p. xxv; b) Gender, relation, and difference in psychoanalytic perspective. Chodorow, Nancy, p.3-19; c) Mother-daughter relationships: Psychodynamics, politics, and philosophy. Flax, Jane, p.20-40; d) The bonds of love: Rational violence and erotic domination. Benjamin, Jessica, p.41-70; e) Language and revolution: The Franco-American Dis-connection. Stanton, Domna C., p.73-87; f) The powers of difference. Féral, Josette, p.88-94; g) To be or not to be ... a feminist speaker. Makward, Christiane, p.95-105; h) Introduction: Psychoanalysis and feminism in France. Gallop, Jane, p.106; i) Rethinking the maternal. Burke, Carolyn G., p.107-114; j) Psychoanalysis in France. Gallop, Jane, p.114-121; k) Poetry is not a luxury. Lorde, Audre, p.125-127; l) For the Etruscans: Sexual difference and artistic production - the debate over a female aesthetic. DuPlessis, Rachel Blau, p.128-156; m) Difference and language: A linguist's perspective. McConnell-Ginet, Sally, p.157-166; n) For a restricted thematics: Writing, speech, and difference in *Madame Bovary*. Schor, Naomi, p.167-192; o) Separation and survival: Mothers, daughters, sisters: - The women's experimental theater. Coss, Clare, Segal, Sondra and Sklar, Roberta, p.193-235; p) Visibility and difference: Black women in history and literature - pieces of a paper and some ruminations. Stadler, Quandra Prettyman, p.239-246; q) Black women and feminism. Omolade, Barbara, p.247-257; r) Androgyny and the psychology of sex differences. Heilbrun, Carolyn G., p.258-266; s) Lesbianism and the social function of taboo. Farley, Pamella, p.267-273; t) In a different voice: Women's conceptions of self and of morality. Gilligan, Carol, p.274-317; u) Women in power and politics. Messinger, Ruth, p.318-326; v) Women and the uses of power. Janeway, Elizabeth, p.327-344.

133. Gayspeak: Gay Male & Lesbian Communication.
Chesebro, James W., ed. New York: Pilgrim Press, 1981.
a) Homosexual labeling and the male role. Karr, Rodney
G., p.3-11; b) Coming out as a communicative process.
Darsey, James and Jandt, Fred E., p.12-27; c) Lesbians,
gay men, and their "languages". Hayes, Joseph J., p.28-
42; d) Gayspeak. Hayes, Joseph J., p.45-57; e)
"Gayspeak": A response. Darsey, James, p.58-67; f)
Recognition among lesbians in straight settings. Painter,
Dorothy S., p.68-79; g) Communication patterns in estab-
lished lesbian relationships. Day, Connie L. and Morse,
Ben W., p.80-86; h) Gay masculinity in the gay disco.
Chesebro, James W. and Klenk, Kenneth L., p.87-103; i)
Gay fantasies in gay publications. Glenn, John D., p.104-
113; j) Male homophobia. Garfinkle, Ellen M. and Morin,
Stephen F., p.117-129; k) The pathogenic secret. Ehrlich,
Larry G., p.130-141; l) Androgyny, sex-role rigidity, and
homophobia. Siegel, Paul, p.142-152; m) Images of the
gay male in contemporary drama. Carlsen, James W.,
p.165-174; n) Views of homosexuality among social scientists. Chesebro, James W., p.175-188; o) Media reaction to
the 1979 gay march on Washington. Nelson, Jeffrey,
p.189-196; p) Educational responsibilities to gay male and
lesbian students. DeVito, Joseph A., p.197-207; q)
Consciousness-raising among gay males. Chesebro, James
W., Cragan, John F. and McCullough, Patricia, p.211-223;
r) From "commies" and "queers" to "gay is good".
Darsey, James, p.224-247; s) Troy Perry: Gay advocate.
Robinson, David J., p.248-259; t) Lesbian feminist
rhetoric as a social movement. Nogle, Vicki, p.260-271; u)
Gay civil rights and the roots of oppression. Gearhart,
Sally Miller, p.275-285; v) Referendum campaigns vs. gay
rights. Park, Jan Carl, p.286-290; w) Ideologies in two gay
rights controversies. Brummett, Barry, p.291-302; x)
Religious fundamentalism and the democratic process.
Fischli, Ronald D., p.303-313.

134. Gender and Generation. McRobbie, Angela and Nava,
Mica, eds. Houndmills, Basingstoke, Hampshire:
Macmillan, 1984.
a) Youth service provision, social order and the question
of girls. Nava, Mica, p.1-30; b) Femininity and adolescence. Hudson, Barbara, p.31-53; c) Groping towards sexism: Boys' sex talk. Wood, Julian, p.54-84; d) Drawing the
line. Nava, Mica, p.85-111; e) Family fortunes. Chappell,
Adrian, p.112-129; f) Dance and social fantasy.
McRobbie, Angela, p.130-161; g) Some day my prince will
come. Walkerdine, Valerie, p.162-184; h) Alice in the consumer wonderland. Carter, Erica, p.185-214.

135. Gender and Literary Voice. Todd, Janet, ed. New York:
Holmes & Meier, 1980.
a) Is there a female voice? Joyce Carol Oates replies.
p.10-11; b) The looking-glass through Alice. Gillman,
Linda, p.12-25; c) Wariness and women's language: Two
modest verbal studies. Caws, Mary Ann, p.26-36; d)
Masculine and feminine personae in the love poetry of
Christine de Pisan. Price, Paola Malpezzi, p.37-53; e) The
Wife of Bath: Narrator as victim. Bolton, W.F., p.54-66; f)
Symbol, mask, and meter in the poetry of Louise Bogan.

Moore, Patrick, p.67-80; g) Olive Schreiner - A note on
sexist language and the feminist writer. Blake, Kathleen,
p.81-86; h) When silence has its way with you: Hazel Hall.
Andrews, Marcia S., p.87-107; i) May Sarton and fictions
of old age. Woodward, Kathleen, p.108-127; j) The
woman at the window: Ann Radcliffe in the novels of
Mary Wollstonecraft and Jane Austen. Butler, Marilyn,
p.128-148; k) Edith Wharton and the ghost story. Smith,
Allan Gardner, p.149-159; l) New directions in the contemporary bildungsroman: Lisa Alther's *Kinflicks*.
Braendlin, Bonnie Hoover, p.160-172; m) The laughter of
maidens, the crackle of matriarchs: Notes on the collision
between comedy and feminism. Wilt, Judith, p.173-196;
n) Mistresses and madonnas in the novels of Margaret
Dabble. Whittier, Gayle, p.197-213; o) Snow beneath
snow: A reconsideration of the virgin of *Villette*. Bledsoe,
Robert, p.214-222; p) Emma Bovary's masculinization:
Convention of clothes and morality of conventions. Festa-
McCormick, Diana, p.223-235; q) Power or sexuality: The
bind of Corneille's *Pulcherie*. Stanton, Domna C., p.236-
247; r) On the birth of death: An *Arrest d'Amour* of
Martial d'Auvergne. Conley, Tom, p.248-257. s) Feminist
criticism reviewed. Auerbach, Nina, p.258-268.

136. Gender and Nonverbal Behavior. Mayo, Clara and
Henley, Nancy M., eds. New York: Springer-Verlag, 1981.
a) Nonverbal behavior: Barrier or agent for sex role
change? Henley, Nancy M. and Mayo, Clara, p.3-13; b)
Gender patterns in touching behavior. Major, Brenda,
p.15-37; c) Women and nonverbal leadership cues: When
seeing is not believing. Geis, Florence and Porter,
Natalie, p.39-61; d) Visual behavior and dominance in
women and men. Dovidio, John F., Ellyson, Steve L. and
Fehr, B. J., p.63-79; e) Sex differences in body movements
and positions. Davis, Martha and Weitz, Shirley, p.81-92;
f) Sex-role influences in dyadic interaction: A theoretical
model. Ickes, William, p.95-128; g) Gender gestures: Sex,
sex-role, and nonverbal communication. LaFrance,
Marianne, p.129-150; h) Gender, androgyny, and conversational assertiveness. Crosby, Faye, Jose, Paul and Wong-
McCarthy, William, p.151-169; i) A feminist critique of
androgyny: Toward the elimination of gender attributions
for learned behavior. Lott, Bernice, p.171-180; j) The
development of sex differences in nonverbal signals:
Fallacies, facts, and fantasies. Haviland, Jeannette Jones
and Malatesta, Carol Zander, p.183-208; k) The seven
ages of woman: A view from American magazine advertisements. Umiker-Sebeok, Jean, p.209-252; l) Nonverbal
behavior and lesbian/gay orientation. Webbink, Patricia,
p.253-259; m) Nonverbal processes in feminist therapy.
Robson, Elizabeth, p.261-269.

137. Gender and Psychopathology. Al-Issa, Ihsan, ed. New
York: Academic Press, 1982.
a) Gender and psychopathology in perspective. Al-Issa,
Ihsan, p.3-29; b) Gender as a model for mental health.
Maffeo, Patricia A., p.31-50; c) Gender and child psy-
chopathology. Al-Issa, Ihsan, p.53-81; d) Gender and
adult psychopathology. Al-Issa, Ihsan, p.83-101; e)
Psychopathology and sex differences in the aged. Hecht,

Elizabeth and Mensh, Ivan N., p.103-129; f) Gender and depression. Hammen, Constance L., p.133-152; g) Gender and schizophrenia. Al-Issa, Ihsan, p.153-177; h) Gender and phobia. Fodor, Iris Goldstein, p.179-197; i) Gender, drinking, and alcohol abuse. Leland, Joy, p.201-220; j) Gender and drug use and abuse. Fidell, Linda S., p.222-236; k) Gender and crime. Campbell, Anne, p.237-254; l) Gender, genes, and psychopathology. Eysenck, Ans J., p.257-278; m) Gender, hormones, and psychopathology. Al-Issa, Ihsan, p.279-304; n) Gender and sexual functioning. Heiman, Julia R. and Verhulst, Johan, p.305-320; o) Gender, psychophysiological disorders, and mortality. Waldron, Ingrid, p.321-335; p) Gender and obesity. Foreyt, John P. and Goodrick, G. Ken, p.337-355.

138. Gender, Class & Education. Walker, Stephen and Barton, Len, eds. Sussex: Falmer Press, 1983.
a) Gender, class and education: A personal view. Barton, Len and Walker, Stephen, p.1-18; b) Intersections of gender and class: Accommodation and resistance by working-class and affluent females to contradictory sex-role ideologies. Anyon, Jean, p.19-37; c) Gender, resistance and power. Davies, Lynn, p.39-52; d) Work, class and teaching. Apple, Michael W., p.53-67; e) A cloud over co-education: An analysis of the forms of transmission of class and gender relations. Arnot, Madeleine, p.69-91; f) The conservative school? Sex roles at home, at work and at school. Delamont, Sara, p.93-105; g) Gender, patriarchy and class in the popular education of women. Deem, Rosemary, p.107-121; h) Women and teaching: A semi-detached sociology of a semi-profession. Acker, Sandra, p.123-139; i) Sex, education and social policy: A new moral economy? David, Miriam, p.141-159; j) Social theory, social relations and education. Culley, Lorraine and Demaine, Jack, p.161-172; k) Gender, class and education: A teaching bibliography of European studies. Coats, Maggie, p.173-182; l) Gender, class and education: A teaching bibliography of Australian and New Zealand studies. Evans, Terry, p.183-189; m) Gender, class and education: A teaching bibliography of American studies. Moskowitz, Emily J., p.191-213.

139. Gender, Class and Work. Gamarnikow, Eva, et al., eds. London: Heinemann, 1983.
a) Introduction: Class and work: Bringing women back in. Morgan, David H.J. and Taylorson, Daphne E., p.1-10; b) Patriarchal exploitation and the rise of English capitalism. Middleton, Chris, p.11-27; c) Not so much a factory, more a form of patriarchy: Gender and class during industrialisation. Lown, Judy, p.28-45; d) Women, men and social class. Britten, Nicky and Heath, Anthony, p.46-60; e) Trends in female social mobility. Chapman, Tony, Payne, Geoff and Payne, Judy, p.61-76; f) Participation in local union organisation. School meals staff: A case study. Cunnison, Sheila, p.77-95; g) Women, gender relations and wage labour. Pollert, Anna, p.96-114; h) 'Getting on'. Gender differences in career development: A case study in the hairdressing industry. Attwood, Margaret and Hatton, Frances, p.115-130; i) Feminisation and unioni-

sation: A case study from banking. Heritage, John, p.131-148; j) Patriarchal structures: The case of unemployment. Walby, Sylvia, p.149-166.

140. The Gender Gap in Psychotherapy: Social Realities and Psychological Processes. Rieker, Patricia Perri and Carmen, Elaine (Hilberman), eds. New York: Plenum Press, 1984.
a) Presidential address: Conceptual ambiguity and morality in modern psychiatry. Stone, Alan A., p.5-12; b) Editorial: Morality in medicine. Halleck, Seymour L., p.15-16; c) Inequality and women's mental health: An overview. Carmen, Elaine (Hilberman), Miller, Jean Baker and Russo, Nancy Felipe, p.17-39; d) The effects of inequality on psychology. Miller, Jean Baker, p.45-51; e) Some effects of proportions on group life: Skewed sex ratios and responses to token women. Kanter, Rosabeth Moss, p.53-78; f) Men's power with women, other men, and society: A men's movement analysis. Pleck, Joseph H., p.79-89; g) Women in positions of authority: A case study of changing sex roles. Mayes, Sharon S., p.91-103; h) Early origins of envy and devaluation of women: Implications for sex-role stereotypes. Lerner, Harriet E., p.111-124; i) Female dependency in context: Some theoretical and technical considerations. Lerner, Harriet E., p.125-134; j) Female masochism and the enforced restriction of choice. Waites, Elizabeth A., p.139-150; k) Roles and role conflict of women in infertile couples. Allison, Janet R., p.151-165; l) Cinderella's stepsisters: A feminist perspective on anorexia nervosa and bulimia. Boskind-Lodahl, Marlene, p.167-180; m) Emotional intimacy among men. Lewis, Robert A., p.181-193; n) Victims of violence and psychiatric illness. Carmen, Elaine (Hilberman), Mills, Trudy and Rieker, Patricia Perri, p.199-211; o) Overview: The "wife-beater's wife" reconsidered. Hilberman, Elaine, p.213-236; p) Father-daughter incest. Herman, Judith and Hirschman, Lisa, p.237-258; q) Families at risk for father-daughter incest. Herman, Judith and Hirschman, Lisa, p.259-264; r) Special issues for women in psychotherapy. Lerner, Harriet E., p.271-284; s) Issues in the psychotherapy of lesbians. Gartrell, Nanette, p.285-299; t) A feminist approach to family therapy. Hare-Mustin, Rachel T., p.301-318; u) Men's new family roles: Some implications for therapists. Berger, Michael, p.319-332; v) Teaching value clarification: The example of gender and psychotherapy. Carmen, Elaine (Hilberman) and Rieker, Patricia Perri, p.337-348; w) Toward an analysis of sex-role-related issues in the therapeutic relationship. Kaplan, Alexandra G., p.349-360; x) Psychiatry's problem with no name: Therapist-patient sex. Davidson, Virginia, p.361-368; y) Sexual misconduct by psychiatrists: The ethical and clinical dilemma of confidentiality. Stone, Alan A., p.369-374.

141. Genetics and Breast Cancer. Lynch, Henry T., ed. New York: Van Nostrand Reinhold Co., 1981.
a) Introduction to breast cancer genetics. Lynch, Henry T., p.1-13; b) Genetic control of breast cancer susceptibility in animals. Henry, Timothy J., Kouri, Richard E. and

McKinney, Cindy E., p.14-48; c) Statistical model for the study of familial breast cancer. Elston, Robert C., Go, Rodney C.P. and King, Mary-Claire, p.49-64; d) Pathologic aspects of familial carcinoma of breast. Mulcahy, Gabriel M. and Platt, Rudolf F., p.65-97; e) Epidemiology of breast cancer. Lynch, Henry T. and Lynch, Jane F., p.98-133; f) Genetic heterogeneity and breast cancer: Variable tumor spectra. Lynch, Henry T., p.134-173; g) Hormones, genetics, and breast cancer. Fishman, Jack and Schneider, Jill, p.174-186; h) Breast cancer in Cowden's syndrome. Brownstein, Martin H., p.187-195; i) Genetic counseling, patient and family management: Familial breast cancer. Lynch, Henry T., et al., p.196-242.

142. George Eliot: A Centenary Tribute. Haight, Gordon S. and VanArsdel, Rosemary T. eds. Totowa, NJ: Barnes & Noble, 1982.
a) George Eliot's bastards. Haight, Gordon S., p.1-10; b) George Eliot's language of the sense. McMaster, Juliet, p.11-27; c) A Meredithian glance at Gwendolen Harleth. Daniels, Elizabeth A., p.28-37; d) *Middlemarch* and the new humanity. ApRoberts, Ruth, p.38-46; e) 'Stealthy convergence' in *Middlemarch*. Heilman, Robert B., p.47-54; f) Antique gems from *Romola* to *Daniel Deronda*. Wiesenfarth, Joseph, p.55-63; g) The choir invisible: The poetics of humanist piety. Vogeler, Martha S., p.64-81; h) How George Eliot's people think. Korg, Jacob, p.82-89; i) George Eliot and the Russians. Berlin, Miriam H., p.90-106; j) George Eliot and her biographers. Nadel, Ira Bruce, p.107-121; k) The ambivalence of *The Mill on the Floss*. Adam, Ian, p.122-136; l) The unity of *Felix Holt*. Sandler, Florence, p.137-152; m) 'This petty medium': In the middle of *Middlemarch*. Hulcoop, John E., p.153-166.

143. George Eliot: Centenary Essays and an Unpublished Fragment. Smith, Anne, ed. London: Vision, 1981.
a) A new George Eliot manuscript. Baker, William, p.9-20; b) Critical approaches to George Eliot. Wright, Terence, p.21-35; c) *The Mill on the Floss* and the unreliable narrator. Martin, Graham, p.36-54; d) *Adam Bede* and "the story of the past". Palliser, Charles, p.55-76; e) *Romola* and the myth of apocalypse. Gezari, Janet K., p.77-102; f) Law, religion and the unity of *Felix Holt*. Vance, Norman, p.103-123; g) Origins, *Middlemarch*, endings: George Eliot's crisis of the antecedent. Gordon, Jan B., p.124-151; h) The hero as dilettante: *Middlemarch* and *Nostromo*. Levine, George, p.152-180; i) Fruit and seed: The finale to *Middlemarch*. Meikle, Susan, p.181-195; j) Gwendolen Harleth and "The girl of the period". Zimmerman, Bonnie, p.196-217.

144. The German Family: Essays on the Social History of the Family in Nineteenth- and Twentieth-Century Germany. Evans, Richard J. and Lee, W. R., eds. London: Croom Helm, 1981.
a) The German family: A critical survey of the current state of historical research. Lee, Robert, p.19-50; b) Family and role-division: The polarisation of sexual stereotypes in the nineteenth century - an aspect of the dissociation of work and family life. Hausen, Karin, p.51-83; c) Family and 'modernisation': The peasant family and social change in nineteenth-century Bavaria. Lee, Robert, p.84-119; d) Family and household: Social structures in a German village between the two World Wars. Wagner, Kurt and Wilke, Gerhard, p.120-147; e) Women, family and death: Excess mortality of women in child-bearing age in four communities in nineteenth-century Germany. Imhof, Arthur E., p.148-174; f) The family life-cycle: A study of factory workers in nineteenth century Württemberg. Schomerus, Heilwig, p.175-193; g) Overcrowding and family life: Working-class families and the housing crisis in late nineteenth-century Duisburg. Jackson, James H., p.194-220; h) Women's work and the family: Women garment workers in Berlin and Hamburg before the First World War. Dasey, Robyn, p.221-255; i) Politics and the family: Social democracy and the working-class family in theory and practice before 1914. Evans, Richard J., p.256-288.

145. German Women in the Nineteenth Century: A Social History. Fout, John C., ed. New York: Holmes & Meier, 1984.
a) Current research on German women's history in the nineteenth century. Fout, John C., p.3-54; b) Enlightened reforms and Bavarian girls' education: Tradition through innovation. Schneider, Joanne, p.55-71; c) Hannah Arendt's *Rahel Varnhagen*. Hertz, Deborah, p.72-87; d) Henriette Schleiermacher: A woman in a traditional role. Jensen, Gwendolyn E., p.88-103; e) The reading habits of women in the *Vormärz*. Möhrmann, Renate, p.104-117; f) Prelude to consciousness: Amalie Sieveking and the Female Association for the Care of the Poor and the Sick. Prelinger, Catherine M., p.118-132; g) Female political opposition in pre-1848 Germany: The role of Kathinka Zitz-Halein. Zucker, Stanley, p.133-150; h) German women writers and the Revolution of 1848. Secci, Lia, p.151-171; i) Self-conscious histories: Biographies of German women in the nineteenth century. Joeres, Ruth-Ellen Boetcher, p.172-196; j) Growing up female in the nineteenth century. Jacobi-Dittrich, Juliane, p.197-217; k) The radicalization of Lily Braun. Meyer, Alfred G., p.218-233; l) The impact of agrarian change on women's work and child care in early-nineteenth-century Prussia. Lee, W. R., p.234-255; m) Domestic industry: Work options and women's choices. Franzoi, Barbara, p.256-269; n) Social insurance and the family work of Oberlausitz home weavers in the late nineteenth century. Quataert, Jean H., p.270-294; o) The woman's role in the German working-class family in the 1890s from the perspective of women's autobiographies. Fout, John C., p.295-319; p) The civilizing tendency of hygiene: Working-class women under medical control in Imperial Germany. Frevert, Ute, p.320-344; q) The female victim: Homicide and women in Imperial Germany. Bergstrom, Randolph E. and Johnson, Eric A., p.345-367; r) An English-language bibliography on European and American women's history. Fout, John C., p.368-423.

146. Handbook of Clinical Intervention in Child Sexual Abuse. Sgroi, Suzanne M., ed. Lexington, MA: LexingtonBooks, 1982.
a) A conceptual framework for child sexual abuse. Blick, Linda Canfield, Porter, Frances Sarnacki and Sgroi, Suzanne M., p.9-37; b) Validation of child sexual abuse. Blick, Linda Canfield, Porter, Frances Sarnacki and Sgroi, Suzanne M., p.39-79; c) An approach to case management. Sgroi, Suzanne M., p.81-108; d) Treatment of the sexually abused child. Blick, Linda Canfield, Porter, Frances Sarnacki and Sgroi, Suzanne M., p.109-145; e) Group therapy with female adolescent incest victims. Blick, Linda Canfield and Porter, Frances Sarnacki, p.147-175; f) Sibling incest. Laredo, Carlos M., p.177-189; g) Individual and group treatment of mothers of incest victims. Dana, Natalie T. and Sgroi, Suzanne M., p.191-214; h) The incest offender. Groth, A. Nicholas, p.215-239; i) Family treatment. Sgroi, Suzanne M., p.241-267; j) Arts therapy with sexually abused children. Naitove, Connie E., p.269-308; k) Law enforcement and child sexual abuse. Graves, Patricia G. and Sgroi, Suzanne M., p.309-333; l) Multidisciplinary team review of child-sexual-abuse cases. Sgroi, Suzanne M., p.335-343; m) Evaluation of child-sexual-abuse programs. Bander, Karen W., Bishop, Gerrie and Fein, Edith, p.345-376; n) How to start a child-sexual-abuse intervention program. Sgroi, Suzanne M., p.377-384.

147. Her Story in Sport: A Historical Anthology of Women in Sports. Howell, Reet, ed. West Point, NY: Leisure Press, 1982.
a) Ball game participation of North American Indian women. Cheska, Alyce, p.19-34; b) Recreational activities of women in colonial America. Howell, Reet, p.35-43; c) The rise and development of women's concern for the physical education of American women, 1776-1885: From independence to the foundation of the American Association for the Advancement of Physical Education. Park, Roberta, p.44-56; d) The ladies' department of the *American Farmer*, 1825-1830: A locus for the advocacy of family health and exercise. Berryman, Jack and Brislin, Joann, p.57-69; e) American women, 1880-1860 (sic): Recreational pursuits and exercise. Howell, Reet, p.70-79; f) Woman's place in nineteenth century Canadian sport. Lindsay, Peter, p.80-86; g) Generalizations on women and sport, games and play in the United States from settlement to 1860. Howell, Reet, p.87-95; h) Sport and the Cult of True Womanhood: A paradox at the turn of the century. Squires, Mary-Lou, p.101-106; i) The realm of sports and the athletic woman, 1850-1900. Kenney, Karen, p.107-140; j) Women's participation in sporting activities as an indicator of a feminist movement in Canada between 1867-1914. Pitters, Marian, p.141-153; k) Women in sport and physical education in the United States 1900-1914. Howell, Maxwell L. and Howell, Reet, p.154-164; l) The effect of changing attitudes toward sexual morality upon the promotion of physical education for women in nineteenth century America. Vertinsky, Patricia, p.165-177; m) The American sportswoman from 1900 to 1920. Noonkester, Barbara, p.178-222; n) An

analysis of humour pertaining to sportswomen in Canadian newspapers from 1910-1920. Pitters, Marian, p.223-233; o) Women's sport: A trial of equality. Lucas, John and Smith, Ron, p.239-265; p) Eleonora Randolph Sears, pioneer in women's sports. Davenport, Joanna, p.266-272; q) Canadian women at the Olympic games. Schrodt, Barbara, p.273-283; r) Canadian women at the Commonwealth games. Schrodt, Barbara, p.284-293; s) Women in sport in the United States, 1945 to 1978. Heistand, Deborah, p.294-329; t) The effect of current sports legislation on women in Canada and the U.S.A. - Title IX. Burke, Peggy, p.330-342; u) Women in the sports halls of fame. Howell, Reet, p.343-350; v) The Eastern legacy - the early history of physical education for women. Davenport, Joanna, p.355-368; w) School physical activity programs for the antebellum southern females. Albertson, Roxanne, p.369-379; x) Adele Parot: Pathfinder for the Dioclesian Lewis school of gymnastic expression in the American west. Barney, Robert, p.380-390; y) The influential Miss Homans. Spears, Betty, p.391-404; z) History and structure of the department of physical education at the University of California with special reference to women's sports. Park, Roberta, p.405-416; aa) The first intercollegiate contest for women: Basketball, April 4, 1896. Emery, Lynne, p.417-423; bb) Interscholastic basketball: Bane of collegiate physical educators. Welch, Paula, p.424-431; cc) The controlled development of collegiate sport for women, 1923-1936. Gerber, Ellen W., p.432-459; dd) The history of women's intercollegiate athletics in Ohio, 1945-1972. Kearney, June Frances, p.460-471; ee) Major influences on the development of high school girls' sports in Ontario. Gurney, Helen, p.472-491; ff) From sidesaddle to rodeo. Remley, Mary-Lou, p.498-508; gg) The contributions of women to the history of competitive tennis in the United States in the twentieth century. Lumpkin, Angela, p.509-526; hh) The establishment of softball for American women, 1900-1940. Fidler, Merrie A., p.527-540; ii) The Edmonton Grads: The team and its social significance from 1915-1940. Dewar, John, p.541-547; jj) The 1930 U.B.C. women's basketball team: Those other world champions. Zerbe, Louisa, p.548-551; kk) The story: Six-player girls' basketball in Iowa. Beran, Janice Ann, p.552-563; ll) The development of women's organized sport in the 1920's: A study of the Canadian Ladies Golf Union. Mitchell, Sheila, p.564-571; mm) American women: Their debut in international track and field. Welch, Paula, p.572-578; nn) Sexual discrimination in youth sport: The case of Margaret Gisolo. Ladd, Tony, p.579-589; oo) The All-American Girls' Baseball League, 1943-1954. Fidler, Merrie A., p.590-607; pp) A historical perspective of women's membership in selected national sports organizations. Fidler, Merrie A., p.608-612.

148. The Hidden Half: Studies of Plains Indian Women. Albers, Patricia and Medicine, Beatrice, eds. Lanham, MD: University Press of America, 1983.
a) Introduction: New perspectives on Plains Indian women. Albers, Patricia, p.1-26; b) Beasts of burden and menial slaves: Nineteenth century observations of

Northern Plains Indian women. Weist, Katherine, p.29-52; c) The shackles of tradition. Kehoe, Alice, p.53-73; d) Male/female task differentiation among the Hidatsa: Toward the development of an archeological approach to the study of gender. Spector, Janet, p.77-99; e) Women's work: An examination of women's roles in Plains Indian arts and crafts. Schneider, Mary Jane, p.101-121; f) The role of Sioux women in the production of ceremonial objects: The case of the star quilt. Albers, Patricia and Medicine, Beatrice, p.123-140; g) The political economy of gender: A 19th century Plains Indian case study. Klein, Alan, p.143-173; h) Sioux women in transition: A study of their changing status in a domestic and capitalist sector of production. Albers, Patricia, p.175-234; i) Male and female in traditional Lakota culture. DeMallie, Raymond, p.237-265; j) "Warrior women" - Sex role alternatives for Plains Indian women. Medicine, Beatrice, p.267-277.

149. Hidden in the Household: Women's Domestic Labour under Capitalism. Fox, Bonnie, ed. Ontario, Canada: Women's Press, 1980.
a) Domestic labour and the working-class household. Seccombe, Wally, p.25-99; b) Capital, the state and the origins of the working-class household. Curtis, Bruce, p.101-134; c) Domestic labour: A methodological discussion. Briskin, Linda, p.135-172; d) Women's double work day: Twentieth-century changes in the reproduction of daily life. Fox, Bonnie, p.173-216; e) The expanded reproduction cycle of labour power in twentieth-century capitalism. Seccombe, Wally, p.217-266; f) Domestic labour and the reproduction of labour power: Towards an analysis of women, the family, and class. Blumenfeld, Emily and Mann, Susan, p.267-307.

150. Home Girls: A Black Feminist Anthology. Smith, Barbara, ed. New York: Kitchen Table: Women of Color Press, 1983.
a) Poem. Hull, Gloria T., p.lvi; b) For a Godchild, Regina, on the occasion of her first love (poem). Derricotte, Toi, p.3-5; c) The damned (poem). Derricotte, Toi, p.6-7; d) Hester's Song (poem). Derricotte, Toi, p.8-9; e) The sisters. Veaux, Alexis de, p.10-12; f) Debra (poem). Clinton, Michelle T., p.13-14; g) If I could write this in fire, I would write this in fire. Cliff, Michelle, p.15-30; h) The blood - yes, the blood: A conversation. Smith, Cenen and Smith, Barbara, p.31-51; i) Something Latino was up with us. Redd, Spring, p.52-56; j) "I used to think" (poem). McCray, Chirlane, p.57-59; k) The black back-ups (poem). Rushin, Donna Kate, p.60-63; l) Home. Smith, Barbara, p.64-69; m) "Under the days": The buried life and poetry of Angelina Weld Grmiké. Hull, Gloria T., p.73-82; n) The black lesbian in American literature: An overview. Shockley, Ann Allen, p.83-93; o) Artists without art form. Weems, Renita, p.94-105; p) I've been thinking of Diana Sands. Jones, Patricia, p.106-109; q) Cultural legacy denied and discovered: Black lesbians in fiction by women. Gomez, Jewelle L., p.110-123; r) What it is I think she's doing anyhow: A reading of Toni Cade Bambara's *The Salt Eaters*. Hull, Gloria T., p.124-142; s)

Tar beach. Lorde, Audre, p.145-158; t) Cat. Carter, Julie, p.159-165; u) Before I dress and soar again (poem). Allegra, Donna, p.166-167; v) LeRoy's birthday. Mays, Raymina Y., p.168-170; w) The wedding. Smith, Beverly, p.171-176; x) Maria de las Rosas (poem). Birtha, Becky, p.177-178; y) Miss Esther's land. Banks, Barbara A., p.179-196; z) The failure to transform: homophobia in the black community. Clarke, Cheryl, p.197-208. aa) What will you be? (poem). Parker, Pat, p.209-213; bb) Among the things that use to be (poem). Coleman, Willie M., p.221-222; cc) From sea to shining sea (poem). Jordan, June, p.223-229; dd) Women of summer. Clarke, Cheryl, p.230-254; ee) The tired poem: Last letter from a typical unemployed black professional woman (poem). Rushin, Donna Kate, p.255-259; ff) Shoes are made for walking. Steele, Shirley O., p.260-269; gg) Billy de Lye (poem). McCalla, Deidre, p.270-271; hh) The Combahee River collective statement. Combahee River Collective, p.272-282; ii) Black macho and black feminism. Powell, Linda C., p.283-292; jj) Black lesbian/feminist organizing: A conversation. Abdulahad, Tania, et al., p.293-319; kk) Reflections on black feminist therapy. Johnson, Eleanor, p.320-324; ll) For strong women (poem). Clinton, Michelle T., p.325-327; mm) The black goddess (poem). Rushin, Donna Kate, p.328-330; nn) Women's spirituality: A household act. Teish, Luisah, p.331-351; oo) Only justice can stop a curse. Walker, Alice, p.352-355; pp) Coalition politics: Turning the century. Reagon, Bernice Johnson, p.356-368.

151. Home, School and Leisure in the Soviet Union. Brine, Jenny, Perrie, Maureen and Sutton, Andrew, eds. London: George Allen & Unwin, 1980.
a) Housing ideals, structural constraints and the emancipation of women. Andrusz, G. D., p.3-25; b) Domestic labour and Soviet society. Holt, Alix, p.26-54; c) 'A woman's right to choose' in the Soviet Union. Holland, Barbara, p.55-69; d) Secondary education for all in a forward-looking society. Koutaissoff, Elisabeth, p.73-91; e) Socialisation in the literature lesson. O'Dell, Felicity, p.92-109; f) Soviet boarding education: Its rise and progress. Dunstan, John, p.110-141; g) Soviet child care: Its organisation at local level. Drake, Madeline, p.142-159; h) Backward children in the USSR: An unfamiliar approach to a familiar problem. Sutton, Andrew, p.160-191; i) Achievements and problems in Soviet recreational planning. Shaw, Denis J. B., p.195-214; j) Sport in Soviet society: Fetish or free play? Riordan, James, p.215-238; k) Reading as a leisure pursuit in the USSR. Brine, Jenny, p.239-269.

152. Homosexuality and the Catholic Church. Gramick, Jeannine, ed. Chicago: Thomas More Press, 1983.
a) Reflections of a gay Catholic. McNaught, Brian, p.21-44; b) Growing up lesbian and Catholic. Borden, Ann, p.45-59; c) New sociological theory on homosexuality. Gramick, Jeannine, p.60-79; d) Overcoming the structured evil of male domination and heterosexism. Zanotti, Barbara, p.80-88; e) Homosexuality, celibacy, religious life and ordination. Nugent, Robert, p.89-120; f) Civil rights in

a church of compassion. Kane, Theresa, p.121-128; g) Gay men and women and the vowed life. Hubbuch, Cornelius, p.129-137; h) Moral theology and homosexuality. Curran, Charles, p.138-168; i) Shifting attitudes toward homosexuality. McGuire, Kenneth, p.169-174.

153. Households and the World-Economy. Smith, Joan, Wallerstein, Immanuel and Evers, Hans-Dieter, eds. Beverly Hills, CA: Sage, 1984.
a) Household structures and labor-force formation in the capitalist world-economy. Wallerstein, Immanuel, p.17-22; b) Subsistence reproduction: A framework for analysis. Clauss, Wolfgang, Evers, Hans-Dieter and Wong, Diana, p.23-36; c) Households as income-pooling units. Friedman, Kathie, p.37-55; d) The limits of using the household as a unit of analysis. Wong, Diana, p.56-63; e) Nonwage labor and subsistence. Smith, Joan, p.64-89; f) Households, modes of living, and production systems. Stauth, Georg, p.90-100; g) Development and underdevelopment of household-based production in Europe. Schiel, Tilman, p.101-130; h) The proletarian is dead: Long live the housewife? von Werlhof, Claudia, p.131-147; i) Beyond the peasant to proletarian debate: African household formation in South Africa. Martin, William G., p.151-167; j) Household economy and financial capital: The case of passbook savings in Brazil. Barbosa, Eva Machado, p.168-172; k) The contribution of public goods to household reproduction: Case study from Brazil. Augel, Johannes, p.173-179; l) State, collective, and household: The process of accumulation in China, 1949-65. Thompson, Lanny, p.180-198; m) Gender division within the U.S. working class: Households in the Philadelphia area, 1870-1945. Dickinson, Torry, p.199-211; n) Working or helping? London working-class children in the domestic economy. Davin, Anna, p.215-232; o) Wages, consumption, and survival: Working class households in Puerto Rico in the 1930's. Baerga, Maria del Carmen, p.233-251; p) Towards a theory of the sexual division of labor. Bennholdt-Thomsen, Veronika, p.252-271; q) Conflicts inside and outside the household: A West African case study. Elwert, Georg, p.272-296.

154. Ideals for Women in the Works of Christine de Pizan. Bornstein, Diane, ed. (Detroit, MI?): Published for Michigan Consortium for Medieval and Early Modern Studies, 1981.
a) Self-consciousness and self concepts in the work of Christine de Pizan. Bornstein, Diane, p.11-28; b) The crowned dame, dame opinion, and dame philosophy: The female characteristics of three ideals in Christine de Pizan's *L'Avision Christine*. Durlay, Maureen Slattery, p.29-50; c) Christine de Pizan and Order of the Rose. Willard, Charity C., p.51-67; d) Virginity as an ideal in Christine de Pizan's *Cité des Dames*. Reno, Christine, p.69-90; e) Christine de Pizan's *Livre des Trois Vertus*: Feminine ideal or practical advice? Willard, Charity C., p.91-116; f) The ideal of the lady of the manor as reflected in Christine de Pizan's *Livre des Trois Vertus*. Bornstein, Diane, p.117-128.

155. The Image of the Prostitute in Modern Literature. Horn, Pierre L. and Pringle, Mary Beth, eds. New York: Frederick Ungar, 1984.
a) The prostitute as scapegoat: Mildred Rogers in Somerset Maugham's *Of Human Bondage*. Braendlin, Bonnie Hoover, p.9-18; b) French feminist theater and the subject of prostitution, 1870-1914. Millstone, Amy, p.19-27; c) Zola's view of prostitution in *Nana*. Warren, Jill, p.29-41; d) The magic circle: The role of the prostitute in Isak Dinesen's *Gothic Tales*. Whissen, Thomas, p.43-51; e) The romantization of the prostitute in Dostoevsky's fiction. Moravcevich, Nicholas, p.53-61; f) The prostitute in Arab and North African fiction. Accad, Evelyne, p.63-75; g) Courtesans and prostitutes in South Asian literature. Weir, Ann Lowry, p.77-89; h) The fate of the fallen woman in *Maggie* and *Sister Carrie*. Hussman, Lawrence E., p.91-100; i) The uncommon prostitute: The contemporary image in an American age of pornography. Hughes, James M., p.101-118; j) Women writing about prostitutes: Amalia Jamilis and Luisa Valenzuela. Kaminsky, Amy Katz, p.119-131.

156. Images of Women in Antiquity. Cameron, Averil and Kuhrt, Amélie, eds. Detroit, MI: Wayne State University Press, 1983.
a) Women: Model for possession by Greek daemons. Padel, Ruth, p.3-19; b) Exit Atossa: Images of women in Greek historiography on Persia. Sancisi-Weerdenburg, Heleen, p.20-33; c) Women and witchcraft in ancient Assyria. Rollin, Sue, p.34-45; d) Influential women. Lefkowitz, Mary R., p.49-64; e) The god's wife of Amun in the 18th dynasty in Egypt. Robins, Gay, p.65-78; f) Women and housing in classical Greece: The archaeological evidence. Walker, Susan, p.81-91; g) Women on Athenian vases: Problems of interpretation. Williams, Dyfri, p.92-106; h) Bound to bleed: Artemis and Greek women. King, Helen, p.109-127; i) Hittite birth rituals. Pringle, Jackie, p.128-141; j) Celtic women in the early middle ages. Davies, Wendy, p.145-165; k) In search of Byzantine women: Three avenues of approach. Herrin, Judith, p.167-190; l) Bridewealth and dowry in Nuzi. Grosz, Katarzyna, p.193-206; m) Infanticide in Hellenistic Greece. Pomeroy, Sarah B., p.207-222; n) Women and wealth. Bremen, Riet Van, p.223-242; o) Goddesses, women and Jezebel. Ackroyd, Peter R., p.245-259; p) The Naditu women of Sippar. Jeyes, Ulla, p.260-272; q) The role of Jewish women in the religion, ritual and cult of Graeco-Roman Palestine. Archer, Léonie J., p.273-287; r) Women in early Syrian Christianity. Harvey, Susan Ashbrook, p.288-298.

157. In Her Own Right: Selected Essays on Women's History in B.C.. Latham, Barbara and Kess, Cathy, eds. Victoria, B.C.: Camosun College, 1980.
a) Writing women into British Columbia's history. Marie, Gillian, p.1-18; b) To Columbia on the Tynemouth: The emigration of single women and girls in 1862. Lay, Jackie, p.19-41; c) Notes on the British Columbia Protestant Orphan's Home. Lupton, Nora, p.43-54; d) British Columbia Women's Institute in the early years: Time to

remember. Zacharias, Alexandra, p.55-78; e) Public and political: Documents of the woman's suffrage campaign in British Columbia, 1871-1917: The view from Victoria. Cramer, Michael H., p.79-100; f) Agnes Deans Cameron: Against the current. Pazdro, Roberta J., p.101-123; g) Maria Grant, 1854-1937: The life and times of an early twentieth century Christian. Whelen, Gloria, p.125-146; h) Evlyn Farris and the University Women's Club. Adilman, Tami, p.147-166; i) Sexism in British Columbia trade unions, 1900-1920. Campbell, Marie, p.167-186; j) Helena Gutteridge: Votes for women and trade unions. Wade, Susan, p.187-203; k) The 'social evil': Prostitution in Vancouver, 1900-1920. Nilsen, Deborah, p.205-228; l) The B.C. Liberal Party and women's reforms, 1916-1928. Crossley, Diane, p.229-253; m) A response to the depression: The local Council of Women of Vancouver. Powell, Mary Patricia, p.255-278; n) Women and reform in British Columbia: Some preliminary suggestions. Weiss, Gillian, p.279-284; o) Postscript: Huntresses. Wozney, Christine, p.285-286; p) Appendix: Votes for women: Profiles of prominent British Columbia suffragists and social reformers. Hale, Linda Louise, p.287-302.

158. In the Shadow of the Past: Psychology Portrays the Sexes: A Social and Intellectual History. Lewin, Miriam, ed. New York: Columbia University Press, 1984.
a) The power of the past: History and the psychology of women. Harris, Barbara J., p.1-25; b) Freud's heritage: Fathers and daughters in German literature (1750- 1850). Wickert, Gabriele, p.26-38; c) The Victorians, the psychologists, and psychic birth control. Lewin, Miriam, p.39-76; d) Leta Hollingworth: Toward a sexless intelligence. Rosenberg, Rosalind, p.77-96; e) Not quite new worlds: Psychologists' conceptions of the ideal family in the twenties. Morawski, J. G., p.97-125; f) "Give me a dozen healthy infants": John B. Watson's popular advice on childrearing, women, and the family. Harris, Ben, p.126-154; g) "Rather worse than folly?" psychology measures femininity and masculinity, 1: From Terman and Miles to the Guilfords. Lewin, Miriam, p.155-178; h) Psychology measures femininity and masculinity, 2: From "13 Gay Men" to the instrumental-expressive distinction. Lewin, Miriam, p.179-204; i) The theory of male sex role identity: Its rise and fall, 1936 to the present. Pleck, Joseph H., p.205-225; j) Mother: Social sculptor and trustee of the faith. Contratto, Susan, p.226-255; k) "To pet, coddle, and 'Do For'": Caretaking and the concept of maternal instinct. Shields, Stephanie A., p.256-273; l) Metatheoretical influences on conceptions of human development. Benack, Suzanne and Gergen, Kenneth J., p.274-294; m) The study of employed mothers over half a century. Hoffman, Lois Wladis, p.295-314.

159. The Incidence of Female Criminality in the Contemporary World. Adler, Freda, ed. New York: New York University Press, 1981.
a) International concern in light of the American experience. Adler, Freda, p.1-13; b) Female criminality in the Netherlands. Bruinsma, G.J.N., Dessaur, C.I. and Van Hezewijk, W.J.V., p.14-63; c) Female criminality in

Finland - What do the statistics show? Anttila, I., p.64-83; d) Norwegian women in court. Jensen, A., p.84-101; e) Female crime in England and Wales. Gibbens, T.C.N., p.102-121; f) Changing patterns of female criminality in Germany. Middendorff, D. and Middendorff, W., p.122-133; g) The criminality of women in Poland. Plenska, D., p.134-144; h) Crimes against life committed by women in Hungary. Rasko, G., p.145-157; i) A preliminary study of female criminality in Nigeria. Oloruntimehin, O., p.158-175; j) Female criminality in Egypt. El Ashmawi, A.W., p.176-187; k) Argentine statistics on female criminality. Kent, J.N., p.188-214; l) Venezuelan female criminality: The ideology of diversity and marginality. Aniyar de Castro, L., p.215-227; m) Criminality amongst women in India: A study of female offenders and female convicts. Bhanot, M.L. and Misra, Surat, p.228-257; n) Emancipation of women and crime in Japan. Sato, K.S., p.258-272.

160. The Incorporated Wife. Callan, Hilary and Ardener, Shirley , eds. London: Croom Helm, 1984.
a) Incorporation and exclusion: Oxford academics' wives. Ardener, Shirley, p.27-49; b) Ambivalence and dedication: Academic wives in Cambridge University, 1870-1970. Sciama, Lidia, p.50-66; c) Police wives: A reflection of police concepts of order and control. Young, Malcolm, p.67-88; d) Camp followers: A note on wives of the armed services. Macmillan, Mona, p.89-105; e) The suitable wife: Preparation for marriage in London and Rhodesia/Zimbabwe. Kirkwood, Deborah, p.106-119; f) Shell wives in limbo. Tremayne, Soraya, p.120-134; g) The negation of structure: A note on British council wives. Clark, Isobel, p.135-142; h) Settler wives in southern Rhodesia: A case study. Kirkwood, Deborah, p.143-164; i) Colonial wives: Villains or victims? Gartrell, Beverley, p.165-185; j) Memsahibs in colonial Malaya: A study of European wives in a British colony and protectorate, 1900-1940. Brownfoot, Janice, p.186-210.

161. Indian Women in Media: A Collection of Essays. WCSRC-CISRS Joint Women's Programme, ed. Delhi: Lithouse, 1984.
a) Movement against the portrayal of women in India. Ramesh, Asha, p.1-3; b) Press coverage of women and women's concerns. Eashwar, Sucharita, p.4-7; c) Applauding servility - Images of women in advertisements. Krishnan, Prabha, p.8-13; d) Portrayal of women in women's journals. Ramesh, Asha, p.14-19; e) Women and Bengali literature. Gangopadhyay, Arati, p.20-25; f) Television and women. Centre for Women's Development Studies Committee of the Portrayal of Women in Media, p.26-39; g) A fallen image - Women in India. H.P., Philomena and Sarkar, Sutapa, p.40-44; h) Women and mass media in Kerala. Velocherry, Joseph, p.45-62.

162. Interest and Emotion: Essays on the Study of Family and Kinship. Medick, Hans and Sabean, David Warren, eds. Cambridge, England: Cambridge University Press, 1984.
a) Interest and emotion in family and kinship studies: A critique of social history and anthropology. Medick, Hans

and Sabean, David Warren, p.9-27; b) Putting kin and kinship to good use: The circulation of goods, labour, and names on Karpathos (Greece). Vernier, Bernard, p.28-76; c) Infanticide in rural Bavaria in the nineteenth century. Schulte, Regina, p.77-102; d) Possession and dispossession: Maternity and mortality in Morocco. Maher, Vanessa, p.103-128; e) 'Avoir sa part': Sibling relations in partible inheritance Brittany. Segalen, Martine, p.129-144; f) Tensions, dissensions, and ruptures inside the family in seventeenth- and eighteenth-century Haute Provence. Collomp, Alain, p.145-170; g) Young bees in an empty hive: Relations between brothers-in-law in a south German village around 1800. Sabean, David Warren, p.171-186; h) 'A brother is a creative thing': Change and conflict in a Melpa family (Papua New Guinea). Strathern, Andrew, p.187-209; i) The Aragonese royal family around 1300. Sablonier, Roger, p.210-239; j) Afro-American kinship before and after emancipation in North America. Gutman, Herbert G., p.241-265; k) Parental strategies: Calculation or sentiment?: Fostering practices among West Africans. Goody, Esther, p.266-277; l) Kinship and class consciousness: Family values and work experience among hospital workers in an American southern town. Sacks, Karen, p.279-299; m) Linen was their life: Family survival strategies and parent-child relations in nineteenth-century France. Tilly, Louise A., p.300-316; n) Village spinning bees: Sexual culture and free time among rural youths in early modern Germany. Medick, Hans, p.317-339; o) Family fun in Starve Harbor: Custom, history and confrontation in village Newfoundland. Sider, Gerald M., p.340-370; p) Mothers, sons, and the sale of symbols and goods: The 'German Mother's Day' 1923-33. Hausen, Karin, p.371-413.

163. International Feminism: Networking against Female Sexual Slavery. Barry, Kathleen, Bunch, Charlotte and Castley, Shirley, eds. New York: International Women's Tribune Centre, 1984.
a) International politics of female sexual slavery. Barry, Kathleen, p.21-31; b) The network defines its issues: Theory, evidence and analysis of female sexual slavery. Barry, Kathleen, p.32-48; c) Network strategies and organizing against female sexual slavery. Bunch, Charlotte, p.49-62; d) Why I oppose Kisaeng tours. Matsui, Yayori, p.64-72; e) The woman, the love, and the power. Olsson, Hanna, p.73-81; f) The devadasi problem. H. P., Philomena and Ramesh, Asha, p.82-87; g) Traffic of children. Bridel, Renee, p.89-93; h) The torture of women political prisoners: A case study in female sexual slavery. Bunster, Ximena, p.94-102.

164. Jane Austen in a Social Context. Monaghan, David, ed. Totowa, NJ: Barnes & Noble, 1981.
a) Introduction: Jane Austen as a social novelist. Monaghan, David, p.1-8; b) Jane Austen and romantic imprisonment. Auerbach, Nina, p.9-27; c) The influence of place: Jane Austen and the novel of social consciousness. Banfield, Ann, p.28-48; d) Disregarded designs: Jane Austen's sense of the volume. Butler, Marilyn, p.49-65; e) Sex and social life in Jane Austen's novels. Fergus,

Jan S., p.66-85; f) 'Real solemn history' and social history. Kent, Christopher, p.86-104; g) Jane Austen and the position of women. Monaghan, David, p.105-121; h) Jane Austen and the problem of leisure. Nardin, Jane, p.122-142; i) *Mansfield Park*: The revolt of the 'feminine' woman. Smith, Leroy W., p.143-158; j) Muted discord: Generational conflict in Jane Austen. Spacks, Patricia Meyer, p.159-179; k) In between - Anne Elliot marries a sailor and Charlotte Heywood goes to the seaside. Tanner, Tony, p.180-194.

165. Judge Lawyer Victim Thief: Women, Gender Roles, and Criminal Justice. Rafter, Nicole Hahn and Stanko, Elizabeth Anne, eds. Boston, MA: Northeastern University, 1982.
a) One hundred years of fear: Rape and the medical profession. Mills, Elizabeth Anne, p.29-62; b) Would you believe this woman? Prosecutorial screening for "credible" witnesses and a problem of justice. Stanko, Anne Elizabeth, p.63-82; c) The dark side of marriage: Battered wives and the domination of women. Klein, Dorie, p.83-107; d) Exploring female crime patterns: Problems and prospects. Parisi, Nicolette, p.111-129; e) Work and the addicted prostitute. Rosenbaum, Marsha, p.131-150; f) Murdered women and women who murder: A critique of the literature. Wilbanks, William, p.151-180; g) Delinquency causation in female offenders. Warren, Marguerite Q., p.181-202; h) Are females treated differently? A review of the theories and evidence on sentencing and parole decisions. Parisi, Nicolette, p.205-220; i) Female delinquents in a suburban court. Fenster, Carol and Mahoney, Anne Rankin, p.221-238; j) Hard times: Custodial prisons for women and the example of the New York State Prison for Women at Auburn, 1893-1933. Rafter, Nicole Hahn, p.237-260; k) Female patients and the medical profession in jails and prisons: A case of quintuple jeopardy. Shaw, Nancy Stoller, p.261-273; l) "The government's unique experiment in salvaging women criminals": Cooperation and conflict in the administration of a women's prison - The case of the Federal Industrial Institution for Women at Alderson. SchWeber, Claudine, p.277-303; m) Women as criminal justice professionals: A challenge to change tradition. Flynn, Edith Elisabeth, p.305-340; n) Sex-role operations: Strategies for women working in the criminal justice system. Baunach, Phyllis Jo and Rafter, Nicole Hahn, p.341-358; o) Women in the criminal justice profession: An analysis of status conflict. Wilson, Nanci Koser, p.359-372.

166. Kartini Centenary: Indonesian Women Then and Now. Zainu'ddin, Ailsa Thomson, ed. Clayton, Victoria, Australia: Monash University, 1980.
a) Kartini - her life, work and influence. Zainu'ddin, Ailsa Thomson, p.1-29; b) Women in a yogyakarta kampung. Lucas, Kadar, p.30-38; c) Women in the workforce. Raharjo, Yulfita, p.56-68; d) The search for women in Indonesian history. Dobbin, Christine, p.56-68; e) Rights and responsibility, power and privilege: Women's roles in contemporary Indonesia. Manderson, Lenore, p.69-92.

167. Keeping the Peace: A Women's Peace Handbook. Jones, Lynne, ed. London: The Women's Press, 1983.
a) Starting a movement: Frauen für frieden (Women for Peace, West Germany). Quistorp, Eva, p.7-13; b) Organising at the grassroots: Vrouwen voor vrede (Women for Peace, the Netherlands). Smid, Frouke, p.14-21; c) Working as a group. Nottingham WONT, p.22-29; d) A national campaign: Women's party for survival. Sheldon, Sayre, p.30-39; e) All is connectedness: Scenes from the Women's Pentagon Action USA. King, Ynestra, p.40-63; f) Babies against the bomb: A statement. Swade, Tamar, p.64-67; g) Children need smiles not missiles: Planning a walk Oxford Mothers for Nuclear Disarmament. Lavelle, Jini, p.68-78; h) On common ground: The women's peace camp at Greenham Common. Jones, Lynne, p.79-97; i) At the foot of the mountain: The Shibokusa women of Kita Fuji. Caldecott, Leonie, p.98-107; j) A women's day for disarmament: Notes on organising a decentralised action. Jones, Lynne and Miller, Margot, p.108-119; k) Organising a mass lobby of Parliament: Families against the bomb. Tutton, Anne, p.120-130.

168. Knowledge Reconsidered: A Feminist Overview. Franklin, Ursula Martius, ed. Ottawa, Ontario: Canadian Research Institute for the Advancement of Women, 1984.
a) The renaissance of women. Smith, Dorothy E., p.1-14; b) From feminism to a new conception of ethics. Sherwin, Susan, p.15-24; c) Hindsight is 20/20: The development, achievements and dilemmas of feminist literary criticism. Lebowitz, Andrea, p.25-41; d) What has the feminist perspective done for Canadian history? Van Kirk, Sylvia, p.43-58; e) Conceptualizing "women" in anthropology and sociology. Luxton, Meg, p.59-75; f) Will women change technology or will technology change women? Franklin, Urusla Martius, p.77-90; g) Production et communication du savior dans une perspective féministe: Enjuex et défis pour les femmes. Jean, Michèle, p.91-101; h) Creating and communicating knowledge from a feminist perspective: Risks and challenges for women. Jean, Michèle, p.102-110.

169. Labor Education for Women Workers. Wertheimer, Barbara Mayer, ed. Philadelphia, PA: Temple University Press, 1981.
a) Labor education and women workers: An historical perspective. Goldfarb, Lyn and Kornbluh, Joyce L., p.15-31; b) Promoting and recruiting: Reaching the target audience. Rozen, Freida Shoenberg, p.32-41; c) The short course. Semel, Rochelle, p.42-53; d) Conferences: The one-day model. Kornbluh, Hy and Kornbluh, Joyce L., p.54-61; e) Training rank and file leaders: A case study. Rachlin, Marjorie B., p.62-70; f) Credit programs for working women. Schrier, Katherine, p.71-82; g) Residential schools. Wertheimer, Barbara M., p.83-97; h) Evaluating programs for working adults. Rosen, Stanley and Samper, Maria-Luz D., p.98-108; i) Discussion method. Rachlin, Marjorie B., p.111-119; j) Case studies: How to develop and use them. Busman, Gloria, p.120-126; k) Using oral history in the classroom. Hoffman,

Alice M., p.127-137; l) Games and other exercises. Nelson, Anne H., p.138-155; m) Labor history through field trips. Adelman, William, p.159-170; n) Training women for political action. Mobley, Donna, p.171-181; o) Grievance handling for women stewards. Torres, Ida, p.182-193; p) Occupational health and safety for women workers: Some teaching models. Bertinuson, Janet and Hricko, Andrea M., p.194-203; q) Education for affirmative action: Two union approaches. Johnson, Gloria T. and Komer, Odessa, p.204-216; r) How to choose and use materials in education for women workers. Wallihan, James, p.217-225; s) Subjects and materials: How to handle controversy. Kopelov, Connie, p.226-230; t) How foundations view funding proposals on working women. Berresford, Susan Vail, p.233-240; u) Funding worker education through tuition refund plans. Abramovitz, Mimi, p.241-251; v) Labor education and women workers: An international comparison. Cook, Alice H. and Till-Retz, Roberta, p.255-264.

170. A Labour of Love: Women, Work and Caring. Finch, Janet and Groves, Dulcie, eds. London: Routledge & Kegan Paul, 1983.
a) Caring: A labour of love. Graham, Hilary, p.13-30; b) Why do women care? Ungerson, Clare, p.31-49; c) Employment, women and their disabled children. Baldwin, Sally and Glendinning, Caroline, p.53-71; d) The caring wife. Oliver, Judith, p.72-88; e) Single careers: Employment, housework and caring. Wright, Fay, p.89-105; f) Care for elderly people: A conflict between women and the state. Walker, Alan, p.106-128; g) The economics of work and caring. Rimmer, Lesley, p.131-147; h) Natural selection: Perspectives on entitlement to the invalid care allowance. Finch, Janet and Groves, Dulcie, p.148-166.

171. Language, Gender and Society. Thorne, Barrie, Kramarae, Cheris and Henley, Nancy, eds. Rowley, MA: Newbury House, 1983.
a) Language, gender and society: Opening a second decade of research. Henley, Nancy, Kramarae, Cheris and Thorne, Barrie, p.7-24; b) Beyond the he/man approach: The case for nonsexist language. Martyna, Wendy, p.25-37; c) Prescriptive grammar and the pronoun problem. MacKay, Donald G., p.38-53; d) Linguistic options and choices for black women in the rural South. Nichols, Patricia C., p.54-68; e) Intonation in a man's world. McConnell-Ginet, Sally, p.69-88; f) Interaction: The work women do. Fishman, Pamela M., p.89-102; g) Small insults: A study of interruptions in cross-sex conversations between unacquainted persons. West, Candace and Zimmerman, Don H., p.103-118; h) Men, inexpressiveness, and power. Sattel, Jack W., p.119-124; i) Consciousness as style: Style as aesthetic. Penelope, Julia (Stanley) and Wolfe, Susan J., p.125-139; j) Men's speech to young children. Gleason, Jean Berko and Greif, Esther Blank, p.140-150; k) Sex similarities and differences in language, speech, and nonverbal communication: An annotated bibliography. Henley, Nancy, Kramarae, Cheris and Thorne, Barrie, p.153-331.

172. Latin American Woman: The Meek Speak Out. Turner, June H., ed. Silver Springs, MD: International Educational Development, 1980.
a) Squatter settlement decision-making: For men only? (Peru). Arimana, Carmen, p.11-24; b) Research experiences with rural women (Costa Rica). Chacón, Isabel, p.25-38; c) The only way (Peru). Carlier, Anita, p.39-50; d) Learning to take hold of one's own destiny (Bolivia). Moor de Crespo, Carmela, p.51-61; e) Our national inferiority complex: A cause for violence? (El Salvador). Moreira, Ana, p.63-72; f) Only you men have your needs satisfied (Ecuador). Luzuriaga, Luz, p.73-83; g) The Chocó woman: Agent for change (Colombia). Arango, Marta, p.85-100; h) It all depends on the teacher (Honduras). Ramirez, Francisca, p.101-110; i) Integrating women into rural cooperatives: Pluses and minuses (Bolivia). Eddy de Arellano, Bambi, p.111-122; j) Where are our campesino brothers? Let the murderers answer! (Nicaragua). Rappaccioli, Myra de, p.123-131; k) Some sow, others reap (Colombia). Briceño, Maria Esperanza, p.133-146; l) The broken wing (Peru). Valcárcel, Jenny, p.147-161; m) Saving money with bio-gas (Colombia). Alvear, Ligia Cock, p.163-174.

173. The Law and Politics of Abortion. Schneider, Carl E. and Vinovskis, Maris A., eds. Lexington, MA: LexingtonBooks, 1980.
a) Rewriting *Roe v. Wade*. Regan, Donald H., p.1-80; b) The juridical status of the fetus: A proposal for legal protection of the unborn. King, Patricia A., p.81-121; c) The abortion-funding cases and population control: An imaginary lawsuit and some reflections on the uncertain limits of reproductive privacy. Appleton, Susan Frelich, p.122-157; d) *Roe v. Wade* and the lesson of the pre-*Roe* case law. Morgan, Richard Gregory, p.158-182; e) Abortion and the presidential election of 1976: A multivariate analysis of voting behavior. Vinovskis, Maris A., p.184-205; f) Public support for pro-choice abortion policies in the nation and states: Changes and stability after the *Roe* and *Doe* decisions. Uslaner, Eric, M. and Weber, Ronald E., p.206-223; g) The politics of abortion in the House of Representatives in 1976. Vinovskis, Maris A., p.224-261.

174. Learning Our Way: Essays in Feminist Education. Bunch, Charlotte and Pollack, Sandra, eds. Trumansburg, NY: Crossing Press, 1983.
a) If the mortarboard fits...radical feminism in academia. Gearhart, Sally Miller, p.2-17; b) The politics of black women's studies. Hull, Gloria T. and Smith, Barbara, p.19-33; c) Teaching writing in prison. Loewenstein, Andrea, p.34-48; d) College for neighborhood women: Innovation and growth. Haywoode, Terry L., p.49-58; e) All-women classes and the struggle for women's liberation. Women's Studies College, SUNY Buffalo, p.59-77; f) The new right challenges women's studies: The Long Beach women's studies program. Brooks, Betty Willis and Sievers, Sharon L., p.78-88; g) Teaching the feminist minority. Davis, Barbara Hillyer, p.89-97; h) Feminist scholarship: The extent of the revolution. Howe, Florence, p.98-111; i) A note on Sagaris. Bunch, Charlotte, p.114-115; j) The ideas and the realities: Sagaris, Session I. St. Joan, Jackie, p.116-128; k) Women and process: The Sagaris split, Session II. Sherman, Susan, p.129-137; l) Califia: An experiment in feminist education Califia community. Murphy, Marilyn, p.138-153; m) Feminist art and education at Califia: My personal experience. Germain, Diane F., p.154-159; n) Women of color Califia. Silva, Carmen, p.160-168; o) Feminist education at the feminist studio workshop. Iskin, Ruth, p.169-186; p) Unlearning complicity, remembering resistance: White women's anti-racism education. Wolverton, Terry, p.187-199; q) The Women's Writer's Center: An interview with the directors. DeVries, Rachel, Gambill, Sue Dove and Speicher, Rita, p.200-209; r) A feminist chautauqua for a rural state. Sands, Diane, Smith, Judy and Thompson, Jennifer, p.210-218; s) Creative teaching spaces: Home movies. Hammer, Barbara, p.219-223; t) The women's school of planning and architecture. Birkby, Noel Phyllis and Weisman, Leslie Kanes, p.224-245; u) Not by degrees: Feminist theory and education. Bunch, Charlotte, p.248-260; v) Feminist values: Guidelines for a teaching methodology in women's studies. Schniedewind, Nancy, p.261-271; w) Black-eyed blues connections: From the inside out. Russell, Michelle Gibbs, p.272-284; x) Self-disclosure and the commitment to social change. Beck, Evelyn Torton, p.285-291; y) What are rights without means? Educating feminists for the future. Zimmerman, Jan, p.292-301; z) Charlotte Bunch and Betty Powell talk about feminism, blacks, and education as politics. Bunch, Charlotte and Powell, Betty, p.302-316; aa) Friends and critics: The feminist academy. Minnich, Elizabeth Kamarck, p.317-329.

175. Legendary Ladies of Texas. Abernethy, Francis Edward, ed. Dallas, TX: E-Heart Press, 1981.
a) María de Agreda: The lady in blue. Abernethy, Francis Edward, p.9-14; b) Angelina. Corbin, Diane H., p.15-20; c) Emily Morgan: Yellow rose of Texas. Turner, Martha Anne, p.21-30; d) The weeping woman: La Llorona. West, John O., p.31-38; e) Belle Starr: The Bandit Queen of Dallas. Winegarten, Ruthe, p.39-50; f) The ghost of Chipita: The crying woman of San Patricio. Underwood, Marilyn, p.51-56; g) The capitol's lady. Bateman, Audray, p.57-58; h) Two sixshooters and a sunbonnet: The story of Sally Skull. Kilgore, Dan, p.59-72; i) Sophia Porter: Texas' own Scarlett O'Hara. Maguire, Jack, p.73-78; j) Elise Waerenskjold: A modern on the prairie. Smith, Sherry A., p.79-84; k) Adah Isaacs Menken: From Texas to Paris. Palmer, Pamela Lynn, p.85-94; l) Elisabet Ney: Texas' first lady of sculpture. Nye, Mary E., p.95-107; m) Mollie Bailey: Circus entrepreneur. Hartzog, Martha, p.107-114; n) Martha White McWhirter and the Belton Sanctificationists. Werden, Frieda, p.115-122; o) Aunt Dicy: Legendary black lady. Byrd, James W., p.123-132; p) El Paso madams. Frost, H. Gordon, p.133-144; q) Pardon me, Governor Ferguson. Paulissen, Maisie, p.145-162; r) "Tell them I don't smoke cigars": The story of Bonnie Parker. Gorzell, André L. and Phillips, John Neal, p.163-172; s) Glamor girl called Electra. Tolbert, Frank X., p.173-174; t) The babe. Knief, Mary Kay, p.175-184; u)

Janis and the Austin scene. Alexander, Stanley G., p.185-194; v) Legends in their own time: The Dallas Cowboy cheerleaders. Lee, James Ward, p.195-202; w) Honky Tonk Angels. McGinity, Sue Simmons, p.203-210; x) Woman as victim in modern folklore. Carpenter, Ann, p.211-216; y) Mrs. Bailey and the bears. Hewett, Margaret L., p.217.

176. Lesbian Studies: Present and Future. Cruikshank, Margaret, ed. Old Westbury, NY: Feminist Press, 1982.
a) Dyke in academe. Bennett, Paula, p.3-8; b) Black lesbians in academia: Visible invisibility. Davenport, Doris, p.9-11; c) "Out" at the university: Myth and reality. McNaron, Toni A. H., p.12-15; d) I lead two lives: Confessions of a closet Baptist. Segrest, Mab, p.16-19; e) Harassment in rural America. Sturtz, Sue, p.20-21; f) Sexual energy in the classroom. Gurko, Jane, p.25-31; g) "Kissing/Against the Light": A look at lesbian poetry. Bulkin, Elly, p.32-54; h) Lesbian literature: A third world feminist perspective. Moraga, Cherrie and Smith, Barbara, p.55-65; i) Homophobia in the classroom. Manahan, Nancy, p.66-69; j) Teaching the psychology of women: A lesbian feminist perspective. Fontaine, Coralyn, p.70-80; k) Teaching about Jewish lesbians in literature: From *Zeitl* and *Richel* to *The Tree of Begats*. Beck, Evelyn Torton, p.81-87; l) Journey into otherness: Teaching *The Well of Loneliness*. McNaron, Toni A.H., p.88-92; m) Learning through teaching: A lesbianism course in 1972. Davis, Madeline, p.93-96; n) But what about men...? Bright, Clare, p.97-99; o) Black lesbians before 1970: A bibliographical essay. Roberts, JR, p.103-109; p) Resources for lesbian history. Freedman, Estelle, p.110-114; q) Who hid lesbian history? Faderman, Lillian, p.115-121; r) Lesbian biography, biography of lesbians. Doughty, Frances, p.122-127; s) One out of thirty: Lesbianism in women's studies textbooks. Zimmerman, Bonnie, p.128-131; t) Lesbian images in women's literature anthologies. Hickok, Kathy, p.132-147; u) Is feminist criticism really feminist? Birtha, Becky, p.148-151; v) The lesbian periodicals index. Potter, Clare, p.152-161; w) Note on "Reading A Subject" in periodical indexes. Red, Ida VSW, p.162-164; x) Older lesbians. Poor, Matile, p.165-173; y) Toward a laboratory of one's own: Lesbians in science. Hynes, H. Patricia, p.174-178; z) Lesbians in physical education and sport. Cobhan, Linn ni, p.179-186; aa) Love between women in prison. Faith, Karlene, p.187-193; bb) A lesbian perspective on women's studies. Frye, Marilyn, p.194-198.

177. Lives: Chinese Working Women. Sheridan, Mary and Salaff, Janet W., eds. Bloomington, IN: Indiana University Press, 1984.
a) The life history method. Sheridan, Mary, p.11-22; b) Historical background on Chinese women. McElderry, Andrea, p.25-50; c) Spinster sisterhoods. Sankar, Andrea, p.51-70; d) Village wives. Davis-Friedman, Deborah, p.71-75; e) Hakka women. Johnson, Elizabeth L., p.76-91; f) Doing fieldwork. Arrigo, Linda Gail, Kung, Lydia and Salaff, Janet W., p.95-108; g) Taiwan garment workers. Kung, Lydia, p.109-122; h) Taiwan electronics workers.

Arrigo, Linda Gail, p.123-145; i) Wage earners in Hong Kong. Salaff, Janet W., p.146-171; j) The Chinese biographical method: A moral and didactic tradition. Ch'en, Jerome, p.175-179; k) Yenan women in revolution. Sheridan, Mary, p.180-196; l) "On the eve of her departure". Ch'en, Jerome, p.197-203; m) Contemporary generations. Sheridan, Mary, p.204-235.

178. Lives in Stress: Women and Depression. Belle, Deborah, ed. Beverly Hills, CA: Sage Publications, 1982.
a) Research methods and sample characteristics. Belle, Deborah and Dill, Diana, p.24-32; b) Sources of stress: Events or conditions? Makosky, Vivian Parker, p.35-53; c) Daily lives. Dill, Diana and Greywolf, Elizabeth, p.54-64; d) Growing up: The impact of loss and change. Reese, Maureen Foley, p.65-80; e) Work: Its meaning for women's lives. Tebbets, Ruth, p.83-95; f) The public welfare system: Regulation and dehumanization. Marshall, Nancy, p.96-108; g) The human cost of discrimination. Steele, Emilie, et al., p.109-119; h) The politics of the poor. Greywolf, Elizabeth, p.120-130; i) Social ties and social support. Belle, Deborah, p.133-144; j) Fathers' support to mothers and children. Longfellow, Cynthia and Zur-Szpiro, Susan, p.145-153; k) Parenting philosophies and practices. Zelkowitz, Phyllis, p.154-162; l) The quality of mother-child relationships. Longfellow, Cynthia, Saunders, Elisabeth and Zelkowitz, Phyllis, p.163-176; m) The challenge of coping. Dill, Diana and Feld, Ellen, p.179-196; n) Mental health problems and their treatment. Belle, Deborah, et al., p.197-210; o) Physical health issues. Ashley, Polly, Greywolf, Elizabeth and Reese, Maureen Foley, p.211-221; p) Families revisited. Reese, Maureen Foley, p.225-235.

179. Loaded Questions: Women in the Military. Chapkis, Wendy, ed. Amsterdam: Transnational Institute, 1981.
a) Militarization/civilianization. Merryfinch, Lesley, p.9-13; b) Patriarchy - A working definition. Elster, Ellen, p.14-15; c) The Private Benjamin syndrome. Chapkis, Wendy and Wings, Mary, p.17-21; d) The military model. Enloe, Cynthia, p.23-29; e) Sexual division of labour. Yuval-Davis, Nira, p.31-35; f) Equal opportunity trap. Tiffany, Jennifer, p.36-39; g) The recruitment of women. Megens, Ine and Wings, Mary, p.41-49; h) NATO: What is it and why should women care? Enloe, Cynthia, p.51-61; i) Nuclear Europe. Ennen, Gisela and Kuik, Jannie, p.63-64; j) NATO: The lesson machine. Enloe, Cynthia, p.65-71; k) The Israeli example. Yuval-Davis, Nira, p.73-77; l) Freedom fighters. Heikens, Carolien, p.79-81; m) The peaceful sex. Albrecht-Heide, Astrid, p.83-87.

180. The Lost Tradition: Mothers and Daughters in Literature. Davidson, Cathy N. and Broner, E. M., eds. New York: Frederick Ungar, 1980.
a) Mothers and daughters in ancient Near Eastern literature. Ochshorn, Judith, p.5-15; b) Kriemhild and Clytemnestra - Sisters in crime or independent women? Tobol, Carol E. W. and Washington, Ida H., p.15-21; c) Eve's orphans: Mothers and daughters in medieval English literature. Stiller, Nikki, p.22-32; d) The new

mother of the English renaissance: Her writings on motherhood. Travitsky, Betty S., p.33-43; e) The great unwritten story: Mothers and daughters in Shakespeare. Schotz, Myra Glazer, p.44-54; f) Jane Austen and the tradition of the absent mother. MacDonald, Susan Peck, p.58-69; g) Unmothered daughter and the radical reformer: Harriet Martineau's career. Myers, Mitzi, p.70-80; h) "The mother's history" in George Eliot's life, literature and political ideology. Zimmerman, Bonnie, p.81-94; i) Mothers and daughters in *Wives and Daughters*: A study of Elizabeth Gaskell's last novel. Berke, Jacqueline and Berke, Laura, p.95-109; j) Mothers and daughters in the fiction of the New Republic. Davidson, Cathy N., p.115-127; k) Reconstruction in the house of art: Emily Dickinson's "I never had a mother". Mossberg, Barbara Ann Clarke, p.128-138; l) Ellen Glasgow: Daughter as justified. Wagner, Linda W., p.139-146; m) Mothers, daughters, and incest in the late novels of Edith Wharton. Tintner, Adeline R., p.147-156; n) Reentering paradise: Cather, Colette, Woolf and their mothers. Lilienfeld, Jane, p.160-175; o) How light a *Lighthouse* for today's women? Dash, Irene G., Kushner, Deena Dash and Moore, Deborah Dash, p.176-188; p) The muse as Medusa. Elias-Button, Karen, p.193-206; q) The nightmare repetition: The mother-daughter conflict in Doris Lessing's *Children of Violence*. Fishburn, Katherine, p.207-216; r) A subtle psychic bond: The mother figure in Sylvia Plath's poetry. Broe, Mary Lynn, p.217-230; s) The hungry Jewish mother. Duncan, Erika, p.231-241; t) A psychological journey: Mothers and daughters in English-Canadian fiction. Irvine, Lorna, p.242-252; u) "Don't never forget the bridge that you crossed over on": The literature of matrilineage. Maglin, Nan Bauer, p.257-267; v) Spider woman's web: Mothers and daughters in Southwestern Native American literature. Bannan, Helen M., p.268-279; w) Mothers and daughters: Another minority group. Rosinsky, Natalie M., p.280-290; x) Heritages: Dimensions of mother-daughter relationships in women's autobiographies. Bloom, Lynn Z., p.291-303; y) Mothers and daughters in literature: A preliminary bibliography. Kessler, Carol Farley, Moore, Ann M. and Rudenstein, Gail M., p.309-322.

181. Machina Ex Dea: Feminist Perspectives on Technology. Rothschild, Joan, ed. New York: Pergamon, 1983.
a) Women hold up two-thirds of the sky: Notes for a revised history of technology. Stanley, Autumn, p.3-22; b) Lillian Moller Gilbreth and the founding of modern industrial engineering. Prescott, Martha Moore, p.23-37; c) Mathematization of engineering: Limits on women and the field. Hacker, Sally L., p.38-58; d) Technology and work degradation: Effects of office automation on women clerical workers. Feldberg, Roslyn L. and Glenn, Evelyn Nakano, p.59-78; e) Technology, housework, and women's liberation: A theoretical analysis. Rothschild, Joan, p.79-93; f) Mining the earth's womb. Merchant, Carolyn, p.99-117; g) Toward an ecological feminism and a feminist ecology. King, Ynestra, p.118-129; h) Women, science, and popular mythology. Keller, Evelyn Fox, p.130-146; i) Women and the assessment of technology: To think, to be,

to unthink, to free. Bush, Corlann Gee, p.151-170; j) An end to technology: A modest proposal. Gearhart, Sally M., p.171-182; k) Reproductive technology: The future for women? Hanmer, Jalna, p.183-197; l) What if...science and technology in feminist utopias. Schweickart, Patrocinio, p.193-211; m) Afterward: Machina ex dea and future research. Rothschild, Joan, p.213-225.

182. Making Space: Women and the Man-Made Environment. MATRIX, ed. London: Pluto Press, 1984.
a) Women, architects and feminism. Darke, Jane, p.11-25; b) Homes fit for heroines: Housing in the twenties. McFarlane, Barbara, p.26-36; c) Women and public space. Boys, Jos, p.37-54; d) House design and women's roles. Boys, Jos, et al., p.55-80; e) Housing the family. Francis, Sue, p.81-88; f) Working with women. Bradshaw, Frances, p.89-105; g) Private kitchens, public cooking. Roberts, Marion, p.106-119; h) House and home. Foo, Benedicte, p.120-136.

183. Malaysian Women: Problems & Issues. Hong, Evelyn, ed. Penang, Malaysia: Consumer Association of Penang, 1983.
a) Rural women in development. Hong, Evelyn, p.5-29; b) Women, economics and the environment. Ghee, Lim Teck, p.31-36; c) Status of rural women. Nye, Ng Sock, p.38-47; d) Women workers in the manufacturing industries. Ariffin, Jamilah, p.49-62; e) Women factory workers and the law. Leng, Tan Pek, p.64-74; f) Hysteria among factory workers. Lee, Raymond, p.76-78; g) Hazards faced by women at work. Eng, Khoo Hoon, p.80-88; h) Women's health. Hong, Evelyn, p.90-121; i) Abused women. Samuel, Charlotte, p.122-125; j) Sexual offences. Teoh, S.K., p.126-134.

184. Marriage and Fertility: Studies in Interdisciplinary History. Rabb, Theodore K. and Rotberg, Robert I., eds. Princeton, N.J.: Princeton University Press, 1980.
a) Medieval marriage characteristics: A neglected factor in the history of medieval serfdom. Coleman, Emily R., p.3-17; b) Childbearing among the lower classes of late medieval England. Hanawalt, Barbara A., p.19-40; c) Dowries and kinsmen in early Renaissance Venice. Chojnacki, Stanley, p.41-70; d) Elizabethan birth control and Puritan attitudes. Schnucker, Robert V., p.71-83; e) Illegitimacy, sexual revolution, and social change in modern Europe. Shorter, Edward, p.85-120; f) Bastardy and socioeconomic structure of south Germany. Lee, W. R., p.121-143; g) Bastardy in south Germany: A comment. Shorter, Edward, p.145-155; h) Bastardy in south Germany: A reply. Lee, W. R., p.157-162; i) Female sexual attitudes and the rise of illegitimacy: A case study. Fairchilds, Cissie, p.163-203; j) A case of naiveté in the use of statistics. Flandrin, Jean-Louis, p.205-211; k) A reply. Fairchilds, Cissie, p.212-218; l) Women's work and European fertility patterns. Cohen, Miriam, Scott, Joan W. and Tilly, Louise A., p.219-248; m) Parisian infants and Norman wet nurses in the early nineteenth century: A statistical study. Sussman, George D., p.249-266; n) The origins of the birth control movement in England in

the early nineteenth century. Langer, William L., p.267-284; o) Age at menarche in Europe since the eighteenth century. Laslett, Peter, p.285-300; p) Toward a theory of remarriage: A case study of Newburyport at the beginning of the nineteenth century. Grigg, Susan, p.301-338; q) Premarital pregnancy in America, 1640-1971: An overview and interpretation. Hindus, Michael S. and Smith, Daniel Scott, p.339-372.

185. Marriage and the Family in the Year 2020. Kirkendall, Lester A. and Gravatt, Arthur E. eds. Buffalo, NY: Prometheus Books, 1984.
a) Looking toward the year 2020. Gravatt, Arthur E. and Kirkendall, Lester A., p.3-10; b) Social forces and the changing family. Clanton, Gordon, p.13-46; c) Marriage and the family: Styles and forms. Gravatt, Arthur E. and Kirkendall, Lester A., p.49-72; d) "Mate" selection in the year 2020. Murstein, Bernard I., p.73-88; e) Transformations in human reproduction. Francoeur, Robert T., p.89-105; f) Growing up slowly: Another century of childhood. Constantine, Larry L., p.106-117; g) Personal and social attitudes toward parenting. Lasswell, Marcia, p.118-133; h) The evolution of sex roles: The transformation of masculine and feminine values. Farrell, Warren, p.134-160; i) The transition from sex to sexuality and intimacy. Kirkendall, Lester A. and Perry, Michael E., p.161-182; j) Moral concepts in the year 2020: The individual, the family, and society. Francoeur, Robert T., p.183-204; k) The work/family connection in the year 2020. Elkin, Larry and Portner, Joyce, p.207-225; l) Physical settings for families in 2020: In space, on earth. Devlin, Ann Sloan, p.226-246; m) Family options, governments, and the social milieu: Viewed from the 21st century. Kirkendall, Lester A., p.247-267; n) Beyond the melting pot: Nationalism, militarism and the family. Boyd, Judith C. and Orthner, Dennis K., p.268-281; o) 2020 and beyond. Alam, Sterling E., p.285-300.

186. May Sarton: Woman and Poet. Hunting, Constance, ed. Orono, ME: National Poetry Foundation, 1982.
a) May Sarton: Reaching the lighthouse. Hunting, Constance, p.15-22; b) An eccentric biography. Hunting, Constance, p.25-30; c) May Sarton: Approaches to autobiography. Frank, Charles E., p.33-41; d) May Sarton's memoirs. Heilbrun, Carolyn G., p.43-52; e) House, home and solitude: Memoirs and journals of May Sarton. Owens, Suzanne, p.53-68; f) A French view of May Sarton. Lydon, Mary, p.71-77; g) "The Action of the beautiful": The concept of balance in the writings of May Sarton. Thyng, Deborah, p.79-84; h) The country of the imagination. Creange, Renée, p.85-99; i) Living rooms: Amity in the novels of May Sarton. Shaw, Sheila, p.101-111; j) Patterns of love and friendship: Five novels by May Sarton. Bakerman, Jane S., p.113-122; k) May Sarton's *The Small Room*: A comparison and an analysis. Bakerman, Jane S., p.123-132; l) Rage for justice: Political, social and moral consciousness in selected novels of May Sarton. Bryan, Mary, p.133-144; m) Perimeters of power: An examination of *As We Are Now*. Bakerman, Jane S., p.145-156; n) Redefinitions of traditional

Christian emblems and outlooks in May Sarton's novels of 1970-1975. Gaskill, Gayle, p.157-169; o) A note on May Sarton's use of form. Fowler, Sigrid H., p.173-178; p) The sculptor and the rock: Some uses of myth in the poetry of May Sarton. Eddy, Darlene Mathis, p.179-186; q) Metaphor in five garden poems by May Sarton. Connelly, Maureen, p.187-192; r) The singing wound: Intensifying paradoxes in May Sarton's " A Divorce of Lovers". Taylor, Henry, p.193-200; s) "The risk is very great": The poetry of May Sarton. Hunting, Constance, p.201-209; t) "Sister of the mirage and echo": An interview with May Sarton. Putney, Paula G., p.213-225; u) To be reborn: An interview with May Sarton. Hammond, Karla, p.227-238; v) A further interview with May Sarton. Hammond, Karla, p.239-248; w) "I live alone in a very beautiful place": An interview with May Sarton. Kaplan, Robin and Neiderbach, Shelley, p.249-260; x) A shining in the dark: May Sarton's accomplishment. Bailin, George, p.263-280; y) A revised bibliography. Blouin, Lenora P., p.283-319.

187. Medieval Religious Women. Nichols, John A. and Shank, Lillian Thomas, eds. Kalamazoo, MI: Cistercian Publications, 1984.
a) Muffled voices: The lives of consecrated women in the fourth century. McNamara, Jo Ann, p.11-29; b) Byzantine asceticism and women's monasteries in early medieval Italy. Abrahamse, Dorothy de F., p.31-49; c) Strict active enclosure and its effects on the female monastic experience (500-1100). Schulenberg, Jane Tibbets, p.51-86; d) Benedictine life for women in central France, 850-1100: A feminist revival. Skinner, Mary, p.87-113; e) Anglo-Saxon nuns in Anglo-Norman hagiography: Humility and power. Millinger, Susan, p.115-129; f) Why English nunneries had no history: A study of the problems of the English nunneries founded after the Conquest. Thompson, Sally, p.131-149; g) Male/female cooperation: The example of fontevrault. Gold, Penny Schine, p.151-168; h) All ages, every condition, and both sexes: The emergence of a Gilbertine identity. Elkins, Sharon K., p.169-182; i) Feminine lay piety in the High Middle Ages: The Beguines. Devlin, Dennis, p.183-196; j) The nun as anchoress: England, 1100-1500. Warren, Ann K., p.197-212; k) Stixwould in the market place. Graves, Coburn V., p.213-235; l) Medieval Cistercian nunneries and English Bishops. Nichols, John A., p.237-249; m) Ten centuries of growth: The Cistercian Abbey of Soleilmont. Conner, Elizabeth, p.251-267; n) Epilogue: Does St Bernard have a specific message for nuns? Leclercq, Jean, p.269-278.

188. Medieval Women Writers. Wilson, Katharina M., ed. Athens, GA: The University of Georgia Press, 1984.
a) The Frankish mother: Dhuoda. Marchand, James, p.1-29; b) The Saxon canoness: Hrotsvit of Gandersheim. Wilson, Katharina M., p.30-63; c) The French courtly poet: Marie de France. Ferrante, Joan M., p.64-89; d) The French scholar-lover: Heloise. Radice, Betty, p.90-108; e) The German visionary: Hildegard of Bingen. Kraft, Kent, p.109-130; f) The provençal *Trobairitz*: Castelloza. Dronke, Peter, p.131-152; g) The German mystic: Mechthild of Magdeburg. Howard, John, p.153-

185; h) The Brabant mystic: Hadewijch. Vanderauwera, Ria, p.186-203; i) The French heretic Beguine: Marguerite Porete. Bryant, Gwendolyn, p.204-226; j) The Swedish visionary: Saint Bridget. Obrist, Barbara, p.227-251; k) The Tuscan visionary: Saint Catherine of Siena. Berrigan, Joseph, p.252-268; l) The English mystic: Julian of Norwich. Jones, Catherine, p.269-296; m) The English religious enthusiast: Margery Kempe. Provost, William, p.297-319; n) The Spanish love poet: Florencia Pinar. Snow, Joseph, p.320-332; o) The Franco-Italian professional writer: Christine de Pizan. Willard, Charity Cannon, p.333-363.

189. Men's Studies Modified: The Impact of Feminism on the Academic Disciplines. Spender, Dale, ed. Oxford: Pergamon Press, 1981.
a) A thief in the house: Women and language. Jenkins, Mercilee M. and Kramarae, Cheris, p.11-22; b) Dancing through the minefield: Some observations on the theory, practice and politics of a feminist literary criticism. Kolodny, Annette, p.23-42; c) Methodocracy, misogyny and bad faith: The response of philosophy. Ruth, Sheila, p.43-53; d) Women lost and found: The impact of feminism on history. Lewis, Jane, p.55-72; e) Some of the boys won't play any more: The impact of feminism on sociology. Roberts, Helen, p.73-81; f) Toward the emasculation of political science: The impact of feminism. Lovenduski, Joni, p.83-97; g) Anthropology - a discipline with a legacy. MacCormack, Carol P., p.99-109; h) Psychology and feminism - if you can't beat them, join them. Walker, Beverly M., p.111-124; i) The oldest, the most established, the most quantitative of the social sciences - and most dominated by men; The impact of feminism on economics. Ferber, Marianne A. and Teiman, Michelle L., p.125-139; j) The impact of feminism on media studies - just another commercial break? Baehr, Helen, p.141-153; k) Education: The patriarchal paradigm and the response to feminism. Spender, Dale, p.155-73; l) Before and after: The impact of feminism on the academic discipline of law. O'Donovan, Katherine, p.175-187; m) Medicine as 'old husbands' tales': The impact of feminism. Elston, Mary Ann, p.189-211; n) The emperor doesn't wear any clothes: The impact of feminism on biology. Hubbard, Ruth, p.213-235; o) Dirty fingers, grime and slag heaps: Purity and the scientific ethic. Overfield, Kathy, p.237-248.

190. Menarche: The Transition from Girl to Woman. Golub, Sharon, ed. Lexington, MA: LexingtonBooks, 1983.
a) Fatness, menarche, and fertility. Frisch, Rose E., p.5-20; b) Endocrine aspects of menarche and menopause - milestones in the woman's life cycle. Dyrenfurth, Inge, p.21-46; c) Age at menarche and year of birth in relation to adult height and weight among Caucasian, Japanese, and Chinese women living in Hawaii. Gilbert, Fred I., Goodman, Madeleine J. and Grove, John S., p.47-58; d) Menarche: Meaning of measures and measuring meaning. Petersen, Anne C., p.63-76; e) Through the looking glass of menarche: What the adolescent girl sees. Koff, Elissa, p.77-86; f) Recollections of menarche, current

menstrual attitudes, and perimenstrual symptoms. Dery, Gretchen Kramer, Most, Ada and Woods, Nancy Fugate, p.87-97; g) Menarche: Its effects on mother-daughter and father-daughter interactions. Danza, Roberta, p.99-105; h) Physical attractiveness and physical stigma: Menstruation and the common cold. Brown, Virginia H., Larson, M. Victoria and Unger, Rhoda K., p.107-111; i) Variations in the experience of menarche as a function of preparedness. Rierdan, Jill, p.119-125; j) Menstrual education: Past, present, and future. Milow, Vera J., p.127-132; k) Menstrual beliefs and experiences of mother-daughter dyads. Menke, Edna M., p.133-137; l) Beliefs and attitudes of young girls regarding menstruation. Williams, Lenore R., p.139-148; m) Virginity rituals and chastity control during puberty: Cross-cultural patterns. Paige, Karen Ericksen, p.155-174; n) Age at menarche and sexual conduct in adolescence and young adulthood. Gagnon, John H., p.175-185; o) Menarche and teenage pregnancy: A misuse of historical data. Bullough, Vern L., p.187-193; p) Menarche and adolescent pregnancy. Leppert, Phyllis C., p.195-199; q) "Oh dear me! Why weren't we all boys, then there wouldn't be any bother": Menarche and popular American fiction. Kincaid-Ehlers, Elizabeth, p.205-228; r) Clinical aspects of menarche: Normal variations and common disorders. Warren, Michelle P., p.229-242; s) Prostaglandins in primary dysmenorrhea: Basis for the new therapy. Chan, W. Y., p.243-249; t) Dysmenorrhea in adolescence. Brooks-Gunn, Jeanne and Ruble, Diane N., p.251-261; u) Steroidal contraceptive use and subsequent development of hyperprolactinemia. Badawy, Shawky Z. A., et al., p.263-266; v) Menarche: A psychoanalytic perspective. Notman, Malkah T., p.271-278; w) The psychological concomitants of menarche in psychiatric patients. Darwin, Jaine L., p.279-286; x) Primary and secondary amenorrhea in anorexia nervosa. Falk, James R., et al., p.287-295; y) Premenstrual affective syndrome in adolescent and adult psychiatric patients. Friedman, Richard C., et al., p.297-306; z) Future directions for research. Parlee, Mary Brown, p.309-313; aa) Implications for women's health and well-being. Golub, Sharon, p.315-320.

191. The Mental Health of Women. Guttentag, Marcia, Salasin, Susan and Belle, Deborah, eds. New York: Academic Press, 1980.
a) Who uses mental health facilities? Belle, Deborah, p.1-20; b) Patterns of diagnoses received by men and women. Belle, Deborah and Goldman, Noreen, p.21-30; c) Community surveys: Sex differences in mental illness. Goldman, Noreen and Ravid, Renee, p.31-55; d) Depressions among women: Their nature and causes. Klerman, Gerald L. and Weissman, Myrna M., p.57-92; e) Risk factors for depression: What do we learn from them? Radloff, Lenore Sawyer, p.93-109; f) Stress and the mental health of women: A discussion of research and issues. Makosky, Vivian Parker, p.111-127; g) Tailoring evaluation to measure the accountability of mental health services to women. Baxter, James W., Kiresuk, Thomas J. and Schultz, Susan K., p.129-154.

192. Mexican Women in the United States: Struggles Past and Present. Mora, Magdalena and Castillo, Adelaida R. Del, eds. Los Angeles, CA: Chicano Studies Research Center Publications, University of California, 1980.
a) Sex, nationality, and class: La obrera Mexicana. Castillo, Adelaida R. Del and Mora, Magdalena, p.1-4; b) Mexican women in organization. Castillo, Adelaida R. Del, p.7-16; c) Lives of Chicana activists: The Chicano student movement (a case study). Hernandez, Patricia, p.17-25; d) Women in the Chicano movement. Vásquez, Carlos, p.27-28; e) Toward a democratic women's movement in the United States. Ortiz, Roxanne Dunbar, p.29-35; f) The rise and demise of women's liberation: A class analysis. Dixon, Marlene, p.37-43; g) Toward a science of women's liberation. Dumoulin, John and Larguia, Isabel, p.45-61; h) Sterilization: An overview. Castillo, Adelaida R. Del, p.65-70; i) Se me acabó la canción: An ethnography of non-consenting sterilizations among Mexican women in Los Angeles. Velez, Carlos G., p.71-91; j) Capital's flight: The apparel industry moves south. NACLA Report of the Americas, p.95-104; k) Silicon Valley: Paradise or paradox? Bernstein, Alan, et al., p.105-112; l) Los Angeles garment district sews a cloak of shame. Schlein, Lisa, p.113-116; m) Women at Farah: An unfinished story. Coyle, Laurie, Hershatter, Gail and Honig, Emily, p.117-143; n) The election day immigration raids at Lilli Diamond Originals and the response of the ILGWU. Vázquez, Mario F., p.145-148; o) Working-class women in nineteenth century Mexico. Hart, John, p.151-157; p) A la mujer (to women). Mágon, Ricardo Flores, p.159-162; q) Sara Estela Ramírez: Una rosa roja en el movimiento. Zamora, Emilio, p.163-169; r) La costura en Los Angeles 1933-1939: The ILGWU and the politics of domination. Monroy, Douglas, p.171-178; s) I'm talking for justice. Moreno, Maria, p.181-182; t) Lucy Duran - Wife, mother, and organizer. Nuestra Lucha, p.183-184; u) Personal chronicle of Crystal City. Castañeda, Irene, p.185-187; v) Señora Flores de Andrade. Gamio, Manuel, p.189-192; w) Appendix: Profile of the Chicana: A statistical fact sheet. Waldman, Elizabeth, p.195-204.

193. The Missing Half: Girls and Science Education. Kelly, Alison, ed. Manchester, England: Manchester University Press, 1981.
a) Girls and science education: Is there a problem? Kelly, Alison, p.1-19; b) Sex differences in science achievement: Some results and hypotheses. Kelly, Alison, p.22-42; c) A biological basis for the sex differences in achievement in science? Gray, J. A., p.43-58; d) Socialisation in patriarchal society. Kelly, Elinor, p.59-72; e) Science achievement as an aspect of sex roles. Kelly, Alison, p.73-84; f) Biological inevitabilities or political choices? The future for girls in science. Griffiths, Dorothy and Saraga, Esther, p.85-97; g) Factors differentially affecting the science subject preferences, choices and attitudes of girls and boys. Ormerod, M. B., p.100-112; h) Science options in a girls' grammar school. Ebbutt, Dave, p.113-122; i) Choosing or channelling? Kelly, Alison, p.123-138; j) Who says girls can't be engineers? Newton, Peggy, p.139-149; k) Predicting specialisation in science. Bradley, Judy, p.150-

163; l) Girls studying science in the sixth form. Collings, John and Smithers, Alan, p.164-179; m) Differential treatment of boy and girl pupils during science lessons. Galton, Maurice, p.180-191; n) Sex differences in science examinations. Harding, Jan, p.192-204; o) Girls' science: Boys' science revisited. Ebbutt, Dave, p.205-215; p) The image of science. Weinreich-Haste, Helen, p.216-229; q) From schoolgirls' essays. p.233-241; r) Girls, physics and sexism. p.242-246; s) Feminism and science teaching: Some classroom observations. Samuel, Judy, p.247-256; t) From teachers' letters. p.257-263; u) Sex typing in schools. Whyte, Judith, p.264-275; v) Retrieving the missing half. Kelly, Alison, p.276-297.

194. Mother Worship: Theme and Variations. Preston, James J., ed. Chapel Hill, NC: University of North Carolina Press, 1982.
a) The Virgin of Guadalupe and the female self-image: A Mexican case history. Campbell, Ena, p.5-24; b) The Tonantsi cult of the Eastern Nahua. Sandstrom, Alan R., p.25-50; c) In quest of the Black Virgin: She is black because she is black. Cappannari, Stephen C. and Moss, Leonard W., p.53-74; d) The cult of Brigid: A study of pagan-Christian syncretism in Ireland. Cathasaigh, Donál Ó, p.75-94; e) An Italian religious feast: The *Fujenti* rites of the Madonna dell'Arco, Naples. Tentori, Tullio, p.95-122; f) The worship of Mother Earth in Russian culture. Hubbs, Joanna, p.123-144; g) Postindustrial Marian pilgrimage. Turner, Edith and Turner, Victor, p.145-173; h) The goddess Kannagi: A dominant symbol of south Indian Tamil society. Pandian, Jacob, p.177-191; i) The village Mother in Bengal. Nicholas, Ralph W., p.192-209; j) The goddess Chandi as an agent of change. Preston, James J., p.210-226; k) Pox and the terror of childlessness: Images and ideas of the smallpox goddess in a north Indian village. Kolenda, Pauline, p.227-250; l) The milk overflowing ceremony in Sri Lanka. Weeramunda, A. J., p.251-262; m) Rangda the witch. McKean, Philip Frick, p.265-282; n) The Great Goddess today in Burma and Thailand: An exploration of her symbolic relevance to monastic and female roles. Ferguson, John P., p.283-303; o) Mother Earth: The great goddess of West Africa. McCall, Daniel F., p.304-324; p) Conclusion: New perspectives on mother worship. Preston, James J., p.325-343.

195. Mothering: Essays in Feminist Theory. Trebilcot, Joyce, ed. Totowa, NJ: Rowman & Allanheld, 1983.
a) The obligations of mothers and fathers. Held, Virginia, p.7-20; b) Why men don't rear children: A power analysis. Polatnick, M. Rivka, p.21-40; c) When women and men mother. Ehrensaft, Diane, p.41-61; d) Against "parenting". Peterson, Susan Rae, p.62-69; e) If all else fails, I'm still a mother. Valeska, Lucia, p.70-78; f) Reproduction, mothering, and the origins of patriarchy. al-Hibri, Azizah, p.81-93; g) Womb envy: An explanatory concept. Kittay, Eva Feder, p.94-128; h) Is male gender identity the cause of male domination? Young, Iris Marion, p.129-146; i) Review of Chodorow's *The Reproduction of Mothering*. Bart, Pauline, p.147-152; j) On conceiving motherhood

and sexuality: A feminist materialist approach. Ferguson, Ann, p.153-182; k) The maternal instinct (1972) & Afterword (1982). Whitbeck, Caroline, p.185-198; l) Parenting and property. Smith, Janet Farrell, p.199-212; m) Maternal thinking. Ruddick, Sara, p.213-230; n) Preservative love and military destruction: Some reflections on mothering and peace. Ruddick, Sara, p.231-262; o) Toward an ethic of nurturance: Luce Irigaray on mothering and power. Kuykendall, Eleanor H., p.263-274; p) The answer is matriarchy. Love, Barbara and Shanklin, Elizabeth, p.275-283; q) Feminism, pronatalism, and motherhood. Gimenez, Martha E., p.287-314; r) Motherhood: The annihilation of women. Allen, Jeffner, p.315-330.

196. Mothering the Mind: Twelve Studies of Writers and Their Silent Partners. Perry, Ruth and Brownley, Martine Watson, eds. New York: Holmes & Meier, 1984.
a) "My idea in your mind": John Locke and Damaris Cudworth Masham. O'Donnell, Sheryl, p.26-46; b) The secrets of Swift and Stella. Carnochan, W.B., p.48-63; c) "Under the dominion of *some* woman": The friendship of Samuel Johnson and Hester Thrale. Brownley, Martine Watson, p.64-79; d) The domestic economy of art: Elizabeth Barrett and Robert Browning. Mermin, Dorothy, p.82-101; e) On exile and fiction: The Leweses and the Shelleys. Knoepflmacher, U. C., p.102-121; f) Gertrice/Altrude: Stein, Toklas, and the paradox of the happy marriage. Stimpson, Catharine R., p.122-139; g) I sign my mother's name: Alice Walker, Dorothy West and Paule Marshall. Washington, Mary Helen, p.142-153; h) The magic spinning wheel: Straw to gold - Colette, Willy and Sido. Lilienfeld, Jane, p.164-178; i) Virginia Woolf and her violin: Mothering, madness, and music. Marcus, Jane, p.180-201; j) Closer than a brother: Swinburne and Watts-Dunton. Jordan, John O., p.204-216; k) Emerson and the angel of midnight: The Legacy of Mary Moody Emerson. Barish, Evelyn, p.218-237; l) "A spirit, yet a woman too!": Dorothy and William Wordsworth. Vogler, Thomas A., p.238-258.

197. Muriel Spark: An Odd Capacity for Vision. Bold, Alan, ed. London: Vision, 1984.
a) Ridiculous demons. Hart, Francis Russell, p.23-43; b) Fun and games with life-stories. Shaw, Valerie, p.44-70; c) Autonomy and fabulation in the fiction of Muriel Spark. Pullin, Faith, p.71-93; d) Calvinism and Catholicism in Muriel Spark. Massie, Allan, p.94-107; e) Muriel Spark: Critic into novelist. Menzies, Janet, p.111-131; f) Muriel Spark and satire. Randisi, Jennifer L., p.132-146; g) Spark and Scotland. Royle, Trevor, p.147-166; h) The liberated instant: Muriel Spark and the short story. Hubbard, Tom, p.167-182; i) Mrs. Spark's verse. Perrie, Walter, p.183-204.

198. Muslim Women. Hussain, Freda, ed. New York: St. Martin's Press, 1984.
a) Introduction: The ideal and contextual realities of Muslim women. Hussain, Freda, p.1-7; b) The status of women in early Islam. Stowasser, Barbara Freyer, p.11-43; c) The Islamic revolution and women: Quest for the Quranic model. Hussain, Freda and Radwan, Kamelia, p.44-67; d) Roles in transition: The evolving position of women in Arab-Islamic countries. Gerner, Debbie J., p.71-99; e) The literary treatment of women in North Africa. Nisbet, Anne- Marie, p.100-110; f) Early feminist movements in Turkey and Egypt. Ahmed, Leila, p.111-123; g) A traditional ceremony in an Islamic milieu in Malaysia. Strange, Heather, p.127-140; h) Islam and the legal status of women in Tunisia. Salem, Norma, p.141-168; i) Female education in Egypt: Changing attitudes over a span of 100 years. Khattab, Hind A. and el-Daeiff, Syeda Greiss, p.169-197; j) The struggle of women in the national development of Pakistan. Hussain, Freda, p.198-220; k) Lessons from fieldwork in the Sudan. Fluehr-Lobban, Carolyn, p.221-228.

199. My Troubles Are Going to Have Trouble with Me: Everyday Trials and Triumphs of Women Workers. Sacks, Karen Brodkin and Remy, Dorothy, eds. New Brunswick, NJ: Rutgers University Press, 1984.
a) Generations of working-class families. Sacks, Karen Brodkin, p.15-38; b) Southern textile women: Generations of survival and struggle. Frankel, Linda, p.39-60; c) Sacrifice, satisfaction, and social change: Employment and the family. Ferree, Myra Marx, p.61-79; d) Housework and domestic labor: Racial and technological change. Palmer, Phyllis, p.80-91; e) Economic stagnation and discrimination. Remy, Dorothy and Sawers, Larry, p.95-112; f) Women in retail sales work: The continuing dilemma of service. Benson, Susan Porter, p.113-123; g) Word processing: Forward for business, backward for women. Machung, Anne, p.124-139; h) Brave new office: The changing world of the legal secretary. Murphree, Mary C., p.140-159; i) Women's work in the library/information sector. Estabrook, Leigh S., p.160-172; j) Computers, ward secretaries, and a walkout in a Southern hospital. Sacks, Karen Brodkin, p.173-190; k) Resistance strategies: The routine struggle for bread and roses. Shapiro-Perl, Nina, p.193-208; l) Women and work in Silicon Valley: Options and futures. Katz, Naomi and Kemnitzer, David S., p.209-218; m) Contrasting sexual harassment in female- and male-dominated occupations. Carothers, Suzanne C. and Crull, Peggy, p.219-228; n) *Maquiladoras*: The view from the inside. Kelly, María Patricia Fernández, p.229-246; o) On the shop floor: Multi-ethnic unity against the conglomerate. Lamphere, Louise, p.247-263.

200. Nature, Culture and Gender. MacCormack, Carol P. and Strathern, Marilyn, eds. Cambridge: Cambridge University Press, 1980.
a) Nature, culture and gender: A critique. MacCormack, Carol P., p.1-24; b) Women and the dialectics of nature in eighteenth-century French thought. Bloch, Jean H. and Bloch, Maurice, p.25-41; c) Natural facts: A historical perspective on science and sexuality. Jordanova, L.J., p.42-69; d) The power of signs: Gender, culture and the wild in the Bolivian Andes. Harris, Olivia, p.70-94; e) Proto-social to adult: A Sherbro transformation. MacCormack, Carol P., p.95-118; f) Gender, sexuality and

marriage: A Kaulong model of nature and culture. Goodale, Jane C., p.119-142; g) Images of nature in Gimi thought. Gillison, Gillian, p.143-173; h) No nature, no culture: The Hagen case. Strathern, Marilyn, p.174-222.

201. A Needle, a Bobbin, a Strike: Women Needleworkers in America. Jensen, Joan M. and Davidson, Sue, eds. Philadelphia, PA: Temple University Press, 1984.
a) Needlework as art, craft, and livelihood before 1900. Jensen, Joan M., p.1-19; b) "If I didn't have my sewing machine...": Women and sewing-machine technology. Baron, Ava and Klepp, Susan E., p.20-59; c) "A paradise of fashion": A. T. Stewart's department store, 1862-1875. Gardner, Deborah S., p.60-80; d) The great uprisings: 1900-1920. Jensen, Joan M., p.83-93; e) The great uprising in Rochester. Jensen, Joan M., p.94-113; f) The uprising in Chicago: The men's garment workers strike, 1910-1911. Weiler, N. Sue, p.114-139; g) The great uprising in Cleveland: When sisterhood failed. Scharf, Lois, p.146-166; h) The uprising of the 20,000: The making of a labor legend. Schofield, Ann, p.167-182; i) Inside and outside the unions: 1920-1980. Jensen, Joan M., p.185-194; j) Dorothy Jacobs Bellanca: Women clothing workers and the runaway shops. Asher, Nina, p.195-226; k) Women at Farah: An unfinished story. Coyle, Laurie, Hershatter, Gail and Honig, Emily, p.227-277; l) A stitch in our time: New York's Hispanic garment workers in the 1980s. Green, Hardy and Weiner, Elizabeth, p.278-296.

202. New Feminist Essays on Virginia Woolf. Marcus, Jane, ed. Lincoln, NE: University of Nebraska Press, 1981.
a) Thinking back through our mothers. Marcus, Jane, p.1-30; b) Woolf's 'Magical garden of women'. Hawkes, Ellen, p.31-60; c) Shakespeare's *other* sister. DeSalvo, Louise A., p.61-81; d) Some female versions of pastoral: *The Voyage Out* and matriarchal mythologies. Moore, Madeline, p.82-104; e) *Jacob's Room* as comedy: Woolf's parodic *Bildungsroman*. Little, Judy, p.105-124; f) *Mrs Dalloway*: The communion of saints. Henke, Suzette A., p.125-147; g) Where the spear plants grew: The Ramsays' marriage in *To the Lighthouse*. Lilienfeld, Jane, p.148-169; h) Why is *Orlando* difficult? Wilson, J.J., p.170-184; i) Private brother, public world. Ruddick, Sara, p.185-215; j) The politics of city space in *The Years*: Street, love, pillar boxes and bridges. Squier, Susan, p.216-237; k) What is to console us?: The politics of deception in Woolf's short stories. Meyerowitz, Selma, p.238-252; l) Virginia Woolf's last words on words: *Between the Acts* and 'Anon'. Eisenberg, Nora, p.253-266.

203. New Space for Women. Wekerle, Gerda R., Peterson, Rebecca and Morley, David, eds. Boulder, CO: Westview Press, 1980.
a) Introduction: The domestic workplace. Peterson, Rebecca, p.37-39; b) The home: A critical problem for changing sex roles. Saegert, Susan and Winkel, Gary, p.41-63; c) The household as workplace: Wives, husbands, and children. Berk, Sarah Fenstermaker, p.65-81; d) The appropriation of the house: Changes in house design and concepts of domesticity. Rock, Cynthia, Torre, Susana

and Wright, Gwendolyn, p.83-100; e) Redesigning the domestic workplace. Hayden, Dolores, p.101-121; f) Introduction: Urban design: The price women pay. Wekerle, Gerda R., p.125-127; g) Women's place in the new suburbia. Fava, Sylvia F., p.129-149; h) Women's travel patterns in a suburban development. Cichocki, Mary K., p.151-163; i) Women in the suburban environment: A U.S.-Sweden comparison. Popenoe, David, p.165-174; j) Swedish women in single-family housing. Werner, Karla, p.175-188; k) Toward supportive neighborhoods: Women's role in changing the segregated city. Stamp, Judy, p.189-198; l) Introduction: Women in environmental decisionmaking: Institutional constraints. Morley, David, p.201-204; m) Architecture: Toward a feminist critique. Berkeley, Ellen Perry, p.205-218; n) Women in planning: There's more to affirmative action than gaining access. Leavitt, Jacqueline, p.219-234; o) No academic matter: Unconscious discrimination in environmental design education. p.235-253; p) From kitchen to storefront: Women in the tenant movement. Barton, Stephen, Joselit, Jenna Weissman and Lawson, Ronald, p.255-271; q) Women at city hall. Butler, Richard W. and Phillips, Susan, p.273-286; r) Introduction: Women as environmental activists. Peterson, Rebecca, p.289-291; s) The Los Angeles Woman's Building: A public center for woman's culture. Bretteville, Sheila Levrant de, p.293-310; t) Emergency shelter: The development of an innovative women's environment. Cools, Anne, p.311-318; u) Housing for single-parent families: A women's design. Soper, Mary, p.319-332.

204. Nontraditional Families: Parenting and Child Development. Lamb, Michael E., ed. Hillsdale, NJ: Lawrence Erlbaum, 1982.
a) Parental behavior and child development in nontraditional families: An introduction. Lamb, Michael E., p.1-12; b) The two-provider family: Problems and potentials. Moen, Phyllis, p.13-43; c) Maternal employment and child development: A review. Lamb, Michael E., p.45-69; d) The ecology of day care. Belsky, Jay, Steinberg, Laurence D. and Walker, Ann, p.71-116; e) Varying degrees of paternal involvement in infant care: Attitudinal and behavioral correlates. Lamb, Michael E., et al., p.117-137; f) Shared-caregiving families: An Australian study. Russell, Graeme, p.139-171; g) Primary caregiving and role-sharing fathers. Radin, Norma, p.173-204; h) Antecedents and consequences of various degrees of paternal involvement in child rearing: The Israeli project. Sagi, Abraham, p.205-232; i) Effects of divorce on parents and children. Cox, Martha, Cox, Roger and Hetherington, E. Mavis, p.233-288; j) Social development and parent-child interaction in father-custody and stepmother families. Elliott, Gary L., Santrock, John W. and Warshak, Richard A., p.289-314; k) Comparative socialization practices in traditional and alternative families. Eiduson, Bernice T., et al., p.315-346.

205. Not Just Pin Money: Selected Essays on the History of Women's Work in British Columbia. Latham, Barbara K. and Pazdro, Roberta J., eds. Victoria, British Columbia:

Camosun College, 1984.
a) "Sundays always make me think of home": Time and place in Canadian women's history. Conrad, Margaret, p.1-16; b) When you don't know the language, listen to the silence: An historical overview of native Indian women in BC. Franklin, Anna and Mitchell, Marjorie, p.17-35; c) Rainbow women of the Fraser Valley: Lifesongs through the generations. Battung, Diane, Buker, Laura and Ravicz, Marilyn, p.37-52; d) A preliminary sketch of Chinese women and work in British Columbia, 1858-1950. Adilman, Tamara, p.53-78; e) The response of the WMS to the immigration of Asian women, 1888-1942. Dieren, Karen van, p.79-97; f) A note on Asian Indian women in British Columbia, 1900-1935. Doman, Mahinder Kaur, p.99-104; g) "Roughing it in the bush" in British Columbia: Mary Moody's pioneer life in New Westminster 1859-1863. Gresko, Jacqueline, p.105-117; h) From pastels to chisel: The changing role of BC women artists. Pazdro, Roberta J., p.119-140; i) The gentlewomen of Queen Mary's coronation hostel. Barber, Marilyn, p.141-158; j) Six saucepans to one: Domestic science vs. the home in British Columbia 1900-1930. Riley, Barbara, p.159-181; k) Women on campus in British Columbia: Strategies for survival, years of war and peace, 1906-1920. Stewart, Lee, p.185-193; l) Postscript: Women in whose honour BC schools have been named. Small, Marion, p.195-198; m) The brightest women of our land: Vancouver clubwomen 1919-1928. Weiss, Gillian, p.199-209; n) They also served: The British Columbia women's institutes in two World Wars. Dennison, Carol J., p.211-219; o) Domesticity and discipline: The Girl Guides in British Columbia 1910-1943. MacQueen, Bonnie, p.221-235; p) "Especially when no one agrees": An interview with May Campbell. Ogg, Kathryn, p.237-247; q) "Services rendered, rearing children for the state": Mothers' pensions in British Columbia 1919-1931. Davies, Megan, p.249-263; r) Sinners or sinned against?: Historical aspects of female juvenile delinquency in British Columbia. Matters, Indiana, p.265-277; s) Last back: Folklore and the telephone operators in the 1919 Vancouver general strike. Bernard, Elaine, p.279-286; t) A union man's wife: The ladies' auxiliary movement in the IWA, the Lake Cowichan experience. Diamond, Sara, p.287-296; u) Cheap at half the price: The history of the fight for equal pay in BC. Bannerman, Josie, Chopik, Kathy and Zurbrigg, Ann, p.297-313; v) The search for legitimacy: Nurses' registration in British Columbia 1913-1935. Whittaker, Jo Ann, p.315-326; w) Vivian Dowding: Birth control activist 1892-. Bishop, Mary F., p.327-335; x) Reducing maternal mortality in British Columbia: An educational process. Lewis, Norah L., p.337-355; y) Mary Ellen Smith: The right woman in the right place at the right time. Norcross, Elizabeth, p.357-364; z) The peacock and the guinea hen: Political profiles of Dorothy Gretchen Steeves and Grace MacInnis. Walsh, Susan, p.365-379; aa) Tilly Jean Rolston: She knew how to throw a party. Proom, Juliette, p.381-388; bb) From home to house: Women in the BC legislature. Carter, Connie and Daoust, Eileen, p.389-405; cc) Joan Kennedy and the British Columbia Women's Service Corps. Wade, Susan,

p.407-428; dd) Women at Cominco during the Second World War. Turnbull, Elsie G., p.429-434.

206. Of Common Cloth: Women in the Global Textile Industry. Chapkis, Wendy and Enloe, Cynthia, eds. Amsterdam: Transnational Institute, 1983.
a) Nimble fingers and other fables. Elson, Diane, p.5-13; b) Restructuring: The cutting edge. Chhachhi, Amrita, Gloster, Margherita and McDevitt, Martha, p.15-23; c) The patriarchal thread - A history of exploitation. Chenut, Helen and Lown, Judy, p.25-37; d) The case of India. Chhachhi, Amrita, p.39-45; e) Iloilo. Bulatao, Beth, p.47; f) Woman worker/working woman. Elson, Diane, p.49-53; g) The double day. Baud, Isa and Joekes, Susan, p.55-59; h) A woman's home is her factory. Luijken, Anneke van and Mitter, Swasti, p.61-76; i) The sewing machine. Chenut, Helen, p.68-69; j) The safety catch. Jackson, Pauline, p.70-73; k) Racism at work. Enloe, Cynthia, p.75-79; l) Working on racism: Centro Obrero. Marin, Patricia and Rodriguez, Cecilia, p.80-85; m) Blue jeans blues. Bradley, Margaret, p.87-90; n) Resistance, strikes and strategies. Cheung, Choi Wan and Karl, Marilee, p.91-97; o) Can the union make us strong. Rankin, Theresa, p.99-105; p) Using sex and Satan to bust the union (an interview with Corky Jennings). Chapkis, Wendy, p.107-113; q) We are what we wear - The dilemma of the feminist consumer. Enloe, Cynthia, p.115-119.

207. Of Marriage and the Market: Women's Subordination in International Perspective. Young, Kate, Wolkowitz, Carol and McCullagh, Roslyn, eds. London: CSE Books, 1981.
a) Gender and economics: The sexual division of labour and the subordination of women. Mackintosh, Maureen, p.1-15; b) Subsistence production and extended reproduction. Bennholdt-Thomsen, Veronika, p.16-29; c) Women's labours: The naturalisation of social inequality and women's subordination. Stolcke, Verena, p.30-48; d) Households as natural units. Harris, Olivia, p.49-68; e) Work, consumption and authority within the household: A Moroccan case. Maher, Vanessa, p.69-87; f) 'I'm hungry, mum': The politics of domestic budgeting. Whitehead, Ann, p.88-111; g) Women, kinship and capitalist development. Stivens, Maila, p.112-126; h) Sexuality and the control of procreation. Morokvasic, Mirjana, p.127-143; i) The subordination of women and the internationalisation of factory production. Elson, Diane and Pearson, Ruth, p.144-166; j) Women in socialist societies: Problems of theory and practice. Molyneux, Maxine, p.167-202.

208. Of Marriage and the Market: Women's Subordination Internationally and Its Lessons. Young, Kate, Wolkowitz, Carol and McCullagh, Roslyn, eds. London: Routledge & Kegan Paul, 1984.
a) Introduction: The continuing subordination of women in the development process. Pearson, Ruth, Whitehead, Ann and Young, Kate, p.ix-xix; b) Gender and economics: The sexual division of labour and the subordination of women. Mackintosh, Maureen, p.3-17; c) The subordination of women and the internationalisation of factory pro-

duction. Elson, Diane and Pearson, Ruth, p.18-40; d) Subsistence production and extended reproduction. Bennholdt-Thomsen, Veronika, p.41-54; e) Women in socialist societies: Problems of theory and practice. Molyneux, Maxine, p.55-90; f) 'I'm hungry, mum': The politics of domestic budgeting. Whitehead, Ann, p.93-116; g) Work, consumption and authority within the household: A Moroccan case. Maher, Vanessa, p.117-135; h) Households as natural units. Harris, Olivia, p.136-155; i) Women's labours: The naturalisation of social inequality and women's subordination. Stolcke, Verena, p.159-177; j) Women, kinship and capitalist development. Stivens, Maila, p.178-192; k) Sexuality and control of procreation. Morokvasic, Mirjana, p.193-209.

209. Office Automation: Jekyll or Hyde? Marschall, Daniel and Gregory, Judith, eds. Cleveland, OH: Working Women Education Fund, 1983.
a) Choices in the development of office automation. Shaiken, Harley, p.5-14; b) Office automation: Jekyll or Hyde? Nussbaum, Karen, p.15-21; c) Bargaining over the social costs of information technology. Ciborra, Claudio, p.22-29; d) Women, technological change and employment levels: The role of trade union policies. Cammell, Helga, p.33-38; e) Government policies on new information technologies and their implications for employment: An overview of EEC countries, with particular reference to women. Henwood, Felicity and Zmroczek, Christine, p.39-49; f) Training: The magic cure for all ills? Dasey, Robyn, p.50-58; g) The issue of employment and office technology from a managerial perspective. Connell, John J., p.59-62; h) The implications of technology for U.S. employment. McKay, Roberta, p.63-68; i) Assessing the myths of the job market. Greenbaum, Joan, p.69-72; j) Productivity and service quality in the private sector. Hammer, Michael, p.73-76; k) Automation and the quality of work life at the Swedish telephone company: A management view. Hermansson, Svea and Tornqvist, Brita, p.79-83; l) Automation and the quality of work life at the Swedish telephone company: A union view. Westman, Berith, p.84-88; m) New technology and its implications in U.S. clerical work. Feldberg, Roslyn and Glenn, Evelyn N., p.89-95; n) The role of common sense in the process of interface design. Suchman, Lucy, p.96-101; o) Staff participation in office systems' design: Two case studies at the World Bank. Barry, Richard E., p.102-108; p) Strengthening group solidarity of clericals: A case study. Morgall, Janine, p.109-113; q) The decline of the "secretary as generalist". Murphree, Mary, p.114-118; r) Turning secretaries into word processors: Some fiction and a fact or two. Machung, Anne, p.119-123; s) Office computerization: Research then and now. Ostberg, Olov, p.127-142; t) Labor legislation in Norway: Its application to the introduction of new technology. Hjort, Lisbet, p.143-149; u) Occupational health and the design of work. Thoresen, Kari, p.150-154; v) An issue of respect: Women workers demand healthy and safe offices. Mitchell, Mary, p.155-157; w) An overview of NIOSH research on clerical workers. Cohen, Barbara, p.158-161; x) Health hazards in the computerized office. Henifin, Mary Sue and Stellman,

Jeanne M., p.162-166; y) The health impacts of low-level radiation on VDT operators. DeMatteo, Bob, p.167-172; z) A union perspective on health hazards of VDTs. Eisen, David, p.173-176; aa) Let the technology adapt! Reinhardt, Elisabeth, p.179-184; bb) Building new partnerships in a high-tech economy. Dukakis, Michael, p.185-189; cc) Experimental approaches towards telecommunications in France. Nora, Hervé, p.190-195; dd) Women and the fight around office automation. Goldet, Madame Cecile, p.196-199; ee) Alternative models of worker participation. Schneider, Leslie, p.200-204; ff) Collective bargaining strategies on new technology: The experience of West German trade unions. Meyer, Regine, p.205-214; gg) Taking the initiative on new technology: Canadian labor approaches. Pomeroy, Fred, p.215-219; hh) Legislative and research options for the U.S. Congress. Houlihan, Dennis, p.220-223; ii) Public policy and the employment impacts of office computerization. Reid, Julyan, p.224-229.

210. Older Women: Issues and Prospects. Markson, Elizabeth W., ed. Lexington, MA: LexingtonBooks, 1983.
a) Changing appearance for women in the middle years of life: Trauma? Berkun, Cleo S., p.11-35; b) The crossroads of menopause: A chance and a risk for the aging process of women. Gognalons-Nicolet, Maryvonne, p.37-48; c) Out of the *Mikvah* into the sauna: A study of women's health clubs. Jacobs, Ruth Harriet, p.49-54; d) The sexuality of older women. Adams, Catherine and Turner, Barbara F., p.55-72; e) Beyond the sweatshop: Older women in blue-collar jobs. Rosen, Ellen, p.75-91; f) Beyond the hearth: Older women and retirement. Szinovacz, Maximiliane E., p.93-120; g) Labor markets and old ladies' homes. Gratton, Brian, p.121-149; h) Shopping-bag women: Aging deviants in the city. Hand, Jennifer, p.155-177; i) Suburban older women. Johnson, Elizabeth S., p.179-193; j) The ever-single elderly woman. Anderson, Donna and Braito, Rita, p.195-225; k) Family relationships of older women: A women's issue. Hess, Beth B. and Waring, Joan, p.227-251; l) Concerns about parental health. Marshall, Victor W., Rosenthal, Carolyn J. and Synge, Jane, p.253-273; m) The final challenge: Facing death. O'Laughlin, Kay, p.275-296; n) Physical changes after menopause. Kerzner, Lawrence J., p.299-313; o) Cardiovascular risk factors in the elderly woman. Brand, Frederick N. and Kannel, William B., p.315-327.

211. On Being a Jewish Feminist: A Reader. Heschel, Susannah, ed. New York: Schocken, 1983.
a) The Jew who wasn't there: *Halakhah* and the Jewish woman. Adler, Rachel, p.12-18; b) The Jewish family: Looking for a usable past. Hyman, Paula, p.19-26; c) The hungry Jewish mother. Duncan, Erika, p.27-39; d) The Lilith question. Cantor, Aviva, p.40-50; e) Marriages made in heaven? Battered Jewish wives. Scarf, Mimi, p.51-64; f) Israeli women: Three myths. Hazleton, Lesley, p.65-87; g) Women-identified women in male-identified Judaism. Bauman, Batya, p.88-95; h) Memories of an Orthodox youth. Kendall, Thena, p.96-104; i) A feminist path to Judaism. Shulman, Gail, p.105-109; j) Notes

toward finding the right question. Ozick, Cynthia, p.120-151; k) Women and power in the Federation. Lipstadt, Deborah E., p.152-166; l) The Noah syndrome. Kaplan, Rosa Felsenburg, p.167-170; m) Scenes from the life of a Jewish lesbian. Bloch, Alice, p.171-176; n) Kaddish from the "wrong" side of the *Mehitzah*. Reguer, Sara, p.177-181; o) Learning to chant the Torah: A first step. Stern, Arleen, p.182-185; p) History, fiction, and the tradition: Creating a Jewish feminist poetic. Satlof, Claire R., p.186-206; q) And Deborah made ten. Lipstadt, Deborah, p.207-209; r) Reactions to a woman Rabbi. Geller, Laura, p.210-213; s) The right question is theological. Plaskow, Judith, p.223-233; t) Steps toward feminine imagery of deity in Jewish theology. Gross, Rita M., p.234-247; u) Bride, spouse, daughter: Images of the feminine in classical Jewish sources. Green, Arthur, p.248-260; v) Feminist Judaism: Restoration of the moon. Waskow, Arthur I., p.261-272; w) The secret Jew: An oral tradition of women (poem). Gottlieb, Lynn, p.273-277; x) Spring cleaning ritual on the eve of full moon Nisan (poem). Gottlieb, Lynn, p.278-280.

212. On the Problem of Men: Two Feminist Conferences. Friedman, Scarlet and Sarah, Elizabeth, eds. London: The Women's Press, 1982.
a) Heterosexuality, couples and parenthood: A 'natural' cycle? Friedman, Scarlet, p.5-20; b) Femininity, masculinity and sexuality. Jackson, Stevi, p.21-28; c) 'On the other side of the billboard...': Pornography, male fantasies and the objectification of women. Faraday, Annabel, p.29-38; d) Towards a revolutionary feminist analysis of rape. London Rape Action Group, p.39-43; e) Rape and marital violence in the maintenance of male power. Hill, Tina, p.44-55; f) The sexual abuse of children in the home. Jeffreys, Sheila, p.56-66; g) The packaging of women: Science and our sexuality. Overfield, Kathy, p.67-81; h) Transsexualism: Can men turn men into women? McNeill, Sandra, p.82-87; i) The politics of monogamy. Lewis, Jill, p.88-100; j) Coping: Or how mothers are seen and not heard. Graham, Hilary, p.101-116; k) Fatherhood: Bringing it all back home. Friedman, Scarlet and Sutton, Jo, p.117-127; l) Female performers on a male stage: The first women's liberation movement and the authority of men. Sarah, Elizabeth, p.135-156; m) Male feminists and divided women. Leonard, Diana, p.157-173; n) Now what are they up to? Men in the 'Men's movement'. Bradshaw, Jan, p.174-189; o) 'Male needs': The problems and problems of working with gay men. Stanley, Liz, p.190-213; p) The 'perks' of male power: Heterosexuality and the oppression of women. Ettorre, Betsy, p.214-226; q) Sexual assumptions in the women's movement. Sebestyen, Amanda, p.227-237; r) What can one do with a son? Feminist politics and male children. Hamblin, Angela, p.238-244; s) Poems on my sons. Astra, p.245-254.

213. One Way Ticket: Migration and Female Labour. Phizacklea, Annie, ed. London: Routledge & Kegan Paul, 1983.
a) Women in migration: Beyond the reductionist outlook.

Morokvasic, Mirjana, p.13-32; b) Motherhood and waged work: West Indian, Asian and white mothers compared. Stone, Karen, p.33-52; c) The second generation: West Indian female school-leavers. Dex, Shirley, p.53-72; d) Sexual divisions and ethnic adaptation: The case of Greek-Cypriot women. Anthias, Floya, p.73-94; e) In the front line. Phizacklea, Annie, p.95-112; f) Living in between: Turkish women in their homeland and in the Netherlands. Brouwer, Lenie and Priester, Marijke, p.113-130; g) Transnational production and women workers. Hancock, Mary, p.131-145.

214. Outsiders on the Inside: Women & Organizations. Forisha, Barbara L. and Goldman, Barbara H., eds. Englewood Cliffs, NJ: Prentice-Hall, 1981.
a) The inside and the outsider: Women in organizations. Forisha, Barbara L., p.9-30; b) Socialization and self-esteem: Women in management. Kosinar, Patricia, p.31-41; c) Different is not lesser: Women in science. Goldman, Barbara H. and Ramey, Estelle R., p.42-54; d) Rhetoric and organizational change: New applications of feminine style. Pearson, Sheryl S., p.55-74; e) Structuring the inside: The impact of organizations on sex differences. Kanter, Rosabeth Moss, p.75-83; f) The view from the bench: The exercise of power. Graves, Helen M., p.91-104; g) An administrator's viewpoint: The interaction of sex and power. Bardwick, Judith M., p.105-113; h) Styles of leadership: Power and feminine values. Hauptman, Anna R., p.114-121; i) Women, men, and professional writing: Signature of power? Goldman, Barbara H., p.122-135; j) The battle of the sexes: Power and sexual aggressiveness. Forisha, Barbara L. and Heady, Judith, p.135-147; k) The minutiae of discrimination: The need for support. Rowe, Mary, p.155-170; l) The probability of redress: Seeking external support. Gleason, Sandra E., p.171-187; m) Women, work and friendship: Personal confirmation and support. Candy, Sandra E., p.188-198; n) Mobilizing resources: Creating a support system. Bunker, Barbara Benedict, p.199-222; o) Ageism vs. sexism: Male models as a source of support. Rosenthal, Marilynn M., p.213-222; p) An attempt at collectivity: Professional confirmation and support. Bowker, Joan P., p.223-230; q) The work — family problem: Overloading the system. Pleck, Joseph H., p.239-254; r) Dual-career families: Intimacy or productivity? Forisha, Barbara L., p.255-271; s) One woman's perspective: Intimacy and productivity. Binford, Martha B., p.272-284; t) Dream vs. drift in women's careers: The question of generativity. Daniels, Pamela, p.285-302; u) Conclusion: Integrating love and power. Forisha, Barbara L. and Goldman, Barbara H., p.303-306.

215. Over Our Dead Bodies: Women Against the Bomb. Thompson, Dorothy, ed. London: Virago, 1983.
a) Beyond the wasteland. Mooney, Bel, p.5-14; b) How I learnt to start worrying and hate the bomb: The effects of a nuclear bombardment. Buirski, Jeanette, p.15-28; c) Three poems. Clifford, Gay, p.29-31; d) The balance of terror: Deterrence and peace-keeping. Ruehl, Beryl, p.32-48; e) The illusion of protection: Civil defence.

Wood, Suzanne, p.49-60; f) Defend us against our defenders: Democracy and security. Thompson, Dorothy, p.61-69; g) Two poems. Dubé, Janet, p.70-72; h) A voice from the peace camps: Greenham Common and Upper Heyford. Lowry, Maggie, p.73-77; i) Fuel for the nuclear arms race: Nuclear power and nuclear weapons. Mowlam, Marjorie, p.78-88; j) Letter to my neighbour: Nuclear war and the countryside. Pettitt, Ann, p.89-107; k) Take the toys from the boys: Competition and the nuclear arms race. Mansueto, Connie, p.108-119; l) Alternative defence: The search for non-nuclear alternatives. Foley, Lisa, p.120-128; m) Alternative defence: Nonviolent struggle and peace building. Solomon, Myrtle, p.129-135; n) The women who wire up the weapons: Workers in armament factories. Wainwright, Hilary, p.136-145; o) Anger in a black landscape. Carter, Angela, p.146-156; p) Building on the positives: The USSR. Porter, Cathy, p.157-161; q) Building on the positives: The USA. Thompson, Dorothy, p.162-166; r) Poem. Dube', Janet, p.167-168; s) Contemplating a nuclear future: Nuclear war, politics and the individual. Soper, Kate, p.169-179; t) The women's peace crusade: The history of a forgotten campaign. Liddington, Jill, p.180-198; u) Womanpower and nuclear politics: Women and the peace movement. Assiter, Alison, p.199-206; v) Interesting times: A chronology of the nuclear age. Sugden, Marian p.207-227.

216. Parenting in a Multicultural Society. Fantini, Mario D. and Cárdenas, René, eds. New York: Longman, 1980.
a) Introduction: Parenting in contemporary society. Fantini, Mario D. and Russo, John B., p.xxix-xxxvi; b) Significant sociocultural factors in effective parenting. Gordon, Ira J., p.3-16; c) A cross-cultural perspective on parenting. LeVine, Robert A., p.17-26; d) Developmental universals and their implications for parental competence. Jordan, Daniel C., p.27-40; e) The black family: An adaptive perspective. Comer, James P., p.43-53; f) Parenting for multiculturalism: A Mexican-American model. Cox, Barbara G. and Ramirez, Manuel, p.54-62; g) Parenting in the Native-American community. Burgess, Bill J., p.63-73; h) The Asian-American family. Suzuki, Bob H., p.74-102; i) The Puerto Rican family: Its role in cultural transition. Fitzpatrick, Joseph P. and Travieso, Lourdes, p.103-119; j) Implications for national policy decisions: The black family perspective. Bowen, Elizabeth and Carney, Magdalene, p.120-137; k) Experts and amateurs: Some unintended consequences of parent education. Hess, Robert D., p.141-159; l) What can "research experts" tell parents about effective socialization? Lamb, Michael E., p.160-169; m) Effective care-giving: The child from birth to three. Carew, Jean V., p.170-184; n) The early education of minority children. Cárdenas, José A. and Zamora, Gloria, p.187-206; o) The parent as educator: A home-school model of socialization. Fantini, Mario D., p.207-222; p) The relationship between home and school: A commentary on the current scene. Bell, Terrell H., p.223-232; q) An alternative perspective on parental

support: Child-care information and referral service. Levine, James A., p.235-242; r) Organizing delivery of parent education. Weikart, David P., p.243-252; s) Toward new methods in parent education. Brocher, Tobias H., p.253-269; t) Parenting in a pluralistic society: Toward a policy of options and choices. Fantini, Mario D. and Russo, John B., p.271-280.

217. Patriarchy in a Welfare Society. Holter, Harriet, ed. Oslo, Norway: Universitetsforlaget, 1984.
a) Women's research and social theory. Holter, Harriet, p.9-25; b) Women and the welfare state: The transition from private to public dependence. Hernes, Helga Maria, p.26-45; c) Women's right to money. Dahl, Tove Stang, p.46-66; d) Caring as women's work in the welfare state. Wœrness, Kari, p.67-87; e) The organizational woman and the trojan-horse effect. Søresen, Bjørg Aase, p.88-105; f) The female working class. Hoel, Marit, p.106-118; g) Women's mutual alliances, altruism as a premise for interaction. Ve, Hildur, p.119-135; h) Love and power in marriage. Haavind, Hanne, p.136-167; i) Gender as forms of value. Holter, Øystein Gullvåg, p.168-204; j) Theoretical ambiguities - A reflection of women's lives? Haukaa, Runa, p.205-222.

218. Perspectives on Power: Women in Africa, Asia, and Latin America. O'Barr, Jean F., ed. Durham, NC: Duke University, Center for International Studies, 1982.
a) An overview of women and power in Africa. Sacks, Karen, p.1-10; b) *Sati* or *Shakti*: Women, culture and politics in India. Mukhopadhyay, Carol, p.11-26; c) Legitimizing political women: Expanding options for female political elites in Latin America. Jacquette, Jane S., p.27-36; d) Tea and power: The anatomy of a conflict. Pharr, Susan J., p.37-49; e) Riot and rebellion among African women: Three examples of women's political clout. Wipper, Audrey, p.50-72; f) Women textile workers in the militarization of southeast Asia. Enloe, Cynthia H., p.73-86; g) Women and social policy: Lessons from Scandinavia. Schirmer, Jennifer G., p.87-101; h) Women in development planning: Advocacy, institutionalization and implementation. Lewis, Barbara, p.102-118.

219. Perspectives on Rape and Sexual Assault. Hopkins, June, ed. London: Harper & Row, 1984.
a) The victim's contribution to sexual offences. West, Donald J., p.1-14; b) Incest and sexual abuse of children. Gibbens, T.C.N., p.15-24; c) Aspects of violence in prostitution. Cunnington, Susan, p.25-36; d) The social uses of sexuality: Symbolic interaction, power and rape. Plummer, Ken, p.37-55; e) Police officer or doctor? Police surgeons' attitudes and opinions about rape. Geis, Gilbert, Geis, Robley and Wright, Richard, p.56-66; f) The role of the judiciary in the failure of the Sexual Offences (Amendment) Act to improve the treatment of the rape victim. Lowe, Marion, p.67-88; g) Crisis intervention with victims of forcible rape: A police perspective. O'Reilly, Harry J., p.89-103; h) Loss and mourning in victims of rape and sexual assault. Hopkins, June and Thompson, Ernestine H., p.104-117.

220. Perspectives on Women in the 1980s. Turner, Joan and Emery, Lois, eds. Winnipeg, Canada: University of Manitoba Press, 1983.
a) There comes a time. Turner, Joan, p.3-13; b) Perspectives on women in the 1980s: The Baird Poskanzer Memorial Lecture. Steinem, Gloria, p.14-27; c) The power politics of motherhood. Levine, Helen, p.28-40; d) Poverty: The feminine complaint. O'Connell, Dorothy, p.41-65; e) Native women and the state. Pierre-Aggamaway, Marlene, p.66-73; f) Feminist counselling: Approach or technique? Levine, Helen, p.74-87; g) Women as providers and consumers. Levine, Helen, O'Connell, Dorothy and Pierre-Aggamaway, Marlene, p.88-98; h) The electronic sweatshop. Gregory, Judith, p.99-112; i) Women, families and the state. Eichler, Margrit, p.113-127; j) Romantic love and reproductive rights. English, Deirdre, p.128-135; k) Strategies for the eighties. Eichler, Margrit, et al., p.136-148; l) Change, hope and celebration. Turner, Joan, p.149-158.

221. Perspectives on Work and the Family. Hansen, James C. and Cramer, Stanley H., eds. Rockville, MD: Aspen Systems, 1984.
a) The family as an influence on career development. Herr, Edwin L. and Lear, Patricia Best, p.1-15; b) Effects of maternal employment on children: Implications for the family therapist. Etaugh, Claire, p.16-39; c) Working mothers: Effects on the marriage and the mother. Hodgson, Mary L., p.40-55; d) Understanding dual career families. Gilbert, Lucia Albino, p.56-71; e) Voluntary mid-life career change: Family effects. Entine, Alan D., p.72-80; f) Family effects of dislocation, unemployment, and discouragement. Cramer, Stanley H. and Keitel, Merle A., p.81-93; g) Burnout and job dissatisfaction: Impact on the family. Freudenberger, Herbert J., p.94-105; h) The process of retirement: Implications for late-life counseling. Brice, Gary C. and Nowak, Carol A., p.106-123.

222. The Ph.D. Experience: A Woman's Point of View. Vartuli, Sue, ed. New York: Praeger, 1982.
a) A professional socialization process. Vartuli, Sue A., p.1-14; b) The ambivalent decision. Bolig, Rosemary A., p.15-26; c) High noon: Surviving the comprehensive exams. McConnell, Mary Ann, p.27-34; d) Taking the giant step: Writing the dissertation. Smith, Bernice D., p.35-44; e) Surviving in a predominantly white male institution. Levy, Phyllis Saltzman, p.45-60; f) New brains for old bodies: The impact of emotional and physical stress during the Ph.D. process. Barnett, Sharon, p.61-70; g) The diary of a web spinner. Tracey, Katherine O., p.71-78; h) In and out of relationships: A serious game for the woman doctoral student. Williams, Rosalind, p.79-92; i) The impossible dream: The Ph.D., marriage, and family. Levstik, Linda S., p.93-104; j) Grandma! What big plans you've got!: The older woman's Ph.D. experience. Wells, Mary Cay, p.105-114; k) The job hunt. McNairy, Marion R., p.115-126; l) Is the Ph.D. experience worth it?: A discussion. p.127-138.

223. Philosophy and Sex (new rev. edition). Baker, Robert and Elliston, Frederick, eds. Buffalo, NY: Prometheus Books, 1984.
a) Love: A feminist critique. Firestone, Shulamith, p.37-52; b) Love and feminism. Solomon, Robert C., p.53-70; c) The ethics of having love affairs. Taylor, Richard, p.71-92; d) Is adultery immoral? Wasserstrom, Richard, p.93-106; e) Monogamy: A critique. McMurty, John, p.107-118; f) The consolation of marriage. Palmer, David, p.119-129; g) Marriage, love, and procreation. Bayles, Michael D., p.130-145; h) Gay marriage. Elliston, Frederick, p.146-166; i) Humanae vitae. Pope Paul VI, p.167-184; j) Sex, birth control, and human life. Cohen, Carl, p.185-200; k) A defense of abortion. Thomson, Judith Jarvis, p.201-217; l) Abortion and a woman's right to decide. Jaggar, Alison, p.218-230; m) Abortion and the golden rule. Hare, R.M., p.231-248; n) "Pricks" and "Chicks": A plea for persons. Baker, Robert, p.249-267; o) Sexual perversion. Nagel, Thomas, p.268-279; p) Better sex. Ruddick, Sara, p.280-299; q) Sexual immorality delineated. Baumrin, Bernard H., p.300-311; r) Pornography and respect for women. Garry, Ann, p.312-326; s) Pornography, feminism, and censorship. Berger, Fred R., p.327-352; t) An essay on "Paederasty". Bentham, Jeremy, p.353-369; u) The morality of homosexuality. Ruse, Michael, p.370-390; v) Curing homosexuality. Suppe, Frederick, p.391-420; w) Taking responsibility for sexuality. Trebilcot, Joyce, p.421-430; x) Adult-child sex. Ehman, Robert, p.431-446; y) Critique. Frye, Marilyn, p.447-456; z) Case studies. Cross, Richard, p.460-470.

224. Pink Triangles: Radical Perspectives on Gay Liberation. Mitchell, Pam, ed. Boston, MA: Alyson Publications, 1980.
a) Culture and politics. Riddiough, Christine, p.14-33; b) Cosmetics as an act of revolution. Shively, Charley, p.34-47; c) Lesbians and gay men: Hetero sexualities, common cause. Mitchell, Pam, p.48-56; d) Looking at pornography: Erotica and the socialist morality. Blachford, Gregg, p.57-71; e) Old and gay. Shively, Charley, p.72-77; f) Happy families? Paedophilia examined. Gay Left Collective, p.78-89; g) Childhood sexuality and paedophilia. Gough, Jamie, p.90-96; h) Why Marxism? Gay Left Collective, p.98-106; i) Lesbianism: A socialist feminist perspective. Williams, Susan, p.107-116; j) Toward a scientific analysis of the gay question. Los Angeles Research Group, p.117-135; k) Some thoughts on gay/lesbian oppression. Riddiough, Christine, p.136-146; l) Towards a Marxist theory of gay liberation. Fernbach, David, p.148-163; m) Revolution in the pursuit of happiness: Love and community-building on the left. MacLean, Judy, p.164-170; n) Lesbian and gay oppression in the '80s: Androgyny, men and power. Killinger, Marc, p.171-187.

225. Pleasure and Danger: Exploring Female Sexuality. Vance, Carol S., ed. Boston, MA: Routledge & Kegan Paul, 1984.
a) Pleasure and danger: Toward a politics of sexuality. Vance, Carole S., p.1-27; b) Seeking ecstasy on the battlefield: Danger and pleasure in nineteenth-century feminist

sexual thought. DuBois, Ellen Carol and Gordon, Linda, p.31-49; c) The taming of the id: Feminist sexual politics, 1968-83. Echols, Alice, p.50-72; d) Interstices: A small drama of words. Spillers, Hortense J., p.73-100; e) Public silence, private terror. Allison, Dorothy, p.103-114; f) Everything they always wanted you to know: The ideology of popular sex literature. Altman, Meryl, p.115-130; g) Above and beyond politics: The sexual socialization of children. Calderone, Mary S., p.131-137; h) Politically correct? Politically incorrect? Dimen, Muriel, p.138-148; i) Cultural and historical influences on sexuality in Hispanic/Latin women: Implications for psychotherapy. Espin, Oliva M., p.149-164; j) The myth of the perfect body. Galler, Roberta, p.165-172; k) The body politic: The defense of sexual restriction by anti-abortion activists. Ginsburg, Faye, p.173-188; l) Variety: The pleasure in looking. Gordon, Bette, p.189-203; m) No more nice girls. Harvey, Brett, p.204-209; n) No progress in pleasure. Kruger, Barbara, p.210-216; o) Beyond politics? Children and sexuality. Millett, Kate, p.217-224; p) Fat and the fantasy of perfection. Munter, Carol, p.225-231; q) The fem question. Nestle, Joan, p.232-241; r) The misunderstanding: Toward a more precise sexual vocabulary. Newton, Esther and Walton, Shirley, p.242-250; s) The historical repression of women's sexuality. Robinson, Patricia Murphy, p.251-266; t) Thinking sex: Notes for a radical theory of the politics of sexuality. Rubin, Gayle, p.267-319; u) *Histoire d'O*: The construction of a female subject. Silverman, Kaja, p.320-349; v) Search for tomorrow: On feminism and the reconstruction of teen romance. Thompson, Sharon, p.350-384; w) The forbidden: Eroticism and taboo. Webster, Paula, p.385-398.

226. Political Women: Current Roles in State and Local Government. Flammang, Janet A. ed. Beverly Hills, CA: Sage, 1984.
a) Women in local government: An overview. Antolini, Denise, p.23-40; b) Women and state politics: An assessment. Githens, Marianne, p.41-63; c) Conceptions of the "political": White activists in Atlanta. Fowlkes, Diane L., p.66-86; d) Filling the party vacuum: Women at the grassroots level in local politics. Flammang, Janet A., p.87-113; e) Women in political parties: Gender differences in motives among California party activists. Bell, Julie Davis and Costantini, Edmond, p.114-138; f) Women as legislative candidates in six states. Clark, Janet, et al., p.141-155; g) Women's organizational strategies in state legislatures. Mueller, Carol, p.156-176; h) Female state senators as cue givers: ERA roll-call voting, 1972-1979. Hill, David B., p.177-190; i) Women on the state bench: Correlates of access. Cook, Beverly B., p.191-218; j) Community responses to violence against women: The case of a battered women's shelter. Wurr, Anne, p.221-241; k) Women's collaborative activities and city life: Politics and policy. Ackelsberg, Martha A., p.242-259; l) State and local policies on motherhood. Stoper, Emily, p.260-276; m) Resources and constraints on women in the policymaking process: States and local arenas. Boneparth, Ellen, p.277-290.

227. The Politics of Housework. Malos, Ellen, ed. London: Allison & Busby, 1980.
a) The history of the housewife. Hall, Catherine, p.44-71; b) The home: Its work and influence. Gilman, Charlotte Perkins, p.72-82; c) Women as domestic workers. Bondfield, Margaret, p.83-87; d) Working-class wives. Rice, Marjorie Spring, p.88-98; e) The politics of housework. Mainardi, Pat, p.99-104; f) The housewife. Gail, Suzanne, p.105-112; g) Women and the family. Bachelli, Ann, Twort, Hazel and Williams, Jan, p.113-118; h) The political economy of women's liberation. Benston, Margaret, p.119-129; i) Women's work is never done. Morton, Peggy, p.130-157; j) The dialectic of sex. Firestone, Shulamith, p.158-159; k) The power of women and the subversion of the community. Costa, Mariarosa Dalla and James, Selma, p.160-195; l) The carrot, the stick and the movement. Rowbotham, Sheila, p.196-201; m) When is a wage not a wage? Freeman, Caroline, p.202-209; n) Oppressed politics. Delmar, Ros, p.210-217; o) 'The housewife and her labour under capitalism' - a critique. Coulson, Margaret, Magas, Branka and Wainwright, Hilary, p.218-234; p) Women's domestic labour. Gardiner, Jean, Himmelweit, Susan and Mackintosh, Maureen, p.235-252; q) Wages against housework. Federici, Silvia, p.253-261; r) Wages for housework - political and theoretical considerations. Landes, Joan, p.262-274.

228. The Politics of the Second Electorate: Women and Public Participation. Lovenduski, Joni and Hills, Jill, eds. London: Routledge & Kegan, 1981.
a) Britain. Hills, Jill, p.8-32; b) USA. Evans, Judith, p.33-51; c) Canada. Brodie, M. Janine and Vickers, Jill McCalla, p.52-83; d) Australia. Simms, Marian, p.83-112; e) France. Mossuz-Lavau, Janine and Sineau, Mariette, p.112-133; f) Spain. Matsell, Catherine, p.134-152; g) West Germany. Hall, Jane, p.153-181; h) Italy. Weber, Maria, p.182-207; i) Sweden. Eduards, Maud, p.208-227; j) Finland. Haavio-Mannila, Elina, p.228-251; k) Eastern Europe. Wolchik, Sharon L., p.252-278; l) USSR. Lovenduski, Joni, p.278-291; m) Japan. Hargadine, Eileen, p.299-319.

229. The Politics of Women's Spirituality: Essays on the Rise of Spiritual Power Within the Feminist Movement. Spretnak, Charlene, ed. Garden City, NY: Anchor Press, 1982.
a) The great goddess: Who was she? Stone, Merlin, p.7-21; b) Women and culture in goddess-oriented old Europe. Gimbutas, Marija, p.22-31; c) Prepatriarchal female/goddess images. Rich, Adrienne, p.32-38; d) The origins of music: Women's goddess worship. Drinker, Sophie, p.39-48; e) Witchcraft as goddess religion. Starhawk, p.49-56; f) From the house of Yemanja: The goddess heritage of black women. Sojourner, Sabrina, p.57-63; g) The three faces of goddess spirituality. Stone, Merlin, p.64-70; h) Why women need the goddess: Phenomenological, psychological, and political reflections. Christ, Carol P., p.71-86; i) Ancient mirrors of womanhood. Stone, Merlin, p.91-96; j) The Amazon legacy.

Chesler, Phyllis, p.97-113; k) Tales of a reincarnated Amazon princess: The invincible wonder woman? Steinem, Gloria, p.114-120; l) Growing up with legends of the Chinese swordswomen. Beh, Siew Hwa, p.121-126; m) Meanings of matriarchy. Adler, Margot, p.127-137; n) Drawing from mythology in women's quest for selfhood. Debrida, Bella, p.138-151; o) Our heritage is our power. Chicago, Judy, p.152-156; p) A consciousness manifesto. Passmore, Nancy F. W., p.163-171; q) Consciousness, politics, and magic. Starhawk, p.172-184; r) The metaphors of power. Starrett, Barbara, p.185-193; s) Womanpower: Energy re-sourcement. Gearhart, Sally, p.194-206; t) Gyn/ecology: Spinning new time/space. Daly, Mary, p.207-212; u) Feminist witchcraft: Controlling our own inner space. Goldenberg, Naomi, p.213-218; v) Contemporary feminist rituals. Turner, Kay, p.219-233; w) Honor and ceremony in women's rituals. Broner, E. M., p.234-244; x) Images and models - in process. Weaver, Juanita, p.249-257; y) Martial art meditations. Culpepper, Emily E., p.258-264; z) From sacred blood to the curse and beyond. Grahn, Judy, p.265-279; aa) The healing powers of women. Glendinning, Chellis, p.280-293; bb) Expanding personal power through meditation. Iglehart, Hallie, p.294-304; cc) Feeding the feminist psyche through ritual theater. Podos, Batya, p.305-311; dd) See for yourself: Women's spirituality in holistic art. Edelson, Mary Beth, p.312-326; ee) Images of spiritual power in women's fiction. Christ, Carol P. and Spretnak, Charlene, p.327-343; ff) Sisterhood as cosmic covenant. Daly, Mary, p.351-361; gg) The personal is political. Collins, Sheila D., p.362-367; hh) Dimensions of spirituality. Davis, Judy and Weaver, Juanita, p.368-372; ii) Politics, spirituality, and models of change. Riddle, Dorothy I., p.373-381; jj) The politics of feminist spirituality. Rush, Anne Kent, p.382-385; kk) Metaphysical feminism. Morgan, Robin, p.386-392; ll) The politics of women's spirituality. Spretnak, Charlene, p.393-398; mm) Feminist spirituality: The politics of the psyche. Antonelli, Judith, p.399-403; nn) The unnatural divorce of spirituality and politics. Iglehart, Hallie, p.404-414; oo) Ethics and justice in goddess religion. Starhawk, p.415-422; pp) WITCH: Spooking the patriarchy during the late sixties. p.427-429; qq) On common ground: Native American and feminist spirituality approaches in the struggle to save mother earth. Todd, Judith, p.430-445; rr) Spiritual dimensions of feminist anti-nuclear activism. Foglia, Gina and Wolffberg, Dorit, p.446-461; ss) Spiritual techniques for re-powering survivors of sexual assault. Shaffer, Carolyn R., p.462-469; tt) The Christian right's "Holy War" against feminism. Spretnak, Charlene, p.470-496; uu) The voice of women's spirituality in futurism. Copper, Baba, p.497-509; vv) Women's collective spirit: Exemplified and envisioned. Shinell, Grace, p.510-528; ww) Spiritual hierarchies: The empress' new clothes? Greenfield, Gloria Z., p.531-534; xx) Myths and matriarchies. Binford, Sally R., p.541-549; yy) Afterword: Feminist politics and the nature of mind. Spretnak, Charlene, p.563-573.

230. Pornography and Sexual Aggression. Malamuth, Neil M. and Donnerstein, Edward, eds. Orlando, FL: Academic Press, 1984.
a) Introduction: Pornography and sex research. Byrne, Donn and Kelley, Kathryn, p.1-18; b) Aggression against women: Cultural and individual causes. Malamuth, Neil M., p.19-52; c) Pornography: Its effect on violence against women. Donnerstein, Edward, p.53-84; d) Arousal, affect, and the aggression-moderating effect of erotica. Sapolsky, Barry S., p.85-113; e) Effects of massive exposure to pornography. Bryant, Jennings and Zillmann, Dolf, p.115-138; f) Sex and violence: A ripple effect. Court, John H., p.143-172; g) Pornography in Japan: Cross-cultural and theoretical considerations. Abramson, Paul R. and Hayashi, Haruo, p.173-183; h) Sexual stratification, pornography, and rape in the United States. Baron, Larry and Straus, Murray A., p.185-209; i) Sexually aggressive men: Empirical findings and theoretical implications. Koss, Mary P. and Leonard, Kenneth E., p.213-232; j) Sexual signaling and sexual aggression in adolescent relationships. Goodchilds, Jacqueline D. and Zellman, Gail L., p.233-243; k) Using psychological research on violent pornography to inform legal change. Linz, Daniel and Penrod, Steven, p.247-275; l) Bases of liability for injuries produced by media portrayals of violent pornography. Linz, Daniel, et al., p.277-304; m) Afterword: Sex, violence, and the media: Where do we stand now? Eysenck, H. J., p.305-318.

231. Powers of Desire: The Politics of Sexuality. Snitow, Ann, Stansell, Christine and Thompson, Sharon, eds. New York: Monthly Review Press, 1983.
a) Sex and society: A research note from social history and anthropology. Rapp, Rayna and Ross, Ellen, p.51-73; b) "Charity girls" and city pleasures: Historical notes on working-class sexuality, 1880-1920. Peiss, Kathy, p.74-87; c) Marching to a different drummer: Lesbian and gay GIs in World War II. Bérubé, Allan, p.88-99; d) Capitalism and gay identity. D'Emilio, John, p.100-113; e) Family, sexual morality, and popular movements in turn-of-the-century America. Epstein, Barbara, p.117-130; f) Feminism, men, and modern love: Greenwich Village, 1900-1925. Trimberger, Ellen Kay, p.131-152; g) The new woman and the rationalization of sexuality in Weimar Germany. Grossmann, Atina, p.153-171; h) Compulsory heterosexuality and lesbian existence. Rich, Adrienne, p.177-205; i) Russian working women: Sexuality in bonding patterns and the politics of daily life. Bobroff, Anne, p.206-227; j) they're always curious. Klepfisz, Irena, p.228; k) The Afro-American female: The historical context of the construction of sexual identity. Simson, Rennie, p.229-235; l) I just came out pregnant. Garcia, Felicita, p.236-244; m) Mass market romance: Pornography for women is different. Snitow, Ann Barr, p.245-263; n) Issues and answers. Goldberg, Myra, p.264-269; o) Garden paths, descents. Thompson, Sharon, p.270-275; p) Master and slave: The fantasy of erotic domination. Benjamin, Jessica, p.280-299; q) Outside the operating room of the sex-change doctor. Olds, Sharon, p.300; r) Movie. Harrison, Nancy, p.301-307; s) Street dream #1 (story). Thompson, Sharon, p.308-308; t) Is the gaze male? Kaplan, E. Ann, p.309-327; u) "The mind that

burns in each body": Women, rape, and racial violence. Hall, Jacquelyn Dowd, p.328-349; v) Hearts of darkness. Omolade, Barbara, p.350-367; w) Gender systems, ideology, and sex research. Vance, Carole S., p.371-384; x) The teacher. Rosenthal, Carole, p.385-393; y) What we're rollin around in bed with: Sexual silences in feminism. Hollibaugh, Amber and Moraga, Cherríe, p.394-405; z) In the morning (poem). Cortez, Jayne, p.406-408; aa) Bestiary (poem). Olds, Sharon, p.409-409; bb) A story of a girl and her dog. Shulman, Alix Kates, p.410-415; cc) Male vice and female virtue: Feminism and the politics of prostitution in nineteenth-century Britain. Walkowitz, Judith R., p.419-438; dd) The new feminism of yin and yang. Echols, Alice, p.439-459; ee) Feminism, moralism, and pornography. Willis, Ellen, p.460-467; ff) My mother liked to fuck. Nestle, Joan, p.468-470; gg) Abortion: Is a woman a person? Willis, Ellen, p.471-476; hh) The fear that feminism will free men first. English, Deirdre, p.477-483.

232. The Powers of Tamil Women. Wadley, Susan S., ed. Syracuse, NY: Syracuse University, 1980.
a) On the meaning of sakti to women in Tamil Nadu. Egnor, Margaret, p.1-34; b) The auspicious married woman. Reynolds, Holly Baker, p.35-60; c) Marriage in Tamil culture: The problem of conflicting "models". Daniel, Sheryl B., p.61-91; d) Hidden powers: Cultural and socio-economic accounts of Jaffna women. David, Kenneth, p.93-136; e) A note on the nobility of women in popular Tamil fiction. Lindholm, James, p.137-151; f) The paradoxical powers of Tamil women. Wadley, Susan S., p.153-170.

233. Pregnant Women at Work. Chamberlain, Geoffrey, ed. London: Macmillan Press, 1984.
a) Women at work in pregnancy. Chamberlain, Geoffrey, p.3-13; b) The effect of work on placental function and fetal growth. Hytten, Frank E., p.15-25; c) The hazards of work in pregnancy. Murray, Robert, p.27-34; d) Women workers at higher risk of reproductive hazards. Adbul-Karim, Raja W., p.35-44; e) Reproductive hazards of the American life style. Gabbe, Steven G., p.45-60; f) Birth defects and parental occupation. Erickson, J. David, p.61-72; g) The epidemiological identification of reproductive hazards. McDowall, Michael E., p.73-85; h) The effects of work in pregnancy: Short- and long-term associations. Peters, Timothy J., et al., p.87-104; i) Occupational fatigue and preterm birth. Laumon, Bernard and Mamelle, Nicole, p.105-115; j) The effect of the mother's work on the infant. Oakley, Ann, p.117-132; k) Mechanisms of teratogenesis: The extrapolation of the results of animal studies to man. Johnson, E. Marshall, p.135-151; l) What evidence is required to identify a chemical as a reproductive hazard? Mattison, Donald R., p.153-165; m) Animal and human studies in genetic toxicology. Legator, Marvin S. and Ward, Jonathan B., p.167-188; n) A trade union view of reproductive health. McKechnie, Sheila, p.191-202; o) A management view of reproductive health. Plaut, Jonathan, p.203-212; p) Legal considerations of reproductive hazards in industry in the United Kingdom. Lorber, Steven J., p.213-224; q) Legal considerations of reproductive hazards in industry in the United States. Ashford, Nicholas A., p.225-239; r) What can be done in antenatal care? Foster, Ann, p.241-247; s) The contribution of the occupational health services. Baker, Frances J. T., p.249-256; t) Educating workers, management and the general public. McEwen, James, p.257-270; u) Future research on work in pregnancy. Elbourne, Diana and Garcia, Jo, p.273-287; v) Adverse influences of the working environment. Chamberlain, Geoffrey, p.289-291.

234. Pre-Industrial Women: Interdisciplinary Perspectives. Dixon, Suzanne and Munford, Theresa, eds. Canberra, Australia: Australian National University, 1984.
a) Theoretical perspectives on pre-industrial women. Dixon, Suzanne, p.2-5; b) Women, politics and the formation of the Chinese state. Munford, Theresa, p.6-8; c) Shamanism as institutionalised ego defense and elite formation associated with transvestism in a Borneo society. Huilgol, Glynn, p.9-14; d) Some perceptions of Indonesian women under Islam. Woodcroft-Lee, Carlien Patricia, p.15-21; e) Evidence concerning Anglo-Saxon women from archaeology. Meaney, Audrey, p.22-29; f) The status of women in old and early middle kingdom Egypt? Callender, Gae, p.30-36; g) Social history and women's history. Aveling, Marian, p.37-39; h) The limitations of demography for women's history. Ifeka, Caroline, p.40-42; i) Women and the concept of change in history. Bashar, Nazife, p.43-50; j) 'Woman-ing' the landscape: East Anglia 1300-1500: A discussion on sources and methodology. Ross, Barbara, p.51-54; k) Summing up: Beyond the 'status of women'. Dixon, Suzanne, p.55-57.

235. Prejudice and Pride: Discrimination Against Gay People in Modern Britain. Galloway, Bruce, ed. London: Routledge & Kegan Paul, 1983.
a) At home. Durell, Anna, p.1-18; b) At school. Dobson, Malcolm, p.19-34; c) At work. Daly, Mike, p.35-61; d) On the streets. Meldrum, Julian, p.62-77; e) Parliament and the law. Warner, Nigel, p.78-101; f) The police and the courts. Galloway, Bruce, p.102-124; g) In prison. Billingham, Nick, p.125-138; h) The church. Green, Robin, p.139-164; i) The medical profession. Marshall, John, p.165-193; j) The media. Howes, Keith, p.194-212; k) The fight for equality. Burns, Roy, p.213-228.

236. The Premenstrual Syndrome. Keep, Pieter A. van and Utian, Wulf H., eds. Lancaster, England: MTP Press, 1981.
a) Aetiology of premenstrual syndrome. Day, J.B. and Taylor, R.W., p.11-29; b) The premenstrual syndrome - an epidemiological and statistical exercise. Keep, P.A. van and Lehert, P., p.31-42; c) Premenstrual syndrome - a holistic approach. Burrows, G., Dennerstein, L. and Spencer-Gardner, C., p.43-49; d) An appraisal of the role of progesterone in the therapy of premenstrual syndrome. Sampson, G. A., p.51-69; e) An explorative study into the clinical effects of dydrogesterone in the treatment of premenstrual syndrome. Strecker, J. R., p.71-79; f) A double-

blind, placebo-controlled, multi-centre study of the efficacy of dydrogesterone (Duphaston®). Haspels, A. A., p.81-92.

237. Premenstrual Tension: A Multidisciplinary Approach. Debrovner, Charles H., ed. New York: Human Sciences Press, 1982.
a) The gynecologist's approach. Sturgis, Somers H., p.13-27; b) The endocrinologist's approach. Ramey, Estelle, p.35-45; c) The psychiatrist's approach. Notman, Malkah, p.51-63; d) The nutritionist's approach. Abraham, Guy E., p.71-91; e) The effect of placebos. Debrovner, Charles H., p.95-99.

238. Procreation or Pleasure?: Sexual Attitudes in American History. Altherr, Thomas L., ed. Malabar, FL: Robert E. Krieger, 1983.
a) The Puritans and sex. Morgan, Edmund S., p.5-16; b) Passionlessness: An interpretation of Victorian sexual ideology, 1790-1850. Cott, Nancy F., p.17-29; c) Davey Crockett as trickster: Pornography, liminality and symbolic inversion in Victorian America. Smith-Rosenberg, Carroll, p.31-45; d) The spermatic economy: A nineteenth-century view of sexuality. Barker-Benfield, G.J., p.47-70; e) From maidenhood to menopause: Sex education for women in Victorian America. Haller, John S., p.71-85; f) The erotic South: Civilization and sexuality in American abolitionism. Walters, Ronald G., p.87-98; g) The awesome power of sex: The polemical campaign against Mormon polygamy. Cannon, Charles A., p.99-113; h) Harlot or heroine? Changing views of prostitution, 1870-1920. Fishbein, Leslie, p.115-125; i) Ideas of the early sex education movement in America, 1890-1920. Strong, Bryan, p.127-144; j) The scientist as sex crusader: Alfred C. Kinsey and American culture. Morantz, Regina M., p.145-166.

239. The Psychobiology of Sex Differences and Sex Roles. Parsons, Jacquelynne E., ed. Washington, D.C.: Hemisphere Publishing Corp., 1980.
a) Psychosexual neutrality: Is anatomy destiny? Parsons, Jacquelynne E., p.3-29; b) Biopsychosocial processes in the development of sex-related differences. Petersen, Anne C., p.31-55; c) Gonadal hormones and cognitive functioning. Broverman, Donald M., Klaiber, Edward L. and Vogel, William, p.57-80; d) Human sex-hormone abnormalities viewed from an androgynous perspective: A reconsideration of the work of John Money. Kaplan, Alexandra G., p.81-91; e) Biochemical and neurophysiological influences on human sexual behavior. Ledwitz-Rigby, Florence, p.95-104; f) Homosexual orientation in women and men: A hormonal basis? Meyer-Bahlburg, Heino F. L., p.105-130; g) A social psychological model of human sexuality. Falbo, Toni, p.131-142; h) American birth practices: A critical review. Hahn, Susan Reed and Paige, Karen Ericksen, p.145-175; i) Sources of maternal stress in the postpartum period: A review of the literature and an alternative view. Magnus, Elisabeth M., p.177-208; j) Adult life cycles: Changing roles and changing hormones. Notman, Malkah, p.209-224; k) Research on men-

strual-related psychological changes: Alternative perspectives. Brooks-Gunn, Jeanne, Clarke, Anne and Ruble, Diane N., p.227-243; l) A social psychological perspective on the menstrual cycle. Sherif, Carolyn Wood, p.245-268; m) Body time and social time: Mood patterns by menstrual cycle phase and day of week. Rossi, Alice S. and Rossi, Peter E., p.269-304.

240. Psychology and Gynaecological Problems. Broome, Annabel and Wallace, Louise, eds. London: Tavistock Publications, 1984.
a) Sterilization. Alder, Elizabeth, p.1-17; b) Regret and reversal of sterilization. Hall, E.V. van, Lambers, K.J. and Trimbos-Kemper, G.C.M., p.18-39; c) Psychosocial aspects of contraception. Clarke, Lynda, p.40-59; d) Termination of pregnancy. Broome, Annabel, p.60-76; e) Infertility and alternative parenting. Humphrey, Michael, p.77-94; f) Chronic pelvic pain. Beard, R. W. and Pearce, Shirley, p.95-116; g) Psychological aspects of gynaecological cancer. Andersen, Barbara L., p.117-141; h) Psychological aspects of hysterectomy. Kincey, John and McFarlane, T., p.142-160; i) Psychological preparation for gynaecological surgery. Wallace, Louise, p.161-188; j) Psychosexual problems. Dodd, Barbara G. and Parsons, Anthony D., p.189-210; k) Psychological aspects of the menstruum and premenstruum. Bosanko, Carole and Fielding, Dorothy, p.211-242; l) A psychosocial study of the climacteric. Cooke, David J., p.243-265; m) A feminist perspective on women and health. Osborne, Kate, p.266-282.

241. The Public and the Private. Gamarnikow, Eva, et al., eds. London: Heinemann, 1983.
a) Social sciences and the state: Fighting like a woman. Stacey, Meg, p.7-11; b) Public and private: Marking the boundaries. Imray, Linda and Middleton, Audrey, p.12-27; c) Blowing the cover of the protective male: A community study of violence to women. Hanmer, Jalna and Saunders, Sheila, p.28-46; d) Men and war: Status, class and the social reproduction of masculinity. Allatt, Patricia, p.47-61; e) Women and caring: Skills, tasks and taboos. Ungerson, Clare, p.62-77; f) 'It's a pleasure to cook for him': Food, mealtimes and gender in some South Wales households. Murcott, Anne, p.78-90; g) 'Women and old boats': The sexual division of labour in a Newfoundland outport. Porter, Marilyn, p.91-105; h) Dividing the rough and the respectable: Working-class women and pre-school playgroups. Finch, Janet, p.106-117; i) Purification or social control? Ideologies of reproduction and the churching of women after childbirth. Rushton, Peter, p.118-131; j) Do her answers fit his questions? Women and the survey method. Graham, Hilary, p.132-146; k) Interviewing men: 'Taking gender seriously'. McKee, Lorna and O'Brien, Margaret, p.147-161.

242. The Representation of Women in Fiction. Heilbrun, Carolyn G. and Higonnet, Margaret R., eds. Baltimore, MD: Johns Hopkins University Press, 1983.
a) Fictional consensus and female casualties. Ermarth, Elizabeth, p.1-18; b) The birth of the artist as heroine:

(Re)production, the *Künstlerroman* tradition, and the fiction of Katherine Mansfield. Gubar, Susan, p.19-59; c) Liberty, sorority, misogyny. Marcus, Jane, p.60-97; d) "Herself against herself": The clarification of Clara Middleton. Miller, J. Hillis, p.98-123; e) Writing (from) the feminine: George Sand and the novel of female pastoral. Miller, Nancy K., p.124-151; f) *Persuasion* and the promises of love. Poovey, Mary, p.152-180.

243. Research in the Interweave of Social Roles: Families and Jobs. Pleck, Joseph H. and Lopata, Helena Z., eds. Greenwich, CT: JAI Press, 1983.
a) Urban and rural working women in Poland today: Between social change and social conflict. Lobodzinska, Barbara, p.3-33; b) Gender and interaction in the workplace. Miller, Jon and Olson, Jon, p.35-58; c) The role and status of women scientific research workers in research groups. Stolte-Heiskanen, Veronica, p.59-87; d) The old world, new rights, and the limited rebellion: Challenges to traditional authority in immigrant families. Pleck, Elizabeth, p.91-112; e) Mothers as social agents: Structuring the community activities of school aged children. O'Donnell, Lydia and Stueve, Ann, p.113-129; f) Black families and childrearing support networks. Malson, Michelene Ridley, p.131-141; g) Katie's place: Women's work, professional work, and social reform. Fowlkes, Martha R., p.143-159; h) Family, work, and individual development in dual-career marriages: Issues for research. Fava, Sylvia F. and Genovese, Rosalie G., p.163-185; i) Work experience and family relations among working-class and lower-middle-class families. Katz, Mitchell H. and Piotrkowski, Chaya S., p.187-200; j) Overtime over the life cycle: A test of the life cycle squeeze hypothesis. Moen, Phyllis and Moorehouse, Martha, p.201-218; k) Weak links in men's worker-earner roles: A descriptive model. Rodman, Hyman and Safilios-Rothschild, Constantina, p.219-238; l) Unemployment and family stress. Voydanoff, Patricia, p.239-250; m) Husbands' paid work and family roles: Current research issues. Pleck, Joseph H., p.251-333.

244. Research in the Interweave of Social Roles: Women and Men. Lopata, Helena Z., ed. Greenwich, CT: JAI Press, 1980.
a) Colombian women in party politics: A token role. Harkess, Shirley, p.1-31; b) White mothers in the American civil rights movements. Blumberg, Rhoda Lois, p.33-50; c) Sex segregation and the women's roles in the economic system: The case of Iran. Touba, Jacquiline Rudolph, p.51-98; d) Occupation-family-linkages as perceived by men in the early stages of professional and managerial careers. Mortimer, Jeylan T., p.99-117; e) The roles of men and women in French families: Change or stability in the patterns and practices? Pitrou, Agnes, p.119-138; f) The roles of Greek husbands and wives: Definitions and fulfillment. Dijkers, Marcellinus and Safilios-Rothschild, Constantina, p.139-166; g) The nurture of adults by children in family settings. Boulding, Elise, p.167-189; h) Sexual customs and gender roles in Sweden and America: An analysis and interpretation.

Reiss, Ira L., p.191-220; i) Traditional sex norms and the innovative function of afternoon dancing. Haavio-Mannila, Elina and Snicker, Raija, p.221-245; j) Synthetic smiles and fabricated faces. Oliver, David B., p.247-263; k) Role loss and manic depression. Glassner, Barry, p.265-282.

245. Rethinking the Family: Some Feminist Questions. Thorne, Barrie and Yalom, Marilyn, eds. New York: Longman, 1982.
a) Feminist rethinking of the family: An overview. Thorne, Barrie, p.1-24; b) Is there a family? New anthropological views. Collier, Jane, Rosaldo, Michelle Z. and Yanagisako, Sylvia, p.25-39; c) Why nineteenth-century feminists did not support "birth control" and twentieth-century feminists do: Feminism, reproduction, and the family. Gordon, Linda, p.40-53; d) The fantasy of the perfect mother. Chodorow, Nancy and Contratto, Susan, p.54-75; e) Maternal thinking. Ruddick, Sara, p.76-94; f) Mothering, fathering, and mental illness. Spiegel, David, p.95-110; g) Shifting perspectives on marital property law. Prager, Susan Westerberg, p.111-130; h) Why men resist. Goode, William J., p.131-150; i) Home production for use in a market economy. Brown, Clair (Vickery), p.151-167; j) Family and class in contemporary America: Notes toward an understanding of ideology. Rapp, Rayna, p.168-187; k) The place of the family in the origins of the welfare state. Zaretsky, Eli, p.188-234; l) The family: The view from a room of her own. Bridenthal, Renate, p.225-239.

246. Rethinking Women's Roles: Perspectives from the Pacific. O'Brien, Denise and Tiffany, Sharon W., eds. Berkeley, CA: University of California Press, 1984.
a) Introduction: Feminist perceptions in anthropology. Tiffany, Sharon W., p.1-11; b) Domesticity and the denigration of women. Strathern, Marilyn, p.13-31; c) Complementarity: The relationship between female and male in the East Sepik village of Bun, Papua New Guinea. McDowell, Nancy, p.32-52; d) "Women never hunt": The portrayal of women in Melanesian ethnography. O'Brien, Denise, p.53-70; e) Revenge suicide by Lusi women: An expression of power. Counts, Dorothy Ayers, p.71-93; f) Women, work, and change in Nagovisi. Nash, Jill, p.94-119; g) Pigs, pearlshells, and 'women's work': Collective response to change in highland Papua New Guinea. Sexton, Lorraine Dusak, p.120-152; h) "Sing to the Lord a New Song": Women in the churches of Oceania. Forman, Charles W., p.153-172; i) European women in the Solomon Islands, 1900-1942: Accommodation and change on the Pacific frontier. Boutilier, James A., p.173-200.

247. Re-Vision: Essays in Feminist Film Criticism. Doane, Mary Ann, Mellencamp, Patricia and Williams, Linda, eds. Frederick, MD: University Publications of America, 1984.
a) Feminist film criticism: An introduction. Doane, Mary Ann, Mellencamp, Patricia and Williams, Linda, p.1-17; b) Developments in feminist film criticism. Gledhill,

Christine, p.18-48; c) The woman at the keyhole: Women's cinema and feminist criticism. Mayne, Judith, p.49-66; d) The "woman's film": Possession and address. Doane, Mary Ann, p.67-82; e) When the woman looks. Williams, Linda, p.83-99; f) From repressive tolerance to erotic liberation: *Maedchen in Uniform*. Rich, B. Ruby, p.100-130; g) Dis-embodying the female voice. Silverman, Kaja, p.131-149; h) Now and nowhere: Roeg's *Bad Timing*. de Lauretis, Teresa, p.150-169.

248. Rewriting Nursing History. Davies, Celia, ed. Totowa, NJ: Barnes & Noble, 1980.
a) Introduction: The contemporary challenge in nursing history. Davies, Celia, p.11-17; b) Nurse recruitment to four provincial hospitals 1881-1921. Maggs, Christopher, p.18-40; c) From Sarah Gamp to Florence Nightingale: A critical study of hospital nursing systems from 1840 to 1897. Williams, Katherine, p.41-75; d) The administration of poverty and the development of nursing practice in nineteenth-century England. Bolton, Gail and Dean, Mitchell, p.76-101; e) A constant casualty: Nurse education in Britain and the USA to 1939. Davies, Celia, p.102-122; f) Asylum nursing before 1914: A chapter in the history of labour. Carpenter, Mick, p.123-146; g) 'The history of the present' - contradiction and struggle in nursing. Bellaby, Paul and Oribabor, Patrick, p.147-174; h) Old wives' tales? Women healers in English history. Versluysen, Margaret Connor, p.175-199; i) Archives and the history of nursing. Foster, Janet and Sheppard, Julia, p.200-214.

249. Rocking the Boat: Academic Women and Academic Processes. DeSole, Gloria and Hoffmann, Leonore, eds. New York: Modern Language Association, 1981.
a) The most important thing for you to know. Lieberman, Marcia R., p.3-7; b) To file of not to file. Weise, Selene Harding-Curd, p.8-14; c) Paying your dues, part-time. Kantrowitz, Joanne Spencer, p.15-36; d) Joan Roberts and the university. Macaulay, Jacqueline and Slavin, Sarah, p.37-49; e) Not by lawyers alone: Ten practical lessons for academic litigants. Rackin, Phyllis, p.50-56; f) I'm not shouting "Jubilee": One black woman's story. Hull, Gloria T., p.57-60; g) The crux: Quality judgment and departmental autonomy. Burkhard, Marianne, p.61-65; h) Fighting for tenure: A bittersweet victory. Rosenthal, Carole, p.66-73; i) Career politics and the practice of women's studies. Coulter, Sara, p.77-81; j) A jury of one's peers. Abramson, Joan, p.82-97; k) The failure of affirmative action for women: One university's experience. Macaulay, Jacqueline, p.98-116; l) A network of one's own. Childers, Karen, et al., p.117-127.

250. Schooling for Women's Work. Deem, Rosemary, ed. London: Routledge & Kegan Paul, 1980.
a) Introduction: Women, work and schooling: The relevance of gender. Deem, Rosemary, p.1-12; b) Socio-cultural reproduction and women's education. MacDonald, Madeleine, p.13-25; c) The importance of being Ernest ... Emma ... Tom ... Jane. The perception and categorization of gender conformity and gender deviation in primary

schools. Clarricoates, Katherine, p.26-41; d) Studying girls at school: The implications of confusion. Llewellyn, Mandy, p.42-51; e) Black girls in a London comprehensive school. Fuller, Mary, p.52-64; f) Education and the individual: Schooling for girls, or mixed schooling - a mixed blessing? Shaw, Jennifer, p.66-75; g) Sex differences in mathematical performance: A review of research and possible action. Weiner, Gaby, p.76-86; h) Sex differences in performance in science examinations. Harding, Jan, p.87-97; i) Into work: Continuity and change. Keil, Teresa and Newton, Peggy, p.98-111; j) Young women in the labour market: Stability and change. Ashton, David and Maguire, M., p.112-125; k) Women in higher education: A case study of the open university. Griffiths, Moira, p.126-141; l) How many women academics 1912-76? Rendel, Margherita, p.142-161; m) The experiences of women graduates in the labour market. Chisholm, Lynne and Woodward, Diana, p.162-176; n) Women, school and work: Some conclusions. Deem, Rosemary, p.177-183.

251. Scientific-Technological Change and the Role of Women in Development. D'Onofrio-Flores, Pamela M. and Pfafflin, Sheila M., eds. Boulder, CO: Westview Press, 1982.
a) Technology, economic development, and the division of labour by sex. D'Onofrio-Flores, Pamela M., p.13-28; b) Women and technology in the industrialized countries. Bergom-Larsson, Maria, p.29-75; c) Women and technology in peripheral countries: An overview. Tadesse, Zenebeworke, p.77-111; d) The impact of science and technology and the role of women in science in Mexico. Srinivasan, Mangalam, p.113-148; e) The power of persistence: Consciousness raising at international fora - the case of UNCSTD. Leet, Mildred Robbins, p.149-178; f) Some reflections on women in science and technology after UNCSTD. Pfafflin, Sheila M., p.179-188.

252. Second Trimester Pregnancy Termination. Keirse, Marc J.N.C., et al., eds. The Hague, Netherlands: Leiden University Press, 1982.
a) Midtrimester abortion: a global view. Tietze, Christopher, p.1-11; b) Second trimester abortion as a social problem: Delay in abortion seeking behaviour and its causes. Ketting, E., p.12-19; c) Legal aspects of pregnancy termination in Europe. Schnabel, Paul, p.20-29; d) A review of abortion practices and their safety. Diggory, Peter, p.30-40; e) The trimester threshold for pregnancy termination: Myth or truth? Cates, Willard and Grimes, David A., p.41-51; f) Aspirotomy for outpatient termination of pregnancy in the second trimester. Beekhuizen, W., et al., p.52-64; g) Instrumental abortion in the second trimester: an overview. Cates, Willard and Grimes, David A., p.65-79; h) Intra-amniotic hypertonic saline instillation in the second trimester. Kerenyi, Thomas D., p.80-87; i) Extra-amniotic ethacridine (Rivanol®)-catheter technique for midtrimester abortion. Ingemanson, Carl-Axel, p.88-93; j) Fact and fancy in the termination of molar pregnancy with particular reference to uterine stimulants. Keirse, Marc J.N.C., p.94-107; k) Natural prostaglandins alone or in combination for termination of

pregnancy. Craft, Ian, p.108-114; l) Termination of second trimester pregnancy with prostaglandin analogues. Amy, Jean-Jacques, p.115-131; m) Prostaglandin therapy for second trimester abortion: An overview of current status and recent trends. Embrey, M.P., p.132-137; n) Termination of pregnancy after intrauterine foetal death. Keirse, Marc J.N.C., p.138-154; o) Complications of second trimester abortion. Berger, Gary S. and Keith, Louis G., p.155-167; p) Prevention of Rhesus (D) isoimmunization after abortion. Gravenhorst, J. Bennebroek, p.168-173; q) Contraception following second trimester abortion. Berger, Gary S. and Keith, Louis G., p.174-183; r) Sterilization combined with midtrimester abortion. Rioux, Jacques E. and Yuzpe, A. Albert, p.184-191; s) Somatic sequelae and future reproduction after pregnancy termination. Hogue, Carol J. Rowland, p.192-201; t) Some considerations on the psychosocial aspects of pregnancy termination. van Hall, E.V., p.202-206.

253. The Second X and Women's Health. Fooden, Myra, ed. New York: Gordian Press, 1983.
a) Genes and gender update. Tobach, Ethel, p.7-28; b) Update on genetics. Freedman, Victoria H., p.29-37; c) What's new in endocrinology? Target: Sex hormones. Gordon, Susan, p.39-48; d) Sex and temperament revisited. Sharff, Jagna Wojcicka, p.49-62; e) The myth of assembly-line hysteria. Harris, Ben, p.65-86; f) Genes and gender in the workplace. Bellin, Judith S. and Rubenstein, Reva, p.87-100; g) Reproductive hazards in the workplace: A course curriculum guide. Chavkin, Wendy, et al., p.101-130; h) Sexism in gynecologic practices. Gold, Marji, p.133-141; i) The effects of childbearing on women's mental health: A critical review of the literature. Bram, Susan, p.143-160; j) Women's mental health. Fooden, Myra, p.161-183; k) The health of older women in our society. Vroman, Georgine M., p.185-204; l) Sexism and racism in health policy. Christmas, June Jackson, p.205-215.

254. Seeing our Way Clear: Feminist Revision of the Academy. Loring, Katherine, ed. Ann Arbor, MI: GLCA Women's Studies Program, 1983.
a) Seeing our way clear: Feminist re-vision of the academy. McIntosh, Peggy, p.1-14; b) The evolution of the woman scientist. Sherman, Laurel, p.15-22; c) The artist as hero in Maxine Hong Kingston's *The Woman Warrior*. Rosenberg, Warren, p.23-26; d) *Song of Solomon*: The hero with a woman's face. Griffin, Gail, p.27-32; e) Images of women in film. Stensaas, Starla, p.33-36; f) Captured angel in the centerfold. Swim, Janet, p.37-44; g) The hurt that lasts forever. Meyer, Karmen, p.45-51; h) Broaching the issue: Homophobia. Dickie, Jane and Glenn, Audrey, p.52-60; i) Increasing female participation in the mathematics classroom. Brunson, Pansy, p.61-66; j) The problem: Idealism and accommodation in the feminist transformation of the academy. Vacca, Linnea, p.67-69; k) Know your heroines. Loux, Ann, p.70-74; l) Communication or collusion?: Maneuvering through the maze of patriarchal theology. Cady, Linell, p.75-77; m) American female dramatists: Show but no go? Jensen,

Julie, p.78-80; n) The whole thing: In search of relevance and integration made dynamic by creativity. Edelson, Mary Beth, p.81-88; o) When we dream together. Zanotti, Barbara, p.89-92.

255. Separate Worlds: Studies of Purdah in South Asia. Papanek, Hanna and Minault, Gail, eds. Delhi: Chanakya Publications, 1982.
a) Purdah: Separate worlds and symbolic shelter. Papanek, Hanna, p.3-53; b) Purdah revisited: A comparison of Hindu and Muslim interpretations of the cultural meaning of purdah in South Asia. Vatuk, Sylvia, p.54-78; c) Purdah and the Hindu family in central India. Jacobson, Doranne, p.81-109; d) The domestic realm in the lives of Hindu women in Calcutta. Beech, Mary Higdon, p.110-138; e) Purdah among the Oswals of Mewar. Mehta, Rama, p.139-163; f) Gradations of purdah and the creation of social boundaries on a Baluchistan oasis. Pastner, Corroll McClure, p.164-189; g) Purdah in Pakistan: Seclusion and modern occupations for women. Papanek, Hanna, p.190-216; h) From purdah to politics: The social feminism of the all-India women's organizations. Forbes, Geraldine H., p.219-244; i) Purdah politics: The role of Muslim women in Indian nationalism, 1911-1924. Minault, Gail, p.245-261; j) Purdah and participation: Women in the politics of Bangladesh. Jahan, Rounaq, p.262-282; k) The status of women in Islam: A modernist interpretation. Rahman, Fazlur, p.285-310.

256. Sex and Class in Women's History. Newton, Judith L., Ryan, Mary P. and Walkowitz, Judith R., eds. London: Routledge & Kegan Paul, 1983.
a) Class and gender in Victorian England. Davidoff, Leonore, p.17-71; b) Freud's Dora, Dora's hysteria. Ramas, Maria, p.72-113; c) Servants, sexual relations and the risks of illegitimacy in London, 1801-1900. Gillis, John R., p.114-145; d) Free black women and the question of matriarchy. Lebsock, Suzanne, p.146-166; e) The power of women's networks. Ryan, Mary P., p.167-186; f) "The men are as bad as their masters...": Socialism, feminism and sexual antagonism in the London tailoring trade in the 1830s. Taylor, Barbara, p.187-220; g) One hand tied behind us: A review essay. Stansell, Christine, p.221-231; h) Examining family history. Bridenthal, Renate, Rapp, Rayna and Ross, Ellen, p.232-258; i) The doubled vision of feminist theory. Kelly, Joan, p.259-270.

257. Sex & Love: New Thoughts on Old Contradictions. Cartledge, Sue and Ryan, Joanna, eds. London: Women's Press, 1983.
a) Purity, motherhood, pleasure or threat? Definitions of female sexuality 1900-1970s. Bland, Lucy, p.8-29; b) Sensual uncertainty, or why the clitoris is not enough. Segal, Lynne, p.30-47; c) Really being in love means wanting to live in a different world. Goodison, Lucy, p.48-66; d) Struggling to change, changing with struggle. Chambers, Jo, p.67-74; e) The daughter is mother of the child: Cycles of lesbian sexuality. Brown, Jill, p.75-88; f) Sex and childbirth. Saunders, Lesley, p.89-104; g) Is a

feminist heterosexuality possible? Hamblin, Angela, p.105-123; h) Heterosexual sex: Power and desire for the other. Hollway, Wendy, p.124-140; i) From where I stand: A case for feminist bisexuality. Gregory, Deborah, p.141-156; j) Women alone. Bickerton, Tricia, p.157-166; k) Duty and desire: Creating a feminist morality. Cartledge, Sue, p.167-179; l) I'll climb the stairway to heaven: Lesbianism in the seventies. Wilson, Elizabeth, p.180-197; m) Psychoanalysis and women loving women. Ryan, Joanna, p.196-209; n) Sexual theory and practice: Another double standard. Ruehl, Sonja, p.210-223.

258. Sex Differences in Britain. Reid, Ivan and Wormald, Eileen, eds. London: Grant McIntyre, 1982.
a) Sex differences and this book. Reid, Ivan and Wormald, Eileen, p.1-11; b) Sex, gender and society. Cooper, Andrew, p.12-28; c) Vital statistics. Reid, Ivan, p.29-58; d) Social security and the family. Kidd, Tony, p.59-84; e) Educational opportunity and achievement. Wilkin, Margaret, p.85-113; f) The labour market. Webb, Michael, p.114-174; g) Political participation. Wormald, Eileen, p.175-203; h) Involvement in crime. Stratta, Erica, p.204-234; i) Sex differences in Britain. Reid, Ivan and Wormald, Eileen, p.235-251.

259. Sex Differentiation and Schooling. Marland, Michael, ed. London: Heinemann, 1983.
a) School as a sexist amplifier. Marland, Michael, p.1-7; b) Boys and girls entering school. Jacklin, Carol Nagy, p.8-17; c) The hidden curriculum: Academic consequences of teacher expectations. Serbin, Lisa A., p.18-41; d) Staffing for sexism: Educational leadership and role models. Marland, Michael, p.42-59; e) Anxiety, aspirations and the curriculum. Sutherland, Margaret B., p.60-71; f) Sex differences in achievement orientations: Consequences for academic choices and attainments. Dweck, Carol S. and Licht, Barbara G., p.72-97; g) 'Telling how it is': Language and gender in the classroom. Spender, Dale, p.98-116; h) Guidance and pastoral care. Marland, Michael, p.117-122; i) Sex differentiation and careers. Bould, Jackie and Hopson, Barrie, p.123-142; j) Curriculum matters. Marland, Michael, p.143-162; k) Success in mathematics. Fennema, Elizabeth, p.163-180; l) Should the sexes be separated? Marland, Michael, p.181-186; m) Equality or equity? - a European overview. Byrne, Eileen M., p.187-201.

260. Sex Discrimination and Equal Opportunity: The Labor Market and Employment Policy. Schmid, Günther and Weitzel, Renate, eds. New York: St. Martin's Press, 1984.
a) Women in the labour market and equal opportunity policy in Sweden, United Kingdom, United States and West Germany. Schmid, Günther, p.1-19; b) A look at the male female unemployment differentials in the Federal Republic of Germany, Sweden, United Kingdom, and the United States of America. Björklund, Anders, p.20-43; c) Patterns of occupational segregation by sex in the labor market. Jonung, Christina, p.44-68; d) Earnings differentials: Empirical evidence and causes. O'Neill, June, p.69-91; e) Equal opportunity and the law in the United States. Braun, Rachel Eisenberg, p.92-106; f) The effects of statutory employment policies on women in the United Kingdom labour market. Glucklich, Pauline, p.107-131; g) Equal opportunity policies in Sweden. Gustafsson, Siv, p.132-154; h) Equal opportunity policies for women in the Federal Republic of Germany. Eitel, Ludwig and Pfarr, Heide M., p.155-190; i) Policies and implementation of anti-discrimination strategies. Jackson, Christine, p.191-201; j) Labour market policy in four countries: Are women adequately represented? MacLennan, Emma and Weitzel, Renate, p.202-248; k) Estimating the impact of labor market policies on women: A discussion of the four-country studies on the employment of women. Cain, Glen, p.249-263; l) The political economy of labor market discrimination: A theoretical and comparative analysis of sex discrimination. Schmid, Günther, p.264-303.

261. Sex Discrimination in Higher Education: Strategies for Equality. Farley, Jennie, ed. Ithaca, NY: New York State School of Industrial and Labor Relations, Cornell University, 1981.
a) Litigation: Strategy of the last resort. Vladeck, Judith P., p.1-22; b) Building mentorship frameworks as part of an effective equal opportunity ecology. Rowe, Mary P., p.23-33; c) Grievances and their redress in the eighties. Davies, Helen C. and Davies, Robert E., p.34-65; d) Strategies for eliminating sex discrimination: Times that try men's souls. Sandler, Bernice R., p.66-89; e) Progress and pitfalls: Reports from participating institutions. p.99-101; f) "Go find yourself a mentor". Rowe, Mary P., p.102-104; g) Faculty grievance procedure. University of Pennsylvania, p.105-121.

262. Sex Equity in Education. Stockard, Jean, et al., eds. New York: Academic Press, 1980.
a) Sex roles in education. Stockard, Jean, p.3-9; b) Sex inequities in the experience of students. Stockard, Jean, p.11-48; c) Why sex inequities exist for students. Stockard, Jean, p.49-77; d) Differentiation by sex in educational professions. Schmuck, Patricia A., p.79-97; e) Why sex inequities exist in the profession of education. Stockard, Jean, p.99-115; f) A social-psychological analysis of the context for change. Kempner, Ken, p.119-141; g) Laws prohibiting sex discrimination in schools. Williams, Peg, p.143-164; h) Context of change: The women's movement as a political process. Schmuck, Patricia A., p.165-183; i) Educational equity: Current and future needs. Stockard, Jean, p.185-194.

263. Sex/Gender Division of Labor: Feminist Perspectives. Duluth, Minnesota: Center for Advanced Feminist Studies, University of Minnesota, 1983.
a) Women and welfare work: Demystifying the myth of disembeddedness. Noble, Barbara Presley and Whelan, Mary K., p.7-12; b) Housework as a comparative advantage: The neoclassical theory of the sexual division of labor. Brown, Lisa Jo, p.13-25; c) Symmetrical families? Changing gender role expectations and the breadwinner role in the contemporary United States. Potuchek, Jean L., p.27-40; d) "Blessed be the tie that binds": YWCA

extension work among industrial women, Minneapolis, 1900-1910. Faue, Elizabeth, p.41-51; e) "For love and money both": Women's work-related decisions in twentieth century Minneapolis. Walsh, Eileen P., p.53-62; f) The sexual division of labor on American farms: 1750-1850. Jensen, Joan M., p.63-70; g) "Mom, it's a losing proposition": The decline of women's subsistence production on Iowa farms. Fink, Deborah, p.71-78; h) Creating a place for women: American book publishing in the nineteenth century. Coultrap-McQuin, Susan, p.79-84; i) "Teacher, teacher": Teachers and educators in a stratified "female" profession. Moss, Rosalind Urbach, p.85-92; j) Professionalism, division of labor by gender, and the control of nursing practice. Allen, David G., p.93-103; k) Industrial social workers in France, 1917-1939: A study in the sex/gender division of labor. Crisler, Jane, p.105-116; l) Men servants and women bosses: The domestic service institution in colonial Zambia. Hansen, Karen Tranberg, p.117-138; m) The new economic readjustment policies: Implications for Chinese urban working women. Dalsimer, Marlyn and Nisonoff, Laurie, p.139-164.

264. Sex, Race, and the Role of Women in the South. Hawks, Joanne V. and Skemp, Sheila L., eds. Jackson, MS: University Press of Mississippi, 1983.
a) Women's history and the revision of Southern history. Friedman, Jean E., p.3-12; b) Sisters under their skins: Southern working women, 1880-1950. Janiewski, Dolores, p.13-35; c) The public role of Southern women. Swain, Martha H., p.37-57; d) Black women in a Southern city: Washington, D.C., 1890-1920. Harley, Sharon, p.59-74; e) Southern literary women as chroniclers of Southern life. Jones, Anne Goodwyn, p.75-93; f) Historians construct the Southern woman. Scott, Anne Firor, p.95-110.

265. Sex Role Attitudes and Cultural Change. Gross, Ira, Downing, John and D'Heurle, Adma, eds. Dordrecht, Holland: D. Reidel, 1982.
a) Parents' sex role attitudes and children's concepts of femininity and masculinity. Rose, Suzanna and Serafica, Felicisima C., p.11-24; b) Ethnic differences in sex stereotyping by mothers: Implications for health care. Johnston, Maxene and Sarty, Merrill, p.25-37; c) The role of schools in developing sex role attitudes. Dwyer, Carol A., p.39-43; d) Review of the literature of non-sexist curriculum and a critique of the underlying assumptions and rationale. Hughes, Selma, p.45-50; e) Language and attitudes toward masculine and feminine sex role. Ernst, Shirley B., p.51-58; f) Does sex stereotyping lead to a higher incidence of male dyslexia? Gross, Alice D., p.57-64; g) Making literacy equally accessible to females and males. Downing, John, p.65-79; h) Sex typing in occupational preferences of high school boys and girls. Brown, Cathleen A., p.81-88; i) Aspirations and sex roles - Are they in conflict? Hutt, Corinne, p.89-91; j) Cross-sex friendship in the elementary school. Cohen, Jeffrey, D'Heurle, Adma and Widmark-Peterson, V., p.93-100; k) Sex differences in children's road accidents. Downing, Charles S., p.100-107; l) Cultural differences in children's

sex role stereotypes. Kleiman, Betty and Leung, Sophia M.R., p.109-120; m) Sex role stereotyping and mental health standards in Israel: A cross-cultural comparison. Dreman, Solly B., p.121-129; n) Sex role images in Lebanese text books. Abu Nasr, J., Kallab, I. and Lorfing, I., p.131-140; o) Strategies of healthy sex role development in modernized India. Pandey, Rama S., p.141-149; p) Effectiveness of self-persuasion in producing healthy attitudes towards polygyny. Ugwuegbu, Denis C., p.151-155; q) Overemphasis of mother role and inflexibility of roles. Niemelä, P., p.157-162; r) Sex without reproduction: Voluntary childlessness as a response to contemporary sex roles. Bram, Susan, p.163-175; s) Changing sex roles reflected in the films of François Truffaut. D'Heurle, Adma, p.175-195; t) Mental health in boys and girls: Awareness of attitudes for positive sex roles. Gross, Ira, p.197-200.

266. Sex Role Research: Measuring Social Change. Richardson, Barbara L. and Wirtenberg, Jeana, eds. New York: Praeger, 1983.
a) New maps of development: New visions of maturity. Gilligan, Carol, p.17-32; b) Social science inquiries into female achievement: Recurrent methodological problems. Kaufman, Debra R. and Richardson, Barbara L., p.33-48; c) Overview of research methods. Wallston, Barbara Strudler, p.51-76; d) Evaluation issues in women's studies. Bagenstos, Naida Tushnet and Millsap, Mary Ann, p.77-91; e) Methodological issues in the study of sex-related differences. Jacklin, Carol Nagy, p.93-100; f) Sampling: Issues and problems in sex role and social change research. Gardner, David W. and Shakeshaft, Charol, p.103-112; g) Instruments and measures in a changing, diverse society. Beere, Carole A., p.113-138; h) All things being equal, a behavior is superior to an attitude: Studies of sex-typed and sex-biased attitudes and behaviors. Vaughter, Reesa M., p.139-150; i) Statistical analysis in sex roles and social change. Rosenthal, Evelyn R., p.153-172; j) Methods for integrative reviews. Jackson, Gregg B., p.173-196; k) The impact of societal biases on research methods. Campbell, Patricia B., p.197-213; l) Causal models: Their import and their triviality. Boruch, Robert F., p.215-248.

267. Sex Role Stereotyping and Affirmative Action Policy. Gutek, Barbara A., ed. Los Angeles, CA: Institute of Industrial Relations, University of California, 1982.
a) Achievement in women: Implications for equal employment opportunity policy. Canter, Rachelle, p.9-64; b) The importance of being right when you think you are: Self-serving bias in equal employment opportunity. Larwood, Laurie, p.65-80; c) Double jeopardy: Resistance to affirmative action from potential beneficiaries. Martin, Joanne and Northcraft, Gregory B., p.81-130; d) A psychological examination of sexual harassment. Gutek, Barbara A., p.131-163; e) Career concepts and human resource management: The case of the dual-career couple. Von Glinow, Mary Ann, p.164-184; f) Equity for women at work: Models of change. Nieva, Veronica F., p.185-227.

268. Sex Roles and Psychopathology. Widom, Cathy Spatz, ed. New York: Plenum, 1984.
a) Sex roles and psychopathology. Widom, Cathy Spatz, p.3-17; b) A historical perspective. Dwyer, Ellen, p.19-48; c) Gender ideology and phobias in women. Wolfe, Barry E., p.51-72; d) Hysteria. Winstead, Barbara Ann, p.73-100; e) Sex roles and psychophysiological disorders: Coronary heart disease. Platt, Jane E., p.101-121; f) Depression in relation to sex roles: Differences in learned susceptibility and precipitating factors. Cox, Sue and Radloff, Lenore Sawyer, p.123-143; g) Suicide. Lester, David, p.145-156; h) Schizophrenia. LaTorre, Ronald A., p.157-179; i) Sex roles, criminality, and psychopathology. Widom, Cathy Spatz, p.183-217; j) A sex-roles perspective on drug and alcohol use by women. Colten, Mary Ellen and Marsh, Jeanne C., p.219-248; k) Sex roles and sexual dysfunction. Stock, Wendy E., p.249-275; l) Sex-related differences in the epidemiology of child psychopathology. Eme, Robert F., p.279-316; m) Sex-role stereotypes and the development of eating disorders. Finn, Stephen and Leon, Gloria R., p.317-337; n) Senescence, sex roles, and stress: Shepherding resources into old age. Datan, Nancy and Holt, Linda, p.339-352; o) Sex roles, psychological assessment, and patient management. Zeldow, Peter B., p.355-374; p) Sex roles in medicine. Fidell, Linda S., p.375-389.

269. Sex Roles and Social Change in Native Lower Central American Societies. Loveland, Christine A. and Loveland, Franklin O., eds. Urbana, IL: University of Illinois Press, 1982.
a) Rama men and women: An ethnohistorical analysis of change. Loveland, Christine A., p.3-22; b) Structural continuity in the division of men's and women's work among black Carib (Garífuna). Kerns, Virginia, p.23-43; c) Sex roles and subsistence: A comparative analysis of three Central American communities. Cominsky, Sheila and Scrimshaw, Mary, p.44-69; d) New economic roles for Cuna males and females: An examination of socioeconomic change in a San Blas community. Costello, Richard W., p.70-87; e) New roles for males in Guaymí society. Bort, John R. and Young, Philip D., p.88-102; f) Being Cuna and female: Ethnicity mediating change in sex roles. Swain, Margaret Byrne, p.103-123; g) Watch that pot or the *waksuk* will eat you up: An analysis of male and female roles in Rama Indian myth. Loveland, Franklin O., p.124-141; h) Symbolic aspects of Bribri roles on the occasions of birth and death. Bozzoli de Wille, M.E., p.142-165.

270. Sex Roles, Family, & Community in Turkey. Kâgitçibasi, Çigdem, ed. Bloomington, IN: Indiana University Turkish Studies, 1982.
a) Duofocal family structure and an alternative model of husband-wife relationship. Olson, Emelie A., p.33-72; b) The significance of family and kinship in urban Turkey. Duben, Alan, p.73-99; c) Urban change and women's roles in Turkey: An overview and evaluation. Kandiyoti, Deniz, p.101-120; d) Dualism in values toward education of Turkish women. Erkut, Sumru, p.121-132; e) Women's education in rural Turkey. Özbay, Ferhunde, p.133-149; f) Sex roles, value of children and fertility in Turkey. Kâgitçibasi, Çigdem, p.151-180; g) Female labor power relations in the urban Turkish family. Kuyas, Nilüfer, p.181-205; h) The effect of international labor migration on women's roles: The Turkish case. Abadan-Unat, Nermin, p.207-236; i) Economic change and the Gecekondu family. Senyapili, Tansi, p.235-248; j) The plight of urban migrants: Dynamics of service procurement in a squatter area. Heper, Metin, p.249-267; k) Changing patterns of patronage: A study in structural change. Kiray, Mübeccel B., p.269-293; l) Psychopathology and the Turkish family: A family systems theory analysis. Fisek, Güler Okman, p.295-321; m) Social change and family crisis: The nature of Turkish divorce. Levine, Ned, p.323-347; n) Social psychological patterns of homicide in Turkey: A comparison of male and female convicted murders. Özgür, Serap and Sunar, Diane, p.349-381; o) Civil violence in Turkey: Its infrastructural, social and cultural foundations. Magnarella, Paul J., p.383-401.

271. Sex Roles: Origins, Influences, and Implications for Women. Stark-Adamec, Cannie, ed. Montreal: Eden Press, 1980.
a) Why? Stark-Adamec, Cannie, p.1-19; b) Androgyny: A dead end or a promise. Pyke, Sandra W., p.20-32; c) Parents and the sex-role development of the preschool child. Tudiver, Judith G., p.33-49; d) Women of South Asian and Anglo-Saxon origins in the Canadian context. Naidoo, Josephine C., p.50-69; e) Perspectives from women on sport and leisure. Butt, Dorcas Susan, p.70-88; f) Sex-role ideology and sex bias in judgments of occupational suitability. Burt, Barbara, Kalin, Rudolf and Stoppard, Janet M., p.89-99; g) A cross-cultural comparison of assertiveness in women. Cammaert, Lorna, p.100-110; h) Assertiveness training for improved conflict resolution style. Emmot, Shelagh, p.111-126; i) Beyond a cognitive/behavioural approach: Congruent assertion training. Greenberg, Leslie S. and Kahn, Sharon E., p.127-138; j) Beyond the fear of success: Observations on women's fears. Rubin, Berte, p.139-147; k) Female superiority in sex difference competence comparisons: A review of the literature. Moses, Barbara, Smye, Marti Diane and Wine, Jeri Dawn, p.148-163; l) Sex differences in assertiveness: Implications for research and treatment. Moses, Barbara, Smye, Marti Diane and Wine, Jeri Dawn, p.164-175; m) Assertiveness: Sex differences in relationships between self-report and behavioural measures. Moses, Barbara, Smye, Marti Diane and Wine, Jeri Dawn, p.176-186; n) Hormones and behaviour: Introduction. Henrik, Elizabeth, p.187-189; o) Mood and behaviour changes in menopausal women receiving gonadal hormones or placebo. Brender, William, Gelfand, Morrie M. and Sherwin, Barbara Brender, p.190-205; p) Feeling states and the menstrual cycle. Vingilis, Evelyn, p.206-216; q) Theoretical/conceptual implications of study design and statistical analysis: Research on the menstrual cycle. Koeske, Randi Daimon, p.217-232.

272. Sex Segregation in the Workplace: Trends, Explanations, Remedies. Reskin, Barbara F., ed. Washington, DC: National Academy Press, 1984.
a) Trends in occupational segregation by sex and race, 1960-1981. Beller, Andrea H., p.11-26; b) A woman's place is with other women: Sex segregation within organizations. Baron, James N. and Bielby, William T., p.27-55; c) Job changing and occupational sex segregation: Sex and race comparisons. Rosenfeld, Rachel A., p.56-86; d) Occupational sex segregation: Prospects for the 1980s. Beller, Andrea H. and Han, Kee-ok Kim, p.91-114; e) Occupational segregation and labor market discrimination. Blau, Francine D., p.117-143; f) Toward a general theory of occupational sex segregation: The case of public school teaching. Strober, Myra H., p.144-156; g) Commentary: Strober's theory of occupational sex segregation. Mason, Karen Oppenheim, p.157-170; h) Work experience, job segregation, and wages. Corcoran, Mary, Duncan, Greg J. and Ponza, Michael, p.171-191; i) Sex typing in occupational socialization. Brinton, Mary C. and Marini, Margaret Mooney, p.192-232; j) Institutional factors contributing to sex segregation in the workplace. Reskin, Barbara F. and Roos, Patricia A., p.235-260; k) Commentary: The need to study the transformation of job structures. Kelley, Maryellen R., p.261-264; l) Job integration strategies: Today's programs and tomorrow's needs. Harlan, Sharon L. and O'Farrell, Brigid, p.267-291; m) Occupational desegregation in CETA programs. Berryman, Sue E. and Waite, Linda J., p.292-307.

273. Sex Selection of Children. Bennett, Neil G., ed. New York: Academic Press, 1983.
a) Sex selection of children: An overview. Bennett, Neil G., p.1-12; b) Measuring sex preferences and their effects on fertility. McClelland, Gary H., p.13-45; c) Sex selection through amniocentesis and selective abortion. Kobrin, Frances E. and Potter, Robert G., p.47-71; d) Timing of fertilization and the sex ratio of offspring. James, William H., p.73-99; e) Decision making and sex selection with biased technologies. Bennett, Neil G. and Mason, Andrew, p.101-111; f) The economics of sex preference and sex selection. Bloom, David E. and Grenier, Gilles, p.113-128; g) Parental sex preferences and sex selection. Williamson, Nancy E., p.129-145; h) Legal aspects of pre-natal sex selection. Evans, V. Jeffery, p.147-200; i) Toward a moral policy for sex choice. Powledge, Tabitha M., p.201-212; j) Ethics and public policy: Should sex choice be discouraged? Fletcher, John C., p.213-252.

274. Sexism in the Secondary Curriculum. Whyld, Janie, ed. London: Haper & Row, 1983.
a) School life - Organization and control. Whyld, Janie, p.28-45; b) Classroom interaction. Clarricoates, Katherine, p.46-64; c) Subject image, examinations and teaching materials. Whyld, Janie, p.65-76; d) English. Rose, Joy, p.77-98; e) Modern languages. Hingley, Phil, p.99-110; f) Mathematics and science - Introduction. Samuel, Judy, p.111-126; g) Mathematics. Sharkey, Sarah, p.127-136; h) Science. Samuel, Judy, p.137-147; i) History. Bruley, Sue, Pollock, Jan and Turnbull,

Annmarie, p.148-164; j) Geography. Larsen, Brekke, p.165-178; k) Social studies. Whyld, Janie, p.179-198; l) Home economics. Wynn, Barbara, p.199-215; m) Craft, design, and technology. Grant, Martin, p.216-227; n) Art. Hatton, Jennifer, p.228-236; o) Business studies. Keeley, Phil and Myers, Kate, p.237-247; p) Careers. Prout, Gillian, p.248-262; q) Sex education. Rocheron, Yvette and Whyld, Janie, p.270-284; r) Physical education. Browne, Pat, Matzen, Lene and Whyld, Janie, p.270-284; s) Remedial education. Winter, Margaret, p.285-294; t) More than one way forward. Whyld, Janie, p.295-314.

275. Sexist Language: A Modern Philosophical Analysis. Vetterling-Braggin, Mary, ed. Totowa, NJ: Rowman and Littlefield, 1981.
a) Male chauvinism: A conceptual analysis. Frye, Marilyn, p.7-22; b) Sexist language and sexism. Shute, Sara, p.23-33; c) Sexist speech: Two basic questions. Grim, Patrick, p.34-51; d) Language and Woman's Place (excerpts). Lakoff, Robin, p.60-67; e) Linguistics and feminism. Valian, Virginia, p.68-80; f) Lakoff on language and women. Fortunata, Jacqueline, p.81-91; g) The myth of the neutral "man". Moulton, Janice, p.100-115; h) The hidden joke: Generic uses of masculine terminology. Korsmeyer, Carolyn, p.116-131; i) Feminist linguistics in philosophy. Kuykendall, Eleanor, p.132-146; j) Gender-neutral terms. Duran, Jane, p.147-154; k) Degenderization. Beardsley, Elizabeth Lane, p.155-160; l) "Pricks" and "chicks": A plea for "persons". Baker, Robert, p.161-182; m) Sex and reference. Moulton, Janice, p.183-193; n) How words hurt: Attitudes, metaphor and oppression. Ross, Stephanie, p.194-216; o) Vs. Ms. Levin, Michael, p.217-222; p) Against "Vs. Ms.". Purdy, L.M., p.223-228; q) Beyond the miserable vision of "Vs. Ms.". Soble, Alan, p.229-248; r) Sexism and racism: Some conceptual differences. Thomas, Laurence, p.256-270; s) Thomas on sexism. Postow, B.C., p.271-278; t) Moral redescription and political self-deception. Ketchum, Sara Ann, p.279-289; u) A note on the ethics of theories of truth. Grim, Patrick, p.290-298; v) A note on logical truth and non-sexist semantics. Stenner, A.J., p.299-306; w) Reference and truth: The case of sexist and racist utterances. Taylor, Kriste, p.307-318.

276. Sexual Aggression and the Law. Verdun-Jones, Simon N. and Keltner, Alfred A., eds. Burnaby, B.C.: Simon Fraser University, 1983.
a) The classification of sexual aggressives and their associated demographic, social, developmental and psychological features. Marshall, William L., p.1-13; b) The relationship between treatment for sex offenders and the court. Abel, Gene G., p.15-26; c) Prediction of recidivism and the evaluation of treatment programs for sex offenders. Quinsey, Vernon L., p.27-40; d) The assessment and treatment of sexual offenders. Abel, Gene G., Marshall, William L. and Quinsey, Vernon L., p.41-52; e) Sexual aggression and the law - implications for the future. Dickens, Bernard M., p.53-72; f) Ethics and ethical dilemmas in the treatment of sex offenders. Gordon, R. and

Verdun-Jones, Simon N., p.73-96; g) Sentencing the sexual offender. Oliver, H.G., p.97-111.

277. Sexual Arousal: New Concepts in Basic Sciences, Diagnosis, and Treatment. Ficher, Miguel, Fishkin, Ralph E. and Jacobs, Joseph A., eds. Springfield, IL: Charles C. Thomas, 1984.
a) Psychological causes of lack of arousal. Fink, Paul J., p.5-14; b) Hormones and sexual arousal. Persky, Harold, p.15-23; c) Physiology of male sexual arousal. Jacobs, Joseph A., p.24-34; d) Mechanisms of sexual arousal in females. Eskin, Bernard A., p.35-56; e) The assessment of sleep erections for diagnosis of erectile disorders. Schiavi, Raul C., et al., p.59-69; f) Psychophysiologic measurement of sexual arousal in females. Abel, Gene G. and Cunningham-Rathner, Jerry, p.70-87; g) The multidisciplinary approach to the diagnosis and treatment of male sexual dysfunction. Fishkin, Ralph E., et al., p.88-97; h) Evaluation and treatment of impotence: The urologist's viewpoint. Arsdalen, Keith N. Van, Malloy, Terrence R. and Wein, Alan J., p.101-115; i) Current approaches in endocrinology. Eskin, Bernard A., p.116-141; j) Current approaches in sex therapy. Eisenstein, Talia and Ficher, Ilda V., p.142-156; k) Study of sexual dysfunction among male diabetics. Ficher, Miguel, et al., p.159-204; l) Sexual arousal responses and disability. Glass, Dorothea D., p.207-217; m) Effects of aging on sexual arousal. Lief, Harold I., p.218-231; n) Effect of drugs on sexual arousal. Marco, Luis A., p.232-252; o) Sexuality with cardiac disease. Naso, Frank, p.253-258.

278. The Sexual Dimension in Literature. Bold, Alan, ed. London: Vision, 1982.
a) Sex and classical literature. Green, Peter, p.19-48; b) 'Last Night's Rambles': Restoration literature and the war between the sexes. Goreau, Angeline, p.49-69; c) The secret nexus: Sex and literature in eighteenth-century Britain. Boucé, Paul-Gabriel, p.70-89; d) Victorian erotica. Webb, Peter, p.90-121; e) Sexual fiction in America, 1955-80. Charney, Maurice, p.122-142; f) Phallic worship: Some personal meditations on a sacred theme. Kirkup, James, p.145-162; g) Homosexuality and literature. Perrie, Walter, p.163-182; h) Erotic poetry in English. Parker, Derek, p.183-201; i) Literature and pornography. Wilson, Colin, p.202-219.

279. Sexual Dimorphism in Homo Sapiens: A Question of Size. Hall, Roberta L., ed. New York: Praeger, 1982.
a) Introduction: Consequences of sexuality. Hall, Roberta L., p.3-9; b) Sexual dimorphism in nonhuman primates. Leutenegger, Walter, p.11-36; c) Sex differences: The female as baseline for species description. McCown, Elizabeth R., p.37-83; d) The fossil record of sex. Krantz, Grover S., p.85-105; e) Sexual dimorphism in skeletal samples. Hamilton, Margaret E., p.107-163; f) Sexual dimorphism and settlement pattern in Middle Eastern skeletal populations. Finkel, David J., p.165-185; g) Studies in modern populations: Unit of analysis. Hall, Roberta L., p.189-196; h) A cross-cultural investigation into the sexual dimorphism of stature. Gray, J. Patrick

and Wolfe, Linda D., p.197-230; i) Sexual dimorphism for size in seven nineteenth-century Northwest coast populations. Hall, Roberta L., p.231-244; j) Size sexual dimorphism and secular trend: Indicators of subclinical malnutrition? Brauer, Gerhard W., p.245-259; k) Normal and abnormal sexual dimorphic patterns of growth and development. Lieberman, Leslie Sue, p.263-316; l) Human proportionality and sexual dimorphism. Ross, William D. and Ward, Richard, p.317-361; m) Absolute and relative sex differences in body composition. Bailey, Stephen M., p.363-390; n) Sexual dimorphism and nutrient reserves. Stini, William A., p.391-419.

280. Sexual Dynamics of Anti-Social Behavior. Schlesinger, Louis B. and Revitch, Eugene, eds. Springfield, IL: Charles C. Thomas, 1983.
a) Prostitution: Profession and pathology. Jolly, Robert William and Sagarin, Edward, p.9-30; b) Pornography: Its consequences on the observer. Donnerstein, Edward and Malamuth, Neil, p.31-50; c) Nymphomania, hostile sex, and superego development. Shainess, Natalie, p.51-74; d) Sexual permissiveness and its consequences. Gershman, Harry, p.75-87; e) Gender dysphoria and dyssocial behavior. Stuntz, Richard C., p.88-112; f) Genital exhibitionism in men and women. Hollender, Marc H., p.118-131; g) The kleptomanias and female criminality. Zavitzianos, George, p.132-158; h) The dynamics of sexual assault. Groth, A. Nicholas and Hobson, William F., p.159-172; i) Burglaries with sexual dynamics. Revitch, Eugene, p.173-191; j) Fire setting (pyromania) and its relationship to sexuality. Fras, Ivan, p.192-200; k) Sexual dynamics in homicide and assault. Revitch, Eugene and Schlesinger, Louis B., p.206-227; l) Erotized repetitive hangings. Resnik, Harvey L.P., p.228-245; m) Necrophilia and antisocial acts. Dimock, John and Smith, Selwyn M., p.246-256; n) Bondage and sadomasochism. Litman, Robert E., p.257-277; o) Vampirism and autovampirism. Bourguignon, André, p.278-301.

281. Sexual Issues in Family Therapy. Hensen, James C., Woody, Jane Divita and Woody, Robert Henley, eds. Rockville, MD: Aspen Systems Corp., 1983.
a) Human sexuality in the life cycle of the family system. Maddock, James W., p.1-31; b) The sexual self and fertility. Brashear, Diane B. and Ebling, John L., p.32-48; c) Sexual disorders and the family therapist. Cole, Collier M., p.49-61; d) Sexuality in divorce and remarriage. Woody, Jane Divita, p.62-81; e) Homosexual and bisexual issues. Collins, Leslie E. and Zimmerman, Nathalia, p.82-100; f) Incest and sexual violence. Authier, Karen, p.101-128; g) Sexuality and disability. Botvin-Madorsky, Julie G., Ward-McKinlay, Thomas and Ward-Mckinlay, Candace, p.129-152; h) Ethical and legal aspects of sexual issues. Woody, Robert Henley, p.153-167.

282. Sexual Meanings: The Cultural Construction of Gender and Sexuality. Ortner, Sherry B. and Whitehead, Harriet, eds. Cambridge: Cambridge University Press, 1981.
a) Introduction: Accounting for sexual meanings. Ortner, Sherry B. and Whitehead, Harriet, p.1-27; b) The gender

revolution and the transition from bisexual horde to patrilocal band: The origins of gender hierarchy. Cucchiari, Salvatore, p.31-79; c) The bow and the burden strap: A new look at institutionalized homosexuality in native North America. Whitehead, Harriet, p.80-115; d) Transforming "natural" woman: Female ritual leaders and gender ideology among Bimin-Kuskusmin. Poole, Fitz John Porter, p.116-165; e) Self-interest and the social good: Some implications of Hagen gender imagery. Strathern, Marilyn, p.166-191; f) Sexuality and gender in Samoa: Conceptions and missed conceptions. Shore, Bradd, p.192-215; g) Like wounded stags: Male sexual ideology in an Andalusian town. Brandes, Stanley, p.216-239; h) Pigs, women, and the men's house in Amazonia: An analysis of six Mundurucú myths. Nadelson, Leslee, p.240-272; i) Politics and gender in simple societies. Collier, Jane F. and Rosaldo, Michelle Z., p.275-329; j) Women, warriors, and patriarchs. Llewelyn-Davies, Melissa, p.330-358; k) Gender and sexuality in hierarchical societies: The case of Polynesia and some comparative implications. Ortner, Sherry B., p.359-409.

283. Sexual Politics, Feminism and Socialism. London: Routledge & Kegan Paul, 1981.
a) When women and men mother. Ehrensaft, Diane, p.21-47; b) Children and parents: Who chooses? Hodges, Jill, p.49-65; c) The genesis of the social. Hirst, Paul, p.67-82; d) Feminists - The degenerates of the social? Bennett, Fran, Campbell, Beatrix and Coward, Rosalind, p.83-92; e) Reply: Feminists - The degenerates of the social? Hirst, Paul, p.93-95; f) Sexist bias and law. Kingdom, Elizabeth F., p.97-114; g) Women's organisation in the Labour Party. Culley, Lorraine, p.115-122; h) Interview with Frances Morrell. Bennett, Fran, Culley, Lorraine and Hindess, Barry, p.123-136; i) Interview with Jo Richardson. Adlam, Diana, Hindess, Barry and Smith, Dan, p.137-152; j) Race, left strategies and the state. Ben-Tovim, Gideon, et al., p.153-181; k) A left strategy for Labour. Hain, Peter, p.183-200; l) Does Labour always fail? Pimlott, Ben, p.201-204; m) The impasse facing CND. Fernbach, David, p.205-218; n) The silences of *New Left Review*. Sassoon, D., p.219-254; o) The socialist economic review project: Progress in the economics of the left. Cobham, David, p.255-267; p) Public expenditure and budgetary policy. Thompson, Grahame, p.269-286; q) Industrial strategy and trade union politics. Lane, Tony, p.287-306.

284. The Sexual Victimology of Youth. Schultz, Leroy G., ed. Springfield, IL: Charles C. Thomas, 1980.
a) The sexual abuse of children and minors: A short history of legal control efforts. Schultz, LeRoy G., p.3-17; b) Sexual victimization of children: An urban mental health center survey. Swift, Carolyn, p.18-24; c) Sexual molestation of children: The last frontier of child abuse. Sgroi, Suzanne M., p.25-35; d) Diagnosis and treatment - an introduction. Schultz, LeRoy G., p.39-42; e) The sexually misused child. Brant, Renee S. T. and Tisza, Veronica B., p.43-59; f) Observations after sexual traumata suffered in childhood. Brunold, Heinz, p.60-66; g) Sexual trauma of

children and adolescents. Burgess, Ann W. and Holmstrom, Lynda L., p.67-82; h) Sexual assault center emergency room protocol: Child/adolescent patients. Sexual Assault Center, p.83-90; i) Incest - an introduction. Schultz, LeRoy G., p.93-96; j) Father-daughter incest. Herman, Judith and Hirschman, Lisa, p.97-124; k) Children not severely damaged by incest with a parent. Kemph, John P. and Yorukoglu, Atalay, p.125-139; l) Humanistic treatment of father-daughter incest. Giarretto, Henry, p.140-161; m) Incest policy recommendations. Schultz, LeRoy G., p.163-167; n) The victim and justice system - an introduction. Schultz, LeRoy G., p.171-174; o) Interviewing child victims of sex offenders. Flammang, C. J., p.175-186; p) The protection of the child victim of a sexual offense in the criminal justice system. Libai, David, p.187-245; q) Special techniques for child witnesses. Berliner, Lucy and Stevens, Doris, p.246-256; r) Courtroom use of hospital records in sexual assault cases. Burgess, Ann W. and Laszlo, Anna T., p.257-269; s) The child sex industry - an introduction. Schultz, LeRoy G., p.273-274; t) The last porno show. Amon, Robert S., p.275-291; u) Preying on playgrounds. Baker, C. David, p.292-334; v) The pederasts. Rossman, Parker, p.335-349; w) Policy recommendations on child pornography control. Schultz, LeRoy G., p.350-352; x) Sexual emancipation - an introduction. Schultz, LeRoy G., p.355-356; y) The age of sexual consent: Fault, friction, freedom. Schultz, LeRoy G., p.357-377.

285. Sexuality and Life-Threatening Illness. Tallmer, Margot, et al., eds. Springfield, IL: Charles C. Thomas, 1984.
a) The impact of sexuality, professional authoritarianism, and health crises on rehabilitation. Francoeur, Robert T., p.5-15; b) Eros and thanatos: Lingering taboos in doctor-patient communication. Lister, Larry, p.16-31; c) The social relation of sex and death. Moller, David E., p.32-35; d) Death and sexuality. Laury, Gabriel V., p.36-43; e) Physical disability, life-threatening illness, and enhancement of sexual health. Bullard, David G., et al., p.44-60; f) Sexual feelings in the terminally ill patient. Patterson, Paul R., p.61-64; g) Is there love before dying? Sharpe, Lawrence, p.65-72; h) Sexuality and cancer. Stager, Gordon L. and Stager, Rae Ellen S., p.75-85; i) Castration and sexual potency. Leiter, Elliot, p.86-89; j) Potency and its effects on patients. Schoenberg, Harry, p.90-94; k) Sexual dysfunction in the chronically ill male. Roberts, Myron S., p.95-99; l) Differential diagnosis and treatment for organogenic and psychogenic erectile dysfunction. Bullard, David G., p.100-105; m) Sexual rehabilitation after gynecologic cancer. Waletzky, Lucy R., p.106-123; n) Sex in institutions. Shore, David A., p.127-147; o) Sexual attitudes and activities in old age. Tallmer, Margot, p.148-159; p) Sex and disability - sociosexual education presentation format. Smith, Don, p.160-165; q) Sexuality and multiple sclerosis - must they be mutually exclusive? Brickley, Terry, p.166-173; r) Sexuality and the spinal cord injured woman: An interview. Becker, Elle Friedman, p.174-185; s) Establishing a women's group for disabled clients. Sherer, Denise and Thornton, Victoria, p.186-190; t) How to stubbornly refuse to disturb oneself emotional-

ly about anything - even about death, dying and sexual mutilation. Ellis, Albert, p.191-204.

286. Sexuality and Victorian Literature. Cox, Don Richard, ed. Knoxville, TN: University of Tennessee Press, 1984.
a) Lewis Carroll and Victorian morality. Cohen, Morton, p.3-19; b) "Dual life": The status of women in Stoker's *Dracula*. Johnson, Alan P., p.20-39; c) Cash and the sex nexus. Calder, Jenni, p.40-53; d) The fallen woman's sexuality: Childbirth and censure. MacPike, Loralee, p.54-71; e) "Other people's prudery": Mary Elizabeth Braddon. Casey, Ellen Miller, p.72-82; f) "Swinburne planteth, Hardy watereth": Victorian views of pain and pleasure in human sexuality. McGhee, Richard, p.83-107; g) Bathsheba's lovers: Male sexuality in *Far from the Madding Crowd*. Beegel, Susan, p.108-127; h) *The Bachelor's Pocket Book for 1851*. Slater, Michael, p.128-140; i) Sexuality and the Victorian artist: Dickens and Swinburne. Carter, Geoffrey, p.141-160; j) On the enrichment of poor monkeys by myth and dream; or how Dickens Rousseauisticized and pre-Freudianized Victorian views of childhood. Spilka, Mark, p.161-179; k) Passion between women in the Victorian novel. Putzell-Korab, Sara, p.180-195; l) Fallen women, lost children: Wilde and the theatre in the nineties. Johnson, Wendell Stacy, p.196-211; m) "Morbid depression alternating with excitement": Sex in Victorian newspapers. Boyle, Thomas F., p.212-233; n) "Here a captive heart busted": From Victorian sentimentality to modern sexuality. Fulweiler, Howard, p.234-250; o) The worlds of Victorian sexuality: Work in progress. Maynard, John, p.251-265.

287. Sexuality in America: Contemporary Perspectives on Sexual Identity, Dysfunction & Treatment. Brown, Donald A. and Clary, Chanda, eds. Ann Arbor, MI: Greenfield Books, 1981.
a) Our sexual heritage. Brownfain, John J., p.1-12; b) Male sexuality: Socio-sexual change and the single status. Cross, Herbert J. and Kimlicka, Thomas M., p.13-42; c) Female sexuality: Singlehood and the problems of intimacy. Silverman, Herbert, p.43-68; d) Marriage. Schoenberg, B. Mark, p.69-84; e) Sexuality verboten: Young and old. Urbick, Thelma, p.85-98; f) Black sexuality. Wheeler, William H., p.99-112; g) Varieties of sexual expression. Mercier, Raymond G., p.113-126; h) Homosexuality. Blair, Ralph, p.127-142; i) In search of a vagina. Petrini, Mario, p.143-168; j) Sources and prevention of dysfunction. Woolson, Allen M., p.169-184; k) Communicating sexuality. Moy, Caryl, p.185-202; l) Selecting a qualified therapist. Schiller, Patricia, p.203-218; m) Psychological aspects of sexual dysfunction. Drake, Lewis W. and Nederlander, Caren, p.219-282; n) Surrogate partners and their use in sex therapy. Roberts, Barbara, p.283-300; o) An interview with a sex surrogate. Brown, Donald A., p.301-318; p) Creative sexuality: Androgyny. Lin, James, p.319-332.

288. Sexuality in Organizations: Romantic and Coercive Behaviors at Work. Neugarten, Dail Ann and Shafritz, Jay M., eds. Oak Park, IL: Moore Publishing, 1980.
a) The executive man and woman: The issue of sexuality. Bradford, David L., Sargent, Alice G. and Sprague, Melinda S., p.17-28; b) Worklife problems for both women and men. Farley, Jennie, p.29-37; c) Coping with Cupid: The formation, impact, and management of romantic relationships in organizations. Quinn, Robert E., p.38-52; d) A proposal: We need taboos on sex at work. Mead, Margaret, p.53-56; e) Women's work. MacKinnon, Catharine A., p.59-66; f) The impact of sexual harassment on the job: A profile of the experiences of 92 women. Crull, Peggy, p.67-71; g) The other side of the coin: Women who exploit their sexuality for gain. Backhouse, Constance and Cohen, Leah, p.72-77; h) Responses of fair employment practice agencies to sexual harassment complaints: A report and recommendations. Working Women's Institute, p.81-85; i) Sexual harassment in the workplace — What should the employer do? Faucher, Mary D. and McCullogh, Kenneth J., p.86-91; j) Action plans for management and unions. Backhouse, Constance and Cohen, Leah, p.92-97; k) Policy statement and definition of sexual harassment. U.S. Office of Personnel Management, p.98-99; l) A federal response to sexual harassment: Policy-making at Johnson Space Center, NASA. Atkinson, Joseph D. and Layden, Dianne R., p.100-106; m) Policy on sexual harassment. Government of the District of Columbia, p.107-108; n) Sexual harassment cases. MacKinnon, Catharine A., p.111-113; o) Sexual harassment and Title VII: The foundation for the elimination of sexual cooperation as an employment condition. Goldberg, Alan, p.114-137; p) Sexual harassment: Finding a cause of action under Title VII. Seymour, William C., p.138-153.

289. Sexuality in the Later Years: Roles and Behavior. Weg, Ruth B., ed. New York: Academic Press, 1983.
a) Introduction: Beyond intercourse and orgasm. Weg, Ruth B., p.1-10; b) The cross-cultural and historical context. Hotvedt, Mary, p.13-37; c) The physiological perspective. Weg, Ruth B., p.40-80; d) The sociological perspective. Robinson, Pauline K., p.82-103; e) Gender identity: A life-span view of sex-role development. Livson, Florine B., p.105-127; f) Old and alone: The unmarried in later life. Corby, Nan and Zarit, Judy Maes, p.131-145; g) Intimacy and adaptation. Weiss, Lawrence J., p.148-166; h) Long-term care institutions. Kassel, Victor, p.167-184; i) Range of alternatives. Avant, W. Ray and Dressel, Paula L., p.185-207; j) Research: Status, gaps, and design. Finkle, Alex, p.211-221; k) Dysfunction: Origins and therapeutic approaches. Felstein, Ivor, p.223-247; l) Continuity of self-actualization: Womanhood in climacterium and old age. Landau, Erika and Maoz, Benjamin, p.251-258; m) Institutional life: The Canadian experience. Schlesinger, Benjamin, p.259-269; n) A view from Sweden. Gustavii, Birgitta, p.271-275; o) Beyond generativity: Toward a sensuality of later life. Datan, Nancy and Rodeheaver, Dean, p.279-288.

290. The Sexuality Papers: Male Sexuality and the Social Control of Women. Coveney, Lal, et al., eds. London: Hutchinson, 1984.

a) 'Free from all uninvited touch of man': Women's campaigns around sexuality, 1880-1914. Jeffreys, Sheila, p.22-44; b) Sexology and the social construction of male sexuality (Havelock Ellis). Jackson, Margaret, p.45-68; c) Sexology and the universalization of male sexuality (from Ellis to Kinsey, and Masters and Johnson). Jackson, Margaret, p.69-84; d) Theory into practice: Sexual liberation or social control? (*Forum* magazine 1968-1981). Coveney, Lal, Kay, Leslie and Mahoney, Pat, p.85-103.

291. Sexually Abused Children and Their Families. Mrazek, Patricia Beezley and Kempe, C. Henry, eds. Oxford: Pergamon, 1981.
a) Definition and recognition of sexual child abuse: Historical and cultural perspectives. Mrazek, Patricia Beezley, p.5-16; b) Psychosexual development within the family. Mrazek, David A. and Mrazek, Patricia Beezley, p.17-32; c) A psychoanalyst's view of sexual abuse by parents. Freud, Anna, p.33-34; d) Recognition of child sexual abuse in the United Kingdom. Bentovim, Arnon, Lynch, Margaret and Mrazek, Patricia Beezley, p.35-50; e) Sexual child abuse: The legislation and the law in the United States. Fraser, Brian G., p.55-74; f) Sexual abuse of children: An examination of European criminal law. Doek, Jack E., p.75-84; g) Sexual deviance: The adult offender. Macdonald, John M., p.89-96; h) The nature of incest: A review of contributing factors. Mrazek, Patricia Beezley, p.97-108; i) Incest: Intake and investigation. Aldridge, David J. and Topper, Anne B., p.109-128; j) Medical assessment of child sexual abuse. Kerns, David L., p.129-142; k) The child psychiatric examination of the sexually abused child. Mrazek, David A., p.143-154; l) Special problems in the treatment of child sexual abuse. Mrazek, Patricia Beezley, p.159-166; m) Incest and dysfunctional family system. Bentovim, Arnon and Mrazek, Patricia Beezley, p.167-178; n) A comprehensive child sexual abuse treatment program. Giarretto, Henry, p.179-198; o) Group psychotherapy with sexually abused children. Mrazek, Patricia Beezley, p.199-210; p) The cotherapy relationship in group treatment of sexually mistreated adolescent girls. Dean, Janet and Gottlieb, Bruce, p.211-218; q) Long-term effects of sexual abuse in childhood. Alexander, Helen and Steele, Brandt F., p.223-234; r) The effects of child sexual abuse: Methodological considerations. Mrazek, David A. and Mrazek, Patricia Beezley, p.235-243.

292. Sisterhood and Solidarity: Workers' Education for Women, 1914-1984. Kornbluh, Joyce L. and Frederickson, Mary, eds. Philadelphia, PA: Temple University Press, 1984.
a) The Women's Trade Union League training school for women organizers, 1914-1926. Jacoby, Robin Miller, p.3-35; b) From soul to strawberries: The International Ladies' Garment Workers' Union and workers' education, 1914-1950. Wong, Susan Stone, p.37-74; c) Citizens for Democracy: The industrial programs of the YWCA. Frederickson, Mary, p.75-106; d) Blue collars and bluestockings: The Bryn Mawr summer school for women workers, 1921-1938. Heller, Rita, p.107-145; e)

Recognizing regional differences: The southern summer school for women workers. Frederickson, Mary, p.147-186; f) Partners in progress: The affiliated schools for women workers, 1928-1939. Roydhouse, Marion W., p.187-221; g) Education in working-class solidarity: The summer school for office workers. Kessler-Harris, Alice, p.223-251; h) The she-she-she camps: An experiment in living and learning, 1934-1937. Kornbluh, Joyce L., p.253-283; i) To rekindle the spirit: Current education programs for women workers. Wertheimer, Barbara Mayer, p.285-323; j) Memories of a movement: A conversation. Goldfarb, Lyn, p.325-342.

294. So Much Hard Work: Women and Prostitution in Australian History. Daniels, Kay, ed. Sydney, Australia: Fontana/Collins: 1984.
a) Prostitution in Tasmania during the transition from penal settlement to 'civilized' society. Daniels, Kay, p.15-86; b) 'More sinned against than sinning'?: Prostitution in South Australia, 1836-1914. Horan, Susan, p.87-126; c) 'Soiled doves': Prostitution in colonial Queensland. Evans, Raymond, p.127-161; d) Dealing with the 'social evil': Prostitution and the police in Perth and on the eastern goldfields, 1895-1924. Davidson, Raelene, p.162-191; e) The making of a prostitute proletariat in early twentieth-century New South Wales. Allen, Judith, p.192-232; f) 'Black Velvet': Aboriginal women and their relations with white men in the Northern Territory, 1910-1940. McGrath, Ann, p.233-297; g) Prostitution and the law: The question of decriminalization. Mills, Helen, p.298-316; h) 'Working': An interview with Betty N. Bickford, Anne, p.317-344; i) Introduction: St. Kilda voices. Daniels, Kay, p.335-338; j) Prostitution: One experience. Johnston, Dorothy, p.338-365; k) From delicacy to dilemma: A feminist perspective. Jackson, Sue and Otto, Dianne, p.366-382.

295. Social and Psychological Problems of Women: Prevention and Crisis Intervention. Rickel, Annette U., Gerrard, Meg and Iscoe, Ira, eds. Washington, DC: Hemisphere Publishing, 1984.
a) Female development and achievement. Gilbert, Lucia Albino, p.5-17; b) Women as competent community builders: The other side of the coin. Reinharz, Shulamit, p.19-43; c) Mothering and the young child. Dorr, Darwin and Friedenberg, Lisa, p.45-60; d) Black women in American society: A resource development perspective. Allen, LaRue and Britt, David W., p.61-84; e) The antecedents and prevention of unwanted pregnancy. Geis, Bill D., Gerrard, Meg and McCann, Lisa, p.85-101; f) Sex differences in separation and divorce: A longitudinal perspective. Bloom, Bernard L, Caldwell, Robert A. and Hodges, William F., p.103-120; g) Enhancing childrearing skills in lower income women. Shure, Myrna B., p.121-138; h) The impact of crime on urban women. Gordon, Margaret T. and Riger, Stephanie, p.139-156; i) Women's health issues. Albino, Judith E. and Tedesco, Lisa A., p.157-172; j) Social support and efficacy in advocacy roles: A case study of two women's organizations. Bond, Meg A. and Kelly, James

G., p.173-196; k) Depression in women: The postpartum experience. Atkinson, A. Kathleen and Rickel, Annette U., p.197-218; l) The relation of stressful life events to gender. Dohrenwend, Barbara Snell and Mulvey, Anne, p.219-237; m) Differential needs and treatment approaches for women in psychotherapy. Broughan, Kathleen G. and Lorion, Raymond P., p.239-252; n) Substance abuse in women: Etiology and prevention. Bry, Brenna H., p.253-272; o) Older women and mental health. Fuentes, Max, Gatz, Margaret and Pearson, Cynthia, p.273-299; p) New directions for women: Moving beyond the 1980s. Rickel, Annette U., et al., p.301-312.

296. Social Power and Influence of Women. Stamm, Liesa and Ryff, Carol D., eds. Boulder, CO: Westview, 1984.
a) Introduction: An interdisciplinary perspective on women's power and influence. Ryff, Carol D. and Stamm, Liesa, p.1-11; b) Differential power of women over the life course: A case study of age-roles as an indicator of power. Stamm, Liesa, p.15-35; c) Women in intergenerational patterns of power and influence. Hagestad, Gunhild O., p.37-55; d) Women's self-perceptions of power and influence across adult life. Ryff, Carol D., p.59-79; e) A three-generational analysis of change in women's achievement motivation and power. Schwartz, Linda S. and Troll, Lillian E., p.81-98; f) Mastery and pleasure: A two-factor model of well-being of women in the middle years. Barnett, Rosalind C. and Baruch, Grace K., p.99-113; g) Racial-ethnic women and work: Towards an analysis of race and gender stratification. Glenn, Evelyn Nakano, p.117-150; h) Powerless by definition: Occupational and pay patterns of women in the workplace. Malveaux, Julianne Marie, p.151-166; i) Women's power in the workplace. Remy, Dorothy and Sawers, Larry, p.167-184; j) Women and power within the historical dynamic of feminist scholarship. Sacks, Karen Brodkin, p.187-190; k) Sources and effects of women's power. Giele, Janet Zollinger, p.191-199.

297. Social Researching: Politics, Problems, Practice. Bell, Colin and Roberts, Helen, eds. London: Routledge & Kegan Paul, 1984.
a) The SSRC: Restructured and defended. Bell, Colin, p.14-31; b) Negotiating the problem: The DHSS and research on violence in marriage. Hanmer, Jalna and Leonard, Diana, p.32-53; c) Researching spoonbending: Concepts and practice of participatory fieldwork. Collins, H.M., p.54-69; d) 'It's great to have someone to talk to': The ethics and politics of interviewing women. Finch, Janet, p.70-87; e) Incidence or incidents: Political and methodological underpinnings of a health research process in a small Italian town. Frankenberg, Ronald, p.88-103; f) Surveying through stories. Graham, Hilary, p.104-124; g) A postscript to nursing. James, Nicky, p.125-146; h) Bringing it all back home: An anthropologist in Belfast. Jenkins, Richard, p.147-164; i) The personable and the powerful: Gender and status in sociological research. Scott, Sue, p.165-178; j) The *Affluent Worker* revisited. Platt, Jennifer, p.179-198; k) Putting the show on

the road: The dissemination of research findings. Roberts, Helen, p.199-212.

298. Social Science Research and Women in the Arab World. London: Frances Pinter, 1984.
a) Arab women: The status of research in the social sciences and the status of women. Rassam, Amal, p.1-13; b) Survey of research on women in the Arab gulf region. Allaghi, Farida and Almana, Aisha, p.14-40; c) Research in the social sciences on North African women: Problems, trends, and needs. Baffoun, Alya, p.41-58; d) Research in the social sciences on women in Morocco. Belarbi, Aicha, p.59-81; e) Human sciences research on Algerian women. Hakiki, Fatiha and Talahite, Claude, p.82-93; f) The history, development, organization and position of women's studies in the Sudan. Kashif-Badri, Hagga, p.94-112; g) The conditions required for women to conduct research on women in the Arab region. Oussedik, Fatma, p.113-121; h) Toward a theoretical framework for the study of women in the Arab world. Rassam, Amal, p.122-138; i) A survey of trends in social sciences research on women in the Arab region, 1960-1980. Kader, Soha Abdel, p.139-175.

299. Socio-Economic Status of Indian Women. Manohar, K. Murali, ed. Delhi, India: Seema Publications, 1983.
a) Socio-economic status of Indian women. Manohar, K. Murali, p.1-30; b) Maid servants. Manohar, K. Murali and Shobha, V., p.31-45; c) Sanitary Workers. Manohar, K. Murali and Sambaiah, P., p.47-61; d) Beedi workers. Manohar, K. Murali, Rao, B. Janardhan and Shobha, V., p.63-75; e) Construction workers. Manohar, K. Murali, Rao, B. Janardhan and Shobha, V., p.77-86; f) Petty traders. Janardhan, K., Manohar, K. Murali and Shobha, V., p.87-100; g) Tribal migrants. Kumari, Chidananda, Manohar, K. Murali and Rao, K. Seetarama, p.101-114.

300. Southeast Asia: Women, Changing Social Structure and Cultural Continuity. Hainsworth, Geoffrey B., ed. Ottawa, Canada: University of Ottawa Press, 1981.
a) Modernization, changing roles of women and expectations for development in southeast Asia. Hollnsteiner, Mary Racelis, p.3-18; b) Women, society and change: Perspectives on the division of labour. Jacobson, Helga E., p.19-25; c) The Minangkabau woman: Cultural centre or ethnic symbol? Prindiville, Joanne, p.26-33; d) The psychology of politeness among the Javanese. Josefowitz, Nina, p.34-41; e) The infant formula controversy in southeast Asia: Advocacy confrontation or applied anthropology? Van Esterik, Penny, p.42-52; f) Changes in women's status associated with modernization in northern Thailand. Mueke, Marjorie, p.53-65; g) Patterns of urbanization in the Philippines. Chen, Anita B., p.66-83; h) Rural-urban linkages and migration: A Philippines case study. Trager, Lillian, p.84-94; i) The public bureaucracy and social change in Singapore. Quah, John, p.95-118; j) The CHIT fund in Singapore: Failure of a large-scale rotating credit fund. Chua, Beng-Huat, p.119-134; k) Buddhist attitudes toward social change in Burma and Thailand. Matthews, Bruce, p.135-149; l) Have stories,

will travel: How Buddhism won the southeast. Amore, Roy C., p.150-156; m) The Thai forest tradition: Local and international manifestations. Placzek, James, p.156-185; n) Church-military relations in the Philippines. Youngblood, Robert L., p.186-207; o) Islamic law in Christian Southeast Asia: The politics of establishing Shari'a courts in the Philippines. Bentley, Carter, p.208-228.

301. Speaking for Ourselves: Women of the South. Alexander, Maxine, ed. New York: Pantheon Books, 1984.
a) Celebrate Emma (poem). Benz, Maudy, p.5-6; b) Legacy: Memories of our foremothers. Gilbert, Dee, p.7-15; c) Pipsissewa, Calamus, and Pennyroyal. Garcia-Barrio, Constance, p.16-17; d) Genealogy (poem). Robson, Ruthann, p.18-19; e) Magnolias grow in dirt: The bawdy lore of southern women. Green, Rayna, p.20-28; f) Tribute to my husband. Nelson, Mattie Mae, p.29-30; g) Corn shuckings, fiddle contests, square dances: Oral history with Lily May Ledford. High, Ellesa Clay, p.34-43; h) Growing up southern & sexy. Jemison, Marie Stokes, p.44-51; i) Three maxims in the life of Mary. Mebane, Mary, p.52-63; j) My Aunt Isadora (fiction). Ettinger, Amelia Diaz, p.64-66; k) The rape of Dona (poem). Howard, Lee, p.67-71; l) Mill village (poem). Ford, Clara D., p.76; m) It seems to help me bear it better when she knows about it. Bolsterli, Margaret Jones, p.77-83; n) Ole black Emelda (fiction). Teish, Luisah, p.84-86; o) Women in the Texas ILGWU, 1933-50. Hield, Melissa, p.87-97; p) Shoulder to shoulder. Braden, Anne, p.98-105; q) Hard times cotton mill girls. Byerly, Victoria Morris, p.106-111; r) Are you looking, cousin Dell? Mandrell, Regina M.K., p.112-113; s) What she aims to be (song). Massek, Sue, p.118-119; t) Coal-mining women. Moore, Marat, p.120-127; u) If you got time to lean, you got time to clean. Blount, Alma, p.128-132; v) It's something inside you. Watriss, Wendy, p.133-142; w) Prostitution I: Trying to make a living. Poliakoff, Phaye, p.143-150; x) Prostitution II: Not no easy business. Wilkerson, Sarah, p.151-155; y) Tessa (poem). Loken, Vivian M., p.156; z) Miss Elsie Riddick. Prioli, Carmine, p.157-162; aa) Dear Mary Catherine. Sewell, Marilyn, p.166-169; bb) Paralyzed (fiction). Smith, Lee, p.170-183; cc) My grandmother's gift (poem). Pender, Glenda Neel, p.184-185; dd) Quilting women. Miller, Jennifer, p.186-192; ee) Two poems for Minnie's boy. Moody, Joycelyn K., p.193-194; ff) Spilled salt (fiction). Neely, Barbara, p.195-201; gg) The prodigal child's homecoming: California to Georgia (poem). Burch, Beverly, p.207; hh) swing through the south journal, fall 1981. gossett, hattie, p.208-219; ii) Delta (fiction). Mays, Ramina Y., p.220-224; jj) Speaking in tongues: A letter to Third World women writers. Anzaldúa, Gloria, p.225-231; kk) Women's consciousness and the southern black. Evans, Sara, p.232-245; ll) The challenge (poem). Davis, Christina, p.250; mm) Mock trial (play). Bright, Susan, p.251-259; nn) The lonesomes ain't no spring picnic (fiction). Miller, Birthalene, p.260-268; oo) Queen of the road. Wheaton, Liz, p.269-271; pp) Listen!! (poem).

Alexander, Maxine, p.272-273; qq) I lead two lives: Confessions of a closet Baptist. Segrest, Mab, p.274-278; rr) There's not a child that can't learn. McCarthy, Rebecca, p.279-280.

302. The Status of Women in Librarianship: Historical, Sociological, and Economic Issues. Heim, Kathleen M., ed. New York: Neal-Schuman, 1983.
a) Revision versus reality: Women in the history of the public library movement, 1876-1920. Hildenbrand, Suzanne, p.7-27; b) Sex-typing in education for librarianship: 1870-1920. Brand, Barbara Elizabeth, p.29-49; c) The recruitment of men into librarianship, following World War II. O'Brien, Nancy Patricia, p.51-66; d) Undergraduate women as potential recruits to the library profession. Reeling, Patricia, p.67-98; e) Assertiveness training for library-school students. Sukiennik, Adelaide Weir, p.99-138; f) Biographical research on women librarians: Its paucity, perils, and pleasures. Grotzinger, Laurel A., p.139-190; g) Profiles of the careers of selected black female librarians. Rhodes, Lelia Gaston, p.191-205; h) The woman academic-library administrator: A career profile. Fennell, Janice C., p.207-241; i) Salary and position levels of females and males in academic libraries. Martin, Jean K., p.243-285; j) Women in academic-library, higher-education, and corporate management: A research review. Irvine, Betty Jo, p.287-320; k) Mobility and professional involvement in librarianship: A study of the "Class of '55". Taylor, Marion R., p.321-344; l) Geographic mobility and career advancement of male and female librarians. Robinson, Judith Schiek, p.345-391; m) An analysis of the study, "Career paths of male and female librarians in Canada". Futas, Elizabeth, p.393-423; n) The reentry professional librarian. Dickson, Katherine Murphy, p.425-435.

303. Stepping Off the Pedestal: Academic Women in the South. Stringer, Patricia A. and Thompson, Irene, eds. New York: Modern Language Association, 1982.
a) A different kind of being. Brett, Sally, p.13-22; b) IWY: Breaking the silence: a fantasy (poem). Pratt, Minnie Bruce, p.23-25; c) Mary Munford and higher education for women in Virginia. Newell, Mary Gathright, p.26-38; d) Women's studies at Vanderbilt: Toward a strategy for the eighties. Langland, Elizabeth, p.41-47; e) New women at Old Dominion. Hassencahl, Fran and Rhodes, Carolyn H., p.48-59; f) A delicate balance: Academic women in Arkansas. Taylor, Barbara G., p.60-70; g) Teaching women's studies at the University of Arkansas. Bolsterli, Margaret Jones, p.71-75; h) Academic women in Mississippi: Oktoberfest 1980. Prenshaw, Peggy W., p.76-88; i) Fair Harvard and the fairer sex. Baker, Susan Read, p.91-98; j) Racial myths and attitudes among white female students at the University of Florida. Gary-Harris, Faye, p.99-108; k) The black female academic: Doubly burdened or doubly blessed? Irvine, Jacqueline Jordan, p.109-117; l) Tilting at windmills in the Quixotic South. Thompson, Irene, p.118-129; m) She who laughs first. Stitzel, Judith, p.130-134; n) To Delois and Willie (poem). Park, Martha Mayes, p.135; o) Scratching at the com-

pound. Stevenson, Mary Lou Kohfeldt, p.136-144; p) The historical perspective: A bibliographical essay. Shadron, Virginia, et al., p.145-168.

304. The Stereotyping of Women: Its Effects on Mental Health. Franks, Violet and Rothblum, Esther D., eds. New York: Springer, 1983.
a) Introduction: Warning! Sex-role stereotypes may be hazardous to your health. Franks, Violet and Rothblum, Esther D., p.3-10; b) Sex-role stereotypes and mental health: Conceptual models in the 1970s and issues for the 1980s. Kelly, Jeffrey A., p.11-29; c) The development of sex-role stereotypes in children: Crushing realities. Brown, Lynda M. and Weinraub, Marsha, p.30-59; d) Sex roles and language use: Implications for mental health. Kirsh, Barbara, p.59-79; e) Sex-role stereotypes and depression in women. Rothblum, Esther D., p.83-111; f) Women and agoraphobia: A case for the etiological significance of the feminine sex-role stereotype. Brehony, Kathleen A., p.112-128; g) Sex-role stereotypes and female sexual dysfunction. Leiblum, Sandra R. and Tevlin, Helen E., p.129-150; h) Women's assertion and the feminine sex-role stereotype. Muehlenhard, Charlene L., p.153-171; i) Women, weight, and health. Zegman, Marilyn A., p.172-200; j) The resocialization of single-again women. Garret-Fulks, Nikki and Worell, Judith, p.201-229; k) Sex-role stereotypes and violence against women. Resick, Patricia A., p.230-256; l) Concluding comments, criticism, and caution: Consistent conservatism or constructive change? Franks, Violet and Rothblum, Esther D., p.259-270.

305. Still Ain't Satisfied! Canadian Feminism Today. Fitzgerald, Maureen, Guberman, Connie and Wolfe, Margie, eds. Toronto: The Women's Press, 1982.
a) The last ten years: A personal/political view. Wall, Naomi, p.15-27; b) Claim no easy victories: The fight for reproductive rights. McDonnell, Kathleen, p.32-42; c) Whose body? Whose self? Beyond pornography. Kostash, Myrna, p.43-54; d) Home sweet home? Cole, Susan G., p.55-67; e) Breaking the hold: Women against rape. James, Barbara, p.68-75; f) Once more with feeling: Heterosexuality and feminist consciousness. Kates, Joanne, p.76-84; g) Shades of lavender: Lesbian sex and sexuality. Zaremba, Eve, p.85-92; h) Providing services the feminist way. Ridington, Jillian, p.93-107; i) The home: A contested terrain. Luxton, Meg, p.112-122; j) Minding the children. Schulz, Pat, p.123-131; k) Getting organized...in the feminist unions. Ainsworth, Jackie, et al., p.132-140; l) Getting organized...in the Confederation of Canadian Unions. Vohanka, Sue, p.141-151; m) Getting organized...in the Canadian Labour Congress. Gallagher, Deirdre, p.152-162; n) Getting organized...in Saskatchewan Working Women. Kouri, Denise, p.163-167; o) Sexual harassment as a form of social control. Kadar, Marlene, p.168-180; p) Is your job hazardous to your health? Langton, Marianne, p.181-194; q) When all the secretaries demand what they are worth. Davitt, Patricia J., p.195-209; r) Rosie the Riveter meets the sexual division of labour. Field, Debbie, p.210-221; s) Women

in trades in British Columbia. Braid, Kate, p.222-229; t) Mothers, sisters, lovers, listen. Gottlieb, Amy, p.234-242; u) A message of solidarity. Women Working with Immigrant Women, p.243-248; v) Immigrant women: The silent partners of the women's movement. Ng, Winnie, p.249-256; w) Beyond barriers: Native women and the women's movement. Lachapelle, Caroline, p.257-264; x) Working with words: Feminist publishing in Canada. Wolfe, Margie, p.265-275; y) More radical with age: Women and education. Tudiver, Sari, p.276-286; z) But is it feminist art? Donegan, Rosemary, Martin, Liz and Read, Daphne, p.287-299.

306. Teaching Women's Literature from a Regional Perspective. Hoffmann, Lenore and Rosenfelt, Deborah, eds. New York: The Modern Language Association of America, 1982.
a) The whole truth: Frameworks for the study of women's noncanonical literature. Meese, Elizabeth, p.15-22; b) The "rooted" landscape and the woman writer. Bader, Julia, p.23-30; c) Cross-cultural perspectives: Creole and Acadian women. Parker, Alice A., p.31-43; d) On the literary uses of private documents. Bolsterli, Margaret Jones, p.44-54; e) Tell me all you know: Reading letters and diaries of rural women. Hampsten, Elizabeth, p.55-63; f) Alice Dunbar-Nelson: A regional approach. Hull, Gloria T., p.64-68; g) "Aunt Amelia's diary": The record of a reluctant pioneer. Armitage, Susan H., p.69-73; h) Dusting the mirror: Researching women's history. Grevatt, Marge, p.74-83; i) Feminist pedagogy: Lost voices of American women. Culley, Margo, p.84-91; j) "Full of memories": Teaching matrilineage. Maglin, Nan Bauer, p.92-104; k) From concept to classroom. Carver, Ann Cathey, p.105-117; l) Southern women's literature and culture: Course development and the pedagogical process. Gladney, Rose, Meese, Elizabeth A. and Parker, Alice, p.118-131; m) The editor and the writer: An approach to archival manuscripts. Brett, Sally Alexander, p.132-139; n) Letters and diaries: Demystifying archival research for undergraduates. Saxton, Ruth O., p.140-149; o) Oral history as a resource in teaching women's studies. Grevatt, Marge, p.150-157; p) Public presentation reports. Culley, Margo and Friedman, Adele, p.158-162; q) New forms for new research. Davis, Barbara Hillyer, p.163-171; r) Authentic voices. Stitzel, Judith, p.172-175.

307. The Technological Woman: Interfacing with Tomorrow. Zimmerman, Jan, ed. New York: Praeger, 1983.
a) Introduction: New technology, old values. Zimmerman, Jan, p.3-6; b) Sex differences, science, and society. Lowe, Marian, p.7-17; c) Gender and industry on Mexico's new frontier. Kelly, María Patricia Fernández, p.18-29; d) Women, nature and domination. Merchant, Carolyn, p.30-37; e) Doubletalk: Sexism in tech talk. Lakoff, Robin Tolmach, p.38-43; f) For women, the chips are down. Benston, Margaret Lowe, p.44-54; g) From Africa to America: Black women inventors. Stanley, Autumn, p.55-64; h) Women and appropriate technology: A feminist assessment. Smith, Judy, p.65-70; i) The GABe self-cleaning house. GABe, Frances, p.75-82; j)

Household technologies: Burden or blessing? Bereano, Philip L. and Bose, Christine E., p.83-93; k) The lonely squandering of urban time. Markusen, Ann R., p.94-101; l) Getting there: Women and transportation. Giuliano, Genevieve, p.102-112; m) Living better vicariously? Horwitz, Jaime and Zimmerman, Jan, p.113-121; n) Putting women in the energy picture. Hunt, Irmgard, p.122-127; o) Abortion: A domestic technology. Luker, Kristin, p.128-135; p) Mother calls herself a housewife, but she buys bulls. Jensen, Katherine, p.136-144; q) Word processing: "This is not a final draft". Levy, Ellen and Otos, Sally, p.149-158; r) Women's work in the office of the future. Gutek, Barbara A., p.159-168; s) Cold solder on a hot stove. Morales, Rebecca, p.169-180; t) Blue collar women. Walshok, Mary Lindenstein, p.181-187; u) New jobs in new technologies: Experienced only need apply. Reynolds, Diane, p.188-190; v) Paths to power in high technology organizations. Josefowitz, Natasha, p.191-200; w) Bambi meets Godzilla: Life in the corporate jungle. Emerson, Sandra, p.201-206; x) A sperm-donor baby grows up. Rubin, Suzanne, p.211-215; y) Surrogate motherhood - an interview. Smith, Karen, p.216-220; z) Engineered conception: The new parenthood. Winters, Barbara, p.221-238; aa) Juggling health care technology and women's needs. Parker, Alberta, p.239-244; bb) Female futures in women's science fiction. Gearhart, Sally Miller, p.245-250; cc) EQUALS in computer technology. Kreinberg, Nancy and Stage, Elizabeth K., p.251-259; dd) The next move: Organizing women in the office. Gregory, Judith, p.260-272; ee) Tomorrow is a woman's issue. Sommers, Tish, p.273-278; ff) Feminism: A catalyst for the future. Huckle, Patricia, p.279-286.

308. Teenage Pregnancy in a Family Context: Implications for Policy. Ooms, Theodora, ed. Philadelphia, PA: Temple University Press, 1981.
a) Teenage women in the United States: Sex, contraception, pregnancy, fertility, and maternal and infant health. Jones, Audrey E. and Placek, Paul J., p.49-72; b) The family's role in adolescent sexual behavior. Fox, Greer Litton, p.73-130; c) Implicating the family: Teenage parenthood and kinship involvement. Furstenberg, Frank F., p.131-164; d) Government policies related to teenage family formation and functioning: An inventory. Moore, Kristin A., p.165-212; e) Sex education and the prevention of teenage pregnancy: An overview of policies and programs in the United States. Scales, Peter, p.213-253; f) Adolescent parent programs and family involvement. Forbush, Janet Bell and Maciocha, Teresa (assistant), p.254-276; g) Ethical and legal issues in teenage pregnancies. Steinfels, Margaret O'Brien, p.277-306; h) Adolescent sexuality and teenage pregnancy from a black perspective. Butts, June Dobbs, p.307-325; i) The impact of adolescent pregnancy on Hispanic adolescents and their families. Martinez, Angel Luis, p.326-344; j) Bringing in the family: Kinship support and contraceptive behavior. Furstenberg, Frank F., Herceg-Baron, Roberta and Jemail, Jay, p.345-370; k) Family involvement, notification, and responsibility: A personal essay. Ooms, Theodora, p.371-398.

309. Teenage Sexuality, Pregnancy, and Childbearing. Furstenberg, Frank F., Lincoln, Richard and Menken, Jane, eds. Philadelphia: University of Pennsylvania Press, 1981.
a) Teenage family formation in postwar America. Berkov, Beth and Sklar, June, p.23-43; b) Teenage illegitimacy: An exchange. Cutright, Phillips, et al., p.44-51; c) The legitimacy status of first births to U.S. women aged 15-24, 1939-1978. Moore, Maurice J. and O'Connell, Martin, p.52-67; d) Sexual and contraceptive experience of young unmarried women in the United States, 1976 and 1971. Kantner, John F. and Zelnik, Melvin, p.68-92; e) First pregnancies to women aged 15-19: 1976 and 1971. Kantner, John F. and Zelnik, Melvin, p.93-111; f) Contraceptive patterns and premarital pregnancy among women aged 15-19 in 1976. Kantner, John F. and Zelnik, Melvin, p.112-135; g) The effect of government policies on out-of-wedlock sex and pregnancy. Caldwell, Steven B. and Moore, Kristin A., p.126-135; h) The risk of adolescent pregnancy in the first months of intercourse. Kantner, John F., Zabin, Laurie Schwab and Zelnik, Melvin, p.136-148; i) Teenage pregnancies: Looking ahead to 1984. Tietze, Christopher, p.149-154; j) Some speculations on the future of marriage and fertility. Westoff, Charles F., p.155-162; k) The health and social consequences of teenage childbearing. Menken, Jane, p.167-183; l) The social consequences of teenage parenthood. Furstenberg, Frank F., p.184-210; m) Teenage mothers and teenage fathers: The impact of early childbearing on the parents' personal and professional lives. Card, Josefina J. and Wise, Lauress L., p.211-222; n) Marriage, remarriage, marital disruption and age at first birth. McCarthy, James and Menken, Jane, p.223-233; o) Early childbearing and subsequent fertility. Menken, Jane and Trussell, James, p.234-250; p) Economic consequences of teenage childbearing. Trussell, James, p.251-264; q) The children of teenage parents. Baldwin, Wendy and Cain, Virginia S., p.265-279; r) Family support: Helping teenage mothers to cope. Crawford, Albert G. and Furstenberg, Frank F., p.280-300; s) Contraception, abortion and venereal disease: Teenagers' knowledge and the effect of education. Reichelt, Paul A. and Werley, Harriet H., p.305-316; t) Guessing and misinformation about pregnancy risk among urban mothers. Presser, Harriet B., p.317-326; u) Sexual and contraceptive knowledge, attitudes and behavior of male adolescents. Finkel, David J. and Finkel, Madelon Lubin, p.327-335; v) Early motherhood: Ignorance or bliss? Presser, Harriet B., p.336-349; w) Psychological vulnerability to unwanted pregnancy. Miller, Warren B., p.350-354; x) Teenagers: Fertility control behavior and attitudes before and after abortion, childbearing or negative pregnancy test. Evans, Jerome R., Selstad, Georgiana and Welcher, Wayne H., p.355-371; y) Adolescent pregnancy prevention services in high school clinics. Edwards, Laura E., et al., p.372-382; z) Misinforming pregnant teenagers. Ambrose, Linda, p.387-393; aa) Contraceptive services for adolescents: An overview. Dryfoos, Joy G. and Heisler, Toni, p.394-408; bb) Teenagers and pregnancy: The law in 1979. Paul, Eve W. and Pilpel, Harriet F., p.409-419.

310. Test-Tube Women: What Future for Motherhood? Arditti, Rita, Duelli-Klein, Renate and Minden, Shelley, eds. London: Pandora Press, 1984.
    a) A yenga tale. Neeley, Barbara, p.11-19; b) The meanings of choice in reproductive technology. Rothman, Barbara Katz, p.23-33; c) Egg snatchers. Corea, Genoveffa, p.37-51; d) Who owns the embryo? Albury, Rebecca, p.54-67; e) Egg farming and women's future. Murphy, Julie, p.68-75; f) From mice to men? Implications of progress in cloning research. Murphy, Jane, p.76-91; g) Designer genes: A view from the factory. Minden, Shelley, p.92-98; h) Inside the surrogate industry. Ince, Susan, p.99-116; i) An interview with Mirtha Quintanales, from the Third World women's archives. Arditti, Rita and Minden, Shelley, p.119-130; j) Teenage oppression and reproductive rights. Trawick, Eleanor, p.131-137; k) Refusing to take women seriously: 'Side effects' and the politics of contraception. Pollock, Scarlet, p.138-152; l) Women as targets in India's family planning policy. Balasubrahmanyan, Vimal, p.153-164; m) Calling the shots? The international politics of depo-provera. Bunkle, Phillida, p.165-187; n) Subtle forms of sterilization abuse: A reproductive rights analysis. Clarke, Adele, p.188-212; o) Abortion, a woman's matter: An explanation of who controls abortion and how and why they do it. Kaufmann, K., p.213-234; p) Technology and prenatal femicide. Holmes, Helen Bequaert and Hoskins, Betty B., p.237-255; q) If you would be the mother of a son (poem). Sangari, Kumkum, p.256-265; r) Abortion of a special kind: Male sex selection in India. Roggencamp, Viola, p.266-276; s) Claiming all of our bodies: Reproductive rights and disabilities. Finger, Anne, p.281-297; t) Born and unborn: The implications of reproductive technologies for people with disabilities. Saxton, Marsha, p.298-312; u) XYLO: A true story. Rapp, Rayna, p.313-328; v) Personal courage is not enough: Some hazards of childbearing in the 1980s. Hubbard, Ruth, p.331-355; w) Reproductive technologies: The final solution to the woman question? Rowland, Robyn, p.356-369; x) Children by donor insemination: A new choice for lesbians. Hornstein, Francie, p.373-381; y) Doing it ourselves: Self insemination. Duelli-Klein, Renate, p.382-390; z) Equal opportunity for babies? Not in Oakland! Coalition to Fight Infant Mortality, p.391-396; aa) Who is going to rock the petri dish? For feminists who have considered parthenogenesis when the movement is not enough. Breeze, Nancy, p.397-401; bb) Taking the initiative: Information versus technology in pregnancy. Ritchie, Maureen, p.402-413; cc) Regaining trust. Holland, Ruth and McKenna, Jill, p.414-418; dd) Through the speculum. Downer, Carol, p.419-426; ee) Feminist ethics, ecology and vision. Raymond, Janice, p.427-437; ff) A womb of one's own. Hanmer, Jalna, p.438-448; gg) The courage of sisters. Newport, Cris, p.449-456.

311. Theories of Women's Studies. Bowles, Gloria and Duelli-Klein, Renate, eds. Berkeley, CA: Women's Studies, University of California, 1980.
    a) Is women's studies an academic discipline? Bowles, Gloria, p.1-11; b) Learning women's studies. Rutenberg, Taly, p.12-17; c) Women's studies as an academic discipline: Why and how to do it. Coyner, Sandra, p.18-40; d) Feminism: A last chance for the humanities? Watkins, Bari, p.41-47; e) How to do what we want to do: Thoughts about feminist methodology. Duelli-Klein, Renate, p.48-64; f) Selected annotated bibliography of articles on theories of women's studies. Bowles, Gloria, Duelli-Klein, Renate and Heckscher, M. Erika, p.65-75.

312. Theories of Women's Studies. Bowles, Gloria and Duelli-Klein, Renate, eds. London: Routledge & Kegan Paul, 1983.
    a) Introduction: Theories of women's studies and the autonomy/integration debate. Bowles, Gloria and Duelli Klein, Renate, p.1-26; b) Theorising about theorising. Spender, Dale, p.27-31; c) Is women's studies an academic discipline? Bowles, Gloria, p.32-45; d) Women's studies as an academic discipline: Why and how to do it. Coyner, Sandra, p.46-71; e) Learning women's studies. Rutenberg, Taly, p.72-78; f) Feminism: A last chance for the humanities? Watkins, Bari, p.79-87; g) How to do what we want to do: Thoughts about feminist methodology. Duelli Klein, Renate, p.88-104; h) Passionate scholarship: Notes on values, knowing and method in feminist social science. Du Bois, Barbara p.105-116; i) Towards a methodology for feminist research. Mies, Maria, p.117-139; j) The value of quantitative methodology for feminist research. Jayaratne, Toby Epstein, p.140-161; k) Experiential analysis: A contribution to feminist research. Reinharz, Shulamit, p.162-191; l) 'Back into the personal' or: Our attempt to construct 'feminist research'. Stanley, Liz and Wise, Sue, p.192-209; m) Women's studies as a strategy for change: Between criticism and vision. Westkott, Marcia, p.210-218; n) In praise of theory: The case for women's studies. Evans, Mary, p.219-228; o) Selected annotated bibliography of articles on theories of women's studies. Bowles, Gloria, Duelli Klein, Renate and Rutenberg, Taly, p.229-268.

313. Theory and Practice of Feminist Literary Criticsm. Mora, Gabriela and Van Hooft, Karen S., eds. Ypsilanti, MI: Bilingual Press/Editorial Bilingüe, 1982.
    a) Crítica feminista: Apuntes sobre definiciones y problemas. Mora, Gabriela, p.2-13; b) The "I" in Adrienne Rich: Individuation and the androgyne archetype. Flowers, Betty S., p.14-35; c) Prisoner in utopia. Pezzuoli, Giovanna, p.36-43; d) Foucault's fantasia for feminists: The woman reading. Thiébaux, Marcelle, p.44-61; e) El ángel del hogar: The cult of domesticity in nineteenth-century Spain. Aldaraca, Bridget, p.62-87; f) Mis brujas favoritas. Valenzuela, Luisa, p.88-95; g) Ideology and *The Mysteries of Udolpho*. Poovey, Mary, p.98-116; h) La poupée perdue: Ordre et désordre dans *Les Petites Filles Modèles* de la Comtesse de Ségur. Mathé, Sylvie, p.117-130; i) The fiction of family: Ideology and narrative in Elsa Morante. Evans, Annette, p.131-137; j) The off-center spatiality of women's discourse. Lamont, Rosette C., p.138-155; k) Narradoras hispanoamericanas: Vieja y nueva problemática en renovadas elaboraciones. Mora, Gabriela, p.156-174; l) Alienation and eros in three sto-

ries by Beatriz Guido, Marta Lynch and Amalia Jamilis. Lewald, Ernest H., p.175-185; m) A feminist reading of "Los ojos verdes". Boyer, H. Patsy, p.188-200; n) "Folly and a woman": Galdos' rhetoric of irony in *Tristana*. Friedman, Edward H., p.201-228; o) "La loca, la tonta, la literata": Women's destiny in Clarin's *La Regenta*. Schyfter, Sara E., p.229-241; p) Women as moral and political alternatives in Conrad's early novels. Nadelhaft, Ruth, p.242-255; q) Vipers, victims, and virgins: Women and their relationships with men in the poetry of Nicanor Parra. Van Hooft, Karen S., p.256-278; r) Hacia un análisis feminista de *Tres Tristes Tigres*. Rivero, Eliana, p.279-291.

314. Toward a Balanced Curriculum: A Sourcebook for Initiating Gender Integration Projects. Spanier, Bonnie, Bloom, Alexander, and Boroviak, Darlene, eds. Cambridge, MA: Schenkman Publishing Co., 1984.
a) Where does integration fit: The development of women's studies. Stimpson, Catharine, p.11-24; b) Interactive phases of curricular re-vision. McIntosh, Peggy, p.25-34; c) The humanities: Redefining the canon. Butler, Johnnella E., p.35-41; d) The social sciences: Establishing gender as a category. Boroviak, Darlene L., p.42-48; e) The natural sciences: Casting a critical eye on 'objectivity'. Spanier, Bonnie, p.49-56; f) Project on women and social change: Smith College. Schuster, Marilyn R. and Van Dyne, Susan R., p.59-72; g) Toward a balanced curriculum: Wheaton College. Spanier, Bonnie, p.73-79; h) Project on women in the curriculum: Montana State University. Schmitz, Betty, p.80-90; i) The women's studies program: Yale University. Cott, Nancy F., p.91-97; j) Appropriate teaching methods for integrating women. Maher, Frances, p.101-108; k) Black studies and women's studies: An overdue partnership. Butler, Johnnella E. and Culley, Margo, p.109-116; l) Moving beyond the curriculum: The 'political' value of an integration strategy. Fritsche, JoAnn M., p.117-123; m) Library resources on women. Bergman, Sherrie S., p.127-134; n) Resources in black women's studies. Sims-Wood, Janet, p.135-141; o) Reconstructing American literature: A strategy for change. Lauter, Paul, p.142-154; p) From issue to action. Schmitz, Betty, p.157-158; q) A view from the funding agencies. Lynch, Felicia, p.159-162; r) In-house resources. Goldsmid, Paula, p.163-169; s) Resource networks. Savage, David, p.170-172; t) Wheaton's assessment process: A case study and its lessons. Tolpin, Martha, p.173-192; u) Women, gender, and the curriculum. Schmidt, Ruth, p.191-193.

315. Toward a Feminist Transformation of the Academy: III: Proceedings of the Seventh Annual GLCA Women's Studies Conference. Reed, Beth, ed. Ann Arbor, MI: GLCA Women's Studies Program, 1982.
a) The emergence of women in twentieth-century Chilean history and literature. Richards, Caroline, p.1-8; b) Attitudes toward gender in two cultures: Puerto Rico and the United States. Berrio, Margaret, et al., p.9-17; c) Still crazy after all these years: The uses of madness in women's fiction. Griffin, Gail, p.18-26; d) Feminist coun-

seling. DiStefano, Anna, p.27-31; e) A dialogue critical issues in women's studies: Race, class, and sexual orientation. DiStefano, Anna and Hooker, Eva, p.32-36; f) Women, reproductive freedom, and the law: A selected annotated bibliography. Langley, Patricia A., p.37-46; g) The art of quilting: Thoughts from a contemporary quilter. Parr, Joyce, p.47-51; h) Two in one, one in two: An exploration of a birth experience and images of the sacred. Massanari, Ronald L., p.52-58; i) Can a man teach women's studies? Banning, Cyrus W., p.59-60; j) Analyzing discrimination against women in the labor market - A few lessons from John Stuart Mill. Klay, Robin, p.61-65; k) Women's studies and the re-vision of liberal education: "What is a nice girl/boy like you doing here?". Dickie, Jane, p.66-67.

316. Toward the Second Decade: The Impact of the Women's Movement on American Institutions. Justice, Betty and Pore, Renate, eds. Westport, CT: Greenwood, 1981.
a) Legitimate theatre is illegitimate. Lee, Maryat, p.11-24; b) Better than a shriveled husk: New forms for the theatre. Jacker, Corinne, p.25-34; c) Playwrights, poets, and novelists: Sisters under the skin. Ginsberg, Elaine, p.35-40; d) Women in the dental profession. Reynolds, Nancy, p.41-48; e) Women in medicine. Phillips, Ruth M., p.49-56; f) Knots in the family tie. Burnett, Marilou, p.59-69; g) Continuing education: A vital process for women. Robertson, Adelle F., p.71-81; h) Toward freedom and self-determination: New directions in mental health services. Breen, Edith, p.83-91; i) The menopause in changing times. Bart, Pauline and Perlmutter, Ellen, p.93-117; j) The lost cause: The aging woman in American feminism. Datan, Nancy, p.119-125; k) Education, girls, and power. Verheyden-Hilliard, Mary Ellen, p.129-139; l) Challenging curricular assumptions: Teaching and studying women's literature from a regional perspective. Stitzel, Judith, p.141-148; m) De jure sex discrimination. Baekey, Carol and Lichtman, Judith L., p.149-161; n) Resistance to the women's movement in the United States: The ERA controversy as prototype. Dunlap, Mary, p.163-169; o) Women's right to full participation in shaping society's course: An evolving constitutional precept. Ginsburg, Ruth Bader, p.171-188; p) Status report on the women's movement as indexed by a "Festival of Women" in West Virginia, Fall 1978. Paterson, Ann, et al., p.189-223.

317. Transitions of Aging. Datan, Nancy and Lohmann, Nancy, eds. New York: Academic Press, 1980.
a) Adaptive dimensions of adult cognition. Labouvie-Vief, Gisela, p.3-26; b) Life satisfaction research in aging: Implications for policy development. Lohmann, Nancy, p.27-40; c) Physical activity as it relates to the health of the aged. Ostrow, Andrew C., p.41-56; d) The competent older woman. Datan, Nancy and Giesen, Carol Boellhoff, p.57-72; e) Intergenerational relations in later life: A family system approach. Troll, Lillian E., p.75-91; f) The widowed family member. Lopata, Helena Znaniecka, p.93-118; g) The clinical psychology of later life: Developmental paradigms. Griffin, Brian, Grunes,

Jerome and Gutmann, David, p.119-131; h) Economic status of late middle-aged widows. Thompson, Gayle B., p.133-149; i) Growing old "inside": Aging and attachment to place in an Appalachian community. Rowles, Graham D., p.153-170; j) Environmental change: The older person as initiator and responder. Lawton, M. Powell, p.171-193; k) Institutionalization of the aged. Tobin, Sheldon S., p.195-211.

318. Twentieth-Century Women Novelists. Staley, Thomas F., ed. Totowa, NJ: Barnes & Noble, 1982.
a) Passionate portrayal of things to come: Doris Lessing's recent fiction. Kaplan, Sydney Janet, p.1-15; b) The wages of intellectuality . . . and the fictional wagers of Iris Murdoch. Widmer, Kingsley, p.16-38; c) Olivia Manning: Witness to history. Mooney, Harry J., p.39-60; d) Women victimised by fiction: Living and loving in the novels of Barbara Pym. Brothers, Barbara, p.61-80; e) Cold enclosures: The fiction of Susan Hill. Jackson, Rosemary, p.81-103; f) The clinical world of P.D. James. Benstock, Bernard, p.104-129; g) Women and children first: The novels of Margaret Drabble. Cunningham, Gail, p.130-152; h) Muriel Spark: The novelist as dandy. McBrien, William, p.153-178; i) Edna O'Brien: A kind of Irish childhood. O'Brien, Darcy, p.179-190; j) The masculine world of Jennifer Johnston. Benstock, Shari, p.191-217.

319. Twice a Minority: Mexican American Women. Melville, Margarita B., ed. St. Louis: C.V. Mosby Co., 1980.
a) Family planning practices of Mexican Americans. Andrade, Sally J., p.17-32; b) Chicana use of abortion: The case of Alcala. Urdaneta, Maria Luisa, p.33-51; c) Mexican, Mexican American, and Chicana childbirth. Kay, Margarita A., p.52-63; d) Breast-feeding and social class mobility: The case of Mexican migrant mothers in Houston, Texas. Johnson, Carmen Acosta, p.66-82; e) "La vieja Inés," a Mexican folk game: A research note. Limón, José E., p.88-94; f) Symbolic strategies for change: A discussion of the Chicana women's movement. Mason, Terry, p.95-108; g) Mexican American women as innovators. Whiteford, Linda, p.109-126; h) "All the good and bad in this world": Women, traditional medicine, and Mexican American culture. Macklin, June, p.127-148; i) Selective acculturation of female Mexican migrants. Melville, Margarita B., p.155-163; j) Cultural styles and adolescent sex role perceptions: An exploration of responses to a value picture projective test. Long, John M. and Vigil, Diego, p.164-172; k) Social networks and survival strategies: An exploratory study of Mexican American, black and Anglo family female heads in San Jose, California. Wagner, Roland M. and Schaffer, Diane M., p.173-190; l) Health and illness perceptions of the Chicana. Lorig, Kate R., Manzanedo, Hector Garcia and Walters, Esperanza Garcia, p.191-207; m) The status of Hispanic women in nursing. Alvarado, Anita L., p.208-216; n) Feminism: The Chicana and the Anglo versions, a historical analysis. Cotera, Marta, p.217-234; o) The non-consenting sterilization of Mexican women in Los Angeles: Issues of psychocultural rupture and legal

redress in paternalistic behavioral-environments. Velez-I., Carlos G., p.235-248; p) To be aged, Hispanic, and female: The triple risk. Blau, Zena Smith, Oser, George T. and Stephens, Richard C., p.249-258.

320. The Undergraduate Woman: Issues in Educational Equity. Perun, Pamela J., ed. Lexington, MA: LexingtonBooks, 1982.
a) The undergraduate woman: Theme and variations. Perun, Pamela J., p.3-14; b) Culture, service, and work: Changing ideals of higher education for women. Antler, Joyce, p.15-41; c) Recent trends in the higher education of women. Bird, Joyce Adair and Heyns, Barbara, p.43-69; d) Mapping the road to academe: A review of research on women, men, and the college-selection process. Hanson, Katherine H. and Litten, Larry H., p.73-97; e) Sex bias in aptitude and achievement tests used in higher education. Lockheed, Marlaine E., p.99-126; f) Sex differences in the significance of economic resources for choosing and attending a college. Hearn, James C. and Rosenfeld, Rachel A., p.127-157; g) Epistemology and agency in the development of undergraduate women. Clinchy, Blythe and Zimmerman, Claire, p.161-181; h) Social psychology looks at but does not see the undergraduate woman. Erkut, Sumru, p.183-204; i) Educational and career progress of Chicana and Native-American college women. Astin, Helen S. and McNamara, Patricia P., p.205-227; j) Sex differences in the impact of college environments on black students. Fleming, Jacqueline, p.229-250; k) Undergraduates and their teachers: An analysis of student evaluations of male and female instructors. Bennett, Sheila Kishler, p.251-273; l) Sex differences in the implications of the links between major departments and the occupational structure. Hearn, James C. and Olzak, Susan, p.275-299; m) Career plans of college women: Patterns and influences. Brown, Marsha D., p.303-335; n) Career commitment of female college graduates: Conceptualization and measurement issues. Bielby, Denise Del Vento, p.337-350; o) Family formation and educational attainment. Alexander, Karl L., Eckland, Bruce K. and Reilly, Thomas W., p.351-373; p) Life after college: Historical links between women's education and women's work. Giele, Janet K. and Perun, Pamela J., p.375-398; q) Issues of educational equity in the 1980s: Multiple perspectives. Perun, Pamela, et al., p.399-419.

321. Unfinished Business: Social Justice for Women in Australia. Broom, Dorothy H., ed. Sydney, Australia: George Allen & Unwin, 1984.
a) Schooling and injustice for girls. Blackburn, Jean, p.3-18; b) Gender and dependency. Tulloch, Patricia, p.19-37; c) Comment: Gender and dependency. Cass, Bettina, p.38-45; d) Natural resources: Health, reproduction and the gender order. Broom, Dorothy, p.46-61; e) Production and consumption: Public versus private. Game, Ann and Pringle, Rosemary, p.65-79; f) Women in the Australian labour force. Eccles, Sandra, p.80-93; g) Comment: Women in the Australian labour force. Moir, Hazel, p.94-100; h) Income inequality. Jones, Frank,

p.101-115; i) Comment: Income inequality. Chapman, Bruce, p.116-119; j) The distribution of income within households. Edwards, Meredith, p.120-136; k) The bureaucrat as usurer. Dowse, Sara, p.139-160; l) The women's movement and social justice. Curthoys, Ann, p.161-176; m) Comment: Women's movement and social justice. Eisenstein, Hester, p.177-180; n) Can there be justice for women under capitalism?: Questions about 'patriarchy'. Magarey, Susan, p.181-187; o) Can there be justice for women under capitalism?: Social justice for whom? Cox, Eva, p.188-193.

322. Unheard Words: Women and Literature in Africa, the Arab World, Asia, the Caribbean and Latin America. Schipper, Mineke, ed. London: Allison & Busby, 1984.
a) Women and literature in Africa. Schipper, Mineke, p.22-58; b) Interview with Miriam Tlali (South Africa). Schipper, Mineke, p.59-68; c) Women and literature in the Arab world. Kilpatrick, Hilary, p.72-90; d) Arab literature in North Africa. Voogd, Lourina de, p.91-101; e) Francophone literature in North Africa. Houwelingen, Flora von, p.102-113; f) Interview with Etel Adnan (Lebanon). Kilpatrick, Hilary, p.114-120; g) Women and literature in Asia: South Asia. Gupta, Sanjukta, p.124-140; h) Women and literature in Asia: South-East Asia. Hellwig, Tineke, p.141-159; i) Interview with Nabaneeta Deb-Sen (India). Gupta, Sajukta, p.160-164; j) Women and literature in the Caribbean. Phaf, Ineke, p.168-200; k) Interview with Astrid Roemer (Surinam). Phaf, Ineke, p.201-210; l) Women and literature in Latin America. Hughes, Psiche, p.215-254; m) Interview with Cristina Peri Rossi (Uruguay). Hughes, Psiche, p.255-274.

323. Union Sisters: Women in the Labour Movement. Briskin, Linda and Yanz, Lynda, eds. Toronto: The Women's Educational Press, 1983.
a) Women at work in Canada. Smith, David and Yanz, Lynda, p.15-27; b) Women and unions in Canada: A statistical overview. Briskin, Linda, p.28-43; c) No proper deal: Women workers and the Canadian labour movement, 1870-1940. Frager, Ruth, p.44-64; d) Out of the ghettos: Affirmative action and unions. Larkin, Jackie, p.67-86; e) "Action Positive" in the Quebec trade union movement. David, Hélène, p.87-102; f) Under attack: Women, unions and microtechnology. Pollock, Marion, p.103-118; g) Part-time work and unions. White, Julie, p.119-135; h) Sexual harassment: An issue for unions. Attenborough, Susan, p.136-143; i) Coercion or male culture: A new look at co-worker harassment. Field, Debbie, p.144-160; j) Lesbians and gays in the union movement. Genge, Susan, p.161-170; k) The right to strike. Darcy, Judy and Lauzon, Catherine, p.171-181; l) Bargaining for equality. Adams, Jane and Griffin, Julie, p.182-197; m) Why are so many women unorganized? Ritchie, Laurell, p.200-211; n) Triple oppression: Immigrant women in the labour force. Cumsille, Alejandra, et al., p.212-221; o) Domestic workers: The experience in B.C.. Epstein, Rachel, p.222-237; p) Organizing freelancers in the arts. Kates, Joanne and Springer, Jane, p.238-255; q) Women's challenge to organized labour. Briskin, Linda, p.259-271;

r) Working, mothering and militancy: Women in the CNTU. Guberman, Nancy, p.272-284; s) Women's committees: The Quebec experience. David, Francoise, p.285-292; t) The dilemma facing women's committees. Field, Debbie, p.293-303; u) Free universal day care: The OFL takes a stand. Colley, Susan, p.307-321; v) Wives supporting the strike. Lane, Arja, p.322-332; w) From ladies' auxiliaries to wives' committees. Luxton, Meg, p.333-347; x) Trade union women and the NDP. Sarra, Janis, p.348-360; y) Building links: Labour and the women's movement. Egan, Carolyn and Yanz, Lynda, p.361-375; z) Women, work and unions: A cineography. Forbes, Dinah, p.377-395; aa) Trade union resources on women. Briskin, Linda, p.396-406; bb) Women and unions: A selected bibliography. Yanz, Lynda, p.407-416.

324. Unplanned Careers: The Working Lives of Middle-Aged Women. Shaw, Lois Banfill, ed. Lexington, MA: LexingtonBooks, 1983.
a) Problems of labor-market reentry. Shaw, Lois B., p.33-44; b) Causes of irregular employment patterns. Shaw, Lois B., p.45-59; c) Occupational atypicality: Changes, causes, and consequences. Daymont, Thomas and Statham, Anne, p.61-75; d) Attitudes toward women working: Changes over time and implications for the labor-force behaviors of husbands and wives. Rhoton, Patricia and Statham, Anne, p.77-92; e) Economic consequences of poor health in mature women. Chirikos, Thomas N. and Nestel, Gilbert, p.93-105; f) Economic consequences of midlife change in marital status. Mercier, Jacqueline, Nestel, Gilbert and Shaw, Lois B., p.109-125.

325. Unspoken Worlds: Women's Religious Lives in Non-Western Cultures. Falk, Nancy Auer and Gross, Rita M., eds. San Francisco: Harper & Row, 1980.
a) Patterns in women's religious lives. p.xi-xviii; b) Julia: An east African diviner. Binford, Martha B., p.3-21; c) Mother Guru: Jnanananda of Madras, India. White, Charles S. J., p.22-37; d) Possession sickness and women shamans in Korea. Harvey, Youngsook Kim, p.41-52; e) Ecstasy and possession: Women of ancient Greece and the cult of Dionysus. Kraemer, Ross S., p.53-69; f) Golden handprints and red-painted feet: Hindu childbirth rituals in central India. Jacobson, Doranne, p.73-93; g) Hindu women's family and household rites in a north Indian village. Wadley, Susan S., p.94-109; h) The ladies of Lord Krishna: Rituals of middle-aged women in eastern India. Freeman, James M., p.110-126; i) Black Carib women and rites of death. Kerns, Virginia, p.127-140; j) The controversial vows of urban Muslim women in Iran. Betteridge, Anne H., p.141-155; k) Islam and tribal women in a village in Iran. Friedl, Erika, p.159-173; l) No women's liberation: The heritage of a woman prophet in modern Japan. Nakamura, Kyoko Motomochi, p.174-190; m) Empress Wu and the historians: A tyrant and saint of classical China. Paul, Diana, p.191-206; n) The case of the vanishing nuns: The fruits of ambivalence in ancient Indian Buddhism. Falk, Nancy Auer, p.207-224; o) Accomplished women in tantric Buddhism of medieval

India and Tibet. Ray, Reginald A., p.227-242; p) Women of influence and prestige among the Native American Iroquois. Shimony, Annemarie, p.243-259; q) Rosinta, rats, and the river: Bad luck is banished in Andean Bolivia. Bastien, Joseph W., p.260-274; r) Menstruation and childbirth as ritual and religious experience among native Australians. Gross, Rita M., p.277-292.

326. Victims of Sexual Aggression: Treatment of Children, Women, and Men. Stuart, Irving R. and Greer, Joanne G., eds. New York: Van Nostrand Reinhold, 1984.
a) Psychodynamics of sexual assault experiences. Nadelson, Carol C. and Notman, Malkah T., p.3-17; b) Working for and with rape victims: Crisis intervention and advocacy. Holmes, Karen A., p.18-35; c) Rape trauma syndrome: Developmental variations. Amanat, Ebrahim, p.36-53; d) Treatment of sexually abused children. Adams, Paul and Adams-Tucker, Christine, p.57-74; e) Network aspects of treatment for incestuously abused children. Carnevale, Patty and Fine, Paul, p.75-90; f) Clinical intervention with boy victims of sexual abuse. Rogers, Carl M. and Terry, Tremaine, p.91-104; g) Group work with preadolescent sexual assault victims. Berliner, Lucy and Ernst, Elise, p.105-124; h) Sexual assault in correctional institutions: Prevention and intervention. Cotton, Donald J. and Groth, A. Nicholas, p.127-156; i) Rape of men in the community. Kaufman, Arthur, p.156-179; j) Sexual assault of the older woman. Hicks, Dorothy J. and Moon, Denise M., p.180-196; k) Marital and sexual dysfunction following rape: Identification and treatment. Miller, William R. and Williams, Ann Marie, p.197-210; l) Behavioral treatment of sexual dysfunctions in sexual assault survivors. Becker, Judith V. and Skinner, Linda J., p.211-233; m) Rape and the college student: Multiple crises in late adolescence. Rowan, Edward L. and Rowan, Judith B., p.234-250; n) Treatment of prostitute victims of sexual assault. Silbert, Mimi H., p.251-269.

327. Violence and the Family. Green, Maurice R., ed. Boulder, CO: Westview Press, 1980.
a) A sociological perspective on the causes of family violence. Straus, Murray A., p.7-31; b) Discussion: Violence in the family. Bloch, Donald A., p.32-36; c) Television viewing, family style and aggressive behavior in preschool children. Singer, Dorothy G. and Singer, Jerome L., p.37-65; d) Discussion: Television violence and the family. Friedrich-Cofer, Lynette K., p.66-77; e) Ethnopsychiatric dimensions in family violence. Spiegel, John P., p.79-89; f) Discussion: Violence and the family in perspective. West, Louis Jolyon, p.90-104; g) Functions of the police and the justice system in family violence. Bard, Morton, p.105-120.

328. Virginia Woolf: A Feminist Slant. Marcus, Jane, ed. Lincoln, NE: University of Nebraska Press, 1983.
a) Introduction: Virginia Woolf aslant. Marcus, Jane, p.1-6; b) The niece of a nun: Virginia Woolf, Caroline Stephen, and the cloistered imagination. Marcus, Jane, p.7-36; c) Virginia liked Elizabeth. Fox, Alice, p.37-52; d) Fathers in general: The patriarchy in Virginia Woolf's fic-

tion. Schlack, Beverly Ann, p.52-77; e) 1897: Virginia Woolf at fifteen. DeSalvo, Louise A., p.78-108; f) Isis unveiled: Virginia Woolf's use of Egyptian myth. Haller, Evelyn, p.109-131; g) Political aesthetics: Virginia Woolf and Dorothy Richardson. Gillespie, Diane Filby, p.132-151; h) An uneasy sisterhood: Virginia Woolf and Katherine Mansfield. McLaughlin, Ann L., p.152-161; i) Clarissa Dalloway's respectable suicide. Jensen, Emily, p.162-179; j) Virginia Woolf and the women's movement. Black, Naomi, p.180-197; k) A track of our own: Typescript drafts of *The Years*. Squier, Susan, p.198-211; l) Theater of war: Virginia Woolf's *Between the Acts*. Sears, Sallie, p.212-235; m) Virginia Woolf in her fifties. Heilbrun, Carolyn G., p.236-254; n) *Three Guineas* before and after: Further answers to correspondents. Silver, Brenda R., p.254-276.

329. Virginia Woolf: Centennial Essays. Ginsberg, Elaine K. and Gottlieb, Laura Moss, eds. Troy, NY: Whitston Publishing, 1983.
a) Virginia Woolf and the intellectual origins of Bloomsbury. Rosenbaum, S. P., p.11-26; b) Virginia Woolf and her violin: Mothering, madness and music. Marcus, Jane, p.27-49; c) Virginia Woolf and Julia Stephen: The distaff side of history. Stemerick, Martine, p.51-80; d) The squirrel's heart beat and the death of a moth. Faris, Wendy B., p.81-91; e) The anti-madonna in the work and thought of Virginia Woolf. Haller, Evelyn, p.93-109; f) Virginia Woolf and the problem of the body. Lyon, George Ella, p.111-125; g) 'The prime minister': A key to *Mrs. Dalloway*. Henke, Suzette A., p.127-141; h) Private and public consciousness in *Mrs. Dalloway* and *To the Lighthouse*. Haring-Smith, Tori, p.143-162; i) Speech acts in *To the Lighthouse*. Libertin, Mary, p.163-185; j) *The Waves*: A utopia of androgyny? Sypher, Eileen B., p.187-213; k) *The Years*: A feminist novel. Gottlieb, Laura Moss, p.215-229; l) A common sitting room: Virginia Woolf's critique of women writers. Klein, Kathleen Gregory, p.231-248; m) 'What right have I, a woman?': Virginia Woolf's reading notes on Sidney and Spenser. Fox, Alice, p.249-256; n) Virginia Woolf and the classics: Every Englishman's prerogative transmuted into fictional art. Herman, William, p.257-268; o) The whole contention between Mr. Bennett and Mrs. Woolf, revisited. Daugherty, Beth Rigel, p.269-294; p) Combining 'the advantages of fact and fiction': Virginia Woolf's biographies of Vita Sackville-West, Flush, and Roger Fry. Lewis, Thomas S. W., p.295-324.

330. Virginia Woolf: Revaluation and Continuity. Freedman, Ralph, ed. Berkeley, CA: University of California Press, 1980.
a) Introduction: Virginia Woolf, the novel, and a chorus of voices. Freedman, Ralph, p.3-12; b) Hunting the moth: Virginia Woolf and the creative imagination. Richter, Harvena, p.13-28; c) Virginia Woolf's narrators and the art of "life itself". Hafley, James, p.29-43; d) Forms of the Woolfian short story. Fleishman, Avrom, p.44-70; e) "Surely order did prevail": Virginia Woolf and *The Voyage Out*. McDowell, Frederick P. W., p.73-96; f) Enchanted

organs, magic bells: *Night and Day* as comic opera. Marcus, Jane, p.97-122; g) The form of fact and fiction: *Jacob's Room* as paradigm. Freedman, Ralph, p.123-140; h) *Mrs. Dalloway*: The unguarded moment. Ruotolo, Lucio, p.141-160; i) *To the Lighthouse*: Virginia Woolf's Winter's Tale. Dibattista, Maria, p.161-188; j) *Orlando* and its genesis: Venturing and experimenting in art, love, and sex. Love, Jean O., p.189-218; k) Nature and community: A study of cyclical reality in *The Waves*. Moore, Madeline, p.219-240; l) Nature and history in *The Years*. Naremore, James, p.241-262; m) Woolf's peculiar comic world: *Between the Acts*. Fussell, B. H., p.263-283.

331. Vox Feminae: Studies in Medieval Woman's Songs. Plummer, John F., ed. Kalamazoo, MI: Medieval Institute Publications, Western Michigan University, 1981.
a) Woman's song in medieval Latin. Schotter, Anne Howland, p.19-33; b) Voice and audience: The emotional world of the *cantigas de amigo*. Ashley, Kathleen, p.35-45; c) The woman's song in medieval German poetry. Jackson, William E., p.47-94; d) The woman's songs of Hartmann von Aue. Heinen, Hubert, p.95-110; e) Woman's songs in Irish, 800-1500. Lehmann, Ruth P.M., p.111-134; f) The woman's song in Middle English and its European backgrounds. Plummer, John F., p.135-154; g) The "other" voice: Woman's song, its satire and its transcendence in late medieval British literature. Fries, Maureen, p.155-178; h) Poems by "The Lady" in *La Chasse et le départ d'amours (1509)*. Winn, Mary Beth, p.179-198.

332. The Voyage In: Fictions of Female Development. Abel, Elizabeth, Hirsch, Marianne and Langland, Elizabeth, eds. Hanover, NH: University Press of New England, 1983.
a) Spiritual *Bildung*: The beautiful soul as paradigm. Hirsch, Marianne, p.23-48; b) The novel of awakening (five novels). Rosowski, Susan J., p.49-68; c) "Fairy-born and human-bred": Jane Eyre's education in romance. Rowe, Karen E., p.69-89; d) The reflecting reader in *Villette*. Silver, Brenda R., p.90-111; e) Female stories of experience: Alcott's *Little Women* in light of *Work*. Langland, Elizabeth, p.112-130; f) The sisterhood of Jane Eyre and Antoinette Cosway. Baer, Elizabeth R., p.131-148; g) Revolutionary turnings: *The Mountain Lion* reread. Gelfant, Blanche H., p.149-160; h) Narrative structure(s) and female development: The case of *Mrs. Dalloway*. Abel, Elizabeth, p.161-185; i) Doris Lessing and the parables of growth. Stimpson, Catharine R., p.186-205; j) Through the looking glass: When women tell fairy tales. Rose, Ellen Cronan, p.209-227; k) The female novel of development and the myth of psyche. Ferguson, Mary Anne, p.228-243; l) Exiting from patriarchy: The lesbian novel of development. Zimmerman, Bonnie, p.244-257; m) "Why are you afraid to have me at your side?": From passivity to power in *Salt of the Earth*. Kasdan, Margo, p.258-269; n) Plain, black, and decently wild: The heroic possibilities of *Maud Martha*. Washington, Mary Helen, p.270-286; o) *Family Ties*: Female development in Clarice Lispector. Peixoto, Marta,

p.287-302; p) Shadowing/surfacing/shedding: Contemporary German writers in search of a female *Bildungsroman*. Frieden, Sandra, p.304-316.

333. We are Bosses Ourselves: The Status and Role of Aboriginal Women Today. Gale, Fay, ed. Canberra, Australia: Australian Instutite of Aboriginal Studies, 1983.
a) Mythical women, past and present. Berndt, Catherine H., p.13-23; b) Consulting with women. Bell, Diane, p.24-28; c) A certain heritage: Women and their children in north Australia. Brandl, Maria, p.29-39; d) The social and economic importance of the women in Jigalong. Chesson, Marlene, p.40-43; e) The conflicting role of aboriginal women in today's society. Boyle, Helen, p.44-47; f) Women and land rights: The Pitjantjatjara land claims. Ilyatjari, Nganyintja, p.55-61; g) The recent history of the Borroloola aboriginal people and their struggle for land rights. Avery, John, p.62-65; h) Borroloola community and land rights. Isaac, Annie and McDinny, Eileen, p.66-67; i) Borroloola women speak. Man and woman: dance. Avery, John, p.68-77; j) Women and land rights: A review. Ludwig, Wendy, p.78-83; k) Women and land rights: Kiuk and Wagaidj women in the Darwin area. Tennant, Lorna, p.84-85; l) Historical factors which have affected aboriginal lifestyles since colonisation. Deuschle, Vi, p.86-88; m) Women in the health role. Tynan, Barbara J., p.93-99; n) Study into the needs of aboriginal women who have been raped or sexually assaulted. Bligh, Vivian, p.100-103; o) Aboriginal women's role today in early childhood school education. Moeckel, Margot J., p.104-121; p) The Yuendumu aboriginal cultural pre-school. Egan, Jeannie Nungarrayi, p.122-123; q) Aboriginal women in education. Koolmatrie, Janis, p.124-125; r) Income and employment for women in remote communities: Examples from the Northern Territory. Young, Elspeth, p.126-135; s) Recording our history. Kartinyeri, Doreen, p.136-157; t) Aboriginal women today. Department of Aboriginal Affairs, p.158-159.

334. The Welsh Law of Women. Jenkins, Dafydd and Owen, Morfydd E., eds. Cardiff, Wales: University of Wales Press, 1980.
a) The normal paradigms of a woman's life in the Irish and Welsh texts. McAll, Christopher, p.7-22; b) Nau Kynywedi Teithiauc. Charles-Edwards, T. M., p.23-39; c) Shame and reparation: Women's place in the kin. Owen, Morfydd E., p.40-68; d) Property interests in the classical Welsh law of women. Jenkins, Dafydd, p.69-92; e) The status of women and the practice of marriage in late-medieval Wales. Davies, R. R., p.93-114; f) The European legal context of the Welsh law of matrimonial property. Walters, D. B., p.115-131.

335. What Is To Be Done About the Family? Segal, Lynne, ed. Harmondsworth, Middlesex: Penguin Books, 1983.
a) 'The most important thing of all' - Rethinking the family: An overview. Segal, Lynne, p.9-24; b) 'Smash the family?' Recalling the 1960s. Segal, Lynne, p.25-64; c) From utopian to scientific feminism? Early feminist critiques of

the family. Nava, Mica, p.65-105; d) Production rules
OK? Waged work and the family. Himmelweit, Susan,
p.106-128; e) 'The serious burdens of love?' Some questions on child-care, feminism and socialism. Riley,
Denise, p.129-156; f) Sex - A family affair. Campbell,
Beatrix, p.157-167; g) Home thoughts from not so far
away: A personal look at family. Clark, Wendy, p.168-189;
h) The state, welfare and women's dependence. Bennett,
Fran, p.190-214; i) No turning back - Thatcherism, the
family and the future. Segal, Lynne, p.215-232.

336. When Biology Became Destiny: Women in Weimar and
Nazi Germany. Bridenthal, Renate, Grossmann, Atina
and Kaplan, Marion, eds. New York: Monthly Review
Press, 1984.
a) Introduction: Women in Weimar and Nazi Germany.
p.1-29; b) Beyond *Kinder, Küche, Kirche*: Weimar women
in politics and work. Bridenthal, Renate and Koonz,
Claudia, p.33-65; c) Abortion and economic crisis: The
1931 campaign against paragraph 218. Grossmann, Atina,
p.66-86; d) The Bremen morality scandal. Meyer-
Renschhausen, Elisabeth, p.87-108; e) Helene Stöcker:
Left-wing intellectual and sex reformer. Hackett, Amy,
p.109-130; f) Mother's day in the Weimar Republic.
Hausen, Karin, p.131-152; g) "Professional" housewives:
Stepsisters of the women's movement. Bridenthal,
Renate, p.153-173; h) Sisterhood under siege: Feminism
and anti-semitism in Germany, 1904-1938. Kaplan,
Marion, p.174-196; i) The competition for women's *leben-
sraum*, 1928-1934. Koonz, Claudia, p.199-236; j) The cre-
ation of a female assembly-line proletariat. Tröger,
Annemarie, p.237-270; k) Racism and sexism in Nazi
Germany: Motherhood, compulsory sterilization, and the
state. Bock, Gisela, p.271-296; l) Women and the
Holocaust: The case of German and German-Jewish
women. Milton, Sybil, p.297-333; m) The story of Ruth.
Kramer, Sylvia and Nebel, Ruth, p.334-348; n) Comrade -
woman - mother - resistance fighter. Jacob, Katharina
and Szepansky, Gerda, p.349-362.

337. Wisconsin Women: Graduate School and the Professions.
Swoboda, Marian J. and Roberts, Audrey J., eds.
Madison, WI: Office of Women, University of Wisconsin,
1980.
a) Vocational aspirations and job realities. Droste, Jean,
p.1-10; b) Women in science. Barnes, Bette and Dickie,
Ruth, p.13-20; c) Women's contributions to the library
school. Fenster, Valmai, p.21-27; d) Women in engineering. Greenfield, Lois, p.29-39; e) Nursing in the UW system. Cooper, Signe, p.41-53; f) Women in the medical
school. Apple, Rima and Leavitt, Judith, p.55-64; g)
Women and the law school. Doyle, Ruth, p.65-73; h)
Women in the school of music. Sylvander, Carolyn, p.75-
78; i) Women in the art department. Mjaanes, Judith,
p.79-87; j) Women and cooperative home economics
extension. Dickie, Ruth, p.89-100; k) Women on the academic staff. Elder, Joann, p.101-108; l) Women and student government. Wright, Buff, p.109-119; m) Socio-economic profile of faculty women at Madison. Freeman,
Bonnie Cook, p.123-134; n) Traditional and non-tradi-

tional choices of disciplines by women. Swoboda, Marian,
p.135-151.

338. Woman in Irish Legend, Life and Literature. Gallagher,
S.F., ed. Gerrards Cross, Buckinghamshire: Colin Smythe,
1983.
a) Irish women in legend, literature and life. Reynolds,
Lorna, p.11-25; b) The female principle in Gaelic poetry.
O'Brien, Maire Cruise, p.26-37; c) Women in the plays of
W.B. Yeats. Parkin, Andrew, p.38-57; d) Synge and the
nature of woman. Saddlemyer, Ann, p.58-73; e) The new
woman and the old goddess: The shaping of Shaw's
mythology. Smith, J. Percy, p.74-90; f) 'Two words for
women': A reassessment of O'Casey's heroines. Ayling,
Ronald, p.91-114; g) The look of a queen. Kenner, Hugh,
p.115-124; h) The dramatic treatment of Robert Emmet
and Sarah Curran. Hawkins, Maureen S.G., p.125-137; i)
Rewriting history: Anna Parnell's *The Tale of a Great
Sham*. Hearne, Dana, p.138-149; j) Appendix: A reply to
the toast to Canada. Laurence, Margaret, p.150-151.

339. The Woman in Management: Career and Family Issues.
Farley, Jennie, ed. Ithaca, NY: ILR Press, 1983.
a) Women in a changing economy. Kreps, Juanita M., p.1-
12; b) Women and men at work: Jockeying for position.
Harragan, Betty Lehan, p.12-20; c) Women managers:
Moving up in a high tech society. Kanter, Rosabeth Moss,
p.21-36; d) Being a manager in a multicultural world.
Johnson, Pam McAllister, p.37-39; e) Coping with illegal
sex discrimination. Bartlett, Linda, p.40-44; f) The single
woman: Moving up by moving around. Kiryluk, Carol,
p.45-48; g) Dual career couples: How the company can
help. Byrnes, Eleanor, p.49-53; h) Working couples and
child care. Oesterle, Patricia M., p.54-56; i) Does becoming a parent mean falling off the fast track? Osterman,
Gail Bryant, p.57-60; j) One family's decision: A leave of
absence. Coffey, Margaret, p.61-64; k) Personal choices.
Smith, Deborah K., p.65-68.

340. Woman the Gatherer. Dahlberg, Frances, ed. New
Haven, CT: Yale University Press, 1981.
a) The female chimpanzee as a human evolutionary prototype. McGrew, W. C., p.35-73; b) Women as shapers of
the human adaptation. Zihlman, Adrienne L., p.75-120;
c) Woman the hunter: The Agta. Estioko-Griffin, Agnes
and Griffin, P. Bion, p.121-151; d) Interpretations and
"facts" in aboriginal Australia. Berndt, Catherine H.,
p.153-203; e) Mbuti womanhood. Turnbull, Colin M.,
p.205-219; f) The null case: The Chipewyan. Sharp, Henry
S., p.221-244.

341. A Woman's Conflict: The Special Relationship Between
Women and Food. Kaplan, Jane Rachel, ed. Englewood
Cliffs, NJ: Prentice-Hall, 1980.
a) Introduction: Beauty and the feast. Kaplan, Jane
Rachel, p.1-14; b) Thin fat people. Bruch, Hilde, p.15-28;
c) A woman's body in a man's world: A review of findings
on body image and weight control. Dyrenforth, Sue R.,
Wooley, Orland W. and Wooley, Susan C., p.29-57; d)
Barbara's foodworld: A case history. Kaplan, Jane

Rachel, p.59-83; e) Women in the kitchen: The feminist boiling point. Sokolov, Raymond, p.85-89; f) Feast and famine: Gifts of the goddess. Downing, Chris, p.91-105; g) Venus as endomorph. Beller, Anne Scott, p.107-138; h) Pregnancy: Is motherhood fattening? Beller, Anne Scott, p.139-158; i) Soul, black women and food. Styles, Marva, p.159-176; j) The nutritional needs of women. Contento, Isobel, p.177-199; k) Working up an appetite. Aronson, Naomi, p.201-231; l) Farming out the home: Women and agribusiness. Hacker, Sally, p.233-263.

342. Woman's Nature: Rationalizations of Inequality. Lowe, Marian and Hubbard, Ruth, eds. New York: Pergamon, 1983.
a) Social effects of some contemporary myths about women. Hubbard, Ruth, p.1-8; b) Women's nature and scientific objectivity. Fee, Elizabeth, p.9-28; c) Black women as producers and reproducers for profit. Burnham, Dorothy, p.29-38; d) The dialectic of biology and culture. Lowe, Marian, p.39-62; e) Indian women: Tribal identity as status quo. Medicine, Beatrice, p.63-74; f) The scientific mystique: Can a white lab coat guarantee purity in the search for knowledge about the nature of women? Messing, Karen, p.75-88; g) Feminist analysis of gender: A critique. Smith, Joan, p.89-110; h) Ideologies of male dominance as divide and rule politics: An anthropologist's view. Leacock, Eleanor, p.111-122; i) Origins of the sexual division of labor. Leibowitz, Lila, p.123-148.

343. The Woman's Part: Feminist Criticism of Shakespeare. Lenz, Carolyn Ruth Swift, Greene, Gayle, and Neely, Carol Thomas, eds. Urbana, IL: University of Illinois Press, 1980.
a) The woman's part: Female sexuality as power in Shakespeare's plays. Berggren, Paula S., p.17-34; b) "Neither mother, wife, nor England's queen": The roles of women in *Richard III*. Miner, Madonne M., p.35-55; c) Shakespeare and the soil of rape. Stimpson, Catharine R., p.56-64; d) Comic structure and the humanizing of Kate in *The Taming of the Shrew*. Bean, John C., p.65-78; e) Those "soft and delicate desires": *Much Ado* and the distrust of women. Hays, Janice, p.79-99; f) As we like it: How a girl can be smart and still popular. Park, Clara Claiborne, p.100-116; g) Counsels of gall and grace: Intimate conversations between women in Shakespeare's plays. McKewin, Carole, p.117-132; h) Shakespeare's Cressida: "A kind of self". Greene, Gayle, p.133-149; i) "I wooed thee with my sword": Shakespeare's tragic paradigms. Gohlke, Madelon, p.150-179; j) Coming of age in Verona. Kahn, Coppélia, p.171-193; k) A heart cleft in twain: The dilemma of Shakespeare's Gertrude. Smith, Rebecca, p.194-210; l) Women and men in *Othello*: "What should such a fool/Do with so good a woman?". Neely, Carol Thomas, p.211-240; m) Lady Macbeth: "Infirm of purpose". Klein, Joan Larsen, p.240-255; n) Shakespeare's female characters as actors and audience. Novy, Marianne, p.256-270; o) A penchant for Perdita on the eighteenth-century stage. Dash, Irene G., p.271-284; p) The Miranda trap: Sexism and racism in Shakespeare's *Tempest*. Leininger, Lorie Jerrell, p.285-294; q) "O sacred, shadowy, cold, and constant queen": Shakespeare's imperiled and chastening daughters of romance. Frey, Charles, p.295-313; r) Women and men in Shakespeare: A selective bibliography. Greene, Gayle, Lenz, Carolyn Ruth Swift and Neely, Carol Thomas, p.314-335.

344. Women: A Feminist Perspective (3rd edition). Freeman, Jo, ed. Palo Alto, CA: Mayfield Publishing, 1984.
a) Sexual terrorism. Sheffield, Carole J., p.3-19; b) The rape culture. Herman, Dianne, p.20-38; c) Abortion: The controversial choice. Bishop, Nadean, p.39-53; d) Sexual harassment: The link between gender stratification, sexuality, and women's economic status. Martin, Susan Ehrlich, p.54-69; e) Women, health, and medicine. Rothman, Barbara Katz, p.70-80; f) The origin of the family. Gough, Kathleen, p.83-99; g) Power in dating relationships. Peplau, Letitia Anne, p.100-112; h) Marital relationships and mental health: The psychic costs of inequality. Steil, Janice M., p.113-123; i) Motherhood: Contemporary conflict for women. Hoffnung, Michele, p.124-138; j) Child care. Norgren, Jill, p.139-153; k) Sex-role socialization: A focus on women. Weitzman, Lenore J., p.157-237; l) Women and higher education: Sex differentials in the status of students and scholars. Fox, Mary Frank, p.238-255; m) The double standard: Age. Bell, Inge Powell, p.256-263; n) The internalization of powerlessness: A case study of the displaced homemaker. Greenwood-Audant, Lois M., p.264-281; o) Women and widowhood: The suffering beyond grief. Stillion, Judith M., p.282-293; p) Women in the labor force: An overview. Blau, Francine D., p.297-315; q) Clerical work: The female occupation. Feldberg, Roslyn L. and Glenn, Evelyn Nakano, p.316-336; r) "Union is power": Sketches from women's labor history. Wertheimer, Barbara M., p.337-352; s) Professional women: How real are the recent gains? Kaufman, Debra Renee, p.353-369; t) Trust, loyalty, and the place of women in the informal organization of work. Lorber, Judith, p.370-378; u) Women, law, and public policy. Freeman, Jo, p.381-401; v) Women and politics: The real majority. Lynn, Naomi B., p.402-422; w) Race and ethnicity in the lives of minority women. Almquist, Elizabeth McTaggart, p.423-453; x) What price independence? Social reactions to lesbians, spinsters, widows, and nuns. Weitz, Rose, p.454-464; y) The sexual politics of interpersonal behavior. Freeman, Jo and Henley, Nancy, p.465-477; z) Sexism and the English language: The linguistic implications of being a woman. Adams, Karen L. and Ware, Norma C., p.478-491; aa) Poverty is a woman's problem. Shortridge, Kathleen, p.492-501; bb) Farewell to alms: Women's fare under welfare. Pearce, Diana M., p.502-515; cc) The historical background. Klein, Viola, p.519-532; dd) The first feminists. Hole, Judith and Levine, Ellen, p.533-542; ee) The women's liberation movement: Its origins, structure, activities, and ideas. Freeman, Jo, p.543-556; ff) Feminist consciousness and black women. Terrelonge, Pauline, p.557-567; gg) Keep us on the pedestal: Women against feminism in twentieth century America. Marshall, Susan E., p.568-581.

345. Women & Alcohol. Camberwell Council on Alcoholism, ed. London: Tavistock Pub., 1980.
a) The causes of increasing drinking problems amongst women. Shaw, Stan, p.1-40; b) The physical effects and metabolism of alcohol. Ghodse, A. Hamid and Tregenza, G. S., p.41-52; c) The foetal alcohol syndrome. Sclare, Astor Balfour, p.53-66; d) Psychological aspects of women and alcohol. Saunders, Bill, p.67-101; e) The family. Wilson, Clare, p.101-132; f) Response and recognition. Sheehan, Margaret and Watson, Jacqui, p.133-158; g) Counselling. Page, Annabel, p.159-175; h) Single homeless women and alcohol. Otto, Shirley, p.176-200.

346. Women and Child Workers in Unorganised Sector: Non-government Organisation's Perspectives. Gangrade, K.D. and Gathia, J.A., eds. New Delhi: Concept Publishing, 1983.
a) Employment of women and child: Battles to fight. Gangrade, K.D., p.49-72; b) Child workers in the informal sector role of the NGOs: Some reflections. Gathia, J.A., p.73-80; c) Making women visible. Jhabvala, Renana, p.81; d) Technologies for poor women. Sharma, Y.K., p.82-84; e) Salient laws on women and children: A selected bibliography. Bakht, M. and Gupta, A.S., p.87-101.

347. Women and Colonization: Anthropological Perspectives. Etienne, Mona and Leacock, Eleanor, eds. New York: Praeger, 1980.
a) Montagnais women and the Jesuit program for colonization. Leacock, Eleanor, p.25-42; b) Sunksquaws, shamans, and tradeswomen: Middle Atlantic coastal Algonkian women during the 17th and 18th centuries. Grumet, Robert Steven, p.43-62; c) The mothers of the nation: Seneca resistance to Quaker intervention. Rothenberg, Diane, p.63-87; d) Contending with colonization: Tlingit men and women in change. Klein, Laura F., p.88-108; e) Forced transition from egalitarianism to male dominance: The Bari of Colombia. Brown, Susan E. and Buenaventura-Posso, Elisa, p.109-133; f) Aztec women: The transition from status to class in empire and colony. Nash, June, p.134-148; g) "The universe has turned inside out...There is no justice for us here": Andean women under Spanish rule. Silverblatt, Irene, p.149-185; h) Daughters of the lakes and rivers: Colonization and the land rights of Luo women. Okeyo, Achola Pala, p.186-213; i) Women and men, cloth and colonization: The transformation of production-distribution relations among the Baule (Ivory Coast). Etienne, Mona, p.214-238; j) Desert politics: Choices in the "marriage market". Bell, Diane, p.239-269; k) Stability in banana leaves: Colonization and women in Kiriwina, Trobriand Islands. Weiner, Annette B., p.270-293; l) Putting down sisters and wives: Tongan women and colonization. Gailey, Christine Ward, p.294-322.

348. Women and Crime. Mukherjee, Satyanshu K. and Scutt, Jocelynne A. eds. Sydney: Allen & Unwin, 1981.
a) Sexism in criminal law. Scutt, Jocelynne A., p.1-21; b) Hidden from history: Women victims of crime. Summers, Anne, p.22-30; c) Women, crime and punishment. Windschuttle, Elizabeth, p.31-50; d) The mythinterpretation of female crime. Omodei, Roslyn, p.51-69; e) Theorizing about female crime. Naffin, Ngaire p.70-91; f) The processing of juveniles in Victoria. Hancock, Linda and Hiller, Anne Edwards, p.92-126; g) The myth of rising female crime. Fitzgerald, R. William and Mukherjee, Satyanshu K., p.127-166; h) Women in constraints. Hartz-Karp, Janette, p.167-195; i) Prisons, prisoners and the community. Willson, Sandra A.K., p.196-204.

349. Women and Crime in America. Bowker, Lee H., ed. New York: Macmillan, 1981.
a) Criminological theory: Its ideology and implications concerning women. Smart, Carol, p.6-18; b) American women and crime. Simon, Rita J., p.18-39; c) Crime and the contemporary woman: An analysis of changing levels of female property crime, 1960-1975. Steffensmeier, Darrell J., p.39-59; d) Patterns of female property crime, 1960-1978: A postscript. Steffensmeier, Darrell J., p.59-65; e) The economics of female criminality: An analysis of police blotters, 1890-1976. Dudley, Sandra, Giordano, Peggy C. and Kerbel, Sandra, p.65-82; f) Gender differences in delinquency: Quantity and quality. Feyerherm, William, p.82-92; g) Aw! Your mother's in the mafia: Women criminals in progressive New York. Block, Alan, p.98-117; h) The woman participant in Washington's riots. Miller, E. Eugene, p.117-125; i) Prostitution in Nevada. Symanski, Richard, p.126-154; j) Women as victims: An examination of the results of L.E.A.A.'s National Crime Survey Program. Bowker, Lee H., p.158-179; k) The victim in a forcible rape case: A feminist view. Wood, Pamela L., p.190-211; l) Rape: Power, anger, and sexuality. Burgess, Ann W., Groth, A. Nicholas and Holmstrom, Lynda L., p.212-223; m) Sexual aggression: A second look at the offended female. Kanin, Eugene J. and Parcell, Stanley R., p.223-233; n) Sex roles, power, and woman battering. Pagelow, Mildred D., p.239-277; o) Secondary battering and alternatives of female victims to spouse abuse. Pagelow, Mildred D., p.277-300; p) The underside of married life: Power, influence, and violence. Adler, Emily Stier, p.300-320; q) An interview with Sara Smith - One woman's experience with the cycle of violence. Anonymous, p.320-328; r) Barriers to becoming a "successful" rape victim. Randall, Susan C. and Rose, Vicki M., p.336-354; s) Judicial paternalism and the female status offender: Training women to know their place. Chesney-Lind, Meda, p.354-366; t) Police processing of female offenders. Moyer, Imogene L. and White, Garland F., p.366-377; u) Sex-role stereotypes and justice for women. Feinman, Clarice, p.383-391; v) Imprisoned women and their children. Blumenthal, Karen I. and McGowan, Brenda G., p.392-408; w) Gender differences in prisoner subcultures. Bowker, Lee H., p.409-419; x) Reform school families. Carter, Barbara, p.419-439.

350. Women and Development: The Sexual Division of Labor in Rural Societies. Benería, Lourdes, ed. New York: Praeger, 1982.
a) The dynamics of the sexual division of labor and inte-

gration of rural women into the world market. Mies, Maria, p.1-28; b) Women workers and the green revolution. Sen, Gita, p.29-64; c) Peasant production, proletarianization, and the sexual division of labor in the Andes. Deere, Carmen Diana and Leal, Magdalena León de, p.65-93; d) Resource allocation and the sexual division of labor: A case study of a Moslem Hausa village in northern Nigeria. Longhurst, Richard, p.95-117; e) Accounting for women's work. Benería, Lourdes, p.119-147; f) The creation of a relative surplus population: A case study from Mexico. Young, Kate, p.149-177; g) From rural subsistence to an industrial peripheral work force: An examination of female Malaysian migrants and capital accumulation in Singapore. Heyzer, Noeleen, p.179-202; h) The impact of land reform on women: The case of Ethiopia. Tadesse, Zenebeworke, p.203-222; i) The sexual division of labor in rural China. Croll, Elisabeth, p.223-247.

351. Women and Education: Equity or Equality? Fennema, Elizabeth and Ayer, M. Jane, eds. Berkeley, CA: McCutchan, 1984.
a) Equity or equality: What shall it be? Bennison, Anne, et al., p.1-18; b) The impacts of irrelevance: Women in the history of American education. Greene, Maxine, p.19-39; c) Career and life satisfactions among Terman's gifted women. Barbee, Ann H. and Sears, Pauline S., p.41-83; d) Biology: Its role in gender-related educational experiences. Crockett, Lisa J. and Petersen, Anne C., p.85-115; e) Sex segregation and male preeminence in elementary classrooms. Lockheed, Marlaine E., p.117-135; f) Girls, women, and mathematics. Fennema, Elizabeth, p.137-164; g) Women's studies at the secondary school level. Kaub, Shirley Jane, p.165-179; h) Women's education and career choice: Disparities between theory and practice. Astin, Helen S. and Snyder, Mary Beth, p.181-195; i) The participation of minority women in higher education. Marrett, Cora Bagley and Matthews, Westina, p.197-220; j) Women, space, and power in higher education. Ayer, M. Jane, p.221-238; k) Studying women's studies: A guide to archival research. Searing, Susan E., p.239-252; l) Women's studies: A discipline takes shape. Merritt, Karen, p.253-262.

352. Women and Educational Leadership. Biklen, Sari Knopp and Brannigan, Marilyn B., eds. Lexington, MA: LexingtonBooks, 1980.
a) Introduction: Barriers to equity - Women, educational leadership, and social change. Biklen, Sari Knopp, p.1-23; b) Prophets, chiefs, commissioners, and queens: The moral and institutional context of leadership. Freedman, Michael, p.27-34; c) The psychology of leadership: Implications for women. Conoley, Jane Close, p.35-46; d) Power and opportunity in the principalship: The case of two women leaders in education. Beam, Amy and Greenfield, William, p.47-62; e) Historical perspectives on women in educational leadership. Burstyn, Joan N., p.65-75; f) Feminism and the woman school administrator. Gribskov, Margaret, p.77-91; g) Single-sex education and leadership: The early years of Simmons College. Kohlstedt, Sally Gregory, p.93-112; h) Coeducation and

the development of leadership skills in women: Historical perspectives from Cornell University, 1868-1900. Haines, Patricia Foster, p.113-128; i) Sex bias in school administration. Clement, Jacqueline, p.131-137; j) Socialization and education of young black girls in school. Lightfoot, Sara Lawrence, p.139-164; k) The black female administrator: Woman in a double bind. Doughtery, Rosie, p.165-174; l) How real is fear of success? Johnson, Marilyn, p.175-182; m) The need for female role models in education. Antonucci, Toni, p.185-195; n) Working and parenting: The male and father role. Keller, Harold R., p.197-207; o) The transition from parenting to working and parenting. Bogdan, Janet, p.209-221; p) Leadership training for increased effectiveness among women educational administrators: Two local models. Winslow, Mary Bowes, p.223-238; q) Changing women's representation in school management: A systems perspective. Schmuck, Patricia A., p.239-259.

353. Women and Health in America: Historical Readings. Leavitt, Judith Walzer, ed. Madison, WI: University of Wisconsin Press, 1984.
a) The female animal: Medical and biological views of woman and her role in nineteenth-century America. Rosenberg, Charles and Smith-Rosenberg, Carroll, p.12-27; b) Women, menstruation, and nineteenth-century medicine. Bullough, Vern and Voght, Martha, p.28-37; c) What ought to be and what was: Women's sexuality in the nineteenth century. Degler, Carl N., p.40-56; d) Passionlessness: An interpretation of Victorian sexual ideology, 1790-1850. Cott, Nancy F., p.57-69; e) The female world of love and ritual: Relations between women in nineteenth-century America. Smith-Rosenberg, Carroll, p.70-89; f) "Imagine my surprise": Women's relationships in historical perspective. Rupp, Leila J., p.90-102; g) Voluntary motherhood: The beginnings of feminist birth control ideas in the United States. Gordon, Linda, p.104-116; h) Patterns of abortion and the response of American physicians, 1790-1930. Mohr, James C., p.117-123; i) Doctors, birth control, and social values, 1830-1970. Reed, James, p.124-139; j) "On the importance of the obstetrick art": Changing customs of childbirth in America, 1760 to 1825. Scholten, Catherine M., p.142-154; k) "Down to death door's": Women's perceptions of childbirth in America. Leavitt, Judith Walzer and Walton, Whitney, p.155-165; l) The Loomis trial: Social mores and obstetrics in the mid-nineteenth century. Drachman, Virginia G., p.166-174; m) Birthing and anesthesia: The debate over twilight sleep. Leavitt, Judith Walzer, p.175-184; n) Chlorotic girls, 1870-1920: A historical perspective on female adolescence. Brumberg, Joan Jacobs, p.186-195; o) Prostitution, venereal disease, and American medicine. Connelly, Mark Thomas, p.196-221; p) "The fashionable diseases": Women's complaints and their treatment in nineteenth-century America. Wood, Ann Douglas, p.222-238; q) The perils of feminist history. Morantz, Regina Markell, p.239-245; r) "All hail to pure cold water!" Sklar, Kathryn Kish, p.246-254; s) The woman behind the trademark. Stage, Sarah, p.255-269; t) The rise and fall of Battey's operation: A fashion in

surgery. Longo, Lawrence D., p.270-284; u) "Safe delivered," but by whom? Midwives and men-midwives in early America. Donegan, Jane B., p.302-317; v) The American midwife controversy: A crisis of professionalization. Kobrin, Frances E., p.318-326; w) Mary Breckinridge, the frontier nursing service, and the introduction of nurse-midwifery in the United States. Dye, Nancy Schrom, p.327-343; x) Making women modern: Middle-class women and health reform in nineteenth-century America. Morantz, Regina Markell, p.346-358; y) Mary Gove Nichols, prophetess of health. Blake, John B., p.359-375; z) Ministries of healing: Mary Baker Eddy, Ellen G. White, and the religion of health. Numbers, Ronald L. and Schoepflin, Rennie B., p.376-389; aa) Feminist showplace. Walsh, Mary Roth, p.392-405; bb) Professionalism, feminism, and gender roles: A comparative study of nineteenth-century medical therapeutics. Morantz, Regina Markell and Zschoche, Sue, p.406-421; cc) Homeopathy and sexual equality: The controversy over coeducation at Cincinnati's Pulte Medical College, 1873-1879. Barlow, William and Powell, David O., p.422-428; dd) On the evolution of women's medical societies. Marrett, Cora Bagley, p.429-437; ee) Doctors or ladies? Women physicians in psychiatric institutions, 1872-1900. McGovern, Constance M., p.438-452; ff) "Neither for the drawing room nor for the kitchen": Private duty nursing in Boston, 1873-1914. Reverby, Susan, p.454-466; gg) "Little world of our own": The Pennsylvania Hospital Training School for Nurses, 1895-1907. Tomes, Nancy, p.467-481; hh) More than "the physician's hand": Skill and authority in twentieth-century nursing. Melosh, Barbara, p.482-496; ii) Mabel K. Staupers and the integration of black nurses into the armed forces. Hine, Darlene Clark, p.497-506.

354. Women and Health: The Politics of Sex in Medicine. Fee, Elizabeth, ed. Farmingdale, NY: Baywood Publishing, 1983.
a) Women and health care: A comparison of theories. Fee, Elizabeth, p.17-34; b) Convenience and the occurrence of births: Induction of labor in the United States and Canada. Rindfuss, Ronald R., et al., p.37-58; c) Vaginal cancer: An iatrogenic disease? Weiss, Kay, p.59-75; d) Sexism and racism in the American health care industry: A comparative analysis. Garrett, Sharon D. and Weaver, Jerry L., p.79-104; e) Women workers in the health service industry. Brown, Carol A., p.105-116; f) Employment and women's health: An analysis of causal relationships. Waldron, Ingrid, p.119-138; g) Do men and women have different jobs because of their biological differences? Messing, Karen, p.139-148; h) The politics of birth control, 1920-1940: The impact of professionals. Gordon, Linda, p.151-175; i) Medicine and patriarchal violence: The social construction of a "private" event. Flitcraft, Anne, Frazier, William and Stark, Evan, p.177-209; j) Chlorosis and chronic disease in 19th-century Britain: The social constitution of somatic illness in a capitalist society. Figlio, Karl, p.213-241; k) Sociobiology: Another biological determinism. Lewontin, R.C., p.243-259.

355. Women and Household Labor. Berk, Sarah Fenstermaker, ed. Beverly Hills, CA: Sage Publications, 1980.
a) Prologue: Reflections on the study of household labor. Oakley, Ann, p.7-14; b) An enlarged human existence? Technology and household work in nineteenth-century America. Strasser, Susan M., p.29-51; c) Housework technology and household work. Robinson, John P., p.53-68; d) Social status of the homemaker. Bose, Christine, p.69-87; e) Satisfaction with housework: The social context. Ferree, Myra Marx, p.89-112; f) The new home economics: An agenda for sociological research. Berk, Richard A., p.113-148; g) Women's life-cycle time allocation: An econometric analysis. Lehrer, Evelyn and Nerlove, Marc, p.149-168; h) Household time: A cross-cultural example. Nelson, Linda, p.169-190; i) Contributions to household labor: Comparing wives' and husbands' reports. Berk, Sarah Fenstermaker and Shih, Anthony, p.191-227; j) Domestic labor as work discipline: The struggle over housework in foster homes. Wittner, Judith G., p.229-247; k) Everyone needs three hands: Doing unpaid and paid work. Glazer, Nona, p.249-274; l) Household work, wage work, and sexual equality. Vanek, Joann, p.275-291.

356. Women and Language in Literature and Society. McConnell-Ginet, Sally, Borker, Ruth and Furman, Nelly, eds. New York: Praeger, 1980.
a) Linguistics and the feminist challenge. McConnell-Ginet, Sally, p.3-25; b) Anthropology: Social and cultural perspectives. Borker, Ruth, p.26-44; c) Textual feminism. Furman, Nelly, p.45-54; d) Proprieters of language. Kramarae, Cheris, p.58-68; e) The psychology of the generic masculine. Martyna, Wendy, p.69-78; f) "Don't 'dear' me!" Manes, Joan and Wolfson, Nessa, p.79-92; g) "Women's language" or "powerless language"? Atkins, Bowman K. and O'Barr, William M., p.93-110; h) How and why are women more polite: Some evidence from a Mayan community. Brown, Penelope, p.111-136; i) Women in their speech communities. Nichols, Patricia C., p.140-149; j) Women's speech: The voice of feminism. Giles, Howard, et al., p.150-156; k) Directive-response speech sequences in girls' and boys' task activities. Goodwin, Marjorie Harness, p.157-173; l) Anger and the politics of naming. Scheman, Naomi, p.174-187; m) Honing a habitable languagescape: Women's images for the new world frontiers. Kolodny, Annette, p.188-204; n) The silence is broken. Donovan, Josephine, p.205-218; o) The "feminine" language of Marianne Moore. Costello, Bonnie, p.222-238; p) The construction of ambiguity in *The Awakening*: A linguistic analysis. Treichler, Paula A., p.239-257; q) Women's autobiography in France: For a dialectics of identification. Miller, Nancy K., p.258-273; r) Snatches of conversation. Gallop, Jane, p.274-283; s) Writing like a woman. Kamuf, Peggy, p.284-299; t) Reading reading: Echo's abduction of language. Greenberg, Caren, p.300-309; u) Unmaking and making in *To the Lighthouse*. Spivak, Gayatri C., p.310-327.

357. Women and Low Pay. Sloane, Peter J., ed. London: Macmillan, 1980.

a) Low pay amongst women - the facts. Siebert, W.S. and Sloane, Peter J., p.9-56; b) Relative female earnings in Great Britain and the impact of legislation. Chiplin, Brian, Curran, Margaret M. and Parsley, C. J., p.57-126; c) The structure of labour markets and low pay for women. Sloane, Peter J., p.127-164; d) Low pay and female employment in Canada with selected references to the USA. Gunderson, Morely and Jain, Harish C., p.165-222; e) Shortcomings and problems in analyses of women and low pay. Siebert, W.S. and Sloane, Peter J., p.223-252.

358. Women and Media. Baehr, Helen, ed. New York: Pergamon Press, 1980.
a) Women in broadcasting (U.S.) *de jure, de facto*. Eddings, Barbara Murray, p.1-13; b) Watching the family. Booth, Jane, p.15-28; c) The 'liberated woman' in television drama. Baehr, Helen, p.29-39; d) Women and radio. Karpf, Anne, p.41-54; e) Feminist art practice and the mass media: A 'personal' account. Dalton, Pen, p.55-57; f) Camerawoman obscura: A 'personal' account, p.59-61; g) 'The advice of a real friend': Codes of intimacy and oppression in women's magazines 1937-1955, p.63-78; h) Overworking the working woman: The double day in a mass magazine. Glazer, Nona, p.79-93; i) Women in Latin American fotonovelas: From Cinderella to Mata Hari. Flora, Cornelia Butler, p.95-104; j) He admits...but she confesses. Stewart, Penni, p.105-114.

359. Women and Mental Health. Howell, Elizabeth and Bayes, Marjorie, eds. New York: Basic Books, 1981.
a) Women: From Freud to the present. Howell, Elizabeth, p.3-25; b) Early origins of envy and devaluation of women: Implications for sex-role stereotypes. Lerner, Harriet E., p.26-40; c) Psychological consequences of sexual inequality. Miller, Jean B. and Mothner, Ira, p.41-50; d) The conflict between nurturance and autonomy in mother-daughter relationships and within feminism. Flax, Jane, p.51-69; e) Psychology of women: Perspectives on theory and research for the eighties. Sobel, Emilie F., p.70-78; f) The prevalence of gender-role bias in mental health services. Bayes, Marjorie, p.83-85; g) Sex-role stereotypes and clinical judgements of mental health. Broverman, Inge K., et al., p.86-97; h) Report of the task force on sex bias and sex-role stereotyping in psychotherapeutic practice. Brodsky, Annette M. and Holroyd, Jean, p.98-112; i) The psychiatrist-woman patient relationship. Stephenson, P. Susan and Walker, Gillian A., p.113-130; j) A review of women's psychotropic drug use. Cooperstock, Ruth, p.131-140; k) Psychiatry's problem with no name: Therapist-patient sex. Davidson, Viriginia, p.141-148; l) The influence of gender on diagnosis and psychopathology. Howell, Elizabeth, p.153-159; m) Sex differences and the epidemiology of depression. Klerman, Gerald L. and Weissman, Myrna M., p.160-195; n) The hysterical personality: A "woman's disease". Lerner, Harriet E., p.196-206; o) Madness in women. Lewis, Helen B., p.207-227; p) Phobias after marriage: Women's declaration of dependence.

Symonds, Alexandra, p.228-239; q) A starving family: An interactional view of anorexia nervosa. Mazur, Dorothy Conrad, p.240-247; r) Cinderella's stepsisters: A feminist perspective on anorexia nervosa and bulimia. Boskind-Lodahl, Marlene, p.248-262; s) Group process for women with orgasmic difficulties. Ayres, Toni and Barbach, Lonnie Garfield, p.263-268; t) Issues in the treatment of female addiction: A review and critique of the literature. Berger, Lisa H., Cuskey, Walter R. and Densen-Gerber, Judianne, p.269-295; u) The female alcoholic. Fraser, Judy, p.296-305; v) Women's treatment needs. Bayes, Marjorie and Howell, Elizabeth, p.309-310; w) A study of attitudes toward menarche in white middle-class American adolescent girls. Whisnant, Lynn and Zegans, Leonard, p.311-324; x) Teenage pregnancy: A research review. Chilman, Catherine S., p.325-339; y) Psychological reactions of postpartum women. Howell, Elizabeth, p.340-346; z) Attitudes toward parenting in dual-career families. Johnson, Colleen Leahy and Johnson, Frank Arvid, p.347-356; aa) Female-headed families: Trends and implications. Reinhardt, Hazel and Wattenberg, Esther, p.357-372; bb) Lesbian families: Cultural and clinical issues. Hall, Marny, p.373-384; cc) Midlife concerns of women: Implications of the menopause. Notman, Malkah T., p.385-394; dd) Abortion counseling. Kahn-Edrington, Marla, p.395-399; ee) Abortion counseling with adolescents. Gedan, Sharon, p.400-405; ff) Divorced women. Carter, Dianne K. and Rawlings, Edna I., p.406-410; gg) Postmastectomy counseling. Fisher, Joan Z. and Joiner, James G., p.411-418; hh) Group work with widows. Toth, Andre and Toth, Susan, p.419-425; ii) Psychosocial aspects of wife battering. Star, Barbara, et al., p.426-439; jj) Wife battering and the maintenance of gender roles: A sociopsychological perspective. Bayes, Marjorie, p.440-448; kk) Rape: Sexual disruption and recovery. Burgess, Ann Wolbert and Holmstrom, Lynda Lytle, p.449-461; ll) Development of a medical center rape crisis intervention program. McCombie, Sharon L., et al., p.462-469; mm) The rape victim: Psychodynamic considerations. Nadelson, Carol C. and Notman, Malkah T., p.470-480; nn) Identification and treatment of incest victims. Gelinas, Denise J., p.481-496; oo) Incest between fathers and daughters. Herman, Judith and Hirschman, Lisa, p.497-504; pp) Psychotherapy with women clients: The impact of feminism. Howell, Elizabeth, p.509-513; qq) Women patients and women therapists: Some issues that come up in psychotherapy. Goz, Rebecca, p.514-533; rr) Adaptive and pathogenic aspects of sex-role stereotypes: Implications for parenting and psychotherapy. Lerner, Harriet E., p.534-543; ss) A feminist works with nontraditional clients. Israel, Joan, p.544-552; tt) A feminist approach to family therapy. Hare-Mustin, Rachel T., p.553-571; uu) The consciousness-raising group as a model for therapy with women. Brodsky, Annette M., p.572-580; vv) The psychotherapeutic impact of women's consciousness-raising groups. Lieberman, Morton A., et al., p.581-599; ww) Where do we go from here? Howell, Elizabeth, p.603-606; xx) A decade of feminist influence on psychotherapy. Brodsky,

Annette M., p.607-619; yy) New directions in counseling women. Worell, Judith, p.620-637.

360. Women and Mental Health Policy. Walker, Lenore E., ed. Beverly Hills, CA: Sage Publications, 1984.
a) Women in the mental health delivery system: Implications for research and public policy. Russo, Nancy Felipe, p.21-41; b) Female psychologists in policymaking positions. Stringer, Donna M. and Welton, Nancy R., p.43-58; c) Women and psychotherapy research. Auerbach, Arthur H. and Johnson, Marilyn, p.59-77; d) The relational self in women: Developmental theory and public policy. Kaplan, Alexandra G. and Surrey, Janet L., p.78-94; e) Women, spirituality, and mental health. Hendricks, Maureen C., p.95-115; f) Reproductive advancements: Theory, research applications, and psychological issues. Nadelson, Carol C. and Notman, Malkah T., p.117-133; g) Inequality and mental health: Low income and minority women. Belle, Deborah, p.135-150; h) Lesbian women and mental health policy. Lyon, Phyllis and Martin, Del, p.151-179; i) Women's mental health in times of transition. Bernard, Jessie, p.181-195; j) Violence against women: Implications for mental health policy. Walker, Lenore E., p.197-206; k) Sexual intimacy between psychotherapists and clients: Policy implications for the future. Bouhoutsos, Jacqueline C., p.207-227; l) Women and work: Implications for mental health. Frieze, Irene Hanson and Sales, Esther, p.229-246; m) New sex therapies: Policy and practice. Cammaert, Lorna P., p.247-266; n) Feminist therapy: Implications for practitioners. Rosewater, Lynne Bravo, p.267-279; o) Media psychology and public policy. Brown, Laura S., p.281-294; p) Professional psychology's response to women's mental health needs. Cummings, Nicholas A., p.295-305.

361. Women and Minorities in Science: Strategies for Increasing Participation. Humphreys, Sheila M., ed. Boulder, CO: Westview Press, 1982.
a) Leverage for equal opportunity through mastery of mathematics. Sells, Lucy W., p.7-26; b) Labor force participation of women baccalaureates in science. Vetter, Betty M., p.27-37; c) EQUALS: Working with educators. Kreinberg, Nancy, p.39-54; d) Improving minority preparation for math-based disciplines. Finnell, Robert A., p.55-64; e) A short-term intervention program: Math-science conferences. Cronkite, Ruth C. and Perl, Teri Hoch, p.65-85; f) Affirmative action programs that work. George, Yolanda Scott, p.87-98; g) Career paths for women in physics. Max, Claire Ellen, p.99-118; h) Increasing the participation of college women in mathematics-related fields. Blum, Lenore and Givant, Steven, p.119-137; i) Women in engineering: A dynamic approach. Daniels, Jane Z. and LeBold, William K., p.139-163; j) Effectiveness of science career conferences. Humphreys, Sheila M., p.165-186; k) Strategies to increase participation of minorities in medicine. Allender, Jeanne G., Epps, A. Cherrie and Pisano, Joseph C., p.187-201; l) An evaluation of programs for reentry women scientists. Ingison, Linda J. and Lantz, Alma E., p.203-218.

362. Women and Politics in Twentieth Century Africa and Asia. Sutlive, Vinson H., Altshuler, Nathan and Zamora, Mario D., eds. Williamsburg, VA: Department of Anthropology, College of William and Mary, 1981.
a) Women's politics in Africa. Staudt, Kathleen A., p.1-28; b) An examination of education, social change, and national development policy: The case of Kenyan women. Lindsay, Beverly, p.29-48; c) Muslim Middle Eastern women's participation in violent political conflict: Causes and characteristics. Danforth, Sandra, p.49-68; d) The mobilization of Iraqi women into the wage labor force. Joseph, Suad, p.69-90; e) Gender, politics and modernization: The Indian case. Bald, Suresht R. and Mukhopadhyay, Carol C., p.91-121; f) "Big women" and politics in a Philippine fishing town. Szanton, M. Cristina Blanc, p.123-141; g) The politics of healing in Malaysia. Laderman, Carol, p.143-158.

363. Women and Politics in Twentieth Century Latin America. McGee, Sandra F., ed. Williamsburg, VA: Dept. of Anthropology, College of William and Mary, 1981.
a) In defense of motherhood: Divorce law in Cuba during the early Republic. Wheeler, Lynn Stoner, p.1-31; b) Working class Afro-Surinamese women and national politics: Traditions and changes in an independent state. Brana-Shute, Rosemary, p.33-56; c) Women and revolution: The brigadas femeninas and the Mexican Cristero Rebellion, 1926-1929. Miller, Barbara, p.57-66; d) Patrons, politics, and schools: An arena for Brazilian women. Miller, Linda, p.67-89; e) Social policy and women in Latin America: The need for a new model. Flora, Cornelia Butler, p.91-105; f) Research on women in Latin America: Problems of networking and comparative analysis in the last decade. Schmidt, Steffen W., p.107-133.

364. Women and Property - Women as Property. Hirschon, Renée, ed. London: Croom Helm, 1984.
a) Introduction: Property, power and gender relations. Hirschon, Renée, p.1-22; b) Cognatic descent, Islamic law and women's property on the East African coast. Caplan, Patricia, p.23-43; c) The exchange of women and property: Marriage in post-revolutionary China. Croll, Elisabeth, p.44-61; d) Dowry in North India: Its consequences for women. Sharma, Ursula, p.62-74; e) Female power and the inequality of wealth and motherhood in north-western Portugal. Pina-Cabral, Joãe, p.75-91; f) The legal and social transformation of rural women in Aegean Turkey. Starr, June, p.92-116; g) Divorce and the disadvantaged: African women in urban South Africa. Burman, Sandra, p.117-139; h) 'Fear woman': Property and modes of production in urban Ghana. Westwood, Sallie, p.140-157; i) Subject or object? Women and the circulation of valuables in highlands New Guinea. Strathern, Marilyn, p.158-175; j) Men and women, kinship and property: Some general issues. Whitehead, Ann, p.176-192.

365. Women and Psychotherapy: An Assessment of Research and Practice. Brodsky, Annette M. and Hare-Mustin, Rachel T., eds. New York: The Guilford Press, 1980.

a) Gender and psychotherapeutic outcome. Howard, Kenneth I. and Orlinsky, David E., p.3-34; b) Therapist attitudes and sex-role stereotyping. Sherman, Julia A., p.35-66; c) Gender and the process of therapy. Johnson, Marilyn and Marecek, Jeanne, p.67-93; d) Depression. Weissman, Myrna M., p.97-112; e) Anxieties: Agoraphobia and hysteria. Chambless, Dianne L. and Goldstein, Alan J., p.113-134; f) Eating disorders: Obesity and anorexia. Wooley, Orland W. and Wooley, Susan C., p.135-158; g) Marital and family conflicts. Gurman, Alan S. and Klein, Marjorie H., p.159-188; h) Psychodynamic perspectives. Kaplan, Alexandra G. and Yasinski, Lorraine, p.191-215; i) Behavior therapies. Blechman, Elaine A., p.217-244; j) Feminist therapy. Gilbert, Lucia Albino, p.245-265; k) Consciousness-raising and self-help. Kravetz, Diane, p.267-283; l) Minority women: Social-cultural issues. Wilkinson, Doris Y., p.285-304; m) Reproductive crises. Nadelson, Carol and Notman, Malkah T., p.307-338; n) Battered women. Walker, Lenore E., p.339-363; o) Women in marital transition. McMahon, Sarah Lynne, p.365-382; p) Psychotherapy and women: Priorities for research. Brodsky, Annette M. and Hare-Mustin, Rachel T., p.385-409.

366. Women and Religion in America - Volume 1: The Nineteenth Century. Ruether, Rosemary Radford and Keller, Rosemary Skinner, eds. San Francisco: Harper & Row, 1981.
a) Women and revivalism. Blauvelt, Martha Tomhave, p.1-45; b) Women in utopian movements. Ruether, Rosemary Radford, p.46-100; c) The leadership of nuns in immigrant Catholicism. Ewens, Mary, p.101-149; d) The Jewish woman's encounter with American culture. Braude, Ann, p.150-192; e) The struggle for the right to preach. Zikmund, Barbara Brown, p.193-241; f) Lay women in the Protestant tradition. Keller, Rosemary Skinner, p.242-293; g) Women in social reform movements. Gifford, Carolyn De Swarte, p.294-340.

367. Women and Religion in America - Volume 2: The Colonial and Revolutionary Periods. Ruether, Rosemary Radford and Keller, Rosemary Skinner, eds. San Francisco, CA: Harper & Row, 1983.
a) American Indian women and religion. Druke, Mary and Peterson, Jacqueline, p.1-41; b) Women and religion in Spanish America. Lavrin, Asunción, p.42-78; c) Women in colonial French America. Allen, Christine, p.79-131; d) New England women: Ideology and experience in first-generation Puritanism (1630-1650). Keller, Rosemary Skinner, p.132-192; e) The religious experience of Southern women. Mathews, Alice E., p.193-232; f) Black women and religion in the colonial period. Webb, Lillian Ashcraft, p.233-259; g) Women in sectarian and utopian groups. Prelinger, Catherine M. and Ruether, Rosemary Radford, p.260-315; h) Women and revivalism: The Puritan and Wesleyan traditions. Blauvelt, Martha Tomhave and Keller, Rosemary Skinner, p.316-367; i) Women, civil religion, and the American Revolution. Keller, Rosemary Skinner, p.368-408.

368. Women and Revolution in Iran. Nashat, Guity, ed. Boulder, CO: Westview Press, 1983.
a) Women in pre-revolutionary Iran: A historical overview. Nashat, Guity, p.5-36; b) Status of women in the Qur'an. Rahman, Fazlur, p.37-54; c) Women in Shi'i Fiqh: Images through the Hadith. Ferdows, Adele K. and Ferdows, Amir H., p.55-68; d) Social and economic change in the role of women, 1956-1978. Mirani, S. Kaveh, p.69-86; e) Fatimeh as a role model in the works of Ali Shari'ati. Hermansen, Marcia K., p.87-96; f) An analysis of Fida'i and Mujahidin positions on women's rights. Sanasarian, Eliz, p.97-108; g) To veil or not to veil: A matter of protest or policy. Betteridge, Anne H., p.109-128; h) Revitalization: Some reflections on the work of Saffar-Zadeh. Milani, Farzaneh, p.129-140; i) Poor women and social consciousness in revolutionary Iran. Bauer, Janet, p.141-170; j) Aliabad women: Revolution as religious activity. Hegland, Mary E., p.171-194; k) Women in the ideology of the Islamic Republic. Nashat, Guity, p.195-216; l) State ideology and village women. Friedl, Erika, p.217-230; m) The institution of Mut'a marriage in Iran: A formal and historical perspective. Haeri, Shahla, p.231-252; n) Family planning in post-revolutionary Iran. Mossavar-Rahmani, Yasmin L., p.253-262; o) Women imprisoned in the kingdom of the Mullahs. Dwyer, Cynthia Brown, p.263-284.

369. Women and Revolution: A Discussion of the Unhappy Marriage of Marxism and Feminism. Sargent, Lydia, ed. London: Pluto Press, 1981.
a) New left women and men: The honeymoon is over. Sargent, Lydia, p.xi-xxxii; b) The unhappy marriage of Marxism and feminism: Towards a more progressive union. Hartmann, Heidi, p.1-41; c) Beyond the unhappy marriage: A critique of the dual systems theory. Young, Iris, p.43-69; d) Socialism, feminism, and gay/lesbian liberation. Riddiough, Christine, p.71-89; e) The incompatible menage à trois: Marxism, feminism, and racism. Joseph, Gloria, p.91-107; f) The unhappy marriage of Marxism and feminism: Can it be saved? Ehrlich, Carol, p.109-133; g) What is the real material base of patriarchy and capital? Harding, Sandra, p.135-163; h) Capitalism is an advanced stage of patriarchy: But Marxism is not feminism. Al-Hibri, Azizah, p.165-193; i) Marxism and feminism: Unhappy marriage, trial separation or something else? Vogel, Lise, p.195-217; j) Cultural Marxism: Nonsynchrony and feminist practice. Hicks, Emily, p.219-237; k) Mothers, fathers, and children: From private to public patriarchy. Brown, Carol, p.239-267; l) The marriage of capitalist and patriarchcal ideologies: Meanings of male bonding and male ranking in U.S. culture. Stewart, Katie, p.269-311; m) The unhappy marriage of patriarchy and capitalism. Ferguson, Ann and Folbre, Nancy, p.313-338; n) Reform and/or revolution: Towards a unified women's movement. Eisenstein, Zillah, p.339-362.

370. Women and Slavery in Africa. Robertson, Claire C. and Klein, Martin A., eds. Madison, WI: University of Wisconsin Press, 1983.

a) Women's importance in African slave systems. Klein, Martin A. and Robertson, Claire C., p.3-25; b) African women in the Atlantic slave trade. Klein, Herbert S., p.29-38; c) Sexual demography: The impact of the slave trade on family structure. Thornton, John, p.39-48; d) Female slavery. Meillassoux, Claude, p.49-66; e) Women in slavery in the western Sudan. Klein, Martin A., p.67-88; f) Sustaining the system: Trading towns along the middle Zaire. Harms, Robert, p.95-110; g) Slavery and reproductive labor in Mombasa. Strobel, Margaret, p.111-129; h) The Songhay-Zarma female slave: Relations of production and ideological status. Olivier de Sardan, Jean-Pierre, p.130-143; i) Women in slavery among the Mangbetu c.1800-1910. Keim, Curtis A., p.144-159; j) Slave wives, free sisters: Bakongo women and slavery c.1700-1850. Broadhead, Susan Herlin, p.160-181; k) The story of Swema: Female vulnerability in nineteenth century East Africa. Alpers, Edward A., p.185-199; l) Post-proclamation slavery in Accra: A female affair? Robertson, Claire C., p.220-242; m) Appendix: A note on Anlo (Ewe) slavery and the history of a slave. Nukunya, G.K., p.243-245; n) Bwanikwa: Consciousness and protest among slave women in Central Africa, 1886-1911. Wright, Marcia, p.246-267; o) Slaves, slave owners, and slave dealers: Sherbro coast and hinterland. MacCormack, Carol P., p.271-294; p) A Nhara of the Guinea-Bissau region: Mãe Aurélia Correia. Brooks, George E., p.295-319; q) Women slavers of Guinea-Conakry. Mouser, Bruce L., p.320-339; r) Servitude and worldly success in the palace of Dahomey. Bay, Edna G., p.340-367.

371. Women and Space: Ground Rules and Social Maps. Ardener, Shirley, ed. London: Croom Helm, 1981.
a) Ground rules and social maps for women: An introduction. Ardener, Shirley, p.11-34; b) Andean women and the concept of space/time. Skar, Sarah, p.35-49; c) Women's space in a men's house: The British House of Commons. Rodgers, Silvia, p.50-71; d) Essential objects and the sacred: Interior and exterior space in an urban Greek locality. Hirschon, Renée, p.72-88; e) The problem of privacy in Mediterranean anthropology. Sciama, Lidia, p.89-111; f) Sexual prohibitions, shared space and fictive marriages in Shi'ite Iran. Khatib-Chahidi, Jane, p.112-133; g) Place and face: Of women in Doshman Ziari, Iran. Wright, Susan, p.136-157; h) The sexual division of domestic space among two Soviet minorities: The Georgians and the Tadjiks. Dragadze, Tamara, p.158-184; i) Spatial domains and women's mobility in Yorubaland, Nigeria. Callaway, Helen, p.168-186; j) Where women must dominate: Response to oppression in a South African urban community. Ridd, Rosemary, p.187-201; k) Private parts in public places: The case of actresses. Blair, Juliet, p.205-228.

372. Women and Sport: An Historical, Biological, Physiological and Sportsmedical Approach. Borms, J., Hebbelinck, M. and Venerando, A., eds. Basel, Switzerland: S. Karger, 1980.
a) Women and sport: A question of freedom. Ferris, E., p.4-10; b) An historical overview. Howell, R., p.11-15; c)

Women and sport in ancient Greece. Lämmer, M., p.16-23; d) Women and sport during the Renaissance. English, E. B., p.24-30; e) Development of women's sport in the 20th century. Simri, U., p.31-44; f) Women and sports in Egypt: History and problems. Badr, S. M., p.45-51; g) An outline of the history of women and western sport in Japan. Seiwa, H., p.52-57; h) The influence of women doctors on the origins of women's sports in Germany. Pfister, G., p.58-65; i) The "sporty" Australians. Jobling, I. F., p.66-72; j) Introduction to the biology of the female athlete. Poortmans, J., p.73-76; k) Physiological and metabolic responses of female athletes during laboratory and field exercises. Berg, A. and Keul, J., p.77-96; l) Is the significance of muscle fibre types to muscle metabolism different in females than in males? Jacobs, I. and Karlsson, J., p.97-101; m) Fundamental performance characteristics in females and males. Komi, P. V., p.102-108; n) Women and sport: An introduction to the physiological aspects. Wilmore, J. H., p.109-111; o) Specificity of swim training on maximal oxygen uptake: An inter-sex comparison. Lavoie, J. M. and Thibault, G., p.112-118; p) Measurement of maximal short-term (anaerobic) power output during cycling. Boreham, A. and Sargeant, A. J., p.119-124; q) Short time, maximal muscular performance: Relation to muscle lactate and fiber type in females. Jacobs, I. and Tesch, P., p.125-132; r) Reproducibility of aerobic power and related physiological variables in women. Keizer, H. A., Kuipers, H. and Verstappen, F. T. J., p.133-140; s) Exercise-induced changes in estradiol metabolism and their possible physiological meaning. Keizer, H. A., et al., p.141-147; t) Effects of training intensity on cardiac output in young women. Avon, G. and Massicotte, D., p.148-154; u) VO2 max and anaerobic threshold in pre- and post-pubescent girls. Girandola, R. N., et al., p.155-161; v) Anaerobic energy metabolism of women. Bachl, N., Iwanoff, I. and Prokop, L., p.162-167; w) Energy cost of ice skating with figure skates for women. Léger, L. A., p.168-174; x) Comparison of exercise between females and males. Maresh, C. M., Noble, B. J. and Ritchey, M., p.175-179; y) Pituitary response to physical exercise: Sex differences. Moretti, C., et al., p.180-186; z) Effect of increased intensity of training on maximum oxygen uptake and muscular performance of young female cross-country skiers. Rahkila, P. and Rusko, H. K., p.187-194; aa) Menstrual effects of athletic training. Mann, G. V., p.195-199; bb) Iron deficiency in female athletes. Strauzenberg, S. E., et al., p.200-208; cc) Sport and reproduction in women. Zichella, L., et al., p.209-215; dd) Foot disorders of female marathon runners before and after a marathon race. Brüggemann, G. and Koring, W., p.216-219; ee) Traumatological aspects of sports of high achievements for women. Mironova, Z., p.220-225.

373. Women and Technological Change in Developing Countries. Dauber, Roslyn and Cain, Melinda L., eds. Boulder, CO: Westview Press, 1981.
a) Foreword: Seeing our global economy whole. Henderson, Hazel, p.xvii-xxii; b) Overview: Women and technology — resources for our future. Cain, Melinda L.,

p.3-8; c) Integration into what? Reflections on development planning for women. Boulding, Elise, p.9-32; d) Women, technology and the development process. International Labor Organization, Office for Women, p.33-47; e) New technologies for food-related activities: An equity strategy. Tinker, Irene, p.51-88; f) Impact of selected industrial technologies on women in Mexico. Srinivasan, Mangalam, p.89-108; g) Women and the development of "underdevelopment": The African experience. Seidman, Ann, p.109-126; h) Java, Indonesia: The introduction of rice processing technology. Cain, Melinda L., p.127-137; i) Baseline study for socio-economic evaluation of Tangaye solar site. Hemmings-Gapihan, Grace S., p.139-148; j) Changing role of Maya mothers and daughters. Elmendorf, Mary, p.149-179; k) Women's work in multinational electronics factories. Lim, Linda Y. C., p.181-190; l) Technologies appropriate for women: Theory, practice and policy. Carr, Marilyn, p.193-203; m) The plight of the invisible farmer: The effect of national agricultural policy on women in Africa. Fortmann, Louise, p.205-214; n) The differential impact of programs and policies on women in development. Papanek, Hanna, p.215-227; o) Roles of women: UNCSTD background discussion paper. Leet, Mildred Robbins, p.229-236; p) Applying policy analysis to women and technology: A framework for consideration. Dauber, Rosyln, p.237-251.

374. Women and the Cuban Revolution: Speeches & Documents by Fidel Castro, Vilma Espin & Others. Stone, Elizabeth, ed. New York: Pathfinder Press, 1981.
a) The early years. Espin, Vilma, p.33-46; b) The revolution within the Revolution. Castro, Fidel, p.48-54; c) The struggle for women's equality. Castro, Fidel, p.55-72; d) Thesis: On the full exercise of women's equality. Communist Party of Cuba, p.74-105; e) Into the third decade. Castro, Fidel, p.107-132; f) Appendix A: Maternity law for working women. Fernández Padilla, Oscar, p.133-139; g) Appendix B: The family code. Cuban Family Code, p.140-151.

375. Women and the Law: Property, Family and the Legal Profession. Weisberg, D. Kelly, ed. Cambridge, MA: Schenkman Publishing, 1982.
a) Women as property in the early Roman empire. Treggiari, Susan, p.7-33; b) Widows' rights in Anglo-Saxon law. Rivers, Theodore John, p.35-43; c) *Merchet* and women's property rights in medieval England. Searle, Eleanor, p.45-68; d) The married women's property acts, 1839-1865: Reform, reaction or revolution? Speth, Linda E., p.69-91; e) Rape in thirteenth-century England: A study of the common-law courts. Kittel, Ruth, p.101-115; f) Under great temptations here: Women and divorce law in puritan Massachusetts. Weisberg, D. Kelly, p.117-131; g) The law of husband and wife in nineteenth-century America: Changing views of divorce. Hindus, Michael S. and Withey, Lynne E., p.133-153; h) Historical background of "protective" labor legislation: *Muller v. Oregon*. Erickson, Nancy S., p.155-186; i) Adult derivative benefits in social security: A women's issue. Blumberg, Grace Ganz, p.187-221; j) Barred from the bar: Women and

legal education in the United States, 1870-1890. Weisberg, D. Kelly, p.231-258; k) Clara Shortridge Foltz: Pioneer in the law. Brandt, Susan L., Milrod, Patience and Schwartz, Mortimer D., p.259-281; l) Women's entry into corporate law firms. Epstein, Cynthia Fuchs, p.283-305.

376. Women and the Law: Women and Criminal Law. Weisberg, D. Kelly, ed. Cambridge, MA: Schenkman Publishing, 1982.
a) The certain wages of sin: Sentence and punishment of female felons in colonial Massachusetts, 1673-1774. Hull, N. E. H., p.7-25; b) Dealing with dependence: Paternalism and tax evasion in eighteenth-century Rhode Island. Crane, Elaine F., p.27-44; c) The crime of precocious sexuality: Female juvenile delinquency and the Progressive Era. Schlossman, Steven and Wallach, Stephanie, p.45-84; d) The weaker vessel: Legal versus social reality in mental commitments in nineteenth-century New York. Dwyer, Ellen, p.85-106; e) Sex-based discrimination in the mental institutionalization of women. Lerner, Judith and Roth, Robert T., p.107-139; f) Nineteenth-century women's prison reform and its legacy. Freedman, Estelle, p.141-157; g) Women before the law: Females as felons and prey in fourteenth-century England. Hanawalt, Barbara A., p.165-195; h) The criminality of women in eighteenth-century England. Beattie, J. M., p.197-238; i) The incarceration of women: A search for answers. Jensen, Gary F., p.239-257; j) Sex differences in the processing of criminal defendants. Cardascia, John, Nagel, Ilene H. and Ross, Catherine E., p.259-282; k) Criminological theory: Its ideology and implications concerning women. Smart, Carol, p.283-296.

377. Women and the Mathematical Mystique. Fox, Lynn H., Brody, Linda and Tobin, Dianne, eds. Baltimore, MD: Johns Hopkins University Press, 1980.
a) Female mathematicians: A contemporary appraisal. Luchins, Abraham S. and Luchins, Edith H., p.7-22; b) The creative woman mathematician. Helson, Ravenna, p.23-54; c) Is mathematics a sexist discipline? Ernest, John, p.57-65; d) The mathematics filter and the education of women and minorities. Sells, Lucy W., p.66-75; e) Sex-related differences in mathematics achievement: Where and why. Fennema, Elizabeth, p.76-93; f) Sex differences in the development of precocious mathematical talent. Cohn, Sanford J. and Fox, Lynn H., p.94-111; g) An experiment in mathematics education at the college level. MacDonald, Carolyn T., p.115-137; h) Factors affecting female participation in advanced placement programs in mathematics, chemistry, and physics. Casserly, Patricia Lund, p.138-163; i) An accelerative intervention program for mathematically gifted girls. Brody, Linda and Fox, Lynn H., p.164-178; j) Career interests and career education: A key to change. Fox, Lynn H. and Tobin, Dianne, p.179-191; k) Conclusions: What do we know and where should we go? Fox, Lynn H., p.195-208.

378. Women and the Public Sphere: A Critique of Sociology and Politics. Siltanen, Janet and Stanworth, Michelle, eds.

London: Hutchinson, 1984.
a) Male and female: Job versus gender models in the sociology of work. Feldberg, Roslyn and Glenn, Evelyn Nakano, p.23-36; b) Industrial radicalism and the domestic division of labor. Watt, Ian, p.37-46; c) Workers side by side: Women and the trade union movement. Hunt, Pauline, p.47-53; d) Militancy and acquiescence among women workers. Purcell, Kate, p.54-67; e) Women as employees: Social consciousness and collective action. Brown, Richard, p.68-74; f) Unions: The men's affair? Beynon, Huw and Blackburn, Robert, p.75-88; g) Unity is strength? Feminism and the labor movement. Barrett, Michèle, p.89-95; h) Politics an unnatural practice: Political science looks at female participation. Bourque, Susan and Grossholtz, Jean, p.103-121; i) Women: If not apolitical, then conservative. Goot, Murray and Reid, Elizabeth, p.122-136; j) Women and voting in Britain. Hills, Jill, p.137-139; k) The party identifications of women: Parkin put to the test. Taylor, Stan, p.140-144; l) Candidate evaluations by men and women. Andersen, Kristi and Shabad, Goldie, p.145-155; m) Gender, levels of political thinking and political action. Farah, Barbara and Jennings, M. Kent, p.156-159; n) Women in positions of political leadership in Britain, France and West Germany. Sanzone, Donna S., p.160-175; o) Beyond leadership. Wainwright, Hilary, p.176-282; p) The politics of private woman and public man. Siltanen, Janet and Stanworth, Michelle, p.185-205.

379. Women and the Structure of Society: Selected Research from the Fifth Berkshire Conference on the History of Women. Harris, Barbara J. and McNamara, JoAnn K., eds. Durham, NC: Duke University Press, 1984.
a) Glimpses of Muslim urban women in classical Islam. Wilson, Boydena R., p.5-11; b) Piety and kin: The limits of antebellum Southern women's reform. Friedman, Jean E., p.12-19; c) The planter's wife revisited: Women, equity law, and the Chancery Court in seventeenth-century Maryland. Gampel, Gwen Victor, p.20-35; d) Aristocratic widows in fifteenth-century England. Rosenthal, Joel T., p.36-47; e) Was she a good mother? Some thoughts on a new issue for feminist biography. Antler, Joyce, p.53-66; f) Linnaeus's daughters: Women and British botany. Shteir, Ann B., p.67-73; g) The holy woman and the urban community in sixteenth-century Avila. Bilinkoff, Jodi, p.74-80; h) Right-wing female activists in Buenos Aires, 1900-1932. McGee, Sandra F., p.85-97; i) The London Biblewomen and Nurses Mission, 1857-1880: Class relations/women's relations. Ducrocq, Françoise, p.98-107; j) The ethnological mirror: American evangelical women and their heathen sisters, 1870-1910. Brumberg, Joan Jacobs, p.108-128; k) "My spirit eye": Some functions of spiritual and visionary experience in the lives of five black women preachers, 1810-1880. Humez, Jean M., p.129-143; l) City mothers, city daughters, and the dance hall girls: The limits of female political power in San Francisco, 1913. Gullett, Gayle, p.149-159; m) The limitations of sisterhood: Elizabeth Cady Stanton and division in the American suffrage movement, 1875-1902. DuBois, Ellen, p.160-169; n) Feminism, professionalism, and

germs: A study of the thought of Mary Putnam Jacobi and Elizabeth Blackwell. Morantz, Regina Markell, p.170-185; o) Jewish involvement in the New York City woman suffrage movement. Lerner, Elinor, p.191-205; p) "If eight hours seems few to you...": Women workers' strikes in Italian rice fields, 1901-1906. Zappi, Elda Gentili, p.206-214; q) Responses to the political activism of Women of the People in revolutionary Paris, 1789-1793. Applewhite, Harriet B. and Levy, Darline Gay, p.215-231; r) The effects of the Chinese Revolution on women and their families. Frenier, Mariam Darce, p.232-252.

380. Women and the World of Work. Hoiberg, Anne, ed. New York: Plenum Press, 1982.
a) Women as world makers. Pintasilgo, Maria de Lourdes, p.21-34; b) The education and employment of women scientists and engineers in the United States. Hornig, Lilli S., p.35-53; c) Elected women: Skewers of the political system. Stiehm, Judith Hicks, p.55-64; d) The relationship between the labor force employment of women and the changing social organization in Canada. Marsden, Lorna R., p.65-76; e) Power and political behaviors in organizations: A new frontier for research on male/female differences. Schein, Virginia E., p.77-84; f) Sex-role stereotypes and personal attributes within a developmental framework. Rosen, Anne-Sofie, p.85-93; g) Bringing down the rear: The decline in the economic position of single-mother families. Brown, Clair (Vickery), p.109-127; h) Job creation and unemployment for Canadian women. Armstrong, Hugh and Armstrong, Pat, p.129-152; i) Poverty viewed as a woman's problem - The U.S. case. Chapman, Gordon R. and Chapman, Jane Roberts, p.153-177; j) Poverty, work, and mental health: The experience of low-income mothers. Belle, Deborah E. and Tebbets, Ruth, p.179-188; k) Microeconomic effects of women entering the labor force. Reagan, Barbara B., p.203-221; l) Women's work and the family wage in Canada. Connelly, M. Patricia, p.223-237; m) A statistical analysis of female participation in work and the effects on the population and socioeconomic development: A case study of Greece. Athanassiou, Stylianos K., p.239-253; n) Labor force participation and earnings of women in Andalusia. Riboud, Michelle, p.255-267; o) Economic aspects of female labor force participation in the Federal Republic of Germany. Franz, Wolfgang, p.269-278; p) Child care use and constraints in the United States. Presser, Harriet B., p.295-304; q) The attitude of Danish mothers to child care, 1975 to 1979. Transgaard, Henning, p.305-320; r) Research on women's work and the family at the urban institute. Tangri, Sandra S., p.321-330; s) Women's work participation and the economic support of children. Bergmann, Barbara R., p.331-339.

381. Women and Theatre: Calling the Shots. Todd, Susan, ed. London: Faber and Faber, 1984.
a) Right out in front. Walter, Harriet, p.11-23; b) But will men like it? Or living as a feminist writer without committing murder. Lavery, Bryony, p.24-32; c) Box of tricks. Seymour, Di, p.33-46; d) Directions. Brighton, Pam, p.47-

61; e) Interpretations. Steed, Maggie, p.62-74; f) Up to now. Hayes, Catherine, p.75-81; g) Covering the ground. Jellicoe, Ann, p.82-96; h) Taking care of everything. Jenkins, Meri, p.97-107; i) Insider. Aukin, Liane, p.108-116.

382. Women and Trade Unions in Eleven Industrialized Countries. Cook, Alice H., Lorwin, Val R. and Daniels, Arlene Kaplan, eds. Philadelphia: Temple University Press, 1984.
a) Denmark. Foged, Brita, Olsen, Anne and Otte, Helle, p.37-62; b) Federal Republic of Germany. Cook, Alice H., p.63-94; c) Finland. Haavio-Mannila, Elina, p.95-119; d) France. Maruani, Margaret, p.120-139; e) Great Britain. Boston, Sarah and Lorwin, Val R., p.140-161; f) Ireland. King, Deborah Schuster, p.162-183; g) Italy. Beccalli, Bianca, p.184-214; h) Japan. Hanami, Tadashi, p.215-238; i) Norway. Holter, Harriet and Sørensen, Bjørg Aase, p.239-260; j) Sweden. Acker, Joan, Lorwin, Val R. and Qvist, Gunmar, p.261-285; k) The United States of America. Wertheimer, Barbara Mayer, p.286-311.

383. Women and Utopia: Critical Interpretations. Barr, Marleen and Smith, Nicholas D., eds. Lanham, MD: University Press of America, 1983.
a) A new anarchism: Social and political ideas in some recent feminist eutopias. Sargent, Lyman, Tower, p.3-33; b) Method in her madness: Feminism in the crazy utopian vision of Tiptree's Courier. Rhodes, Carolyn, p.34-42; c) Utopia at the end of a male chauvinist dystopian world: Suzy McKee Charnas's feminist science fiction. Barr, Marleen, p.43-66; d) World views in utopian novels by women. Freibert, Lucy M., p.67-84; e) The heavenly utopia of Elizabeth Stuart Phelps. Kessler, Carol Farley, p.85-95; f) Wright's *Islandia*: Utopia with problems. Flieger, Verlyn, p.96-107; g) The *Left Hand of Darkness*: Androgyny and the feminist utopia. Rhodes, Jewell Parker, p.108-120; h) Truth and art in women's worlds: Doris Lessing's *Marriages Between Zones Three, Four, and Five*. Khanna, Lee Cullen, p.121-134; i) Opposing necessity and truth: The argument against politics in Doris Lessing's utopian vision. White, Thomas I., p.134-147; j) Beyond defensiveness: Feminist research strategies. Patai, Daphne, p.148-169.

384. Women and Western American Literature. Stauffer, Helen Winter and Rosowski, Susan J., eds. Troy, NY: Whitston Publishing Co., 1982.
a) The civilizers: Women's organizations and western American literature. Underwood, June O., p.3-16; b) Marie Louise Ritter: The pioneer woman in fact and fiction. Ritter, Darlene, p.17-27; c) A study of feminism as a motif in *A Journey to Pike's Peak and New Mexico* by Julia Archibald Holmes. Solomon, Margaret, p.28-39; d) Reluctant pioneers. Armitage, Susan H., p.40-51; e) Women in western American fiction: Images or real women? Meldrum, Barbara Howard, p.55-69; f) Sacajawea of myth and history. Remley, David, p.70-89; g) Miscegenation in popular western history and fiction. Deming, Caren J., p.90-99; h) The emergence of

Helen Chalmers. Malpezzi, Frances M., p.100-113; i) The western roots of feminism in Agnes Smedley's *Daughter of Earth*. Nichols, Kathleen L., p.114-123; j) Pioneer women in the works of two Montana authors: Interviews with Dorothy M. Johnson and A. B. Guthrie, Jr., Mathews, Sue, p.124-131; k) Hamlin Garland's feminism. Kaye, Frances W., p.135-161; l) The Virginian and Antonia Shimerda: Different sides of the western coin. Murphy, John J., p.162-178; m) Beret as the Norse mythological goddess Freya/Gurthr. Farmer, Catherine D., p.179-193; n) Marian Forrester and Moll Flanders: Fortunes and misfortunes. Yongue, Patricia Lee, p.194-211; o) Wright Morris, women, and American culture. Wydeven, Joseph, p.212-229; p) The young girl in the West: Disenchantment in Jean Stafford's short fiction. Walsh, Mary Ellen Williams, p.230-243; q) Toward a new paradigm: Mari Sandoz's study of red and white myth in *Cheyenne Autumn*. Rippey, Barbara, p.247-266; r) Where the West begins: Constance Rourke's images of her own frontierland. Bellman, Samuel I., p.267-282; s) Pioneering the imagination: Eudora Welty's *The Robber Bridegroom*. Graulich, Melody, p.283-296; t) The moral in Austin's *The Land of Little Rain*. Work, James C., p.297-310; u) A laddered, rain-bearing rug: Paula Gunn Allen's poetry. Jahner, Elaine, p.311-326.

385. Women and Work in Africa. Bay, Edna G., ed. Boulder, CO: Westview Press, 1982.
a) Women, work, and ethnicity: The Sierra Leone case. White, E. Frances, p.19-33; b) Control of land, labor, and capital in rural southern Sierra Leone. MacCormack, Carol P., p.35-53; c) Dependence and autonomy: The economic activities of secluded Hausa women in Kano, Nigeria. Schildkrout, Enid, p.55-81; d) Women and agricultural change in the railway region of Zambia: Dispossession and counterstrategies, 1930-1970. Muntemba, Maud Shimwaayi, p.83-103; e) Marginal lives: Conflict and contradiction in the position of female traders in Lusaka, Zambia. Schuster, Ilsa, p.105-126; f) Colonialism, education, and work: Sex differentiation in colonial Zaire. Yates, Barbara A., p.127-152; g) Reinventing the past and circumscribing the future: *Authenticité* and the negative image of women's work in Zaire. Wilson, Francille Rusan, p.153-170; h) International development and the evolution of women's economic roles: A case study from northern Gulma, Upper Volta. Hemmings-Gapihan, Grace S., p.171-189; i) Women's work in a communal setting: The Tanzanian policy of *Ujamaa*. Fortmann, Louise, p.191-205; j) Women farmers and inequities in agricultural services. Staudt, Kathleen A., p.207-224; k) Women's employment and development: A conceptual framework applied to Ghana. Campbell, Claudia and Steel, William F., p.225-248; l) Fertility and employment: An assessment of role incompatibility among African urban women. Lewis, Barbara, p.249-276; m) The child-care dilemma of working mothers in African cities: The case of Lagos, Nigeria. Fapohunda, Eleanor R., p.277-288; n) Women's cooperative thrift and credit societies: An element of women's

programs in the Gambia. Ceesay-Marenah, Coumba, p.289-295.

386. Women and Work in India: Continuity and Change. Lebra, Joyce, Paulson, Joy and Everett, Jana, eds. New Delphi, India: Promilla & Co., 1984. a) Housewives. Paulson, Joy, p.25-62; b) Agricultural laborers. Gulati, Leela, p.63-77; c) Sweepers. Karlekar, Malavika, p.78-99; d) Women in education. Trembour, Mary, p.100-125; e) Women in medicine. Lebra, Joyce, p.126-156; f) Women in the arts. Jones, Diane and Kaimal, Padma, p.157-183; g) Street vendors. Per-Lee, Dianne A., p.184-200; h) Construction workers. Ghosh, Chitra, p.201-211; i) Women and political leadership. Everett, Jana, p.212-236; j) Women in law and administration. Everett, Jana, p.237-262; k) Women in media. Costelli, Helen, p.263-286.

387. Women and Work: Problems and Perspectives. Kahn-Hut, Rachel, Daniels, Arlene Kaplan and Colvard, Richard, eds. New York: Oxford University Press, 1982. a) Women and the division of labor: Limiting assumptions. p.17-23; b) Toward a sociotechnological theory of the women's movement. Huber, Joan, p.24-28; c) Women in the occupational world: Social disruption and conflict. Coser, Rose Laub and Rokoff, Gerald, p.39-53; d) Sex discrimination and employment practices: An experiment with unconventional job inquires. Levinson, Richard M., p.54-64; e) Male and female: Job versus gender models in the sociology of work. Feldberg, Roslyn L. and Glenn, Evelyn Nakano, p.65-80; f) Home work and market work: Systematic segregation. p.81-87; g) Industrialization and femininity: A case study of nineteenth-century New England. Epstein, Barbara, p.88-100; h) The work-family role system. Pleck, Joseph H., p.101-110; i) Commitment and cultural mandate: Women in medicine. Bourne, Patricia Gerald and Wikler, Norma Juliet, p.111-122; j) Dilemmas of Japanese professional women. Osako, Masako Murakami, p.123-135; k) Invisible work: Unacknowledged contributions. p.137-143; l) The future of American fertility. Ryder, Norman B., p.144-152; m) Stay home, little Sheba: On placement, displacement, and social change. Coser, Rose Laub, p.153-160; n) The inexpressive male: Tragedy or sexual politics? Sattel, Jack W., p.160-169; o) Interaction: The work women do. Fishman, Pamela M., p.170-180; p) Dilemmas and contradictions of status: The case of the dual-career family. Hunt, Janet G. and Hunt, Larry L., p.181-191; q) Degraded and deskilled: The proletarianization of clerical work. Feldberg, Roslyn L. and Glenn, Evelyn Nakano, p.202-217; r) Job opportunities of black and white working-class women. Hillsman, Sally T. and Levenson, Bernard, p.218-233; s) The impact of hierarchical structures on the work behavior of women and men. Kanter, Rosabeth Moss, p.234-247; t) Sex stratification, technology and organization change: A longitudinal case study of AT&T. Hacker, Sally L., p.248-266; u) Unresolved questions: Three feminist perspectives. Colvard, Richard, Daniels, Arlene Kaplan and Kahn-Hut, Rachel, p.267-271.

388. Women and World Change: Equity Issues in Development. Black, Naomi and Cottrell, Ann Baker, eds. Beverly Hills, CA: Sage, 1981. a) Development with equity for women. McCormack, Thelma, p.15-30; b) Rural women in development. Blumberg, Rae Lesser, p.32-56; c) Singapore women: Work and the family. Salaff, Janet, p.57-82; d) Household economic strategies in Kingston, Jamaica. Bolles, A. Lynn, p.83-96; e) Women's work and worth in an Acadian maritime village. Davis, Nanciellen, p.97-119; f) Women and law: Land tenure in Africa. Newman, Katherine S., p.120-138; g) Women in Communist countries: Comparative public policy. Jancar, Barbara, p.139-158; h) Public day care in Britain and Sweden: A sociological perspective. Ruggie, Mary, p.159-182; i) Rural women and development planning in Peru. Bourque, Susan C. and Warren, Kay Barbara, p.183-197; j) Women's organizations and social change: The age-of-marriage issue in India. Ramusack, Barbara N., p.198-216; k) Social feminism in France: A case study. Black, Naomi, p.217-238; l) The contemporary American women's movement. Cottrell, Ann Baker, p.239-264; m) The future for women and development. Black, Naomi, p.265-286.

389. Women as Interpreters of the Visual Arts, 1820-1979. Sherman, Claire Richter and Holcomb, Adele M., eds. Westport, CT: Greenwood Press, 1981. a) Precursors and pioneers (1820-1890). Sherman, Claire Richter, p.3-26; b) Widening horizons (1890-1930). Sherman, Claire Richter, p.27-59; c) The tradition continues (1930-1979). Sherman, Claire Richter, p.61-90; d) Anna Jameson (1794-1860): Sacred art and social vision. Holcomb, Adele M., p.93-121; e) Margaret Fuller (1810-1850): Her work as an art critic. Holcomb, Adele M. and Walker, Corlette R., p.123-146; f) Lady Dilke (1840-1904): The six lives of an art historian. Eisler, Colin, p.147-180; g) Mariana Griswold Van Rensselaer (1851-1934): America's first professional woman art critic. Kinnard, Cythnia D., p.181-205; h) Georgiana Goddard King (1871-1939): Educator and pioneer in medieval Spanish art. Saunders, Susanna Terrell, p.209-238; i) Margarete Bieber (1879-1978): An archaeologist in two worlds. Bonfante, Larissa, p.239-274; j) Gisela Marie Augusta Richter (1882-1972): Scholar of classical art and museum archaeologist. Edlund, Ingrid E., McCann, Anna Marguerite and Sherman, Claire Richter, p.275-300; k) Erica Tietze-Conrat (1883-1958): Productive scholar in renaissance and baroque art. Kahr, Madlyn Millner, p.301-326; l) Sirarpie Der Nersessian (b. 1896): Educator and scholar in Byzantine and Armenian art. Allen, Jelisaveta Stanojevich, p.329-356; m) Dorothy Burr Thompson (b. 1900): Classical archaeologist. Havelock, Christine Mitchell, p.357-375; n) Dorothy Eugenia Miner (1904-1973): The varied career of a medievalist: Scholar and keeper of manuscripts, librarian and editor at the Walters Art Gallery. Sherman, Claire Richter, p.377-409; o) Agnes Mongan (b. 1905): Connoisseur of old master drawings. Bohlin, Diane DeGrazia, p.411-434.

390. Women, Class and History: Feminist Perspectives on Australia 1788-1978. Windschuttle, Elizabeth, ed. Auckland, New Zealand: Fontana/Collins, 1980.
a) Women and the family in Australian history. Grimshaw, Patricia, p.37-52; b) 'Feeding the poor and sapping their strength': The public role of ruling-class women in eastern Australia, 1788-1850. Windshuttle, Elizabeth, p.53-80; c) Women and labour, 1880-1900. Markey, Ray, p.83-111; d) Educated and white-collar women in the 1880s. Garner, Coral Chambers, p.112-131; e) Evolution, eugenics and women: The impact of scientific theories on attitudes towards women, 1870-1920. Bacchi, Carol, p.132-156; f) Women in mining communities. Mitchell, Winifred, p.157-170; g) Homes are divine workshops. Willis, Sabine, p.173-191; h) 'I have never liked trade unionism': The development of the Royal Australian Nursing Federation, Queensland Branch, 1904-1945. Law, Glenda, p.192-215; i) The Women's Peace Army. Gowland, Pat, p.216-234; j) 'Spinifex fairies': Aboriginal workers in the Northern territory, 1911-39. McGrath, Ann, p.237-267; k) 'Without fear or favour' - Lucie Barnes. Stevens, Joyce, p.268-286; l) The Australian women's Guild of Empire. Castle, Josie, p.287-312; m) The memoirs of 'Cleopatra Sweatfigure'. Gollan, Daphne, p.313-329; n) Rooms of their own: The domestic situation of Australian women writers between the wars. Modjeska, Drusilla, p.330-352; o) From balaclavas to bayonets: Women's voluntary war work, 1939-41. Shute, Carmel, p.353-387; p) The unwritten history of Adela Pankhurst Walsh. Summers, Anne, p.388-404; q) Sally Bowen: Political and social experiences of a working-class woman. Robertson, Mavis, p.405-422; r) Equal pay case, 1951. Marchisotti, Daisy, p.423-429; s) Right-wing union officials versus married women workers. Nord, Stella, p.430-436; t) Women's struggle to become tram drivers in Melbourne, 1956-75. Bevege, Margaret, p.437-452; u) Revolution and machismo: Women in the New South Wales Builders Labourers' Federation, 1961-75. Burgmann, Meredith, p.453-491; v) Women and economic crises: The Great Depression and the present crisis. Power, Margaret, p.492-513; w) Women, work and technological change. Rubinstein, Linda, p.514-530; x) Crime and sexual politics. Scutt, Jocelynne, p.531-557; y) Sexism and health care. Wyndham, Diana, p.558-591.

391. Women, Communication, and Careers. Grewe-Partsch, Marianne and Robinson, Gertrude J., eds. München, Germany: K. G. Saur, 1980.
a) Early childhood experiences and women's achievement motives. Hoffman, Lois Wladis, p.10-35; b) Career awareness in young children. Dorr, Aimee and Lesser, Gerald S., p.36-75; c) Children's impressions of television mothers. Wartella, Ellen, p.76-84; d) Time, television, and women's career perspectives. Grewe-Partsch, Marianne and Sturm, Hertha, p.85-92; e) Changing Canadian and US magazine portrayals of women and work: Growing opportunities for choice. Robinson, Gertrude J., p.93-113; f) Career management and women. Jelinek, Mariann, p.114-125; g) The influence of female and male communi-

cation styles on conflict strategies: Problem areas. Frost, Joyce Hocker, p.126-136.

392. Women, Crime, and Justice. Datesman, Susan K. and Scarpitti, Frank R., eds. New York: Oxford University Press, 1980.
a) The extent and nature of female crime. Datesman, Susan K. and Scarpitti, Frank R., p.3-64; b) The etiology of female crime: A review of the literature. Klein, Dorie, p.70-105; c) Female deviance and the female sex role: A preliminary investigation. Rosenblum, Karen E., p.106-128; d) Female delinquency and broken homes: A reassessment. Datesman, Susan K. and Scarpitti, Frank R., p.129-149; e) The interaction between women's emancipation and female criminality: A cross-cultural perspective. Adler, Freda, p.150-166; f) Crimes of violence by women. Jackson, Maurice, Ward, David A. and Ward, Reneé E., p.171-191; g) Searching for women in organized crime. Block, Alan, p.192-213; h) Women, heroin, and property crime. Inciardi, James A., p.214-222; i) The economics of prostitution. Sheehy, Gail, p.223-237; j) The molls. Miller, Walter B., p.238-248; k) Discriminatory sentencing of women offenders: The argument for ERA in a nutshell. Temin, Carolyn Engel, p.255-276; l) Chivalry and paternalism: Disparities of treatment in the criminal justice system. Moulds, Elizabeth F., p.277-299; m) Unequal protection of males and females in the juvenile court. Datesman, Susan K. and Scarpitti, Frank R., p.300-319; n) Women in prison: Discriminatory practices and some legal solutions. Haft, Marilyn G., p.320-338; o) Mothers behind bars: A look at the parental rights of incarcerated women. Haley, Kathleen, p.339-354.

393. Women, Education and Modernization of the Family in West Africa. Ware, Helen, ed. Canberra, Australia: Australian National University, 1981.
a) Wage earner and mother: Compatibility of roles on a Cameroon plantation. De Lancey, Virginia, p.1-21; b) Education and socio-demographic change in Nigeria. Orubuloye, Israel, p.22-41; c) Women and work: A study of female and male attitudes in the modern sector of an African metropolis (Lagos). Karanja, Wambui Wa, p.42-66; d) Worlds apart? A comparative study of European and African traditional family life as depicted in the novels of Laurie Lee and Camara Laye. Soyinka, Susan, p.67-87; e) The stable African family: Traditional and modern family structures in two African societies (Basa and Manding). Koenig, Dolores, p.88-111; f) Plural marriage, fertility and the problem of multiple causation. Arowolo, Oladele, p.112-133; g) Education and fertility among Cameroonian working women. Koenig, Dolores, p.134-153; h) The relationship between education and fertility. Cochrane, Susan, p.154-178.

394. Women Emerge in the Seventies. Swoboda, Marian J. and Roberts, Audrey J., eds. Madison, WI: Office of Women, University of Wisconsin, 1980.
a) The women's movement and the university. Freeman, Bonnie Cook, p.1- 9; b) History of the Association of Faculty Women at Madison. Bleier, Ruth, p.11-22; c) A

history of the Wisconsin Coordinating Council of Women in Higher Education. Macaulay, Jacqueline, p.23-34; d) Committee on the Status of Women at Milwaukee. Crisler, Jane, p.35-38; e) Graduate women assess the campus. Dyke, Jane Van, p.39-49; f) A women's studies plan for Wisconsin. Merritt, Karen, p.53-58; g) The women's studies program at Milwaukee. Skalitzky, Rachel I., p.59-62; h) Sedition in a sexist society: The Platteville paradigm. Parsons, Barbara, p.63-73; i) Chair, chairman, chairperson. Sylvander, Carolyn, p.75-79; j) Women's athletics at Madison and Title IX. Saunders, Kit, p.81-92; k) Merging two careers and marriage. Krouse, Agate and Krouse, Harry, p.93-95; l) We have hired couples for years. Moore, Nancy Newell, p.97-105; m) The president's wife: A changing role - observations of a chancellor's wife. Guskin, Judith T., p.107-111; n) Child care and the university. Kiefer, Irene, p.113-119; o) Continuing education: A personal view. Clarenbach, Kathryn F., p.121-129; p) An E.B. Fred Fellow. Hicklin, Fannie, p.131-132; q) Continuing education services in the UW system. Geisler, Peg, p.133-139; r) Meeting the needs of re-entering students. Stelmahoske, Isabelle, p.141-147; s) A remarkable woman: Grace Pilgrim Bloom. Hinz, JoAnn, p.149-150; t) From undergraduate to judge at sixty. Brown Betty D., p.151-153.

395. Women, Health, and International Development. Aguwa, Margaret I., ed. East Lansing, MI: Michigan State University, 1983.
a) Genocide can be bloodless. Mernissi, Fatima, p.1-5; b) Women as promoters of health in the developing world. Bender, Deborah, p.7-19; c) Women and health care personnel planning. Butter, Irene, p.21-32; d) Women, food and health in Tanzania: A crisis of the 1980s. Turshen, Meredeth, p.33-42; e) Water and sanitation-related health constraints on women's contribution to the economic development of communities. Elemendorf, Mary and Isely, Raymond B., p.43-58; f) Perceptions of a family planning campaign in rural Mexico. Millard, Ann V., p.59-67; g) The political economy of population policy in South Africa. Brown, Barbara, p.69-85; h) Family planning in rural China. Ren-Ying, Yan, p.87-90; i) Women's understanding about reproductive physiology and their choice of herbal medicines in Cali, Colombia. Browner, Carol, p.91-103; j) Health beliefs and behaviors of middle class urban women in Lahore, Pakistan. Eickmeier, Janice L., p.105-112; k) Obstetrical complications associated with traditional medical practices at Nsukka. Aguwa, C. Nze, Aguwa, Margaret and Aguwa, Okechukwu, p.113-120; l) Anger sickness: Social stress and native diagnosis among Ecuadorian Indians. Butler, Barbara, p.121-132.

396. Women, Health and Reproduction. Roberts, Helen, ed. London: Routledge & Kegan Paul, 1981.
a) Male hegemony in family planning. Roberts, Helen, p.1-17; b) Midwives, medical men and 'poor women labouring of child': Lying-in hospitals in eighteenth-century London. Versluysen, Margaret Connor, p.18-49; c) Competing ideologies of reproduction: Medical and maternal perspectives on pregnancy. Graham, Hilary and

Oakley, Ann, p.50-74; d) Depo-provera: The extent of the problem: A case study in the politics of birth control. Rakusen, Jill, p.75-108; e) Seizing the means of reproduction: An illegal feminist abortion collective — how and why it worked. Bart, Pauline, p.109-128; f) Well woman clinics: A positive approach to women's health. Gardner, Katy, p.129-143; g) A woman in medicine: Reflections from the inside. Young, Gail, p.144-162; h) Sex predetermination, artificial insemination and the maintenance of male-dominated culture. Hanmer, Jalna, p.163-190.

397. Women-Identified Women. Darty, Trudy and Potter, Sandee, eds. Palo Alto, CA: Mayfield Pub. Co., 1984.
a) Changing theories of lesbianism: Challenging the stereotypes. Browning, Christine, p.11-30; b) Developing a lesbian identity. Gramick, Jeannine, p.31-44; c) The coming-out process: Violence against lesbians. Baetz, Ruth, p.45-50; d) Lesbian relationships: A struggle toward partner equality. Sang, Barbara, p.51-65; e) The older lesbian: Love relationships and friendship patterns. Raphael, Sharon and Robinson, Mina, p.67-82; f) Beloved women: The lesbian in American Indian culture. Allen, Paula Gunn, p.83-96; g) Reclamation: A lesbian Indian story. Brant, Beth, p.97-103; h) The Puerto Rican lesbian in the United States. Hidalgo, Hilda, p.105-115; i) Compulsory heterosexuality and lesbian existence. Rich, Adrienne, p.119-148; j) Lesbians and the law: Where sexism and heterosexism meet. Gould, Meredith, p.149-162; k) Lesbianism and motherhood: Implications for child custody. Lewin, Ellen, p.163-183; l) Lesbian childbirth and woman-controlled conception. Wolf, Deborah Goleman, p.185-193; m) Lesbians and contemporary health care systems: Oppression and opportunity. Darty, Trudy and Potter, Sandee, p.195-210; n) Peril and promise: Lesbians' workplace participation. Schneider, Beth, p.211-230; o) From accommodation to rebellion: The politicization of lesbianism. Weitz, Rose, p.233-248; p) Culture-making: Lesbian classics in the year 2000. Kaye/Kantrowitz, Melanie, p.249-265; q) The black lesbian in American literature: An overview. Shockley, Ann Allen, p.267-275; r) Without approval: The lesbian poetry tradition. Steinshouer, Betty, p.277-285; s) Lesbians and women's music. Tilchen, Maida, p.287-303.

398. Women in Academe. Dudovitz, Resa L., ed. Oxford, England: Pergamon Press, 1984.
a) Power and empowerment. Moglen, Helene, p.131-134; b) Work in the interstices: Woman in academe. Adams, Harriet Farwell, p.135-141; c) Black woman professor — white university. McKay, Nellie, p.143-147; d) Survival in the 'master's house': The role of graduate teaching assistants in effecting curriculum change. Dudovitz, Resa L., et al., p.149-157; e) Self-disclosure and the commitment to social change. Beck, Evelyn Torton, p.159-163; f) 'They shared a laboratory together': Feminist collaboration in the academy. Abel, Elizabeth, Hirsch, Marianne and Langland, Elizabeth, p.165-167; g) Is 'Chloe liked Olivia' a lesbian plot? Zimmerman, Bonnie, p.169-175; h) Beyond defensiveness: A feminist research strategies. Patai, Daphne, p.177-189; i) Women, the other acade-

mics. Acker, Sandra, p.191-201; j) Women's studies and men's careers: How the 'social problem' of women in education maintained the academic status of men in the 1970s. Lockheed, Marlaine E. and Stein, Sandra L., p.203-209; k) On the bottom rung: A discussion of women's work in sociology. Porter, Mary and Scott, Sue, p.211-221; l) Academic women, affirmative action, and mid-America in the eighties. Lattin, Patricia Hopkins, p.223-230; m) Hard truths for strategic change: Dilemmas of implementing affirmative action. Chertos, Cynthia H., p.231-241.

399. Women in American Theatre: Careers, Images, Movements: An Illustrated Anthology and Sourcebook. Chinoy, Helen Krich and Jenkins, Linda Walsh, eds. New York: Crown, 1981.
a) Sex roles and shamans. Jenkins, Linda Walsh, p.12-18; b) Trampling out the vintage. Lee, Susan Dye, p.19-24; c) Friendship and ritual in the WTUL. Moore, Elizabeth Payne, p.25-28; d) Rites and rights. Patterson, Cynthia and Watkins, Bari J., p.29-33; e) Crowning Miss California, again. Bierman, James H., p.33-40; f) Murshida Ivy O. Duce. Star, Sandra Inez, p.41-43; g) *The Story of a Mother* (play). Boesing, Martha and At the Foot of the Mountain (theater), p.44-50; h) "Lesson I Bleed". Curb, Rosemary K., p.50-56; i) Anne Brunton Merry: First star. Doty, Gresdna, p.60-65; j) Enter the harlot. Johnson, Claudia D., p.66-74; k) Women in male roles: Charlotte Cushman and others. Shafer, Yvonne, p.74-81; l) Adah Isaacs Menken in *Mazeppa*. Adler, Lois, p.81-87; m) Lydia Thompson and the "British Blondes". Moses, Marlie, p.88-92; n) Henrietta Vinton Davis: Shakespearean actress. Hill, Errol, p.92-97; o) Mary Shaw: A fighting champion. Schanke, Robert A., p.98-107; p) Aileen Stanley, Her life and times. Burian, Grayce Susan, p.107-113; q) The art of Ruth Draper. McKenna, Muriel, p.114-119; r) Uta Hagen and Eva Le Gallienne. Spector, Susan and Urkowitz, Steven, p.119-123; s) Women mimes in America. Rolfe, Bari, p.123-128; t) Mercy Warren, satirist of the revolution. Robinson, Alice Mc Donnell, p.131-137; u) Looking to women: Rachel Crothers and the feminist heroine. Gottlieb, Lois, p.137-145; v) Apropos of women and the folk play. France, Rachel, p.145-153; w) Anne Nichols: $1,000,000.00 playwright. Abramson, Doris and Harris, Laurilyn, p.153-157; x) Sophie Treadwell: Agent for change. Heck-Rabi, Louise, p.157-162; y) The comic muse of Mary Chase. Wertheim, Albert, p.163-170; z) Lillian Hellman's memorial drama. Billson, Marcus K. and Smith, Sidonie A., p.171-178; aa) Sylvia Plath, a dramatic poet. Devlin, Diana, p.179-184; bb) Woman alone, women together. Moore, Honor, p.184-190; cc) Women open Augusta's first theatre. Curtis, Mary Julia, p.193-197; dd) Art theatre in Hull-House. Rich, J. Dennis, p.197-203; ee) The adventure of life: Writing for children. Chorpenning, Charlotte, p.204-207; ff) Alvina Krause: A great teacher of acting. Downs, David and McCants, Billie, p.208-211; gg) Peggy Clark Kelley: Reminiscences of a "designing" woman. Kelley, Peggy Clark, p.211-217; hh) Matriarchs of the regional theatre. Magnus, Dorothy B., p.217-224; ii)

The lady is a critic. Latta, Caroline J. Dodge, p.224-231; jj) "Casting by Juliet Taylor" (Interview). Chinoy, Helen Krich, p.232-235; kk) The second face of the idol: Women in melodrama. Bank, Rosemarie K., p.238-243; ll) Women in Pulitzer Prize plays, 1918-1949. Stephens, Judith Louise, p.243-251; mm) The women's world of Glaspell's *Trifles*. Stein, Karen F., p.251-254; nn) Black women in plays by black playwrights. Miller, Jeanne-Marie A., p.254-260; oo) Who put the "Tragic" in the Tragic Mulatto? Fletcher, Winona L., p.260-266; pp) Creative drama: Sex role stereotyping? Wright, Lin, p.266-273; qq) Feminist theatre: A rhetorical phenomenon. Gillespie, Patti P., p.276-285; rr) Megan Terry (Interview). Leavitt, Dinah L., p.285-292; ss) The Washington area feminist theatre. Schurr, Cathleen and Wilkins, Mary Catherine, p.293-300; tt) New York feminist theater troupe. Charbonneau, Claudette and Winer, Lucy, p.300-307; uu) The Lavender Cellar theatre. Leavitt, Dinah L., p.308-311; vv) *Rebeccah*: Rehearsal notes. Malpede, Karen, p.311-315; ww) *Fefu and Her Friends*. Pevitts, Beverley Byers, p.316-320; xx) A rainbow of voices. Mael, Phyllis, p.320-324.

400. Women in Bangladesh: Some Socio-economic Issues. Huq, Jahanara, et al., eds. Dhaka, Bangladesh: Women for Women, 1983.
a) Women's employment and agriculture: Extracts from a case study. Begum, Saleha and Greeley, Martin, p.1-16; b) Rural pauperization: Its impact on the economic role and status of rural women in Bangladesh. Westergaard, Kirsten, p.17-35; c) Women's income earning activities and family welfare in Bangladesh. Qadir, Sayeda Rowshan, p.36-45; d) Impact of male migration on rural housewives. Islam, Mahmuda, p.46-53; e) Population planning and rural women's co-operative in IRDP women's programme: Some critical issues. Akhtar, Farida, Banu, Fazila and Feldman, Shelley, p.54-69; f) Life cycle, food behaviour and nutrition of women in Bangladesh. Rizvi, Najma, p.70-79; g) Some aspects of mental health of women in Bangladesh. Tuckwell, Sue, p.80-88; h) Energy needs of poor households: An abstract. Tinker, Irene, p.89-92.

401. Women in China: Current Directions in Historical Scholarship. Guisso, Richard W. and Johannesen, Stanley, eds. Youngstown, NY: Philo Press, 1981.
a) The Chinese Buddhist monastic order for women: The first two centuries. Tsai, Kathryn A., p.1-20; b) Taoism and the androgynous ideal. Ames, Roger T., p.21-45; c) Thunder over the lake: The five classics and the perception of woman in early China. Guisso, Richard W., p.47-61; d) The Chinese Lieh-nü tradition. Sung, Marina H., p.63-74; e) The many faces of Cui Yingying. Dong, Lorraine, p.75-98; f) Power and prestige: Palace women in the Northern Sung (960-1126). Chung, Priscilla Ching, p.99-112; g) Women in the kinship system of the Southern Song upper class. Ebrey, Patricia, p.113-128; h) Widows and remarriage in Ming and early Qing China. Waltner, Ann, p.129-146; i) One woman's rise to power: Cheng I's wife and the pirates. Murray, Dian, p.147-161; j) Female

infanticide in China. Lee, Bernice J., p.163-177; k) The influence of western women on the anti-footbinding movement 1840-1911. Drucker, Alison R., p.179-199; l) Catholic sisters in China: An effort to raise the status of women. Bradshaw, Sue, p.210-213; m) In the public eye: Women in early twentieth-century China. Beahan, Charlotte L., p.215-238.

402. Women in Contemporary India and South Asia. de Souza, Alfred, ed. New Delhi: Manohar Publications, 1980.
a) Women in India and South Asia: An introduction. de Souza, Alfred, p.1-29; b) The data base for studies on women: Sex biases in national data systems. D'Souza, Stan, p.31-60; c) The study of women in South Asia: Some current methodological and research issues. Singh, Andrea Menefee, p.61-93; d) Trends and structure of female labour force participation in rural and urban Pakistan. Shah, Makhdoom A. and Shah, Nasra M., p.95-123; e) Family status and female work participation. D'Souza, Victor S., p.125-139; f) Women in Bangladesh: Food-for-work and socioeconomic change. Chen, Marty and Ghuznari, Ruby, p.141-164; g) Women and the law: Constitutional rights and continuing inequalities. Minattur, Joseph, p.165-178; h) Women and religion: The status and image of women in some major religious traditions. King, Ursula, p.179-197; i) Muslim women in Uttar Pradesh: Social mobility and directions of change. Bhatty, Zarina, p.199-211; j) Purdah and public space. Sharma, Ursula M., p.213-239; k) Etiquette among women in Karnataka: Forms of address in the village and the family. Ullrich, Helen E., p.241-261; l) Asian women in Britain: Strategies of adjustment of Indian and Pakistani migrants. Khan, Verity Saifullah, p.263-285; m) The aging woman in India: Self-perceptions and changing roles. Vatuk, Sylvia, p.287-309.

403. Women in Contemporary Muslim Societies. Smith, Jane I., ed. Lewisburg, PA: Bucknell University Press, 1980.
a) The religious lives of Muslim women. Beck, Lois, p.27-60; b) Traditional affirmations concerning the role of women as found in contemporary Arab Islamic literature. Haddad, Yvonne Yazbeck, p.61-86; c) The determinants of social position among rural Moroccan women. Davis, Susan Schaefer, p.87-99; d) The social and political roles of Arab women: A study of conflict. Shilling, Nancy Adams, p.100-145; e) Access to property and the states of women in Islam. Pastner, Carroll McClure, p.146-185; f) Ritual status of Muslim women in rural India. Fruzzetti, Lina M., p.186-208; g) Women, law, and social change in Iran. Haeri, Shahla, p.209-235; h) The political mobilization of women in the Arab world. Fluehr-Lobban, Carolyn, p.235-252.

404. Women in Crisis. Russianoff, Penelope, ed. New York: Human Sciences Press, 1981.
a) Women in crisis: The issue. Norton, Eleanor Holmes, p.24-31; b) Learned helplessness. Russianoff, Penelope, p.33-37; c) Learned helplessness, depression, and alcohol problems of women. Gomberg, Edith S. Lisansky, p.38-

43; d) The stigmatized woman. Leone, Rose, p.44-48; e) The double bind: Minority women. Saunders, Marguerite, p.49-55; f) The sparse ghetto: Service delivery in a rural area. Weitzel, Joan, p.56-63; g) Reaching the middle class female. Duffié, Nikki N., p.64-68; h) Reaching the middle class alcoholic. Seixas, Judith, p.69-73; i) Holistic approaches for women. Milton, Catherine, p.77-79; j) The woman in treatment: Evaluation and diagnostic implications. Freudenberger, Herbert J., p.80-84; k) Sexism in treatment. Lewis, Barbara A., p.85-91; l) Sexism in drug abuse treatment programs. Levy, Stephen J., p.92-100; m) Women and substance abuse: Treatment issues. Buxton, Millicent E. and Smith, David E., p.101-107; n) Plenary session: Intervention/service delivery systems. Austin, Severa, p.108-115; o) Plenary session: Intervention/service delivery systems. Lazar, Joyce, p.116-121; p) Innovative alcoholism programs for women. Finkelstein, Norma, p.122-127; q) Motivation and the alcoholic woman. Blume, Sheila B., p.128-132; r) Breaking cycles of victimization: The shelter as an affirmative institution. McGarry, Peggy Ann and McGrath, Dennis, p.133-144; s) The mythology of rape. Halpern, Susan, p.145-147; t) In the pursuit of justice in sentencing and prison. Fogel, David, p.148-155; u) The role of the family in teenage pregnancy: Support or sabotage. Cherry, Violet Padayachi, p.156-171; v) Pregnancy and drinking. Robe, Lucy Barry, p.172-175; w) Prostitution and sexual violence. James, Jennifer, p.176-217; x) Young female offenders in Massachusetts: Toward leaving the juvenile justice system successfully. Peacock, Carol, p.218-220; y) The unique employment problems of female offenders returning to the community and labor market. Taylor, Barbara, p.221-224; z) Vocational rehabilitation: Options for women. Cappelli, Denise, p.225-228; aa) Stereotypes and stigma: Barriers to recovery. Hall, Jacquelyn H., p.229-235; bb) Making change. Abzug, Bella S., p.236-242; cc) Postintervention and support systems. Messinger, Ruth W., p.243-246; dd) Establishing interdisciplinary treatment networks. Koppel, Flora, p.247-251; ee) Self-power and leadership. Mainker, Marlene Crosby, p.252-256; ff) Federal support: Understanding and utilizing the federal dollar. Grygelko, Marilee, p.257-260.

405. Women in Eastern Europe and the Soviet Union. Yedlin, Tova, ed. New York: Praeger, 1980.
a) Marxism, feminism, and sex equality. Heitlinger, Alena, p.9-20; b) The women's liberation issue in nineteenth century Russia. Stites, Richard, p.21-30; c) Women revolutionaries: The personal and the political. Engel, Barbara Alpern, p.31-43; d) Socialism and feminism: The first stages of women's organizations in the eastern part of the Austrian empire. Bohachevsky-Chomiak, Martha, p.44-64; e) Bolshevik women: The first generation. Clements, Barbara Evans, p.65-74; f) The early decrees of Zhenotdel. McNeal, Robert H., p.75-86; g) Marxism and women's oppression: Bolshevik theory and practice in the 1920's. Holt, Alix, p.87-114; h) Soviet women in combat in World War II: The ground/air defense forces. Cottam, K. Jean, p.115-127; i) The anti-fascist front of women and the Communist Party in Croatia: Conflicts within the

resistance. Reed, Mary E., p.128-139; j) Have women's chances for political recruitment in the USSR really improved? Harasymiw, Bohdan, p.140-184; k) The social composition of women deputies in Soviet elective politics: A preliminary analysis of official biographies. Maher, Janet E., p.185-211; l) Women in contemporary Poland: Their social and occupational position and attitudes toward work. Adamski, Wladylsaw W., p.212-225; m) Procreation and new definitions in the role of women in a Soviet bloc country: The case of Poland. Mazur, D. Peter, p.226-238; n) Some demographic, particularly fertility, correlates of female status in Eastern Europe and the republics of the Soviet Union. Krótki, Karol J., p.239-269.

406. Women in Film Noir. Kaplan, E. Ann, ed. London: BFI Publishing, 1980.
a) Klute 1: A contemporary film noir and feminist criticism. Gledhill, Christine, p.6-21; b) Woman's place: The absent family of film noir. Harvey, Sylvia, p.22-34; c) Women in film noir. Place, Janey, p.35-54; d) Duplicity in Mildred Pierce. Cook, Pam, p.68-82; e) The place of women in Fritz Lang's *The Blue Gardenia*. Kaplan, E. Ann, p.83-90; f) Resistance through charisma: Rita Hayworth and Gilda. Dyer, Richard, p.91-99; g) Double indemnity. Johnston, Claire, p.100-111; h) Klute 2: Feminism and Klute. Gledhill, Christine, p.112-128.

407. Women in Higher Education Administration. Tinsley, Adrian, Secor, Cynthia, and Kaplan, Sheila, eds. San Francisco: Jossey-Bass Inc., 1984.
a) Careers in college and university administration: How are women affected? Moore, Kathryn M., p.5-15; b) Career mapping and the professional development process. Tinsley, Adrian, p.17-24; c) Preparing the individual for institutional leadership: The summer institute. Secor, Cynthia, p.25-33; d) The administrative skills program: What have we learned? Speizer, Jeanne J., p.35-45; e) Toward a new era of leadership: The national identification program. Shavlik, Donna and Touchton, Judy, p.47-58; f) Lifting as we climb: Networks for minority women. Wilkerson, Margaret B., p.59-67; g) An agenda for senior women administrators. Helly, Dorothy O. and Kaplan, Sheila, p.67-75; h) Foundation support for administrative advancement: A mixed record. Bernstein, Alison R., p.77-84; i) Getting the best: Conclusions, recommendations, and selected resources. Kaplan, Sheila, Secor, Cynthia and Tinsley, Adrian, p.85-91.

408. Women in Hispanic Literature: Icons and Fallen Idols. Miller, Beth, ed. Berkeley, CA: University of California Press, 1983.
a) Spain's first women writers. Deyermond, Alan, p.27-52; b) Echoes of the Amazon myth in medieval Spanish literature. Irizarry, Estelle, p.53-66; c) Sexual humor in misogynist medieval exampla. Goldberg, Harriet, p.67-83; d) Women in the *Book of Good Love*. Gimeno, Rosalie, p.84-96; e) Marina/Malinche: Masks and shadows. Phillips, Rachel, p.97-114; f) Women against wedlock: The reluctant brides of Golden Age drama. McKendrick, Melveena, p.115-146; g) The convent as catalyst for

autonomy: Two Hispanic nuns of the seventeenth century. Arenal, Electa, p.147-183; h) A school for wives: Women in eighteenth-century Spanish theater. Kish, Kathleen, p.184-200; i) Gertrude the Great: Avellaneda, nineteenth-century feminist. Miller, Beth, p.201-214; j) Notes toward a definition of Gabriela Mistral's ideology. Alegría, Fernando, p.215-226; k) Female archetypes in Mexican literature. Leal, Luis, p.227-242; l) Sara de Etcheverts: The contradictions of literary feminism. Masiello, Francine, p.243-258; m) The greatest punishment: Female and male in Lorca's tragedies. Burton, Julianne, p.259-279; n) The changing face of woman in Latin American fiction. Welles, Marcia L., p.280-288; o) The censored sex: Woman as author and character in Franco's Spain. Levine, Linda Gould, p.289-315; p) Sexual politics and the theme of sexuality in Chicana poetry. Ordóñez, Elizabeth, p.316-339; q) From mistress to murderess: The metamorphosis of Buñuel's Tristana. Miller, Beth, p.340-360.

409. Women in Joyce. Henke, Suzette and Unkeless, Elaine, eds. Urbana, IL: University of Illinois Press, 1982.
a) The woman hidden in James Joyce's *Chamber Music*. Boyle, Robert, p.3-30; b) *Dubliners*: Women in Irish society. Walzl, Florence L., p.31-56; c) Emma Clery in *Stephen Hero*: A young woman walking proudly through the decayed city. Scott, Bonnie Kime, p.57-81; d) Stephen Dedalus and women: A portrait of the artist as a young misogynist. Henke, Suzette, p.82-107; e) Bertha's role in *Exiles*. Bauerle, Ruth, p.108-131; f) Gerty MacDowell: Joyce's sentimental heroine. Henke, Suzette, p.132-149; g) The conventional Molly Bloom. Unkeless, Elaine, p.150-168; h) The genuine Christine: Psychodynamics of Issy. Benstock, Shari, p.169-196; i) Anna Livia Plurabelle: The dream woman. Norris, Margot, p.197-214; j) Afterword. Heilbrun, Carolyn G., p.215-216.

410. Women in Local Politics. Stewart, Debra W., ed. Metuchen, NJ: Scarecrow, 1980.
a) The invisible hands: Sex roles and the division of labor in two local political parties. Margolis, Diane, p.22-41; b) Political culture and selection of women judges in trial courts. Cook, Beverly Blair, p.42-60; c) The effects of sex on recruitment: Connecticut local offices. Mezey, Susan Gluck, p.61-85; d) Recruitment of women to suburban city councils: Higgins vs. Chevalier. Merritt, Sharyne, p.86-105; e) Sex differences in role behavior and policy orientations of suburban officeholders: The effect of women's employment. Merritt, Sharyne, p.115-129; f) Women judges and public policy in sex integration. Cook, Beverly Blair, p.130-148; g) Organizational role orientations on female-dominant commissions: Focus on staff-commissioner interaction. Stewart, Debra W., p.149-176; h) Perceptions of women's roles on local councils in Connecticut. Mezey, Susan Gluck, p.177-197; i) Commissions on the status of women and building a local policy agenda. Stewart, Debra W., p.198-214.

411. Women in Midlife. Baruch, Grace and Brooks-Gunn, Jeanne, eds. New York: Plenum Press, 1984.

a) Introduction: The study of women in midlife. Baruch, Grace K. and Brooks-Gunn, Jeanne, p.1-8; b) Life events and the boundaries of midlife for women. Brooks-Gunn, Jeanne and Kirsh, Barbara, p.11-30; c) Methods for a life-span developmental approach to women in the middle years. Lachman, Margie E., p.31-68; d) Middle-aged women in literature. Heilbrun, Carolyn G., p.69-79; e) The middle years: Changes and variations in social-role commitments. Barnewolt, Debra and Lopata, Helena Z., p.83-108; f) Multiple roles of midlife women: A case for new directions in theory, research, and policy. Long, Judy and Porter, Karen L., p.109-159; g) The psychological well-being of women in the middle years. Baruch, Grace K., p.161-180; h) Social change and equality: The roles of women and economics. Alington, Diane E. and Troll, Lillian E., p.181-202; i) The daughter of aging parents. O'Donnell, Lydia and Stueve, Ann, p.203-225; j) Motherhood in the middle years: Women and their adult children. Hay, Julia, Traupmann, Jane and Wood, Vivian, p.227-244; k) Black women in the middle years. Spurlock, Jeanne, p.245-260; l) Problems of American middle-class women in their middle years: A comparative approach. Whiting, Beatrice Blyth, p.261-273; m) Health care and midlife women. DeLorey, Catherine, p.277-301; n) Reproductive issues, including menopause. Parlee, Mary Brown, p.303-313; o) Midlife woman as student. Schlossberg, Nancy K., p.315-339; p) The anxiety of the unknown - choice, risk, responsibility: Therapeutic issues for today's adult women. Barnett, Rosalind C., p.341-357; q) Reflections and perspectives on 'therapeutic issues for today's adult women'. Notman, Malkah T., p.359-369; r) Sexuality and the middle-aged woman. Luria, Zella and Meade, Robert G., p.371-397.

412. Women in New Worlds: Historical Perspectives on the Wesleyan Tradition. Thomas, Hilah F. and Keller, Rosemary Skinner, eds. Nashville, TN: Abingdon, 1981.
a) Women's history/everyone's history. Mathews, Donald G., p.29-47; b) The last fifteen years: Historians' changing views of American women in religion and society. Sklar, Kathryn Kish, p.48-65; c) Women of the word: Selected leadership roles of women in Mr. Wesley's Methodism. Brown, Earl Kent, p.69-87; d) Minister as prophet? or as mother?: Two nineteenth-century models. Hardesty, Nancy A., p.88-101; e) Mary McLeod Bethune as religionist. Newsome, Clarence G., p.102-116; f) Georgia Harkness: Social activist and/or mystic. Scott, Martha L., p.117-140; g) Ministry through marriage: Methodist clergy wives on the trans-Mississippi frontier. Jeffrey, Julie Roy, p.143-160; h) Hispanic clergy wives: Their contribution to United Methodism in the southwest, later nineteenth century to the present. Náñez, Clotilde Falcón, p.161-177; i) Preparing women for the Lord's work: The story of three Methodist training schools, 1880-1940. Brereton, Virginia Lieson, p.178-199; j) The social gospel according to Phoebe: Methodist deaconesses in the metropolis, 1885-1918. Dougherty, Mary Agnes, p.200-216; k) Laity rights and leadership: Winning them for women in the Methodist Protestant church, 1860-1900. Noll, William T., p.219-

232; l) "A new impulse": Progress in lay leadership and service by women of the United Brethren in Christ and the Evangelical Association, 1870-1910. Gorrell, Donald K., p.233-245; m) Creating a sphere for women: The Methodist Episcopal church, 1869-1906. Keller, Rosemary Skinner, p.246-260; n) The laity rights movement, 1906-1918: Women's suffrage in the Methodist Episcopal Church, South. Shadron, Virginia, p.261-275; o) Nineteenth-century A.M.E. preaching women: Cutting edge of women's inclusion in church polity. Dodson, Jualynne, p.276-289; p) Evangelical domesticity: The woman's temperance crusade of 1873-1874. Lee, Susan Dye, p.293-309; q) For god and home and native land: the W.C.T.U.'s image of woman in the late nineteenth century. Gifford, Carolyn De Swarte, p.310-327; r) Korean women in Hawaii, 1903-1945: The role of Methodism in their liberation and in their participation in the Korean independence movement. Chai, Alice, p.328-344; s) Shaping a new society: Methodist women and industrial reform in the south, 1880-1940. Frederickson, Mary E., p.345-361; t) Winifred L. Chappell: Everybody on the left knew her. Crist, Miriam J., p.362-378.

413. Women in New Zealand Society. Bunkle, Phillida and Hughes, Beryl, eds. Sydney, Australia: George Allen & Unwin, 1980.
a) Women in the political life of New Zealand. Aitken, Judith, p.11-33; b) The role and status of Maori women. Blank, Arapera, p.34-51; c) The origins of the women's movement in New Zealand: The Women's Christian Temperance Union 1885-1895. Bunkle, Phillida, p.52-76; d) Fertility, sexuality and social control in New Zealand. Fenwick, Penny, p.77-98; e) The road ahead for the women's movement - out of the womb and into the world. Gillespie, Christine, p.99-117; f) Women and the professions in New Zealand. Hughes, Beryl, p.118-138; g) Education and the movement towards equality. McDonald, Geraldine, p.139-158; h) Women, work and family: 1880-1926. Olssen, Erik, p.159-183; i) Women artists in New Zealand. Paul, Janet, p.184-216; j) Mummy's boys: Pakeha men and male culture in New Zealand. Phillips, Jock, p.217-243; k) Pioneer into feminist: Jane Mander's heroines. Wevers, Lydia, p.244-260.

414. Women in Oklahoma: A Century of Change. Thurman, Melvena K., ed. Oklahoma City, OK: Oklahoma Historical Society, 1983.
a) Women in literature of the West. Morrison, Daryl, p.3-44; b) Cherokee women. Milam, Virginia, p.45-56; c) Women of the Osage: A century of change, 1874-1982. Wilson, Terry P., p.57-102; d) Patient and useful servants: Women missionaries in Indian territory. Peterson, Susan, p.103-123; e) Pioneer women: A photographic perspective. Prose, Maryruth, p.124-139; f) Women in Oklahoma education. Hubbell, Joe W., p.140-161; g) College life in Oklahoma territory. Cresswell, John and Segall, William E., p.162-181; h) Woman's suffrage, Oklahoma style, 1890-1918. James, Louise Boyd, p.182-198; i) The gender

liberation: Black women as elected officials in Oklahoma. Williams, Nudie, p.199-210.

415. Women in Organizations: Barriers and Breakthroughs. Pilotta, Joseph J., ed. Prospect Heights, IL: Waveland Press, 1983.
a) Trust and power in the organization: An overview. Pilotta, Joseph J., p.1-10; b) Internal barriers. Deaux, Kay, p.11-22; c) Sexual harassment in the organization. Jones, Tricia S., p.23-37; d) Lady you're trapped: Breaking out of conflict cycles. Putnam, Linda L., p.39-53; e) Women in organizations: The impact of law. Baum, Lawrence, p.55-71; f) Effective interpersonal communication for women of the corporation: Think like a man, talk like a lady. Fitzpatrick, Mary Anne, p.73-84; g) Breakthrough: Making it happen with women's networks. DeWine, Sue, p.85-101.

416. Women in Scientific and Engineering Professions. Haas, Violet B. and Perrucci, Carolyn C., eds. Ann Arbor, MI: University of Michigan Press, 1984.
a) Central issues facing women in the science-based professions. Perrucci, Carolyn C., p.1-16; b) Professional women in developing nations: The United States and the Third World compared. Gonzalez, Nancie L., p.19-42; c) Professional women in transition. Hornig, Lilli S., p.43-58; d) Changing patterns of recruitment and employment. Vetter, Betty M., p.59-74; e) Planning strategies for women in scientific professions. Cobb, Jewel Plummer, p.75-85; f) Academic career mobility for women and men psychologists. Rosenfeld, Rachel A., p.89-127; g) Responsibilities of women faculty in engineering schools. Dresselhaus, Mildred S., p.128-134; h) Alternative development of a scientific career. Hopkins, Esther A. H., p.137-146; i) Scientific sexism: The world of chemistry. Briscoe, Anne M., p.147-159; j) You've come a long way baby: The myth and the reality. McAfee, Naomi J., p.160-169; k) Early socialization: Causes and cures of mathematics anxiety. Campbell, Patricia F. and Geller, Susan C., p.173-180; l) Women engineers in history: Profiles in holism and persistence. Trescott, Martha M., p.181-204; m) Should professional women be like professional men? Hubbard, Ruth, p.205-211; n) Class, race, sex, scientific objects of knowledge: A socialist-feminist perspective on the social construction of productive nature and some political consequences. Haraway, Donna J., p.212-229; o) Evolving views of women's professional roles. Haas, Violet B., p.230-240.

417. Women in Search of Utopia: Mavericks and Mythmakers. Rohrlich, Ruby and Baruch, Elaine Hoffman, eds. New York: Schocken, 1984.
a) Rethinking matriliny among the Hopi. LeBow, Diane, p.8-20; b) Women of the Celtic Tuath. McNelly, Geraldine Day, p.21-29; c) Women in transition: Crete and Sumer. Rohrlich, Ruby, p.30-42; d) Al dente (poem). Burke, France, p.43-44; e) The Shakers: Gender equality in hierarchy. Rohrlich, Ruby, p.54-61; f) Frances Wright: Utopian feminist. Bensman, Marilyn, p.62-69; g) A song of Sojourner Truth (poem). Jordan, June, p.70-72; h)

Housework and utopia: Women and the Owenite socialist communities. Harsin, Jill, p.73-84; i) What's that smell in the kitchen? (poem). Piercy, Marge, p.85; j) The Woman's Commonwealth: Utopia in nineteenth-century Texas. Andreadis, A. Harriette, p.86-96; k) A utopian female support network: The case of the Henry Street Settlement. Cook, Blanche Wiesen, p.109-115; l) *Mujeres Libres* and the role of women in anarchist revolution. Ackelsberg, Martha A., p.116-127; m) A litany for survival (poem). Lorde, Audre, p.128-129; n) Women in the Children of God: "Revolutionary women" or "Mountin' maids"? Wangerin, Ruth Elizabeth, p.130-139; o) Tulsa (poem). Shange, Ntozake, p.140-145; p) Findhorn, Scotland: The people who talk to plants. Sheer, Arlene, p.146-156; q) Twin Oaks: A feminist looks at indigenous socialism in the United States. Weinbaum, Batya, p.157-167; r) Utopia in question: Programming women's needs into the technology of tomorrow. Zimmerman, Jan, p.168-176; s) The craft of their hands. Whyatt, Frances, p.177-179; t) Imagining a different world of talk. Henley, Nancy, Kramarae, Cheris and Thorne, Barrie, p.180-188; u) The linguistic transformation of womanhood. Gershuny, H. Lee, p.189-200; v) Women in men's utopias. Baruch, Elaine Hoffman, p.209-218; w) Motherhood in feminist utopias. Lees, Susan H., p.219-232; x) Realities and fictions: Lesbian visions of utopia. Farley, Tucker, p.233-246; y) Neither Arcadia nor Elysium: E. M. Broner's *A Weave of Women*. Pladott, Dinnah, p.247-256; z) The land of ordinary people: For John Lennon (poem). Arnason, Eleanor, p.257-259; aa) Of time and revolution: Theories of social change in contemporary feminist science fiction. Pearson, Carol S., p.260-265; bb) Change and art in women's worlds: Doris Lessing's *Canopus in Argos: Archives*. Khanna, Lee Cullen, p.269-279; cc) Therrillium (story). Adams, Mischa, p.280-288; dd) Outcome of the matter: The sun (poem). Piercy, Marge, p.289-290; ee) A women's museum of art. Harris, Ann Sutherland, p.291-295; ff) Future visions: Today's politics: Feminist utopias in review. Gearhart, Sally Miller, p.296-309.

418. Women in Society: Interdisciplinary Essays. The Cambridge Women's Studies Group, ed. London: Virago, 1981.
a) Work and the family: Who gets 'the best of both worlds'? Wajcman, Judy, p.9-24; b) A commentary on theories of female wage labour. Siltanen, Janet, p.25-40; c) The history of the family. Jordanova, L.J., p.41-54; d) Motherhood and mothering. Antonis, Barbie, p.55-74; e) Left critiques of the family. Riley, Denise, p.75-91; f) Mental illness, mental health: Changing norms and expectations. Jordanova, L.J., p.95-114; g) Domestic violence: Battered women in Britain in the 1970s. Binney, Val, p.115-126; h) 'A daughter: A thing to be given away'. Brown, Penelope, et al., p.127-145; i) Sexuality and homosexuality. Caplan, Jane, p.149-167; j) Contraception and abortion. Greenwood, Karen and King, Lucy, p.168-184; k) Feminist thought and reproductive control: The state and 'the right to choose'. Riley, Denise, p.185-199; l) 'If it's natural, we can't change it'. Lieven, Elena, p.203-223;

m) Oppressive dichotomies: The nature/culture debate. Brown, Penelope and Jordanova, L.J., p.224-241; n) Universals and particulars in the position of women. Brown, Penelope, p.242-256; o) Subjectivity, materialism and patriarchy. Lieven, Elena, p.257-275.

419. Women in the Ancient World: The *Arethusa Papers*. Peradotto, John and Sullivan, J.P., eds. Albany, NY: State University of New York Press, 1984.
a) Early Greece: The origins of the western attitude toward women. Arthur, Marylin B., p.7-58; b) "Reverse similes" and sex roles in the *Odyssey*. Foley, Helene P., p.59-78; c) Workers and drones: Labor, idleness and gender definition in Hesiod's beehive. Sussman, Linda S., p.79-93; d) Sappho and Helen. duBois, Page, p.95-105; e) The maenad in early Greek art. McNally, Sheila, p.107-141; f) Classical Greek attitudes to sexual behavior. Dover, K.J., p.143-157; g) The dynamics of misogyny: Myth and mythmaking in the *Oresteia*. Zeitlin, Froma I., p.159-194; h) The menace of Dionysus: Sex roles and reversals in Euripides' *Bacchae*. Segal, Charles, p.195-212; i) Plato: Misogynist, phaedophile, and feminist. Wender, Dorothea, p.213-228; j) The women of Etruria. Warren, Larissa Bonfante, p.229-239; k) The role of women in Roman elegy: Counter-cultural feminism. Hallett, Judith P., p.241-262; l) Rape and rape victims in the *Metamorphoses*. Curran, Leo C., p.263-286; m) Theodora and Antonina in the *Historia Arcana*: History and/or fiction? Fisher, Elizabeth A., p.287-313; n) Selected bibliography on women in classical Antiquity, p.315-471.

420. Women in the Cities of Asia: Migration and Urban Adaptation. Fawcett, James T., Khoo, Siew-Ean and Smith, Peter C., eds. Boulder, CO: Westview Press, 1984.
a) Urbanization, migration and the status of women. Fawcett, James T., Khoo, Siew-Ean and Smith, Peter C., p.3-11; b) The migration of women to cities: A comparative perspective. Go, Stella P., Khoo, Siew-Ean and Smith, Peter C., p.15-35; c) Female migration: A conceptual framework. Thadani, Veena N. and Todaro, Michael P., p.36-59; d) Women in rural-urban circulation networks: Implications for social structural change. Strauch, Judith, p.60-77; e) Rural-to-urban migration of women in India: Patterns and implications. Singh, Menefee Andrea, p.81-107; f) The female migrant in Pakistan. Shah, Nasra M., p.108-124; g) Female rural-to-urban migration in peninsular Malaysia. Khoo, Siew-Ean and Pirie, Peter, p.125-142; h) Female migration in Thailand. Arnold, Fred and Piampiti, Suwanlee, p.143-164; i) The migration of women in the Philippines. Eviota, Elizabeth U. and Smith, Peter C., p.165-190; j) Urban migrant women in the Republic of Korea. Hong, Sawon, p.191-210; k) Migration of women workers in peninsular Malaysia: Impact and implications. Ariffin, Jamilah, p.213-226; l) Female migrants in Bangkok metropolis. Piampiti, Suwanlee, p.227-246; m) The migration of rural women to Taipei. Huang, Nora Chiang, p.247-268; n) New models and traditional networks: Migrant women in Tehran. Bauer, Janet, p.269-293; o) Migrant women at work in

Asia. Shah, Nasra M. and Smith, Peter C., p.297-322; p) Female Asian immigrants in Honolulu: Adaptation and success. Gardner, Robert W. and Wright, Paul A., p.323-346; q) Philippine urbanism and the status of women. Bulatao, Rodolfo A., p.347-364; r) Adaptation of Polynesian female migrants in New Zealand. Graves, Nancy B., p.365-393; s) Women in Asian cites: Policies, public services, and research. Khoo, Siew-Ean, et al., p.397-406.

421. Women in the Family and the Economy: An International Comparative Survey. Kurian, George and Ghosh, Ratna, eds. Westport, CT: Greenwood, 1981.
a) Cultural determinants of power for women within the family: A neglected aspect of family research. Conklin, George H., p.9-27; b) Female-headed households and domestic organization in San Isidro, Guatemala: A test of Hammel and Laslett's comparative typology. Kendall, Carl, p.29-41; c) A causal interpretation of the effect of mother's education and employment status on parental decision-making role patterns in the Korean family. Kim, Kyong-Dong and Kim, On-Jook Lee, p.43-57; d) Social and economic integration of South Asian women in Montreal, Canada. Ghosh, Ratna, p.59-71; e) Planning for women in the new towns: New concepts and dated roles. Goldstein, Joan, p.73-80; f) Birth order and alienation among college women in Lebanon. Tomeh, Aida K., p.81-106; g) Education of Muslim women: Tradition versus modernity. Menon, M. Indu, p.107-115; h) The effect of religious affiliation on woman's role in Middle Eastern Arab Society. Dodd, Peter C., p.117-129; i) Attitudes of women towards certain selected cultural practices in Kerala state, India. John, Mariam and Kurian, George, p.131-142; j) Attitudes and ideology: Correlates of liberal attitudes towards the role of women. Gibbins, Roger, Ponting, J. Rick and Symons, Gladys L., p.143-164; k) Feminist egalitarianism, social action orientation and occupational roles: A cross-national study. Caupin, Benedicte, DeHaan, Neil and Geismar, Ludwig L., p.165-178; l) English-Canadian and French-Canadian attitudes towards women: Results of the Canadian Gallup polls. Boyd, Monica, p.179-196; m) Comparative attitudes about marital sex among Negro women in the United States, Great Britain and Trinidad. Bell, Robert R., p.197-207; n) Working wives in the United States and Venezuela: A cross-national study of decision making. Cunningham, Isabella C. M. and Green, Robert T., p.217-230; o) Wife-employment and the emergence of egalitarian marital role prescriptions: 1900-1974. Brown, Bruce W., p.231-244; p) Changes in Canadian female labour force participation and some possible implications for conjugal power. Pool, D. Ian, p.245-256; q) Sex role attitudes, female employment, and marital satisfaction. Bahr, Stephen J. and Day, Randal D., p.257-272; r) Some aspirations of lower class black mothers. Jackson, Roberta H., p.273-284; s) Labor force participation and fertility, contraceptive knowledge, attitude and practice of the women of Barbados. Ebanks, G.E., George, P.M. and Nobbe, Charles, p.285-296; t) Fertility and family economy in the Iranian rural communities. Aghajanian, Akbar, p.297-306;

u) The impact of children on female earnings. Niemi, Albert W., p.307-316; v) Some comments on the home roles of businesswomen in India, Australia and Canada. Ross, Aileen D., p.317-330; w) The demands of work and the human quality of marriage: An exploratory study of professionals in two socialist societies. Rueschemeyer, Marilyn, p.331-344; x) Occupational choice among female academicians - The Israeli case. Chopp-Tibon, Shira, Etzioni-Halevy, Eva and Shapira, Rina, p.345-358; y) Variations in women's roles and family life under the socialist regime in China. Liu, William T. and Yu, Elena S.H., p.359-374; z) Women in the Cuban bureaucracies: 1968-1974. Aguirre, Benigno E., p.375-392; aa) Career constraints among women graduate students in a developing society: West Pakistan. A study in the changing status of women. Korson, J. Henry, p.393-412; bb) Minority within a minority: On being South Asian and female in Canada. Ghosh, Ratna, p.413-426.

422. Women in the Indian Labour Force. Bangkok, Thailand: Asian Regional Team for Employment Promotion, 1981.
a) Women in the labour force of India: A macro-level statistical profile. Seal, K. C., p.21-92; b) Women workers of India: A case of market segmentation. Mukhopadhyay, Swapna, p.93-119; c) Women in the labour force in India. Parthasarathy, G. and Rao, G. Dasaradharama, p.121-137.

423. Women in the Middle Years: Current Knowledge and Directions for Research and Policy. Giele, Janet Zollinger, ed. New York: John Wiley, 1982.
a) Women in adulthood: Unanswered questions. Giele, Janet Zollinger, p.1-35; b) Women and health: The social dimensions of biomedical data. Lorenz, Gerda and Nathanson, Constance A., p.37-87; c) Adult development and women's development: Arrangements for a marriage. Gilligan, Carol, p.89-114; d) Women's work and family roles. Giele, Janet Zollinger, p.115-150; e) Women in the German Democratic Republic: Impact of culture and social policy. Ecklein, Joan, p.151-197; f) Future research and policy questions. Giele, Janet Zollinger, p.199-240; g) Longitudinal and cross-sectional data sources on women in the middle years. Antonucci, Toni C., p.241-274.

424. Women in the Urban and Industrial Workforce: Southeast and East Asia. Jones, Gavin W., ed. Canberra, Australia: Australian National University, 1984.
a) Economic growth and changing female employment structure in the cities of Southeast and East Asia. Jones, Gavin W., p.17-59; b) Trends in female labour force participation and occupational shifts in urban Korea. Koo, Sung-Yeal, p.61-73; c) Trends in female labour force participation in Taiwan: The transition toward higher technology activities. Liu, Paul K.C., p.75-99; d) Employment patterns of educated women in Indonesian cities. Hull, Valerie and Raharjo, Yulfita, p.101-126; e) Towards meeting the needs of urban female factory workers in peninsular Malaysia. Lean, Lim Lin, p.129-148; f) Constraints on the organization of women industrial workers. Blake, Myrna, p.149-162; g) Islamic attitudes to female employ-

ment in industrializing economies: Some notes from Malaysia. Siraj, Mehrun, p.163-173; h) Occupational health hazards of female industrial workers in Malaysia. Hoon, Lee Siew, p.175-187; i) Women's work: Factory, family and social class in an industrializing order. Salaff, Janet and Wong, Aline, p.189-214; j) Making the bread and bringing it home: Female factory workers and the family economy. Wolf, Diane L., p.215-231; k) Female domestic servants in Cagayan de Oro, Philippines: Social and economic implications of employment in a 'premodern' occupational role. Palabrica-Costello, Marilou, p.235-250; l) The Bangkok masseuses: Origins, status and prospects. Phongpaichit, Pasuk, p.251-257; m) Growth of the bazaar economy and its significance for women's employment: Trends of the 1970s in Davao City, Philippines. Barth, Gerald and Hackenberg, Beverly, p.259-273; n) Urbanward migration and employment of women in Southeast and East Asian cities: Patterns and policy issues. Khoo, Siew-Ean, p.277-291; o) Employment structure of female migrants to the cities in the Philippines. Engracia, Luisa and Herrin, Alejandro, p.293-303; p) Women migrants in Bangkok: An economic analysis of their employment and earnings. Tongudai, Pawadee, p.305-323; q) Effect of female labour force participation on fertility: The case of construction workers in Chiang Mai City. Singhanetra-Renard, Anchalee, p.325-335; r) Women, work and the family in a developing society: Taiwan. Lu, Yu-Hsia, p.339-367; s) The impact of female employment on household management. Miralao, Virginia A., p.369-386; t) Female employment and the family: A case study of the Bataan Export Processing Zone. Zosa-Feranil, Imelda, p.387-403.

425. Women in the Work Force. Bernardin, H. John, ed. New York: Praeger, 1982.
a) An overview of the research on women in management: A typology and a prospectus. Wortman Jr., Max S., p.1-28; b) Hard-hatted women: Reflections on blue-collar employment. Deaux, Kay and Ullman, Joseph C., p.29-47; c) Women and the psychology of achievement: Implications for personal and social change. Mednick Martha T., p.48-69; d) Career progress of women: Getting in and staying in. Rosen, Benson, p.70-99; e) Trying hurts women, helps men: The meaning of effort. Hansen, Ranald D. and O'Leary, Virginia E., p.100-123; f) Socialization experiences of women and men graduate students in male sex-typed career fields. Terborg, James R., Tubbs, Mark E. and Zalesny, Mary D., p.124-155; g) Estimating benefits and costs of antisexist training programs in organizations. Dunnette, Marvin d. and Motowidlo, Stephan J., p.156-182; h) Causal determinants of job satisfaction in dual career couples. Klenke-Hamel, Karen, p.183-204; i) Job evaluation and discrimination: Legal, economic, and measurement perspectives on comparable worth and women's pay. Beatty, James R. and Beatty, Richard W., p.205-234.

426. Women in the Workplace. Wallace, Phyllis A., ed. Boston, MA: Auburn House Publishing Company, 1982.
a) Increased labor force participation of women and affir-

mative action. Wallace, Phyllis A., p.1-24; b) The MBA: Same passport to success for women and men? Strober, Myra H., p.25-44; c) The apprenticeship model of organizational careers: A response to changes in the relation between work and family. Bailyn, Lotte, p.45-58; d) Sex differences in factors affecting managerial career advancement. Harlan, Anne and Weiss, Carol L., p.59-100; e) Moving forward, standing still: Women in white collar jobs. Malveaux, Julianne M., p.101-133; f) Women and nontraditional blue collar jobs in the 1980s: An overview. O'Farrell, Brigid, p.135-165; g) Corporate experiences in improving women's job opportunities. Lynton, Edith F. and Shaeffer, Ruth Gilbert, p.167-213.

427. Women in the Workplace: Effects on Families. Borman, Kathryn M., Quarm, Daisy and Gideonse, Sarah, eds. Norwood, NJ: Ablex Publishing Corp., 1984.
a) Introduction: Government response to working women and their families: Values, the policy-making process, and research utilization. Gideonse, Sarah, p.1-32; b) The importance of early care. Sroufe, L. Alan and Ward, Mary J., p.35-60; c) Fathers, mothers, and childcare in the 1980s: Family influences on child development. Lamb, Michael E., p.61-88; d) Child care options and decisions: Facts and figurings for families. Honig, Alice Sterling, p.89-111; e) Gender inequities in childhood social life and adult work life. Borman, Kathryn M. and Frankel, Judith, p.113-135; f) Men, women, work, and family. Mortimer, Jeylan T. and Sorensen, Glorian, p.139-167; g) Paid and unpaid work: Contradictions in American women's lives today. Glazer, Nona Y., p.169-186; h) Sexual inequality: The high cost of leaving parenting to women. Quarm, Daisy, p.187-208; i) Conceptions of kinship and the family reproduction cycle. Farber, Bernard, p.211-232; j) Gender roles and the state. Grubb, W. Norton and Lazerson, Marvin, p.233-256.

428. Women, Men, and the International Division of Labor. Fernández-Kelly, María Patricia and Nash, June, eds. Albany, NY: State University of New York Press, 1983.
a) The impact of the changing international division of labor on different sectors of the labor force. Nash, June, p.3-38; b) The new international division of labor and the U.S. work force: The case of the electronics industry. Snow, Robert T., p.39-69; c) Capitalism, imperialism, and patriarchy: The dilemma of third-world women workers in multinational factories. Lim, Linda Y.C., p.70-91; d) Women, production, and reproduction in industrial capitalism: A comparison of Brazilian and U.S. factory workers. Safa, Helen I., p.95-116; e) Household, community, national, and multinational industrial development. Aguiar, Neuma, p.117-137; f) Kitchens hit by priorities: Employed working-class Jamaican women confront the IMF. Bolles, Lynn, p.138-160; g) The domestic clothing workers in the Mexican metropolis and their relation to dependent capitalism. Alonso, José Antonio, p.161-173; h) Labor migration and the new industrial division of labor. Sassen-Koob, Saskia, p.175-204; i) Mexican border industrialization, female labor force participation, and migration.

Fernández-Kelly, María Patricia, p.205-223; j) *Maquiladoras*: A new face of international capitalism on Mexico's northern frontier. Bustamante, Jorge A., p.224-256; k) The formation of an ethnic group: Colombian female workers in Venezuela. Berlin, Magalit, p.257-270; l) Silicon Valley's women workers: A theoretical analysis of sex-segregation in the electronics industry labor market. Green, Susan S., p.273-331; m) Fast forward: The internationalization of Silicon Valley. Katz, Naomi and Kemnitzer, David S., p.332-345; n) The division of labor in electronics. Keller, John F., p.346-373; o) The impact of industrialization on women: A Caribbean case. Abraham-Van der Mark, Eve E., p.374-386; p) The emergence of small-scale industry in a Taiwanese rural community. Tai-Li, Hu, p.387-406; q) Women textile workers in the militarization of Southeast Asia. Enloe, Cynthia H., p.407-425; r) Global industries and Malay peasants in peninsular Malaysia. Ong, Aihwa, p.426-439.

429. Women Ministers. Weidman, Judith L., ed. San Francisco: Harper & Row, 1981.
a) Growing toward effective ministry. Pollock, M. Helene, p.13-31; b) Small church — big family. Barksdale, Virginia, p.33-47; c) Preaching through metaphor. Huie, Janice Riggle, p.49-66; d) Preaching in the black tradition. Kelly, Leontine T.C., p.67-76; e) Women and liturgy. Park, Patricia, p.77-87; f) A ministry of presence. Gill, Brita, p.89-106; g) Bearing the good news. Bell, Dianna Pohlman, p.107-121; h) Unboxing Christian education. Rowlett, Martha Graybeal, p.123-134; i) The embodied church. Gross, Lora, p.135-157; j) The task of enabling. Otaño-Rivera, Blanqui, p.159-168; k) Colleagues in marriage and ministry. Allen, Ronald J. and McKiernan-Allen, Linda, p.169-182.

430. Women of Iran: The Conflict with Fundamentalist Islam. Azari, Farah, ed. London: Ithaca Press, 1983.
a) Islam's appeal to women in Iran: Illusions and reality. Azari, Farah, p.1-71; b) The economic base for the revival of Islam in Iran. Afshar, Soraya, p.72-89; c) Sexuality and women's oppression in Iran. Azari, Farah, p.90-156; d) The attitude of the Iranian left to the women's question. Afshar, Soraya, p.157-169; e) A historical background to the women's movement in Iran. Bahar, Sima, p.170-189; f) The post-revolutionary women's movement in Iran. Azari, Farah, p.190-225.

431. Women of Southeast Asia. Van Esterik, Penny, ed. DeKalb, IL: Northern Illinois University, 1982.
a) Buddhism, sex-roles and the Thai economy. Kirsch, Thomas, p.16-41; b) Women meditation teachers in Thailand. Van Esterik, John, p.42-54; c) Laywomen in Theravada Buddhism. Van Esterik, Penny, p.55-78; d) Putting Malay women in their place. Laderman, Carol C., p.76-99; e) Women in Java's rural middle class: Progress or regress. Hull, Valerie L., p.100-123; f) Women and men in Iloilo, Philippines: 1903-1970. Szanton, M. Cristina Blanc, p.124-153; g) Sex roles in the Philippines: The ambiguous Cebuana. Neher, Clark D., p.154-175; h)

Sexual status in Southeast Asia: Comparative perspectives on women, agriculture and political organization. Winzeler, Robert L., p.176-213.

432. Women, Philosophy, and Sport: A Collection of New Essays. Postow, Betsy C., ed. Metuchen, NJ: Scarecrow, 1983.
a) Justice and gender in school sports. Warren, Mary Anne, p.12-37; b) Education and sports: A reply to "Justice and gender in school sports". Moulton, Janice, p.38-45; c) Athletics, gender, and justice. Lemos, Ramon M., p.46-56; d) Reply to Moulton and Lemos. Warren, Mary Anne, p.57-60; e) Afterword on equal opportunity. Postow, Betsy, p.61-68; f) Employment for women in athletics: What is fair play? Heizer, Ruth B., p.70-93; g) Sports, sex-equality, and the media. Belliotti, Raymond A., p.96-114; h) Cooperative competition in sport. Vetterling-Braggin, Mary, p.123-132; i) Equality and competition: Can sports make a women of a girl? Addelson, Kathryn Pyne, p.133-161; j) Competition, friendship, and human nature. Hyland, Drew A., p.162-176; k) The overemphasis on winning: A philosophical look. Hundley, Joan, p.177-200; l) Philosophy of education, physical education, and the sexes. Klein, J. Theodore, p.207-232; m) Education for equality. Atherton, Margaret, p.233-245; n) Women's physical education: A gender-sensitive perspective. Diller, Ann and Houston, Barbara, p.246-277; o) The ethics of gender discrimination: A response to Ann Diller and Barbara Houston's "Women's Physical Education". Nicholson, Linda J., p.278-286; p) Putting away the pom-poms: An educational psychologist's view of females and sports. Nielsen, Linda, p.287-303.

433. Women, Politics, and Literature in Bengal. Seely, Clinton B., ed. East Lansing, MI: Michigan State University, 1981.
a) Goddesses or rebels: The women revolutionaries of Bengal. Forbes, Geraldine H., p.3-17; b) Conditions influencing rural and town women's participation in the labor force. Feldman, Shelley and McCarthy, Florence E., p.19-30; c) Madness as entropy: A Bengali view. Bhattacharyya, Deborah P., p.31-40; d) British tradesmen of Calcutta, 1830-1900: A preliminary study of their economic and political roles. Furedy, Chris, p.43-62; e) Bengal politics of the first decade of the present century: A defence of extremism. Goswami, Chitta R., p.63-68; f) Bengal election, 1937: Fazlul Huq and M. A. Jinnah: A study in leadership stress in Bengal politics. Rahim, Enayetur, p.69-89; g) Inequality and radical land reform: Some notes from west Bengal. Bhattacharyya, Jnanabrata, p.91-98; h) Forms of the Indian notion of sexuality and an interpretation of the Mymensing ballad of Kajalrekha. Bahl, Kali Charan, p.101-117; i) British response to Bengali literature in the nineteenth century. Basu, Shubhra, p.119-127; j) Some poems from *Citra* by Radindranath Tagore. Rogers, Kristine M., p.129-137; k) Radindranath Tagore: Cultural ambassador of India to the United States. Borra, Ranjan, p.139-145; l) Say it with structure: Tagore and *Mangala Kavya*. Seely, Clinton B., p.147-155; m) The image of Bengal in the emerging liter-

ature of Bangladesh: The fiction of Hasan Azizul Huq. Kopf, David M., p.157-167.

434. Women, Power, and Change. Weick, Ann and Vandiver, Susan T., eds. Washington, D.C.: National Association of Social Workers, 1980.
a) Redefining concepts of mental health. Wetzel, Janice Wood, p.3-16; b) Depression in women: Explanations and prevention. De Lange, Janice M., p.17-26; c) Therapy with battered women. Henson, Deborah M. and Schinderman, Janet L., p.27-37; d) Rape crisis theory revisited. Baum, Martha, Sales, Esther and Shore, Barbara K., p.38-48; e) Older women as victims of violence. FallCreek, Stephanie and Hooyman, Nancy, p.49-66; f) Black women: The resilient victims. White, Barbara W., p.69-77; g) Asian-American women: A historical and cultural perspective. Ryan, Angela Shen, p.78-88; h) The Chicana in transition. Fimbres, Martha Molina, p.89-95; i) Observations on social work with American Indian women. Blanchard, Evelyn Lance, p.96-103; j) Homophobia and social work practice with lesbians. Cummerton, Joan M., p.104-113; k) Social work with lesbian couples. Woodman, Natalie Jane, p.114-124; l) Dilemmas in role identification for low-income women. Cassella, Marie, Groves, Betsy McAlister and Jacobs, Jane, p.127-136; m) Work requirements for AFDC mothers. Hill, Kathleen Spangler, p.137-145; n) Toward a feminist model for planning for and with women. Ellsworth, Cheryl, et al., p.146-157; o) Toward androgyny in community and organizational practice. Brandwein, Ruth A., p.158-170; p) Issues of power in social work practice. Weick, Ann, p.173-185; q) Beyond advocacy. Sancier, Betty, p.186-196; r) Issues for women in a 'woman's' profession. Meyer, Carol H., p.197-205; s) Social work values and skills to empower women. Solomon, Barbara Bryant, p.206-214.

435. Women, Power and Policy. Boneparth, Ellen, ed. New York: Pergamon, 1982.
a) Representing women: The transition from social movement to interest group. Costain, Anne N., p.19-37; b) Representing women at the state and local levels: Commissions on the status of women. Rosenberg, Rina, p.38-46; c) Women and public policy: An overview. Freeman, Jo, p.47-67; d) Pay equity: Beyond equal pay for equal work. Grune, Joy Ann and Kahn, Wendy, p.75-89; e) Alternative work patterns and the double life. Stoper, Emily, p.90-108; f) Women and housing: The limitations of liberal reform. Diamond, Irene, p.109-117; g) In search of a national child-care policy: Background and prospects. Norgren, Jill, p.124-143; h) The womb factor: Pregnancy policies and employment of women. Huckle, Patricia, p.144-161; i) Antiobscenity: A comparison of the legal and feminist perspectives. Bessmer, Sue, p.167-183; j) Battered women and public policy. Wexler, Sandra, p.184-204; k) Women's crime, women's justice. Moulds, Elizabeth Fry, p.205-231; l) The foreign policy beliefs of women in leadership positions. Holsti, Ole R. and Rosenau, James N., p.238-262; m) Bureaucratic resistance to women's programs: The case of women in devel-

opment. Staudt, Kathleen A., p.263-281; n) Women, men, and military service: Is protection necessarily a racket? Stiehm, Judith Hicks, p.282-293.

436. Women, Power and Political Systems. Rendel, Margherita, ed. London: Croom Helm, 1981.
a) Women, power and political systems. Rendel, Margherita, p.15-49; b) Women and citizenship: Mobilisation, participation, representation. Stiehm, Judith, p.50-65; c) Women's role in the formulation of public policies in Brazil. Tabak, Fanny, p.66-80; d) Women's education and participation in the labour force: The case of Nigeria. Awosika, Keziah, p.81-93; e) Women in government as policy-makers and bureaucrats: The Turkish case. Abadan-Unat, Nermin, p.94-115; f) Creating employment opportunities for rural women: Some issues affecting attitudes and policy. Sachak, Najma, p.116-134; g) Demography, political reform and women's issues in Czechoslovakia. Wolchik, Sharon L., p.135-150; h) A hard day's night: Women, reproduction and service society. Kickbusch, Ilona, p.151-159; i) Technology, 'women's work' and the social control of women. Rothschild, Joan, p.160-183; j) Women's employment networks: Strategies for development. Col, Jeanne Marie, p.184-194; k) The impact of the women's movement and legislative activity of women MPs on social development. Haavio-Mannila, Elina and Sinkkonen, Sirkka, p.195-215; l) Will women judges make a difference in women's legal rights? A prediction from attitudes and simulated behaviour. Cook, Beverly B., p.216-239; m) Future perspectives. Rendel, Margherita, p.240-241.

437. Women Returning to Work: Policies and Progress in Five Countries. Yohalem, Alice M., ed. Montclair, NJ: Allanheld, Osmun, 1980.
a) Federal Republic of Germany. Langkau, Jochem and Langkau-Herrmann, Monika, p.17-58; b) France. Gontier, Geneviève and Labourie-Racape, Annie, p.59-106; c) Sweden. Jonung, Christina and Thordarsson, Bodil, p.107-159; d) United Kingdom. Rothwell, Sheila, p.160-216; e) United States. Yohalem, Alice M., p.217-287.

438. Women Scientists: The Road to Liberation. Richter, Derek, ed. London: Macmillan, 1982.
a) Opportunities for women in science. Richter, Derek, p.1-13; b) Opportunities for women scientists in India. Sohonie, Kamala, p.14-23; c) It takes more than luck (United States). Kies, Marian W., p.24-44; d) Becoming an anthropologist (Japan). Nakane, Chie, p.45-60; e) The wild cat (France and Italy). Bolis, Liana, p.61-74; f) The achievement of Iranian women in science. Rahmani, Tahereh M.Z., p.75-98; g) Reflections on a scientific adventure (Italy and United States). Levi-Montalcini, Rita, p.99-117; h) Women scientists in Sweden. Fischer-Hjalmars, Inga, p.118-136; i) A little about myself, and more about a more important matter - the brain (USSR). Bechtereva, Natalia P., p.137-157; j) Women in Cambridge biochemistry (United Kingdom). Needham, Dorothy, p.158-163; k) The progress of science in Africa.

Maathai, W. Muta, p.164-184; l) Autobiography of an unknown woman (India). Rajalakshmi, R., p.185-210.

439. Women: Sex and Sexuality. Stimpson, Catharine R. and Person, Ethel Spector, eds. Chicago, IL: University of Chicago Press, 1980.
a) Who is Sylvia? On the loss of sexual paradigms. Janeway, Elizabeth, p.4-20; b) Sex and power: Sexual bases of radical feminism. Shulman, Alix Kates, p.21-35; c) Sexuality as the mainstay of identity: Psychoanalytic perspectives. Person, Ethel Spector, p.36-61; d) Compulsory heterosexuality and lesbian existence. Rich, Adrienne, p.62-91; e) Reproductive freedom: Beyond "A woman's right to choose". Petchesky, Rosalind Pollack, p.92-116; f) Menstruation and reproduction: An Oglala case. Powers, Marla N., p.117-128; g) Pornography and repression: A reconsideration. Diamond, Irene, p.129-144; h) The politics of prostitution. Walkowitz, Judith, p.145-157; i) The front line: Notes on sex in novels by women, 1969-1979. Snitow, Ann, Barr, p.158-174; j) Biological influences on human sex and gender. Baker, Susan W., p.175-191; k) Behavior and the menstrual cycle. Friedman, Richard C., et al., p.192-211; l) Pregnancy. Leifer, Myra, p.212-223; m) Maternal sexuality and asexual motherhood. Contratto, Susan Weisskopf, p.224-240; n) Toward a biology of menopause. Goodman, Madeleine, p.241-255; o) Social and behavioral constructions of female sexuality. Fowlkes, Martha R. and Miller, Patricia Y., p.256-273; p) "The love crisis": Couples advice books of the late 1970s. Ross, Ellen, p.274-287; q) *Homosexuality in Perspective* by William H. Masters and Virginia E. Johnson. Cooper, Arnold M., p.288-294; r) *The Hosken Report: Genital and Sexual Mutilation of Females* by Fran P. Hosken. Fee, Elizabeth, p.294-296; s) *Sexual Excitement* by Robert J. Stoller. Michels, Robert, p.296-299; t) *The History of Sexuality*. Vol. 1: *An Introduction* by Michel Foucault. Shaffer, Elinor, p.299-307; u) "I am not contented": Female masochism and lesbianism in early twentieth-century New England. Duberman, Martin Bauml, p.308-324; v) Female sexuality and the Catholic confessional. Zaretsky, Eli, p.325-333.

440. Women, Social Welfare and the State in Australia. Baldock, Cora V. and Cass, Bettina, eds. Sydney: Allen & Unwin, 1983.
a) The end is where we start from: Women and welfare since 1901. Roe, Jill, p.1-19; b) Public policies and the paid work of women. Baldock, Cora V., p.20-53; c) Redistribution to children and to mothers: A history of child endowment and family allowances. Cass, Bettina, p.54-84; d) Women and consumer capitalism. Pringle, Rosemary, p.85-103; e) Capitalism, patriarchy and the city. Harman, Elizabeth J., p.104-129; f) Women as welfare recipients: Women, poverty and the state. Bryson, Lois, p.130-145; g) Sex and money in the welfare state. Shaver, Sheila, p.146-163; h) Population policies and family policies: State construction of domestic life. Cass, Bettina, p.164-185; i) Pater-patria: Child-rearing and the state. Cox, Eva, p.186-200; j) The women's movement's fandango with the state: The movement's role in public

policy since 1972. Dowse, Sara, p.201-222; k) Legislating for the right to be equal. Scutt, Jocelynne A., p.223-245; l) Social policy, education and women. Porter, Paige, p.246-261; m) In sickness and in health: Social policy and the control of women. Broom, Dorothy H., p.262-278; n) Volunteer work as work: Some theoretical considerations. Baldock, Cora V., p.279-297.

441. Women, Technology and Innovation. Rothschild, Joan, ed. Oxford: Pergamon, 1982.
a) Daughters of Isis, daughters of Demeter: When women sowed and reaped. Stanley, Autumn, p.289-304; b) Women and technology in ancient Alexandria: Maria and Hypatia. Alic, Margaret, p.305-312; c) The machine in utopia: Shaker women and technology. Irvin, Helen Deiss, p.313-319; d) Women and microelectronics: The case of word processors. Arnold, Erik, Birke, Lynda and Faulkner, Wendy, p.321-340; e) The culture of engineering: Woman, workplace and machine. Hacker, Sally L., p.341-353; f) Technology and the future of women: Haven't we met somewhere before? Zimmerman, Jan, p.355-367; g) Teaching and learning about women and technology. Rothschild, Joan, p.369; h) Feminist pedagogy and technology: Reflections on the Goddard feminism and ecology summer program. King, Ynestra, p.370-372; i) A preview of AAUW's biennial study/action topic 'Taking hold of technology'. Bush, Corlann Gee, p.373-374; j) Teaching women and technology at the University of Washington. Bereano, Philip, Bose, Christine and Durslag, Ivy, p.374-377; k) Women and technology project, Missoula, Montana. University of Montana, p.378-379.

442. Women, the Arts, and the 1920's in Paris and New York. Wheeler, Kenneth W. and Lussier, Virginia Lee, eds. New Brunswick, NJ: Transaction, 1982.
a) Colette's literary reputation. Cottrell, Robert D., p.8-13; b) Willa Cather: A problematic ideal. Douglas, Ann, p.14-19; c) Louisa May Alcott: The influence of *Little Women*. Heilbrun, Carolyn G., p.20-26; d) Gertrude Stein: The complex force of her femininity. Secor, Cynthia, p.27-35; e) City of words. Howard, Maureen, p.42-48; f) Shapes of the feminine experience in art. Pais, Sara Via, p.49-55; g) Salonists and chroniclers. Hahn, Emily, p.56-64; h) Publishing in Paris. Ford, Hugh D., p.65-73; i) Poets and versifiers, singers and signifiers: Women of the Harlem Renaissance. Wall, Cheryl A., p.74-98; j) Women and fashion. Hollander, Anne, p.109-125; k) Suppressed desires: Women in the theater. Chinoy, Helen Krich, p.126-132; l) Women and dance. Kendall, Elizabeth, p.133-137; m) Women's voices. Rorem, Ned, p.138-141; n) Women and politics: The obscured dimension. Cook, Blanche Wiesen, p.147-152; o) Reflections on feminism: Implications for today. O'Neill, William, p.153-155.

443. Women Therapists Working with Women: New Theory and Process of Feminist Therapy. Brody, Claire M., ed. New York: Springer Publishing Co., 1984.
a) Authenticity in feminist therapy. Brody, Claire M.,

p.11-21; b) The therapist as imposter. Gibbs, Margaret S., p.22-33; c) The convergence of psychoanalysis and feminism: Gender identity and autonomy. Benjamin, Jessica, p.37-45; d) Feminist psychoanalysis: Theory and practice. Eichenbaum, Luise and Orbach, Susie, p.46-54; e) Female role socialization: The analyst and the analysis. Schlachet, Barbara Cohn, p.56-65; f) Treatment of the imposter phenomenon in high-achieving women. Clance, Pauline Rose and Imes, Suzanne, p.69-85; g) Strategies for dealing with sex-role stereotypes. Fodor, Iris and Rothblum, Esther D., p.86-95; h) Psychotherapy with black women and the dual effects of racism and sexism. Trotman, Frances K., p.96-108; i) Feminist therapy with minority clients. Brody, Claire M., p.109-115; j) Hidden assumptions in theory and research on women. Unger, Rhoda Kesler, p.119-134; k) Working women and stress. Solomon, Laura J., p.135-143; l) A feminist approach to math-anxiety reduction. Deitch, Irene, p.144-156; m) Some feminist concerns in an age of networking. Kaufman, Debra R., p.157-164.

444. Women, War, and Revolution. Berkin, Carol R. and Lovett, Clara M., eds. New York: Holmes & Meier, 1980.
a) Women of the popular classes in revolutionary Paris, 1789-1795. Applewhite, Harriet Branson and Levy, Darline Gay, p.9-35; b) "I don't call that *Volksgemeinschaft*": Women, class, and war in Nazi Germany. Rupp, Leila J., p.37-53; c) The job he left behind: American women in the shipyards during World War II. Skold, Karen Beck, p.55-75; d) "Life, liberty, and dower": The legal status of women after the American Revolution. Salmon, Marylynn, p.85-106; e) Old wine in new bottles: The institutional changes for women of the people during the French revolution. Johnson, Mary Durham, p.107-143; f) Communist feminism: Its synthesis and demise. Farnsworth, Beatrice Brodsky, p.145-163; g) Women in the Chinese communist revolution: The question of political equality. Maloney, Joan M., p.165-181; h) Revolution and *conciencia*: Women in Cuba. Casal, Lourdes, p.183-206; i) Revolution and retreat: Upper-class French women after 1789. Pope, Barbara Corrado, p.215-236; j) Patriot mothers in the post-risorgimento: Women after the Italian revolution. Howard, Judith Jeffrey, p.237-258; k) "The mother half of humanity": American women in the peace and preparedness movements in World War I. Steinson, Barbara J., p.259-284.

445. Women, Women Writers, and the West. Lee, L. L. and Lewis, Merrill, eds. Troy, NY: Whitston Publishing, 1980.
a) The old one and the wind (poem). Short, Clarice, p.3-3; b) Women's literature and the American frontier: A new perspective on the frontier myth. Armitage, Susan H., p.5-13; c) The Tonopah ladies. Ronald, Ann, p.15-24; d) American dream, nightmare underside: Diaries, letters and fiction of women on the American frontier. McKnight, Jeannie, p.25-44; e) Homestead home. Lenz, Elinor, p.45-54; f) Mari Sandoz and western biography. Stauffer, Helen, p.55-69; g) Women poets and the "Northwest School". Bangs, Carol Jane, p.71-82; h) Hamlin Garland and the cult of true womanhood. Carp,

Roger E., p.83-99; i) Gertrude Atherton's California woman: From love story to psychological drama. McClure, Charlotte S., p.101-109; j) Madness and personification in *Giants in the Earth*. Grider, Sylvia, p.111-117; k) Conrad Richter's southwestern ladies. Meldrum, Barbara, p.119-129; l) Westering and woman: A thematic study of Kesey's *One Flew Over the Cuckoo's Nest* and Fisher's *Mountain Man*. Flora, Joseph M., p.131-141; m) Heroes vs women: Conflict and duplicity in Stegner. Ahearn, Kerry, p.143-159; n) Willa Cather and the sense of history. Slote, Bernice, p.161-171; o) Dorothy Scarborough's critique of the frontier experience in *The Wind*. Quissell, Barbara, p.173-195; p) Folk narrative in Caroline Gordon's frontier fiction. Rodenberger, M. Lou, p.197-208; q) The Mormon novel: Virginia Sorensen's *The Evening and the Morning*. Lee, Sylvia B., p.209-218; r) "On the *other* side of the mountains": The westering experiences in the fiction of Ethel Wilson. Mitchell, Beverley, p.219-231; s) Tradition of the exile: Judith Wright's Australian "West". Tatum, Stephen, p.233-247.

446. Women, Work, and Family in the Soviet Union. Lapidus, Gail Warshofsky, ed. Armonk, NY: M. E. Sharpe, 1982. a) Women, work, and family: New Soviet perspectives. Lapidus, Gail W., p.ix-xlvi; b) Current problems of female labor in the USSR. Rzhanitsyna, L., p.3-21; c) Socioeconomic problems of female employment. Sonin, M. Ia., p.22-32; d) Features of the development of female employment. Kostakov, V. G., p.33-68; e) The educational and occupational skill level of industrial workers. Kotliar, A. E. and Turchaninova, S. Ia., p.69-120; f) Raising the skill level of women workers. Shishkan, N. M., p.121-130; g) The utilization of female labor in agriculture. Fedorova, M., p.131-146; h) The twenty-fifth congress of the CPSU and current problems of employment of female labor in the republics of central Asia. Ubaidullaeva, R. A., p.147-155; i) Protection of female labor. Sheptulina, N. N., p.156-162; j) Women's work and the family. Iankova, Z. A., Iazykova, V. S. and Novikova, E. E., p.165-190; k) Changing family roles and marital instability. Kharchev, A. G. and Matskovskii, M. S., p.191-218; l) Changes in the status of women and the demographic development of the family. Volkov, A. G., p.218-229; m) Maternal care of infants. Katkova, I., p.230-239; n) Women with large families: A sociodemographic analysis. Ata-Mirzaev, O., p.240-249; o) The quantity and quality of work: A round table. Kutyrev, B. P. and Novikova, E. E., p.253-266; p) How working women combine work and household duties. Porokhniuk, V. and Shepeleva, M. S., p.267-276; q) Part-time employment of women. Kuleshova, L. M. and Mamontova, T. I., p.277-281; r) The position of women and demographic policy. Kiseleva, G., p.282-295.

447. Women, Work, and Health: Challenges to Corporate Policy. Egdahl, Richard H. and Walsh, Diana Chapman, eds. New York: Springer-Verlag, 1980. a) Genesis and highlights of a conference. Walsh, Diana Chapman, p.3-26; b) Overview: The health of working

women. Lebowitz, Ann, p.27-72; c) The state of the art of strength testing. Hogan, Joyce C., p.75-98; d) Moving women into outside craft jobs. Reilly, Richard R., p.99-111; e) Changing roles and mental health in women. Duff, Jean F., p.115-131; f) Employee health services for women workers. Warshaw, Leon J., p.132-144; g) Special needs of women in health examinations. Morrison, Donna, et al., p.145-155; h) Sex discrimination in group pensions. Blum, John D., p.156-167; i) A legal perspective on workplace reproductive hazards. Stillman, Nina G., p.171-178; j) The biology of toxic effects on reproductive outcomes. Stellman, Jeanne M., p.179-189; k) Evaluation and control of embryofetotoxic substances. Karrh, Bruce W., p.190-197; l) Fetotoxicity and fertile female employees. Clyne, Robert M., p.198-207; m) The control of hazardous exposures in the workplace. Bernacki, Edward J., p.208-210; n) A legal perspective on pregnancy leave and benefits. Stillman, Nina G., p.213-230; o) Non-medical issues presented by the pregnant worker. Warshaw, Leon J., p.231-242; p) Challenges to corporate policy. Walsh, Diana Chapman, p.245-256.

448. Women Writers and the City: Essays in Feminist Literary Criticism. Squier, Susan Merrill, ed. Knoxville, TN: University of Tennessee Press, 1984. a) The city as catalyst for Flora Tristan's vision of social change. Dijkstra, Sandra, p.13-34; b) Marguerite Duras: Women's language in men's cities. Rava, Susan, p.35-44; c) Return to Mytilène: Renée Vivien and the city of women. Blankley, Elyse, p.45-67; d) George Eliot and the city: The imprisonment of culture. Paxton, Nancy L., p.71-96; e) Every woman is an island: Vita Sackville-West, the image of the city and the pastoral idyll. Desalvo, Louise A., p.97-113; f) Tradition and revision: The classic city novel and Virginia Woolf's *Night and Day*. Squier, Susan Merrill, p.114-133; g) A wilderness of one's own: Feminist fantasy novels of the twenties: Rebecca West and Sylvia Townsend Warner. Marcus, Jane, p.134-160; h) "A gigantic mother": Katherine Mansfield's London. Kaplan, Sydney Janet, p.161-175; i) Reading the city as palimpsest: The experiential perception of the city in Doris Lessing's *The Four-Gated City*. Sizemore, Christine W., p.176-190; j) Quest for the peaceable kingdom: Urban/rural codes in Roy, Laurence, and Atwood. Grace, Sherrill E., p.193-209; k) Willa Cather's lost Chicago sisters. Bremer, Sidney H., p.210-229; l) "A laying on of hands": Transcending the city in Ntozake Shange's *for colored girls who have considered suicide/when the rainbow is enuf*. Mitchell, Carolyn, p.230-248; m) Another view of the "City upon a Hill": The prophetic vision of Adrienne Rich. Martin, Wendy, p.249-264; n) Sister to Faust: The city's "hungry" woman as heroine. Gelfant, Blanche H., p.265-287; o) Literature and the city: A checklist of relevant secondary works. Squier, Susan Merrill, p.288-294.

449. Women Writers of 20th-Century China. Palandri, Angela Jung, ed. Eugene, OR: Asian Studies Program, University of Oregon, 1982. a) Introduction: A historical perspective. Palandri,

Angela Jung, p.1-17; b) Images of women in Ping Hsin's fiction. Bien, Gloria, p.19-40; c) Portraits by a lady: The fictional world of Ling Shuhua. Cuadrado, Clara Y., p.41-62; d) Feminism and literary technique in Ting Ling's early short stories. Barlow, Tani E., p.63-110; e) The shaping of life: Structure and narrative process in Eileen Chang's *The Rouge of the North*. Kao, Hsin-Sheng C., p.111-136; f) A woman's voice: The poetry of Yungtzu. Lin, Julia C., p.137-162.

450. Women Writers of the Contemporary South. Prenshaw, Peggy Whitman, ed. Jackson, MS: University Press of Mississippi, 1984.
a) The fiction of Anne Tyler. Betts, Doris, p.23-37; b) Alice Walker's celebration of self in southern generations. Davis, Thadious M., p.39-53; c) Gail Godwin and the ideal of southern womanhood. Rhodes, Carolyn, p.55-68; d) Eating the moment absolutely up: The fiction of Beverly Lowry. Skaggs, Merrill Maguire, p.67-82; e) Shirley Ann Grau and the short story. Rohrberger, Mary, p.83-101; f) Lisa Alther: The irony of return? Ferguson, Mary Anne, p.103-115; g) Ellen Douglas: Moralist and realist. Manning, Carol S., p.117-134; h) Doris Bett's Nancy Finch: A heroine for the 1980s. Scura, Dorothy M., p.135-145; i) Mermaids, angels and free women: The heroines of Elizabeth Spencer's fiction. Prenshaw, Peggy Whitman, p.147-164; j) Mary Lee Settle's connections: Class and clothes in the Beulah quintet. Joyner, Nancy Carol, p.165-178; k) The androgynous, bi-racial vision of Berry Morgan. Bolsterli, Margaret Jones, p.179-193; l) Rita Mae Brown: Feminist theorist and southern novelist. Chew, Martha, p.195-213; m) Youth in Toni Cade Bambara's *Gorilla, My Love*. Hargrove, Nancy D., p.215-232; n) The miracle of realism: The bid for self-knowledge in the fiction of Ellen Gilchrist. Garner, Anita Miller and Thompson, Jeanie, p.233-247; o) The world of Lee Smith. Jones, Anne Goodwyn, p.249-272; p) The career of Joan Williams: Problems in assessment. Wittenberg, Judith Bryant, p.273-282; q) Stopping places: Bobbie Ann Mason's short stories. Ryan, Maureen, p.283-294; r) Why there are no southern writers. Athas, Daphne, p.295-306.

451. Women Writers of the Short Story. Silberfeld, Heath, ed. Englewood Cliffs, NJ: Prentice-Hall, 1980.
a) The art of Jewett's *Pointed Firs*. Berthoff, Warner, p.11-31; b) Introduction to *The Collected Short Stories of Edith Wharton*. Lewis, R.W.B., p.32-49; c) Reflections on Willa Cather. Porter, Katherine Anne, p.50-60; d) Willa Cather. Trilling, Lionel, p.61-68; e) Irony with a center: Katherine Anne Porter. Warren, Robert Penn, p.69-85; f) The eye of the story. Welty, Eudora, p.86-95; g) The world of love: The fiction of Eudora Welty. Jones, Alun R., p.96-111; h) Love and separateness in Eudora Welty. Warren, Robert Penn, p.112-123; i) Introduction to *Everything That Rises Must Converge*. Fitzgerald, Robert, p.124-135; j) Flannery O'Connor, a realist of distances. Quinn, M. Bernetta, p.136-144; k) The other side of despair. Merton, Thomas, p.145-149; l) The visionary art of Flannery O'Connor. Oates, Joyce Carol, p.150-162.

452. Women's Autobiography: Essays in Criticism. Jelinek, Estelle C., ed. Bloomington, IN: Indiana University Press, 1980.
a) Introduction: Women's autobiography and the male tradition. Jelinek, Estelle C., p.1-20; b) The emergence of women's autobiography in England. Pomerleau, Cynthia S., p.21-38; c) Quest for community: Spiritual autobiographies of eighteenth-century Quaker and Puritan women in America. Edkins, Carol, p.39-52; d) *Harriet Martineau's Autobiography*: The making of a female philosopher. Myers, Mitzi, p.53-70; e) The paradox and success of Elizabeth Cady Stanton. Jelinek, Estelle C., p.71-92; f) The autobiographer and her readers: From apology to affirmation. Winston, Elizabeth, p.93-111; g) Selves in hiding. Spacks, Patricia Meyer, p.112-132; h) In search of the black female self: African-American women's autobiographies and ethnicity. Blackburn, Regina, p.133-148; i) Gertrude Stein and the problems of autobiography. Breslin, James E., p.149-162; j) Lillian Hellman and the strategy of the "other". Billson, Marcus K. and Smith, Sidonie A., p.163-179; k) The metaphysics of matrilinearism in women's autobiography: Studies of Mead's *Blackberry Winter*, Hellman's *Pentimento*, Angelou's *I Know Why the Caged Bird Sings*, and Kingston's *The Woman Warrior*. Demetrakopoulos, Stephanie A., p.180-205; l) Anaïs Nin's *Diary* in context. Bloom, Lynn Z. and Holder, Orlee, p.206-220; m) Towards a theory of form in feminist autobiography: Kate Millett's *Flying* and *Sita*; Maxine Hong Kingston's *The Woman Warrior*. Juhasz, Suzanne, p.221-237; n) The lady's not for spurning: Kate Millett and the critics. Kolodny, Annette, p.238-260.

453. Women's Culture: The Women's Renaissance of the Seventies. Kimball, Gayle, ed. Metuchen, NJ: Scarecrow Press, 1981.
a) Women's culture: Themes and images. Kimball, Gayle, p.2-29; b) Defining women's culture. Morgan, Robin, p.30-40; c) Women's imagery/women's art. Roos, Sandra, p.42-59; d) A female form language. Chicago, Judy, p.60-71; e) Humor in California underground women's comix. Mitchell, Dolores, p.72-90; f) Goddess imagery in ritual. Edelson, Mary Beth, p.91-105; g) Women's theatre: Creating the dream now. Suntree, Susan, p.106-116; h) Women's images in film. Hammer, Barbara, p.117-129; i) Women and fashion. Kimball, Barbara, p.130-146; j) Women's music. Scovill, Ruth, p.148-162; k) Female composition. Gardner, Kay, p.163-176; l) Madonna or witch: Women's muse in contemporary American poetry. Ashworth, Debora, p.178-186; m) Mirror images. Piercy, Marge, p.187-194; n) The use of story in women's novels of the seventies. Megibow, Carol Burr, p.195-214; o) Characteristics of women's dreams. King, Johanna, p.215-228; p) Feminist theology. Kimball, Gayle, p.230-237; q) Goddess worship in Wicce. Budapest, Z., p.238-248; r) Feminist therapy. Kaschak, Ellyn, p.250-263; s) Feminist women's health centers. Hasper, Dido, p.264-279; t) Institutions of women's culture. Iskin, Ruth, p.280-291.

454. Women's Experience in America: An Historical Anthology. Katz, Esther and Rapone, Anita, eds. New Brunswick, NJ: Transaction Books, 1980.
a) American women and domestic culture: An approach to women's history. Katz, Esther and Rapone, Anita, p.3-14; b) The case of the American Jezebels: Anne Hutchinson and female agitation during the years of the Antinomian turmoil, 1636-1640. Koehler, Lyle W., p.21-45; c) Widowhood in eighteenth-century Massachusetts: A problem in the history of the family. Keyssar, Alexander, p.47-78; d) The lady and the mill girl: Changes in the status of women in the Age of Jackson. Lerner, Gerda, p.87-99; e) Ladies bountiful: Organized women's benevolence in early nineteenth-century America. Melder, Keith, p.101-123; f) The war within a war: Women nurses in the Union Army. Wood, Ann Douglas, p.125-143; g) The spiritualist medium: A study of female professionalization in Victorian America. Moore, R. Laurence, p.145-168; h) Cultural hybrid in the slums: The college woman and the Settlement House, 1889-1894. Rousmaniere, John P., p.169-191; i) The cult of true womanhood: 1820-1860. Welter, Barbara, p.193-218; j) Catharine Beecher and the education of American women. Burstyn, Joan, p.219-235; k) Family limitation, sexual control, and domestic feminism in Victorian America. Smith, Daniel Scott, p.235-257; l) The female world of love and ritual: Relations between women in nineteenth-century America. Smith-Rosenberg, Carroll, p.259-291; m) Women and their families on the Overland Trail, 1842-1867. Faragher, Johnny and Stansell, Christine, p.293-314; n) The hysterical woman: Sex roles and role conflict in nineteenth century America. Smith-Rosenberg, Carroll, p.315-337; o) The American woman's pre-World War I freedom in manners and morals. McGovern, James R., p.345-365; p) Prosperity's child: Some thoughts on the flapper. Yellis, Kenneth A., p.367-388; q) Cookbooks and law books: The hidden history of career women in twentieth-century America. Stricker, Frank, p.389-411.

455. Women's Issues and Social Work Practice. Mancuso, Arlene and Norman, Elaine, eds. Itasca, IL: F.E. Peacock, 1980.
a) Sex roles and sexism. Norman, Elaine, p.11-20; b) A herstory of women in social work. Vandiver, Susan T., p.21-38; c) No drums, no trumpets: Working-class women. Mancuso, Arlene, p.41-56; d) Aging and old age: The last sexist rip-off. Faulkner, Audrey, p.57-90; e) Ain't I a woman. Joseph, Barbara, p.91-112; f) The social work profession encounters the battered woman. Kremen, Eleanor, p.113-132; g) New knowledge and the drinking woman. Corrigan, Eileen, p.133-152; h) Some mothers are lesbians. Goodman, Bernice, p.153-180; i) Women and the health care system: Implications for social work practice. Polansky, Elinor, p.183-200; j) Women and the mental health system. Donadello, Gloria, p.201-218; k) Women and income maintenance programs. Chambré, Susan Maizel, p.219-240; l) Women administrators in social work. Chernesky, Roslyn, p.241-262.

456. Women's Problems in General Practice. McPherson, Ann and Anderson, Anne, eds. Oxford: Oxford University Press, 1983.
a) Why women's health? McPherson, Ann, p.1-12; b) Menstrual problems. Anderson, Anne and McPherson, Ann, p.13-41; c) Premenstrual tension. Sanders, Diana, p.42-62; d) Menopause. Anderson, Anne and McPherson, Ann, p.63-83; e) Breast cancer and benign breast disease. Adam, Sheila and Roberts, Maureen, p.84-106; f) The 'ectomies'. Anderson, Anne and McPherson, Ann, p.106-117; g) Contraception. Law, Barbara, p.118-149; h) Unwanted pregnancy and abortion. Bury, Judith, p.150-178; i) Cervical cytology. McPherson, Ann and Savage, Wendy, p.179-202; j) Depression. Greenwood, Judy, p.203-223; k) Sexual problems. Hawton, Keith and Oppenheimer, Catherine, p.224-260; l) Infertility. Charnock, Mark, p.261-288; m) Vaginal discharge. Barlow, David, p.289-302; n) Cystitis. Elliott, Shirley and Mayon-White, Richard, p.303-321; o) Migraine. Peet, Katharine, p.322-336; p) Health education. Graham, Hilary, p.337-348; q) Eating problems. Mitchell, Elizabeth, p.349-380.

457. Women's Religious Experience. Holden, Pat, ed. London: Croom Helm, 1983.
a) Mediums, controls and eminent men. Skultans, Vieda, p.15-26; b) Theosophy and feminism: Some explorations in nineteenth century biography. Burfield, Diana, p.27-56; c) Doves and magpies: Village women in the Greek Orthodox Church. Rushton, Lucy, p.57-70; d) Gender and religion in a Turkish town: A comparison of two types of formal women's gatherings. Tapper, Nancy, p.71-83; e) Essence and existence: Women and religion in ancient Indian texts. Leslie, Julia, p.89-112; f) Women, fertility and the worship of gods in a Hindu village. Thompson, Catherine, p.113-132; g) Women in Judaism: The fact and the fiction. Neuberger, Julia, p.132-142; h) Between law and custom: Women's experience of Judaism. Webber, Jonathan, p.143-162; i) Women excluded? Masking and masquerading in West Africa. Tonkin, Elizabeth, p.163-174; j) Men, women and misfortune in Bunyole. Whyte, Susan Reynolds, p.175-192.

458. Women's Retirement: Policy Implications of Recent Research. Szinovacz, Maximiliane, ed. Beverly Hills, CA: Sage Publications, 1982.
a) Introduction: Research on women's retirement. Szinovacz, Maximiliane, p.13-21; b) Midlife work history and retirement income. Henretta, John C. and O'Rand, Angela, p.25-44; c) Life satisfaction among aging women: A causal model. Riddick, Carol Cutler, p.45-59; d) Employment status and social support: The experience of the mature woman. Depner, Charlene and Ingersoll, Berit, p.61-76; e) Working women versus homemakers: Retirement resources and correlates of well-being. Keith, Pat M., p.77-91; f) Preretirement preparation: Sex differences in access, sources, and use. Kroeger, Naomi, p.95-111; g) Retirement expectations and plans: A comparison of professional men and women. Higgins, Claire E., Newman, Evelyn S. and Sherman, Susan R., p.113-122; h)

Attitudes toward retirement: A comparison of professional and nonprofessional married women. Johnson, Carolyn Kitchings and Price-Bonham, Sharon, p.123-138; i) Retirement plans and retirement adjustment. Szinovacz, Maximiliane, p.139-150; j) The process of retirement: Comparing women and men. Atchley, Robert C., p.153-168; k) After retirement: An exploratory study of the professional woman. Jewson, Ruth Hathaway, p.169-181; l) Professional women: Work pattern as a correlate of retirement satisfaction. Block, Marilyn R., p.183-194; m) Personal problems and adjustment to retirement. Szinovacz, Maximiliane, p.195-203; n) Responsibility for household tasks: Comparing dual-earner and dual-retired marriages. Brubaker, Timothy H. and Hennon, Charles B., p.205-219; o) Conclusion: Service needs of women retirees. Szinovacz, Maximiliane, p.221-233.

459. Women's Roles and Population Trends in the Third World. Anker, Richard, Buvinic Mayra and Youssef, Nadia H., eds. London: Croom Helm, 1982.
a) Demographic change and the role of women: A research programme in developing countries. Anker, Richard, p.29-51; b) The allocation of women's time and its relation to fertility. Mueller, Eva, p.55-86; c) Class and historical analysis for the study of women and economic change. Deere, Carmen Diana, Humphries, Jane and Leal, Magdalena León de, p.87-114; d) Female power, autonomy and demographic change in the Third World. Safilios-Rothschild, Constantina, p.117-132; e) Family structure and women's reproductive and productive roles: Some conceptual and methodological issues. Oppong, Christine, p.133-150; f) A social anthropological approach to women's roles and status in developing countries: The domestic cycle. Epstein, T. Scarlett, p.151-170; g) The interrelationship between the division of labour in the household, women's roles and their impact on fertility. Youssef, Nadia H., p.173-201; h) Women's work and their status: Rural Indian evidence of labour market and environment effects on sex differences in childhood mortality. Schultz, T. Paul, p.202-236; i) Women and the urban labour market. Jelin, Elizabeth, p.239-267; j) Sex discrimination in the urban labour markets: Some propositions based on Indian evidence. Papola, T.S., p.268-280.

460. Women's Sexual Development: Explorations of *Inner Space*. Kirkpatrick, Martha, ed. New York: Plenum Press, 1980.
a) "Role, Jenny Jenkins, Roll": Little girls and maidens in American folksongs - an analysis of sexual attitudes. Oaks, Priscilla, p.1-18; b) The history of female sexuality in the United States. Lewis, Myrna I., p.19-38; c) Discussion: A historian's approach. Geltner, Sharon Ordman, p.39-43; d) Physiological aspects of female sexual development: Conception through puberty. Baill, Cori and Money, John, p.45-59; e) Physiological aspects of female sexual development: Gestation, lactation, menopause, and erotic physiology. Baill, Cori and Money, John, p.61-76; f) Psychological and physiological concepts in female sexuality: A discussion of physiologoical aspects of female sexual development. Rubin,

Lynne, p.77-81; g) Some suggested revisions concerning early female development. Galenson, Eleanor and Roiphe, Herman, p.83-105; h) The early stages of female psychosexual development: A Kleinian view. Elmhirst, Susanna Isaacs, p.107-125; i) Femininity. Stoller, Robert J., p.127-145; j) Masturbation in women. Clower, Virginia Lawson, p.147-166; k) Discussion: Another point of view. Golden, Joshua, p.167-170; l) The misnamed female sex organ. Ash, Mildred, p.171-179; m) Finding self in the lesbian community. Ponse, Barbara, p.181-200; n) Discussion: Random comments. Riess, B.F., p.201-206; o) Daughters and lovers: Reflections on the life cycle of father-daughter relationships. Ekstein, Rudolph, p.207-221; p) Role of the father. Adams, Paul L. and Adams-Tucker, Christine, p.223-237; q) Sex education versus sexual learning. Roberts, Elizabeth J., p.239-250; r) A sex-information switchboard. Rila, Margo and Steinhart, Judith, p.251-254; s) Self-help for sex. Downer, Carol, p.255-271; t) Self-help in gynecological practice. Edwards, Laura and Lawrence, Allen, p.273-279; u) Young women and the sexual revolution. Canfield, Elizabeth K., p.281-289.

461. Women's Sexual Experience: Explorations of the *Dark Continent*. Kirkpatrick, Martha, ed. New York: Plenum Press, 1982.
a) Women's sexual response. Kaplan, Helen S. and Sucher, Erica, p.3-16; b) The sexual experience of Afro-American women: A middle-income sample. Wyatt, Gail Elizabeth, p.17-39; c) Discussion: Further thoughts on a group discussion by black women about sexuality. Butts, June Dobbs, p.41-43; d) Sexual consequences of acculturation of American Indian women. Echohawk, Marlene, p.45-55; e) Discussion: Myths in the midst of missing data. Weibel, Joan Crofut, p.57-60; f) Sex and sexuality: Women at midlife. Rubin, Lillian B., p.61-82; g) Discussion: Midlife women: Lessons for sex therapy. Schover, Leslie R., p.83-86; h) In praise of older women. Genevay, B., p.87-101; i) Discussion: Aging and female sexuality. Bragonier, J. Robert, p.103-105; j) The cradle of sexual politics: Incest. Armstrong, Louise, p.109-125; k) Beyond belief: The reluctant discovery of incest. Summit, Roland, p.127-150; l) Effects of teenage motherhood. Church, Merle G., p.151-166; m) Does motherhood mean maturity? Sugar, Max, p.167-177; n) Discussion: Some developmental aspects of adolescent mothers. Tasini, Miriam, p.179-184; o) Female sexuality and pregnancy. Pape, Rachel Edgarde, p.185-197; p) Discussion: The developmental crisis of pregnancy. Vida, Judith E., p.199-204; q) Voluntary childlessness. Benedek, Elissa and Vaughn, Richard, p.205-222; r) Discussion: Voluntary sterilization in childless women. Rubinstein, Lidia M., p.223-226; s) Women in swinging: America's Amazon society? Levin, Lloyd M., p.227-237; t) Discussion: Extramarital sex: A multifaceted experience. Sandlin, Joann DeLora, p.239-245; u) Wife beating: A product of sociosexual development. Martin, Del, p.247-261; v) Discussion: Psychoanalytic reflections on the "beaten wife syndrome". Blum, Harold P., p.263-267; w) The prostitute

as victim. James, Jennifer, p.269-292; x) Discussion: Legal victim or social victim? Lee, Lois, p.293-294; y) Women - victims of the VD rip-off. Brecher, Edward M., p.295-313; z) Discussion: Prophylaxis of sexually transmitted diseases: An overview. Holmes, King K., p.315-319.

462. Women's Spirit Bonding. Kalven, Janet and Buckley, Mary I., eds. New York: The Pilgrim Press, 1984.
a) Women, poverty, and economic justice. Buckley, Mary I., p.3-10; b) Class, gender, and religion: A theoretical overview and some political implications. Salvo, Jackie Di, p.11-34; c) The great chain of being and the chain of command. Scanzoni, Letha Dawson, p.41-55; d) Making the world live: Feminism and the domination of nature. King, Ynestra, p.56-64; e) Racism and the bonding of women. Phelps, Jamie, p.70-74; f) A historical addendum. Johnson, Rebecca, p.75-84; g) "Las Marías" of the feminist movement. Isasi-Diaz, Ada Maria and Tarango, Yolanda, p.85-88; h) Anti-semitism: The unacknowledged racism. Plaskow, Judith, p.89-96; i) White women and racism. Golden, Renny, p.97-105; j) A black response to feminist theology. Grant, Jacquelyn, p.117-124; k) Women as makers of literature. Williams, Delores S., p.139-145; l) Political oppression and creative survival. Hunt, Mary E., p.164-172; m) Patriarchy and death. Condren, Mary, p.173-189; n) Why women need the war god. Brown, Karen McCarthy, p.190-201; o) Feminist liberation theology and Yahweh as holy warrior: An analysis of symbol. Christ, Carol P., p.202-212; p) Women responding to the Arab-Israeli conflict. Abu-Saba, Mary Bentley, Plaskow, Judith and Ruether, Rosemary Radford, p.221-233; q) My voice...and many others. Wilson, Lynn, p.240-242; r) A religious perspective. Scanzoni, Letha Dawson, p.243-248; s) A political perspective. Hunt, Mary E., p.249-254; t) Affirming diversity and Biblical tradition. Wakeman, Mary K., p.267-280; u) Reclaiming our past. Ochshorn, Judith, p.281-292; v) Claiming the center: A critical feminist theology of liberation. Fiorenza, Elisabeth Schüssler, p.293-309; w) Immanence: Uniting the spiritual and political. Starhawk, p.310-317; x) Envisioning our hopes: Some models of the future. Ruether, Rosemary Radford, p.325-335; y) A feminist approach to alternative enterprises. Coston, Carol, p.336-343; z) Guidelines for planners of ritual. Neu, Diann and Upton, Julia, p.347-348; aa) Reflections on the creation of a ritual meal. Umansky, Ellen M., p.351-352.

463. Women's Travel Issues: Research Needs and Priorities. Rosenbloom, Sandra, ed. Washington, D.C.: U.S. Department of Transportation, GPO, 1980.
a) Women's travel issues: The research and policy environment. Rosenbloom, Sandra, p.1-40; b) Intra-household implications of the involvement of women in the paid labor force. Rosenbloom, Sandra, p.43-47; c) The movement of women into the labor force. Smith, Ralph E., p.49-73; d) Influence of employment and children on intra-household travel behavior. McGinnis, Richard G., p.75-103; e) Shopping trips: Who makes them and when? Borlaug, Karen L. and Skinner, Louise E., p.105-126; f) The impact of women's employment on household travel

patterns: A Swedish example. Hanson, Perry and Hanson, Susan, p.127-169; g) Analysis of activity schedules along the dimension of gender. Damm, David, p.171-196; h) Women's work trips: An empirical and theoretical overview. Madden, Janice Fanning and White, Michelle J., p.201-242; i) Individual spatial behavior. Betak, John F. and Harman, Elizabeth J., p.243-284; j) Residential location and transportation analyses: Married women workers. Hock, Carolyn, p.285-303; k) Role influence in transportation decision making. Koppelman, Frank S., Syskowski, David F. and Tybout, Alice M., p.309-353; l) Women's travel behavior and attitudes: An empirical analysis. Kerpelman, Larry C., Ott, Marian T. and Studenmund, A.H., p.355-379; m) Sex differences in travel preferences and decision making. Recker, Wilfred and Schuler, Harry J., p.381-416; n) Travel patterns and behavior of women in urban areas. Sen, Lalita, p.417-436; o) Perceived safety and security in transportation systems as determined by the gender of the traveler. Richards, Larry G., et al., p.441-477; p) The transportation implications of women's fear of assault. Klein, Frieda, p.479-483; q) Gender differences in reactions to vehicle environments. Jacobson, Ira D. and Richards, Larry G., p.489-513; r) A comparative survey of women car buyers. Hunt, Martin F., p.515-543; s) Can current transportation planning methods analyze women's travel issues? Hartgen, David T., p.551-568; t) Gender-role identification in the methodology of transportation planning. Cleveland, Donald E. and Kostyniuk, Lydia P., p.569-606; u) The transportation planning process. Paaswell, Robert E. and Paaswell, Rosalind S., p.607-631; v) An alternative approach to travel demand modeling: Constraints-oriented theories and societal roles. Burnett, K. Patricia, p.633-677; w) Speech. Butchman, Alan D., p.713-718; x) Speech. Shalala, Donna E., p.719-732; y) Speech. Feingold, Ellen B., p.733-738; z) Speech. Bowers, Karl S., p.739-741; aa) Speech. Gianturco, Adriana, p.743-755; bb) Speech. Liburdi, Lillian C., p.757-766; cc) Speech. Turner, Carmen, p.767-779.

464. Women's Views of the Political World of Men. Stiehm, Judith Hicks, ed. Dobbs Ferry, NY: Transnational Publishers, 1982.
a) Power as ideology: A feminist analysis. Jaquette, Jane S., p.7-29; b) Overcoming the barriers: An approach to the study of how women's issues are kept from the political agenda. Dahlerup, Drude, p.31-66; c) The shame of the marriage contract. Pateman, Carole, p.67-97; d) Women and authoritarian regimes. Tabak, Fanny, p.99-119; e) Prologue to a feminist critique of war and politics. Hartsock, Nancy C.M., p.121-150; f) Despotism and civil society: The limits of patriarchcal citizenship. Yeatman, Anna, p.151-176; g) Consequences of seizing the reins in the household: A Marxist-feminist critique of Marx and Engels. Clark, Lorenne M.G., p.177-204; h) The man question. Stiehm, Judith Hicks, p.205-223.

465. Women's Welfare Women's Rights. Lewis, Jane, ed. London: Croom Helm, 1983.
a) Dealing with dependency: State practices and social

realities, 1870-1945. Lewis, Jane, p.17-37; b) Members and survivors: Women and retirement-pensions legislation. Groves, Dulcie, p.38-63; c) Who still cares for the family? Recent developments in income maintenance, taxation and family law. Land, Hilary, p.64-85; d) Sex equality and social security. Abel-Smith, Brian, p.86-102; e) Women and health policy. Oakley, Ann, p.103-129; f) Women's employment, legislation and the labour-market. Bruegel, Irene, p.130-169; g) Equal opportunity policies: Some implications for women of contrasts between enforcement bodies in Britain and the USA. Meehan, Elizabeth, p.170-192; h) The new right, sex, education and social policy: Towards a new moral economy in Britain and the USA. David, Miriam E., p.193-218.

466. Women's Work and Women's Roles: Economics and Everyday Life in Indonesia, Malaysia and Singapore. Manderson, Lenore, ed. Canberra, Australia: Australian National University, 1983.
a) Women as cultural intermediaries in nineteenth-century Batavia. Abeyasekere, Susan, p.15-29; b) The Peranankan Chinese woman at a crossroad. Bocquet-Siek, Margaret, p.31-52; c) Healing as women's work in Bali. Connor, Linda H., p.53-72; d) Land ownership in Negri Sembilan, 1900-1977. Fett, Ione, p.73-96; e) Rich woman, poor woman: Occupation differences in a textile producing village in Central Java. Price, Susanna, p.97-110; f) Women and work in an Indonesian mining town. Robinson, Kathy, p.111-127; g) Housewives and farmers: Malay women in the Muda Irrigation Scheme. Barnard, Rosemary, p.129-145; h) Indonesian women in development: State theory and urban kampung practice. Sullivan, Norma, p.147-171; i) Separate but equal: Indonesian Muslim perceptions of the roles of women. Woodcroft-Lee, Carlien Patricia, p.173-192; j) Four paces behind: Women's work in peninsular Malaysia. O'Brien, Leslie N., p.193-215; k) The feminization of the teaching profession in Singapore. Inglis, Christine, p.217-238.

467. Work and the Family. Moss, Peter and Fonda, Nickie, eds. London: Temple Smith, 1980.
a) Parents at work. Moss, Peter, p.22-67; b) Employment prospects and equal opportunity. Elias, Peter, p.68-86; c) Managing work and family life: A comparative policy overview. Kamerman, Sheila, p.87-109; d) Statutory maternity leave in the United Kingdom: A case study. Fonda, Nickie, p.110-134; e) The stance of Britain's major parties and interest groups. Coote, Anna and Hewitt, Patricia, p.135-157; f) The impact of work on the family. Rapoport, Rhona and Rapoport, Robert, p.158-185; g) The future prospect. Fonda, Nickie and Moss, Peter, p.186-202.

468. Work and Womanhood: Norwegian Studies. Leira, Arnlaug, ed. Oslo, Norway: Institute for Social Research, 1983.
a) The making of a female occupation: A case study of cleaning work. Kalleberg, Annemor, p.15-47; b) Working hours and segmentation in the Norwegian labour market. Strømsheim, Gunvor, p.48-65; c) Trade union participa-

tion of women in Norway: Structural changes, dilemmas and challenges. Berg, Anne Marie, p.66-87; d) Women's attempts to break down sex barriers in the labour market. Aga, Synnøva, p.88-124; e) Women's work strategies: An analysis of the organisation of everyday life in an urban neighbourhood. Leira, Arnlaug, p.125-160; f) On work, art and women: A discussion of the ambiguous position of women artists. Berg, Mie, p.161-189; g) Conceptualising domestic work: Comments on definitions of "work" in some Norwegian studies. Haugen, Inger, p.190-214; h) Love and power: The division of household labour. Berg, Anne Marie, p.215-233; i) Perspectives on work and reproduction with special reference to women's opportunities and adaptation. Houg, Tora, p.234-261.

469. Work, Family, and Health: Latina Women in Transition. Zambrana, Ruth E., ed. New York: Hispanic Research Center, Fordham University, 1982.
a) Introduction: Latina women in transition. Zambrana, Ruth E., p.ix-xiii; b) Mental health needs of Puerto Rican women in the United States. Comas-Diaz, Lillian, p.1-10; c) The self-perception of Puerto Rican women toward their societal roles. Rosario, Lillian M., p.11-16; d) Hispanic women in suburbia. Press, Sylvia Peña, p.17-26; e) Transactional family patterns: A preliminary exploration of Puerto Rican female adolescents. Canino, Glorisa, p.27-36; f) Cultural attitudes toward mental illness among Puerto Rican migrant women. Gil, Rosa Maria, p.37-45; g) "La operacion": An analysis of sterilization in a Puerto Rican community in Connecticut. Gonzalez, Maria, et al., p.47-61; h) The utilization of pediatric health services by Hispanic mothers. Irigoyen, Matilde and Zambrana, Ruth E., p.63-73; i) A preliminary historical analysis of women and work in Puerto Rico: 1899-1975. Burgos, Nilsa M., p.75-86; j) The emerging Cuban women of Florida's Dade County. Rodriguez, Angela M. and Vila, Mayra E., p.87-94; k) Family roles of Hispanic women: Stereotypes, empirical findings, and implications for research. Andrade, Sally J., p.95-106.

470. Work, Women and the Labour Market. West, Jackie, ed. London: Routledge & Kegan Paul, 1982.
a) Sex and skill in the organisation of the clothing industry. Coyle, Angela, p.10-26; b) 'If it's only women it doesn't matter so much'. Armstrong, Peter, p.27-43; c) Contemporary clerical work: A case study of local government. Crompton, Rosemary, Jones, Gareth and Reid, Stuart, p.44-60; d) New technology and women's office work. West, Jackie, p.61-79; e) Contemporary clothing 'sweatshops', Asian female labour and collective organisation. Hoel, Barbro, p.80-98; f) Migrant women and wage labour: The case of West Indian women in Britain. Phizacklea, Annie, p.99-116; g) Standing on the edge: Working class housewives and the world of work. Porter, Marilyn, p.117-134; h) The 'understanding' employer. Freeman, Caroline, p.135-153; i) A woman's place is her union. Hunt, Judith, p.154-171.

471. Working Women: An International Survey. Davidson, Marilyn J. and Cooper, Cary L., eds. New York: Wiley,

1984.
a) Women at work in Great Britain. Knowles, Wilf and Lockwood, Betty, p.3-38; b) Women at work in Ireland. Murdoch, Henry, p.39-62; c) Women at work in the Federal Republic of Germany. Hesse, Beate, p.63-81; d) Women at work in Holland. Rijk, Tineke de, p.83-102; e) Women at work in Italy: Legislation - evolution and prospects. Ballestrero, Maria Vittoria, p.103-122; f) Women at work in Greece: The sociological and legal perspectives. Moussourou, Loukia M. and Spiliotopoulos, Sophia, p.123-150; g) Women at work in Sweden. Scriven, Jeannie, p.153-181; h) Women at work in Finland. Haavio-Mannila, Elina, Kandolin, Irja and Kauppinen-Toropainen, Kaisa, p.183-208; i) Women at work in Portugal. Carmo Nunes, Maria do, p.209-233; j) Women at work in the USA. Gutek, Barbara A. and Larwood, Laurie, p.237-267; k) Women at work in the USSR. Attwood, Lynne and McAndrew, Maggie, p.269-304.

472. The World of the Older Woman: Conflicts and Resolutions. Lesnoff-Caravaglia, Gari, ed. New York: Human Sciences Press, 1984.
a) Double stigmata: Female and old. Lesnoff-Caravaglia, Gari, p.11-20; b) The psychosocial problems of older women. Troll, Lillian E., p.21-35; c) Social class and the older family member. Trager, Natalie P., p.36-48; d) The abused older woman: A discussion of abuses and rape. Rathbone-McCuan, Eloise, p.49-70; e) Legal issues affecting older women. Nathanson, Paul S., p.71-91; f) Institutionalized women: Some classic types, some common problems, and some partial solutions. Knapp, Nancy Mayer, p.92-126; g) The "babushka" or older woman in Soviet society. Lesnoff-Caravaglia, Gari, p.127-136; h) Widowhood: The last stage in wifedom. Lesnoff-Caravaglia, Gari, p.137-143; i) Widow-to-widow: The elderly widow and mutual help. Cooperband, Adele and Silverman, Phyllis R., p.144-161; j) Now for the feminist menopause that refreshes. Heide, Wilma Scott, p.162-174; k) Policy directions and program design: Issues and implications in services for the older woman. Auslander, Stefanie S. and Steinhauer, Marcia B., p.175-186.

473. A World of Women: Anthropological Studies of Women in the Societies of the World. Bourguignon, Erika, ed. New York: Praeger, 1980.

a) The contemporary Saudi woman. Deaver, Sherri, p.19-42; b) Women of Brunei. Kimball, Linda A., p.43-56; c) Women's role in a Muslim Hausa town (Mirria, Republic of Niger). Saunders, Margaret O., p.57-86; d) Dioula women in town: A view of intra-ethnic variation (Ivory Coast). Ellovich, Risa S., p.87-103; e) Spirit magic in the social relations between men and women (Saõ Paulo, Brazil). Pressel, Esther, p.107-128; f) Spirit mediums in Umbanda Evangelizada of Porto Alegre, Brazil: Dimensions of power and authority. Lerch, Patricia Barker, p.129-159; g) Sex and status: Women in St. Vincent. Henney, Jeannette H., p.161-183; h) Adaptive strategies and social networks of women in St. Kitts. Gussler, Judith D., p.185-209; i) Women in Yucatán. Goodman, Felicitas D., p.213-233; j) The uses of traditional concepts in the development of new urban roles: Cuban women in the United States. Boone, Margaret S., p.235-269; k) The life of Sarah Penfield, rural Ohio grandmother: Tradition maintained, tradition threatened. Joyce, Rosemary, p.271-303; l) The economic role of women in Alaskan Eskimo society. Ager, Lynn Price, p.305-317; m) Comparisons and implications: What have we learned? Bourguignon, Erika, p.321-342.

474. The Writer on Her Work. Sternburg, Janet, ed. New York: W.W. Norton, 1980.
a) Still just writing. Tyler, Anne, p.3-16; b) Why I write. Didion, Joan, p.17-25; c) The parable of the cave or: In praise of watercolors. Gordon, Mary, p.27-32; d) *De memoria*. Milford, Nancy, p.33-43; e) My grandmother who painted. Moore, Honor, p.45-70; f) Creating oneself from scratch. Murray, Michele, p.71-93; g) On being female, black, and free. Walker, Margaret, p.95-106; h) Thoughts on writing: A diary. Griffin, Susan, p.107-120; i) *One* child of one's own: A meaningful digression within the work(s). Walker, Alice, p.121-140; j) The middle period. Bengis, Ingrid, p.141-152; k) What it is I think I'm doing anyhow. Bambara, Toni Cade, p.153-168; l) Blood and guts: The tricky problem of being a woman writer in the late twentieth century. Jong, Erica, p.169-179; m) The coming book. Kingston, Maxine Hong, p.181-185; n) *Opening nights*: The opening days. Burroway, Janet, p.187-215; o) The education of a poet. Rukeyser, Muriel, p.217-230; p) Becoming a writer. Godwin, Gail, p.231-255.

SUBJECT INDEX

Subject Headings Used

Abortion
Anthropology and Folklore
Art and Architecture
Athletics and Sports
Children and Adolescents
Communications/Media/Publishing
Crime
Economics/Employment/Business
Education
Feminist Theory/Women's Studies
Film and Theater
History and Area Studies: Africa
History and Area Studies: Asia
History and Area Studies: Australia and Oceania
History and Area Studies: Canada
History and Area Studies: Europe
History and Area Studies: Latin America
History and Area Studies: Middle East
History and Area Studies: United States
History: General Collections
International Studies
Language and Linguistics
Law
Lesbianism and Homosexuality
Library Science
Literature and Literary Criticism
Medicine/Health/Biology
Older and Middle Age Women
Philosophy
Political Science/Public Policy/Politics
Psychology
Religion
Science and Mathematics
Sexuality
Sociology
Women of Color in the United States

Abortion
2 Abortion: Moral and Legal Perspectives
3 Abortion: Understanding Differences
173 The Law and Politics of Abortion
252 Second Trimester Pregnancy Termination

Anthropology and Folklore
68 Comparative Perspectives of Third World Women: The Impact of Race, Sex, and Class
98 Exploring the Other Half: Field Research with Rural Women in Bangladesh
162 Interest and Emotion: Essays on the Study of Family and Kinship
194 Mother Worship: Theme and Variations
200 Nature, Culture and Gender
234 Pre-industrial Women: Interdisciplinary Perspectives
246 Rethinking Women's Roles: Perspectives from the Pacific
269 Sex Roles and Social Change in Native Lower Central American Societies

282 Sexual Meanings: The Cultural Construction of Gender and Sexuality
333 We Are Bosses Ourselves: The Status and Role of Aboriginal Women Today
340 Woman the Gatherer
347 Women and Colonization: Anthropological Perspectives
350 Women and Development: The Sexual Division of Labor in Rural Societies
371 Women and Space: Ground Rules and Social Maps
471 A World of Women: Anthropological Studies of Women in the Societies of the World

Art and Architecture
117 Feminism and Art History: Questioning the Litany
182 Making Space: Women and the Man-Made Environment
203 New Space for Women
371 Women and Space: Ground Rules and Social Maps
389 Women as Interpreters of the Visual Arts, 1820-1979
442 Women, the Arts, and the 1920's in Paris and New York
453 Women's Culture: The Women's Renaissance of the Seventies

Athletics and Sports
107 The Female Athlete: A Socio-Psychological and Kinanthropometric Approach
147 Her Story in Sport: A Historical Anthology of Women in Sports
372 Women and Sport: An Historical, Biological, Physiological and Sportsmedical Approach
432 Women, Philosophy, and Sport: A Collection of New Essays

Children & Adolescents
55 Child Pornography and Sex Rings
57 Childhood Sexual Learning: The Unwritten Curriculum
79 The Custom-Made Child?: Women-Centered Perspectives
80 Day Care: Scientific and Social Policy Issues
146 Handbook of Clinical Intervention in Child Sexual Abuse
265 Sex Role Attitudes and Cultural Change
284 The Sexual Victimology of Youth
291 Sexually Abused Children and Their Families
309 Teenage Sexuality, Pregnancy, and Childbearing
326 Victims of Sexual Aggression: Treatment of Children, Women, and Men
346 Women and Child Workers in Unorganised Sector: Non-Government Organisation's Perspectives

Communications/Media/Publishing
15 Alternative Materials in Libraries
161 Indian Women in Media: A Collection of Essays
358 Women and Media
391 Women, Communication and Careers

Crime
55 Child Pornography and Sex Rings
63 Coed Prison
159 The Incidence of Female Criminality in the Contemporary World
163 International Feminism: Networking against Female Sexual Slavery
165 Judge Lawyer Victim Thief: Women, Gender Roles, and Criminal Justice
219 Perspectives on Rape and Sexual Assault
230 Pornography and Sexual Aggression
276 Sexual Aggression and the Law
284 The Sexual Victimology of Youth
326 Victims of Sexual Aggression: Treatment of Children, Women, and Men
348 Women and Crime
349 Women and Crime in America
392 Women, Crime, and Justice

Economics/Employment/Business
13 All Her Labours
44 Careers of Professional Women
46 A Challenge to Social Security: The Changing Roles of Women and Men in American Society
49 The Changing Composition of the Workforce: Implications for Future Research and Its Application
65 Comparable Worth and Wage Discrimination: Technical Possibilities and Political Realities
66 Comparable Worth: Issues and Alternatives
67 Comparable Worth: Issues and Alternatives (2nd edition)
86 Double Exposure: Women's Health Hazards on the Job and at Home
87 Dual-Career Couples
89 The Economics of Women and Work
93 Equal Employment Policy for Women: Strategies for Implementation in the United States, Canada, and Western Europe
104 Family and Work in Rural Societies: Perspectives on Non-Wage Labour
110 Female Labor Supply: Theory and Estimation
139 Gender, Class and Work
149 Hidden in the Household: Women's Domestic Labour under Capitalism
153 Households and the World-Economy
160 The Incorporated Wife
169 Labor Education for Women Workers
170 A Labour of Love: Women, Work and Caring
179 Loaded Questions: Women in the Military
199 My Troubles are Going to have Trouble with Me: Everyday Trials and Triumphs of Women Workers
201 A Needle, a Bobbin, a Strike: Women Needleworkers in America
205 Not Just Pin Money: Selected Essays on the History of Women's Work in British Columbia
206 Of Common Cloth: Women in the Global Textile Industry
208 Of Marriage and the Market: Women's Subordination Internationally and Its Lessons

209 Office Automation: Jekyll or Hyde?

213 One Way Ticket: Migration and Female Labour

214 Outsiders on the Inside: Women & Organizations

221 Perspectives on Work and the Family

233 Pregnant Women at Work

243 Research in the Interweave of Social Roles: Families and Jobs

260 Sex Discrimination and Equal Opportunity: The Labor Market and Employment Policy

263 Sex/Gender Division of Labor: Feminist Perspectives

267 Sex Role Stereotyping and Affirmative Action Policy

272 Sex Segregation in the Workplace: Trends, Explanations, Remedies

288 Sexuality in Organizations: Romantic and Coercive Behaviors at Work

292 Sisterhood and Solidarity: Workers' Education for Women, 1914-1984

299 Socio-Economic Status of Indian Women

323 Union Sisters: Women in the Labour Movement

324 Unplanned Careers: The Working Lives of Middle-Aged Women

339 The Woman in Management: Career and Family Issues

346 Women and Child Workers in Unorganised Sector: Non-Government Organisation's Perspectives

355 Women and Household Labor

357 Women and Low Pay

378 Women and the Public Sphere: A Critique of Sociology and Politics

380 Women and the World of Work

382 Women and Trade Unions in Eleven Industrialized Countries

385 Women and Work in Africa

386 Women and Work in India: Continuity and Change

387 Women and Work: Problems and Perspectives

391 Women, Communication and Careers

415 Women in Organizations: Barriers and Breakthroughs

421 Women in the Family and the Economy: An International Comparative Survey

422 Women in the Indian Labour Force

424 Women in the Urban and Industrial Workforce: Southeast and East Asia

425 Women in the Work Force

426 Women in the Workplace

427 Women in the Workplace: Effects on Families

428 Women, Men, and the International Division of Labor

436 Women, Power and Political Systems

437 Women Returning to Work: Policies and Progress in Five Countries

446 Women, Work, and Family in the Soviet Union

447 Women, Work and Health: Challenges to Corporate Policy

458 Women's Retirement: Policy Implications of Recent Research

463 Women's Travel Issues: Research Needs and Priorities

466 Women's Work and Women's Roles: Economics and Everyday Life in Indonesia, Malaysia and Singapore

467 Work and the Family

468 Work and Womanhood: Norwegian Studies

469 Work, Family, and Health: Latina Women in Transition

470 Work, Women and the Labour Market

471 Working Women: An International Survey

Education

45   The Challenge of Change: Perspectives on Family, Work, and Education

62   Co-Education Reconsidered

70   Conference on the Educational and Occupational Needs of American Indian Women

71   Conference on the Educational and Occupational Needs of Asian-Pacific-American Women

72   Conference on the Educational and Occupational Needs of Hispanic Women

90   Educational Policy and Management: Sex Differentials

97   Excellence, Reform and Equity in Education: An International Perspective

100 Expressions of Power in Education: Studies of Class, Gender and Race

122 Feminist Pedagogy and the Learning Climate

126 Feminist Visions: Toward a Transformation of the Liberal Arts Curriculum

138 Gender, Class & Education

169 Labor Education for Women Workers

174 Learning Our Way: Essays in Feminist Education

189 Men's Studies Modified: The Impact of Feminism on the Academic Disciplines

193 The Missing Half: Girls and Science Education

222 The Ph.D. Experience: A Woman's Point of View

249 Rocking the Boat: Academic Women and Academic Processes

250 Schooling for Women's Work

259 Sex Differentiation and Schooling

261 Sex Discrimination in Higher Education: Strategies for Equality

262 Sex Equity in Education

265 Sex Role Attitudes and Cultural Change

274 Sexism in the Secondary Curriculum

303 Stepping Off the Pedestal: Academic Women in the South

306 Teaching Women's Literature from a Regional Perspective

312 Theories of Women's Studies

314 Toward a Balanced Curriculum: A Sourcebook for Initiating Gender Integration Projects

320 The Undergraduate Woman: Issues in Educational Equity

337 Wisconsin Women: Graduate School and the Professions

351 Women and Education: Equity or Equality?

352 Women and Educational Leadership

394 Women Emerge in the Seventies

398 Women in Academe

407 Women in Higher Education Administration

418 Women in Society: Interdisciplinary Essays

432 Women, Philosophy, and Sport: A Collection of New Essays

Feminist Theory/Women's Studies

7   Against Sadomasochism: A Radical Feminist Analysis

14   All the Women are White, All the Blacks are Men, But Some of Us are Brave: Black Women's Studies

31   Beyond Domination: New Perspectives on Women and Philosophy

34   Biological Woman - The Convenient Myth: A Collection of Feminist Essays and a Comprehensive Bibliography

43   Building Feminist Theory: Essays from Quest

60   Class, Race, and Sex: The Dynamics of Control

76   A Creative Tension: Key Issues of Socialist-Feminism

84   Discovering Reality: Feminist Perspectives on Epistemology, Metaphysics, Methodology, and Philosophy of Science

85   Doing Feminist Research

99   Exploring Women's Past: Essays in Social History

102 Face to Face: Fathers, Mothers, Masters, Monsters - Essays for a Nonsexist Future

116 "Femininity", "Masculinity", and "Androgyny": A Modern Philosophical Discussion

118 Feminism and Process Thought: The Harvard Divinity School/Claremont Center for Process Studies Symposium Papers

119 Feminism, Culture and Politics

120 Feminism in Canada: From Pressure to Politics

122 Feminist Pedagogy and the Learning Climate

123 A Feminist Perspective in the Academy: The Difference It Makes

124 Feminist Re-Visions: What has Been and Might Be

125 Feminist Theorists: Three Centuries of Women's Intellectual Traditions

126 Feminist Visions: Toward a Transformation of the Liberal Arts Curriculum

128 Flawed Liberation: Socialism and Feminism

129 Freedom, Feminism, and the State: An Overview of Individualist Feminism

132 The Future of Difference

168 Knowledge Reconsidered: A Feminist Overview

176 Lesbian Studies: Present and Future

189 Men's Studies Modified: The Impact of Feminism on the Academic Disciplines

195 Mothering: Essays in Feminist Theory

200 Nature, Culture and Gender

207 Of Marriage and the Market: Women's Subordination in International Perspective

212 On the Problem of Men: Two Feminist Conferences

214 Outsiders on the Inside: Women & Organizations

220 Perspectives on Women in the 1980s

229 The Politics of Women's Spirituality: Essays on the Rise of Spiritual Power Within the Feminist Movement

241 The Public and the Private

247 Re-vision: Essays in Feminist Film Criticism

254 Seeing Our Way Clear: Feminist Revision of the Academy

256 Sex and Class in Women's History

263 Sex/Gender Division of Labor: Feminist Perspectives

282 Sexual Meanings: The Cultural Construction of Gender and Sexuality

283 Sexual Politics, Feminism and Socialism

296 Social Power and Influence of Women

305 Still Ain't Satisfied! Canadian Feminism Today

311 Theories of Women's Studies (1980)

312 Theories of Women's Studies (1983)

313 Theory and Practice of Feminist Literary Criticism

314 Toward a Balanced Curriculum: A Sourcebook for Initiating Gender Integration Projects

315 Toward a Feminist Transformation of the Academy: III: Proceedings of the Seventh Annual GLCA Women's Studies Conference

342 Woman's Nature: Rationalizations of Inequality

344 Women: A Feminist Perspective

369 Women and Revolution: A Discussion of the Unhappy Marriage of Marxism and Feminism

379 Women and the Structure of Society: Selected Research from the Fifth Berkshire Conference on the History of Women

417 Women in Search of Utopia: Mavericks and Mythmakers

439 Women: Sex and Sexuality

453 Women's Culture: The Women's Renaissance of the Seventies

464 Women's Views of the Political World of Men

Film and Theater

247 Re-vision: Essays in Feminist Film Criticism

399 Women in American Theatre: Careers, Images, Movements: An Illustrated Anthology and Sourcebook

406 Women in Film Noir

History and Area Studies: Africa

5 African Women in the Development Process

6 African Women South of the Sahara

218 Perspectives on Power: Women in Africa, Asia, and Latin America

322 Unheard Words: Women and Literature in Africa, the Arab World, Asia, the Caribbean and Latin America

362 Women and Politics in Twentieth Century Africa and Asia

370 Women and Slavery in Africa

385 Women and Work in Africa

393 Women, Education and Modernization of the Family in West Africa

History and Area Studies: Asia

21 Asian Women in Transition

58 Chinese Women in Southeast Asia

75 Country Papers on Career Services for Women in Asia

92 The Endless Day: Some Case Material on Asian Rural Women

101 The Extended Family: Women and Political Participation in India and Pakistan

161 Indian Women in Media: A Collection of Essays

166 Kartini Centenary: Indonesian Women Then and Now

177 Lives: Chinese Working Women

183 Malaysian Women: Problems & Issues

218 Perspectives on Power: Women in Africa, Asia, and Latin America

232 The Powers of Tamil Women

255 Separate Worlds: Studies of Purdah in South Asia

299 Socio-Economic Status of Indian Women

300 Southeast Asia: Women, Changing Social Structure and Cultural Continuity

322 Unheard Words: Women and Literature in Africa, the Arab World, Asia, the Caribbean and Latin America

362 Women and Politics in Twentieth Century Africa and Asia

386 Women and Work in India: Continuity and Change

400 Women in Bangladesh: Some Socio-Economic Issues

401 Women in China: Current Directions in Historical Scholarship

402 Women in Contemporary India and South Asia

420 Women in the Cities of Asia: Migration and Urban Adaptation

422 Women in the Indian Labour Force

424 Women in the Urban and Industrial Workforce: Southeast and East Asia

431 Women of Southeast Asia

433 Women, Politics, and Literature in Bengal

466 Women's Work and Women's Roles: Economics and Everyday Life in Indonesia, Malaysia and Singapore

History and Area Studies: Australia and Oceania

23 Australian Women and the Political System

94 Ethnicity, Class and Gender in Australia

246 Rethinking Women's Roles: Perspectives from the Pacific

294 So Much Hard Work: Women and Prostitution in Australian History

321 Unfinished Business: Social Justice for Women in Australia

348 Women and Crime

390 Women, Class and History: Feminist Perspectives on Australia 1788-1978

440 Women, Social Welfare and the State in Australia

History and Area Studies: Canada

120 Feminism in Canada: From Pressure to Politics

157 In Her Own Right: Selected Essays on Women's History in B.C.

205 Not Just Pin Money: Selected Essays on the History of Women's Work in British Columbia

220 Perspectives on Women in the 1980s

305 Still Ain't Satisfied! Canadian Feminism Today

323 Union Sisters: Women in the Labour Movement

History and Area Studies: Europe

22 Aspects of Female Existence: Proceedings from the St. Gertrud Symposium "Women in the Middle Ages"

33 Beyond Their Sex: Learned Women of the European Past

50 The Changing Experience of Women

95 European Women on the Left: Socialism, Feminism, and the Problems Faced by Political Women, 1880 to the Present

130 French Women and the Age of Enlightenment

144 The German Family: Essays on the Social History of the Family in Nineteenth- and Twentieth-Century Germany

145 German Women in the Nineteenth Century: A Social History

151 Home, School and Leisure in the Soviet Union

156 Images of Women in Antiquity

248 Rewriting Nursing History

258 Sex Differences in Britain

331 Vox Feminae: Studies in Medieval Woman's Songs

334 The Welsh Law of Women

336 When Biology Became Destiny: Women in Weimar and Nazi Germany

338 Woman in Irish Legend, Life and Literature

405 Women in Eastern Europe and the Soviet Union

408 Women in Hispanic Literature: Icons and Fallen Idols

419 Women in the Ancient World: The *Arethusa Papers*

442 Women, the Arts, and the 1920's in Paris and New York

446 Women, Work, and Family in the Soviet Union

465 Women's Welfare Women's Rights

471 Working Women: An International Survey

History and Area Studies: Latin America

74 Contemporary Women Authors of Latin America: Introductory Essays

172 Latin American Woman: The Meek Speak Out

218 Perspectives on Power: Women in Africa, Asia, and Latin America

269 Sex Roles and Social Change in Native Lower Central American Societies

322 Unheard Words: Women and Literature in Africa, the Arab World, Asia, the Caribbean and Latin America

363 Women and Politics in Twentieth Century Latin America

374 Women and the Cuban Revolution: Speeches & Documents by Fidel Castro, Vilma Espin & Others

408 Women in Hispanic Literature: Icons and Fallen Idols

History and Area Studies: Middle East

156 Images of Women in Antiquity

198 Muslim Women

270 Sex Roles, Family, & Community in Turkey

298 Social Science Research and Women in the Arab World

322 Unheard Words: Women and Literature in Africa, the Arab World, Asia, the Caribbean and Latin America

368 Women and Revolution in Iran

403 Women in Contemporary Muslim Societies

430 Women of Iran: The Conflict with Fundamentalist Islam

History and Area Studies: United States

19 Anne Hutchinson: Troubler of the Puritan Zion

61 Clio was a Woman: Studies in the History of American Women

73 Conference on the Educational and Occupational Needs of White Ethnic Women

81 Decades of Discontent: The Women's Movement, 1920-1940

148 The Hidden Half: Studies of Plains Indian Women

175 Legendary Ladies of Texas

201 A Needle, a Bobbin, a Strike: Women Needleworkers in America

226 Political Women: Current Roles in State and Local Government

238 Procreation or Pleasure?: Sexual Attitudes in American History

264 Sex, Race, and the Role of Women in the South

292 Sisterhood and Solidarity: Workers' Education for Women, 1914-1984

301 Speaking for Ourselves: Women of the South

316 Toward the Second Decade: The Impact of the Women's Movement on American Institutions

349 Women and Crime in America

353 Women and Health in America: Historical Readings

366 Women and Religion in America - Volume 1: The Nineteenth Century

367 Women and Religion in America - Volume 2: The Colonial and Revolutionary Periods

414 Women in Oklahoma: A Century of Change

442 Women, the Arts, and the 1920's in Paris and New York

454 Women's Experience in America: an Historical Anthology

History: General Collections

99 Exploring Women's Past: Essays in Social History

112 Female Scholars: A Tradition of Learned Women before 1800

113 Female Soldiers - Combatants or Noncombatants? Historical and Contemporary Perspectives

184 Marriage and Fertility: Studies in Interdisciplinary History

234 Pre-Industrial Women: Interdisciplinary Perspectives

256 Sex and Class in Women's History

International Studies

39 The Black Woman Cross-Culturally

52 The Changing Position of Women in Family and Society: A Cross-National Comparison

68 Comparative Perspectives of Third World Women: The Impact of Race, Sex, and Class

77 Creative Women in Changing Societies: A Quest for Alternatives

82 Developing Nations: Challenges Involving Women

83 A Dialogue on Third World Women: Learning through the Humanities

104 Family and Work in Rural Societies: Perspectives on Non-Wage Labour

153 Households and the World-Economy

159 The Incidence of Female Criminality in the Contemporary World

163 International Feminism: Networking against Female Sexual Slavery

179 Loaded Questions: Women in the Military

200 Nature, Culture and Gender

206 Of Common Cloth: Women in the Global Textile Industry

207 Of Marriage and the Market: Women's Subordination in International Perspective

208 Of Marriage and the Market: Women's Subordination Internationally and its Lessons

213 One Way Ticket: Migration and Female Labour

228 The Politics of the Second Electorate: Women and Public Participation

244 Research in the Interweave of Social Roles: Women and Men

251 Scientific-Technological Change and the Role of Women in Development

325 Unspoken Worlds: Women's Religious Lives in Non-Western Cultures

350 Women and Development: The Sexual Division of Labor in Rural Societies

371 Women and Space: Ground Rules and Social Maps

373 Women and Technological Change in Developing Countries

382 Women and Trade Unions in Eleven Industrialized Countries

388 Women and World Change: Equity Issues in Development

395 Women, Health, and International Development

403 Women in Contemporary Muslim Societies

421 Women in the Family and the Economy: An International Comparative Survey

428 Women, Men, and the International Division of Labor

457 Women's Religious Experience

Language and Linguistics

133 Gayspeak: Gay Male & Lesbian Communication

136 Gender and Nonverbal Behavior

171 Language, Gender and Society

275 Sexist Language: A Modern Philosophical Analysis

356 Women and Language in Literature and Society

Law

78 The Criminal Justice System and Women: Women Offenders, Victims, Workers

111 The Female Offender

173 The Law and Politics of Abortion

276 Sexual Aggression and the Law

334 The Welsh Law of Women

364 Women and Property - Women as Property

375 Women and the Law: Property, Family and the Legal Profession

376 Women and the Law: Women and Criminal Law

Lesbianism and Homosexuality

7 Against Sadomasochism: A Radical Feminist Analysis

133 Gayspeak: Gay Male & Lesbian Communication

150 Home Girls: A Black Feminist Anthology

152 Homosexuality and the Catholic Church

176 Lesbian Studies: Present and Future

224 Pink Triangles: Radical Perspectives on Gay Liberation

235 Prejudice and Pride: Discrimination against Gay People in Modern Britain

397 Women-Identified Women

Library Science

15 Alternative Materials in Libraries

302 The Status of Women in Librarianship: Historical, Sociological, and Economic Issues

Literature and Literary Criticism

1 10 women of Mystery

17 American Novelists Revisited: Essays in Feminist Criticism

20 The Art of Margaret Atwood: Essays in Criticism

27 Be Good, Sweet Maid: An Anthology of Women & Literature

30 Between Women: Biographers, Novelists, Critics, Teachers and Artists Write about Their Work on Women

32 Beyond the Eternal Feminine: Critical Essays on Women and German Literature

40 Black Women Writers (1950-1980): A Critical Evaluation

64 Colette: The Woman, the Writer

74 Contemporary Women Authors of Latin America: Introductory Essays

108 The Female Autograph

109 The Female Gothic

114 The Feminine Eye: Science Fiction and the Women Who Write It

121 Feminist Critics Read Emily Dickinson

127 Fiction by American Women: Recent Views

131 Future Females: A Critical Anthology

135 Gender and Literary Voice

142 George Eliot: A Centenary Tribute

143 George Eliot: Centenary Essays and an Unpublished Fragment

155 The Image of the Prostitute in Modern Literature

164 Jane Austen in a Social Context

180 The Lost Tradition: Mothers and Daughters in Literature

186 May Sarton: Woman and Poet

188 Medieval Women Writers

196 Mothering the Mind: Twelve Studies of Writers and Their Silent Partners

197 Muriel Spark: An Odd Capacity for Vision

202 New Feminist Essays on Virginia Woolf

232 The Powers of Tamil Women

242 The Representation of Women in Fiction

278 The Sexual Dimension in Literature

286 Sexuality and Victorian Literature

301 Speaking for Ourselves: Women of the South

306 Teaching Women's Literature from a Regional Perspective

313 Theory and Practice of Feminist Literary Criticism

318 Twentieth-Century Women Novelists

322 Unheard Words: Women and Literature in Africa, the Arab World, Asia, the Caribbean and Latin America

328 Virginia Woolf: A Feminist Slant

329 Virginia Woolf: Centennial Essays

330 Virginia Woolf: Revaluation and Continuity

331 Vox Feminae: Studies in Medieval Woman's Songs

332 The Voyage In: Fictions of Female Development

338 Woman in Irish Legend, Life and Literature

343 The Woman's Part: Feminist Criticism of Shakespeare

381 Women and Theatre: Calling the Shots

383 Women and Utopia: Critical Interpretations

384 Women and Western American Literature

408 Women in Hispanic Literature: Icons and Fallen Idols

409 Women in Joyce

419 Women in the Ancient World: The *Arethusa Papers*

433 Women, Politics, and Literature in Bengal

442 Women, the Arts, and the 1920's in Paris and New York

445 Women, Women Writers, and the West

448 Women Writers and the City: Essays in Feminist Literary Criticism

449 Women Writers of 20th-Century China

450 Women Writers of the Contemporary South

451 Women Writers of the Short Story

452 Women's Autobiography: Essays in Criticism

453 Women's Culture: The Women's Renaissance of the Seventies

474 The Writer on Her Work

Medicine/Health/Biology

4 Adolescent Pregnancy: Perspectives for the Health Professional

9 Alcohol and Drug Problems in Women

10 Alcohol Problems in Women: Antecedents, Consequences, and Intervention

11 Alcoholism in Women

16 Alternative Social Services for Women

28 Behavior and the Menstrual Cycle

34 Biological Woman - the Convenient Myth: A Collection of Feminist Essays and a Comprehensive Bibliography

36 Birth Control and Controlling Birth: Women-Centered Perspectives

51 Changing Perspectives on Menopause

53 The Changing Risk of Disease in Women: An Epidemiologic Approach

56 Childbirth: Alternatives to Medical Control

79 The Custom-Made Child?: Women-Centered Perspectives

86 Double Exposure: Women's Health Hazards on the Job and at Home

137 Gender and Psychopathology

141 Genetics and Breast Cancer

190 Menarche: The Transition from Girl to Woman

191 The Mental Health of Women

233 Pregnant Women at Work

236 The Premenstrual Syndrome

237 Premenstrual Tension: A Multidisciplinary Approach

239 The Psychobiology of Sex Differences and Sex Roles

240 Psychology and Gynaecological Problems

248 Rewriting Nursing History

252 Second Trimester Pregnancy Termination

253 The Second X and Women's Health

273 Sex Selection of Children

279 Sexual Dimorphism in Homo Sapiens: A Question of Size

285 Sexuality and Life-Threatening Illness

309 Teenage Sexuality, Pregnancy, and Childbearing

310 Test-Tube Women: What Future for Motherhood?

341 A Woman's Conflict: The Special Relationship between Women and Food

345 Women & Alcohol

353 Women and Health in America: Historical Readings

354 Women and Health: The Politics of Sex in Medicine

360 Women and Mental Health Policy

395 Women, Health, and International Development

396 Women, Health and Reproduction

447 Women, Work, and Health: Challenges to Corporate Policy

456 Women's Problems in General Practice

469 Work, Family, and Health: Latina Women in Transition

Older and Middle Age Women

47 Change and Choice: Women and Middle Age

210 Older Women: Issues and Prospects

289 Sexuality in the Later Years: Roles and Behavior

317 Transitions of Aging

324 Unplanned Careers: the Working Lives of Middle-Aged Women

423 Women in the Middle Years: Current Knowledge and Directions for Research and Policy

472 The World of the Older Woman: Conflicts and Resolutions

Philosophy

31 Beyond Domination: New Perspectives on Women and Philosophy

84 Discovering Reality: Feminist Perspectives on Epistemology, Metaphysics, Methodology, and Philosophy of Science

106 The Family in Political Thought

116 "Femininity", "Masculinity", and "Androgyny": A Modern Philosophical Discussion

154 Ideals for Women in the Works of Christine de Pizan

223 Philosophy and Sex

275 Sexist Language: A Modern Philosophical Analysis

Political Science/Public Policy/Politics

23 Australian Women and the Political System

35 Biopolitics and Gender

95 European Women on the Left: Socialism, Feminism, and the Problems Faced by Political Women, 1880 to the Present

103 Families, Politics, and Public Policy: A Feminist Dialogue on Women and the State

106 The Family in Political Thought

119 Feminism, Culture and Politics

128 Flawed Liberation: Socialism and Feminism

129 Freedom, Feminism, and the State: An Overview of Individualist Feminism

167 Keeping the Peace: A Women's Peace Handbook

173 The Law and Politics of Abortion

179 Loaded Questions: Women in the Military

215 Over Our Dead Bodies: Women Against the Bomb

218 Perspectives on Power: Women in Africa, Asia, and Latin America

226 Political Women: Current Roles in State and Local Government

227 The Politics of Housework

228 The Politics of the Second Electorate: Women and Public Participation

336 When Biology Became Destiny: Women in Weimar and Nazi Germany

360 Women and Mental Health Policy

362 Women and Politics in Twentieth Century Africa and Asia

363 Women and Politics in Twentieth Century Latin America

369 Women and Revolution: A Discussion of the Unhappy Marriage of Marxism and Feminism

374 Women and the Cuban Revolution: Speeches & Documents by Fidel Castro, Vilma Espin & Others

378 Women and the Public Sphere: A Critique of Sociology and Politics

410 Women in Local Politics

433 Women, Politics, and Literature in Bengal

435   Women, Power and Policy
436   Women, Power and Political Systems
444   Women, War, and Revolution
464   Women's Views of the Political World of Men

Psychology

8   Aggression, Adaptations, and Psychotherapy
16   Alternative Social Services for Women
29   Behavior Modification with Women
57   Childhood Sexual Learning: The Unwritten Curriculum
69   Concepts of Femininity and the Life Cycle
76   A Creative Tension: Key Issues of Socialist-Feminism
88   Early Female Development: Current Psychoanalytic Views
96   The Evolving Female: Women in Psychosocial Context
136   Gender and Nonverbal Behavior
137   Gender and Psychopathology
140   The Gender Gap in Psychotherapy: Social Realities and Psychological Processes
146   Handbook of Clinical Intervention in Child Sexual Abuse
158   In the Shadow of the Past: Psychology Portrays the Sexes: A Social and Intellectual History
178   Lives in Stress: Women and Depression
221   Perspectives on Work and the Family
230   Pornography and Sexual Aggression
239   The Psychobiology of Sex Differences and Sex Roles
240   Psychology and Gynaecological Problems
268   Sex Roles and Psychopathology
271   Sex Roles: Origins, Influences, and Implications for Women
277   Sexual Arousal: New Concepts in Basic Sciences, Diagnosis, and Treatment
280   Sexual Dynamics of Anti-Social Behavior
281   Sexual Issues in Family Therapy
285   Sexuality and Life-Threatening Illness
287   Sexuality in America: Contemporary Perspectives on Sexual Identity, Dysfunction & Treatment
291   Sexually Abused Children and Their Families
295   Social and Psychological Problems of Women: Prevention and Crisis Intervention
304   The Stereotyping of Women: Its Effects on Mental Health
326   Victims of Sexual Aggression: Treatment of Children, Women, and Men
341   A Woman's Conflict: The Special Relationship Between Women and Food
359   Women and Mental Health
360   Women and Mental Health Policy
365   Women and Psychotherapy: An Assessment of Research and Practice
411   Women in Midlife
443   Women Therapists Working with Women: New Theory and Process of Feminist Therapy
460   Women's Sexual Development: Explorations of *Inner Space*

Religion

19   Anne Hutchinson: Troubler of the Puritan Zion
42   Blueprint for Living: Perspectives for Latter-Day Saint Women
59   Christian Feminism: Visions of a New Humanity
91   The Emerging Christian Woman: Church and Society Perspectives
115   Feminine in the Church
152   Homosexuality and the Catholic Church
187   Medieval Religious Women
194   Mother Worship: Theme and Variations
211   On Being a Jewish Feminist: A Reader
229   The Politics of Women's Spirituality: Essays on the Rise of Spiritual Power within the Feminist Movement
325   Unspoken Worlds: Women's Religious Lives in Non-Western Cultures
366   Women and Religion in America - Volume 1: The Nineteenth Century
367   Women and Religion in America - Volume 2: The Colonial and Revolutionary Periods
412   Women in New Worlds: Historical Perspectives on the Wesleyan Tradition
429   Women Ministers
457   Women's Religious Experience
462   Women's Spirit Bonding

Science and Mathematics

12   Alice Through the Microscope: The Power of Science over Women's Lives
181   Machina Ex Dea: Feminist Perspectives on Technology
193   The Missing Half: Girls and Science Education
251   Scientific-Technological Change and the Role of Women in Development
307   The Technological Woman: Interfacing with Tomorrow
361   Women and Minorities in Science: Strategies for Increasing Participation
377   Women and the Mathematical Mystique
416   Women in Scientific and Engineering Professions
438   Women Scientists: The Road to Liberation
441   Women, Technology and Innovation

Sexuality

24   The Bases of Human Sexual Attraction
48   Changing Boundaries: Gender Roles and Sexual Behavior
134   Gender and Generation
225   Pleasure and Danger: Exploring Female Sexuality
231   Powers of Desire: The Politics of Sexuality
238   Procreation or Pleasure?: Sexual Attitudes in American History
257   Sex & Love: New Thoughts on Old Contradictions
271   Sex Roles: Origins, Influences, and Implications for Women
277   Sexual Arousal: New Concepts in Basic Sciences, Diagnosis, and Treatment
280   Sexual Dynamics of Anti-Social Behavior
281   Sexual Issues in Family Therapy
285   Sexuality and Life-Threatening Illness

287   Sexuality in America: Contemporary Perspectives on Sexual Identity, Dysfunction & Treatment
289   Sexuality in the Later Years: Roles and Behavior
290   The Sexuality Papers: Male Sexuality and the Social Control of Women
309   Teenage Sexuality, Pregnancy, and Childbearing
397   Women-Identified Women
439   Women: Sex and Sexuality
460   Women's Sexual Development: Explorations of *Inner Space*
461   Women's Sexual Experience: Explorations of the *Dark Continent*

Sociology

5   African Women in the Development Process
16   Alternative Social Services for Women
18   And the Poor Get Children: Radical Perspectives on Population Dynamics
25   The Battered Woman Syndrome
26   Battered Women and Their Families: Intervention Strategies and Treatment Programs
37   Black Families
38   The Black Woman
45   The Challenge of Change: Perspectives on Family, Work, and Education
46   A Challenge to Social Security: The Changing Roles of Women and Men in American Society
48   Changing Boundaries: Gender Roles and Sexual Behavior
50   The Changing Experience of Women
52   The Changing Position of Women in Family and Society: A Cross-National Comparison
54   Chicanas and Alcoholism: A Socio-Cultural Perspective of Women
76   A Creative Tension: Key Issues of Socialist-Feminism
80   Day Care: Scientific and Social Policy Issues
87   Dual-Career Couples
92   The Endless Day: Some Case Material on Asian Rural Women
94   Ethnicity, Class and Gender in Australia
100   Expressions of Power in Education: Studies of Class, Gender and Race
101   The Extended Family: Women and Political Participation in India and Pakistan
102   Face to Face: Fathers, Mothers, Masters, Monsters - Essays for a Nonsexist Future
103   Families, Politics, and Public Policy: A Feminist Dialogue on Women and the State
104   Family and Work in Rural Societies: Perspectives on Non-Wage Labour
105   The Family in Change
138   Gender, Class & Education
140   The Gender Gap in Psychotherapy: Social Realities and Psychological Processes
144   The German Family: Essays on the Social History of the Family in Nineteenth- and Twentieth-Century Germany

149 Hidden in the Household: Women's Domestic Labour Under Capitalism

151 Home, School and Leisure in the Soviet Union

160 The Incorporated Wife

162 Interest and Emotion: Essays on the Study of Family and Kinship

170 A Labour of Love: Women, Work and Caring

177 Lives: Chinese Working Women

184 Marriage and Fertility: Studies in Interdisciplinary History

185 Marriage and the Family in the Year 2020

195 Mothering: Essays in Feminist Theory

204 Nontraditional Families: Parenting and Child Development

207 Of Marriage and the Market: Women's Subordination in International Perspective

210 Older Women: Issues and Prospects

212 On the Problem of Men: Two Feminist Conferences

216 Parenting in a Multicultural Society

217 Patriarchy in a Welfare Society

227 The Politics of Housework

231 Powers of Desire: The Politics of Sexuality

239 The Psychobiology of Sex Differences and Sex Roles

241 The Public and the Private

243 Research in the Interweave of Social Roles: Families and Jobs

244 Research in the Interweave of Social Roles: Women and Men

245 Rethinking the Family: Some Feminist Questions

246 Rethinking Women's Roles: Perspectives from the Pacific

255 Separate Worlds: Studies of Purdah in South Asia

258 Sex Differences in Britain

265 Sex Role Attitudes and Cultural Change

266 Sex Role Research: Measuring Social Change

267 Sex Role Stereotyping and Affirmative Action Policy

269 Sex Roles and Social Change in Native Lower Central American Societies

270 Sex Roles, Family, & Community in Turkey

291 Sexually Abused Children and Their Families

294 So Much Hard Work: Women and Prostitution in Australian History

295 Social and Psychological Problems of Women: Prevention and Crisis Intervention

297 Social Researching: Politics, Problems, Practice

298 Social Science Research and Women in the Arab World

301 Speaking for Ourselves: Women of the South

308 Teenage Pregnancy in a Family Context: Implications for Policy

310 Test-Tube Women: What Future for Motherhood?

319 Twice a Minority: Mexican American Women

327 Violence and the Family

335 What is to Be Done About the Family?

355 Women and Household Labor

364 Women and Property - Women as Property

388 Women and World Change: Equity Issues in Development

393 Women, Education and Modernization of the Family in West Africa

403 Women in Contemporary Muslim Societies

404 Women in Crisis

411 Women in Midlife

413 Women in New Zealand Society

418 Women in Society: Interdisciplinary Essays

420 Women in the Cities of Asia: Migration and Urban Adaptation

427 Women in the Workplace: Effects on Families

434 Women, Power, and Change

455 Women's Issues and Social Work Practice

458 Women's Retirement: Policy Implications of Recent Research

459 Women's Roles and Population Trends in the Third World

465 Women's Welfare Women's Rights

466 Women, Work and Women's Roles: Economics and Everyday Life in Indonesia, Malaysia and Singapore

469 Work, Family, and Health: Latina Women in Transition

Women of Color in the United States

14 All the Women are White, All the Blacks Are Men, But Some of Us Are Brave: Black Women's Studies

37 Black Families

38 The Black Woman

39 The Black Woman Cross-Culturally

40 Black Women Writers (1950-1980): A Critical Evaluation

41 Black Working Women Debunking the Myths: A Multidisciplinary Approach

54 Chicanas and Alcoholism: A Socio-Cultural Perspective of Women

60 Class, Race, and Sex: The Dynamics of Control

70 Conference on the Educational and Occupational Needs of American Indian Women

71 Conference on the Educational and Occupational Needs of Asian-Pacific-American Women

72 Conference on the Educational and Occupational Needs of Hispanic Women

148 The Hidden Half: Studies of Plains Indian Women

150 Home Girls: A Black Feminist Anthology

192 Mexican Women in the United States: Struggles Past and Present

216 Parenting in a Multicultural Society

264 Sex, Race, and the Role of Women in the South

319 Twice a Minority: Mexican American Women

361 Women and Minorities in Science: Strategies for Increasing Participation

469 Work, Family, and Health: Latina Women in Transition

EDITOR INDEX

Abel, Elizabeth
332 The Voyage In: Fictions of Female Development

Abernethy, Francis Edward
175 Legendary Ladies of Texas

Adler, Freda
159 The incidence of female criminality in the contemporary world

Aguwa, Margaret I.
395 Women, Health, and International Development

Albers, Patricia
148 The hidden half: studies of plains indian women

Alexander, Anna Vareed
91 The Emerging Christian Woman: Church and Society Perspectives

Alexander, Maxine
301 Speaking for Ourselves: Women of the South

Al-Issa, Ihsan
137 Gender and Psychopathology

Allgeier, Elizabeth Rice
48 Changing Boundaries: Gender Roles and Sexual Behavior

Altherr, Thomas L.
238 Procreation or Pleasure?: Sexual Attitudes in American History

Altshuler, Nathan
362 Women and Politics in Twentieth Century Africa and Asia

Amsden, Alice H.
89 The Economics of Women and Work

Anderson, Anne
456 Women's Problems in General Practice

Anker, Richard
459 Women's Roles and Population Trends in the Third World

Ardener, Shirley
160 The Incorporated Wife
371 Women and Space: Ground Rules and Social Maps

Arditti, Rita
310 Test-Tube Women: What Future for Motherhood?

Arevalo, Rodolfo
54 Chicanas and Alcoholism: A Socio-Cultural Perspective of Women

Ascher, Carol
30 Between Women: Biographers, Novelists, Critics, Teachers and Artists Write about Their Work on Women

Ayer, M. Jane
351 Women and education: equity or equality?

Azari, Farah
430 Women of Iran: The Conflict with Fundamentalist Islam

Baehr, Helen
358 Women and Media

Baker, Robert
223 Philosophy and Sex

Baldock, Cora V.
440 Women, Social Welfare and the State in Australia

Bargainnier, Earl F.
1 10 Women of Mystery

Barr, Marleen
131 Future Females: A Critical Anthology
383 Women and Utopia: Critical Interpretations

Barry, Kathleen
163 International Feminism: Networking against Female Sexual Slavery

Barton, Len
138 Gender Class & Education

Baruch, Elaine Hoffman
417 Women in Search of Utopia: Mavericks and Mythmakers

Baruch, Grace
411 Women in Midlife

Bay, Edna G.
385 Women and Work in Africa

Bayes, Marjorie
359 Women and Mental Health

Beckman, Linda J.
10 Alcohol Problems in Women: Antecedents, Consequences, and Intervention

Bell, Colin
297 Social Researching: Politics, Problems, Practice

Belle, Deborah
178 Lives in Stress: Women and Depression
191 The Mental Health of Women

Benería, Lourdes
350 Women and Development: The Sexual Division of Labor in Rural Societies

Bennett, Neil G.
273 Sex Selection of Children

Berk, Sarah Fenstermaker
355 Women and Household Labor

Berkin, Carol R.
444 Women, War, And Revolution

Bernardin, H. John
425 Women in the Work Force

Bevilacqua, Winifred Farrant
127 Fiction by American Women: Recent Views

Biklen, Sari Knopp
352 Women and Educational Leadership

Birke, Lynda
12 Alice through the Microscope: The Power of Science over Women's Lives

Black, Naomi
388 Women and World Change: Equity Issues in Development

Blechman, Elaine A.
29 Behavior Modification with Women

Bloom, Alexander
314 Toward a Balanced Curriculum: A Sourcebook for Initiating Gender Integration Projects

Bold, Alan
197 Muriel Spark: An Odd Capacity for Vision
278 The Sexual Dimension in Literature

Boneparth, Ellen
435 Women, Power and Policy

Borker, Ruth
356 Women and Language in Literature and Society

Borman, Kathryn M.
427 Women in the Workplace: Effects on Families

Borms, J.
107 The Female Athlete: A Socio-Psychological and Kinanthropometric Approach
372 Women and Sport: An Historical, Biological, Physiological and Sportsmedical Approach

Bornstein, Diane
154 Ideals for Women in the Works of Christine De Pizan

Boroviak, Darlene
314 Toward a Balanced Curriculum: A Sourcebook for Initiating Gender Integration Projects

Bottomley, Gill
94 Ethnicity, Class and Gender in Australia

Bourguignon, Erika
473 A World of Women: Anthropological Studies of Women in the Societies of the World

Bowker, Lee H.
349 Women and Crime in America

Bowles, Gloria
311 Theories of Women's Studies (1980)
312 Theories of Women's Studies (1983)

Brannigan, Marilyn B.
352 Women And Educational Leadership

Bremer, Francis J.
19 Anne Hutchinson: Troubler of the Puritan Zion

Bridenthal, Renate
336 When Biology Became Destiny: Women in Weimar and Nazi Germany

Brine, Jenny
151 Home, School and Leisure in the Soviet Union

Brink, J. R.
112 Female Scholars: A Tradition of Learned Women Before 1800

Briskin, Linda
323 Union Sisters: Women in the Labour Movement

Brodsky, Annette M.
365 Women and Psychotherapy: An Assessment of Research and Practice

Brody, Claire M.
443 Women Therapists Working with Women: New Theory and Process of Feminist Therapy

Brody, Linda
377 Women and the Mathematical Mystique

Broner, E. M.
180   The Lost Tradition: Mothers and
      Daughters in Literature

Brooks-Gunn, Jeanne
411   Women in Midlife

Broom, Dorothy H.
321   Unfinished Business: Social Justice for
      Women in Australia

Broome, Annabel
240   Psychology and Gynaecological Problems

Broude, Norma
117   Feminism and Art History: Questioning
      the Litany

Brown, Donald A.
287   Sexuality in America: Contemporary
      Perspectives on Sexual Identity,
      Dysfunction & Treatment

Brownley, Martine Watson
196   Mothering the Mind: Twelve Studies of
      Writers and Their Silent Partners

Brunt, Rosalind
119   Feminism, Culture and Politics

Buckley, Mary I.
462   Women's Spirit Bonding

Bunch, Charlotte
163   International Feminism: Networking
      against Female Sexual Slavery
174   Learning Our Way: Essays in feminist
      Education

Bunkle, Phillida
413   Women in New Zealand Society

Burgess, Ann Wolbert
55   Child Pornography and Sex Rings

Burkhauser, Richard V.
46   A Challenge to Social Security: The
     Changing Roles of Women and Men in
     American Society

Buvinic Mayra
459   Women's Roles and Population Trends in
      the Third World

Cain, Melinda L.
373   Women and Technological Change in
      Developing Countries

Callahan, Daniel
3   Abortion: Understanding Differences

Callahan, Sidney
3   Abortion: Understanding Differences

Callan, Hilary
160   The Incorporated Wife

Camberwell Council on Alcoholism
345   Women & Alcohol

The Cambridge Women's Studies Group
418   Women in Society: Interdisciplinary Essays

Cameron, Averil
156   Images of Women in Antiquity

Cárdenas, René
216   Parenting in a Multicultural Society

Carlé, Birte
22   Aspects of Female Existence: Proceedings
     from the St. Gertrud Symposium "Women
     in the Middle Ages"

Carlson, Richard O.
90   Educational Policy and Management: Sex
     Differentials

Carmen, Elaine (Hilberman)
140   The Gender Gap in Psychotherapy: Social
      Realities and Psychological Processes

Cartledge, Sue
257   Sex & Love: New Thoughts on Old
      Contradictions

Cass, Bettina
440   Women, Social Welfare and the State in
      Australia

Castillo, Adelaida R. Del
192   Mexican Women in the United States:
      Struggles Past and Present

Castley, Shirley
163   International Feminism: Networking
      Against Female Sexual Slavery

Chamberlain, Geoffrey
233   Pregnant Women at Work

Chapkis, Wendy
179   Loaded Questions: Women in the Military
206   Of Common Cloth: Women in the Global
      Textile Industry

Charters, W. W.
90   Educational Policy and Management: Sex
     Differentials

Chavkin, Wendy
86   Double Exposure: Women's Health
     Hazards on the Job and at Home

Chesebro, James W.
133   Gayspeak: Gay Male & Lesbian
      Communication

Chinoy, Helen Krich
399   Women in American Theatre: Careers,
      Images, Movements: An Illustrated
      Anthology and Sourcebook

Chipp, Sylvia A.
21   Asian Women in Transition

Clark, Marieanne Lindeqvist
55   Child Pornography and Sex Rings

Clary, Chanda
287   Sexuality in America: Contemporary
      Perspectives on Sexual Identity,
      Dysfunction & Treatment

Cocalis, Susan L.
32   Beyond the Eternal Feminine: Critical
     Essays on Women and German Literature

Colvard, Richard
387   Women and Work: Problems and
      Perspectives

Cook, Alice H.
382   Women and Trade Unions in Eleven
      Industrialized Countries

Cook, Mark
24   The Bases of Human Sexual Attraction

Cooper, Cary L.
471   Working Women: An International Survey

Cottrell, Ann Baker
388   Women and World Change: Equity Issues
      in Development

Coveney, Lal
290   The Sexuality Papers: Male Sexuality and
      the Social Control of Women

Cox, Don Richard
286   Sexuality and Victorian Literature

Cramer, Stanley H.
221   Perspectives on Work and the Family

Crawford, Patricia
99   Exploring Women's Past: Essays in Social
     History

Cruikshank, Margaret
176   Lesbian Studies: Present and Future

Dahlberg, Frances
340   Woman the Gatherer

Daniels, Arlene Kaplan
382   Women and Trade Unions in Eleven
      Industrialized Countries
387   Women and Work: Problems and
      Perspectives

Daniels, Kay
294   So Much Hard Work: Women and
      Prostitution in Australian History

Danky, James P.
15   Alternative Materials in Libraries

Darty, Trudy
397   Women-Identified Women

Datan, Nancy
317   Transitions of Aging

Datesman, Susan K.
392   Women, Crime, and Justice

Dauber, Roslyn
373   Women and Technological Change in
      Developing Countries

Davaney, Sheila Greeve
118   Feminism and Process Thought: The
      Harvard Divinity School/Claremont
      Center for Process Studies Symposium
      Papers

Davidson, Arnold E.
20   The Art of Margaret Atwood: Essays in
     Criticism

Davidson, Cathy N.
20   The Art of Margaret Atwood: Essays in
     Criticism
180   The Lost Tradition: Mothers and
      Daughters in Literature

Davidson, Marilyn J.
471   Working Women: An International Survey

Davidson, Sue
201   A Needle, a Bobbin, a Strike: Women
      Needleworkers in America

Davies, Celia
248   Rewriting Nursing History

de Souza, Alfred
402   Women in Contemporary India and South
      Asia

Debrovner, Charles H.
237   Premenstrual Tension: A Multidisciplinary
      Approach

Deem, Rosemary
62   Co-Education Reconsidered
250   Schooling for Women's Work

DeSalvo, Louise
30 Between Women: Biographers, Novelists, Critics, Teachers and Artists Write about Their Work on Women

DeSole, Gloria
249 Rocking the Boat: Academic Women and Academic Processes

Deutrich, Mabel E.
61 Clio Was a Woman: Studies in the History of American Women

D'Heurle, Adma
265 Sex Role Attitudes and Cultural Change

Diamond, Irene
103 Families, Politics, and Public Policy: A Feminist Dialogue on Women and the State

Dinnerstein, Myra
51 Changing Perspectives on Menopause

Dixon, Suzanne
234 Pre-Industrial Women: Interdisciplinary Perspectives

Doane, Mary Ann
247 Re-Vision: Essays in Feminist Film Criticism

Donnerstein, Edward
230 Pornography and Sexual Aggression

D'Onofrio-Flores, Pamela M.
251 Scientific-Technological Change and the Role of Women in Development

Downing, John
265 Sex Role Attitudes and Cultural Change

Dudovitz, Resa L.
398 Women in Academe

Duelli-Klein, Renate
310 Test-Tube Women: What Future for Motherhood?
311 Theories of Women's Studies (1980)
312 Theories of Women's Studies (1983)

Eddy, Cristen C.
11 Alcoholism in Women

Egdahl, Richard H.
447 Women, Work, and Health: Challenges to Corporate Policy

Eisenstein, Hester
132 The Future of Difference

Eisinger, Erica Mendelson
64 Colette: The Woman, The Writer

Elliston, Frederick
223 Philosophy and Sex

Elshtain, Jean Bethke
106 The Family in Political Thought

Emery, Lois
220 Perspectives on Women in the 1980s

Enloe, Cynthia
206 Of Common Cloth: Women in the Global Textile Industry

Epstein, T. Scarlett
92 The Endless Day: Some Case Material on Asian Rural Women

Etienne, Mona
347 Women and Colonization: Anthropological Perspectives

Evans, Mari
40 Black Women Writers (1950-1980): A Critical Evaluation

Evans, Richard J.
144 The German Family: Essays on the Social History of the Family in Nineteenth- and Twentieth-Century Germany

Everett, Jana
386 Women and Work in India: Continuity and Change

Evers, Hans-Dieter
153 Households and the World-Economy

Falk, Nancy Auer
325 Unspoken Worlds: Women's Religious Lives in Non-Western Cultures

Fantini, Mario D.
216 Parenting in a Multicultural Society

Faria, Stella
91 The Emerging Christian Woman: Church and Society Perspectives

Farley, Jennie
261 Sex Discrimination in Higher Education: Strategies for Equality
339 The Woman in Management: Career and Family Issues

Fawcett, James T.
420 Women in the Cities of Asia: Migration and Urban Adaptation

Fee, Elizabeth
354 Women and Health: The Politics of Sex in Medicine

Fennema, Elizabeth
351 Women and Education: Equity or Equality?

Fernández-Kelly, María Patricia
428 Women, Men, and the International Division of Labor

Fernández Olmos, Margarite
74 Contemporary Women Authors of Latin America: Introductory Essays

Ficher, Miguel
277 Sexual Arousal: New Concepts in Basic Sciences, Diagnosis, and Treatment

Finch, Janet
170 A Labour of Love: Work and Caring

Finn, Geraldine
120 Feminism in Canada: From Pressure to Politics

Fishkin, Ralph E.
277 Sexual Arousal: New Concepts in Basic Sciences, Diagnosis, and Treatment

Fitzgerald, Maureen
305 Still Ain't Satisfied! Canadian Feminism Today

Flaming, Janet A.
226 Political Women: Current Roles in State and Local Government

Fleenor, Juliann E.
109 The Female Gothic

Fleischmann, Fritz
17 American Novelists Revisited: Essays in Feminist Criticism

Fonda, Nickie
467 Work and the Family

Fooden, Myra
253 The Second X and Women's Health

Ford, John L.
11 Alcoholism in Women

Forisha, Barbara L.
214 Outsiders on the Inside: Women & Organizations

Fout, John C.
145 German Women in the Nineteenth Century: A Social History

Fowlkes, Diane L.
126 Feminist Visions: Toward a Transformation of the Liberal Arts Curriculum

Fox, Bonnie
149 Hidden in the Household: Women's Domestic Labour Under Capitalism

Fox, Lynn H.
377 Women and the Mathematical Mystique

Franklin, Ursula Martius
168 Knowledge Reconsidered: A Feminist Overview

Franks, Violet
304 The Stereotyping of Women: Its Effects on Mental Health

Frederickson, Mary
292 Sisterhood and Solidarity: Workers' Education for Women, 1914-1984

Freedman, Ralph
330 Virginia Woolf: Revaluation and Continuity

Freeman, Jo
344 Women: A Feminist Perspective

Fried, Barbara
34 Biological Woman - The Convenient Myth: A Collection of Feminist Essays and a Comprehensive Bibliography

Friedman, Richard C.
28 Behavior and the Menstrual Cycle

Friedman, Scarlet
212 On the problem of Men: Two Feminist Conferences

Furlong, Monica
115 Feminine in the Church

Furman, Nelly
356 Women and Language in Literature and Society

Furstenberg, Frank F.
309 Teenage Sexuality, Pregnancy, and Childbearing

Gale, Fay
333 We are Bosses Ourselves: The Status and Role of Aboriginal Women Today

Gallagher, S. F.
338 Woman in Irish Legend, Life and Literature

Galloway, Bruce
235 Prejudice and Pride: Discrimination Against Gay People in Modern Britain

Gamarnikow, Eva
139 Gender, Class and Work

241 The Public and the Private

Gangrade, K. D.
346 Women and Child Workers in
Unorganised Sector: Non-Government
Organisation's Perspectives

Garfield, Jay L.
2 Abortion: Moral and Legal Perspectives

Garrard, Mary D.
117 Feminism and Art History: Questioning
the Litany

Gathia, J.A.
346 Women and Child Workers in
Unorganised Sector: Non-Government
Organisation's Perspectives

Gerrard, Meg
295 Social and Psychological Problems of
Women: Prevention and Crisis
Intervention

Ghosh, Ratna
421 Women in the Family and the Economy:
An International Comparative Survey

Gideonse, Sarah
427 Women In the Workplace: Effects on
Families

Giele, Janet Zollinger
423 Women in the Middle Years: Current
Knowledge and Directions for Research
and Policy

Ginsberg, Elaine K.
329 Virginia Woolf: Centennial Essays

Glickman, Albert S.
49 The Changing Composition of the
Workforce: Implications for Future
Research and Its Application

Gold, Ellen B.
53 The Changing Risk of Disease in Women:
An Epidemiologic Approach

Goldman, Barbara H.
214 Outsiders on the Inside: Women &
Organizations

Goldman, Nancy Loring
113 Female Soldiers - Combatants or
Noncombatants? Historical and
Contemporary Perspective

Golub, Sharon
190 Menarche: The Transition from Girl to
Woman

Goodman, Kay
32 Beyond the Eternal Feminine: Critical
Essays on Women and German Literature

Gordon, Edmund W.
80 Day Care: Scientific and Social Policy
Issues

Gott, S. Edna
82 Developing Nations: Challenges Involving
Women

Gottlieb, Laura Moss
329 Virginia Woolf: Centennial Essays

Gottlieb, Naomi
16 Alternative Social Services for Women

Gould, Carol C.
31 Beyond Domination: New Perspectives on
Women and Philosophy

Gove, Walter
123 A Feminist Perspective in the Academy:
The Difference it Makes

Gramick, Jeannine
152 Homosexuality and the Catholic Church

Gravatt, Arthur E.
185 Marriage and the Family in the Year 2020

Green, Justin J.
21 Asian Women in Transition

Green, Maurice R.
327 Violence and the Family

Greene, Gayle
343 The Woman's Part: Feminist Criticism of
Shakespeare

Greer, Joanne G.
326 Victims of Sexual Aggression: Treatment
of Children, Women, and Men

Gregory, Judith
209 Office automation: Jekyll or Hyde?

Grewe-Partsch, Marianne
391 Women, Communication and Careers

Griffiths, Curt Taylor
111 The Female Offender

Gross, Ira
265 Sex Role Attitudes and Cultural Change

Gross, Michael
36 Birth Control and Controlling Birth:
Women-Centered Perspectives
79 The Custom-Made Child?: Women-
Centered Perspectives

Gross, Rita M.
325 Unspoken Worlds: Women's Religious
Lives in Non-Western Cultures

Grossmann, Atina
336 When Biology Became Destiny: Women in
Weimar and Nazi Germany

Groves, Dulcie
170 A Labour of Love: Women, Work and
Caring

Guberman, Connie
305 Still Ain't Satisfied! Canadian Feminism
Today

Guisso, Richard W.
401 Women in China: Current Directions in
Historical Scholarship

Gumbert, Edgar B.
100 Expressions of Power in Education:
Studies of Class, Gender and Race

Gutek, Barbara A.
267 Sex Role Stereotyping and Affirmative
Action Policy

Guttentag, Marcia
191 The Mental Health of Women

Haas, Violet B.
416 Women in Scientific and Engineering
Professions

Haight, Gordon S.
142 George Eliot: A Centenary Tribute

Hainsworth, Geoffrey B.
300 Southeast Asia: Women, Changing Social
Structure and Cultural Continuity

Hall, Roberta L.
279 Sexual Dimorphism in Homo Sapiens: A
Question of Size

Hansen, James C.
221 Perspectives on Work and the Family

Harding, Sandra
84 Discovering Reality: Feminist Perspectives
on Epistemology, Metaphysics, Methodology, and Philosophy of Science

Hare-Mustin, Rachel T.
365 Women and Psychotherapy: An
Assessment of Research and Practice

Harris, Barbara J.
379 Women and the Structure of Society:
Selected Research from the Fifth Berkshire Conference on the History of
Women

Hawks, Joanne V.
264 Sex, Race, and the Role of Women in the
South

Hay, Margaret Jean
6 African Women South of the Sahara

Hebbelinck, M.
107 The Female Athlete: A Socio-
Psychological and Kinanthropometric
Approach
372 Women and Sport: An Historical,
Biological, Physiological and Sportsmedical Approach

Heckerman, Carol Landau
96 The Evolving Female: Women in
Psychosocial Contex

Heilbrun, Carolyn G.
242 The Representation of Women in Fiction

Heim, Kathleen M.
302 The Status of Women in Librarianship:
Historical, Sociological, and Economic
Issues

Henifin, Mary Sue
34 Biological Woman - The Convenient
Myth: A Collection of Feminist Essays and
a Comprehensive Bibliography

Henke, Suzette
409 Women in Joyce

Henley, Nancy
136 Gender and Nonverbal Behavior
171 Language, Gender and Society

Hennessey, Patricia
2 Abortion: Moral and Legal Perspectives

Hensen, James C.
281 Sexual Issues in Family Therapy

Heschel, Susannah
211 On Being a Jewish Feminist: A Reader

Higonnet, Margaret R.
242 The Representation of Women in Fiction

Hills, Jill
228 The Politics of the Second Electorate:
Women and Public Participation

Hintikka, Merrill B.
84 Discovering Reality: Feminist Perspectives
on Epistemology, Metaphysics,
Methodology, and Philosophy of Science

Hirsch, Marianne
332 The Voyage In: Fictions of Female Development

Hirschon, Renée
364 Women and Property - Women as Property

Hoffmann, Leonore
249 Rocking the Boat: Academic Women and Academic Processes
306 Teaching Women's Literature from a Regional Perspective

Hoiberg, Anne
380 Women and the World of Work

Holcomb, Adele M.
389 Women as Interpreters of the Visual Arts, 1820-1979

Holden, Karen C.
46 A Challenge to Social Security: The Changing Roles of Women and Men in American Society

Holden, Pat
457 Women's Religious Experience

Holmes, Helen B.
36 Birth Control and Controlling Birth: Women-Centered Perspectives
79 The Custom-Made Child?: Women-Centered Perspectives

Holter, Harriet
217 Patriarchy in a Welfare Society

Hong, Evelyn
183 Malaysian Women: Problems & Issues

Hopkins, June
219 Perspectives on Rape and Sexual Assault

Horn, Pierre L.
155 The Image of the Prostitute in Modern Literature

Horner, Matina
45 The Challenge of Change: Perspectives on Family, Work, and Education

Hoskins, Betty B.
36 Birth Control and Controlling Birth: Women-Centered Perspectives
79 The Custom-Made Child?: Women-Centered Perspectives

Howell, Elizabeth
359 Women and mental health

Howell, Reet
147 Her Story in Sport: A Historical Anthology of Women in Sports

Hubbard, Ruth
34 Biological Woman - The Convenient Myth: A Collection of Feminist Essays and a Comprehensive Bibliography
342 Woman's Nature: Rationalizations of Inequality

Hughes, Beryl
413 Women in New Zealand Society

Hull, Gloria T.
14 All the Women are White, All the Blacks are Men, But Some of Us are Brave: Black Women's Studies

Humphreys, Sheila M.
361 Women and Minorities in Science: Strategies for Increasing Participation

Hunting, Constance
186 May Sarton: Woman and Poet

Huq, Jahanara
400 Women in Bangladesh: Some Socio-Economic Issues

Hussain, Freda
198 Muslim Women

Iscoe, Ira
295 Social and Psychological Problems of Women: Prevention and Crisis Intervention

Islam, Shamima
98 Exploring the Other Half: Field Research with Rural Women in Bangladesh

Jacobs, Joseph A.
277 Sexual Arousal: New Concepts in Basic Sciences, Diagnosis, and Treatment

Jardine, Alice
132 The Future of Difference

Jelinek, Estelle C.
452 Women's Autobiography: Essays in Criticism

Jenkins, Dafydd
334 The Welsh Law of Women

Jenkins, Linda Walsh
399 Women in American Theatre: Careers, Images, Movements: An Illustrated Anthology and Sourcebook

Jensen, Joan M.
81 Decades of Discontent: The Women's Movement, 1920-1940
201 A Needle, a Bobbin, a Strike: Women Needleworkers in America

Johannesen, Stanley
401 Women in China: Current Directions in Historical Scholarship

Jones, Gavin W.
424 Women in the Urban and Industrial Workforce: Southeast and East Asia

Jones, Lynne
167 Keeping the Peace: A Women's Peace Handbook

Juhasz, Suzanne
121 Feminist Critics Read Emily Dickinson

Justice, Betty
316 Toward the Second Decade: The Impact of the Women's Movement on American Institutions

Kâgitçibasi, Çigdem
270 Sex Roles, Family, & Community in Turkey

Kahn-Hut, Rachel
387 Women and Work: Problems and Perspectives

Kalant, Oriana Josseau
9 Alcohol and Drug Problems in Women

Kalven, Janet
462 Women's Spirit Bonding

Kaplan, E. Ann
406 Women in Film Noir

Kaplan, Jane Rachel
341 A Woman's Conflict: The Special Relationship Between Women and Food

Kaplan, Marion
336 When Biology Became Destiny: Women in Weimar and Nazi Germany

Kaplan, Sheila
407 Women in Higher Education Administration

Katz, Esther
454 Women's Experience in America: An Historical Anthology

Keep, Pieter A. van
236 The Premenstrual Syndrome

Keirse, Marc J.N.C.
252 Second Trimester Pregnancy Termination

Keller, Rosemary Skinner
366 Women and Religion in America - Volume 1: The Nineteenth Century
367 Women and Religion in America - Volume 2: The Colonial and Revolutionary Periods
412 Women in New Worlds: Historical Perspectives on the Wesleyan Tradition

Kelly, Alison
193 The Missing Half: Girls and Science Education

Kelly, Gail P.
97 Excellence, Reform and Equity in Education: An International Perspective

Keltner, Alfred A.
276 Sexual Aggression and the Law

Kempe, C. Henry
291 Sexually Abused Children and their Families

Kern, Robert
95 European Women on the Left: Socialism, Feminism, and the Problems Faced by Political Women, 1880 to the Present

Kess, Cathy
157 In Her Own Right: Selected Essays on Women's History in B.C.

Khoo, Siew-Ean
420 Women in the Cities of Asia: Migration and Urban Adaptation

Kimball, Gayle
453 Women's Culture: The Women's Renaissance of the Seventies

Kirkendall, Lester A.
185 Marriage and the Family in the Year 2020

Kirkpatrick, Martha
460 Women's Sexual Development: Explorations of *Inner Space*
461 Women's Sexual Experience: Explorations of the *Dark Continent*

Klein, Martin A.
370 Women and Slavery in Africa

Kornbluh, Joyce L.
292 Sisterhood and Solidarity: Workers' Education for Women, 1914-1984

Kramarae, Cheris
171 Language, Gender and Society

Kuhrt, Amélie
156 Images of Women in Antiquity

Kurian, George
421 Women in the Family and the Economy: An International Comparative Survey

Labalme, Patricia H.
33 Beyond Their Sex: Learned Women of the European Past

Lamb, Michael E.
204 Nontraditional Families: Parenting and Child Development

Langland, Elizabeth
123 A Feminist Perspective in the Academy: The Difference it Makes
332 The Voyage In: Fictions of Female Development

Lapidus, Gail Warshofsky
446 Women, Work, and Family in the Soviet Union

Latham, Barbara
157 In Her Own Right: Selected Essays on Women's History in B.C.
205 Not Just Pin Money: Selected Essays on the History of Women's Work in British Columbia

Leacock, Eleanor
347 Women and Colonization: Anthropological Perspectives

Leavitt, Judith Walzer
353 Women and Health in America: Historical Readings

Lebra, Joyce
58 Chinese Women in Southeast Asia
386 Women and Work in India: Continuity and Change

Lee, L. L.
445 Women, Women Writers, and the West

Lee, W. R.
144 The German Family: Essays on the Social History of the Family in Nineteenth- and Twentieth-Century Germany

Leira, Arnlaug
468 Work and Womanhood: Norwegian Studies

Lenz, Carolyn Ruth Swift
343 The Woman's Part: Feminist Criticism of Shakespeare

Lepervanche, Marie M. de
94 Ethnicity, Class and Gender in Australia

Lesnoff-Caravaglia, Gari
472 The World of the Older Woman: Conflicts and Resolutions

Lessinger, Hanna
60 Class, Race, and Sex: The Dynamics of Control

Lewin, Miriam
158 In the Shadow of the Past: Psychology Portrays the Sexes: A Social and Intellectual History

Lewis, Jane
465 Women's Welfare Women's Rights

Lewis, Merrill
445 Women, Women Writers, and the West

Lincoln, Richard
309 Teenage Sexuality, Pregnancy, and Childbearing

Linden, Robin Ruth
7 Against Sadomasochism: A Radical Feminist Analysis

Lindsay, Beverly
68 Comparative Perspectives of Third World Women: The Impact of Race, Sex, and Class

Livernash, E. Robert
66 Comparable Worth: Issues and Alternatives
67 Comparable Worth: Issues and Alternatives (2nd edition)

Lohmann, Nancy
317 Transitions of Aging

Long, Norman
104 Family and Work in Rural Societies: Perspectives on Non-Wage Labour

Lopata, Helena Z.
243 Research in the Interweave of Social Roles: Families and Jobs
244 Research in the Interweave of Social Roles: Women and Men

Loring, Katherine
122 Feminist Pedagogy and the Learning Climate
254 Seeing our Way Clear: Feminist Revision of the Academy

Lorwin, Val R.
382 Women and Trade Unions in Eleven Industrialized Countries

Loveland, Christine A.
269 Sex Roles and Social Change in Native Lower Central American Societies

Loveland, Franklin O.
269 Sex Roles and Social Change in Native Lower Central American Societies

Lovenduski, Joni
228 The Politics of the Second Electorate: Women and Public Participation

Lovett, Clara M.
444 Women, War, and Revolution

Lowe, Marian
342 Woman's Nature: Rationalizations of Inequality

Lupri, Eugen
52 The Changing Position of Women in Family and Society: A Cross-National Comparison

Lussier, Virginia Lee
442 Women, the Arts, and the 1920's in Paris and New York

Lynch, Henry T.
141 Genetics and Breast Cancer

MacCormack, Carol P.
200 Nature, Culture and Gender

Malamuth, Neil M.
230 Pornography and Sexual Aggression

Malos, Ellen
227 The Politics of Housework

Mancuso, Arlene
455 Women's Issues and Social Work Practice

Manderson, Lenore
466 Women's Work and Women's Roles: Economics and Everyday Life in Indonesia, Malaysia and Singapore

Manohar, K. Murali
299 Socio-Economic Status of Indian Women

Marcus, Jane
202 New Feminist Essays on Virginia Woolf
328 Virginia Woolf: A Feminist Slant

Markson, Elizabeth W.
210 Older Women: Issues and Prospects

Marland, Michael
259 Sex Differentiation and Schooling

Marschall, Daniel
209 Office Automation: Jekyll or Hyde?

MATRIX (Architectural Co-operative)
182 Making space: Women and the man-made environment

Mayo, Clara
136 Gender and Nonverbal Behavior

McAdoo, Harriette Pipes
37 Black Families

McCarty, Mari Ward
64 Colette: The Woman, the Writer

McClure, Charlotte S.
126 Feminist Visions: Toward a Transformation of the Liberal Arts Curriculum

McConnell-Ginet, Sally
356 Women and Language in Literature and Society

McCormick, Naomi B.
48 Changing Boundaries: Gender Roles and Sexual Behavior

McCullagh, Roslyn
207 Of Marriage and the Market: Women's Subordination in International Perspective
208 Of Marriage and the Market: Women's Subordination Internationally and Its Lessons

McElroy, Wendy
129 Freedom, Feminism, and the State: An Overview of Individualist Feminism

McGee, Sandra F.
363 Women and Politics in Twentieth Century Latin America

McNamara JoAnn K.
379 Women and the Structure of Society: Selected Research from the Fifth Berkshire Conference on the History of Women

McPherson, Ann
456 Women's Problems in General Practice

McRobbie, Angela
134 Gender and Generation

Medicine, Beatrice
148 The Hidden Half: Studies of Plains Indian Women

Medick, Hans
162 Interest and Emotion: Essays on the Study of Family and Kinship

Mellencamp, Patricia
247 Re-vision: Essays in Feminist Film Criticism

Melville, Margarita B.
319 Twice a Minority: Mexican American Women

Mendell, Dale
88 Early Female Development: Current Psychoanalytic Views

Menell, Zoë
47 Change and Choice: Women and Middle Age

Menken, Jane
309 Teenage Sexuality, Pregnancy, and Childbearing

Meulenbelt, Anja
76 A Creative Tension: Key Issues of Socialist-Feminism

Meyer, Doris
74 Contemporary Women Authors of Latin America: Introductory Essays

Michaelson, Karen L.
18 And the Poor Get Children: Radical Perspectives on Population Dynamics

Miles, Angela R.
120 Feminism in Canada: From Pressure to Politics

Miller, Beth
408 Women in Hispanic Literature: Icons and Fallen Idols

Miller, Sally M.
128 Flawed Liberation: Socialism and Feminism

Minault, Gail
101 The Extended Family: Women and Political Participation in India and Pakistan

255 Separate Worlds: Studies of Purdah in South Asia

Minden, Shelley
310 Test-Tube Women: What Future for Motherhood?

Minor, Marianne
54 Chicanas and Alcoholism: A Socio-Cultural Perspective of Women

Mitchell, Pam
224 Pink Triangles: Radical Perspectives on Gay Liberation

Monaghan, David
164 Jane Austen in a Social Context

Montgomery Evelyn I.
82 Developing Nations: Challenges Involving Women

Mora, Gabriela
313 Theory and Practice of Feminist Literary Criticism

Mora, Magdalena
192 Mexican Women in the United States: Struggles Past and Present

Morgan, Robin
293 Sisterhood is Global: The International Women's Movement Anthology

Morley, David
203 New Space for Women

Moss, Peter
467 Work and the Family

Mouritsen, Maren M.
42 Blueprint for Living: Perspectives for Latter-Day Saint Women

Mrazek, Patricia Beezley
291 Sexually Abused Children and Their Families

Mukherjee, Satyanshu K.
348 Women and Crime

Mumford, David M.
4 Adolescent Pregnancy: Perspectives for the Health Professional

Munford, Theresa
234 Pre-Industrial Women: Interdisciplinary Perspectives

Murray, Meg McGavran
102 Face to Face: Fathers, Mothers, Masters, Monsters - Essays for a Nonsexist Future

Musgrave, Beatrice
47 Change and Choice: Women and Middle Age

Nadelson, Carol C.
8 Aggression, Adaptations, and Psychotherapy

45 The Challenge of Change: Perspectives on Family, Work, and Education

69 Concepts of Femininity and the Life Cycle

Nance, Margit
111 The Female Offender

Nash, June
428 Women, Men and the International Division of Labor

Nashat, Guity
368 Women and Revolution in Iran

Nava, Mica
134 Gender and Generation

Neely, Carol Thomas
343 The Woman's Part: Feminist Criticism of Shakespeare

Nelson, Nici
5 African Women in the Development Process

Neugarten, Dail Ann
288 Sexuality in Organizations: Romantic and Coercive Behaviors at Work

Newton, Judith L.
256 Sex and Class in Women's History

Nichols, John A.
187 Medieval Religious Women

Nicol, Davidson
77 Creative Women in Changing Societies: A Quest for Alternatives

Norman, Elaine
455 Women's Issues and Social Work Practice

Notman, Malkah T.
8 Aggression, Adaptations, and Psychotherapy

45 The Challenge of Change: Perspectives on Family, Work, and Education

69 Concepts of Femininity and the Life Cycle

O'Barr, Jean F.
218 Perspectives on Power: Women in Africa, Asia, and Latin America

O'Brien, Denise
246 Rethinking Women's Roles: Perspectives from the Pacific

O'Donnell, Sheryl R.
51 Changing Perspectives on Menopause

Ooms, Theodora
308 Teenage Pregnancy in a Family Context: Implications for Policy

Ortner, Sherry B.
282 Sexual Meanings: The Cultural Construction of Gender and Sexuality

Owen, Morfydd E.
334 The Welsh Law of Women

Pagano, Darlene R.
7 Against Sadomasochism: A Radical Feminist Analysis

Palandri, Angela Jung
449 Women Writers of 20th-Century China

Papanek, Hanna
255 Separate Worlds: Studies of Purdah in South Asia

Parsons, Jacquelynne E.
239 The Psychobiology of Sex Differences and Sex Roles

Patraka, Vivian
124 Feminist Re-Visions: What has Been and Might Be

Paulson, Joy
58 Chinese Women in Southeast Asia

386 Women and Work in India: Continuity and Change

Pazdro, Roberta J.
205 Not Just Pin Money: Selected Essays on the History of Women's Work in British Columbia

Pepitone-Rockwell, Fran
87 Dual-Career Couples

Peradotto, John
419 Women in the Ancient World: The *Arethusa Papers*

Perrie, Maureen
151 Home, School and Leisure in the Soviet Union

Perrucci, Carolyn C.
416 Women in Scientific and Engineering Professions

Perry, Ruth
196 Mothering the Mind: Twelve Studies of Writers and Their Silent Partners

Person, Ethel Spector
439 Women: Sex and Sexuality

Perun, Pamela J.
320 The Undergraduate Woman: Issues in Educational Equity

Peterson, Rebecca
203 New Space for Women

Pfafflin, Sheila M.
251 Scientific-Technological Change and the Role of Women in Development

Phizacklea, Annie
213 One Way Ticket: Migration and Female Labour

Pilotta, Joseph J.
415 Women in Organizations: Barriers and Breakthroughs

Pleck, Joseph H.
243 Research in the Interweave of Social Roles: Families and Jobs

Plottel, Jeanine Parisier
108 The Female Autograph

Plummer, John F.
331 Vox Feminae: Studies in Medieval Woman's Songs

Pollack, Sandra
174 Learning Our Way: Essays in Feminist Education

Pore, Renate
316 Toward the Second Decade: The Impact of the Women's Movement on American Institutions

Postow, Betsy C.
432 Women, Philosophy, and Sport: A Collection of New Essays

Potter, Sandee
397 Women-Identified Women

Prenshaw, Peggy Whitman
450 Women Writers of the Contemporary South

Preston, James J.
194 Mother Worship: Theme and Variations

Price, Barbara Raffel
78 The Criminal Justice System and Women: Women Offenders, Victims, Workers

Pringle, Mary Beth
155 The Image of the Prostitute in Modern Literature

Purdy, Virginia C.
61 Clio was a Woman: Studies in the History of American Women

Quarm, Daisy
427 Women in the Workplace: Effects on Families

Rabb, Theodore K.
184 Marriage and Fertility: Studies in Interdisciplinary History

Rafter, Nicole Hahn
165 Judge Lawyer Victim Thief: Women, Gender Roles, and Criminal Justice

Rapone, Anita
454 Women's Experience in America: An Historical Anthology

Ratner, Ronnie Steinberg
93 Equal Employment Policy for Women: Strategies for Implementation in the United States, Canada, and Western Europe

Reed, Beth
315 Toward a Feminist Transformation of the Academy: III: Proceedings of the Seventh Annual GLCA Women's Studies Conference

Reid, Ivan
258 Sex Differences in Britain

Remick, Helen
65 Comparable Worth and Wage Discrimination: Technical Possibilities and Political Realities

Remy, Dorothy
199 My Troubles are Going to Have Trouble with Me: Everyday Trials and Triumphs of Women Workers

Rendel, Margherita
436 Women, Power and Political Systems

Reskin, Barbara F.
272 Sex Segregation in the Workplace: Trends, Explanations, Remedies

Revitch, Eugene
280 Sexual Dynamics of Anti-Social Behavior

Richardson, Barbara L.
266 Sex Role Research: Measuring Social Change

Richter, Derek
438 Women Scientists: The Road to Liberation

Rickel, Annette U.
295 Social and Psychological Problems of Women: Prevention and Crisis Intervention

Rieker, Patricia Perri
140 The Gender Gap in Psychotherapy: Social Realities and Psychological Processes

Roberts, Albert R.
26 Battered Women and Their Families: Intervention Strategies and Treatment Programs

Roberts, Audrey J.
337 Wisconsin Women: Graduate School and the Professions
394 Women Emerge in the Seventies

Roberts, Elizabeth J.
57 Childhood Sexual Learning: The Unwritten Curriculum

Roberts, Helen
85 Doing Feminist Research
297 Social Researching: Politics, Problems, Practice
396 Women, Health and Reproduction

Robertson, Claire C.
370 Women and Slavery in Africa

Robinson, Gertrude J.
391 Women, Communication and Careers

Rodgers-Rose, La Frances
38 The Black Woman

Rohrlich, Ruby
417 Women in Search of Utopia: Mavericks and Mythmakers

Romalis, Shelly
56 Childbirth: Alternatives to Medical Control

Rosenbloom, Sandra
463 Women's Travel Issues: Research Needs and Priorities

Rosenfelt, Deborah
306 Teaching Women's Literature from a Regional Perspective

Rosowski, Susan J.
384 Women and Western American Literature

Rotberg, Robert I.
184 Marriage and Fertility: Studies in Interdisciplinary History

Rothblum, Esther D.
304 The stereotyping of women: its effects on mental health

Rothschild, Joan
181 Machina ex dea: feminist perspectives on technology
441 Women, technology and innovation

Rowan, Caroline
119 Feminism, culture and politics

Ruddick, Sara
30 Between Women: Biographers, Novelists, Critics, Teachers and Artists Write about Their Work on Women

Ruether, Rosemary Radford
366 Women and Religion in America - Volume 1: The Nineteenth Century
367 Women and Religion in America - Volume 2: The Colonial and Revolutionary periods

Russell, Diana E. H.
7 Against Sadomasochism: A Radical Feminist Analysis

Russianoff, Penelope
404 Women in Crisis

Ryan, Joanna
257 Sex & Love: New Thoughts on Old Contradictions

Ryan, Mary P.
256 Sex and Class in Women's History

Ryff, Carol D.
296 Social Power and Influence of Women

Sabean, David Warren
162 Interest and Emotion: Essays on the Study of Family and Kinship

Sacks, Karen Brodkin
199 My Troubles are Going to Have Trouble With Me: Everyday Trials and Triumphs of Women Workers

Salaff, Janet W.
177 Lives: Chinese Working Women

Salasin, Susan
191 The Mental Health of Women

Sarah, Elizabeth
212 On the Problem of Men: Two Feminist Conferences

Sargent, Lydia
369 Women and Revolution: A Discussion of the Unhappy Marriage of Marxism and Feminism

Scarpitti, Frank R.
392 Women, Crime, and Justice

Scharf, Lois
81 Decades of Discontent: The Women's Movement, 1920-1940

Schipper, Mineke
322 Unheard Words: Women and Literature in Africa, the Arab World, Asia, the Caribbean and Latin America

Schlesinger, Louis B.
280 Sexual Dynamics of Anti-Social Behavior

Schmid, Günther
260 Sex Discrimination and Equal Opportunity: The Labor Market and Employment Policy

Schmuck, Patricia A.
90 Educational Policy and Management: Sex Differentials

Schneider, Carl E.
173 The Law and Politics of Abortion

Schultz, Leroy G.
284 The Sexual Victimology of Youth

Scott, Patricia Bell
14 All the Women are White, All the Blacks are Men, But Some of Us Are Brave: Black Women's Studies

Scutt, Jocelynne A.
348 Women and Crime

Secor, Cynthia
407 Women in Higher Education Administration

Seely, Clinton B.
433 Women, Politics, and Literature in Bengal

Segal, Lynne
335 What Is to Be Done About the Family?

Sgroi, Suzanne M.
146 Handbook of Clinical Intervention in Child Sexual Abuse

Shafritz, Jay M.
288 Sexuality in Organizations: Romantic and Coercive Behaviors at Work

Shank, Lillian Thomas
187 Medieval Religious Women

Shaw, Lois Banfill
324 Unplanned Careers: The Working Lives of Middle-Aged Women

Sheridan, Mary
177 Lives: Chinese Working Women

Sherman, Claire Richter
389 Women as Interpreters of the Visual Arts, 1820-1979

Shipstone, Norah
75 Country Papers on Career Services for Women in Asia

Shore, Elliott
15 Alternative Materials in Libraries

Silberfeld, Heath
451 Women Writers of the Short Story

Siltanen, Janet
378 Women and the Public Sphere: A Critique of Sociology and Politics

Silverstone, Rosalie
44 Careers of Professional Women

Simms, Marian
23 Australian Women and the Political System

Skemp, Sheila L.
264 Sex, Race, and the Role of Women in the South

Slaughter, Jane
95 European Women on the Left: Socialism, Feminism, and the Problems Faced by Political Women, 1880 to the Present

Sloane, Peter J.
357 Women and Low Pay

Smith, Anne
143 George Eliot: Centenary Essays and an Unpublished Fragment

Smith, Barbara
14 All the Women are White, All the Blacks are Men, but Some of Us Are Brave: Black Women's Studies
150 Home Girls: A Black Feminist Anthology

Smith, James P.
110 Female Labor Supply: Theory and Estimation

Smith, Jane I.
403 Women in Contemporary Muslim Societies

Smith, Joan
153 Households and the World-Economy

Smith, Nicholas D.
383 Women and Utopia: Critical Interpretations

Smith, Peggy B.
4 Adolescent Pregnancy: Perspectives for the Health Professional

Smith, Peter C.
420 Women in the Cities of Asia: Migration and Urban Adaptation

Smykla, John Ortiz
63 Coed Prison

Snitow, Ann
231 Powers of Desire: The Politics of Sexuality

Sokoloff, Natalie J.
78 The Criminal Justice System and Women: Women Offenders, Victims, Workers

Spanier, Bonnie
314 Toward a Balanced Curriculum: A Sourcebook for Initiating Gender Integration Projects

Spencer, Samia I.
130 French Women and the Age of Enlightenment

Spender, Dale
125 Feminist Theorists: Three Centuries of Women's Intellectual Traditions
189 Men's Studies Modified: The Impact of Feminism on the Academic Disciplines

Spretnak, Charlene
229 The Politics of Women's Spirituality: Essays on the Rise of Spiritual Power Within the Feminist Movement

Squier, Susan Merrill
448 Women Writers and the City: Essays in Feminist Literary Criticism

Staicar, Tom
114 The Feminine Eye: Science Fiction and the Women Who Write it

Staley, Thomas F.
318 Twentieth-Century Women Novelists

Stamm, Liesa
296 Social Power and Influence of Women

Stanko, Elizabeth Anne
165 Judge Lawyer Victim Thief: Women, Gender Roles, and Criminal Justice

Stansell, Christine
231 Powers of Desire: The Politics of Sexuality

Stanton, Domna C.
108 The Female Autograph

Stanworth, Michelle
378 Women and the Public Sphere: A Critique of Sociology and Politics

Star, Susan Leigh
7 Against Sadomasochism: A Radical Feminist Analysis

Stark-Adamec, Cannie
271 Sex Roles: Origins, Influences, and Implications for Women

Stauffer, Helen Winter
384 Women and Western American Literature

Steady, Filomina Chioma
39 The Black Woman Cross-Culturally

Sternburg, Janet
474 The Writer on Her Work

Stewart, Debra W.
410 Women in Local Politics

Stichter, Sharon
6 African Women South of the Sahara

Stiehm, Judith Hicks
464 Women's Views of the Political World of Men

Stimpson, Catharine R.
439 Women: Sex and Sexuality

Stockard, Jean
262 Sex Equity in Education

Stoecker, Barbara J.
82 Developing Nations: Challenges Involving Women

Stokland, Torill
77 Creative Women in Changing Societies: A Quest for Alternatives

Stone, Elizabeth
374 Women and the Cuban Revolution: Speeches & Documents by Fidel Castro, Vilma Espin & Others

Strathern, Marilyn
200 Nature, Culture and Gender

Stringer, Patricia A.
303 Stepping Off the Pedestal: Academic Women in the South

Stuart, Irving R.
326 Victims of Sexual Aggression: Treatment of Children, Women, and Men

Sullivan, J.P.
419 Women in the Ancient World: *The Arethusa Papers*

Sutlive, Vinson H.
362 Women and Politics in Twentieth Century Africa and Asia

Sutton, Andrew
151 Home, School and Leisure in the Soviet Union

Swerdlow, Amy
60 Class, Race, and Sex: The Dynamics of Control

Swoboda, Marian J.
337 Wisconsin Women: Graduate School and the Professions
394 Women Emerge in the Seventies

Szinovacz, Maximiliane
458 Women's Retirement: Policy Implications of Recent Research

Tallmer, Margot
285 Sexuality and Life-Threatening Illness

Tellis-Nayak, Jessie B.
91 The Emerging Christian Woman: Church and Society Perspectives

Thomas, Hilah F.
412 Women in New Worlds: Historical Perspectives on the Wesleyan Tradition

Thompson, Dorothy
215 Over Our Dead Bodies: Women Against the Bomb

Thompson, Irene
303 Stepping Off the Pedestal: Academic Women in the South

Thompson, Sharon
231 Powers of Desire: The Politics of Sexuality

Thorne, Barrie
171 Language, Gender and Society
245 Rethinking the Family: Some Feminist Questions

Thurman, Melvena K.
414 Women in Oklahoma: A Century of Change

Tiffany, Sharon W.
246 Rethinking Women's Roles: Perspectives from the Pacific

Tilly, Louise A.
124 Feminist Re-Visions: What has Been and Might Be

Tinsley, Adrian
407 Women in Higher Education Administration

Tobin, Dianne
377 Women and the Mathematical Mystique

Todd, Janet
27 Be Good, Sweet Maid: An Anthology of Women & Literature
135 Gender and Literary Voice

Todd, Susan
381 Women and Theatre: Calling the Shots

Trebilcot, Joyce
195 Mothering: Essays in Feminist Theory

Trost, Jan
105 The Family in Change

Turner, Joan
220 Perspectives on Women in the 1980s

Turner, June H.
172 Latin American Woman: The Meek Speak

Unkeless, Elaine
409 Women in Joyce

Utian, Wulf H.
236 The Premenstrual Syndrome

Vajrathon, Mallica
77 Creative Women in Changing Societies: A Quest for Alternatives

Van Esterik, Penny
431 Women of Southeast Asia

Van Hooft, Karen S.
313 Theory and Practice of Feminist Literary Criticism

VanArsdel, Rosemary T.
142 George Eliot: A Centenary Tribute

Vance, Carol S.
225 Pleasure and Danger: Exploring Female Sexuality

Vandiver, Susan T.
434 Women, Power, and Change

Vartuli, Sue
222 The Ph.D. Experience: A Woman's Point of View

Venerando, A.
107 The Female Athlete: A Socio-Psychological and Kinanthropometric Approach
372 Women and Sport: An Historical, Biological, Physiological and Sportsmedical Approach

Verdun-Jones, Simon N.
276 Sexual Aggression and the Law

Vetterling-Braggin, Mary
116 "Femininity", "Masculinity", and "Androgyny": A Modern Philosophical Discussion
275 Sexist Language: A Modern Philosophical Analysis

Vinovskis, Maris A.
173 The Law and Politics of Abortion

Voda, Ann M.
51 Changing Perspectives on Menopause

Wadley, Susan S.
232 The Powers of Tamil Women

Walker, Lenore E.
25 The Battered Woman Syndrome
360 Women and Mental Health Policy

Walker, Stephen
138 Gender Class & Education

Walkowitz, Judith R.
256 Sex and Class in Women's History

Wallace, Louise
240 Psychology and Gynaecological Problems

Wallace, Phyllis A.
426 Women in the Workplace

Wallerstein, Immanuel
153 Households and the World-Economy

Walsh, Diana Chapman
447 Women, Work, and Health: Challenges to Corporate Policy

Ward, Audrey
44 Careers of Professional Women

Ware, Helen
393 Women, Education and Modernization of the Family in West Africa

Watts, Meredith W.
35 Biopolitics and Gender

Watts, Rosemary A.
92 The Endless Day: Some Case Material on Asian Rural Women

WCSRC-CISRS Joint Women's Programme
161 Indian Women in Media: A Collection of Essays

Weg, Ruth B.
289 Sexuality in the Later Years: Roles and Behavior

Weick, Ann
434 Women, Power, and Change

Weidman, Judith L.
59 Christian Feminism: Visions of a New Humanity
429 Women Ministers

Weisberg, D. Kelly
375 Women and the Law: Property, Family and the Legal Profession
376 Women and the Law: Women and Criminal Law

Weitzel, Renate
260 Sex Discrimination and Equal Opportunity: The Labor Market and Employment Policy

Wekerle, Gerda R.
203 New Space for Women

Wertheimer, Barbara Mayer
169 Labor Education for Women Workers

West, Jackie
470 Work, Women and the Labour Market

Wheeler, Kenneth W.
442 Women, the Arts, and the 1920's in Paris and New York

Whitehead, Harriet
282 Sexual Meanings: The Cultural Construction of Gender and Sexuality

Whitelegg, Elizabeth
50 The Changing Experience of Women

Whyld, Janie
274 Sexism in the Secondary Curriculum

Widom, Cathy Spatz
268 Sex Roles and Psychopathology

Williams, Linda
247 Re-Vision: Essays in Feminist Film Criticism

Wilsnack, Sharon C.
10 Alcohol Problems in Women: Antecedents, Consequences, and Intervention

Wilson, Katharina M.
188 Medieval Women Writers

Windschuttle, Elizabeth
390 Women, Class and History: Feminist Perspectives on Australia 1788-1978

Wirtenberg, Jeana
266 Sex Role Research: Measuring Social Change

Wolfe, Margie
305 Still Ain't Satisfied! Canadian Feminism Today

Wolkowitz, Carol
207 Of Marriage and the Market: Women's Subordination in International Perspective
208 Of Marriage and the Market: Women's Subordination Internationally and its Lessons

Women and Labour Publications Collective
13 All Her Labours

Woody, Jane Divita
281 Sexual Issues in Family Therapy

Woody, Robert Henley
281 Sexual Issues in Family Therapy

Wormald, Eileen
258 Sex Differences in Britain

Wu, Rosalind
70 Conference on the Educational and Occupational Needs of American Indian Women

71 Conference on the Educational and Occupational Needs of Asian-Pacific-American Women

72 Conference on the Educational and Occupational Needs of Hispanic Women

73 Conference on the Educational and Occupational Needs of White Ethnic Women

Yalom, Marilyn
245 Rethinking the Family: Some Feminist Questions

Yanz, Lynda
323 Union Sisters: Women in the Labour Movement

Yedlin, Tova
405 Women in Eastern Europe and the Soviet Union

Yohalem, Alice M.
437 Women Returning to Work: Policies and Progress in Five Countries

Young, Kate
207 Of Marriage and the Market: Women's Subordination in International perspective

208 Of Marriage and the Market: Women's Subordination Internationally and its Lessons

Youssef, Nadia H.
459 Women's Roles and Population Trends in the Third World

Zainu'ddin, Ailsa Thomson
166 Kartini Centenary: Indonesian Women Then and Now

Zambrana, Ruth E.
469 Work, Family, and Health: Latina Women in Transition

Zamora, Mario D.
362 Women and Politics in Twentieth Century Africa and Asia

Zigler, Edward F.
80 Day Care: Scientific and Social Policy Issues

Zimmerman, Jan
307 The Technological Woman: Interfacing with Tomorrow

AUTHOR INDEX

Abadan-Unat, Nermin
270h The effect of international labor migration on women's roles: The Turkish case
436e Women in government as policy-makers and bureaucrats: The Turkish case

Abdulahad, Tania
150jj Black lesbian/feminist organizing: A conversation

Abdullah, Tahrunnessa
98k Action research with rural women in Bangladesh: Some observations and experiences

Abel, Elizabeth
332h Narrative structure(s) and female development: The case of *Mrs. Dalloway*
398f 'They shared a laboratory together': Feminist collaboration in the academy

Abel, Gene G.
276b The relationship between treatment for sex offenders and the court
276d The assessment and treatment of sexual offenders
277f Psychophysiologic measurement of sexual arousal in females

Abel-Smith, Brian
465d Sex equality and social security

Abernethy, Francis Edward
175a María de Agreda: The lady in blue

Abernethy, Virginia
3g Children, personhood, and a pluralistic society
3r Commentary to chapter 10 (chapter q)

Abeyasekere, Susan
466a Women as cultural intermediaries in nineteenth-century Batavia

Aboulafia, Mitchell
31i From domination to recognition

Abraham, Guy E.
237d The nutritionist's approach (prementrual tension)

Abraham-Van der Mark, Eve E.
428o The impact of industrialization on women: A Caribbean case

Abrahams, Ray G.
104d Co-operation on and between eastern Finnish family farms

Abrahamse, Dorothy de F.
187b Byzantine asceticism and women's monasteries in early medieval Italy

Abramovitz, Mimi
169u Funding worker education through tuition refund plans

Abramson, Doris
399w Anne Nichols: $1,000,000.00 playwright

Abramson, Fredric D.
79k Policy decisions in prenatal diagnosis: The example of fetal alcoholism syndrome

Abramson, Joan
249j A jury of one's peers

Abramson, Paul R.
230g Pornography in Japan: Cross-cultural and theoretical considerations

Abu Nasr, J.
265n Sex role images in Lebanese text books

Abu-Saba, Mary Bentley
462p Women responding to the Arab-Israeli conflict

Abzug, Bella S.
404bb Making change

Accad, Evelyne
155f The prostitute in Arab and North African fiction

Ackelsberg, Martha A.
103u "Sisters" or "comrades"? The politics of friends and families
226k Women's collaborative activities and city life: Politics and policy
417l *Mujeres Libres* and the role of women in anarchist revolution

Acker, Joan
382j Sweden

Acker, Sandra
138h Women and teaching: A semi-detached sociology of a semi-profession
398i Women, the other academics

Ackroyd, Peter R.
156o Goddesses, women and Jezebel

Adam, Ian
142k The ambivalence of *The Mill on the Floss*

Adam, Sheila
456e Breast cancer and benign breast disease

Adams, Catherine
210d The sexuality of older women

Adams, Harriet Farwell
398b Work in the interstices: Woman in academeme

Adams, Jane
323l Bargaining for equality

Adams, Karen L.
344z Sexism and the English language: The linguistic implications of being a woman

Adams, Lois
68d Women in Zaire: Disparate status and roles

Adams, Mischa
417cc Therrillium (story)

Adams, Paul
326d Treatment of sexually abused children
460p Role of the father

Adams-Tucker, Christine
326d Treatment of sexually abused children
460p Role of the father

Adamski, Wladyslaw W.
405l Women in contemporary Poland: Their social and occupational position and attitudes toward work

Adbul-Karim, Raja W.
233d Women workers at higher risk of reproductive hazards

Addelson, Kathryn Pyne
84j The man of professional wisdom
432i Equality and competition: Can sports make a women of a girl?

Adelman, William
169m Labor history through field trips

Adelson, Leslie
32n The question of a feminist aesthetic and Karin Struck's *Klassenliebe*

Adilman, Tamara
157h Evlyn Farris and the University Women's Club
205d A preliminary sketch of Chinese women and work in British Columbia, 1858-1950

Adlam, Diana
283i Interview with Jo Richardson

Adler, Emily Stier
349p The underside of married life: Power, influence, and violence

Adler, Freda
159a International concern in light of the American experience
392e The interaction between women's emancipation and female criminality: A cross-cultural perspective

Adler, Lois
399l Adah Isaacs Menken in *Mazeppa*

Adler, Margot
229m Meanings of matriarchy

Adler, Rachel
211a The Jew who wasn't there: *Halakhah* and the Jewish woman

Afshar, Soraya
430b The economic base for the revival of Islam in Iran
430d The attitude of the Iranian left to the women's question

Aga, Synnøva
468d Women's attempts to break down sex barriers in the labour market

Ager, Lynn Price
473l The economic role of women in Alaskan Eskimo society

Aghajanian, Akbar
421t Fertility and family economy in the Iranian rural communities

Aguiar, Neuma
428e Household, community, national, and multinational industrial development

Aguirre, Benigno E.
421z Women in the Cuban bureaucracies: 1968-1974

Aguwa, C. Nze
395k Obstetrical complications associated with traditional medical practices at Nsukka

Aguwa, Margaret
395k Obstetrical complications associated with traditional medical practices at Nsukka

Aguwa, Okechukwu
395k Obstetrical complications associated with traditional medical practices at Nsukka

Ahearn, Kerry
445m Heroes vs women: Conflict and duplicity in Stegner

Ahmed, Leila
198f Early feminist movements in Turkey and Egypt

Ahmed, Zeenat
92c Pakistan: *Mor* and *Tor*: Binary and opposing models of Pukhtun womanhood

Aidoo, Agnes Akosua
39c Asante queen mothers in government and politics in the nineteenth century

Ainsworth, Jackie
305k Getting organized...in the feminist unions

Aitken, Judith
413a Women in the political life of New Zealand

Akbar, S.
92c Pakistan: *Mor* and *Tor*: Binary and opposing models of Pukhtun womanhood

Akhtar, Farida
400e Population planning and rural women's cooperative in IRDP women's programme: Some critical issues

Alam, Sterling E.
185o 2020 and beyond

Albers, Patricia
148a Introduction: New perspectives on Plains Indian women
148f The role of Sioux women in the production of ceremonial objects: The case of the star quilt
148h Sioux women in transition: A study of their changing status in a domestic and capitalist sector of production

Albertson, Roxanne
147w School physical activity programs for the antebellum southern females

Albin, Robert C.
82j Livestock and range management

Albino, Judith E.
295i Women's health issues

Albrecht-Heide, Astrid
179m The peaceful sex

Albury, Rebecca
23m 'Law reform and human reproduction': Implications for women
310d Who owns the embryo?

Aldaraca, Bridget
313e El ángel del hogar: The cult of domesticity in nineteenth century Spain

Alder, Christine
111s Issues in the application of parole guidelines to females

Alder, Elizabeth
240a Sterilization

Alderfer, C. P.
49k Reflections on polarities and bias

Aldridge, David J.
291i Incest: Intake and investigation

Aldridge, Delores P.
38r Black female suicides: Is the excitement justified?

Alegría, Fernando
408j Notes toward a definition of Gabriela Mistral's ideology

Alessi, Joseph J.
26c Group treatment of children in shelters for battered women

Alexander, Anna Vareed
91i Through the feminist looking glass: Images of women

Alexander, Cheryl S.
53f Women as victims of crime

Alexander, Helen
291q Long-term effects of sexual abuse in childhood

Alexander, James F.
29o Female delinquents

Alexander, Karl L.
320o Family formation and educational attainment

Alexander, Maxine
301pp Listen! (poem)

Alexander, Sally
50c Women's work in nineteenth-century London: A study of the years 1820-1850

Alexander, Stanley G.
175u Janis and the Austin scene

al-Hibri, Azizah
195f Reproduction, mothering, and the origins of patriarchy
369h Capitalism is an advanced stage of patriarchy: But Marxism is not feminism

Alic, Margaret
441b Women and technology in ancient Alexandria: Maria and Hypatia

Alington, Diane E.
411h Social change and equality: The roles of women and economics

Al-Issa, Ihsan
137a Gender and psychopathology in perspective
137c Gender and child psychopathology
137d Gender and adult psychopathology
137g Gender and schizophrenia
137m Gender, hormones, and psychopathology

Allaghi, Farida
298b Survey of research on women in the Arab gulf region

Allatt, Patricia
241d Men and war: Status, class and the social reproduction of masculinity

Allawy, M. H.
107g Differences in athletic aggression among Egyptian female athletes

Allegra, Donna
150u Before I dress and soar again (poem)

Allen, Anita L.
31m Women and their privacy: What is at stake?

Allen, Christine
367c Women in colonial French America

Allen, D. W.
49l We can influence the future!

Allen, David G.
263j Professionalism, division of labor by gender, and the control of nursing practice

Allen, Jeffner
195r Motherhood: The annihilation of women

Allen, Jelisaveta Stanojevich
389l Sirarpie Der Nersessian (b. 1896): Educator and scholar in Byzantine and Armenian art

Allen, Judith
294e The making of a prostitute proletariat in early twentieth-century New South Wales

Allen, LaRue
295d Black women in American society: A resource development perspective

Allen, Pat
12j Reproductive engineering: The final solution?

Allen, Paula Gunn
397f Beloved women: The lesbian in American Indian culture

Allen, Ronald J.
429k Colleagues in marriage and ministry

Allender, Jeanne G.
361k Strategies to increase participation of minorities in medicine

Allgeier, A. R.
48g Sexuality and gender roles in the second half of life

Allgeier, Elizabeth Rice
48a The intimate relationship between gender roles and sexuality
48h Reproduction, roles, and responsibilities
48n Future influences on the interaction of gender and human sexual expression

Allin, Paul
50w Women in official statistics

Allison, Dorothy
225e Public silence, private terror

Allison, Janet R.
140k Roles and role conflict of women in infertile couples

Almana, Aisha
298b Survey of research on women in the Arab gulf region

Almquist, Elizabeth
41c Sources of life satisfaction: The different worlds of black women and white women
44w Race and ethnicity in the lives of minority women

Almy, Linda
63e A study of a coeducational correctional facility

Almy, Millie
80x Day care and early childhood education

Alonso, José Antonio
428g The domestic clothing workers in the Mexican metropolis and their relation to dependent capitalism

Alpers, Edward A.
370k The story of Swema: Female vulnerability in nineteenth century East Africa

Alpers, Svetlana
117k Art history and its exclusions: The example of Dutch art

Alpert, Geoffrey P.
78j Women prisoners and the law: Which way will the pendulum swing?

Altman, Leslie
112a Christine de Pisan: First professional woman of letters (French, 1364-1430?)

Altman, Meryl
225f Everything they always wanted you to know: The ideology of popular sex literature

Alvarado, Anita L.
319m The status of Hispanic women in nursing

Alvear, Ligia Cock
172m Saving money with bio-gas (Colombia)

Alves, Maria Helena
83h The church, the unions, women and the opposition in Brazil

Amanat, Ebrahim
326c Rape trauma syndrome: Developmental variations

Amaro, Hortensia
10k Patterns of women's use of alcohol treatment agencies

Amatniek, Joan Cindy
34m Bibliography: Women, science, and health

Ambrose, Linda
309z Misinforming pregnant teenagers

Ames, Roger T.
401b Taoism and the androgynous ideal

Ammons, Elizabeth
17i Cool Diana and the Blood-red muse: Edith Wharton on innocence and art

Amon, Robert S.
284t The last porno show

Amore, Roy C.
300l Have stories, will travel: How Buddhism won the southeast

Ampola, Mary G.
79i Prenatal diagnosis

Amrane, Djamila
113f Algeria: Anticolonial war

Amy, Jean-Jacques
252l Termination of second trimester pregnancy with prostaglandin analogues

Andersen, Barbara L.
240g Psychological aspects of gynaecological cancer

Andersen, Kristi
378l Candidate evaluations by men and women

Anderson, Anne
456b Menstrual problems
456d Menopause
456f The 'ectomies'

Anderson, Donna
210j The ever-single elderly woman

Anderson, Helene M.
74c Rosario Castellanos and the structures of power

Anderson, Kathleen M.
110o Managing the female offender: Crisis and change in the California Institution for Women

Anderson, Margaret
99c 'Helpmeet for man': Women in mid-nineteenth century western Australia

Anderson, Roxanne
24g Human sexuality in cross-cultural perspective

Andrade, Sally J.
319a Family planning practices of Mexican Americans
469k Family roles of Hispanic women: Stereotypes, empirical findings, and implications for research

Andreadis, A. Harriette
417j The Woman's Commonwealth: Utopia in nineteenth-century Texas

Andrews, Marcia S.
135h When silence has its way with you: Hazel Hall

Andrews, Stephen Pearl
129m Love, marriage and divorce

Andrisani, P. J.
49c The age mix of the labor force in 1990: Implications for labor market research

Andrusz, G. D.
151a Housing ideals, structural constraints and the emancipation of women

Angelou, Maya
40a Shades and slashes of light

Anglin, Mary
126j Redefining the family and women's status within the family: The case of southern Appalachia

Angress, Ruth
32d Kleist's nation of amazons

Aniyar de Castro, L.
159l Venezuelan female criminality: The ideology of diversity and marginality

Anker, Richard
459a Demographic change and the role of women: A research programme in developing countries

Annis, Helen M.
9k Alcoholism in women: Treatment modalities and outcomes

Ans, Jacki
36e Status of contraceptive technology development

Anson, Cynthia
82f Appropriate technology

Anthias, Floya
213d Sexual divisions and ethnic adaptation: The case of Greek-Cypriot women

Anthony, Susan
129v Trade unionism and women's work

Antler, Joyce
320b Culture, service, and work: Changing ideals of higher education for women
379e Was she a good mother? Some thoughts on a new issue for feminist biography

Antolini, Denise
226a Women in local government: An overview

Antonelli, Judith
229mm Feminist spirituality: The politics of the psyche

Antonis, Barbie
418d Motherhood and mothering

Antonucci, Toni
352m The need for female role models in education
423g Longitudinal and cross-sectional data sources on women in the middle years

Anttila, I.
159c Female criminality in Finland - What do the statistics show?

Anyon, Jean
138b Intersections of gender and class: Accommodation and resistance by working-class and affluent females to contradictory sex-role ideologies

Anzaldúa, Gloria
301jj Speaking in tongues: A letter to Third World women writers

ApRoberts, Ruth
142d *Middlemarch* and the new humanity

Apple, Michael W.
97c The political economy of text publishing
100b Teaching and 'women's work': A comparative historical and ideological analysis
138d Work, class and teaching

Apple, Rima
337f Women in the medical school

Appleton, Susan Frelich
173c The abortion-funding cases and population control: An imaginary lawsuit and some reflections on the uncertain limits of reproductive privacy

Applewhite, Harriet B.
130c Women, democracy, and revolution in Paris, 1789-1794
379q Responses to the political activism of Women of the People in revolutionary Paris, 1789-1793
444a Women of the popular classes in revolutionary Paris, 1789-1795

Apuzzo, Ginny
43s Confrontation: Black/white

Arango, Marta
172g The Chocó woman: Agent for change (Colombia)

Arbur, Rosemarie
114a Leigh Brackett: No "long goodbye" is good enough

Archer, David F.
51c Biochemical findings and medical management of the menopause

Archer, Léonie J.
156q The role of Jewish women in the religion, ritual and cult of Graeco-Roman Palestine

Ardener, Shirley
160a Incorporation and exclusion: Oxford academics' wives
371a Ground rules and social maps for women: An introduction

Arditi, Ralph R.
63m The ERA and coed prisons

Arditti, Rita
50i Feminism and science
310i An interview with Mirtha Quintanales, from the Third World women's archives

Arenal, Electa
408g The convent as catalyst for autonomy: Two Hispanic nuns of the seventeenth century

Arens, Jenneke
98e Learning from poor women: A method of village study

Ariffin, Jamilah
183d Women workers in the manufacturing industries
420k Migration of women workers in peninsular Malaysia: Impact and implications

Arimana, Carmen
172a Squatter settlement decision-making: For men only? (Peru)

Armitage, Susan H.
306g "Aunt Amelia's diary": The record of a reluctant pioneer
384d Reluctant pioneers
445b Women's literature and the American frontier: A new perspective on the frontier myth

Armstrong, Gail
78c Females under the law: 'Protected' but unequal

Armstrong, Hugh
380h Job creation and unemployment for Canadian women

Armstrong, Louise
461j The cradle of sexual politics: Incest

Armstrong, Pamela
103m Daddy's right: Incestuous assault

Armstrong, Pat
380h Job creation and unemployment for Canadian women

Armstrong, Peter
470b 'If it's only women it doesn't matter so much'

Arnason, Eleanor
417z The land of ordinary people: For John Lennon (poem)

Arnold, Erik
441d Women and microelectronics: The case of word processors

Arnold, Fred
420h Female migration in Thailand

Arnot, Madeleine
62d How shall we educate our sons?
138e A cloud over co-education: An analysis of the forms of transmission of class and gender relations

Aronson, Lisa
6h Women in the arts

Aronson, Naomi
341k Working up an appetite

Arowolo, Oladele
393f Plural marriage, fertility and the problem of multiple causation

Arrigo, Linda Gail
177f Doing fieldwork
177h Taiwan electronics workers

Arsdalen, Keith N. Van
277h Evaluation and treatment of impotence: The urologist's viewpoint

Arthur, Marylin B.
419a Early Greece: The origins of the western attitude toward women

Ascher, Carol
30f On "Clearing the Air": My letter to Simone de Beauvoir

Ash, Mildred
460l The misnamed female sex organ

Asher, Nina
201j Dorothy Jacobs Bellanca: Women clothing workers and the runaway shops

Ashford, Nicholas A.
233q Legal considerations of reproductive hazards in industry in the United States

Ashley, Kathleen
331b Voice and audience: The emotional world of the *cantigas de amigo*

Ashley, Mary Jane
53g Women, alcohol, and the risk of disease

Ashley, Polly
178o Physical health issues

Ashton, David
250j Young women in the labour market: Stability and change

Ashworth, Debora
453l Madonna or witch: Women's muse in contemporary American poetry

Assiter, Alison
215u Womanpower and nuclear politics: Women and the peace movement

Astin, Helen S.
49m College student values and the world of work
320i Educational and career progress of Chicana and Native-American college women
351h Women's education and career choice: Disparities between theory and practice

Astra
212s Poems on my sons

Aswad, Barbara C.
18d Rural family size and economic change: A Middle Eastern case

Ata-Mirzaev, O.
446n Women with large families: A sociodemographic analysis

Atchley, Robert C.
458j The process of retirement: Comparing women and men

Athanassiou, Stylianos K.
380m A statistical analysis of female participation in work and the effects on the population and socioeconomic development: A case study of Greece

Athas, Daphne
450r Why there are no southern writers

Atherton, Margaret
432m Education for equality

Atkeson, Beverly M.
29h Parenting: Training mothers as behavior therapists for their children

Atkins, Bowman K.
356g "Women's language" or "powerless language"?

Atkinson, A. Kathleen
295k Depression in women: The postpartum experience

Atkinson, Joseph D.
288l A federal response to sexual harassment: Policy-making at Johnson Space Center, NASA

Atkinson, Linda E.
36e Status of contraceptive technology development

Atkinson, Ti-Grace
7i Why I'm against S/M liberation

Attenborough, Susan
323h Sexual harassment: An issue for unions

Attneave, Carolyn L.
70h Indian boarding schools and Indian women: Blessing or curse?

Attwood, Lynne
471k Women at work in the USSR

Attwood, Margaret
139h 'Getting on'. Gender differences in career development: A case study in the hairdressing industry

Auerbach, Arthur H.
360c Women and psychotherapy research

Auerbach, Nina
17h *The Bostonians*: Feminists and the new world
27a Artists and mothers: A false alliance
135s Feminist criticism reviewed
164b Jane Austen and romantic imprisonment

Augel, Johannes
153k The contribution of public goods to household reproduction: Case study from Brazil

Aukin, Liane
381i Insider

Auslander, Stefanie S.
472k Policy directions and program design: Issues and implications in services for the older woman

Austin, Severa
404n Plenary session: Intervention/service delivery systems

Authier, Karen
281f Incest and sexual violence

Avant, W. Ray
289i Range of alternatives

Aveling, Marian
234g Social history and women's history

Averill, Mary Beth
84e Evolution and patriarchal myths of scarcity and competition

Avery, Byllye Y.
36t Contrasts in the birthing place: Hospital and birth center

Avery, John
333i Borroloola women speak. Man and woman: dance

333g The recent history of the Borroloola aboriginal people and their struggle for land rights

Avon, G.
372t Effects of training intensity on cardiac output in young women

Awosika, Keziah
436d Women's education and participation in the labour force: The case of Nigeria

Axelsen, Diana E.
79p Decisions about handicapped newborns: Values and procedures

Ayala-Vázquez, Nancy
72g Guidance and counseling of Spanish-background girls

Ayer, M. Jane
351j Women, space, and power in higher education

Ayling, Ronald
338t 'Two words for women': A reassessment of O'Casey's heroines

Ayres, Toni
359s Group process for women with orgasmic difficulties

Azari, Farah
430a Islam's appeal to women in Iran: Illusions and reality
430c Sexuality and women's oppression in Iran
430f The post-revolutionary women's movement in Iran

Bacchi, Carol
390e Evolution, eugenics and women: The impact of scientific theories on attitudes towards women, 1870-1920

Bachelli, Ann
227g Women and the family

Bachl, N.
372v Anaerobic energy metabolism of women

Backhouse, Constance
288g The other side of the coin: Women who exploit their sexuality for gain
288j Action plans for management and unions

Badawy, Shawky Z. A.
190u Steroidal contraceptive use and subsequent development of hyperprolactinemia

Bader, Julia
306b The "rooted" landscape and the woman writer

Badr, S. M.
372f Women and sports in Egypt: History and problems

Baehr, Helen
189j The impact of feminism on media studies - just another commercial break?
358c The 'liberated woman' in television drama

Baekey, Carol
316m De jure sex discrimination

Baer, Denise L.
35b Biology, gender, and politics: An assessment and critique

Baer, Elizabeth R.
332f The sisterhood of Jane Eyre and Antoinette Cosway

Baerga, Maria del Carmen
153o Wages, consumption, and survival: Working class households in Puerto Rico in the 1930's

Baetz, Ruth
397c The coming-out process: Violence against lesbians

Baffoun, Alya
298c Research in the social sciences on North African women: Problems, trends, and needs

Bagby, Thomas R.
67g The legal framework

Bagenstos, Naida Tushnet
266d Evaluation issues in women's studies

Bahar, Sima
430e A historical background to the women's movement in Iran

Bahl, Kali Charan
433h Forms of the Indian notion of sexuality and an interpretation of the Mymensing ballad of Kajalrekha

Bahr, Howard M.
11g Women on skid row

Bahr, Stephen J.
421q Sex role attitudes, female employment, and marital satisfaction

Bailey, Stephen M.
279m Absolute and relative sex differences in body composition

Bailin, George
186x A shining in the dark: May Sarton's accomplishment

Baill, Cori
460d Physiological aspects of female sexual development: Conception through puberty
460e Physiological aspects of female sexual development: Gestation, lactation, menopause, and erotic physiology

Bailyn, Lotte
426c The apprenticeship model of organizational careers: A response to changes in the relation between work and family

Bainton, Roland H.
33e Learned women in the Europe of the sixteenth century

Bair, Deirdre
108o *My life...this curious object*: Simone de Beauvoir on autobiography

Baker, C. David
284u Preying on playgrounds

Baker, Frances J. T.
233s The contribution of the occupational health services

Baker, John Austin
115k The right time

Baker, Robert
223n "Pricks" and "Chicks": A plea for persons
275l "Pricks" and "chicks": A plea for "persons"

Baker, Robin
86a The clean, light image of the electronics industry: Miracle or mirage?

Baker, Susan Read
303i Fair Harvard and the fairer sex

Baker, Susan W.
439j Biological influences on human sex and gender

Baker, William
143a A new George Eliot manuscript

Bakerman, Jane S.
1e Ruth Rendell
186j Patterns of love and friendship: Five novels by May Sarton
186k May Sarton's *The Small Room*: A comparison and an analysis
186m Perimeters of power: An examination of *As We Are Now*

Bakht, M.
346e Salient laws on women and children: A selected bibliography

Balasubrahmanyan, Vimal
310l Women as targets in India's family planning policy

Bald, Suresht R.
362e Gender, politics and modernization: The Indian case

Baldock, Cora V.
440b Public policies and the paid work of women
440n Volunteer work as work: Some theoretical considerations

Baldwin, Sally
170c Employment, women and their disabled children

Baldwin, Wendy
309q The children of teenage parents

Bale, P.
107o Body composition and somatotype characteristics of sportswomen

Ballestrero, Maria Vittoria
471e Women at work in Italy: Legislation - evolution and prospects

Ballorain, Rolande
17f Mark Twain's capers: A chameleon in King Carnival's court

Bambara, Toni Cade
40d Salvation is the issue
474k What it is I think I'm doing anyhow

Bander, Karen W.
146m Evaluation of child-sexual-abuse programs

Bane, Mary Jo
45g The American divorce rate: What does it mean? What should we worry about?
57g Social services and sexual learning

Banfield, Ann
164c The influence of place: Jane Austen and the novel of social consciousness

Bangs, Carol Jane
445g Women poets and the "Northwest School"

Bangun, Masliana
92g The advantages of functional education and credit facilities for Javanese rural women

Bank, Rosemarie K.
399kk The second face of the idol: Women in melodrama

Banks, Barbara A.
150y Miss Esther's land

Bannan, Helen M.
180v Spider woman's web: Mothers and daughters in Southwestern Native American literature

Bannerman, Josie
205u Cheap at half the price: The history of the fight for equal pay in BC

Banning, Cyrus W.
315i Can a man teach women's studies?

Banta, David
36p Benefits and risks of electronic fetal monitoring

Banu, Fazila
400e Population planning and rural women's cooperative in IRDP women's programme: Some critical issues

Bar On, Bat-Ami
7g Feminism and sadomasochism: Self-critical notes

Barbach, Lonnie Garfield
359s Group process for women with orgasmic difficulties

Barbee, Ann H.
351c Career and life satisfactions among Terman's gifted women

Barber, Marilyn
205i The gentlewomen of Queen Mary's coronation hostel

Barbosa, Eva Machado
153j Household economy and financial capital: The case of passbook savings in Brazil

Bard, Morton
327g Functions of the police and the justice system in family violence

Bardaglio, Peter
103d The transformation of patriarchy: The historic role of the state

Bardwick, Judith M.
214g An administrator's viewpoint: The interaction of sex and power

Bargainnier, Earl F.
1c Ngaio Marsh

Barish, Evelyn
196k Emerson and the angel of midnight: The Legacy of Mary Moody Emerson

Barker-Benfield, Ben
19k Anne Hutchinson and the Puritan attitude toward women

Barker-Benfield, G.J.
238d The spermatic economy: A nineteenth-century view of sexuality

Barksdale, Virginia
429b Small church — big family

Barlow, David
456m Vaginal discharge

Barlow, David H.
29b Unraveling the nature of sex roles

Barlow, Sally
42m A response, and more questions

Barlow, Tani E.
449d Feminism and literary technique in Ting Ling's early short stories

Barlow, William
353cc Homeopathy and sexual equality: The controversy over coeducation at Cincinnati's Pulte Medical College, 1873-1879

Barnard, Rosemary
466g Housewives and farmers: Malay women in the Muda Irrigation Scheme

Barnes, Bette
337b Women in science

Barnett, Rosalind C.
296f Mastery and pleasure: A two-factor model of well-being of women in the middle years
411p The anxiety of the unknown - choice, risk, responsibility: Therapeutic issues for today's adult women

Barnett, Sharon
222f New brains for old bodies: The impact of emotional and physical stress during the Ph.D. process

Barnewolt, Debra
87f Spouses' contributions to each other's roles
411e The middle years: Changes and variations in social-role commitments

Barney, Robert
147x Adele Parot: Pathfinder for the Dioclesian Lewis school of gymnastic expression in the American west

Baron, Ava
201b "If I didn't have my sewing machine...": Women and sewing-machine technology

Baron, James N.
272b A woman's place is with other women: Sex segregation within organizations

Baron, Larry
230h Sexual stratification, pornography, and rape in the United States

Barr, Marleen
114f Holding fast to feminism and moving beyond: Suzy McKee Charnas's *The Vampire Tapestry*
131l Charles Bronson, Samurai, and other feminine images: A transactive response to *The Left Hand of Darkness*
383c Utopia at the end of a male chauvinist dystopian world: Suzy McKee Charnas's feminist science fiction

Barragán, Polly Baca
72a The lack of political involvement of Hispanic women as it relates to their educational background and occupational opportunities

Barrett, Michèle
50e The 'family wage'
119b Feminism and the definition of cultural politics
378g Unity is strength? Feminism and the labor movement

Barrett, Nancy S.
123f How the study of women has restructured the discipline of economics

Barrett-Connor, Elizabeth
53t Sex differences in diabetes mellitus

Barry, Kathleen
7e On the history of cultural sadism
163a International politics of female sexual slavery
163b The network defines its issues: Theory, evidence and analysis of female sexual slavery

Barry, Richard E.
209o Staff participation in office systems' design: Two case studies at the World Bank

Bart, Pauline
34h Taking the men out of menopause
195i Review of Chodorow's *The Reproduction of Mothering*
316i The menopause in changing times
396e Seizing the means of reproduction: An illegal feminist abortion collective — how and why it worked

Bart, Pauline B.
51m Changing views of "the change": A critical review and suggestions for an attributional approach

Bartels, Else
50q Biological sex differences and sex stereotyping

Barth, Gerald
424m Growth of the bazaar economy and its significance for women's employment: Trends of the 1970s in Davao City, Philippines

Bartlett, Linda
339e Coping with illegal sex discrimination

Barton, Len
138a Gender, class and education: A personal view

Barton, Stephen
203p From kitchen to storefront: Women in the tenant movement

Baruch, Elaine Hoffman
417v Women in men's utopias

Baruch, Grace K.
296f Mastery and pleasure: A two-factor model of well-being of women in the middle years
411a Introduction: The study of women in midlife
411g The psychological well-being of women in the middle years

Basen, Neil K.
128e The "Jennie Higginses" of the "New South in the West": A regional survey of socialist activists, agitators, and organizers, 1901-1917

Bashar, Nazife
234i Women and the concept of change in history

Bass, B. M.
49j Leadership and management in the 1990's

Bastien, Joseph W.
325q Rosinta, rats, and the river: Bad luck is banished in Andean Bolivia

Basu, Amrita
101i Two faces of protest: Alternative forms of women's mobilization in West Bengal and Maharashtra

Basu, Shubhra
433i British response to Bengali literature in the nineteenth century

Bateman, Audray
175g The capitol's lady

Battis, Emery
19a Thine eyes shall see thy teachers
19b Mrs. Hutchinson's behavior in terms of menopausal symptoms

Battung, Diane
205c Rainbow women of the Fraser Valley: Lifesongs through the generations

Baud, Isa
206g The double day

Bauer, Janet
368i Poor women and social consciousness in revolutionary Iran
420n New models and traditional networks: Migrant women in Tehran

Bauerle, Ruth
409e Bertha's role in *Exiles*

Baum, Lawrence
415e Women in organizations: The impact of law

Baum, Martha
434d Rape crisis theory revisited

Bauman, Batya
211g Women-identified women in male-identified Judaism

Baumrin, Bernard H.
223q Sexual immorality delineated

Baunach, Phyllis Jo
78i You can't be a mother and be in prison...can you? Impacts of the mother-child separation
165n Sex-role operations: Strategies for women working in the criminal justice system

Baxter, James W.
191g Tailoring evaluation to measure the accountability of mental health services to women

Baxter, Vee
16m Battered women

Bay, Edna G.
370r Servitude and worldly success in the palace of Dahomey

Bayes, Marjorie
359f The prevalence of gender-role bias in mental health services
359v Women's treatment needs
359jj Wife battering and the maintenance of gender roles: A sociopsychological perspective

Bayles, Michael D.
223g Marriage, love, and procreation

Baym, Nina
17c Thwarted nature: Nathaniel Hawthorne as feminist

Bazemore, Gordon
111s Issues in the application of parole guidelines to females

Bérubé, Allan
231c Marching to a different drummer: Lesbian and gay GIs in World War II

Beahan, Charlotte L.
401m In the public eye: Women in early twentieth-century China

Beam, Amy
352d Power and opportunity in the principalship: The case of two women leaders in education

Bean, John C.
343d Comic structure and the humanizing of Kate in *The Taming of the Shrew*

Beard, R. W.
240f Chronic pelvic pain

Beardsley, Elizabeth Lane
116k On curing conceptual confusion: Response to Mary Anne Warren
275k Degenderization

Beattie, J. M.
376h The criminality of women in eighteenth-century England

Beatty, James R.
65d Some problems with contemporary job evaluation systems
425i Job evaluation and discrimination: Legal, economic, and measurement perspectives on comparable worth and women's pay

Beatty, Richard W.
65d Some problems with contemporary job evaluation systems
425i Job evaluation and discrimination: Legal, economic, and measurement perspectives on comparable worth and women's pay

Beccalli, Bianca
382g Italy

Bechtereva, Natalia P.
438i A little about myself, and more about a more important matter - the brain (USSR)

Beck, Evelyn Torton
174x Self-disclosure and the commitment to social change
176k Teaching about Jewish lesbians in literature: From *Zeitl* and *Richel* to *The Tree of Begats*
398e Self-disclosure and the commitment to social change

Beck, J. Gayle
29b Unraveling the nature of sex roles

Beck, Lois
403a The religious lives of Muslim women

Beck, Rochelle
80p Beyond the stalemate in child care public policy

Becker, Elle Friedman
285r Sexuality and the spinal cord injured woman: An interview

Becker, Gary
89b A theory of the allocation of time

Becker, Judith V.
326l Behavioral treatment of sexual dysfunctions in sexual assault survivors

Becker, Susan
81j International feminism between the wars: The National Woman's Party versus the League of Women Voters

Beckman, Linda J.
10k Patterns of women's use of alcohol treatment agencies

Bedell, Jeanne F.
1i Emma Lathen

Beech, Mary Higdon
255d The domestic realm in the lives of Hindu women in Calcutta

Beegel, Susan
286g Bathsheba's lovers: Male sexuality in *Far from the Madding Crowd*

Beekhuizen, W.
252f Aspirotomy for outpatient termination of pregnancy in the second trimester

Beere, Carole A.
266g Instruments and measures in a changing, diverse society

Begum, Saleha
98h Personal account of the role of a supervisor in the Bangladesh fertility survey
400a Women's employment and agriculture: Extracts from a case study

Begus, Sarah
103m Daddy's right: Incestuous assault

Beh, Siew Hwa
229l Growing up with legends of the Chinese swordswomen

Belanger, Albert J.
55b Scope of the problem: Investigation and prosecution
55c Typology of sex rings exploiting children

Belarbi, Aicha
298d Research in the social sciences on women in Morocco

Belfiglio, Genevieve
17b Fenimore Cooper's heroines

Bell, Colin
297a The SSRC: Restructured and defended

Bell, David S.
9l Dependence on psychotropic drugs and analgesics in men and women

Bell, Diane
333b Consulting with women
347j Desert politics: Choices in the "marriage market"

Bell, Dianna Pohlman
429g Bearing the good news

Bell, Inge Powell
344m The double standard: Age

Bell, Julie Davis
226e Women in political parties: Gender differences in motives among California party activists

Bell, Norma
57d Television as a sphere of influence on the c

Bell, Robert R.
421m Comparative attitudes about marital sex among Negro women in the United States, Great Britain and Trinidad

Bell, Susan E.
79b The DES controversy: Discovery, distribution and regulation

Bell, Terrell H.
216p The relationship between home and school: A commentary on the current scene

Bellaby, Paul
248g 'The history of the present' - contradiction and struggle in nursing

Bellace, Janice R.
66e A foreign perspective
67e A foreign perspective

Belle, Deborah
96d Mothers and their children: A study of low-income families
178a Research methods and sample characteristics
178i Social ties and social support
178n Mental health problems and their treatment
191a Who uses mental health facilities?
191b Patterns of diagnoses received by men and women
360g Inequality and mental health: Low income and minority women

Belle, Deborah E.
380j Poverty, work, and mental health: The experience of low-income mothers

Beller, Andrea H.
272a Trends in occupational segregation by sex and race, 1960-1981
272d Occupational sex segregation: Prospects for the 1980s

Beller, Anne Scott
341g Venus as endomorph
341h Pregnancy: Is motherhood fattening?

Bellin, Judith S.
253f Genes and gender in the workplace

Belliotti, Raymond A.
432g Sports, sex-equality, and the media

Bellman, Samuel I.
384r Where the West begins: Constance Rourke's images of her own frontierland

Belovitch, Tamara E.
96e The experience of abortion

Belsky, Jay
204d The ecology of day care

Ben-Tovim, Gideon
283j Race, left strategies and the state

Benack, Suzanne
158l Metatheoretical influences on conceptions of human development

Bender, Deborah
395b Women as promoters of health in the developing world

Bendix, Helga M.
79r Rights of a handicapped neonate: What every parent and professional should know

Benedek, E. P.
8c Women and violence

Benedek, Elissa
461q Voluntary childlessness

Benería, Lourdes
5a Conceptualizing the labor force: The underestimation of women's economic activities
60p Women's role in economic development: Practical and theoretical implications of class and gender inequalities
350e Accounting for women's work

Bengis, Ingrid
474j The middle period

Benjamin, Jessica
132d The bonds of love: Rational violence and erotic domination
231p Master and slave: The fantasy of erotic domination
443c The convergence of psychoanalysis and feminism: Gender identity and autonomy

Bennett, Fran
283d Feminists - The degenerates of the social?
283h Interview with Frances Morrell
335h The state, welfare and women's dependence

Bennett, Neil G.
273a Sex selection of children: An overview
273e Decision making and sex selection with biased technologies

Bennett, Paula
176a Dyke in academe

Bennett, Sheila Kishler
320k Undergraduates and their teachers: An analysis of student evaluations of male and female instructors

Bennett, Susan E.
28q Oral contraceptives and the menstrual cycle

Bennett, William F.
82r Curriculum: Preparation for involvement

Bennholdt-Thomsen, Veronika
153p Towards a theory of the sexual division of labor
207b Subsistence production and extended reproduction
208d Subsistence production and extended reproduction

Bennison, Anne
351a Equity or equality: What shall it be?

Benshoof, Janet
2b The legacy of *Roe v Wade*

Bensman, Marilyn
417f Frances Wright: Utopian feminist

Benson, Susan Porter
199f Women in retail sales work: The continuing dilemma of service

Benstock, Bernard
318f The clinical world of P. D. James

Benstock, Shari
318j The masculine world of Jennifer Johnston
409h The genuine Christine: Psychodynamics of Issy

Benston, Margaret
120b Feminism and the critique of scientific method
227h The political economy of women's liberation
307f For women, the chips are down

Bentham, Jeremy
223t An essay on "paederasty"

Bentley, Carter
300o Islamic law in Christian Southeast Asia: The politics of establishing Shari'a courts in the Philippines

Bentovim, Arnon
291d Recognition of child sexual abuse in the United Kingdom
291m Incest and dysfunctional family system

Benz, Maudy
301a Celebrate Emma (poem)

Beran, Janice Ann
147kk The story: Six-player girls' basketball in Iowa

Beranbaum, Tina M.
55a Child pornography in the 1970s

Bereano, Philip
307j Household technologies: Burden or blessing?
441j Teaching women and technology at the University of Washington

Berendes, Heinz W.
53h Health hazards associated with oral contraceptives

Berg, A.
372k Physiological and metabolic responses of female athletes during laboratory and field exercises

Berg, Anne Marie
468c Trade union participation of women in Norway: Structural changes, dilemmas and challenges
468h Love and power: The division of household labour

Berg, Mie
468f On work, art and women: A discussion of the ambiguous position of women artists

Berger, Arthur Asa
131n A personal response to Whetmore's "A female captain's enterprise"

Berger, Fred R.
223s Pornography, feminism, and censorship

Berger, Gary S.
252o Complications of second trimester abortion
252q Contraception following second trimester abortion

Berger, Lisa H.
359t Issues in the treatment of female addiction: A review and critique of the literature

Berger, Michael
140u Men's new family roles: Some implications for therapists

Berggren, Paula S.
343a The woman's part: Female sexuality as power in Shakespeare's plays

Bergman, Anni
88c Considerations about the development of the girl during the separation-individuation process

Bergman, Sherrie S.
314m Library resources on women

Bergmann, Barbara R.
46h The housewife and social security reform: A feminist perspective

65j Economic models as a means of calculating legal compensation claims

89l Occupational segregation, wages and profits when employers discriminate by race and sex

89o Curing high unemployment rates among blacks and women

93u The contribution of labor market data in combating employment discrimination

380s Women's work participation and the economic support of children

Bergmann, Maria V.
88f The female oedipus complex: Its antecedents and evolution

Bergom-Larsson, Maria
251b Women and technology in the industrialized countries

Bergstrom, Randolph E.
145q The female victim: Homicide and women in Imperial Germany

Berk, Richard A.
355f The new home economics: An agenda for sociological research

Berk, Sarah Fenstermaker
203c The household as workplace: Wives, husbands, and children

355i Contributions to household labor: Comparing wives' and husbands' reports

Berke, Jacqueline
180i Mothers and daughters in *Wives and Daughters*: A study of Elizabeth Gaskell's last novel

Berke, Laura
180i Mothers and daughters in *Wives and Daughters*: A study of Elizabeth Gaskell's last novel

Berkeley, Ellen Perry
203m Architecture: Toward a feminist critique

Berkman, Joyce Avrech
36b Historical styles of contraceptive advocacy

Berkov, Beth
309a Teenage family formation in postwar America

Berkun, Cleo S.
210a Changing appearance for women in the middle years of life: Trauma?

Berlin, Magalit
428k The formation of an ethnic group: Colombian female workers in Venezuela

Berlin, Miriam H.
142i George Eliot and the Russians

Berliner, Lucy
284q Special techniques for child witnesses

326g Group work with preadolescent sexual assault victims

Berman, Jeffrey
131o Where's all the fiction in science fiction?

Berman, Sanford
15d Access to alternatives: New approaches in cataloging

Bernacki, Edward J.
447m The control of hazardous exposures in the workplace

Bernard, Elaine
205s Last back: Folklore and the telephone operators in the 1919 Vancouver general strike

Bernard, Jessie
45e Ground rules for marriage: Perspectives on the pattern of an era

102g The good-provider role: Its rise and fall

360i Women's mental health in times of transition

Berndt, Catherine H.
333a Mythical women, past and present

340d Interpretations and "facts" in aboriginal Australia

Bernstein, Alan
192k Silicon Valley: Paradise or paradox?

Bernstein, Alison R.
407h Foundation support for administrative advancement: A mixed record

Bernstein, Stanley
122f The social determination of science: Some implications for women's studies

Berresford, Susan Vail
169t How foundations view funding proposals on working women

Berrigan, Joseph
188k The Tuscan visionary: Saint Catherine of Siena

Berrio, Margaret
315b Attitudes toward gender in two cultures: Puerto Rico and the United States

Berry, David E.
46e The double-decker alternative for eliminating dependency under social security

Berryman, Jack
147d The ladies' department of the *American Farmer*, 1825-1830: A locus for the advocacy of family health and exercise

Berryman, Sue E.
272m Occupational desegregation in CETA programs

Berthoff, Warner
451a The art of Jewett's *Pointed Firs*

Bertinuson, Janet
169p Occupational health and safety for women workers: Some teaching models

Bessmer, Sue
435i Antiobscenity: A comparison of the legal and feminist perspectives

Best, Sandy
12d The tyrannical womb: Menstruation and menopause

34g Changing minds: Women, biology, and the menstrual cycle

Betak, John F.
463i Individual spatial behavior

Bethel, Lorraine
14q "This infinity of conscious pain": Zora Neale Hurston and the black female literary tradition

Betteridge, Anne H.
325j The controversial vows of urban Muslim women in Iran

368g To veil or not to veil: A matter of protest or policy

Betts, Doris
450a The fiction of Anne Tyler

Beunen, G.
107q Somatic and motor characteristics of female gymnasts

Bevege, Margaret
390t Women's struggle to become tram drivers in Melbourne, 1956-75

Beyer, Janice M.
11f Women employees and job-based alcoholism programs

Beynon, Huw
378f Unions: The men's affair?

Bhanot, M. L.
159m Criminality amongst women in India: A study of female offenders and female convicts

Bhattacharyya, Deborah P.
433c Madness as entropy: A Bengali view

Bhattacharyya, Jnanabrata
433g Inequality and radical land reform: Some notes from west Bengal

Bhatty, Zarina
402i Muslim women in Uttar Pradesh: Social mobility and directions of change

Bickerton, Tricia
257j Women alone

Bickford, Anne
294h 'Working': An interview with Betty N.

Bielby, Denise Del Vento
320n Career commitment of female college graduates: Conceptualization and measurement issues

Bielby, William T.
272b A woman's place is with other women: Sex segregation within organizations

Bien, Gloria
449b Images of women in Ping Hsin's fiction

Bierman, James H.
399e Crowning Miss California, again

Biklen, Sari Knopp
352a Introduction: Barriers to equity - women, educational leadership, and social change

Bilby, Kenneth
39x Black women and survival: A Maroon case

Bilinkoff, Jodi
379g The holy woman and the urban community in sixteenth-century Avila

Billingham, Nick
235g In prison

Billson, Marcus K.
399z Lillian Hellman's memorial drama
452j Lillian Hellman and the strategy of the "other"

Binford, Martha B.
214s One woman's perspective: Intimacy and productivity
325b Julia: An east African diviner

Binford, Sally R.
229xx Myths and matriarchies

Binney, Val
418g Domestic violence: Battered women in Britain in the 1970s

Bird, Joyce Adair
320c Recent trends in the higher education of women

Birkby, Noel Phyllis
174t The women's school of planning and architecture

Birke, Lynda
12d The tyrannical womb: Menstruation and menopause
12e From zero to infinity: Scientific views of lesbians
34c From sin to sickness: Hormonal theories of lesbianism
34g Changing minds: Women, biology, and the menstrual cycle
441d Women and microelectronics: The case of word processors

Birtha, Becky
150x Maria de las Rosas (poem)
176u Is feminist criticism really feminist?

Bishop, Gerrie
146m Evaluation of child-sexual-abuse programs

Bishop, Mary F.
205w Vivian Dowding: Birth control activist 1892-

Bishop, Nadean
344c Abortion: The controversial choice

Bithorn, María Angélica
72h Hispanic women move forward - Out of a marginal status

Björklund, Anders
260b A look at the male female unemployment differentials in the Federal Republic of Germany, Sweden, United Kingdom, and the United States of America

Blachford, Gregg
224d Looking at pornography: Erotica and the socialist morality

Black, Naomi
125r Virginia Woolf: The life of natural happiness
328j Virginia Woolf and the women's movement
388k Social feminism in France: A case study
388m The future for women and development

Blackburn, Jean
321a Schooling and injustice for girls

Blackburn, Regina
452h In search of the black female self: African-American women's autobiographies and ethnicity

Blackburn, Robert
378f Unions: the men's affair?

Blackwell, Henry
129j Marriage contract

Blair, Juliet
371k Private parts in public places: The case of actresses

Blair, Ralph
287h Homosexuality

Blaisdell, C. J.
112c Marguerite de Navarre and her circle (French, 1492-1549)

Blake, John B.
353y Mary Gove Nichols, prophetess of health

Blake, Kathleen
135g Olive Schreiner - A note on sexist language and the feminist writer

Blake, Myrna
424f Constraints on the organization of women industrial workers

Blanchard, Evelyn Lance
70d Organizing American Indian women
434i Observations on social work with American Indian women

Blanchet, Therese
98d Becoming an 'insider': Women's privileges in village field work

Bland, Lucy
50y 'Guardians of the race' or 'vampires upon the nation's health'? Female sexuality and its regulation in early twentieth century Britain
257a Purity, motherhood, pleasure or threat? Definitions of female sexuality 1900-1970s

Blank, Arapera
413b The role and status of Maori women

Blankley, Elyse
448c Return to Mytilène: Renée Vivien and the city of women

Blask, David E.
51i Potential role of the pineal gland in the human menstrual cycle

Blau, Francine D.
272e Occupational segregation and labor market discrimination
344p Women in the labor force: An overview

Blau, Zena Smith
319p To be aged, Hispanic, and female: The triple risk

Blauvelt, Martha Tomhave
366a Women and revivalism
367h Women and revivalism: The Puritan and Wesleyan traditions

Blechman, Elaine A.
29a Women's behavior in a man's world: Sex differences in competence
365i Behavior therapies

Bledsoe, Robert
135o Snow beneath snow: A reconsideration of the virgin of *Villette*

Bleier, Ruth
394b History of the Association of Faculty Women at Madison

Blick, Linda Canfield
146a A conceptual framework for child sexual abuse
146b Validation of child sexual abuse
146d Treatment of the sexually abused child
146e Group therapy with female adolescent incest victims

Bligh, Vivian
333n Study into the needs of aboriginal women who have been raped or sexually assaulted

Bloch, Alice
211m Scenes from the life of a Jewish lesbian

Bloch, Donald A.
327b Discussion: Violence in the family

Bloch, Jean H.
200b Women and the dialectics of nature in eighteenth-century French thought

Bloch, Maurice
200b Women and the dialectics of nature in eighteenth-century French thought

Block, Alan
349g Aw! Your mother's in the mafia: Women criminals in progressive New York
392g Searching for women in organized crime

Block, Jeanne H.
45i Assessing personal and social change in two generations

Block, Marilyn R.
458l Professional women: Work pattern as a correlate of retirement satisfaction

Bloom, Anne R.
113g Israel: The longest war

Bloom, Bernard L
295f Sex differences in separation and divorce: A longitudinal perspective

Bloom, David E.
273f The economics of sex preference and sex selection

Bloom, Lynn Z.
180x Heritages: Dimensions of mother-daughter relationships in women's autobiographies
452l Anai"s Nin's *Diary* in context

Blouin, Lenora P.
186y A revised bibliography

Blount, Alma
301u If you got time to lean, you got time to clean

Blum, Harold P.
461v Discussion: Psychoanalytic reflections on the "beaten wife syndrome"

Blum, John D.
447h Sex discrimination in group pensions

Blum, Lenore
361h Increasing the participation of college women in mathematics-related fields

Blumberg, Grace Ganz
375i Adult derivative benefits in social security: A women's issue

Blumberg, Rae Lesser
388b Rural women in development

Blumberg, Rhoda Lois
244b White mothers in the American civil rights movements

Blume, Sheila B.
11i Diagnosis, casefinding, and treatment of alcohol problems in women
404q Motivation and the alcoholic woman

Blumenfeld, Emily
149f Domestic labour and the reproduction of labour power: Towards an analysis of women, the family, and class

Blumenthal, Karen I.
349v Imprisoned women and their children

Bobroff, Anne
231i Russian working women: Sexuality in bonding patterns and the politics of daily life

Bock, Gisela
336k Racism and sexism in Nazi Germany: Motherhood, compulsory sterilization, and the state

Bocquet-Siek, Margaret
466b The Peranankan Chinese woman at a crossroad

Boddy, Julie
81g Photographing women: The Farm Security Administration work of Marion Post Wolcott

Boesing, Martha
399g *The Story of a Mother* (play)

Bogdan, Janet
352o The transition from parenting to working and parenting

Bohachevsky-Chomiak, Martha
405d Socialism and feminism: The first stages of women's organizations in the eastern part of the Austrian empire

Bohlin, Diane DeGrazia
389o Agnes Mongan (b. 1905): Connoisseur of old master drawings

Boles, Janet K.
103s The family impact statement: Ideology and feasibility

Bolig, Rosemary A.
222b The ambivalent decision

Bolis, Liana
438e The wild cat (France and Italy)

Bolles, Lynn
83e Working class Jamaican women: Trade unions and political activity
388d Household economic strategies in Kingston, Jamaica
428f Kitchens hit by priorities: Employed working-class Jamaican women confront the IMF

Bollinger, Sharon L.
112j Mercy Otis Warren: Playwright, poet, and historian of the American revolution

Bolsterli, Margaret Jones
301m It seems to help me bear it better when she knows about it
303g Teaching women's studies at the University of Arkansas
306d On the literary uses of private documents

450k The androgynous, bi-racial vision of Berry Morgan

Bolton, Gail
248d The administration of poverty and the development of nursing practice in nineteenth-century England

Bolton, W. F.
135e *The Wife of Bath*: Narrator as victim

Bond, Gary R.
96l The role and function of women's consciousness raising: Self-help, psychotherapy, or political activation?

Bond, Meg A.
295j Social support and efficacy in advocacy roles: A case study of two women's organizations

Bondfield, Margaret
227c Women as domestic workers

Boneparth, Ellen
103o Work, gender, and technological innovation
226m Resources and constraints on women in the policymaking process: States and local arenas

Bonfante, Larissa
389i Margarete Bieber (1879-1978): An archaeologist in two worlds

Boone, Carroll
65n Comparable worth under various federal and state laws

Boone, Margaret S.
473j The uses of traditional concepts in the development of new urban roles: Cuban women in the United States

Boone, Sylvia Ardyn
77d Creative women in artistic and literary change

Booth, Jane
358b Watching the family

Boothroyd, Wilfred E.
9h Nature and development of alcoholism in women

Borden, Ann
152b Growing up lesbian and Catholic

Boreham, A.
372p Measurement of maximal short-term (anaerobic) power output during cycling

Boris, Eileen
103d The transformation of patriarchy: The historic role of the state

Borker, Ruth
356b Anthropology: Social and cultural perspectives

Borlaug, Karen L.
463e Shopping trips: Who makes them and when?

Borman, Kathryn M.
427e Gender inequities in childhood social life and adult work life

Bornstein, Diane
154a Self-consciousness and self concepts in the work of Christine de Pizan

154f The ideal of the lady of the manor as reflected in Christine de Pizan's *Livre des Trois Vertus*

Boroviak, Darlene L.
314d The social sciences: Establishing gender as a category

Borra, Ranjan
433k Radindranath Tagore: Cultural ambassador of India to the United States

Bort, John R.
269e New roles for males in Guaymí society

Boruch, Robert F.
266l Causal models: Their import and their triviality

Bosanko, Carole
240k Psychological aspects of the menstruum and premenstruum

Bose, Christine
50o Technology and changes in the division of labour in the American home
307h Household technologies: Burden or blessing
355d Social status of the homemaker
441j Teaching women and technology at the University of Washington

Bositis, David A.
35b Biology, gender, and politics: An assessment and critique

Boskind-Lodahl, Marlene
140l Cinderella's stepsisters: A feminist perspective on anorexia nervosa and bulimia
359r Cinderella's stepsisters: A feminist perspective on anorexia nervosa and bulimia

Boston, Sarah
382e Great Britain

Bottomley, Gill
94f Women on the move: Migration and feminism

Botvin-Madorsky, Julie G.
281g Sexuality and disability

Boucé, Paul-Gabriel
278c The secret nexus: Sex and literature in eighteenth-century Britain

Bouhoutsos, Jacqueline C.
360k Sexual intimacy between psychotherapists and clients: Policy implications for the future

Bould, Jackie
259i Sex differentiation and careers

Boulding, Elise
102o Public nurturance and the man on horseback
244g The nurture of adults by children in family settings
373c Integration into what? Reflections on development planning for women

Bouquet, Mary
104g Women's work in rural south-west England

Bourguignon, André
280o Vampirism and autovampirism

Bourguignon, Erika
473m Comparisons and implications: What have we learned?

Bourne, Patricia Gerald
387i   Commitment and cultural mandate:
       Women in medicine

Bourque, Susan
378h   Politics an unnatural practice: Political sci-
       ence looks at female participation
388i   Rural women and development planning
       in Peru

Boutilier, James A.
246i   European women in the Solomon Islands,
       1900-1942: Accommodation and change
       on the Pacific frontier

Bowen, Elizabeth
216j   Implications for national policy decisions:
       The black family perspective

Bowers, Karl S.
463z   Speech

Bowes, Alison M.
104i   The organization of labour in an Israeli
       kibbutz

Bowker, Joan P.
214p   An attempt at collectivity: Professional
       confirmation and support

Bowker, Lee H.
26i   Coping with wife abuse: Personal and
       social networks
349j   Women as victims: An examination of the
       results of L.E.A.A.'s National Crime
       Survey Program
349w   Gender differences in prisoner subcultures

Bowles, Gloria
311a   Is women's studies an academic discipline?
311f   Selected annotated bibliography of articles
       on theories of women's studies
312a   Introduction: Theories of women's studies
       and the autonomy/integration debate
312c   Is women's studies an academic discipline?
312o   Selected annotated bibliography of articles
       on theories of women's studies

Bowman, Barbara
109c   Victoria Holt's gothic romances: A struc-
       turalist inquiry

Bowring, Richard
108c   The female hand in Heian Japan: A first
       reading

Boxer, Marilyn J.
95c   When radical and socialist feminism were
       joined: The extraordinary failure of
       Madeleine Pelletier

Boyd, Judith C.
185n   Beyond the melting pot: Nationalism, mili-
       tarism and the family

Boyd, Monica
421l   English-Canadian and French-Canadian
       attitudes towards women: Results of the
       Canadian Gallup polls

Boyd, Vicki D.
26a   Emergency room intervention: Detection,
       assessment, and treatment

Boyd-Franklin, Nancy
60l   Black family life-styles: A lesson in survival

Boyer, Debra
111g   Juvenile prostitution

Boyer, H. Patsy
313m   A feminist reading of "Los ojos verdes"

Boyle, Helen
333e   The conflicting role of aboriginal women
       in today's society

Boyle, Robert
409a   The woman hidden in James Joyce's
       Chamber Music

Boyle, Thomas F.
286m   "Morbid depression alternating with
       excitement": Sex in Victorian newspapers

Boys, Jos
182c   Women and public space
182d   House design and women's roles

Bozzoli de Wille, M.E.
269h   Symbolic aspects of Bribri roles on the
       occasions of birth and death

Bracey, Dorothy H.
78p   Concurrent and consecutive abuse: The
       juvenile prostitute

Bracht, Dona Lansing
16s   The displaced homemaker

Brack, Datha Clapper
34i   Displaced - the midwife by the male physi-
       cian

Brackbill, Yvonne
36o   Drugs, birth, and ethics

Braden, Anne
301p   Shoulder to shoulder

Bradford, David L.
288a   The executive man and woman: The issue
       of sexuality

Bradley, Judy
193k   Predicting specialisation in science

Bradley, Margaret
206m   Blue jeans blues

Bradshaw, Frances
182f   Working with women

Bradshaw, Jan
212n   Now what are they up to? Men in the
       'Men's movement'

Bradshaw, Sue
401l   Catholic sisters in China: An effort to raise
       the status of women

Braendlin, Bonnie Hoover
135l   New directions in the contemporary bil-
       dungsroman: Lisa Alther's *Kinflicks*
155a   The prostitute as scapegoat: Mildred
       Rogers in Somerset Maugham's *Of Human
       Bondage*

Brager, Marilyn
111f   The female juvenile offender

Bragonier, J. Robert
461i   Discussion: Aging and female sexuality

Braid, Kate
305s   Women in trades in British Columbia

Braiker, Harriet B.
10l   Therapeutic issues in the treatment of
       alcoholic women

Braito, Rita
210j   The ever-single elderly woman

Bram, Susan
253i   The effects of childbearing on women's
       mental health: A critical review of the lit-
       erature
265r   Sex without reproduction: Voluntary child-
       lessness as a response to contemporary sex
       roles

Brana-Shute, Rosemary
363b1 Working class Afro-Surinamese women
       and national politics: Traditions and
       changes in an independent state

Brand, Barbara Elizabeth
302b   Sex-typing in education for librarianship:
       1870-1920

Brand, Frederick N.
210o   Cardiovascular risk factors in the elderly
       woman

Brandes, Stanley
282g   Like wounded stags: Male sexual ideology
       in an Andalusian town

Brandl, Maria
333c   A certain heritage: Women and their chil-
       dren in north Australia

Brandt, Susan L.
375k   Clara Shortridge Foltz: Pioneer in the law

Brandwein, Ruth A.
434o   Toward androgyny in community and orga-
       nizational practice

Brant, Beth
397g   Reclamation: A lesbian Indian story

Brant, Renee S. T.
284e   The sexually misused child

Brashear, Diane B.
281b   The sexual self and fertility

Braude, Ann
366d   The Jewish woman's encounter with
       American culture

Brauer, Gerhard W.
279j   Size sexual dimorphism and secular trend:
       Indicators of subclinical malnutrition?

Braun, Rachel Eisenberg
260e   Equal opportunity and the law in the
       United States

Braybon, Gail
50f   The need for women's labour in the First
       World War

Brazelton, T. Berry
69e   The early mother-child relationship: A
       developmental view of woman as mother

Brecher, Edward M.
461y   Women - victims of the VD rip-off

Breen, Edith
316h   Toward freedom and self-determination:
       New directions in mental health services

Breeze, Nancy
310aa Who is going to rock the petri dish? For
       feminists who have considered partheno-
       genesis when the movement is not enough

Brehony, Kathleen A.
304f   Women and agoraphobia: A case for the
       etiological significance of the feminine sex-
       role stereotype

Brehony, Kevin
62b Co-education: Perspectives and debates in the early twentieth century

Bremen, Riet Van
156n Women and wealth

Bremer, Sidney H.
448k Willa Cather's lost Chicago sisters

Brender, William
271o Mood and behaviour changes in menopausal women receiving gonadal hormones or placebo

Brereton, Virginia Lieson
412i Preparing women for the Lord's work: The story of three Methodist training schools, 1880-1940

Breslin, James E.
452i Gertrude Stein and the problems of autobiography

Brett, Sally
303a A different kind of being

Brett, Sally Alexander
306m The editor and the writer: An approach to archival manuscripts

Bretteville, Sheila Levrant de
203s The Los Angeles Woman's Building: A public center for woman's culture

Brice, Gary C.
221h The process of retirement: Implications for late-life counseling

Briceño, Maria Esperanza
172k Some sow, others reap (Colombia)

Brickley, Terry
285q Sexuality and multiple sclerosis - must they be mutually exclusive?

Bridel, Renee
163g Traffic of children

Bridenthal, Renate
60a Notes toward a feminist dialectic
245l The family: The view from a room of her own
256h Examining family history
336b Beyond *Kinder, Küche, Kirche*: Weimar women in politics and work
336g "Professional" housewives: Stepsisters of the women's movement

Bright, Clare
176n But what about men...?

Bright, Susan
301mm Mock trial (play)

Brighton Women and Science Group
12h Technology in the lying-in room

Brighton, Pam
381d Directions

Brine, Jenny
151k Reading as a leisure pursuit in the USSR

Brink, J. R.
112f Bathsua Makin: Educator and linguist (English, 1608?-1675?)

Brinkley-Carter, Christina
38c Black fertility: Recent demographic and sociological influences

Brinton, Louise A.
53o Etiologic factors for invasive and noninvasive cervical abnormalities

Brinton, Mary C.
272i Sex typing in occupational socialization

Briscoe, Anne M.
416i Scientific sexism: The world of chemistry

Briskin, Linda
149c Domestic labour: A methodological discussion
323b Women and unions in Canada: A statistical overview
323q Women's challenge to organized labour
323aa Trade union resources on women

Brislin, Joann
147d The ladies' department of the *American Farmer*, 1825-1830: A locus for the advocacy of family health and exercise

Britt, David W.
295d Black women in American society: A resource development perspective

Britten, Nicky
139d Women, men and social class

Brizzi, Mary T.
114d C. J. Cherryh and tomorrow's new sex roles

Broadhead, Susan Herlin
370j Slave wives, free sisters: Bakongo women and slavery c.1700-1850

Brocher, Tobias H.
216s Toward new methods in parent education

Brock, Rita Nakashima
59c The feminist redemption of Christ

Brodie, M. Janine
228c Canada

Brodsky, Annette M.
16d Therapeutic aspects of consciousness-raising groups
359h Report of the task force on sex bias and sex-role stereotyping in psychotherapeutic practice
359uu The consciousness-raising group as a model for therapy with women
359xx A decade of feminist influence on psychotherapy
365p Psychotherapy and women: Priorities for research

Brody, Claire M.
443a Authenticity in feminist therapy
443i Feminist therapy with minority clients

Brody, Linda
377i An accelerative intervention program for mathematically gifted girls

Brody, Miriam
125c Mary Wollstonecraft: Sexuality and women's rights

Broe, Mary Lynn
180r A subtle psychic bond: The mother figure in Sylvia Plath's poetry

Bromberg, Joann
56a Having a baby: A story essay

Broner, E. M.
229w Honor and ceremony in women's rituals

Brooks, Betty Willis
174f The new right challenges women's studies: The Long Beach women's studies program

Brooks, Evelyn
60c The feminist theology of the black Baptist church, 1880-1900

Brooks, George E.
370p A Nhara of the Guinea-Bissau region: Mãe Aurélia Correia

Brooks, Gwendolyn
40g The field of the fever, the time of the tall-walkers

Brooks, Jerome
40z In the name of the father: The poetry of Audre Lord

Brooks-Gunn, Jeanne
28i A developmental analysis of menstrual distress in adolescence
51n A sociocultural approach
51o Expectations regarding menstrual symptoms: Effects on evaluation and behavior of women
190t Dysmenorrhea in adolescence
239k Research on menstrual-related psychological changes: Alternative perspectives
411a Introduction: The study of women in midlife
411b Life events and the boundaries of midlife for women

Broom, Dorothy
321d Natural resources: Health, reproduction and the gender order
440m In sickness and in health: Social policy and the control of women

Broome, Annabel
240d Termination of pregnancy

Brophy, Julia
50n From disregard to disrepute: The position of women in family law

Brothers, Barbara
318d Women victimised by fiction: Living and loving in the novels of Barbara Pym

Broude, Norma
117a Introduction: Feminism and art history
117n Degas's "Misogyny"
117q Miriam Schapiro and "femmage": Reflections on the conflict between decoration and abstraction in twentieth-century art

Broughan, Kathleen G.
295m Differential needs and treatment approaches for women in psychotherapy

Brouwer, Lenie
213f Living in between: Turkish women in their homeland and in the Netherlands

Broverman, Donald M.
239c Gonadal hormones and cognitive functioning

Broverman, Inge K.
359g Sex-role stereotypes and clinical judgements of mental health

Brown Betty D.
394t From undergraduate to judge at sixty

Brown, Barbara
395g The political economy of population policy in South Africa

Brown, Bruce W.
421o Wife-employment and the emergence of egalitarian marital role prescriptions: 1900-1974

Brown, Carol
369k Mothers, fathers, and children: From private to public patriarchy

Brown, Carol A.
354e Women workers in the health service industry

Brown, Cathleen A.
265h Sex typing in occupational preferences of high school boys and girls

Brown, Clair (Vickery)
245i Home production for use in a market economy
380g Bringing down the rear: The decline in the economic position of single-mother families

Brown, Donald A.
287o An interview with a sex surrogate

Brown, Earl Kent
412c Women of the word: Selected leadership roles of women in Mr. Wesley's Methodism

Brown, James
113h Greece: Reluctant presence

Brown, Jill
257e The daughter is mother of the child: Cycles of lesbian sexuality

Brown, Judith K.
51d A cross-cultural exploration of the end of the childbearing years

Brown, Karen McCarthy
462n Why women need the war god

Brown, Laura S.
360o Media psychology and public policy

Brown, Lisa Jo
263b Housework as a comparative advantage: The neoclassical theory of the sexual division of labor

Brown, Lynda M.
304c The development of sex-role stereotypes in children: Crushing realities

Brown, Marsha D.
320m Career plans of college women: Patterns and influences

Brown, Martha H.
14z A listing of non-print materials on black women

Brown, Penelope
50z Oppressive dichotomies: The nature/culture debate
356h How and why are women more polite: Some evidence from a Mayan community
418h 'A daughter: A thing to be given away'
418m Oppressive dichotomies: The nature/culture debate
418n Universals and particulars in the position of women

Brown, Richard
378e Women as employees: Social consciousness and collective action

Brown, Susan E.
347e Forced transition from egalitarianism to male dominance: The Bari of Colombia

Brown, Virginia H.
190h Physical attractiveness and physical stigma: Menstruation and the common cold

Brown, Wendy
103t Reproductive freedom and the right to privacy: A paradox for feminists

Browne, Pat
274r Physical education

Browner, Carol
395i Women's understanding about reproductive physiology and their choice of herbal medicines in Cali, Colombia

Brownfain, John J.
287a Our sexual heritage

Brownfoot, Janice
160j Memsahibs in colonial Malaya: A study of European wives in a British colony and protectorate, 1900-1940

Browning, Christine
397a Changing theories of lesbianism: Challenging the stereotypes

Brownley, Martine Watson
196c "Under the dominion of *some* woman": The friendship of Samuel Johnson and Hester Thrale

Brownstein, Martin H.
141h Breast cancer in Cowden's syndrome

Brubaker, Timothy H.
458n Responsibility for household tasks: Comparing dual-earner and dual-retired marriages

Bruch, Hilde
341b Thin fat people

Bruegel, Irene
50g Women as a reserve army of labour: A note on recent British experience
465f Women's employment, legislation and the labour-market

Brüggemann, G.
372dd Foot disorders of female marathon runners before and after a marathon race

Bruinsma, G.J.N.
159b Female criminality in the Netherlands

Bruley, Sue
274i History

Brumberg, Joan Jacobs
353n Chlorotic girls, 1870-1920: A historical perspective on female adolescence
379j The ethnological mirror: American evangelical women and their heathen sisters, 1870-1910

Brummett, Barry
133w Ideologies in two gay rights controversies

Brunold, Heinz
284f Observations after sexual traumata suffered in childhood

Brunson, Pansy
254i Increasing female participation in the mathematics classroom

Brunt, Rosalind
119g 'An immense verbosity': Permissive sexual advice in the 1970s

Bry, Brenna H.
295n Substance abuse in women: Etiology and prevention

Bryan, Mary
186l Rage for justice: Political, social and moral consciousness in selected novels of May Sarton

Bryant, Fred C.
82j Livestock and range management

Bryant, Gwendolyn
188i The French heretic Beguine: Marguerite Porete

Bryant, Jennings
230e Effects of massive exposure to pornography

Bryson, Jeff B.
87l Salary and job performance differences in dual-career couples

Bryson, Judy C.
5b Women and agriculture in sub-Saharan Africa: Implications for development

Bryson, Lois
440f Women as welfare recipients: Women, poverty and the state

Bryson, Rebecca
87l Salary and job performance differences in dual-career couples

Buckley, Mary I.
462a Women, poverty, and economic justice

Budapest, Z.
453q Goddess worship in Wicce

Budd, Karen S.
29r Mentally retarded mothers

Buenaventura-Posso, Elisa
347e Forced transition from egalitarianism to male dominance: The Bari of Colombia

Buenker, John D.
128f The politics of mutual frustration: Socialists and suffragists in New York and Wisconsin

Buhle, Mari Jo
128d Lena Morrow Lewis: Her rise and fall

Buirski, Jeanette
215b How I learnt to start worrying and hate the bomb: The effects of a nuclear bombardment

Buker, Laura
205c Rainbow women of the Fraser Valley: Lifesongs through the generations

Bulatao, Beth
206e Iloilo

Bulatao, Rodolfo A.
420q Philippine urbanism and the status of women

Bulkin, Elly
176g "Kissing/Against the Light": A look at lesbian poetry

Bullard, David G.

285e Physical disability, life-threatening illness, and enhancement of sexual health

285l Differential diagnosis and treatment for organogenic and psychogenic erectile dysfunction

Bullough, Vern

190o Menarche and teenage pregnancy: A misuse of historical data

353b Women, menstruation, and nineteenth-century medicine

Bunch, Charlotte

43d Beyond either/or: Feminist options

43f Not for lesbians only

43q The reform tool kit

163c Network strategies and organizing against female sexual slavery

174i A note on Sagaris

174u Not by degrees: Feminist theory and education

174z Charlotte Bunch and Betty Powell talk about feminism, blacks, and education as politics

Bunch, Peggy L.

4j Legal aspects of adolescent pregnancy

Bunker, Barbara Benedict

214n Mobilizing resources: Creating a support system

Bunkle, Phillida

310m Calling the shots? The international politics of depo-provera

413c The origins of the women's movement in New Zealand: The Women's Christian Temperance Union 1885-1895

Bunster, Ximena

83f Working women in Latin America

163h The torture of women political prisoners: A case study in female sexual slavery

Burch, Beverly

301gg The prodigal child's homecoming: California to Georgia (poem)

Burden, Dianne

16p Women as single parents: Alternative services for a neglected population

Burfield, Diana

457b Theosophy and feminism: Some explorations in nineteenth century biography

Burfield, William B.

46f Disability insurance under proposed reforms

Burgess, Ann W.

55e Typology of collectors

55f Impact of child pornography and sex rings on child victims and their families

55j Treatment issues with children involved in pornography and sex rings

284g Sexual trauma of children and adolescents

284r Courtroom use of hospital records in sexual assault cases

349l Rape: Power, anger, and sexuality

359kk Rape: Sexual disruption and recovery

Burgess, Bill J.

216g Parenting in the Native-American community

Burgmann, Meredith

23b Black sisterhood: The situation of urban aboriginal women and their relationship to the white women's movement

390u Revolution and machismo: Women in the New South Wales Builders Labourers' Federation, 1961-75

Burgos, Nilsa M.

469i A preliminary historical analysis of women and work in Puerto Rico: 1899-1975

Burian, Grayce Susan

399p Aileen Stanley, Her life and times

Buric, Olivera

52o Change in the system of social power: Conditions for the social equality of women in Yugoslavia

Burke, Carolyn G.

132i Rethinking the maternal

Burke, France

417d Al dente (poem)

Burke, Peggy

147t The effect of current sports legislation on women in Canada and the U.S.A. - Title IX

Burkhard, Marianne

249g The crux: Quality judgment and departmental autonomy

Burkhauser, Richard V.

46c Earnings sharing: Incremental and fundamental reform

Burks, Ruth Elizabeth

40e From baptism to resurrection: Toni Cade Bambara and the incongruity of language

Burman, Sandra

364g Divorce and the disadvantaged: African women in urban South Africa

Burnett, K. Patricia

463v An alternative approach to travel demand modeling: Constraints-oriented theories and societal roles

Burnett, Marilou

316f Knots in the family tie

Burnham, Dorothy

342c Black women as producers and reproducers for profit

Burns, Roy

235k The fight for equality

Burroway, Janet

474n *Opening nights*: The opening days

Burrows, G.

236c Premenstrual syndrome - a holistic approach

Burstyn, Joan

352e Historical perspectives on women in educational leadership

454j Catharine Beecher and the education of American women

Burt, Barbara

271f Sex-role ideology and sex bias in judgments of occupational suitability

Burton, Julianne

408m The greatest punishment: Female and male in Lorca's tragedies

Bury, Judith

456h Unwanted pregnancy and abortion

Bush, Corlann Gee

181i Women and the assessment of technology: To think, to be, to unthink, to free

441i A preview of AAUW's biennial study/action topic 'Taking hold of technology'

Busman, Gloria

169j Case studies: How to develop and use them

Bustamante, Jorge A.

428j *Maquiladoras*: A new face of international capitalism on Mexico's northern frontier

Butchman, Alan D.

463w Speech

Butler, Barbara

395l Anger sickness: Social stress and native diagnosis among Ecuadorian Indians

Butler, Johnnella E.

122b Black studies/women's studies: Points of convergence

314c The humanities: Redefining the canon

314k Black studies and women's studies: An overdue partnership

Butler, Judy

7v Lesbian S & M: The politics of dis-illusion

Butler, Marilyn

135j The woman at the window: Ann Radcliffe in the novels of Mary Wollstonecraft and Jane Austen

164d Disregarded designs: Jane Austen's sense of the volume

Butler, Matilda

87j Coordinated-career couples: Convergence and divergence

Butler, Richard W.

203q Women at city hall

Butler, Sandra

78q Incest: Whose reality, whose theory?

Butt, Dorcas Susan

271e Perspectives from women on sport and leisure

Butter, Irene

395c Women and health care personnel planning

Butts, June Dobbs

308h Adolescent sexuality and teenage pregnancy from a black perspective

461c Discussion: Further thoughts on a group discussion by black women about sexuality

Buxton, Millicent E.

404m Women and substance abuse: Treatment issues

Byerly, Victoria Morris

301q Hard times cotton mill girls

Byrd, James W.

175o Aunt Dicy: Legendary black lady

Byrne, Donn

24b Social background, attitudes and sexual attraction

230a Introduction: Pornography and sex research

Byrne, Eileen M.
259m Equality or equity? - a European overview

Byrnes, Eleanor
339g Dual career couples: How the company can help

Byron, Egeland
80e Developmental consequences of out-of-home care for infants in a low-income population

Cabezas, Amado Y.
71k Economic and employment status of Asian-Pacific women

Cadieux, Rita
65k Canada's equal pay for work of equal value law

Cady, Linell
254l Communication or collusion?: Maneuvering through the maze of patriarchal theology

Cahill, Lisa Sowle
3n Commentary to chapter 8 (chapter m)
3q Abortion, autonomy, and community

Cain, Glen
260k Estimating the impact of labor market policies on women: A discussion of the four-country studies on the employment of women

Cain, Melinda L.
373b Overview: Women and technology — resources for our future
373h Java, Indonesia: The introduction of rice processing technology

Cain, Virginia S.
309q The children of teenage parents

Caldecott, Leonie
167i At the foot of the mountain: The Shibokusa women of Kita Fuji

Calder, Jenni
286c Cash and the sex nexus

Calderone, Mary S.
225g Above and beyond politics: The sexual socialization of children

Caldwell, Patricia
19j The Antinomian language controversy

Caldwell, Robert A.
295f Sex differences in separation and divorce: A longitudinal perspective

Caldwell, Steven B.
309g The effect of government policies on out-of-wedlock sex and pregnancy

Calhoun, Karen S.
291 Physiological and reproductive disorders

Callahan, Daniel
3t Commentary to chapter 11 (chapter s)
3u The abortion debate: Is progress possible?

Callahan, Sidney
3s Value choices in abortion
3v Commentary to chapter 12 (chapter u)

Callaway, Helen
371i Spatial domains and women's mobility in Yorubaland, Nigeria

Callender, Gae
234f The status of women in old and early middle kingdom Egypt?

Cammaert, Lorna
271g A cross-cultural comparison of assertiveness in women
360m New sex therapies: Policy and practice

Cammell, Helga
209d Women, technological change and employment levels: The role of trade union policies

Cammett, John M.
95h Communist women and the fascist experience

Campbell, Anne
137k Gender and crime

Campbell, Beatrix
283d Feminists - The degenerates of the social?
335f Sex - A family affair

Campbell, Charles F.
63c Co-corrections - FCI Forth Worth after three years

Campbell, Claudia
385k Women's employment and development: A conceptual framework applied to Ghana

Campbell, Ena
194a The Virgin of Guadalupe and the female self-image: A Mexican case history

Campbell, Julie
16r Women in midstream

Campbell, Marie
157i Sexism in British Columbia trade unions, 1900-1920

Campbell, Patricia B.
266k The impact of societal biases on research methods

Campbell, Patricia F.
416k Early socialization: Causes and cures of mathematics anxiety

Campbell, Robert G.
82k Land tenure and cooperatives: Origin, development and persistence of Navajo matrifocality in subsistence, production, exchange and tenure

Candy, Sandra E.
214m Women, work and friendship: Personal confirmation and support

Canfield, Elizabeth K.
460u Young women and the sexual revolution

Canino, Glorisa
469e Transactional family patterns: A preliminary exploration of Puerto Rican female adolescents

Cannon, Charles A.
238g The awesome power of sex: The polemical campaign against Mormon polygamy

Cannon, Elaine A.
42h Daughters of God

Canter, Rachelle
267a Achievement in women: Implications for equal employment opportunity policy

Cantomi, Lucile
26g Family trouble clinic: Family service of Detroit and Wayne County

Cantor, Aviva
211d The Lilith question

Caplan, Jane
418i Sexuality and homosexuality

Caplan, Patricia
5f Development policies in Tanzania - some implications for women
364b Cognatic descent, Islamic law and women's property on the East African coast

Cappannari, Stephen C.
194c In quest of the Black Virgin: She is black because she is black

Cappelli, Denise
404z Vocational rehabilitation: Options for women

Card, Josefina J.
309m Teenage mothers and teenage fathers: The impact of early childbearing on the parents' personal and professional lives

Cardascia, John
376j Sex differences in the processing of criminal defendants

Cárdenas, José A.
216n The early education of minority children

Carew, Jan R.
100c The Indian and African presence in the Americas: Some aspects of historical distortion

Carew, Jean V.
216m Effective care-giving: The child from birth to three

Carey, George
115c Women and authority in the scriptures

Carlé, Birte
22g Structural patterns in the legends of the holy women of Christianity

Carlier, Anita
172c The only way (Peru)

Carlsen, James W.
133m Images of the gay male in contemporary drama

Carlson, Bonnie E.
26h Children's observations of interparental violence

Carlson, Richard O.
90g The sex dimension of careers in educational management: Overview and synthesis

Carlton, Wendy
79o Perfectibility and the neonate: The burden of expectations on mothers and their health providers

Carmen, Elaine (Hilberman)
8d Wife abuse: Culture as destiny
140c Inequality and women's mental health: An overview
140n Victims of violence and psychiatric illness
140v Teaching value clarification: The example of gender and psychotherapy

Carmo Nunes, Maria do
471i Women at work in Portugal

Carnevale, Patty
326e Network aspects of treatment for incestuously abused children

Carney, Magdalene
216j Implications for national policy decisions: The black family perspective

Carnochan, W.B.
196b The secrets of Swift and Stella

Carnoy, Martin
100a The dialectic of education: An alternative approach to education and social change in developing countries

Carol, M.
91t Women religious and the new society

Carothers, Suzanne C.
199m Contrasting sexual harassment in female- and male-dominated occupations

Carp, Roger E.
445h Hamlin Garland and the cult of true womanhood

Carpenter, Ann
175x Woman as victim in modern folklore

Carpenter, Mick
248f Asylum nursing before 1914: A chapter in the history of labour

Carr, Marilyn
373l Technologies appropriate for women: Theory, practice and policy

Carrera, Michael
57e Sexual learning in the elementary school

Carrington, Christine H.
38q Depression in black women: A theoretical appraisal

Carroll, Constance M.
14m Three's a crowd: The dilemma of the black woman in higher education

Carson, Barbara Harrell
127f Winning: Katherine Anne Porter's women

Carter, Angela
215o Anger in a black landscape

Carter, Barbara
349x Reform school families

Carter, Connie
205bb From home to house: Women in the BC legislature

Carter, Dianne K.
359ff Divorced women

Carter, Erica
134h Alice in the consumer wonderland

Carter, Geoffrey
286i Sexuality and the Victorian artist: Dickens and Swinburne

Carter, J. E. L.
107j Somatotypes of female athletes

Carter, Julie
150t Cat

Carter, Steven F.
1j Amanda Cross

Cartledge, Sue
257k Duty and desire: Creating a feminist morality

Carver, Ann Cathey
306k From concept to classroom

Carver, Cynthia
56d The deliverers: A woman doctor's reflections on medical socialization

Casal, Lourdes
444h Revolution and concienciaital: Women in Cuba

Case, Patricia J.
15l Collections of contemporary alternative materials in libraries: A directory

Casey, Ellen Miller
286e "Other people's prudery": Mary Elizabeth Braddon

Cass, Bettina
321c Comment: Gender and dependency
440c Redistribution to children and to mothers: A history of child endowment and family allowances
440h Population policies and family policies: State construction of domestic life

Cassella, Marie
434l Dilemmas in role identification for low-income women

Casserly, Patricia Lund
377h Factors affecting female participation in advanced placement programs in mathematics, chemistry, and physics

Cassidy, Marie M.
36h Depo-provera and sterilization abuse overview

Castañeda, Irene
192u Personal chronicle of Crystal City

Castillo, Adelaida R. Del
192a Sex, nationality, and class: La obrera Mexicana
192b Mexican women in organization
192h Sterilization: An overview

Castle, Josie
390l The Australian women's Guild of Empire

Castro, Fidel
374b The revolution within the Revolution
374c The struggle for women's equality
374e Into the third decade

Castro, Laura
54d Program planning for Hispanic women: One ideal model

Cates, Willard
252e The trimester threshold for pregnancy termination: Myth or truth?
252g Instrumental abortion in the second trimester: an overview

Cathasaigh, Dona'l O'
194d The cult of Brigid: A study of pagan-Christian syncretism in Ireland

Caupin, Benedicte
421k Feminist egalitarianism, social action orientation and occupational roles: A cross-national study

Cavalli, Alessandro
52g The changing role of women: The case of Italy

Cavior, Helene Enid
63h The development of a scale to assess inmate and staff attitudes toward co-corrections

Caws, Mary Ann
135c Wariness and women's language: Two modest verbal studies

Cazenave, Noel A.
37k Black men in America: The quest for "manhood"

Ceesay-Marenah, Coumba
385n Women's cooperative thrift and credit societies: An element of women's programs in the Gambia

Celentano, David D.
10d Multiple substance abuse among women with alcohol-related problems

Centre for Women's Development Studies
Committee of the Portrayal of Women in Media
161f Television and women

Cepeda, Rita
16v Social services and the Hispanic woman

Ch'en, Jerome
177j The Chinese biographical method: A moral and didactic tradition
177l "On the eve of her departure"

Chabran, Myrtha
30j Exiles

Chacón, Isabel
172b Research experiences with rural women (Costa Rica)

Chafe, William H.
45b The challenge of sex equality: Old values revisited or a new culture?
61a What we wish we knew about women: A dialog

Chai, Alice
412r Korean women in Hawaii, 1903-1945: The role of Methodism in their liberation and in their participation in the Korean independence movement

Chalou, George C.
61e Women in the American revolution: Vignettes or profiles?

Chamberlain, Geoffrey
233a Women at work in pregnancy
233v Adverse influences of the working environment

Chambers, Jo
257d Struggling to change, changing with struggle

Chambers, Marjorie Bell
102l A political diary of an assertive woman

Chambless, Dianne L.
365e Anxieties: Agoraphobia and hysteria

Chambré, Susan Maizel
455k Women and income maintenance programs

Chan, W. Y.
190s Prostaglandins in primary dysmenorrhea: Basis for the new therapy

Chapkis, Wendy
179c The Private Benjamin syndrome
206p Using sex and Satan to bust the union (an interview with Corky Jennings)

Chapman, Bruce
321i Comment: Income inequality

Chapman, Edgar L.
114h Sex, satire, and feminism in the science fiction of Suzette Haden Elgin

Chapman, Gordon R.
380i Poverty viewed as a woman's problem - The U.S. case

Chapman, Jane Roberts
111k The treatment of convicted female offenders in the criminal justice system
380i Poverty viewed as a woman's problem - The U.S. case

Chapman, Tony
139e Trends in female social mobility

Chappell, Adrian
134e Family fortunes

Charbonneau, Claudette
399tt New York feminist theater troupe

Charles-Edwards, T. M.
334b Nau Kynywedi Teithiauc

Charnas, Suzy McKee
131i A woman appeared

Charney, Maurice
278e Sexual fiction in America, 1955-80

Charnock, Mark
456l Infertility

Charters, W. W.
90a The sex dimension - An overview
90c Sex equity in educational policies and practices
90r The gender of principals and principal/teacher relations in elementary schools

Chavkin, Wendy
86e Closed office-building syndrome
86l Walking a tightrope: Pregnancy, parenting, and work
253g Reproductive hazards in the workplace: A course curriculum guide

Chen, Anita B.
300g Patterns of urbanization in the Philippines

Chen, Marty
402f Women in Bangladesh: Food-for-work and socioeconomic change

Chenut, Helen
206c The patriarchal thread - A history of exploitation
206i The sewing machine

Cheong, Jacqueline Leong
71j The early socialization of Asian-American female children

Chernesky, Roslyn
455l Women administrators in social work

Cherry, Frances
48l Gender roles and sexual violence

Cherry, Violet Padayachi
404u The role of the family in teenage pregnancy: Support or sabotage

Chertos, Cynthia H.
398m Hard truths for strategic change: Dilemmas of implementing affirmative action

Chesebro, James W.
133h Gay masculinity in the gay disco
133n Views of homosexuality among social scientists
133q Consciousness-raising among gay males

Cheska, Alyce
107a Women's sports - the unlikely myth of equality
147a Ball game participation of North American Indian women

Chesler, Phyllis
229j The Amazon legacy

Chesney-Lind, Meda
78d Guilty by reason of sex: Young women and the juvenile justice system
349s Judicial paternalism and the female status offender: Training women to know their place

Chesson, Marlene
333d The social and economic importance of the women in Jigalong

Cheung, Choi Wan
206n Resistance, strikes and strategies

Chevigny, Bell Gale
30u Daughters writing: Toward a theory of women's biography

Chew, Martha
450l Rita Mae Brown: Feminist theorist and southern novelist

Chhachhi, Amrita
206b Restructuring: The cutting edge
206d The case of India

Chicago, Judy
229o Our heritage is our power
453d A female form language

Childers, Karen
249l A network of one's own

Childress, Alice
40j A candle in a gale wind

Chilman, Catherine S.
359x Teenage pregnancy: A research review

Chinnery, Doug
111n Managing the female offender: Some observations

Chinoy, Helen Krich
399jj "Casting by Juliet Taylor" (Interview)
442k Suppressed desires: Women in the theater

Chiplin, Brian
89m Sexual discrimination in the labour market
357b Relative female earnings in Great Britain and the impact of legislation

Chipp, Sylvia A.
21i The modern Pakistani woman in a Muslim society
101j The All-Pakistan Women's Association and the 1961 Muslim family laws ordinance

Chirikos, Thomas N.
324e Economic consequences of poor health in mature women

Chisholm, Lynne
85g The expert's view? The sociological analysis of graduates' occupational and domestic roles
250m The experiences of women graduates in the labour market

Cho, Hyoung
75c Working women in Korea

Chodorow, Nancy
132b Gender, relation, and difference in psychoanalytic perspective
245d The fantasy of the perfect mother

Chojnacki, Stanley
184c Dowries and kinsmen in early Renaissance Venice

Chopik, Kathy
205u Cheap at half the price: The history of the fight for equal pay in BC

Chopp-Tibon, Shira
421x Occupational choice among female academicians - The Israeli case

Chorpenning, Charlotte
399ee The adventure of life: Writing for children

Christ, Carol P.
229ee Images of spiritual power in women's fiction
229h Why women need the goddess: Phenomenological, psychological, and political reflections
462o Feminist liberation theology and Yahweh as holy warrior: An analysis of symbol

Christensen, Harold T.
105d Recent data reflecting upon the sexual revolution in America

Christian, Barbara
40nn Alice Walker: The black woman artist as wayward
41b The concept of class in the novels of black women

Christmas, June Jackson
253l Sexism and racism in health policy

Chua, Beng-Huat
300j The CHIT fund in Singapore: Failure of a large-scale rotating credit fund

Chung, Jinyoung
75b Employment of Korean women

Chung, Priscilla Ching
401f Power and prestige: Palace women in the Northern Sung (960-1126)

Church, Merle G.
461l Effects of teenage motherhood

Ciborra, Claudio
209c Bargaining over the social costs of information technology

Cicero, Theodore J.
9o   Sex differences in the effects of alcohol and other psychoactive drugs on endocrine function: Clinical and experimental evidence

Cichocki, Mary K.
203h Women's travel patterns in a suburban development

Citron, Marcia J.
108j Fanny Mendelssohn Hensel: Musician in her brother's shadow

Claessens, A.
107q Somatic and motor characteristics of female gymnasts

Clance, Pauline Rose
443f Treatment of the imposter phenomenon in high-achieving women

Clanton, Gordon
185b Social forces and the changing family

Clarenbach, Kathryn F.
394o Continuing education: A personal view

Clark, Garcia
43u   The Beguines: A medieval women's community

Clark, Isobel
160g The negation of structure: A note on British council wives

Clark, Janet
226f Women as legislative candidates in six states

Clark, Lorenne M. G.
464g Consequences of seizing the reins in the household: A Marxist-feminist critique of Marx and Engels

Clark, Peter
115l Snakes and ladders: Reflections on hierarchy and The Fall

Clark, Wendy
335g Home thoughts from not so far away: A personal look at family

Clarke, Adele
310n Subtle forms of sterilization abuse: A reproductive rights analysis

Clarke, Anne
239k Research on menstrual-related psychological changes: Alternative perspectives

Clarke, Cheryl
150z Failure to transform: homophobia in the black community
150dd Women of summer

Clarke, Jocelyn
23c   Losing the numbers game: Women, tokenism and power

Clarke, Lynda
240c Psychosocial aspects of contraception

Clarricoates, Katherine
250c The importance of being Ernest ... Emma ... Tom ... Jane. The perception and categorization of gender conformity and gender deviation in primary schools
274b Classroom interaction

Clausen, Jeanette
32p   Our language, our selves: Verena Stefan's critique of patriarchal language

Clauss, Wolfgang
153b Subsistence reproduction: A framework for analysis

Clement, Jacqueline
352i Sex bias in school administration

Clements, Barbara Evans
405e Bolshevik women: The first generation

Clements, Helen
82w   Practicalities of participation

Cleveland, Donald E.
463t Gender-role identification in the methodology of transportation planning

Cleyre, Voltairine de
129c Anarchism and American traditions
129aa The economic tendency of freethought

Cliff, Michelle
30r   Sister/outsider: Some thoughts on Simone Weil
150g If I could write this in fire, I would write this in fire

Clifford, Gay
215c Three poems

Clifton, Lucille
40m   A simple language

Clinchy, Blythe
320g Epistemology and agency in the development of undergraduate women

Clinton, Michelle T.
150f Debra (poem)
150ll For strong women (poem)

Cloud, Kathleen
82b   AID and women in development
82p   Views of women in international development

Clower, Virginia Lawson
460j Masturbation in women

Clyne, Robert M.
447l Fetotoxicity and fertile female employees

Coalition to Fight Infant Mortality
310z Equal opportunity for babies? Not in Oakland!

Coats, Maggie
138k Gender, class and education: A teaching bibliography of European studies

Cobb, Jewel Plummer
416e Planning strategies for women in scientific professions

Cobb, John B.
118b Feminism and process thought: A two-way relationship

Cobham, David
283o The socialist economic review project: Progress in the economics of the left

Cobhan, Linn ni
176z Lesbians in physical education and sport

Cocalis, Susan L.
32a   The eternal feminine is leading us on

Cochrane, Susan
393h The relationship between education and fertility

Coffey, Margaret
339j One family's decision: A leave of absence

Cogan, John
110b Married women's labor supply: A comparison of alternative estimation procedures
110g Labor supply with costs of labor market entry

Coghlan, Mary
47f   The family

Cohen, Barbara
209w An overview of NIOSH research on clerical workers

Cohen, Carl
223j Sex, birth control, and human life

Cohen, Jeffrey
265j Cross-sex friendship in the elementary school

Cohen, Karen A.
8k   Emotional reactions to miscarriage

Cohen, Leah
288g The other side of the coin: Women who exploit their sexuality for gain
288j Action plans for management and unions

Cohen, Marjorie
120d The problem of studying "economic man"

Cohen, Miriam
184l Women's work and European fertility patterns

Cohen, Morton
286a Lewis Carroll and Victorian morality

Cohen, Stanley H.
63h   The development of a scale to assess inmate and staff attitudes toward co-corrections

Cohen, Yolande
120j Thoughts on women and power

Cohn, Jan
1g   Mary Roberts Rinehart

Cohn, Sanford J.
377f Sex differences in the development of precocious mathematical talent

Col, Jeanne Marie
436j Women's employment networks: Strategies for development

Colacurcio, Michael
19m   Footsteps of Anne Hutchinson

Cole, Collier M.
281c Sexual disorders and the family therapist

Cole, Johnetta
68i   Women in Cuba: The revolution within the revolution
83i   Racism and sexism: They ain't genetic you know!

Cole, Susan G.
305d Home sweet home?

Coleman, Emily R.
184a Medieval marriage characteristics: A neglected factor in the history of medieval serfdom

Coleman, Linda
86b   The risks of healing: The hazards of the nursing profession

Coleman, Willie M.
150bb Among the things that use to be (poem)

Coll, Regina
91c Feminist liberation theology: Its past and future

Colley, Susan
323u Free universal day care: The OFL takes a stand

Collier, Eugenia
40bb The closing of the circle: Movement from division to wholeness in Paule Marshall's fiction
40pp Fields watered with blood: Myth and ritual in the poetry of Margaret Walker

Collier, Jane
245b Is there a family? New anthropological views
282i Politics and gender in simple societies

Collings, John
193l Girls studying science in the sixth form

Collins, H.M.
297c Researching spoonbending: Concepts and practice of participatory fieldwork

Collins, Jock
94a Immigration and class: The Australian experience

Collins, Leslie E.
281e Homosexual and bisexual issues

Collins, Sheila
57h Religion and sexual learning of children
102d Religion and the fearful father: Vision of liberation or American-style fascism?

Collins, Sheila D.
229gg The personal is political

Collomp, Alain
162f Tensions, dissensions, and ruptures inside the family in seventeenth- and eighteenth-century Haute Provence

Colten, Mary Ellen
268j A sex-roles perspective on drug and alcohol use by women

Colvard, Richard
387u Unresolved questions: Three feminist perspectives

Comas-Diaz, Lillian
469b Mental health needs of Puerto Rican women in the United States

Combahee River Collective
14c A black feminist statement
150hh Combahee River collective statement

Combs, Beverly J.
129p If you liked gun control, you'll love the antiabortion amendment

Comer, James P.
216e The black family: An adaptive perspective

Comer, Lee
50l Monogamy, marriage and economic dependence

Comini, Alessandra
117o Gender or genius? The women artists of German expressionism

Cominsky, Sheila
269c Sex roles and subsistence: A comparative analysis of three Central American communities

Commaille, Jacques
105i Towards a new definition of divorce

Communist Party of Cuba
374d Thesis: On the full exercise of women's equality

Condren, Mary
462m Patriarchy and death

Conger, Syndy McMillen
109e The reconstruction of the gothic feminine ideal in Emily Brontë's *Wuthering Heights*

Conklin, George H.
421a Cultural determinants of power for women within the family: A neglected aspect of family research

Conley, Tom
135r On the birth of death: *An Arrest d'Amour* of Martial d'Auvergne

Connell, John J.
209g The issue of employment and office technology from a managerial perspective

Connelly, M. Patricia
380l Women's work and the family wage in Canada

Connelly, Mark Thomas
353o Prostitution, venereal disease, and American medicine

Connelly, Maureen
186q Metaphor in five garden poems by May Sarton

Conner, Elizabeth
187m Ten centuries of growth: The Cistercian Abbey of Soleilmont

Conner, Susan P.
130b Women and politics

Connor, Linda H.
466c Healing as women's work in Bali

Connors, Denise
79y Response

Connors, Lyndsay
23j The politics of the National Women's Advisory Council

Conoley, Jane Close
352c The psychology of leadership: Implications for women

Conrad, Margaret
205a "Sundays always make me think of home": Time and place in Canadian women's history

Conroy, Mary Alice
111q Sex-role concepts among federal female offenders

Constantine, Larry L.
185f Growing up slowly: Another century of childhood

Contento, Isobel
341j The nutritional needs of women

Contratto, Susan
124g Psychology views mothers and mothering: 1897-1980
158j Mother: Social sculptor and trustee of the faith
245d The fantasy of the perfect mother
439m Maternal sexuality and asexual motherhood

Cook, Alice H.
65o Developments in selected states
93b Collective bargaining as a strategy for achieving equal opportunity and equal pay: Sweden and West Germany
93i Vocational training, the labor market, and the unions
169v Labor education and women workers: An international comparison
382b Federal Republic of Germany

Cook, Beverly Blair
226i Women on the state bench: Correlates of access
410b Political culture and selection of women judges in trial courts
410f Women judges and public policy in sex integration
436l Will women judges make a difference in women's legal rights? A prediction from attitudes and simulated behaviour

Cook, Blanche Wiesen
30w Biographer and subject: A critical connection
417k A utopian female support network: The case of the Henry Street Settlement
442n Women and politics: The obscured dimension

Cook, Katsi
36w A Native American response

Cook, Mark
24e Social skill and human sexual attraction

Cook, Pam
406d Duplicity in Mildred Pierce

Cooke, David J.
240l A psychosocial study of the climacteric

Cools, Anne
203t Emergency shelter: The development of an innovative women's environment

Cooper, Andrew
258b Sex, gender and society

Cooper, Arnold M.
439q *Homosexuality in Perspective* by William H. Masters and Virginia E. Johnson

Cooper, Signe
337e Nursing in the UW system

Cooperband, Adele
472i Widow-to-widow: The elderly widow and mutual help

Cooperstock, Ruth
359j A review of women's psychotropic drug use

Coote, Anna
467e The stance of Britain's major parties and interest groups

Cope, Bill
94e Multiculturalism and education policy

Copper, Baba
229uu The voice of women's spirituality in futurism

Corbin, Diane H.
175b Angelina

Corby, Nan
289f Old and alone: The unmarried in later life

Corcoran, Mary
272h Work experience, job segregation, and wages

Cordova, Dorothy L.
71f Educational alternatives for Asian-Pacific women

Corea, Genoveffa
36j The depo-provera weapon
310c Egg snatchers

Corrado, Raymond R.
111b Female terrorists: Competing perspectives

Correa, Gladys
72b Puerto Rican women in education and potential impact on occupational patterns

Corrigan, Eileen
455g New knowledge and the drinking woman

Corrigan, Philip
97b In/Forming schooling: Space/time/textuality in compulsory state provided "mass" schooling systems

Cortez, Jayne
231z In the morning (poem)

Coser, Rose Laub
387c Women in the occupational world: Social disruption and conflict
387m Stay home, little Sheba: On placement, displacement, and social change

Coss, Clare
132o Separation and survival: Mothers, daughters, sisters: - The women's experimental theater

Costa, Mariarosa Dalla
227k The power of women and the subversion of the community

Costain, Anne N.
435a Representing women: The transition from social movement to interest group

Costantini, Edmond
226e Women in political parties: Gender differences in motives among California party activists

Costelli, Helen
386k Women in media

Costello, Bonnie
356o The "feminine" language of Marianne Moore

Costello, Richard W.
269d New economic roles for Cuna males and females: An examination of socioeconomic change in a San Blas community

Coston, Carol
462y A feminist approach to alternative enterprises

Cotera, Marta
319n Feminism: The Chicana and the Anglo versions, a historical analysis

Cothran, Ann
64p Image structure, codes, and recoding in *The Pure and the Impure*

Cott, Nancy F.
108k Women as law clerks: Catherine G. Waugh
238b Passionlessness: An interpretation of Victorian sexual ideology, 1790-1850
314i The women's studies program: Yale University
353d Passionlessness: An interpretation of Victorian sexual ideology, 1790-1850

Cottam, K. Jean
405h Soviet women in combat in World War II: The ground/air defense forces

Cotton, Donald J.
326h Sexual assault in correctional institutions: Prevention and intervention

Cottrell, Ann Baker
388l The contemporary American women's movement

Cottrell, Robert D.
442a Colette's literary reputation

Coulson, Margaret
227o 'The housewife and her labour under capitalism' - a critique

Coulter, Sara
249i Career politics and the practice of women's studies

Coultrap-McQuin, Susan
263h Creating a place for women: American book publishing in the nineteenth century

Counts, Dorothy Ayers
246e Revenge suicide by Lusi women: An expression of power

Court, John H.
230f Sex and violence: A ripple effect

Coveney, Lal
290d Theory into practice: Sexual liberation or social control? (*Forum* magazine 1968-1981)

Cowan, Belita
36c Ethical problems in government-funded contraceptive research

Cowan, Ruth Schwartz
81h Two washes in the morning and a bridge party at night: The American housewife between the wars

Coward, Rosalind
119h Sexual politics and psychoanalysis: Some notes on their relation
283d Feminists - The degenerates of the social?

Cox, Barbara G.
216f Parenting for multiculturalism: A Mexican-American model

Cox, Eva
321o Can there be justice for women under capitalism?: Social justice for whom?
440i Pater-patria: Child-rearing and the state

Cox, Martha
204i Effects of divorce on parents and children

Cox, Roger
204i Effects of divorce on parents and children

Cox, Sue
268f Depression in relation to sex roles: Differences in learned susceptibility and precipitating factors

Coyle, Angela
470a Sex and skill in the organisation of the clothing industry

Coyle, Laurie
192m Women at Farah: An unfinished story
201k Women at Farah: An unfinished story

Coyner, Sandra
311c Women's studies as an academic discipline: Why and how to do it
312d Women's studies as an academic discipline: Why and how to do it

Craft, Ian
252k Natural prostaglandins alone or in combination for termination of pregnancy

Cragan, John F.
133q Consciousness-raising among gay males

Cramer, Michael H.
157e Public and political: Documents of the woman's suffrage campaign in British Columbia, 1871-1917: The view from Victoria

Cramer, Stanley H.
221f Family effects of dislocation, unemployment, and discouragement

Crane, Elaine F.
376b Dealing with dependence: Paternalism and tax evasion in eighteenth-century Rhode Island

Crawford, Albert G.
4e Social implications of teenage childbearing
309r Family support: Helping teenage mothers to cope

Crawford, Jacqueline K.
63l Two losers don't make a winner: The case against the co-correctional institution

Crawford, Patricia
99b From the woman's view: Pre-industrial England, 1500-1750

Creange, Renée
186h The country of the imagination

Crescy, John
91r New wine in new skins: Women in secular institutes

Cresswell, John
414g College life in Oklahoma territory

Crisler, Jane
263k Industrial social workers in France, 1917-1939: A study in the sex/gender division of labor
394d Committee on the Status of Women at Milwaukee

Crist, Miriam J.
412t Winifred L. Chappell: Everybody on the left knew her

Crockett, Lisa J.
351d Biology: Its role in gender-related educational experiences

Croll, Elisabeth
350i The sexual division of labor in rural China
364c The exchange of women and property: Marriage in post-revolutionary China

Crompton, Rosemary
470c Contemporary clerical work: A case study of local government

Cronkite, Ruth C.
361e A short-term intervention program: Math-science conferences

Crosby, Faye
136h Gender, androgyny, and conversational assertivness

Crosland, Margaret
64k Colette and Ravel: The enchantress and the illusionist

Cross, Herbert J.
287b Male sexuality: Socio-sexual change and the single status

Cross, Richard
223z Case studies

Cross, Tia
14h Face-to-face, day-to-day - racism CR

Crossley, Diane
157l The B.C. Liberal Party and women's reforms, 1916-1928

Crowder, Diane
64p Image structure, codes, and recoding in *The Pure and the Impure*

Crowley, John W.
17g W.D. Howells: The ever-womanly

Crull, Peggy
86g Sexual harassment and women's health
199m Contrasting sexual harassment in female- and male-dominated occupations
288f The impact of sexual harassment on the job: A profile of the experiences of 92 women

Crumpacker, Laurie
17d Four novels of Harriet Beecher Stowe: A study in nineteenth-century androgyny

Cseh-Szombathy, László
105b Modern and traditional elements in the expectations of young married couples regarding their marital life

Cuadrado, Clara Y.
449c Portraits by a lady: The fictional world of Ling Shuhua

Cuban Family Code
374g Appendix B: The family code

Cucchiari, Salvatore
282b The gender revolution and the transition from bisexual horde to patrilocal band: The origins of gender hierarchy

Cudjoe, Selwyn R.
40b Maya Angelou and the autobiographical statement

Culley, Lorraine
138j Social theory, social relations and education
283g Women's organisation in the Labour Party
283h Interview with Frances Morrell

Culley, Margo
306i Feminist pedagogy: Lost voices of American women
306p Public presentation reports
314k Black studies and women's studies: An overdue partnership

Culpepper, Emily Erwin
79aa Sex preselection: Discussion moderator's remarks

79nn Reflections: Uncovering patriarchal agendas and exploring woman-oriented values
229y Martial art meditations

Cummerton, Joan M.
434j Homophobia and social work practice with lesbians

Cummings, Nicholas A.
360p Professional psychology's response to women's mental health needs

Cumsille, Alejandra
323n Triple oppression: Immigrant women in the labour force

Cunningham, Gail
318g Women and children first: The novels of Margaret Drabble

Cunningham, Isabella C. M.
421n Working wives in the United States and Venezuela: A cross-national study of decision making

Cunningham-Rathner, Jerry
277f Psychophysiologic measurement of sexual arousal in females

Cunnington, Susan
219c Aspects of violence in prostitution

Cunnison, Sheila
139f Participation in local union organisation. School meals staff: A case study

Curb, Rosemary K.
399h "Lesson I Bleed"

Curlewis, Joan
13h Women working in heavy industry in World War II

Curran, Charles
152h Moral theology and homosexuality

Curran, Leo C.
419l Rape and rape victims in the *Metamorphoses*

Curran, Libby
12a Science education: Did she drop out or was she pushed?

Curran, Margaret M.
357b Relative female earnings in Great Britain and the impact of legislation

Curthoys, Ann
321l The women's movement and social justice

Curtis, Bruce
149b Capital, the state and the origins of the working-class household

Curtis, Judith
130n The epistolières

Curtis, Mary Julia
399cc Women open Augusta's first theatre

Cuskey, Walter R.
359t Issues in the treatment of female addiction: A review and critique of the literature

Cutright, Phillips
309b Teenage illegitimacy: An exchange

Cuza Malé, Belkis
74h A woman and her poems (essay)

Dahl, Tove Stang
217c Women's right to money

Dahlerup, Drude
464b Overcoming the barriers: An approach to the study of how women's issues are kept from the political agenda

Dally, Ann
47a A time of change

Dalsimer, Marlyn
263m The new economic readjustment policies: Implications for Chinese urban working women

Dalton, Katharina
28k Premenstrual tension: An overview

Daly, Mary
229ff Sisterhood as cosmic covenant
229t Gyn/ecology: Spinning new time/space

Daly, Mike
235c At work

Damm, David
463g Analysis of activity schedules along the dimension of gender

Damsholt, Nanna
22e Women in Latin Medieval literature in Denmark e.g. annals and chronicles

Dan, Alice J.
51z The Interdisciplinary Society for Menstrual Cycle Research: Creating knowledge from our experience

Dana, Natalie T.
146g Individual and group treatment of mothers of incest victims

Dandridge, Rita B.
14w On the novels written by selected black women: A bibliographical essay

Danforth, Sandra
362c Muslim Middle Eastern women's participation in violent political conflict: Causes and characteristics

Daniel, Sheryl B.
232c Marriage in Tamil culture: The problem of conflicting "models"

Daniels, Arlene Kaplan
387u Unresolved questions: Three feminist perspectives

Daniels, Elizabeth A.
142c A Meredithian glance at Gwendolen Harleth

Daniels, Jane Z.
361i Women in engineering: A dynamic approach

Daniels, Kay
294a Prostitution in Tasmania during the transition from penal settlement to 'civilized' society
294i Introduction: St. Kilda voices

Daniels, Pamela
214t Dream vs. drift in women's careers: The question of generativity

Danky, James P.
15c The acquisition of alternative materials

Danza, Roberta
190g Menarche: Its effects on mother-daughter and father-daughter interactions

Daoust, Eileen
205bb From home to house: Women in the BC legislature

Darcy, Judy
323k The right to strike

Darke, Jane
182a Women, architects and feminism

Darsey, James
133b Coming out as a communicative process
133e "Gayspeak": A response
133r From "commies" and "queers" to "gay is good"

Darty, Trudy
397m Lesbians and contemporary health care systems: Oppression and opportunity

Darwin, Jaine L.
190w The psychological concomitants of menarche in psychiatric patients

Dasey, Robyn
144h Women's work and the family: Women garment workers in Berlin and Hamburg before the First World War
209f Training: The magic cure for all ills?

Dash, Irene G.
180o How light a *Lighthouse* for today's women?
343o A penchant for Perdita on the eighteenth-century stage

Dass, Tehrim
75e Working women in India

Datan, Nancy
268n Senescence, sex roles, and stress: Shepherding resources into old age
289o Beyond generativity: Toward a sensuality of later life
316j The lost cause: The aging woman in American feminism
317d The competent older woman

Datesman, Susan K.
392a The extent and nature of female crime
392d Female delinquency and broken homes: A reassessment
392m Unequal protection of males and females in the juvenile court

Dauber, Rosyln
373p Applying policy analysis to women and technology: A framework for consideration

Daubler-Gmelin, Herta
93o Equal employment opportunity for women in West Germany today

Daugherty, Beth Rigel
329o The whole contention between Mr. Bennett and Mrs. Woolf, revisited

Dauster, Frank
74b Success and the Latin American writer

Davenport, Doris
176b Black lesbians in academia: Visible invisibility

Davenport, Joanna
147p Eleonora Randolph Sears, pioneer in women's sports
147v The eastern legacy - the early history of physical education for women

David, Francoise
323s Women's committees: The Quebec experience

David, Hélène
323e "Action Positive" in the Quebec trade union movement

David, Kenneth
232d Hidden powers: Cultural and socio-economic accounts of Jaffna women

David, Miriam E.
97d Parents, children and the state
138i Sex, education and social policy: A new moral economy?
465h The new right, sex, education and social policy: Towards a new moral economy in Britain and the USA

Davidoff, Leonore
256a Class and gender in Victorian England

Davidson, Arnold E.
20l Prospects and retrospects in *Life Before Man*

Davidson, Cathy N.
20l Prospects and retrospects in *Life Before Man*
180j Mothers and daughters in the fiction of the New Republic

Davidson, Clara Dixon
129q Relations between parents and children

Davidson, Howard A.
55l Appendix A: Legal resources on sexual exploitation of children
55n Appendix C: Cases related to obscenity issues

Davidson, Raelene
99e 'As good a bloody woman as any other woman...': Prostitutes in western Australia, 1895-1939
294d Dealing with the 'social evil': Prostitution and the police in Perth and on the eastern goldfields, 1895-1924

Davidson, Virginia
140x Psychiatry's problem with no name: Therapist-patient sex
359k Psychiatry's problem with no name: Therapist-patient sex

Davies, Celia
248a Introduction: The contemporary challenge in nursing history
248e A constant casualty: Nurse education in Britain and the USA to 1939

Davies, Helen C.
261c Grievances and their redress in the eighties

Davies, Lynn
138c Gender, resistance and power

Davies, Megan
205q "Services rendered, rearing children for the state": Mothers' pensions in British Columbia 1919-1931

Davies, R. R.
334e The status of women and the practice of marriage in late-medieval Wales

Davies, Robert E.
261c Grievances and their redress in the eighties

Davies, Wendy
156j Celtic women in the early middle ages

Davin, Anna
153n Working or helping? London working-class children in the domestic economy

Davis, Barbara Hillyer
174g Teaching the feminist minority
306q New forms for new research

Davis, Christina
301ll The challenge (poem)

Davis, Frank G.
37g Economics and mobility: A theoretical rationale for urban black family well-being

Davis, Judy
229hh Dimensions of spirituality

Davis, Madeline
176m Learning through teaching: A lesbianism course in 1972

Davis, Martha
136e Sex differences in body movements and positions

Davis, Nanciellen
388e Women's work and worth in an Acadian maritime village

Davis, Nancy
2j Abortion and self-defense

Davis, Natalie Zemon
33g Gender and genre: Women as historical writers, 1400-1820

Davis, Paula G.
28c Neuroendocrine regulation of sexual behavior

Davis, Susan Schaefer
403c The determinants of social position among rural Moroccan women

Davis, Thadious M.
450b Alice Walker's celebration of self in southern generations

Davis, Tricia
119d 'What kind of woman is she?' Women and Communist Party politics, 1941-1955

Davis-Friedman, Deborah
177d Village wives

Davitt, Patricia J.
305q When all the secretaries demand what they are worth

Day, Connie L.
133g Communication patterns in established lesbian relationships

Day, J. B.
236a Aetiology of premenstrual syndrome

Day, Randal D.
421q Sex role attitudes, female employment, and marital satisfaction

Day, Stanley
129o The persecution of Moses Harman

Daymont, Thomas N.
49c The age mix of the labor force in 1990: Implications for labor market research
324c Occupational atypicality: Changes, causes, and consequences

De Lancey, Virginia
393a Wage earner and mother: Compatibility of roles on a Cameroon plantation

De Lange, Janice M.
434b Depression in women: Explanations and prevention

de Lauretis, Teresa
247h Now and nowhere: Roeg's *Bad Timing*

de Souza, Alfred
402a Women in India and South Asia: An introduction

Deacon, Desley
23k The employment of women in the commonwealth public service: The creation and reproduction of a dual labour market

Dean, Janet
291p The co-therapy relationship in group treatment of sexually mistreated adolescent girls

Dean, Mitchell
248d The administration of poverty and the development of nursing practice in nineteenth-century England

Dean, Virginia
65n Comparable worth under various federal and state laws

Deaux, Kay
415b Internal barriers
425b Hard-hatted women: Reflections on blue-collar employment

Deaver, Sherri
473a The contemporary Saudi woman

Debrida, Bella
229n Drawing from mythology in women's quest for selfhood

Debrovner, Charles H.
237e The effect of placebos (prementrual tension)

Deem, Rosemary
62a Introduction: Co-education reconsidered - reviving the debate
62g Conclusion: Co-education, equal educational opportunity and change
97a Women, educational reform and the process of change
138g Gender, patriarchy and class in the popular education of women
250a Introduction: Women, work and schooling: The relevance of gender
250n Women, school and work: Some conclusions

Deere, Carmen Diana
350c Peasant production, proletarianization, and the sexual division of labor in the Andes
459c Class and historical analysis for the study of women and economic change

Dege, Kristi
51e Attitudes of families toward menopause

Degler, Carl N.
123d What the women's movement has done to American history
353c What ought to be and what was: Women's sexuality in the nineteenth century

DeHaan, Neil
421k Feminist egalitarianism, social action orientation and occupational roles: A cross-national study

Dehon, Claire
64j Colette and art nouveau

Deitch, Irene
443l A feminist approach to math-anxiety reduction

Delamont, Sara
138f The conservative school? Sex roles at home, at work and at school

Delmar, Ros
227n Oppressed politics

DeLorey, Catherine
411m Health care and midlife women

Delphy, Christine
85e Women in stratification studies

Demaine, Jack
138j Social theory, social relations and education

DeMallie, Raymond
148i Male and female in traditional Lakota culture

DeMatteo, Bob
209y The health impacts of low-level radiation on VDT operators

Demetrakopoulos, Stephanie A.
452k The metaphysics of matrilinearism in women's autobiography: Studies of Mead's *Blackberry Winter*, Hellman's *Pentimento*, Angelou's *I Know Why the Caged Bird Sings* and Kingston's *The Woman Warrior*

Dembinska, Maria
22d Le rôle et la place de la femme provenant de la classe sociale inférieure dans la vie quotidienne du Moyen-Age

D'Emilio, John
231d Capitalism and gay identity

Deming, Caren J.
384g Miscegenation in popular western history and fiction

Denis, Ann B.
52t Wife and/or worker: Sex role concepts of Canadian female students

Dennerstein, L.
236c Premenstrual syndrome - a holistic approach

Dennis, Philip A.
82u NEMOW: A project that stumbled and why

Dennison, Carol J.
205n They also served: The British Columbia women's institutes in two World Wars

Densen-Gerber, Judianne
359t Issues in the treatment of female addiction: A review and critique of the literature

Department of Aboriginal Affairs
333t Aboriginal women today

Depner, Charlene
458d Employment status and social support: The experience of the mature woman

Derricotte, Toi
150b For a Godchild, Regina, on the occasion of her first love (poem)
150c The damned (poem)
150d Hester's Song (poem)

Dery, Gretchen Kramer
190f Recollections of menarche, current menstrual attitudes, and perimenstrual symptoms

Desalvo, Louise A.
30c A portrait of the *Puttana* as a middle-aged Woolf scholar
202c Shakespeare's *other* sister
328e 1897: Virginia Woolf at fifteen
448e Every woman is an island: Vita Sackville-West, the image of the city and the pastoral idyll

Desposito, Lisa
60i The New Right and the abortion issue

Dessaur, C.I.
159b Female criminality in the Netherlands

Detre, Katherine M.
53s Hypertension in women - a review

Deuschle, Vi
333l Historical factors which have affected aboriginal lifestyles since colonisation

Devesa, Susan S.
53m Time trends of cancer incidence and mortality among women

DeVito, Joseph A.
133p Educational responsibilities to gay male and lesbian students

Devlin, Ann Sloan
185l Physical settings for families in 2020: In space, on earth

Devlin, Dennis
187i Feminine lay piety in the High Middle Ages: The Beguines

Devlin, Diana
399aa Sylvia Plath, a dramatic poet

Devon, Tonia K.
68g Up from the harem? The effects of class and sex on political life in northern India

DeVries, Rachel
174q The Women's Writer's Center: An interview with the directors

Dewar, John
147ii The Edmonton Grads: The team and its social significance from 1915-1940

DeWine, Sue
415g Breakthrough: Making it happen with women's networks

Dex, Shirley
213c The second generation: West Indian female school-leavers

Dey, Jennie
5g Gambian women: Unequal partners in rice development projects?

Deyermond, Alan
408a Spain's first women writers

D'Heurle, Adma
265j Cross-sex friendship in the elementary school

265s Changing sex roles reflected in the films of François Truffaut

Diamond, Irene
78r Pornography and repression: A reconsideration
435f Women and housing: The limitations of liberal reform
439g Pornography and repression: A reconsideration

Diamond, Sara
205t A union man's wife: The ladies' auxiliary movement in the IWA, the Lake Cowichan experience

Dibattista, Maria
330i *To the Lighthouse*: Virginia Woolf's Winter's Tale

Dickason, Anne
116a The feminine as a universal

Dickens, Bernard M.
276e Sexual aggression and the law - implications for the future

Dickie, Jane
122q Marital metaphors in the Judeo-Christian tradition: A feminist critique
254h Broaching the issue: Homophobia
315k Women's studies and the re-vision of liberal education: "What is a nice girl/boy like you doing here?"

Dickie, Ruth
337b Women in science
337j Women and cooperative home economics extension

Dickinson, Cindy
86b The risks of healing: The hazards of the nursing profession

Dickinson, Torry
153m Gender division within the U.S. working class: Households in the Philadelphia area, 1870-1945

Dickson, Katherine Murphy
302n The reentry professional librarian

Didion, Joan
474b Why I write

Diehl, Joanne Feit
121i "Ransom in a voice": Language as defense in Dickinson's poetry

Dieren, Karen van
205e The response of the WMS to the immigration of Asian women, 1888-1942

Dietrick, Ellen Battelle
129z Cardinal Gibbons's ignorance

Diggory, Peter
252d A review of abortion practices and their safety

Dijkers, Marcellinus
52h Changing sex roles in the Greek family and society
244f The roles of Greek husbands and wives: Definitions and fulfillment

Dijkstra, Sandra
448a The city as catalyst for Flora Tristan's vision of social change

Dilatush, Lois
58g Women in medicine

58h Family planning and population policies

Dill, Agnes
70h Indian boarding schools and Indian women: Blessing or curse?

Dill, Bonnie Thornton
38g "The means to put my children through": Child-rearing goals and strategies among black female domestic servants
60k "On the hem of life": Race, class, and the prospects for sisterhood

Dill, David L.
55i Victim advocacy as therapy

Dill, Diana
178a Research methods and sample characteristics
178c Daily lives
178m The challenge of coping

Diller, Ann
432n Women's physical education: A gender-sensitive perspective

Dimen, Muriel
225h Politically correct? Politically incorrect?

Dimock, John
280m Necrophilia and anti-social acts

Dinaburg, Daniel
11k Marital therapy of women alcoholics

Dingman, Maurice
91g Challenge of feminism to the church: A Bishop's perspective

Dinnerstein, Dorothy
102p Afterword: Toward the mobilization of Eros

Dion, Karen
24a Physical attractiveness, sex roles and heterosexual attraction

DiStefano, Anna
315d Feminist counseling
315e A dialogue critical issues in women's studies: Race, class, and sexual orientation

Divine, Donna Robinson
108n *Difficult journey - mountainous journey*, the memoirs of Fadwa Tuqan

Dixon, Marlene
192f The rise and demise of women's liberation: A class analysis

Dixon, Melvin
40w Singing a deep song: Language as evidence in the novels of Gayl Jones

Dixon, Suzanne
234a Theoretical perspectives on pre-industrial women
234k Summing up: Beyond the 'status of women'

Djwa, Sandra
20a The where of here: Margaret Atwood and a Canadian tradition

Doane, Mary Ann
247a Feminist film criticism: An introduction
247d The "woman's film": Possession and address

Dobash, Rebecca
50m The violent event

Dobash, Russell
50m The violent event

Dobbin, Christine
166d The search for women in Indonesian history

Dobson, Joanne A.
121e "Oh, Susie, it is dangerous": Emily Dickinson and the archetype of the masculine

Dobson, Malcolm
235b At school

Dodd, Barbara G.
240j Psychosexual problems

Dodd, Peter C.
421h The effect of religious affiliation on woman's role in Middle Eastern Arab Society

Dodson, Jualynne
37a Conceptualizations of black families
412o Nineteenth-century A.M.E. preaching women: Cutting edge of women's inclusion in church polity

Doek, Jack E.
291f Sexual abuse of children: An examination of European criminal law

Doeringer, Peter B.
89i Determinants of the structure of industrial type labor markets

Dohrenwend, Barbara Snell
295l The relation of stressful life events to gender

Doman, Mahinder Kaur
205f A note on Asian Indian women in British Columbia, 1900-1935

Dominian, Jack
47e Married life

Donadello, Gloria
455j Women and the mental health system

Donady, Bonnie
96n Math anxiety and female mental health: Some unexpected links

Donchin, Anne
31e Concepts of woman in psychoanalytic theory: The nature-nurture controversy revisited

Donegan, Jane B.
353u "Safe delivered," but by whom? Midwives and men-midwives in early America

Donegan, Rosemary
305z But is it feminist art?

Dong, Lorraine
401e The many faces of Cui Yingying

Donnerstein, Edward
230c Pornography: Its effect on violence against women
280b Pornography: Its consequences on the observer

D'Onofrio-Flores, Pamela M.
251a Technology, economic development, and the division of labour by sex

Donovan, Josephine
356n The silence is broken

Dooley, Fred
82w Practicalities of participation

Dorr, Aimee
391b Career awareness in young children

Dorr, Darwin
295c Mothering and the young child

Dorsey, David
40q The art of Mari Evans

Doty, Gresdna
399i Anne Brunton Merry: First star

Doudna, Christine
102j Women at the top

Dougherty, Mary Agnes
412j The social gospel according to Phoebe: Methodist deaconesses in the metropolis, 1885-1918

Doughtery, Rosie
352k The black female administrator: Woman in a double bind

Doughty, Frances
176r Lesbian biography, biography of lesbians

Douglas, Ann
442b Willa Cather: A problematic ideal

Douglas, Stephen A.
21f Women in Indonesian politics: The myth of functional interest

Douvan, Elizabeth
45h Family roles in a twenty-year perspective
124l Women and peace

Dover, K.J.
419f Classical Greek attitudes to sexual behavior

Dovidio, John F.
136d Visual behavior and dominance in women and men

Dowben, Carla W.
4j Legal aspects of adolescent pregnancy

Downer, Carol
310dd Through the speculum
460s Self-help for sex

Downing, Charles S.
265k Sex differences in children's road accidents

Downing, Chris
341f Feast and famine: Gifts of the goddess

Downing, John
265g Making literacy equally accessible to females and males

Downs, David
399ff Alvina Krause: A great teacher of acting

Dowse, Sara
321k The bureaucrat as usurer
440j The women's movement's fandango with the state: The movement's role in public policy since 1972

Doyle, Eric
115b The ordination of women in the Roman Catholic Church

Doyle, Ruth
337g Women and the law school

Drachman, Virginia G.
353l The Loomis trial: Social mores and obstetrics in the mid-nineteenth century

Dragadze, Tamara
371h The sexual division of domestic space among two Soviet minorities: The Georgians and the Tadjiks

Drake, Lewis W.
287m Psychological aspects of sexual dysfunction

Drake, Madeline
151g Soviet child care: Its organisation at local level

Drego, Pearl
91d The feminist viewpoint

Dreifus, Claudia
78x Why two women cops were convicted of cowardice

Dreman, Solly B.
265m Sex role stereotyping and mental health standards in Israel: A cross-cultural comparison

Dressel, Paula L.
289i Range of alternatives

Dresselhaus, Mildred S.
416g Responsibilities of women faculty in engineering schools

Drinker, Sophie
229d The origins of music: Women's goddess worship

Dronke, Peter
188f The provençal *Trobairitz*: Castelloza

Droste, Jean
337a Vocational aspirations and job realities

Drucker, Alison R.
401k The influence of western women on the anti-footbinding movement 1840-1911

Druke, Mary
367a American Indian women and religion

Dryfoos, Joy G.
309aa Contraceptive services for adolescents: An overview

D'Souza, Stan
402b The data base for studies on women: Sex biases in national data systems

D'Souza, Victor S.
402e Family status and female work participation

Du Bois, Barbara
312h Passionate scholarship: Notes on values, knowing and method in feminist social science

DuBois, Ellen
225b Seeking ecstasy on the battlefield: Danger and pleasure in nineteenth-century feminist sexual thought
379m The limitations of sisterhood: Elizabeth Cady Stanton and division in the American suffrage movement, 1875-1902

duBois, Page
419d Sappho and Helen

DuPlessis, Rachel Blau
132l For the Etruscans: Sexual difference and artistic production - the debate over a female aesthetic

Dubé, Janet
215g Two poems
215r Poem

Duben, Alan
270b The significance of family and kinship in urban Turkey

Duberman, Martin Bauml
439u "I am not contented": Female masochism and lesbianism in early twentieth-century New England

Ducrocq, Franc,oise
379i The London Biblewomen and Nurses Mission, 1857-1880: Class relations/women's relations

Dudley, Carol A.
28d Hypothalamic peptides and sexual behavior

Dudley, Sandra
349e The economics of female criminality: An analysis of police blotters, 1890-1976

Dudovitz, Resa L.
398d Survival in the 'master's house': The role of graduate teaching assistants in effecting curriculum change

Duelli-Klein, Renate
125j Hedwig Dohm: Passionate theorist
310y Doing it ourselves: Self insemination
311e How to do what we want to do: Thoughts about feminist methodology
311f Selected annotated bibliography of articles on theories of women's studies
312a Introduction: Theories of women's studies and the autonomy/integration debate
312g How to do what we want to do: Thoughts about feminist methodology
312o Selected annotated bibliography of articles on theories of women's studies

Duff, Jean F.
447e Changing roles and mental health in women

Duffié, Nikki N.
404g Reaching the middle class female

Duggan, Lisa
60e The social enforcement of heterosexuality and lesbian resistance in the 1920's

Duiker, William J.
113e Vietnam: War of insurgency

Dukakis, Michael
209bb Building new partnerships in a high-tech economy

Dulac, Liliane
22i Un écrit militant de Christine de Pizan: *Le Ditié de Jehanne d'Arc*

Duley-Morrow, Margot
124n The ERA campaign: Reflections on interpretation and practice

Dumas, Rhetaugh Graves
38m Dilemmas of black females in leadership

Dumoulin, John
192g Toward a science of women's liberation

Duncan, Carol
117l Happy mothers and other new ideas in eighteenth-century French art

117p Virility and domination in early twentieth-century vanguard painting

Duncan, Erika
180s The hungry Jewish mother
211c The hungry Jewish mother

Duncan, Greg J.
272h Work experience, job segregation, and wages

Dunlap, Mary
316n Resistance to the women's movement in the United States: The ERA controversy as prototype

Dunn, Mary Maples
19n Saints and sisters

Dunnette, Marvin d.
425g Estimating benefits and costs of antisexist training programs in organizations

Dunstan, John
151f Soviet boarding education: Its rise and progress

Duran, Jane
116c Nurture theories: A critique
275j Gender-neutral terms

Durell, Anna
235a At home

Durka, Gloria
91n Is partnership possible? Ordained men and unordained women in ministry

Durlay, Maureen Slattery
154b The crowned dame, dame opinion, and dame philosophy: the female characteristics of three ideals in Christine de Pizan's *L'Avision Christine*

Durslag, Ivy
441j Teaching women and technology at the University of Washington

Dutton, Donald G.
111e Social-psychological research and relevant speculation on the issue of domestic violence

Dweck, Carol S.
259f Sex differences in achievement orientations: Consequences for academic choices and attainments

Dwyer, Carol A.
265c The role of schools in developing sex role attitudes

Dwyer, Cynthia Brown
368o Women imprisoned in the kingdom of the Mullahs

Dwyer, Ellen
268b A historical perspective
376d The weaker vessel: Legal versus social reality in mental commitments in nineteenth-century New York

Dye, Nancy Schrom
353w Mary Breckinridge, the frontier nursing service, and the introduction of nurse-midwifery in the United States

Dyer, Richard
406f Resistance through charisma: Rita Hayworth and Gilda

Dyke, Jane Van
394e Graduate women assess the campus

Dyrenforth, Sue R.
341c A woman's body in a man's world: A review of findings on body image and weight control

Dyrenfurth, Inge
51v Endocrine functions in the woman's second half of life
190b Endocrine aspects of menarche and menopause - milestones in the woman's life cycle

Eaker, Elaine D.
53c The effect of employment, family and job stress on coronary heart disease patterns in women

Eashwar, Sucharita
161b Press coverage of women and women's concerns

Ebanks, G. E.
421s Labor force participation and fertility, contraceptive knowledge, attitude and practice of the women of Barbados

Ebbutt, Dave
193h Science options in a girls' grammar school
193o Girls' science: Boys' science revisited

Ebling, John L.
281b The sexual self and fertility

Ebrey, Patricia
401g Women in the kinship system of the Southern Song upper class

Eccles, Sandra
321f Women in the Australian labour force

Echohawk, Marlene
461d Sexual consequences of acculturation of American Indian women

Echols, Alice
225c The taming of the id: Feminist sexual politics, 1968-83
231dd The new feminism of yin and yang

Eckland, Bruce K.
320o Family formation and educational attainment

Ecklein, Joan
423e Women in the German Democratic Republic: Impact of culture and social policy

Eddings, Barbara Murray
358a Women in broadcasting (U.S.) *de jure, de facto*

Eddy, Cristen C.
11d The effects of alcohol on anxiety in problem and nonproblem drinking women
11h Fetal alcohol syndrome and drinking during pregnancy

Eddy, Darlene Mathis
186p The sculptor and the rock: Some uses of myth in the poetry of May Sarton

Eddy de Arellano, Bambi
172i Integrating women into rural cooperatives: Pluses and minuses (Bolivia)

Edelman, Marian Wright
37t An advocacy agenda for black families and children

Edelson, Mary Beth
229dd See for yourself: Women's spirituality in holistic art
254n The whole thing: In search of relevance and integration made dynamic by creativity
453f Goddess imagery in ritual

Edholm, Felicity
50k The unnatural family

Edinburg, Golda M.
69k Women and aging

Edkins, Carol
452c Quest for community: Spiritual autobiographies of eighteenth-century Quaker and Puritan women in America

Edlund, Ingrid E.
389j Gisela Marie Augusta Richter (1882-1972): Scholar of classical art and museum archaeologist

Edmondson, Linda
95d Sylvia Pankhurst: Suffragist, feminist, or socialist?

Edmunds, Marianna
18g Population dynamics and migrant labor in South Africa

Edson, Sakre K.
90j "If they can, I can": Women aspirants to administrative positions in public schools

Eduards, Maud
228i Sweden

Edwards, Kathryn
122c Seeking feminist transformation of the sciences and the teaching of science

Edwards, Laura E.
309y Adolescent pregnancy prevention services in high school clinics
460t Self-help in gynecological practice

Edwards, Maureen
79n Neonatology: Directions and goals

Edwards, Meredith
321j The distribution of income within households

Edwards, Richard C.
89j A theory of labor market segmentation

Edwards, Solomon
40r Affirmation in the works of Mari Evans

Egan, Carolyn
323y Building links: Labour and the women's movement

Egan, Jeannie Nungarrayi
333p The Yuendumu aboriginal cultural preschool

Egnor, Margaret
232a On the meaning of sakti to women in Tamil Nadu

Ehlers, Tracy Bachrach
82t The female family business: A Guatemalan example

Ehman, Robert
223x Adult-child sex

Ehrenreich, Barbara
129y Women and the rise of the American medical profession

Ehrensaft, Diane
195c When women and men mother
283a When women and men mother

Ehrlich, Carol
369f The unhappy marriage of Marxism and feminism: Can it be saved?

Ehrlich, Larry G.
133k The pathogenic secret

Eiben, O. G.
107l Physique of female athletes - anthropological and proportional analysis

Eichenbaum, Luise
443d Feminist psychoanalysis: Theory and practice

Eichler, Margrit
52u The industrialization of housework
220i Women, families and the state
220k Strategies for the eighties

Eickmeier, Janice L.
395j Health beliefs and behaviors of middle class urban women in Lahore, Pakistan

Eiduson, Bernice T.
204k Comparative socialization practices in traditional and alternative families

Eisen, David
209z A union perspective on health hazards of VDTs

Eisenberg, Nora
202l Virginia Woolf's last words on words: *Between the Acts* and 'Anon'

Eisenstein, Hester
321m Comment: Women's movement and social justice

Eisenstein, Talia
277j Current approaches in sex therapy

Eisenstein, Zillah
60g Antifeminism and the New Right
103b The state, the patriarchal family, and working mothers
369n Reform and/or revolution: Towards a unified women's movement

Eisinger, Erica
64i *The Vagabond*: A vision of androgyny

Eisler, Colin
389f Lady Dilke (1840-1904): The six lives of an art historian

Eitel, Ludwig
260h Equal opportunity policies for women in the Federal Republic of Germany

Ekstein, Rudolph
460o Daughters and lovers: Reflections on the life cycle of father-daughter relationships

Ekstrom, Susan Cope
36r A report on birth in three cultures

El Ashmawi, A. W.
159j Female criminality in Egypt

Elbourne, Diana
233u Future research on work in pregnancy

Elbow, Gary S.
82m Participation by women in Guatemalan cooperatives

el-Daeiff, Syeda Greiss
198i Female education in Egypt: Changing attitudes over a span of 100 years

Elder, Joann
337k Women on the academic staff

Eldredge, Yoshie Akimoto
42o The stewardship of talents

Elemendorf, Mary
395e Water and sanitation-related health constraints on women's contribution to the economic development of communities

Elias, Peter
467b Employment prospects and equal opportunity

Elias-Button, Karen
180p The muse as Medusa

Elkin, Larry
185k The work/family connection in the year 2020

Elkins, Sharon K.
187h All ages, every condition, and both sexes: The emergence of a Gilbertine identity

Elliott, Gary L.
204j Social development and parent-child interaction in father-custody and stepmother families

Elliott, Shirley
456n Cystitis

Ellis, Albert
285t How to stubbornly refuse to disturb oneself emotionally about anything - even about death, dying and sexual mutilation

Elliston, Frederick
223h Gay marriage

Ellovich, Risa S.
473d Dioula women in town: A view of intra-ethnic variation (Ivory Coast)

Ellsworth, Cheryl
434n Toward a feminist model for planning for and with women

Ellyson, Steve L.
136d Visual behavior and dominance in women and men

Elmendorf, Mary
373j Changing role of Maya mothers and daughters

Elmhirst, Susanna Isaacs
460h The early stages of female psychosexual development: A Kleinian view

Elshtain, Jean Bethke
3c Reflections on abortion, values, and the family
3h Commentary to chapter 5 (chapter g)
103r Antigone's daughters: Reflections on female identity and the state
106a Introduction: Toward a theory of the family and politics
106c Aristotle, the public-private split, and the case of the suffragists
106n "Thank heaven for little girls": The dialectics of development
129e Antigone's daughters

Elson, Diane
206a Nimble fingers and other fables

206f Woman worker/working woman
207i The subordination of women and the internationalisation of factory production
208c The subordination of women and the internationalisation of factory production

Elster, Ellen
179b Patriarchy - A working definition

Elston, Mary Ann
44e Medicine
189m Medicine as 'old husbands' tales': The impact of feminism

Elston, Robert C.
141c Statistical model for the study of familial breast cancer

Elwert, Georg
153q Conflicts inside and outside the household: A West African case study

Embrey, M. P.
252m Prostaglandin therapy for second trimester abortion: An overview of current status and recent trends

Eme, Robert F.
268l Sex-related differences in the epidemiology of child psychopathology

Emerson, Sandra
307w Bambi meets Godzilla: Life in the corporate jungle

Emery, Lynne
147aa The first intercollegiate contest for women: Basketball, April 4, 1896

Emmot, Shelagh
271h Assertiveness training for improved conflict resolution style

Endicott, Jean
28l Classification of premenstrual syndromes

Eng, Khoo Hoon
183g Hazards faced by women at work

Engel, Barbara Alpern
405c Women revolutionaries: The personal and the political

Engelberg, Laurie
78u Women in a male-dominated profession: The women lawyers

England, Paula
65b Socioeconomic explanations of job segregation

English, Deirdre
129y Women and the rise of the American medical profession
220j Romantic love and reproductive rights
231hh The fear that feminism will free men first

English, E. B.
372d Women and sport during the Renaissance

English, Jane
116o Sex equality in sports

Engracia, Luisa
424o Employment structure of female migrants to the cities in the Philippines

Engram, Eleanor
38k Role transition in early adulthood: Orientations of young black women

Enloe, Cynthia
179d The military model

179h NATO: What is it and why should women care?

179j NATO: The lesson machine

206k Racism at work

206q We are what we wear - The dilemma of the feminist consumer

218f Women textile workers in the militarization of southeast Asia

428q Women textile workers in the militarization of Southeast Asia

Ennen, Gisela

179i Nuclear Europe

Entine, Alan D.

221e Voluntary mid-life career change: Family effects

Epps, A. Cherrie

361k Strategies to increase participation of minorities in medicine

Epstein, Barbara

231e Family, sexual morality, and popular movements in turn-of-the-century America

387g Industrialization and femininity: A case study of nineteenth-century New England

Epstein, Cynthia Fuchs

123i Women in sociological analysis: New scholarship versus old paradigms

375l Women's entry into corporate law firms

Epstein, Rachel

323o Domestic workers: The experience in B.C.

Epstein, T. Scarlett

92a An action-oriented study of the role of women in rural development

92h Rural women and their multiple roles

459f A social anthropological approach to women's roles and status in developing countries: The domestic cycle

Erhart, Robin

79e DES and drugs in pregnancy: A consumer reaction

Erickson, J. David

233f Birth defects and parental occupation

Erickson, Nancy S.

375h Historical background of "protective" labor legislation: *Muller v. Oregon*

Erie, Steven P.

103e Women and the Reagan revolution: Thermidor for the social welfare economy

Erikson, Kai T.

19i Wayward Puritans

Erkut, Sumru

270d Dualism in values toward education of Turkish women

320h Social psychology looks at but does not see the undergraduate woman

Ermarth, Elizabeth

242a Fictional consensus and female casualties

Ernest, John

377c Is mathematics a sexist discipline?

Ernst, Elise

326g Group work with preadolescent sexual assault victims

Ernst, Shirley B.

265e Language and attitudes toward masculine and feminine sex role

Ernster, Virginia L.

53n Risk factors for benign and malignant breast disease

Ervin, Cynthia H.

10f Alcohol use and reproduction

Eskin, Bernard A.

277d Mechanisms of sexual arousal in females

277i Current approaches in endocrinology

Espin, Oliva M.

225i Cultural and historical influences on sexuality in Hispanic/Latin women: Implications for psychotherapy

Espin, Vilma

374a The early years

Estabrook, Leigh S.

199i Women's work in the library/information sector

Estioko-Griffin, Agnes

340c Woman the hunter: The Agta

Etaugh, Claire

221b Effects of maternal employment on children: Implications for the family therapist

Etienne, Mona

347i Women and men, cloth and colonization: The transformation of production-distribution relations among the Baule (Ivory Coast)

Ettinger, Amelia Diaz

301j My Aunt Isadora (fiction)

Ettorre, Betsy

212p The 'perks' of male power: Heterosexuality and the oppression of women

Etzioni-Halevy, Eva

421x Occupational choice among female academicians - The Israeli case

Evans, Annette

313i The fiction of family: Ideology and narrative in Elsa Morante

Evans, Jerome R.

309x Teenagers: Fertility control behavior and attitudes before and after abortion, childbearing or negative pregnancy test

Evans, Judith

228b USA

Evans, Mari

40p My father's passage

Evans, Mary

125u Simone de Beauvoir: Dilemmas of a feminist radical

312n In praise of theory: The case for women's studies

Evans, Raymond

294c 'Soiled doves': Prostitution in colonial Queensland

Evans, Richard J.

144i Politics and the family: Social democracy and the working-class family in theory and practice before 1914

Evans, Sara

301kk Women's consciousness and the southern black

Evans, Terry

138l Gender, class and education: A teaching bibliography of Australian and New Zealand studies

Evans, V. Jeffery

273h Legal aspects of prenatal sex selection

Everett, Jana

386i Women and political leadership

386j Women in law and administration

Evers, Hans-Dieter

153b Subsistence reproduction: A framework for analysis

Eviota, Elizabeth U.

420i The migration of women in the Philippines

Ewens, Mary

366c The leadership of nuns in immigrant Catholicism

Eysenck, Ans J.

137l Gender, genes, and psychopathology

Eysenck, H. J.

230m Afterword: Sex, violence, and the media: Where do we stand now?

Faderman, Lillian

176q Who hid lesbian history?

Fairchilds, Cissie

130e Women and family

184i Female sexual attitudes and the rise of illegitimacy: A case study

184k A reply

Faith, Karlene

176aa Love between women in prison

Falbo, Toni

239g A social psychological model of human sexuality

Falk, James R.

190x Primary and secondary amenorrhea in anorexia nervosa

Falk, Nancy Auer

325n The case of the vanishing nuns: The fruits of ambivalence in ancient Indian Buddhism

FallCreek, Stephanie

434e Older women as victims of violence

Fantini, Mario D.

216a Introduction: Parenting in contemporary society

216o The parent as educator: A home-school model of socialization

216t Parenting in a pluralistic society: Toward a policy of options and choices

Fapohunda, Eleanor R.

385m The child-care dilemma of working mothers in African cities: The case of Lagos, Nigeria

Faraday, Annabel

212c 'On the other side of the billboard...': Pornography, male fantasies and the objectification of women

Faragher, Johnny
454m Women and their families on the Overland Trail, 1842-1867

Farah, Barbara
378m Gender, levels of political thinking and political action

Farber, Bernard
427i Conceptions of kinship and the family reproduction cycle

Farber, Ellen A.
80e Developmental consequences of out-of-home care for infants in a low-income population

Faris, Wendy B.
329d The squirrel's heart beat and the death of a moth

Farley, G. A.
8c Women and violence

Farley, Jennie
288b Worklife problems for both women and men

Farley, Pamella
132s Lesbianism and the social function of taboo

Farley, Tucker
417x Realities and fictions: Lesbian visions of utopia

Farmer, Catherine D.
384m Beret as the Norse mythological goddess Freya/Gurthr

Farnsworth, Beatrice Brodsky
444f Communist feminism: Its synthesis and demise

Farrell, Warren
185h The evolution of sex roles: The transformation of masculine and feminine values

Fasting, K.
107d The influence of the traditional sex roles on women's participation and engagement in sport

Faucher, Mary D.
288i Sexual harassment in the workplace — What should the employer do?

Faue, Elizabeth
263d "Blessed be the tie that binds": YWCA extension work among industrial women, Minneapolis, 1900-1910

Faulkner, Audrey
455d Aging and old age: The last sexist rip-off

Faulkner, Wendy
12g The obsessive orgasm: Science, sex and female sexuality
441d Women and microelectronics: The case of word processors

Fava, Sylvia F.
203g Women's place in the new suburbia
243h Family, work, and individual development in dual-career marriages: Issues for research

Fawcett, James T.
420a Urbanization, migration and the status of women

Féral, Josette
132f The powers of difference

Federici, Silvia
227q Wages against housework

Fedorova, M.
446g The utilization of female labor in agriculture

Fee, Elizabeth
342b Women's nature and scientific objectivity
354a Women and health care: A comparison of theories
439r *The Hosken Report: Genital and Sexual Mutilation of Females* by Fran P. Hosken

Fehr, B. J.
136d Visual behavior and dominance in women and men

Fehr, Kevin O'Brien
9q The effects of opiates, sedative-hypnotics, amphetamines, cannabis, and other psychoactive drugs on the fetus and newborn

Feigenbaum, Elliot
11k Marital therapy of women alcoholics

Fein, Edith
146m Evaluation of child-sexual-abuse programs

Feingold, Ellen B.
463y Speech

Feinman, Clarice
78g Sex role stereotypes and justice for women
349u Sex-role stereotypes and justice for women

Feld, Ellen
178m The challenge of coping

Feldberg, Roslyn L.
181d Technology and work degradation: Effects of office automation on women clerical workers
209m New technology and its implications in U.S. clerical work
344q Clerical work: The female occupation
378a Male and female: Job versus gender models in the sociology of work
387e Male and female: Job versus gender models in the sociology of work
387q Degraded and deskilled: The proletarianization of clerical work

Feldman, Shelley
98n Methodological interventions in programme assessment and evaluation research
400e Population planning and rural women's co-operative in IRDP women's programme: Some critical issues
433b Conditions influencing rural and town women's participation in the labor force

Felstein, Ivor
289k Dysfunction: Origins and therapeutic approaches

Fennell, Janice C.
302h The woman academic-library administrator: A career profile

Fennema, Elizabeth
259k Success in mathematics
351f Girls, women, and mathematics
377e Sex-related differences in mathematics achievement: Where and why

Fenster, Carol
165i Female delinquents in a suburban court

Fenster, Valmai
337c Women's contributions to the library school

Fenwick, Penny
413d Fertility, sexuality and social control in New Zealand

Ferber, Marianne A.
189i The oldest, the most established, the most quantitative of the social sciences - and most dominated by men; The impact of feminism on economics

Ferdows, Adele K.
368c Women in Shi'i Fiqh: Images through the Hadith

Ferdows, Amir H.
368c Women in Shi'i Fiqh: Images through the Hadith

Fergus, Jan S.
164e Sex and social life in Jane Austen's novels

Ferguson, Ann
195j On conceiving motherhood and sexuality: A feminist materialist approach
369m The unhappy marriage of patriarchy and capitalism

Ferguson, John P.
194n The Great Goddess today in Burma and Thailand: An exploration of her symbolic relevance to monastic and female roles

Ferguson, Mary Anne
102n "No more squeezing into one"
332k The female novel of development and the myth of psyche
450f Lisa Alther: The irony of return?

Ferin, Michel
28b The neuroendocrinologic control of the menstrual cycle

Fernández Olmos, Margarite
74g From a woman's perspective: The short stories of Rosario Ferré and Ana Lydia Vega

Fernández Padilla, Oscar
374f Appendix A: Maternity law for working women

Fernández-Kelly, María Patricia
428i Mexican border industrialization, female labor force participation, and migration

Fernando, Chitra
91f The role of the church in the oppression of women

Fernbach, David
224l Towards a Marxist theory of gay liberation
283m The impasse facing CND

Ferrante, Joan M.
33a The education of women in the Middle Ages in theory, fact, and fantasy
188c The French courtly poet: Marie de France

Ferree, Myra Marx
103h Housework: Rethinking the costs and benefits
199c Sacrifice, satisfaction, and social change: Employment and the family
355e Satisfaction with housework: The social context

Ferrence, Roberta G.
9c Sex differences in the prevalence of problem drinking
9d Sex differences in psychoactive drug use: Recent epidemiology
10n Prevention of alcohol problems in women

Ferris, E.
107b Attitudes to women in sport: Preface towards a sociological theory
372a Women and sport: A question of freedom

Festa-McCormick, Diana
135p Emma Bovary's masculinization: Convention of clothes and morality of conventions

Fett, Ione
466d Land ownership in Negri Sembilan, 1900-1977

Fetterley, Judith
127c "The temptation to be a beautiful object": Double standard and double bind in *The House of Mirth*

Feuerwerker, Yi-Tsi Mei
30b In quest of Ding Ling (In quest of myself)

Feyerherm, William
349f Gender differences in delinquency: Quantity and quality

Ficher, Ilda V.
277j Current approaches in sex therapy

Ficher, Miguel
277k Study of sexual dysfunction among male diabetics

Fidell, Linda S.
137j Gender and drug use and abuse
268p Sex roles in medicine

Fidler, Merrie A.
147hh The establishment of softball for American women, 1900-1940
147oo The All-American Girls' Baseball League, 1943-1954
147pp A historical perspective of women's membership in selected national sports organizations

Field, Debbie
305r Rosie the Riveter meets the sexual division of labour
323i Coercion or male culture: A new look at co-worker harassment
323t The dilemma facing women's committees

Fielding, Dorothy
240k Psychological aspects of the menstruum and premenstruum

Figlio, Karl
354j Chlorosis and chronic disease in 19th-century Britain: The social constitution of somatic illness in a capitalist society

Fillmore, Kaye Middleton
10a "When angels fall": Women's drinking as cultural preoccupation and as reality

Fillmore, Lily Wong
71j The early socialization of Asian-American female children

Fimbres, Martha Molina
434h The Chicana in transition

Finch, Janet
170h Natural selection: Perspectives on entitlement to the invalid care allowance
241h Dividing the rough and the respectable: Working-class women and pre-school playgroups
297d 'It's great to have someone to talk to': The ethics and politics of interviewing women

Fine, Paul
326e Network aspects of treatment for incestuously abused children

Finger, Anne
310s Claiming all of our bodies: Reproductive rights and disabilities

Fink, Beatrice
27d Ambivalence in the Gynogram: Sade's utopian woman

Fink, Deborah
263g "Mom, it's a losing proposition": The decline of women's subsistence production on Iowa farms

Fink, Paul J.
277a Psychological causes of lack of arousal

Finkel, David J.
279f Sexual dimorphism and settlement pattern in Middle Eastern skeletal populations
309u Sexual and contraceptive knowledge, attitudes and behavior of male adolescents

Finkel, Madelon Lubin
309u Sexual and contraceptive knowledge, attitudes and behavior of male adolescents

Finkelstein, Norma
404p Innovative alcoholism programs for women

Finkle, Alex
289j Research: Status, gaps, and design

Finn, Geraldine
120g On the oppression of women in philosophy — or, Whatever happened to objectivity?

Finn, Stephen
268m Sex-role stereotypes and the development of eating disorders

Finnegan, Loretta P.
9q The effects of opiates, sedative-hypnotics, amphetamines, cannabis, and other psychoactive drugs on the fetus and newborn

Finnell, Robert A.
361d Improving minority preparation for math-based disciplines

Fiorenza, Elisabeth Schüssler
59b Emerging issues in feminist biblical interpretation
462v Claiming the center: A critical feminist theology of liberation

Firestone, Shulamith
223a Love: A feminist critique
227j The dialectic of sex

Fischer, Clare B.
59f Liberating work

Fischer-Hjalmars, Inga
438h Women scientists in Sweden

Fischli, Ronald D.
133x Religious fundamentalism and the democratic process

Fisek, Güler Okman
270l Psychopathology and the Turkish family: A family systems theory analysis

Fish, Margaret
87d Young marrieds: Wives' employment and family role structure

Fishbein, Leslie
238h Harlot or heroine? Changing views of prostitution, 1870-1920

Fishburn, Katherine
180q The nightmare repetition: The mother-daughter conflict in Doris Lessing's *Children of Violence*

Fisher, Elizabeth A.
419m Theodora and Antonina in the *Historia Arcana*: History and/or fiction?

Fisher, Joan Z.
359gg Postmastectomy counseling

Fisher, Susan M.
8g Juvenile delinquency in girls

Fisher, William
24b Social background, attitudes and sexual attraction
48m Gender, gender-role identification, and response to erotica

Fisher-Manick, Beverly
43n Race and class: Beyond personal politics
43r Put your money where your movement is

Fishkin, Ralph E.
277g The multidisciplinary approach to the diagnosis and treatment of male sexual dysfunction

Fishman, Jack
141g Hormones, genetics, and breast cancer

Fishman, Pamela M.
171f Interaction: The work women do
387o Interaction: The work women do

Fitzgerald, R. William
348g The myth of rising female crime

Fitzgerald, Robert
451i Introduction to *Everything That Rises Must Converge*

Fitzpatrick, Joseph P.
216i The Puerto Rican family: Its role in cultural transition

Fitzpatrick, Mary Anne
415f Effective interpersonal communication for women of the corporation: Think like a man, talk like a lady

Flammang, C. J.
284o Interviewing child victims of sex offenders

Flammang, Janet A.
226d Filling the party vacuum: Women at the grassroots level in local politics

Flanagan, Owen J.
116d Freud: Masculinity, femininity, and the philosophy of mind

Flanders, Jane
126i The fallen woman in fiction

Flandrin, Jean-Louis
184j A case of naiveté in the use of statistics

Flax, Jane
43p   Do feminists need Marxism?
84n   Political philosophy and the patriarchal unconscious: A psychoanalytic perspective on epistemology and metaphysics
103a Contemporary American families: Decline or transformation?
106k The family in contemporary feminist thought: A critical review
132c Mother-daughter relationships: Psychodynamics, politics, and philosophy
359d The conflict between nurturance and autonomy in mother-daughter relationships and within feminism

Fleenor, Juliann E.
109n The gothic prism: Charlotte Perkins Gilman's gothic stories and her autobiography

Fleischmann, Fritz
17a   Charles Brockden Brown: Feminism in fiction

Fleishman, Avrom
330d Forms of the Woolfian short story

Fleishman, Jane
86c   The health hazards of office work

Fleming, Jacqueline
45l   Sex differences in the educational and occupational goals of black college students: Continued inquiry into the black matriarchy theory
320j Sex differences in the impact of college environments on black students

Fletcher, John C.
273j Ethics and public policy: Should sex choice be discouraged?

Fletcher, Winona L.
399oo Who put the "Tragic" in the Tragic Mulatto?

Flieger, Verlyn
383f Wright's *Islandia*: Utopia with problems

Flint, Marcha
51y   Male and female menopause: A cultural put-on

Flitcraft, Anne
354i Medicine and patriarchal violence: The social construction of a "private" event

Flora, Cornelia Butler
363e Social policy and women in Latin America: The need for a new model

Flora, Joseph M.
445l Westering and woman: A thematic study of Kesey's *One Flew Over the Cuckoo's Nest* and Fisher's *Mountain Man*

Flowers, Betty S.
313b The "I" in Adrienne Rich: Individuation and the androgyne archetype

Fluehr-Lobban, Carolyn
198k Lessons from fieldwork in the Sudan
403h The political mobilization of women in the Arab world

Flynn, Edith Elisabeth
165m Women as criminal justice professionals: A challenge to change tradition

Flynn, Gerard
112h Sor Juana Inés de la Cruz: Mexico's tenth muse (Mexican, 1651-1695)

Foa, Sandra M.
112d María de Zayas y Sotomayor: Sibyl of Madrid (Spanish, 1590?-1661?)

Fodor, Iris Goldstein
29n   Weight disorders: Overweight and anorexia
137h Gender and phobia
443g Strategies for dealing with sex-role stereotypes

Foerstel, Lenora
83b   Women, art and community in Papua New Guinea

Foged, Brita
382a Denmark

Fogel, David
404t In the pursuit of justice in sentencing and prison

Foglia, Gina
229rr Spiritual dimensions of feminist antinuclear activism

Folbre, Nancy
369m The unhappy marriage of patriarchy and capitalism

Foley, Helene P.
419b "Reverse similes" and sex roles in *The Odyssey*

Foley, Lisa
215l Alternative defence: The search for nonnuclear alternatives

Fonda, Nickie
467d Statutory maternity leave in the United Kingdom: A case study
467g The future prospect

Fong, Pauline L.
71k   Economic and employment status of Asian-Pacific women

Fontaine, Coralyn
176j Teaching the psychology of women: A lesbian feminist perspective

Foo, Benedicte
182h House and home

Fooden, Myra
253j Women's mental health

Foot, Philippa
2i   Killing and letting die

Forbes, Dinah
323z Women, work and unions: A cineography

Forbes, Geraldine
101c The Indian women's movement: A struggle for women's rights or national liberation?
255h From purdah to politics: The social feminism of the all-India women's organizations
433a Goddesses or rebels: The women revolutionaries of Bengal

Forbush, Janet Bell
308f Adolescent parent programs and family involvement

Ford, Clara D.
301l Mill village (poem)

Ford, Hugh D.
442h Publishing in Paris

Ford, Kimberly
42l   Gospel principles and women

Foreyt, John P.
29i   Health maintenance: Exercise and nutrition
137p Gender and obesity

Forisha, Barbara L.
214a The inside and the outsider: Women in organizations
214j The battle of the sexes: Power and sexual aggressiveness
214r Dual-career families: Intimacy or productivity?
214u Conclusion: Integrating love and power

Forman, Charles W.
246h "Sing to the Lord a New Song": Women in the churches of Oceania

Formanek, Ruth
88a   On the origins of gender identity

Fortmann, Louise
373m The plight of the invisible farmer: The effect of national agricultural policy on women in Africa
385i Women's work in a communal setting: The Tanzanian policy of Ujamaaunder

Fortunata, Jacqueline
275f Lakoff on language and women

Foster, Ann
233r What can be done in antenatal care?

Foster, Frances Smith
108i Neither auction block nor pedestal: *The life and Religious Experience of Jaren Lee, a Coloured Lady*

Foster, Janet
248i Archives and the history of nursing

Fout, John C.
145a Current research on German women's history in the nineteenth century
145o The woman's role in the German working-class family in the 1890s from the perspective of women's autobiographies
145r An English-language bibliography on European and American women's history

Fowler, Sigrid H.
186o A note on May Sarton's use of form

Fowlkes, Diane L.
126a The genesis of feminist visions for transforming the liberal arts curriculum
126c Women knowing: Feminist theory and perspectives on pedagogy
226c Conceptions of the "political": White activists in Atlanta

Fowlkes, Martha R.
243g Katie's place: Women's work, professional work, and social reform
439o Social and behavioral constructions of female sexuality

Fox, Alice
328c Virginia liked Elizabeth

329m 'What right have I, a woman?': Viriginia Woolf's reading notes on Sidney and Spenser

Fox, Bonnie
149d Women's double work day: Twentieth-century changes in the reproduction of daily life

Fox, Brenda
44d Dentistry

Fox, Greer Litton
308b The family's role in adolescent sexual behavior

Fox, Lynn H.
377f Sex differences in the development of precocious mathematical talent
377i An accelerative intervention program for mathematically gifted girls
377j Career interests and career education: A key to change
377k Conclusions: What do we know and where should we go?

Fox, Mary Frank
344l Women and higher education: Sex differentials in the status of students and scholars

Fox-Genovese, Elizabeth
130f Women and work

Frager, Ruth
323c No proper deal: Women workers and the Canadian labour movement, 1870-1940

France, Rachel
399v Apropos of women and the folk play

Francis, Sue
182e Housing the family

Francoeur, Robert T.
185e Transformations in human reproduction
185j Moral concepts in the year 2020: The individual, the family, and society
285a The impact of sexuality, professional authoritarianism, and health crises on rehabilitation

Frank, Charles E.
186c May Sarton: Approaches to autobiography

Frank, Ellen
29j Physical aggression: Treating the victims

Frank, Miriam
32j Ricarda Huch: Myth and reality

Frankel, Judith
427e Gender inequities in childhood social life and adult work life

Frankel, Linda
199b Southern textile women: Generations of survival and struggle

Frankenberg, Ronald
297e Incidence or incidents: Political and methodological underpinnings of a health research process in a small Italian town

Franklin, Anna
205b When you don't know the language, listen to the silence: An historical overview of native Indian women in BC

Franklin, Urusla Martius
168f Will women change technology or will technology change women?

Franks, Violet
304a Introduction: Warning! Sex-role stereotypes may be hazardous to your health
304l Concluding comments, criticism, and caution: Consistent conservatism or constructive change?

Franz, Wolfgang
380o Economic aspects of female labor force participation in the Federal Republic of Germany

Franzoi, Barbara
145m Domestic industry: Work options and women's choices

Fras, Ivan
280j Fire setting (pyromania) and its relationship to sexuality

Fraser, Brian G.
291e Sexual child abuse: The legislation and the law in the United States

Fraser, Judy
359u The female alcoholic

Frazier, William
354i Medicine and patriarchal violence: The social construction of a "private" event

Frederickson, Mary
292c Citizens for Democracy: The industrial programs of the YWCA
292e Recognizing regional differences: The southern summer school for women workers
412s Shaping a new society: Methodist women and industrial reform in the south, 1880-1940

Frederiksen, Elke
32g German women writers in the nineteenth century: Where are they?

Fredricks, Shirley
95f Feminism: The essential ingredient in Federica Montseny's anarchist theory

Freedman, Estelle
81a The new woman: Changing views of women in the 1920s
176p Resources for lesbian history
376f Nineteenth-century women's prison reform and its legacy

Freedman, Michael
352b Prophets, chiefs, commissioners, and queens: The moral and institutional context of leadership

Freedman, Ralph
330a Introduction: Virginia Woolf, the novel, and a chorus of voices
330g The form of fact and fiction: *Jacob's Room* as paradigm

Freedman, Victoria H.
253b Update on genetics

Freeman, Alexa
43x Building feminist organizations

Freeman, Bonnie Cook
337m Socio-economic profile of faculty women at Madison
394a The women's movement and the university

Freeman, Caroline
227m When is a wage not a wage?

470h The 'understanding' employer

Freeman, James M.
325h The ladies of Lord Krishna: Rituals of middle-aged women in eastern India

Freeman, Jo
344ee The women's liberation movement: Its origins, structure, activities, and ideas
344u Women, law, and public policy
344y The sexual politics of interpersonal behavior
435c Women and public policy: An overview

Freibert, Lucy M.
383d World views in utopian novels by women

French, Laurence
39s The incarcerated black female: The case of social double jeopardy

Frenier, Mariam Darce
379r The effects of the Chinese Revolution on women and their families

Freud, Anna
291c A psychoanalyst's view of sexual abuse by parents

Freud, Sigmund
50s Female sexuality

Freudenberg, Nicholas
86n From grassroots activism to political power: Women organizing against environmental hazards

Freudenberger, Herbert J.
221g Burnout and job dissatisfaction: Impact on the family
404j The woman in treatment: Evaluation and diagnostic implications

Freudiger, Patricia
41c Sources of life satisfaction: The different worlds of black women and white women

Frevert, Ute
145p The civilizing tendency of hygiene: Working-class women under medical control in Imperial Germany

Frey, Charles
343q "O sacred, shadowy, cold, and constant queen": Shakespeare's imperiled and chastening daughters of romance

Fried, Barbara
34b Boys will be boys will be boys: The language of sex and gender

Frieden, Sandra
32m The left-handed compliment: Perspectives and stereotypes in criticism
332p Shadowing/surfacing/shedding: Contemporary German writers in search of a female *Bildungsroman*

Friedenberg, Lisa
295c Mothering and the young child

Friederich, Mary Anna
51w Aging, menopause, and estrogens: The clinician's dilemma

Friedl, Erika
325k Islam and tribal women in a village in Iran
368l State ideology and village women

Friedman, Adele
306p Public presentation reports

Friedman, Edward H.
313n "Folly and a woman": Galdos' rhetoric of irony in *Tristana*

Friedman, Jean E.
264a Women's history and the revision of southern history
379b Piety and kin: The limits of antebellum Southern women's reform

Friedman, Kathie
153c Households as income-pooling units

Friedman, Richard C.
190y Premenstrual affective syndrome in adolescent and adult psychiatric patients
439k Behavior and the menstrual cycle

Friedman, Rochelle
8k Emotional reactions to miscarriage

Friedman, Scarlet
212a Heterosexuality, couples and parenthood: A 'natural' cycle?
212k Fatherhood: Bringing it all back home

Friedrich-Cofer, Lynette K.
327d Discussion: Television violence and the family

Fries, Maureen
331g The "other" voice: Woman's song, its satire and its transcendence in late medieval British literature

Frieze, Irene Hanson
10i Alcohol use and marital violence: Female and male differences in reactions to alcohol
360l Women and work: Implications for mental health

Frisch, Adam J.
114e Toward new sexual identities: James Tiptree, Jr.

Frisch, Rose E.
190a Fatness, menarche, and fertility

Fritsche, JoAnn M.
314l Moving beyond the curriculum: The 'political' value of an integration strategy

Frost, H. Gordon
175p El Paso madams

Frost, Joyce Hocker
391g The influence of female and male communication styles on conflict strategies: Problem areas

Frouman-Smith, Erica
74e The paradoxes of Silvina Bullrich

Fruzzetti, Lina M.
403f Ritual status of Muslim women in rural India

Frye, Douglas
80k The problem of infant day care

Frye, Marilyn
43i Who wants a piece of the pie?
176bb A lesbian perspective on women's studies
223y Critique
275a Male chauvinism: A conceptual analysis

Fuchs, Fritz
28j Dysmenorrhea and dyspareunia

Fuentes, Max
295o Older women and mental health

Fujii, Sharon M.
71m Elderly Pacific Island and Asian-American women: A framework for understanding

Fuller, Mary
250e Black girls in a London comprehensive school

Fulweiler, Howard
286n "Here a captive heart busted": From Victorian sentimentality to modern sexuality

Furedy, Chris
433d British tradesmen of Calcutta, 1830-1900: A preliminary study of their economic and political roles

Furman, Nelly
356c Textual feminism

Furstenberg, Frank F.
4e Social implications of teenage childbearing
308c Implicating the family: Teenage parenthood and kinship involvement
308j Bringing in the family: Kinship support and contraceptive behavior
309l The social consequences of teenage parenthood
309r Family support: Helping teenage mothers to cope

Fussell, B. H.
330m Woolf's peculiar comic world: *Between the Acts*

Futas, Elizabeth
302m An analysis of the study, "Career paths of male and female librarians in Canada"

GABe, Frances
307i The GABe self-cleaning house

Gabbe, Steven G.
233e Reproductive hazards of the American life style

Gaertner, Karen N.
90l Administrative careers in public school organizations

Gagnon, John H.
190n Age at menarche and sexual conduct in adolescence and young adulthood

Gagnon, Madeleine
120l My body in writing

Gail, Suzanne
227f The housewife

Gailey, Christine Ward
347l Putting down sisters and wives: Tongan women and colonization

Galebach, Stephen H.
2g A human life statute

Galenson, Eleanor
460g Some suggested revisions concerning early female development

Galindo, Antonio Sanchez
111p Prison treatment of female offenders in Mexico

Gallagher, Deirdre
305m Getting organized...in the Canadian Labour Congress

Galler, Roberta
225j The myth of the perfect body

Gallop, Jane
132h Introduction: Psychoanalysis and feminism in France
132j Psychoanalysis in France
356r Snatches of conversation

Galloway, Bruce
235f The police and the courts

Galton, Maurice
193m Differential treatment of boy and girl pupils during science lessons

Gambill, Sue Dove
174q The Women's Writer's Center: An interview with the directors

Gambrill, Eileen D.
96k Assertion training for women

Game, Ann
321e Production and consumption: Public versus private

Gamio, Manuel
192v Señora Flores de Andrade

Gampel, Gwen Victor
379c The planter's wife revisited: Women, equity law, and the Chancery Court in seventeenth-century Maryland

Gangopadhyay, Arati
161e Women and Bengali literature

Gangrade, K. D.
346a Employment of women and child: Battles to fight

Garcia, Felicita
231l I just came out pregnant

García, Frieda
72c The cult of virginity

Garcia, Jo
233u Future research on work in pregnancy

Garcia-Barrio, Constance
301c Pipsissewa, Calamus, and Pennyroyal

Gardiner, Jean
227p Women's domestic labour

Gardiner, Linda
130k Women in science

Gardner, David W.
266f Sampling: Issues and problems in sex role and social change research

Gardner, Deborah S.
201c "A paradise of fashion": A. T. Stewart's department store, 1862-1875

Gardner, Katy
396f Well woman clinics: A positive approach to women's health

Gardner, Kay
453k Female composition

Gardner, Robert W.
420p Female Asian immigrants in Honolulu: Adaptation and success

Garfinkel, Irwin
46e The double-decker alternative for eliminating dependency under social security

Garfinkle, Ellen M.
133j Male homophobia

Garner, Anita Miller
450n The miracle of realism: The bid for self-knowledge in the fiction of Ellen Gilchrist

Garner, Coral Chambers
390d Educated and white-collar women in the 1880s

Garrard, Mary D.
108f Artemisia Gentileschi: The artist's autograph in letters and paintings
117a Introduction: Feminism and art history
117i Artemisia and Susanna

Garret-Fulks, Nikki
304j The resocialization of single-again women

Garrett, Gerald A.
11g Women on skid row

Garrett, Sharon D.
354d Sexism and racism in the American health care industry: A comparative analysis

Garry, Ann
223r Pornography and respect for women

Gartrell, Beverley
160i Colonial wives: Villains or victims?

Gartrell, Nanette
140s Issues in the psychotherapy of lesbians

Gary-Harris, Faye
303j Racial myths and attitudes among white female students at the University of Florida

Gaskill, Gayle
186n Redefinitions of traditional Christian emblems and outlooks in May Sarton's novels of 1970-1975

Gaskin, Ina May
36s Community alternatives to high technology birth

Gathia, J. A.
346b Child workers in the informal sector role of the NGOs: Some reflections

Gatz, Margaret
295o Older women and mental health

Gavin, Susan
78v A century of women in policing

Gay Left Collective
224f Happy families? Paedophilia examined
224h Why Marxism?

Gayle, Addison
40h Gwendolyn Brooks: Poet of the whirlwind

Gearhart, Sally Miller
133u Gay civil rights and the roots of oppression
174a If the mortarboard fits...radical feminism in academia
181j An end to technology: A modest proposal
229s Womanpower: Energy re-sourcement
307bb Female futures in women's science fiction
417ff Future visions: Today's politics: Feminist utopias in review

Gedan, Sharon
359ee Abortion counseling with adolescents

Geis, Bill D.
295e The antecedents and prevention of unwanted pregnancy

Geis, Florence
136c Women and nonverbal leadership cues: When seeing is not believing

Geis, Gilbert
219e Police officer or doctor? Police surgeons' attitudes and opinions about rape

Geis, Robley
219e Police officer or doctor? Police surgeons' attitudes and opinions about rape

Geisler, Peg
394q Continuing education services in the UW system

Geismar, Ludwig L.
421k Feminist egalitarianism, social action orientation and occupational roles: A cross-national study

Gelb, Joyce
103n The politics of wife abuse

Gelfand, Morrie M.
271o Mood and behaviour changes in menopausal women receiving gonadal hormones or placebo

Gelfant, Blanche H.
127d The forgotten reaping-hook: Sex in *My Antonia*
332g Revolutionary turnings: *The Mountain Lion* reread
448n Sister to Faust: The city's "hungry" woman as heroine

Gelinas, Denise J.
359nn Identification and treatment of incest victims

Geller, Janet A.
26b Conjoint therapy for the treatment of domestic violence

Geller, Laura
211r Reactions to a woman Rabbi

Geller, Susan C.
416k Early socialization: Causes and cures of mathematics anxiety

Gelles, Richard J.
105l Physical violence in a nationally representative sample of American families

Geltner, Sharon Ordman
460c Discussion: A historian's approach

Genack, Abraham
8p Research on gender and psychotherapy

Genevay, B.
461h In praise of older women

Genge, Susan
323j Lesbians and gays in the union movement

Genovese, Rosalie G.
243h Family, work, and individual development in dual-career marriages: Issues for research

George, Diana Hume
102e Toward psychoanalytic feminism: The mother in dream-stealing, the father in dreams

George, P. M.
421s Labor force participation and fertility, contraceptive knowledge, attitude and practice of the women of Barbados

George, Yolanda Scott
361f Affirmative action programs that work

Gerber, Ellen W.
147cc The controlled development of collegiate sport for women, 1923-1936

Gergen, Kenneth J.
158l Metatheoretical influences on conceptions of human development

Gerlach-Nielsen, Merete
22j New trends in the Danish women's movement, 1970-1978

Germain, Diane F.
174m Feminist art and education at Califia: My personal experience

Gerner, Debbie J.
198d Roles in transition: The evolving position of women in Arab-Islamic countries

Gerrard, Meg
295e The antecedents and prevention of unwanted pregnancy

Gershman, Harry
280d Sexual permissiveness and its consequences

Gershuny, H. Lee
417u The linguistic transformation of womanhood

Gezari, Janet K.
143e *Romola* and the myth of apocalypse

Ghee, Lim Teck
183b Women, economics and the environment

Ghodse, A. Hamid
345b The physical effects and metabolism of alcohol

Ghosh, Chitra
386h Construction workers

Ghosh, Ratna
421d Social and economic integration of South Asian women in Montreal, Canada
421bb Minority within a minority: On being South Asian and female in Canada

Ghuznari, Ruby
402f Women in Bangladesh: Food-for-work and socioeconomic change

Gianturco, Adriana
463aa Speech

Giarretto, Henry
284l Humanistic treatment of father-daughter incest
291n A comprehensive child sexual abuse treatment program

Gibbens, T. C. N.
159e Female crime in England and Wales
219b Incest and sexual abuse of children

Gibbins, Roger
421j Attitudes and ideology: Correlates of liberal attitudes towards the role of women

Gibbs, Margaret S.
443b The therapist as imposter

Giddings, Paula
40t Nikki Giovanni: Taking a chance on feeling

Gideonse, Sarah
427a Introduction: Government response to working women and their families: Values, the policy-making process, and research utilization

Giele, Janet K.
320p Life after college: Historical links between women's education and women's work

Giele, Janet Zollinger
296k Sources and effects of women's power
423a Women in adulthood: Unanswered questions
423d Women's work and family roles
423f Future research and policy questions

Giese, W. K.
107s Measures of body size and form of elite female basketball players

Giesen, Carol Boellhoff
317d The competent older woman

Gifford, Carolyn De Swarte
366g Women in social reform movements
412q For god and home and native land: the W.C.T.U.'s image of woman in the late nineteenth century

Gil, Rosa Maria
469f Cultural attitudes toward mental illness among Puerto Rican migrant women

Gilbert, Dee
301b Legacy: Memories of our foremothers

Gilbert, Fred I.
190c Age at menarche and year of birth in relation to adult height and weight among Caucasian, Japanese, and Chinese women living in Hawaii

Gilbert, Lucia Albino
221d Understanding dual career families
295a Female development and achievement
365j Feminist therapy

Gilbert, Sandra M.
108b Ceremonies of the alphabet: Female grandmatologies and the female autograph
121b The wayward nun beneath the hill: Emily Dickinson and the mysteries of womanhood

Gilbertson, Marilyn
90q The influence of gender on the verbal interactions among principals and staff members: An exploratory study

Giles, Howard
356j Women's speech: The voice of feminism

Gilkes, Cheryl Townsend
38n "Holding back the ocean with a broom": Black women and community work
60s From slavery to social welfare: Racism and the control of black women

Gill, Brita
429f A ministry of presence

Gillespie, Christine
413e The road ahead for the women's movement - out of the womb and into the world

Gillespie, Diane Filby
27j Virginia Woolf's Miss Latrobe: The artist's last struggle against masculine values

328g Political aesthetics: Virginia Woolf and Dorothy Richardson

Gillespie, Patti P.
399qq Feminist theatre: A rhetorical phenomenon

Gilligan, Carol
45c Do changes in women's rights change women's moral judgements?
132t In a different voice: Women's conceptions of self and of morality
266a New maps of development: New visions of maturity
423c Adult development and women's development: Arrangements for a marriage

Gillis, John R.
256c Servants, sexual relations and the risks of illegitimacy in London, 1801-1900

Gillison, Gillian
200g Images of nature in Gimi thought

Gillman, Linda
135b The looking-glass through Alice

Gilman, Charlotte Perkins
227b The home: Its work and influence

Gilmartin, David
101f Kinship, women, and politics in twentieth-century Punjab

Gimbutas, Marija
229b Women and culture in goddess-oriented old Europe

Gimenez, Martha E.
195q Feminism, pronatalism, and motherhood

Gimeno, Rosalie
408d Women in the *Book of Good Love*

Ginsberg, Elaine
316c Playwrights, poets, and novelists: Sisters under the skin

Ginsburg, Faye
225k The body politic: The defense of sexual restriction by anti-abortion activists

Ginsburg, Ruth Bader
316o Women's right to full participation in shaping society's course: An evolving constitutional precept

Giordano, Peggy C.
349e The economics of female criminality: An analysis of police blotters, 1890-1976

Giovanni, Nikki
40s An answer to some questions on how I write: In three parts

Girandola, R. N.
372u VO2 max and anaerobic threshold in pre- and post- pubescent girls

Giroux, Henry
97e Public education and the discourse of crisis, power and vision

Githens, Marianne
226b Women and state politics: An assessment

Giuliano, Genevieve
307l Getting there: Women and transportation

Givant, Steven
361h Increasing the participation of college women in mathematics-related fields

Gladney, Rose
306l Southern women's literature and culture: Course development and the pedagogical process

Glass, Dorothea D.
277l Sexual arousal responses and disability

Glass, James
106m Kafka and Laing on the trapped consciousness: The family as political life

Glasser, Leah Blatt
301l "She is the one you call sister": Discovering Mary Wilkins Freeman

Glassner, Barry
244k Role loss and manic depression

Glavanis, Kathy R.G.
104a Aspects of non-capitalist social relations in rural Egypt: The small peasant household in an Egyptian delta village

Glazer, Nona
355k Everyone needs three hands: Doing unpaid and paid work
427g Paid and unpaid work: Contradictions in American women's lives today

Gleason, Jean Berko
171j Men's speech to young children

Gleason, Sandra E.
214l The probability of redress: Seeking external support

Gledhill, Christine
247b Developments in feminist film criticism
406a Klute 1: A contemporary film noir and feminist criticism
406h Klute 2: Feminism and Klute

Glendinning, Caroline
170c Employment, women and their disabled children

Glendinning, Chellis
229aa The healing powers of women

Glenn, Audrey
254h Broaching the issue: Homophobia

Glenn, Evelyn Nakano
181d Technology and work degradation: Effects of office automation on women clerical workers
209m New technology and its implications in U.S. clerical work
296g Racial-ethnic women and work: Towards an analysis of race and gender stratification
344q Clerical work: The female occupation
378a Male and female: Job versus gender models in the sociology of work
387e Male and female: Job versus gender models in the sociology of work
387q Degraded and deskilled: The proletarianization of clerical work

Glenn, John D.
133i Gay fantasies in gay publications

Glennon, Theresa
80t Considering proprietary child care

Glick, Ira
28q Oral contraceptives and the menstrual cycle

Glick, Ira D.
11k Marital therapy of women alcoholics

Glick, Paul C.
37f A demographic picture of black families

Glick, Ruth M.
78h National study of women's correctional programs

Glickman, A. S.
49a Charting a course

Gloster, Margherita
206b Restructuring: The cutting edge

Glover, Laurice
88e A suggested developmental sequence for a preoedipal genital phase

Gluck, Sherna
81m Socialist feminism between the two World Wars: Insights from oral history

Glucklich, Pauline
260f The effects of statutory employment policies on women in the United Kingdom labour market

Gnanadason, Aruna
91q Women ... Where are you? Women in the Protestant churches

Go, Rodney C. P.
141c Statistical model for the study of familial breast cancer

Go, Stella P.
420b The migration of women to cities: A comparative perspective

Godwin, Gail
474p Becoming a writer

Gognalons-Nicolet, Maryvonne
210b The crossroads of menopause: A chance and a risk for the aging process of women

Gohlke, Madelon
343i "I wooed thee with my sword": Shakespeare's tragic paradigms

Gold, Ellen B.
53l Epidemiology of pituitary adenomas

Gold, Marji
253h Sexism in gynecologic practices

Gold, Penny Schine
187g Male/female cooperation: The example of fontevrault

Goldberg, Alan
288o Sexual harassment and Title VII: The foundation for the elimination of sexual cooperation as an employment condition

Goldberg, Evelyn L.
53d Health effects of becoming widowed

Goldberg, Harriet
408c Sexual humor in misogynist medieval exampla

Goldberg, Myra
231n Issues and answers

Golden, Joshua
460k Discussion: Another point of view

Golden, Renny
462i White women and racism

Goldenberg, Naomi
229u Feminist witchcraft: Controlling our own inner space

Goldet, Madame Cecile
209dd Women and the fight around office automation

Goldfarb, Lyn
169a Labor education and women workers: An historical perspective
292j Memories of a movement: A conversation

Goldfried, Marvin R.
29m Anxiety-related disorders, fears, and phobias

Goldman, Barbara H.
214c Different is not lesser: Women in science
214i Women, men, and professional writing: Signature of power?
214u Conclusion: Integrating love and power

Goldman, Emma
129dd Patriotism: A menace to liberty

Goldman, Nancy Loring
113a Great Britain and the World Wars

Goldman, Noreen
191b Patterns of diagnoses received by men and women
191c Community surveys: Sex differences in mental illness

Goldsmid, Paula
314r In-house resources

Goldsmith, Elizabeth C.
108g Giving weight to words: Madame de Sévigné's letters to her daughter

Goldstein, Alan J.
365e Anxieties: Agoraphoria and hysteria

Goldstein, Joan
421e Planning for women in the new towns: New concepts and dated roles

Gollan, Daphne
390m The memoirs of 'Cleopatra Sweatfigure'

Golub, Sharon
190aa Implications for women's health and well-being

Gomberg, Edith S. Lisansky
10h Antecedents of alcohol problems in women
404c Learned helplessness, depression, and alcohol problems of women

Gomez, Jewelle L.
150q Cultural legacy denied and discovered: Black lesbians in fiction by women

Gontier, Geneviève
437b France

Gonzales, Sylvia
68m La chicana: Guadalupe or malinche
72i Chicana evolution (poem)
72j La Chicana: An overview

Gonzalez, Maria
469g "La operacion": An analysis of sterilization in a Puerto Rican community in Connecticut

Gonzalez, Nancie L.
416b Professional women in developing nations: The United States and the Third World compared

Gonzalez, Nancie Solien
39v Household and family in the Caribbean: Some definitions and concepts
39cc West Indian characteristics of the black Carib

González, Rosalinda M.
81c Chicanas and Mexican immigrant families 1920-1940: Women's subordination and family exploitation

Good, Barbara J.
102m Women in the U.S. Foreign Service: A quiet revolution

Goodale, Jane C.
200f Gender, sexuality and marriage: A Kaulong model of nature and culture

Goodchilds, Jacqueline D.
48c Becoming sexual in adolescence
230j Sexual signaling and sexual aggression in adolescent relationships

Goode, William J.
245h Why men resist

Goodison, Lucy
257c Really being in love means wanting to live in a different world

Goodman, Bernice
455h Some mothers are lesbians

Goodman, Charlotte
27m Women and madness in the fiction of Joyce Carol Oates

Goodman, Felicitas D.
473i Women in Yucatán

Goodman, Jody
80q The battle for day care in America: A view from the trenches

Goodman, Kay
32a The eternal feminine is leading us on

Goodman, Madeleine J.
51t A critique of menopause research
190c Age at menarche and year of birth in relation to adult height and weight among Caucasian, Japanese, and Chinese women living in Hawaii
439n Toward a biology of menopause

Goodrick, G. Ken
29i Health maintenance: Exercise and nutrition
137p Gender and obesity

Goodwin, Marjorie Harness
356k Directive-response speech sequences in girls' and boys' task activities

Goody, Esther
162k Parental strategies: Calculation or sentiment?: Fostering practices among West Africans

Goot, Murray
378i Women: If not apolitical, then conservative

Gordis, Leon
53v Implications of epidemiologic data for developing health policy for women

Gordon, Bette
2251 Variety: The pleasure in looking

Gordon, David M.
89j A theory of labor market segmentation

Gordon, Elizabeth
5d An analysis of the impact of labour migration on the lives of women in Lesotho

Gordon, Ira J.
216b Significant sociocultural factors in effective parenting

Gordon, Jan B.
143g Origins, *Middlemarch*, endings: George Eliot's crisis of the antecedent

Gordon, Linda
225b Seeking ecstasy on the battlefield: Danger and pleasure in nineteenth-century feminist sexual thought

245c Why nineteenth-century feminists did not support "birth control" and twentieth-century feminists do: Feminism, reproduction, and the family

353g Voluntary motherhood: The beginnings of feminist birth control ideas in the United States

354h The politics of birth control, 1920-1940: The impact of professionals

Gordon, Margaret T.
295h The impact of crime on urban women

Gordon, Mary
474c The parable of the cave or: In praise of watercolors

Gordon, R.
276f Ethics and ethical dilemmas in the treatment of sex offenders

Gordon, Steven L.
48k The intimate relationships of lesbians and gay men

Gordon, Susan
253c What's new in endocrinology? Target: Sex hormones

Gordon-McCord, Sue
122d The learning climate and the non-traditional student

Goreau, Angeline
125a Aphra Behn: A scandal to modesty

278b 'Last Night's Rambles': Restoration literature and the war between the sexes

Gorrell, Donald K.
412l "A new impulse": Progress in lay leadership and service by women of the United Brethren in Christ and the Evangelical Association, 1870-1910

Gorzell, André L.
175r "Tell them I don't smoke cigars": The story of Bonnie Parker

Gosselin, Chris
24c The influence of special sexual desires

gossett, hattie
301hh swing through the south journal, fall 1981

Goswami, Chitta R.
433e Bengal politics of the first decade of the present century: A defence of extremism

Gottlieb, Amy
305t Mothers, sisters, lovers, listen

Gottlieb, Bruce
291p The co-therapy relationship in group treatment of sexually mistreated adolescent girls

Gottlieb, Laura Moss
329k *The Years*: A feminist novel

Gottlieb, Lois
399u Looking to women: Rachel Crothers and the feminist heroine

Gottlieb, Lynn
211w The secret Jew: An oral tradition of women (poem)

211x Spring cleaning ritual on the eve of full moon Nisan (poem)

Gottlieb, Naomi
16a Women and mental health: The problem of depression

16e Women and health care

16i Women and chemical dependency

16q The older woman

Gough, Jamie
224g Childhood sexuality and paedophilia

Gough, Kathleen
344f The origin of the family

Gould, Carol C.
31a Private rights and public virtues: Women, the family, and democracy

Gould, David
111i The Hillcrest School of Oregon: Guided group interaction in a juvenile institution

Gould, Meredith
397j Lesbians and the law: Where sexism and heterosexism meet

Government of the District of Columbia
288m Policy on sexual harassment

Gowland, Pat
390i The Women's Peace Army

Goz, Rebecca
359qq Women patients and women therapists: Some issues that come up in psychotherapy

Grace, Sherrill E.
20c Margaret Atwood and the poetics of duplicity

448j Quest for the peaceable kingdom: Urban/rural codes in Roy, Laurence, and Atwood

Graham, Hilary
50u Competing ideologies of reproduction: Medical and maternal perspectives on pregnancy

170a Caring: A labour of love

212j Coping: Or how mothers are seen and not heard

241j Do her answers fit his questions? Women and the survey method

297f Surveying through stories

396c Competing ideologies of reproduction: Medical and maternal perspectives on pregnancy

456p Health education

Graham, Ruth
130g Women versus clergy, women pro clergy

Grahn, Judy
229z From sacred blood to the curse and beyond

Gramick, Jeannine
152c New sociological theory on homosexuality

397b Developing a lesbian identity

Grant, Jacquelyn
14o Black women and the church

462j A black response to feminist theology

Grant, Martin
274m Craft, design, and technology

Grant, Sara
91v Sammelan of the spirit

Gratton, Brian
210g Labor markets and old ladies' homes

Graulich, Melody
384s Pioneering the imagination: Eudora Welty's *The Robber Bridegroom*

Gravatt, Arthur E.
185a Looking toward the year 2020

185c Marriage and the family: Styles and forms

Gravenhorst, J. Bennebroek
252p Prevention of Rhesus(D) isoimmunization after abortion

Graves, Coburn V.
187k Stixwould in the market place

Graves, Helen M.
214f The view from the bench: The exercise of power

Graves, Nancy B.
420r Adaptation of Polynesian female migrants in New Zealand

Graves, Patricia G.
146k Law enforcement and child sexual abuse

Gray, J. A.
193c A biological basis for the sex differences in achievement in science?

Gray, J. Patrick
279h A cross-cultural investigation into the sexual dimorphism of stature

Gray, Mary Jane
36x An obstetrician's perspective

Gray, Mary W.
65j Economic models as a means of calculating legal compensation claims

Gray, Ronald H.
53i Pelvic inflammatory disease: Causes and consequences

Greeley, Martin
400a Women's employment and agriculture: Extracts from a case study

Green, Arthur
211u Bride, spouse, daughter: Images of the feminine in classical Jewish sources

Green, Carol Hurd
17j Stephen Crane and the fallen women

Green, Hardy
201l A stitch in our time: New York's Hispanic garment workers in the 1980s

Green, Judith
28r Recent trends in the treatment of premenstrual syndrome: A critical review

Green, Justin J.
21d Female elite goals and national development: Some data from the Philippines

Green, Mary Elizabeth
112i Elizabeth Elstob: The Saxon nymph (English, 1683-1765)

Green, Peter
278a Sex and classical literature

Green, Rayna
301e Magnolias grow in dirt: The bawdy lore of southern women

Green, Robert T.
421n Working wives in the United States and Venezuela: A cross-national study of decision making

Green, Robin
235h The church

Green, Susan S.
428l Silicon Valley's women workers: A theoretical analysis of sex-segregation in the electronics industry labor market

Greenbaum, Joan
209i Assessing the myths of the job market

Greenberg, Caren
356t Reading reading: Echo's abduction of language

Greenberg, Leslie S.
271i Beyond a cognitive/behavioural approach: Congruent assertion training

Greenberger, Marcia
93d The effectiveness of federal laws prohibiting sex discrimination in employment in the United States

Greenblat, Cathy Stein
57c Work, the family, and children's sexual learning

Greene, Gayle
343h Shakespeare's Cressida: "A kind of self"
343r Women and men in Shakespeare: A selective bibliography

Greene, Maxine
351b The impacts of irrelevance: Women in the history of American education

Greenfield, Gloria Z.
229ww Spiritual hierarchies: The empress' new clothes?

Greenfield, Lois
337d Women in engineering

Greenfield, William
352d Power and opportunity in the principalship: The case of two women leaders in education

Greenspan, Stephen
29r Mentally retarded mothers

Greenwood, Janet
13d Besides our size it's because we are women: The strike by the laundry workers union 15 January - 5 February 1982

Greenwood, Judy
456j Depression

Greenwood, Karen
418j Contraception and abortion

Greenwood-Audant, Lois M.
344n The internalization of powerlessness: A case study of the displaced homemaker

Gregory, Chester W.
61d Black women in pre-federal America

Gregory, Deborah
257i From where I stand: A case for feminist bisexuality

Gregory, Judith
220h The electronic sweatshop
307dd The next move: Organizing women in the office

Greif, Esther Blank
171j Men's speech to young children

Grenier, Gilles
273f The economics of sex preference and sex selection

Gresko, Jacqueline
205g "Roughing it in the bush" in British Columbia: Mary Moody's pioneer life in New Westminster 1859-1863

Gretzinger, Jacqueline
51e Attitudes of families toward menopause

Grevatt, Marge
306h Dusting the mirror: Researching women's history
306o Oral history as a resource in teaching women's studies

Grewe-Partsch, Marianne
391d Time, television, and women's career perspectives

Greywolf, Elizabeth
178c Daily lives
178h The politics of the poor
178o Physical health issues

Gribskov, Margaret
352f Feminism and the woman school administrator

Grider, Sylvia
445j Madness and personification in *Giants in the Earth*

Griesse, Anne Eliot
113c Russia: Revolution and war

Griffen, Joyce
51r Cultural models for coping with menopause

Griffin, Brian
317g The clinical psychology of later life: Developmental paradigms

Griffin, Gail
254d *Song of Solomon*: The hero with a woman's face
315c Still crazy after all these years: The uses of madness in women's fiction

Griffin, Julie
323l Bargaining for equality

Griffin, P. Bion
340c Woman the hunter: The Agta

Griffin, Susan
7x Sadomasochism and the erosion of self: A critical reading of *Story of O*
78l Rape: The all-American crime
474h Thoughts on writing: A diary

Griffiths, Dorothy
193f Biological inevitabilities or political choices? The future for girls in science

Griffiths, Moira
250k Women in higher education: A case study of the open university

Grigg, Susan
184p Toward a theory of remarriage: A case study of Newburyport at the beginning of the nineteenth century

Grim, Patrick
116g Sex and social roles: How to deal with the data
275c Sexist speech: Two basic questions
275u A note on the ethics of theories of truth

Grimes, David A.
252e The trimester threshold for pregnancy termination: Myth or truth?
252g Instrumental abortion in the second trimester: an overview

Grimké, Angelina
129b Human rights not founded on sex

Grimké, Sarah
129k Legal disabilities of women

Grimshaw, Patricia
390a Women and the family in Australian history

Gritz, Ellen R.
9n Problems related to the use of tobacco by women

Grontkowski, Christine R.
84l The mind's eye

Groome, Thomas H.
91j From chauvinism and clericalism to priesthood: The long march

Gross, Alice D.
265f Does sex stereotyping lead to a higher incidence of male dyslexia?

Gross, Ira
265t Mental health in boys and girls: Awareness of attitudes for positive sex roles

Gross, Lora
429i The embodied church

Gross, Michael
84e Evolution and patriarchal myths of scarcity and competition

Gross, Rita M.
211t Steps toward feminine imagery of deity in Jewish theology
325r Menstruation and childbirth as ritual and religious experience among native Australians

Grossholtz, Jean
103c Battered women's shelters and the political economy of sexual violence
378h Politics an unnatural practice: Political science looks at female participation

Grossman, Marlyn
34h Taking the men out of menopause

Grossmann, Atina
60d Crisis, reaction, and resistance: Women in Germany in the 1920's and 1930's
231g The new woman and the rationalization of sexuality in Weimar Germany

336c Abortion and economic crisis: The 1931 campaign against paragraph 218

Grosz, Katarzyna
156l Bridewealth and dowry in Nuzi

Groth, A. Nicholas
146h The incest offender
280h The dynamics of sexual assault
326h Sexual assault in correctional institutions: Prevention and intervention
349l Rape: Power, anger, and sexuality

Grotzinger, Laurel A.
302f Biographical research on women librarians: Its paucity, perils, and pleasures

Grove, John S.
190c Age at menarche and year of birth in relation to adult height and weight among Caucasian, Japanese, and Chinese women living in Hawaii

Groves, Betsy McAlister
434l Dilemmas in role identification for low-income women

Groves, Dulcie
170h Natural selection: Perspectives on entitlement to the invalid care allowance
465b Members and survivors: Women and retirement-pensions legislation

Grubb, W. Norton
427j Gender roles and the state

Grumet, Robert Steven
347b Sunksquaws, shamans, and tradeswomen: Middle Atlantic coastal Algonkian women during the 17th and 18th centuries

Grune, Joy Ann
65m The role of labor
435d Pay equity: Beyond equal pay for equal work

Grunes, Jerome
317g The clinical psychology of later life: Developmental paradigms

Grygelko, Marilee
404ff Federal support: Understanding and utilizing the federal dollar

Gubar, Susan
108b Ceremonies of the alphabet: Female grandmatologies and the female autograph
242b The birth of the artist as heroine: (Re)production, the *Künstlerroman* tradition, and the fiction of Katherine Mansfield

Guberman, Nancy
323r Working, mothering and militancy: Women in the CNTU

Guenther, Margaret B.
32c Faustunder: The tragedy reexamined

Gugler, Josef
39h The second sex in town

Guisso, Richard W.
401c Thunder over the lake: The five classics and the perception of woman in early China

Gulati, Leela
386b Agricultural laborers

Gullett, Gayle
379l City mothers, city daughters, and the dance hall girls: The limits of female political power in San Francisco, 1913

Gundersheimer, Werner L.
33b Women, learning, and power: Eleonora of Aragon and the Court of Ferrara

Gunderson, Morely
357d Low pay and female employment in Canada with selected references to the USA

Gupta, A. S.
346e Salient laws on women and children: A selected bibliography

Gupta, Sanjukta
322g Women and literature in Asia: South Asia
322i Interview with Nabaneeta Deb-Sen (India)

Gurin, Gerald
37q Group identity development within black families

Gurko, Jane
176f Sexual energy in the classroom

Gurman, Alan S.
29g Marriage and the family: An unconscious male bias in behavioral treatment?
365g Marital and family conflicts

Gurney, Helen
147ee Major influences on the development of high school girls' sports in Ontario

Guskin, Judith T.
394m The president's wife: A changing role — observations of a chancellor's wife

Gussler, Judith D.
473h Adaptive strategies and social networks of women in St. Kitts

Gustafsson, Siv
260g Equal opportunity policies in Sweden

Gustavii, Birgitta
289n A view from Sweden

Gutek, Barbara A.
48i Gender roles and sexuality in the world of work
267d A psychological examination of sexual harassment
307r Women's work in the office of the future
471j Women at work in the USA

Gutman, Herbert G.
162j Afro-American kinship before and after emancipation in North America

Gutmann, David
317g The clinical psychology of later life: Developmental paradigms

Guyer, Jane I.
6b Women in the rural economy: Contemporary variations

H. P., Philomena
161g A fallen image - Women in India
163f The devadasi problem

Haas, Violet B.
416o Evolving views of women's professional roles

Haavind, Hanne
217h Love and power in marriage

Haavio-Mannila, Elina
52k Economic and family roles of men and women in Northern Europe: A historical cross-national comparison
228j Finland
244i Traditional sex norms and the innovative function of afternoon dancing
382c Finland
436k The impact of the women's movement and legislative activity of women MPs on social development
471h Women at work in Finland

Hackenberg, Beverly
424m Growth of the bazaar economy and its significance for women's employment: Trends of the 1970s in Davao City, Philippines

Hacker, Sally L.
181c Mathematization of engineering: Limits on women and the field
341l Farming out the home: Women and agribusiness
387t Sex stratification, technology and organization change: A longitudinal case study of AT&T
441e The culture of engineering: Woman, workplace and machine

Hackett, Amy
336e Helene Stöcker: Left-wing intellectual and sex reformer

Haddad, Yvonne Yazbeck
403b Traditional affirmations concerning the role of women as found in contemporary Arab Islamic literature

Haeri, Shahla
368m The institution of Mut'a marriage in Iran: A formal and historical perspective
403g Women, law, and social change in Iran

Hafley, James
330c Virginia Woolf's narrators and the art of "life itself"

Haft, Marilyn G.
392n Women in prison: Discriminatory practices and some legal solutions

Hagestad, Gunhild O.
296c Women in intergenerational patterns of power and influence

Hahn, Emily
442g Salonists and chroniclers

Hahn, Susan Reed
239h American birth practices: A critical review

Haight, Gordon S.
142a George Eliot's bastards

Hailes, Jean
47c Questions women want to ask about the menopause

Hain, Peter
283k A left strategy for Labour

Haines, Patricia Foster
352h Coeducation and the development of leadership skills in women: Historical perspectives from Cornell University, 1868-1900

Hakiki, Fatiha
298e Human sciences research on Algerian women

Halbreich, Uriel
281 Classification of premenstrual syndromes

Hale, Janice
38e The black woman and child rearing

Hale, Linda Louise
157p Appendix: Votes for women: Profiles of prominent British Columbia suffragists and social reformers

Haley, Kathleen
392o Mothers behind bars: A look at the parental rights of incarcerated women

Hall, Catherine
50a The butcher, the baker, the candlestick-maker: The shop and the family in the Industrial Revolution
50b The home turned upside down? The working-class family in cotton textiles 1780-1850
227a The history of the housewife

Hall, David
19c The Antinomian controversy

Hall, E. V. van
240b Regret and reversal of sterilization

Hall, Jacquelyn Dowd
231u "The mind that burns in each body": Women, rape, and racial violence

Hall, Jacquelyn H.
404aa Stereotypes and stigma: Barriers to recovery

Hall, Jane
228g West Germany

Hall, Marny
359bb Lesbian families: Cultural and clinical issues

Hall, Roberta L.
279a Introduction: Consequences of sexuality
279g Studies in modern populations: Unit of analysis
279i Sexual dimorphism for size in seven nineteenth-century Northwest coast populations

Halleck, Seymour L.
140b Editorial: Morality in medicine

Haller, Evelyn
328f Isis unveiled: Virginia Woolf's use of Egyptian myth
329e The anti-madonna in the work and thought of Virginia Woolf

Haller, John S.
238e From maidenhood to menopause: Sex education for women in Victorian America

Hallett, Judith P.
419k The role of women in Roman elegy: Counter-cultural feminism

Halmi, Katherine A.
28n The menstrual cycle in anorexia nervosa

Halpern, Susan
404s The mythology of rape

Hamblin, Angela
212r What can one do with a son? Feminist politics and male children
257g Is a feminist heterosexuality possible?

Hamilton, Margaret E.
279e Sexual dimorphism in skeletal samples

Hammen, Constance L.
137f Gender and depression

Hammer, Barbara
174s Creative teaching spaces: Home movies
453 Women's images in film

Hammer, Michael
209j Productivity and service quality in the private sector

Hammond, Karla
186u To be reborn: An interview with May Sarton
186v A further interview with May Sarton

Hampel, Bill
94j Generations and class: Sicilian-Australians in Melbourne

Hampsten, Elizabeth
306e Tell me all you know: Reading letters and diaries of rural women

Han, Kee-ok Kim
272d Occupational sex segregation: Prospects for the 1980s

Hanami, Tadashi
382h Japan

Hanawalt, Barbara A.
184b Childbearing among the lower classes of late medieval England
376g Women before the law: Females as felons and prey in fourteenth-century England

Hancock, Linda
348f The processing of juveniles in Victoria

Hancock, Mary
213g Transnational production and women workers

Hand, Jennifer
210h Shopping-bag women: Aging deviants in the city

Hanmer, Jalna
12j Reproductive engineering: The final solution?
181k Reproductive technology: The future for women?
241c Blowing the cover of the protective male: A community study of violence to women
297b Negotiating the problem: The DHSS and research on violence in marriage
310ff A womb of one's own
396h Sex predetermination, artificial insemination and the maintenance of male-dominated culture

Hanneman, Kathleen
111i The Hillcrest School of Oregon: Guided group interaction in a juvenile institution

Hanoch, Giora
110c Hours and weeks in the theory of labor supply
110f A multivariate model of labor supply: Methodology and estimation

Hansen, Karen Tranberg
263l Men servants and women bosses: The domestic service institution in colonial Zambia

Hansen, Ranald D.
425e Trying hurts women, helps men: The meaning of effort

Hanson, Katherine H.
320d Mapping the road to academe: A review of research on women, men, and the college-selection process

Hanson, Perry
463f The impact of women's employment on household travel patterns: A Swedish example

Hanson, Susan
463f The impact of women's employment on household travel patterns: A Swedish example

Harasymiw, Bohdan
405j Have women's chances for political recruitment in the USSR really improved?

Haraway, Donna J.
416n Class, race, sex, scientific objects of knowledge: A socialist-feminist perspective on the social construction of productive nature and some political consequences

Hardesty, Nancy A.
412d Minister as prophet? or as mother?: Two nineteenth-century models

Harding, Jan
193n Sex differences in science examinations
250h Sex differences in performance in science examinations

Harding, Sandra
3d Commentary to chapter 3 (chapter c)
3m Beneath the surface of the abortion dispute: Are women fully human?
31c Is gender a variable in conceptions of rationality? A survey of issues
84p Why has the sex/gender system become visible only now?
369g What is the real material base of patriarchy and capital?

Hare, R.M.
223m Abortion and the golden rule

Hare-Mustin, Rachel T.
140t A feminist approach to family therapy
359tt A feminist approach to family therapy
365p Psychotherapy and women: Priorities for research

Hargadine, Eileen
228m Japan

Hargreaves, Mary W.M.
61j Darkness before the dawn: The status of women in the Depression years

Hargrove, Nancy D.
450m Youth in Toni Cade Bambara's *Gorilla, My Love*

Haring-Smith, Tori
329h Private and public consciousness in *Mrs. Dalloway* and *To the Lighthouse*

Harkess, Shirley
244a Colombian women in party politics: A token role

Harlan, Anne
426d Sex differences in factors affecting managerial career advancement

Harlan, Sharon L.
2721 Job integration strategies: Today's pro-
        grams and tomorrow's needs

Harley, Sharon
264d Black women in a southern city:
        Washington, D.C., 1890-1920

Harman, Elizabeth J.
440e Capitalism, patriarchy and the city
463i Individual spatial behavior

Harman, Lillian
129g An "age of consent" symposium
129s Some problems of social freedom

Harms, Robert
370f Sustaining the system: Trading towns along
        the middle Zaire

Harper, Anne L.
103l Teenage sexuality and public policy: An
        agenda for gender education
126p Human sexuality: New insights from
        women's history

Harragan, Betty Lehan
339b Women and men at work: Jockeying for
        position

Harré, Rom
24h The dramaturgy of sexual relations

Harris, Ann Sutherland
417ee A women's museum of art

Harris, Barbara J.
158a The power of the past: History and the
        psychology of women

Harris, Ben
158f "Give me a dozen healthy infants": John
        B. Watson's popular advice on childrear-
        ing, women, and the family
253e The myth of assembly-line hysteria

Harris, D. V.
107e Personality research: Implications for
        women in sport

Harris, Elizabeth
7j Sadomasochism: A personal experience

Harris, Holly
111d Family violence: Women as offenders or
        victims

Harris, Laurilyn
399w Anne Nichols: $1,000,000.00 playwright

Harris, Olivia
200d The power of signs: Gender, culture and
        the wild in the Bolivian Andes
207d Households as natural units
208h Households as natural units

Harris, William J.
40u Sweet soft essence of possibility: The poet-
        ry of Nikki Giovanni

Harrison, Algea
37m Attitudes toward procreation among black
        adults

Harrison, Beverly Wildung
59g Human sexuality and mutuality

Harrison, Nancy
231r Movie

Harrison, Ted
111t Recent development in probation and
        parole in British Columbia

Harsin, Jill
417h Housework and utopia: Women and the
        Owenite socialist communities

Hart, Francis Russell
197a Ridiculous demons

Hart, John
192o Working-class women in nineteenth centu-
        ry Mexico

Hartgen, David T.
463s Can current transportation planning meth-
        ods analyze women's travel issues?

Hartman, Carol R.
55e Typology of collectors
55j Treatment issues with children involved in
        pornography and sex rings

Hartmann, Heidi
65i Assessing pay discrimination using nation-
        al data
369b The unhappy marriage of Marxism and
        feminism: Towards a more progressive
        union

Hartmann, Susan M.
61k Women in the military service

Hartsock, Nancy
43a Political change: Two perspectives on pow-
        er
43c Fundamental feminism: Process and per-
        spective
43k Staying alive
60j Difference and domination in the women's
        movement: The dialectic of theory and
        practice
84o The feminist standpoint: Developing the
        ground for a specifically feminist historical
        materialism
464e Prologue to a feminist critique of war and
        politics

Hartz-Karp, Janette
348h Women in constraints

Hartzog, Martha
175m Mollie Bailey: Circus entrepreneur

Harvey, Brett
225m No more nice girls

Harvey, Susan Ashbrook
156r Women in early Syrian Christianity

Harvey, Sylvia
406b Woman's place: The absent family of film
        noir

Harvey, Youngsook Kim
325d Possession sickness and women shamans in
        Korea

Hasan, Yousuf
98i Working through local female investiga-
        tors: Experiences in a broad survey

Haselgrove, Margaret
13c Photo essay: Women and work

Hasna, Mahbuba Kaneez
98j Survey research with rural women in
        Bangladesh

Haspels, A. A.
236f A double-blind, placebo-controlled, multi-
        centre study of the efficacy of dydroges-
        terone (Duphaston R)

Hasper, Dido
453s Feminist women's health centers

Hassencahl, Fran
303e New women at Old Dominion

Hatch, Maureen
86j Mother, father, worker: Men and women
        and the reproduction risks of work

Hatch, Orrin G.
80m Families, children, and child care

Hatfield, Elaine
48f What do women and men want from love
        and sex?

Hatton, Frances
139h 'Getting on'. Gender differences in career
        development: A case study in the hair-
        dressing industry

Hatton, Jennifer
274n Art

Haugen, Inger
468g Conceptualising domestic work:
        Comments on definitions of "work" in
        some Norwegian studies

Haukaa, Runa
217j Theoretical ambiguities - A reflection of
        women's lives?

Hauptman, Anna R.
214h Styles of leadership: Power and feminine
        values

Hausen, Karin
144b Family and role-division: The polarisation
        of sexual stereotypes in the nineteenth
        century - an aspect of the dissociation of
        work and family life
162p Mothers, sons, and the sale of symbols and
        goods: The 'German Mother's Day' 1923-
        33
336f Mother's day in the Weimar Republic

Hauser, Barbara B.
16c Issues in feminist therapy: The work of a
        woman's study group

Hauser, Stuart T.
8p Research on gender and psychotherapy

Havelock, Christine Mitchell
117d Mourners on Greek vases: Remarks on the
        social history of women
389m Dorothy Burr Thompson (b. 1900):
        Classical archaeologist

Haviland, Jeannette Jones
136j The development of sex differences in
        nonverbal signals: Fallacies, facts, and fan-
        tasies

Hawkes, Ellen
202b Woolf's 'Magical garden of women'

Hawkes, Glenn R.
87d Young marrieds: Wives' employment and
        family role structure

Hawkins, Maureen S.G.
338h The dramatic treatment of Robert Emmet
        and Sarah Curran

Hawkins, Patricia A.
55o Appendix D: Fighting adult entertainment centers at the grassroots level

Hawton, Keith
456k Sexual problems

Hay, Julia
411j Motherhood in the middle years: Women and their adult children

Hay, Samuel A.
40k Alice Childress's dramatic structure

Hayashi, Haruo
230g Pornography in Japan: Cross-cultural and theoretical considerations

Hayden, Dolores
203e Redesigning the domestic workplace

Hayes, Catherine
381f Up to now

Hayes, Joseph J.
133c Lesbians, gay men, and their "languages"
133d Gayspeak

Hayne, Barrie
1f Anna Katharine Green

Haynes, Suzanne G.
53c The effect of employment, family and job stress on coronary heart disease patterns in women

Hays, Janice
343e Those "soft and delicate desires": *Much Ado* and the distrust of women

Haywoode, Terry L.
174d College for neighborhood women: Innovation and growth

Hazleton, Lesley
211f Israeli women: Three myths

Heady, Judith
214j The battle of the sexes: Power and sexual aggressiveness

Hearn, James C.
320f Sex differences in the significance of economic resources for choosing and attending a college
320l Sex differences in the implications of the links between major departments and the occupational structure

Hearn, Kristin
26c Group treatment of children in shelters for battered women

Hearne, Dana
338i Rewriting history: Anna Parnell's *The Tale of a Great Sham*

Heath, Anthony
139d Women, men and social class

Hebbelinck, M.
107t Body build of female Olympic rowers

Hecht, Elizabeth
137e Psychopathology and sex differences in the aged

Heck-Rabi, Louise
399x Sophie Treadwell: Agent for change

Heckman, James
110e Sample selection bias as a specification error

Heckscher, M. Erika
311f Selected annotated bibliography of articles on theories of women's studies

Heen, Mary
65l A review of federal court decisions under Title VII of the Civil Rights Act of 1964

Heffernan, Esther
63d A coed prison
63k Women in a coed joint

Hegland, Mary E.
368j Aliabad women: Revolution as religious activity

Heiberg, Astrid No/klebye
8m The myofascial pain dysfunction syndrome: An unheeded neuromuscular disorder

Heide, Wilma Scott
472j Now for the feminist menopause that refreshes

Heikens, Carolien
179l Freedom fighters

Heilbrun, Carolyn G.
132r Androgyny and the psychology of sex differences
186d May Sarton's memoirs
328m Virginia Woolf in her fifties
409j Afterword
411d Middle-aged women in literature
442c Louisa May Alcott: The influence of *Little Women*

Heilman, Robert B.
142e 'Stealthy convergence' in *Middlemarch*

Heiman, Julia R.
137n Gender and sexual functioning

Hein, Hilde
7h Sadomasochism and the liberal tradition
31g Liberating philosophy: An end to the dichotomy of matter and spirit

Heinen, Hubert
331d The woman's songs of Hartmann von Aue

Heisler, Toni
309aa Contraceptive services for adolescents: An overview

Heiss, Jerold
37l Women's values regarding marriage and the family

Heistand, Deborah
147s Women in sport in the United States, 1945 to 1978

Heitlinger, Alena
405a Marxism, feminism, and sex equality

Heizer, Ruth B.
432f Employment for women in athletics: What is fair play?

Helberger, Christof
93v Work analysis as a means to achieve equal pay for working women: The Federal Republic of Germany

Held, Thomas
52r Economic recession and Swiss women's attitudes towards marital role segregation

Held, Virginia
116n The obligations of mothers and fathers

195a The obligations of mothers and fathers

Helen
91m Moral theology from a feminist perspective

Heller, Rita
292d Blue collars and bluestockings: The Bryn Mawr summer school for women workers, 1921-1938

Hellwig, Tineke
322h Women and literature in Asia: South-East Asia

Helly, Dorothy O.
407g An agenda for senior women administrators

Helöe, Berit
8m The myofascial pain dysfunction syndrome: An unheeded neuromuscular disorder

Helson, Ravenna
377b The creative woman mathematician

Hemmings-Gapihan, Grace S.
373i Baseline study for socio-economic evaluation of Tangaye solar site
385h International development and the evolution of women's economic roles: A case study from northern Gulma, Upper Volta

Hemmons, Willa Mae
38s The women's liberation movement: Understanding black women's attitudes

Henderson, Hazel
373a Foreword: Seeing our global economy whole

Henderson, Helen K.
82j Livestock and range management

Hendricks, Maureen C.
360e Women, spirituality, and mental health

Henifin, Mary Sue
34e No fertile women need apply: Employment discrimination and reproductive hazards in the workplace
34m Bibliography: Women, science, and health
86d The particular problems of video display terminals
209x Health hazards in the computerized office

Henke, Suzette
202f *Mrs Dalloway*: The communion of saints
329g 'The prime minister': A key to *Mrs. Dalloway*
409d Stephen Dedalus and women: A portrait of the artist as a young misogynist
409f Gerty MacDowell: Joyce's sentimental heroine

Henley, Nancy
136a Nonverbal behavior: Barrier or agent for sex role change?
171a Language, gender and society: Opening a second decade of research
171k Sex similarities and differences in language, speech, and nonverbal communication: An annotated bibliography
344y The sexual politics of interpersonal behavior
417t Imagining a different world of talk

Henn, Jeanne K.
6a   Women in the rural economy: Past, present and future

Henney, Jeannette H.
473g   Sex and status: Women in St. Vincent

Hennon, Charles B.
458n   Responsibility for household tasks: Comparing dual-earner and dual-retired marriages

Henretta, John C.
458b   Midlife work history and retirement income

Henrik, Elizabeth
51h   Neuroendocrine mechanisms of reproductive aging in women and female rats
271n   Hormones and behaviour: Introduction

Henry, Timothy J.
141b   Genetic control of breast cancer susceptibility in animals

Henson, Deborah M.
434c   Therapy with battered women

Henwood, Felicity
209e   Government policies on new information technologies and their implications for employment: An overview of EEC countries, with particular reference to women

Heper, Metin
270j   The plight of urban migrants: Dynamics of service procurement in a squatter area

Herceg-Baron, Roberta
308j   Bringing in the family: Kinship support and contraceptive behavior

Heritage, John
139i   Feminisation and unionisation: A case study from banking

Herlands, Rosalind L.
79cc   Biological manipulations for producing and nurturing mammalian embryos

Herman, Debra
126n   Does equality mean sameness? A historical perspective on the college curriculum for women with reflections on the current situation

Herman, Dianne
344b   The rape culture

Herman, Judith
140p   Father-daughter incest
140q   Families at risk for father-daughter incest
284j   Father-daughter incest
359oo   Incest between fathers and daughters

Herman, William
329n   Virginia Woolf and the classics: Every Englishman's prerogative transmuted into fictional art

Hermansen, Marcia K.
368e   Fatimeh as a role model in the works of Ali Shari'ati

Hermansson, Svea
209k   Automation and the quality of work life at the Swedish telephone company: A management view

Hernandez, Aileen
41d   Black women and the political process in the United States

Hernandez, Enrique
53q   Risk factors for ovarian cancer

Hernandez, Patricia
192c   Lives of Chicana activists: The Chicano student movement (a case study)

Hernes, Helga Maria
217b   Women and the welfare state: The transition from private to public dependence

Herr, Edwin L.
221a   The family as an influence on career development

Herrin, Alejandro
424o   Employment structure of female migrants to the cities in the Philippines

Herrin, Judith
156k   In search of Byzantine women: Three avenues of approach

Hershatter, Gail
192m   Women at Farah: An unfinished story
201k   Women at Farah: An unfinished story

Hertz, Deborah
145c   Hannah Arendt's *Rahel Varnhagen*

Hess, Beth B.
210k   Family relationships of older women: A women's issue

Hess, Robert D.
216k   Experts and amateurs: Some unintended consequences of parent education

Hesse, Beate
471c   Women at work in the Federal Republic of Germany

Hetherington, E. Mavis
204i   Effects of divorce on parents and children

Hewett, Margaret L.
175y   Mrs. Bailey and the bears

Hewitt, Patricia
467e   The stance of Britain's major parties and interest groups

Heyns, Barbara
320c   Recent trends in the higher education of women

Heywood, Angela
129n   Body housekeeping

Heywood, Ezra H.
129l   Cupid's yokes
129cc   Perpetual vassalage

Heyzer, Noeleen
350g   From rural subsistence to an industrial peripheral work force: An examination of female Malaysian migrants and capital accumulation in Singapore

Hicklin, Fannie
394p   An E.B. Fred Fellow

Hickok, Kathy
176t   Lesbian images in women's literature anthologies

Hicks, Dorothy J.
326j   Sexual assault of the older woman

Hicks, Emily
369j   Cultural Marxism: Nonsynchrony and feminist practice

Hidalgo, Hilda
397h   The Puerto Rican lesbian in the United States

Hield, Melissa
301o   Women in the Texas ILGWU, 1933-50

Higginbotham, Elizabeth
14k   Two representative issues in contemporary sociological work on black women
60m   Laid bare by the system: Work and survival for black and Hispanic women

Higgins, Claire E.
458g   Retirement expectations and plans: A comparison of professional men and women

Higgins, Millicent W.
53e   Changing patterns of smoking and risk of disease

High, Ellesa Clay
301g   Corn shuckings, fiddle contests, square dances: Oral history with Lily May Ledford

Hilberman, Elaine
140o   Overview: The "wife-beater's wife" reconsidered

Hildebrand, George
66c   The market system
67c   The market system

Hildenbrand, Suzanne
302a   Revision versus reality: Women in the history of the public library movement, 1876-1920

Hill, David B.
226h   Female state senators as cue givers: ERA roll-call voting, 1972-1979

Hill, Errol
399n   Henrietta Vinton Davis: Shakespearean actress

Hill, Frances
82f   Appropriate technology

Hill, Judith
51k   Smoking, alcohol, and body mass relationships to early menopause: Implications for risk of cardiovascular disease

Hill, Kathleen Spangler
434m   Work requirements for AFDC mothers

Hill, Robert B.
37r   Multiple public benefits and poor black families

Hill, Shirley Y.
10e   Vulnerability to the biomedical consequences of alcoholism and alcohol-related problems among women

Hill, Tina
212e   Rape and marital violence in the maintenance of male power

Hiller, Anne Edwards
348f   The processing of juveniles in Victoria

Hills, Jill
228a   Britain
378j   Women and voting in Britain

Hillsman, Sally T.
387r   Job opportunities of black and white working-class women

Himmelweit, Hilde T.
57d Television as a sphere of influence on the child's learning about sexuality

Himmelweit, Susan
227p Women's domestic labour
335d Production rules OK? Waged work and the family

Hindess, Barry
283h Interview with Frances Morrell
283i Interview with Jo Richardson

Hinding, Andrea
61b An abundance of riches: The women's history sources survey

Hindus, Michael S.
184q Premarital pregnancy in America, 1640-1971: An overview and interpretation
375g The law of husband and wife in nineteenth-century America: Changing views of divorce

Hine, Darlene Clark
39n Female slave resistance: The economics of sex
353ii Mabel K. Staupers and the integration of black nurses into the armed forces

Hingley, Phil
274e Modern languages

Hintikka, Jaakko
84h How can language be sexist?

Hintikka, Merrill B.
84h How can language be sexist?

Hinz, JoAnn
394s A remarkable woman: Grace Pilgrim Bloom

Hirata, Lucie Cheng
711 Social mobility of Asian women in America: A critical review

Hirsch, Marianne
332a Spiritual *Bildung*: The beautiful soul as paradigm
398f 'They shared a laboratory together': Feminist collaboration in the academy

Hirschman, Lisa
140p Father-daughter incest
140q Families at risk for father-daughter incest
284j Father-daughter incest
359oo Incest between fathers and daughters

Hirschon, Renée
364a Introduction: Property, power and gender relations
371d Essential objects and the sacred: Interior and exterior space in an urban Greek locality

Hirst, Paul
283c The genesis of the social
283e Reply: Feminists - The degenerates of the social?

Hjort, Lisbet
209t Labor legislation in Norway: Its application to the introduction of new technology

Hoad, Anne
115g Crumbs from the table: Towards a whole priesthood

Hoagland, Sarah Lucia
7s Sadism, masochism, and lesbian-feminism
116e "Femininity," resistance and sabotage

Hobson, William F.
280h The dynamics of sexual assault

Hock, Carolyn
463j Residential location and transportation analyses: Married women workers

Hodges, Jill
283b Children and parents: Who chooses?

Hodges, William F.
295f Sex differences in separation and divorce: A longitudinal perspective

Hodgson, Mary L.
221c Working mothers: Effects on the marriage and the mother

Hoel, Barbro
470e Contemporary clothing 'sweatshops', Asian female labour and collective organisation

Hoel, Marit
217f The female working class

Hoffman, Alice M.
169k Using oral history in the classroom

Hoffman, Lois Wladis
158m The study of employed mothers over half a century
391a Early childhood experiences and women's achievement motives

Hoffnung, Michele
344i Motherhood: Contemporary conflict for women

Hofrichter, Frima Fox
117j Judith Leyster's *Proposition* - Between virtue and vice

Hogan, Joyce C.
447c The state of the art of strength testing

Hogan, Judy
15i Publishers on libraries: Small presses and the library

Hogsett, A. Charlotte
126e Darwin and sexism: Victorian causes, contemporary effects

Hogue, Carol J. Rowland
252s Somatic sequelae and future reproduction after pregnancy termination

Holcomb, Adele M.
389d Anna Jameson (1794-1860): Sacred art and social vision
389e Margaret Fuller (1810-1850): Her work as an art critic

Holden, Karen C.
46b Supplemental OASI benefits to homemakers through current spouse benefits, a homemaker credit, and child-care drop-out years

Holder, Orlee
4521 Anaïs Nin's *Diary* in context

Hole, Judith
344dd The first feminists

Holland, Barbara
151c 'A woman's right to choose' in the Soviet Union

Holland, Norman N.
131k You, U.K. Le Guin

Holland, Ruth
310cc Regaining trust

Hollander, Anne
442j Women and fashion

Hollender, Marc H.
280f Genital exhibitionism in men and women

Hollibaugh, Amber
231y What we're rollin around in bed with: Sexual silences in feminism

Hollnsteiner, Mary Racelis
300a Modernization, changing roles of women and expectations for development in southeast Asia

Hollway, Wendy
257h Heterosexual sex: Power and desire for the other

Holmes, Helen B.
31n A feminist analysis of the Universal Declaration of Human Rights
36a Reproductive technologies: The birth of a women-centered analysis
36y Policymaking and projections overview
79a Reproductive technologies: The birth of a women-centered analysis
310p Technology and prenatal femicide

Holmes, Karen A.
326b Working for and with rape victims: Crisis intervention and advocacy

Holmes, King K.
461z Discussion: Prophylaxis of sexually transmitted diseases: An overview

Holmstrom, Lynda L.
284g Sexual trauma of children and adolescents
3491 Rape: Power, anger, and sexuality
359kk Rape: Sexual disruption and recovery

Holroyd, Jean
359h Report of the task force on sex bias and sex-role stereotyping in psychotherapeutic practice

Holsti, Ole R.
4351 The foreign policy beliefs of women in leadership positions

Holt, Alix
151b Domestic labour and Soviet society
405g Marxism and women's oppression: Bolshevik theory and practice in the 1920's

Holt, Linda
268n Senescence, sex roles, and stress: Shepherding resources into old age

Holt, Steven A.
57g Social services and sexual learning

Holter, Harriet
217a Women's research and social theory
382i Norway

Holter, Øystein Gullvåg
217i Gender as forms of value

Holtzman, Joan Hirsch
79f DES: Ten points of controversy

Homans, Margaret
109p Dreaming of children: Literalization in *Jane Eyre* and *Wuthering Heights*
121g "Oh, vision of language!": Dickinson's poems of love and death

Homma-True, Reiko
71c Mental health issues among Asian-American women

Honeycut, Karen
95b Clara Zetkin: A Socialist approach to the problem of women's oppression

Hong, Evelyn
183a Rural women in development
183h Women's health

Hong, Sawon
420j Urban migrant women in the Republic of Korea

Honig, Alice Sterling
427d Child care options and decisions: Facts and figurings for families

Honig, Emily
192m Women at Farah: An unfinished story
201k Women at Farah: An unfinished story

Hoogenboom, Annemiek
76f Women's struggles in the third world

Hooker, Eva
315e A dialogue critical issues in women's studies: Race, class, and sexual orientation

Hoon, Emily Franck
29e Sexuality

Hoon, Lee Siew
424h Occupational health hazards of female industrial workers in Malaysia

Hooyman, Nancy
434e Older women as victims of violence

Hopkins, Esther A. H.
416h Alternative development of a scientific career

Hopkins, June
219h Loss and mourning in victims of rape and sexual assault

Hopson, Barrie
259i Sex differentiation and careers

Horan, Susan
294b 'More sinned against than sinning'?: Prostitution in South Australia, 1836-1914

Horne, Alan J.
20n A checklist of writings by and about Margaret Atwood

Hornig, Lilli S.
380b The education and employment of women scientists and engineers in the United States
416c Professional women in transition

Hornstein, Francie
310x Children by donor insemination: A new choice for lesbians

Horsley, Ritta Jo
32b A critical appraisal of Goethe's *Iphigenie*

Horwitz, Jaime
307m Living better vicariously?

Hoskins, Betty B.
310p Technology and prenatal femicide

Hoskins, Marilyn W.
82i Agriculture, forestry, conservation and women
82q Issues and alternatives in planning projects for women

Hotvedt, Mary
289b The cross-cultural and historical context

Houg, Tora
468i Perspectives on work and reproduction with special reference to women's opportunities and adaptation

Houlihan, Dennis
209hh Legislative and research options for the U.S. Congress

House, Kay
17b Fenimore Cooper's Heroines

Houston, Barbara
432n Women's physical education: A gender-sensitive perspective

Houwelingen, Flora von
322e Francophone literature in North Africa

Howard, John
188g The German mystic: Mechthild of Magdeburg

Howard, Judith Jeffrey
444j Patriot mothers in the post-risorgimento: Women after the Italian revolution

Howard, June
124d Widening the dialogue on feminist science fiction

Howard, Kenneth I.
365a Gender and psychotherapeutic outcome

Howard, Lee
301k The rape of Dona (poem)

Howard, Maureen
442e City of words

Howe, Florence
174h Feminist scholarship: The extent of the revolution

Howell, Elizabeth
359a Women: From Freud to the present
359l The influence of gender on diagnosis and psychopathology
359v Women's treatment needs
359y Psychological reactions of postpartum women
359pp Psychotherapy with women clients: The impact of feminism
359ww Where do we go from here?

Howell, Maxwell L.
147k Women in sport and physical education in the United States 1900-1914

Howell, Reet
147b Recreational activities of women in colonial America
147e American women, 1880-1860 (sic): Recreational pursuits and exercise
147g Generalizations on women and sport, games and play in the United States from settlement to 1860
147k Women in sport and physical education in the United States 1900-1914

147u Women in the sports halls of fame
372b An historical overview

Howes, Keith
235j The media

Howett, Catherine M.
126m Careers in landscape architecture: Recovering for women what the "ladies" won and lost

Hricko, Andrea M.
169p Occupational health and safety for women workers: Some teaching models

Huang, Nora Chiang
420m The migration of rural women to Taipei

Hubbard, Ruth
34a Have only men evolved?
79gg The case against in vitro fertilization and implantation
84d Have only men evolved?
189n The emperor doesn't wear any clothes: The impact of feminism on biology
310v Personal courage is not enough: Some hazards of childbearing in the 1980s
342a Social effects of some contemporary myths about women
416m Should professional women be like professional men?

Hubbard, Tom
197h The liberated instant: Muriel Spark and the short story

Hubbell, Joe W.
414f Women in Oklahoma education

Hubbs, Joanna
194f The worship of Mother Earth in Russian culture

Hubbuch, Cornelius
152g Gay men and women and the vowed life

Huber, Joan
387b Toward a sociotechnological theory of the women's movement

Huckle, Patricia
307ff Feminism: A catalyst for the future
435h The womb factor: Pregnancy policies and employment of women

Hudson, Ann
54e Commonalities among female alcoholics

Hudson, Barbara
134b Femininity and adolescence

Hug, Jim
91e Theological issues raised by feminism

Hughes, Beryl
413f Women and the professions in New Zealand

Hughes, James M.
155i The uncommon prostitute: The contemporary image in an American age of pornography

Hughes, Patricia
120m Fighting the good fight: Separation or integration?

Hughes, Psiche
322l Women and literature in Latin America
322m Interview with Cristina Peri Rossi (Uruguay)

Hughes, Selma
265d Review of the literature of non-sexist curriculum and a critique of the underlying assumptions and rationale

Huie, Janice Riggle
429c Preaching through metaphor

Huilgol, Glynn
234c Shamanism as institutionalised ego defense and elite formation associated with transvestism in a Borneo society

Hulcoop, John E.
142m 'This petty medium': In the middle of *Middlemarch*

Hulka, Barbara S.
53p Estrogens and endometrial cancer

Hull, Gloria T.
14a Introduction: The politics of black women's studies

14r Researching Alice Dunbar-Nelson: A personal and literary perspective

30g Alice Dunbar-Nelson: A personal and literary perspective

150a Poem

150m "Under the days": The buried life and poetry of Angelina Weld Grmiké

150r What it is I think she's doing anyhow: A reading of Toni Cade Bambara's *The Salt Eaters*

174b The politics of black women's studies

249f I'm not shouting "Jubilee": One black woman's story

306f Alice Dunbar-Nelson: A regional approach

Hull, N. E. H.
376a The certain wages of sin: Sentence and punishment of female felons in colonial Massachusetts, 1673-1774

Hull, Valerie
424d Employment patterns of educated women in Indonesian cities

431e Women in Java's rural middle class: Progress or regress

Humez, Jean M.
379k "My spirit eye": Some functions of spiritual and visionary experience in the lives of five black women preachers, 1810-1880

Humphrey, Michael
94k Religion, law and family disputes in a Lebanese Muslim community in Sydney

240e Infertility and alternative parenting

Humphreys, Sheila M.
361j Effectiveness of science career conferences

Humphries, Jane
89f Class struggle and the persistence of the working-class family

106j The working-class family: A Marxist perspective

459c Class and historical analysis for the study of women and economic change

Hundley, Joan
432k The overemphasis on winning: A philosophical look

Hunt, Audrey
50w Women in official statistics

Hunt, Irmgard
307n Putting women in the energy picture

Hunt, Janet G.
387p Dilemmas and contradictions of status: The case of the dual-career family

Hunt, JoJo
70k American Indian women: Their relationship to the federal government

Hunt, Judith
470i A woman's place is her union

Hunt, Larry L.
387p Dilemmas and contradictions of status: The case of the dual-career family

Hunt, Martin F.
463r A comparative survey of women car buyers

Hunt, Mary E.
462l Political oppression and creative survival

462s A political perspective

Hunt, Pauline
378c Workers side by side: Women and the trade union movement

Hunter, Nan D.
103k Women and child support

Hunting, Constance
186a May Sarton: Reaching the lighthouse

186b An eccentric biography

186s "The risk is very great": The poetry of May Sarton

Hurt, Stephen W.
28o Psychopathology and the menstrual cycle

Hurwitz, Irving
8g Juvenile delinquency in girls

Hussain, Freda
198a Introduction: The ideal and contextual realities of Muslim women

198c The Islamic revolution and women: Quest for the Quranic model

198j The struggle of women in the national development of Pakistan

Hussman, Lawrence E.
155h The fate of the fallen woman in *Maggie* and *Sister Carrie*

Hutchins, Trova
16m Battered women

Hutchison, Barbara
90f The problem of sex bias in curriculum materials

Hutt, Corinne
265i Aspirations and sex roles - Are they in conflict?

Hyde, Janet
122g Bem's gender schema theory

Hyland, Drew A.
432j Competition, friendship, and human nature

Hyman, Paula
211b The Jewish family: Looking for a usable past

Hynes, H. Patricia
176y Toward a laboratory of one's own: Lesbians in science

Hytten, Frank E.
233b The effect of work on placental function and fetal growth

Iankova, Z. A.
446j Women's work and the family

Iazykova, V. S.
446j Women's work and the family

Ickes, William
136f Sex-role influences in dyadic interaction: A theoretical model

Ifeka, Caroline
234h The limitations of demography for women's history

Iglehart, Hallie
229bb Expanding personal power through meditation

229nn The unnatural divorce of spirituality and politics

Ilyatjari, Nganyintja
333f Women and land rights: The Pitjantjatjara land claims

Imes, Suzanne
443f Treatment of the imposter phenomenon in high-achieving women

Imhof, Arthur E.
144e Women, family and death: Excess mortality of women in child-bearing age in four communities in nineteenth-century Germany

Imray, Linda
241b Public and private: Marking the boundaries

Ince, Susan
310h Inside the surrogate industry

Inciardi, James A.
392h Women, heroin, and property crime

Ingemanson, Carl-Axel
252i Extra-amniotic ethacridine (Rivanol)-catheter technique for midtrimester abortion

Ingersoll, Berit
458d Employment status and social support: The experience of the mature woman

Ingersoll, Ralph W.
4b Administrative concerns

Ingison, Linda J.
361l An evaluation of programs for reentry women scientists

Inglis, Christine
466k The feminization of the teaching profession in Singapore

Ingold, Tim
104e The estimation of work in a northern Finnish farming community

International Labor Organization, Office for Women
373d Women, technology and the development process

Irigoyen, Matilde
469h The utilization of pediatric health services by Hispanic mothers

Irizarry, Estelle
408b Echoes of the Amazon myth in medieval Spanish literature

Irvin, Helen Deiss
441c The machine in utopia: Shaker women and technology

Irvine, Betty Jo
302j Women in academic-library, higher-education, and corporate management: A research review

Irvine, Jacqueline Jordan
303k The black female academic: Doubly burdened or doubly blessed?

Irvine, Lorna
20f One woman leads to another
180t A psychological journey: Mothers and daughters in English-Canadian fiction

Irwin, Joyce L.
112e Anna Maria van Schurman: The star of Utrecht (Dutch, 1607-1678)

Isaac, Annie
333h Borroloola community and land rights

Isasi-Diaz, Ada Maria
462g "Las Marías" of the feminist movement

Isely, Raymond B.
395e Water and sanitation-related health constraints on women's contribution to the economic development of communities

Iskin, Ruth
174o Feminist education at the feminist studio workshop
453t Institutions of women's culture

Islam, Mahmuda
98f Anthropological approach to study of rural women in Bangladesh: Experience of a female researcher
400d Impact of male migration on rural housewives

Islam, Shamima
98c Access to village women: Experiences in breaking barriers

Israel, Joan
359ss A feminist works with nontraditional clients

Iwanoff, I.
372v Anaerobic energy metabolism of women

Jacker, Corinne
316b Better than a shriveled husk: New forms for the theatre

Jacklin, Carol Nagy
259b Boys and girls entering school
266e Methodological issues in the study of sex-related differences

Jacklin, Pamela
90d The concept of sex equity in jurisprudence

Jackowitz, Ann
30p Anna O./Bertha Pappenheim and me

Jackson, Christine
260i Policies and implementation of anti-discrimination strategies

Jackson, Gregg B.
266j Methods for integrative reviews

Jackson, James H.
144g Overcrowding and family life: Working-class families and the housing crisis in late nineteenth-century Duisburg

Jackson, James S.
37q Group identity development within black families

Jackson, Laura
58b Prostitution

Jackson, Margaret
290b Sexology and the social construction of male sexuality (Havelock Ellis)
290c Sexology and the universalization of male sexuality (from Ellis to Kinsey, and Masters and Johnson)

Jackson, Maurice
392f Crimes of violence by women

Jackson, Pauline
206j The safety catch

Jackson, Roberta H.
421r Some aspirations of lower class black mothers

Jackson, Rosemary
318e Cold enclosures: The fiction of Susan Hill

Jackson, Stevi
212b Femininity, masculinity and sexuality

Jackson, Sue
294k From delicacy to dilemma: A feminist perspective

Jackson, William E.
331c The woman's song in medieval German poetry

Jackson-Brown, Irene V.
39t Black women and music: A survey from Africa to the new world

Jacob, Katharina
336n Comrade - woman - mother - resistance fighter

Jacobi-Dittrich, Juliane
145j Growing up female in the nineteenth century

Jacobs, I.
372l Is the significance of muscle fibre types to muscle metabolism different in females than in males?
372q Short time, maximal muscular performance: Relation to muscle lactate and fiber type in females

Jacobs, Jane
434l Dilemmas in role identification for low-income women

Jacobs, Joseph A.
277c Physiology of male sexual arousal

Jacobs, Ruth Harriet
210c Out of the *Mikvah* into the sauna: A study of women's health clubs

Jacobsen, Florence S.
42d Our heritage

Jacobson, Doranne
255c Purdah and the Hindu family in central India
325f Golden handprints and red-painted feet: Hindu childbirth rituals in central India

Jacobson, Helga E.
300b Women, society and change: Perspectives on the division of labour

Jacobson, Ira D.
463q Gender differences in reactions to vehicle environments

Jacoby, Robin Miller
124j The Women's Trade Union League school for women organizers
292a The Women's Trade Union League training school for women organizers, 1914-1926

Jacquette, Jane S.
218c Legitimizing political women: Expanding options for female political elites in Latin America

Jaggar, Alison
31b Human biology in feminist theory: Sexual equality reconsidered
223l Abortion and a woman's right to decide

Jahan, Rounaq
21j Women in politics: A case study of Bangladesh
255j Purdah and participation: Women in the politics of Bangladesh

Jahner, Elaine
384u A laddered, rain-bearing rug: Paula Gunn Allen's poetry

Jain, Harish C.
357d Low pay and female employment in Canada with selected references to the USA

Jakubowicz, Andrew
94b Ethnicity, multiculturalism and neo-conservatism

Jalland, Patricia
99d Victorian spinsters: Dutiful daughters, desperate rebels and the transition to the new women

James, Barbara
305e Breaking the hold: Women against rape

James, Edith
61m Edith Bolling Wilson: A documentary view

James, Jennifer
78o The prostitute as victim
111g Juvenile prostitution
404w Prostitution and sexual violence
461w The prostitute as victim

James, Louise Boyd
414h Woman's suffrage, Oklahoma style, 1890-1918

James, Nicky
297g A postscript to nursing

James, Selma
227k The power of women and the subversion of the community

James, Sibyl
109h Gothic transformations: Isak Dinesen and the gothic

James, William H.
273d Timing of fertilization and the sex ratio of offspring

Jameson, Penny
1221 Finding one's way through the labyrinth: A symposium on women's lives: Introduction
122m Finding one's way through the labyrinth: A symposium on women's lives: Methodology

Jamison, Angelene
40hh Imagery in the women poems: The art of Carolyn Rodgers

Janardhan, K.
299f Petty traders

Jancar, Barbara
113d Yugoslavia: War of resistance
388g Women in Communist countries: Comparative public policy

Jandt, Fred E.
133b Coming out as a communicative process

Janeway, Elizabeth
132v Women and the uses of power
439a Who is Sylvia? On the loss of sexual paradigms

Janiewski, Dolores
81d Flawed victories: The experiences of black and white women workers in Durham during the 1930s
264b Sisters under their skins: Southern working women, 1880-1950

Janis, Juel M.
80v Health care services for children in day care programs

Janowsky, David S.
28s Premenstrual tension: Etiology

Janson-Smith, Deirdre
12c Sociobiology: So what?

Janus, Mark-David
55g Youth prostitution

Jaquette, Jane S.
464a Power as ideology: A feminist analysis

Jardine, Alice
132a Prelude: The future of difference

Jaros, Dean
35e Sex, endocrines, and political behavior

Jasso, Sonia
86f Following the harvest: The health hazards of migrant and seasonal farmworking women

Jayaratne, Toby Epstein
312j The value of quantitative methodology for feminist research

Jean, Michèle
168g Production et communication du savior dans une perspective féministe: Enjuex et défis pour les femmes
168h Creating and communicating knowledge from a feminist perspective: Risks and challenges for women

Jeffrey, Julie Roy
412g Ministry through marriage: Methodist clergy wives on the trans-Mississippi frontier

Jeffreys, Sheila
212f The sexual abuse of children in the home
290a 'Free from all uninvited touch of man': Women's campaigns around sexuality, 1880-1914

Jelin, Elizabeth
459i Women and the urban labour market

Jelinek, Estelle C.
452a Introduction: Women's autobiography and the male tradition
452e The paradox and success of Elizabeth Cady Stanton

Jelinek, Mariann
391f Career management and women

Jellicoe, Ann
381g Covering the ground

Jemail, Jay
308j Bringing in the family: Kinship support and contraceptive behavior

Jemison, Marie Stokes
301h Growing up southern & sexy

Jenkins, Dafydd
334d Property interests in the classical Welsh law of women

Jenkins, Linda Walsh
399a Sex roles and shamans

Jenkins, Mercilee M.
189a A thief in the house: Women and language

Jenkins, Meri
381h Taking care of everything

Jenkins, Richard
297h Bringing it all back home: An anthropologist in Belfast

Jennings, M. Kent
378m Gender, levels of political thinking and political action

Jensen, A.
159d Norwegian women in court

Jensen, Emily
328i Clarissa Dalloway's respectable suicide

Jensen, Gary F.
376i The incarceration of women: A search for answers

Jensen, Gwendolyn E.
145d Henriette Schleiermacher: A woman in a traditional role

Jensen, Joan M.
81i All pink sisters: The War Department and the feminist movement in the 1920s
201a Needlework as art, craft, and livelihood before 1900
201d The great uprisings: 1900-1920
201e The great uprising in Rochester
201i Inside and outside the unions: 1920-1980
263f The sexual division of labor on American farms: 1750-1850

Jensen, Julie
254m American female dramatists: Show but no go?

Jensen, Katherine
307p Mother calls herself a housewife, but she buys bulls

Jesser, Clinton J.
48d The courtship game: Power in the sexual encounter

Jewson, Ruth Hathaway
458k After retirement: An exploratory study of the professional woman

Jexlev, Thelma
22b Wills, deeds, and charters as sources for the history of medieval women

Jeyes, Ulla
156p The Naditu women of Sippar

Jhabvala, Renana
346c Making women visible

Jiménez-Vázquez, Rosa
72k Social issues confronting Hispanic-American women

Jobling, I. F.
372i The "sporty" Australians

Joekes, Susan
206g The double day

Joeres, Ruth-Ellen Boetcher
145i Self-conscious histories: Biographies of German women in the nineteenth century

Joffe, Carole
103i Why the United States has no child-care policy

Johannesson, Russell
65h A policy-capturing application in a union setting

John, Mariam
421i Attitudes of women towards certain selected cultural practices in Kerala state, India

Johnson, Alan P.
286b "Dual life": The status of women in Stoker's *Dracula*

Johnson, Belinda A.
29k Depression: A behavioral-cognitive approach

Johnson, Carmen Acosta
319d Breast-feeding and social class mobility: The case of Mexican migrant mothers in Houston, Texas

Johnson, Carol
13j Some problems and developments in Marxist feminist theory

Johnson, Carolyn Kitchings
458h Attitudes toward retirement: A comparison of professional and nonprofessional married women

Johnson, Claudia D.
399j Enter the harlot

Johnson, Colleen Leahy
87g Parenthood, marriage, and careers: Situational constraints and role strain
359z Attitudes toward parenting in dual-career families

Johnson, E. Marshall
233k Mechanisms of teratogenesis: The extrapolation of the results of animal studies to man

Johnson, Elaine Dorough
108e To restore honor and fortune: *The Autobiography of Lenor López de Córdoba*

Johnson, Eleanor
150kk Reflections on black feminist therapy

Johnson, Elizabeth L.
177e Hakka women

Johnson, Elizabeth S.
210i Suburban older women

Johnson, Eric A.
145q The female victim: Homicide and women in Imperial Germany

Johnson, Eve
65m The role of labor
87g Parenthood, marriage, and careers: Situational constraints and role strain

Johnson, Frank Arvid
359z Attitudes toward parenting in dual-career families

Johnson, Gloria T.
169q Education for affirmative action: Two union approaches

Johnson, Kay Ann
21c Women in the People's Republic of China

Johnson, Leanor Boulin
37e Perspectives on black family empirical research: 1965-1978

Johnson, Marie
104h Domestic work in rural Iceland: An historical overview

Johnson, Marilyn
352l How real is fear of success?
360c Women and psychotherapy research
365c Gender and the process of therapy

Johnson, Mary Durham
444e Old wine in new bottles: The institutional changes for women of the people during the French revolution

Johnson, Miriam
90n The sources and dynamics of sexual inequality in the profession of education

Johnson, Pam McAllister
339d Being a manager in a multicultural world

Johnson, Rebecca
462f A historical addendum

Johnson, Richard L.
32i Gabriele Reuter: Romantic and realist

Johnson, Sharon M.
111m Beyond incarceration: A women's alternative

Johnson, Wendell Stacy
286l Fallen women, lost children: Wilde and the theatre in the nineties

Johnson, William G.
46f Disability insurance under proposed reforms

Johnston, Claire
406g Double indemnity

Johnston, Dorothy
294j Prostitution: One experience

Johnston, Maxene
265b Ethnic differences in sex stereotyping by mothers: Implications for health care

Joiner, James G.
359gg Postmastectomy counseling

Jolly, Robert William
280a Prostitution: Profession and pathology

Jonel, Marissa
7b Letter from a former masochist

Jones, Alun R.
451g The world of love: The fiction of Eudora Welty

Jones, Anne Goodwyn
264e Southern literary women as chroniclers of southern life
450o The world of Lee Smith

Jones, Anne Hudson
131b Alexei Panshin's almost non-sexist *Rite of Passage*

Jones, Audrey E.
308a Teenage women in the United States: Sex, contraception, pregnancy, fertility, and maternal and infant health

Jones, Catherine
188l The English mystic: Julian of Norwich

Jones, Diane
386f Women in the arts

Jones, Diane Carlson
35f Power structures and perceptions of power holders in same-sex groups of young children

Jones, Frank
321h Income inequality

Jones, Gareth
470c Contemporary clerical work: A case study of local government

Jones, Gavin W.
424a Economic growth and changing female employment structure in the cities of Southeast and East Asia

Jones, Gayl
40v About my work

Jones, Lynne
167h On common ground: The women's peace camp at Greenham Common
167j A women's day for disarmament: Notes on organising a decentralised action

Jones, Patricia
150p I've been thinking of Diana Sands

Jones, Tricia S.
415c Sexual harassment in the organization

Jong, Erica
474l Blood and guts: The tricky problem of being a woman writer in the late twentieth century

Jonung, Christina
260c Patterns of occupational segregation by sex in the labor market
437c Sweden

Jordan, Brigitte
56f Studying childbirth: The experience and methods of a woman anthropologist

Jordan, Daniel C.
216d Developmental universals and their implications for parental competence

Jordan, John O.
196j Closer than a brother: Swinburne and Watts-Dunton

Jordan, June
150cc From sea to shining sea (poem)
417g A song of Sojourner Truth (poem)

Jordanova, L.
50z Oppressive dichotomies: The nature/culture debate
200c Natural facts: A historical perspective on science and sexuality
418c The history of the family
418f Mental illness, mental health: Changing norms and expectations
418m Oppressive dichotomies: The nature/culture debate

Jorge, Angela
60n Issues of race and class in women's studies: A Puerto Rican woman's thoughts

Josantony
91m Moral theology from a feminist perspective

Jose, Paul
136h Gender, androgyny, and conversational assertiveness

Josefowitz, Natasha
307v Paths to power in high technology organizations

Josefowitz, Nina
300d The psychology of politeness among the Javanese

Joselit, Jenna Weissman
203p From kitchen to storefront: Women in the tenant movement

Joseph, Barbara
455e Ain't I a woman

Joseph, Gloria
68h Caribbean women: The impact of race, sex, and class
369e The incompatible menage à trois: Marxism, feminism, and racism

Joseph, Suad
362d The mobilization of Iraqi women into the wage labor force

Jovick, Thomas D.
90i Ambitions and the opportunity for professionals in the elementary school
90r The gender of principals and principal/teacher relations in elementary schools

Jowell, Jeffrey
93g The enforcement of laws against sex discrimination in England: Problems of institutional design

Joyce, Robin
13l Feminism: An early tradition amongst western Australian labor women
23e Labor women: Political housekeepers or politicians?

Joyce, Rosemary
473k The life of Sarah Penfield, rural Ohio grandmother: Tradition maintained, tradition threatened

Joyner, Nancy C.
1d P. D. James
450j Mary Lee Settle's connections: Class and clothes in the Beulah quintet

Juhasz, Suzanne
121a Introduction: Feminist critics read Emily Dickinson
452m Towards a theory of form in feminist autobiography: Kate Millett's *Flying* and *Sita*; Maxine Hong Kingston's *The Woman Warrior*

Jules-Rosette, Benetta
39i Women in indigenous African cults and churches

Justus, Joyce Bennett
39w Women's role in West Indian society

Kaboolian, Linda
124l Women and peace

Kadar, Marlene
305o Sexual harassment as a form of social control

Kader, Soha Abdel
298i A survey of trends in social sciences research on women in the Arab region, 1960-1980

Kagan, Sharon L.
80t Considering proprietary child care

Kâgitçibasi, Çigdem
270f Sex roles, value of children and fertility in Turkey

Kahane, Claire
109o The maternal legacy: The grotesque tradition in Flannery O'Connor's female gothic

Kahn, Coppélia
343j Coming of age in Verona

Kahn, Janet
57b Toward an understanding of sexual learning and communication: An examination of social learning theory and nonschool learning environments

Kahn, Sharon E.
271i Beyond a cognitive/behavioural approach: Congruent assertion training

Kahn, Wendy
435d Pay equity: Beyond equal pay for equal work

Kahn-Edrington, Marla
359dd Abortion counseling

Kahn-Hut, Rachel
387u Unresolved questions: Three feminist perspectives

Kahr, Madlyn Millner
117h Delilah
389k Erica Tietze-Conrat (1883-1958): Productive scholar in renaissance and baroque art

Kail, Andreé
58d Housewives

Kaimal, Padma
386f Women in the arts

Kakakios, Michael
94i Migrant communities and class politics: The Greek community in Australia

Kalant, Oriana Josseau
9a Sex differences in alcohol and drug problems - some highlights

Kalantzis, Mary
94e Multiculturalism and education policy

Kalin, Rudolf
271f Sex-role ideology and sex bias in judgments of occupational suitability

Kallab, I.
265n Sex role images in Lebanese text books

Kalleberg, Annemor
468a The making of a female occupation: A case study of cleaning work

Kallgren, Joyce K.
21a Women in Asian cities, their political and economic roles: Research problems and strategies

Kamerman, Sheila
467c Managing work and family life: A comparative policy overview

Kaminsky, Amy Katz
108e To restore honor and fortune: *The Autobiography of Lenor López de Córdoba*
155j Women writing about prostitutes: Amalia Jamilis and Luisa Valenzuela

Kampen, Natalie Boymel
117e Social status and gender in Roman art: The case of the saleswoman

Kamuf, Peggy
356s Writing like a woman

Kandiyoti, Deniz
270c Urban change and women's roles in Turkey: An overview and evaluation

Kandolin, Irja
471h Women at work in Finland

Kane, Theresa
152f Civil rights in a church of compassion

Kanin, Eugene J.
349m Sexual aggression: A second look at the offended female

Kannel, William B.
210o Cardiovascular risk factors in the elderly woman

Kanter, Rosabeth Moss
93n The impact of organizational structure: Models and methods for change
140e Some effects of proportions on group life: Skewed sex ratios and responses to token women
214e Structuring the inside: The impact of organizations on sex differences
339c Women managers: Moving up in a high tech society
387s The impact of hierarchical structures on the work behavior of women and men

Kantner, John F.
309d Sexual and contraceptive experience of young unmarried women in the United States, 1976 and 1971
309e First pregnancies to women aged 15-19: 1976 and 1971
309f Contraceptive patterns and premarital pregnancy among women aged 15-19 in 1976
309h The risk of adolescent pregnancy in the first months of intercourse

Kantrowitz, Joanne Spencer
249c Paying your dues, part-time

Kao, Hsin-Sheng C.
449e The shaping of life: Structure and narrative process in Eileen Chang's *The Rouge of the North*

Kaplan, Alexandra G.
140w Toward an analysis of sex-role-related issues in the therapeutic relationship
239d Human sex-hormone abnormalities viewed from an androgynous perspective: A reconsideration of the work of John Money
360d The relational self in women: Developmental theory and public policy
365h Psychodynamic perspectives

Kaplan, E. Ann
231t Is the gaze male?
406e The place of women in Fritz Lang's *The Blue Gardenia*

Kaplan, Helen S.
461a Women's sexual response

Kaplan, Jane Rachel
341a Introduction: Beauty and the feast
341d Barbara's foodworld: A case history

Kaplan, Marion
336h Sisterhood under siege: Feminism and anti-semitism in Germany, 1904-1938

Kaplan, Robin
186w "I live alone in a very beautiful place": An interview with May Sarton

Kaplan, Rosa Felsenburg
211l The Noah syndrome

Kaplan, Sheila
407g An agenda for senior women administrators
407i Getting the best: Conclusions, recommendations, and selected resources

Kaplan, Sydney Janet
318a Passionate portrayal of things to come: Doris Lessing's recent fiction
448h "A gigantic mother": Katherine Mansfield's London

Kapp, Ardeth Greene
42i Drifting, dreaming, directing

Karanja, Wambui Wa
393c Women and work: A study of female and male attitudes in the modern sector of an African metropolis (Lagos)

Karl, Marilee
206n Resistance, strikes and strategies

Karlekar, Malavika
386c Sweepers

Karlsson, J.
372l Is the significance of muscle fibre types to muscle metabolism different in females than in males?

Karpf, Anne
358d Women and radio

Karr, Rodney G.
133a Homosexual labeling and the male role

Karrh, Bruce W.
447k Evaluation and control of embryofetotoxic substances

Kartinyeri, Doreen
333s Recording our history

Kaschak, Ellyn
453r Feminist therapy

Kasdan, Margo
332m "Why are you afraid to have me at your side?": From passivity to power in *Salt of the Earth*

Kashif-Badri, Hagga
298f The history, development, organization and position of women's studies in the Sudan

Kassel, Victor
289h Long-term care institutions

Kates, Joanne
305f Once more with feeling: Heterosexuality and feminist consciousness
323p Organizing freelancers in the arts

Katkova, I.
446m Maternal care of infants

Katoppo, Marianne
91h Woman's image of herself

Katz, Esther
454a American women and domestic culture: An approach to women's history

Katz, Joseph
45j The past and future of the undergraduate woman

Katz, Mitchell H.
243i Work experience and family relations among working-class and lower-middle-class families

Katz, Naomi
199l Women and work in Silicon Valley: Options and futures
428m Fast forward: The internationalization of Silicon Valley

Katzenstein, Mary Fainsod
101k Towards equality? Cause and consequence of the political prominence of women in India

Kaub, Shirley Jane
351g Women's studies at the secondary school level

Kaufman, Arthur
326i Rape of men in the community

Kaufman, Debra R.
266b Social science inquiries into female achievement: Recurrent methodological problems
344s Professional women: How real are the recent gains?
443m Some feminist concerns in an age of networking

Kaufman, Raymond H.
4h Issues surrounding adolescent pregnancy terminations

Kaufmann, K.
310o Abortion, a woman's matter: An explanation of who controls abortion and how and why they do it

Kauppinen-Toropainen, Kaisa
471h Women at work in Finland

Kay, Leslie
290d Theory into practice: Sexual liberation or social control? (*Forum* magazine 1968-1981)

Kay, Margarita A.
319c Mexican, Mexican American, and Chicana childbirth

Kay, Susan Ann
35c Political ideology, sociobiology, and the U.S. women's rights movement

Kaye, Frances W.
384k Hamlin Garland's feminism

Kaye/Kantrowitz, Melanie
397p Culture-making: Lesbian classics in the year 2000

Kearney, June Frances
147dd The history of women's intercollegiate athletics in Ohio, 1945-1972

Kearns, Bessie Jean Ruley
51f Perceptions of menopause by Papago women

Kearns, Deborah
23n *A Theory of Justice* and love: Rawls on the family

Keefer, Constance H.
69e The early mother-child relationship: A developmental view of woman as mother

Keeley, Phil
274o Business studies

Keep, P.A. van
236b The premenstrual syndrome - an epidemiological and statistical exercise

Kehoe, Alice
148c The shackles of tradition

Keil, Teresa
250i Into work: Continuity and change

Keim, Curtis A.
370i Women in slavery among the Mangbetu c. 1800-1910

Keirse, Marc J.N.C.
252j Fact and fancy in the termination of molar pregnancy with particular reference to uterine stimulants
252n Termination of pregnancy after intrauterine foetal death

Keitel, Merle A.
221f Family effects of dislocation, unemployment, and discouragement

Keith, Louis G.
252o Complications of second trimester abortion
252q Contraception following second trimester abortion

Keith, Pat M.
458e Working women versus homemakers: Retirement resources and correlates of well-being

Keizer, H. A.
372r Reproducibility of aerobic power and related physiological variables in women

372s Exercise-induced changes in estradiol metabolism and their possible physiological meaning

Keller, Evelyn Fox
84k Gender and science
84l The mind's eye
181h Women, science, and popular mythology

Keller, Harold R.
352n Working and parenting: The male and father role

Keller, John F.
428n The division of labor in electronics

Keller, Karl
121d Notes on sleeping with Emily Dickinson

Keller, Rosemary Skinner
366f Lay women in the Protestant tradition
367d New England women: Ideology and experience in first-generation Puritanism (1630-1650)
367h Women and revivalism: The Puritan and Wesleyan traditions
367i Women, civil religion, and the American Revolution
412m Creating a sphere for women: The Methodist Episcopal church, 1869-1906

Kelley, Kathryn
230a Introduction: Pornography and sex research

Kelley, Mary
127a The sentimentalists: Promise and betrayal in the home

Kelley, Maryellen R.
272k Commentary: The need to study the transformation of job structures

Kelley, Peggy Clark
399gg Peggy Clark Kelley: Reminiscences of a "designing" woman

Kelly, Alison
193a Girls and science education: Is there a problem?
193b Sex differences in science achievement: Some results and hypotheses
193e Science achievement as an aspect of sex roles
193i Choosing or channelling?
193v Retrieving the missing half

Kelly, Elinor
193d Socialisation in patriarchal society

Kelly, Gail P.
68o The schooling of Vietnamese immigrants: Internal colonialism and its impact on women

Kelly, Gertrude
129x State aid to science

Kelly, James G.
295j Social support and efficacy in advocacy roles: A case study of two women's organizations

Kelly, Jeffrey A.
304b Sex-role stereotypes and mental health: Conceptual models in the 1970s and issues for the 1980s

Kelly, Joan
256i The doubled vision of feminist theory

Kelly, Leontine T.C.
429d Preaching in the black tradition

Kelly, María Patricia Fernández
199n *Maquiladoras*: The view from the inside
307c Gender and industry on Mexico's new frontier

Kelsall, R. Keith
44h Teaching

Kelsey, Jennifer L.
53u Epidemiology of osteoporosis

Kemnitzer, David S.
199l Women and work in Silicon Valley: Options and futures
428m Fast forward: The internationalization of Silicon Valley

Kemph, John P.
284k Children not severely damaged by incest with a parent

Kempner, Ken
262f A social-psychological analysis of the context for change

Kendall, Carl
421b Female-headed households and domestic organization in San Isidro, Guatemala: A test of Hammel and Laslett's comparative typology

Kendall, Elizabeth
442l Women and dance

Kendall, Thena
211h Memories of an Orthodox youth

Kenen, Regina H.
79h A look at prenatal diagnosis within the context of changing parental and reproductive norms

Kennedy, Edward M.
80n Child care - A commitment to be honored

Kenner, Hugh
338g The look of a queen

Kenney, Karen
147i The realm of sports and the athletic woman, 1850-1900

Kent, Christopher
164f 'Real solemn history' and social history

Kent, George
40i Gwendolyn Brooks' poetic realism: A developmental survey

Kent, J. N.
159k Argentine statistics on female criminality

Keohane, Nannerl O.
123e Speaking from silence: Women and the science of politics

Ker, Margaret
99a Brides of Christ and poor mortals: Women in medieval society

Kerbel, Sandra
349e The economics of female criminality: An analysis of police blotters, 1890-1976

Kerenyi, Thomas D.
252h Intra-amniotic hypertonic saline instillation in the second trimester

Kern, Robert
95g Margarita Nelken: Women and the crisis of Spanish politics

Kerns, David L.
291j Medical assessment of child sexual abuse

Kerns, Virginia
269b Structural continuity in the division of men's and women's work among black Carib (Garífuna)
325i Black Carib women and rites of death

Kerpelman, Larry C.
463l Women's travel behavior and attitudes: An empirical analysis

Kerzner, Lawrence J.
210n Physical changes after menopause

Keshena, Rita
70i Relevancy of tribal interests and tribal diversity in determining the educational needs of American Indians

Kessler, Carol Farley
180y Mothers and daughters in literature: A preliminary bibliography
383e The heavenly utopia of Elizabeth Stuart Phelps

Kessler, Suzanne
50r Developmental aspects of gender

Kessler-Harris, Alice
86i Protection for women: Trade unions and labor laws
292g Education in working-class solidarity: The summer school for office workers

Kestenberg, Judith S.
88d The inner-genital phase - prephallic and preoedipal

Ketchum, Anne Duhamel
64c Colette and the enterprise of writing: A reappraisal

Ketchum, Sara Ann
275t Moral redescription and political self-deception

Kettering, Terri A.
15b The alternative press and the mass media: Two case studies

Ketting, E.
252b Second trimester abortion as a social problem: Delay in abortion seeking behaviour and its causes

Keul, J.
372k Physiological and metabolic responses of female athletes during laboratory and field exercises

Keyfitz, Nathan
45a American demographic directions

Keyssar, Alexander
454c Widowhood in eighteenth-century Massachusetts: A problem in the history of the family

Keyworth, Florence
119f Invisible struggles: The politics of ageing

Khan, Verity Saifullah
402l Asian women in Britain: Strategies of adjustment of Indian and Pakistani migrants

Khanna, Lee Cullen
383h Truth and art in women's worlds: Doris Lessing's *Marriages Between Zones Three, Four, and Five*

417bb Change and art in women's worlds: Doris Lessing's *Canopus in Argos: Archives*

Kharchev, A. G.
446k Changing family roles and marital instability

Khatib-Chahidi, Jane
371f Sexual prohibitions, shared space and fictive marriages in Shi'ite Iran

Khattab, Hind A.
198i Female education in Egypt: Changing attitudes over a span of 100 years

Khoo, Siew-Ean
420a Urbanization, migration and the status of women
420b The migration of women to cities: A comparative perspective
420g Female rural-to-urban migration in peninsular Malaysia
420s Women in Asian cites: Policies, public services, and research
424n Urbanward migration and employment of women in Southeast and East Asian cities: Patterns and policy issues

Kickbusch, Ilona
436h A hard day's night: Women, reproduction and service society

Kidd, Tony
258d Social security and the family

Kidwell, Clara Sue
70c The status of American Indian women in higher education

Kiefer, Irene
394n Child care and the university

Kies, Marian W.
438c It takes more than luck (United States)

Kilgore, Dan
175h Two sixshooters and a sunbonnet: The story of Sally Skull

Killens, John O.
40l The literary genius of Alice Childress

Killinger, Marc
224n Lesbian and gay oppression in the '80s: Androgyny, men and power

Kilpatrick, Hilary
322c Women and literature in the Arab world
322f Interview with Etel Adnan (Lebanon)

Kim, Bok-Lim C.
71n Asian wives of U.S. servicemen: Women in triple jeopardy

Kim, Kyong-Dong
421c A causal interpretation of the effect of mother's education and employment status on parental decision-making role patterns in the Korean family

Kim, On-Jook Lee
421c A causal interpretation of the effect of mother's education and employment status on parental decision-making role patterns in the Korean family

Kim, Yung-Chung
75c Working women in Korea

Kimball, Barbara
453i Women and fashion

Kimball, Camilla E.
42c   Keys for a woman's progression

Kimball, Gayle
453a   Women's culture: Themes and images
453p   Feminist theology

Kimball, Linda A.
473b   Women of Brunei

Kimball, Spencer W.
42a   Our sisters in the church

Kimlicka, Thomas M.
287b   Male sexuality: Socio-sexual change and
       the single status

Kincaid-Ehlers, Elizabeth
51b   Bad maps for an unknown region:
       Menopause from a literary perspective
190q   "Oh dear me! Why weren't we all boys,
       then there wouldn't be any bother":
       Menarche and popular American fiction

Kincey, John
240h   Psychological aspects of hysterectomy

King, Deborah Schuster
382f   Ireland

King, Francis P.
46g   Occupational pension plans and spouse
       benefits

King, Helen
156h   Bound to bleed: Artemis and Greek
       women

King, Johanna
453o   Characteristics of women's dreams

King, Lucy
418j   Contraception and abortion

King, Margaret L.
33c   Book-lined cells: Women and humanism in
       the early Italian Renaissance

King, Mary-Claire
141c   Statistical model for the study of familial
       breast cancer

King, Patricia A.
2d   The juridical status of the fetus: A propos-
       al for legal protection of the unborn
173b   The juridical status of the fetus: A propos-
       al for legal protection of the unborn

King, Ursula
402h   Women and religion: The status and image
       of women in some major religious tradi-
       tions

King, Ynestra
167e   All is connectedness: Scenes from the
       Women's Pentagon Action USA
181g   Toward an ecological feminism and a femi-
       nist ecology
441h   Feminist pedagogy and technology:
       Reflections on the Goddard feminism and
       ecology summer program
462d   Making the world live: Feminism and the
       domination of nature

Kingdom, Elizabeth F.
283f   Sexist bias and law

Kingston, Maxine Hong
474m   The coming book

Kinksy, Lynn
129f   Government is women's enemy

Kinnaird, Joan K.
125b   Mary Astell: Inspired by ideas

Kinnard, Cythnia D.
389g   Mariana Griswold Van Rensselaer (1851-
       1934): America's first professional woman
       art critic

Kinsey, Susan R.
130m   The memorialists

Kiray, Mübeccel B.
270k   Changing patterns of patronage: A study
       in structural change

Kiresuk, Thomas J.
191g   Tailoring evaluation to measure the
       accountability of mental health services to
       women

Kirkendall, Lester A.
185a   Looking toward the year 2020
185c   Marriage and the family: Styles and forms
185i   The transition from sex to sexuality and
       intimacy
185m   Family options, governments, and the
       social milieu: Viewed from the 21st centu-
       ry

Kirkpatrick, Jean
11m   Women and alcohol

Kirkup, James
278f   Phallic worship: Some personal medita-
       tions on a sacred theme

Kirkwood, Deborah
160e   The suitable wife: Preparation for mar-
       riage in London and Rhodesia/Zimbabwe
160h   Settler wives in southern Rhodesia: A case
       study

Kirsch, Thomas
431a   Buddhism, sex-roles and the Thai economy

Kirsh, Barbara
304d   Sex roles and language use: Implications
       for mental health
411b   Life events and the boundaries of midlife
       for women

Kirshner, Lewis A.
8p   Research on gender and psychotherapy

Kiryluk, Carol
339f   The single woman: Moving up by moving
       around

Kiseleva, G.
446r   The position of women and demographic
       policy

Kish, Kathleen
408h   A school for wives: Women in eighteenth-
       century Spanish theater

Kishwar, Madhu
91o   Bondage: Denial or fundamental rights to
       women

Kittay, Eva Feder
31h   Pornography and the erotics of domination
195g   Womb envy: An explanatory concept

Kittel, Ruth
375e   Rape in thirteenth-century England: A
       study of the common-law courts

Klaiber, Edward L.
28m   Estrogens and central nervous system
       function: Electroencephalography, cogni-
       tion, and depression

239c   Gonadal hormones and cognitive function-
       ing

Klapholz, Henry
36n   The electronic fetal monitor in perina-
       tology

Klay, Robin
315j   Analyzing discrimination against women in
       the labor market - A few lessons from
       John Stuart Mill

Kleiman, Betty
265l   Cultural differences in children's sex role
       stereotypes

Klein, Alan
148g   The political economy of gender: A 19th
       century Plains Indian case study

Klein, Dorie
78b   The etiology of female crime: A review of
       the literature
78k   Violence against women: Some considera-
       tions regarding its causes and eliminations
165c   The dark side of marriage: Battered wives
       and the domination of women
392b   The etiology of female crime: A review of
       the literature

Klein, Frieda
463p   The transportation implications of
       women's fear of assault

Klein, Herbert S.
370b   African women in the Atlantic slave trade

Klein, J. Theodore
432l   Philosophy of education, physical educa-
       tion, and the sexes

Klein, Joan Larsen
343m   Lady Macbeth: "Infirm of purpose"

Klein, Kathleen Gregory
1a   Dorothy Sayers
329l   A common sitting room: Virginia Woolf's
       critique of women writers

Klein, Laura F.
347d   Contending with colonization: Tlingit men
       and women in change

Klein, Marjorie H.
29g   Marriage and the family: An unconscious
       male bias in behavioral treatment?
365g   Marital and family conflicts

Klein, Martin A.
370a   Women's importance in African slave sys-
       tems
370e   Women in slavery in the western Sudan

Klein, Viola
344cc   The historical background

Klenk, Kenneth L.
133h   Gay masculinity in the gay disco

Klenke-Hamel, Karen
425h   Causal determinants of job satisfaction in
       dual career couples

Klepfisz, Irena
231j   they're always curious

Klepp, Susan E.
201b   "If I didn't have my sewing machine...":
       Women and sewing-machine technology

Klerman, Gerald L.

81 Depression in women: Epidemiology, explanations, and impact on the family

191d Depressions among women: Their nature and causes

359m Sex differences and the epidemiology of depression

Klerman, Lorraine V.

10j Female alcohol abuse: Its effects on the family

Kline, David

57b Toward an understanding of sexual learning and communication: An examination of social learning theory and nonschool learning environments

Kline, Jennie

53j Environmental exposures and spontaneous abortion

Klingbeil, Karil S.

26a Emergency room intervention: Detection, assessment, and treatment

Knapp, Mona

32k "Eine frau, aber mehr als das, eine Persönlichkeit, aber mehr als das: eine frau": The structural analysis of the female characters in the novels of Max Frisch

Knapp, Nancy Mayer

472f Institutionalized women: Some classic types, some common problems, and some partial solutions

Knief, Mary Kay

175t The babe

Knoepflmacher, U. C.

196e On exile and fiction: The Leweses and the Shelleys

Knowles, Wilf

471a Women at work in Great Britain

Knuckman, Paul

55h The role of community health centers

Koadlow, Elsie

47d Sex

Kobrin, Frances E.

273c Sex selection through amniocentesis and selective abortion

353v The American midwife controversy: A crisis of professionalization

Kocik, Lucjan

104f A note on the custom of 'paying off' on family farms in Poland

Köckeis-Stangl, Eva

52f The position of Austrian women in the family: Some data, many questions, and a few interpretations

Koehler, Lyle

19l The case of the American Jezebels

454b The case of the American Jezebels: Anne Hutchinson and female agitation during the years of the Antinomian turmoil, 1636-1640

Koenig, Dolores

393e The stable African family: Traditional and modern family structures in two African societies (Basa and Manding)

393g Education and fertility among Cameroonian working women

Koeske, Randi Daimon

51a Toward a biosocial paradigm for menopause research: Lessons and contributions from the behavioral sciences

51aa Beyond oppositional analysis: Concluding remarks

271q Theoretical/conceptual implications of study design and statistical analysis: Research on the menstrual cycle

Koff, Elissa

190e Through the looking glass of menarche: What the adolescent girl sees

Kogelman, Stanley

96n Math anxiety and female mental health: Some unexpected links

Kohlstedt, Sally Gregory

352g Single-sex education and leadership: The early years of Simmons College

Kohn, Lawrence

190u Steroidal contraceptive use and subsequent development of hyperprolactinemia

Kolenda, Konstantin

4k Ethical issues of adolescent pregnancy

Kolenda, Pauline

194k Pox and the terror of childlessness: Images and ideas of the smallpox goddess in a north Indian village

Kollias, Karen

43l Class realities: Create a new power base

Kolodny, Annette

189b Dancing through the minefield: Some observations on the theory, practice and politics of a feminist literary criticism

356m Honing a habitable languagescape: Women's images for the new world frontiers

452n The lady's not for spurning: Kate Millett and the critics

Komer, Odessa

169q Education for affirmative action: Two union approaches

Komi, P. V.

372m Fundamental performance characteristics in females and males

Komter, Aafke

76d Feminism and psychoanalysis

Konie, Gwendoline

77e An eclectic workshop

Koo, Sung-Yeal

424b Trends in female labour force participation and occupational shifts in urban Korea

Koolish, Lynda

30h This is who she is to me: On photographing women

Koolmatrie, Janis

333q Aboriginal women in education

Koonz, Claudia

336b Beyond *Kinder, Küche, Kirche*: Weimar women in politics and work

336i The competition for women's *lebensraum*, 1928-1934

Kopelov, Connie

169s Subjects and materials: How to handle controversy

Kopf, David M.

433m The image of Bengal in the emerging literature of Bangladesh: The fiction of Hasan Azizul Huq

Koppel, Flora

404dd Establishing interdisciplinary treatment networks

Koppelman, Frank S.

463k Role influence in transportation decision making

Korenbrot, Carol

36d Value conflicts in biomedical research into future contraceptives

Korg, Jacob

142h How George Eliot's people think

Koring, W.

372dd Foot disorders of female marathon runners before and after a marathon race

Korman, A. K.

49g Commentary on studies of gender-mix in labor market research

Kornbluh, Hy

169d Conferences: The one-day model

Kornbluh, Joyce L.

169a Labor education and women workers: An historical perspective

169d Conferences: The one-day model

292h The she-she-she camps: An experiment in living and learning, 1934-1937

Korsmeyer, Carolyn

275h The hidden joke: Generic uses of masculine terminology

Korson, J. Henry

421aa Career constraints among women graduate students in a developing society: West Pakistan. A study in the changing status of women

Koshal, Manjulika

21k Indira Gandhi as head of government

Kosinar, Patricia

214b Socialization and self-esteem: Women in management

Koss, Mary P.

230i Sexually aggressive men: Empirical findings and theoretical implications

Kostakov, V. G.

446d Features of the development of female employment

Kostash, Myrna

305c Whose body? Whose self? Beyond pornography

Kostyniuk, Lydia P.

463t Gender-role identification in the methodology of transportation planning

Kotliar, A. E.

446e The educational and occupational skill level of industrial workers

Kouri, Denise

305n Getting organized...in Saskatchewan Working Women

Kouri, Richard E.

141b Genetic control of breast cancer susceptibility in animals

Koutaissoff, Elisabeth
151d Secondary education for all in a forward-looking society

Koziara, Karen Shallcross
65h A policy-capturing application in a union setting

Kra, Pauline
130q Montesquieu and women

Kraemer, Ross S.
325e Ecstasy and possession: Women of ancient Greece and the cult of Dionysus

Kraft, Kent
188e The German visionary: Hildegard of Bingen

Kramarae, Cheris
171a Language, gender and society: Opening a second decade of research
171k Sex similarities and differences in language, speech, and nonverbal communication: An annotated bibliography
189a A thief in the house: Women and language
356d Proprieters of language
417t Imagining a different world of talk

Kramer, David
95j Ulrike Meinhof: An emancipated terrorist?

Kramer, Sylvia
336m The story of Ruth

Krantz, Grover S.
279d The fossil record of sex

Krasnick, Mark
111u Problems of policy development in criminal justice

Kraus, Henry
117f Eve and Mary: Conflicting images of medieval woman

Kravetz, Diane
365k Consciousness-raising and self-help

Kreinberg, Nancy
307cc EQUALS in computer technology
361c EQUALS: Working with educators

Kremen, Eleanor
455f The social work profession encounters the battered woman

Kreps, Juanita M.
339a Women in a changing economy

Kress, Susan
131j In and out of time: The form of Marge Piercy's novels

Kreuter, Gretchen
128c May Wood Simons: Party theorist

Kreuter, Kent
128c May Wood Simons: Party theorist

Krickus, Mary Ann
73e The status of East European women in the family: Tradition and change

Krippel, Elizabeth
63d A coed prison

Krishnan, Prabha
161c Applauding servility - Images of women in advertisements

Kristeller, Paul Oskar
33d Learned women of early modern Italy: Humanists and university scholars

Kristeva, Julia
108q My memory's hyperbole

Kroeger, Naomi
458f Preretirement preparation: Sex differences in access, sources, and use

Krop, Harry D.
29e Sexuality

Krótki, Karol J.
405n Some demographic, particularly fertility, correlates of female status in Eastern Europe and the republics of the Soviet Union

Krouse, Agate
394k Merging two careers and marriage

Krouse, Harry
394k Merging two careers and marriage

Krouse, Richard W.
106h Patriarchal liberalism and beyond: From John Stuart Mill to Harriet Taylor

Kruchkow, Diane
15g Publishers on libraries: Walking through walls

Kruger, Barbara
225n No progress in pleasure

Kuhns, E. D.
49i The setting and the reality for labor relations in the 90's

Kuik, Jannie
179i Nuclear Europe

Kuipers, H.
372r Reproducibility of aerobic power and related physiological variables in women

Kuleshova, L. M.
446q Part-time employment of women

Kumari, Chidananda
299g Tribal migrants

Kung, Lydia
177f Doing fieldwork
177g Taiwan garment workers

Kurian, George
421i Attitudes of women towards certain selected cultural practices in Kerala state, India

Kushner, Deena Dash
180o How light a *Lighthouse* for today's women?

Kutyrev, B. P.
446o The quantity and quality of work: A round table

Kuyas, Nilüfer
270g Female labor power relations in the urban Turkish family

Kuykendall, Eleanor
195o Toward an ethic of nurturance: Luce Irigaray on mothering and power
275i Feminist linguistics in philosophy

La Follette, Suzanne
129u The economic position of women

Labalme, Patricia H.
33f Women's roles in early modern Venice: An exceptional case

Laborde, Alice M.
130v The problem of sexual equality in Sadean prose

Labourie-Racape, Annie
437b France

Labouvie-Vief, Gisela
317a Adaptive dimensions of adult cognition

Lachapelle, Caroline
305w Beyond barriers: Native women and the women's movement

Lachman, Margie E.
411c Methods for a life-span developmental approach to women in the middle years

Lachmann, Frank M.
88h Narcissistic development

Ladd, Florence C.
57i Human sexuality: Messages in public environments

Ladd, Tony
147nn Sexual discrimination in youth sport: The case of Margaret Gisolo

Laderman, Carol
362g The politics of healing in Malaysia
431d Putting Malay women in their place

Ladipo, Patricia
5h Developing women's cooperatives: An experiment in rural Nigeria

Ladner, Joyce
39e Tanzanian women in nation building
39m Racism and tradition: Black womanhood in historical perspective

LaFrance, Marianne
136g Gender gestures: Sex, sex-role, and nonverbal communication

Lakoff, Robin Tolmach
275d *Language and Woman's Place* (excerpts)
307e Doubletalk: Sexism in tech talk

Lamanna, Mary Ann
3a Social science and ethical issues: The policy implications of poll data on abortion

Lamb, Catherine
122k How women and men write about themselves (less differently than you might expect)

Lamb, Michael E.
204a Parental behavior and child development in nontraditional families: An introduction
204c Maternal employment and child development: A review
204e Varying degrees of paternal involvement in infant care: Attitudinal and behavioral correlates
216l What can "research experts" tell parents about effective socialization?
427c Fathers, mothers, and childcare in the 1980s: Family influences on child development

Lamb, Neven P.
82g Nutrition and health

Lambers, K. J.
240b Regret and reversal of sterilization

Lambert, Jean
118e Becoming human: A contextual approach to decisions about pregnancy and abortion

Lambiotte, Joellen
63j Sex-role differentiation in a co-correctional setting

Lämmer, M.
372c Women and sport in ancient Greece

Lamont, Rosette C.
313j The off-center spatiality of womens' discourse

Lamphere, Louise
73h The economic struggles of female factory workers: A comparison of French, Polish, and Portuguese immigrants
199o On the shop floor: Multi-ethnic unity against the conglomerate

Lampman, Robert J.
46a Concepts underlying the current controversy about women's social security benefits

Land, Hilary
93q Social policies and the family: Their effect on women's paid employment in Great Britain
465c Who still cares for the family? Recent developments in income maintenance, taxation and family law

Landau, Erika
289l Continuity of self-actualization: Womanhood in climacterium and old age

Landes, Joan
106g Hegel's conception of the family
227r Wages for housework - political and theoretical considerations

Lane, Ann J.
125l Charlotte Perkins Gilman: The personal is political
125t Mary Ritter Beard: Women as force

Lane, Arja
323v Wives supporting the strike

Lane, Rose Wilder
129d Give me liberty

Lane, Tony
283q Industrial strategy and trade union politics

Lange, Lynda
84a Woman is not a rational animal: On Aristotle's biology of reproduction

Langer, Sandra L.
126h Against the grain: A working feminist art criticism

Langer, William L.
184n The origins of the birth control movement in England in the early nineteenth century

Langkau, Jochem
437a Federal Republic of Germany

Langkau-Herrmann, Monika
437a Federal Republic of Germany

Langland, Elizabeth
303d Women's studies at Vanderbilt: Toward a strategy for the eighties
332e Female stories of experience: Alcott's *Little Women* in light of *Work*

398f 'They shared a laboratory together': Feminist collaboration in the academy

Langley, Patricia A.
315f Women, reproductive freedom, and the law: A selected annotated bibliography

Langton, Marianne
305p Is your job hazardous to your health?

Lanning, Kenneth V.
55d Collectors
55e Typology of collectors

Lantz, Alma E.
361l An evaluation of programs for reentry women scientists

Lapchik, Richard E.
391l The role of women in the struggle against *apartheid* in South Africa

Lapham, E. Virginia Sheppard
79s Living with an impaired neonate and child: A feminist issue

Lapidus, Gail W.
446a Women, work, and family: New Soviet perspectives

LaPin, Deirdre
6g Women in African literature

Laredo, Carlos M.
146f Sibling incest

Larguia, Isabel
192g Toward a science of women's liberation

Larkin, Jackie
323d Out of the ghettos: Affirmative action and unions

Larsen, Brekke
274j Geography

Larson, Eric H.
18h The effects of plantation economy on a Polynesian population

Larson, M. Victoria
190h Physical attractiveness and physical stigma: Menstruation and the common cold

Larwood, Laurie
267b The importance of being right when you think you are: Self-serving bias in equal employment opportunity
471j Women at work in the USA

Larzelere, Robert E.
105j Some correlates of marital trust

Lasch, Christopher
102a A society without fathers: Cooperative commonwealth or harmonious ant-heap?

Lash, Joseph P.
61n Eleanor Roosevelt's role in women's history

Lashof, Joyce
36z Forces impacting on the policymaker

Laslett, Peter
184o Age at menarche in Europe since the eighteenth century

Lasswell, Marcia
185g Personal and social attitudes toward parenting

Laszlo, Anna T.
284r Courtroom use of hospital records in sexual assault cases

Lateef, Shahida
101h The Indian women's movement and national development: An overview

LaTorre, Ronald A.
268h Schizophrenia

Latortue, Regine
39bb The black woman in Haitian society and literature

Latta, Caroline J. Dodge
399ii The lady is a critic

Lattin, Patricia Hopkins
398l Academic women, affirmative action, and mid-America in the eighties

Laumon, Bernard
233i Occupational fatigue and preterm birth

Laurence, Margaret
338j Appendix: A reply to the toast to Canada

Laury, Gabriel V.
285d Death and sexuality

Lauter, Paul
102i Beyond consciousness raising: Changing sexist institutions
314o Reconstructing American literature: A strategy for change

Lauzon, Catherine
323k The right to strike

Lavelle, Jini
167g Children need smiles not missiles: Planning a walk Oxford Mothers for Nuclear Disarmament

Lavery, Bryony
381b But will men like it? Or living as a feminist writer without committing murder

Lavoie, J. M.
372o Specificity of swim training on maximal oxygen uptake: An inter-sex comparison

Lavrin, Asunción
367b Women and religion in Spanish America

Law, Barbara
456g Contraception

Law, Glenda
390h 'I have never liked trade unionism': The development of the Royal Australian Nursing Federation, Queensland Branch, 1904-1945

Lawe, Barbara
87i The balancing act: Coping strategies for emerging family lifestyles

Lawe, Charles
87i The balancing act: Coping strategies for emerging family lifestyles

Lawhead, Helen D.
98l Towards the making of a documentary film on rural women in Bangladesh

Lawrence, Allen
460t Self-help in gynecological practice

Lawson, Ronald
203p From kitchen to storefront: Women in the tenant movement

Lawton, M. Powell
317j Environmental change: The older person as initiator and responder

Lay, Jackie
157b To Columbia on the Tynemouth: The emigration of single women and girls in 1862

Layden, Dianne R.
288l A federal response to sexual harassment: Policy-making at Johnson Space Center, NASA

Lazar, Joyce
404o Plenary session: Intervention/service delivery systems

Lazarre, Jane
30n "Charlotte's Web": Reading *Jane Eyre* over time

Lazerson, Marvin
427j Gender roles and the state

Leacock, Eleanor
342h Ideologies of male dominance as divide and rule politics: An anthropologist's view
347a Montagnais women and the Jesuit program for colonization

Leader, Shelah Gilbert
103g Fiscal policy and family structure

Leal, Luis
408k Female archetypes in Mexican literature

Leal, Magdalena León de
350c Peasant production, proletarianization, and the sexual division of labor in the Andes
459c Class and historical analysis for the study of women and economic change

Lean, Lim Lin
424e Towards meeting the needs of urban female factory workers in peninsular Malaysia

Lear, Patricia Best
221a The family as an influence on career development

Leavitt, Dinah L.
399rr Megan Terry (Interview)
399uu The Lavender Cellar theatre

Leavitt, Jacqueline
203n Women in planning: There's more to affirmative action than gaining access

Leavitt, Judith
337f Women in the medical school
353k "Down to death door's": Women's perceptions of childbirth in America
353m Birthing and anesthesia: The debate over twilight sleep

Lebacqz, Karen
36bb The ethicist in policymaking

LeBold, William K.
361i Women in engineering: A dynamic approach

LeBow, Diane
417 Rethinking matriliny among the Hopi

Lebowitz, Andrea
168c Hindsight is 20/20: The development, achievements and dilemmas of feminist literary criticism

Lebowitz, Ann
447b Overview: The health of working women

Lebra, Joyce
58a Immigration to Southeast Asia
58c Bazaar and service occupations
386e Women in medicine

Lebsock, Suzanne
256d Free black women and the question of matriarchy

Lecker, Robert
20k Janus through the looking glass: Atwood's first three novels

Leclercq, Jean
187n Epilogue: Does St Bernard have a specific message for nuns?

Ledwitz-Rigby, Florence
239e Biochemical and neurophysiological influences on human sexual behavior

Lee, Bernice J.
401j Female infanticide in China

Lee, Dorothy H.
40ee The quest for self: Triumph and failure in the works of Toni Morrison

Lee, James Ward
175v Legends in their own time: The Dallas Cowboy cheerleaders

Lee, Lois
461x Discussion: Legal victim or social victim?

Lee, Maryat
316a Legitimate theatre is illegitimate

Lee, Raymond
183f Hysteria among factory workers

Lee, Robert
144a The German family: A critical survey of the current state of historical research
144c Family and 'modernisation': The peasant family and social change in nineteenth-century Bavaria

Lee, Sirkka Tuomi
73f The role of learning in the lives of Finnish and other ethnic women and a proposal for self-education

Lee, Susan Dye
399b Trampling out the vintage
412p Evangelical domesticity: The woman's temperance crusade of 1873-1874

Lee, Sylvia B.
445q The Mormon novel: Virginia Sorensen's *The Evening and the Morning*

Lee, Vera G.
130w The edifying examples

Lee, W. R.
145l The impact of agrarian change on women's work and child care in early nineteenth-century Prussia
184f Bastardy and socioeconomic structure of south Germany
184h Bastardy in south Germany: A reply

Lees, Susan H.
417w Motherhood in feminist utopias

Leet, Mildred Robbins
251e The power of persistence: Consciousness raising at international fora - the case of UNCSTD
373o Roles of women: UNCSTD background discussion paper

Leeuwen, Gerwin van
91k Women in ministries

Lefkowitz, Mary R.
156d Influential women

Legator, Marvin S.
233m Animal and human studies in genetic toxicology

Léger, L. A.
372w Energy cost of ice skating with figure skates for women

Leggon, Cheryl Bernadette
38l Black female professionals: Dilemmas and contradictions of status

Lehert, P.
236b The premenstrual syndrome - an epidemiological and statistical exercise

Lehmann, Ruth P. M.
331e Woman's songs in Irish, 800-1500

Lehrer, Evelyn
355g Women's life-cycle time allocation: An econometric analysis

Leiblum, Sandra R.
304g Sex-role stereotypes and female sexual dysfunction

Leibowitz, Lila
342i Origins of the sexual division of labor

Leifer, Myra
439l Pregnancy

Leininger, Lorie Jerrell
343p The Miranda trap: Sexism and racism in Shakespeare's *Tempest*

Leira, Arnlaug
468e Women's work strategies: An analysis of the organisation of everyday life in an urban neighbourhood

Leiter, Elliot
285i Castration and sexual potency

Lejeune, Philippe
108p Women and autobiography at author's expense

Leland, Joy
10c Alcohol use and abuse in ethnic minority women
137i Gender, drinking, and alcohol abuse

Lemaire, Ria
22h La lyrique portugaise primitive de "Cantigas de Amigo"

Lemkau, Jeanne Parr
96f Women and employment: Some emotional hazards

Lemos, Ramon M.
432c Athletics, gender, and justice

Leng, Tan Pek
183e Women factory workers and the law

Lennane, Jean

50t Alleged psychogenic disorders in women - a possible manifestation of sexual prejudice

Lennane, John

50t Alleged psychogenic disorders in women - a possible manifestation of sexual prejudice

Lenz, Carolyn Ruth Swift

343r Women and men in Shakespeare: A selective bibliography

Lenz, Elinor

445e Homestead home

Leon, Gloria R.

268m Sex-role stereotypes and the development of eating disorders

Leonard, Diana

212m Male feminists and divided women

297b Negotiating the problem: The DHSS and research on violence in marriage

Leonard, John G.

101 Social reform and women's participation in political culture: Andhra and Madras

Leonard, Karen I.

101b Social reform and women's participation in political culture: Andhra and Madras

Leonard, Kenneth E.

230i Sexually aggressive men: Empirical findings and theoretical implications

Leone, Rose

404d The stigmatized woman

Lepervanche, Marie de

94c The 'naturalness' of inequality

Leppert, Phyllis C.

190p Menarche and adolescent pregnancy

Lerch, Patricia Barker

473f Spirit mediums in Umbanda Evangelizada of Porto Alegre, Brazil: Dimensions of power and authority

Lerner, Elinor

379o Jewish involvement in the New York City woman suffrage movement

Lerner, Gerda

454d The lady and the mill girl: Changes in the status of women in the Age of Jackson

Lerner, Harriet E.

8q Special issues for women in psychotherapy

140h Early origins of envy and devaluation of women: Implications for sex-role stereotypes

140i Female dependency in context: Some theoretical and technical considerations

140r Special issues for women in psychotherapy

359b Early origins of envy and devaluation of women: Implications for sex-role stereotypes

359n The hysterical personality: A "woman's disease"

359rr Adaptive and pathogenic aspects of sex-role stereotypes: Implications for parenting and psychotherapy

Lerner, Judith

376e Sex-based discrimination in the mental institutionalization of women

Lesh, Cheri

7y Hunger and thirst in the house of distorted mirrors

Leslie, Julia

457e Essence and existence: Women and religion in ancient Indian texts

Lesnoff-Caravaglia, Gari

472a Double stigmata: Female and old

472g The "babushka" or older woman in Soviet society

472h Widowhood: The last stage in wifedom

Lesser, Gerald S.

391b Career awareness in young children

Lester, David

268g Suicide

Leung, Sophia M.R.

265l Cultural differences in children's sex role stereotypes

Leutenegger, Walter

279b Sexual dimorphism in nonhuman primates

Levenson, Bernard

387r Job opportunities of black and white working-class women

Levi-Montalcini, Rita

438g Reflections on a scientific adventure (Italy and United States)

Levin, Lloyd M.

461s Women in swinging: America's Amazon society?

Levin, Michael

275o Vs. Ms.

Levine, Carol

36i Depo-provera: Some ethical questions about a controversial contraceptive

Levine, Ellen

344dd The first feminists

Levine, George

143h The hero as dilettante: *Middlemarch* and *Nostromo*

Levine, Harry Gene

9b Temperance and women in 19th-century United States

Levine, Helen

120h The personal is political: Feminism and the helping professions

220c The power politics of motherhood

220f Feminist counselling: Approach or technique?

220g Women as providers and consumers

Levine, Irma

16r Women in midstream

Levine, James A.

80s The prospects and dilemmas of child care information and referral

216q An alternative perspective on parental support: Child-care information and referral service

Levine, Linda Gould

408o The censored sex: Woman as author and character in Franco's Spain

Levine, Ned

270m Social change and family crisis: The nature of Turkish divorce

LeVine, Robert A.

216c A cross-cultural perspective on parenting

Levinson, Richard M.

387d Sex discrimination and employment practices: An experiment with unconventional job inquires

Levstik, Linda S.

222i The impossible dream: The Ph.D., marriage, and family

Levy, Darline Gay

130c Women, democracy, and revolution in Paris, 1789-1794

379q Responses to the political activism of Women of the People in revolutionary Paris, 1789-1793

444a Women of the popular classes in revolutionary Paris, 1789-1795

Levy, Ellen

307q Word processing: "This is not a final draft"

Levy, Judith M.

36t Contrasts in the birthing place: Hospital and birth center

Levy, Phyllis Saltzman

222e Surviving in a predominantly white male institution

Levy, René

52r Economic recession and Swiss women's attitudes towards marital role segregation

Levy, Stephen J.

404l Sexism in drug abuse treatment programs

Lewald, Ernest H.

313l Alienation and eros in three stories by Beatriz Guido, Marta Lynch and Amalia Jamilis

Lewin, Ellen

397k Lesbianism and motherhood: Implications for child custody

Lewin, Miriam

158c The Victorians, the psychologists, and psychic birth control

158g "Rather worse than folly?" psychology measures femininity and masculinity, 1: From Terman and Miles to the Guilfords

158h Psychology measures femininity and masculinity, 2: From "13 Gay Men" to the instrumental-expressive distinction

Lewis, Barbara

6k The impact of development policies on women

218h Women in development planning: Advocacy, institutionalization and implementation

385l Fertility and employment: An assessment of role incompatibility among African urban women

Lewis, Barbara A.

404k Sexism in treatment

Lewis, Helen B.

359o Madness in women

Lewis, Jane

189d Women lost and found: The impact of feminism on history

465a Dealing with dependency: State practices and social realities, 1870-1945

Lewis, Jill
212i   The politics of monogamy

Lewis, Myrna I.
460b   The history of female sexuality in the United States

Lewis, Norah L.
205x   Reducing maternal mortality in British Columbia: An educational process

Lewis, R. W. B.
451b   Introduction to *The Collected Short Stories of Edith Wharton*

Lewis, Robert A.
105j   Some correlates of marital trust
140m   Emotional intimacy among men

Lewis, Shelby
68c   African women and national development

Lewis, Thomas S. W.
329p   Combining 'the advantages of fact and fiction': Virginia Woolf's biographies of Vita Sackville-West, Flush, and Roger Fry

Lewontin, R.C.
354k   Sociobiology: Another biological determinism

Libai, David
284p   The protection of the child victim of a sexual offense in the criminal justice system

Liban, Carolyn B.
9k   Alcoholism in women: Treatment modalities and outcomes

Libertin, Mary
329i   Speech acts in *To the Lighthouse*

Liburdi, Lillian C.
463bb   Speech

Licht, Barbara G.
259f   Sex differences in achievement orientations: Consequences for academic choices and attainments

Lichtman, Judith L.
316m   De jure sex discrimination

Liddington, Jill
215t   The women's peace crusade: The history of a forgotten campaign

Lidoff, Joan
109f   Domestic gothic: The imagery of anger in Christina Stead's *The Man Who Loved Children*

Lieberman, Leslie Sue
279k   Normal and abnormal sexual dimorphic patterns of growth and development

Lieberman, Marcia R.
249a   The most important thing for you to know

Lieberman, Morton A.
96l   The role and function of women's consciousness raising: Self-help, psychotherapy, or political activation?
359vv   The psychotherapeutic impact of women's consciousness-raising groups

Lief, Harold I.
277m   Effects of aging on sexual arousal

Lieven, Elena
418l   'If it's natural, we can't change it'
418o   Subjectivity, materialism and patriarchy

Lightfoot, Sara Lawrence
352j   Socialization and education of young black girls in school

Lilienfeld, Jane
180n   Reentering paradise: Cather, Colette, Woolf and their mothers
196h   The magic spinning wheel: Straw to gold - Colette, Willy and Sido
202g   Where the spear plants grew: The Ramsays' marriage in *To the Lighthouse*

Liljestrom, Rita
93r   Integration of family policy and labor market policy in Sweden

Lim, Linda Y. C.
373k   Women's work in multinational electronics factories
428c   Capitalism, imperialism, and patriarchy: The dilemma of third-world women workers in multinational factories

Limón, José E.
319e   "La vieja Inés," a Mexican folk game: A research note

Lin, James
287p   Creative sexuality: Androgyny

Lin, Julia C.
449f   A woman's voice: The poetry of Yungtzu

Lind, Meda Chesney
111a   Re-discovering Lilith: Misogyny and the "new" female criminal

Linden, Robin Ruth
7a   Introduction: Against sadomasochism

Lindholm, James
232e   A note on the nobility of women in popular Tamil fiction

Lindsay, Beverly
68a   Perspectives of third world women: An introduction
68b   Introduction: Women in developing countries
68e   Issues confronting professional African women: Illustrations from Kenya
68k   Introduction: Minority women in the United States
68p   Third world women and social reality: A conclusion
362b   An examination of education, social change, and national development policy: The case of Kenyan women

Lindsay, Peter
147f   Woman's place in nineteenth century Canadian sport

Linehan, Marsha M.
29f   Interpersonal effectiveness in assertive situations

Linkie, Daniel M.
28a   The physiology of the menstrual cycle

Linz, Daniel
230k   Using psychological research on violent pornography to inform legal change
230l   Bases of liability for injuries produced by media portrayals of violent pornography

Lipman-Blumen, Jean
45d   Emerging patterns of female leadership in formal organizations, or must the female leader go formal?

Lipsitt, Don R.
8j   The painful woman: Complaints, symptoms, and illness

Lipsitz, Joan Scheff
4a   Adolescent psychosexual development

Lipstadt, Deborah
211k   Women and power in the Federation
211q   And Deborah made ten

Lisansky, Judith M.
10h   Antecedents of alcohol problems in women

Lister, Larry
285b   Eros and thanatos: Lingering taboos in doctor-patient communication

Litman, Robert E.
280n   Bondage and sadomasochism

Litten, Larry H.
320d   Mapping the road to academe: A review of research on women, men, and the college-selection process

Little, Judy
202e   *Jacob's Room* as comedy: Woolf's parodic *Bildungsroman*

Little, Ruth E.
10f   Alcohol use and reproduction

Liu, Paul K. C.
424c   Trends in female labour force participation in Taiwan: The transition toward higher technology activities

Liu, William T.
421y   Variations in women's roles and family life under the socialist regime in China

Livingston, Dennis
79kk   The biology of utopia: Science fiction perspectives on ectogenesis

Livson, Florine B.
289e   Gender identity: A life-span view of sex-role development

Llewellyn, Catriona
85f   Occupational mobility and the use of the comparative method

Llewellyn, Mandy
250d   Studying girls at school: The implications of confusion

Llewelyn-Davies, Melissa
282j   Women, warriors, and patriarchs

Lobodzinska, Barbara
243a   Urban and rural working women in Poland today: Between social change and social conflict

Locke, Elaine
79j   Antenatal diagnosis: The physician-patient relationship

Locke, Mamie
126k   Sexism and racism: Obstacles to the development of black women in South Africa

Lockheed, Marlaine E.
320e   Sex bias in aptitude and achievement tests used in higher education
351e   Sex segregation and male preeminence in elementary classrooms
398j   Women's studies and men's careers: How the 'social problem' of women in educa-

tion maintained the academic status of men in the 1970s

Lockwood, Betty
471a Women at work in Great Britain

Loewenstein, Andrea
174c Teaching writing in prison

Loewenstein, Sophie Freud
96c Passion as a mental health hazard
96h Toward choice and differentiation in the midlife crises of women

Logan, Rebecca L.
79ll Ectogenesis and ideology

Lohmann, Nancy
317b Life satisfaction research in aging: Implications for policy development

Loken, Vivian M.
301y Tessa (poem)

London Rape Action Group
212d Towards a revolutionary feminist analysis of rape

Long, John M.
319j Cultural styles and adolescent sex role perceptions: An exploration of responses to a value picture projective test

Long, Judy
411f Multiple roles of midlife women: A case for new directions in theory, research, and policy

Longfellow, Cynthia
178j Fathers' support to mothers and children
178l The quality of mother-child relationships

Longhurst, Richard
350d Resource allocation and the sexual division of labor: A case study of a Moslem Hausa village in northern Nigeria

Longo, Lawrence D.
353t The rise and fall of Battey's operation: A fashion in surgery

Loo, Fe V.
71e Asian women in professional health schools, with emphasis on nursing

Lopata, Helena Z.
87f Spouses' contributions to each other's roles
317f The widowed family member
411e The middle years: Changes and variations in social-role commitments

Lorber, Judith
344t Trust, loyalty, and the place of women in the informal organization of work

Lorber, Steven J.
233p Legal considerations of reproductive hazards in industry in the United Kingdom

Lorde, Audre
7f Interview with Audre Lorde
40y My words will be there
132k Poetry is not a luxury
150s Tar beach
417m A litany for survival (poem)

Loree, Marguerite J.
93c Equal pay and equal opportunity law in France

Lorenz, Gerda
423b Women and health: The social dimensions of biomedical data

Lorfing, I.
265n Sex role images in Lebanese text books

Lorig, Kate R.
319l Health and illness perceptions of the Chicana

Lorion, Raymond P.
295m Differential needs and treatment approaches for women in psychotherapy

Lorwin, Val R.
382e Great Britain
382j Sweden

Los Angeles Research Group
224j Toward a scientific analysis of the gay question

Lott, Bernice
136i A feminist critique of androgyny: Toward the elimination of gender attributions for learned behavior

Lott, Juanita Tamayo
71a Keynote address

Loux, Ann
122o Finding one's way through the labyrinth: A symposium on women's lives: Meals — chaos or community
254k Know your heroines

Love, Barbara
195p The answer is matriarchy

Love, Jean O.
330j *Orlando* and its genesis: Venturing and experimenting in art, love, and sex

Loveland, Christine A.
269a Rama men and women: An ethnohistorical analysis of change

Loveland, Franklin O.
269g Watch that pot or the *waksuk* will eat you up: An analysis of male and female roles in Rama Indian myth

Lovenduski, Joni
189f Toward the emasculation of political science: The impact of feminism
228l USSR

Lovinfosse, Lee
54e Commonalities among female alcoholics

Lowe, Marian
34d Social bodies: The interaction of culture and women's biology
307b Sex differences, science, and society
342d The dialectic of biology and culture

Lowe, Marion
219f The role of the judiciary in the failure of the Sexual Offences (Amendment) Act to improve the treatment of the rape victim

Lowenstein, Wendy
13g Tribute to Joan Curlewis

Lown, Judy
139c Not so much a factory, more a form of patriarchy: Gender and class during industrialisation
206c The patriarchal thread - A history of exploitation

Lowry, I. Elaine
73b Organizing neighborhood women for political and social action

Lowry, Maggie
215h A voice from the peace camps: Greenham Common and Upper Heyford

Lu, Yu-Hsia
424r Women, work and the family in a developing society: Taiwan

Lubic, Ruth Watson
56g Alternative maternity care: Resistance and change

Lucas, John
147o Women's sport: A trial of equality

Lucas, Kadar
166b Women in a yogyakarta kampung

Luce, Judith Dickson
36u Ethical issues relating to childbirth as experienced by the birthing woman and midwife

Luce, Nancy A.
102e Toward psychoanalytic feminism: The mother in dream-stealing, the father in dreams

Luchins, Abraham S.
377a Female mathematicians: A contemporary appraisal

Luchins, Edith H.
377a Female mathematicians: A contemporary appraisal

Ludwig, Thomas E.
122q Marital metaphors in the Judeo-Christian tradition: A feminist critique

Ludwig, Wendy
333j Women and land rights: A review

Luijken, Anneke van
206h A woman's home is her factory

Luker, Kristin
3b Abortion and the meaning of life
307o Abortion: A domestic technology

Lumpkin, Angela
147gg The contributions of women to the history of competitive tennis in the United States in the twentieth century

Luomala, Nancy
117b Matrilineal reinterpretation of some Egyptian sacred cows

Lupri, Eugen
52a The changing positions of women and men in comparative perspective
52b The changing roles of Canadian women in family and work: An overview

Lupton, Nora
157c Notes on the British Columbia Protestant Orphan's Home

Luria, Zella
411r Sexuality and the middle-aged woman

Luxton, Meg
168e Conceptualizing "women" in anthropology and sociology
305i The home: A contested terrain
323w From ladies' auxiliaries to wives' committees

Luzuriaga, Luz
172f   Only you men have your needs satisfied (Ecuador)

Lydon, Mary
186f   A French view of May Sarton

Lynch, Felicia
314q   A view from the funding agencies

Lynch, Henry T.
141a   Introduction to breast cancer genetics
141e   Epidemiology of breast cancer
141f   Genetic heterogeneity and breast cancer: Variable tumor spectra
141i   Genetic counseling, patient and family management: Familial breast cancer

Lynch, Jane F.
141e   Epidemiology of breast cancer

Lynch, Margaret
291d   Recognition of child sexual abuse in the United Kingdom

Lynn, David B.
87c   Intellectual development of women

Lynn, Naomi B.
344v   Women and politics: The real majority

Lynton, Edith F.
426g   Corporate experiences in improving women's job opportunities

Lyon, George Ella
329f   Virginia Woolf and the problem of the body

Lyon, Phyllis
360h   Lesbian women and mental health policy

Maathai, W. Muta
438k   The progress of science in Africa

Macaulay, Jacqueline
249d   Joan Roberts and the university
249k   The failure of affirmative action for women: One university's experience
394c   A history of the Wisconsin Coordinating Council of Women in Higher Education

MacCormack, Carol P.
189g   Anthropology - a discipline with a legacy
200a   Nature, culture and gender: A critique
200e   Proto-social to adult: A Sherbro transformation
370o   Slaves, slave owners, and slave dealers: Sherbro coast and hinterland
385b   Control of land, labor, and capital in rural southern Sierra Leone

MacDonald, Carolyn T.
377g   An experiment in mathematics education at the college level

Macdonald, John M.
291g   Sexual deviance: The adult offender

MacDonald, Madeleine
250b   Socio-cultural reproduction and women's education

MacDonald, Marian L.
29c   Behavioral assessment of women clients

MacDonald, Maurice
46a   Concepts underlying the current controversy about women's social security benefits

MacDonald, Nancy
43w   The feminist workplace

MacDonald, Susan Peck
180f   Jane Austen and the tradition of the absent mother

MacGuire, Jillian
44f   Nursing

Machung, Anne
199g   Word processing: Forward for business, backward for women
209r   Turning secretaries into word processors: Some fiction and a fact or two

Maciocha, Teresa
308f   Adolescent parent programs and family involvement

Mack, Delores
82w   Practicalities of participation

MacKay, Donald G.
171c   Prescriptive grammar and the pronoun problem

MacKinnon, Catharine A.
2c   *Roe v Wade*: A study in male ideology
78s   Sexual harassment: The experience
288e   Women's work
288n   Sexual harassment cases

Mackintosh, Maureen
207a   Gender and economics: The sexual division of labour and the subordination of women
208b   Gender and economics: The sexual division of labour and the subordination of women
227p   Women's domestic labour

Macklin, June
319h   "All the good and bad in this world": Women, traditional medicine, and Mexican American culture

Macklin, Ruth
2e   Personhood and the abortion debate

MacLean, Judy
224m   Revolution in the pursuit of happiness: Love and community-building on the left

MacLennan, Emma
260j   Labour market policy in four countries: Are women adequately represented?

MacMillan, Jackie
43x   Building feminist organizations

MacMillan, Margaret
111l   Women in court: Assisting the female offender

Macmillan, Mona
160d   Camp followers: A note on wives of the armed services

MacPike, Loralee
286d   The fallen woman's sexuality: Childbirth and censure

MacQueen, Bonnie
205o   Domesticity and discipline: The Girl Guides in British Columbia 1910-1943

Madden, Janice Fanning
463h   Women's work trips: An empirical and theoretical overview

Maddock, James W.
281a   Human sexuality in the life cycle of the family system

Madhubuti, Haki
40o   Lucille Clifton: Warm water, greased legs, and dangerous poetry
40kk   Sonia Sanchez: The bringer of memories

Mael, Phyllis
399xx A rainbow of voices

Maffeo, Patricia A.
137b   Gender as a model for mental health

Magarey, Susan
321n   Can there be justice for women under capitalism?: Questions about 'patriarchy'

Magas, Branka
227o   'The housewife and her labour under capitalism' - a critique

Maggs, Christopher
248b   Nurse recruitment to four provincial hospitals 1881-1921

Maglin, Nan Bauer
180u   "Don't never forget the bridge that you crossed over on": The literature of matrilineage
306j   "Full of memories": Teaching matrilineage

Magnarella, Paul J.
270o   Civil violence in Turkey: Its infrastructural, social and cultural foundations

Magnus, Dorothy B.
399hh Matriarchs of the regional theatre

Magnus, Elisabeth M.
239i   Sources of maternal stress in the postpartum period: A review of the literature and an alternative view

Mágon, Ricardo Flores
192p   A la mujer (to women)

Maguire, Jack
175i   Sophia Porter: Texas' own Scarlett O'Hara

Maguire, M.
250j   Young women in the labour market: Stability and change

Maher, Frances
314j   Appropriate teaching methods for integrating women

Maher, Janet E.
405k   The social composition of women deputies in Soviet elective politics: A preliminary analysis of official biographies

Maher, Vanessa
162d   Possession and dispossession: Maternity and mortality in Morocco
207e   Work, consumption and authority within the household: A Moroccan case
208g   Work, consumption and authority within the household: A Moroccan case

Mahoney, Anne Rankin
165i   Female delinquents in a suburban court

Mahoney, Pat
290d   Theory into practice: Sexual liberation or social control? (*Forum* magazine 1968-1981)

Mahowald, Mary B.
3f   Commentary to chapter 4 (chapter e)

3k   Abortion and equality

Mainardi, Patricia
117r   Quilts: The great American art
227e   The politics of housework

Mainker, Marlene Crosby
404ee   Self-power and leadership

Maio, Kathleen L.
109d   Had-I-but-known: The marriage of gothic terror and detection

Major, Brenda
136b   Gender patterns in touching behavior

Makiesky-Barrow, Susan
39y   Social inequality and sexual status in Barbados

Makosky, Vivian Parker
178b   Sources of stress: Events or conditions?
191f   Stress and the mental health of women: A discussion of research and issues

Makward, Christiane
27o   Quebec women writers
64q   Colette and signs: A partial reading of a writer "born *not* to write"
132g   To be or not to be ... a feminist speaker

Malamuth, Neil
230b   Aggression against women: Cultural and individual causes
280b   Pornography: Its consequences on the observer

Malan, Nancy E.
61o   Photographs as historical documents (American women through the camera's eye)

Malatesta, Carol Zander
136j   The development of sex differences in nonverbal signals: Fallacies, facts, and fantasies

Mallet-Joris, Françoise
64a   A womanly vocation (Colette)

Malloy, Terrence R.
277h   Evaluation and treatment of impotence: The urologist's viewpoint

Maloney, Joan M.
444g   Women in the Chinese communist revolution: The question of political equality

Malpede, Karen
399vv   *Rebeccah*: Rehearsal notes

Malpezzi, Frances M.
384h   The emergence of Helen Chalmers

Malson, Michelene Ridley
243f   Black families and childrearing support networks

Malueg, Sara Ellen Procious
130p   Women and the Encyclopédie

Malveaux, Julianne M.
41e   Shifts in the occupational and employment status of black women: Current trends and future implications
296h   Powerless by definition: Occupational and pay patterns of women in the workplace
426e   Moving forward, standing still: Women in white collar jobs

Mamdani, Mahmood
18b   The ideology of population control

Mamelle, Nicole
233i   Occupational fatigue and preterm birth

Mamontova, T. I.
446q   Part-time employment of women

Manahan, Nancy
176i   Homophobia in the classroom

Mancuso, Arlene
455c   No drums, no trumpets: Working-class women

Manderson, Lenore
166e   Rights and responsibility, power and privilege: Women's roles in contemporary Indonesia

Mandrell, Regina M.K.
301r   Are you looking, cousin Dell?

Manes, Joan
356f   "Don't 'dear' me!"

Mangkuprawira, Sjafri
92e   Indonesia: Married women's work pattern in rural Java

Mann, G. V.
372aa   Menstrual effects of athletic training

Mann, Susan
149f   Domestic labour and the reproduction of labour power: Towards an analysis of women, the family, and class

Manning, Aubrey
24i   Sexual attraction in animals

Manning, Carol S.
450g   Ellen Douglas: Moralist and realist

Manns, Wilhelmina
37p   Support systems of significant others in black families

Manohar, K. Murali
299a   Socio-economic status of Indian women
299b   Maid servants
299c   Sanitary Workers
299d   Beedi workers
299e   Construction workers
299f   Petty traders
299g   Tribal migrants

Mansueto, Connie
215k   Take the toys from the boys: Competition and the nuclear arms race

Manzanedo, Hector Garcia
319l   Health and illness perceptions of the Chicana

Maoz, Benjamin
289l   Continuity of self-actualization: Womanhood in climacterium and old age

Marchand, James
188a   The Frankish mother: Dhuoda

Marchisotti, Daisy
390r   Equal pay case, 1951

Marcil-Lacoste, Louise
84g   The trivialization of the notion of equality

Marco, Luis A.
277n   Effect of drugs on sexual arousal

Marcus, Jane
30v   Invisible mending

196i   Virginia Woolf and her violin: Mothering, madness, and music
202a   Thinking back through our mothers
242c   Liberty, sorority, misogyny
328a   Introduction: Virginia Woolf aslant
328b   The niece of a nun: Virginia Woolf, Caroline Stephen, and the cloistered imagination
329b   Virginia Woolf and her violin: Mothering, madness and music
330f   Enchanted organs, magic bells: *Night and Day* as comic opera
448g   A wilderness of one's own: Feminist fantasy novels of the twenties: Rebecca West and Sylvia Townsend Warner

Marecek, Jeanne
365c   Gender and the process of therapy

Maresh, C. M.
372x   Comparison of exercise between females and males

Margolis, Diane
410a   The invisible hands: Sex roles and the division of labor in two local political parties

Marie, Gillian
157a   Writing women into British Columbia's history

Marin, Patricia
206l   Working on racism: Centro Obrero

Marini, Margaret Mooney
272i   Sex typing in occupational socialization

Märker, K.
107k   Influence of athletic training on the maturity process of girls

Markey, Ray
390c   Women and labour, 1880-1900

Markusen, Ann R.
307k   The lonely squandering of urban time

Marland, Michael
259a   School as a sexist amplifier
259d   Staffing for sexism: Educational leadership and role models
259h   Guidance and pastoral care
259j   Curriculum matters
259l   Should the sexes be separated?

Marrett, Cora Bagley
351i   The participation of minority women in higher education
353dd   On the evolution of women's medical societies

Marsden, Lorna R.
93k   The role of the National Action Committee on the Status of Women in facilitating equal pay policy in Canada
380d   The relationship between the labor force employment of women and the changing social organization in Canada

Marsh, Jeanne C.
268j   A sex-roles perspective on drug and alcohol use by women

Marshall, John
235i   The medical profession

Marshall, Nancy
178f   The public welfare system: Regulation and dehumanization

Marshall, Susan E.
344gg Keep us on the pedestal: Women against feminism in twentieth century America

Marshall, Victor W.
210l Concerns about parental health

Marshall, William L.
276a The classification of sexual aggressives and their associated demographic, social, developmental and psychological features
276d The assessment and treatment of sexual offenders

Martelet, Penny
61h The Woman's Land Army, World War I

Martínez, Margaret
72e Puerto Rican women in higher education in the United States

Martin, Biddy
32r Irmtraud Morgner's *Leben und Abenteuer der Trobadora Beatriz*

Martin, Catherine A.
9m Opiate dependence in women

Martin, Del
78n Battered women: Society's problem
360h Lesbian women and mental health policy
461u Wife beating: A product of sociosexual development

Martin, Graham
143c *The Mill on the Floss* and the unreliable narrator

Martin, Jane
116q Sex equality and education in Plato's Just State

Martin, Jean K.
302i Salary and position levels of females and males in academic libraries

Martin, Jeannie
94g Non English-speaking women: Production and social reproduction

Martin, Joan
40aa The unicorn is black: Audre Lorde in retrospect

Martin, Joanne
267c Double jeopardy: Resistance to affirmative action from potential beneficiaries

Martin, Liz
305z But is it feminist art?

Martin, Susan Ehrlich
344d Sexual harassment: The link between gender stratification, sexuality, and women's economic status

Martin, Wendy
448m Another view of the "City upon a Hill": The prophetic vision of Adrienne Rich

Martin, William G.
153i Beyond the peasant to proletarian debate: African household formation in South Africa

Martin, William R.
9m Opiate dependence in women

Martin-Shelton, Darla
16j The first two years: A profile of women entering Women, Inc.

Martinez, Angel Luis
308i The impact of adolescent pregnancy on Hispanic adolescents and their families

Martinson, Floyd
105f The family, the child, and social change

Martyna, Wendy
171b Beyond the he/man approach: The case for nonsexist language
356e The psychology of the generic masculine

Maruani, Margaret
382d France

Marum, M. Elizabeth
98j Survey research with rural women in Bangladesh

Marvin, Bertha
129h Irrelevancies

Masiello, Francine
408l Sara de Etcheverts: The contradictions of literary feminism

Masnick, Barbara R.
16c Issues in feminist therapy: The work of a woman's study group

Mason, Andrew
273e Decision making and sex selection with biased technologies

Mason, Karen Oppenheim
272g Commentary: Strober's theory of occupational sex segregation

Mason, Rose
7l Racism and sadomasochism: A conversation with two black lesbians

Mason, Terry
319f Symbolic strategies for change: A discussion of the Chicana women's movement

Massanari, Ronald L.
315h Two in one, one in two: An exploration of a birth experience and images of the sacred

Massek, Sue
301s What she aims to be (song)

Massicotte, D.
372t Effects of training intensity on cardiac output in young women

Massie, Allan
197d Calvinism and Catholicism in Muriel Spark

Masters, Roger D.
35g Explaining "male chauvinism" and "feminism": Cultural differences in male and female reproductive strategies

Mathe, Mirjam
8f The adolescent girl in a group home

Mathé, Sylvie
313h La poupée perdue: Ordre et désordre dans *Les Petites Filles Modèles* de la Comtesse de Ségur

Mathews, Alice E.
367e The religious experience of Southern women

Mathews, Donald G.
412a Women's history/everyone's history

Mathews, Mary Alice
69i Marriage and midlife: The impact of social change

Mathews, Patricia
114b C. L. Moore's classic science fiction

Mathews, Sue
384j Pioneer women in the works of two Montana authors: Interviews with Dorothy M. Johnson and A. B. Guthrie, Jr.

Mathia, Gene A.
82l Tenure and the role of the female

Mathis, Melissa Bay
7u New expanded-type version lesbian handkerchief code

Matlock, Gerald
82c Participation through Title XII, consortia, and the project process in AID

Matsell, Catherine
228f Spain

Matskovskii, M. S.
446k Changing family roles and marital instability

Matsui, Yayori
163d Why I oppose Kisaeng tours

Matters, Indiana
205r Sinners or sinned against?: Historical aspects of female juvenile delinquency in British Columbia

Matthews, Bruce
300k Buddhist attitudes toward social change in Burma and Thailand

Matthews, Jacquie
125f Barbara Bodichon: Integrity in diversity

Matthews, Janet R.
87m Going shopping: The professional couple in the job market

Matthews, Jill Julius
13a Deconstructing the masculine universe: The case of women's work

Matthews, Lee H.
87m Going shopping: The professional couple in the job market

Matthews, Westina
351i The participation of minority women in higher education

Mattison, Donald R.
233l What evidence is required to identify a chemical as a reproductive hazard?

Matzen, Lene
274r Physical education

Max, Claire Ellen
361g Career paths for women in physics

Maxwell, Colleen
42n The traditional role of the Mormon woman

May, Gita
130t Rousseau's "antifeminism" reconsidered

Mayes, Sharon S.
140g Women in positions of authority: A case study of changing sex roles

Maynard, John
286o The worlds of Victorian sexuality: Work in progress

Mayne, Judith
247c The woman at the keyhole: Women's cinema and feminist criticism

Mayo, Clara
136a Nonverbal behavior: Barrier or agent for sex role change?

Mayon-White, Richard
456n Cystitis

Mayrand, Theresa
79ee Response

Mays, Ramina Y.
150v LeRoy's birthday
301ii Delta (fiction)

Mazorra, Maria
86f Following the harvest: The health hazards of migrant and seasonal farmworking women

Mazur, D. Peter
405m Procreation and new definitions in the role of women in a Soviet bloc country: The case of Poland

Mazur, Dorothy Conrad
359q A starving family: An interactional view of anorexia nervosa

McAdoo, Harriette Pipes
37i Patterns of upward mobility in black families
38h Black mothers and the extended family support network
41f Stress and support networks of working single black mothers

McAdoo, John L.
37o Involvement of fathers in the socialization of black children

McAfee, Naomi J.
416j You've come a long way baby: The myth and the reality

McAlister-Hermann, Judith
32q Literary emasculation: Household imagery in Christa Reinig's *Entmannung*

McAll, Christopher
334a The normal paradigms of a woman's life in the Irish and Welsh texts

McAndrew, Maggie
471k Women at work in the USSR

McBrien, William
318h Muriel Spark: The novelist as dandy

McCall, Daniel F.
194o Mother Earth: The great goddess of West Africa

McCalla, Deidre
150gg Billy de Lye (poem)

McCann, Anna Marguerite
389j Gisela Marie Augusta Richter (1882-1972): Scholar of classical art and museum archaeologist

McCann, Lisa
295e The antecedents and prevention of unwanted pregnancy

McCants, Billie
399ff Alvina Krause: A great teacher of acting

McCarthy, Florence E.
98m Methodological issues in longitudinal and comparative research in Bangladesh
433b Conditions influencing rural and town women's participation in the labor force

McCarthy, James
309n Marriage, remarriage, marital disruption and age at first birth

McCarthy, Rebecca
301rr There's not a child that can't learn

McCartney, Kathleen
80f Environmental differences among day care centers and their effects on children's development

McCarty, Mari
64l The theatre as literary model: Role-playing in *Chéri* and *The Last of Chéri*

McCay, Mary A.
17n Fitzgerald's women: Beyond winter dreams

McClelland, Gary H.
273b Measuring sex preferences and their effects on fertility

McClure, Charlotte S.
126a The genesis of feminist visions for transforming the liberal arts curriculum
126c Women knowing: Feminist theory and perspectives on pedagogy
445i Gertrude Atherton's California woman: From love story to psychological drama

McCluskey, John
40cc And called every generation blessed: Theme, setting, and ritual in the works of Paule Marshall

McCluskey, Audrey T.
40n Tell the good news: A view of the works of Lucille Clifton

McCombie, Sharon L.
359ll Development of a medical center rape crisis intervention program

McCombs, Judith
20b Atwood's haunted sequences: *The Circle Game*, *The Journals of Susanna Moodie, and Power Politics*

McConnell, Mary Ann
222c High noon: Surviving the comprehensive exams

McConnell-Ginet, Sally
132m Difference and language: A linguist's perspective
171e Intonation in a man's world
356a Linguistics and the feminist challenge

McCormack, Thelma
388a Development with equity for women

McCormick, Nancy
4g Venereal disease and the adolescent

McCormick, Naomi B.
48a The intimate relationship between gender roles and sexuality
48d The courtship game: Power in the sexual encounter

48n Future influences on the interaction of gender and human sexual expression

McCourt, Kathleen
73i Irish, Italian, and Jewish women at the grassroots level: A historical and sociological perspective

McCown, Elizabeth R.
279c Sex differences: The female as baseline for species description

McCrady, Barbara S.
8n Women and alcohol abuse
29p Women and alcoholism

McCray, Carrie Allen
38d The black woman and family roles

McCray, Chirlane
150j "I used to think" (poem)

McCubbin, Hamilton I.
105h Developing family invulnerability to stress: Coping patterns and strategies wives employ in managing family separations

McCullogh, Kenneth J.
288i Sexual harassment in the workplace — What should the employer do?

McCullough, Patricia
133q Consciousness-raising among gay males

McCullough, Wayne R.
37q Group identity development within black families

McDevitt, Martha
206b Restructuring: The cutting edge

McDinny, Eileen
333h Borroloola community and land rights

McDonald, Geraldine
413g Education and the movement towards equality

McDonnell, Kathleen
305b Claim no easy victories: The fight for reproductive rights

McDowall, Michael E.
233g The epidemiological identification of reproductive hazards

McDowell, Douglas S.
66g The legal framework
67h An analysis of the National Academy of Sciences' comparable worth study

McDowell, Frederick P. W.
330e "Surely order did prevail": Virgina Woolf and *The Voyage Out*

McDowell, Nancy
246c Complementarity: The relationship between female and male in the East Sepik village of Bun, Papua New Guinea

McElderry, Andrea
177b Historical background on Chinese Women

McElroy, Wendy
129a The roots of individualist feminism in 19th-century America

McEwen, Bruce S.
28c Neuroendocrine regulation of sexual behavior

McEwen, James
233t Educating workers, management and the general public

McFarlane, Barbara
182b Homes fit for heroines: Housing in the twenties

McFarlane, T.
240h Psychological aspects of hysterectomy

McGarry, Peggy Ann
404r Breaking cycles of victimization: The shelter as an affirmative institution

McGee, Sandra F.
379h Right-wing female activists in Buenos Aires, 1900-1932

McGhee, Richard
286f "Swinburne planteth, Hardy watereth": Victorian views of pain and pleasure in human sexuality

McGinity, Sue Simmons
175w Honky Tonk Angels

McGinnis, Richard G.
463d Influence of employment and children on intra-household travel behavior

McGovern, Constance M.
353ee Doctors or ladies? Women physicians in psychiatric institutions, 1872-1900

McGovern, James R.
454o The American woman's pre-World War I freedom in manners and morals

McGowan, Brenda G.
349v Imprisoned women and their children

McGrath, Ann
294f 'Black Velvet': Aboriginal women and their relations with white men in the Northern Territory, 1910-1940
390j 'Spinifex fairies': Aboriginal workers in the Northern territory, 1911-39

McGrath, Dennis
404r Breaking cycles of victimization: The shelter as an affirmative institution

McGrew, W. C.
340a The female chimpanzee as a human evolutionary prototype

McGuire, Kenneth
152i Shifting attitudes toward homosexuality

McIntosh, Mary
50e The 'family wage'
119e The family in socialist-feminist politics

McIntosh, Peggy
254a Seeing our way clear: Feminist re-vision of the academy
314b Interactive phases of curricular re-vision

McKay, Nellie
398c Black woman professor — white university

McKay, Roberta
209h The implications of technology for U.S. employment

McKean, Philip Frick
194m Rangda the witch

McKechnie, Sheila
233n A trade union view of reproductive health

McKee, Lorna
241k Interviewing men: 'Taking gender seriously'

McKendrick, Melveena
408f Women against wedlock: The reluctant brides of Golden Age drama

McKenna, Jill
310cc Regaining trust

McKenna, Muriel
399q The art of Ruth Draper

McKenna, Wendy
50r Developmental aspects of gender

McKenney, Mary
43m Class attitudes and professionalism

McKewin, Carole
343g Counsels of gall and grace: Intimate conversations between women in Shakespeare's plays

McKiernan-Allen, Linda
429k Colleagues in marriage and ministry

McKinney, Cindy E.
141b Genetic control of breast cancer susceptibility in animals

McKnight, Jeannie
445d American dream, nightmare underside: Diaries, letters and fiction of women on the American frontier

McLaughlin, Ann L.
328h An uneasy sisterhood: Virginia Woolf and Katherine Mansfield

McLaughlin, Blandine L.
130s Diderot and women

McLay, Catherine
20h The dark voyage: *The Edible Woman* as romance

McMahan, Eva M.
126d Research on women's communication: Critical assessment and recommendations

McMahon, Sarah Lynne
365o Women in marital transition

McMaster, Juliet
142b George Eliot's language of the sense

McMurty, John
223e Monogamy: A critique

McNairy, Marion R.
222k The job hunt

McNally, Sheila
419e The maenad in early Greek art

McNamara, Jo Ann
187a Muffled voices: The lives of consecrated women in the fourth century

McNamara, Patricia P.
320i Educational and career progress of Chicana and Native-American college women

McNaron, Toni A. H.
176h "Out" at the university: Myth and reality
176l Journey into otherness: Teaching The Well of Lonelinessital

McNaught, Brian
152a Reflections of a gay Catholic

McNeal, Robert H.
405f The early decrees of Zhenotdel

McNeill, Sandra
212h Transsexualism: Can men turn men into women?

McNelly, Geraldine Day
417b Women of the Celtic Tuath

McPherson, Ann
456a Why women's health?
456b Menstrual problems
456d Menopause
456f The 'ectomies'
456i Cervical cytology

McQueen, David V.
10d. Multiple substance abuse among women with alcohol-related problems

McRobbie, Angela
134f Dance and social fantasy

Mead, Margaret
288d A proposal: We need taboos on sex at work

Meade, Robert G.
411r Sexuality and the middle-aged woman

Meaney, Audrey
234e Evidence concerning Anglo-Saxon women from archaeology

Mebane, Mary
301i Three maxims in the life of Mary

Medicine, Beatrice
70e The interaction of culture and sex roles in the schools
148f The role of Sioux women in the production of ceremonial objects: The case of the star quilt
148j "Warrior women" - Sex role alternatives for Plains Indian women
342e Indian women: Tribal identity as status quo

Medick, Hans
162a Interest and emotion in family and kinship studies: A critique of social history and anthropology
162n Village spinning bees: Sexual culture and free time among rural youths in early modern Germany

Mednick Martha T.
425c Women and the psychology of achievement: Implications for personal and social change

Meehan, Elizabeth
465g Equal opportunity policies: Some implications for women of contrasts between enforcement bodies in Britain and the USA

Meehan, Mary
3i More trouble than they're worth? Children and abortion
3p Commentary to chapter 9 (chapter o)

Meese, Elizabeth
306a The whole truth: Frameworks for the study of women's noncanonical literature
306l Southern women's literature and culture: Course development and the pedagogical process

Megens, Ine
179g The recruitment of women

Megibow, Carol Burr
453n The use of story in women's novels of the seventies

Meguro, Yoriko
52i The changing status and role of women in Japan

Mehta, Rama
255e Purdah among the Oswals of Mewar

Meikle, Douglas B.
35c Political ideology, sociobiology, and the U.S. women's rights movement

Meikle, Susan
143i Fruit and seed: The finale to *Middlemarch*

Meillassoux, Claude
370d Female slavery

Melder, Keith
454e Ladies bountiful: Organized women's benevolence in early nineteenth-century America

Meldrum, Barbara
384e Women in western American fiction: Images or real women?
445k Conrad Richter's southwestern ladies

Meldrum, Julian
235d On the streets

Melhuus, Marit
104b Cash crop production and family labour: Tobacco growers in Corrientes, Argentina

Mellencamp, Patricia
247a Feminist film criticism: An introduction

Mello, Nancy K.
9g Some behavioral and biological aspects of alcohol problems in women

Mellown, Muriel
125s Vera Brittain: Feminist in a new age

Melosh, Barbara
353hh More than "the physician's hand": Skill and authority in twentieth-century nursing

Melville, Margarita B.
319i Selective acculturation of female Mexican migrants

Mendell, Dale
88e A suggested developmental sequence for a preoedipal genital phase

Menke, Edna M.
190k Menstrual beliefs and experiences of mother-daughter dyads

Menken, Jane
309k The health and social consequences of teenage childbearing
309n Marriage, remarriage, marital disruption and age at first birth
309o Early childbearing and subsequent fertility

Menning, Barbara
79hh In defense of in vitro fertilization

Menon, M. Indu
421g Education of Muslim women: Tradition versus modernity

Mensh, Ivan N.
137e Psychopathology and sex differences in the aged

Menzies, Janet
197e Muriel Spark: Critic into novelist

Merchant, Carolyn
181f Mining the earth's womb
307d Women, nature and domination

Mercier, Jacqueline
324f Economic consequences of midlife change in marital status

Mercier, Raymond G.
287g Varieties of sexual expression

Meredith, Jesse
7k A response to Samois

Mermin, Dorothy
196d The domestic economy of art: Elizabeth Barrett and Robert Browning

Merni, F.
107p Differences in males and females in joint movement range during growth

Mernissi, Fatima
395a Genocide can be bloodless

Merritt, James D.
131c "She pluck'd, she eat"

Merritt, Karen
351l Women's studies: A discipline takes shape
394f A women's studies plan for Wisconsin

Merritt, Sharyne
410d Recruitment of women to suburban city councils: Higgins vs. Chevalier
410e Sex differences in role behavior and policy orientations of suburban officeholders: The effect of women's employment

Merryfinch, Lesley
179a Militarization/civilianization

Merton, Thomas
451k The other side of despair

Messing, Karen
342f The scientific mystique: Can a white lab coat guarantee purity in the search for knowledge about the nature of women?
354g Do men and women have different jobs because of their biological differences?

Messinger, Ruth
132u Women in power and politics
404cc Postintervention and support systems

Meyer, Alfred G.
145k The radicalization of Lily Braun

Meyer, Carol H.
434r Issues for women in a 'woman's' profession

Meyer, Doris
74a "Feminine" testimony in the works of Teresa de la Parra, María Luisa Bombal, and Victoria Ocampo

Meyer, Karmen
254g The hurt that lasts forever

Meyer, Marsha
32e *Wally, die Zweiflerin* and *Madonna*: A discussion of sex-socialization in the nineteenth century

Meyer, Regine
209ff Collective bargaining strategies on new technology: The experience of West German trade unions

Meyer-Bahlburg, Heino F. L.
239f Homosexual orientation in women and men: A hormonal basis?

Meyer-Renschhausen, Elisabeth
336d The Bremen morality scandal

Meyerowitz, Selma
202k What is to console us?: The politics of deception in Woolf's short stories

Mezey, Susan Gluck
410c The effects of sex on recruitment: Connecticut local offices
410h Perceptions of women's roles on local councils in Connecticut

Michaels, Meredith W.
2k Abortion and the claims of samaritanism

Michaelson, Karen L.
18a Introduction: Population theory and the political economy of population processes
18e Population policy, family size, and the reproduction of the labor force in India: The case of Bombay

Michel, Andrée
52e Female marital behaviour in French society

Michels, Robert
439s *Sexual Excitement* by Robert J. Stoller

Middendorff, D.
159f Changing patterns of female criminality in Germany

Middendorff, W.
159f Changing patterns of female criminality in Germany

Middleton, Audrey
241b Public and private: Marking the boundaries

Middleton, Chris
139b Patriarchal exploitation and the rise of English capitalism

Mies, Maria
312i Towards a methodology for feminist research
350a The dynamics of the sexual division of labor and integration of rural women into the world market

Milam, Virginia
414b Cherokee women

Milani, Farzaneh
368h Revitalization: Some reflections on the work of Saffar-Zadeh

Miles, Angela R.
120i Ideological hegemony in political discourse: Women's specificity and equality

Milford, Nancy
474d De memoria

Milkovich, George T.
66a The emerging debate
67a The emerging debate

Millard, Ann V.
395f Perceptions of a family planning campaign in rural Mexico

Miller, Barbara
363c Women and revolution: The brigadas femeninas and the Mexican Cristero Rebellion, 1926-1929

Miller, Beth
408i Gertrude the Great: Avellaneda, nineteenth-century feminist
408q From mistress to murderess: The metamorphosis of Buñuel's Tristana

Miller, Birthalene
301nn The lonesomes ain't no spring picnic (fiction)

Miller, Brenda A.
111r Drug abuse and criminality among women in detention

Miller, Cristanne
121h How "low feet" stagger: Disruptions of language in Dickinson's poetry

Miller, D. I.
107u Body segment contributions of female athletes to translational and rotational requirements of non-twisting springboard dive takeoffs

Miller, E. Eugene
349h The woman participant in Washington's riots

Miller, Ivan W.
29k Depression: A behavioral-cognitive approach

Miller, J. Hillis
242d "Herself against herself": The clarification of Clara Middleton

Miller, Jean B.
359c Psychological consequences of sexual inequality

Miller, Jean Baker
8b Aggression in women: Conceptual issues and clinical implications
8r Conflict and psychological development: Women in the family
102f Why the fathers cannot solve the problems: Some possible clues
140c Inequality and women's mental health: An overview
140d The effects of inequality on psychology

Miller, Jeanne-Marie A.
14x Black women playwrights from Grimke' to Shange: Selected synopses of their works
399nn Black women in plays by black playwrights

Miller, Jennifer
301dd Quilting women

Miller, Jon
243b Gender and interaction in the workplace

Miller, Linda
363d Patrons, politics, and schools: An arena for Brazilian women

Miller, Margot
167j A women's day for disarmament: Notes on organising a decentralised action

Miller, Nancy K.
64o The anamnesis of a female "I": In the margins of self-portrayal (Colette)
242e Writing (from) the feminine: George Sand and the novel of female pastoral
356q Women's autobiography in France: For a dialectics of identification

Miller, Patricia Y.
439o Social and behavioral constructions of female sexuality

Miller, Sally M.
128b Women in the party bureaucracy: Subservient functionaries
128h Commentary

Miller, Walter B.
392j The molls

Miller, Warren B.
309w Psychological vulnerability to unwanted pregnancy

Miller, William R.
326k Marital and sexual dysfunction following rape: Identification and treatment

Millett, Kate
225o Beyond politics? Children and sexuality

Millinger, Susan
187e Anglo-Saxon nuns in Anglo-Norman hagiography: Humility and power

Mills, Donald L.
52b The changing roles of Canadian women in family and work: An overview

Mills, Elizabeth Anne
165a One hundred years of fear: Rape and the medical profession

Mills, Helen
294g Prostitution and the law: The question of decriminalization

Mills, Trudy
140n Victims of violence and psychiatric illness

Millsap, Mary Ann
266d Evaluation issues in women's studies

Millstone, Amy
155b French feminist theater and the subject of prostitution, 1870-1914

Milow, Vera J.
190j Menstrual education: Past, present, and future

Milrod, Patience
375k Clara Shortridge Foltz: Pioneer in the law

Milton, Catherine
404i Holistic approaches for women

Milton, Sybil
336l Women and the Holocaust: The case of German and German-Jewish women

Minattur, Joseph
402g Women and the law: Constitutional rights and continuing inequalities

Minault, Gail
21h Political change: Muslim women in conflict with Parda: Their role in the Indian Nationalist Movement
101a Introduction: The extended family as metaphor and the expansion of women's realm
101d Sisterhood or separation? The All-India Muslim Ladies' Conference and the Nationalist Movement
255i Purdah politics: The role of Muslim women in Indian nationalism, 1911-1924

Mincer, Jacob
89a Labor force participation of married women: A study of labor supply
89g Family investments in human capital: Earnings of women

Minden, Shelley
310g Designer genes: A view from the factory
310i An interview with Mirtha Quintanales, from the Third World women's archives

Miner, Madonne M.
343b "Neither mother, wife, nor England's queen": The roles of women in *Richard III*

Minnich, Elizabeth Kamarck
30k Hannah Arendt: Thinking as we are
174aa Friends and critics: The feminist academy

Minor, Marianne
54a A systems model for planning culturally specific programs

Mintz, Sidney W.
39aa Economic role and cultural tradition

Miralao, Virginia A.
424s The impact of female employment on household management

Mirani, S. Kaveh
368d Social and economic change in the role of women, 1956-1978

Mironova, Z.
372ee Traumatological aspects of sports of high achievements for women

Misra, Surat
159m Criminality amongst women in India: A study of female offenders and female convicts

Mitchell, Beverley
445r "On the otherital side of the mountains": The westering experiences in the fiction of Ethel Wilson

Mitchell, Carolyn
448l "A laying on of hands": Transcending the city in Ntozake Shange's *for colored girls who have considered suicide/when the rainbow is enuf*

Mitchell, Dolores
453e Humor in California underground women's comix

Mitchell, Elizabeth
456q Eating problems

Mitchell, Marjorie
205b When you don't know the language, listen to the silence: An historical overview of native Indian women in BC

Mitchell, Mary
209v An issue of respect: Women workers demand healthy and safe offices

Mitchell, Pam
224c Lesbians and gay men: Hetero sexualities, common cause

Mitchell, Sheila
147ll The development of women's organized sport in the 1920's: A study of the Canadian Ladies Golf Union

Mitchell, Valory
45i Assessing personal and social change in two generations

Mitchell, Winifred
390f Women in mining communities

Mitter, Swasti
206h A woman's home is her factory

Mittman, Barbara G.
130i Women and the theatre arts

Mjaanes, Judith
337i Women in the art department

Mobley, Donna
169n Training women for political action

Modjeska, Drusilla
390n Rooms of their own: The domestic situation of Australian women writers between the wars

Moeckel, Margot J.
333o Aboriginal women's role today in early childhood school education

Moen, Phyllis
204b The two-provider family: Problems and potentials
243j Overtime over the life cycle: A test of the life cycle squeeze hypothesis

Mogey, John
105c Marital expectations of wives in contemporary Poland

Moglen, Helene
398a Power and empowerment

Mohr, James C.
353h Patterns of abortion and the response of American physicians, 1790-1930

Möhrmann, Renate
145e The reading habits of women in the *Vormärz*

Moir, Hazel
321g Comment: Women in the Australian labour force

Moller, David E.
285c The social relation of sex and death

Molyneux, Maxine
207j Women in socialist societies: Problems of theory and practice
208e Women in socialist societies: Problems of theory and practice

Monaghan, David
164a Introduction: Jane Austen as a social novelist
164g Jane Austen and the position of women

Money, John
460d Physiological aspects of female sexual development: Conception through puberty
460e Physiological aspects of female sexual development: Gestation, lactation, menopause, and erotic physiology

Monroy, Douglas
192r La costura en Los Angeles 1933-1939: The ILGWU and the politics of domination

Monteiro, Rita
91a A new outlook on women: Psychological and biological

Montgomery, Evelyn I.
82u NEMOW: A project that stumbled and why

Moody, Joycelyn K.
301ee Two poems for Minnie's boy

Moon, Denise M.
326j Sexual assault of the older woman

Mooney, Bel
215a Beyond the wasteland

Mooney, Harry J.
318c Olivia Manning: Witness to history

Moor de Crespo, Carmela
172d Learning to take hold of one's own destiny (Bolivia)

Moore, Ann M.
180y Mothers and daughters in literature: A preliminary bibliography

Moore, Deborah Dash
180o How light a *Lighthouse* for today's women?

Moore, Donna M.
87k Equal opportunity laws and dual-career couples

Moore, Elizabeth Payne
399c Friendship and ritual in the WTUL

Moore, Evelyn
37s Policies affecting the status of black children and families
80u Day care: A black perspective

Moore, Honor
399bb Woman alone, women together
474e My grandmother who painted

Moore, J. W.
49n Whom should the schools serve, When...?

Moore, Kathryn M.
407a Careers in college and university administration: How are women affected?

Moore, Kristin A.
308d Government policies related to teenage family formation and functioning: An inventory
309g The effect of government policies on out-of-wedlock sex and pregnancy

Moore, Madeline
202d Some female versions of pastoral: *The Voyage Out* and matriarchal mythologies
330k Nature and community: A study of cyclical reality in *The Waves*

Moore, Marat
301t Coal-mining women

Moore, Maurice J.
309c The legitimacy status of first births to U.S. women aged 15-24, 1939-1978

Moore, Nancy Newell
394l We have hired couples for years

Moore, Patrick
135f Symbol, mask, and meter in the poetry of Louise Bogan

Moore, R. Laurence
454g The spiritualist medium: A study of female professionalization in Victorian America

Moorehouse, Martha
243j Overtime over the life cycle: A test of the life cycle squeeze hypothesis

Mora, Gabriela
313a Crítica feminista: Apuntes sobre definiciones y problemas
313k Narradoras hispanoamericanas: Vieja y nueva problemática en renovadas elaboraciones

Mora, Magdalena
192a Sex, nationality, and class: La obrera Mexicana

Moraga, Cherríe
176h Lesbian literature: A third world feminist perspective
231y What we're rollin around in bed with: Sexual silences in feminism

Morales, Rebecca
307s Cold solder on a hot stove

Morantz, Regina Markell
238j The scientist as sex crusader: Alfred C. Kinsey and American culture
353q The perils of feminist history
353x Making women modern: Middle-class women and health reform in nineteenth-century America
353bb Professionalism, feminism, and gender roles: A comparative study of nineteenth-century medical therapeutics
379n Feminism, professionalism, and germs: A study of the thought of Mary Putnam Jacobi and Elizabeth Blackwell

Moravcevich, Nicholas
155e The romantization of the prostitute in Dostoevsky's fiction

Morawski, J. G.
158e Not quite new worlds: Psychologists' conceptions of the ideal family in the twenties

Moreira, Ana
172e Our national inferiority complex: A cause for violence? (El Salvador)

Moreno, Maria
192s I'm talking for justice

Moretti, C.
372y Pituitary response to physical exercise: Sex differences

Morgall, Janine
50h Typing our way to freedom: Is it true that new office technology can liberate women?
209p Strengthening group solidarity of clericals: A case study

Morgan, David
85d Men, masculinity and the process of sociological enquiry

Morgan, David H. J.
139a Introduction: Class and work: Bringing women back in

Morgan, Edmund S.
19f The case against Anne Hutchinson
238a The Puritans and sex

Morgan, Richard Gregory
173d *Roe v. Wade* and the lesson of the pre-*Roe* case law

Morgan, Robin
7n The politics of sado-masochistic fantasies
229kk Metaphysical feminism
453b Defining women's culture

Morin, Stephen F.
133j   Male homophobia

Morioka, Kiyomi
52i   The changing status and role of women in Japan

Morley, David
203l   Introduction: Women in environmental decisionmaking: Institutional constraints

Morley, Janet
115d   'The faltering words of men': Exclusive language in the liturgy

Morokvasic, Mirjana
207h   Sexuality and the control of procreation
208k   Sexuality and control of procreation
213a   Women in migration: Beyond the reductionist outlook

Morris, Adalaide
121f   "The love of thee-a prism be": Men and women in the love poetry of Emily Dickinson

Morris, Joan
22c   Iconography as a means of research on the history of the status of women

Morris, Naomi M.
28g   Epidemiological patterns of sexual behavior in the menstrual cycle

Morris, Norman
47b   The menopause: Physiological, pathological, and psychological aspects

Morris, Richard B.
19g   Jezebel before the judges

Morris-Farber, Nina
321   Sociological implications of Gabriele Wohmann's critical reception

Morrison, Daryl
414a   Women in literature of the West

Morrison, Donna
447g   Special needs of women in health examinations

Morrison, Toni
40dd   Rootedness: The ancestor as foundation

Morrissey, Michael
94d   Migrantness, culture and ideology

Morse, Ben W.
133g   Communication patterns in established lesbian relationships

Mortimer, Jeylan T.
244d   Occupation-family-linkages as perceived by men in the early stages of professional and managerial careers
427f   Men, women, work, and family

Morton, Peggy
227i   Women's work is never done

Moses, Arnold
190u   Steroidal contraceptive use and subsequent development of hyperprolactinemia

Moses, Barbara
271k   Female superiority in sex difference competence comparisons: A review of the literature
271l   Sex differences in assertiveness: Implications for research and treatment

271m   Assertiveness: Sex differences in relationships between self-report and behavioural measures

Moses, Claire G.
130bb   Conclusion: The legacy of the eighteenth century: A look at the future

Moses, Marlie
399m   Lydia Thompson and the "British Blondes"

Moses, Yolanda T.
39z   Female status, the family and male dominance in a West Indian community

Moskowitz, Emily J.
138m   Gender, class and education: A teaching bibliography of American studies

Moss, Leonard W.
194c   In quest of the Black Virgin: She is black because she is black

Moss, Peter
467a   Parents at work
467g   The future prospect

Moss, Robert L.
28d   Hypothalamic peptides and sexual behavior

Moss, Rosalind Urbach
263i   "Teacher, teacher": Teachers and educators in a stratified "female" profession

Mossavar-Rahmani, Yasmin L.
368n   Family planning in post-revolutionary Iran

Mossberg, Barbara Antonina Clarke
121c   Emily Dickinson's nursery rhymes
180k   Reconstruction in the house of art: Emily Dickinson's "I never had a mother"

Mossink, Marijke
76b   Domestic and public

Mossuz-Lavau, Janine
228e   France

Most, Ada
190f   Recollections of menarche, current menstrual attitudes, and perimenstrual symptoms

Mothner, Ira
359c   Psychological consequences of sexual inequality

Motowidlo, Stephan J.
425g   Estimating benefits and costs of antisexist training programs in organizations

Moulds, Elizabeth F.
392l   Chivalry and paternalism: Disparities of treatment in the criminal justice system
435k   Women's crime, women's justice

Moulton, Janice
31j   Women's work and sex roles
84i   A paradigm of philosophy: The adersary method
116m   Sex roles and the sexual division of labor
275g   The myth of the neutral "man"
275m   Sex and reference
432b   Education and sports: A reply to "Justice and gender in school sports"

Mouser, Bruce L.
370q   Women slavers of Guinea-Conakry

Moussourou, Loukia M.
471f   Women at work in Greece: The sociological and legal perspectives

Mowlam, Marjorie
215i   Fuel for the nuclear arms race: Nuclear power and nuclear weapons

Moy, Caryl
287k   Communicating sexuality

Moyer, Imogene L.
349t   Police processing of female offenders

Mrazek, David A.
291b   Psychosexual development within the family
291k   The child psychiatric examination of the sexually abused child
291r   The effects of child sexual abuse: Methodological considerations

Mrazek, Patricia Beezley
291a   Definition and recognition of sexual child abuse: Historical and cultural perspectives
291b   Psychosexual development within the family
291d   Recognition of child sexual abuse in the United Kingdom
291h   The nature of incest: A review of contributing factors
291l   Special problems in the treatment of child sexual abuse
291m   Incest and dysfunctional family system
291o   Group psychotherapy with sexually abused children
291r   The effects of child sexual abuse: Methodological considerations

Muehlenhard, Charlene L.
304h   Women's assertion and the feminine sex-role stereotype

Mueke, Marjorie
300f   Changes in women's status associated with modernization in northern Thailand

Mueller, Carol
226g   Women's organizational strategies in state legislatures

Mueller, Eva
459b   The allocation of women's time and its relation to fertility

Mueller, Janel M.
108d   Autobiography of a new 'creatur': Female spirituality, selfhood, and authorship in *The Book of Margery Kempe*

Muhlenfeld, Elisabeth S.
126l   Of paradigm and paradox: The case of Mary Boykin Chesnut

Mukherjee, Satyanshu K.
348g   The myth of rising female crime

Mukhopadhyay, Carol
218b   *Sati* or *Shakti*: Women, culture and politics in India
362e   Gender, politics and modernization: The Indian case

Mukhopadhyay, Swapna
422b   Women workers of India: A case of market segmentation

Mulcahy, Elena Berezaluce
72d   Latinas in educational leadership: Chicago, Illinois

Mulcahy, Gabriel M.
141d Pathologic aspects of familial carcinoma of breast

Mulford, Harold A.
11c Women and men problem drinkers: Sex differences in patients served by Iowa's community alcoholism centers

Mullings, Leith
83c Gender, race and class in the United States: Lessons from third world women
86h Minority women, work, and health

Mulvey, Anne
295l The relation of stressful life events to gender

Mumford, David M.
4g Venereal disease and the adolescent

Munford, Theresa
234b Women, politics and the formation of the Chinese state

Munnel, Alicia H.
46d Women and a two-tier social security system

Muntemba, Maud Shimwaayi
385d Women and agricultural change in the railway region of Zambia: Dispossession and counterstrategies, 1930-1970

Munter, Carol
225p Fat and the fantasy of perfection

Muramatsu, Yasuko
75a Women's employment in Japan

Murcott, Anne
241f 'It's a pleasure to cook for him': Food, mealtimes and gender in some South Wales households

Murdoch, Henry
471b Women at work in Ireland

Murphree, Mary
199h Brave new office: The changing world of the legal secretary
209q The decline of the "secretary as generalist"

Murphy, Jane
310f From mice to men? Implications of progress in cloning research

Murphy, John J.
384l The Virginian and Antonia Shimerda: Different sides of the western coin

Murphy, Julie
310e Egg farming and women's future

Murphy, Marilyn
174l Califia: An experiment in feminist education Califia community

Murray, Dian
401i One woman's rise to power: Cheng I's wife and the pirates

Murray, Meg McGavran
102b Breaking free of symbolic bondage: From feminine submission to a vision of equality
102k The work got done: An interview with Clara Mortenson Beyer

Murray, Michele
474f Creating oneself from scratch

Murray, Robert F.
79ii In vitro fertilization and embryo transfer: The process of making public policy
233c The hazards of work in pregnancy

Murstein, Bernard
24f Process, filter and stage theories of attraction
185d "Mate" selection in the year 2020

Mussell, Kay J.
109b "But why do they read those things?" The female audience and the gothic novel

Mutukwa, Gladys
77a Creative women in political change

Myers, Kate
274o Business studies

Myers, Lena Wright
38j On marital relations: Perceptions of black women

Myers, Mitzi
180g Unmothered daughter and the radical reformer: Harriet Martineau's career
452d Harriet Martineau's *Autobiography*: The making of a female philosopher

Myers, Robert J.
46i Incremental change in social security needed to result in equal and fair treatment of men and women

NACLA Report of the Americas
192j Capital's flight: The apparel industry moves south

Nadel, Ira Bruce
142j George Eliot and her biographers

Nadelhaft, Ruth
313p Women as moral and political alternatives in Conrad's early novels

Nadelson, Carol C.
8a Social change and psychotherapeutic implications
8b Aggression in women: Conceptual issues and clinical implications
69b Changing views of the relationship between femininity and reproduction
69f To marry or not to marry
69g Maternal work and children
69i Marriage and midlife: The impact of social change
87e Dual-career marriages: Benefits and costs
326a Psychodynamics of sexual assault experiences
359mm The rape victim: Psychodynamic considerations
360f Reproductive advancements: Theory, research applications, and psychological issues
365m Reproductive crises

Nadelson, Leslee
282h Pigs, women, and the men's house in Amazonia: An analysis of six Mundurucú myths

Nadelson, Theodore
8i The organic-functional controversy
87e Dual-career marriages: Benefits and costs

Naffin, Ngaire
348e Theorizing about female crime

Nagel, Ilene H.
376j Sex differences in the processing of criminal defendants

Nagel, Thomas
223o Sexual perversion

Naidoo, Josephine C.
271d Women of South Asian and Anglo-Saxon origins in the Canadian context

Naitove, Connie E.
146j Arts therapy with sexually abused children

Nakamura, Charles Y.
48i Gender roles and sexuality in the world of work

Nakamura, Kyoko Motomochi
325l No women's liberation: The heritage of a woman prophet in modern Japan

Nakane, Chie
438d Becoming an anthropologist (Japan)

Nandy, Dipak
93f Administering anti-discrimination legislation in Great Britain

Náñez, Clotilde Falcón
412h Hispanic clergy wives: Their contribution to United Methodism in the southwest, later nineteenth century to the present

Nardelli-Haight, Giuliana
73d The Museo Italo Americano: My involvement with the Italian American community in San Francisco

Nardin, Jane
164h Jane Austen and the problem of leisure

Naremore, James
330l Nature and history in The *Years*

Nash, Jill
246f Women, work, and change in Nagovisi

Nash, June
83g Class consciousness and world view of a Bolivian mining woman
347f Aztec women: The transition from status to class in empire and colony
428a The impact of the changing international division of labor on different sectors of the labor force

Nashat, Guity
368a Women in pre-revolutionary Iran: A historical overview
368k Women in the ideology of the Islamic Republic

Naso, Frank
277o Sexuality with cardiac disease

Natalizia, Elena M.
78z Marxist feminism: Implications for criminal justice

Nath, Jharna
92b Bangladesh: Beliefs and customs observed by Muslim rural women during their life cycle

Nathanson, Constance A.
423b Women and health: The social dimensions of biomedical data

Nathanson, Paul S.
472e Legal issues affecting older women

Nava, Mica
134a Youth service provision, social order and the question of girls
134d Drawing the line
335c From utopian to scientific feminism? Early feminist critiques of the family

Navarro, Marysa
108m Of sparrows and condors: The autobiography of Eva Perón

Naveed-I-Rahat
92d Pakistan: The role of women in reciprocal relationships in a Punjab village

Naylor, Audrey
80i The Yale Child Welfare Research Program: Description and results

Nebel, Ruth
336m The story of Ruth

Nederlander, Caren
287m Psychological aspects of sexual dysfunction

Needham, Dorothy
438j Women in Cambridge biochemistry (United Kingdom)

Neely, Barbara
301ff Spilled salt (fiction)
310a A yenga tale

Neely, Carol Thomas
343l Women and men in *Othello*: "What should such a fool/Do with so good a woman?"
343r Women and men in Shakespeare: A selective bibliography

Neher, Clark D.
431g Sex roles in the Philippines: The ambiguous Cebuana

Neiderbach, Shelley
186w "I live alone in a very beautiful place": An interview with May Sarton

Nelson, Anne H.
169l Games and other exercises

Nelson, Jeffrey
133o Media reaction to the 1979 gay march on Washington

Nelson, John R.
80o The politics of federal day care regulation

Nelson, Linda
355h Household time: A cross-cultural example

Nelson, Mattie Mae
301f Tribute to my husband

Nelson, Nici
5c Mobilizing village women: Some organizational and management considerations

Nentwig, M. Ruth
79u Technical aspects of sex preselection

Nerlove, Marc
355g Women's life-cycle time allocation: An econometric analysis

Ness, Susan
78t A sexist selection process keeps qualified women off the bench

Nestel, Gilbert
324e Economic consequences of poor health in mature women
324f Economic consequences of midlife change in marital status

Nestle, Joan
225q The fem question
231ff My mother liked to fuck

Neto, Virginia V.
78h National study of women's correctional programs

Neu, Diann
462z Guidelines for planners of ritual

Neuberger, Julia
457g Women in Judaism: The fact and the fiction

Newell, Mary Gathright
303c Mary Munford and higher education for women in Virginia

Newman, Evelyn S.
458g Retirement expectations and plans: A comparison of professional men and women

Newman, Katherine S.
388f Women and law: Land tenure in Africa

Newport, Cris
310gg The courage of sisters

Newsome, Clarence G.
412e Mary McLeod Bethune as religionist

Newton, Esther
225r The misunderstanding: Toward a more precise sexual vocabulary

Newton, Peggy
193j Who says girls can't be engineers?
250i Into work: Continuity and change

Ng, Winnie
305v Immigrant women: The silent partners of the women's movement

Nibley, Hugh W.
42f Patriarchy and matriarchy

Nicholas, Ralph W.
194i The village Mother in Bengal

Nichols, Jeanette
7q Is sadomasochism feminist? A critique of the Samois position

Nichols, John A.
187l Medieval Cistercian nunneries and English Bishops

Nichols, Kathleen L.
384i The western roots of feminism in Agnes Smedley's *Daughter of Earth*

Nichols, Nina da Vinci
109l Place and eros in Radcliffe, Lewis, and Brontë

Nichols, Patricia C.
171d Linguistic options and choices for black women in the rural South
356i Women in their speech communities

Nichols, Rosalie
129t Are feminist businesses capitalistic?

Nicholson, Linda
31l Feminist theory: The private and the public
116l Women's work: Views from the history of philosophy
432o The ethics of gender discrimination: A response to Ann Diller and Barbara Houston's "Women's Physical Education"

Nicola, JoAnn
87d Young marrieds: Wives' employment and family role structure

Nielsen, Eva Trein
22f Une contribution au débat concernant le status de la femme dans les villes du Danemark au Moyen-Age

Nielsen, Linda
432p Putting away the pom-poms: An educational psychologist's view of females and sports

Nielsen, Ruth
103q Family responsibilities as a labor market issue: A Scandinavian perspective

Niemelä, P.
265q Overemphasis of mother role and inflexibility of roles

Niemi, Albert W.
421u The impact of children on female earnings

Niemi, Beth
89n The female-male differential in unemployment rates

Nieto, Consuelo
72l Chicana identity: Interaction of culture and sex roles

Nieva, Veronica F.
49f The feminization of the labor force: Research for industrial/organizational psychology
267f Equity for women at work: Models of change

Nievera, Fe C.
71b Some effects of childrearing practices on the value systems of Asian-American women

Nieves, Josephine
72e Puerto Rican women in higher education in the United States

Nilsen, Deborah
157k The 'social evil': Prostitution in Vancouver, 1900-1920

Nisbet, Anne-Marie
198e The literary treatment of women in North Africa

Nishi, Setsuko Matsunaga
71g Chairperson's report

Nisonoff, Laurie
263m The new economic readjustment policies: Implications for Chinese urban working women

Nobbe, Charles
421s Labor force participation and fertility, contraceptive knowledge, attitude and practice of the women of Barbados

Noble, B. J.
372x Comparison of exercise between females and males

Noble, Barbara Presley
263a Women and welfare work: Demystifying the myth of disembeddedness

Nobles, Wade W.
37d African-American family life: An instrument of culture

Nochlin, Linda
117m Lost and *found*: Once more the fallen woman

Nogle, Vicki
133t Lesbianfeminist rhetoric as a social movement

Noll, William T.
412k Laity rights and leadership: Winning them for women in the Methodist Protestant church, 1860-1900

Noonkester, Barbara
147m The American sportswoman from 1900 to 1920

Nora, Hervé
209cc Experimental approaches towards telecommunications in France

Norcross, Elizabeth
205y Mary Ellen Smith: The right woman in the right place at the right time

Nord, Stella
390s Right-wing union officials versus married women workers

Norell, Donna
64f The relationship between meaning and structure in Colette's *Rain-moon*

Norgren, Jill
344j Child care
435g In search of a national child-care policy: Background and prospects

Norman, Elaine
455a Sex roles and sexism

Norman, William H.
29k Depression: A behavioral-cognitive approach

Norr, Kathleen
87f Spouses' contributions to each other's roles

Norris, Margot
409i Anna Livia Plurabelle: The dream woman

Norris, Maryel
7m An opinionated piece on sadomasochism

Norris, R. A.
115e The ordination of women and the 'maleness' of the Christ

Northcraft, Gregory B.
267c Double jeopardy: Resistance to affirmative action from potential beneficiaries

Northrup, Herbert R.
66d Wage setting and collective bargaining
67d Wage setting and collective bargaining

Norton, Eleanor Holmes
404a Women in crisis: The issue

Norton, Theodore Mills
106l Contemporary critical theory and the family: Private world and public crisis

Noschese, Christine
73a Ethnic women and the media

Notman, Malkah T.
8a Social change and psychotherapeutic implications
8b Aggression in women: Conceptual issues and clinical implications

69a Feminine development: Changes in psychoanalytic theory
69b Changing views of the relationship between femininity and reproduction
69f To marry or not to marry
69g Maternal work and children
69h Midlife concerns of women: Implications of menopause
190v Menarche: A psychoanalytic perspective
237c The psychiatrist's approach (premenstrual tension)
239j Adult life cycles: Changing roles and changing hormones
326a Psychodynamics of sexual assault experiences
359cc Midlife concerns of women: Implications of the menopause
359mm The rape victim: Psychodynamic considerations
360f Reproductive advancements: Theory, research applications, and psychological issues
365m Reproductive crises
411q Reflections and perspectives on 'therapeutic issues for today's adult women'

Nottingham WONT
167c Working as a group

Novikova, E. E.
446j Women's work and the family
446o The quantity and quality of work: A round table

Novy, Marianne
343n Shakespeare's female characters as actors and audience

Nowak, Carol A.
221h The process of retirement: Implications for late-life counseling

Nuestra Lucha
192t Lucy Duran - Wife, mother, and organizer

Nugent, Robert
152e Homosexuality, celibacy, religious life and ordination

Nukunya, G.K.
370m Appendix: A note on Anlo (Ewe) slavery and the history of a slave

Numbers, Ronald L.
353z Ministries of healing: Mary Baker Eddy, Ellen G. White, and the religion of health

Nunes, Maria Luisa
39ee Images of the woman of color in Brazilian literature: O Cortico, Clara Dos Anjos, Gabriela Cravo E Canela, and O Quinze

Nussbaum, Karen
209b Office automation: Jekyll or Hyde?

Nye, Mary E.
175l Elisabet Ney: Texas' first lady of sculpture

Nye, Ng Sock
183c Status of rural women

O'Barr, Jean
6i African women in politics

O'Barr, William M.
356g "Women's language" or "powerless language"?

O'Brien, Darcy
318i Edna O'Brien: A kind of Irish childhood

O'Brien, Denise
246d "Women never hunt": The portrayal of women in Melanesian ethnography

O'Brien, Leslie N.
466j Four paces behind: Women's work in peninsular Malaysia

O'Brien, Maire Cruise
338b The female principle in Gaelic poetry

O'Brien, Margaret
241k Interviewing men: 'Taking gender seriously'

O'Brien, Mary
120k Feminist praxis

O'Brien, Nancy Patricia
302c The recruitment of men into librarianship, following World War II

O'Brien, Sharon
17l Mothers, daughters, and the "art necessity": Willa Cather and the creative process

O'Connell, Dorothy
220d Poverty: The feminine complaint
220g Women as providers and consumers

O'Connell, Martin
309c The legitimacy status of first births to U.S. women aged 15-24, 1939-1978

O'Dell, Felicity
151e Socialisation in the literature lesson

O'Donnell, Lydia
243e Mothers as social agents: Structuring the community activities of school aged children
411i The daughter of aging parents

O'Donnell, Sheryl
196a "My idea in your mind": John Locke and Damaris Cudworth Masham

O'Donovan, Katherine
189l Before and after: The impact of feminism on the academic discipline of law

O'Farrell, Brigid
272l Job integration strategies: Today's programs and tomorrow's needs
426f Women and nontraditional blue collar jobs in the 1980s: An overview

O'Laughlin, Kay
210m The final challenge: Facing death

O'Leary, Virginia E.
425e Trying hurts women, helps men: The meaning of effort

O'Neale, Sondra
40c Reconstruction of the composite self: New images of black women in Maya Angelou's continuing autobiography

O'Neill, June
260d Earnings differentials: Empirical evidence and causes

O'Neill, William
442o Reflections on feminism: Implications for today

O'Rand, Angela
458b Midlife work history and retirement income

O'Reilly, Harry J.
219g Crisis intervention with victims of forcible rape: A police perspective

Oakley, Ann
50u   Competing ideologies of reproduction: Medical and maternal perspectives on pregnancy
85b   Interviewing women: A contradiction in terms
125k Millicent Garrett Fawcett: Duty and determination
233j The effect of the mother's work on the infant
355a Prologue: Reflections on the study of household labor
396c Competing ideologies of reproduction: Medical and maternal perspectives on pregnancy
465e Women and health policy

Oaks, Priscilla
460a "Role, Jenny Jenkins, Roll": Little girls and maidens in American folksongs - an analysis of sexual attitudes

Oates, Joyce Carol
127g The visionary art of Flannery O'Connor
135a Is there a female voice? Joyce Carol Oates replies
451l The visionary art of Flannery O'Connor

Oates, Richard P.
190u Steroidal contraceptive use and subsequent development of hyperprolactinemia

Obrist, Barbara
188j The Swedish visionary: Saint Bridget

Ochshorn, Judith
126g The contest between androgyny and patriarchy in early western tradition
180a Mothers and daughters in ancient Near Eastern literature
462u Reclaiming our past

Oda, Yukiko
75a   Women's employment in Japan

Oesterle, Patricia M.
339h Working couples and child care

Ogbu, John U.
37h   Black education: A cultural-ecological perspective

Ogg, Kathryn
205p "Especially when no one agrees": An interview with May Campbell

Ojala, Jeanne A.
112g Madame de Sévigné: Chronicler of an age (French, 1626-1696)

Okeyo, Achola Pala
347h Daughters of the lakes and rivers: Colonization and the land rights of Luo women

Okin, Susan Moller
106b Philosopher queens and private wives: Plato on women and the family

Okonjo, Kamene
39d   Women's political participation Nigeria

Olds, Sharon
231q Outside the operating room of the sex-change doctor

231aa Bestiary (poem)

Olesen, Virginia
51x   Sociological observations on ethical issues implicated in estrogen replacement therapy at menopause

Oliner, Marion Michel
88b   The anal phase

Oliver, David B.
244j Synthetic smiles and fabricated faces

Oliver, H. G.
276g Sentencing the sexual offender

Oliver, Judith
170d The caring wife

Olivier de Sardan, Jean-Pierre
370h The Songhay-Zarma female slave: Relations of production and ideological status

Oloruntimehin, O.
159i A preliminary study of female criminality in Nigeria

Olsen, Anne
382a Denmark

Olson, Christine M.
11h   Fetal alcohol syndrome and drinking during pregnancy

Olson, Emelie A.
270a Duofocal family structure and an alternative model of husband-wife relationship

Olson, Jon
243b Gender and interaction in the workplace

Olson, Robert C.
111h Contingency management in a juvenile treatment setting

Olssen, Erik
413h Women, work and family: 1880-1926

Olsson, Hanna
163e The woman, the love, and the power

Olzak, Susan
320l Sex differences in the implications of the links between major departments and the occupational structure

Omodei, Roslyn
348d The mythinterpretation of female crime

Omolade, Barbara
132q Black women and feminism
231v Hearts of darkness

Ong, Aihwa
428r Global industries and Malay peasants in peninsular Malaysia

Ooms, Theodora
3e   A family perspective on abortion
3j   Commentary to chapter 6 (chapter i)
308k Family involvement, notification, and responsibility: A personal essay

Oppenheimer, Catherine
456k Sexual problems

Oppenheimer, Helen
47h   Moral choice

Oppong, Christine
52p   Women's roles and conjugal family systems in Ghana

459e Family structure and women's reproductive and productive roles: Some conceptual and methodological issues

Orbach, Susie
443d Feminist psychoanalysis: Theory and practice

Ordóñez, Elizabeth
408p Sexual politics and the theme of sexuality in Chicana poetry

Organisation for Economic Co-operation and Development
89p   The 1974-1975 recession and the employment of women

Oribabor, Patrick
248g 'The history of the present' - contradiction and struggle in nursing

Orlinsky, David E.
365a Gender and psychotherapeutic outcome

Ormerod, M.B.
193g Factors differentially affecting the science subject preferences, choices and attitudes of girls and boys

Orthner, Dennis K.
185n Beyond the melting pot: Nationalism, militarism and the family

Ortiz, Roxanne Dunbar
192e Toward a democratic women's movement in the United States

Ortner, Sherry B.
124e The founding of the first Sherpa nunnery, and the problem of "women" as an analytic category
282a Introduction: Accounting for sexual meanings
282k Gender and sexuality in hierarchical societies: The case of Polynesia and some comparative implications

Orubuloye, Israel
393b Education and socio-demographic change in Nigeria

Osako, Masako Murakami
71i   The effects of Asian-American kinship systems on women's educational and occupational attainment
387j Dilemmas of Japanese professional women

Osborne, Kate
240m A feminist perspective on women and health

Oser, George T.
319p To be aged, Hispanic, and female: The triple risk

Ostberg, Olov
209s Office computerization: Research then and now

Osterman, Gail Bryant
339i Does becoming a parent mean falling off the fast track?

Ostrow, Andrew C.
317c Physical activity as it relates to the health of the aged

Otaño-Rivera, Blanqui
429j The task of enabling

Otos, Sally
307q Word processing: "This is not a final draft"

Ott, Marian T.
463l Women's travel behavior and attitudes: An empirical analysis

Otte, Helle
382a Denmark

Otto, Dianne
294k From delicacy to dilemma: A feminist perspective

Otto, Shirley
345h Single homeless women and alcohol

Oussedik, Fatma
298g The conditions required for women to conduct research on women in the Arab region

Outshoorn, Joyce
76c The dual heritage

Overfield, Kathy
189o Dirty fingers, grime and slag heaps: Purity and the scientific ethic
212g The packaging of women: Science and our sexuality

Owen, Morfydd E.
334c Shame and reparation: Women's place in the kin

Owens, Suzanne
186e House, home and solitude: Memoirs and journals of May Sarton

Özbay, Ferhunde
270e Women's education in rural Turkey

Özgür, Serap
270n Social psychological patterns of homicide in Turkey: A comparison of male and female convicted murders

Ozick, Cynthia
211j Notes toward finding the right question

Paaswell, Robert E.
463u The transportation planning process

Paaswell, Rosalind S.
463u The transportation planning process

Padawer, Wendy J.
29m Anxiety-related disorders, fears, and phobias

Paddock, Susan C.
90k Male and female career paths in school administration

Padel, Ruth
156a Women: Model for possession by Greek daemons

Paffenbarger Jr., Ralph S.
53k An epidemiologic perspective of mental illness and childbirth

Pagano, Darlene
7l Racism and sadomasochism: A conversation with two black lesbians
7q Is sadomasochism feminist? A critique of the Samois position

Page, Annabel
345g Counselling

Page, Jane
16r Women in midstream

Pagelow, Mildred D.
349n Sex roles, power, and woman battering
349o Secondary battering and alternatives of female victims to spouse abuse

Paige, Karen Ericksen
190m Virginity rituals and chastity control during puberty: Cross-cultural patterns
239h American birth practices: A critical review

Painter, Dorothy S.
133f Recognition among lesbians in straight settings

Pais, Sara Via
442f Shapes of the feminine experience in art

Paisley, William
87j Coordinated-career couples: Convergence and divergence

Pala, Achola O.
39j Definitions of women and development: An African perspective

Palabrica-Costello, Marilou
424k Female domestic servants in Cagayan de Oro, Philippines: Social and economic implications of employment in a 'premodern' occupational role

Palandri, Angela Jung
449a Introduction: A historical perspective

Palliser, Charles
143d *Adam Bede* and "the story of the past"

Palmer, David
223f The consolation of marriage

Palmer, Pamela Lynn
175k Adah Isaacs Menken: From Texas to Paris

Palmer, Phyllis
199d Housework and domestic labor: Racial and technological change

Palmeri, Ann
84f Charlotte Perkins Gilman: Forerunner of a feminist social science

Pandey, Rama S.
265o Strategies of healthy sex role development in modernized India

Pandian, Jacob
194h The goddess Kannagi: A dominant symbol of south Indian Tamil society

Papanek, Hanna
255a Purdah: Separate worlds and symbolic shelter
255g Purdah in Pakistan: Seclusion and modern occupations for women
373n The differential impact of programs and policies on women in development

Pape, Rachel Edgarde
461o Female sexuality and pregnancy

Papola, T. S.
459j Sex discrimination in the urban labour markets: Some propositions based on Indian evidence

Parcell, Stanley R.
349m Sexual aggression: A second look at the offended female

Parisi, Nicolette
165d Exploring female crime patterns: Problems and prospects

165h Are females treated differently? A review of the theories and evidence on sentencing and parole decisions

Park, Clara Claiborne
343f As we like it: How a girl can be smart and still popular

Park, Jan Carl
133v Referendum campaigns vs. gay rights

Park, Martha Mayes
303n To Delois and Willie (poem)

Park, Patricia
429e Women and liturgy

Park, Roberta
147c The rise and development of women's concern for the physical education of American women, 1776-1885: From independence to the foundation of the AAAPE
147z History and structure of the department of physical education at the University of California with special reference to women's sports

Park, Sun Ai
91b Religion and menstruation

Parker, Alberta
307aa Juggling health care technology and women's needs

Parker, Alice
306c Cross-cultural perspectives: Creole and Acadian women
306l Southern women's literature and culture: Course development and the pedagogical process

Parker, Derek
278h Erotic poetry in English

Parker, Frederick B.
11a Sex-role adjustment in women alcoholics

Parker, Pat
150aa What will you be? (poem)

Parker-Smith, Bettye J.
40ii Running wild in her soul: The poetry of Carolyn Rodgers
40oo Alice Walker's women: In search of some peace of mind

Parkin, Andrew
338c Women in the plays of W.B. Yeats

Parlee, Mary Brown
28e The psychology of the menstrual cycle: Biological and physiological perspectives
190z Future directions for research
411n Reproductive issues, including menopause

Parr, Joyce
315g The art of quilting: Thoughts from a contemporary quilter

Parry, Susan M.
102h A primer on women and the democratization of the workplace

Parsley, C. J.
357b Relative female earnings in Great Britain and the impact of legislation

Parsons, Anthony D.
240j Psychosexual problems

Parsons, Barbara
394h   Sedition in a sexist society: The Platteville paradigm

Parsons, Jacquelynne E.
48b   Sexual socialization and gender roles in childhood
239a   Psychosexual neutrality: Is anatomy destiny?

Parthasarathy, G.
422c   Women in the labour force in India

Parvey, Constance F.
59h   Re-membering: A global perspective on women

Passmore, Nancy F. W.
229p   A consciousness manifesto

Pastner, Carroll McClure
255f   Gradations of purdah and the creation of social boundaries on a Baluchistan oasis
403e   Access to property and the states of women in Islam

Patai, Daphne
383j   Beyond defensiveness: Feminist research strategies
398h   Beyond defensiveness: A feminist research strategies

Pateman, Carole
464c   The shame of the marriage contract

Paterson, Ann
316p   Status report on the women's movement as indexed by a "Festival of Women" in West Virginia, Fall 1978

Patraka, Vivian
124c   Notes on technique in feminist drama: *Apple Pie* and *Signs of Life*

Patterson, Cynthia
399d   Rites and rights

Patterson, Michelle
78u   Women in a male-dominated profession: The women lawyers

Patterson, Paul R.
285f   Sexual feelings in the terminally ill patient

Patterson-Black, Gene
17e   On Herman Melville

Paul, Diana
325m   Empress Wu and the historians: A tyrant and saint of classical China

Paul, Eve W.
309bb   Teenagers and pregnancy: The law in 1979

Paul, Janet
413i   Women artists in New Zealand

Paulissen, Maisie
175q   Pardon me, Governor Ferguson

Paulson, Joy
58f   Women in modern occupations
386a   Housewives

Paxton, Nancy L.
448d   George Eliot and the city: The imprisonment of culture

Payne, Geoff
139e   Trends in female social mobility

Payne, Judy
139e   Trends in female social mobility

Pazdro, Roberta J.
157f   Agnes Deans Cameron: Against the current
205h   From pastels to chisel: The changing role of BC women artists

Peacock, Carol
404x   Young female offenders in Massachusetts: Toward leaving the juvenile justice system successfully

Pearce, Diana M.
344bb   Farewell to alms: Women's fare under welfare

Pearce, Shirley
240f   Chronic pelvic pain

Pearson, Carol
131e   Coming Home: Four feminist utopias and patriarchal experience
417aa   Of time and revolution: Theories of social change in contemporary feminist science fiction

Pearson, Cynthia
295o   Older women and mental health

Pearson, Gail
101g   Nationalism, universalization, and the extended female space in Bombay City

Pearson, Ruth
207i   The subordination of women and the internationalisation of factory production
208a   Introduction: The continuing subordination of women in the development process
208c   The subordination of women and the internationalisation of factory production

Pearson, Sheryl S.
214d   Rhetoric and organizational change: New applications of feminine style

Peattie, Noel
15h   Publishers on libraries: Stake your claim

Peet, Katharine
456o   Migraine

Peiss, Kathy
231b   "Charity girls" and city pleasures: Historical notes on working-class sexuality, 1880-1920

Peixoto, Marta
332o   *Family Ties*: Female development in Clarice Lispector

Pence, Ellen
14f   Racism - a white issue

Pender, Glenda Neel
301cc   My grandmother's gift (poem)

Penelope, Julia (Stanley)
171i   Consciousness as style: Style as aesthetic

Penrod, Steven
230k   Using psychological research on violent pornography to inform legal change

Pepitone-Rockwell, Fran
87b   Catalytic movements: Civil rights and women

Peplau, Letitia Anne
48k   The intimate relationships of lesbians and gay men
344g   Power in dating relationships

Per-Lee, Dianne A.
386g   Street vendors

Perkins, Linda
39p   Black women and racial "uplift" prior to emancipation

Perl, Teri Hoch
361e   A short-term intervention program: Math-science conferences

Perlmutter, Ellen
51m   Changing views of "the change": A critical review and suggestions for an attributional approach
316i   The menopause in changing times

Perloff, Marjorie G.
127h   "A ritual for being born twice": Sylvia Plath's *The Bell Jar*

Perreault, Geraldine
31q   Contemporary feminist perspectives on women and higher education

Perrie, Walter
197i   Mrs. Spark's verse
278g   Homosexuality and literature

Perrucci, Carolyn C.
416a   Central issues facing women in the science-based professions

Perry, Michael E.
185i   The transition from sex to sexuality and intimacy

Persky, Harold
277b   Hormones and sexual arousal

Person, Ethel Spector
439c   Sexuality as the mainstay of identity: Psychoanalytic perspectives

Persyn, U.
107n   Some differences between men and women in various factors which determine swimming performance

Perun, Pamela J.
320a   The undergraduate woman: Theme and variations
320p   Life after college: Historical links between women's education and women's work
320q   Issues of educational equity in the 1980's: Multiple perspectives

Petchesky, Rosalind Pollack
18c   "Reproductive choice" in the contemporary United States: A social analysis of female sterilization
60o   Reproduction and class divisions among women
439e   Reproductive freedom: Beyond "A woman's right to choose"

Peters, Marie F.
37n   Parenting in black families with young children: A historical perspective

Peters, Timothy J.
233h   The effects of work in pregnancy: Short- and long-term associations

Petersen, Anne C.
190d   Menarche: Meaning of measures and measuring meaning
239b   Biopsychosocial processes in the development of sex-related differences

351d Biology: Its role in gender-related educational experiences

Petersen, Cheryl Bowser
78y Doing time with the boys: An analysis of women correctional officers in all-male facilities

Peterson, Jacqueline
367a American Indian women and religion

Peterson, Rebecca
203a Introduction: The domestic workplace
203r Introduction: Women as environmental activists

Peterson, Susan
414d Patient and useful servants: Women missionaries in Indian territory

Peterson, Susan Rae
79l The politics of prenatal diagnosis: A feminist ethical analysis
195d Against "parenting"

Petras, Elizabeth McLean
18f Cross-national labor migrants: Actors in the international division of labor

Petrini, Mario
287i In search of a vagina

Pettigrew, Joyce
85c Reminiscences of fieldwork among the Sikhs

Pettitt, Ann
215j Letter to my neighbour: Nuclear war and the countryside

Pevitts, Beverley Byers
399w *Fefu and Her Friends*

Pezzuoli, Giovanna
313c Prisoner in utopia

Pfafflin, Sheila M.
77c Creative women in scientific-technological and medical change
251f Some reflections on women in science and technology after UNCSTD

Pfarr, Heide M.
260h Equal opportunity policies for women in the Federal Republic of Germany

Pfeffer, Cynthia R.
8h Childhood and adolescent suicidal behavior, with an emphasis on girls

Pfister, G.
372h The influence of women doctors on the origins of women's sports in Germany

Phaf, Ineke
322j Women and literature in the Caribbean
322k Interview with Astrid Roemer (Surinam)

Phanuel, Mirabai
75d Career counselling for poor rural and urban women of South India

Pharr, Susan J.
21b The Japanese woman: Evolving views of life and role
218d Tea and power: The anatomy of a conflict

Phelps, Edmund S.
89h The statistical theory of racism and sexism

Phelps, Jamie
462e Racism and the bonding of women

Phelps, Linda
43o Patriarchy and capitalism

Phillips, Jock
413j Mummy's boys: Pakeha men and male culture in New Zealand

Phillips, John Neal
175r "Tell them I don't smoke cigars": The story of Bonnie Parker

Phillips, Rachel
408e Marina/Malinche: Masks and shadows

Phillips, Ruth M.
316e Women in medicine

Phillips, Susan
203q Women at city hall

Phillis, Diane E.
48j Sink or swing? The lifestyles of single adults

Phizacklea, Annie
213e In the front line
470f Migrant women and wage labour: The case of West Indian women in Britain

Phongpaichit, Pasuk
424l The Bangkok masseuses: Origins, status and prospects

Piampiti, Suwanlee
420h Female migration in Thailand
420l Female migrants in Bangkok metropolis

Pian, Canta
71h Immigration of Asian women and the status of recent Asian women immigrants

Pielke, Robert G.
116j Are androgyny and sexuality compatible?

Piercy, Marge
417i What's that smell in the kitchen? (poem)
417dd Outcome of the matter: The sun (poem)
453m Mirror images

Pierre-Aggamaway, Marlene
220e Native women and the state
220g Women as providers and consumers

Pierson, David
65h A policy-capturing application in a union setting

Pierson, Ruth
120e Feminism and the writing and teaching of history

Pilotta, Joseph J.
415a Trust and power in the organization: An overview

Pilpel, Harriet F.
309bb Teenagers and pregnancy: The law in 1979

Pimlott, Ben
283l Does Labour always fail?

Pina-Cabral, João de
364e Female power and the inequality of wealth and motherhood in north-western Portugal

Pintasilgo, Maria de Lourdes
380a Women as world makers

Piotrkowski, Chaya S.
243i Work experience and family relations among working-class and lower-middle-class families

Piotrowski, Jerzy
105c Marital expectations of wives in contemporary Poland

Pipes, William Harrison
37c Old-time religion: Benches can't say "Amen"

Pirie, Peter
420g Female rural-to-urban migration in peninsular Malaysia

Pisano, Joseph C.
361k Strategies to increase participation of minorities in medicine

Pitner, Nancy J.
90p Hormones and harems: Are the activities of superintending different for a woman?

Pitrou, Agnes
244e The roles of men and women in French families: Change or stability in the patterns and practices?

Pitters, Marian
147j Women's participation in sporting activities as an indicator of a feminist movement in Canada between 1867-1914
147n An analysis of humour pertaining to sportswomen in Canadian newspapers from 1910-1920

Pizarro, Agueda
74j The arc of paradox (essay)

Place, Janey
406c Women in film noir

Placek, Paul J.
308a Teenage women in the United States: Sex, contraception, pregnancy, fertility, and maternal and infant health

Placzek, James
300m The Thai forest tradition: Local and international manifestations

Pladott, Dinnah
417y Neither Arcadia nor Elysium: E. M. Broner's *A Weave of Women*

Plaskow, Judith
211s The right question is theological
462h Anti-semitism: The unacknowledged racism
462p Women responding to the Arab-Israeli conflict

Platt, Jane E.
268e Sex roles and psychophysiological disorders: Coronary heart disease

Platt, Jennifer
297j The *Affluent Worker* re-visited

Platt, Rudolf F.
141d Pathologic aspects of familial carcinoma of breast

Plaut, Jonathan
233o A management view of reproductive health

Pleck, Elizabeth
124m The defeat of the Equal Rights Amendment
243d The old world, new rights, and the limited rebellion: Challenges to traditional authority in immigrant families

Pleck, Joseph H.
124h How psychology constructed masculinity: The theory of male sex role identity
140f Men's power with women, other men, and society: A men's movement analysis
158i The theory of male sex role identity: Its rise and fall, 1936 to the present
214q The work — family problem: Overloading the system
243m Husbands' paid work and family roles: Current research issues
387h The work-family role system

Plenska, Danuta
111c Women's criminality in Poland
159g The criminality of women in Poland

Plummer, John F.
331f The woman's song in Middle English and its European backgrounds

Plummer, Ken
219d The social uses of sexuality: Symbolic interaction, power and rape

Podos, Batya
229cc Feeding the feminist psyche through ritual theater

Poindexter, Alfred N.
4h Issues surrounding adolescent pregnancy terminations

Polachek, Solomon
89g Family investments in human capital: Earnings of women

Polansky, Elinor
455i Women and the health care system: Implications for social work practice

Polatnick, M. Rivka
195b Why men don't rear children: A power analysis

Poliakoff, Phaye
301w Prostitution I: Trying to make a living

Polikoff, Nancy D.
103j Gender and child-custody determinations: Exploding the myths

Pollert, Anna
139g Women, gender relations and wage labour

Pollock, Jan
274i History

Pollock, M. Helene
429a Growing toward effective ministry

Pollock, Marion
323f Under attack: Women, unions and microtechnology

Pollock, Scarlet
310k Refusing to take women seriously: 'Side effects' and the politics of contraception

Polonsky, Derek C.
69i Marriage and midlife: The impact of social change

Pomerleau, Cynthia S.
452b The emergence of women's autobiography in England

Pomeroy, Fred
209gg Taking the initiative on new technology: Canadian labor approaches

Pomeroy, Sarah B.
156m Infanticide in Hellenistic Greece
419n Selected bibliography on women in classical Antiquity

Ponse, Barbara
460m Finding self in the lesbian community

Ponting, J. Rick
421j Attitudes and ideology: Correlates of liberal attitudes towards the role of women

Ponza, Michael
272h Work experience, job segregation, and wages

Pool, D. Ian
421p Changes in Canadian female labour force participation and some possible implications for conjugal power

Poole, Fitz John Porter
282d Transforming "natural" woman: Female ritual leaders and gender ideology among Bimin-Kuskusmin

Poor, Matile
176x Older lesbians

Poortmans, J.
372j Introduction to the biology of the female athlete

Poovey, Mary
242f *Persuasion* and the promises of love
313g Ideology and *The Mysteries of Udolpho*

Pope Paul VI
223i Humanae vitae

Pope, Barbara Corrado
444i Revolution and retreat: Upper-class French women after 1789

Popenoe, David
203i Women in the suburban environment: A U.S.- Sweden comparison

Popham, Robert E.
9j Sex differences in mortality: A comparison of male and female alcoholics

Porokhniuk, V.
446p How working women combine work and household duties

Porter, Cathy
215p Building on the positives: The USSR

Porter, Frances Sarnacki
146a A conceptual framework for child sexual abuse
146b Validation of child sexual abuse
146d Treatment of the sexually abused child
146e Group therapy with female adolescent incest victims

Porter, Karen L.
411f Multiple roles of midlife women: A case for new directions in theory, research, and policy

Porter, Katherine Anne
451c Reflections on Willa Cather

Porter, Marilyn
241g 'Women and old boats': The sexual division of labour in a Newfoundland outport
470g Standing on the edge: Working class housewives and the world of work

Porter, Mary
398k On the bottom rung: A discussion of women's work in sociology

Porter, Natalie
136c Women and nonverbal leadership cues: When seeing is not believing

Porter, Paige
440l Social policy, education and women

Portman, Lisa
65m The role of labor

Portner, Joyce
185k The work/family connection in the year 2020

Postow, B. C.
116p Women and "masculine" sports: Androgyny qualified
275s Thomas on sexism

Postow, Betsy
432e Afterword on equal opportunity

Potter, Clare
176v The lesbian periodicals index

Potter, Robert G.
273c Sex selection through amniocentesis and selective abortion

Potter, Sandee
397m Lesbians and contemporary health care systems: Oppression and opportunity

Potuchek, Jean L.
263c Symmetrical families? Changing gender role expectations and the breadwinner role in the contemporary United States

Powell, Betty
43s Confrontation: Black/white
174z Charlotte Bunch and Betty Powell talk about feminism, blacks, and education as politics

Powell, David O.
353cc Homeopathy and sexual equality: The controversy over coeducation at Cincinnati's Pulte Medical College, 1873-1879

Powell, Linda C.
150ii Black macho and black feminism

Powell, Mary Patricia
157m A response to the depression: The local Council of Women of Vancouver

Power, Margaret
390v Women and economic crises: The Great Depression and the present crisis

Powers, Marla N.
439f Menstruation and reproduction: An Oglala case

Powers, Patricia
55j Treatment issues with children involved in pornography and sex rings

Powledge, Tabitha M.
79w Unnatural selection: On choosing children's sex
273i Toward a moral policy for sex choice

Prager, Susan Westerberg
245g Shifting perspectives on marital property law

Prather, Charlotte C.
130y The view from Germany

Pratt, Annis
20i *Surfacing* and the rebirth journey

Pratt, Minnie Bruce
303b IWY: Breaking the silence: a fantasy (poem)

Pratt, Norma Fain
81f Culture and radical politics: Yiddish women writers in America, 1890-1940

Pratt, William C.
128g Women socialists and their male comrades: The Reading experience, 1927-1936

Preisinger, Arthur A.
82v How your organization can participate

Prelinger, Catherine M.
145f Prelude to consciousness: Amalie Sieveking and the Female Association for the Care of the Poor and the Sick
367g Women in sectarian and utopian groups

Prenshaw, Peggy W.
303h Academic women in Mississippi: Oktoberfest 1980
450i Mermaids, angels and free women: The heroines of Elizabeth Spencer's fiction

Prentice, Alison
120e Feminism and the writing and teaching of history

Prescott, Martha Moore
181b Lillian Moller Gilbreth and the founding of modern industrial engineering

Presley, Sharon
129f Government is women's enemy

Press, Sylvia Peña
469d Hispanic women in suburbia

Pressel, Esther
473e Spirit magic in the social relations between men and women (Saõ Paulo, Brazil)

Presser, Harriet B.
309t Guessing and misinformation about pregnancy risk among urban mothers
309v Early motherhood: Ignorance or bliss?
380p Child care use and constraints in the United States

Prestage, Jewel L.
380o Political behavior of American black women: An overview

Preston, James J.
194j The goddess Chandi as an agent of change
194p Conclusion: New perspectives on mother worship

Price, Barbara Raffel
78a The criminal law and women
78v A century of women in policing
78aa Postscript: The future of women and the criminal law

Price, Paola Malpezzi
135d Masculine and feminine personae in the love poetry of Christine de Pisan

Price, Susanna
466e Rich woman, poor woman: Occupation differences in a textile producing village in Central Java

Price, Virginia
55g Youth prostitution

Price-Bonham, Sharon
458h Attitudes toward retirement: A comparison of professional and nonprofessional married women

Priester, Marijke
213f Living in between: Turkish women in their homeland and in the Netherlands

Prindiville, Joanne
300c The Minangkabau woman: Cultural centre or ethnic symbol?

Pringle, Jackie
156i Hittite birth rituals

Pringle, Rosemary
13b Capitalism, gender and the labour process: Two case studies
321e Production and consumption: Public versus private
440d Women and consumer capitalism

Prioli, Carmine
301z Miss Elsie Riddick

Prokop, L.
372v Anaerobic energy metabolism of women

Proom, Juliette
205aa Tilly Jean Rolston: She knew how to throw a party

Propper, Alice M.
111j Prison homosexuality: Re-examining conventional wisdom

Prose, Maryruth
414e Pioneer women: A photographic perspective

Prout, Gillian
274p Careers

Provence, Sally
80b Infant day care: Relationships between theory and practice
80i The Yale Child Welfare Research Program: Description and results

Provost, William
188m The English religious enthusiast: Margery Kempe

Pullin, Faith
197c Autonomy and fabulation in the fiction of Muriel Spark

Punnett, Laura
36f Women-controlled research

Purcell, Kate
378d Militancy and acquiescence among women workers

Purdy, L. M.
275p Against "Vs. Ms."

Purdy, Virginia C.
61c National Archives resources for research in the history of American women

Puryear, Gwendolyn Randall
68n The black woman: Liberated or oppressed?

Putnam, Linda L.
415d Lady you're trapped: Breaking out of conflict cycles

Putney, Paula G.
186t "Sister of the mirage and echo": An interview with May Sarton

Putzell-Korab, Sara
286k Passion between women in the Victorian novel

Pyke, Sandra W.
271b Androgyny: A dead end or a promise

Qadir, Sayeda Rowshan
400c Women's income earning activities and family welfare in Bangladesh

Quaglio, Francine
60t Religion as an instrument of social control

Quah, John
300i The public bureaucracy and social change in Singapore

Quarm, Daisy
427h Sexual inequality: The high cost of leaving parenting to women

Quataert, Jean H.
145n Social insurance and the family work of Oberlausitz home weavers in the late nineteenth century

Quester, George H.
113l The problem

Quinn, M. Bernetta
451j Flannery O'Connor, a realist of distances

Quinn, Robert E.
288c Coping with Cupid: The formation, impact, and management of romantic relationships in organizations

Quinsey, Vernon L.
276c Prediction of recidivism and the evaluation of treatment programs for sex offenders
276d The assessment and treatment of sexual offenders

Quissell, Barbara
445o Dorothy Scarborough's critique of the frontier experience in *The Wind*

Quistorp, Eva
167a Starting a movement: Frauen für frieden (Women for Peace, West Germany)

Qvist, Gunmar
382j Sweden

Rabine, Leslie
27e George Sand and the myth of femininity

Rabinowitz, Paula
124b Naming, magic and documentary: The subversion of the narrative in *Song of Solomon*, *Ceremony*, and *China Men*

Rabkin, Eric S.
131a Science fiction women before liberation

Rabun Jr., John B.
55k Combating child pornography and prostitution: One county's approach

Rachlin, Marjorie B.
169e Training rank and file leaders: A case study
169i Discussion method

Rackin, Phyllis
249e Not by lawyers alone: Ten practical lessons for academic litigants

Radice, Betty
188d The French scholar-lover: Heloise

Radin, Norma
204g Primary caregiving and role-sharing fathers

Radloff, Lenore Sawyer
191e Risk factors for depression: What do we learn from them?
268f Depression in relation to sex roles: Differences in learned susceptibility and precipitating factors

Radlove, Shirley
48e Sexual response and gender roles

Radov, Carol G.
16c Issues in feminist therapy: The work of a woman's study group

Radwan, Kamelia
198c The Islamic revolution and women: Quest for the Quranic model

Rafter, Nicole Hahn
78z Marxist feminism: Implications for criminal justice
165j Hard times: Custodial prisons for women and the example of the New York State Prison for Women at Auburn, 1893-1933
165n Sex-role operations: Strategies for women working in the criminal justice system

Raharjo, Yulfita
166c Women in the workforce
424d Employment patterns of educated women in Indonesian cities

Rahim, Enayetur
433f Bengal election, 1937: Fazlul Huq and M. A. Jinnah: A study in leadership stress in Bengal politics

Rahkila, P.
372z Effect of increased intensity of training on maximum oxygen uptake and muscular performance of young female cross-country skiers

Rahman, Fazlur
255k The status of women in Islam: A modernist interpretation
368b Status of women in the Qur'an

Rahmani, Tahereh M. Z.
438f The achievement of Iranian women in science

Rainone, Francine
31j Women's work and sex roles
116m Sex roles and the sexual division of labor

Rajalakshmi, R.
438l Autobiography of an unknown woman (India)

Rakusen, Jill
396d Depo-provera: The extent of the problem: A case study in the politics of birth control

Ramas, Maria
256b Freud's Dora, Dora's hysteria

Ramesh, Asha
161a Movement against the portrayal of women in India
161d Portrayal of women in women's journals
163f The devadasi problem

Ramey, Estelle R.
53b The relationship of the sex hormone/prostaglandin interaction to female and male longevity
214c Different is not lesser: Women in science
237b The endocrinologist's approach (premenstrual tension)

Ramirez, Francisca
172h It all depends on the teacher (Honduras)

Ramirez, Manuel
216f Parenting for multiculturalism: A Mexican-American model

Ramusack, Barbara N.
101e Catalysts or helpers? British feminists, Indian women's rights, and Indian independence
388j Women's organizations and social change: The age-of-marriage issue in India

Ramwell, Peter
53b The relationship of the sex hormone/prostaglandin interaction to female and male longevity

Randall, Susan C.
349r Barriers to becoming a "successful" rape victim

Randisi, Jennifer L.
197f Muriel Spark and satire

Rankin, Theresa
206o Can the union make us strong

Rao, B. Janardhan
299d Beedi workers
299e Construction workers

Rao, G. Dasaradharama
422c Women in the labour force in India

Rao, K. Seetarāma
299g Tribal migrants

Raphael, Sharon
397e The older lesbian: Love relationships and friendship patterns

Rapone, Anita
454a American women and domestic culture: An approach to women's history

Rapoport, Rhona
45m Change and constancy: A hundred years' tale
87a Three generations of dual-career family research
467f The impact of work on the family

Rapoport, Robert
45m Change and constancy: A hundred years' tale
87a Three generations of dual-career family research
467f The impact of work on the family

Rapp, Rayna
60f The twenties' backlash: Compulsory heterosexuality, the consumer family, and the waning of feminism
231a Sex and society: A research note from social history and anthropology
245j Family and class in contemporary America: Notes toward an understanding of ideology
256h Examining family history
310u XYLO: A true story

Rappaccioli, Myra de
172j Where are our campesino brothers? Let the murderers answer! (Nicaragua)

Rasko, G.
159h Crimes against life committed by women in Hungary

Rasmus, Carolyn J.
42p Women in the light of the Gospel

Rassam, Amal
298a Arab women: The status of research in the social sciences and the status of women
298h Toward a theoretical framework for the study of women in the Arab world

Rathbone-McCuan, Eloise
472d The abused older woman: A discussion of abuses and rape

Ratner, Ronnie Steinberg
93a The policy and problem: Overview of seven countries
93t Equal employment policy for women: Summary of themes and issues

Rausch, Jeffrey L.
28s Premenstrual tension: Etiology

Rava, Susan
448b Marguerite Duras: Women's language in men's cities

Ravicz, Marilyn
205c Rainbow women of the Fraser Valley: Lifesongs through the generations

Ravid, Renee
191c Community surveys: Sex differences in mental illness

Rawlings, Edna I.
359ff Divorced women

Ray, Reginald A.
325o Accomplished women in tantric Buddhism of medieval India and Tibet

Raymond, Janice
43e The illusion of androgyny
79z Sex preselection: A response
310ee Feminist ethics, ecology and vision

Read, Daphne
305z But is it feminist art?

Reagan, Barbara B.
380k Microeconomic effects of women entering the labor force

Reagon, Bernice Johnson
150pp Coalition politics: Turning the century

Reardon, Joan
127j *Fear of Flying*: Developing the feminist novel

Reardon, Richard
24d Perceptual and cognitive mechanisms in human sexual attraction

Rebscher, Frances
190u Steroidal contraceptive use and subsequent development of hyperprolactinemia

Recker, Wilfred
463m Sex differences in travel preferences and decision making

Red, Ida VSW
176w Note on "Reading A Subject" in periodical indexes

Redd, Spring
150i Something Latino was up with us

Reed, James
353i Doctors, birth control, and social values, 1830-1970

Reed, Mary E.
405i The anti-fascist front of women and the Communist Party in Croatia: Conflicts within the resistance

Reeling, Patricia
302d Undergraduate women as potential recruits to the library profession

Reese, Maureen Foley
178d Growing up: The impact of loss and change
178o Physical health issues
178p Families revisited

Refshauge, Chloe
13e Bearers of burdens: Occupational safety without discrimination

Regalado, Rose
54c New approaches for prevention and education of alcoholism among Hispanic women

Regan, Donald H.
173a Rewriting *Roe v. Wade*

Reguer, Sara
211n Kaddish from the "wrong" side of the *Mehitzah*

Reich, Michael
89j A theory of labor market segmentation

Reichelt, Paul A.
309s Contraception, abortion and venereal disease: Teenagers' knowledge and the effect of education

Reid, Elizabeth
378i Women: If not apolitical, then conservative

Reid, Ivan
258a Sex differences and this book
258c Vital statistics
258i Sex differences in Britain

Reid, Julyan
209ii Public policy and the employment impacts of office computerization

Reid, Stuart
470c Contemporary clerical work: A case study of local government

Reilly, John M.
1h Margaret Millar

Reilly, Richard R.
447d Moving women into outside craft jobs

Reilly, Thomas W.
320o Family formation and educational attainment

Rein, Martin
103e Women and the Reagan revolution: Thermidor for the social welfare economy

Reinhardt, Elisabeth
209aa Let the technology adapt!

Reinhardt, Hazel
359aa Female-headed families: Trends and implications

Reinhardt, Nancy S.
123b New directions for feminist criticism in theatre and the related arts

Reinharz, Shulamit
124i Feminist research methodology groups: Origins, forms, functions
295b Women as competent community builders: The other side of the coin
312k Experiential analysis: A contribution to feminist research

Reiss, Ira L.
105e Toward a theory of extramarital sexual relationships
244h Sexual customs and gender roles in Sweden and America: An analysis and interpretation

Relyea, Suzanne
64n Polymorphemic perversity: Colette's illusory "real"

Remick, Helen
65f Dilemmas of implementation: The case of nursing
65g Major issues in *a priori* applications
65p Technical possibilities and political realities: Concluding remarks
93s Beyond equal pay for equal work: Comparable worth in the state of Washington

Remley, David
384f Sacajawea of myth and history

Remley, Mary-Lou
147ff From sidesaddle to rodeo

Rempel, Ursula M.
130j Women and music: Ornament of the profession?

Remy, Dorothy
199e Economic stagnation and discrimination
296i Women's power in the workplace

Rendel, Margherita
250l How many women academics 1912-76?
436a Women, power and political systems
436m Future perspectives

Reno, Christine
154d Virginity as an ideal in Christine de Pizan's *Cite' des Dames*

Ren-Ying, Yan
395h Family planning in rural China

Resch, Yannick
64m Writing, language, and the body

Rescorla, Leslie A.
80i The Yale Child Welfare Research Program: Description and results

Resick, Patricia A.
304k Sex-role stereotypes and violence against women

Reskin, Barbara F.
272j Institutional factors contributing to sex segregation in the workplace

Resnik, Harvey L.P.
280l Erotized repetitive hangings

Resnik, Mindy
16n Counselor's roles

Reuter, Jeanette
51l Erik Erikson and Doris Lessing: Psychological theory and the female novel of development

Reverby, Susan
353ff "Neither for the drawing room nor for the kitchen": Private duty nursing in Boston, 1873-1914

Revitch, Eugene
280i Burglaries with sexual dynamics
280k Sexual dynamics in homicide and assault

Reynierse, J. H.
49h Human resource planning and the intuitive manager: Models for the 1990's

Reynolds, Diane
307u New jobs in new technologies: Experienced only need apply

Reynolds, Holly Baker
232b The auspicious married woman

Reynolds, Lorna
338a Irish women in legend, literature and life

Reynolds, Nancy
316d Women in the dental profession

Rhodes, Carolyn
303e New women at Old Dominion
383b Method in her madness: Feminism in the crazy utopian vision of Tiptree's courier
450c Gail Godwin and the ideal of southern womanhood

Rhodes, Jewell Parker
383g *The Left Hand of Darkness*: Androgyny and the feminist utopia

Rhodes, Lelia Gaston
302g Profiles of the careers of selected black female librarians

Rhoton, Patricia
324d Attitudes toward women working: Changes over time and implications for the labor-force behaviors of husbands and wives

Rian, Karen
7d Sadomasochism and the social construction of desire

Riboud, Michelle
380n Labor force participation and earnings of women in Andalusia

Rice, Danielle
130o Women and the visual arts

Rice, Dorothy P.
53a Sex differences in disease risk

Rice, Marjorie Spring
227d Working-class wives

Rich, Adrienne
50p Anger and tenderness: The experience of motherhood
229c Prepatriarchal female/goddess images
231h Compulsory heterosexuality and lesbian existence
397i Compulsory heterosexuality and lesbian existence
439d Compulsory heterosexuality and lesbian existence

Rich, B. Ruby
247f From repressive tolerance to erotic liberation: *Maedchen in Uniform*

Rich, J. Dennis
399dd Art theatre in Hull-House

Richards, Caroline
315a The emergence of women in twentieth-century Chilean history and literature

Richards, David A. J.
2h Constitutional privacy, religious disestablishment, and the abortion decisions

Richards, Evelyn L.
75g Current status of employment of women in Lebanon

Richards, Larry G.
463o Perceived safety and security in transportation systems as determined by the gender of the traveler

463q Gender differences in reactions to vehicle environments

Richardson, Barbara L.
266b Social science inquiries into female achievement: Recurrent methodological problems

Richey, Cheryl A.
16b Cognitive-behavioral strategies for the treatment of depression in women

96k Assertion training for women

Richmond, Julius B.
80v Health care services for children in day care programs

Richter, Derek
438a Opportunities for women in science

Richter, Harvena
330b Hunting the moth: Virginia Woolf and the creative imagination

Rickel, Annette U.
295k Depression in women: The postpartum experience

295p New directions for women: Moving beyond the 1980s

Ridd, Rosemary
371j Where women must dominate: Response to oppression in a South African urban community

Riddick, Carol Cutler
458c Life satisfaction among aging women: A causal model

Riddiough, Christine
224a Culture and politics

224k Some thoughts on gay/lesbian oppression

369d Socialism, feminism, and gay/lesbian liberation

Riddle, Dorothy I.
229ii Politics, spirituality, and models of change

Ridington, Jillian
305h Providing services the feminist way

Rieker, Patricia Perri
140n Victims of violence and psychiatric illness

140v Teaching value clarification: The example of gender and psychotherapy

Rierdan, Jill
190i Variations in the experience of menarche as a function of preparedness

Riess, B. F.
460n Discussion: Random comments

Riger, Stephanie
295h The impact of crime on urban women

Rijk, Tineke de
471d Women at work in Holland

Rila, Margo
460r A sex-information switchboard

Riley, Barbara
205j Six saucepans to one: Domestic science vs. the home in British Columbia 1900-1930

Riley, Denise
335e 'The serious burdens of love?' Some questions on child-care, feminism and socialism

418e Left critiques of the family

418k Feminist thought and reproductive control: The state and 'the right to choose'

Rimmer, Lesley
170g The economics of work and caring

Rindfuss, Ronald R.
354b Convenience and the occurrence of births: Induction and labor in the United States and Canada

Riordan, James
151j Sport in Soviet society: Fetish or free play?

Rioux, Jacques E.
252r Sterilization combined with midtrimester abortion

Rippey, Barbara
384q Toward a new paradigm: Mari Sandoz's study of red and white myth in *Cheyenne Autumn*

Ritchey, M.
372x Comparison of exercise between females and males

Ritchie, Laurell
323m Why are so many women unorganized?

Ritchie, Maureen
310bb Taking the initiative: Information versus technology in pregnancy

Ritter, Darlene
384b Marie Louise Ritter: The pioneer woman in fact and fiction

Rivero, Eliana
313r Hacia un análisis feminista de *Tres Tristes Tigres*

Rivers, Theodore John
375b Widows' rights in Anglo-Saxon law

Rivkin, Elizabeth Thaele
39k The black woman in South Africa: An Azanian profile

Rizvi, Najma
98a Getting to know a rural community in Bangladesh

400f Life cycle, food behaviour and nutrition of women in Bangladesh

Robbert, Louise Buenger
112b Caterina Corner, Queen of Cyprus (Venetian, 1454?-1510)

Robbins, Kittye Delle
102c Tiamat and her children: An inquiry into the persistence of mythic archetypes of woman as monster/villainess/victim

Robe, Lucy Barry
404v Pregnancy and drinking

Roberts, Albert R.
26d Crisis intervention with battered women

26e Intervention with the abusive partner

26f Police intervention

Roberts, Barbara
287n Surrogate partners and their use in sex therapy

Roberts, Don
15f Alternative roads to alternative media

Roberts, Elizabeth J.
57a Dimensions of sexual learning in childhood

57j Sexuality and social policy: The unwritten curriculum

460q Sex education versus sexual learning

Roberts, Harry V.
66f Statistical biases in the measurement of employment discrimination

67f Statistical biases in the measurement of employment discrimination

Roberts, Helen
85a Women and their doctors: Power and powerlessness in the research process

189e Some of the boys won't play any more: The impact of feminism on sociology

297k Putting the show on the road: The dissemination of research findings

396a Male hegemony in family planning

Roberts, JR
176o Black lesbians before 1970: A bibliographical essay

Roberts, Marion
182g Private kitchens, public cooking

Roberts, Maureen
456e Breast cancer and benign breast disease

Roberts, Myron S.
285k Sexual dysfunction in the chronically ill male

Roberts, Nanette M.
59e American women and life-style change

Roberts, Patti
65n Comparable worth under various federal and state laws

Robertson, Adelle F.
316g Continuing education: A vital process for women

Robertson, Anne
80g Day care and children's responsiveness to adults

Robertson, Claire C.
6c Women in the urban economy

370a Women's importance in African slave systems

370l Post-proclamation slavery in Accra: A female affair?

Robertson, Mavis
390q Sally Bowen: Political and social experiences of a working-class woman

Robertson, Peter C.
93e Strategies for improving the economic situation of women in the United States: Systemic thinking, systemic discrimination, and systematic enforcement

Robin, Gerald D.
78m Forcible rape: Institutionalized sexism in the criminal justice system

Robins, Gay
156e The god's wife of Amun in the 18th dynasty in Egypt

Robins, Lee N.
9e Longitudinal studies of alcohol and drug problems: Sex differences

Robinson, Alice Mc Donnell
399t Mercy Warren, satirist of the revolution

Robinson, David J.
133s Troy Perry: Gay advocate

Robinson, Gertrude J.
391e Changing Canadian and US magazine portrayals of women and work: Growing opportunities for choice

Robinson, Jean C.
103p Women in a revolutionary society: The state and family policy in China

Robinson, John P.
355c Housework technology and household work

Robinson, Judith Schiek
302l Geographic mobility and career advancement of male and female librarians

Robinson, Kathy
466f Women and work in an Indonesian mining town

Robinson, Lillian S.
60u Women, media, and the dialectics of resistance

Robinson, Marcelle
111i The Hillcrest School of Oregon: Guided group interaction in a juvenile institution

Robinson, Mina
397e The older lesbian: Love relationships and friendship patterns

Robinson, Patricia Murphy
225s The historical repression of women's sexuality

Robinson, Pauline K.
289d The sociological perspective

Robson, Elizabeth
136m Nonverbal processes in feminist therapy

Robson, Jill
115h Mary: My sister

Robson, Ruthann
301d Genealogy (poem)

Rocheron, Yvette
274q Sex education

Rock, Cynthia
203d The appropriation of the house: Changes in house design and concepts of domesticity

Rodeheaver, Dean
289o Beyond generativity: Toward a sensuality of later life

Rodenberger, M. Lou
445p Folk narrative in Caroline Gordon's frontier fiction

Rodgers, Carolyn
40gg An amen arena

Rodgers, Silvia
371c Women's space in a men's house: The British House of Commons

Rodgers-Rose, La Frances
38a The black woman: A historical overview
38b Some demographic characteristics of the black woman: 1940 to 1975
38p Dialectics of black male-female relationships

Rodman, Hyman
243k Weak links in men's worker-earner roles: A descriptive model

Rodriguez, Angela M.
469j The emerging Cuban women of Florida's Dade County

Rodriguez, Cecilia
206l Working on racism: Centro Obrero

Rodriguez-Trias, Helen
34f Sterilization abuse

Roe, Jill
440a The end is where we start from: Women and welfare since 1901

Rogers, Adrienne
130a Women and the law

Rogers, Carl M.
326f Clinical intervention with boy victims of sexual abuse

Rogers, Everett M.
57f Peer communication and sexuality

Rogers, Gwendolyn
150jj Black lesbian/feminist organizing: A conversation

Rogers, Katharine M.
130x The view from England

Rogers, Kristine M.
433j Some poems from *Citra* by Radindranath Tagore

Roggencamp, Viola
310r Abortion of a special kind: Male sex selection in India

Rohrberger, Mary
450e Shirley Ann Grau and the short story

Rohrlich, Ruby
417c Women in transition: Crete and Sumer
417e The Shakers: Gender equality in hierarchy

Roiphe, Herman
460g Some suggested revisions concerning early female development

Rokoff, Gerald
387c Women in the occupational world: Social disruption and conflict

Rolfe, Bari
399s Women mimes in America

Rollen, Berit
93h Equality between men and women in the labor market: The Swedish National Labor Market Board

Rollin, Sue
156c Women and witchcraft in ancient Assyria

Romalis, Coleman
56c Taking care of the little woman: Father-physician relations during pregnancy and childbirth

Romalis, Shelly
56b Natural childbirth and the reluctant physician

Romanowski, Sylvie
64g A typology of women in Colette's novels

Ronald, Ann
109k Terror-gothic: Nightmare and dream in Ann Radcliffe and Charlotte Brontë
445c The Tonopah ladies

Rooke, Constance
27h Beauty in distress: *Daniel Deronda* and *The House of Mirth*

Roos, Patricia A.
65i Assessing pay discrimination using national data
272j Institutional factors contributing to sex segregation in the workplace

Roos, Sandra
453c Women's imagery/women's art

Rorem, Ned
442m Women's voices

Rosaldo, Michelle Z.
245b Is there a family? New anthropological views
282i Politics and gender in simple societies

Rosario, Lillian M.
469c The self-perception of Puerto Rican women toward their societal roles

Rose, Ellen Cronan
332j Through the looking glass: When women tell fairy tales

Rose, Hilary
50x Making science feminist

Rose, Joy
274d English

Rose, Suzanna
265a Parents' sex role attitudes and children's concepts of femininity and masculinity

Rose, Vicki M.
349r Barriers to becoming a "successful" rape victim

Rosen, Anne-Sofie
380f Sex-role stereotypes and personal attributes within a developmental framework

Rosen, Benson
425d Career progress of women: Getting in and staying in

Rosen, Ellen
210e Beyond the sweatshop: Older women in blue-collar jobs

Rosen, Stanley
169h Evaluating programs for working adults

Rosenau, James N.
435l The foreign policy beliefs of women in leadership positions

Rosenbaum, Marsha
165e Work and the addicted prostitute

Rosenbaum, S. P.
329a Virginia Woolf and the intellectual origins of Bloomsbury

Rosenberg, Charles
353a The female animal: Medical and biological views of woman and her role in nineteenth-century America

Rosenberg, Harriet G.
86m The home is the workplace: Hazards, stress, and pollutants in the household

Rosenberg, Jan
60h Feminism, the family, and the New Right

Rosenberg, Rina
435b Representing women at the state and local levels: Commissions on the status of women

Rosenberg, Rosalind
158d Leta Hollingworth: Toward a sexless intelligence

Rosenberg, Warren
254c The artist as hero in Maxine Hong Kingston's *The Woman Warrior*

Rosenblatt, Karin
53q Risk factors for ovarian cancer

Rosenblatt, Paul
24g Human sexuality in cross-cultural perspective

Rosenbloom, Sandra
463a Women's travel issues: The research and policy environment
463b Intra-household implications of the involvement of women in the paid labor force

Rosenblum, Karen E.
392c Female deviance and the female sex role: A preliminary investigation

Rosenfeld, Rachel A.
272c Job changing and occupational sex segregation: Sex and race comparisons
320f Sex differences in the significance of economic resources for choosing and attending a college
416f Academic career mobility for women and men psychologists

Rosenmeier, Jesper
19e The image of Adam and the image of Christ

Rosenshein, Neil B.
53q Risk factors for ovarian cancer

Rosenthal, Carole
231x The teacher
249h Fighting for tenure: A bittersweet victory

Rosenthal, Carolyn J.
210l Concerns about parental health

Rosenthal, Evelyn R.
266i Statistical analysis in sex roles and social change

Rosenthal, Joel T.
379d Aristocratic widows in fifteenth-century England

Rosenthal, Marilynn M.
214o Ageism vs. sexism: Male models as a source of support

Rosett, Henry L.
9p The effects of alcohol on the fetus and offspring

Rosewater, Lynne Bravo
360n Feminist therapy: Implications for practitioners

Rosinsky, Natalie M.
180w Mothers and daughters: Another minority group

Rosowski, Susan J.
332b The novel of awakening

Ross, Aileen D.
421v Some comments on the home roles of businesswomen in India, Australia and Canada

Ross, Barbara
234j 'Woman-ing' the landscape: East Anglia 1300-1500: A discussion on sources and methodology

Ross, Catherine E.
376j Sex differences in the processing of criminal defendants

Ross, Ellen
60f The twenties' backlash: Compulsory heterosexuality, the consumer family, and the waning of feminism
231a Sex and society: A research note from social history and anthropology
256h Examining family history
439p "The love crisis": Couples advice books of the late 1970s

Ross, James
63b Characteristics of co-correctional institutions
63i Co-correctional models
63k Women in a coed joint

Ross, Stanford G.
46j The changing nature of social security

Ross, Stephanie
275n How words hurt: Attitudes, metaphor and oppression

Ross, William D.
107i Proportionality and body composition in male and female Olympic athletes: A kinanthropometric overview
279l Human proportionality and sexual dimorphism

Rosser, Sue V.
126e Darwin and sexism: Victorian causes, contemporary effects

Rossi, Alice S.
239m Body time and social time: Mood patterns by menstrual cycle phase and day of week

Rossi, Peter E.
239m Body time and social time: Mood patterns by menstrual cycle phase and day of week

Rossman, Parker
284v The pederasts

Rossoff, Margaret
7q Is sadomasochism feminist? A critique of the Samois position

Rota, S.
107h Machover test applied to 130 Italian female top athletes

Roth, Robert T.
376e Sex-based discrimination in the mental institutionalization of women

Rothblum, Esther D.
304a Introduction: Warning! Sex-role stereotypes may be hazardous to your health
304e Sex-role stereotypes and depression in women
304l Concluding comments, criticism, and caution: Consistent conservatism or constructive change?
443g Strategies for dealing with sex-role stereotypes

Rothenberg, Diane
347c The mothers of the nation: Seneca resistance to Quaker intervention

Rothenberg, Paula
31k The political nature of relations between the sexes

Rothman, Barbara Katz
56e Awake and aware, or false consciousness: The cooption of childbirth reform in America
310b The meanings of choice in reproductive technology
344e Women, health, and medicine

Rothschild, Joan
181e Technology, housework, and women's liberation: A theoretical analysis
181m Afterward: Machina ex dea and future research
436i Technology, 'women's work' and the social control of women
441g Teaching and learning about women and technology

Rothwell, Sheila
437d United Kingdom

Rousmaniere, John P.
454h Cultural hybrid in the slums: The college woman and the Settlement House, 1889-1894

Rowan, Caroline
119c 'Mothers, vote labour!' The state, the labour movement and working-class mothers, 1900-1918

Rowan, Edward L.
326m Rape and the college student: Multiple crises in late adolescence

Rowan, Judith B.
326m Rape and the college student: Multiple crises in late adolescence

Rowbotham, Sheila
227l The carrot, the stick and the movement

Rowe, Karen E.
332c "Fairy-born and human-bred": Jane Eyre's education in romance

Rowe, Mary P.
214k The minutiae of discrimination: The need for support
261b Building mentorship frameworks as part of an effective equal opportunity ecology
261f "Go find yourself a mentor"

Rowland, Robyn
310w Reproductive technologies: The final solution to the woman question?

Rowles, Graham D.
317i Growing old "inside": Aging and attachment to place in an Appalachian community

Rowlett, Martha Graybeal
429h Unboxing Christian education

Roydhouse, Marion W.
292f Partners in progress: The affiliated schools for women workers, 1928-1939

Royle, Trevor
197g Spark and Scotland

Rozen, Freida Shoenberg
169b Promoting and recruiting: Reaching the target audience

Rozovsky, Fay A.
79d The legal aspects of the DES case: What can be done

Ruback, Barry
63a The sexually integrated prison: A legal and policy evaluation

Rubbo, Ann
39dd The spread of capitalism in rural Colombia: Effects on poor women

Rubenstein, Reva
253f Genes and gender in the workplace

Rubery, Jill
89k Structured labour markets, worker organization and low pay

Rubin, Berte
271j Beyond the fear of success: Observations on women's fears

Rubin, Gayle
225t Thinking sex: Notes for a radical theory of the politics of sexuality

Rubin, Lillian B.
461f Sex and sexuality: Women at midlife

Rubin, Suzanne
307x A spermdonor baby grows up

Rubinstein, Lidia M.
461r Discussion: Voluntary sterilization in childless women

Rubinstein, Linda
390w Women, work and technological change

Ruble, Diane N.
28i A developmental analysis of menstrual distress in adolescence
51o Expectations regarding menstrual symptoms: Effects on evaluation and behavior of women
190t Dysmenorrhea in adolescence
239k Research on menstrual-related psychological changes: Alternative perspectives

Rudat, Eva M. Kahiluoto
130aa The view from Spain: Rocco *finesse* and *espirit* versus plebian manners

Ruddick, Sara
30i New combinations: Learning from Virginia Woolf
195m Maternal thinking
195n Preservative love and military destruction: Some reflections on mothering and peace
202i Private brother, public world
223p Better sex

245e Maternal thinking

Rudenstein, Gail M.
180y Mothers and daughters in literature: A preliminary bibliography

Rudes, Nancy
8f The adolescent girl in a group home

Rudhart, Blanca-Maria
22a "Glory is like a circle in the water"...Thoughts and suggestions towards a definition of feminine historical research

Ruehl, Beryl
215d The balance of terror: Deterrence and peace-keeping

Ruehl, Sonja
119a Inverts and experts: Radclyffe Hall and the lesbian identity
257n Sexual theory and practice: Another double standard

Rueschemeyer, Marilyn
421w The demands of work and the human quality of marriage: An exploratory study of professionals in two socialist societies

Ruether, Rosemary Radford
31f Sexism, religion, and the social and spiritual liberation of women today
59a Feminist theology and spirituality
91l Preacher and priest: Typologies of ministry and ordination of women
123c The feminist critique in religious studies
366b Women in utopian movements
367g Women in sectarian and utopian groups
462p Women responding to the Arab-Israeli conflict
462x Envisioning our hopes: Some models of the future

Ruggie, Mary
388h Public day care in Britain and Sweden: A sociological perspective

Rukeyser, Muriel
474o The education of a poet

Runte, Roseann
130h Women as muse

Ruopp, Richard R.
80d Janus faces day care: Perspectives on quality and cost

Ruotolo, Lucio
330h *Mrs. Dalloway*: The unguarded moment

Rupp, Leila J.
353f "Imagine my surprise": Women's relationships in historical perspective
444b "I don't call that *Volksgemeinschaft*": Women, class, and war in Nazi Germany

Ruse, Michael
223u The morality of homosexuality

Rush, Anne Kent
229jj The politics of feminist spirituality

Rushin, Donna Kate
150k The black back-ups (poem)
150ee Tired poem: Last letter from a typical unemployed black professional woman (poem)
150mm Black goddess (poem)

Rushing, Andrea Benton
39u Images of black women in Afro-American poetry

Rushton, Lucy
457c Doves and magpies: Village women in the Greek Orthodox Church

Rushton, Peter
241i Purification or social control? Ideologies of reproduction and the churching of women after childbirth

Rusko, H. K.
372z Effect of increased intensity of training on maximum oxygen uptake and muscular performance of young female cross-country skiers

Russ, Joanna
43v Reflections on science fiction
109a Somebody's trying to kill me and I think it's my husband: The modern gothic
131f Recent feminist utopias

Russell, Diana
50v Rape and the masculine mystique

Russell, Diana E. H.
7w Sadomasochism: A contra-feminist activity

Russell, Graeme
204f Shared-caregiving families: An Australian study

Russell, Letty M.
59d Women and ministry: Problem or possibility?

Russell, Michelle
14n Slave codes and liner notes
14s Black-eyed blues connections: Teaching black women
43j An open letter to the academy
174w Black-eyed blues connections: From the inside out

Russianoff, Penelope
404b Learned helplessness

Russo, Gloria M.
130r Voltaire and women

Russo, John B.
216a Introduction: Parenting in contemporary society
216t Parenting in a pluralistic society: Toward a policy of options and choices

Russo, Nancy Felipe
140c Inequality and women's mental health: An overview
360a Women in the mental health delivery system: Implications for research and public policy

Rutenberg, Taly
311b Learning women's studies
312e Learning women's studies
312o Selected annotated bibliography of articles on theories of women's studies

Ruth, Sheila
189c Methodocracy, misogyny and bad faith: The response of philosophy

Ruthchild, Geraldine
122e The best feminist criticism is a new criticism

Rutledge, Essie Manuel
38i Marital interaction goals of black women: Strengths and effects

Rutter, Michael
80a Social-emotional consequences of day care for preschool children

Ruzek, Sheryl Burt
36q Ethical issues in childbirth technology

Ryan, Angela Shen
434g Asian-American women: A historical and cultural perspective

Ryan, Joanna
257m Psychoanalysis and women loving women

Ryan, Mary P.
61p Retrospect and prospect
81e The projection of a new womanhood: The movie moderns in the 1920's
256e The power of women's networks

Ryan, Maureen
450q Stopping places: Bobbie Ann Mason's short stories

Ryder, Norman B.
387l The future of American fertility

Ryff, Carol D.
296a Introduction: An interdisciplinary perspective on women's power and influence
296d Women's self-perceptions of power and influence across adult life

Rzhanitsyna, L.
446b Current problems of female labor in the USSR

Sabean, David Warren
162a Interest and emotion in family and kinship studies: A critique of social history and anthropology
162g Young bees in an empty hive: Relations between brothers-in-law in a south German village around 1800

Sablonier, Roger
162i The Aragonese royal family around 1300

Sachak, Najma
436f Creating employment opportunities for rural women: Some issues affecting attitudes and policy

Sacks, Karen Brodkin
83a Science and the status quo
162l Kinship and class consciousness: Family values and work experience among hospital workers in an American southern town
199a Generations of working-class families
199j Computers, ward secretaries, and a walk-out in a Southern hospital
218a An overview of women and power in Africa
296j Women and power within the historical dynamic of feminist scholarship

Saddlemyer, Ann
338d Synge and the nature of woman

Saegert, Susan
203b The home: A critical problem for changing sex roles

Safa, Helen
83d Woman and the international division of labor
428d Women, production, and reproduction in industrial capitalism: A comparison of Brazilian and U.S. factory workers

Safilios-Rothschild, Constantina
52h Changing sex roles in the Greek family and society
113h Greece: Reluctant presence
243k Weak links in men's worker-earner roles: A descriptive model
244f The roles of Greek husbands and wives: Definitions and fulfillment
459d Female power, autonomy and demographic change in the Third World

Safro, Ivor L.
4d Adolescent sexuality, pregnancy, and childbearing

Sagarin, Edward
280a Prostitution: Profession and pathology

Sagi, Abraham
204h Antecedents and consequences of various degrees of paternal involvement in child rearing: The Israeli project

Saiving, Valerie C.
118a Androgynous life: A feminist appropriation of process thought

Salaff, Janet
177f Doing fieldwork
177i Wage earners in Hong Kong
388c Singapore women: Work and the family
424i Women's work: Factory, family and social class in an industrializing order

Salem, Norma
198h Islam and the legal status of women in Tunisia

Sales, Esther
360l Women and work: Implications for mental health
434d Rape crisis theory revisited

Salladay, Susan Anthony
79dd Ethics and reproductive technology

Salmela, J. H.
107f Sugar and spice and everything nice: Is that what female athletes behave like?

Salmon, Marylynn
444d "Life, liberty, and dower": The legal status of women after the American Revolution

Salt, Patricia
45k Changing sex roles: College graduates of the 1960's and 1970's

Salvo, Jackie Di
462b Class, gender, and religion: A theoretical overview and some political implications

Salzman, Leon
96j A new look at the psychoanalytic view of the female

Sambaiah, P.
299c Sanitary Workers

Samper, Maria-Luz D.
169h Evaluating programs for working adults

Sampson, G. A.
236d An appraisal of the role of progesterone in the therapy of premenstrual syndrome

Samuel, Charlotte
183i Abused women

Samuel, Judy
193s Feminism and science teaching: Some classroom observations
274f Mathematics and science - Introduction
274h Science

Sanasarian, Eliz
368f An analysis of Fida'i and Mujahidin positions on women's rights

Sanchez, Sonia
40jj Ruminations/Reflections

Sancier, Betty
434q Beyond advocacy

Sancisi-Weerdenburg, Heleen
156b Exit Atossa: Images of women in Greek historiography on Persia

Sanders, Diana
456c Premenstrual tension

Sanders, Scott
131d Woman as nature in science fiction

Sandler, Bernice R.
261d Strategies for eliminating sex discrimination: Times that try men's souls

Sandler, Florence
142l The unity of *Felix Holt*

Sandlin, Joann DeLora
461t Discussion: Extramarital sex: A multifaceted experience

Sandmaier, Marian
11l Women helping women: Opening the door to treatment

Sands, Diane
174r A feminist chautauqua for a rural state

Sandstrom, Alan R.
194b The Tonantsi cult of the Eastern Nahua

Sang, Barbara
397d Lesbian relationships: A struggle toward partner equality

Sangari, Kumkum
310q If you would be the mother of a son (poem)

Sankar, Andrea
177c Spinster sisterhoods

Santer, Henriette
115i Stereotyping the sexes in society and in the Church

Santrock, John W.
204j Social development and parent-child interaction in father-custody and stepmother families

Sanzone, Donna S.
378n Women in positions of political leadership in Britain, France and West Germany

Sapolsky, Barry S.
230d Arousal, affect, and the aggression-moderating effect of erotica

Saraga, Esther
193f Biological inevitabilities or political choices? The future for girls in science

Sarah, Elizabeth
125p Christabel Pankhurst: Reclaiming her power
212l Female performers on a male stage: The first women's liberation movement and the authority of men

Sarde, Michèle Blin
64b The first steps in a writer's career

Sargeant, A. J.
372p Measurement of maximal short-term (anaerobic) power output during cycling

Sargent, Alice G.
288a The executive man and woman: The issue of sexuality

Sargent, Lydia
369a New left women and men: The honeymoon is over

Sargent, Lyman Tower
131h An ambiguous legacy: The role and position of women in the English Eutopia
383a A new anarchism: Social and political ideas in some recent feminist eutopias

Sarkar, Sutapa
161g A fallen image-Women in India

Sarra, Janis
323x Trade union women and the NDP

Sarty, Merrill
265b Ethnic differences in sex stereotyping by mothers: Implications for health care

Sassen-Koob, Saskia
428h Labor migration and the new industrial division of labor

Sassoon, D.
283n The silences of *New Left Review*

Satlof, Claire R.
211p History, fiction, and the tradition: Creating a Jewish feminist poetic

Sato, K.S.
159n Emancipation of women and crime in Japan

Sattel, Jack W.
171h Men, inexpressiveness, and power
387n The inexpressive male: Tragedy or sexual politics?

Saunders, Bill
345d Psychological aspects of women and alcohol

Saunders, Elisabeth
178l The quality of mother-child relationships

Saunders, Kit
394j Women's athletics at Madison and Title IX

Saunders, Laverna
122h In search of excellence in academic libraries, or, challenging the henhouse model

Saunders, Lesley
257f Sex and childbirth

Saunders, Margaret O.
473c Women's role in a Muslim Hausa town (Mirria, Republic of Niger)

Saunders, Marguerite
404e The double bind: Minority women

Saunders, Sheila
241c Blowing the cover of the protective male: A community study of violence to women

Saunders, Susanna Terrell
389h Georgiana Goddard King (1871-1939): Educator and pioneer in medieval Spanish art

Savage, David
314s Resource networks

Savage, Wendy
456i Cervical cytology

Sawer, Marian
13k Conditions of entry: Women and politics in Australia
23g 'Women candidates speak'
23h Women and women's issues in the 1980 federal elections

Sawers, Larry
199e Economic stagnation and discrimination
296i Women's power in the workplace

Sawhill, Isabel V.
89e Economic perspectives on the family

Saxton, Marsha
310t Born and unborn: The implications of reproductive technologies for people with disabilities

Saxton, Ruth O.
306n Letters and diaries: Demystifying archival research for undergraduates

Sayers, Janet
12b Psychological sex differences

Scales, Peter
308e Sex education and the prevention of teenage pregnancy: An overview of policies and programs in the United States

Scanlon, Barbara
55g Youth prostitution

Scanlon, Laura Polla
73g Changing needs of ethnic women in higher education

Scanzoni, Letha Dawson
462c The great chain of being and the chain of command
462r A religious perspective

Scarf, Mimi
211e Marriages made in heaven? Battered Jewish wives

Scarpitti, Frank R.
392a The extent and nature of female crime
392d Female delinquency and broken homes: A reassessment
392m Unequal protection of males and females in the juvenile court

Schafer, Patricia Cooney
10i Alcohol use and marital violence: Female and male differences in reactions to alcohol

Schaffer, Diane M.
319k Social networks and survival strategies: An exploratory study of Mexican American, black, and Anglo female family heads in San Jose, California

Schanke, Robert A.
399o Mary Shaw: A fighting champion

Scharf, Lois
81k "The forgotten woman": Working women, the New Deal, and women's organizations
201g The great uprising in Cleveland: When sisterhood failed

Schein, Virginia E.
380e Power and political behaviors in organizations: A new frontier for research on male/female differences

Scheirbeck, Helen Maynor
70b Current educational status of American Indian girls

Scheman, Naomi
84m Individualism and the objects of psychology
356l Anger and the politics of naming

Scherini, Rose
73d The Museo Italo Americano: My involvement with the Italian American community in San Francisco

Schiavi, Raul C.
277e The assessment of sleep erections for diagnosis of erectile disorders

Schiel, Tilman
153g Development and underdevelopment of household-based production in Europe

Schildkrout, Enid
385c Dependence and autonomy: The economic activities of secluded Hausa women in Kano, Nigeria

Schiller, Patricia
4m Sexual counseling for adolescents
287l Selecting a qualified therapist

Schinderman, Janet L.
434c Therapy with battered women

Schipper, Mineke
322a Women and literature in Africa
322b Interview with Miriam Tlali (South Africa)

Schirmer, Jennifer G.
218g Women and social policy: Lessons from Scandinavia

Schlachet, Barbara Cohn
443e Female role socialization: The analyst and the analysis

Schlack, Beverly Ann
328d Fathers in general: The patriarchy in Virginia Woolf's fiction

Schlein, Lisa
192l Los Angeles garment district sews a cloak of shame

Schlesinger, Benjamin
289m Institutional life: The Canadian experience

Schlesinger, Louis B.
280k Sexual dynamics in homicide and assault

Schlobin, Roger C.
114c Andre Norton: Humanity amid the hardware
131p The future females: A selected checklist through 1979

Schlossberg, Nancy K.
411o Midlife woman as student

Schlossman, Steven
376c The crime of precocious sexuality: Female juvenile delinquency and the Progressive Era

Schmid, Günther
260a Women in the labour market and equal opportunity policy in Sweden, United Kingdom, United States and West Germany
260l The political economy of labor market discrimination: A theoretical and comparative analysis of sex discrimination

Schmidt, Ruth
314u Women, gender, and the curriculum

Schmidt, Steffen W.
363f Research on women in Latin America: Problems of networking and comparative analysis in the last decade

Schmidt, Wolfgang
9j Sex differences in mortality: A comparison of male and female alcoholics

Schmitz, Betty
314h Project on women in the curriculum: Montana State University
314p From issue to action

Schmuck, Patricia A.
90a The sex dimension - An overview
90e Clues to sex bias in the selection of school administrators: A report from the Oregon network
90g The sex dimension of careers in educational management: Overview and synthesis
90m The sex dimension of school organization: Overview and synthesis
262d Differentiation by sex in educational professions
262h Context of change: The women's movement as a political process
352q Changing women's representation in school management: A systems perspective

Schnabel, Paul
252c Legal aspects of pregnancy termination in Europe

Schneider, Beth
397n Peril and promise: Lesbians' workplace participation

Schneider, Jill
141g Hormones, genetics, and breast cancer

Schneider, Joanne
145b Enlightened reforms and Bavarian girls' education: Tradition through innovation

Schneider, Leslie
209ee Alternative models of worker participation

Schneider, Mary Jane
148e Women's work: An examination of women's roles in Plains Indian arts and crafts

Schniedewind, Nancy
174v Feminist values: Guidelines for a teaching methodology in women's studies

Schnucker, Robert V.
184d Elizabethan birth control and Puritan attitudes

Schoenberg, B. Mark
287d Marriage

Schoenberg, Harry
285j Potency and its effects on patients

Schoepf, Brooke
82n Dynamics of social and cultural change

Schoepflin, Rennie B.
353z Ministries of healing: Mary Baker Eddy, Ellen G. White, and the religion of health

Schofield, Ann
201h The uprising of the 20,000: The making of a labor legend

Scholes, Robert
131g A footnote to Russ's "Recent feminist utopias"

Scholten, Catherine M.
353j "On the importance of the obstetrick art": Changing customs of childbirth in America, 1760 to 1825

Schomerus, Heilwig
144f The family life-cycle: A study of factory workers in nineteenth century Württemberg

School-Age Child Care Project
80w School-age child care

Schoonenboom, I.J.
52d The position of women in the Netherlands: Marginal change

Schor, Naomi
132n For a restricted thematics: Writing, speech, and difference in *Madame Bovary*

Schotter, Anne Howland
331a Woman's song in medieval Latin

Schotz, Myra Glazer
180e The great unwritten story: Mothers and daughters in Shakespeare

Schover, Leslie R.
461g Discussion: Midlife women: Lessons for sex therapy

Schrier, Katherine
169f Credit programs for working women

Schrodt, Barbara
147q Canadian women at the Olympic games
147r Canadian women at the Commonwealth games

Schubert, Glendon
35d The biopolitics of sex: Gender, genetics, and epigenetics

Schulenberg, Jane Tibbets
187c Strict active enclosure and its effects on the female monastic experience (500-1100)

Schuler, Harry J.
463m Sex differences in travel preferences and decision making

Schulte, Regina
162c Infanticide in rural Bavaria in the nineteenth century

Schultz, LeRoy G.
284a The sexual abuse of children and minors: A short history of legal control efforts
284d Diagnosis and treatment - an introduction
284i Incest - an introduction
284m Incest policy recommendations

284n The victim and justice system - an introduction
284s The child sex industry - an introduction
284w Policy recommendations on child pornography control
284x Sexual emancipation - an introduction
284y The age of sexual consent: Fault, friction, freedom

Schultz, Susan K.
191g Tailoring evaluation to measure the accountability of mental health services to women

Schultz, T. Paul
110a Estimating labor supply functions for married women
459h Women's work and their status: Rural Indian evidence of labour market and environment effects on sex differences in childhood mortality

Schulz, Pat
305j Minding the children

Schuman, Patricia Glass
15a Libraries and alternatives

Schurr, Cathleen
399ss The Washington area feminist theatre

Schuster, Ilsa
5e Perspectives in development: The problem of nurses and nursing in Zambia
385e Marginal lives: Conflict and contradiction in the position of female traders in Lusaka, Zambia

Schuster, Marilyn R.
314f Project on women and social change: Smith College

Schwab, Donald P.
66b Job evaluation and pay setting: Concepts and practices
67b Job evaluation and pay setting: Concepts and practices

Schwartz, Jack
19h The political trial

Schwartz, Linda S.
296e A three-generational analysis of change in women's achievement motivation and power

Schwartz, Mortimer D.
375k Clara Shortridge Foltz: Pioneer in the law

SchWeber, Claudine
165l "The government's unique experiment in salvaging women criminals": Cooperation and conflict in the administration of a women's prison - The case of the Federal Industrial Institution for Women at Alderson

Schweickart, Patrocinio
181l What if...science and technology in feminist utopias

Schwingl, Pamela J.
16j The first two years: A profile of women entering Women, Inc.

Schyfter, Sara E.
313o "La loca, la tonta, la literata": Women's destiny in Clarín's *La Regenta*

Sciama, Lidia
160b Ambivalence and dedication: Academic wives in Cambridge University, 1870-1970
371e The problem of privacy in Mediterranean anthropology

Sclare, Astor Balfour
345c The foetal alcohol syndrome

Scott, Anne F.
61a What we wish we knew about women: A dialog
264f Historians construct the Southern woman

Scott, Bonnie Kime
409c Emma Clery in *Stephen Hero*: A young woman walking proudly through the decayed city

Scott, Joan W.
50d Women's work and the family in nineteenth-century Europe
89d Women's work and the family in nineteenth-century Europe
184l Women's work and European fertility patterns

Scott, Judith A.
86k Keeping women in their place: Exclusionary policies and reproduction

Scott, Martha L.
412f Georgia Harkness: Social activist and/or mystic

Scott, Patricia Bell
14d Selected bibliography on black feminism
14j Debunking Sapphire: Toward a non-racist and non-sexist social science

Scott, Sue
297i The personable and the powerful: Gender and status in sociological research
398k On the bottom rung: A discussion of women's work in sociology

Scott-Jones, Marilyn
32h Laura Marholm and the question of female nature

Scovill, Ruth
453j Women's music

Scrimshaw, Mary
269c Sex roles and subsistence: A comparative analysis of three Central American communities

Scriven, Jeannie
471g Women at work in Sweden

Scully, Vincent
117c The great goddess and the palace architecture of Crete

Scura, Dorothy M.
450h Doris Bett's Nancy Finch: A heroine for the 1980s

Scutt, Jocelynne A.
348a Sexism in criminal law
390x Crime and sexual politics
440k Legislating for the right to be equal

Seal, K. C.
422a Women in the labour force of India: A macro-level statistical profile

Searing, Susan E.
351k Studying women's studies: A guide to archival research

Searle, Eleanor
375c *Merchet* and women's property rights in medieval England

Sears, Pauline S.
351c Career and life satisfactions among Terman's gifted women

Sears, Sallie
328l Theater of war: Virginia Woolf's *Between the Acts*

Sebestyen, Amanda
212q Sexual assumptions in the women's movement

Secci, Lia
145h German women writers and the Revolution of 1848

Seccombe, Wally
149a Domestic labour and the working-class household
149e The expanded reproduction cycle of labour power in twentieth-century capitalism

Secor, Cynthia
17m The question of Gertrude Stein
127e *Ida, A* great American novel
407c Preparing the individual for institutional leadership: The summer institute
407i Getting the best: Conclusions, recommendations, and selected resources
442d Gertrude Stein: The complex force of her femininity

Secor, Marie
27l Violet Hunt's *Tales of the Uneasy*: Ghost stories of a worldly woman

Secor, Robert
27l Violet Hunt's *Tales of the Uneasy*: Ghost stories of a worldly woman

Seear, Nancy
93l Implementing equal pay and equal opportunity legislation in Great Britain

Seely, Clinton B.
433l Say it with structure: Tagore and Mangala Kavyaital

Segal, Charles
419h The menace of Dionysus: Sex roles and reversals in Euripides' *Bacchae*

Segal, Lynne
257b Sensual uncertainty, or why the clitoris is not enough
335a 'The most important thing of all' - Rethinking the family: An overview
335b 'Smash the family?' Recalling the 1960s
335i No turning back - Thatcherism, the family and the future

Segal, Mady Wechsler
113n The argument for female combatants

Segal, Sondra
132o Separation and survival: Mothers, daughters, sisters: - The women's experimental theater

Segalen, Martine
162e 'Avoir sa part': Sibling relations in partible inheritance Brittany

Segall, William E.
414g College life in Oklahoma territory

Segers, Mary C.
3l Commentary to chapter 7 (chapter k)
3o Abortion and the culture: Toward a feminist perspective

Segrest, Mab
176d I lead two lives: Confessions of a closet Baptist
301qq I lead two lives: Confessions of a closet Baptist

Seiden, Anne E.
87h Time management and the dual-career couple

Seidman, Ann
373g Women and the development of "underdevelopment": The African experience

Seitz, Victoria
80l A methodological comment on "The problem of infant day care"

Seiwa, H.
372g An outline of the history of women and western sport in Japan

Seixas, Judith
404h Reaching the middle class alcoholic

Sells, Lucy W.
361a Leverage for equal opportunity through mastery of mathematics
377d The mathematics filter and the education of women and minorities

Selstad, Georgiana
309x Teenagers: Fertility control behavior and attitudes before and after abortion, childbearing or negative pregnancy test

Semel, Rochelle
169c The short course

Sen, Gita
60p Women's role in economic development: Practical and theoretical implications of class and gender inequalities
350b Women workers and the green revolution

Sen, Lalita
463n Travel patterns and behavior of women in urban areas

Senyapili, Tansi
270i Economic change and the Gecekondu family

Serafica, Felicisima C.
265a Parents' sex role attitudes and children's concepts of femininity and masculinity

Serbin, Lisa A.
259c The hidden curriculum: Academic consequences of teacher expectations

Seretan, L. Glen
128a Daniel DeLeon and the woman question

Sevenhuijsen, Selma
76a The women's movement and motherhood
76e 'The policing of families'

Severne, Liesbeth
51q Psychosocial aspects of the menopause

Seward, Margaret
44d Dentistry

Sewell, Marilyn
301aa Dear Mary Catherine

Sewell, Sandra Serrano
36k Sterilization abuse and Hispanic women

Sexton, Lorraine Dusak
246g Pigs, pearlshells, and 'women's work':
Collective response to change in highland
Papua New Guinea

Sexual Assault Center
284h Sexual assault center emergency room protocol: Child/adolescent patients

Seymour, Di
381c Box of tricks

Seymour, William C.
288p Sexual harassment: Finding a cause of
action under Title VII

Sgroi, Suzanne M.
146a A conceptual framework for child sexual
abuse
146b Validation of child sexual abuse
146c An approach to case management
146d Treatment of the sexually abused child
146g Individual and group treatment of mothers
of incest victims
146i Family treatment
146k Law enforcement and child sexual abuse
146l Multidisciplinary team review of child-sexual-abuse cases
146n How to start a child-sexual-abuse intervention program
284c Sexual molestation of children: The last
frontier of child abuse

Shabad, Goldie
378l Candidate evaluations by men and women

Shadron, Virginia
303p The historical perspective: A bibliographical essay
412n The laity rights movement, 1906-1918:
Women's suffrage in the Methodist
Episcopal Church, South

Shaeffer, Ruth Gilbert
93m Improving job opportunities for women
from a U.S. corporate perspective
426g Corporate experiences in improving
women's job opportunities

Shafer, Yvonne
399k Women in male roles: Charlotte Cushman
and others

Shaffer, Carolyn R.
229ss Spiritual techniques for re-powering survivors of sexual assault

Shaffer, Elinor
439t The History of Sexuality. Vol. 1: An
Introductionital by Michel Foucault

Shah, Makhdoom A.
402d Trends and structure of female labour
force participation in rural and urban
Pakistan

Shah, Nasra M.
402d Trends and structure of female labour
force participation in rural and urban
Pakistan
420f The female migrant in Pakistan
420o Migrant women at work in Asia

Shaiken, Harley
209a Choices in the development of office
automation

Shainess, Natalie
280c Nymphomania, hostile sex, and superego
development

Shakeshaft, Charol
90b Women in educational administration: A
descriptive analysis of dissertation
research and paradigm for future research
266f Sampling: Issues and problems in sex role
and social change research

Shalala, Donna E.
463x Speech

Shange, Ntozake
417o Tulsa (poem)

Shanklin, Elizabeth
195p The answer is matriarchy

Shanley, Mary Lyndon
103v Afterword: Feminism and families in a liberal policy
106d Political and marital despotism:
Montesquieu's *Persian Letters*
106e Marriage contract and social contract in
seventeenth-century English political
thought

Shapira, Rina
421x Occupational choice among female academicians - The Israeli case

Shapiro, Judith
123g Anthropology and the study of gender

Shapiro-Perl, Nina
199k Resistance strategies: The routine struggle
for bread and roses

Sharff, Jagna Wojcicka
253d Sex and temperament revisited

Sharkey, Sarah
274g Mathematics

Sharma, Ursula
364d Dowry in North India: Its consequences
for women
402j Purdah and public space

Sharma, Y. K.
346d Technologies for poor women

Sharp, Henry S.
340f The null case: The Chipewyan

Sharpe, Lawrence
285g Is there love before dying?

Shaver, Sheila
440g Sex and money in the welfare state

Shavlik, Donna
407e Toward a new era of leadership: The
national identification program

Shaw, Denis J. B.
151i Achievements and problems in Soviet
recreational planning

Shaw, Jennifer
62c The politics of single-sex schools
250f Education and the individual: Schooling
for girls, or mixed schooling - a mixed
blessing?

Shaw, Lois B.
324a Problems of labor-market reentry
324b Causes of irregular employment patterns
324f Economic consequences of midlife change
in marital status

Shaw, Nancy Stoller
165k Female patients and the medical profession in jails and prisons: A case of quintuple jeopardy

Shaw, Sheila
186i Living rooms: Amity in the novels of May
Sarton

Shaw, Stan
345a The causes of increasing drinking problems amongst women

Shaw, Valerie
197b Fun and games with life-stories

Shearer, Beth
36aa C/SEC: A special-interest interpersonal
group brings about change

Sheehan, Margaret
345f Response and recognition

Sheehy, Gail
392i The economics of prostitution

Sheer, Arlene
417p Findhorn, Scotland: The people who talk
to plants

Sheffield, Carole J.
344a Sexual terrorism

Sheldon, Sayre
167d A national campaign: Women's party for
survival

Shelley, Dolores
27n A conversation with May Sarton

Shepela, Sharon Toffey
65c Some psychological factors affecting job
segregation and wages

Shepeleva, M. S.
446p How working women combine work and
household duties

Sheppard, H. L.
49b When is old?

Sheppard, Julia
248i Archives and the history of nursing

Shepro, Theresa Aragón
72f Impediments to Hispanic women organizing

Sheptulina, N. N.
446i Protection of female labor

Sherer, Denise
285s Establishing a women's group for disabled
clients

Sheridan, Mary
177a The life history method
177k Yenan women in revolution
177m Contemporary generations

Sherif, Carolyn Wood
239l A social psychological perspective on the
menstrual cycle

Sherman, Claire Richter
117g Taking a second look: Observations on the
iconography of a French queen, Jeanne de
Bourbon (1338-1378)
389a Precursors and pioneers (1820-1890)
389b Widening horizons (1890-1930)
389c The tradition continues (1930-1979)

389j Gisela Marie Augusta Richter (1882-1972): Scholar of classical art and museum archaeologist

389n Dorothy Eugenia Miner (1904-1973): The varied career of a medievalist: Scholar and keeper of manuscripts, librarian and editor at the Walters Art Gallery

Sherman, Joan R.

14v Afro-American women poets of the nineteenth century: A guide to research and bio-bibliographies of the poets

Sherman, Julia A.

365b Therapist attitudes and sex-role stereotyping

Sherman, Laurel

254b The evolution of the woman scientist

Sherman, Susan

174k Women and process: The Sagaris split, Session II

Sherman, Susan R.

458g Retirement expectations and plans: A comparison of professional men and women

Sherwin, Barbara Brender

271o Mood and behaviour changes in menopausal women receiving gonadal hormones or placebo

Sherwin, Susan

168b From feminism to a new conception of ethics

Shields, Stephanie A.

158k "To pet, coddle, and 'Do For'": Caretaking and the concept of maternal instinct

Shih, Anthony

355i Contributions to household labor: Comparing wives' and husbands' reports

Shilling, Nancy Adams

403d The social and political roles of Arab women: A study of conflict

Shimony, Annemarie

325p Women of influence and prestige among the Native American Iroquois

Shinell, Grace

229vv Women's collective spirit: Exemplified and envisioned

Shishkan, N. M.

446f Raising the skill level of women workers

Shively, Charley

224b Cosmetics as an act of revolution

224e Old and gay

Shobha, V.

299b Maid servants

299d Beedi workers

299e Construction workers

299f Petty traders

Shockley, Ann Allen

150n The black lesbian in American literature: An overview

397q The black lesbian in American literature: An overview

Shore, Barbara K.

434d Rape crisis theory revisited

Shore, Bradd

282f Sexuality and gender in Samoa: Conceptions and missed conceptions

Shore, David A.

285n Sex in institutions

Shore, Elliott

15e Reference service for alternative publications

Short, Clarice

445a The old one and the wind (poem)

Shorter, Edward

184e Illegitimacy, sexual revolution, and social change in modern Europe

184g Bastardy in south Germany: A comment

Shortridge, Kathleen

344aa Poverty is a woman's problem

Showalter, Elaine

27k *A Passage to India* as "marriage fiction": Forster's sexual politics

Shteir, Ann B.

379f Linnaeus's daughters: Women and British botany

Shuey, William A.

96g From renunciation to rebellion: The female in literature

Shulman, Alix Kates

30a Living our life

125m Emma Goldman: Anarchist Queen

231bb A story of a girl and her dog

439b Sex and power: Sexual bases of radical feminism

Shulman, Gail

211i A feminist path to Judaism

Shumway, Naomi M.

42g Except you become as little children

Shure, Myrna B.

295g Enhancing childrearing skills in lower income women

Shute, Carmel

390o From balaclavas to bayonets: Women's voluntary war work, 1939-41

Shute, Sara

275b Sexist language and sexism

Shwartz, Susan M.

114g Marion Zimmer Bradley's ethic of freedom

Sider, Gerald M.

162o Family fun in Starve Harbor: Custom, history and confrontation in village Newfoundland

Siebert, W. S.

357a Low pay amongst women - the facts

357e Shortcomings and problems in analyses of women and low pay

Siegel, Paul

133l Androgyny, sex-role rigidity, and homophobia

Siegler, Ava L.

80c Changing aspects of the family: A psychoanalytic perspective on early intervention

Siemienska, Renata

52m Women and the family in Poland

Sievers, Sharon L.

174f The new right challenges women's studies: The Long Beach women's studies program

Silber, Earle

8o The therapeutic alliance in psychoanalytic treatment

Silbert, Mimi H.

326n Treatment of prostitute victims of sexual assault

Silkey, Beryl

53i Pelvic inflammatory disease: Causes and consequences

Siltanen, Janet

378p The politics of private woman and public man

418b A commentary on theories of female wage labour

Silva, Carmen

174n Women of color Califia

Silver, Brenda R.

328n *Three Guineas* before and after: Further answers to correspondents

332d The reflecting reader in *Villette*

Silverblatt, Irene

347g "The universe has turned inside out...There is no justice for us here": Andean women under Spanish rule

Silverman, Deirdre

43h Sexual harassment, working women's dilemma

Silverman, Herbert

287c Female sexuality: Singlehood and the problems of intimacy

Silverman, Kaja

225u *Histoire d'O*: The construction of a female subject

247g Dis-embodying the female voice

Silverman, Martin A.

88g The latency period

Silverman, Phyllis R.

472i Widow-to-widow: The elderly widow and mutual help

Silverstone, Rosalie

44a The bimodal career

44b Accountancy

44i Summing Up

Similes, Kurt

55m Appendix B: Review of legal cases regarding US Code, Section 1461 (mailing obscene or crime-inciting matter)

Simms, Margaret C.

103f Women and housing: The impact of government housing policy

Simms, Marian

23a Political science, women and feminism

23i 'A woman's place is in the House and in the Senate': Women and the 1983 elections

228d Australia

Simms, Ruth

39g The African woman as entrepreneur: Problem and perspectives on their roles

Simon, Rita J.

349b American women and crime

Simons, May Wood
128i   Appendix: Woman and the social problem

Simri, U.
372e   Development of women's sport in the 20th century

Sims, Karen
71   Racism and sadomasochism: A conversation with two black lesbians

Sims-Wood, Janet
314n   Resources in black women's studies

Simson, Rennie
231k   The Afro-American female: The historical context of the construction of sexual identity

Sineau, Mariette
228e   France

Singer, Dorothy G.
327c   Television viewing, family style and aggressive behavior in preschool children

Singer, Jerome L.
327c   Television viewing, family style and aggressive behavior in preschool children

Singh, Andrea Menefee
402c   The study of women in South Asia: Some current methodological and research issues

Singh, Menefee Andrea
420e   Rural-to-urban migration of women in India: Patterns and implications

Singha, Santosh
75f   Career and employment of women in Pakistan

Singhanetra-Renard, Anchalee
424q   Effect of female labour force participation on fertility: The case of construction workers in Chiang Mai City

Sinkkonen, Sirkka
436k   The impact of the women's movement and legislative activity of women MPs on social development

Siraj, Mehrun
424g   Islamic attitudes to female employment in industrializing economies: Some notes from Malaysia

Sizemore, Christine W.
448i   Reading the city as palimpsest: The experiential perception of the city in Doris Lessing's *The Four-Gated City*

Sjafri, Aida
92f   Indonesia: Socio-economic aspects of food consumption in rural Java

Skaggs, Merrill Maguire
450d   Eating the moment absolutely up: The fiction of Beverly Lowry

Skalitzky, Rachel I.
394g   The women's studies program at Milwaukee

Skar, Sarah
104c   Interhousehold co-operation in Peru's southern Andes: A case of multiple sibling-group marriage
371b   Andean women and the concept of space/time

Skinner, Linda J.
326l   Behavioral treatment of sexual dysfunctions in sexual assault survivors

Skinner, Louise E.
463e   Shopping trips: Who makes them and when?

Skinner, Mary
187d   Benedictine life for women in central France, 850-1100: A feminist revival

Sklar, June
309a   Teenage family formation in postwar America

Sklar, Kathryn Kish
353r   "All hail to pure cold water!"
412b   The last fifteen years: Historians' changing views of American women in religion and society

Sklar, Roberta
132o   Separation and survival: Mothers, daughters, sisters: - The women's experimental theater

Skold, Karen Beck
444c   The job he left behind: American women in the shipyards during World War II

Skultans, Vieda
457a   Mediums, controls and eminent men

Slater, Michael
286h   *The Bachelor's Pocket Book for 1851*

Slaughter, Jane
95i   Humanism versus feminism in the socialist movement: The life of Angelica Balabanoff

Slaughter, M. H.
107r   Physique of college women athletes in five sports

Slavin, Sarah
249d   Joan Roberts and the university

Slesarev, G.A.
52l   Soviet women in family and society

Sloane, Peter J.
89m   Sexual discrimination in the labour market
357a   Low pay amongst women - the facts
357c   The structure of labour markets and low pay for women
357e   Shortcomings and problems in analyses of women and low pay

Slote, Bernice
445n   Willa Cather and the sense of history

Small, Marion
205l   Postscript: Women in whose honour BC schools have been named

Smart, Carol
50n   From disregard to disrepute: The position of women in family law
78e   The new female offender: Reality or myth?
349a   Criminological theory: Its ideology and implications concerning women
376k   Criminological theory: Its ideology and implications concerning women

Smid, Frouke
167b   Organising at the grassroots: Vrouwen voor vrede (Women for Peace, the Netherlands)

Smith, Allan Gardner
135k   Edith Wharton and the ghost story

Smith, Barbara
14a   Introduction: The politics of black women's studies
14g   Racism and women's studies
14h   Face-to-face, day-to-day - racism CR
14p   Toward a black feminist criticism
150g   The bood - yes, the blood: A conversation
150l   Home
150jj   Black lesbian/feminist organizing: A conversation
174b   The politics of black women's studies
176h   Lesbian literature: A third world feminist perspective

Smith, Barbara B.
42e   Blueprints for living

Smith, Bernice D.
222d   Taking the giant step: Writing the dissertation

Smith, Betty Jo
82g   Nutrition and health

Smith, Beverly
14h   Face-to-face, day-to-day - racism CR
14l   Black women's health: Notes for a course
34j   Black women's health: Notes for a course
150w   Wedding

Smith, Cenen
150h   The blood - yes, the blood: A conversation

Smith, Dan
283i   Interview with Jo Richardson

Smith, Daniel Scott
184q   Premarital pregnancy in America, 1640-1971: An overview and interpretation
454k   Family limitation, sexual control, and domestic feminism in Victorian America

Smith, David
323a   Women at work in Canada

Smith, David E.
404m   Women and substance abuse: Treatment issues

Smith, Deborah K.
339k   Personal choices

Smith, Don
285p   Sex and disability - sociosexual education presentation format

Smith, Dorothy E.
168a   The renaissance of women

Smith, Elaine M.
61i   Mary McLeod Bethune and the National Youth Administration

Smith, Elizabeth M.
9e   Longitudinal studies of alcohol and drug problems: Sex differences

Smith, Ida
42k   A woman's role and destiny

Smith, J. Percy
338e   The new woman and the old goddess: The shaping of Shaw's mythology

Smith, James P.
110d   Assets and labor supply

Smith, Janet Farrell
31o Rights-conflict, pregnancy, and abortion
195l Parenting and property

Smith, Joan
153e Nonwage labor and subsistence
342g Feminist analysis of gender: A critique

Smith, Judy
174r A feminist chautauqua for a rural state
307h Women and appropriate technology: A feminist assessment

Smith, Karen
307y Surrogate motherhood - an interview

Smith, Lee
301bb Paralyzed (fiction)

Smith, Leroy W.
164i *Mansfield Park*: The revolt of the 'feminine' woman

Smith, Peggy B.
4f Programs for sexually active teens
4i Parenting education
4l Sex education

Smith, Peter C.
420a Urbanization, migration and the status of women
420b The migration of women to cities: A comparative perspective
420i The migration of women in the Philippines
420o Migrant women at work in Asia

Smith, Ralph E.
93p Women's stake in a high-growth economy in the United States
463c The movement of women into the labor force

Smith, Rebecca
343k A heart cleft in twain: The dilemma of Shakespeare's Gertrude

Smith, Ron
147o Women's sport: A trial of equality

Smith, Selwyn M.
280m Necrophilia and anti-social acts

Smith, Sherry A.
175j Elise Waerenskjold: A modern on the prairie

Smith, Sidonie A.
399z Lillian Hellman's memorial drama
452j Lillian Hellman and the strategy of the "other"

Smith, Stuart
62f Single-sex setting

Smith-Rosenberg, Carroll
238c Davey Crockett as trickster: Pornography, liminality and symbolic inversion in Victorian America
353a The female animal: Medical and biological views of woman and her role in nineteenth-century America
353e The female world of love and ritual: Relations between women in nineteenth-century America
454l The female world of love and ritual: Relations between women in nineteenth-century America
454n The hysterical woman: Sex roles and role conflict in nineteenth century America

Smithers, Alan
193l Girls studying science in the sixth form

Smye, Marti Diane
271k Female superiority in sex difference competence comparisons: A review of the literature
271l Sex differences in assertiveness: Implications for research and treatment
271m Assertiveness: Sex differences in relationships between self-report and behavioural measures

Smykla, John Ortiz
63g Problems with research in co-corrections

Snicker, Raija
244i Traditional sex norms and the innovative function of afternoon dancing

Snitow, Ann Barr
231m Mass market romance: Pornography for women is different
439i The front line: Notes on sex in novels by women, 1969-1979

Snow, Joseph
188n The Spanish love poet: Florencia Pinar

Snow, Robert T.
428b The new international division of labor and the U.S. work force: The case of the electronics industry

Snyder, Mary Beth
351h Women's education and career choice: Disparities between theory and practice

Sobel, Emilie F.
359e Psychology of women: Perspectives on theory and research for the eighties

Soble, Alan
116f The political epistemology of "masculine" and "feminine"
275q Beyond the miserable vision of "Vs. Ms."

Sohonie, Kamala
438b Opportunities for women scientists in India

Sojourner, Sabrina
229f From the house of Yemanja: The goddess heritage of black women

Sokoloff, Natalie J.
78a The criminal law and women
78aa Postscript: The future of women and the criminal law

Sokolov, Raymond
341e Women in the kitchen: The feminist boiling point

Solomon, Barbara
16u Alternative social services and the black woman
434s Social work values and skills to empower women

Solomon, Laura J.
443k Working women and stress

Solomon, Margaret
384c A study of feminism as a motif in *A Journey to Pike's Peak and New Mexico* by Julia Archibald Holmes

Solomon, Myrtle
215m Alternative defence: Nonviolent struggle and peace building

Solomon, Robert C.
223b Love and feminism

Sommer, Barbara
28f Cognitive behavior and the menstrual cycle

Sommers, Tish
307ee Tomorrow is a woman's issue

Sonin, M. Ia.
446c Socioeconomic problems of female employment

Soper, Kate
215s Contemplating a nuclear future: Nuclear war, politics and the individual

Soper, Mary
203u Housing for single-parent families: A women's design

Sorensen, Glorian
427f Men, women, work, and family

Søresen, Bjørg Aase
217e The organizational woman and the trojan-horse effect
382i Norway

Sorensen, Henning
113j Denmark: The small NATO nation

Soyinka, Susan
393d Worlds apart? A comparative study of European and African traditional family life as depicted in the novels of Laurie Lee and Camara Laye

Spacks, Patricia Meyer
27i Rebellions of good women
123a The difference it makes
164j Muted discord: Generational conflict in Jane Austen
452g Selves in hiding

Spafford, Belle S.
42b The American Woman's Movement

Spanier, Bonnie
314e The natural sciences: Casting a critical eye on 'objectivity'
314g Toward a balanced curriculum: Wheaton College

Spears, Betty
147y The influential Miss Homans

Spector, Janet
148d Male/female task differentiation among the Hidatsa: Toward the development of an archeological approach to the study of gender

Spector, Susan
399r Uta Hagen and Eva Le Gallienne

Speicher, Rita
174q The Women's Writer's Center: An interview with the directors

Speizer, Jeanne J.
407d The administrative skills program: What have we learned?

Spelman, Elizabeth V.
84b Aristotle and the politicization of the soul

Spence, Janet T.
123h Changing conceptions of men and women: A psychologist's perspective

Spencer, Samia I.
130d Women and education

Spencer-Gardner, C.
236c Premenstrual syndrome - a holistic approach

Spender, Dale
85h The gatekeepers: A feminist critique of academic publishing
125v Modern feminist theorists: Reinventing rebellion
189k Education: The patriarchal paradigm and the response to feminism
259g 'Telling how it is': Language and gender in the classroom
312b Theorising about theorising

Spender, Lynne
125h Matilda Joslyn Gage: Active intellectual

Sperazi, Laura
16j The first two years: A profile of women entering Women, Inc.

Speth, Linda E.
375d The married women's property acts, 1839-1865: Reform, reaction or revolution?

Spiegel, David
245f Mothering, fathering, and mental illness

Spiegel, John P.
327e Ethnopsychiatric dimensions in family violence

Spiliotopoulos, Sophia
471f Women at work in Greece: The sociological and legal perspectives

Spilka, Mark
17p Hemingway and Fauntleroy: An androgynous pursuit
286j On the enrichment of poor monkeys by myth and dream; or how Dickens Rousseauisticized and pre-Freudianized Victorian views of childhood

Spillers, Hortense J.
225d Interstices: A small drama of words

Spivak, Gayatri C.
356u Unmaking and making in *To the Lighthouse*

Spooner, Lysander
129bb A right to make laws?

Sprague, Melinda S.
288a The executive man and woman: The issue of sexuality

Spretnak, Charlene
229ee Images of spiritual power in women's fiction
229ll The politics of women's spirituality
229tt The Christian right's "Holy War" against feminism
229yy Afterword: Feminist politics and the nature of mind

Springer, Beverly Tanner
95a Anna Kuliscioff: Russian revolutionist, Italian feminist

Springer, Jane
323p Organizing freelancers in the arts

Spurgeon, J. H.
107s Measures of body size and form of elite female basketball players

Spurgeon, N. L.
107s Measures of body size and form of elite female basketball players

Spurlock, Jeanne
411k Black women in the middle years

Squier, Susan
202j The politics of city space in *The Years*: Street, love, pillar boxes and bridges
328k A track of our own: Typescript drafts of *The Years*
448f Tradition and revision: The classic city novel and Virginia Woolf's *Night and Day*
448o Literature and the city: A checklist of relevant secondary works

Squires, Mary-Lou
147h Sport and the Cult of True Womanhood: A paradox at the turn of the century

Srinivasan, Mangalam
251d The impact of science and technology and the role of women in science in Mexico
373f Impact of selected industrial technologies on women in Mexico

Sroufe, L. Alan
427b The importance of early care

St. Joan, Jackie
43t Female leaders: Who was Rembrandt's mother?
174j The ideas and the realities: Sagaris, Session I

Stacey, Meg
241a Social sciences and the state: Fighting like a woman

Stack, Carol B.
39r Sex roles and survival strategies in the urban black community

Stacks, Don W.
126d Research on women's communication: Critical assessment and recommendations

Stadler, Quandra Prettyman
132p Visibility and difference: Black women in history and literature - pieces of a paper and some ruminations

Stage, Elizabeth K.
307cc EQUALS in computer technology

Stage, Sarah
353s The woman behind the trademark

Stager, Gordon L.
285h Sexuality and cancer

Stager, Rae Ellen S.
285h Sexuality and cancer

Stagner, R.
49d Postscripts and prospects

Stamm, Liesa
296a Introduction: An interdisciplinary perspective on women's power and influence
296b Differential power of women over the life course: A case study of age-roles as an indicator of power

Stamp, Judy
203k Toward supportive neighborhoods: Women's role in changing the segregated city

Standing, Hilary
12f 'Sickness is a woman's business?': Reflections on the attribution of illness

Stanko, Anne Elizabeth
165b Would you believe this woman? Prosecutorial screening for "credible" witnesses and a problem of justice

Stanley, Autumn
181a Women hold up two-thirds of the sky: Notes for a revised history of technology
307g From Africa to America: Black women inventors
441a Daughters of Isis, daughters of Demeter: When women sowed and reaped

Stanley, Liz
125n Olive Schreiner: New women, free women, all women
212o 'Male needs': The problems and problems of working with gay men
312l 'Back into the personal' or: Our attempt to construct 'feminist research'

Stansell, Christine
256g One hand tied behind us: A review essay
454m Women and their families on the Overland Trail, 1842-1867

Stanton, Domna C.
108a Autogynography: Is the subject different?
132e Language and revolution: The Franco-American Dis-connection
135q Power or sexuality: The bind of Corneille's *Pulcherie*

Stantonbury Campus Sexism in Education Group, Bridgewater Hall School
62e The realities of mixed schooling

Stanworth, Michelle
378p The politics of private woman and public man

Staples, Robert
37j Race and marital status: An overview
39q The myth of the black matriarchy
41g Invited presentation: The black professional woman — career success and interpersonal failure

Star, Barbara
359ii Psychosocial aspects of wife battering

Star, Sandra Inez
399f Murshida Ivy O. Duce

Star, Susan Leigh
7f Interview with Audre Lorde
7p Swastikas: The street and the university

Starcevic, Elizabeth
74f Elena Poniatowska: Witness for the people

Starhawk
229e Witchcraft as goddess religion
229q Consciousness, politics, and magic
229oo Ethics and justice in goddess religion
462w Immanence: Uniting the spiritual and political

Stark, Evan
354i Medicine and patriarchal violence: The social construction of a "private" event

Stark-Adamec, Cannie
271a Why?

Starr, June
364f The legal and social transformation of rural women in Aegean Turkey

Starrett, Barbara
229r The metaphors of power

Statham, Anne
324c Occupational atypicality: Changes, causes, and consequences
324d Attitudes toward women working: Changes over time and implications for the labor-force behaviors of husbands and wives

Staudt, Kathleen
82c Participation through Title XII, consortia, and the project process in AID
82d AID: Promise and performance
82s Household structure in Africa
362a Women's politics in Africa
385j Women farmers and inequities in agricultural services
435m Bureaucratic resistance to women's programs: The case of women in development

Stauffer, Helen
445f Mari Sandoz and western biography

Stauth, Georg
153f Households, modes of living, and production systems

Steady, Filomina Chioma
39a The black woman cross-culturally: An overview
39x Black women and survival: A Maroon case

Steed, Maggie
381e Interpretations

Steel, William F.
385k Women's employment and development: A conceptual framework applied to Ghana

Steele, Brandt F.
291q Long-term effects of sexual abuse in childhood

Steele, Emilie
178g The human cost of discrimination

Steele, Shirley O.
150ff Shoes are made for walking

Steffensmeier, Darrell J.
78f Trends in female crime: It's still a man's world
349c Crime and the contemporary woman: An analysis of changing levels of female property crime, 1960-1975
349d Patterns of female property crime, 1960-1978: A postscript

Steil, Janice M.
344h Marital relationships and mental health: The psychic costs of inequality

Stein, Karen F.
109g Monsters and madwomen: Changing female gothic
399mm The women's world of Glaspell's *Trifles*

Stein, Peter J.
48j Sink or swing? The lifestyles of single adults

Stein, Sandra L.
398j Women's studies and men's careers: How the 'social problem' of women in education maintained the academic status of men in the 1970s

Steinbacher, Roberta
31p Sex preselection: From here to fraternity
79v Futuristic implications of sex preselection

Steinberg, Laurence D.
204d The ecology of day care

Steinberg, Ronnie J.
65a "A want of harmony": Perspectives on wage discrimination and comparable worth
65p Technical possibilities and political realities: Concluding remarks

Steinem, Gloria
220b Perspectives on women in the 1980s: The Baird Poskanzer Memorial Lecture
229k Tales of a reincarnated Amazon princess: The invincible wonder woman?

Steinfels, Margaret O'Brien
308g Ethical and legal issues in teenage pregnancies

Steinhart, Clara
54b The unidentified problem of alcoholism among Hispanic women

Steinhart, Judith
460r A sex-information switchboard

Steinhauer, Marcia B.
472k Policy directions and program design: Issues and implications in services for the older woman

Steinmetz, Suzanne K.
105l Physical violence in a nationally representative sample of American families

Steinshouer, Betty
397r Without approval: The lesbian poetry tradition

Steinson, Barbara J.
444k "The mother half of humanity": American women in the peace and preparedness movements in World War I

Stellman, Jeanne M.
34e No fertile women need apply: Employment discrimination and reproductive hazards in the workplace
209x Health hazards in the computerized office
447j The biology of toxic effects on reproductive outcomes

Stelmahoske, Isabelle
394r Meeting the needs of re-entering students

Stemerick, Martine
329c Virginia Woolf and Julia Stephen: The distaff side of history

Stenner, A.J.
275v A note on logical truth and non-sexist semantics

Stensaas, Starla
254e Images of women in film

Stephens, Judith Louise
399ll Women in Pulitzer Prize plays, 1918-1949

Stephens, Richard C.
319p To be aged, Hispanic, and female: The triple risk

Stephenson, P. Susan
359i The psychiatrist-woman patient relationship

Stern, Arleen
211o Learning to chant the Torah: A first step

Sternburg, Janet
30m Farewell to the farm

Stetson, Erlene
14i Studying slavery: Some literary and pedagogical considerations on the black female slave
30o Silence: Access and aspiration

Stevens, Doris
16o Rape victims
284q Special techniques for child witnesses

Stevens, Joyce
390k 'Without fear or favour' - Lucie Barnes

Stevens, May
30q Ordinary. Extraordinary.

Stevenson, Mary Lou Kohfeldt
303o Scratching at the compound

Stewart, Abigail
45k Changing sex roles: College graduates of the 1960's and 1970's

Stewart, Barbara Duffy
29j Physical aggression: Treating the victims

Stewart, Debra W.
410g Organizational role orientations on female-dominant commissions: Focus on staff-commissioner interaction
410i Commissions on the status of women and building a local policy agenda

Stewart, Joan Hinde
64e Colette and the epistolary novel
130l The novelists and their fictions

Stewart, Katie
369l The marriage of capitalist and patriarchical ideologies: Meanings of male bonding and male ranking in U.S. culture

Stewart, Lee
205k Women on campus in British Columbia: Strategies for survival, years of war and peace, 1906-1920

Steyn, Anna F.
52q The changing position of black women in South Africa

Stichter, Sharon
6l Appendix: Some selected statistics on African women

Stiehm, Judith Hicks
84c The unit of political analysis: Our Aristotelian hangover
380c Elected women: Skewers of the political system
435n Women, men, and military service: Is protection necessarily a racket?
436b Women and citizenship: Mobilisation, participation, representation
464h The man question

Stiglin, Laura E.
46d   Women and a two-tier social security system

Stiller, Nikki
180c   Eve's orphans: Mothers and daughters in medieval English literature

Stillion, Judith M.
344o   Women and widowhood: The suffering beyond grief

Stillman, Nina G.
447i   A legal perspective on workplace reproductive hazards
447n   A legal perspective on pregnancy leave and benefits

Stillman, Peter G.
106d   Political and marital despotism: Montesquieu's *Persian Letters*

Stimpson, Catharine R.
51s   The fallacy of bodily reductionism
108l   The female sociograph: The theater of Virigina Woolf's letters
126b   Women as knowers
196f   Gertrice/Altrude: Stein, Toklas, and the paradox of the happy marriage
314a   Where does integration fit: The development of women's studies
332i   Doris Lessing and the parables of growth
343c   Shakespeare and the soil of rape

Stini, William A.
279n   Sexual dimorphism and nutrient reserves

Stites, Richard
95e   Alexandra Kollontai and the Russian Revolution
113a   Great Britain and the World Wars
113c   Russia: Revolution and war
405b   The women's liberation issue in nineteenth century Russia

Stitzel, Judith
303m   She who laughs first
306r   Authentic voices
316l   Challenging curricular assumptions: Teaching and studying women's literature from a regional perspective

Stivens, Maila
207g   Women, kinship and capitalist development
208j   Women, kinship and capitalist development

Stock, Wendy E.
268k   Sex roles and sexual dysfunction

Stockard, Jean
90n   The sources and dynamics of sexual inequality in the profession of education
262a   Sex roles in education
262b   Sex inequities in the experience of students
262c   Why sex inequities exist for students
262e   Why sex inequities exist in the profession of education
262i   Educational equity: Current and future needs

Stockinger, Jacob
64h   The test of love and nature: Colette and lesbians

Stoever, William K.B.
19d   The theological dimension

Stolcke, Verena
207c   Women's labours: The naturalisation of social inequality and women's subordination
208i   Women's labours: The naturalisation of social inequality and women's subordination

Stoller, Robert J.
460i   Femininity

Stolte-Heiskanen, Veronica
243c   The role and status of women scientific research workers in research groups

Stoltenberg, John
7o   Sadomasochism: Eroticized violence, eroticized powerlessness

Stolz, Stephanie B.
29d   Dissemination of behavioral interventions with women: Needed - a technology

Stone, Alan A.
140a   Presidential address: Conceptual ambiguity and morality in modern psychiatry
140y   Sexual misconduct by psychiatrists: The ethical and clinical dilemma of confidentiality

Stone, Karen
213b   Motherhood and waged work: West Indian, Asian and white mothers compared

Stone, Lucy
129j   Marriage contract

Stone, Merlin
229a   The great goddess: Who was she?
229g   The three faces of goddess spirituality
229i   Ancient mirrors of womanhood

Stone, Michael H.
28p   Premenstrual tension in borderline and related disorders

Stoper, Emily
103o   Work, gender, and technological innovation
226l   State and local policies on motherhood
435e   Alternative work patterns and the double life

Stoppard, Janet M.
271f   Sex-role ideology and sex bias in judgments of occupational suitability

Stowasser, Barbara Freyer
198b   The status of women in early Islam

Strange, Heather
21e   Some changing socioeconomic roles of village women in Malaysia
198g   A traditional ceremony in an Islamic milieu in Malaysia

Strasser, Susan M.
355b   An enlarged human existence? Technology and household work in nineteenth-century America

Strathern, Andrew
162h   'A brother is a creative thing': Change and conflict in a Melpa family (Papua New Guinea)

Strathern, Marilyn
200h   No nature, no culture: The Hagen case
246b   Domesticity and the denigration of women
282e   Self-interest and the social good: Some implications of Hagen gender imagery
364i   Subject or object? Women and the circulation of valuables in highlands New Guinea

Stratta, Erica
258h   Involvement in crime

Straub, Eleanor F.
61l   Women in the civilian labor force

Strauch, Judith
420d   Women in rural-urban circulation networks: Implications for social structural change

Straus, Murray A.
105l   Physical violence in a nationally representative sample of American families
230h   Sexual stratification, pornography, and rape in the United States
327a   A sociological perspective on the causes of family violence

Strauss, Cyd C.
29h   Parenting: Training mothers as behavior therapists for their children

Strauzenberg, S. E.
372bb Iron deficiency in female athletes

Strecker, J. R.
236e   An explorative study into the clinical effects of dydrogesterone in the treatment of premenstrual syndrome

Stricker, Frank
454q   Cookbooks and law books: The hidden history of career women in twentieth-century America

Stringer, Donna M.
360b   Female psychologists in policymaking positions

Strømsheim, Gunvor
468b   Working hours and segmentation in the Norwegian labour market

Strobel, Margaret
6f   Women in religion and in secular ideology
370g   Slavery and reproductive labor in Mombasa

Strober, Myra H.
89q   Wives' labor force behavior and family consumption patterns
90h   Jobs and gender: A history of the structuring of educational employment by sex
272f   Toward a general theory of occupational sex segregation: The case of public school teaching
426b   The MBA: Same passport to success for women and men?

Strong, Bryan
238i   Ideas of the early sex education movement in America, 1890-1920

Strong, Tracy B.
106i   Oedipus as hero: Family and family metaphors in Nietzsche

Strover, Sharon L.
57f   Peer communication and sexuality

Studenmund, A.H.
4631 Women's travel behavior and attitudes: An empirical analysis

Stueve, Ann
243e Mothers as social agents: Structuring the community activities of school aged children

411i The daughter of aging parents

Stuntz, Richard C.
280e Gender dysphoria and dyssocial behavior

Sturgis, Ellie T.
291 Physiological and reproductive disorders

Sturgis, Somers H.
237a The gynecologist's approach (premenstrual tension)

Sturm, Hertha
391d Time, television, and women's career perspectives

Sturtz, Sue
176e Harassment in rural America

Styles, Marva
341i Soul, black women and food

Sucher, Erica
461a Women's sexual response

Suchman, Lucy
209n The role of common sense in the process of interface design

Suchocki, Marjorie
118c Openness and mutuality in process thought and feminist action

Sudarkasa, Niara
37b Interpreting the African heritage in Afro-American family organization

39b Female employment and family organization in West Africa

Sugar, Max
461m Does motherhood mean maturity?

Sugden, Marian
215v Interesting times: A chronology of the nuclear age

Sukiennik, Adelaide Weir
302e Assertiveness training for library-school students

Sullivan, Norma
466h Indonesian women in development: State theory and urban kampung practice

Summers, Anne
348b Hidden from history: Women victims of crime

390p The unwritten history of Adela Pankhurst Walsh

Summit, Roland
461k Beyond belief: The reluctant discovery of incest

Sunar, Diane
270n Social psychological patterns of homicide in Turkey: A comparison of male and female convicted murders

Sung, Marina H.
401d The Chinese Lieh-nü tradition

Suntree, Susan
453g Women's theatre: Creating the dream now

Suppe, Frederick
223v Curing homosexuality

Surrey, Janet L.
360d The relational self in women: Developmental theory and public policy

Sussman, George D.
184m Parisian infants and Norman wet nurses in the early nineteenth century: A statistical study

Sussman, Linda S.
419c Workers and drones: Labor, idleness and gender definition in Hesiod's beehive

Sutherland, Margaret B.
259e Anxiety, aspirations and the curriculum

Sutton, Andrew
151h Backward children in the USSR: An unfamiliar approach to a familiar problem

Sutton, Constance
39y Social inequality and sexual status in Barbados

Sutton, Jo
212k Fatherhood: Bringing it all back home

Suzuki, Bob H.
216h The Asian-American family

Swade, Tamar
167f Babies against the bomb: A statement

Swain, Margaret Byrne
269f Being Cuna and female: Ethnicity mediating change in sex roles

Swain, Martha H.
264c The public role of southern women

Swallow, Helen
36v Midwives in many settings

Sweet, James A.
89r The employment of wives and the inequality of family income

Swift, Carolyn
284b Sexual victimization of children: An urban mental health center survey

Swim, Janet
254f Captured angel in the centerfold

Swinson, Richard P.
9f Sex differences in the inheritance of alcoholism

Swoboda, Marian
337n Traditional and non-traditional choices of disciplines by women

Sylvander, Carolyn
337h Women in the school of music

394i Chair, chairman, chairperson

Symanski, Richard
349i Prostitution in Nevada

Symonds, Alexandra
359p Phobias after marriage: Women's declaration of dependence

Symons, Gladys L.
52s Egalitarianism in marriage? Graduate education and the sexual division of labour in the Canadian family

421j Attitudes and ideology: Correlates of liberal attitudes towards the role of women

Synge, Jane
2101 Concerns about parental health

Sypher, Eileen B.
329j *The Waves*: A utopia of androgyny?

Syskowski, David F.
463k Role influence in transportation decision making

Szanton, M. Cristina Blanc
362f "Big women" and politics in a Philippine fishing town

431f Women and men in Iloilo, Philippines: 1903-1970

Szepansky, Gerda
336n Comrade - woman - mother - resistance fighter

Szinovacz, Maximiliane
210f Beyond the hearth: Older women and retirement

458a Introduction: Research on women's retirement

458i Retirement plans and retirement adjustment

458m Personal problems and adjustment to retirement

458o Conclusion: Service needs of women retirees

Szklo, Moyses
53r Epidemiology of coronary heart disease in women

Tabak, Fanny
436c Women's role in the formulation of public policies in Brazil

464d Women and authoritarian regimes

Tadesse, Zenebeworke
251c Women and technology in peripheral countries: An overview

350h The impact of land reform on women: The case of Ethiopia

Tai-Li, Hu
428p The emergence of small-scale industry in a Taiwanese rural community

Talahite, Claude
298e Human sciences research on Algerian women

Talbot, M. J.
107c Women and sport: A leisure studies perspective

Talburt, Nancy Ellen
1b Josephine Tey

Tallman, Irving
105g Social structure, family socialization, and children's achievement goals: A comparative analysis

Tallmer, Margot
285o Sexual attitudes and activities in old age

Tangen, J. O.
107d The influence of the traditional sex roles on women's participation and engagement in sport

Tangri, Sandra S.
380r Research on women's work and the family at the urban institute

Tanner, Mary
115j Called to priesthood: Interpreting women's experience

Tanner, Tony
106f Julie and "La Maison Paternelle": Another look at Rousseau's *La Nouvelle Heloise*
164k In between - Anne Elliot marries a sailor and Charlotte Heywood goes to the seaside

Tapper, Nancy
457d Gender and religion in a Turkish town: A comparison of two types of formal women's gatherings

Tarango, Yolanda
462g "Las Marías" of the feminist movement

Tasini, Miriam
461n Discussion: Some developmental aspects of adolescent mothers

Tatenberg, Taly
312o Selected annotated bibliography of articles on theories of women's studies

Tatum, Stephen
445s Tradition of the exile: Judith Wright's Australian "West"

Taub, Nadine
60q Defining and combating sexual harassment

Tax, Meredith
30t I had been hungry all the years

Taylor, Barbara
256f "The men are as bad as their masters...": Socialism, feminism and sexual antagonism in the London tailoring trade in the 1830s
404y The unique employment problems of female offenders returning to the community and labor market

Taylor, Barbara G.
303f A delicate balance: Academic women in Arkansas

Taylor, Henry
186r The singing wound: Intensifying paradoxes in May Sarton's "A Divorce of Lovers"

Taylor, Jean
42j Happily ever after

Taylor, Joan Kennedy
129w Protective labor legislation

Taylor, Kriste
275w Reference and truth: The case of sexist and racist utterances

Taylor, Marion R.
302k Mobility and professional involvement in librarianship: A study of the "Class of '55"

Taylor, Nancy
54g Structural family therapy: The Sanchez family

Taylor, R. W.
236a Aetiology of premenstrual syndrome

Taylor, Richard
223c The ethics of having love affairs

Taylor, Stan
378k The party identifications of women: Parkin put to the test

Taylorson, Daphne E.
139a Introduction: Class and work: Bringing women back in

Tebbets, Ruth
178e Work: Its meaning for women's lives
380j Poverty, work, and mental health: The experience of low-income mothers

Tedesco, Lisa A.
295i Women's health issues

Tedesco, Marie
126f A feminist challenge to Darwinism: Antoinette L. B. Blackwell on the relations of the sexes in nature and society

Teiman, Michelle L.
189i The oldest, the most established, the most quantitative of the social sciences - and most dominated by men; The impact of feminism on economics

Teish, Luisah
150nn Women's spirituality: A household act
301n Ole black Emelda (fiction)

Tellis, Bernie
91p Sex roles defined: As others see us

Tellis-Nayak, Jessie B.
91u Women community workers

Temin, Carolyn Engel
392k Discriminatory sentencing of women offenders: The argument for ERA in a nutshell

Tennant, Lorna
333k Women and land rights: Kiuk and Wagaidj women in the Darwin area

Tenopyr, M. L.
49e Implications of the increasing participation of women in the work force in the 1990's

Tentori, Tullio
194e An Italian religious feast: The *Fujenti* rites of the Madonna dell'Arco, Naples

Teoh, S.K.
183j Sexual offences

Terborg, James R.
425f Socialization experiences of women and men graduate students in male sex-typed career fields

Terborg-Penn, Rosalyn
39o Discrimination against Afro-American women in the woman's movement, 1830-1920
81l Discontented black feminists: Prelude and postscript to the passage of the nineteenth amendment

Terrelonge, Pauline
344ff Feminist consciousness and black women

Terry, Tremaine
326f Clinical intervention with boy victims of sexual abuse

Tesch, P.
372q Short time, maximal muscular performance: Relation to muscle lactate and fiber type in females

Tesser, Abraham
24d Perceptual and cognitive mechanisms in human sexual attraction

Tevlin, Helen E.
304g Sex-role stereotypes and female sexual dysfunction

Thadani, Veena N.
420c Female migration: A conceptual framework

Thal, Jodi
29n Weight disorders: Overweight and anorexia

Thibault, G.
372o Specificity of swim training on maximal oxygen uptake: An inter-sex comparison

Thiébaux, Marcelle
313d Foucault's fantasia for feminists: The woman reading

Thomas, Clara
20j *Lady Oracle*: The narrative of a fool-heroine

Thomas, Gerald W.
82e The development process: A holistic approach

Thomas, Kath
13f Queensland public service women

Thomas, Laurence
2l Abortion, slavery, and the law: A study in moral character
275r Sexism and racism: Some conceptual differences

Thomas, Ruth P.
130u The death of an ideal: Female suicides in the eighteenth-century French novel

Thompson, Catherine
457f Women, fertility and the worship of gods in a Hindu village

Thompson, Dorothy
215f Defend us against our defenders: Democracy and security
215q Building on the positives: The USA

Thompson, Ernestine H.
219h Loss and mourning in victims of rape and sexual assault

Thompson, Gayle B.
317h Economic status of late middle-aged widows

Thompson, Grahame
283p Public expenditure and budgetary policy

Thompson, Irene
303l Tilting at windmills in the Quixotic South

Thompson, Jeanie
450n The miracle of realism: The bid for self-knowledge in the fiction of Ellen Gilchrist

Thompson, Jennifer
174r A feminist chautauqua for a rural state

Thompson, Kevin M.
10b Drinking and drinking problems among female adolescents: Patterns and influences

Thompson, Lanny
153l State, collective, and household: The process of accumulation in China, 1949-65

Thompson, Lee Briscoe
20g Minuets and madness: Margaret Atwood's *Dancing Girls*

Thompson, Sally
187f Why English nunneries had no history: A study of the problems of the English nunneries founded after the Conquest

Thompson, Sharon
225v Search for tomorrow: On feminism and the reconstruction of teen romance
231o Garden paths, descents
231s Street dream #1 (story)

Thomson, Judith Jarvis
223k A defense of abortion

Thordarsson, Bodil
437c Sweden

Thoresen, Kari
209u Occupational health and the design of work

Thorne, Barrie
122a Rethinking the ways we teach
171a Language, gender and society: Opening a second decade of research
171k Sex similarities and differences in language, speech, and nonverbal communication: An annotated bibliography
245a Feminist rethinking of the family: An overview
417t Imagining a different world of talk

Thornton, John
370c Sexual demography: The impact of the slave trade on family structure

Thornton, Merle
23l Psychoanalysis and feminist social theory of gender

Thornton, Victoria
285s Establishing a women's group for disabled clients

Thyng, Deborah
186g "The Action of the beautiful": The concept of balance in the writings of May Sarton

Tietze, Christopher
252a Midtrimester abortion: a global view
309i Teenage pregnancies: Looking ahead to 1984

Tiffany, Jennifer
179f Equal opportunity trap

Tiffany, Sharon W.
246a Introduction: Feminist perceptions in anthropology

Tiklicorect, Paula
7t Smokers protest healthism

Tilchen, Maida
397s Lesbians and women's music

Till-Retz, Roberta
169v Labor education and women workers: An international comparison

Tilley, Barbara C.
79c Assessment of risks from DES: An analysis of research on those exposed during pregnancy or in utero

Tillotson, Marcia
109j "A forced solitude": Mary Shelley and the creation of Frankenstein's monster

Tilly, Louise A.
50d Women's work and the family in nineteenth-century Europe
89d Women's work and the family in nineteenth-century Europe
162m Linen was their life: Family survival strategies and parent-child relations in nineteenth-century France
184l Women's work and European fertility patterns

Tinker, Irene
373e New technologies for food-related activities: An equity strategy
400h Energy needs of poor households: An abstract

Tinsley, Adrian
407b Career mapping and the professional development process
407i Getting the best: Conclusions, recommendations, and selected resources

Tintner, Adeline R.
180m Mothers, daughters, and incest in the late novels of Edith Wharton

Tisza, Veronica
8e Incest
284e The sexually misused child

Tobach, Ethel
253a Genes and gender update

Tobias, Sheila
96n Math anxiety and female mental health: Some unexpected links

Tobin, Dianne
377j Career interests and career education: A key to change

Tobin, Sheldon S.
317k Institutionalization of the aged

Tobol, Carol E. W.
180b Kriemhild and Clytemnestra - Sisters in crime or independent women?

Todaro, Michael P.
420c Female migration: A conceptual framework

Todd, Janet
27c Frankenstein's daughter: Mary Shelley and Mary Wollstonecraft

Todd, Judith
229qq On common ground: Native American and feminist spirituality approaches in the struggle to save mother earth

Tolbert, Frank X.
175s Glamor girl called Electra

Tolpin, Martha
314t Wheaton's assessment process: A case study and its lessons

Tomeh, Aida K.
52c A comparative view on the changing position of women in the United States
421f Birth order and alienation among college women in Lebanon

Tomes, Nancy
353gg "Little world of our own": The Pennsylvania Hospital Training School for Nurses, 1895-1907

Tongudai, Pawadee
424p Women migrants in Bangkok: An economic analysis of their employment and earnings

Tonkin, Elizabeth
457i Women excluded? Masking and masquerading in West Africa

Topper, Anne B.
291i Incest: Intake and investigation

Tornqvist, Brita
209k Automation and the quality of work life at the Swedish telephone company: A management view

Törnqvist, Kurt
113k Sweden: The neutral nation

Torre, Susana
203d The appropriation of the house: Changes in house design and concepts of domesticity

Torres, Ida
169o Grievance handling for women stewards

Toth, Andre
359hh Group work with widows

Toth, Susan
359hh Group work with widows

Touba, Jacquiline Rudolph
244c Sex segregation and the women's roles in the economic system: The case of Iran

Touchton, Judy
407e Toward a new era of leadership: The national identification program

Townsey, Roi D.
78w Female patrol officers: A review of the physical capability issue

Tracey, Katherine O.
222g The diary of a web spinner

Tracy, Constance Lever
94h A new Australian working class leadership: The case of Ford Broadmeadows

Trager, Lillian
300h Rural-urban linkages and migration: A Philippines case study

Trager, Natalie P.
472c Social class and the older family member

Transgaard, Henning
380q The attitude of Danish mothers to child care, 1975 to 1979

Traupmann, Jane
411j Motherhood in the middle years: Women and their adult children

Travers, Jeffrey
80d Janus faces day care: Perspectives on quality and cost

Travieso, Lourdes
216i The Puerto Rican family: Its role in cultural transition

Travitsky, Betty S.
180d The new mother of the English renaissance: Her writings on motherhood

Trawick, Eleanor
310j Teenage oppression and reproductive rights

Traylor, Eleanor
40f Music as theme: The jazz mode in the works of Toni Cade Bambara
40qq Music as theme: The blues mode in the works of Margaret Walker

Trebilcot, Joyce
116b Sex roles: The argument from nature
116h Two forms of androgynism
223w Taking responsibility for sexuality

Tregenza, G. S.
345b The physical effects and metabolism of alcohol

Treggiari, Susan
375a Women as property in the early Roman empire

Treichler, Paula A.
356p The construction of ambiguity in *The Awakening*: A linguistic analysis

Treiman, Donald J.
65e Effect of choice of factors and factor weights in job evaluation
65i Assessing pay discrimination using national data

Treloar, Alan E.
51u Predicting the close of menstrual life

Tremayne, Soraya
160f Shell wives in limbo

Trembour, Mary
386d Women in education

Trescott, Martha M.
416l Women engineers in history: Profiles in holism and persistence

Trice, Harrison M.
11f Women employees and job-based alcoholism programs

Trickett, Penelope K.
80j A five-year follow-up of participants in the Yale Child Welfare Research Program

Trilling, Lionel
451d Willa Cather

Trimberger, Ellen Kay
231f Feminism, men, and modern love: Greenwich Village, 1900-1925

Trimbos-Kemper, G. C. M.
240b Regret and reversal of sterilization

Tröger, Annemarie
336j The creation of a female assembly-line proletariat

Troll, Lillian E.
296e A three-generational analysis of change in women's achievement motivation and power
317e Intergenerational relations in later life: A family system approach
411h Social change and equality: The roles of women and economics
472b The psychosocial problems of older women

Trost, Jan
52j The changing role of Swedish women in family and society
105a Changing family and changing society

Trotman, Frances K.
443h Psychotherapy with black women and the dual effects of racism and sexism

Trussell, James
309o Early childbearing and subsequent fertility
309p Economic consequences of teenage childbearing

Tsai, Kathryn A.
401a The Chinese Buddhist monastic order for women: The first two centuries

Tsang, Daniel
15e Reference service for alternative publications
15k Alternative and small publishers view libraries: An empirical study

Tubach, Sally Patterson
32o Verena Stefan's Häutungen: Homoeroticism and feminism

Tubbs, Mark E.
425f Socialization experiences of women and men graduate students in male sex-typed career fields

Tuckwell, Sue
400g Some aspects of mental health of women in Bangladesh

Tudiver, Judith G.
271c Parents and the sex-role development of the preschool child

Tudiver, Sari
18j Country roads take me home: The political economy of wage-labor migration in an eastern Kentucky community
305y More radical with age: Women and education

Tulloch, Patricia
321b Gender and dependency

Tunnadine, Prudence
47d Sex

Turchaninova, S. Ia.
446e The educational and occupational skill level of industrial workers

Turnbull, Annmarie
274i History

Turnbull, Colin M.
340e Mbuti womanhood

Turnbull, Elsie G.
205dd Women at Cominco during the Second World War

Turner, Barbara F.
210d The sexuality of older women

Turner, Carmen
463cc Speech

Turner, Darwin T.
40ff Theme, characterization, and style in the works of Toni Morrison

Turner, Edith
194g Postindustrial Marian pilgrimage

Turner, Joan
220a There comes a time
220l Change, hope and celebration

Turner, Kay
229v Contemporary feminist rituals

Turner, Martha Anne
175c Emily Morgan: Yellow rose of Texas

Turner, Pauline
80h Parents and day care workers: A failed partnership?

Turner, Victor
194g Postindustrial Marian pilgrimage

Turshen, Meredeth
395d Women, food and health in Tanzania: A crisis of the 1980s

Tuten, Jeff M.
113b Germany and the World Wars
113m The argument against female combatants

Tutton, Anne
167k Organising a mass lobby of Parliament: Families against the bomb

Twort, Hazel
227g Women and the family

Tyack, David B.
90h Jobs and gender: A history of the structuring of educational employment by sex

Tybout, Alice M.
463k Role influence in transportation decision making

Tyler, Anne
474a Still just writing

Tynan, Barbara J.
333m Women in the health role

Ubaidullaeva, R. A.
446h The twenty-fifth congress of the CPSU and current problems of employment of female labor in the republics of central Asia

Udry, J. Richard
28g Epidemiological patterns of sexual behavior in the menstrual cycle

Uffen, Ellen Serlen
27b The art of *Mansfield Park*

Uglow, Jenny
125i Josephine Butler: From sympathy to theory

Ugwuegbu, Denis C.
265p Effectiveness of self-persuasion in producing healthy attitudes towards polygyny

Ullman, Joseph C.
425b Hard-hatted women: Reflections on blue-collar employment

Ullrich, Helen E.
402k Etiquette among women in Karnataka: Forms of address in the village and the family

Umansky, Ellen M.
462aa Reflections on the creation of a ritual meal

Umiker-Sebeok, Jean
136k The seven ages of woman: A view from American magazine advertisements

Underwood, June O.
384a The civilizers: Women's organizations and western American literature

Underwood, Marilyn
175f The ghost of Chipita: The crying woman of San Patricio

Unger, Rhoda Kesler
190h Physical attractiveness and physical stigma: Menstruation and the common cold
443j Hidden assumptions in theory and research on women

Ungerson, Clare
170b Why do women care?
241e Women and caring: Skills, tasks and taboos

United States Office of Personnel Management
288k Policy statement and definition of sexual harassment

University of Montana
441k Women and technology project, Missoula, Montana

University of Pennsylvania
261g Faculty grievance procedure

Unkeless, Elaine
409g The conventional Molly Bloom

Upton, Julia
462z Guidelines for planners of ritual

Urbanski, Marie Mitchell Olesen
125e Margaret Fuller: Feminist writer and revolutionary

Urbick, Thelma
287e Sexuality verboten: Young and old

Urdaneta, Maria-Luisa
82h Income-generating projects
319b Chicana use of abortion: The case of Alcala

Urdang, Stephanie
6j Women in contemporary national liberation movements
39f The role of women in the revolution in Guinea-Bissau

Urkowitz, Steven
399r Uta Hagen and Eva Le Gallienne

Uslaner, Eric, M.
173f Public support for pro-choice abortion policies in the nation and states: Changes and stability after the *Roe* and *Doe* decisions

Uys, J.M.
52q The changing position of black women in South Africa

Vacca, Linnea
122n Finding one's way through the labyrinth: A symposium on women's lives: Life stories
254j The problem: Idealism and accommodation in the feminist transformation of the academy

Vajrathon, Mallica
77b Creative women in economic and social change

Valcárcel, Jenny
172l The broken wing (Peru)

Valentine, Bettylou
60r Women on welfare: Public policy and institutional racism

Valenzuela, Luisa
74i The word, that milk cow (essay)
313f Mis brujas favoritas

Valeska, Lucia
43b The future of female separatism
43g If all else fails, I'm still a mother
195e If all else fails, I'm still a mother

Valian, Virginia
275e Linguistics and feminism

Valverde, Lucia
54f Feminist therapy with female alcoholics

Van Der Velden, John
94i Migrant communities and class politics: The Greek community in Australia

Van Dyne, Susan R.
314f Project on women and social change: Smith College

van Esser, M.
107q Somatic and motor characteristics of female gymnasts

Van Esterik, John
431b Women meditation teachers in Thailand

Van Esterik, Penny
300e The infant formula controversy in southeast Asia: Advocacy confrontation or applied anthropology?
431c Laywomen in Theravada Buddhism

van Hall, E. V.
252t Some considerations on the psychosocial aspects of pregnancy termination

Van Hezewijk, W. J. V.
159b Female criminality in the Netherlands

Van Hooft, Karen S.
313q Vipers, victims, and virgins: Women and their relationships with men in the poetry of Nicanor Parra

Van Kirk, Sylvia
168d What has the feminist perspective done for Canadian history?

Vance, Carole S.
225a Pleasure and danger: Toward a politics of sexuality
231w Gender systems, ideology, and sex research

Vance, Norman
143f Law, religion and the unity of *Felix Holt*

Vanderauwera, Ria
188h The Brabant mystic: Hadewijch

Vandiver, Susan T.
455b A herstory of women in social work

Vanek, Joann
89c Time spent in housework
355l Household work, wage work, and sexual equality

Vannicelli, Marsha
10m Treatment outcome of alcoholic women: The state of the art in relation to sex bias and expectancy effects

Vartuli, Sue A.
222a A professional socialization process

Vásquez, Carlos
192d Women in the Chicano movement

Vatuk, Sylvia
255b Purdah revisited: A comparison of Hindu and Muslim interpretations of the cultural meaning of purdah in South Asia

402m The aging woman in India: Self-perceptions and changing roles

Vaughn, Richard
461q Voluntary childlessness

Vaught, Bonny
30d Trying to make things real

Vaughter, Reesa M.
266h All things being equal, a behavior is superior to an attitude: Studies of sex-typed and sex-biased attitudes and behaviors

Vázquez, Mario F.
192n The election day immigration raids at Lilli Diamond Originals and the response of the ILGWU

Ve, Hildur
217g Women's mutual alliances, altruism as a premise for interaction

Veaux, Alexis de
150e The sisters

Velamkunnel, Joseph
91s Religious women in North India

Veld-Langeveld, H. M. in't
52d The position of women in the Netherlands: Marginal change

Velez, Carlos G.
192i Se me acabó la canción: An ethnography of non-consenting sterilizations among Mexican women in Los Angeles
319o The nonconsenting sterilization of Mexican women in Los Angeles: Issues of psychocultural rupture and legal redress in paternalistic behavioral environments

Velocherry, Joseph
161h Women and mass media in Kerala

Vengroff, Linda
82r Curriculum: Preparation for involvement

Vengroff, Richard
82r Curriculum: Preparation for involvement

Verdun-Jones, Simon N.
276f Ethics and ethical dilemmas in the treatment of sex offenders

Verheyden-Hilliard, Mary Ellen
73k Achieving the dreams beyond tradition: Counseling white ethnic American girls
316k Education, girls, and power

Verhulst, Johan
137n Gender and sexual functioning

Vernier, Bernard
162b Putting kin and kinship to good use: The circulation of goods, labour, and names on Karpathos (Greece)

Veroff, Joseph
45f Psychological orientations to the work role: 1957-1976

Versluysen, Margaret Connor
248h Old wives' tales? Women healers in English history
396b Midwives, medical men and 'poor women labouring of child': Lying-in hospitals in eighteenth-century London

Verstappen, F. T. J.
372r Reproducibility of aerobic power and related physiological variables in women

Vertinsky, Patricia
147l The effect of changing attitudes toward sexual morality upon the promotion of physical education for women in nineteenth century America

Vervaecke, H.
107n Some differences between men and women in various factors which determine swimming performance

Vetter, Betty M.
361b Labor force participation of women baccalaureates in science
416d Changing patterns of recruitment and employment

Vetterling-Braggin, Mary
432h Cooperative competition in sport

Vicinus, Martha
124a Rediscovering the "New Woman" of the 1890's: The stories of "George Egerton"

Vickers, Jill McCalla
120a Memoirs of an ontological exile: The methodological rebellions of feminist research
228c Canada

Vida, Judith E.
461p Discussion: The developmental crisis of pregnancy

Viera, Silvia
72m The need for an anthropological and cognitive approach to the education of Hispanic women

Vigil, Diego
319j Cultural styles and adolescent sex role perceptions: An exploration of responses to a value picture projective test

Vila, Mayra E.
469j The emerging Cuban women of Florida's Dade County

Vincent, Sybil Korff
109i The mirror and the cameo: Margaret Atwood's comic/gothic novel, *Lady Oracle*

Vingilis, Evelyn
271p Feeling states and the menstrual cycle

Vinovskis, Maris A.
173e Abortion and the presidential election of 1976: A multivariate analysis of voting behavior
173g The politics of abortion in the House of Representatives in 1976

Viviano, Ann T.
65c Some psychological factors affecting job segregation and wages

Vladeck, Judith P.
261a Litigation: Strategy of the last resort

Voda, Ann M.
51j Menopausal hot flash

Voets, Annemieke
76f Women's struggles in the third world

Vogel, Lise
369i Marxism and feminism: Unhappy marriage, trial separation or something else?

Vogel, William
239c Gonadal hormones and cognitive functioning

Vogeler, Martha S.
142g The choir invisible: The poetics of humanist piety

Voght, Martha
353b Women, menstruation, and nineteenth-century medicine

Vogler, Thomas A.
196l "A spirit, yet a woman too!": Dorothy and William Wordsworth

Vohanka, Sue
305l Getting organized...in the Confederation of Canadian Unions

Volkov, A. G.
446l Changes in the status of women and the demographic development of the family

Von Glinow, Mary Ann
267e Career concepts and human resource management: The case of the dual-career couple

Von-Harder, Gudrun Martius
98g Field research on women in the Comilla District, Bangladesh

von Werlhof, Claudia
153h The proletarian is dead: Long live the housewife?

Voogd, Lourina de
322d Arab literature in North Africa

Voydanoff, Patricia
243l Unemployment and family stress

Vries, Petra de
76a The women's movement and motherhood

Vroman, Georgine M.
253k The health of older women in our society

Wade, Susan
157j Helena Gutteridge: Votes for women and trade unions
205cc Joan Kennedy and the British Columbia Women's Service Corps

Wade-Gayles, Gloria
38f She who is black and mother: In sociology and fiction, 1940-1970

Wadley, Susan S.
232f The paradoxical powers of Tamil women
325g Hindu women's family and household rites in a north Indian village

Wagner, Kurt
144d Family and household: Social structures in a German village between the two World Wars

Wagner, Linda W.
20e The making of *Selected Poems*, the process of surfacing
180l Ellen Glasgow: Daughter as justified

Wagner, Maria M.
32f A German writer and feminist in nineteenth century America: An archival study of Mathilde Franziska Anneke

Wagner, Roland M.
319k Social networks and survival strategies: An exploratory study of Mexican American, black and Anglo family female heads in San Jose, California

Wagner, Sally Roesch
7c Pornography and the sexual revolution: The backlash of sadomasochism

Wagnerová, Alena K.
52n Women in Czechoslovakia

Waheed, Jameelah
150jj Black lesbian/feminist organizing: A conversation

Wahlstrom, Billie J.
124k Split brain research and its implications for feminist education

Wainwright, Hilary
215n The women who wire up the weapons: Workers in armament factories
227o 'The housewife and her labour under capitalism' - a critique
378o Beyond leadership

Waite, Linda J.
272m Occupational desegregation in CETA programs

Waites, Elizabeth A.
140j Female masochism and the enforced restriction of choice

Wajcman, Judy
418a Work and the family: Who gets 'the best of both worlds'?

Wakeman, Mary K.
462t Affirming diversity and Biblical tradition

Walby, Sylvia
139j Patriarchal structures: The case of unemployment

Waldman, Elizabeth
192w Appendix: Profile of the Chicana: A statistical fact sheet

Waldman, Gloria Feiman
74d Affirmation and resistance: Women poets from the Caribbean

Waldron, Ingrid
137o Gender, psychophysiological disorders, and mortality
354f Employment and women's health: An analysis of causal relationships

Waletzky, Lucy R.
285m Sexual rehabilitation after gynecologic cancer

Walker, Alan
170f Care for elderly people: A conflict between women and the state

Walker, Alice
7z A letter of the times, or should this sadomasochism be saved?
14e One child of one's own: A meaningful digression within the work(s) - an excerpt
30y Looking for Zora
40mm *Writing The Color Purple*
150oo Only justice can stop a curse
474i *One* child of one's own: A meaningful digression within the work(s)

Walker, Ann
204d The ecology of day care

Walker, Beverly M.
189h Psychology and feminism - if you can't beat them, join them

Walker, Corlette R.
389e Margaret Fuller (1810-1850): Her work as an art critic

Walker, Gillian A.
359i The psychiatrist-woman patient relationship

Walker, Lenore E.
360j Violence against women: Implications for mental health policy
365n Battered women

Walker, Margaret
474g On being female, black, and free

Walker, Stephen
138a Gender, class and education: A personal view

Walker, Susan
156f Women and housing in classical Greece: The archaeological evidence

Walker, Tillie
70g American Indian children: Foster care and adoptions

Walker-Crawford, Vivienne
7r The saga of Sadie O. Massey

Walkerdine, Valerie
134g Some day my prince will come

Walkowitz, Judith R.
60b Male vice and female virtue: Feminism and the politics of prostitution in nineteenth-century Britain
231cc Male vice and female virtue: Feminism and the politics of prostitution in nineteenth-century Britain
439h The politics of prostitution

Wall, Cheryl A.
17q Zora Neale Hurston: Changing her own words
442i Poets and versifiers, singers and signifiers: Women of the Harlem Renaissance

Wall, Naomi
305a The last ten years: A personal/political view

Wallace, Irene
75e Working women in India

Wallace, Louise
240i Psychological preparation for gynaecological surgery

Wallace, Michele
14b A black feminist's search for sisterhood

Wallace, Phyllis A.
426a Increased labor force participation of women and affirmative action

Wallach, Stephanie
376c The crime of precocious sexuality: Female juvenile delinquency and the progressive era

Wallerstein, Immanuel
153a Household structures and labor-force formation in the capitalist world-economy

Wallihan, James
169r How to choose and use materials in education for women workers

Wallsgrove, Ruth
12k The masculine face of science

Wallston, Barbara Strudler
266c Overview of research methods

Walmsley, Robyn
23d Women, feminism and the political process

Walsh, Diana Chapman
447a Genesis and highlights of a conference
447p Challenges to corporate policy

Walsh, Eileen P.
263e "For love and money both": Women's work-related decisions in twentieth century Minneapolis

Walsh, Mary Ellen Williams
384p The young girl in the West: Disenchantment in Jean Stafford's short fiction

Walsh, Mary Roth
34k The quirks of a woman's brain
353aa Feminist showplace

Walsh, Susan
205z The peacock and the guinea hen: Political profiles of Dorothy Gretchen Steeves and Grace MacInnis

Walsh, Vivien
12i Contraception: The growth of a technology

Walshok, Mary Lindenstein
307t Blue collar women

Walter, Harriet
381a Right out in front

Walters, D. B.
334f The European legal context of the Welsh law of matrimonial property

Walters, Esperanza Garcia
319l Health and illness perceptions of the Chicana

Walters, Ronald G.
238f The erotic South: Civilization and sexuality in American abolitionism

Waltner, Ann
401h Widows and remarriage in Ming and early Qing China

Walton, Shirley
225r The misunderstanding: Toward a more precise sexual vocabulary

Walton, Whitney
353k "Down to death door's": Women's perceptions of childbirth in America

Walzl, Florence L.
409b *Dubliners*: Women in Irish society

Wandersee, Winifred D.
81b The economics of middle-income family life: Working women during the Great Depression

Wang, Bee-Lan Chan
68f Chinese women: The relative influences of ideological revolution, economic growth, and cultural change

Wangerin, Ruth Elizabeth
417n Women in the Children of God: "Revolutionary women" or "Mountin' maids"?

Warburton, Janet R.
29o Female delinquents

Ward Jr., Jerry W.
40x Escape from Trublem: The fiction of Gayl Jones

Ward, Audrey
44a The bimodal career
44g Physiotherapy
44i Summing Up

Ward, David A.
392f Crimes of violence by women

Ward, Jonathan B.
233m Animal and human studies in genetic toxicology

Ward, Mary J.
427b The importance of early care

Ward, Reneé E.
392f Crimes of violence by women

Ward, Richard
279l Human proportionality and sexual dimorphism

Ward, Shirley
58e Women in education

Ward-Mckinlay, Candace
281g Sexuality and disability

Ward-McKinlay, Thomas
281g Sexuality and disability

Ware, Norma C.
344z Sexism and the English language: The linguistic implications of being a woman

Waring, Joan
210k Family relationships of older women: A women's issue

Warlick, Jennifer L.
46e The double-decker alternative for eliminating dependency under social security

Warner, Nigel
235e Parliament and the law

Warren, Ann K.
187j The nun as anchoress: England, 1100-1500

Warren, Jill
155c Zola's view of prostitution in *Nana*

Warren, Kay Barbara
388i Rural women and development planning in Peru

Warren, Larissa Bonfante
419j The women of Etruria

Warren, Marguerite Q.
165g Delinquency causation in female offenders

Warren, Mary Anne
116i Is androgyny the answer to sexual stereotyping?
432a Justice and gender in school sports
432d Reply to Moulton and Lemos

Warren, Michelle P.
190r Clinical aspects of menarche: Normal variations and common disorders

Warren, Robert Penn
451e Irony with a center: Katherine Anne Porter
451h Love and separateness in Eudora Welty

Warshak, Richard A.
204j   Social development and parent-child interaction in father-custody and stepmother families

Warshaw, Leon J.
447f   Employee health services for women workers

447o   Non-medical issues presented by the pregnant worker

Wartella, Ellen
391c   Children's impressions of television mothers

Washbourn, Penelope
118d   The dynamics of female experience: Process models and human values

Washington, Ida H.
180b   Kriemhild and Clytemnestra - Sisters in crime or independent women?

Washington, Mary Helen
14t   Teaching *Black-eyed Susans*: An approach to the study of black women writers

196g   I sign my mother's name: Alice Walker, Dorothy West and Paule Marshall

332n   Plain, black, and decently wild: The heroic possibilities of *Maud Martha*

Waskow, Arthur I.
211v   Feminist Judaism: Restoration of the moon

Wasserstrom, Janice
26b   Conjoint therapy for the treatment of domestic violence

Wasserstrom, Richard
223d   Is adultery immoral?

Watkins, Bari
311d   Feminism: A last chance for the humanities?

312f   Feminism: A last chance for the humanities?

399d   Rites and rights

Watriss, Wendy
301v   It's something inside you

Watson, Dwight
122p   Ibsen's *A Doll's House*: A directorial perspective on performing Nora

Watson, Jacqui
345f   Response and recognition

Watt, Ian
378b   Industrial radicalism and the domestic division of labor

Wattenberg, Esther
359aa   Female-headed families: Trends and implications

Watts, Meredith W.
35a   Introduction: Biopolitics and gender

Weathers, Brenda
11j   Alcoholism and the lesbian community

16k   Alcoholism and the lesbian community

Weaver, Jerry L.
354d   Sexism and racism in the American health care industry: A comparative analysis

Weaver, Juanita
229x   Images and models - in process

229hh   Dimensions of spirituality

Webb, Lillian Ashcraft
367f   Black women and religion in the colonial period

Webb, Michael
258f   The labour market

Webb, Peter
278d   Victorian erotica

Webber, Jonathan
457h   Between law and custom: Women's experience of Judaism

Webbink, Patricia
136l   Nonverbal behavior and lesbian/gay orientation

Weber, Maria
228h   Italy

Weber, Ronald E.
173f   Public support for pro-choice abortion policies in the nation and states: Changes and stability after the *Roe* and *Doe* decisions

Webster, Ellen Low
91w   Church and women: A course

Webster, John C. B.
91w   Church and women: A course

Webster, Paula
225w   The forbidden: Eroticism and taboo

Weems, Renita
150o   Artists without art form

Weeramunda, A. J.
194l   The milk overflowing ceremony in Sri Lanka

Weg, Ruth B.
289a   Introduction: Beyond intercourse and orgasm

289c   The physiological perspective

Weibel, Joan Crofut
461e   Discussion: Myths in the midst of missing data

Weick, Ann
434p   Issues of power in social work practice

Weikart, David P.
216r   Organizing delivery of parent education

Weiler, N. Sue
201f   The uprising in Chicago: The men's garment workers strike, 1910-1911

Wein, Alan J.
277h   Evaluation and treatment of impotence: The urologist's viewpoint

Weinbaum, Batya
417q   Twin Oaks: A feminist looks at indigenous socialism in the United States

Weiner, Annette B.
347k   Stability in banana leaves: Colonization and women in Kiriwina, Trobriand Islands

Weiner, Elizabeth
201l   A stitch in our time: New York's Hispanic garment workers in the 1980s

Weiner, Gaby
125d   Harriet Martineau: A reassessment

125o   Vida Goldstein: The women's candidate

Weinraub, Marsha
304c   The development of sex-role stereotypes in children: Crushing realities

Weinreich-Haste, Helen
193p   The image of science

Weir, Ann Lowry
155g   Courtesans and prostitutes in South Asian literature

Weir, Lorraine
20d   Meridians of perception: A reading of *The Journals of Susanna Moodie*

Weisberg, D. Kelly
375f   Under great temptations here: Women and divorce law in puritan Massachusetts

375j   Barred from the bar: Women and legal education in the United States, 1870-1890

Weise, Selene Harding-Curd
249b   To file of not to file

Weisman, Ellen
122j   A comparison of the movements toward equality in Yugoslavia and England

Weisman, Leslie Kanes
174t   The women's school of planning and architecture

Weiss, Carol L.
426d   Sex differences in factors affecting managerial career advancement

Weiss, Gillian
157n   Women and reform in British Columbia: Some preliminary suggestions

205m   The brightest women of our land: Vancouver clubwomen 1919-1928

Weiss, Kay
354c   Vaginal cancer: An iatrogenic disease?

Weiss, Lawrence J.
289g   Intimacy and adaptation

Weissman, Judith
27g   "Old maids have friends": The unmarried heroine of Trollope's Barsetshire novels

Weissman, Myrna M.
8l   Depression in women: Epidemiology, explanations, and impact on the family

96m   The treatment of depressed women: The efficacy of psychotherapy

191d   Depressions among women: Their nature and causes

359m   Sex differences and the epidemiology of depression

365d   Depression

Weisstein, Naomi
34l   Adventures of a woman in science

Weist, Katherine
148b   Beasts of burden and menial slaves: Nineteenth century observations of Northern Plains Indian women

Weitz, Rose
344x   What price independence? Social reactions to lesbians, spinsters, widows, and nuns

397o   From accommodation to rebellion: The politicization of lesbianism

Weitz, Shirley
136e Sex differences in body movements and positions

Weitzel, Joan
404f The sparse ghetto: Service delivery in a rural area

Weitzel, Renate
260j Labour market policy in four countries: Are women adequately represented?

Weitzman, Lenore J.
344k Sex-role socialization: A focus on women

Wekerle, Gerda R.
203f Introduction: Urban design: The price women pay

Welch, Paula
147bb Interscholastic basketball: Bane of collegiate physical educators
147mm American women: Their debut in international track and field

Welcher, Wayne H.
309x Teenagers: Fertility control behavior and attitudes before and after abortion, childbearing or negative pregnancy test

Welles, Marcia L.
408n The changing face of woman in Latin American fiction

Wellman, Judith
61g Women and radical reform in antebellum upstate New York: A profile of grassroots female abolitionists

Wells, Mary Cay
222j Grandma! What big plans you've got!: The older woman's Ph.D. experience

Welter, Barbara
454i The cult of true womanhood: 1820-1860

Welton, Nancy R.
360b Female psychologists in policymaking positions

Welty, Eudora
451f The eye of the story

Wender, Dorothea
419i Plato: Misogynist, phaedophile, and feminist

Werden, Frieda
175n Martha White McWhirter and the Belton Sanctificationists

Werley, Harriet H.
309s Contraception, abortion and venereal disease: Teenagers' knowledge and the effect of education

Werner, Karla
203j Swedish women in single-family housing

Wertheim, Albert
399y The comic muse of Mary Chase

Wertheimer, Barbara M.
93j Leadership training for union women in the United States: Route to equal opportunity
169g Residential schools
292i To rekindle the spirit: Current education programs for women workers
344r "Union is power": Sketches from women's labor history
382k The United States of America

Wertheimer, Roger
2f Understanding Blackmun's argument: The reasoning of *Roe v Wade*

Wertz, Dorothy C.
36m Man-midwifery and the rise of technology: The problem and proposals for resolution

Wessman, James W.
18i Neo-Malthusian ideology and colonial capitalism: Population dynamics in southwestern Puerto Rico

West, Candace
171g Small insults: A study of interruptions in cross-sex conversations between unacquainted persons

West, Celeste
15j Publishers on libraries: The library as motherlode: A feminist view

West, Donald J.
219a The victim's contribution to sexual offences

West, Jackie
470d New technology and women's office work

West, John O.
175d The weeping woman: La Llorona

West, Louis Jolyon
327f Discussion: Violence and the family in perspective

Westergaard, Kirsten
98b Research on women in Bangladesh: Notes on experiences from the field
400b Rural pauperization: Its impact on the economic role and status of rural women in Bangladesh

Westkott, Marcia
312m Women's studies as a strategy for change: Between criticism and vision

Westman, Berith
209l Automation and the quality of work life at the Swedish telephone company: A union view

Westoff, Charles F.
309j Some speculations on the future of marriage and fertility

Westwood, Sallie
364h 'Fear woman': Property and modes of production in urban Ghana

Wetzel, Janice Wood
434a Redefining concepts of mental health

Wevers, Lydia
413k Pioneer into feminist: Jane Mander's heroines

Wexler, Sandra
435j Battered women and public policy

Whatley, Janet
64d Colette and the art of survival

Wheatley, Margaret
90o The impact of organizational structures on issues of sex equity

Wheaton, Liz
301oo Queen of the road

Wheeler, Leslie
125g Lucy Stone: Radical beginnings

Wheeler, Lynn Stoner
363a In defense of motherhood: Divorce law in Cuba during the early republic

Wheeler, William H.
287f Black sexuality

Wheeler-Bennett, Joan
47g Work

Wheelock, Martha
30x May Sarton: A metaphor for my life, my work, and my art

Whelan, Mary K.
263a Women and welfare work: Demystifying the myth of disembeddedness

Whelen, Gloria
157g Maria Grant, 1854-1937: The life and times of an early twentieth century Christian

Whetmore, Edward
131m A female captain's enterprise: The implications of *Star Trek's* "Turnabout Intruder"

Whip, Rosemary
23f The Parliamentary wife: Participant in the 'two-person single career'

Whisnant, Lynn
359w A study of attitudes toward menarche in white middle-class American adolescent girls

Whissen, Thomas
155d The magic circle: The role of the prostitute in Isak Dinesen's *Gothic Tales*

Whitbeck, Caroline
31d A different reality: Feminist ontology
79q Response
195k The maternal instinct (1972) & Afterword (1982)

White, Barbara W.
434f Black women: The resilient victims

White, Charles S. J.
325c Mother Guru: Jnanananda of Madras, India

White, E. Frances
385a Women, work, and ethnicity: The Sierra Leone case

White, Elizabeth S.
35e Sex, endocrines, and political behavior

White, Garland F.
349t Police processing of female offenders

White, Julie
323g Part-time work and unions

White, Kate
13i Women and unions in Australia

White, Luise
6d Women in the changing African family

White, Michelle J.
463h Women's work trips: An empirical and theoretical overview

White, Thomas I.
383i Opposing necessity and truth: The argument against politics in Doris Lessing's utopian vision

Whiteford, Linda
319g Mexican American women as innovators

Whitehead, Ann
207f   'I'm hungry, mum': The politics of domestic budgeting
208a   Introduction: The continuing subordination of women in the development process
208f   'I'm hungry, mum': The politics of domestic budgeting
364j   Men and women, kinship and property: Some general issues

Whitehead, Harriet
282a   Introduction: Accounting for sexual meanings
282c   The bow and the burden strap: A new look at institutionalized homosexuality in native North America

Whitehead, Paul C.
9d   Sex differences in psychoactive drug use: Recent epidemiology

Whiteman, Henrietta V.
70a   Insignificance of humanity, "Man is tampering with the moon and the stars": The employment status of American Indian women

Whiting, Beatrice Blyth
411l   Problems of American middle-class women in their middle years: A comparative approach

Whittaker, Jo Ann
205v   The search for legitimacy: Nurses' registration in British Columbia 1913-1935

Whittier, Gayle
135n   Mistresses and madonnas in the novels of Margaret Dabble

Whyatt, Frances
417s   The craft of their hands

Whyld, Janie
274a   School life - Organization and control
274c   Subject image, examinations and teaching materials
274k   Social studies
274q   Sex education
274r   Physical education
274t   More than one way forward

Whyte, Judith
193u   Sex typing in schools

Whyte, Susan Reynolds
457j   Men, women and misfortune in Bunyole

Wickert, Gabriele
158b   Freud's heritage: Fathers and daughters in German literature (1750-1850)

Wickham, Ann
50j   The state and training programmes for women

Widmark-Peterson, V.
265j   Cross-sex friendship in the elementary school

Widmer, Kingsley
318b   The wages of intellectuality . . . and the fictional wagers of Iris Murdoch

Widom, Cathy Spatz
268a   Sex roles and psychopathology
268i   Sex roles, criminality, and psychopathology

Wiegand, Karl L.
113i   Japan: Cautious utilization

Wiesenfarth, Joseph
142f   Antique Gems from *Romola* to *Daniel Deronda*

Wieser, Nora Jasquez
68j   Ancient song, new melody in Latin America: Women and film

Wiget, Barbara
103e   Women and the Reagan revolution: Thermidor for the social welfare economy

Wigfall, Valerie
44c   Architecture

Wikler, Daniel
2m   Abortion, privacy, and personhood: From *Roe v Wade* to the human life statute

Wikler, Norma Juliet
387i   Commitment and cultural mandate: Women in medicine

Wilbanks, William
165f   Murdered women and women who murder: A critique of the literature

Wilberger, Carolyn Hope
130z   The view from Russia

Wilke, Gerhard
144d   Family and household: Social structures in a German village between the two World Wars

Wilkerson, Margaret B.
41a   Working women in the United States: A look at the facts
407f   Lifting as we climb: Networks for minority women

Wilkerson, Sarah
301x   Prostitution II: Not no easy business

Wilkin, Margaret
258e   Educational opportunity and achievement

Wilkins, Mary Catherine
399ss   The Washington area feminist theatre

Wilkinson, Doris Y.
365l   Minority women: Social-cultural issues

Wilkinson, Patricia
9i   Sex differences in morbidity of alcoholics

Willams, Carol N.
10j   Female alcohol abuse: Its effects on the family

Willard, Charity C.
154c   Christine de Pizan and Order of the Rose
154e   Christine de Pizan's *Livre des Trois Vertus*: Feminine ideal or practical advice?
188o   The Franco-Italian professional writer: Christine de Pizan

Williams, Agnes F.
70j   Transition from the reservation to an urban setting and the changing roles of American Indian women

Williams, Ann Marie
28h   Sexual behavior and the menstrual cycle
326k   Marital and sexual dysfunction following rape: Identification and treatment

Williams, David
40ll   The poetry of Sonia Sanchez

Williams, Delores S.
462k   Women as makers of literature

Williams, Dyfri
156g   Women on Athenian vases: Problems of interpretation

Williams, Gregory D.
28h   Sexual behavior and the menstrual cycle

Williams, Jan
227g   Women and the family

Williams, Jane
115f   Jesus the Jew and women

Williams, Katherine
248c   From Sarah Gamp to Florence Nightingale: A critical study of hospital nursing systems from 1840 to 1897

Williams, Lenore R.
190l   Beliefs and attitudes of young girls regarding menstruation

Williams, Linda
247a   Feminist film criticism: An introduction
247e   When the woman looks

Williams, Nudie
414i   The gender liberation: Black women as elected officials in Oklahoma

Williams, Ora
14y   American black women composers: A selected annotated bibliography

Williams, Peg
262g   Laws prohibiting sex discrimination in schools

Williams, Robert E.
66g   The legal framework
67g   The legal framework

Williams, Rosalind
222h   In and out of relationships: A serious game for the woman doctoral student

Williams, Rowan
115a   Women and the ministry: A case for theological seriousness

Williams, Sherley Anne
17r   Papa Dick and Sister-Woman: Reflections on women in the fiction of Richard Wright

Williams, Susan
224i   Lesbianism: A socialist feminist perspective

Williams, Yvonne
122i   Levels of female criminal activity as a correlate of female societal power

Williamson, Nancy E.
273g   Parental sex preferences and sex selection

Willis, Ellen
60v   The challenge of profamily politics: A feminist defense of sexual freedom
231ee   Feminism, moralism, and pornography
231gg   Abortion: Is a woman a person?

Willis, Jean L.
125q   Alice Paul: The quintessential feminist

Willis, Sabine
390g   Homes are divine workshops

Willis, Susan
127i   Eruptions of funk: Historicizing Toni Morrison

Willner, Ann Ruth
21g Expanding women's horizons in Indonesia: Toward maximum equality with minimum conflict

Willson, Sandra A.K.
348i Prisons, prisoners and the community

Wilmore, J. H.
372n Women and sport: An introduction to the physiological aspects

Wilsnack, Richard W.
10b Drinking and drinking problems among female adolescents: Patterns and influences

Wilsnack, Sharon C.
10g Drinking, sexuality, and sexual dysfunction in women
11b Femininity by the bottle
11e Prevention of alcohol problems in women: Current status

Wilson, Boydena R.
379a Glimpses of Muslim urban women in classical Islam

Wilson, Clare
345e The family

Wilson, Colin
278i Literature and pornography

Wilson, Elaine
73c Developing a neighborhood-based health facility

Wilson, Elizabeth
257l I'll climb the stairway to heaven: Lesbianism in the seventies

Wilson, Francille Rusan
385g Reinventing the past and circumscribing the future: *Authenticité* and the negative image of women's work in Zaire

Wilson, Geraldine L.
38t The self/group actualization of black women

Wilson, J. J.
30s Carrington revisited
202h Why is *Orlando* difficult?

Wilson, Joan Hoff
112j Mercy Otis Warren: Playwright, poet, and historian of the American revolution (American, 1728-1814)

Wilson, Katharina M.
188b The Saxon canoness: Hrotsvit of Gandersheim

Wilson, Lynn
462q My voice...and many others

Wilson, Nanci Koser
63f Styles of doing time in a coed prison: Masculine and feminine alternatives
165o Women in the criminal justice profession: An analysis of status conflict

Wilson, Terry P.
414c Women of the Osage: A century of change, 1874-1982

Wilt, Judith
135m The laughter of maidens, the crackle of matriarchs: Notes on the collision between comedy and feminism

Wincze, John P.
29e Sexuality

Windschuttle, Elizabeth
348c Women, crime and punishment
390b 'Feeding the poor and sapping their strength': The public role of ruling-class women in eastern Australia, 1788-1850

Wine, Jeri Dawn
120c Gynocentric values and feminist psychology
271k Female superiority in sex difference competence comparisons: A review of the literature
271l Sex differences in assertiveness: Implications for research and treatment
271m Assertiveness: Sex differences in relationships between self-report and behavioural measures

Winegarten, Ruthe
175e Belle Starr: The Bandit Queen of Dallas

Winer, Lucy
399tt New York feminist theater troupe

Wingard, Deborah L.
53t Sex differences in diabetes mellitus

Winget, W. Gary
80r The dilemma of affordable child care

Wings, Mary
179c The Private Benjamin syndrome
179g The recruitment of women

Winkel, Gary
203b The home: A critical problem for changing sex roles

Winn, Mary Beth
331h Poems by "The Lady" in *La Chasse et le départ d'amours* (1509)

Winslow, Mary Bowes
352p Leadership training for increased effectiveness among women educational administrators: Two local models

Winstead, Barbara Ann
268d Hysteria

Winston, Elizabeth
452f The autobiographer and her readers: From apology to affirmation

Winter, Margaret
274s Remedial education

Winters, Barbara
307z Engineered conception: The new parenthood

Winzeler, Robert L.
431h Sexual status in Southeast Asia: Comparative perspectives on women, agriculture and political organization

Wipper, Audrey
6e Women's voluntary associations
218e Riot and rebellion among African women: Three examples of women's political clout

Wise, Lauress L.
309m Teenage mothers and teenage fathers: The impact of early childbearing on the parents' personal and professional lives

Wise, Sue
312l 'Back into the personal' or: Our attempt to construct 'feminist research'

Wiseman, Jacqueline P.
105k Marriage, estrangement, sobriety and recidivism: Some crucial process variables in the case of alcoholic men and their wives

Wisocki, Patricia A.
29q Aging women

Withey, Lynne E.
375g The law of husband and wife in nineteenth-century America: Changing views of divorce

Withington, Anne F.
19h The political trial

Withuis, Jolande
76e 'The policing of families'

Wittenberg, Judith Bryant
17o William Faulkner: A feminist consideration
450p The career of Joan Williams: Problems in assessment

Wittenstein, Kate
39n Female slave resistance: The economics of sex

Wittner, Judith G.
355j Domestic labor as work discipline: The struggle over housework in foster homes

Wittstock, Laura Waterman
68l Native American women: Twilight of a long maidenhood

Woehrer, Carol
73j Family roles and identities of Scandinavian and German women

Wœrness, Kari
217d Caring as women's work in the welfare state

Wolchik, Sharon L.
228k Eastern Europe
436g Demography, political reform and women's issues in Czechoslovakia

Wolf, Deborah Goleman
397l Lesbian childbirth and woman-controlled conception

Wolf, Diane L.
424j Making the bread and bringing it home: Female factory workers and the family economy

Wolfe, Barry E.
268c Gender ideology and phobias in women

Wolfe, Honor
190u Steroidal contraceptive use and subsequent development of hyperprolactinemia

Wolfe, Linda D.
279h A cross-cultural investigation into the sexual dimorphism of stature

Wolfe, Margie
305x Working with words: Feminist publishing in Canada

Wolfe, Susan J.
171i Consciousness as style: Style as aesthetic

Wolff, Cynthia Griffin
109m The Radcliffean gothic model: A form for feminine sexuality
127b Thanatos and Eros: Kate Chopin's *The Awakening*

Wolffberg, Dorit
229rr Spiritual dimensions of feminist anti-
      nuclear activism

Wolfson, Nessa
356f "Don't 'dear' me!"

Wolstenholme, Susan
17k Brother Theodore, hell on women

Wolverton, Terry
174p Unlearning complicity, remembering resis-
      tance: White women's anti-racism educa-
      tion

Women Working with Immigrant Women
305u A message of solidarity

Women's Community Health Center
16h A pelvic teaching program
36g Woman-controlled birth control: A femi-
      nist analysis of natural birth control

Women's Studies College, SUNY Buffalo
174e All-women classes and the struggle for
      women's liberation

Wong, Aline
424i Women's work: Factory, family and social
      class in an industrializing order

Wong, Diana
153b Subsistence reproduction: A framework
      for analysis
153d The limits of using the household as a unit
      of analysis

Wong, Germaine Q.
71d Impediments to Asian-Pacific-American
      women organizing

Wong, Susan Stone
292b From soul to strawberries: The
      International Ladies' Garment Workers'
      Union and workers' education, 1914-1950

Wong-McCarthy, William
136h Gender, androgyny, and conversational
      assertiveness

Wood, Ann Douglas
353p "The fashionable diseases": Women's com-
      plaints and their treatment in nineteenth-
      century America
454f The war within a war: Women nurses in
      the Union Army

Wood, Elizabeth
30e Music into words

Wood, Julia T.
126d Research on women's communication:
      Critical assessment and recommendations

Wood, Julian
134c Groping towards sexism: Boys' sex talk

Wood, Pamela L.
349k The victim in a forcible rape case: A femi-
      nist view

Wood, Rosemary
70f Health problems facing American Indian
      women

Wood, Suzanne
215e The illusion of protection: Civil defence

Wood, Vivian
411j Motherhood in the middle years: Women
      and their adult children

Woodcock, George
20m Bashful but bold: Notes on Margaret
      Atwood as critic

Woodcroft-Lee, Carlien Patricia
234d Some perceptions of Indonesian women
      under Islam
466i Separate but equal: Indonesian Muslim
      perceptions of the roles of women

Woodman, Natalie Jane
434k Social work with lesbian couples

Woodrow, Sharon
86a The clean, light image of the electronics
      industry: Miracle or mirage?

Woods, Nancy Fugate
51p Menopausal distress: A model for epi-
      demiologic investigation
190f Recollections of menarche, current men-
      strual attitudes, and perimenstrual symp-
      toms

Woodward, Diana
85g The expert's view? The sociological analy-
      sis of graduates' occupational and domes-
      tic roles
250m The experiences of women graduates in
      the labour market

Woodward, Kathleen
135i May Sarton and fictions of old age

Woody, Jane Divita
281d Sexuality in divorce and remarriage

Woody, Robert Henley
281h Ethical and legal aspects of sexual issues

Wooley, Orland W.
341c A woman's body in a man's world: A
      review of findings on body image and
      weight control
365f Eating disorders: Obesity and anorexia

Wooley, Susan C.
341c A woman's body in a man's world: A
      review of findings on body image and
      weight control
365f Eating disorders: Obesity and anorexia

Woolson, Allen M.
287j Sources and prevention of dysfunction

Worell, Judith
304j The resocialization of single-again women
359yy New directions in counseling women

Work, James C.
384t The moral in Austin's *The Land of Little
      Rain*

Working Women's Institute
288h Responses of fair employment practice
      agencies to sexual harassment complaints:
      A report and recommendations

Wormald, Eileen
258a Sex differences and this book
258g Political participation
258i Sex differences in Britain

Wortman, Max S.
425a An overview of the research on women in
      management: A typology and a prospectus

Wozney, Christine
157o Postscript: Huntresses

Wright, Ann L.
51g Variation in Navajo menopause: Toward
      an explanation

Wright, Buff
337l Women and student government

Wright, Fay
170e Single careers: Employment, housework
      and caring

Wright, Gwendolyn
203d The appropriation of the house: Changes
      in house design and concepts of domestici-
      ty

Wright, Lin
399pp Creative drama: Sex role stereotyping?

Wright, Marcia
370n Bwanikwa: Consciousness and protest
      among slave women in Central Africa,
      1886-1911

Wright, Paul A.
420p Female Asian immigrants in Honolulu:
      Adaptation and success

Wright, Richard
219e Police officer or doctor? Police surgeons'
      attitudes and opinions about rape

Wright, Susan
371g Place and face: Of women in Doshman
      Ziari, Iran

Wright, Terence
143b Critical approaches to George Eliot

Wundram, Ina Jane
126o Sex differences in the brain: Implications
      for curriculum change

Wurr, Anne
226j Community responses to violence against
      women: The case of a battered women's
      shelter

Wyant, Spencer H.
90e Clues to sex bias in the selection of school
      administrators: A report from the Oregon
      network

Wyatt, Gail Elizabeth
461b The sexual experience of Afro-American
      women: A middle-income sample

Wydeven, Joseph
384o Wright Morris, women, and American cul-
      ture

Wyndham, Diana
390y Sexism and health care

Wynn, Barbara
274l Home economics

Yanagisako, Sylvia
245b Is there a family? New anthropological
      views

Yankova, Z.A.
52l Soviet women in family and society

Yanz, Lynda
323a Women at work in Canada
323y Building links: Labour and the women's
      movement
323bb Women and unions: A selected bibliogra-
      phy

Yasinski, Lorraine
365h Psychodynamic perspectives

Yates, Barbara A.
385f Colonialism, education, and work: Sex differentiation in colonial Zaire

Yawney, Carole
120f To grow a daughter: Cultural liberation and the dynamics of oppression in Jamaica

Yeatman, Anna
464f Despotism and civil society: The limits of patriarchal citizenship

Yellin, Jean Fagan
14u Afro-American women 1800-1910: A selected bibliography

Yellis, Kenneth A.
454p Prosperity's child: Some thoughts on the flapper

Yengoyan, Aram
124f Transvestitism and the ideology of gender: Southeast Asia and beyond

Yohalem, Alice M.
437e United States

Yoke, Carl
114i From alienation to personal triumph: The science fiction of Joan D. Vinge

Yongue, Patricia Lee
384n Marian Forrester and Moll Flanders: Fortunes and misfortunes

Yorukoglu, Atalay
284k Children not severely damaged by incest with a parent

Young, Elspeth
333r Income and employment for women in remote communities: Examples from the Northern Territory

Young, Gail
396g A woman in medicine: Reflections from the inside

Young, Iris
369c Beyond the unhappy marriage: A critique of the dual systems theory

Young, Iris Marion
195h Is male gender identity the cause of male domination?

Young, Kate
208a Introduction: The continuing subordination of women in the development process
350f The creation of a relative surplus population: A case study from Mexico

Young, Malcolm
160c Police wives: A reflection of police concepts of order and control

Young, Mary E.
61f Women, civilization, and the Indian question

Young, Philip D.
269e New roles for males in Guaymí society

Youngblood, Robert L.
300n Church-military relations in the Philippines

Youngs, David D.
4c Psychiatric aspects of adolescent pregnancy

Youssef, Nadia
82a Critical issues in women in development

Yu, Elena S.H.
421y Variations in women's roles and family life under the socialist regime in China

Yuval-Davis, Nira
179e Sexual division of labour
179k The Israeli example

Yuzpe, A. Albert
252r Sterilization combined with midtrimester abortion

Zabin, Laurie Schwab
30h The risk of adolescent pregnancy in the first months of intercourse

Zacharias, Alexandra
157d British Columbia Women's Institute in the early years: Time to remember

Zaharieva, E.
107m Asymmetry of limb circumferences in female athletes

Zainu'ddin, Ailsa Thomson
166a Kartini - her life, work and influence

Zak, Michele W.
51l Erik Erikson and Doris Lessing: Psychological theory and the female novel of development

Zalesny, Mary D.
425f Socialization experiences of women and men graduate students in male sex-typed career fields

Zaltzberg, Ellen
86n From grassroots activism to political power: Women organizing against environmental hazards

Zambrana, Ruth E.
469a Introduction: Latina women in transition
469h The utilization of pediatric health services by Hispanic mothers

Zamora, Emilio
192q Sara Estela Ramírez: Una rosa roja en el movimiento

Zamora, Gloria
216n The early education of minority children

Zanotti, Barbara
152d Overcoming the structured evil of male domination and heterosexism
254o When we dream together

Zappi, Elda Gentili
379p "If eight hours seems few to you...": Women workers' strikes in Italian rice fields, 1901-1906

Zaremba, Eve
305g Shades of lavender: Lesbian sex and sexuality

Zaretsky, Eli
245k The place of the family in the origins of the welfare state
439v Female sexuality and the Catholic confessional

Zarit, Judy Maes
289f Old and alone: The unmarried in later life

Zavitzianos, George
280g The kleptomanias and female criminality

Zegans, Leonard
359w A study of attitudes toward menarche in white middle-class American adolescent girls

Zegman, Marilyn A.
304i Women, weight, and health

Zeitlin, Froma I.
419g The dynamics of misogyny: Myth and mythmaking in the *Oresteia*

Zeldow, Peter B.
268o Sex roles, psychological assessment, and patient management

Zelkowitz, Phyllis
178k Parenting philosophies and practices
178l The quality of mother-child relationships

Zellman, Gail L.
48c Becoming sexual in adolescence
230j Sexual signaling and sexual aggression in adolescent relationships

Zelnik, Melvin
309d Sexual and contraceptive experience of young unmarried women in the United States, 1976 and 1971
309e First pregnancies to women aged 15-19: 1976 and 1971
309f Contraceptive patterns and premarital pregnancy among women aged 15-19 in 1976
309h The risk of adolescent pregnancy in the first months of intercourse

Zerbe, Louisa
147jj The 1930 U.B.C. women's basketball team: Those other world champions

Zichella, L.
372cc Sport and reproduction in women

Zigler, Edward F.
80h Parents and day care workers: A failed partnership?
80q The battle for day care in America: A view from the trenches

Zihlman, Adrienne L.
340b Women as shapers of the human adaptation

Zikmund, Barbara Brown
366e The struggle for the right to preach

Zilbach, Joan
8b Aggression in women: Conceptual issues and clinical implications
69j Separation: A family developmental process of midlife

Zillmann, Dolf
230e Effects of massive exposure to pornography

Zimmerman, Bonnie
143j Gwendolen Harleth and "The girl of the period"
176s One out of thirty: Lesbianism in women's studies textbooks
180h "The mother's history" in George Eliot's life, literature and political ideology
332l Exiting from patriarchy: The lesbian novel of development
398g Is 'Chloe liked Olivia' a lesbian plot?

Zimmerman, Claire

320g Epistemology and agency in the development of undergraduate women

Zimmerman, Don H.

171g Small insults: A study of interruptions in cross-sex conversations between unacquainted persons

Zimmerman, Jan

174y What are rights without means? Educating feminists for the future

307a Introduction: New technology, old values

307m Living better vicariously?

417r Utopia in question: Programming women's needs into the technology of tomorrow

441f Technology and the future of women: Haven't we met somewhere before?

Zimmerman, Nathalia

281e Homosexual and bisexual issues

Zimmerman, Susan

27f *Sonnets from the Portuguese*: A negative and a positive context

Zimmerman, Veva H.

69d The black woman growing up

Zinberg, Norman E.

69c Changing sex stereotypes

Zirin, Mary Fleming

108h *My childhood years*: A memoir by the czarist cavalry officer, Nadezhda Durova

Zmroczek, Christine

209e Government policies on new information technologies and their implications for employment: An overview of EEC countries, with particular reference to women

Zosa-Feranil, Imelda

424t Female employment and the family: A case study of the Bataan Export Processing Zone

Zschoche, Sue

353bb Professionalism, feminism, and gender roles: A comparative study of nineteenth-century medical therapeutics

Zucker, Stanley

145g Female political opposition in pre-1848 Germany: The role of Kathinka Zitz-Halein

Zurbrigg, Ann

205u Cheap at half the price: The history of the fight for equal pay in BC

Zur-Szpiro, Susan

178j Fathers' support to mothers and children

KEYWORD INDEX

Thirteen of the keywords serve as broad umbrella terms providing "see also" references to a large number of related terms and concepts. Each of these related terms has a single "see also" reference to the umbrella term. For example, Discriminate has ten "see also" references, while Sex Bias has a single "see also" reference to Discriminate.

The following keywords have been used as umbrella terms:

Abuse

Age

Child

Class

Crime

Discriminate

Education

Employment

Family

Law

Pay

Reproduce

Religion

A Priori

65g   Major issues in *a priori* applications

AAUW

see American Association of University Women

Ángel del Hogar

313e   El Ángel del hogar: The cult of domesticity in nineteenth century Spain

A.M.E.

see African Methodist Episcopal

Abnormal

53o   Etiologic factors for invasive and noninvasive cervical abnormalities

279k   Normal and abnormal sexual dimorphic patterns of growth and development

Abolition

61g   Women and radical reform in antebellum upstate New York: A profile of grassroots female abolitionists

238f   The erotic South: Civilization and sexuality in American abolitionism

Aborigine

23b   Black sisterhood: The situation of urban aboriginal women and their relationship to the white women's movement

294f   'Black Velvet': Aboriginal women and their relations with white men in the Northern Territory, 1910-1940

333e   The conflicting role of aboriginal women in today's society

333g   The recent history of the Borroloola aboriginal people and their struggle for land rights

333l   Historical factors which have affected aboriginal lifestyles since colonisation

333n   Study into the needs of aboriginal women who have been raped or sexually assaulted

333o   Aboriginal women's role today in early childhood school education

333p   The Yuendumu aboriginal cultural preschool

333q   Aboriginal women in education

333t   Aboriginal women today

340d   Interpretations and "facts" in aboriginal Australia

390j   'Spinifex fairies': Aboriginal workers in the Northern territory, 1911-39

Abortion

see also Roe v Wade

2e   Personhood and the abortion debate

2h   Constitutional privacy, religious disestablishment, and the abortion decisions

2j   Abortion and self-defense

2k   Abortion and the claims of samaritanism

2l   Abortion, slavery, and the law: A study in moral character

3a   Social science and ethical issues: The policy implications of poll data on abortion

3b   Abortion and the meaning of life

3c   Reflections on abortion, values, and the family

3e   A family perspective on abortion

3i   More trouble than they're worth? Children and abortion

3k   Abortion and equality

3m   Beneath the surface of the abortion dispute: Are women fully human?

3o   Abortion and the culture: Toward a feminist perspective

3q   Abortion, autonomy, and community

3s   Value choices in abortion

3u   The abortion debate: Is progress possible?

31o   Rights-conflict, pregnancy, and abortion

53j   Environmental exposures and spontaneous abortion

60i   The New Right and the abortion issue

96e   The experience of abortion

118e   Becoming human: A contextual approach to decisions about pregnancy and abortion

129p   If you liked gun control, you'll love the antiabortion amendment

173c   The abortion-funding cases and population control: An imaginary lawsuit and some reflections on the uncertain limits of reproductive privacy

173e   Abortion and the presidential election of 1976: A multivariate analysis of voting behavior

173g   The politics of abortion in the House of Representatives in 1976

223k   A defense of abortion

223l   Abortion and a woman's right to decide

223m   Abortion and the golden rule

225k   The body politic: The defense of sexual restriction by anti-abortion activists

231gg   Abortion: Is a woman a person?

252a   Midtrimester abortion: A global view

252b   Second trimester abortion as a social problem: Delay in abortion seeking behaviour and its causes

252d   A review of abortion practices and their safety

252g   Instrumental abortion in the second trimester: An overview

252i   Extra-amniotic ethacridine (Rivanol)-catheter technique for midtrimester abortion

252m   Prostaglandin therapy for second trimester abortion: An overview of current status and recent trends

252o   Complications of second trimester abortion

252p   Prevention of Rhesus (D) isoimmunization after abortion

252q   Contraception following second trimester abortion

252r   Sterilization combined with midtrimester abortion

273c   Sex selection through amniocentesis and selective abortion

307o   Abortion: A domestic technology

309s   Contraception, abortion and venereal disease: Teenagers' knowledge and the effect of education

309x   Teenagers: Fertility control behavior and attitudes before and after abortion, childbearing or negative pregnancy test

310o   Abortion, a woman's matter: An explanation of who controls abortion and how and why they do it

310r   Abortion of a special kind: Male sex selection in India

319b   Chicana use of abortion: The case of Alcala

336c   Abortion and economic crisis: The 1931 campaign against paragraph 218

344c   Abortion: The controversial choice

353h   Patterns of abortion and the response of American physicians, 1790-1930

359ee   Abortion counseling with adolescents

359dd   Abortion counseling

396e   Seizing the means of reproduction: An illegal feminist abortion collective — how and why it worked

418j   Contraception and abortion

456h   Unwanted pregnancy and abortion

Absence

180f   Jane Austen and the tradition of the absent mother

339j   One family's decision: A leave of absence

Abuse

see also Assault, Batter, Beat, Child Abuse, Misuse, Molest, Sexual Abuse, Sexual Assault, Sexual Violence, Violence

8d   Wife abuse: Culture as destiny

8n   Women and alcohol abuse

10c   Alcohol use and abuse in ethnic minority women

10d   Multiple substance abuse among women with alcohol-related problems

10j   Female alcohol abuse: Its effects on the family

26e   Intervention with the abusive partner

26i   Coping with wife abuse: Personal and social networks

34f   Sterilization abuse

36h   Depo-provera and sterilization abuse overview

36k   Sterilization abuse and Hispanic women

36l   Depo-provera and sterilization abuse discussion

78p   Concurrent and consecutive abuse: The juvenile prostitute

103n   The politics of wife abuse

111r   Drug abuse and criminality among women in detention

183i   Abused women

212f   The sexual abuse of children in the home

219b   Incest and sexual abuse of children

295n   Substance abuse in women: Etiology and prevention

310n   Subtle forms of sterilization abuse: A reproductive rights analysis

349o   Secondary battering and alternatives of female victims to spouse abuse

472d   The abused older woman: A discussion of abuses and rape

Academic

see also Education

85h   The gatekeepers: A feminist critique of academic publishing

122h   In search of excellence in academic libraries, or, challenging the henhouse model

160a   Incorporation and exclusion: Oxford academics' wives

160b   Ambivalence and dedication: Academic wives in Cambridge University, 1870-1970

174a   If the mortarboard fits...radical feminism in academia

176a   Dyke in Academe

176b   Black lesbians in academia: Visible invisibility

189l Before and after: The impact of feminism on the academic discipline of law

203o No academic matter: Unconscious discrimination in environmental design education

249e Not by lawyers alone: Ten practical lessons for academic litigants

250l How many women academics 1912-76?

259c The hidden curriculum: Academic consequences of teacher expectations

259f Sex differences in achievement orientations: Consequences for academic choices and attainments

302h The woman academic-library administrator: A career profile

302i Salary and position levels of females and males in academic libraries

302j Women in academic-library, higher-education, and corporate management: A research review

303f A delicate balance: Academic women in Arkansas

303h Academic women in Mississippi: Oktoberfest 1980

303k The black female academic: Doubly burdened or doubly blessed?

311a Is women's studies an academic discipline?

311c Women's studies as an academic discipline: Why and how to do it

312c Is women's studies an academic discipline?

312d Women's studies as an academic discipline: Why and how to do it

320d Mapping the road to academe: A review of research on women, men, and the college-selection process

337k Women on the academic staff

398b Work in the interstices: Woman in academe

398i Women, the other academics

398j Women's studies and men's careers: How the 'social problem' of women in education maintained the academic status of men in the 1970s

398l Academic women, affirmative action, and mid-America in the eighties

416f Academic career mobility for women and men psychologists

421x Occupational choice among female academicians - The Israeli case

Academy

43j An open letter to the academy

174aa Friends and critics: The feminist academy

254a Seeing our way clear: Feminist re-vision of the academy

254j The problem: Idealism and accommodation in the feminist transformation of the academy

398f 'They shared a laboratory together': Feminist collaboration in the academy

Acadia, Canada

306c Cross-cultural perspectives: Creole and Acadian women

388e Women's work and worth in an Acadian maritime village

Access

15d Access to alternatives: New approaches in cataloging

30o Silence: Access and aspiration

98c Access to village women: Experiences in breaking barriers

203n Women in planning: There's more to affirmative action than gaining access

265g Making literacy equally accessible to females and males

Accident

265k Sex differences in children's road accidents

Accommodate

138b Intersections of gender and class: Accommodation and resistance by working-class and affluent females to contradictory sex-role ideologies

254j The problem: Idealism and accommodation in the feminist transformation of the academy

397o From accommodation to rebellion: The politicization of lesbianism

Accomplish

186x A shining in the dark: May Sarton's accomplishment

Accountability

191g Tailoring evaluation to measure the accountability of mental health services to women

Accountancy

44b Accountancy

Accra, Ghana

370l Post-proclamation slavery in Accra: A female affair?

Acculturation

319i Selective acculturation of female Mexican migrants

461d Sexual consequences of acculturation of American Indian women

Achieve

see also Success

93b Collective bargaining as a strategy for achieving equal opportunity and equal pay: Sweden and West Germany

93v Work analysis as a means to achieve equal pay for working women: The Federal Republic of Germany

105g Social structure, family socialization, and children's achievement goals: A comparative analysis

193b Sex differences in science achievement: Some results and hypotheses

193c A biological basis for the sex differences in achievement in science?

193e Science achievement as an aspect of sex roles

258e Educational opportunity and achievement

259f Sex differences in achievement orientations: Consequences for academic choices and attainments

266b Social science inquiries into female achievement: Recurrent methodological problems

267a Achievement in women: Implications for equal employment opportunity policy

295a Female development and achievement

296e A three-generational analysis of change in women's achievement motivation and power

320e Sex bias in aptitude and achievement tests used in higher education

377e Sex-related differences in mathematics achievement: Where and why

391a Early childhood experiences and women's achievement motives

425c Women and the psychology of achievement: Implications for personal and social change

438f The achievement of Iranian women in science

443f Treatment of the imposter phenomenon in high-achieving women

Acquaint

171g Small insults: A study of interruptions in cross-sex conversations between unacquainted persons

Acquiescence

378d Militancy and acquiescence among women workers

Acquisition

15c The acquisition of alternative materials

Act

280m Necrophilia and anti-social acts

329i Speech acts in *To the Lighthouse*

Acting

399ff Alvina Krause: A great teacher of acting

Action

see also Affirmative Action

73b Organizing neighborhood women for political and social action

98k Action research with rural women in Bangladesh: Some observations and experiences

169n Training women for political action

288j Action plans for management and unions

288p Sexual harassment: Finding a cause of action under Title VII

314p From issue to action

378e Women as employees: Social consciousness and collective action

378m Gender, levels of political thinking and political action

421k Feminist egalitarianism, social action orientation and occupational roles: A cross-national study

Activation

96l The role and function of women's consciousness raising: Self-help, psychotherapy, or political activation?

Activist

86n From grassroots activism to political power: Women organizing against environmental hazards

128e The "Jennie Higginses" of the "New South in the West": A regional survey of socialist activists, agitators, and organizers, 1901-1917

192c Lives of Chicana activists: The Chicano student movement (a case study)

203r Introduction: Women as environmental activists

205w Vivian Dowding: Birth control activist 1892-

225k The body politic: The defense of sexual restriction by anti-abortion activists

226c Conceptions of the "Political": White activists in Atlanta

226e Women in political parties: Gender differences in motives among California party activists

229rr Spiritual dimensions of feminist antinuclear activism

379h Right-wing female activists in Buenos Aires, 1900-1932

379q Responses to the political activism of Women of the People in revolutionary Paris, 1789-1793

412f Georgia Harkness: Social activist and/or mystic

Activity

90p Hormones and harems: Are the activities of superintending different for a woman?

122i Levels of female criminal activity as a correlate of female societal power

147b Recreational activities of women in colonial America

147w School physical activity programs for the antebellum southern females

226k Women's collaborative activities and city life: Politics and policy

243e Mothers as social agents: Structuring the community activities of school aged children

317c Physical activity as it relates to the health of the aged

463g Analysis of activity schedules along the dimension of gender

Actor

see also Drama, Theater, names of individual playwrights

343n Shakespeare's female characters as actors and audience

Actress

see also Drama, Theater, names of individual playwrights

371k Private parts in public places: The case of actresses

399n Henrietta Vinton Davis: Shakespearean actress

Actualization

38t The self/group actualization of black women

289l Continuity of self-actualization: Womanhood in climacterium and old age

Adam

19e The image of Adam and the image of Christ

Adam Bede

143d *Adam Bede* and "the story of the past"

Adapt

209aa Let the technology adapt!

213d Sexual divisions and ethnic adaptation: The case of Greek-Cypriot women

289g Intimacy and adaptation

340b Women as shapers of the human adaptation

Addict

165e Work and the addicted prostitute

359t Issues in the treatment of female addiction: A review and critique of the literature

Address (Speech)

402k Etiquette among women in Karnataka: Forms of address in the village and the family

Adenoma

53l Epidemiology of pituitary adenomas

Adjustment

458i Retirement plans and retirement adjustment

458m Personal problems and adjustment to retirement

Administrate

4b Administrative concerns

90b Women in educational administration: A descriptive analysis of dissertation research and paradigm for future research

90j "If they can, I can": Women aspirants to administrative positions in public schools

90k Male and female career paths in school administration

90l Administrative careers in public school organizations

352i Sex bias in school administration

386j Women in law and administration

407a Careers in college and university administration: How are women affected?

407d The administrative skills program: What have we learned?

407h Foundation support for administrative advancement: A mixed record

Administrator

90e Clues to sex bias in the selection of school administrators: A report from the Oregon network

214g An administrator's viewpoint: The interaction of sex and power

302h The woman academic-library administrator: A career profile

352f Feminism and the woman school administrator

352k The black female administrator: Woman in a double bind

352p Leadership training for increased effectiveness among women educationaly administrators: Two local models

407g An agenda for senior women administrators

455l Women administrators in social work

Adnan, Etel

322f Interview with Etel Adnan (Lebanon)

Adolescent

see also Child, Young

4a Adolescent psychosexual development

4c Psychiatric aspects of adolescent pregnancy

4d Adolescent sexuality, pregnancy, and childbearing

4e Social implications of teenage childbearing

4f Programs for sexually active teens

4g Venereal disease and the adolescent

4h Issues surrounding adolescent pregnancy terminations

4j Legal aspects of adolescent pregnancy

4k Ethical issues of adolescent pregnancy

4m Sexual counseling for adolescents

8f The adolescent girl in a group home

8h Childhood and adolescent suicidal behavior, with an emphasis on girls

10b Drinking and drinking problems among female adolescents: Patterns and influences

28i A developmental analysis of menstrual distress in adolescence

48c Becoming sexual in adolescence

55g Youth prostitution

103l Teenage sexuality and public policy: An agenda for gender education

134a Youth service provision, social order and the question of girls

134b Femininity and adolescence

146e Group therapy with female adolescent incest victims

147nn Sexual discrimination in youth sport: The case of Margaret Gisolo

162n Village spinning bees: Sexual culture and free time among rural youths in early modern Germany

190e Through the looking glass of menarche: What the adolescent girl sees

190n Age at menarche and sexual conduct in adolescence and young adulthood

190o Menarche and teenage pregnancy: A misuse of historical data

190p Menarche and adolescent pregnancy

190t Dysmenorrhea in adolescence

190y Premenstrual affective syndrome in adolescent and adult psychiatric patients

211h Memories of an Orthodox youth

225v Search for tomorrow: On feminism and the reconstruction of teen romance

230j Sexual signaling and sexual aggression in adolescent relationships

284g Sexual trauma of children and adolescents

284h Sexual assault center emergency room protocol: Child/adolescent patients

291p The co-therapy relationship in group treatment of sexually mistreated adolescent girls

308a Teenage women in the United States: Sex, contraception, pregnancy, fertility, and maternal and infant health

308b The family's role in adolescent sexual behavior

308c Implicating the family: Teenage parenthood and kinship involvement

308d Government policies related to teenage family formation and functioning: An inventory

308e Sex education and the prevention of teenage pregnancy: An overview of policies and programs in the United States

308f Adolescent parent programs and family involvement

308g Ethical and legal issues in teenage pregnancies

308h Adolescent sexuality and teenage pregnancy from a black perspective

308i The impact of adolescent pregnancy on Hispanic adolescents and their families

309a Teenage family formation in postwar America

309b Teenage illegitimacy: An exchange

309c The legitimacy status of first births to U.S. women aged 15-24, 1939-1978

309e First pregnancies to women aged 15-19: 1976 and 1971

309f Contraceptive patterns and premarital pregnancy among women aged 15-19 in 1976

309h The risk of adolescent pregnancy in the first months of intercourse

309i Teenage pregnancies: Looking ahead to 1984

309k The health and social consequences of teenage childbearing

309l The social consequences of teenage parenthood

309m Teenage mothers and teenage fathers: The impact of early childbearing on the parents' personal and professional lives

309p Economic consequences of teenage childbearing

309q The children of teenage parents

309r Family support: Helping teenage mothers to cope

309s Contraception, abortion and venereal disease: Teenagers' knowledge and the effect of education

309u Sexual and contraceptive knowledge, attitudes and behavior of male adolescents

309x Teenagers: Fertility control behavior and attitudes before and after abortion, childbearing or negative pregnancy test

309y Adolescent pregnancy prevention services in high school clinics

309z Misinforming pregnant teenagers

309aa Contraceptive services for adolescents: An overview

309bb Teenagers and pregnancy: The law in 1979

310j Teenage oppression and reproductive rights

319j Cultural styles and adolescent sex role perceptions: An exploration of responses to a value picture projective test

326g Group work with preadolescent sexual assault victims

326m Rape and the college student: Multiple crises in late adolescence

328e 1897: Virginia Woolf at fifteen

353n Chlorotic girls, 1870-1920: A historical perspective on female adolescence

359w A study of attitudes toward menarche in white middle-class American adolescent girls

359x Teenage pregnancy: A research review

359ee Abortion counseling with adolescents

404u The role of the family in teenage pregnancy: Support or sabotage

404x Young female offenders in Massachusetts: Toward leaving the juvenile justice system successfully

450m Youth in Toni Cade Bambara's *Gorilla, My Love*

461l Effects of teenage motherhood

461n Discussion: Some developmental aspects of adolescent mothers

469e Transactional family patterns: A preliminary exploration of Puerto Rican female adolescents

Adopt

70g American Indian children: Foster care and adoptions

Adult

see also Age

37m Attitudes toward procreation among black adults

38k Role transition in early adulthood: Orientations of young black women

48j Sink or swing? The lifestyles of single adults

80g Day care and children's responsiveness to adults

137d Gender and adult psychopathology

169h Evaluating programs for working adults

190c Age at menarche and year of birth in relation to adult height and weight among Caucasian, Japanese, and Chinese women living in Hawaii

190n Age at menarche and sexual conduct in adolescence and young adulthood

190y Premenstrual affective syndrome in adolescent and adult psychiatric patients

200e Proto-social to adult: A Sherbro transformation

223x Adult-child sex

239j Adult life cycles: Changing roles and changing hormones

244g The nurture of adults by children in family settings

291g Sexual deviance: The adult offender

296d Women's self-perceptions of power and influence across adult life

309c The legitimacy status of first births to U.S. women aged 15-24, 1939-1978

317a Adaptive dimensions of adult cognition

375i Adult derivative benefits in social security: A women's issue

411j Motherhood in the middle years: Women and their adult children

411p The anxiety of the unknown - choice, risk, responsibility: Therapeutic issues for today's adult women

411q Reflections and perspectives on 'therapeutic issues for today's adult women'

423a Women in adulthood: Unanswered questions

423c Adult development and women's development: Arrangements for a marriage

427e Gender inequities in childhood social life and adult work life

Adultery

223d Is adultery immoral?

Advancement

407h Foundation support for administrative advancement: A mixed record

Adventure

34l Adventures of a woman in science

399ee The adventure of life: Writing for children

Adversary

84i A paradigm of philosophy: The adversary method

Adverse

233v Adverse influences of the working environment

Advertisement

136k The seven ages of woman: A view from American magazine advertisements

161c Applauding servility - Images of women in advertisements

Advice

119g 'An immense verbosity': Permissive sexual advice in the 1970s

158f "Give me a dozen healthy infants": John B. Watson's popular advice on childrearing, women, and the family

439p "The love crisis": Couples advice books of the late 1970s

Advocacy

36b Historical styles of contraceptive advocacy

55i Victim advocacy as therapy

133s Troy Perry: Gay advocate

295j Social support and efficacy in advocacy roles: A case study of two women's organizations

300e The infant formula controversy in Southeast Asia: Advocacy confrontation or applied anthropology?

326b Working for and with rape victims: Crisis intervention and advocacy

434q Beyond advocacy

Aegean

364f The legal and social transformation of rural women in Aegean Turkey

Aerobic

372r Reproducibility of aerobic power and related physiological variables in women

Aeschylus

419g The dynamics of misogyny: Myth and mythmaking in the *Oresteia*

Aesthetic

171i Consciousness as style: Style as aesthetic

32n The question of a feminist aesthetic and Karin Struck's *Klassenliebe*

132l For the Etruscans: Sexual difference and artistic production - the debate over a female aesthetic

AFDC

see Aid to Families with Dependent Children

Affect

230d Arousal, affect, and the aggression-moderating effect of erotica

Affirm

40r Affirmation in the works of Mari Evans

74d Affirmation and resistance: Women poets from the Caribbean

404r Breaking cycles of victimization: The shelter as an affirmative institution

Affirmative Action

see also Discriminate

169q Education for affirmative action: Two union approaches

203n Women in planning: There's more to affirmative action than gaining access

249k The failure of affirmative action for women: One university's experience

267c Double jeopardy: Resistance to affirmative action from potential beneficiaries

323d Out of the ghettos: Affirmative action and unions

361f Affirmative action programs that work

398l Academic women, affirmative action, and mid-America in the eighties

398m Hard truths for strategic change: Dilemmas of implementing affirmative action

426a Increased labor force participation of women and affirmative action

Affluent

138b Intersections of gender and class: Accommodation and resistance by working-class and affluent females to contradictory sex-role ideologies

Affluent Worker

297j The *Affluent Worker* re-visited

Afford

80r The dilemma of affordable child care

Africa

see also individual countries

5b Women and agriculture in sub-Saharan Africa: Implications for development

6d Women in the changing African family

6g Women in African literature

6i African women in politics

6l Appendix: Some selected statistics on African women

39b Female employment and family organization in West Africa

39g The African woman as entrepreneur: Problem and perspectives on their roles

39i Women in indigenous African cults and churches

39j Definitions of women and development: An African perspective

39t Black women and music: A survey from Africa to the new world

52q The changing position of black women in South Africa

68c African women and national development

68e Issues confronting professional African women: Illustrations from Kenya

82s Household structure in Africa

100c The Indian and African presence in the Americas: Some aspects of historical distortion

153i Beyond the peasant to proletarian debate: African household formation in South Africa

153q Conflicts inside and outside the household: A West African case study

155f The prostitute in Arab and North African fiction

162k Parental strategies: Calculation or sentiment?: Fostering practices among West Africans

194o Mother Earth: The great goddess of West Africa

198e The literary treatment of women in North Africa

218a An overview of women and power in Africa

218e Riot and rebellion among African women: Three examples of women's political clout

298c Research in the social sciences on North African women: Problems, trends, and needs

307g From Africa to America: Black women inventors

322a Women and literature in Africa

322d Arab literature in north Africa

322e Francophone literature in north Africa

325b Julia: An east African diviner

362a Women's politics in Africa

364b Cognatic descent, Islamic law and women's property on the East African coast

364g Divorce and the disadvantaged: African women in urban South Africa

370a Women's importance in African slave systems

370b African women in the Atlantic slave trade

370k The story of Swema: Female vulnerability in nineteenth century East Africa

370n Bwanikwa: Consciousness and protest among slave women in Central Africa, 1886-1911

373g Women and the development of "underdevelopment": The African experience

373m The plight of the invisible farmer: The effect of national agriculture policy on women in Africa

385l Fertility and employment: An assessment of role incompatibility among African urban women

385m The child-care dilemma of working mothers in African cities: The case of Lagos, Nigeria

388f Women and law: Land tenure in Africa

393c Women and work: A study of female and male attitudes in the modern sector of an African metropolis (Lagos)

393d Worlds apart? A comparative study of European and African traditional family life as depicted in the novels of Laurie Lee and Camara Laye

393e The stable African family: Traditional and modern family structures in two African societies (Basa and Manding)

438k The progress of science in Africa

457i Women excluded? Masking and masquerading in West Africa

African

37b Interpreting the African heritage in Afro-American family organization

African American

see also Ethnic, Minority, Race

37a Conceptualizations of black families

37b Interpreting the African heritage in Afro-American family organization

37d African-American family life: An instrument of culture

37e Perspectives on black family empirical research: 1965-1978

37f A demographic picture of black families

37g Economics and mobility: A theoretical rationale for urban black family well-being

37h Black education: A cultural-ecological perspective

37i Patterns of upward mobility in black families

37m Attitudes toward procreation among black adults

37p Support systems of significant others in black families

37q Group identity development within black families

37r Multiple public benefits and poor black families

38c Black fertility: Recent demographic and sociological influences

39r Sex roles and survival strategies in the urban black community

43s Confrontation: Black/white

45l Sex differences in the educational and occupational goals of black college students: Continued inquiry into the black matriarchy theory

60l Black family life-styles: A lesson in survival

80u Day care: A black perspective

89o Curing high unemployment rates among blacks and women

150z Failure to transform: Homophobia in the black community

150ii Black macho and black feminism

162j Afro-American kinship before and after emancipation in North America

174z Charlotte Bunch and Betty Powell talk about feminism, blacks, and education as politics

216e The black family: An adaptive perspective

216j Implications for national policy decisions: The black family perspective

243f Black families and childrearing support networks

287f Black sexuality

301kk Women's consciousness and the southern black

308h Adolescent sexuality and teenage pregnancy from a black perspective

320j Sex differences in the impact of college environments on black students

353ii Mabel K. Staupers and the integration of black nurses into the armed forces

429d Preaching in the black tradition

462j A black response to feminist theology

African American Child

37n Parenting in black families with young children: A historical perspective

37o Involvement of fathers in the socialization of black children

37s Policies affecting the status of black children and families

37t An advocacy agenda for black families and children

352j Socialization and education of young black girls in school

African American Man

37k Black men in America: The quest for "manhood"

37o Involvement of fathers in the socialization of black children

38p Dialectics of black male-female relationships

African American Woman

7l Racism and sadomasochism: A conversation with two black lesbians

14a Introduction: The politics of black women's studies

14b A black feminist's search for sisterhood

14c A black feminist statement

14d Selected bibliography on black feminism

14i Studying slavery: Some literary and pedagogical considerations on the black female slave

14k Two representative issues in contemporary sociological work on black women

14l Black women's health: Notes for a course

14m Three's a crowd: The dilemma of the black woman in higher education

14o   Black women and the church

14p   Toward a black feminist criticism

14q   "This infinity of conscious pain": Zora Neale Hurston and the black female literary tradition

14s   Black-eyed blues connections: Teaching black women

14t   Teaching *Black-eyed Susans*: An approach to the study of black women writers

14u   Afro-American women 1800-1910: A selected bibliography

14v   Afro-American women poets of the nineteenth century: A guide to research and bio-bibliographies of the poets

14w   On the novels written by selected black women: A bibliographical essay

14x   Black women playwrights from Grimké to Shange: Selected synopses of their works

14y   American black women composers: A selected annotated bibliography

14z   A listing of non-print materials on black women

16u   Alternative social services and the black woman

34j   Black women's health: Notes for a course

38a   The black woman: A historical overview

38b   Some demographic characteristics of the black woman: 1940 to 1975

38d   The black woman and family roles

38e   The black woman and child rearing

38f   She who is black and mother: In sociology and fiction, 1940-1970

38g   "The means to put my children through": Child-rearing goals and strategies among black female domestic servants

38h   Black mothers and the extended family support network

38i   Marital interaction goals of black women: Strengths and effects

38j   On marital relations: Perceptions of black women

38k   Role transition in early adulthood: Orientations of young black women

38l   Black female professionals: Dilemmas and contradictions of status

38m   Dilemmas of black females in leadership

38n   "Holding back the ocean with a broom": Black women and community work

38o   Political behavior of American black women: An overview

38p   Dialectics of black male-female relationships

38q   Depression in black women: A theoretical appraisal

38r   Black female suicides: Is the excitement justified?

38s   The women's liberation movement: Understanding black women's attitudes

38t   The self/group actualization of black women

39a   The black woman cross-culturally: An overview

39o   Discrimination against Afro-American women in the woman's movement, 1830-1920

39p   Black women and racial "uplift" prior to emancipation

39s   The incarcerated black female: The case of social double jeopardy

39u   Images of black women in Afro-American poetry

40c   Reconstruction of the composite self: New images of black women in Maya Angelou's continuing autobiography

40nn Alice Walker: The black woman artist as wayward

41b   The concept of class in the novels of black women

41c   Sources of life satisfaction: The different worlds of black women and white women

41d   Black women and the political process in the United States

41e   Shifts in the occupational and employment status of black women: Current trends and future implications

41f   Stress and support networks of working single black mothers

41g   Invited presentation: The black professional woman — career success and interpersonal failure

60c   The feminist theology of the black Baptist church, 1880-1900

60m   Laid bare by the system: Work and survival for black and Hispanic women

60s   From slavery to social welfare: Racism and the control of black women

61d   Black women in pre-federal America

68n   The black woman: Liberated or oppressed?

69d   The black woman growing up

81d   Flawed victories: The experiences of black and white women workers in Durham during the 1930s

81l   Discontented black feminists: Prelude and postscript to the passage of the nineteenth amendment

126k Sexism and racism: Obstacles to the development of black women in South Africa

132p Visibility and difference: Black women in history and literature - pieces of a paper and some ruminations

132q Black women and feminism

150n Black lesbian in American literature: An overview

150q Cultural legacy denied and discovered: Black lesbians in fiction by women

150jj Black lesbian/feminist organizing: A conversation

150kk Reflections on black feminist therapy

171d Linguistic options and choices for black women in the rural South

174b The politics of black women's studies

175o Aunt Dicy: Legendary black lady

176b Black lesbians in academia: Visible invisibility

176o Black lesbians before 1970: A bibliographical essay

229f From the house of Yemanja: The goddess heritage of black women

231k The Afro-American female: The historical context of the construction of sexual identity

249f I'm not shouting "Jubilee": One black woman's story

256d Free black women and the question of matriarchy

264d Black women in a southern city: Washington, D.C., 1890-1920

295d Black women in American society: A resource development perspective

302g Profiles of the careers of selected black female librarians

303k The black female academic: Doubly burdened or doubly blessed?

307g From Africa to America: Black women inventors

314n Resources in black women's studies

319k Social networks and survival strategies: An exploratory study of Mexican American, black and Anglo family female heads in San Jose, California

341i Soul, black women and food

342c Black women as producers and reproducers for profit

344ff Feminist consciousness and black women

352k The black female administrator: Woman in a double bind

367f Black women and religion in the colonial period

379k "My spirit eye": Some functions of spiritual and visionary experience in the lives of five black women preachers, 1810-1880

387r Job opportunities of black and white working-class women

397q The black lesbian in American literature: An overview

398c Black woman professor — white university

399nn Black women in plays by black playwrights

411k Black women in the middle years

414i The gender liberation: Black women as elected officials in Oklahoma

421m Comparative attitudes about marital sex among Negro women in the United States, Great Britain and Trinidad

421r Some aspirations of lower class black mothers

434f Black women: The resilient victims

443h Psychotherapy with black women and the dual effects of racism and sexism

452h In search of the black female self: African-American women's autobiographies and ethnicity

461b The sexual experience of Afro-American women: A middle-income sample

461c Discussion: Further thoughts on a group discussion by black women about sexuality

474g On being female, black, and free

African Methodist Episcopal (A.M.E.)

412o Nineteenth-century A.M.E. preaching women: Cutting edge of women's inclusion in church polity

African Woman

250e Black girls in a London comprehensive school

Afro-Surinamese

363b Working class Afro-Surinamese women and national politics: Traditions and changes in an independent state

Age

see also Adult, Aging, Middle Age, Midlife, Older, Older Woman

49c   The age mix of the labor force in 1990: Implications for labor market research

129g An "age of consent" symposium

184o Age at menarche in Europe since the eighteenth century

190c Age at menarche and year of birth in relation to adult height and weight among Caucasian, Japanese, and Chinese women living in Hawaii

190n Age at menarche and sexual conduct in adolescence and young adulthood

214o Ageism vs. sexism: Male models as a source of support

296b Differential power of women over the life course: A case study of age-roles as an indicator of power

305y More radical with age: Women and education

309n Marriage, remarriage, marital disruption and age at first birth

343j Coming of age in Verona

344m The double standard: Age

388j Women's organizations and social change: The age-of-marriage issue in India

Age of Jackson

454d The lady and the mill girl: Changes in the status of women in the Age of Jackson

Agency

10k Patterns of women's use of alcohol treatment agencies

314q A view from the funding agencies

320g Epistemology and agency in the development of undergraduate women

Agency for International Development (AID)

82b AID and women in development

82c Participation through Title XII, consortia, and the project process in AID

82d AID: Promise and performance

Agenda

37t An advocacy agenda for black families and children

79nn Reflections: Uncovering patriarchal agendas and exploring woman-oriented values

407g An agenda for senior women administrators

410i Commissions on the status of women and building a local policy agenda

Agent

243e Mothers as social agents: Structuring the community activities of school aged children

399x Sophie Treadwell: Agent for change

Aggression

8b Aggression in women: Conceptual issues and clinical implications

29j Physical aggression: Treating the victims

107g Differences in athletic aggression among Egyptian female athletes

214j The battle of the sexes: Power and sexual aggressiveness

230b Aggression against women: Cultural and individual causes

230d Arousal, affect, and the aggression-moderating effect of erotica

230i Sexually aggressive men: Empirical findings and theoretical implications

230j Sexual signaling and sexual aggression in adolescent relationships

276a The classification of sexual aggressives and their associated demographic, social, developmental and psychological features

276e Sexual aggression and the law - implications for the future

327c Television viewing, family style and aggressive behavior in preschool children

349m Sexual aggression: A second look at the offended female

Aging

see also Age

29q Aging women

51h Neuroendocrine mechanisms of reproductive aging in women and female rats

51w Aging, menopause, and estrogens: The clinician's dilemma

69k Women and aging

119f Invisible struggles: The politics of ageing

210b The crossroads of menopause: A chance and a risk for the aging process of women

210h Shopping-bag women: Aging deviants in the city

277m Effects of aging on sexual arousal

317b Life satisfaction research in aging: Implications for policy development

317i Growing old "inside": Aging and attachment to place in an Appalachian community

411i The daughter of aging parents

458c Life satisfaction among aging women: A causal model

461i Discussion: Aging and female sexuality

Agitator

128e The "Jennie Higginses" of the "New South in the West": A regional survey of socialist activists, agitators, and organizers, 1901-1917

Agoraphobia

304f Women and agoraphobia: A case for the etiological significance of the feminine sex-role stereotype

365e Anxieties: Agoraphobia and hysteria

Agrarian

145l The impact of agrarian change on women's work and child care in early-nineteenth-century Prussia

Agreda, María de

175a María de Agreda: The lady in blue

Agriculture

see also Farm, Farmer

5b Women and agriculture in sub-Saharan Africa: Implications for development

82i Agriculture, forestry, conservation and women

341l Farming out the home: Women and agribusiness

373m The plight of the invisible farmer: The effect of national agriculture policy on women in Africa

385d Women and agricultural change in the railway region of Zambia: Dispossession and counterstrategies, 1930-1970

385j Women farmers and inequities in agricultural services

386b Agricultural laborers

400a Women's employment and agriculture: Extracts from a case study

431h Sexual status in Southeast Asia: Comparative perspectives on women, agriculture and political organization

446g The utilization of female labor in agriculture

Agta

340c Woman the hunter: The Agta

AID (Agency for International Development)

see Agency for International Development

Aid to Families with Dependent Children (AFDC)

434m Work requirements for AFDC mothers

Ain't

455e Ain't I a woman

Alas, Leopoldo

313o "La loca, la tonta, la literata": Women's destiny in Clarin's *La Regenta*

Alaska

347d Contending with colonization: Tlingit men and women in change

473l The economic role of women in Alaskan Eskimo society

Alcala

319b Chicana use of abortion: The case of Alcala

Alcohol

see also Alcoholism, Drink

8n Women and alcohol abuse

9a Sex differences in alcohol and drug problems - some highlights

9e Longitudinal studies of alcohol and drug problems: Sex differences

9g Some behavioral and biological aspects of alcohol problems in women

9o Sex differences in the effects of alcohol and other psychoactive drugs on endocrine function: Clinical and experimental evidence

9p The effects of alcohol on the fetus and offspring

10c Alcohol use and abuse in ethnic minority women

10d Multiple substance abuse among women with alcohol-related problems

10f Alcohol use and reproduction

10h Antecedents of alcohol problems in women

10i Alcohol use and marital violence: Female and male differences in reactions to alcohol

10j Female alcohol abuse: Its effects on the family

10k Patterns of women's use of alcohol treatment agencies

10n Prevention of alcohol problems in women

11d The effects of alcohol on anxiety in problem and nonproblem drinking women

11e Prevention of alcohol problems in women: Current status

11h Fetal alcohol syndrome and drinking during pregnancy

11i Diagnosis, casefinding, and treatment of alcohol problems in women

11m Women and alcohol

51k Smoking, alcohol, and body mass relationships to early menopause: Implications for risk of cardiovascular disease

53g Women, alcohol, and the risk of disease

137i   Gender, drinking, and alcohol abuse

268j   A sex-roles perspective on drug and alcohol use by women

345b   The physical effects and metabolism of alcohol

345c   The foetal alcohol syndrome

345d   Psychological aspects of women and alcohol

345h   Single homeless women and alcohol

404c   Learned helplessness, depression, and alcohol problems of women

Alcoholism
see also Alcohol, Drink

9f   Sex differences in the inheritance of alcoholism

9h   Nature and development of alcoholism in women

9i   Sex differences in morbidity of alcoholics

9j   Sex differences in mortality: A comparison of male and female alcoholics

9k   Alcoholism in women: Treatment modalities and outcomes

10e   Vulnerability to the biomedical consequences of alcoholism and alcohol-related problems among women

10l   Therapeutic issues in the treatment of alcoholic women

10m   Treatment outcome of alcoholic women: The state of the art in relation to sex bias and expectancy effects

11a   Sex-role adjustment in women alcoholics

11c   Women and men problem drinkers: Sex differences in patients served by Iowa's community alcoholism centers

11f   Women employees and job-based alcoholism programs

11j   Alcoholism and the lesbian community

11k   Marital therapy of women alcoholics

16k   Alcoholism and the lesbian community

16l   CASPAR: A women's alcoholism program

29p   Women and alcoholism

54b   The unidentified problem of alcoholism among Hispanic women

54c   New approaches for prevention and education of alcoholism among Hispanic women

54e   Commonalities among female alcoholics

54f   Feminist therapy with female alcoholics

79k   Policy decisions in prenatal diagnosis: The example of fetal alcoholism syndrome

105k   Marriage, estrangement, sobriety and recidivism: Some crucial process variables in the case of alcoholic men and their wives

359u   The female alcoholic

404h   Reaching the middle class alcoholic

404p   Innovative alcoholism programs for women

404q   Motivation and the alcoholic woman

Alcott, Louisa May

332e   Female stories of experience: Alcott's *Little Women* in light of *Work*

442c   Louisa May Alcott: The influence of *Little Women*

Alexandria, Egypt

441b   Women and technology in ancient Alexandria: Maria and Hypatia

Algeria

113f   Algeria: Anticolonial war

298e   Human sciences research on Algerian women

Algonkian
see also American Indian

347b   Sunksquaws, shamans, and tradeswomen: Middle Atlantic coastal Algonkian women during the 17th and 18th centuries

Aliabad

368j   Aliabad women: Revolution as religious activity

Alice

134h   Alice in the consumer wonderland

135b   The looking-glass through Alice

Alienate

114i   From alienation to personal triumph: The science fiction of Joan D. Vinge

313l   Alienation and eros in three stories by Beatriz Guido, Marta Lynch and Amalia Jamilis

421f   Birth order and alienation among college women in Lebanon

Alive

43k   Staying alive

All-American Girls' Baseball League

147oo   The All-American Girls' Baseball League, 1943-1954

All-India Muslim Ladies' Conference

101d   Sisterhood or separation? The All-India Muslim Ladies' Conference and the Nationalist Movement

All-Pakistan Women's Association

101j   The All-Pakistan Women's Association and the 1961 Muslim family laws ordinance

Allen, Paula Gunn

384u   A laddered, rain-bearing rug: Paula Gunn Allen's poetry

Alliance

27a   Artists and mothers: A false alliance

217g   Women's mutual alliances, altruism as a premise for interaction

Allocate

89b   A theory of the allocation of time

355g   Women's life-cycle time allocation: An econometric analysis

459b   The allocation of women's time and its relation to fertility

Allowance

170h   Natural selection: Perspectives on entitlement to the invalid care allowance

440c   Redistribution to children and to mothers: A history of child endowment and family allowances

Alone

257j   Women alone

399bb   Woman alone, women together

Alphabet

108b   Ceremonies of the alphabet: Female grandmatologies and the female autograph

Alternative

15a   Libraries and alternatives

15b   The alternative press and the mass media: Two case studies

15c   The acquisition of alternative materials

15d   Access to alternatives: New approaches in cataloging

15e   Reference service for alternative publications

15f   Alternative roads to alternative media

15k   Alternative and small publishers view libraries: An empirical study

15l   Collections of contemporary alternative materials in libraries: A directory

36s   Community alternatives to high technology birth

96i   From traditional psychoanalysis to alternatives to psychotherapy

100a   The dialectic of education: An alternative approach to education and social change in developing countries

209ee   Alternative models of worker participation

289i   Range of alternatives

Alther, Lisa

135l   New directions in the contemporary bildungsroman: Lisa Alther's *Kinflicks*

450f   Lisa Alther: The irony of return?

Altruism

217g   Women's mutual alliances, altruism as a premise for interaction

Amateur

216k   Experts and amateurs: Some unintended consequences of parent education

Amazon

32d   Kleist's nation of amazons

229j   The Amazon legacy

229k   Tales of a reincarnated Amazon princess: The invincible wonder woman?

282h   Pigs, women, and the men's house in Amazonia: An analysis of six Mundurucú myths

408b   Echoes of the Amazon myth in medieval Spanish literature

461s   Women in swinging: America's Amazon society?

Ambassador

433k   Radindranath Tagore: Cultural ambassador of India to the United States

Ambiguity

140a   Presidential address: Conceptual ambiguity and morality in modern psychiatry

217j   Theoretical ambiguities - A reflection of women's lives?

356p   The construction of ambiguity in *The Awakening*: A linguistic analysis

Ambition

90i   Ambitions and the opportunity for professionals in the elementary school

Ambivalence

27d   Ambivalence in the Gynogram: Sade's utopian woman

222b   The ambivalent decision

Amen

37c   Old-time religion: Benches can't say "Amen"

40gg   An amen arena

Amendment

129p If you liked gun control, you'll love the antiabortion amendment

Amenorrhea

190x Primary and secondary amenorrhea in anorexia nervosa

America

see also United States and other names of individual countries

100c The Indian and African presence in the Americas: Some aspects of historical distortion

269c Sex roles and subsistence: A comparative analysis of three Central American communities

282c The bow and the burden strap: A new look at institutionalized homosexuality in native North America

367b Women and religion in Spanish America

367c Women in colonial French America

American Association for the Advancement of Physical Education

147c The rise and development of women's concern for the physical education of American women, 1776-1885: From independence to the foundation of the American Association for the Advancement of Physical Education

American Association of University Women (AAUW)

441i A preview of AAUW's biennial study/action topic 'Taking hold of technology'

American Farmer

147d The ladies' department of the *American Farmer*, 1825-1830: A locus for the advocacy of family health and exercise

American Indian

see also individual tribes

36w A Native American response

61f Women, civilization, and the Indian question

70b Current educational status of American Indian girls

70g American Indian children: Foster care and adoptions

70i Relevancy of tribal interests and tribal diversity in determining the educational needs of American Indians

216g Parenting in the Native-American community

229qq On common ground: Native American and feminist spirituality approaches in the struggle to save mother earth

282c The bow and the burden strap: A new look at institutionalized homosexuality in native North America

325p Women of influence and prestige among the Native American Iroquois

414d Patient and useful servants: Women missionaries in Indian territory

American Indian Woman

68l Native American women: Twilight of a long maidenhood

70a Insignificance of humanity, "Man is tampering with the moon and the stars": The employment status of American Indian women

70c The status of American Indian women in higher education

70d Organizing American Indian women

70f Health problems facing American Indian women

70h Indian boarding schools and Indian women: Blessing or curse?

70j Transition from the reservation to an urban setting and the changing roles of American Indian women

70k American Indian women: Their relationship to the federal government

147a Ball game participation of North American Indian women

148a Introduction: New perspectives on Plains Indian women

148b Beasts of burden and menial slaves: Nineteenth century observations of Northern Plains Indian women

148e Women's work: An examination of women's roles in Plains Indian arts and crafts

148j "Warrior women" - Sex role alternatives for Plains Indian women

180v Spider woman's web: Mothers and daughters in Southwestern Native American literature

305w Beyond barriers: Native women and the women's movement

320i Educational and career progress of Chicana and Native-American college women

342e Indian women: Tribal identity as status quo

347b Sunksquaws, shamans, and tradeswomen: Middle Atlantic coastal Algonkian women during the 17th and 18th centuries

347c The mothers of the nation: Seneca resistance to Quaker intervention

347d Contending with colonization: Tlingit men and women in change

367a American Indian women and religion

397f Beloved women: The lesbian in American Indian culture

397q Reclamation: A lesbian Indian story

434i Observations on social work with American Indian women

461d Sexual consequences of acculturation of American Indian women

American Revolution

367i Women, civil religion, and the American Revolution

American Telephone & Telegraph (AT&T)

387t Sex stratification, technology and organization change: A longitudinal case study of AT&T

Amity

186i Living rooms: Amity in the novels of May Sarton

Amniocentesis

273c Sex selection through amniocentesis and selective abortion

Amniotic

252h Intra-amniotic hypertonic saline instillation in the second trimester

252i Extra-amniotic ethacridine (Rivanol)-catheter technique for midtrimester abortion

Amphetamine

9q The effects of opiates, sedative-hypnotics, amphetamines, cannabis, and other psychoactive drugs on the fetus and newborn

Amun

156e The god's wife of Amun in the 18th dynasty in Egypt

Anaerobic

372p Measurement of maximal short-term (anaerobic) power output during cycling

372u VO2 max and anaerobic threshold in pre- and post-pubescent girls

372v Anaerobic energy metabolism of women

Anal

88b The anal phase

Analgesic

9l Dependence on psychotropic drugs and analgesics in men and women

Analogue

252l Termination of second trimester pregnancy with prostaglandin analogues

Analyst

443e Female role socialization: The analyst and the analysis

Anamnesis

64o The anamnesis of a female "I": In the margins of self-portrayal (Colette)

Anarchism

129c Anarchism and American traditions

383a A new anarchism: Social and political ideas in some recent feminist eutopias

Anarchist

95f Feminism: The essential ingredient in Federica Montseny's anarchist theory

125m Emma Goldman: Anarchist Queen

417l *Mujeres Libres* and the role of women in anarchist revolution

Anatomy

218d Tea and power: The anatomy of a conflict

239a Psychosexual neutrality: Is anatomy destiny?

Ancestor

40dd Rootedness: The ancestor as foundation

Anchoress

187j The nun as anchoress: England, 1100-1500

Ancient

180a Mothers and daughters in ancient Near Eastern literature

457e Essence and existence: Women and religion in ancient Indian texts

Andalusia, Spain

282g Like wounded stags: Male sexual ideology in an Andalusian town

380n Labor force participation and earnings of women in Andalusia

Andes

104c Interhousehold co-operation in Peru's southern Andes: A case of multiple sibling-group marriage

200d The power of signs: Gender, culture and the wild in the Bolivian Andes

325q Rosinta, rats, and the river: Bad luck is banished in Andean Bolivia

347g "The universe has turned inside out...There is no justice for us here": Andean women under Spanish rule

350c Peasant production, proletarianization, and the sexual division of labor in the Andes

371b Andean women and the concept of space/time

Andhra, India

101b Social reform and women's participation in political culture: Andhra and Madras

Androgyny

see also Gender, Role, Sex Role

17d Four novels of Harriet Beecher Stowe: A study in nineteenth-century androgyny

17p Hemingway and Fauntleroy: An androgynous pursuit

43e The illusion of androgyny

64i The *Vagabond*: A vision of androgyny

116h Two forms of androgynism

116i Is androgyny the answer to sexual stereotyping?

116j Are androgyny and sexuality compatible?

116p Women and "masculine" sports: Androgyny qualified

118a Androgynous life: A feminist appropriation of process thought

126g The contest between androgyny and patriarchy in early western tradition

132r Androgyny and the psychology of sex differences

133l Androgyny, sex-role rigidity, and homophobia

136h Gender, androgyny, and conversational assertiveness

136i A feminist critique of androgyny: Toward the elimination of gender attributions for learned behavior

224n Lesbian and gay oppression in the '80s: Androgyny, men and power

239d Human sex-hormone abnormalities viewed from an androgynous perspective: A reconsideration of the work of John Money

271b Androgyny: A dead end or a promise

287p Creative sexuality: Androgyny

313b The "I" in Adrienne Rich: Individuation and the androgyne archetype

329j The *Waves*: A utopia of androgyny?

383g The *Left Hand of Darkness*: Androgyny and the feminist utopia

401b Taoism and the androgynous ideal

434o Toward androgyny in community and organizational practice

450k The androgynous, bi-racial vision of Berry Morgan

Anesthesia

353m Birthing and anesthesia: The debate over twilight sleep

Angel

175w Honky Tonk Angels

254f Captured angel in the centerfold

Angelina

175b Angelina

Angelou, Maya

40b Maya Angelou and the autobiographical statement

40c Reconstruction of the composite self: New images of black women in Maya Angelou's continuing autobiography

452k The metaphysics of matrilinearism in women's autobiography: Studies of Mead's *Blackberry Winter*, Hellman's *Pentimento*, Angelou's *I Know Why the Caged Bird Sings*, and Kingston's *The Woman Warrior*

Anger

see also Emotion

50p Anger and tenderness: The experience of motherhood

109f Domestic gothic: The imagery of anger in Christina Stead's *The Man Who Loved Children*

215o Anger in a black landscape

349l Rape: Power, anger, and sexuality

356l Anger and the politics of naming

395l Anger sickness: Social stress and native diagnosis among Ecuadorian Indians

Anglo

319k Social networks and survival strategies: An exploratory study of Mexican American, black and Anglo family female heads in San Jose, California

319n Feminism: The Chicana and the Anglo versions, a historical analysis

Anglo Saxon

see also England

187e Anglo-Saxon nuns in Anglo-Norman hagiography: Humility and power

234e Evidence concerning Anglo-Saxon women from archaeology

271d Women of South Asian and Anglo-Saxon origins in the Canadian context

375b Widows' rights in Anglo-Saxon law

Animal

24i Sexual attraction in animals

84a Women is not a rational animal: On Aristotle's biology of reproduction

141b Genetic control of breast cancer susceptibility in animals

233k Mechanisms of teratogenesis: The extrapolation of the results of animal studies to man

233m Animal and human studies in genetic toxicology

353a The female animal: Medical and biological views of woman and her role in nineteenth-century America

Anjos, Clara Dos

39ee Images of the woman of color in Brazilian literature: O Cortico, Clara Dos Anjos, Gabriela Cravo E Canela, and O Quinze

Anlo (Ewe)

370m Appendix: A note on Anlo (Ewe) slavery and the history of a slave

Anna O.

30p Anna O./Bertha Pappenheim and me

Annals

22e Women in Latin Medieval literature in Denmark e.g. annals and chronicles

Anneke, Mathilde Franziska

32f A German writer and feminist in nineteenth century America: An archival study of Mathilde Franziska Anneke

Annihilation

195r Motherhood: The annihilation of women

Anorexia Nervosa

28n The menstrual cycle in anorexia nervosa

29n Weight disorders: Overweight and anorexia

140l Cinderella's stepsisters: A feminist perspective on anorexia nervosa and bulimia

190x Primary and secondary amenorrhea in anorexia nervosa

359q A starving family: An interactional view of anorexia nervosa

359r Cinderella's stepsisters: A feminist perspective on anorexia nervosa and bulimia

365f Eating disorders: Obesity and anorexia

Another

20f One woman leads to another

Answer

40s An answer to some questions on how I write: In three parts

116i Is androgyny the answer to sexual stereotyping?

231n Issues and answers

241j Do her answers fit his questions? Women and the survey method

Antagonism

256f "The men are as bad as their masters...": Socialism, feminism and sexual antagonism in the London tailoring trade in the 1830s

Antebellum

61g Women and radical reform in antebellum upstate New York: A profile of grassroots female abolitionists

379b Piety and kin: The limits of antebellum Southern women's reform

Antecedent

10h Antecedents of alcohol problems in women

Antenatal

79j Antenatal diagnosis: The physician-patient relationship

233r What can be done in antenatal care?

Anthropology

see also Fieldwork, names of individual cultures

56f Studying childbirth: The experience and methods of a woman anthropologist

72m The need for an anthropological and cognitive approach to the education of Hispanic women

98f Anthropological approach to study of rural women in Bangladesh: Experience of a female researcher

107l Physique of female athletes - anthropological and proportional analysis

123g Anthropology and the study of gender

162a Interest and emotion in family and kinship studies: A critique of social history and anthropology

168e Conceptualizing "women" in anthropology and sociology

189g Anthropology - a discipline with a legacy

231a Sex and society: A research note from social history and anthropology

245b Is there a family? New anthropological views

246a   Introduction: Feminist perceptions in anthropology

297h   Bringing it all back home: An anthropologist in Belfast

300e   The infant formula controversy in Southeast Asia: Advocacy confrontation or applied anthropology?

342h   Ideologies of male dominance as divide and rule politics: An anthropologist's view

356b   Anthropology: Social and cultural perspectives

371e   The problem of privacy in Mediterranean anthropology

438d   Becoming an anthropologist (Japan)

459f   A social anthropological approach to women's roles and status in developing countries: The domestic cycle

Antifeminism
60g   Antifeminism and the New Right
130t   Rousseau's "antifeminism" reconsidered

Antigone
103r   Antigone's daughters: Reflections on female identity and the state
129e   Antigone's daughters

Antinomian
19c   The Antinomian controversy
19j   The Antinomian language controversy
454b   The case of the American Jezebels: Anne Hutchinson and female agitation during the years of the Antinomian turmoil, 1636-1640

Antonina
419m   Theodora and Antonina in the *Historia Arcana*: History and/or fiction?

Antiquity
419n   Selected bibliography on women in classical antiquity

Anxiety
see also Emotion
11d   The effects of alcohol on anxiety in problem and nonproblem drinking women
29m   Anxiety-related disorders, fears, and phobias
96n   Math anxiety and female mental health: Some unexpected links
259e   Anxiety, aspirations and the curriculum
365e   Anxieties: Agoraphobia and hysteria
411p   The anxiety of the unknown - choice, risk, responsibility: Therapeutic issues for today's adult women
416k   Early socialization: Causes and cures of mathematics anxiety
443l   A feminist approach to math-anxiety reduction

Anyhow
474k   What it is I think I'm doing anyhow

Apartheid
39l   The role of women in the struggle against *apartheid* in South Africa

Apocalypse
143e   *Romola* and the myth of apocalypse

Apolitical
378i   Women: If not apolitical, then conservative

Appalachia
126j   Redefining the family and women's status within the family: The case of southern Appalachia
317i   Growing old "inside": Aging and attachment to place in an Appalachian community

Apparel
192j   Capital's flight: The apparel industry moves south

Appear
131i   A woman appeared
210a   Changing appearance for women in the middle years of life: Trauma?

Appetite
341k   Working up an appetite

Apple Pie
124c   Notes on technique in feminist drama: *Apple Pie* and *Signs of Life*

Application
65g   Major issues in *a priori* applications

Apply
307u   New jobs in new technologies: Experienced only need apply

Apprenticeship
426c   The apprenticeship model of organizational careers: A response to changes in the relation between work and family

Approach
404i   Holistic approaches for women

Appropriation
203d   The appropriation of the house: Changes in house design and concepts of domesticity

Aptitude
320e   Sex bias in aptitude and achievement tests used in higher education

Arab
see also Islam, Middle East
155f   The prostitute in Arab and North African fiction
198d   Roles in transition: The evolving position of women in Arab-Islamic countries
298a   Arab women: The status of research in the social sciences and the status of women
298b   Survey of research on women in the Arab gulf region
298g   The conditions required for women to conduct research on women in the Arab region
298h   Toward a theoretical framework for the study of women in the Arab world
298i   A survey of trends in social sciences research on women in the Arab region, 1960-1980
322c   Women and literature in the Arab world
322d   Arab literature in north Africa
403b   Traditional affirmations concerning the role of women as found in contemporary Arab Islamic literature
403d   The social and political roles of Arab women: A study of conflict
403h   The political mobilization of women in the Arab world

421h   The effect of religious affiliation on woman's role in Middle Eastern Arab Society
462p   Women responding to the Arab-Israeli conflict

Aragon
162i   The Aragonese royal family around 1300

Arcadia
417y   Neither Arcadia nor Elysium: E.M. Broner's *A Weave of Women*

Archaeology
148d   Male/female task differentiation among the Hidatsa: Toward the development of an archeological approach to the study of gender
156f   Women and housing in classical Greece: The archaeological evidence
234e   Evidence concerning Anglo-Saxon women from archaeology
389i   Margarete Bieber (1879-1978): An archaeologist in two worlds
389j   Gisela Marie Augusta Richter (1882-1972): Scholar of classical art and museum archaeologist
389m   Dorothy Burr Thompson (b. 1900): Classical archaeologist

Archetype
102c   Tiamat and her children: An inquiry into the persistence of mythic archetypes of woman as monster/villainess/victim
121e   "Oh, Susie, it is dangerous": Emily Dickinson and the archetype of the masculine
313b   The "I" in Adrienne Rich: Individuation and the androgyne archetype
408k   Female archetypes in Mexican literature

Architecture
44c   Architecture
117c   The great goddess and the palace architecture of Crete
126m   Careers in landscape architecture: Recovering for women what the "ladies" won and lost
174t   The women's school of planning and architecture
182a   Women, architects and feminism
203m   Architecture: Toward a feminist critique

Archive
61c   National Archives resources for research in the history of American women
306m   The editor and the writer: An approach to archival manuscripts
306n   Letters and diaries: Demystifying archival research for undergraduates
310i   An interview with Mirtha Quintanales, from the Third World women's archives
351k   Studying women's studies: A guide to archival research

Arena
40gg   An amen arena

Arendt, Hannah
30k   Hannah Arendt: Thinking as we are
145c   Hannah Arendt's *Rahel Varnhagen*

Argentina
104b   Cash crop production and family labour: Tobacco growers in Corrientes, Argentina

159k Argentine statistics on female criminality

379h Right-wing female activists in Buenos Aires, 1900-1932

Argument

2f Understanding Blackmun's argument: The reasoning of *Roe v Wade*

113m The argument against female combatants

113n The argument for female combatants

116b Sex roles: The argument from nature

383i Opposing necessity and truth: The argument against politics in Doris Lessing's utopian vision

Aristocrat

379d Aristocratic widows in fifteenth-century England

Aristotle

84a Women is not a rational animal: On Aristotle's biology of reproduction

84b Aristotle and the politicization of the soul

84c The unit of political analysis: Our Aristotelian hangover

106c Aristotle, the public-private split, and the case of the suffragists

Arkansas

303f A delicate balance: Academic women in Arkansas

Arm

215k Take the toys from the boys: Competition and the nuclear arms race

Armament

215n The women who wire up the weapons: Workers in armament factories

Armed Forces

see also Army, Combatant, GI, Military, War, names of wars

160d Camp followers: A note on wives of the armed services

353ii Mabel K. Staupers and the integration of black nurses into the armed forces

Armenia

389l Sirarpie Der Nersessian (b. 1896): Educator and scholar in Byzantine and Armenian art

Arms Race

215i Fuel for the nuclear arms race: Nuclear power and nuclear weapons

Army

see also Armed Forces, Combatant, GI, Military, War, names of wars

50g Women as a reserve army of labour: A note on recent British experience

61h The Woman's Land Army, World War I

Arouse

230d Arousal, affect, and the aggression-moderating effect of erotica

277a Psychological causes of lack of arousal

277b Hormones and sexual arousal

277c Physiology of male sexual arousal

277d Mechanisms of sexual arousal in females

277f Psychophysiologic measurement of sexual arousal in females

277l Sexual arousal responses and disability

277m Effects of aging on sexual arousal

277n Effect of drugs on sexual arousal

Arrest d'Amour

135r On the birth of death: An *Arrest d'Amour* of Martial d'Auvergne

Art

see also Artist, individual art forms

6h Women in the arts

17i Cool Diana and the Blood-red muse: Edith Wharton on innocence and art

17l Mothers, daughters, and the "art necessity": Willa Cather and the creative process

30x May Sarton: A metaphor for my life, my work, and my art

40hh Imagery in the women poems: The art of Carolyn Rodgers

40q The art of Mari Evans

64j Colette and art nouveau

83b Women, art and community in Papua New Guinea

117a Introduction: Feminism and art history

117e Social status and gender in Roman art: The case of the saleswoman

117k Art history and its exclusions: The example of Dutch art

117l Happy mothers and other new ideas in eighteenth-century French art

117q Miriam Schapiro and "femmage": Reflections on the conflict between decoration and abstraction in twentieth-century art

117r Quilts: The great American art

123b New directions for feminist criticism in theatre and the related arts

126a The genesis of feminist visions for transforming the liberal arts curriculum

126h Against the grain: A working feminist art criticism

130i Women and the theatre arts

130o Women and the visual arts

148e Women's work: An examination of women's roles in Plains Indian arts and crafts

150o Artists without art form

174m Feminist art and education at Califia: My personal experience creative process

196d The domestic economy of art: Elizabeth Barrett and Robert Browning

201a Needlework as art, craft, and livelihood before 1900

229y Martial art meditations

229dd See for yourself: Women's spirituality in holistic art

274n Art

305z But is it feminist art?

323p Organizing freelancers in the arts

329n Virginia Woolf and the classics: Every Englishman's prerogative transmuted into fictional art

330j *Orlando* and its genesis: Venturing and experimenting in art, love, and sex

337i Women in the art department

386f Women in the arts

389d Anna Jameson (1794-1860): Sacred art and social vision

389e Margaret Fuller (1810-1850): Her work as an art critic

389f Lady Dilke (1840-1904): The six lives of an art historian

389g Mariana Griswold Van Rensselaer (1851-1934): America's first professional woman art critic

389h Georgiana Goddard King (1871-1939): Educator and pioneer in medieval Spanish art

389j Gisela Marie Augusta Richter (1882-1972): Scholar of classical art and museum archaeologist

389k Erica Tietze-Conrat (1883-1958): Productive scholar in renaissance and baroque art

389l Sirarpie Der Nersessian (b. 1896): Educator and scholar in Byzantine and Armenian art

399dd Art theatre in Hull-House

417bb Change and art in women's worlds: Doris Lessing's *Canopus in Argos: Archives*

417ee A women's museum of art

419e The maenad in early Greek art

442f Shapes of the feminine experience in art

453c Women's imagery/women's art

468f On work, art and women: A discussion of the ambiguous position of women artists

Art Therapy

see also Therapy

146j Arts therapy with sexually abused children

Artemis

156h Bound to bleed: Artemis and Greek women

Artificial Insemination

396h Sex predetermination, artificial insemination and the maintenance of male-dominated culture

Artist

see also Art

27a Artists and mothers: A false alliance

40nn Alice Walker: The black woman artist as wayward

108f Artemisia Gentileschi: The artist's autograph in letters and paintings

117o Gender or genius? The women artists of German expressionism

150o Artists without art form

205h From pastels to chisel: The changing role of BC women artists

242b The birth of the artist as heroine: (Re)production, the *Künslerroman* tradition, and the fiction of Katherine Mansfield

254c The artist as hero in Maxine Hong Kingston's *The Woman Warrior*

286i Sexuality and the Victorian artist: Dickens and Swinburne

409d Stephen Dedalus and women: A portrait of the artist as a young misogynist

413i Women artists in New Zealand

468f On work, art and women: A discussion of the ambiguous position of women artists

Artistic

77d Creative women in artistic and literary change

132l For the Etruscans: Sexual difference and artistic production - the debate over a female aesthetic

As We Are Now

186m Perimeters of power: An examination of *As We Are Now*

Asante
39c Asante queen mothers in government and politics in the nineteenth century

Asceticism
187b Byzantine asceticism and women's monasteries in early medieval Italy

Asexual
439m Maternal sexuality and asexual motherhood

Asia
see also individual countries
21a Women in Asian cities, their political and economic roles: Research problems and strategies
58a Immigration to Southeast Asia
124f Transvestitism and the ideology of gender: Southeast Asia and beyond
155g Courtesans and prostitutes in South Asian literature
205e The response of the WMS to the immigration of Asian women, 1888-1942
205f A note on Asian Indian women in British Columbia, 1900-1935
213b Motherhood and waged work: West Indian, Asian and white mothers compared
218f Women textile workers in the militarization of Southeast Asia
255b Purdah revisited: A comparison of Hindu and Muslim interpretations of the cultural meaning of purdah in South Asia
255f Gradations of purdah and the creation of social boundaries on a Baluchistan oasis
271d Women of South Asian and Anglo-Saxon origins in the Canadian context
300a Modernization, changing roles of women and expectations for development in Southeast Asia
300e The infant formula controversy in Southeast Asia: Advocacy confrontation or applied anthropology?
300o Islamic law in Christian Southeast Asia: The politics of establishing Shari'a courts in the Philippines
322g Women and literature in Asia: South Asia
322h Women and literature in Asia: South-East Asia
402a Women in India and South Asia: An introduction
402c The study of women in South Asia: Some current methodological and research issues
420o Migrant women at work in Asia
420p Female Asian immigrants in Honolulu: Adaptation and success
420s Women in Asian cites: Policies, public services, and research
424a Economic growth and changing female employment structure in the cities of Southeast and East Asia
424n Urbanward migration and employment of women in Southeast and East Asian cities: Patterns and policy issues
428q Women textile workers in the militarization of Southeast Asia
431h Sexual status in Southeast Asia: Comparative perspectives on women, agriculture and political organization

446h The twenty-fifth congress of the CPSU and current problems of employment of female labor in the republics of central Asia

Asian American
see also Minority, Race
216h The Asian-American family

Asian American Woman
71b Some effects of childrearing practices on the value systems of Asian-American women
71c Mental health issues among Asian-American women
71e Asian women in professional health schools, with emphasis on nursing
71f Educational alternatives for Asian-Pacific women
71i The effects of Asian-American kinship systems on women's educational and occupational attainment
71j The early socialization of Asian-American female children
71k Economic and employment status of Asian-Pacific women
71l Social mobility of Asian women in America: A critical review
71m Elderly Pacific Island and Asian-American women: A framework for understanding
434g Asian-American women: A historical and cultural perspective

Asian Woman
71h Immigration of Asian women and the status of recent Asian women immigrants
71n Asian wives of U.S. servicemen: Women in triple jeopardy
402l Asian women in Britain: Strategies of adjustment of Indian and Pakistani migrants
421d Social and economic integration of South Asian women in Montreal, Canada
421bb Minority within a minority: On being South Asian and female in Canada
470e Contemporary clothing `sweatshops', Asian female labour and collective organisation

Asian-Pacific American Woman
71d Impediments to Asian-Pacific-American women organizing

Aspire
30o Silence: Access and aspiration
259e Anxiety, aspirations and the curriculum
265i Aspirations and sex roles - Are they in conflict?
421r Some aspirations of lower class black mothers

Aspirotomy
252f Aspirotomy for outpatient termination of pregnancy in the second trimester

Assault
see also Abuse
103m Daddy's right: Incestuous assault
219h Loss and mourning in victims of rape and sexual assault
280h The dynamics of sexual assault
280k Sexual dynamics in homicide and assault
284h Sexual assault center emergency room protocol: Child/adolescent patients

326a Psychodynamics of sexual assault experiences
326g Group work with preadolescent sexual assault victims
326h Sexual assault in correctional institutions: Prevention and intervention
326j Sexual assault of the older woman
326l Behavioral treatment of sexual dysfunction in sexual assault survivors
326n Treatment of prostitute victims of sexual assault
463p The transportation implications of women's fear of assault

Assembly Line
53e The myth of assembly-line hysteria
336j The creation of a female assembly-line proletariat

Assert
29f Interpersonal effectiveness in assertive situations
96k Assertion training for women
102l A political diary of an assertive woman
136h Gender, androgyny, and conversational assertiveness
271g A cross-cultural comparison of assertiveness in women
271h Assertiveness training for improved conflict resolution style
271i Beyond a cognitive/behavioural approach: Congruent assertion training
271l Sex differences in assertiveness: Implications for research and treatment
271m Assertiveness: Sex differences in relationships between self-report and behavioural measures
302e Assertiveness training for library-school students
304h Women's assertion and the feminine sex-role stereotype

Assess
26a Emergency room intervention: Detection, assessment, and treatment
29c Behavioral assessment of women clients
45i Assessing personal and social change in two generations
63h The development of a scale to assess inmate and staff attitudes toward co-corrections
98n Methodological interventions in programme assessment and evaluation research
126d Research on women's communication: Critical assessment and recommendations
181i Women and the assessment of technology: To think, to be, to unthink, to free
268o Sex roles, psychological assessment, and patient management
276d The assessment and treatment of sexual offenders

Asset
110d Assets and labor supply

Assistant
398d Survival in the 'master's house': The role of graduate teaching assistants in effecting curriculum change

Association
6e Women's voluntary associations

Assumption

212q Sexual assumptions in the women's movement

265d Review of the literature of non-sexist curriculum and a critique of the underlying assumptions and rationale

443j Hidden assumptions in theory and research on women

Assyria

156c Women and witchcraft in ancient Assyria

Astell, Mary

125b Mary Astell: Inspired by ideas

Asylum

248f Asylum nursing before 1914: A chapter in the history of labour

Asymmetry

107m Asymmetry of limb circumferences in female athletes

AT&T

see American Telephone & Telegraph

Athens, Greece

156g Women on Athenian vases: Problems of interpretation

Atherton, Gertrude

445i Gertrude Atherton's California woman: From love story to psychological drama

Athlete

see also Collegiate, Intercollegiate, Sport, Title IX

107f Sugar and spice and everything nice: Is that what female athletes behave like?

107g Differences in athletic aggression among Egyptian female athletes

107h Machover test applied to 130 Italian female top athletes

107i Proportionality and body composition in male and female Olympic athletes: A kinanthropometric overview

107j Somatotypes of female athletes

107k Influence of athletic training on the maturity process of girls

107l Physique of female athletes - anthropological and proportional analysis

107m Asymmetry of limb circumferences in female athletes

107r Physique of college women athletes in five sports

107u Body segment contributions of female athletes to translational and rotational requirements of non-twisting springboard dive takeoffs

147i The realm of sports and the athletic woman, 1850-1900

147dd The history of women's intercollegiate athletics in Ohio, 1945-1972

372j Introduction to the biology of the female athlete

372k Physiological and metabolic responses of female athletes during laboratory and field exercises

372aa Menstrual effects of athletic training

372bb Iron deficiency in female athletes

394j Women's athletics at Madison and Title IX

432c Athletics, gender, and justice

432f Employment for women in athletics: What is fair play?

Atlanta, GA

226c Conceptions of the "Political": White activists in Atlanta

Atlantic

347b Sunksquaws, shamans, and tradeswomen: Middle Atlantic coastal Algonkian women during the 17th and 18th centuries

370b African women in the Atlantic slave trade

Atossa

156b Exit Atossa: Images of women in Greek historiography on Persia

Attach

317i Growing old "inside": Aging and attachment to place in an Appalachian community

Attack

323f Under attack: Women, unions and microtechnology

Attitude

19k Anne Hutchinson and the Puritan attitude toward women

24b Social background, attitudes and sexual attraction

37m Attitudes toward procreation among black adults

38s The women's liberation movement: Understanding black women's attitudes

43m Class attitudes and professionalism

51e Attitudes of families toward menopause

52r Economic recession and Swiss women's attitudes towards marital role segregation

63h The development of a scale to assess inmate and staff attitudes toward co-corrections

107b Attitudes to women in sport: Preface towards a sociological theory

147l The effect of changing attitudes toward sexual morality upon the promotion of physical education for women in nineteenth century America

152i Shifting attitudes toward homosexuality

184d Elizabethan birth control and Puritan attitudes

184i Female sexual attitudes and the rise of illegitimacy: A case study

185g Personal and social attitudes toward parenting

190f Recollections of menarche, current menstrual attitudes, and perimenstrual symptoms

190l Beliefs and attitudes of young girls regarding menstruation

193g Factors differentially affecting the science subject preferences, choices and attitudes of girls and boys

198i Female education in Egypt: Changing attitudes over a span of 100 years

204e Varying degrees of paternal involvement in infant care: Attitudinal and behavioral correlates

219e Police officer or doctor? Police surgeons' attitudes and opinions about rape

265a Parents' sex role attitudes and children's concepts of femininity and masculinity

265c The role of schools in developing sex role attitudes

265e Language and attitudes toward masculine and feminine sex role

265p Effectiveness of self-persuasion in producing healthy attitudes towards polygyny

265t Mental health in boys and girls: Awareness of attitudes for positive sex roles

266h All things being equal, a behavior is superior to an attitude: Studies of sex-typed and sex-biased attitudes and behaviors

275n How words hurt: Attitudes, metaphor and oppression

285o Sexual attitudes and activities in old age

303j Racial myths and attitudes among white female students at the University of Florida

309u Sexual and contraceptive knowledge, attitudes and behavior of male adolescents

309x Teenagers: Fertility control behavior and attitudes before and after abortion, childbearing or negative pregnancy test

324d Attitudes toward women working: Changes over time and implications for the labor-force behaviors of husbands and wives

390e Evolution, eugenics and women: The impact of scientific theories on attitudes towards women, 1870-1920

393c Women and work: A study of female and male attitudes in the modern sector of an African metropolis (Lagos)

419a Early Greece: The origins of the western attitude toward women

421i Attitudes of women towards certain selected cultural practices in Kerala state, India

421j Attitudes and ideology: Correlates of liberal attitudes towards the role of women

421l English-Canadian and French-Canadian attitudes towards women: Results of the Canadian Gallup polls

421m Comparative attitudes about marital sex among Negro women in the United States, Great Britain and Trinidad

421q Sex role attitudes, female employment, and marital satisfaction

421s Labor force participation and fertility, contraceptive knowledge, attitude and practice of the women of Barbados

430d The attitude of the Iranian left to the women's question

436f Creating employment opportunities for rural women: Some issues affecting attitudes and policy

436l Will women judges make a difference in women's legal rights? A prediction from attitudes and simulated behaviour

460a "Role, Jenny Jenkins, Roll": Little girls and maidens in American folksongs - an analysis of sexual attitudes

463l Women's travel behavior and attitudes: An empirical analysis

469f Cultural attitudes toward mental illness among Puerto Rican migrant women

Attorney

see Lawyer

Attract

24a Physical attractiveness, sex roles and heterosexual attraction

24b Social background, attitudes and sexual attraction

24d Perceptual and cognitive mechanisms in human sexual attraction

24e Social skill and human sexual attraction

24f Process, filter and stage theories of attraction

24i Sexual attraction in animals

190h Physical attractiveness and physical stigma: Menstruation and the common cold

Attribute

12f 'Sickness is a woman's business?': Reflections on the attribution of illness

51m Changing views of "the change": A critical review and suggestions for an attributional approach

Atwood, Margaret

20a The where of here: Margaret Atwood and a Canadian tradition

20b Atwood's haunted sequences: *The Circle Game*, *The Journals of Susanna Moodie*, and *Power Politics*

20c Margaret Atwood and the poetics of duplicity

20d Meridians of perception: A reading of *The Journals of Susanna Moodie*

20e The making of *Selected Poems*, the process of surfacing

20g Minuets and madness: Margaret Atwood's *Dancing Girls*

20j *Lady Oracle*: The narrative of a fool-heroine

20k Janus through the looking glass: Atwood's first three novels

20l Prospects and retrospects in *Life Before Man*

20m Bashful but bold: Notes on Margaret Atwood as critic

20n A checklist of writings by and about Margaret Atwood

109i The mirror and the cameo: Margaret Atwood's comic/gothic novel, *Lady Oracle*

448j Quest for the peaceable kingdom: Urban/rural codes in Roy, Laurence, and Atwood

Auburn, NY

165j Hard times: Custodial prisons for women and the example of the New York State Prison for Women at Auburn, 1893-1933

Auction

108i Neither auction block nor pedestal: *The Life and Religious Experience of Jaren Lee, A Coloured Lady*

Audience

109b "But why do they read those things?" The female audience and the gothic novel

169b Promoting and recruiting: Reaching the target audience

331b Voice and audience: The emotional world of the *cantigas de amigo*

343n Shakespeare's female characters as actors and audience

Aue, Hartmann von

331d The woman's songs of Hartmann von Aue

Augusta, GA

399cc Women open Augusta's first theatre

Aunt Dicy

175o Aunt Dicy: Legendary black lady

Auspicious

232b The auspicious married woman

Austen, Jane

27b The art of *Mansfield Park*

135j The woman at the window: Ann Radcliffe in the novels of Mary Wollstonecraft and Jane Austen

164a Introduction: Jane Austen as a social novelist

164b Jane Austen and romantic imprisonment

164c The influence of place: Jane Austen and the novel of social consciousness

164d Disregarded designs: Jane Austen's sense of the volume

164e Sex and social life in Jane Austen's novels

164g Jane Austen and the position of women

164h Jane Austen and the problem of leisure

164i *Mansfield Park*: The revolt of the 'feminine' woman

164j Muted discord: Generational conflict in Jane Austen

164k In between - Anne Elliot marries a sailor and Charlotte Heywood goes to the seaside

180f Jane Austen and the tradition of the absent mother

242f *Persuasion* and the promises of love

Austin, Mary Hunter

384t The moral in Austin's *The Land of Little Rain*

Austin, TX

175u Janis and the Austin scene

Australia

see also Aborigine

13f Queensland public service women

13i Women and unions in Australia

13k Conditions of entry: Women and politics in Australia

13l Feminism: An early tradition amongst western Australian labor women

94a Immigration and class: The Australian experience

94h A new Australian working class leadership: The case of Ford Broadmeadows

94i Migrant communities and class politics: The Greek community in Australia

94j Generations and class: Sicilian-Australians in Melbourne

94k Religion, law and family disputes in a Lebanese Muslim community in Sydney

99c 'Helpmeet for man': Women in mid-nineteenth century western Australia

99e 'As good a bloody woman as any other woman...': Prostitutes in western Australia, 1895-1939

138l Gender, class and education: A teaching bibliography of Australian and New Zealand studies

204f Shared-caregiving families: An Australian study

228d Australia

234j 'Woman-ing' the landscape: East Anglia 1300-1500: A discussion on sources and methodology

241f 'It's a pleasure to cook for him': Food, mealtimes and gender in some South Wales households

294b 'More sinned against than sinning'?: Prostitution in South Australia, 1836-1914

294c 'Soiled doves': Prostitution in colonial Queensland

294d Dealing with the 'social evil': Prostitution and the police in Perth and on the eastern goldfields, 1895-1924

294e The making of a prostitute proletariat in early twentieth-century New South Wales

294f 'Black Velvet': Aboriginal women and their relations with white men in the Northern Territory, 1910-1940

294i Introduction: St. Kilda voices

321f Women in the Australian labour force

325r Menstruation and childbirth as ritual and religious experience among native Australians

333c A certain heritage: Women and their children in north Australia

333d The social and economic importance of the women in Jigalong

333f Women and land rights: The Pitjantjatjara land claims

333g The recent history of the Borroloola aboriginal people and their struggle for land rights

333h Borroloola community and land rights

333i Borroloola women speak. Man and woman: Dance

333k Women and land rights: Kiuk and Wagaidj women in the Darwin area

333r Income and employment for women in remote communities: Examples from the Northern Territory

340d Interpretations and "facts" in aboriginal Australia

347j Desert politics: Choices in the "marriage market"

348f The processing of juveniles in Victoria

372i The "sporty" Australians

390a Women and the family in Australian history

390b 'Feeding the poor and sapping their strength': The public role of ruling-class women in eastern Australia, 1788-1850

390h 'I have never liked trade unionism': The development of the Royal Australian Nursing Federation, Queensland Branch, 1904-1945

390j 'Spinifex fairies': Aboriginal workers in the Northern territory, 1911-39

390l The Australian women's Guild of Empire

390n Rooms of their own: The domestic situation of Australian women writers between the wars

390t Women's struggle to become tram drivers in Melbourne, 1956-75

390u Revolution and machismo: Women in the New South Wales Builders Labourers' Federation, 1961-75

421v Some comments on the home roles of businesswomen in India, Australia and Canada

445s Tradition of the exile: Judith Wright's Australian "West"

Austria

52f The position of Austrian women in the family: Some data, many questions, and a few interpretations

405d Socialism and feminism: The first stages of women's organizations in the eastern part of the Austrian empire

Authentic

306r Authentic voices

443a Authenticity in feminist therapy

Author

see also Literature, Novelist, Writer; individual authors

108d Autobiography of a new 'creatur': Female spirituality, selfhood, and authorship in *The Book of Margery Kempe*

108p Women and autobiography at author's expense

384j Pioneer women in the works of two Montana authors: Interviews with Dorothy M. Johnson and A. B. Guthrie, Jr.

408o The censored sex: Woman as author and character in Franco's Spain

Authoritarian

285a The impact of sexuality, professional authoritarianism, and health crises on rehabilitation

464d Women and authoritarian regimes

Authority

115c Women and authority in the scriptures

140g Women in positions of authority: A case study of changing sex roles

207e Work, consumption and authority within the household: A Moroccan case

208g Work, consumption and authority within the household: A Moroccan case

212l Female performers on a male stage: The first women's liberation movement and the authority of men

243d The old world, new rights, and the limited rebellion: Challenges to traditional authority in immigrant families

353hh More than "the physician's hand": Skill and authority in twentieth-century nursing

473f Spirit mediums in Umbanda Evangelizada of Porto Alegre, Brazil: Dimensions of power and authority

Autobiography

40b Maya Angelou and the autobiographical statement

40c Reconstruction of the composite self: New images of black women in Maya Angelou's continuing autobiography

108d Autobiography of a new 'creatur': Female spirituality, selfhood, and authorship in *The Book of Margery Kempe*

108m Of sparrows and condors: The autobiography of Eva Perón

108o "My life...this curious object": Simone de Beauvoir on autobiography

108p Women and autobiography at author's expense

109n The gothic prism: Charlotte Perkins Gilman's gothic stories and her autobiography

145o The woman's role in the German working-class family in the 1890s from the perspective of women's autobiographies

180x Heritages: Dimensions of mother-daughter relationships in women's autobiographies

186c May Sarton: Approaches to autobiography

356q Women's autobiography in France: For a dialectics of identification

438l Autobiography of an unknown woman (India)

452a Introduction: Women's autobiography and the male tradition

452b The emergence of women's autobiography in England

452c Quest for community: Spiritual autobiographies of eighteenth-century Quaker and Puritan women in America

452f The autobiographer and her readers: From apology to affirmation

452h In search of the black female self: African-American women's autobiographies and ethnicity

452i Gertrude Stein and the problems of autobiography

452k The metaphysics of matrilinearism in women's autobiography: Studies of Mead's *Blackberry Winter*, Hellman's *Pentimento*, Angelou's *I Know Why the Caged Bird Sings*, and Kingston's *The Woman Warrior*

452m Towards a theory of form in feminist autobiography: Kate Millett's *Flying* and *Sita*; Maxine Hong Kingston's *The Woman Warrior*

The Autobiography of Lenor López de Córdoba

108e To restore honor and fortune: *The Autobiography of Lenor López de Córdoba*

Autograph

108b Ceremonies of the alphabet: Female grandmatologies and the female autograph

108f Artemisia Gentileschi: The artist's autograph in letters and paintings

Autogynography

108a Autogynography: Is the subject different?

Automate

181d Technology and work degradation: Effects of office automation on women clerical workers

209a Choices in the development of office automation

209b Office automation: Jekyll or Hyde?

209k Automation and the quality of work life at the Swedish telephone company: A management view

209l Automation and the quality of work life at the Swedish telephone company: A union view

209dd Women and the fight around office automation

Autonomy

3q Abortion, autonomy, and community

197c Autonomy and fabulation in the fiction of Muriel Spark

249g The crux: Quality judgment and departmental autonomy

312a Introduction: Theories of women's studies and the autonomy/integration debate

359d The conflict between nurturance and autonomy in mother-daughter relationships and within feminism

385c Dependence and autonomy: The economic activities of secluded Hausa women in Kano, Nigeria

408g The convent as catalyst for autonomy: Two Hispanic nuns of the seventeenth century

443c The convergence of psychoanalysis and feminism: Gender identity and autonomy

459d Female power, autonomy and demographic change in the Third World

Autovampirism

280o Vampirism and autovampirism

Auxiliary

323w From ladies' auxiliaries to wives' committees

Avellaneda, Gertrudis Gómez de

408i Gertrude the Great: Avellaneda, nineteenth-century feminist

Avila, Spain

379g The holy woman and the urban community in sixteenth-century Avila

The Awakening

127b Thanatos and Eros: Kate Chopin's *The Awakening*

332b The novel of awakening (five novels)

356p The construction of ambiguity in *The Awakening*: A linguistic analysis

Azanian

39k The black woman in South Africa: An Azanian profile

Aztec

347f Aztec women: The transition from status to class in empire and colony

Babushka

472g The "babushka" or older woman in Soviet society

Baby

see also Child

56a Having a baby: A story essay

167f Babies against the bomb: A statement

307x A spermdonor baby grows up

310z Equal opportunity for babies? Not in Oakland!

Babylonia

156p The Naditu women of Sippar

Baccalaureate

361b Labor force participation of women baccalaureates in science

Bacchae

419h The menace of Dionysus: Sex roles and reversals in Euripides' *Bacchae*

The Bachelor's Pocket Book

286h *The Bachelor's Pocket Book for 1851*

Backlash

7c Pornography and the sexual revolution: The backlash of sadomasochism

60f The twenties' backlash: Compulsory heterosexuality, the consumer family, and the waning of feminism

Bad Timing

247h Now and nowhere: Roeg's *Bad Timing*

Bailey, Bemie

175y Mrs. Bailey and the bears

Bailey, Mollie

175m Mollie Bailey: Circus entrepreneur

Baird Poskanzer Memorial Lecture

220b Perspectives on women in the 1980s: The Baird Poskanzer Memorial Lecture

Baker, Polly

129r The Speech of Polly Baker

Bakongo

370j Slave wives, free sisters: Bakongo women and slavery c.1700-1850

Balabanoff, Angelica

95i Humanism versus feminism in the socialist movement: The life of Angelica Balabanoff

Balaclava

390o From balaclavas to bayonets: Women's voluntary war work, 1939-41

Bali

466c Healing as women's work in Bali

Baluchistan

255f Gradations of purdah and the creation of social boundaries on a Baluchistan oasis

Bambara, Toni Cade

40e From baptism to resurrection: Toni Cade Bambara and the incongruity of language

40f Music as theme: The jazz mode in the works of Toni Cade Bambara

150r What it is I think she's doing anyhow: A reading of Toni Cade Bambara's *The Salt Eaters*

450m Youth in Toni Cade Bambara's *Gorilla, My Love*

Bambi

307w Bambi meets Godzilla: Life in the corporate jungle

Banana

347k Stability in banana leaves: Colonization and women in Kiriwina, Trobriand Islands

Bandit Queen

175e Belle Starr: The Bandit Queen of Dallas

Bangkok, Thailand

420l Female migrants in Bangkok metropolis

424l The Bangkok masseuses: Origins, status and prospects

424p Women migrants in Bangkok: An economic analysis of their employment and earnings

Bangladesh

21j Women in politics: A case study of Bangladesh

92b Bangladesh: Beliefs and customs observed by Muslim rural women during their life cycle

98a Getting to know a rural community in Bangladesh

98b Research on women in Bangladesh: Notes on experiences from the field

98f Anthropological approach to study of rural women in Bangladesh: Experience of a female researcher

98g Field research on women in the Comilla District, Bangladesh

98h Personal account of the role of a supervisor in the Bangladesh fertility survey

98j Survey research with rural women in Bangladesh

98k Action research with rural women in Bangladesh: Some observations and experiences

98l Towards the making of a documentary film on rural women in Bangladesh

98m Methodological issues in longitudinal and comparative research in Bangladesh

255j Purdah and participation: Women in the politics of Bangladesh

400b Rural pauperization: Its impact on the economic role and status of rural women in Bangladesh

400c Women's income earning activities and family welfare in Bangladesh

400f Life cycle, food behaviour and nutrition of women in Bangladesh

400g Some aspects of mental health of women in Bangladesh

402f Women in Bangladesh: Food-for-work and socioeconomic change

433m The image of Bengal in the emerging literature of Bangladesh: The fiction of Hasan Azizul Huq

Bank

139i Feminisation and unionisation: A case study from banking

Baptism

40e From baptism to resurrection: Toni Cade Bambara and the incongruity of language

Baptist

see also Religion

60c The feminist theology of the black Baptist church, 1880-1900

176d I lead two lives: Confessions of a closet Baptist

301qq I lead two lives: Confessions of a closet Baptist

Bar

375j Barred from the bar: Women and legal education in the United States, 1870-1890

392o Mothers behind bars: A look at the parental rights of incarcerated women

Barbados

39y Social inequality and sexual status in Barbados

421s Labor force participation and fertility, contraceptive knowledge, attitude and practice of the women of Barbados

Barbara

341d Barbara's foodworld: A case history

Bargain

66d Wage setting and collective bargaining

67d Wage setting and collective bargaining

93b Collective bargaining as a strategy for achieving equal opportunity and equal pay: Sweden and West Germany

209ff Collective bargaining strategies on new technology: The experience of West German trade unions

323l Bargaining for equality

Bari

347e Forced transition from egalitarianism to male dominance: The Bari of Colombia

Barnes, Lucie

390k 'Without fear or favour' - Lucie Barnes

Baroque

389k Erica Tietze-Conrat (1883-1958): Productive scholar in renaissance and baroque art

Barrett, Elizabeth

196d The domestic economy of art: Elizabeth Barrett and Robert Browning

Barrier

98c Access to village women: Experiences in breaking barriers

349r Barriers to becoming a "successful" rape victim

415b Internal barriers

464b Overcoming the barriers: An approach to the study of how women's issues are kept from the political agenda

468d Women's attempts to break down sex barriers in the labour market

Barsetshire

27g "Old maids have friends": The unmarried heroine of Trollope's Barsetshire novels

Basa

393e The stable African family: Traditional and modern family structures in two African societies (Basa and Manding)

Baseball

147oo The All-American Girls' Baseball League, 1943-1954

Bashful

20m Bashful but bold: Notes on Margaret Atwood as critic

Basketball

107s Measures of body size and form of elite female basketball players

147aa The first intercollegiate contest for women: Basketball, April 4, 1896

147bb Interscholastic basketball: Bane of collegiate physical educators

147jj The 1930 U.B.C. women's basketball team: Those other world champions

147kk The story: Six-player girls' basketball in Iowa

Bastard

142a George Eliot's bastards

184f Bastardy and socioeconomic structure of south Germany

184g Bastardy in south Germany: A comment

184h Bastardy in south Germany: A reply

Bataan

424t Female employment and the family: A case study of the Bataan Export Processing Zone

Batavia

466a Women as cultural intermediaries in nineteenth-century Batavia

Bathsheba

286g Bathsheba's lovers: Male sexuality in *Far from the Madding Crowd*

Batter

see also Abuse

16m Battered women

26c Group treatment of children in shelters for battered women

26d Crisis intervention with battered women

78n Battered women: Society's problem

103c Battered women's shelters and the political economy of sexual violence

165c The dark side of marriage: Battered wives and the domination of women

211e Marriages made in heaven? Battered Jewish wives

226j Community responses to violence against women: The case of a battered women's shelter

349n Sex roles, power, and woman battering

349o   Secondary battering and alternatives of female victims to spouse abuse

359ii Psychosocial aspects of wife battering

359jj Wife battering and the maintenance of gender roles: A sociopsychological perspective

365n   Battered women

418g   Domestic violence: Battered women in Britain in the 1970s

434c   Therapy with battered women

435j   Battered women and public policy

455f   The social work profession encounters the battered woman

Battey

353t   The rise and fall of Battey's operation: A fashion in surgery

Bauer, Ida

256b   Freud's Dora, Dora's hysteria

Baule

347i   Women and men, cloth and colonization: The transformation of production-distribution relations among the Baule (Ivory Coast)

Bavaria

144c   Family and 'modernisation': The peasant family and social change in nineteenth-century Bavaria

145b   Enlightened reforms and Bavarian girls' education: Tradition through innovation

162c   Infanticide in rural Bavaria in the nineteenth century

Bawdy

301e   Magnolias grow in dirt: The bawdy lore of southern women

Bazaar

58c   Bazaar and service occupations

424m   Growth of the bazaar economy and its significance for women's employment: Trends of the 1970s in Davao City, Philippines

Bear

175y   Mrs. Bailey and the bears

301m   It seems to help me bear it better when she knows about it

Beard, Mary Ritter

125t   Mary Ritter Beard: Women as force

Beast

148b   Beasts of burden and menial slaves: Nineteenth century observations of Northern Plains Indian women

Beat

see also Abuse

140o   Overview: The "wife-beater's wife" reconsidered

461u   Wife beating: A product of sociosexual development

461v   Discussion: Psychoanalytic reflections on the "beaten wife syndrome"

Beauchamp, Christine

409h   The genuine Christine: Psychodynamics of Issy

Beauty

41a   Introduction: Beauty and the feast

Beauvoir, Simone de

30f   On "Clearing the Air": My letter to Simone de Beauvoir

108o   "My life...this curious object": Simone de Beauvoir on autobiography

125u   Simone de Beauvoir: Dilemmas of a feminist radical

Becquer, Gustavo Adolfo

313m   A feminist reading of "Los ojos verdes"

Beecher, Catharine

454j   Catharine Beecher and the education of American women

Beedi

299d   Beedi workers

Beguines

43u   The Beguines: A medieval women's community

187i   Feminine lay piety in the High Middle Ages: The Beguines

188i   The French heretic Beguine: Marguerite Porete

Behavior

see also Psychology

8h   Childhood and adolescent suicidal behavior, with an emphasis on girls

9g   Some behavioral and biological aspects of alcohol problems in women

16b   Cognitive-behavioral strategies for the treatment of depression in women

19b   Mrs. Hutchinson's behavior in terms of menopausal symptoms

28f   Cognitive behavior and the menstrual cycle

29a   Women's behavior in a man's world: Sex differences in competence

29c   Behavioral assessment of women clients

29d   Dissemination of behavioral interventions with women: Needed - a technology

29g   Marriage and the family: An unconscious male bias in behavioral treatment?

29h   Parenting: Training mothers as behavior therapists for their children

35e   Sex, endocrines, and political behavior

38o   Political behavior of American black women: An overview

51a   Toward a biosocial paradigm for menopause research: Lessons and contributions from the behavioral sciences

51o   Expectations regarding menstrual symptoms: Effects on evaluation and behavior of women

52e   Female marital behaviour in French society

89q   Wives' labor force behavior and family consumption patterns

136a   Nonverbal behavior: Barrier or agent for sex role change?

136b   Gender patterns in touching behavior

136d   Visual behavior and dominance in women and men

136i   A feminist critique of androgyny: Toward the elimination of gender attributions for learned behavior

136l   Nonverbal behavior and lesbian/gay orientation

173e   Abortion and the presidential election of 1976: A multivariate analysis of voting behavior

204a   Parental behavior and child development in nontraditional families: An introduction

204e   Varying degrees of paternal involvement in infant care: Attitudinal and behavioral correlates

239e   Biochemical and neurophysiological influences on human sexual behavior

252b   Second trimester abortion as a social problem: Delay in abortion seeking behaviour and its causes

266h   All things being equal, a behavior is superior to an attitude: Studies of sex-typed and sex-biased attitudes and behaviors

271i   Beyond a cognitive/behavioural approach: Congruent assertion training

271n   Hormones and behaviour: Introduction

271o   Mood and behaviour changes in menopausal women receiving gonadal hormones or placebo

280e   Gender dysphoria and dyssocial behavior

308b   The family's role in adolescent sexual behavior

308j   Bringing in the family: Kinship support and contraceptive behavior

309u   Sexual and contraceptive knowledge, attitudes and behavior of male adolescents

309x   Teenagers: Fertility control behavior and attitudes before and after abortion, childbearing or negative pregnancy test

324d   Attitudes toward women working: Changes over time and implications for the labor-force behaviors of husbands and wives

326l   Behavioral treatment of sexual dysfunction in sexual assault survivors

327c   Television viewing, family style and aggressive behavior in preschool children

344y   The sexual politics of interpersonal behavior

365i   Behavior therapies

380e   Power and political behaviors in organizations: A new frontier for research on male/female differences

387s   The impact of hierarchical structures on the work behavior of women and men

400f   Life cycle, food behaviour and nutrition of women in Bangladesh

410e   Sex differences in role behavior and policy orientations of suburban officeholders: The effect of women's employment

419f   Classical Greek attitudes to sexual behavior

436l   Will women judges make a difference in women's legal rights? A prediction from attitudes and simulated behaviour

439k   Behavior and the menstrual cycle

439o   Social and behavioral constructions of female sexuality

463i   Individual spatial behavior

463l   Women's travel behavior and attitudes: An empirical analysis

463n   Travel patterns and behavior of women in urban areas

Behavioral-Cognitive

29k   Depression: A behavioral-cognitive approach

Behn, Aphra

125a   Aphra Behn: A scandal to modesty

Being

303a   A different kind of being

462c The great chain of being and the chain of command

Belfast, Ireland

297h Bringing it all back home: An anthropologist in Belfast

Belief

92b Bangladesh: Beliefs and customs observed by Muslim rural women during their life cycle

190k Menstrual beliefs and experiences of mother-daughter dyads

190l Beliefs and attitudes of young girls regarding menstruation

435l The foreign policy beliefs of women in leadership positions

Belize

269b Structural continuity in the division of men's and women's work among black Carib (Garífuna)

The Bell Jar

127h "A ritual for being born twice": Sylvia Plath's *The Bell Jar*

Bellanca, Dorothy Jacobs

201j Dorothy Jacobs Bellanca: Women clothing workers and the runaway shops

Belton, TX

175n Martha White McWhirter and the Belton Sanctificationists

Bem

122g Bem's gender schema theory

Bench

78t A sexist selection process keeps qualified women off the bench

214f The view from the bench: The exercise of power

226i Women on the state bench: Correlates of access

Benedictine

187d Benedictine life for women in central France, 850-1100: A feminist revival

Beneficiary

267c Double jeopardy: Resistance to affirmative action from potential beneficiaries

Benefit

36p Benefits and risks of electronic fetal monitoring

37r Multiple public benefits and poor black families

46a Concepts underlying the current controversy about women's social security benefits

46b Supplemental OASI benefits to homemakers through current spouse benefits, a homemaker credit, and child-care drop-out years

46g Occupational pension plans and spouse benefits

103h Housework: Rethinking the costs and benefits

375i Adult derivative benefits in social security: A women's issue

425g Estimating benefits and costs of antisexist training programs in organizations

447n A legal perspective on pregnancy leave and benefits

Benevolence

454e Ladies bountiful: Organized women's benevolence in early nineteenth-century America

Bengal, India

161l Women and Bengali literature

194i The village Mother in Bengal

433a Goddesses or rebels: The women revolutionaries of Bengal

433c Madness as entropy: A Bengali view

433e Bengal politics of the first decade of the present century: A defence of extremism

433f Bengal election, 1937: Fazlul Huq and M. A. Jinnah: A study in leadership stress in Bengal politics

433g Inequality and radical land reform: Some notes from west Bengal

433i British response to Bengali literature in the nineteenth century

433m The image of Bengal in the emerging literature of Bangladesh: The fiction of Hasan Azizul Huq

Benign

53n Risk factors for benign and malignant breast disease

Bennett, Arnold

329o The whole contention between Mr. Bennett and Mrs. Woolf, revisited

Beret

384m Beret as the Norse mythological goddess Freya/Gurthr

Berlin, Germany

144h Women's work and the family: Women garment workers in Berlin and Hamburg before the First World War

Bertha

409e Bertha's role in *Exiles*

Best

407i Getting the best: Conclusions, recommendations, and selected resources

Bethune, Mary Mcleod

61i Mary McLeod Bethune and the National Youth Administration

412e Mary McLeod Bethune as religionist

Betray

127a The sentimentalists: Promise and betrayal in the home

Bett, Doris

450h Doris Bett's Nancy Finch: A heroine for the 1980s

Between the Acts

202l Virginia Woolf's last words on words: *Between the Acts* and 'Anon'

328l Theater of war: Virginia Woolf's *Between the Acts*

330m Woolf's peculiar comic world: *Between the Acts*

Beulah

450j Mary Lee Settle's connections: Class and clothes in the Beulah quintet

Beyer, Clara Mortenson

102k The work got done: An interview with Clara Mortenson Beyer

Bias

see also Discriminate

29g Marriage and the family: An unconscious male bias in behavioral treatment?

49k Reflections on polarities and bias

66f Statistical biases in the measurement of employment discrimination

67f Statistical biases in the measurement of employment discrimination

90e Clues to sex bias in the selection of school administrators: A report from the Oregon network

90f The problem of sex bias in curriculum materials

110e Sample selection bias as a specification error

266h All things being equal, a behavior is superior to an attitude: Studies of sex-typed and sex-biased attitudes and behaviors

266k The impact of societal biases on research methods

271f Sex-role ideology and sex bias in judgments of occupational suitability

273e Decision making and sex selection with biased technologies

283f Sexist bias and the law

359f The prevalence of gender-role bias in mental health services

402b The data base for studies on women: Sex biases in national data systems

Bible

see also Scripture, Religion

59b Emerging issues in feminist biblical interpretation

462t Affirming diversity and Biblical tradition

Biblewomen

379i The London biblewomen and nurses mission, 1857-1880: Class relations/women's relations

Bibliography

4m Bibliography: Women, science, and health

14d Selected bibliography on black feminism

14u Afro-American women 1800-1910: A selected bibliography

14v Afro-American women poets of the nineteenth century: A guide to research and bio-bibliographies of the poets

14w On the novels written by selected black women: A bibliographical essay

14y American black women composers: A selected annotated bibliography

138k Gender, class and education: A teaching bibliography of European studies

138l Gender, class and education: A teaching bibliography of Australian and New Zealand studies

138m Gender, class and education: A teaching bibliography of American studies

145r An English-language bibliography on European and American women's history

171k Sex similarities and differences in language, speech, and nonverbal communication: An annotated bibliography

176o Black lesbians before 1970: A bibliographical essay

180y Mothers and daughters in literature: A preliminary bibliography

186y A revised bibliography

303p The historical perspective: A bibliographical essay

311f Selected annotated bibliography of articles on theories of women's studies

312o Selected annotated bibliography of articles on theories of women's studies

315f Women, reproductive freedom, and the law: A selected annotated bibliography

323bb Women and unions: A selected bibliography

343r Women and men in Shakespeare: A selective bibliography

346e Salient laws on women and children: A selected bibliography

419n Selected bibliography on women in classical antiquity

Bieber, Margarete

389i Margarete Bieber (1879-1978): An archaeologist in two worlds

Bildung

332a Spiritual *Bildung*: The beautiful soul as paradigm

Bildungsroman

135l New directions in the contemporary bildungsroman: Lisa Alther's *Kinflicks*

202e *Jacob's Room* as comedy: Woolf's parodic Bildungsroman

332p Shadowing/surfacing/shedding: Contemporary German writers in search of a female Bildungsroman

Billboard

212c 'On the other side of the billboard...': Pornography, male fantasies and the objectification of women

Bimin-Kuskusmin

282d Transforming "natural" woman: Female ritual leaders and gender ideology among Bimin-Kuskusmin

Bind

404e The double bind: Minority women

Biobibliography

14v Afro-American women poets of the nineteenth century: A guide to research and bio-bibliographies of the poets

Biochemistry

51c Biochemical findings and medical management of the menopause

239e Biochemical and neurophysiological influences on human sexual behavior

438j Women in Cambridge biochemistry (United Kingdom)

Biogas

172m Saving money with bio-gas (Colombia)

Biography

30u Daughters writing: Toward a theory of women's biography

30w Biographer and subject: A critical connection

142j George Eliot and her biographers

145i Self-conscious histories: Biographies of German women in the nineteenth century

176r Lesbian biography, biography of lesbians

177j The Chinese biographical method: A moral and didactic tradition

186b An eccentric biography

302f Biographical research on women librarians: Its paucity, perils, and pleasures

329p Combining 'the advantages of act and fiction': Virginia Woolf's biographies of Vita Sackville-West, Flush, and Roger Fry

379e Was she a good mother? Some thoughts on a new issue for feminist biography

445f Mari Sandoz and western biography

457b Theosophy and feminism: Some explorations in nineteenth century biography

Biology

9g Some behavioral and biological aspects of alcohol problems in women

28e The psychology of the menstrual cycle: Biological and physiological perspectives

31b Human biology in feminist theory: Sexual equality reconsidered

34d Social bodies: The interaction of culture and women's biology

34g Changing minds: Women, biology, and the menstrual cycle

35b Biology, gender, and politics: An assessment and critique

50q Biological sex differences and sex stereotyping

79cc Biological manipulations for producing and nurturing mammalian embryos

79kk The biology of utopia: Science fiction perspectives on ectogenesis

84a Women is not a rational animal: On Aristotle's biology of reproduction

91a A new outlook on women: Psychological and biological

189n The emperor doesn't wear any clothes: The impact of feminism on biology

193c A biological basis for the sex differences in achievement in science?

193f Biological inevitabilities or political choices? The future for girls in science

342d The dialectic of biology and culture

351d Biology: Its role in gender-related educational experiences

353a The female animal: Medical and biological views of woman and her role in nineteenth-century America

354g Do men and women have different jobs because of their biological differences?

354k Sociobiology: Another biological determinism

372j Introduction to the biology of the female athlete

439j Biological influences on human sex and gender

439n Toward a biology of menopause

447j The biology of toxic effects on reproductive outcomes

Biomedicine

10e Vulnerability to the biomedical consequences of alcoholism and alcohol-related problems among women

36d Value conflicts in biomedical research into future contraceptives

423b Women and health: The social dimensions of biomedical data

Biopolitics

35a Introduction: Biopolitics and gender

35d The biopolitics of sex: Gender, genetics, and epigenetics

Biopsychosocial

239b Biopsychosocial processes in the development of sex-related differences

Biosocial

51a Toward a biosocial paradigm for menopause research: Lessons and contributions from the behavioral sciences

Birth

see also Reproduce

36a Reproductive technologies: The birth of a women-centered analysis

36o Drugs, birth, and ethics

36r A report on birth in three cultures

36s Community alternatives to high technology birth

36t Contrasts in the birthing place: Hospital and birth center

36u Ethical issues relating to childbirth as experienced by the birthing woman and midwife

79a Reproductive technologies: The birth of a women-centered analysis

135r On the birth of death: An *Arrest d'Amour* of Martial d'Auvergne

156i Hittite birth rituals

190c Age at menarche and year of birth in relation to adult height and weight among Caucasian, Japanese, and Chinese women living in Hawaii

233f Birth defects and parental occupation

233i Occupational fatigue and preterm birth

239h American birth practices: A critical review

269h Symbolic aspects of Bribri roles on the occasions of birth and death

309c The legitimacy status of first births to U.S. women aged 15-24, 1939-1978

309n Marriage, remarriage, marital disruption and age at first birth

315h Two in one, one in two: An exploration of a birth experience and images of the sacred

353m Birthing and anesthesia: The debate over twilight sleep

354b Convenience and the occurrence of births: Induction and labor in the United States and Canada

Birth Control

see also Contraception, Reproduce

36g Woman-controlled birth control: A feminist analysis of natural birth control

158c The Victorians, the psychologists, and psychic birth control

184d Elizabethan birth control and Puritan attitudes

184n The origins of the birth control movement in England in the early nineteenth century

205w Vivian Dowding: Birth control activist 1892-

223j Sex, birth control, and human life

245c Why nineteenth-century feminists did not support "birth control" and twentieth-century feminists do: Feminism, reproduction, and the family

353g Voluntary motherhood: The beginnings of feminist birth control ideas in the United States

353i Doctors, birth control, and social values, 1830-1970

354h The politics of birth control, 1920-1940: The impact of professionals

396d Depo-provera: The extent of the problem: A case study in the politics of birth control

Birth Order

421f Birth order and alienation among college women in Lebanon

Birthday

150v LeRoy's birthday

Bisexuality

257i From where I stand: A case for feminist bisexuality

281e Homosexual and bisexual issues

282b The gender revolution and the transition from bisexual horde to patrilocal band: The origins of gender hierarchy

Bishop

91g Challenge of feminism to the church: A Bishop's perspective

187l Medieval Cistercian nunneries and English Bishops

Black

see also African American, Minority, Race

39q The myth of the black matriarchy

39cc West Indian characteristics of the black Carib

40aa The unicorn is black: Audre Lorde in retrospect

174w Black-eyed blues connections: From the inside out

194c In quest of the Black Virgin: She is black because she is black

269b Structural continuity in the division of men's and women's work among black Carib (Garífuna)

325i Black Carib women and rites of death

474g On being female, black, and free

Black Studies

122b Black studies/women's studies: Points of convergence

314k Black studies and women's studies: An overdue partnership

Black Virgin

194c In quest of the Black Virgin: She is black because she is black

Black Woman

see also African American Woman

23b Black sisterhood: The situation of urban aboriginal women and their relationship to the white women's movement

39k The black woman in South Africa: An Azanian profile

39m Racism and tradition: Black womanhood in historical perspective

39t Black women and music: A survey from Africa to the new world

39x Black women and survival: A Maroon case

39bb The black woman in Haitian society and literature

52q The changing position of black women in South Africa

Black-eyed

14s Black-eyed blues connections: Teaching black women

Black-eyed Susans

14t Teaching *Black-eyed Susans*: An approach to the study of black women writers

Blackberry Winter

452k The metaphysics of matrilinearism in women's autobiography: Studies of Mead's *Blackberry Winter*, Hellman's *Pentimento*, Angelou's *I Know Why the Caged Bird Sings*, and Kingston's *The Woman Warrior*

Blackmun, Hugo

2f Understanding Blackmun's argument: The reasoning of *Roe v Wade*

Blackwell, Antoinette L. B.

126f A feminist challenge to Darwinism: Antoinette L. B. Blackwell on the relations of the sexes in nature and society

Blackwell, Elizabeth

379n Feminism, professionalism, and germs: A study of the thought of Mary Putnam Jacobi and Elizabeth Blackwell

Blessing

70h Indian boarding schools and Indian women: Blessing or curse?

303k The black female academic: Doubly burdened or doubly blessed?

Blond

399m Lydia Thompson and the "British Blondes"

Blood

150h The blood - yes, the blood: A conversation

156h Bound to bleed: Artemis and Greek women

229z From sacred blood to the curse and beyond

Bloom, Grace Pilgrim

394s A remarkable woman: Grace Pilgrim Bloom

Bloom, Molly

409g The conventional Molly Bloom

Bloomsbury

329a Virginia Woolf and the intellectual origins of Bloomsbury

Blue

174w Black-eyed blues connections: From the inside out

206m Blue jeans blues

Blue Collar

see also Employment

210e Beyond the sweatshop: Older women in blue-collar jobs

307t Blue collar women

425b Hard-hatted women: Reflections on blue-collar employment

426f Women and nontraditional blue collar jobs in the 1980s: An overview

The Blue Gardenia

406e The place of women in Fritz Lang's *The Blue Gardenia*

Blueprint

42e Blueprints for living

Blues

14s Black-eyed blues connections: Teaching black women

40qq Music as theme: The blues mode in the works of Margaret Walker

Boarding

70h Indian boarding schools and Indian women: Blessing or curse?

Boat

241g 'Women and old boats': The sexual division of labour in a Newfoundland outport

Bodichon, Barbara

125f Barbara Bodichon: Integrity in diversity

Body

34d Social bodies: The interaction of culture and women's biology

51k Smoking, alcohol, and body mass relationships to early menopause: Implications for risk of cardiovascular disease

51s The fallacy of bodily reductionism

64m Writing, language, and the body

107i Proportionality and body composition in male and female Olympic athletes: A kinanthropometric overview

107o Body composition and somatotype characteristics of sportswomen

107s Measures of body size and form of elite female basketball players

107t Body build of female Olympic rowers

107u Body segment contributions of female athletes to translational and rotational requirements of non-twisting springboard dive takeoffs

120l My body in writing

129n Body housekeeping

136e Sex differences in body movements and positions

222f New brains for old bodies: The impact of emotional and physical stress during the Ph.D. process

225j The myth of the perfect body

225k The body politic: The defense of sexual restriction by anti-abortion activists

239m Body time and social time: Mood patterns by menstrual cycle phase and day of week

279m Absolute and relative sex differences in body composition

305c Whose body? Whose self? Beyond pornography

310s Claiming all of our bodies: Reproductive rights and disabilities

329f Virginia Woolf and the problem of the body

341c A woman's body in a man's world: A review of findings on body image and weight control

Bogan, Louise

135f Symbol, mask, and meter in the poetry of Louise Bogan

Bold

20m Bashful but bold: Notes on Margaret Atwood as critic

Bolivia

83g Class consciousness and world view of a Bolivian mining woman

172d Learning to take hold of one's own destiny (Bolivia)

172i Integrating women into rural cooperatives: Pluses and minuses (Bolivia)

200d The power of signs: Gender, culture and the wild in the Bolivian Andes

325q   Rosinta, rats, and the river: Bad luck is banished in Andean Bolivia

Bolshevik

405e   Bolshevik women: The first generation

405g   Marxism and women's oppression: Bolshevik theory and practice in the 1920's

Bomb

167f   Babies against the bomb: A statement

167k   Organising a mass lobby of Parliament: Families against the bomb

215b   How I learnt to start worrying and hate the bomb: The effects of a nuclear bombardment

Bombal, María Luisa

74a   "Feminine" testimony in the works of Teresa de la Parra, María Luisa Bombal, and Victoria Ocampo

Bombay, India

18e   Population policy, family size, and the reproduction of the labor force in India: The case of Bombay

101g   Nationalism, universalization, and the extended female space in Bombay City

Bond

132d   The bonds of love: Rational violence and erotic domination

180r   A subtle psychic bond: The mother figure in Sylvia Plath's poetry

369l   The marriage of capitalist and patriarchical ideologies: Meanings of male bonding and male ranking in U.S. culture

462e   Racism and the bonding of women

Bondage

91o   Bondage: Denial or fundamental rights to women

102b   Breaking free of symbolic bondage: From feminine submission to a vision of equality

280n   Bondage and sadomasochism

Book

see also Read, Textbook

33c   Book-lined cells: Women and humanism in the early Italian Renaissance

258a   Sex differences and this book

263h   Creating a place for women: American book publishing in the nineteenth century

265n   Sex role images in Lebanese text books

439p   "The love crisis": Couples advice books of the late 1970s

474m   The coming book

Book of Good Love

408d   Women in the *Book of Good Love*

The Book of Margery Kempe

108d   Autobiography of a new 'creatur': Female spirituality, selfhood, and authorship in *The Book of Margery Kempe*

Border

428i   Mexican border industrialization, female labor force participation, and migration

Borderline

28p   Premenstrual tension in borderline and related disorders

"Born not to Write"

64q   Colette and signs: A partial reading of a writer "Born *not* to Write"

Borneo

234c   Shamanism as institutionalised ego defense and elite formation associated with transvestism in a Borneo society

Borroloola, Australia

333g   The recent history of the Borroloola aboriginal people and their struggle for land rights

333h   Borroloola community and land rights

333i   Borroloola women speak. Man and woman: Dance

Boss

263l   Men servants and women bosses: The domestic service institution in colonial Zambia

Boston, MA

353ff   "Neither for the drawing room nor for the kitchen": Private duty nursing in Boston, 1873-1914

Bostonians

17h   The *Bostonians*: Feminists and the new world

Botany

379f   Linnaeus's daughters: Women and British botany

Bottle

11b   Femininity by the bottle

Boundary

255f   Gradations of purdah and the creation of social boundaries on a Baluchistan oasis

Bountiful

454e   Ladies bountiful: Organized women's benevolence in early nineteenth-century America

Bovary, Emma

135p   Emma Bovary's masculinization: Convention of clothes and morality of conventions

Bow

282c   The bow and the burden strap: A new look at institutionalized homosexuality in native North America

Bowen, Sally

390q   Sally Bowen: Political and social experiences of a working-class woman

Box

202j   The politics of city space in *The Years*: Street, love, pillar boxes and bridges

Boy

see also Child, Male, Man, Masculine

34b   Boys will be boys will be boys: The language of sex and gender

78y   Doing time with the boys: An analysis of women correctional officers in all-male facilities

134c   Groping towards sexism: Boys' sex talk

193g   Factors differentially affecting the science subject preferences, choices and attitudes of girls and boys

193m   Differential treatment of boy and girl pupils during science lessons

193o   Girls' science: Boys' science revisited

259b   Boys and girls entering school

265h   Sex typing in occupational preferences of high school boys and girls

265t   Mental health in boys and girls: Awareness of attitudes for positive sex roles

326f   Clinical intervention with boy victims of sexual abuse

356k   Directive-response speech sequences in girls' and boys' task activities

Brabant

188h   The Brabant mystic: Hadewijch

Brackett, Leigh

114a   Leigh Brackett: No "long goodbye" is good enough

Braddon, Mary Elizabeth

286e   "Other people's prudery": Mary Elizabeth Braddon

Bradley, Marion Zimmer

114g   Marion Zimmer Bradley's ethic of freedom

Brain

34k   The quirks of a woman's brain

124k   Split brain research and its implications for feminist education

126o   Sex differences in the brain: Implications for curriculum change

222f   New brains for old bodies: The impact of emotional and physical stress during the Ph.D. process

438i   A little about myself, and more about a more important matter - the brain (USSR)

Braun, Lily

145k   The radicalization of Lily Braun

Brazil

39ee   Images of the woman of color in Brazilian literature: O Cortico, Clara Dos Anjos, Gabriela Cravo E Canela, and O Quinze

83h   The church, the unions, women and the opposition in Brazil

153j   Household economy and financial capital: The case of passbook savings in Brazil

153k   The contribution of public goods to household reproduction: Case study from Brazil

363d   Patrons, politics, and schools: An arena for Brazilian women

428d   Women, production, and reproduction in industrial capitalism: A comparison of Brazilian and U.S. factory workers

436c   Women's role in the formulation of public policies in Brazil

473e   Spirit magic in the social relations between men and women (São Paulo, Brazil)

473f   Spirit mediums in Umbanda Evangelizada of Porto Alegre, Brazil: Dimensions of power and authority

Breast

53n   Risk factors for benign and malignant breast disease

141a   Introduction to breast cancer genetics

141b   Genetic control of breast cancer susceptibility in animals

141c   Statistical model for the study of familial breast cancer

141d   Pathologic aspects of familial carcinoma of breast

141e   Epidemiology of breast cancer

141f   Genetic heterogeneity and breast cancer: Variable tumor spectra

141g   Hormones, genetics, and breast cancer

141h   Breast cancer in Cowden's syndrome

141i   Genetic counseling, patient and family management: Familial breast cancer

319d   Breast-feeding and social class mobility: The case of Mexican migrant mothers in Houston, Texas

456e   Breast cancer and benign breast disease

Breckinridge, Mary

353w   Mary Breckinridge, the frontier nursing service, and the introduction of nurse-mid-wifery in the United States

Bremen

336d   The Bremen morality scandal

Bribri Indians

269h   Symbolic aspects of Bribri roles on the occasions of birth and death

Bride

see also Dowry, Marriage, Wedding

99a   Brides of Christ and poor mortals: Women in medieval society

211u   Bride, spouse, daughter: Images of the feminine in classical Jewish sources

408f   Women against wedlock: The reluctant brides of Golden Age drama

Bridewealth

156l   Bridewealth and dowry in Nuzi

Bridge

81h   Two washes in the morning and a bridge party at night: The American housewife between the wars

202j   The politics of city space in *The Years*: Street, love, pillar boxes and bridges

Brigadas

363c   Women and revolution: The brigadas femeninas and the Mexican Cristero Rebellion, 1926-1929

Bright, Mary Chavelita Dunne

124a   Rediscovering the "New Woman" of the 1890's: The stories of "George Egerton"

Brigid

194d   The cult of Brigid: A study of pagan-Christian syncretism in Ireland

Britain

see England

British Blondes

399m   Lydia Thompson and the "British Blondes"

British Columbia

111t   Recent development in probation and parole in British Columbia

157a   Writing women into British Columbia's history

157b   To Columbia on the Tynemouth: The emi-gration of single women and girls in 1862

157c   Notes on the British Columbia Protestant Orphan's Home

157d   British Columbia Women's Institute in the early years: Time to remember

157i   Sexism in British Columbia trade unions, 1900-1920

157l   The B.C. Liberal Party and women's reforms, 1916-1928

157n   Women and reform in British Columbia: Some preliminary suggestions

157p   Appendix: Votes for women: Profiles of prominent British Columbia suffragists and social reformers

205b   When you don't know the language, listen to the silence: An historical overview of native Indian women in BC

205c   Rainbow women of the Fraser Valley: Lifesongs through the generations

205d   A preliminary sketch of Chinese women and work in British Columbia, 1858-1950

205f   A note on Asian Indian women in British Columbia, 1900-1935

205g   "Roughing it in the bush" in British Columbia: Mary Moody's pioneer life in New Westminster 1859-1863

205h   From pastels to chisel: The changing role of BC women artists

205j   Six saucepans to one: Domestic science vs. the home in British Columbia 1900-1930

205k   Women on campus in British Columbia: Strategies for survival, years of war and peace, 1906-1920

205l   Postscript: Women in whose honour BC schools have been named

205m   The brightest women of our land: Vancouver clubwomen 1919-1928

205n   They also served: The British Columbia women's institutes in two World Wars

205o   Domesticity and discipline: The Girl Guides in British Columbia 1910-1943

205q   "Services rendered, rearing children for the state": Mothers' pensions in British Columbia 1919-1931

205r   Sinners or sinned against?: Historical aspects of female juvenile delinquency in British Columbia

205s   Last back: Folklore and the telephone operators in the 1919 Vancouver general strike

205t   A union man's wife: The ladies' auxiliary movement in the IWA, the Lake Cowichan experience

205u   Cheap at half the price: The history of the fight for equal pay in BC

205v   The search for legitimacy: Nurses' registra-tion in British Columbia 1913-1935

205x   Reducing maternal mortality in British Columbia: An educational process

205bb   From home to house: Women in the BC legislature

205cc   Joan Kennedy and the British Columbia Women's Service Corps

205dd   Women at Cominco during the second World War

305s   Women in trades in British Columbia

323o   Domestic workers: The experience in B.C.

British Columbia Women's Institute

157d   British Columbia Women's Institute in the early years: Time to remember

Brittain, Vera

125s   Vera Brittain: Feminist in a new age

Brittany

162e   'Avoir sa part': Sibling relations in partible inheritance Brittany

Broadcast

358a   Women in broadcasting (U.S.) de jure, de facto

Broner, E.M.

417y   Neither Arcadia nor Elysium: E.M. Broner's *A Weave of Women*

Bronson, Charles

131l   Charles Bronson, Samurai, and other fem-inine images: A transactive response to *The Left Hand of Darkness*

Brontë, Charlotte

109k   Terror-gothic: Nightmare and dream in Ann Radcliffe and Charlotte Brontë

109l   Place and eros in Radcliffe, Lewis, and Brontë

109p   Dreaming of children: Literalization in *Jane Eyre* and *Wuthering Heights*

135o   Snow beneath snow: A reconsideration of the virgin of *Villette*

332c   "Fairy-born and human-bred": Jane Eyre's education in romance

332d   The reflecting reader in *Villette*

332f   The sisterhood of Jane Eyre and Antoinette Cosway

Brontë, Emily

109e   The reconstruction of the gothic feminine ideal in Emily Brontë's *Wuthering Heights*

109p   Dreaming of children: Literalization in *Jane Eyre* and *Wuthering Heights*

Brooks, Gwendolyn

40h   Gwendolyn Brooks: Poet of the whirlwind

40i   Gwendolyn Brooks' poetic realism: A developmental survey

332n   Plain, black, and decently wild: The heroic possibilities of *Maud Martha*

Brother

see also Family

17k   Brother Theodore, hell on women

108j   Fanny Mendelssohn Hensel: Musician in her brother's shadow

162g   Young bees in an empty hive: Relations between brothers-in-law in a south German village around 1800

172j   Where are our campesino brothers? Let the murderers answer! (Nicaragua)

196j   Closer than a brother: Swinburne and Watts-Dunton

202i   Private brother, public world

Brown, Charles Brockden

17a   Charles Brockden Brown: Feminism in fic-tion

Brown, Rita Mae

450l   Rita Mae Brown: Feminist theorist and southern novelist

Browning, Elizabeth Barrett

27f   *Sonnets from the Portuguese*: A negative and a positive context

Browning, Robert

196d   The domestic economy of art: Elizabeth Barrett and Robert Browning

Bruja

313f   Mis brujas favoritas

Brunei

473b   Women of Brunei

Bryant, Dorothy

131e   Coming Home: Four feminist utopias and patriarchal experience

Bryn Mawr

292d   Blue collars and bluestockings: The Bryn Mawr summer school for women workers, 1921-1938

Buddhism
see also Religion

300k Buddhist attitudes toward social change in Burma and Thailand

300l Have stories, will travel: How Buddhism won the southeast

325n The case of the vanishing nuns: The fruits of ambivalence in ancient Indian Buddhism

325o Accomplished women in tantric Buddhism of medieval India and Tibet

401a The Chinese Buddhist monastic order for women: The first two centuries

431a Buddhism, sex-roles and the Thai economy

431c Laywomen in Theravada Buddhism

Budget

207f 'I'm hungry, mum': The politics of domestic budgeting

208f 'I'm hungry, mum': The politics of domestic budgeting

283p Public expenditure and budgetary policy

Buenos Aires, Argentina

379h Right-wing female activists in Buenos Aires, 1900-1932

Build

43x Building feminist organizations

86e Closed office-building syndrome

107t Body build of female Olympic rowers

203s The Los Angeles woman's building: A public center for woman's culture

295b Women as competent community builders: The other side of the coin

Bulimia

140l Cinderella's stepsisters: A feminist perspective on anorexia nervosa and bulimia

359r Cinderella's stepsisters: A feminist perspective on anorexia nervosa and bulimia

Bullrich, Silvina

74e The paradoxes of Silvina Bullrich

Bun, Papua New Guinea

246c Complementarity: The relationship between female and male in the East Sepik village of Bun, Papua New Guinea

Bunch, Charlotte

174z Charlotte Bunch and Betty Powell talk about feminism, blacks, and education as politics

Bunyole, Uganda

457j Men, women and misfortune in Bunyole

Buñuel, Luis

408q From mistress to murderess: The metamorphosis of Buñuel's Tristana

Burden

148b Beasts of burden and menial slaves: Nineteenth century observations of Northern Plains Indian women

282c The bow and the burden strap: A new look at institutionalized homosexuality in native North America

303k The black female academic: Doubly burdened or doubly blessed?

Bureaucracy

128b Women in the party bureaucracy: Subservient functionaries

321k The bureaucrat as usurer

300i The public bureaucracy and social change in Singapore

421z Women in the Cuban bureaucracies: 1968-1974

435m Bureaucratic resistance to women's programs: The case of women in development

436e Women in government as policy-makers and bureaucrats: The Turkish case

Burglary

280i Burglaries with sexual dynamics

Burma

194n The Great Goddess today in Burma and Thailand: An exploration of her symbolic relevance to monastic and female roles

300k Buddhist attitudes toward social change in Burma and Thailand

Burnout

221g Burnout and job dissatisfaction: Impact on the family

Business
see also Company, Corporation, Factory, Industry, Management

82t The female family business: A Guatemalan example

129t Are feminist businesses capitalist?

199g Word processing: Forward for business, backward for women

274o Business studies

Businesswoman

421v Some comments on the home roles of businesswomen in India, Australia and Canada

Butler, Josephine

125i Josephine Butler: From sympathy to theory

Buy

463r A comparative survey of women car buyers

Bwanikwa

370n Bwanikwa: Consciousness and protest among slave women in Central Africa, 1886-1911

Byzantine

156k In search of Byzantine women: Three avenues of approach

187b Byzantine asceticism and women's monasteries in early medieval Italy

389l Sirarpie Der Nersessian (b. 1896): Educator and scholar in Byzantine and Armenian art

Cagayan de Oro, Philippines

424k Female domestic servants in Cagayan de Oro, Philippines: Social and economic implications of employment in a 'premodern' occupational role

Calamus

301c Pipsissewa, Calamus, and Pennyroyal

Calcutta, India

255d The domestic realm in the lives of Hindu women in Calcutta

433d British tradesmen of Calcutta, 1830-1900: A preliminary study of their economic and political roles

Cali, Colombia

395i Women's understanding about reproductive physiology and their choice of herbal medicines in Cali, Colombia

Califia

174l Califia: An experiment in feminist education Califia community

174m Feminist art and education at Califia: My personal experience

174n Women of color Califia

California

73d The Museo Italo Americano: My involvement with the Italian American community in San Francisco

111o Managing the female offender: Crisis and change in the California Institution for Women

192i Se me acabó la canción: An ethnography of non-consenting sterilizations among Mexican women in Los Angeles

192l Los Angeles garment district sews a cloak of shame

192r La costura en Los Angeles 1933-1939: The ILGWU and the politics of domination

203s The Los Angeles woman's building: A public center for woman's culture

226e Women in political parties: Gender differences in motives among California party activists

310z Equal opportunity for babies? Not in Oakland!

319k Social networks and survival strategies: An exploratory study of Mexican American, black and Anglo family female heads in San Jose, California

319o The nonconsenting sterilization of Mexican women in Los Angeles: Issues of psychocultural rupture and legal redress in paternalistic behavior

379l City mothers, city daughters, and the dance hall girls: The limits of female political power in San Francisco, 1913

399e Crowning Miss California, again

445c The Tonopah ladies

445i Gertrude Atherton's California woman: From love story to psychological drama

453e Humor in California underground women's comix

California Institution for Women

111o Managing the female offender: Crisis and change in the California Institution for Women

Calvinism
see also Religion

197d Calvinism and Catholicism in Muriel Spark

Cambridge University

160b Ambivalence and dedication: Academic wives in Cambridge University, 1870-1970

438j Women in Cambridge biochemistry (United Kingdom)

Cameo

109i The mirror and the cameo: Margaret Atwood's comic/gothic novel, *Lady Oracle*

Camera

61o Photographs as historical documents (American women through the camera's eye)

Cameron, Agnes Deans

157f Agnes Deans Cameron: Against the current

Cameroon

393a Wage earner and mother: Compatibility of roles on a Cameroon plantation

393g Education and fertility among Cameroonian working women

Camp

160d Camp followers: A note on wives of the armed services

167h On common ground: The women's peace camp at Greenham Common

215h A voice from the peace camps: Greenham Common and Upper Heyford

Campaign

133v Referendum campaigns vs. gay rights

167d A national campaign: Women's party for survival

238g The awesome power of sex: The polemical campaign against Mormon polygamy

290a 'Free from all uninvited touch of man': Women's campaigns around sexuality, 1880-1914

Campaign for Nuclear Disarmament (CND)

283m The impasse facing CND

Campbell, May

205p "Especially when no one agrees": An interview with May Campbell

Campesino

172j Where are our campesino brothers? Let the murderers answer! (Nicaragua)

Campus

see also Education

205k Women on campus in British Columbia: Strategies for survival, years of war and peace, 1906-1920

394e Graduate women assess the campus

Canada

see also individual provinces

20a The where of here: Margaret Atwood and a Canadian tradition

27o Quebec women writers

52b The changing roles of Canadian women in family and work: An overview

52s Egalitarianism in marriage? Graduate education and the sexual division of labour in the Canadian family

52t Wife and/or worker: Sex role concepts of Canadian female students

65k Canada's equal pay for work of equal value law

93k The role of the National Action Committee on the Status of Women in facilitating equal pay policy in Canada

147f Woman's place in nineteenth century Canadian sport

147j Women's participation in sporting activities as an indicator of a feminist movement in Canada between 1867-1914

147n An analysis of humour pertaining to sportswomen in Canadian newspapers from 1910-1920

147q Canadian women at the Olympic games

147r Canadian women at the Commonwealth games

147t The effect of current sports legislation on women in Canada and the U.S.A. - Title IX

147ii The Edmonton Grads: The team and its social significance from 1915-1940

157b To Columbia on the Tynemouth: The emigration of single women and girls in 1862

157k The 'social evil': Prostitution in Vancouver, 1900-1920

157m A response to the depression: The local Council of Women of Vancouver

168d What has the feminist perspective done for Canadian history?

180t A psychological journey: Mothers and daughters in English-Canadian fiction

205a "Sundays always make me think of home": Time and place in Canadian women's history

209gg Taking the initiative on new technology: Canadian labor approaches

228c Canada

271d Women of South Asian and Anglo-Saxon origins in the Canadian context

289m Institutional life: The Canadian experience

302m An analysis of the study, "Career paths of male and female librarians in Canada"

305x Working with words: Feminist publishing in Canada

323a Women at work in Canada

323b Women and unions in Canada: A statistical overview

323c No proper deal: Women workers and the Canadian labour movement, 1870-1940

323e "Action Positive" in the Quebec trade union movement

338j Appendix: A reply to the toast to Canada

347a Montagnais women and the Jesuit program for colonization

354b Convenience and the occurrence of births: Induction and labor in the United States and Canada

357d Low pay and female employment in Canada with selected references to the USA

380d The relationship between the labor force employment of women and the changing social organization in Canada

380h Job creation and unemployment for Canadian women

380l Women's work and the family wage in Canada

388e Women's work and worth in an Acadian maritime village

391e Changing Canadian and US magazine portrayals of women and work: Growing opportunities for choice

421d Social and economic integration of South Asian women in Montreal, Canada

421l English-Canadian and French-Canadian attitudes towards women: Results of the Canadian Gallup polls

421p Changes in Canadian female labour force participation and some possible implications for conjugal power

421v Some comments on the home roles of businesswomen in India, Australia and Canada

421bb Minority within a minority: On being South Asian and female in Canada

Canadian Labour Congress

305m Getting organized...in the Canadian Labour Congress

Canadian Ladies Golf Union

147ll The development of women's organized sport in the 1920's: A study of the Canadian Ladies Golf Union

Cancer

see also Carcinoma, Disease

53m Time trends of cancer incidence and mortality among women

53p Estrogens and endometrial cancer

53q Risk factors for ovarian cancer

141a Introduction to breast cancer genetics

141b Genetic control of breast cancer susceptibility in animals

141c Statistical model for the study of familial breast cancer

141e Epidemiology of breast cancer

141f Genetic heterogeneity and breast cancer: Variable tumor spectra

141g Hormones, genetics, and breast cancer

141h Breast cancer in Cowden's syndrome

141i Genetic counseling, patient and family management: Familial breast cancer

240g Psychological aspects of gynaecological cancer

285h Sexuality and cancer

285m Sexual rehabilitation after gynecologic cancer

354c Vaginal cancer: An iatrogenic disease?

456e Breast cancer and benign breast disease

Candidate

23g 'Women candidates speak'

125o Vida Goldstein: The women's candidate

226f Women as legislative candidates in six states

378l Candidate evaluations by men and women

Candle

40j A candle in a gale wind

Cannabis

9q The effects of opiates, sedative-hypnotics, amphetamines, cannabis, and other psychoactive drugs on the fetus and newborn

Canon

306a The whole truth: Frameworks for the study of women's noncanonical literature

314c The humanities: Redefining the canon

Canoness

188b The Saxon canoness: Hrotsvit of Gandersheim

Canopus in Argos: Archives

417bb Change and art in women's worlds: Doris Lessing's *Canopus in Argos: Archives*

Cantigas de Amigo

22h La lyrique portugaise primitive de "Cantigas de Amigo"

331b Voice and audience: The emotional world of the *cantigas de amigo*

Capital

89g Family investments in human capital: Earnings of women

149b Capital, the state and the origins of the working-class household

153j Household economy and financial capital: The case of passbook savings in Brazil

192j Capital's flight: The apparel industry moves south

350g From rural subsistence to an industrial peripheral work force: An examination of female Malaysian migrants and capital accumulation in Singapore

369g What is the real material base of patriarchy and capital?

385b Control of land, labor, and capital in rural southern Sierra Leone

Capitalism
see also Industrial

13b Capitalism, gender and the labour process: Two case studies

18i Neo-Malthusian ideology and colonial capitalism: Population dynamics in southwestern Puerto Rico

39dd The spread of capitalism in rural Colombia: Effects on poor women

43o Patriarchy and capitalism

104a Aspects of non-capitalist social relations in rural Egypt: The small peasant household in an Egyptian delta village

129t Are feminist businesses capitalistic?

139b Patriarchal exploitation and the rise of English capitalism

148h Sioux women in transition: A study of their changing status in a domestic and capitalist sector of production

149e The expanded reproduction cycle of labour power in twentieth-century capitalism

153a Household structures and labor-force formation in the capitalist world-economy

207g Women, kinship and capitalist development

208j Women, kinship and capitalist development

227o 'The housewife and her labour under capitalism' - a critique

231d Capitalism and gay identity

321n Can there be justice for women under capitalism?: Questions about 'patriarchy'

321o Can there be justice for women under capitalism?: Social justice for whom?

354j Chlorosis and chronic disease in 19th-century Britain: The social constitution of somatic illness in a capitalist society

369h Capitalism is an advanced stage of patriarchy: But Marxism is not feminism

369l The marriage of capitalist and patriarchical ideologies: Meanings of male bonding and male ranking in U.S. culture

369m The unhappy marriage of patriarchy and capitalism

428c Capitalism, imperialism, and patriarchy: The dilemma of Third-World women workers in multinational factories

428d Women, production, and reproduction in industrial capitalism: A comparison of Brazilian and U.S. factory workers

428g The domestic clothing workers in the Mexican metropolis and their relation to dependent capitalism

428j *Maquiladoras*: A new face of international capitalism on Mexico's northern frontier

440d Women and consumer capitalism

440e Capitalism, patriarchy and the city

Capitol
175g The capitol's lady

Captain
131m A female captain's enterprise: The implications of *Star Trek's* "Turnabout Intruder"

Capture
254f Captured angel in the centerfold

Car
463r A comparative survey of women car buyers

Carcinoma
see also Cancer, Disease

141d Pathologic aspects of familial carcinoma of breast

Cardiac
277o Sexuality with cardiac disease

372t Effects of training intensity on cardiac output in young women

Cardinal Gibbons
129z Cardinal Gibbons's ignorance

Cardiovascular
51k Smoking, alcohol, and body mass relationships to early menopause: Implications for risk of cardiovascular disease

210o Cardiovascular risk factors in the elderly woman

Care
see also Child Care, Day Care, Health Care

56g Alternative maternity care: Resistance and change

70g American Indian children: Foster care and adoptions

145f Prelude to consciousness: Amalie Sieveking and the Female Association for the Care of the Poor and the Sick

170a Caring: A labour of love

170b Why do women care?

170d The caring wife

170e Single careers: Employment, housework and caring

170f Care for elderly people: A conflict between women and the state

170g The economics of work and caring

170h Natural selection: Perspectives on entitlement to the invalid care allowance

204e Varying degrees of paternal involvement in infant care: Attitudinal and behavioral correlates

217d Caring as women's work in the welfare state

233r What can be done in antenatal care?

241e Women and caring: Skills, tasks and taboos

259h Guidance and pastoral care

289h Long-term care institutions

381h Taking care of everything

427b The importance of early care

Care Giving
204f Shared-caregiving families: An Australian study

204g Primary caregiving and role-sharing fathers

216m Effective care-giving: The child from birth to three

Care Taking
158k "To pet, coddle, and 'Do For'": Caretaking and the concept of maternal instinct

Career
see also Dual Career, Employment, individual careers

23f The Parliamentary wife: Participant in the 'two-person single career'

41g Invited presentation: The black professional woman — career success and interpersonal failure

44a The bimodal career

64b The first steps in a writer's career

75d Career counselling for poor rural and urban women of South India

75f Career and employment of women in Pakistan

87g Parenthood, marriage, and careers: Situational constraints and role strain

87j Coordinated-career couples: Convergence and divergence

90g The sex dimension of careers in educational management: Overview and synthesis

90k Male and female career paths in school administration

90l Administrative careers in public school organizations

126m Careers in landscape architecture: Recovering for women what the "ladies" won and lost

139h 'Getting on'. Gender differences in career development: A case study in the hairdressing industry

170e Single careers: Employment, housework and caring

214t Dream vs. drift in women's careers: The question of generativity

221a The family as an influence on career development

221e Voluntary mid-life career change: Family effects

244d Occupation-family-linkages as perceived by men in the early stages of professional and managerial careers

249i Career politics and the practice of women's studies

259i Sex differentiation and careers

267e Career concepts and human resource management: The case of the dual-career couple

274p Careers

302g Profiles of the careers of selected black female librarians

302h The woman academic-library administrator: A career profile

302l Geographic mobility and career advancement of male and female librarians

302m An analysis of the study, "Career paths of male and female librarians in Canada"

320i Educational and career progress of Chicana and Native-American college women

320m Career plans of college women: Patterns and influences

320n Career commitment of female college graduates: Conceptualization and measurement issues

351c Career and life satisfactions among Terman's gifted women

351h Women's education and career choice: Disparities between theory and practice

361g Career paths for women in physics

361j Effectiveness of science career conferences

377j Career interests and career education: A key to change

391b Career awareness in young children

391d Time, television, and women's career perspectives

391f Career management and women

394k Merging two careers and marriage

398j Women's studies and men's careers: How the 'social problem' of women in education maintained the academic status of men in the 1970s

407a Careers in college and university administration: How are women affected?

407b Career mapping and the professional development process

416f Academic career mobility for women and men psychologists

416h Alternative development of a scientific career

421aa Career constraints among women graduate students in a developing society: West Pakistan. A study in the changing status of women

425d Career progress of women: Getting in and staying in

425f Socialization experiences of women and men graduate students in male sex-typed career fields

426c The apprenticeship model of organizational careers: A response to changes in the relation between work and family

426d Sex differences in factors affecting managerial career advancement

450p The career of Joan Williams: Problems in assessment

454q Cookbooks and law books: The hidden history of career women in twentieth-century America

Caribbean

39v Household and family in the Caribbean: Some definitions and concepts

39cc West Indian characteristics of the black Carib

68h Caribbean women: The impact of race, sex, and class

74d Affirmation and resistance: Women poets from the Caribbean

269b Structural continuity in the division of men's and women's work among black Carib (Garífuna)

322j Women and literature in the Caribbean

428o The impact of industrialization on women: A Caribbean case

473g Sex and status: Women in St. Vincent

Carrington, Dora

30s Carrington revisited

Carroll, Lewis

286a Lewis Carroll and Victorian morality

Carrot

227l The carrot, the stick and the movement

Case History

341d Barbara's foodworld: A case history

Case Law

173d *Roe v. Wade* and the lesson of the pre-*Roe* case law

Case Management

146c An approach to case management

Case Study

13b Capitalism, gender and the labour process: Two case studies

15b The alternative press and the mass media: Two case studies

21j Women in politics: A case study of Bangladesh

139f Participation in local union organisation. School meals staff: A case study

139h 'Getting on'. Gender differences in career development: A case study in the hairdressing industry

139i Feminisation and unionisation: A case study from banking

140g Women in positions of authority: A case study of changing sex roles

148g The political economy of gender: A 19th century Plains Indian case study

153k The contribution of public goods to household reproduction: Case study from Brazil

153q Conflicts inside and outside the household: A West African case study

160h Settler wives in southern Rhodesia: A case study

163h The torture of women political prisoners: A case study in female sexual slavery

169e Training rank and file leaders: A case study

169j Case studies: How to develop and use them

184i Female sexual attitudes and the rise of illegitimacy: A case study

184p Toward a theory of remarriage: A case study of Newburyport at the beginning of the nineteenth century

192c Lives of Chicana activists: The Chicano student movement (a case study)

209o Staff participation in office systems' design: Two case studies at the World Bank

209p Strengthening group solidarity of clericals: A case study

223z Case studies

250k Women in higher education: A case study of the open university

295j Social support and efficacy in advocacy roles: A case study of two women's organizations

296b Differential power of women over the life course: A case study of age-roles as an indicator of power

300h Rural-urban linkages and migration: A Philippines case study

314t Wheaton's assessment process: A case study and its lessons

344n The internalization of powerlessness: A case study of the displaced homemaker

350d Resource allocation and the sexual division of labor: A case study of a Moslem Hausa village in northern Nigeria

350f The creation of a relative surplus population: A case study from Mexico

380m A statistical analysis of female participation in work and the effects on the population and socioeconomic development: A case study of Greece

385h International development and the evolution of women's economic roles: A case study from northern Gulma, Upper Volta

387g Industrialization and femininity: A case study of nineteenth-century New England

387t Sex stratification, technology and organization change: A longitudinal case study of AT&T

388k Social feminism in France: A case study

396d Depo-provera: The extent of the problem: A case study in the politics of birth control

400a Women's employment and agriculture: Extracts from a case study

424t Female employment and the family: A case study of the Bataan Export Processing Zone

467d Statutory maternity leave in the United Kingdom: A case study

468a The making of a female occupation: A case study of cleaning work

470c Contemporary clerical work: A case study of local government

Cash

104b Cash crop production and family labour: Tobacco growers in Corrientes, Argentina

286c Cash and the sex nexus

CASPAR

16l CASPAR: A women's alcoholism program

Cast

399jj "Casting by Juliet Taylor" (Interview)

Castellanos, Rosario

74c Rosario Castellanos and the structures of power

Castelloza

188f The provençal *Trobairitz*: Castelloza

Castrate

285i Castration and sexual potency

Casuality

242a Fictional consensus and female casualties

Cat

150t Cat

438e The wild cat (France and Italy)

Cataloging

15d Access to alternatives: New approaches in cataloging

Catalyst

307ff Feminism: A catalyst for the future

448a The city as catalyst for Flora Tristan's vision of social change

Catalytic

87b Catalytic movements: Civil rights and women

Catch

206j The safety catch

Cather, Willa

17l Mothers, daughters, and the "art necessity": Willa Cather and the creative process

127d The forgotten reaping-hook: Sex in *My Antonia*

180n Reentering paradise: Cather, Colette, Woolf and their mothers

332b The novel of awakening (five novels)

384l The Virginian and Antonia Shimerda: Different sides of the western coin

384n Marian Forrester and Moll Flanders: Fortunes and misfortunes
442b Willa Cather: A problematic ideal
445n Willa Cather and the sense of history
448k Willa Cather's lost Chicago sisters
451c Reflections on Willa Cather
451d Willa Cather

Catheter
252i Extra-amniotic ethacridine (Rivanol)-catheter technique for mid-trimester abortion

Catholicism
see also Religion
115b The ordination of women in the Roman Catholic Church
152a Reflections of a gay Catholic
152b Growing up lesbian and Catholic
197d Calvinism and Catholicism in Muriel Spark
366c The leadership of nuns in immigrant Catholicism
401l Catholic sisters in China: An effort to raise the status of women
439v Female sexuality and the Catholic confessional

Caucasian
see also Race, White
190c Age at menarche and year of birth in relation to adult height and weight among Caucasian, Japanese, and Chinese women living in Hawaii

Causal
266l Causal models: Their import and their triviality

Cause
78k Violence against women: Some considerations regarding its causes and eliminations
191d Depressions among women: Their nature and causes
324b Causes of irregular employment patterns
324c Occupational atypicality: Changes, causes, and consequences
327a A sociological perspective on the causes of family violence

Cavalry
108h *My Childhood Years*: A memoir by the czarist cavalry officer, Nadezhda Durova

Cave
474c The parable of the cave or: In praise of watercolors

Cebuana
431g Sex roles in the Philippines: The ambiguous Cebuana

Celebrate
220l Change, hope and celebration

Celibate
152e Homosexuality, celibacy, religious life and ordination

Cell
33c Book-lined cells: Women and humanism in the early Italian Renaissance

Celtic
156j Celtic women in the early middle ages
417b Women of the Celtic Tuath

Censor
223s Pornography, feminism, and censorship
408o The censored sex: Woman as author and character in Franco's Spain

Censure
286d The fallen woman's sexuality: Childbirth and censure

Center
36t Contrasts in the birthing place: Hospital and birth center
55h The role of community health centers
55o Appendix D: Fighting adult entertainment centers at the grassroots level
174q The women's writer's center: An interview with the directors
203s The Los Angeles woman's building: A public center for woman's culture
284b Sexual victimization of children: An urban mental health center survey
359ll Development of a medical center rape crisis intervention program
453s Feminist women's health centers
462v Claiming the center: A critical feminist theology of liberation

Centerfold
254f Captured angel in the centerfold

Central America
269c Sex roles and subsistence: A comparative analysis of three Central American communities

Centro Obrero
206l Working on racism: Centro Obrero

Century
78v A century of women in policing
401a The Chinese Buddhist monastic order for women: The first two centuries

Ceremony
108b Ceremonies of the alphabet: Female grandmatologies and the female autograph
148f The role of Sioux women in the production of ceremonial objects: The case of the star quilt
198g A traditional ceremony in an Islamic milieu in Malaysia
194l The milk overflowing ceremony in Sri Lanka
229w Honor and ceremony in women's rituals

Ceremony
124b Naming, magic and documentary: The subversion of the narrative in *Song of Solomon*, *Ceremony*, and *China Men*

Cervix
53o Etiologic factors for invasive and noninvasive cervical abnormalities
456i Cervical cytology

Caesarian
36aa C/SEC: A special-interest interpersonal group brings about change

CETA
see Comprehensive Employment Training Act

Chain
462c The great chain of being and the chain of command

Chair
394i Chair, chairman, chairperson

Chairman
394i Chair, chairman, chairperson

Chairperson
394i Chair, chairman, chairperson

Challenge
178m The challenge of coping
210m The final challenge: Facing death
323q Women's challenge to organized labour
447p Challenges to corporate policy

Chalmers, Helen
384h The emergence of Helen Chalmers

Chamber Music
409a The woman hidden in James Joyce's *Chamber Music*

Chameleon
17f Mark Twain's capers: A chameleon in King Carnival's court

Champion
399o Mary Shaw: A fighting champion

Chancellor
394m The president's wife: A changing role — observations of a chancellor's wife

Chancery
379c The planter's wife revisited: Women, equity law, and the Chancery Court in seventeenth-century Maryland

Chandi
194j The goddess Chandi as an agent of change

Chang, Eileen
449e The shaping of life: Structure and narrative process in Eileen Chang's *The Rouge of the North*

Change
45m Change and constancy: A hundred years' tale
47a A time of change
82n Dynamics of social and cultural change
220l Change, hope and celebration
234i Women and the concept of change in history
262f A social-psychological analysis of the context for change
404bb Making change
418l 'If it's natural, we can't change it'

Channel
193i Choosing or channelling?

Chant
211o Learning to chant the Torah: A first step

Chaos
122o Finding one's way through the labyrinth: A symposium on women's lives: Meals — chaos or community

Chappell, Winifred L.
412t Winifred L. Chappell: Everybody on the left knew her

Character
32k "Eine frau, aber mehr als das, eine Persönlichkeit, aber mehr als das: eine frau: The structural analysis of the female characters in the novels of Max Frisch
40ff Theme, characterization, and style in the works of Toni Morrison

343n Shakespeare's female characters as actors and audience

408o The censored sex: Woman as author and character in Franco's Spain

Characteristic

39cc West Indian characteristics of the black Carib

63b Characteristics of co-correctional institutions

Charisma

406f Resistance through charisma: Rita Hayworth and Gilda

Charlotte's Web

30n "Charlotte's Web": Reading *Jane Eyre* over time

Charnas, Suzy McKee

114f Holding fast to feminism and moving beyond: Suzy McKee Charnas's *The Vampire Tapestry*

383c Utopia at the end of a male chauvinist dystopian world: Suzy McKee Charnas's feminist science fiction

Chart

49a Charting a course

Charter

22b Wills, deeds, and charters as sources for the history of medieval women

Chase, Mary

399y The comic muse of Mary Chase

Chastity

190m Virginity rituals and chastity control during puberty: Cross-cultural patterns

Chaucer, Geoffrey

135e The Wife of Bath: Narrator as victim

Chautauqua

174r A feminist chautauqua for a rural state

Chauvinism

35g Explaining "male chauvinism" and "feminism": Cultural differences in male and female reproductive strategies

91j From chauvinism and clericalism to priesthood: The long march

275a Male chauvinism: A conceptual analysis

383c Utopia at the end of a male chauvinist dystopian world: Suzy McKee Charnas's feminist science fiction

Chéri

64l The theatre as literary model: Role-playing in *Chéri* and *The Last of Chéri*

Checklist

20n A checklist of writings by and about Margaret Atwood

131p The future females: A selected checklist through 1979

Cheerleader

175v Legends in their own time: The Dallas Cowboy cheerleaders

Chemical Dependency

16i Women and chemical dependency

Chemistry

233l What evidence is required to identify a chemical as a reproductive hazard?

377h Factors affecting female participation in advanced placement programs in mathematics, chemistry, and physics

416i Scientific sexism: The world of chemistry

Cheng I

401i One woman's rise to power: Cheng I's wife and the pirates

Cherokee

see also American Indian

414b Cherokee women

Cherryh, C.J.

114d C. J. Cherryh and tomorrow's new sex roles

Chesnut, Mary Boykin

126l Of paradigm and paradox: The case of Mary Boykin Chesnut

Chevalier, Maurice

410d Recruitment of women to suburban city councils: Higgins vs. Chevalier

Cheyenne Autumn

384q Toward a new paradigm: Mari Sandoz's study of red and white myth in *Cheyenne Autumn*

Chiang Mai City

424q Effect of female labour force participation on fertility: The case of construction workers in Chiang Mai City

Chicago, IL

72d Latinas in educational leadership: Chicago, Illinois

201f The uprising in Chicago: The men's garment workers strike, 1910-1911

448k Willa Cather's lost Chicago sisters

Chicana

see Hispanic

Chick

223n "Pricks" and "Chicks": A plea for persons

275l "Pricks" and "chicks": A plea for "persons"

Child

see also Adolescent, African American Child, Baby, Boy, Childhood, Girl, Infant, School-Age, Young

3g Children, personhood, and a pluralistic society

3i More trouble than they're worth? Children and abortion

14e One child of one's own: A meaningful digression within the work(s) - an excerpt

26c Group treatment of children in shelters for battered women

26h Children's observations of interparental violence

29h Parenting: Training mothers as behavior therapists for their children

35f Power structures and perceptions of power holders in same-sex groups of young children

42g Except you become as little children

55a Child pornography in the 1970s

55c Typology of sex rings exploiting children

55f Impact of child pornography and sex rings on child victims and their families

55j Treatment issues with children involved in pornography and sex rings

55k Combating child pornography and prostitution: One county's approach

55l Appendix A: Legal resources on sexual exploitation of children

57c Work, the family, and children's sexual learning

57d Television as a sphere of influence on the child's learning about sexuality

57h Religion and sexual learning of children

69e The early mother-child relationship: A developmental view of woman as mother

69g Maternal work and children

70g American Indian children: Foster care and adoptions

71j The early socialization of Asian-American female children

78i You can't be a mother and be in prison...can you? Impacts of the mother-child separation

79s Living with an impaired neonate and child: A feminist issue

79w Unnatural selection: On choosing children's sex

80a Social-emotional consequences of day care for preschool children

80g Day care and children's responsiveness to adults

80i The Yale Child Welfare Research Program: Description and results

80m Families, children, and child care

80v Health care services for children in day care programs

96d Mothers and their children: A study of low-income families

97d Parents, children and the state

102c Tiamat and her children: An inquiry into the persistence of mythic archetypes of woman as monster/villainess/victim

103j Gender and child-custody determinations: Exploding the myths

105f The family, the child, and social change

105g Social structure, family socialization, and children's achievement goals: A comparative analysis

109p Dreaming of children: Literalization in *Jane Eyre* and *Wuthering Heights*

129q Relations between parents and children

137c Gender and child psychopathology

151h Backward children in the USSR: An unfamiliar approach to a familiar problem

162m Linen was their life: Family survival strategies and parent-child relations in nineteenth-century France

163g Traffic of children

167g Children need smiles not missiles: Planning a walk Oxford mothers for nuclear disarmament

170c Employment, women and their disabled children

171j Men's speech to young children

178j Fathers' support to mothers and children

178l The quality of mother-child relationships

195b Why men don't rear children: A power analysis

203c The household as workplace: Wives, husbands, and children

204i Effects of divorce on parents and children

204j Social development and parent-child interaction in father-custody and stepmother families

212r What can one do with a son? Feminist politics and male children

216m Effective care-giving: The child from birth to three

216n The early education of minority children

221b Effects of maternal employment on children: Implications for the family therapist

223x Adult-child sex

225g Above and beyond politics: The sexual socialization of children

225o Beyond politics? Children and sexuality

243e Mothers as social agents: Structuring the community activities of school aged children

244g The nurture of adults by children in family settings

257e The daughter is mother of the child: Cycles of lesbian sexuality

265a Parents' sex role attitudes and children's concepts of femininity and masculinity

265k Sex differences in children's road accidents

265l Cultural differences in children's sex role stereotypes

268l Sex-related differences in the epidemiology of child psychopathology

270f Sex roles, value of children and fertility in Turkey

273a Sex selection of children: An overview

283b Children and parents: Who chooses?

284q Special techniques for child witnesses

284s The child sex industry - an introduction

284w Policy recommendations on child pornography control

286l Fallen women, lost children: Wilde and the theatre in the nineties

295c Mothering and the young child

301rr There's not a child that can't learn

304c The development of sex-role stereotypes in children: Crushing realities

305j Minding the children

309q The children of teenage parents

310x Children by donor insemination: A new choice for lesbians

318g Women and children first: The novels of Margaret Drabble

333c A certain heritage: Women and their children in north Australia

346a Employment of women and child: Battles to fight

346b Child workers in the informal sector role of the NGOs: Some reflections

346e Salient laws on women and children: A selected bibliography

349v Imprisoned women and their children

369k Mothers, fathers, and children: From private to public patriarchy

380s Women's work participation and the economic support of children

391b Career awareness in young children

391c Children's impressions of television mothers

397k Lesbianism and motherhood: Implications for child custody

399ee The adventure of life: Writing for children

411j Motherhood in the middle years: Women and their adult children

421u The impact of children on female earnings

440c Redistribution to children and to mothers: A history of child endowment and family allowances

463d Influence of employment and children on intra-household travel behavior

474i *One* child of one's own: A meaningful digression within the work(s)

Child Abuse

see also Abuse

146a A conceptual framework for child sexual abuse

146b Validation of child sexual abuse

146d Treatment of the sexually abused child

146j Arts therapy with sexually abused children

146k Law enforcement and child sexual abuse

146l Multidisciplinary team review of child-sexual-abuse cases

146m Evaluation of child-sexual-abuse programs

146n How to start a child-sexual-abuse intervention program

212f The sexual abuse of children in the home

219b Incest and sexual abuse of children

284a The sexual abuse of children and minors: A short history of legal control efforts

284b Sexual victimization of children: An urban mental health center survey

284c Sexual molestation of children: The last frontier of child abuse

284e The sexually misused child

284g Sexual trauma of children and adolescents

284h Sexual assault center emergency room protocol: Child/adolescent patients

284k Children not severely damaged by incest with a parent

284o Interviewing child victims of sex offenders

284p The protection of the child victim of a sexual offense in the criminal justice system

291a Definition and recognition of sexual child abuse: Historical and cultural perspectives

291d Recognition of child sexual abuse in the United Kingdom

291e Sexual child abuse: The legislation and the law in the United States

291f Sexual abuse of children: An examination of European criminal law

291j Medical assessment of child sexual abuse

291k The child psychiatric examination of the sexually abused child

291l Special problems in the treatment of child sexual abuse

291n A comprehensive child sexual abuse treatment program

291o Group psychotherapy with sexually abused children

291r The effects of child sexual abuse: Methodological considerations

326d Treatment of sexually abused children

326e Network aspects of treatment for incestuously abused children

Child Care

see also Care, Day Care

46b Supplemental OASI benefits to homemakers through current spouse benefits, a homemaker credit, and child-care dropout years

80m Families, children, and child care

80n Child care - A commitment to be honored

80p Beyond the stalemate in child care public policy

80r The dilemma of affordable child care

80s The prospects and dilemmas of child care information and referral

80t Considering proprietary child care

80w School-age child care

103i Why the United States has no child-care policy

145l The impact of agrarian change on women's work and child care in early-nineteenth-century Prussia

151g Soviet child care: Its organisation at local level

216q An alternative perspective on parental support: Child-care information and referral service

335e 'The serious burdens of love?' Some questions on child-care, feminism and socialism

339h Working couples and child care

344j Child care

380p Child care use and constraints in the United States

380q The attitude of Danish mothers to child care, 1975 to 1979

385m The child-care dilemma of working mothers in African cities: The case of Lagos, Nigeria

394n Child care and the university

427c Fathers, mothers, and childcare in the 1980s: Family influences on child development

427d Child care options and decisions: Facts and figurings for families

435g In search of a national child-care policy: Background and prospects

Child Development

80e Developmental consequences of out-of-home care for infants in a low-income population

80f Environmental differences among day care centers and their effects on children's development

88c Considerations about the development of the girl during the separation-individuation process

106n "Thank heaven for little girls": The dialectics of development

204a Parental behavior and child development in nontraditional families: An introduction

204c Maternal employment and child development: A review

271c Parents and the sex-role development of the preschool child

427c Fathers, mothers, and childcare in the 1980s: Family influences on child development

Child Rearing

38e The black woman and child rearing

38g "The means to put my children through": Child-rearing goals and strategies among black female domestic servants

71b Some effects of childrearing practices on the value systems of Asian-American women

158f "Give me a dozen healthy infants": John B. Watson's popular advice on childrearing, women, and the family

204h Antecedents and consequences of various degrees of paternal involvement in child rearing: The Israeli project

243f Black families and childrearing support networks

295g Enhancing childrearing skills in lower income women

440i Pater-patria: Child-rearing and the state

Child Support

103k Women and child support

Childbearing

see also Reproduce

4d Adolescent sexuality, pregnancy, and childbearing

4e Social implications of teenage childbearing

51d A cross-cultural exploration of the end of the childbearing years

144e Women, family and death: Excess mortality of women in child-bearing age in four communities in nineteenth-century Germany

184b Childbearing among the lower classes of late medieval England

253i The effects of childbearing on women's mental health: A critical review of the literature

309k The health and social consequences of teenage childbearing

309m Teenage mothers and teenage fathers: The impact of early childbearing on the parents' personal and professional lives

309o Early childbearing and subsequent fertility

309p Economic consequences of teenage childbearing

309x Teenagers: Fertility control behavior and attitudes before and after abortion, childbearing or negative pregnancy test

310v Personal courage is not enough: Some hazards of childbearing in the 1980s

Childbirth

see also Reproduce

36q Ethical issues in childbirth technology

36u Ethical issues relating to childbirth as experienced by the birthing woman and midwife

53k An epidemiologic perspective of mental illness and childbirth

56b Natural childbirth and the reluctant physician

56c Taking care of the little woman: Father-physician relations during pregnancy and childbirth

56e Awake and aware, or false consciousness: The cooption of childbirth reform in America

56f Studying childbirth: The experience and methods of a woman anthropologist

241i Purification or social control? Ideologies of reproduction and the churching of women after childbirth

257f Sex and childbirth

286d The fallen woman's sexuality: Childbirth and censure

319c Mexican, Mexican American, and Chicana childbirth

325f Golden handprints and red-painted feet: Hindu childbirth rituals in central India

325r Menstruation and childbirth as ritual and religious experience among native Australians

353j "On the importance of the obstetrick art": Changing customs of childbirth in America, 1760 to 1825

353k "Down to death door's": Women's perceptions of childbirth in America

397l Lesbian childbirth and woman-controlled conception

Childhood

see also Child

8h Childhood and adolescent suicidal behavior, with an emphasis on girls

48b Sexual socialization and gender roles in childhood

57a Dimensions of sexual learning in childhood

80x Day care and early childhood education

185f Growing up slowly: Another century of childhood

224g Childhood sexuality and paedophilia

284f Observations after sexual traumata suffered in childhood

286j On the enrichment of poor monkeys by myth and dream; or how Dickens Rousseauisticized and pre-Freudianized Victorian views of childhood

291q Long-term effects of sexual abuse in childhood

318i Edna O'Brien: A kind of Irish childhood

333o Aboriginal women's role today in early childhood school education

391a Early childhood experiences and women's achievement motives

427e Gender inequities in childhood social life and adult work life

459h Women's work and their status: Rural Indian evidence of labour market and environment effects on sex differences in childhood mortality

Childless

194k Pox and the terror of childlessness: Images and ideas of the smallpox goddess in a north Indian village

265r Sex without reproduction: Voluntary childlessness as a response to contemporary sex roles

461q Voluntary childlessness

461r Discussion: Voluntary sterilization in childless women

Children of God

417n Women in the Children of God: "Revolutionary women" or "Mountin' maids"?

Children of Violence

180q The nightmare repetition: The mother-daughter conflict in Doris Lessing's *Children of Violence*

Childress, Alice

40k Alice Childress's dramatic structure

40l The literary genius of Alice Childress

Chile

315a The emergence of women in twentieth-century Chilean history and literature

Chimpanzee

340a The female chimpanzee as a human evolutionary prototype

China

21c Women in the People's Republic of China

68f Chinese women: The relative influences of ideological revolution, economic growth, and cultural change

103p Women in a revolutionary society: The state and family policy in China

153l State, collective, and household: The process of accumulation in China, 1949-65

177b Historical background on Chinese Women

177j The Chinese biographical method: A moral and didactic tradition

177k Yenan women in revolution

190c Age at menarche and year of birth in relation to adult height and weight among Caucasian, Japanese, and Chinese women living in Hawaii

205d A preliminary sketch of Chinese women and work in British Columbia, 1858-1950

229l Growing up with legends of the Chinese swordswomen

234b Women, politics and the formation of the Chinese state

263m The new economic readjustment policies: Implications for Chinese urban working women

325m Empress Wu and the historians: A tyrant and saint of classical China

350i The sexual division of labor in rural China

364c The exchange of women and property: Marriage in post-revolutionary China

379r The effects of the Chinese Revolution on women and their families

395h Family planning in rural China

401a The Chinese Buddhist monastic order for women: The first two centuries

401c Thunder over the lake: The five classics and the perception of woman in early China

401d The Chinese Lieh-nü tradition

401f Power and prestige: Palace women in the Northern Sung (960-1126)

401h Widows and remarriage in Ming and early Qing China

401j Female infanticide in China

401l Catholic sisters in China: An effort to raise the status of women

401m In the public eye: Women in early twentieth-century China

421y Variations in women's roles and family life under the socialist regime in China

444g Women in the Chinese communist revolution: The question of political equality

China Men

124b Naming, magic and documentary: The subversion of the narrative in *Song of Solomon*, *Ceremony*, and *China Men*

Chinese Woman

466b The Peranankan Chinese woman at a crossroad

Chip

307f For women, the chips are down

Chipewyan

see also American Indian

340f The null case: The Chipewyan

Chipita

see Rodriguez, Chipita

CHIT

300j The CHIT fund in Singapore: Failure of a large-scale rotating credit fund

Chivalry

392l Chivalry and paternalism: Disparities of treatment in the criminal justice system

Chlorosis

353n Chlorotic girls, 1870-1920: A historical perspective on female adolescence

354j Chlorosis and chronic disease in 19th-century Britain: The social constitution of somatic illness in a capitalist society

Chocó

172g The Chocó woman: Agent for change (Colombia)

Chodorow, Nancy

195i Review of Chodorow's *The Reproduction of Mothering*

Choice

see also Pro-Choice

3s   Value choices in abortion

18c   "Reproductive choice" in the contemporary United States: A social analysis of female sterilization

47h   Moral choice

96h   Toward choice and differentiation in the midlife crises of women

140j Female masochism and the enforced restriction of choice

145m Domestic industry: Work options and women's choices

151c 'A woman's right to choose' in the Soviet Union

193g Factors differentially affecting the science subject preferences, choices and attitudes of girls and boys

193i Choosing or channelling?

209a Choices in the development of office automation

259f Sex differences in achievement orientations: Consequences for academic choices and attainments

273i Toward a moral policy for sex choice

273j Ethics and public policy: Should sex choice be discouraged?

310b The meanings of choice in reproductive technology

310x Children by donor insemination: A new choice for lesbians

337n Traditional and non-traditional choices of disciplines by women

339k Personal choices

344c Abortion: The controversial choice

347j Desert politics: Choices in the "marriage market"

351h Women's education and career choice: Disparities between theory and practice

411p The anxiety of the unknown - choice, risk, responsibility: Therapeutic issues for today's adult women

418k Feminist thought and reproductive control: The state and 'the right to choose'

421x Occupational choice among female academicians - The Israeli case

439e Reproductive freedom: Beyond "A woman's right to choose"

Choir

142g The choir invisible: The poetics of humanist piety

Choose

see Choice

Chopin, Kate

127b Thanatos and Eros: Kate Chopin's *The Awakening*

332b The novel of awakening (five novels)

356p The construction of ambiguity in *The Awakening*: A linguistic analysis

Christ

19e   The image of Adam and the image of Christ

59c   The feminist redemption of Christ

99a   Brides of Christ and poor mortals: Women in medieval society

115e The ordination of women and the 'maleness' of the Christ

Christianity

see also Religion

22g   Structural patterns in the legends of the holy women of Christianity

122q Marital metaphors in the Judeo-Christian tradition: A feminist critique

156r Women in early Syrian Christianity

157g Maria Grant, 1854-1937: The life and times of an early twentieth century Christian

186n Redefinitions of traditional Christian emblems and outlooks in May Sarton's novels of 1970-1975

194d The cult of Brigid: A study of pagan-Christian syncretism in Ireland

229tt The Christian right's "Holy War" against feminism

300o Islamic law in Christian Southeast Asia: The politics of establishing Shari'a courts in the Philippines

429h Unboxing Christian education

Christine, de Pisan

22i   Un écrit militant de Christine de Pizan: *Le Ditié de Jehanne d'Arc*

112a Christine de Pisan: First professional woman of letters (French, 1364-1430?)

135d Masculine and feminine personae in the love poetry of Christine dePisan

154a Self-consciousness and self concepts in the work of Christine de Pizan

154b The crowned dame, dame opinion, and dame philosophy: The female characteristics of three ideals in Christine de Pizan's *L'Avision Christine*

154c Christine de Pizan and Order of the Rose

154d Virginity as an ideal in Christine de Pizan's *Cité des Dames*

154e Christine de Pizan's *Livre des Trois Vertus*: Feminine ideal or practical advice?

154f The ideal of the lady of the manor as reflected in Christine de Pizan's *Livre des Trois Vertus*

188o The Franco-Italian professional writer: Christine de Pizan

Chronicle

22e   Women in Latin Medieval literature in Denmark e.g. annals and chronicles

112g Madame de Sévigné: Chronicler of an age (French, 1626-1696)

192u Personal chronicle of Crystal City

264e Southern literary women as chroniclers of southern life

442g Salonists and chroniclers

Chronology

215v Interesting times: A chronology of the nuclear age

Church

see also Religion

14o   Black women and the church

39i   Women in indigenous African cults and churches

42a   Our sisters in the church

60c   The feminist theology of the black Baptist church, 1880-1900

83h   The church, the unions, women and the opposition in Brazil

91f   The role of the church in the oppression of women

91g   Challenge of feminism to the church: A Bishop's perspective

91q   Women ... Where are you? Women in the Protestant churches

91w   Church and women: A course

115b The ordination of women in the Roman Catholic Church

115i Stereotyping the sexes in society and in the Church

152f Civil rights in a church of compassion

235h The church

241i Purification or social control? Ideologies of reproduction and the churching of women after childbirth

246h "Sing to the Lord a New Song": Women in the churches of Oceania

300n Church-military relations in the Philippines

412k Laity rights and leadership: Winning them for women in the Methodist Protestant church, 1860-1900

412m Creating a sphere for women: The Methodist Episcopal church, 1869-1906

412n The laity rights movement, 1906-1918: Women's suffrage in the Methodist Episcopal Church, South

412o Nineteenth-century A.M.E. preaching women: Cutting edge of women's inclusion in church polity

429b Small church — big family

429i The embodied church

457c Doves and magpies: Village women in the Greek Orthodox Church

Cincinnati, OH

353cc Homeopathy and sexual equality: The controversy over coeducation at Cincinnati's Pulte Medical College, 1873-1879

Cinderella

140l Cinderella's stepsisters: A feminist perspective on anorexia nervosa and bulimia

359r Cinderella's stepsisters: A feminist perspective on anorexia nervosa and bulimia

Cinema

247c The woman at the keyhole: Women's cinema and feminist criticism

Cineography
323z Women, work and unions: A cineography

The Circle Game
20b Atwood's haunted sequences: *The Circle Game*, *The Journals of Susanna Moodie*, and *Power Politics*

Circulation
364i Subject or object? Women and the circulation of valuables in highlands New Guinea

Circumference
107m Asymmetry of limb circumferences in female athletes

Circus
175m Mollie Bailey: Circus entrepreneur

Cistercian
187l Medieval Cistercian nunneries and English Bishops

Cistercian Abbey
187m Ten centuries of growth: The Cistercian Abbey of Soleilmont

Cité de Dames
154d Virginity as an ideal in Christine de Pizan's *Cité des Dames*

Citizen
292c Citizens for Democracy: The industrial programs of the YWCA
436b Women and citizenship: Mobilisation, participation, representation
464f Despotism and civil society: The limits of patriarchical citizenship

Citra
433j Some poems from *Citra* by Radindranath Tagore

City
see also Local, Metropolis, Rural, Suburb, Town, Urban, Village
21a Women in Asian cities, their political and economic roles: Research problems and strategies
22f Une contribution au débat concernant le status de la femme dans les villes du Danemark au Moyen-Age
202j The politics of city space in *The Years*: Street, love, pillar boxes and bridges
203k Toward supportive neighborhoods: Women's role in changing the segregated city
203q Women at city hall
210h Shopping-bag women: Aging deviants in the city
226k Women's collaborative activities and city life: Politics and policy
231b "Charity girls" and city pleasures: Historical notes on working-class sexuality, 1880-1920
264d Black women in a southern city: Washington, D.C., 1890-1920
379l City mothers, city daughters, and the dance hall girls: The limits of female political power in San Francisco, 1913
385m The child-care dilemma of working mothers in African cities: The case of Lagos, Nigeria
409c Emma Clery in *Stephen Hero*: A young woman walking proudly through the decayed city

410d Recruitment of women to suburban city councils: Higgins vs. Chevalier
420b The migration of women to cities: A comparative perspective
420s Women in Asian cites: Policies, public services, and research
424a Economic growth and changing female employment structure in the cities of Southeast and East Asia
424d Employment patterns of educated women in Indonesian cities
424n Urbanward migration and employment of women in Southeast and East Asian cities: Patterns and policy issues
424o Employment structure of female migrants to the cities in the Philippines
440e Capitalism, patriarchy and the city
442e City of words
448a The city as catalyst for Flora Tristan's vision of social change
448b Marguerite Duras: Women's language in men's cities
448c Return to Mytilène: Renée Vivien and the city of women
448d George Eliot and the city: The imprisonment of culture
448e Every woman is an island: Vita Sackville-West, the image of the city and the pastoral idyll
448f Tradition and revision: The classic city novel and Virginia Woolf's *Night and Day*
448i Reading the city as palimpsest: The experiential perception of the city in Doris Lessing's *The Four-Gated City*
448l "A laying on of hands": Transcending the city in Ntozake Shange's *for colored girls who have considered suicide/when the rainbow is enuf*
448n Sister to Faust: The city's "hungry" woman as heroine
448o Literature and the city: A checklist of relevant secondary works

City upon the Hill
448m Another view of the "City upon a Hill": The prophetic vision of Adrienne Rich

Civil
215e The illusion of protection: Civil defence
270o Civil violence in Turkey: Its infrastructural, social and cultural foundations
367i Women, civil religion, and the American Revolution
464f Despotism and civil society: The limits of patriarchical citizenship

Civil Rights
see also Right
87b Catalytic movements: Civil rights and women
133u Gay civil rights and the roots of oppression
152f Civil rights in a church of compassion
244b White mothers in the American civil rights movements

Civil Rights Act
65l A review of federal court decisions under Title VII of the Civil Rights Act of 1964

Civil War (United States)
454f The war within a war: Women nurses in the Union Army

Civilian
61l Women in the civilian labor force
179a Militarization/civilianization

Civilization
61f Women, civilization, and the Indian question
238f The erotic South: Civilization and sexuality in American abolitionism

Civilize
145p The civilizing tendency of hygiene: Working-class women under medical control in Imperial Germany
384a The civilizers: Women's organizations and western American literature

Claim
65j Economic models as a means of calculating legal compensation claims

Clarin
313o "La loca, la tonta, la literata": Women's destiny in Clarin's *La Regenta*

Class
see also Lower Class, Lower Middle Class, Middle Class, Social Class, Upper Class, Working Class
41b The concept of class in the novels of black women
43l Class realities: Create a new power base
43m Class attitudes and professionalism
43n Race and class: Beyond personal politics
60k "On the hem of life": Race, class, and the prospects for sisterhood
60n Issues of race and class in women's studies: A Puerto Rican woman's thoughts
60o Reproduction and class divisions among women
60p Women's role in economic development: Practical and theoretical implications of class and gender inequalities
68g Up from the harem? The effects of class and sex on political life in northern India
68h Caribbean women: The impact of race, sex, and class
83c Gender, race and class in the United States: Lessons from Third World women
83g Class consciousness and world view of a Bolivian mining woman
89f Class struggle and the persistence of the working-class family
94a Immigration and class: The Australian experience
94i Migrant communities and class politics: The Greek community in Australia
94j Generations and class: Sicilian-Australians in Melbourne
138a Gender, class and education: A personal view
138b Intersections of gender and class: Accommodation and resistance by working-class and affluent females to contradictory sex-role ideologies
138d Work, class and teaching
138e A cloud over co-education: An analysis of the forms of transmission of class and gender relations
138g Gender, patriarchy and class in the popular education of women
138k Gender, class and education: A teaching bibliography of European studies

138l Gender, class and education: A teaching bibliography of Australian and New Zealand studies

138m Gender, class and education: A teaching bibliography of American studies

139a Introduction: Class and work: Bringing women back in

139c Not so much a factory, more a form of patriarchy: Gender and class during industrialisation

149f Domestic labour and the reproduction of labour power: Towards an analysis of women, the family, and class

162l Kinship and class consciousness: Family values and work experience among hospital workers in an American southern town

174e All-women classes and the struggle for women's liberation

192a Sex, nationality, and class: La obrera Mexicana

192f The rise and demise of women's liberation: A class analysis

241d Men and war: Status, class and the social reproduction of masculinity

245j Family and class in contemporary America: Notes toward an understanding of ideology

256a Class and gender in Victorian England

315e A dialogue critical issues in women's studies: Race, class, and sexual orientation

347f Aztec women: The transition from status to class in empire and colony

379i The London biblewomen and nurses mission, 1857-1880: Class relations/women's relations

416n Class, race, sex, scientific objects of knowledge: A socialist-feminist perspective on the social construction of productive nature and some political consequences

444a Women of the popular classes in revolutionary Paris, 1789-1795

444b "I don't call that *Volksgemeinschaft*": Women, class, and war in Nazi Germany

450j Mary Lee Settle's connections: Class and clothes in the Beulah quintet

459c Class and historical analysis for the study of women and economic change

462b Class, gender, and religion: A theoretical overview and some political implications

Class of '55
302k Mobility and professional involvement in librarianship: A study of the "Class of '55"

Classe Social
22d Le rôle et la place de la femme provenant de la classe sociale inférieure dans la vie quotidienne du Moyen-Age

Classic
278a Sex and classical literature

329n Virginia Woolf and the classics: Every Englishman's prerogative transmuted into fictional art

334d Property interests in the classical Welsh law of women

379a Glimpses of Muslim urban women in classical Islam

397p Culture-making: Lesbian classics in the year 2000

401c Thunder over the lake: The five classics and the perception of woman in early China

419n Selected bibliography on women in classical antiquity

Classification
276a The classification of sexual aggressives and their associated demographic, social, developmental and psychological features

Classroom
see also Education
169k Using oral history in the classroom

176f Sexual energy in the classroom

176i Homophobia in the classroom

193s Feminism and science teaching: Some classroom observations

254i Increasing female participation in the mathematics classroom

259g 'Telling how it is': Language and gender in the classroom

274b Classroom interaction

306k From concept to classroom

351e Sex segregation and male preeminence in elementary classrooms

Clean
301u If you got time to lean, you got time to clean

307i The GABe self-cleaning house

468a The making of a female occupation: A case study of cleaning work

Clemens, Samuel
17f Mark Twain's capers: A chameleon in King Carnival's court

Cleopatra Sweatfigure
390m The memoirs of 'Cleopatra Sweatfigure'

Clergy
see also Religion
130g Women versus clergy, women pro clergy

412g Ministry through marriage: Methodist clergy wives on the trans-Mississippi frontier

412h Hispanic clergy wives: Their contribution to United Methodism in the southwest, later nineteenth century to the present

Cleric
91j From chauvinism and clericalism to priesthood: The long march

Clerical
181d Technology and work degradation: Effects of office automation on women clerical workers

209m New technology and its implications in U.S. clerical work

209p Strengthening group solidarity of clericals: A case study

209w An overview of NIOSH research on clerical workers

344q Clerical work: The female occupation

387q Degraded and deskilled: The proletarianization of clerical work

470c Contemporary clerical work: A case study of local government

Clerk
108k Women as law clerks: Catherine G. Waugh

Clery, Emma
409c Emma Clery in *Stephen Hero*: A young woman walking proudly through the decayed city

Cleveland, OH
201g The great uprising in Cleveland: When sisterhood failed

Client
29c Behavioral assessment of women clients

285s Establishing a women's group for disabled clients

359pp Psychotherapy with women clients: The impact of feminism

359ss A feminist works with nontraditional clients

360k Sexual intimacy between psychotherapists and clients: Policy implications for the future

443i Feminist therapy with minority clients

Clifton, Lucille
40n Tell the good news: A view of the works of Lucille Clifton

40o Lucille Clifton: Warm water, greased legs, and dangerous poetry

Climacteric
240l A psychosocial study of the climacteric

289l Continuity of self-actualization: Womanhood in climacterium and old age

Climate
122d The learning climate and the non-traditional student

Clinic
309y Adolescent pregnancy prevention services in high school clinics

396f Well woman clinics: A positive approach to women's health

Clinical
8b Aggression in women: Conceptual issues and clinical implications

9o Sex differences in the effects of alcohol and other psychoactive drugs on endocrine function: Clinical and experimental evidence

140y Sexual misconduct by psychiatrists: The ethical and clinical dilemma of confidentiality

190r Clinical aspects of menarche: Normal variations and common disorders

236e An explorative study into the clinical effects of dydrogesterone in the treatment of premenstrual syndrome

359bb Lesbian families: Cultural and clinical issues

359g Sex-role stereotypes and clinical judgements of mental health

Clinician
51w Aging, menopause, and estrogens: The clinician's dilemma

Clitoria
257b Sensual uncertainty, or why the clitoris is not enough

Clone
310f From mice to men? Implications of progress in cloning research

Closet

176d I lead two lives: Confessions of a closet Baptist

301qq I lead two lives: Confessions of a closet Baptist

Cloth

see also Garment, Textile

135p Emma Bovary's masculinization: Convention of clothes and morality of conventions

201j Dorothy Jacobs Bellanca: Women clothing workers and the runaway shops

347i Women and men, cloth and colonization: The transformation of production-distribution relations among the Baule (Ivory Coast)

428g The domestic clothing workers in the Mexican metropolis and their relation to dependent capitalism

450j Mary Lee Settle's connections: Class and clothes in the Beulah quintet

470a Sex and skill in the organisation of the clothing industry

470e Contemporary clothing 'sweatshops', Asian female labour and collective organisation

Club

210c Out of the *Mikvah* into the sauna: A study of women's health clubs

Clubwomen

205m The brightest women of our land: Vancouver clubwomen 1919-1928

Clytemnestra

180b Kriemhild and Clytemnestra - Sisters in crime or independent women?

CND

see Campaign for Nuclear Disarmament

CNTU

see Confederation of National Trade Unions

Coal Mining

301t Coal-mining women

Coalition

150pp Coalition politics: Turning the century

Coast

279i Sexual dimorphism for size in seven nineteenth-century Northwest coast populations

Coat

342f The scientific mystique: Can a white lab coat guarantee purity in the search for knowledge about the nature of women?

Code

7u New expanded-type version lesbian handkerchief code

64p Image structure, codes, and recoding in *The Pure and the Impure*

374g Appendix B: The family code

Co-Education

see also Education

62a Introduction: Co-education reconsidered - reviving the debate

62b Co-education: Perspectives and debates in the early twentieth century

62g Conclusion: Co-education, equal educational opportunity and change

63d A coed prison

63e A study of a coeducational correctional facility

63f Styles of doing time in a coed prison: Masculine and feminine alternatives

63k Women in a coed joint

63m The ERA and coed prisons

138e A cloud over co-education: An analysis of the forms of transmission of class and gender relations

352h Coeducation and the development of leadership skills in women: Historical perspectives from Cornell University, 1868-1900

353cc Homeopathy and sexual equality: The controversy over coeducation at Cincinnati's Pulte Medical College, 1873-1879

Coercion

323i Coercion or male culture: A new look at co-worker harassment

Cognatic

364b Cognatic descent, Islamic law and women's property on the East African oast

Cognition

16b Cognitive-behavioral strategies for the treatment of depression in women

24d Perceptual and cognitive mechanisms in human sexual attraction

28f Cognitive behavior and the menstrual cycle

28m Estrogens and central nervous system function: Electroencephalography, cognition, and depression

29k Depression: A behavioral-cognitive approach

72m The need for an anthropological and cognitive approach to the education of Hispanic women

239c Gonadal hormones and cognitive functioning

271i Beyond a cognitive/behavioural approach: Congruent assertion training

317a Adaptive dimensions of adult cognition

Cold

190h Physical attractiveness and physical stigma: Menstruation and the common cold

Colette

64d Colette and the art of survival

64e Colette and the epistolary novel

64f The relationship between meaning and structure in Colette's *Rain-moon*

64g A typology of women in Colette's novels

64h The test of love and nature: Colette and lesbians

64j Colette and art nouveau

64k Colette and Ravel: The enchantress and the illusionist

64n Polymorphemic perversity: Colette's illusory "real"

64q Colette and signs: A partial reading of a writer "Born *not* to Write"

180d Reentering paradise: Cather, Colette, Woolf and their mothers

196h The magic spinning wheel: Straw to gold - Colette, Willy and Sido

442a Colette's literary reputation

Collaborate

226k Women's collaborative activities and city life: Politics and policy

398f 'They shared a laboratory together': Feminist collaboration in the academy

Colleague

429k Colleagues in marriage and ministry

The Collected Short Stories of Edith Wharton

451b Introduction to *The Collected Short Stories of Edith Wharton*

Collective

66d Wage setting and collective bargaining

67d Wage setting and collective bargaining

93b Collective bargaining as a strategy for achieving equal opportunity and equal pay: Sweden and West Germany

153l State, collective, and household: The process of accumulation in China, 1949-65

209ff Collective bargaining strategies on new technology: The experience of West German trade unions

214p An attempt at collectivity: Professional confirmation and support

229vv Women's collective spirit: Exemplified and envisioned

378e Women as employees: Social consciousness and collective action

396e Seizing the means of reproduction: An illegal feminist abortion collective — how and why it worked

470e Contemporary clothing 'sweatshops', Asian female labour and collective organisation

Collector

55d Collectors

55e Typology of collectors

College

see also Education

45k Changing sex roles: College graduates of the 1960's and 1970's

45l Sex differences in the educational and occupational goals of black college students: Continued inquiry into the black matriarchy theory

49m College student values and the world of work

107r Physique of college women athletes in five sports

126n Does equality mean sameness? A historical perspective on the college curriculum for women with reflections on the current situation

174d College for neighborhood women: Innovation and growth

320d Mapping the road to academe: A review of research on women, men, and the college-selection process

320f Sex differences in the significance of economic resources for choosing and attending a college

320i Educational and career progress of Chicana and Native-American college women

320j Sex differences in the impact of college environments on black students

320m Career plans of college women: Patterns and influences

320n Career commitment of female college graduates: Conceptualization and measurement issues

320p   Life after college: Historical links between women's education and women's work

326m   Rape and the college student: Multiple crises in late adolescence

361h   Increasing the participation of college women in mathematics-related fields

377g   An experiment in mathematics education at the college level

407a   Careers in college and university administration: How are women affected?

414g   College life in Oklahoma territory

421f   Birth order and alienation among college women in Lebanon

454h   Cultural hybrid in the slums: The college woman and the Settlement House, 1889-1894

Collegiate
see also Athlete, Intercollegiate, Sport

147bb   Interscholastic basketball: Bane of collegiate physical educators

147cc   The controlled development of collegiate sport for women, 1923-1936

Collusion

254l   Communication or collusion?: Maneuvering through the maze of patriarchal theology

Colombia

39dd   The spread of capitalism in rural Colombia: Effects on poor women

172g   The Chocó woman: Agent for change (Colombia)

172k   Some sow, others reap (Colombia)

172m   Saving money with bio-gas (Colombia)

244a   Colombian women in party politics: A token role

347e   Forced transition from egalitarianism to male dominance: The Bari of Colombia

395i   Women's understanding about reproductive physiology and their choice of herbal medicines in Cali, Colombia

Colombian Women

428k   The formation of an ethnic group: Colombian female workers in Venezuela

Colonial

18i   Neo-Malthusian ideology and colonial capitalism: Population dynamics in southwestern Puerto Rico

68o   The schooling of Vietnamese immigrants: Internal colonialism and its impact on women

113f   Algeria: Anticolonial war

147b   Recreational activities of women in colonial America

160i   Colonial wives: Villains or victims?

263l   Men servants and women bosses: The domestic service institution in colonial Zambia

294c   'Soiled doves': Prostitution in colonial Queensland

367c   Women in colonial French America

367f   Black women and religion in the colonial period

376a   The certain wages of sin: Sentence and punishment of female felons in colonial Massachusetts, 1673-1774

385f   Colonialism, education, and work: Sex differentiation in colonial Zaire

Colonize

333l   Historical factors which have affected aboriginal lifestyles since colonisation

347a   Montagnais women and the Jesuit program for colonization

347d   Contending with colonization: Tlingit men and women in change

347h   Daughters of the lakes and rivers: Colonization and the land rights of Luo women

347i   Women and men, cloth and colonization: The transformation of production-distribution relations among the Baule (Ivory Coast)

347k   Stability in banana leaves: Colonization and women in Kiriwina, Trobriand Islands

347l   Putting down sisters and wives: Tongan women and colonization

Colony

160j   Memsahibs in colonial Malaya: A study of European wives in a British colony and protectorate, 1900-1940

347f   Aztec women: The transition from status to class in empire and colony

Color

174n   Women of color Califia

The Color Purple

40mm   Writing The Color Purple

Combahee River Collective

150hh   Combahee River collective statement

Combat

55k   Combating child pornography and prostitution: One county's approach

60q   Defining and combating sexual harassment

93u   The contribution of labor market data in combating employment discrimination

405h   Soviet women in combat in World War II: The ground/air defense forces

Combatant
see also Armed Forces, Army, GI, War

113m   The argument against female combatants

113n   The argument for female combatants

Comedy

135m   The laughter of maidens, the crackle of matriarchs: Notes on the collision between comedy and feminism

202e   Jacob's Room as comedy: Woolf's parodic Bildungsroman

Comic

109i   The mirror and the cameo: Margaret Atwood's comic/gothic novel, Lady Oracle

330m   Woolf's peculiar comic world: Between the Acts

343d   Comic structure and the humanizing of Kate in The Taming of the Shrew

399y   The comic muse of Mary Chase

Comic Opera

330f   Enchanted organs, magic bells: Night and Day as comic opera

Comilla District, Bangladesh

98g   Field research on women in the Comilla District, Bangladesh

Cominco

205dd   Women at Cominco during the second World War

Coming Out

133b   Coming out as a communicative process

397c   The coming-out process: Violence against lesbians

Comix

453e   Humor in California underground women's comix

Command

462c   The great chain of being and the chain of command

Commie

133r   From "commies" and "queers" to "gay is good"

Commission

410g   Organizational role orientations on female-dominant commissions: Focus on staff-commissioner interaction

410i   Commissions on the status of women and building a local policy agenda

435b   Representing women at the state and local levels: Commissions on the status of women

Commitment

376d   The weaker vessel: Legal versus social reality in mental commitments in nineteenth-century New York

387i   Commitment and cultural mandate: Women in medicine

411e   The middle years: Changes and variations in social-role commitments

Committee

323s   Women's committees: The Quebec experience

323t   The dilemma facing women's committees

323w   From ladies' auxiliaries to wives' committees

Committee on the Status of Women

394d   Committee on the Status of Women at Milwaukee

Common Sense

209n   The role of common sense in the process of interface design

Commonality

54e   Commonalities among female alcoholics

Commonwealth

23k   The employment of women in the commonwealth public service: The creation and reproduction of a dual labour market

102a   A society without fathers: Cooperative commonwealth or harmonious ant-heap?

147r   Canadian women at the Commonwealth games

Communal

385i   Women's work in a communal setting: The Tanzanian policy of Ujamaa

Communication

57b   Toward an understanding of sexual learning and communication: An examination of social learning theory and nonschool learning environments

57f   Peer communication and sexuality

126d   Research on women's communication: Critical assessment and recommendations

133b   Coming out as a communicative process

133g   Communication patterns in established lesbian relationships

136g Gender gestures: Sex, sex-role, and non-verbal communication

168g Production et communication du savior dans une perspective féministe: enjuex et défis pour les femmes

168h Creating and communicating knowledge from a feminist perspective: Risks and challenges for women

171k Sex similarities and differences in language, speech, and nonverbal communication: An annotated bibliography

254l Communication or collusion?: Maneuvering through the maze of patriarchal theology

285b Eros and thanatos: Lingering taboos in doctor-patient communication

287k Communicating sexuality

391g The influence of female and male communication styles on conflict strategies: Problem areas

415f Effective interpersonal communication for women of the corporation: Think like a man, talk like a lady

Communism

95h Communist women and the fascist experience

388g Women in Communist countries: Comparative public policy

444f Communist feminism: Its synthesis and demise

444g Women in the Chinese communist revolution: The question of political equality

Communist Party

119d 'What kind of woman is she?' Women and Communist Party politics, 1941- 1955

405i The anti-fascist front of women and the Communist Party in Croatia: Conflicts within the resistance

Communist Party of the Soviet Union (CPSU)

446h The twenty-fifth congress of the CPSU and current problems of employment of female labor in the republics of central Asia

Community

3q Abortion, autonomy, and community

11c Women and men problem drinkers: Sex differences in patients served by Iowa's community alcoholism centers

11j Alcoholism and the lesbian community

16k Alcoholism and the lesbian community

18j Country roads take me home: The political economy of wage-labor migration in an eastern Kentucky community

36s Community alternatives to high technology birth

38n "Holding back the ocean with a broom": Black women and community work

39r Sex roles and survival strategies in the urban black community

39z Female status, the family and male dominance in a West Indian community

43u The Beguines: A medieval women's community

55h The role of community health centers

73d The Museo Italo Americano: My involvement with the Italian American community in San Francisco

83b Women, art and community in Papua New Guinea

91u Women community workers

94i Migrant communities and class politics: The Greek community in Australia

94k Religion, law and family disputes in a Lebanese Muslim community in Sydney

98a Getting to know a rural community in Bangladesh

104e The estimation of work in a northern Finnish farming community

122o Finding one's way through the labyrinth: A symposium on women's lives: Meals — chaos or community

150z Failure to transform: Homophobia in the black community

174l Califia: An experiment in feminist education Califia community

191c Community surveys: Sex differences in mental illness

216g Parenting in the Native-American community

224m Revolution in the pursuit of happiness: Love and community-building on the left

226j Community responses to violence against women: The case of a battered women's shelter

227k The power of women and the subversion of the community

241c Blowing the cover of the protective male: A community study of violence to women

243e Mothers as social agents: Structuring the community activities of school aged children

269c Sex roles and subsistence: A comparative analysis of three Central American communities

269d New economic roles for Cuna males and females: An examination of socioeconomic change in a San Blas community

295b Women as competent community builders: The other side of the coin

317i Growing old "inside": Aging and attachment to place in an Appalachian community

326i Rape of men in the community

330k Nature and community: A study of cyclical reality in *The Waves*

333h Borroloola community and land rights

333r Income and employment for women in remote communities: Examples from the Northern Territory

348i Prisons, prisoners and the community

356h How and why are women more polite: Some evidence from a Mayan community

356i Women in their speech communities

371j Where women must dominate: Response to oppression in a South African urban community

379g The holy woman and the urban community in sixteenth-century Avila

395e Water and sanitation-related health constraints on women's contribution to the economic development of communities

404y The unique employment problems of female offenders returning to the community and labor market

417h Housework and utopia: Women and the Owenite socialist communities

421t Fertility and family economy in the Iranian rural communities

428e Household, community, national, and multinational industrial development

428p The emergence of small-scale industry in a Taiwanese rural community

434o Toward androgyny in community and organizational practice

452c Quest for community: Spiritual autobiographies of eighteenth-century Quaker and Puritan women in America

460m Finding self in the lesbian community

469g "La operacion": An analysis of sterilization in a Puerto Rican community in Connecticut

Company
see also Business, Corporation, Factory, Industry, Management

209k Automation and the quality of work life at the Swedish telephone company: A management view

209l Automation and the quality of work life at the Swedish telephone company: A union view

339g Dual career couples: How the company can help

Comparable Worth
see also Pay

65a "A want of harmony": Perspectives on wage discrimination and comparable worth

65n Comparable worth under various federal and state laws

67h An analysis of the National Academy of Sciences' comparable worth study

93s Beyond equal pay for equal work: Comparable worth in the state of Washington

425i Job evaluation and discrimination: Legal, economic, and measurement perspectives on comparable worth and women's pay

Comparison
473m Comparisons and implications: What have we learned?

Compassion
152f Civil rights in a church of compassion

Compensation
65j Economic models as a means of calculating legal compensation claims

Competence
29a Women's behavior in a man's world: Sex differences in competence

216d Developmental universals and their implications for parental competence

271k Female superiority in sex difference competence comparisons: A review of the literature

317d The competent older woman

Competition
84e Evolution and patriarchal myths of scarcity and competition

215k Take the toys from the boys: Competition and the nuclear arms race

336i The competition for women's *lebensraum*, 1928-1934

432h Cooperative competition in sport

432i Equality and competition: Can sports make a women of a girl?

432j Competition, friendship, and human nature

Complaint

8j   The painful woman: Complaints, symp-
      toms, and illness

288h Responses of fair employment practice
      agencies to sexual harassment complaints:
      A report and recommendations

353p "The fashionable diseases": Women's com-
      plaints and their treatment in nineteenth-
      century America

Complementarity

246c Complementarity: The relationship
      between female and male in the East Sepik
      village of Bun, Papua New Guinea

Complex

88f   The female oedipus complex: Its
      antecedents and evolution

Complication

252o Complications of second trimester abor-
      tion

Compliment

32m   The left-handed compliment: Perspectives
      and stereotypes in criticism

Composer

see also Music

14y   American black women composers: A
      selected annotated bibliography

Composition

107i Proportionality and body composition in
      male and female Olympic athletes: A
      kinanthropometric overview

107o Body composition and somatotype charac-
      teristics of sportswomen

279m Absolute and relative sex differences in
      body composition

453k Female composition

Compound

303o Scratching at the compound

Comprehensive

222c High noon: Surviving the comprehensive
      exams

**Comprehensive Employment Training Act
(CETA)**

272m Occupational desegregation in CETA pro-
      grams

Compulsory

60f   The twenties' backlash: Compulsory het-
      erosexuality, the consumer family, and the
      waning of feminism

97b   In/Forming schooling: Space/time/textuali-
      ty in compulsory state provided "mass"
      schooling systems

Computer

199j Computers, ward secretaries, and a walk-
      out in a Southern hospital

209s Office computerization: Research then
      and now

209x Health hazards in the computerized office

209ii Public policy and the employment impacts
      of office computerization

307cc EQUALS in computer technology

Comrade

103u "Sisters" or "comrades"? The politics of
      friends and families

128g Women socialists and their male com-
      rades: The Reading experience, 1927-1936

336n Comrade-woman-mother-resistance fight-
      er

Conceive

195j On conceiving motherhood and sexuality:
      A feminist materialist approach

Conception

see also Reproduce

307z Engineered conception: The new parent-
      hood

397l Lesbian childbirth and woman-controlled
      conception

460d Physiological aspects of female sexual
      development: Conception through puberty

Concern

159a International concern in light of the
      American experience

161b Press coverage of women and women's
      concerns

Conclusion

407i Getting the best: Conclusions, recommen-
      dations, and selected resources

Condor

108m Of sparrows and condors: The autobiogra-
      phy of Eva Perón

Conduct

140y Sexual misconduct by psychiatrists: The
      ethical and clinical dilemma of confiden-
      tiality

Confederation of Canadian Unions

305l Getting organized...in the Confederation
      of Canadian Unions

**Confederation of National Trade Unions
(CNTU)**

323r Working, mothering and militancy:
      Women in the CNTU

Conference

169d Conferences: The one-day model

361j Effectiveness of science career confer-
      ences

447a Genesis and highlights of a conference

Confession

176d I lead two lives: Confessions of a closet
      Baptist

301qq I lead two lives: Confessions of a closet
      Baptist

Confessional

439v Female sexuality and the Catholic confes-
      sional

Confidential

140y Sexual misconduct by psychiatrists: The
      ethical and clinical dilemma of confiden-
      tiality

Confirmation

214m Women, work and friendship: Personal
      confirmation and support

214p An attempt at collectivity: Professional
      confirmation and support

Conflict

8r   Conflict and psychological development:
      Women in the family

21g   Expanding women's horizons in Indonesia:
      Toward maximum equality with minimum
      conflict

21h   Political change: Muslim women in conflict
      with Parda: Their role in the Indian
      Nationalist Movement

31o   Rights-conflict, pregnancy, and abortion

36d   Value conflicts in biomedical research into
      future contraceptives

117f Eve and Mary: Conflicting images of
      medieval woman

140k Roles and role conflict of women in infer-
      tile couples

153q Conflicts inside and outside the house-
      hold: A West African case study

162h 'A brother is a creative thing': Change and
      conflict in a Melpa family (Papua New
      Guinea)

164j Muted discord: Generational conflict in
      Jane Austen

165l "The government's unique experiment in
      salvaging women criminals": Cooperation
      and conflict in the administration of a
      women's prison - The case of the Federal
      Industrial Instutition for Women at
      Alderson

165o Women in the criminal justice profession:
      An analysis of status conflict

218d Tea and power: The anatomy of a conflict

243a Urban and rural working women in Poland
      today: Between social change and social
      conflict

271h Assertiveness training for improved con-
      flict resolution style

344i Motherhood: Contemporary conflict for
      women

362c Muslim Middle Eastern women's partici-
      pation in violent political conflict: Causes
      and characteristics

365g Marital and family conflicts

385e Marginal lives: Conflict and contradiction
      in the position of female traders in Lusaka,
      Zambia

387c Women in the occupational world: Social
      disruption and conflict

403d The social and political roles of Arab
      women: A study of conflict

415d Lady you're trapped: Breaking out of con-
      flict cycles

445m Heroes vs women: Conflict and duplicity in
      Stegner

462p Women responding to the Arab-Israeli
      conflict

Conformity

250c The importance of being Ernest ... Emma
      ... Tom ... Jane. The perception and catego-
      rization of gender conformity and gender
      deviation in primary schools

Confrontation

43s   Confrontation: Black/white

162o Family fun in Starve Harbor: Custom, his-
      tory and confrontation in village
      Newfoundland

Confusion

116k On curing conceptual confusion: Response
      to Mary Anne Warren

Conglomerate

199o On the shop floor: Multi-ethnic unity
      against the conglomerate

Congress

209hh Legislative and research options for the
      U.S. Congress

Congruent
271i Beyond a cognitive/behavioural approach: Congruent assertion training

Conjoint
26b Conjoint therapy for the treatment of domestic violence

Conjugal
52p Women's roles and conjugal family systems in Ghana

421p Changes in Canadian female labour force participation and some possible implications for conjugal power

Connecticut
410c The effects of sex on recruitment: Connecticut local offices

410h Perceptions of women's roles on local councils in Connecticut

469g "La operacion": An analysis of sterilization in a Puerto Rican community in Connecticut

Connect
167e All is connectedness: Scenes from the Women's Pentagon Action USA

174w Black-eyed blues connections: From the inside out

Conrad, Joesph
313p Women as moral and political alternatives in Conrad's early novels

Consciousness
see also Social Consciousness

56e Awake and aware, or false consciousness: The cooption of childbirth reform in America

83g Class consciousness and world view of a Bolivian mining woman

145f Prelude to consciousness: Amalie Sieveking and the Female Association for the Care of the Poor and the Sick

145i Self-conscious histories: Biographies of German women in the nineteenth century

154a Self-consciousness and self concepts in the work of Christine de Pizan

162l Kinship and class consciousness: Family values and work experience among hospital workers in an American southern town

171i Consciousness as style: Style as aesthetic

229p A consciousness manifesto

229q Consciousness, politics, and magic

301kk Women's consciousness and the southern black

305f Once more with feeling: Heterosexuality and feminist consciousness

329h Private and public consciousness in *Mrs. Dalloway* and *To the Lighthouse*

344ff Feminist consciousness and black women

370n Bwanikwa: Consciousness and protest among slave women in Central Africa, 1886-1911

444h Revolution and *conciencia*: Women in Cuba

Consciousness Raising
14h Face-to-face, day-to-day - racism CR

16d Therapeutic aspects of consciousness-raising groups

96l The role and function of women's consciousness raising: Self-help, psychotherapy, or political activation?

102i Beyond consciousness raising: Changing sexist institutions

133q Consciousness-raising among gay males

251e The power of persistence: Consciousness raising at international fora - the case of UNCSTD

359uu The consciousness-raising group as a model for therapy with women

359vv The psychotherapeutic impact of women's consciousness-raising groups

365k Consciousness-raising and self-help

Consecration
187a Muffled voices: The lives of consecrated women in the fourth century

Consensus
242a Fictional consensus and female casualties

Consent
129g An "age of consent" symposium

192i Se me acabó la canción: An ethnography of non-consenting sterilizations among Mexican women in Los Angeles

284y The age of sexual consent: Fault, friction, freedom

319o The nonconsenting sterilization of Mexican women in Los Angeles: Issues of psychocultural rupture and legal redress in paternalistic behavior

Conservation
82i Agriculture, forestry, conservation and women

Conservatism
94b Ethnicity, multiculturalism and neo-conservatism

138f The conservative school? Sex roles at home, at work and at school

304l Concluding comments, criticism, and caution: Consistent conservatism or constructive change?

378i Women: If not apolitical, then conservative

Constancy
45m Change and constancy: A hundred years' tale

Constitution
2h Constitutional privacy, religious disestablishment, and the abortion decisions

316o Women's right to full participation in shaping society's course: An evolving constitutional precept

354j Chlorosis and chronic disease in 19th-century Britain: The social constitution of somatic illness in a capitalist society

402g Women and the law: Constitutional rights and continuing inequalities

Constraint
203l Introduction: Women in environmental decisionmaking: Institutional constraints

226m Resources and constraints on women in the policymaking process: States and local arenas

348h Women in constraints

Construction
7d Sadomasochism and the social construction of desire

225u *Histoire d'O*: The construction of a female subject

231k The Afro-American female: The historical context of the construction of sexual identity

290b Sexology and the social construction of male sexuality (Havelock Ellis)

299e Construction workers

312l 'Back into the personal' or: Our attempt to construct 'feminist research'

354i Medicine and patriarchal violence: The social construction of a "private" event

386h Construction workers

424q Effect of female labour force participation on fertility: The case of construction workers in Chiang Mai City

Consult
333b Consulting with women

Consumer
60f The twenties' backlash: Compulsory heterosexuality, the consumer family, and the waning of feminism

79e DES and drugs in pregnancy: A consumer reaction

134h Alice in the consumer wonderland

206q We are what we wear - The dilemma of the feminist consumer

220g Women as providers and consumers

440d Women and consumer capitalism

Consumption
89q Wives' labor force behavior and family consumption patterns

92f Indonesia: Socio-economic aspects of food consumption in rural Java

153o Wages, consumption, and survival: Working class households in Puerto Rico in the 1930's

207q Work, consumption and authority within the household: A Moroccan case

208g Work, consumption and authority within the household: A Moroccan case

321e Production and consumption: Public versus private

Contest
305i The home: A contested terrain

Contextual
198a Introduction: The ideal and contextual realities of Muslim women

Continuing Education
see also Education

316g Continuing education: A vital process for women

394o Continuing education: A personal view

394q Continuing education services in the UW system

Continuity
250i Into work: Continuity and change

Contraception
see also Birth Control, Reproduce

12i Contraception: The growth of a technology

28q Oral contraceptives and the menstrual cycle

36b Historical styles of contraceptive advocacy

36c Ethical problems in government-funded contraceptive research

36d Value conflicts in biomedical research into future contraceptives

36e   Status of contraceptive technology development

36i   Depo-provera: Some ethical questions about a controversial contraceptive

53h   Health hazards associated with oral contraceptives

190u   Steroidal contraceptive use and subsequent development of hyperprolactinemia

240c   Psychosocial aspects of contraception

252q   Contraception following second trimester abortion

308a   Teenage women in the United States: Sex, contraception, pregnancy, fertility, and maternal and infant health

308j   Bringing in the family: Kinship support and contraceptive behavior

309d   Sexual and contraceptive experience of young unmarried women in the United States, 1976 and 1971

309f   Contraceptive patterns and premarital pregnancy among women aged 15-19 in 1976

309s   Contraception, abortion and venereal disease: Teenagers' knowledge and the effect of education

309u   Sexual and contraceptive knowledge, attitudes and behavior of male adolescents

309aa Contraceptive services for adolescents: An overview

310k   Refusing to take women seriously: 'Side effects' and the politics of contraception

418j   Contraception and abortion

421s   Labor force participation and fertility, contraceptive knowledge, attitude and practice of the women of Barbados

456g   Contraception

Contract

106e   Marriage contract and social contract in seventeenth-century English political thought

129j   Marriage contract

464c   The shame of the marriage contract

Contradiction

85b   Interviewing women: A contradiction in terms

385e   Marginal lives: Conflict and contradiction in the position of female traders in Lusaka, Zambia

387p   Dilemmas and contradictions of status: The case of the dual-career family

408l   Sara de Etcheverts: The contradictions of literary feminism

Contribute

87f   Spouses' contributions to each other's roles

291h   The nature of incest: A review of contributing factors

337c   Women's contributions to the library school

387k   Invisible work: Unacknowledged contributions

Control

see also Social Control

18b   The ideology of population control

28b   The neuroendocrinologic control of the menstrual cycle

36f   Women-controlled research

36g   Woman-controlled birth control: A feminist analysis of natural birth control

129p   If you liked gun control, you'll love the antiabortion amendment

160c   Police wives: A reflection of police concepts of order and control

207h   Sexuality and the control of procreation

223j   Sex, birth control, and human life

310o   Abortion, a woman's matter: An explanation of who controls abortion and how and why they do it

341c   A woman's body in a man's world: A review of findings on body image and weight control

418k   Feminist thought and reproductive control: The state and 'the right to choose'

440m   In sickness and in health: Social policy and the control of women

447k   Evaluation and control of embryofetotoxic substances

447m   The control of hazardous exposures in the workplace

457a   Mediums, controls and eminent men

Controversy

8i   The organic-functional controversy

19j   The Antinomian language controversy

31e   Concepts of woman in psychoanalytic theory: The nature-nurture controversy revisited

36i   Depo-provera: Some ethical questions about a controversial contraceptive

46a   Concepts underlying the current controversy about women's social security benefits

79b   The DES controversy: Discovery, distribution and regulation

79f   DES: Ten points of controversy

133w   Ideologies in two gay rights controversies

169s   Subjects and materials: How to handle controversy

Convent

408g   The convent as catalyst for autonomy: Two Hispanic nuns of the seventeenth century

Convention

135p   Emma Bovary's masculinization: Convention of clothes and morality of conventions

Convergence

122b   Black studies/women's studies: Points of convergence

Conversation

27n   A conversation with May Sarton

150h   The blood - yes, the blood: A conversation

150jj Black lesbian/feminist organizing: A conversation

171g   Small insults: A study of interruptions in cross-sex conversations between unacquainted persons

292j   Memories of a movement: A conversation

343g   Counsels of gall and grace: Intimate conversations between women in Shakespeare's plays

356r   Snatches of conversation

Convict

see also Crime

78x   Why two women cops were convicted of cowardice

111k   The treatment of convicted female offenders in the criminal justice system

159m   Criminality amongst women in India: A study of female offenders and female convicts

Cook

182g   Private kitchens, public cooking

241f   'It's a pleasure to cook for him': Food, mealtimes and gender in some South Wales households

Cookbook

454q   Cookbooks and law books: The hidden history of career women in twentieth-century America

Cooper, James Fenimore

17b   Fenimore Cooper's Heroines

Cooperate

104c   Interhousehold co-operation in Peru's southern Andes: A case of multiple sibling-group marriage

104d   Co-operation on and between eastern Finnish family farms

165l   "The government's unique experiment in salvaging women criminals": Cooperation and conflict in the administration of a women's prison - The case of the Federal Industrial Institution for Women at Alderson

187g   Male/female cooperation: The example of fontevrault

288o   Sexual harassment and Title VII: The foundation for the elimination of sexual cooperation as an employment condition

Cooperative

5h   Developing women's cooperatives: An experiment in rural Nigeria

82k   Land tenure and cooperatives: Origin, development and persistence of Navajo matrifocality in subsistence, production, exchange and tenure

82m   Participation by women in Guatemalan cooperatives

102a   A society without fathers: Cooperative commonwealth or harmonious ant-heap?

172i   Integrating women into rural cooperatives: Pluses and minuses (Bolivia)

385n   Women's cooperative thrift and credit societies: An element of women's programs in the Gambia

400e   Population planning and rural women's co-operative in IRDP women's programme: Some critical issues

432h   Cooperative competition in sport

Coordinated Career

see also Dual Career

87j   Coordinated-career couples: Convergence and divergence

Coordinating Council of Women in Higher Education

394c   A history of the Wisconsin Coordinating Council of Women in Higher Education

Cop

78x   Why two women cops were convicted of cowardice

Cope

26i   Coping with wife abuse: Personal and social networks

87i The balancing act: Coping strategies for emerging family lifestyles

105h Developing family invulnerability to stress: Coping patterns and strategies wives employ in managing family separations

178m The challenge of coping

212j Coping: Or how mothers are seen and not heard

309r Family support: Helping teenage mothers to cope

Córdoba, Lenor López de

108e To restore honor and fortune: *The Autobiography of Lenor López de Córdobä*

Corneille, Pierre

135q Power or sexuality: The bind of Corneille's *Pulcherie*

Cornell University

352h Coeducation and the development of leadership skills in women: Historical perspectives from Cornell University, 1868-1900

Corner, Caterina

112b Caterina Corner, Queen of Cyprus (Venetian, 1454?-1510)

Coronary

53c The effect of employment, family and job stress on coronary heart disease patterns in women

53r Epidemiology of coronary heart disease in women

268e Sex roles and psychophysiological disorders: Coronary heart disease

Corporation

see also Business, Company, Factory, Industry, Management

93m Improving job opportunities for women from a U.S. corporate perspective

302j Women in academic-library, higher-education, and corporate management: A research review

307w Bambi meets Godzilla: Life in the corporate jungle

375l Women's entry into corporate law firms

415f Effective interpersonal communication for women of the corporation: Think like a man, talk like a lady

426g Corporate experiences in improving women's job opportunities

447p Challenges to corporate policy

Correct

63b Characteristics of co-correctional institutions

63c Co-corrections-FCI Forth Worth after three years

63e A study of a coeducational correctional facility

63g Problems with research in co-corrections

63h The development of a scale to assess inmate and staff attitudes toward co-corrections

63i Co-correctional models

63j Sex-role differentiation in a co-correctional setting

63l Two losers don't make a winner: The case against the co-correctional institution

78h National study of women's correctional programs

78y Doing time with the boys: An analysis of women correctional officers in all-male facilities

225h Politically correct? Politically incorrect?

326h Sexual assault in correctional institutions: Prevention and intervention

Correia, Mãe Aurélia

370p A Nhara of the Guinea-Bissau region: Mãe Aurélia Correia

Correspondent

328n *Three Guineas* before and after: Further answers to correspondents

Corrientes, Argentina

104b Cash crop production and family labour: Tobacco growers in Corrientes, Argentina

Cosmetics

224b Cosmetics as an act of revolution

Cosmic

229ff Sisterhood as cosmic covenant

Cost

80d Janus faces day care: Perspectives on quality and cost

87e Dual-career marriages: Benefits and costs

103h Housework: Rethinking the costs and benefits

110g Labor supply with costs of labor market entry

209c Bargaining over the social costs of information technology

344h Marital relationships and mental health: The psychic costs of inequality

425g Estimating benefits and costs of antisexist training programs in organizations

Costa Rica

172b Research experiences with rural women (Costa Rica)

269h Symbolic aspects of Bribri roles on the occasions of birth and death

Cosway, Antoinette

332f The sisterhood of Jane Eyre and Antoinette Cosway

Cotton

50b The home turned upside down? The working-class family in cotton textiles 1780-1850

301q Hard times cotton mill girls

Council

160g The negation of structure: A note on British council wives

410d Recruitment of women to suburban city councils: Higgins vs. Chevalier

410h Perceptions of women's roles on local councils in Connecticut

Council of Women

157m A response to the depression: The local Council of Women of Vancouver

Counsel

4m Sexual counseling for adolescents

16n Counselor's roles

72g Guidance and counseling of Spanish-background girls

73k Achieving the dreams beyond tradition: Counseling white ethnic American girls

75d Career counselling for poor rural and urban women of South India

141i Genetic counseling, patient and family management: Familial breast cancer

220f Feminist counselling: Approach or technique?

221h The process of retirement: Implications for late-life counseling

315d Feminist counseling

345g Counselling

359dd Abortion counseling

359ee Abortion counseling with adolescents

359gg Postmastectomy counseling

359yy New directions in counseling women

Country

see also Nation, State, individual countries

93a The policy and problem: Overview of seven countries

186h The country of the imagination

251b Women and technology in the industrialized countries

251c Women and technology in peripheral countries: An overview

260j Labour market policy in four countries: Are women adequately represented?

260k Estimating the impact of labor market policies on women: A discussion of the four-country studies on the employment of women

388g Women in Communist countries: Comparative public policy

The Country of the Pointed Fir

451a The art of Jewett's *Pointed Firs*

Countryside

215j Letter to my neighbour: Nuclear war and the countryside

Couple

see also Family

87h Time management and the dual-career couple

87j Coordinated-career couples: Convergence and divergence

87k Equal opportunity laws and dual-career couples

87l Salary and job performance differences in dual-career couples

87m Going shopping: The professional couple in the job market

105b Modern and traditional elements in the expectations of young married couples regarding their marital life

140k Roles and role conflict of women in infertile couples

212a Heterosexuality, couples and parenthood: A 'natural' cycle?

267e Career concepts and human resource management: The case of the dual-career couple

339g Dual career couples: How the company can help

339h Working couples and child care

394l We have hired couples for years

425h Causal determinants of job satisfaction in dual career couples

434k Social work with lesbian couples

439p "The love crisis": Couples advice books of the late 1970s

Courage

310gg The courage of sisters

Courier
383b Method in her madness: Feminism in the crazy utopian vision of Tiptree's Courier

Course
49a   Charting a course
169c The short course

Court
see also Law
17f   Mark Twain's capers: A chameleon in King Carnival's court
33b   Women, learning, and power: Eleonora of Aragon and the Court of Ferrara
65l   A review of federal court decisions under Title VII of the Civil Rights Act of 1964
111l Women in court: Assisting the female offender
159d Norwegian women in court
165i Female delinquents in a suburban court
188c The French courtly poet: Marie de France
235f The police and the courts
276b The relationship between treatment for sex offenders and the court
300o Islamic law in Christian Southeast Asia: The politics of establishing Sharía courts in the Philippines
375e Rape in thirteenth-century England: A study of the common-law courts
379c The planter's wife revisited: Women, equity law, and the Chancery Court in seventeenth-century Maryland
392m Unequal protection of males and females in the juvenile court
410b Political culture and selection of women judges in trial courts

Courtesan
155g Courtesans and prostitutes in South Asian literature

Courtroom
284r Courtroom use of hospital records in sexual assault cases

Courtship
48d   The courtship game: Power in the sexual encounter

Covenant
229ff Sisterhood as cosmic covenant

Cover
381g Covering the ground

Cow
117b Matrilineal reinterpretation of some Egyptian sacred cows

Cowardice
78x   Why two women cops were convicted of cowardice

Cowden's Syndrome
141h Breast cancer in Cowden's syndrome

CPSU
see Communist Party of the Soviet Union

Crackle
135m The laughter of maidens, the crackle of matriarchs: Notes on the collision between comedy and feminism

Craft
148e Women's work: An examination of women's roles in Plains Indian arts and crafts

201a Needlework as art, craft, and livelihood before 1900
274m Craft, design, and technology
417s The craft of their hands
447d Moving women into outside craft jobs

Crane, Stephen
17j   Stephen Crane and the fallen women
155h The fate of the fallen woman in *Maggie* and *Sister Carrie*

Cravo e Canela, Gabriela
39ee Images of the woman of color in Brazilian literature: O Cortico, Clara Dos Anjos, Gabriela Cravo E Canela, and O Quinze

Crazy
315c Still crazy after all these years: The uses of madness in women's fiction
383b Method in her madness: Feminism in the crazy utopian vision of Tiptree's Courier

Create
43l   Class realities: Create a new power base
109j "A forced solitude": Mary Shelley and the creation of Frankenstein's monster
168h Creating and communicating knowledge from a feminist perspective: Risks and challenges for women
254n The whole thing: In search of relevance and integration made dynamic by creativity
462aa Reflections on the creation of a ritual meal
474f Creating oneself from scratch

Creative
17l   Mothers, daughters, and the "art necessity": Willa Cather and the creative process
77a   Creative women in political change
77b   Creative women in economic and social change
77c   Creative women in scientific-technological and medical change
77d   Creative women in artistic and literary change
174s Creative teaching spaces: Home movies
287p Creative sexuality: Androgyny
330b Hunting the moth: Virginia Woolf and the creative imagination
462l Political oppression and creative survival

Credible
165b Would you believe this woman? Prosecutorial screening for "credible" witnesses and a problem of justice

Credit
46b   Supplemental OASI benefits to homemakers through current spouse benefits, a homemaker credit, and child-care dropout years
92g   The advantages of functional education and credit facilities for Javanese rural women
300j The CHIT fund in Singapore: Failure of a large-scale rotating credit fund

Creole
306c Cross-cultural perspectives: Creole and Acadian women

Cressida
343h Shakespeare's Cressida: "A kind of self"

Crete
117c The great goddess and the palace architecture of Crete

417c Women in transition: Crete and Sumer

Crime
see also Convict, Criminal, Criminology, Delinquency, Incarcerate, Inmate, Jail, Law, Offender, Parole, Prison, Sentence, Victim, various types of crime
53f   Women as victims of crime
55m   Appendix B: Review of legal cases regarding US Code, Section 1461 (mailing obscene or crime-inciting matter)
78b   The etiology of female crime: A review of the literature
78f   Trends in female crime: It's still a man's world
78l   Rape: The all-American crime
137k Gender and crime
159e Female crime in England and Wales
159h Crimes against life committed by women in Hungary
159n Emancipation of women and crime in Japan
165d Exploring female crime patterns: Problems and prospects
180b Kriemhild and Clytemnestra - Sisters in crime or independent women?
258h Involvement in crime
295h The impact of crime on urban women
348b Hidden from history: Women victims of crime
348c Women, crime and punishment
348d The mythinterpretation of female crime
348e Theorizing about female crime
348g The myth of rising female crime
349b American women and crime
349c Crime and the contemporary woman: An analysis of changing levels of female property crime, 1960-1975
349d Patterns of female property crime, 1960-1978: A postscript
376c The crime of precocious sexuality: Female juvenile delinquency and the progressive era
390x Crime and sexual politics
392a The extent and nature of female crime
392b The etiology of female crime: A review of the literature
392f Crimes of violence by women
392g Searching for women in organized crime
392h Women, heroin, and property crime
435k Women's crime, women's justice

Criminal
see also Crime
78a   The criminal law and women
78m   Forcible rape: Institutionalized sexism in the criminal justice system
78z   Marxist feminism: Implications for criminal justice
78aa Postscript: The future of women and the criminal law
111a Re-discovering Lilith: Misogyny and the "new" female criminal
111c Women's criminality in Poland
111k The treatment of convicted female offenders in the criminal justice system
111r Drug abuse and criminality among women in detention

111u Problems of policy development in criminal justice

122i Levels of female criminal activity as a correlate of female societal power

159b Female criminality in the Netherlands

159c Female criminality in Finland - What do the statistics show?

159f Changing patterns of female criminality in Germany

159g The criminality of women in Poland

159i A preliminary study of female criminality in Nigeria

159j Female criminality in Egypt

159k Argentine statistics on female criminality

159l Venezuelan female criminality: The ideology of diversity and marginality

159m Criminality amongst women in India: A study of female offenders and female convicts

165l "The government's unique experiment in salvaging women criminals": Cooperation and conflict in the administration of a women's prison - The case of the Federal Industrial Institution for Women at Alderson

165m Women as criminal justice professionals: A challenge to change tradition

165n Sex-role operations: Strategies for women working in the criminal justice system

165o Women in the criminal justice profession: An analysis of status conflict

268i Sex roles, criminality, and psychopathology

280g The kleptomanias and female criminality

284p The protection of the child victim of a sexual offense in the criminal justice system

291f Sexual abuse of children: An examination of European criminal law

348a Sexism in criminal law

349e The economics of female criminality: An analysis of police blotters, 1890-1976

349g Aw! Your mother's in the mafia: Women criminals in progressive New York

376h The criminality of women in eighteenth-century England

376j Sex differences in the processing of criminal defendants

392e The interaction between women's emancipation and female criminality: A cross-cultural perspective

392l Chivalry and paternalism: Disparities of treatment in the criminal justice system

Criminology
see also Crime

349a Criminological theory: Its ideology and implications concerning women

376k Criminological theory: Its ideology and implications concerning women

Crisis

26d Crisis intervention with battered women

60d Crisis, reaction, and resistance: Women in Germany in the 1920's and 1930's

96h Toward choice and differentiation in the midlife crises of women

97e Public education and the discourse of crisis, power and vision

219g Crisis intervention with victims of forcible rape: A police perspective

326b Working for and with rape victims: Crisis intervention and advocacy

336c Abortion and economic crisis: The 1931 campaign against paragraph 218

365m Reproductive crises

390v Women and economic crises: The Great Depression and the present crisis

404a Women in crisis: The issue

434d Rape crisis theory revisited

Cristero Rebellion, 1926-1929

363c Women and revolution: The brigadas femeninas and the Mexican Cristero Rebellion, 1926-1929

Critic

20m Bashful but bold: Notes on Margaret Atwood as critic

121a Introduction: Feminist critics read Emily Dickinson

174aa Friends and critics: The feminist academy

197e Muriel Spark: Critic into Novelist

200a Nature, culture and gender: A critique

223a Love: A feminist critique

389e Margaret Fuller (1810-1850): Her work as an art critic

389g Mariana Griswold Van Rensselaer (1851-1934): America's first professional woman art critic

399ii The lady is a critic

452n The lady's not for spurning: Kate Millett and the critics

Critica

313a Crítica feminista: Apuntes sobre definiciones y problemas

Criticism
see Critique

Critique
see also Feminist Critique

7q Is sadomasochism feminist? A critique of the Samois position

7x Sadomasochism and the erosion of self: A critical reading of *Story of O*

14p Toward a black feminist criticism

32b A critical appraisal of Goethe's *Iphigenie*

32l Sociological implications of Gabriele Wohmann's critical reception

32m The left-handed compliment: Perspectives and stereotypes in criticism

32p Our language, our selves: Verena Stefan's critique of patriarchal language

35b Biology, gender, and politics: An assessment and critique

51m Changing views of "the change": A critical review and suggestions for an attributional approach

51t A critique of menopause research

85h The gatekeepers: A feminist critique of academic publishing

106l Contemporary critical theory and the family: Private world and public crisis

116c Nuture theories: A critique

120b Feminism and the critique of scientific method

122e The best feminist criticism is a new criticism

122q Marital metaphors in the Judeo-Christian tradition: A feminist critique

123b New directions for feminist criticism in theatre and the related arts

123c The feminist critique in religious studies

126h Against the grain: A working feminist art criticism

135s Feminist criticism reviewed

136i A feminist critique of androgyny: Toward the elimination of gender attributions for learned behavior

143b Critical approaches to George Eliot

162a Interest and emotion in family and kinship studies: A critique of social history and anthropology

165f Murdered women and women who murder: A critique of the literature

168c Hindsight is 20/20: The development, achievements and dilemmas of feminist literary criticism

176u Is feminist criticism really feminist?

189b Dancing through the minefield: Some observations on the theory, practice and politics of a feminist literary criticism

203m Architecture: Toward a feminist critique

223y Critique

227o 'The housewife and her labour under capitalism' - a critique

247a Feminist film criticism: An introduction

247b Developments in feminist film criticism

247c The woman at the keyhole: Women's cinema and feminist criticism

265d Review of the literature of non-sexist curriculum and a critique of the underlying assumptions and rationale

312m Women's studies as a strategy for change: Between criticism and vision

314e The natural sciences: Casting a critical eye on 'objectivity'

329l A common sitting room: Virginia Woolf's critique of women writers

335c From utopian to scientific feminism? Early feminist critiques of the family

342g Feminist analysis of gender: A critique

359t Issues in the treatment of female addiction: A review and critique of the literature

369c Beyond the unhappy marriage: A critique of the dual systems theory

406a Klute 1: A contemporary film noir and feminist criticism

418e Left critiques of the family

445o Dorothy Scarborough's critique of the frontier experience in *The Wind*

464e Prologue to a feminist critique of war and politics

464g Consequences of seizing the reins in the household: A Marxist-feminist critique of Marx and Engels

Croatia

405i The anti-fascist front of women and the Communist Party in Croatia: Conflicts within the resistance

Crockett, Davey

238c Davey Crockett as trickster: Pornography, liminality and symbolic inversion in Victorian America

Crop

104b Cash crop production and family labour: Tobacco growers in Corrientes, Argentina

Cross Cultural

see also Cross National, Culture

24g Human sexuality in cross-cultural perspective

39a The black woman cross-culturally: An overview

51d A cross-cultural exploration of the end of the childbearing years

190m Virginity rituals and chastity control during puberty: Cross-cultural patterns

216c A cross-cultural perspective on parenting

230g Pornography in Japan: Cross-cultural and theoretical considerations

265m Sex role stereotyping and mental health standards in Israel: A cross-cultural comparison

271g A cross-cultural comparison of assertiveness in women

279h A cross-cultural investigation into the sexual dimorphism of stature

289b The cross-cultural and historical context

306c Cross-cultural perspectives: Creole and Acadian women

355h Household time: A cross-cultural example

392e The interaction between women's emancipation and female criminality: A cross-cultural perspective

Cross National

see also Cross Cultural

18f Cross-national labor migrants: Actors in the international division of labor

52k Economic and family roles of men and women in Northern Europe: A historical cross-national comparison

421k Feminist egalitarianism, social action orientation and occupational roles: A cross-national study

421n Working wives in the United States and Venezuela: A cross-national study of decision making

Cross, Amanda

1j Amanda Cross

Cross Section

423g Longitudinal and cross-sectional data sources on women in the middle years

Cross Sex

171s Small insults: A study of interruptions in cross-sex conversations between unacquainted persons

265j Cross-sex friendship in the elementary school

Crothers, Rachel

399u Looking to women: Rachel Crothers and the feminist heroine

Crown

399e Crowning Miss California, again

Crusade

215t The women's peace crusade: The history of a forgotten campaign

238j The scientist as sex crusader: Alfred C. Kinsey and American culture

Crux

249g The crux: Quality judgment and departmental autonomy

Cry

175f The ghost of Chipita: The crying woman of San Patricio

Crystal City, TX

192u Personal chronicle of Crystal City

Cuba

68i Women in Cuba: The revolution within the revolution

363a In defense of motherhood: Divorce law in Cuba during the early republic

374a The early years

374b The revolution within the Revolution

374c The struggle for women's equality

374d Thesis: On the full exercise of women's equality

374e Into the third decade

421z Women in the Cuban bureaucracies: 1968-1974

444h Revolution and *conciencia*: Women in Cuba

469j The emerging Cuban women of Florida's Dade County

473j The uses of traditional concepts in the development of new urban roles: Cuban women in the United States

Cui Yingying

401e The many faces of Cui Yingying

Cult

39i Women in indigenous African cults and churches

72c The cult of virginity

156q The role of Jewish women in the religion, ritual and cult of Graeco-Roman Palestine

194b The Tonantsi cult of the Eastern Nahua

194d The cult of Brigid: A study of pagan-Christian syncretism in Ireland

313e El ángel del hogar: The cult of domesticity in nineteenth century Spain

325e Ecstasy and possession: Women of ancient Greece and the cult of Dionysus

Cult of True Womanhood

147h Sport and the Cult of True Womanhood: A paradox at the turn of the century

445h Hamlin Garland and the cult of true womanhood

454i The cult of true womanhood: 1820-1860

Culture

see also Cross Cultural, Psychocultural, Society

3o Abortion and the culture: Toward a feminist perspective

7e On the history of cultural sadism

8d Wife abuse: Culture as destiny

10a "When angels fall": Women's drinking as cultural preoccupation and as reality

34d Social bodies: The interaction of culture and women's biology

35g Explaining "male chauvinism" and "feminism": Cultural differences in male and female reproductive strategies

36r A report on birth in three cultures

37d African-American family life: An instrument of culture

37h Black education: A cultural-ecological perspective

39aa Economic role and cultural tradition

45b The challenge of sex equality: Old values revisited or a new culture?

50z Oppressive dichotomies: The nature/culture debate

51r Cultural models for coping with menopause

51y Male and female menopause: A cultural put-on

54a A systems model for planning culturally specific programs

68f Chinese women: The relative influences of ideological revolution, economic growth, and cultural change

70e The interaction of culture and sex roles in the schools

72l Chicana identity: Interaction of culture and sex roles

81f Culture and radical politics: Yiddish women writers in America, 1890-1940

82n Dynamics of social and cultural change

82o Women's roles and culturally sensitive programs

94d Migrantness, culture and ideology

101b Social reform and women's participation in political culture: Andhra and Madras

119b Feminism and the definition of cultural politics

120f To grow a daughter: Cultural liberation and the dynamics of oppression in Jamaica

148i Male and female in traditional Lakota culture

150q Cultural legacy denied and discovered: Black lesbians in fiction by women

162n Village spinning bees: Sexual culture and free time among rural youths in early modern Germany

194f The worship of Mother Earth in Russian culture

200a Nature, culture and gender: A critique

200d The power of signs: Gender, culture and the wild in the Bolivian Andes

200f Gender, sexuality and marriage: A Kaulong model of nature and culture

200h No nature, no culture: The Hagen case

203s The Los Angeles woman's building: A public center for woman's culture

216i The Puerto Rican family: Its role in cultural transition

218b *Sati* or *Shakti*: Women, culture and politics in India

224a Culture and politics

225i Cultural and historical influences on sexuality in Hispanic/Latin women: Implications for psychotherapy

229b Women and culture in goddess-oriented old Europe

230b Aggression against women: Cultural and individual causes

232c Marriage in Tamil culture: The problem of conflicting "models"

232d Hidden powers: Cultural and socio-economic accounts of Jaffna women

238j The scientist as sex crusader: Alfred C. Kinsey and American culture

250b Socio-cultural reproduction and women's education

255b Purdah revisited: A comparison of Hindu and Muslim interpretations of the cultural meaning of purdah in South Asia

265l Cultural differences in children's sex role stereotypes

270o Civil violence in Turkey: Its infrastructural, social and cultural foundations

291a Definition and recognition of sexual child abuse: Historical and cultural perspectives

300c The Minangkabau woman: Cultural centre or ethnic symbol?

306l Southern women's literature and culture: Course development and the pedagogical process

315b Attitudes toward gender in two cultures: Puerto Rico and the United States

319h "All the good and bad in this world": Women, traditional medicine, and Mexican American culture

319j Cultural styles and adolescent sex role perceptions: An exploration of responses to a value picture projective test

320b Culture, service, and work: Changing ideals of higher education for women

323i Coercion or male culture: A new look at co-worker harassment

333p The Yuendumu aboriginal cultural preschool

342d The dialectic of biology and culture

344b The rape culture

356b Anthropology: Social and cultural perspectives

359bb Lesbian families: Cultural and clinical issues

365l Minority women: Social-cultural issues

366d The Jewish woman's encounter with American culture

369j Cultural Marxism: Nonsynchrony and feminist practice

369l The marriage of capitalist and patriarchal ideologies: Meanings of male bonding and male ranking in U.S. culture

384o Wright Morris, women, and American culture

387i Commitment and cultural mandate: Women in medicine

396h Sex predetermination, artificial insemination and the maintenance of male-dominated culture

397f Beloved women: The lesbian in American Indian culture

397p Culture-making: Lesbian classics in the year 2000

410b Political culture and selection of women judges in trial courts

413j Mummy's boys: Pakeha men and male culture in New Zealand

418m Oppressive dichotomies: The nature/culture debate

419k The role of women in Roman elegy: Counter-cultural feminism

421a Cultural determinants of power for women within the family: A neglected aspect of family research

421i Attitudes of women towards certain selected cultural practices in Kerala state, India

423e Women in the German Democratic Republic: Impact of culture and social policy

433k Radindranath Tagore: Cultural ambassador of India to the United States

434g Asian-American women: A historical and cultural perspective

441e The culture of engineering: Woman, workplace and machine

448d George Eliot and the city: The imprisonment of culture

453a Women's culture: Themes and images

453b Defining women's culture

453t Institutions of women's culture

454a American women and domestic culture: An approach to women's history

454h Cultural hybrid in the slums: The college woman and the Settlement House, 1889-1894

466a Women as cultural intermediaries in nineteenth-century Batavia

469f Cultural attitudes toward mental illness among Puerto Rican migrant women

Cuna

269d New economic roles for Cuna males and females: An examination of socioeconomic change in a San Blas community

269f Being Cuna and female: Ethnicity mediating change in sex roles

Cupid

129l Cupid's yokes

288c Coping with Cupid: The formation, impact, and management of romantic relationships in organizations

Cure

116k On curing conceptual confusion: Response to Mary Anne Warren

223v Curing homosexuality

Curious

231j they're always curious

Curlewis, Joan

13g Tribute to Joan Curlewis

Curran, Sarah

338h The dramatic treatment of Robert Emmet and Sarah Curran

Curriculum

see also Education

57j Sexuality and social policy: The unwritten curriculum

82r Curriculum: Preparation for involvement

90f The problem of sex bias in curriculum materials

126a The genesis of feminist visions for transforming the liberal arts curriculum

126n Does equality mean sameness? A historical perspective on the college curriculum for women with reflections on the current situation

126o Sex differences in the brain: Implications for curriculum change

253g Reproductive hazards in the workplace: A course curriculum guide

259e Anxiety, aspirations and the curriculum

259j Curriculum matters

265d Review of the literature of non-sexist curriculum and a critique of the underlying assumptions and rationale

314b Interactive phases of curricular re-vision

314g Toward a balanced curriculum: Wheaton College

314h Project on women in the curriculum: Montana State University

314l Moving beyond the curriculum: The 'political' value of an integration strategy

314u Women, gender, and the curriculum

316l Challenging curricular assumptions: Teaching and studying women's literature from a regional perspective

398d Survival in the 'master's house': The role of graduate teaching assistants in effecting curriculum change

Curse

70h Indian boarding schools and Indian women: Blessing or curse?

150oo Only justice can stop a curse

229z From sacred blood to the curse and beyond

Cushman, Charlotte

399k Women in male roles: Charlotte Cushman and others

Custody

103j Gender and child-custody determinations: Exploding the myths

165j Hard times: Custodial prisons for women and the example of the New York State Prison for Women at Auburn, 1893-1933

204j Social development and parent-child interaction in father-custody and stepmother families

397k Lesbianism and motherhood: Implications for child custody

Custom

92b Bangladesh: Beliefs and customs observed by Muslim rural women during their life cycle

162o Family fun in Starve Harbor: Custom, history and confrontation in village Newfoundland

244h Sexual customs and gender roles in Sweden and America: An analysis and interpretation

353j "On the importance of the obstetrick art": Changing customs of childbirth in America, 1760 to 1825

457h Between law and custom: Women's experience of Judaism

Cutting Edge

206b Restructuring: The cutting edge

Cycle

28a The physiology of the menstrual cycle

28b The neuroendocrinologic control of the menstrual cycle

28e The psychology of the menstrual cycle: Biological and physiological perspectives

28f Cognitive behavior and the menstrual cycle

28g Epidemiological patterns of sexual behavior in the menstrual cycle

28h Sexual behavior and the menstrual cycle

28n The menstrual cycle in anorexia nervosa

28o Psychopathology and the menstrual cycle

28q Oral contraceptives and the menstrual cycle

34g Changing minds: Women, biology, and the menstrual cycle

51i Potential role of the pineal gland in the human menstrual cycle

190b Endocrine aspects of menarche and menopause - milestones in the woman's life cycle

239j   Adult life cycles: Changing roles and changing hormones

239l   A social psychological perspective on the menstrual cycle

239m   Body time and social time: Mood patterns by menstrual cycle phase and day of week

271p   Feeling states and the menstrual cycle

271q   Theoretical/conceptual implications of study design and statistical analysis: Research on the menstrual cycle

281a   Human sexuality in the life cycle of the family system

355g   Women's life-cycle time allocation: An econometric analysis

400f   Life cycle, food behaviour and nutrition of women in Bangladesh

404r   Breaking cycles of victimization: The shelter as an affirmative institution

415d   Lady you're trapped: Breaking out of conflict cycles

427i   Conceptions of kinship and the family reproduction cycle

439k   Behavior and the menstrual cycle

460o   Daughters and lovers: Reflections on the life cycle of father-daughter relationships

Cycling
372p   Measurement of maximal short-term (anaerobic) power output during cycling

Cyprus
112b   Caterina Corner, Queen of Cyprus (Venetian, 1454?-1510)

213d   Sexual divisions and ethnic adaptation: The case of Greek-Cypriot women

Cystitis
456n   Cystitis

Cytology
456i   Cervical cytology

Czarist
108h   *My Childhood Years*: A memoir by the czarist cavalry officer, Nadezhda Durova

Czechoslovakia
52n   Women in Czechoslovakia

436g   Demography, political reform and women's issues in Czechoslovakia

Dade County, FL
469j   The emerging Cuban women of Florida's Dade County

Dahomey
370r   Servitude and worldly success in the palace of Dahomey

Dallas Cowboys
175v   Legends in their own time: The Dallas Cowboy cheerleaders

Dallas, TX
175e   Belle Starr: The Bandit Queen of Dallas

175v   Legends in their own time: The Dallas Cowboy cheerleaders

Dalloway, Clarissa
328i   Clarissa Dalloway's respectable suicide

Dame
154b   The crowned dame, dame opinion, and dame philosophy: The female characteristics of three ideals in Christine de Pizan's *L'Avision Christine*

Dance
134f   Dance and social fantasy

244i   Traditional sex norms and the innovative function of afternoon dancing

333i   Borroloola women speak. Man and woman: Dance

379l   City mothers, city daughters, and the dance hall girls: The limits of female political power in San Francisco, 1913

442l   Women and dance

Dancing Girls
20g   Minuets and madness: Margaret Atwood's *Dancing Girls*

Daniel Deronda
27h   Beauty in distress: *Daniel Deronda* and *The House of Mirth*

142c   A Meredithian glance at Gwendolen Harleth

142f   Antique gems from *Romola* to *Daniel Deronda*

143j   Gwendolen Harleth and "The girl of the period"

Dark
20h   The dark voyage: *The Edible Woman* as romance

231v   Hearts of darkness

Darwin, Australia
333k   Women and land rights: Kiuk and Wagaidj women in the Darwin area

Darwin, Charles
126e   Darwin and sexism: Victorian causes, contemporary effects

126f   A feminist challenge to Darwinism: Antoinette L. B. Blackwell on the relations of the sexes in nature and society

Date
344g   Power in dating relationships

Daughter
see also Family

17l   Mothers, daughters, and the "art necessity": Willa Cather and the creative process

27c   Frankenstein's daughter: Mary Shelley and Mary Wollstonecraft

30u   Daughters writing: Toward a theory of women's biography

42h   Daughters of God

99d   Victorian spinsters: Dutiful daughters, desperate rebels and the transition to the new women

103r   Antigone's daughters: Reflections on female identity and the state

108g   Giving weight to words: Madame de Sévigné's letters to her daughter

120f   To grow a daughter: Cultural liberation and the dynamics of oppression in Jamaica

129e   Antigone's daughters

132c   Mother-daughter relationships: Psychodynamics, politics, and philosophy

132o   Separation and survival: Mothers, daughters, sisters: - The women's experimental theater

140p   Father-daughter incest

140q   Families at risk for father-daughter incest

158b   Freud's heritage: Fathers and daughters in German literature (1750-1850)

180a   Mothers and daughters in ancient Near Eastern literature

180c   Eve's orphans: Mothers and daughters in medieval English literature

180e   The great unwritten story: Mothers and daughters in Shakespeare

180g   Unmothered daughter and the radical reformer: Harriet Martineau's career

180i   Mothers and daughters in *Wives and Daughters*: A study of Elizabeth Gaskell's last novel

180j   Mothers and daughters in the fiction of the New Republic

180l   Ellen Glasgow: Daughter as justified

180m   Mothers, daughters, and incest in the late novels of Edith Wharton

180q   The nightmare repetition: The mother-daughter conflict in Doris Lessing's *Children of Violence*

180t   A psychological journey: Mothers and daughters in English-Canadian fiction

180v   Spider woman's web: Mothers and daughters in Southwestern Native American literature

180w   Mothers and daughters: Another minority group

180y   Mothers and daughters in literature: A preliminary bibliography

190g   Menarche: Its effects on mother-daughter and father-daughter interactions

190k   Menstrual beliefs and experiences of mother-daughter dyads

211u   Bride, spouse, daughter: Images of the feminine in classical Jewish sources

257e   The daughter is mother of the child: Cycles of lesbian sexuality

284j   Father-daughter incest

284l   Humanistic treatment of father-daughter incest

343q   "O sacred, shadowy, cold, and constant queen": Shakespeare's imperiled and chastening daughters of romance

347h   Daughters of the lakes and rivers: Colonization and the land rights of Luo women

359d   The conflict between nurturance and autonomy in mother-daughter relationships and within feminism

359oo   Incest between fathers and daughters

373j   Changing role of Maya mothers and daughters

379f   Linnaeus's daughters: Women and British botany

379l   City mothers, city daughters, and the dance hall girls: The limits of female political power in San Francisco, 1913

411i   The daughter of aging parents

418h   'A daughter: A thing to be given away'

441a   Daughters of Isis, daughters of Demeter: When women sowed and reaped

460o   Daughters and lovers: Reflections on the life cycle of father-daughter relationships

Daughter of Earth
332b   The novel of awakening (five novels)

384i   The western roots of feminism in Agnes Smedley's *Daughter of Earth*

Davao City, Philippines
424m   Growth of the bazaar economy and its significance for women's employment: Trends of the 1970s in Davao City, Philippines

Davis, Henrietta Vinton
399n Henrietta Vinton Davis: Shakespearean actress

Day
206g The double day
474n *Opening nights*: The opening days

Day Care
see also Care, Child Care
80a Social-emotional consequences of day care for preschool children
80b Infant day care: Relationships between theory and practice
80d Janus faces day care: Perspectives on quality and cost
80f Environmental differences among day care centers and their effects on children's development
80g Day care and children's responsiveness to adults
80h Parents and day care workers: A failed partnership?
80k The problem of infant day care
80l A methodological comment on "The problem of infant day care"
80o The politics of federal day care regulation
80q The battle for day care in America: A view from the trenches
80u Day care: A black perspective
80v Health care services for children in day care programs
80x Day care and early childhood education
204d The ecology of day care
323u Free universal day care: The OFL takes a stand
388h Public day care in Britain and Sweden: A sociological perspective

De Facto
358a Women in broadcasting (U.S.) *de jure, de facto*

De Jure
316m De jure sex discrimination
358a Women in broadcasting (U.S.) *de jure, de facto*

De la Parra, Teresa
74a "Feminine" testimony in the works of Teresa de la Parra, María Luisa Bombal, and Victoria Ocampo

Deaconess
412j The social gospel according to Phoebe: Methodist deaconesses in the metropolis, 1885-1918

Dead
271b Androgyny: A dead end or a promise

Dealer
370o Slaves, slave owners, and slave dealers: Sherbro coast and hinterland

Dear
356f "Don't 'dear' me!"

Death
121g "Oh, vision of language!": Dickinson's poems of love and death
135r On the birth of death: An *Arrest d'Amour* of Martial d'Auvergne
144e Women, family and death: Excess mortality of women in child-bearing age in four

communities in nineteenth-century Germany
210m The final challenge: Facing death
252n Termination of pregnancy after intrauterine foetal death
269h Symbolic aspects of Bribri roles on the occasions of birth and death
285c The social relation of sex and death
285d Death and sexuality
285t How to stubbornly refuse to disturb oneself emotionally about anything - even about death, dying and sexual mutilation
325i Black Carib women and rites of death
462m Patriarchy and death

Deb-Sen, Nabaneeta
322i Interview with Nabaneeta Deb-Sen (India)

Debate
2e Personhood and the abortion debate
3u The abortion debate: Is progress possible?
50z Oppressive dichotomies: The nature/culture debate
62a Introduction: Co-education reconsidered - reviving the debate
62b Co-education: Perspectives and debates in the early twentieth century
66a The emerging debate
67a The emerging debate
132l For the Etruscans: Sexual difference and artistic production - the debate over a female aesthetic
353m Birthing and anesthesia: The debate over twilight sleep

Deborah
211q And Deborah made ten

Debunk
14j Debunking Sapphire: Toward a non-racist and non-sexist social science

Decade
374e Into the third decade

Decay
409c Emma Clery in *Stephen Hero*: A young woman walking proudly through the decayed city

Decentralize
167j A women's day for disarmament: Notes on organising a decentralised action

Deception
202k What is to console us?: The politics of deception in Woolf's short stories
275t Moral redescription and political self-deception

Decision
2h Constitutional privacy, religious disestablishment, and the abortion decisions
65l A review of federal court decisions under Title VII of the Civil Rights Act of 1964
79p Decisions about handicapped newborns: Values and procedures
118e Becoming human: A contextual approach to decisions about pregnancy and abortion
165h Are females treated differently? A review of the theories and evidence on sentencing and parole decisions
173f Public support for pro-choice abortion policies in the nation and states: Changes

and stability after the *Roe* and *Doe* decisions
216j Implications for national policy decisions: The black family perspective
222b The ambivalent decision
339j One family's decision: A leave of absence

Decision Making
172a Squatter settlement decision-making: For men only? (Peru)
203l Introduction: Women in environmental decisionmaking: Institutional constraints
273e Decision making and sex selection with biased technologies
421c A causal interpretation of the effect of mother's education and employment status on parental decision-making role patterns in the Korean family
421n Working wives in the United States and Venezuela: A cross-national study of decision making
463k Role influence in transportation decision making
463m Sex differences in travel preferences and decision making

Deconstruct
13a Deconstructing the masculine universe: The case of women's work

Decoration
117q Miriam Schapiro and "femmage": Reflections on the conflict between decoration and abstraction in twentieth-century art

Decriminalize
294g Prostitution and the law: The question of decriminalization

Dedalus, Stephen
409d Stephen Dedalus and women: A portrait of the artist as a young misogynist

Deeds
22b Wills, deeds, and charters as sources for the history of medieval women

Defeat
124m The defeat of the Equal Rights Amendment

Defect
233f Birth defects and parental occupation

Defend
215f Defend us against our defenders: Democracy and security

Defendant
376j Sex differences in the processing of criminal defendants

Defense
2j Abortion and self-defense
215l Alternative defence: The search for non-nuclear alternatives
215m Alternative defence: Nonviolent struggle and peace building
223k A defense of abortion
225k The body politic: The defense of sexual restriction by anti-abortion activists
383j Beyond defensiveness: Feminist research strategies
398h Beyond defensiveness: A feminist research strategies

Define
22a "Glory is like a circle in the water"...Thoughts and suggestions towards a definition of feminine historical research
60q Defining and combating sexual harassment
105i Towards a new definition of divorce
291a Definition and recognition of sexual child abuse: Historical and cultural perspectives
296h Powerless by definition: Occupational and pay patterns of women in the workplace

Defoe, Daniel
384n Marian Forrester and Moll Flanders: Fortunes and misfortunes

Degas, Edgar
117n Degas's "Misogyny"

Degenderization
275k Degenderization

Degenerate
283d Feminists - The degenerates of the social?
283e Reply: Feminists - The degenerates of the social?

Degrade
387q Degraded and deskilled: The proletarianization of clerical work

Dehumanize
178f The public welfare system: Regulation and dehumanization

Deity
see also Religion
211t Steps toward feminine imagery of deity in Jewish theology

DeLeon, L. Glen
128a Daniel DeLeon and the woman question

Delicacy
294k From delicacy to dilemma: A feminist perspective

Delilah
117h Delilah

Delinquency
see also Crime
8g Juvenile delinquency in girls
29o Female delinquents
165g Delinquency causation in female offenders
165i Female delinquents in a suburban court
205r Sinners or sinned against?: Historical aspects of female juvenile delinquency in British Columbia
349f Gender differences in delinquency: Quantity and quality
376c The crime of precocious sexuality: Female juvenile delinquency and the progressive era
392d Female delinquency and broken homes: A reassessment

Deliver
56d The deliverers: A woman doctor's reflections on medical socialization
360a Women in the mental health delivery system: Implications for research and public policy
404f The sparse ghetto: Service delivery in a rural area
404n Plenary session: Intervention/service delivery systems

404o Plenary session: Intervention/service delivery systems

Delta
104a Aspects of non-capitalist social relations in rural Egypt: The small peasant household in an Egyptian delta village

Demeter
441a Daughters of Isis, daughters of Demeter: When women sowed and reaped

Democracy
31a Private rights and public virtues: Women, the family, and democracy
102h A primer on women and the democratization of the workplace
130c Women, democracy, and revolution in Paris, 1789-1794
133x Religious fundamentalism and the democratic process
144i Politics and the family: Social democracy and the working-class family in theory and practice before 1914
192e Toward a democratic women's movement in the United States
215f Defend us against our defenders: Democracy and security
292c Citizens for Democracy: The industrial programs of the YWCA

Demography
see also Fertility, Household, Population
37f A demographic picture of black families
38b Some demographic characteristics of the black woman: 1940 to 1975
38c Black fertility: Recent demographic and sociological influences
45a American demographic directions
234h The limitations of demography for women's history
276a The classification of sexual aggressives and their associated demographic, social, developmental and psychological features
370c Sexual demography: The impact of the slave trade on family structure
393b Education and socio-demographic change in Nigeria
405n Some demographic, particularly fertility, correlates of female status in eastern Europe and the republics of the Soviet Union
436g Demography, political reform and women's issues in Czechoslovakia
446l Changes in the status of women and the demographic development of the family
446r The position of women and demographic policy
459a Demographic change and the role of women: A research programme in developing countries
459d Female power, autonomy and demographic change in the Third World

Demon
156a Women: Model for possession by Greek daemons
197a Ridiculous demons

Demystify
306n Letters and diaries: Demystifying archival research for undergraduates

Denigration
246b Domesticity and the denigration of women

Denmark
see also Scandanavia
22e Women in Latin Medieval literature in Denmark e.g. annals and chronicles
22f Une contribution au débat concernant le status de la femme dans les villes du Danemark au Moyen-Age
22j New trends in the Danish women's movement, 1970-1978
113j Denmark: The small NATO nation
382a Denmark

Dentistry
44d Dentistry
316d Women in the dental profession

Department
81i All pink sisters: The War Department and the feminist movement in the 1920s
249g The crux: Quality judgment and departmental autonomy
320l Sex differences in the implications of the links between major departments and the occupational structure
337i Women in the art department

Department of Health and Social Service
297b Negotiating the problem: The DHSS and research on violence in marriage

Departure
177l "On the eve of her departure"

Dependence
9l Dependence on psychotropic drugs and analgesics in men and women
9m Opiate dependence in women
16i Women and chemical dependency
46e The double-decker alternative for eliminating dependency under social security
50l Monogamy, marriage and economic dependence
140i Female dependency in context: Some theoretical and technical considerations
217b Women and the welfare state: The transition from private to public dependence
321b Gender and dependency
335h The state, welfare and women's dependence
359p Phobias after marriage: Women's declaration of dependence
376b Dealing with dependence: Paternalism and tax evasion in eighteenth-century Rhode Island
385c Dependence and autonomy: The economic activities of secluded Hausa women in Kano, Nigeria
465a Dealing with dependency: State practices and social realities, 1870-1945

Depo Provera
36h Depo-provera and sterilization abuse overview
36i Depo-provera: Some ethical questions about a controversial contraceptive
36j The depo-provera weapon
36l Depo-provera and sterilization abuse discussion
310m Calling the shots? The international politics of depo-provera

396d Depo-provera: The extent of the problem: A case study in the politics of birth control

Depression
see also Emotion

81 Depression in women: Epidemiology, explanations, and impact on the family

16a Women and mental health: The problem of depression

16b Cognitive-behavioral strategies for the treatment of depression in women

28m Estrogens and central nervous system function: Electroencephalography, cognition, and depression

29k Depression: A behavioral-cognitive approach

38q Depression in black women: A theoretical appraisal

96m The treatment of depressed women: The efficacy of psychotherapy

137f Gender and depression

191d Depressions among women: Their nature and causes

191e Risk factors for depression: What do we learn from them?

244k Role loss and manic depression

268f Depression in relation to sex roles: Differences in learned susceptibility and precipitating factors

295k Depression in women: The postpartum experience

304e Sex-role stereotypes and depression in women

359m Sex differences and the epidemiology of depression

365d Depression

404c Learned helplessness, depression, and alcohol problems of women

434b Depression in women: Explanations and prevention

456j Depression

Depression (Historical)
see also Great Depression

61j Darkness before the dawn: The status of women in the Depression years

81b The economics of middle-income family life: Working women during the Great Depression

157m A response to the depression: The local Council of Women of Vancouver

390v Women and economic crises: The Great Depression and the present crisis

Deputy
405k The social composition of women deputies in Soviet elective politics: A preliminary analysis of official biographies

DES
see Diethylstilbestrol

Descent
231o Garden paths, descents

364b Cognatic descent, Islamic law and women's property on the East African coast

Description
279c Sex differences: The female as baseline for species description

Desegregate
272m Occupational desegregation in CETA programs

Design
164d Disregarded designs: Jane Austen's sense of the volume

182d House design and women's roles

203d The appropriation of the house: Changes in house design and concepts of domesticity

203e Redesigning the domestic workplace

203f Introduction: Urban design: The price women pay

203o No academic matter: Unconscious discrimination in environmental design education

203u Housing for single-parent families: A women's design

209n The role of common sense in the process of interface design

209o Staff participation in office systems' design: Two case studies at the World Bank

209u Occupational health and the design of work

271q Theoretical/Conceptual implications of study design and statistical analysis: Research on the menstrual cycle

274m Craft, design, and technology

399gg Peggy Clark Kelley: Reminiscences of a "designing" woman

Desire
7d Sadomasochism and the social construction of desire

24c The influence of special sexual desires

257h Heterosexual sex: Power and desire for the other

257k Duty and desire: Creating a feminist morality

Despair
451k The other side of despair

Despotism
106d Political and marital despotism: Montesquieu's *Persian Letters*

464f Despotism and civil society: The limits of patriarchal citizenship

Destiny
8d Wife abuse: Culture as destiny

42k A woman's role and destiny

172d Learning to take hold of one's own destiny (Bolivia)

313o "La loca, la tonta, la literata": Women's destiny in Clarin's *La Regenta*

Destruction
195n Preservative love and military destruction: Some reflections on mothering and peace

Detection
26a Emergency room intervention: Detection, assessment, and treatment

109d Had-I-but-known: The marriage of gothic terror and detection

Detention
111r Drug abuse and criminality among women in detention

Deterrence
215d The balance of terror: Deterrence and peace-keeping

Determinant
403c The determinants of social position among rural Moroccan women

421a Cultural determinants of power for women within the family: A neglected aspect of family research

Determination
316h Toward freedom and self-determination: New directions in mental health services

Determinism
354k Sociobiology: Another biological determinism

Detroit, MI
26g Family trouble clinic: Family service of Detroit and Wayne County

Devadasi
163f The devadasi problem

Devaluation
359b Early origins of envy and devaluation of women: Implications for sex-role stereotypes

140h Early origins of envy and devaluation of women: Implications for sex-role stereotypes

Developing Country
see also Development (Economic), Third World, individual countries

68b Introduction: Women in developing countries

100a The dialectic of education: An alternative approach to education and social change in developing countries

395b Women as promoters of health in the developing world

421aa Career constraints among women graduate students in a developing society: West Pakistan. A study in the changing status of women

459a Demographic change and the role of women: A research programme in developing countries

459f A social anthropological approach to women's roles and status in developing countries: The domestic cycle

Development
see also Third World, individual countries

21d Female elite goals and national development: Some data from the Philippines

37q Group identity development within black families

50r Developmental aspects of gender

51l Erik Erikson and Doris Lessing: Psychological theory and the female novel of development

69a Feminine development: Changes in psychoanalytic theory

82e The development process: A holistic approach

87c Intellectual development of women

158l Metatheoretical influences on conceptions of human development

203h Women's travel patterns in a suburban development

204j Social development and parent-child interaction in father-custody and stepmother families

216d Developmental universals and their implications for parental competence

266a New maps of development: New visions of maturity

279k Normal and abnormal sexual dimorphic patterns of growth and development

295a Female development and achievement

332k The female novel of development and the myth of psyche

332l Exiting from patriarchy: The lesbian novel of development

332o *Family Ties*: Female development in Clarice Lispector

360d The relational self in women: Developmental theory and public policy

362b An examination of education, social change, and national development policy: The case of Kenyan women

377f Sex differences in the development of precocious mathematical talent

407b Career mapping and the professional development process

423c Adult development and women's development: Arrangements for a marriage

436j Women's employment networks: Strategies for development

436k The impact of the women's movement and legislative activity of women MPs on social development

460g Some suggested revisions concerning early female development

Development (Economic)
see also Economy

5b Women and agriculture in sub-Saharan Africa: Implications for development

5e Perspectives in development: The problem of nurses and nursing in Zambia

5f Development policies in Tanzania - some implications for women

5g Gambian women: Unequal partners in rice development projects?

6k The impact of development policies on women

39j Definitions of women and development: An African perspective

68c African women and national development

82a Critical issues in women in development

82b AID and women in development

82p Views of women in international development

92a An action-oriented study of the role of women in rural development

101h The Indian women's movement and national development: An overview

153g Development and underdevelopment of household-based production in Europe

183a Rural women in development

198j The struggle of women in the national development of Pakistan

208a Introduction: The continuing subordination of women in the development process

208j Women, kinship and capitalist development

218h Women in development planning: Advocacy, institutionalization and implementation

251a Technology, economic development, and the division of labour by sex

300a Modernization, changing roles of women and expectations for development in Southeast Asia

373c Integration into what? Reflections on development planning for women

373d Women, technology and the development process

373g Women and the development of "underdevelopment": The African experience

373n The differential impact of programs and policies on women in development

380m A statistical analysis of female participation in work and the effects on the population and socioeconomic development: A case study of Greece

385h International development and the evolution of women's economic roles: A case study from northern Gulma, Upper Volta

385k Women's employment and development: A conceptual framework applied to Ghana

388a Development with equity for women

388b Rural women in development

388i Rural women and development planning in Peru

388m The future for women and development

395e Water and sanitation-related health constraints on women's contribution to the economic development of communities

428e Household, community, national, and multinational industrial development

435m Bureaucratic resistance to women's programs: The case of women in development

466h Indonesian women in development: State theory and urban kampung practice

Development (Psychological)

4a Adolescent psychosexual development

8r Conflict and psychological development: Women in the family

88h Narcissistic development

136j The development of sex differences in nonverbal signals: Fallacies, facts, and fantasies

239b Biopsychosocial processes in the development of sex-related differences

Development (Psychosexual)

4a Adolescent psychosexual development

460h The early stages of female psychosexual development: A Kleinian view

Development (Sexual)

460d Physiological aspects of female sexual development: Conception through puberty

460e Physiological aspects of female sexual development: Gestation, lactation, menopause, and erotic physiology

460f Psychological and physiological concepts in female sexuality: A discussion of physiological aspects of female sexual development

Development (Sociosexual)

461u Wife beating: A product of sociosexual development

Deviance

210h Shopping-bag women: Aging deviants in the city

291g Sexual deviance: The adult offender

392c Female deviance and the female sex role: A preliminary investigation

Deviation

250c The importance of being Ernest ... Emma ... Tom ... Jane. The perception and catego-

rization of gender conformity and gender deviation in primary schools

DHSS
see Department of Health and Social Service

Dhuoda

188a The Frankish mother: Dhuoda

Diabetes Mellitus

53t Sex differences in diabetes mellitus

277k Study of sexual dysfunction among male diabetics

Diagnosis

11i Diagnosis, casefinding, and treatment of alcohol problems in women

79h A look at prenatal diagnosis within the context of changing parental and reproductive norms

79i Prenatal diagnosis

79j Antenatal diagnosis: The physician-patient relationship

79k Policy decisions in prenatal diagnosis: The example of fetal alcoholism syndrome

79l The politics of prenatal diagnosis: A feminist ethical analysis

79m Prenatal diagnosis discussion

191b Patterns of diagnoses received by men and women

277e The assessment of sleep erections for diagnosis of erectile disorders

277g The multidisciplinary approach to the diagnosis and treatment of male sexual dysfunction

284d Diagnosis and treatment - an introduction

285l Differential diagnosis and treatment for organogenic and psychogenic erectile dysfunction

359l The influence of gender on diagnosis and psychopathology

404j The woman in treatment: Evaluation and diagnostic implications

Dialectic

60a Notes toward a feminist dialectic

60j Difference and domination in the women's movement: The dialectic of theory and practice

60u Women, media, and the dialectics of resistance

100a The dialectic of education: An alternative approach to education and social change in developing countries

106n "Thank heaven for little girls": The dialectics of development

227j The dialectic of sex

342d The dialectic of biology and culture

Diana

17i Cool Diana and the Blood-red muse: Edith Wharton on innocence and art

Diary

222g The diary of a web spinner

306e Tell me all you know: Reading letters and diaries of rural women

306g "Aunt Amelia's diary": The record of a reluctant pioneer

306n Letters and diaries: Demystifying archival research for undergraduates

445d American dream, nightmare underside: Diaries, letters and fiction of women on the American frontier

452l Anaïs Nin's *Diary* in context

474h Thoughts on writing: A diary

Dichotomy

31g Liberating philosophy: An end to the dichotomy of matter and spirit

50z Oppressive dichotomies: The nature/culture debate

418m Oppressive dichotomies: The nature/culture debate

Dickens, Charles

286i Sexuality and the Victorian artist: Dickens and Swinburne

286j On the enrichment of poor monkeys by myth and dream; or how Dickens Rousseauisticized and pre-Freudianized Victorian views of childhood

Dickinson, Emily

121a Introduction: Feminist critics read Emily Dickinson

121b The wayward nun beneath the hill: Emily Dickinson and the mysteries of womanhood

121c Emily Dickinson's nursery rhymes

121d Notes on sleeping with Emily Dickinson

121e "Oh, Susie, it is dangerous": Emily Dickinson and the archetype of the masculine

121f "The love of thee-a prism be": Men and women in the love poetry of Emily Dickinson

121g "Oh, vision of language!": Dickinson's poems of love and death

121h How "Low feet" stagger: Disruptions of language in Dickinson's poetry

121i "Ransom in a voice": Language as defense in Dickinson's poetry

180k Reconstruction in the house of art: Emily Dickinson's "I never had a mother"

Diderot, Denis

130p Women and the Encyclopédie

130s Diderot and women

Didrikson, Babe

175t The babe

Die

2i Killing and letting die

Diethylstilbestrol (DES)

79b The DES controversy: Discovery, distribution and regulation

79c Assessment of risks from DES: An analysis of research on those exposed during pregnancy or in utero

79d The legal aspects of the DES case: What can be done

79e DES and drugs in pregnancy: A consumer reaction

79f DES: Ten points of controversy

Difference

see also Gender Difference, Sex Difference

35g Explaining "male chauvinism" and "feminism": Cultural differences in male and female reproductive strategies

60j Difference and domination in the women's movement: The dialectic of theory and practice

63j Sex-role differentiation in a co-correctional setting

80f Environmental differences among day care centers and their effects on children's development

87l Salary and job performance differences in dual-career couples

89n The female-male differential in unemployment rates

96h Toward choice and differentiation in the midlife crises of women

123a The difference it makes

132a Prelude: The future of difference

132b Gender, relation, and difference in psychoanalytic perspective

132f The powers of difference

132m Difference and language: A linguist's perspective

132n For a restricted thematics: Writing, speech, and difference in *Madame Bovary*

132p Visibility and difference: Black women in history and literature - pieces of a paper and some ruminations

148d Male/female task differentiation among the Hidatsa: Toward the development of an archeological approach to the study of gender

260b A look at the male female unemployment differentials in the Federal Republic of Germany, Sweden, United Kingdom, and the United States of America

260d Earnings differentials: Empirical evidence and causes

292e Recognizing regional differences: The southern summer school for women workers

303a A different kind of being

354d Do men and women have different jobs because of their biological differences?

436l Will women judges make a difference in women's legal rights? A prediction from attitudes and simulated behaviour

Difficult Journey - Mountainous Journey

180n *Difficult Journey - Mountainous Journey*, The memoirs of Fadwa Tuqan

Digression

14e One child of one's own: A meaningful digression within the work(s) - an excerpt

474i *One* child of one's own: A meaningful digression within the work(s)

Dilke, Lady

389f Lady Dilke (1840-1904): The six lives of an art historian

Diller, Ann

432o The ethics of gender discrimination: A response to Ann Diller and Barbara Houston's "Women's Physical Education"

Dimension

90a The sex dimension - An overview

Dimorphism

279b Sexual dimorphism in nonhuman primates

279e Sexual dimorphism in skeletal samples

279f Sexual dimorphism and settlement pattern in Middle Eastern skeletal populations

279h A cross-cultural investigation into the sexual dimorphism of stature

279j Size sexual dimorphism and secular trend: Indicators of subclinical malnutrition?

279k Normal and abnormal sexual dimorphic patterns of growth and development

279l Human proportionality and sexual dimorphism

279n Sexual dimorphism and nutrient reserves

Dinesen, Isak

109h Gothic transformations: Isak Dinesen and the gothic

155d The magic circle: The role of the prostitute in Isak Dinesen's *Gothic Tales*

Ding Ling

30b In quest of Ding Ling (In quest of myself)

Dionysus

325e Ecstasy and possession: Women of ancient Greece and the cult of Dionysus

419h The menace of Dionysus: Sex roles and reversals in Euripides' *Bacchae*

Dioula, Ivory Coast

473d Dioula women in town: A view of intraethnic variation (Ivory Coast)

Direct

42i Drifting, dreaming, directing

135l New directions in the contemporary bildungsroman: Lisa Alther's *Kinflicks*

190z Future directions for research

295p New directions for women: Moving beyond the 1980s

381d Directions

Disability

see also Handicap

46f Disability insurance under proposed reforms

129k Legal disabilities of women

170c Employment, women and their disabled children

277l Sexual arousal responses and disability

281g Sexuality and disability

285e Physical disability, life-threatening illness, and enhancement of sexual health

285p Sex and disability - sociosexual education presentation format

285s Establishing a women's group for disabled clients

310s Claiming all of our bodies: Reproductive rights and disabilities

310t Born and unborn: The implications of reproductive technologies for people with disabilities

Disadvantage

364g Divorce and the disadvantaged: African women in urban South Africa

Disarmament

167g Children need smiles not missiles: Planning a walk Oxford mothers for nuclear disarmament

167j A women's day for disarmament: Notes on organising a decentralised action

Discharge

456m Vaginal discharge

Discipline

189g Anthropology - a discipline with a legacy

189l Before and after: The impact of feminism on the academic discipline of law

205o Domesticity and discipline: The Girl Guides in British Columbia 1910-1943

311b Learning women's studies

311c Women's studies as an academic discipline: Why and how to do it

312c Is women's studies an academic discipline?

312d Women's studies as an academic discipline: Why and how to do it

337n Traditional and non-traditional choices of disciplines by women

351l Women's studies: A discipline takes shape

355j Domestic labor as work discipline: The struggle over housework in foster homes

361d Improving minority preparation for math-based disciplines

377c Is mathematics a sexist discipline?

Disclosure

174x Self-disclosure and the commitment to social change

398e Self-disclosure and the commitment to social change

Disco

133h Gay masculinity in the gay disco

Discord

164j Muted discord: Generational conflict in Jane Austen

Discourage

221f Family effects of dislocation, unemployment, and discouragement

273j Ethics and public policy: Should sex choice be discouraged?

Discourse

120i Ideological hegemony in political discourse: Women's specificity and equality

313j The off-center spatiality of womens' discourse

Discover

30l "She is the one you call sister": Discovering Mary Wilkins Freeman

79b The DES controversy: Discovery, distribution and regulation

461k Beyond belief: The reluctant discovery of incest

Discriminate

see also Bias, Affirmative Action, Equal Opportunity, Equal Employment, Segregate, Sex Bias, Sex Discrimination, Sexism, Title VII, Title IX

13e Bearers of burdens: Occupational safety without discrimination

34e No fertile women need apply: Employment discrimination and reproductive hazards in the workplace

65a "A want of harmony": Perspectives on wage discrimination and comparable worth

65i Assessing pay discrimination using national data

66f Statistical biases in the measurement of employment discrimination

67f Statistical biases in the measurement of employment discrimination

89l Occupational segregation, wages and profits when employers discriminate by race and sex

93e Strategies for improving the economic situation of women in the United States: Systemic thinking, systemic discrimination, and systemic enforcement

93f Administering anti-discrimination legislation in Great Britain

93u The contribution of labor market data in combating employment discrimination

178g The human cost of discrimination

199e Economic stagnation and discrimination

203o No academic matter: Unconscious discrimination in environmental design education

214k The minutiae of discrimination: The need for support

260i Policies and implementation of anti-discrimination strategies

260l The political economy of labor market discrimination: A theoretical and comparative analysis of sex discrimination

272e Occupational segregation and labor market discrimination

315j Analyzing discrimination against women in the labor market - A few lessons from John Stuart Mill

392k Discriminatory sentencing of women offenders: The argument for ERA in a nutshell

392n Women in prison: Discriminatory practices and some legal solutions

425i Job evaluation and discrimination: Legal, economic, and measurement perspectives on comparable worth and women's pay

432o The ethics of gender discrimination: A response to Ann Diller and Barbara Houston's "Women's Physical Education"

Discussion

169i Discussion method

Disease

see also Illness, Sickness, specific diseases

51k Smoking, alcohol, and body mass relationships to early menopause: Implications for risk of cardiovascular disease

53a Sex differences in disease risk

53c The effect of employment, family and job stress on coronary heart disease patterns in women

53e Changing patterns of smoking and risk of disease

53g Women, alcohol, and the risk of disease

53i Pelvic inflammatory disease: Causes and consequences

53n Risk factors for benign and malignant breast disease

53r Epidemiology of coronary heart disease in women

268e Sex roles and psychophysiological disorders: Coronary heart disease

277o Sexuality with cardiac disease

309s Contraception, abortion and venereal disease: Teenagers' knowledge and the effect of education

353p "The fashionable diseases": Women's complaints and their treatment in nineteenth-century America

354c Vaginal cancer: An iatrogenic disease?

354j Chlorosis and chronic disease in 19th-century Britain: The social constitution of somatic illness in a capitalist society

359n The hysterical personality: A "woman's disease"

456e Breast cancer and benign breast disease

461z Discussion: Prophylaxis of sexually transmitted diseases: An overview

Disenchantment

384p The young girl in the West: Disenchantment in Jean Stafford's short fiction

Dislocate

221f Family effects of dislocation, unemployment, and discouragement

Displace

34i Displaced - the midwife by the male physician

387m Stay home, little Sheba: On placement, displacement, and social change

Displaced Homemaker

16s The displaced homemaker

344n The internalization of powerlessness: A case study of the displaced homemaker

Dispute

3m Beneath the surface of the abortion dispute: Are women fully human?

Disrupt

121h How "Low feet" stagger: Disruptions of language in Dickinson's poetry

309n Marriage, remarriage, marital disruption and age at first birth

387c Women in the occupational world: Social disruption and conflict

Disseminate

29d Dissemination of behavioral interventions with women: Needed - a technology

297k Putting the show on the road: The dissemination of research findings

Dissertation

90b Women in educational administration: A descriptive analysis of dissertation research and paradigm for future research

222d Taking the giant step: Writing the dissertation

Distress

28i A developmental analysis of menstrual distress in adolescence

51p Menopausal distress: A model for epidemiologic investigation

Distribute

79b The DES controversy: Discovery, distribution and regulation

321j The distribution of income within households

347i Women and men, cloth and colonization: The transformation of production-distribution relations among the Baule (Ivory Coast)

Distrust

343e Those "soft and delicate desires": *Much Ado* and the distrust of women

Dive

107u Body segment contributions of female athletes to translational and rotational requirements of non-twisting springboard dive takeoffs

Diversity

70i Relevancy of tribal interests and tribal diversity in determining the educational needs of American Indians

159l Venezuelan female criminality: The ideology of diversity and marginality

266g Instruments and measures in a changing, diverse society

462t Affirming diversity and Biblical tradition

Diviner

325b Julia: An east African diviner

Division of Labor

see also Employment

18f Cross-national labor migrants: Actors in the international division of labor

50o Technology and changes in the division of labour in the American home

52s Egalitarianism in marriage? Graduate education and the sexual division of labour in the Canadian family

83d Woman and the international division of labor

116m Sex roles and the sexual division of labor

153p Towards a theory of the sexual division of labor

179e Sexual division of labour

207a Gender and economics: The sexual division of labour and the subordination of women

208b Gender and economics: The sexual division of labour and the subordination of women

241g 'Women and old boats': The sexual division of labour in a Newfoundland outport

251a Technology, economic development, and the division of labour by sex

263b Housework as a comparative advantage: The neoclassical theory of the sexual division of labor

263f The sexual division of labor on American farms: 1750-1850

263j Professionalism, division of labor by gender, and the control of nursing practice

263k Industrial social workers in France, 1917-1939: A study in the sex/gender division of labor

300b Women, society and change: Perspectives on the division of labour

305r Rosie the Riveter meets the sexual division of labour

342i Origins of the sexual division of labor

350a The dynamics of the sexual division of labor and integration of rural women into the world market

350c Peasant production, proletarianization, and the sexual division of labor in the Andes

350d Resource allocation and the sexual division of labor: A case study of a Moslem Hausa village in northern Nigeria

350i The sexual division of labor in rural China

378b Industrial radicalism and the domestic division of labor

387a Women and the division of labor: Limiting assumptions

410a The invisible hands: Sex roles and the division of labor in two local political parties

428a The impact of the changing international division of labor on different sectors of the labor force

428b The new international division of labor and the U.S. work force: The case of the electronics industry

428h Labor migration and the new industrial division of labor

428n The division of labor in electronics

459g The interrelationship between the division of labour in the household, women's roles and their impact on fertility

468h Love and power: The division of household labor

Divorce

45g The American divorce rate: What does it mean? What should we worry about?

105i Towards a new definition of divorce

129m Love, marriage and divorce

204i Effects of divorce on parents and children

270m Social change and family crisis: The nature of Turkish divorce

281d Sexuality in divorce and remarriage

295f Sex differences in separation and divorce: A longitudinal perspective

359ff Divorced women

363a In defense of motherhood: Divorce law in Cuba during the early republic

364g Divorce and the disadvantaged: African women in urban South Africa

375f Under great temptations here: Women and divorce law in puritan Massachusetts

375g The law of husband and wife in nineteenth-century America: Changing views of divorce

Do

474k What it is I think I'm doing anyhow

Doctor

see also Medicine, Physician

56d The deliverers: A woman doctor's reflections on medical socialization

85a Women and their doctors: Power and powerlessness in the research process

219e Police officer or doctor? Police surgeons' attitudes and opinions about rape

231q Outside the operating room of the sex-change doctor

285b Eros and thanatos: Lingering taboos in doctor-patient communication

353i Doctors, birth control, and social values, 1830-1970

353ee Doctors or ladies? Women physicians in psychiatric institutions, 1872-1900

372h The influence of women doctors on the origins of women's sports in Germany

Doctoral

222h In and out of relationships: A serious game for the woman doctoral student

Document

61o Photographs as historical documents (American women through the camera's eye)

306d On the literary uses of private documents

Documentary

98l Towards the making of a documentary film on rural women in Bangladesh

Doe v. Bolton

173f Public support for pro-choice abortion policies in the nation and states: Changes and stability after the *Roe* and *Doe* decisions

Dog

231bb A story of a girl and her dog

Dohm, Hedwig

125j Hedwig Dohm: Passionate theorist

A Doll's House

122p Ibsen's *A Doll's House*: A directorial perspective on performing Nora

Domain

371i Spatial domains and women's mobility in Yorubaland, Nigeria

Domestic

see also Homemaker, Housewife, Housework

26b Conjoint therapy for the treatment of domestic violence

38g "The means to put my children through": Child-rearing goals and strategies among black female domestic servants

76b Domestic and public

85g The expert's view? The sociological analysis of graduates' occupational and domestic roles

104h Domestic work in rural Iceland: An historical overview

109f Domestic gothic: The imagery of anger in Christina Stead's *The Man Who Loved Children*

111e Social-psychological research and relevant speculation on the issue of domestic violence

145m Domestic industry: Work options and women's choices

148h Sioux women in transition: A study of their changing status in a domestic and capitalist sector of production

149a Domestic labour and the working-class household

149c Domestic labour: A methodological discussion

149f Domestic labour and the reproduction of labour power: Towards an analysis of women, the family, and class

151b Domestic labour and Soviet society

153n Working or helping? London working-class children in the domestic economy

196d The domestic economy of art: Elizabeth Barrett and Robert Browning

199d Housework and domestic labor: Racial and technological change

203a Introduction: The domestic workplace

203d The appropriation of the house: Changes in house design and concepts of domesticity

203e Redesigning the domestic workplace

205j Six saucepans to one: Domestic science vs. the home in British Columbia 1900-1930

205o Domesticity and discipline: The Girl Guides in British Columbia 1910-1943

207f 'I'm hungry, mum': The politics of domestic budgeting

208f 'I'm hungry, mum': The politics of domestic budgeting

227c Women as domestic workers

227p Women's domestic labour

246b Domesticity and the denigration of women

255d The domestic realm in the lives of Hindu women in Calcutta

307o Abortion: A domestic technology

313e El ángel del hogar: The cult of domesticity in nineteenth century Spain

323o Domestic workers: The experience in B.C.

355j   Domestic labor as work discipline: The struggle over housework in foster homes

371h   The sexual division of domestic space among two Soviet minorities: The Georgians and the Tadjiks

378b   Industrial radicalism and the domestic division of labor

390n   Rooms of their own: The domestic situation of Australian women writers between the wars

412p   Evangelical domesticity: The woman's temperance crusade of 1873-1874

418g   Domestic violence: Battered women in Britain in the 1970s

421b   Female-headed households and domestic organization in San Isidro, Guatemala: A test of Hammel and Laslett's comparative typology

424k   Female domestic servants in Cagayan de Oro, Philippines: Social and economic implications of employment in a 'premodern' occupational role

428g   The domestic clothing workers in the Mexican metropolis and their relation to dependent capitalism

440h   Population policies and family policies: State construction of domestic life

454a   American women and domestic culture: An approach to women's history

454k   Family limitation, sexual control, and domestic feminism in Victorian America

459f   A social anthropological approach to women's roles and status in developing countries: The domestic cycle

468g   Conceptualising domestic work: Comments on definitions of "work" in some Norwegian studies

Dominate

31h   Pornography and the erotics of domination

31i   From domination to recognition

39z   Female status, the family and male dominance in a West Indian community

60j   Difference and domination in the women's movement: The dialectic of theory and practice

78u   Women in a male-dominated profession: The women lawyers

117p   Virility and domination in early twentieth-century vanguard painting

132d   The bonds of love: Rational violence and erotic domination

136d   Visual behavior and dominance in women and men

152d   Overcoming the structured evil of male domination and heterosexism

165c   The dark side of marriage: Battered wives and the domination of women

189i   The oldest, the most established, the most quantitative of the social sciences - and most dominated by men; The impact of feminism on economics

192r   La costura en Los Angeles 1933-1939: The ILGWU and the politics of domination

195h   Is male gender identity the cause of male domination?

199m   Contrasting sexual harassment in female- and male-dominated occupations

231p   Master and slave: The fantasy of erotic domination

307d   Women, nature and domination

342h   Ideologies of male dominance as divide and rule politics: An anthropologist's view

347e   Forced transition from egalitarianism to male dominance: The Bari of Colombia

371j   Where women must dominate: Response to oppression in a South African urban community

410g   Organizational role orientations on female-dominant commissions: Focus on staff-commissioner interaction

462d   Making the world live: Feminism and the domination of nature

Donor

310x   Children by donor insemination: A new choice for lesbians

Dora

256b   Freud's Dora, Dora's hysteria

Doshman Ziari, Iran

371g   Place and face: Of women in Doshman Ziari, Iran

Dostoevsky, Fyodor

155e   The romantization of the prostitute in Dostoevsky's fiction

Double

206g   The double day

257n   Sexual theory and practice: Another double standard

404e   The double bind: Minority women

435e   Alternative work patterns and the double life

Doubletalk

307e   Doubletalk: Sexism in tech talk

Douglas, Ellen

450g   Ellen Douglas: Moralist and realist

Dove

457c   Doves and magpies: Village women in the Greek Orthodox Church

Dowding, Vivian

205w   Vivian Dowding: Birth control activist 1892-

Down

307f   For women, the chips are down

Dowry

see also Bride, Marriage, Wedding

156l   Bridewealth and dowry in Nuzi

184c   Dowries and kinsmen in early Renaissance Venice

364d   Dowry in North India: Its consequences for women

Drabble, Margaret

135n   Mistresses and madonnas in the novels of Margaret Dabble

318g   Women and children first: The novels of Margaret Drabble

Dracula

286b   "Dual life": The status of women in Stoker's *Dracula*

Drama

see also Theater, names of individual playwrights

124c   Notes on technique in feminist drama: *Apple Pie* and *Signs of Life*

133m   Images of the gay male in contemporary drama

254m   American female dramatists: Show but no go?

358c   The 'liberated woman' in television drama

399z   Lillian Hellman's memorial drama

399pp   Creative drama: Sex role stereotyping?

408f   Women against wedlock: The reluctant brides of Golden Age drama

445i   Gertrude Atherton's California woman: From love story to psychological drama

Dramatic

40k   Alice Childress's dramatic structure

338h   The dramatic treatment of Robert Emmet and Sarah Curran

399aa   Sylvia Plath, a dramatic poet

Dramaturgy

24h   The dramaturgy of sexual relations

Draper, Ruth

399q   The art of Ruth Draper

Drawing

see also Art

134d   Drawing the line

389o   Agnes Mongan (b. 1905): Connoisseur of old master drawings

Dream

17n   Fitzgerald's women: Beyond winter dreams

42i   Drifting, dreaming, directing

102e   Toward psychoanalytic feminism: The mother in dream-stealing, the father in dreams

109k   Terror-gothic: Nightmare and dream in Ann Radcliffe and Charlotte Brontë

109p   Dreaming of children: Literalization in *Jane Eyre* and *Wuthering Heights*

254o   When we dream together

409i   Anna Livia Plurabelle: The dream woman

453o   Characteristics of women's dreams

Dreiser, Theodore

17k   Brother Theodore, hell on women

Drift

42i   Drifting, dreaming, directing

Drink

see also Alcohol, Alcoholism

9c   Sex differences in the prevalence of problem drinking

10a   "When angels fall": Women's drinking as cultural preoccupation and as reality

10b   Drinking and drinking problems among female adolescents: Patterns and influences

10g   Drinking, sexuality, and sexual dysfunction in women

11c   Women and men problem drinkers: Sex differences in patients served by Iowa's community alcoholism centers

11d   The effects of alcohol on anxiety in problem and nonproblem drinking women

11h   Fetal alcohol syndrome and drinking during pregnancy

137i   Gender, drinking, and alcohol abuse

345a   The causes of increasing drinking problems amongst women

404v   Pregnancy and drinking

455g   New knowledge and the drinking woman

Driver
390t Women's struggle to become tram drivers in Melbourne, 1956-75

Drone
419c Workers and drones: Labor, idleness and gender definition in Hesiod's beehive

Drop Out
46b Supplemental OASI benefits to homemakers through current spouse benefits, a homemaker credit, and child-care drop-out years

Drug
9a Sex differences in alcohol and drug problems - some highlights
9d Sex differences in psychoactive drug use: Recent epidemiology
9e Longitudinal studies of alcohol and drug problems: Sex differences
9l Dependence on psychotropic drugs and analgesics in men and women
9o Sex differences in the effects of alcohol and other psychoactive drugs on endocrine function: Clinical and experimental evidence
9q The effects of opiates, sedative-hypnotics, amphetamines, cannabis, and other psychoactive drugs on the fetus and newborn
36o Drugs, birth, and ethics
79e DES and drugs in pregnancy: A consumer reaction
268j A sex-roles perspective on drug and alcohol use by women
277n Effect of drugs on sexual arousal
359j A review of women's psychotropic drug use

Drug Abuse
111r Drug abuse and criminality among women in detention
137j Gender and drug use and abuse
404l Sexism in drug abuse treatment programs

Drum
455c No drums, no trumpets: Working-class women

Dual
76c The dual heritage

Dual Career
see also Coordinated Career
87a Three generations of dual-career family research
87e Dual-career marriages: Benefits and costs
87h Time management and the dual-career couple
87k Equal opportunity laws and dual-career couples
87l Salary and job performance differences in dual-career couples
214r Dual-career families: Intimacy or productivity?
221d Understanding dual career families
267e Career concepts and human resource management: The case of the dual-career couple
339g Dual career couples: How the company can help
359z Attitudes toward parenting in dual-career families

387p Dilemmas and contradictions of status: The case of the dual-career family
425h Causal determinants of job satisfaction in dual career couples

Dual Earner
458n Responsibility for household tasks: Comparing dual-earner and dual-retired marriages

Dubliners
409b *Dubliners*: Women in Irish society

Duce, Ivy O.
399f Murshida Ivy O. Duce

Duisburg, Germany
144g Overcrowding and family life: Working-class families and the housing crisis in late nineteenth-century Duisburg

Dunbar-Nelson, Alice
14r Researching Alice Dunbar-Nelson: A personal and literary perspective
30g Alice Dunbar-Nelson: A personal and literary perspective
306f Alice Dunbar-Nelson: A regional approach

Duplicity
20c Margaret Atwood and the poetics of duplicity
445m Heroes vs women: Conflict and duplicity in Stegner

Duran, Lucy
192t Lucy Duran - Wife, mother, and organizer

Duras, Marguerite
448b Marguerite Duras: Women's language in men's cities

Durham, NC
81d Flawed victories: The experiences of black and white women workers in Durham during the 1930s

Durova, Nadezhda
108h *My Childhood Years*: A memoir by the czarist cavalry officer, Nadezhda Durova

Duty
257k Duty and desire: Creating a feminist morality

Dyad
136f Sex-role influences in dyadic interaction: A theoretical model
190k Menstrual beliefs and experiences of mother-daughter dyads

Dydrogesterone
236e An explorative study into the clinical effects of dydrogesterone in the treatment of premenstrual syndrome
236f A double-blind, placebo-controlled, multi-centre study of the efficacy of dydrogesterone (Duphaston®)

Dying
285g Is there love before dying?
285t How to stubbornly refuse to disturb oneself emotionally about anything - even about death, dying and sexual mutilation

Dyke
176a Dyke in Academe

Dynamic
82n Dynamics of social and cultural change

120f To grow a daughter: Cultural liberation and the dynamics of oppression in Jamaica
254n The whole thing: In search of relevance and integration made dynamic by creativity
280h The dynamics of sexual assault
280i Burglaries with sexual dynamics
280k Sexual dynamics in homicide and assault

Dyphaston®
236f A double-blind, placebo-controlled, multi-centre study of the efficacy of dydrogesterone (Duphaston®)

Dysfunction
8m The myofascial pain dysfunction syndrome: An unheeded neuromuscular disorder
10g Drinking, sexuality, and sexual dysfunction in women
268k Sex roles and sexual dysfunction
277g The multidisciplinary approach to the diagnosis and treatment of male sexual dysfunction
277k Study of sexual dysfunction among male diabetics
285k Sexual dysfunction in the chronically ill male
285l Differential diagnosis and treatment for organogenic and psychogenic erectile dysfunction
287j Sources and prevention of dysfunction
287m Psychological aspects of sexual dysfunction
289k Dysfunction: Origins and therapeutic approaches
291m Incest and dysfunctional family system
304g Sex-role stereotypes and female sexual dysfunction
326k Marital and sexual dysfunction following rape: Identification and treatment
326l Behavioral treatment of sexual dysfunction in sexual assault survivors

Dyslexia
265f Does sex stereotyping lead to a higher incidence of male dyslexia?

Dysmenorrhea
28j Dysmenorrhea and dyspareunia
190s Prostaglandins in primary dysmenorrhea: Basis for the new therapy
190t Dysmenorrhea in adolescence

Dyspareunia
28j Dysmenorrhea and dyspareunia

Dysphoria
280e Gender dysphoria and dyssocial behavior

Dyssocial
280e Gender dysphoria and dyssocial behavior

Dystopia
383c Utopia at the end of a male chauvinist dystopian world: Suzy McKee Charnas's feminist science fiction

E.R.A.
see Equal Rights Amendment

Early Childhood Education
see also Education
80x Day care and early childhood education
333o Aboriginal women's role today in early childhood school education

Earn

see also Pay

46c   Earnings sharing: Incremental and funda-
       mental reform

89g   Family investments in human capital:
       Earnings of women

177i   Wage earners in Hong Kong

243k   Weak links in men's worker-earner roles:
       A descriptive model

260d   Earnings differentials: Empirical evidence
       and causes

357b   Relative female earnings in Great Britain
       and the impact of legislation

380n   Labor force participation and earnings of
       women in Andalusia

393a   Wage earner and mother: Compatibility of
       roles on a Cameroon plantation

400c   Women's income earning activities and
       family welfare in Bangladesh

421u   The impact of children on female earnings

424p   Women migrants in Bangkok: An econom-
       ic analysis of their employment and earn-
       ings

Earth

181f   Mining the earth's womb

185l   Physical settings for families in 2020: In
       space, on earth

194f   The worship of Mother Earth in Russian
       culture

194o   Mother Earth: The great goddess of West
       Africa

229qq On common ground: Native American and
       feminist spirituality approaches in the
       struggle to save mother earth

East Anglia, Australia

234j   'Woman-ing' the landscape: East Anglia
       1300-1500: A discussion on sources and
       methodology

East Sepil, Papua New Guinea

246c   Complementarity: The relationship
       between female and male in the East Sepik
       village of Bun, Papua New Guinea

Eat

131c   "She pluck'd, she eat"

268m   Sex-role stereotypes and the development
       of eating disorders

365f   Eating disorders: Obesity and anorexia

456q   Eating problems

Eccentric

186b   An eccentric biography

Eclectic

77e   An eclectic workshop

Ecology

37h   Black education: A cultural-ecological per-
       spective

181g   Toward an ecological feminism and a femi-
       nist ecology

204d   The ecology of day care

310ee Feminist ethics, ecology and vision

441h   Feminist pedagogy and technology:
       Reflections on the Goddard feminism and
       ecology summer program

Econometric

355g   Women's life-cycle time allocation: An
       econometric analysis

Economic

see also Socioeconomic

5a   Conceptualizing the labor force: The
       underestimation of women's economic
       activities

18d   Rural family size and economic change: A
       Middle Eastern case

21a   Women in Asian cities, their political and
       economic roles: Research problems and
       strategies

37g   Economics and mobility: A theoretical
       rationale for urban black family well-being

39n   Female slave resistance: The economics of
       sex

39aa   Economic role and cultural tradition

50l   Monogamy, marriage and economic
       dependence

52k   Economic and family roles of men and
       women in Northern Europe: A historical
       cross-national comparison

52r   Economic recession and Swiss women's
       attitudes towards marital role segregation

60p   Women's role in economic development:
       Practical and theoretical implications of
       class and gender inequalities

65j   Economic models as a means of calculat-
       ing legal compensation claims

68f   Chinese women: The relative influences of
       ideological revolution, economic growth,
       and cultural change

71k   Economic and employment status of
       Asian-Pacific women

73h   The economic struggles of female factory
       workers: A comparison of French, Polish,
       and Portuguese immigrants

77b   Creative women in economic and social
       change

81b   The economics of middle-income family
       life: Working women during the Great
       Depression

89e   Economic perspectives on the family

93e   Strategies for improving the economic sit-
       uation of women in the United States:
       Systemic thinking, systemic discrimination,
       and systemic enforcement

120d   The problem of studying "economic man"

123f   How the study of women has restructured
       the discipline of economics

129u   The economic position of women

129aa The economic tendency of freethought

170g   The economics of work and caring

183b   Women, economics and the environment

189i   The oldest, the most established, the most
       quantitative of the social sciences - and
       most dominated by men; The impact of
       feminism on economics

199e   Economic stagnation and discrimination

207a   Gender and economics: The sexual divi-
       sion of labour and the subordination of
       women

208b   Gender and economics: The sexual divi-
       sion of labour and the subordination of
       women

244c   Sex segregation and the women's roles in
       the economic system: The case of Iran

251a   Technology, economic development, and
       the division of labour by sex

263m   The new economic readjustment policies:
       Implications for Chinese urban working
       women

269d   New economic roles for Cuna males and
       females: An examination of socioeconomic
       change in a San Blas community

270i   Economic change and the Gecekondu
       family

273f   The economics of sex preference and sex
       selection

283o   The socialist economic review project:
       Progress in the economics of the left

309p   Economic consequences of teenage child-
       bearing

317h   Economic status of late middle-aged wid-
       ows

320f   Sex differences in the significance of eco-
       nomic resources for choosing and attend-
       ing a college

324e   Economic consequences of poor health in
       mature women

324f   Economic consequences of midlife change
       in marital status

333d   The social and economic importance of
       the women in Jigalong

336c   Abortion and economic crisis: The 1931
       campaign against paragraph 218

337j   Women and cooperative home economics
       extension

344d   Sexual harassment: The link between gen-
       der stratification, sexuality, and women's
       economic status

349e   The economics of female criminality: An
       analysis of police blotters, 1890-1976

368d   Social and economic change in the role of
       women, 1956-1978

380g   Bringing down the rear: The decline in the
       economic position of single-mother fami-
       lies

380o   Economic aspects of female labor force
       participation in the Federal Republic of
       Germany

380s   Women's work participation and the eco-
       nomic support of children

385c   Dependence and autonomy: The econom-
       ic activities of secluded Hausa women in
       Kano, Nigeria

385h   International development and the evolu-
       tion of women's economic roles: A case
       study from northern Gulma, Upper Volta

388d   Household economic strategies in
       Kingston, Jamaica

390v   Women and economic crises: The Great
       Depression and the present crisis

392i   The economics of prostitution

400b   Rural pauperization: Its impact on the
       economic role and status of rural women
       in Bangladesh

411h   Social change and equality: The roles of
       women and economics

421d   Social and economic integration of South
       Asian women in Montreal, Canada

424a   Economic growth and changing female
       employment structure in the cities of
       Southeast and East Asia

424k   Female domestic servants in Cagayan de
       Oro, Philippines: Social and economic
       implications of employment in a 'premod-
       ern' occupational role

424p   Women migrants in Bangkok: An econom-
       ic analysis of their employment and earn-
       ings

425i Job evaluation and discrimination: Legal, economic, and measurement perspectives on comparable worth and women's pay

430b The economic base for the revival of Islam in Iran

433d British tradesmen of Calcutta, 1830-1900: A preliminary study of their economic and political roles

459c Class and historical analysis for the study of women and economic change

462a Women, poverty, and economic justice

473l The economic role of women in Alaskan Eskimo society

Economy
see also Development, Development (Economic), Employment

6a Women in the rural economy: Past, present and future

6b Women in the rural economy: Contemporary variations

6c Women in the urban economy

18a Introduction: Population theory and the political economy of population processes

18h The effects of plantation economy on a Polynesian population

18j Country roads take me home: The political economy of wage-labor migration in an eastern Kentucky community

93p Women's stake in a high-growth economy in the United States

97c The political economy of text publishing

103c Battered women's shelters and the political economy of sexual violence

103e Women and the Reagan revolution: Thermidor for the social welfare economy

138i Sex, education and social policy: A new moral economy?

148g The political economy of gender: A 19th century Plains Indian case study

153a Household structures and labor-force formation in the capitalist world-economy

153j Household economy and financial capital: The case of passbook savings in Brazil

153n Working or helping? London working-class children in the domestic economy

196d The domestic economy of art: Elizabeth Barrett and Robert Browning

209bb Building new partnerships in a high-tech economy

227h The political economy of women's liberation

238d The spermatic economy: A nineteenth-century view of sexuality

245i Home production for use in a market economy

260l The political economy of labor market discrimination: A theoretical and comparative analysis of sex discrimination

339a Women in a changing economy

373a Foreword: Seeing our global economy whole

395g The political economy of population policy in South Africa

421t Fertility and family economy in the Iranian rural communities

424g Islamic attitudes to female employment in industrializing economies: Some notes from Malaysia

424j Making the bread and bringing it home: Female factory workers and the family economy

424m Growth of the bazaar economy and its significance for women's employment: Trends of the 1970s in Davao City, Philippines

431a Buddhism, sex-roles and the Thai economy

465h The new right, sex, education and social policy: Towards a new moral economy in Britain and the USA

Ecstasy
225b Seeking ecstasy on the battlefield: Danger and pleasure in nineteenth-century feminist sexual thought

325e Ecstasy and possession: Women of ancient Greece and the cult of Dionysus

Ectogenesis
79kk The biology of utopia: Science fiction perspectives on ectogenesis

79ll Ectogenesis and ideology

Ectomies
456f The 'ectomies'

Ecuador
172f Only you men have your needs satisfied (Ecuador)

395l Anger sickness: Social stress and native diagnosis among Ecuadorian Indians

Eddy, Mary Baker
353z Ministries of healing: Mary Baker Eddy, Ellen G. White, and the religion of health

Edge
206b Restructuring: The cutting edge

The Edible Woman
20h The dark voyage: *The Edible Woman* as romance

Edify
130w The edifying examples

Editor
306m The editor and the writer: An approach to archival manuscripts

389n Dorothy Eugenia Miner (1904-1973): The varied career of a medievalist: Scholar and keeper of manuscripts, librarian and editor at the Walters Art Gallery

Edmonton Grads
147ii The Edmonton Grads: The team and its social significance from 1915-1940

Education
see also Academic, Co-Education, Curriculum, Learn, School, Student, Teach, individual types and levels of education

4i Parenting education

12a Science education: Did she drop out or was she pushed?

33a The education of women in the Middle Ages in theory, fact, and fantasy

37h Black education: A cultural-ecological perspective

45l Sex differences in the educational and occupational goals of black college students: Continued inquiry into the black matriarchy theory

52s Egalitarianism in marriage? Graduate education and the sexual division of labour in the Canadian family

54c New approaches for prevention and education of alcoholism among Hispanic women

58e Women in education

62d How shall we educate our sons?

70b Current educational status of American Indian girls

70i Relevancy of tribal interests and tribal diversity in determining the educational needs of American Indians

71f Educational alternatives for Asian-Pacific women

71i The effects of Asian-American kinship systems on women's educational and occupational attainment

72a The lack of political involvement of Hispanic women as it relates to their educational background and occupational opportunities

72b Puerto Rican women in education and potential impact on occupational patterns

72d Latinas in educational leadership: Chicago, Illinois

72m The need for an anthropological and cognitive approach to the education of Hispanic women

73f The role of learning in the lives of Finnish and other ethnic women and a proposal for self-education

90b Women in educational administration: A descriptive analysis of dissertation research and paradigm for future research

90c Sex equity in educational policies and practices

90g The sex dimension of careers in educational management: Overview and synthesis

90h Jobs and gender: A history of the structuring of educational employment by sex

90n The sources and dynamics of sexual inequality in the profession of education

92g The advantages of functional education and credit facilities for Javanese rural women

94e Multiculturalism and education policy

97a Women, educational reform and the process of change

97e Public education and the discourse of crisis, power and vision

100a The dialectic of education: An alternative approach to education and social change in developing countries

103l Teenage sexuality and public policy: An agenda for gender education

116q Sex equality and education in Plato's Just State

124k Split brain research and its implications for feminist education

130d Women and education

133p Educational responsibilities to gay male and lesbian students

138a Gender, class and education: A personal view

138g Gender, patriarchy and class in the popular education of women

138i Sex, education and social policy: A new moral economy?

138j Social theory, social relations and education

138k Gender, class and education: A teaching bibliography of European studies

138l   Gender, class and education: A teaching bibliography of Australian and New Zealand studies

138m   Gender, class and education: A teaching bibliography of American studies

145b   Enlightened reforms and Bavarian girls' education: Tradition through innovation

151f   Soviet boarding education: Its rise and progress

169a   Labor education and women workers: An historical perspective

169q   Education for affirmative action: Two union approaches

169r   How to choose and use materials in education for women workers

169u   Funding worker education through tuition refund plans

169v   Labor education and women workers: An international comparison

174l   Califia: An experiment in feminist education Califia community

174m   Feminist art and education at Califia: My personal experience

174o   Feminist education at the feminist studio workshop

174p   Unlearning complicity, remembering resistance: White women's anti-racism education

174u   Not by degrees: Feminist theory and education

174y   What are rights without means? Educating feminists for the future

174z   Charlotte Bunch and Betty Powell talk about feminism, blacks, and education as politics

189k   Education: The patriarchal paradigm and the response to feminism

190j   Menstrual education: Past, present, and future

193a   Girls and science education: Is there a problem?

198i   Female education in Egypt: Changing attitudes over a span of 100 years

203o   No academic matter: Unconscious discrimination in environmental design education

205x   Reducing maternal mortality in British Columbia: An educational process

216k   Experts and amateurs: Some unintended consequences of parent education

216n   The early education of minority children

216r   Organizing delivery of parent education

216s   Toward new methods in parent education

233t   Educating workers, management and the general public

248e   A constant casualty: Nurse education in Britain and the USA to 1939

250b   Socio-cultural reproduction and women's education

250f   Education and the individual: Schooling for girls, or mixed schooling - a mixed blessing?

258e   Educational opportunity and achievement

259d   Staffing for sexism: Educational leadership and role models

262a   Sex roles in education

262d   Differentiation by sex in educational professions

262e   Why sex inequities exist in the profession of education

262i   Educational equity: Current and future needs

270d   Dualism in values toward education of Turkish women

270e   Women's education in rural Turkey

274s   Remedial education

285p   Sex and disability - sociosexual education presentation format

292b   From soul to strawberries: The International Ladies' Garment Workers' Union and workers' education, 1914-1950

292g   Education in working-class solidarity: The summer school for office workers

292i   To rekindle the spirit: Current education programs for women workers

302b   Sex-typing in education for librarianship: 1870-1920

305y   More radical with age: Women and education

309s   Contraception, abortion and venereal disease: Teenagers' knowledge and the effect of education

315k   Women's studies and the re-vision of liberal education: "What is a nice girl/boy like you doing here?"

316k   Education, girls, and power

320i   Educational and career progress of Chicana and Native-American college women

320o   Family formation and educational attainment

320p   Life after college: Historical links between women's education and women's work

320q   Issues of educational equity in the 1980s: Multiple perspectives

332c   "Fairy-born and human-bred": Jane Eyre's education in romance

333q   Aboriginal women in education

351b   The impacts of irrelevance: Women in the history of American education

351d   Biology: Its role in gender-related educational experiences

351h   Women's education and career choice: Disparities between theory and practice

352a   Introduction: Barriers to equity - women, educational leadership, and social change

352d   Power and opportunity in the principalship: The case of two women leaders in education

352e   Historical perspectives on women in educational leadership

352g   Single-sex education and leadership: The early years of Simmons College

352j   Socialization and education of young black girls in school

352m   The need for female role models in education

352p   Leadership training for increased effectiveness among women educational administrators: Two local models

362b   An examination of education, social change, and national development policy: The case of Kenyan women

375j   Barred from the bar: Women and legal education in the United States, 1870-1890

377d   The mathematics filter and the education of women and minorities

377g   An experiment in mathematics education at the college level

377j   Career interests and career education: A key to change

380b   The education and employment of women scientists and engineers in the United States

385f   Colonialism, education, and work: Sex differentiation in colonial Zaire

386d   Women in education

390d   Educated and white-collar women in the 1880s

393b   Education and socio-demographic change in Nigeria

393g   Education and fertility among Cameroonian working women

393h   The relationship between education and fertility

398j   Women's studies and men's careers: How the 'social problem' of women in education maintained the academic status of men in the 1970s

413g   Education and the movement towards equality

414f   Women in Oklahoma education

421c   A causal interpretation of the effect of mother's education and employment status on parental decision-making role patterns in the Korean family

421g   Education of Muslim women: Tradition versus modernity

424d   Employment patterns of educated women in Indonesian cities

429h   Unboxing Christian education

432b   Education and sports: A reply to "Justice and gender in school sports"

432m   Education for equality

432p   Putting away the pom-poms: An educational psychologist's view of females and sports

436d   Women's education and participation in the labour force: The case of Nigeria

440l   Social policy, education and women

446e   The educational and occupational skill level of industrial workers

454j   Catharine Beecher and the education of American women

456p   Health education

465h   The new right, sex, education and social policy: Towards a new moral economy in Britain and the USA

474o   The education of a poet

Educator

112f   Bathsua Makin: Educator and linguist (English, 1608?-1675?)

216o   The parent as educator: A home-school model of socialization

263i   "Teacher, teacher": Teachers and educators in a stratified "female" profession

361c   EQUALS: Working with educators

389h   Georgiana Goddard King (1871-1939): Educator and pioneer in medieval Spanish art

389l   Sirarpie Der Nersessian (b. 1896): Educator and scholar in Byzantine and Armenian art

EEC

see European Economic Community

Egalitarian

52s Egalitarianism in marriage? Graduate education and the sexual division of labour in the Canadian family

347e Forced transition from egalitarianism to male dominance: The Bari of Colombia

421k Feminist egalitarianism, social action orientation and occupational roles: A cross-national study

421o Wife-employment and the emergence of egalitarian marital role prescriptions: 1900-1974

Egerton, George (Pseudonym)

124a Rediscovering the "New Woman" of the 1890's: The stories of "George Egerton"

Egg

310c Egg snatchers

310e Egg farming and women's future

Ego

234c Shamanism as institutionalised ego defense and elite formation associated with transvestism in a Borneo society

Egypt

104a Aspects of non-capitalist social relations in rural Egypt: The small peasant household in an Egyptian delta village

107g Differences in athletic aggression among Egyptian female athletes

117b Matrilineal reinterpretation of some Egyptian sacred cows

156e The god's wife of Amun in the 18th dynasty in Egypt

159j Female criminality in Egypt

198f Early feminist movements in Turkey and Egypt

198i Female education in Egypt: Changing attitudes over a span of 100 years

234f The status of women in old and early middle kingdom Egypt?

328f Isis unveiled: Virginia Woolf's use of Egyptian myth

372f Women and sports in Egypt: History and problems

441b Women and technology in ancient Alexandria: Maria and Hypatia

Eighteenth Century

50b The home turned upside down? The working-class family in cotton textiles 1780-1850

61d Black women in pre-federal America

61e Women in the American revolution: Vignettes or profiles?

99b From the woman's view: Pre-industrial England, 1500-1750

112i Elizabeth Elstob: The Saxon nymph (English, 1683-1765)

112j Mercy Otis Warren: Playwright, poet, and historian of the American revolution (American, 1728-1814)

117l Happy mothers and other new ideas in eighteenth-century French art

130c Women, democracy, and revolution in Paris, 1789-1794

130u The death of an ideal: Female suicides in the eighteenth-century French novel

130bb Conclusion: The legacy of the eighteenth century: A look at the future

147c The rise and development of women's concern for the physical education of American women, 1776-1885: From independence to the foundation of the American Association for the Advancement of Physical Education

158b Freud's heritage: Fathers and daughters in German literature (1750-1850)

162f Tensions, dissensions, and ruptures inside the family in seventeenth- and eighteenth-century Haute Provence

184o Age at menarche in Europe since the eighteenth century

184q Premarital pregnancy in America, 1640-1971: An overview and interpretation

200b Women and the dialectics of nature in eighteenth-century French thought

238b Passionlessness: An interpretation of Victorian sexual ideology, 1790-1850

263f The sexual division of labor on American farms: 1750-1850

278c The secret nexus: Sex and literature in eighteenth-century Britain

343o A penchant for Perdita on the eighteenth-century stage

347b Sunksquaws, shamans, and tradeswomen: Middle Atlantic coastal Algonkian women during the 17th and 18th centuries

353d Passionlessness: An interpretation of Victorian sexual ideology, 1790-1850

353h Patterns of abortion and the response of American physicians, 1790-1930

353j "On the importance of the obstetrick art": Changing customs of childbirth in America, 1760 to 1825

370j Slave wives, free sisters: Bakongo women and slavery c.1700-1850

376a The certain wages of sin: Sentence and punishment of female felons in colonial Massachusetts, 1673-1774

376b Dealing with dependence: Paternalism and tax evasion in eighteenth-century Rhode Island

376h The criminality of women in eighteenth-century England

379q Responses to the political activism of Women of the People in revolutionary Paris, 1789-1793

389d Anna Jameson (1794-1860): Sacred art and social vision

390b 'Feeding the poor and sapping their strength': The public role of ruling-class women in eastern Australia, 1788-1850

396b Midwives, medical men and 'poor women labouring of child': Lying-in hospitals in eighteenth-century London

408h A school for wives: Women in eighteenth-century Spanish theater

444a Women of the popular classes in revolutionary Paris, 1789-1795

444i Revolution and retreat: Upper-class French women after 1789

452c Quest for community: Spiritual autobiographies of eighteenth-century Quaker and Puritan women in America

454c Widowhood in eighteenth-century Massachusetts: A problem in the history of the family

Eighteenth Dynasty

156e The god's wife of Amun in the 18th dynasty in Egypt

El Paso, TX

175p El Paso madams

El Salvador

172e Our national inferiority complex: A cause for violence? (El Salvador)

Elder

see Older

Elect

23h Women and women's issues in the 1980 federal elections

23i 'A woman's place is in the House and in the Senate': Women and the 1983 elections

173e Abortion and the presidential election of 1976: A multivariate analysis of voting behavior

192n The election day immigration raids at Lilli Diamond Originals and the response of the ILGWU

380c Elected women: Skewers of the political system

405k The social composition of women deputies in Soviet elective politics: A preliminary analysis of official biographies

414i The gender liberation: Black women as elected officials in Oklahoma

433f Bengal election, 1937: Fazlul Huq and M. A. Jinnah: A study in leadership stress in Bengal politics

Electra

see Waggoner, Electra

Electroencephalography

28m Estrogens and central nervous system function: Electroencephalography, cognition, and depression

Electronic

36n The electronic fetal monitor in perinatology

36p Benefits and risks of electronic fetal monitoring

86a The clean, light image of the electronics industry: Miracle or mirage?

220h The electronic sweatshop

373k Women's work in multinational electronics factories

428b The new international division of labor and the U.S. work force: The case of the electronics industry

428l Silicon Valley's women workers: A theoretical analysis of sex-segregation in the electronics industry labor market

428n The division of labor in electronics

Elegy

419k The role of women in Roman elegy: Counter-cultural feminism

Elementary School

see also Education

57e Sexual learning in the elementary school

90i Ambitions and the opportunity for professionals in the elementary school

90r The gender of principals and principal/teacher relations in elementary schools

265j Cross-sex friendship in the elementary school

351e Sex segregation and male preeminence in elementary classrooms

Eleonora of Aragon

33b Women, learning, and power: Eleonora of Aragon and the Court of Ferrara

Eleventh Century

187d Benedictine life for women in central France, 850-1100: A feminist revival

401f Power and prestige: Palace women in the Northern Sung (960-1126)

Elgin, Suzette Haden

114h Sex, satire, and feminism in the science fiction of Suzette Haden Elgin

Eliot, George

27h Beauty in distress: *Daniel Deronda* and *The House of Mirth*

142a George Eliot's bastards

142b George Eliot's language of the sense

142d *Middlemarch* and the new humanity

142e 'Stealthy convergence' in *Middlemarch*

142f Antique gems from *Romola* to *Daniel Deronda*

142h How George Eliot's people think

142i George Eliot and the Russians

142j George Eliot and her biographers

142k The ambivalence of *The Mill on the Floss*

142l The unity of *Felix Holt*

142m 'This petty medium': In the middle of *Middlemarch*

143a A new George Eliot manuscript

143b Critical approaches to George Eliot

143c *The Mill on the Floss* and the unreliable narrator

143e *Adam Bede* and "the story of the past"

143e *Romola* and the myth of apocalypse

143f Law, religion and the unity of *Felix Holt*

143g Origins, *Middlemarch*, endings: George Eliot's crisis of the antecedent

143h The hero as dilettante: *Middlemarch* and *Nostromo*

143i Fruit and seed: The finale to *Middlemarch*

143j Gwendolen Harleth and "The girl of the period"

180h "The mother's history" in George Eliot's life, literature and political ideology

196e On exile and fiction: The Leweses and the Shelleys

332b The novel of awakening (five novels)

448d George Eliot and the city: The imprisonment of culture

Elite

21d Female elite goals and national development: Some data from the Philippines

107s Measures of body size and form of elite female basketball players

218c Legitimizing political women: Expanding options for female political elites in Latin America

234c Shamanism as institutionalised ego defense and elite formation associated with transvestism in a Borneo society

Elizabeth I, Queen of England

328c Virginia liked Elizabeth

Elizabethan

184d Elizabethan birth control and Puritan attitudes

Elliot, Anne

164k In between - Anne Elliot marries a sailor and Charlotte Heywood goes to the seaside

Ellis, Havelock

290b Sexology and the social construction of male sexuality (Havelock Ellis)

290c Sexology and the universalization of male sexuality (from Ellis to Kinsey, and Masters and Johnson)

Elstob, Elizabeth

112i Elizabeth Elstob: The Saxon nymph (English, 1683-1765)

Elysium

417y Neither Arcadia nor Elysium: E.M. Broner's *A Weave of Women*

Emancipate

see also Freedom, Liberate, Women's Liberation

39p Black women and racial "uplift" prior to emancipation

151a Housing ideals, structural constraints and the emancipation of women

159n Emancipation of women and crime in Japan

162j Afro-American kinship before and after emancipation in North America

284x Sexual emancipation - an introduction

392e The interaction between women's emancipation and female criminality: A cross-cultural perspective

Emasculate

32q Literary emasculation: Household imagery in Christa Reinig's *Entmannung*

189f Toward the emasculation of political science: The impact of feminism

Embody

247g Dis-embodying the female voice

Embryo

79cc Biological manipulations for producing and nurturing mammalian embryos

79ii In vitro fertilization and embryo transfer: The process of making public policy

310d Who owns the embryo?

Embryofetotoxic

447k Evaluation and control of embryofetotoxic substances

Emergency

26a Emergency room intervention: Detection, assessment, and treatment

203t Emergency shelter: The development of an innovative women's environment

284h Sexual assault center emergency room protocol: Child/adolescent patients

Emerge

67a The emerging debate

Emerson, Mary Moody

196k Emerson and the angel of midnight: The Legacy of Mary Moody Emerson

Emerson, Ralph Waldo

196k Emerson and the angel of midnight: The Legacy of Mary Moody Emerson

Emigrate

157b To Columbia on the Tynemouth: The emigration of single women and girls in 1862

Emmet, Robert

338h The dramatic treatment of Robert Emmet and Sarah Curran

Emotion

see also individual emotions

8k Emotional reactions to miscarriage

80a Social-emotional consequences of day care for preschool children

96f Women and employment: Some emotional hazards

140m Emotional intimacy among men

162a Interest and emotion in family and kinship studies: A critique of social history and anthropology

222f New brains for old bodies: The impact of emotional and physical stress during the Ph.D. process

285t How to stubbornly refuse to disturb oneself emotionally about anything - even about death, dying and sexual mutilation

331b Voice and audience: The emotional world of the *cantigas de amigo*

Emphasis

432k The overemphasis on winning: A philosophical look

Empire

347f Aztec women: The transition from status to class in empire and colony

Employee

see also Employment, Worker

11f Women employees and job-based alcoholism programs

378e Women as employees: Social consciousness and collective action

Employer

89l Occupational segregation, wages and profits when employers discriminate by race and sex

288i Sexual harassment in the workplace — What should the employer do?

470h The 'understanding' employer

Employment

see also Career, Division of Labor, Employee, Equal Employment, Job, Labor, Labor Force, Labor Market, Occupation, Profession, Unemployment, Vocation, Work, Worker, individual occupations

23k The employment of women in the commonwealth public service: The creation and reproduction of a dual labour market

34e No fertile women need apply: Employment discrimination and reproductive hazards in the workplace

39b Female employment and family organization in West Africa

41e Shifts in the occupational and employment status of black women: Current trends and future implications

53c The effect of employment, family and job stress on coronary heart disease patterns in women

66f Statistical biases in the measurement of employment discrimination

67f Statistical biases in the measurement of employment discrimination

70a Insignificance of humanity, "Man is tampering with the moon and the stars": The employment status of American Indian women

71k Economic and employment status of Asian-Pacific women

75a Women's employment in Japan

75b Employment of Korean women

75f Career and employment of women in Pakistan

75g Current status of employment of women in Lebanon

87d Young marrieds: Wives' employment and family role structure

89p The 1974-1975 recession and the employment of women

89r The employment of wives and the inequality of family income

90h Jobs and gender: A history of the structuring of educational employment by sex

93d The effectiveness of federal laws prohibiting sex discrimination in employment in the United States

93q Social policies and the family: Their effect on women's paid employment in Great Britain

93u The contribution of labor market data in combating employment discrimination

96f Women and employment: Some emotional hazards

158m The study of employed mothers over half a century

170c Employment, women and their disabled children

170e Single careers: Employment, housework and caring

199c Sacrifice, satisfaction, and social change: Employment and the family

204c Maternal employment and child development: A review

209d Women, technological change and employment levels: The role of trade unions policies

209e Government policies on new information technologies and their implications for employment: An overview of EEC countries, with particular reference to women

209g The issue of employment and office technology from a managerial perspective

209h The implications of technology for U.S. employment

209ii Public policy and the employment impacts of office computerization

221b Effects of maternal employment on children: Implications for the family therapist

260f The effects of statutory employment policies on women in the United Kingdom labour market

260k Estimating the impact of labor market policies on women: A discussion of the four-country studies on the employment of women

288h Responses of fair employment practice agencies to sexual harassment complaints: A report and recommendations

288o Sexual harassment and Title VII: The foundation for the elimination of sexual cooperation as an employment condition

324b Causes of irregular employment patterns

333r Income and employment for women in remote communities: Examples from the Northern Territory

346a Employment of women and child: Battles to fight

354f Employment and women's health: An analysis of causal relationships

357d Low pay and female employment in Canada with selected references to the USA

380b The education and employment of women scientists and engineers in the United States

380d The relationship between the labor force employment of women and the changing social organization in Canada

385k Women's employment and development: A conceptual framework applied to Ghana

385l Fertility and employment: An assessment of role incompatibility among African urban women

387d Sex discrimination and employment practices: An experiment with unconventional job inquires

400a Women's employment and agriculture: Extracts from a case study

404y The unique employment problems of female offenders returning to the community and labor market

410e Sex differences in role behavior and policy orientations of suburban officeholders: The effect of women's employment

416d Changing patterns of recruitment and employment

421c A causal interpretation of the effect of mother's education and employment status on parental decision-making role patterns in the Korean family

421o Wife-employment and the emergence of egalitarian marital role prescriptions: 1900-1974

421q Sex role attitudes, female employment, and marital satisfaction

424a Economic growth and changing female employment structure in the cities of Southeast and East Asia

424d Employment patterns of educated women in Indonesian cities

424g Islamic attitudes to female employment in industrializing economies: Some notes from Malaysia

424k Female domestic servants in Cagayan de Oro, Philippines: Social and economic implications of employment in a 'premodern' occupational role

424m Growth of the bazaar economy and its significance for women's employment: Trends of the 1970s in Davao City, Philippines

424n Urbanward migration and employment of women in Southeast and East Asian cities: Patterns and policy issues

424o Employment structure of female migrants to the cities in the Philippines

424p Women migrants in Bangkok: An economic analysis of their employment and earnings

424s The impact of female employment on household management

424t Female employment and the family: A case study of the Bataan Export Processing Zone

425b Hard-hatted women: Reflections on blue-collar employment

428f Kitchens hit by priorities: Employed working-class Jamaican women confront the IMF

432f Employment for women in athletics: What is fair play?

435h The womb factor: Pregnancy policies and employment of women

436f Creating employment opportunities for rural women: Some issues affecting attitudes and policy

436j Women's employment networks: Strategies for development

446c Socioeconomic problems of female employment

446d Features of the development of female employment

446h The twenty-fifth congress of the CPSU and current problems of employment of female labor in the republics of central Asia

446q Part-time employment of women

447f Employee health services for women workers

447l Fetotoxicity and fertile female employees

458d Employment status and social support: The experience of the mature woman

463d Influence of employment and children on intra-household travel behavior

463f The impact of women's employment on household travel patterns: A Swedish example

465f Women's employment, legislation and the labour-market

467b Employment prospects and equal opportunity

Empower

434s Social work values and skills to empower women

Empress Wu

325m Empress Wu and the historians: A tyrant and saint of classical China

Enable

429j The task of enabling

Enchantress

64k Colette and Ravel: The enchantress and the illusionist

Enclosure

187c Strict active enclosure and its effects on the female monastic experience (500-1100)

Encyclopédie, ou Dictionnaire des Sciences, des Arts et des Métiers

130p Women and the Encyclopédie

Endocrine

9o Sex differences in the effects of alcohol and other psychoactive drugs on endocrine function: Clinical and experimental evidence

35e Sex, endocrines, and political behavior

51v Endocrine functions in the woman's second half of life

190b Endocrine aspects of menarche and menopause - milestones in the woman's life cycle

Endocrinology

237b The endocrinologist's approach (premenstrual tension)

253c   What's new in endocrinology? Target: Sex hormones

277i   Current approaches in endocrinology

Endometrial

53p   Estrogens and endometrial cancer

Endomorph

341g   Venus as endomorph

Endowment

440c   Redistribution to children and to mothers: A history of child endowment and family allowances

Enemy

129f   Government is women's enemy

Energy

176f   Sexual energy in the classroom

229s   Womanpower: Energy re-sourcement

307n   Putting women in the energy picture

372v   Anaerobic energy metabolism of women

372w   Energy cost of ice skating with figure skates for women

400h   Energy needs of poor households: An abstract

Enforce

60e   The social enforcement of heterosexuality and lesbian resistance in the 1920's

93e   Strategies for improving the economic situation of women in the United States: Systemic thinking, systemic discrimination, and systemic enforcement

93g   The enforcement of laws against sex discrimination in England: Problems of institutional design

146k   Law enforcement and child sexual abuse

465g   Equal opportunity policies: Some implications for women of contrasts between enforcement bodies in Britain and the USA

Engels, Friedrich

464g   Consequences of seizing the reins in the household: A Marxist-feminist critique of Marx and Engels

Engineering

12j   Reproductive engineering: The final solution?

181b   Lillian Moller Gilbreth and the founding of modern industrial engineering

181c   Mathematization of engineering: Limits on women and the field

193j   Who says girls can't be engineers?

307z   Engineered conception: The new parenthood

337d   Women in engineering

361i   Women in engineering: A dynamic approach

380b   The education and employment of women scientists and engineers in the United States

416g   Responsibilities of women faculty in engineering schools

416l   Women engineers in history: Profiles in holism and persistence

441e   The culture of engineering: Woman, workplace and machine

England

see also Anglo Saxon

50c   Women's work in nineteenth-century London: A study of the years 1820-1850

50g   Women as a reserve army of labour: A note on recent British experience

50y   'Guardians of the race' or 'vampires upon the nation's health'? Female sexuality and its regulation in early twentieth century Britain

60b   Male vice and female virtue: Feminism and the politics of prostitution in nineteenth-century Britain

93f   Administering anti-discrimination legislation in Great Britain

93g   The enforcement of laws against sex discrimination in England: Problems of institutional design

93l   Implementing equal pay and equal opportunity legislation in Great Britain

93q   Social policies and the family: Their effect on women's paid employment in Great Britain

99b   From the woman's view: Pre-industrial England, 1500-1750

101e   Catalysts or helpers? British feminists, Indian women's rights, and Indian independence

104g   Women's work in rural south-west England

106e   Marriage contract and social contract in seventeenth-century English political thought

112f   Bathsua Makin: Educator and linguist (English, 1608?-1675?)

112i   Elizabeth Elstob: The Saxon nymph (English, 1683-1765)

113a   Great Britain and the World Wars

122j   A comparison of the movements toward equality in Yugoslavia and England

130x   The view from England

131h   An ambiguous legacy: The role and position of women in the English Eutopia

139b   Patriarchal exploitation and the rise of English capitalism

153n   Working or helping? London working-class children in the domestic economy

159e   Female crime in England and Wales

160e   The suitable wife: Preparation for marriage in London and Rhodesia/Zimbabwe

160g   The negation of structure: A note on British council wives

160j   Memsahibs in colonial Malaya: A study of European wives in a British colony and protectorate, 1900-1940

180d   The new mother of the English renaissance: Her writings on motherhood

184b   Childbearing among the lower classes of late medieval England

184d   Elizabethan birth control and Puritan attitudes

184n   The origins of the birth control movement in England in the early nineteenth century

187f   Why English nunneries had no history: A study of the problems of the English nunneries founded after the conquest

187j   The nun as anchoress: England, 1100-1500

187l   Medieval Cistercian nunneries and English Bishops

188l   The English mystic: Julian of Norwich

188m   The English religious enthusiast: Margery Kempe

215h   A voice from the peace camps: Greenham Common and Upper Heyford

228a   Britain

231cc   Male vice and female virtue: Feminism and the politics of prostitution in nineteenth-century Britain

233p   Legal considerations of reproductive hazards in industry in the United Kingdom

248d   The administration of poverty and the development of nursing practice in nineteenth-century England

248e   A constant casualty: Nurse education in Britain and the USA to 1939

248h   Old wives' tales? Women healers in English history

250e   Black girls in a London comprehensive school

256a   Class and gender in Victorian England

256c   Servants, sexual relations and the risks of illegitimacy in London, 1801-1900

258i   Sex differences in Britain

260a   Women in the labour market and equal opportunity policy in Sweden, United Kingdom, United States and West Germany

260b   A look at the male female unemployment differentials in the Federal Republic of Germany, Sweden, United Kingdom, and the United States of America

260f   The effects of statutory employment policies on women in the United Kingdom labour market

260j   Labour market policy in four countries: Are women adequately represented?

260k   Estimating the impact of labor market policies on women: A discussion of the four-country studies on the employment of women

278c   The secret nexus: Sex and literature in eighteenth-century Britain

291d   Recognition of child sexual abuse in the United Kingdom

331g   The "other" voice: Woman's song, its satire and its transcendence in late medieval British literature

354j   Chlorosis and chronic disease in 19th-century Britain: The social constitution of somatic illness in a capitalist society

357b   Relative female earnings in Great Britain and the impact of legislation

371c   Women's space in a men's house: The British House of Commons

375c   *Merchet* and women's property rights in medieval England

375e   Rape in thirteenth-century England: A study of the common-law courts

376g   Women before the law: Females as felons and prey in fourteenth-century England

376h   The criminality of women in eighteenth-century England

378j   Women and voting in Britain

378n   Women in positions of political leadership in Britain, France and West Germany

379d   Aristocratic widows in fifteenth-century England

379f   Linnaeus's daughters: Women and British botany

379i   The London biblewomen and nurses mission, 1857-1880: Class relations/women's relations

382e Great Britain

388h Public day care in Britain and Sweden: A sociological perspective

396b Midwives, medical men and 'poor women labouring of child': Lying-in hospitals in eighteenth-century London

402l Asian women in Britain: Strategies of adjustment of Indian and Pakistani migrants

418g Domestic violence: Battered women in Britain in the 1970s

421m Comparative attitudes about marital sex among Negro women in the United States, Great Britain and Trinidad

433d British tradesmen of Calcutta, 1830-1900: A preliminary study of their economic and political roles

433i British response to Bengali literature in the nineteenth century

437d United Kingdom

438j Women in Cambridge biochemistry (United Kingdom)

448h "A gigantic mother": Katherine Mansfield's London

452b The emergence of women's autobiography in England

465g Equal opportunity policies: Some implications for women of contrasts between enforcement bodies in Britain and the USA

465h The new right, sex, education and social policy: Towards a new moral economy in Britain and the USA

467d Statutory maternity leave in the United Kingdom: A case study

467e The stance of Britain's major parties and interest groups

470f Migrant women and wage labour: The case of West Indian women in Britain

471a Women at work in Great Britain

English
274d English

English (Language)
180c Eve's orphans: Mothers and daughters in medieval English literature

180t A psychological journey: Mothers and daughters in English-Canadian fiction

278h Erotic poetry in English

331f The woman's song in Middle English and its European backgrounds

344z Sexism and the English language: The linguistic implications of being a woman

English Canadian
421l English-Canadian and French-Canadian attitudes towards women: Results of the Canadian Gallup polls

English Speaking
94g Non English-speaking women: Production and social reproduction

Enterprise
462y A feminist approach to alternative enterprises

Entertainment
55o Appendix D: Fighting adult entertainment centers at the grassroots level

Enthusiast
188m The English religious enthusiast: Margery Kempe

Entitle
170h Natural selection: Perspectives on entitlement to the invalid care allowance

Entmannung
32q Literary emasculation: Household imagery in Christa Reinig's *Entmannung*

Entrepreneur
39g The African woman as entrepreneur: Problem and perspectives on their roles

175m Mollie Bailey: Circus entrepreneur

Entropy
433c Madness as entropy: A Bengali view

Environment
53j Environmental exposures and spontaneous abortion

80f Environmental differences among day care centers and their effects on children's development

86n From grassroots activism to political power: Women organizing against environmental hazards

183b Women, economics and the environment

203i Women in the suburban environment: A U.S.-Sweden comparison

203l Introduction: Women in environmental decisionmaking: Institutional constraints

203o No academic matter: Unconscious discrimination in environmental design education

203r Introduction: Women as environmental activists

203t Emergency shelter: The development of an innovative women's environment

233v Adverse influences of the working environment

317j Environmental change: The older person as initiator and responder

459h Women's work and their status: Rural Indian evidence of labour market and environment effects on sex differences in childhood mortality

463q Gender differences in reactions to vehicle environments

Envy
140h Early origins of envy and devaluation of women: Implications for sex-role stereotypes

195g Womb envy: An explanatory concept

359b Early origins of envy and devaluation of women: Implications for sex-role stereotypes

Epidemiology
8l Depression in women: Epidemiology, explanations, and impact on the family

9d Sex differences in psychoactive drug use: Recent epidemiology

28g Epidemiological patterns of sexual behavior in the menstrual cycle

51p Menopausal distress: A model for epidemiologic investigation

53k An epidemiologic perspective of mental illness and childbirth

53l Epidemiology of pituitary adenomas

53r Epidemiology of coronary heart disease in women

53u Epidemiology of osteoporosis

53v Implications of epidemiologic data for developing health policy for women

141e Epidemiology of breast cancer

233g The epidemiological identification of reproductive hazards

236b The premenstrual syndrome - an epidemiological and statistical exercise

268l Sex-related differences in the epidemiology of child psychopathology

359m Sex differences and the epidemiology of depression

Epigenetics
35d The biopolitics of sex: Gender, genetics, and epigenetics

Episcopal
see also Religion

412m Creating a sphere for women: The Methodist Episcopal church, 1869-1906

412n The laity rights movement, 1906-1918: Women's suffrage in the Methodist Episcopal Church, South

Epistemology
84n Political philosophy and the patriarchal unconscious: A psychoanalytic perspective on epistemology and metaphysics

116f The political epistemology of "masculine" and "feminine"

320g Epistemology and agency in the development of undergraduate women

Epistolary
64e Colette and the epistolary novel

Epistoliére
130n The epistoliéres

Equal
see also Equality

5g Gambian women: Unequal partners in rice development projects?

46i Incremental change in social security needed to result in equal and fair treatment of men and women

78c Females under the law: 'Protected' but unequal

265g Making literacy equally accessible to females and males

307cc EQUALS in computer technology

392m Unequal protection of males and females in the juvenile court

435d Pay equity: Beyond equal pay for equal work

440k Legislating for the right to be equal

466i Separate but equal: Indonesian Muslim perceptions of the roles of women

Equal Employment
see also Discriminate, Employment

93o Equal employment opportunity for women in West Germany today

93t Equal employment policy for women: Summary of themes and issues

267a Achievement in women: Implications for equal employment opportunity policy

267b The importance of being right when you think you are: Self-serving bias in equal employment opportunity

Equal Opportunity
see also Discriminate

62g Conclusion: Co-education, equal educational opportunity and change

87k Equal opportunity laws and dual-career couples

93b Collective bargaining as a strategy for achieving equal opportunity and equal pay: Sweden and West Germany

93c Equal pay and equal opportunity law in France

93j Leadership training for union women in the United States: Route to equal opportunity

93l Implementing equal pay and equal opportunity legislation in Great Britain

93o Equal employment opportunity for women in West Germany today

179f Equal opportunity trap

260a Women in the labour market and equal opportunity policy in Sweden, United Kingdom, United States and West Germany

260e Equal opportunity and the law in the United States

260g Equal opportunity policies in Sweden

260h Equal opportunity policies for women in the Federal Republic of Germany

261b Building mentorship frameworks as part of an effective equal opportunity ecology

310z Equal opportunity for babies? Not in Oakland!

361a Leverage for equal opportunity through mastery of mathematics

432e Afterword on equal opportunity

465g Equal opportunity policies: Some implications for women of contrasts between enforcement bodies in Britain and the USA

467b Employment prospects and equal opportunity

Equal Pay
see also Comparable Worth, Pay

65k Canada's equal pay for work of equal value law

93b Collective bargaining as a strategy for achieving equal opportunity and equal pay: Sweden and West Germany

93c Equal pay and equal opportunity law in France

93k The role of the National Action Committee on the Status of Women in facilitating equal pay policy in Canada

93l Implementing equal pay and equal opportunity legislation in Great Britain

93s Beyond equal pay for equal work: Comparable worth in the state of Washington

93v Work analysis as a means to achieve equal pay for working women: The Federal Republic of Germany

205u Cheap at half the price: The history of the fight for equal pay in BC

390r Equal pay case, 1951

435d Pay equity: Beyond equal pay for equal work

Equal Rights Amendment (ERA)
see also Equality, Equity, Right

63m The ERA and coed prisons

124m The defeat of the Equal Rights Amendment

124n The ERA campaign: Reflections on interpretation and practice

226h Female state senators as cue givers: ERA roll-call voting, 1972-1979

316n Resistance to the women's movement in the United States: The ERA controversy as prototype

392k Discriminatory sentencing of women offenders: The argument for ERA in a nutshell

Equality
see also Equity, Gender Equity, Right, Sex Equality, Social Inequality

3k Abortion and equality

21g Expanding women's horizons in Indonesia: Toward maximum equality with minimum conflict

52o Change in the system of social power: Conditions for the social equality of women in Yugoslavia

84g The trivialization of the notion of equality

89r The employment of wives and the inequality of family income

93h Equality between men and women in the labor market: The Swedish National Labor Market Board

94c The 'naturalness' of inequality

101k Towards equality? Cause and consequence of the political prominence of women in India

102b Breaking free of symbolic bondage: From feminine submission to a vision of equality

107a Women's sports - the unlikely myth of equality

120i Ideological hegemony in political discourse: Women's specificity and equality

122j A comparison of the movements toward equality in Yugoslavia and England

126n Does equality mean sameness? A historical perspective on the college curriculum for women with reflections on the current situation

140c Inequality and women's mental health: An overview

140d The effects of inequality on psychology

147o Women's sport: A trial of equality

235k The fight for equality

259m Equality or equity? - a European overview

321h Income inequality

323l Bargaining for equality

344h Marital relationships and mental health: The psychic costs of inequality

351a Equity or equality: What shall it be?

353cc Homeopathy and sexual equality: The controversy over coeducation at Cincinnati's Pulte Medical College, 1873-1879

360g Inequality and mental health: Low income and minority women

364e Female power and the inequality of wealth and motherhood in north-western Portugal

374c The struggle for women's equality

374d Thesis: On the full exercise of women's equality

397d Lesbian relationships: A struggle toward partner equality

402g Women and the law: Constitutional rights and continuing inequalities

411h Social change and equality: The roles of women and economics

413g Education and the movement towards equality

432i Equality and competition: Can sports make a women of a girl?

432m Education for equality

433g Inequality and radical land reform: Some notes from west Bengal

444g Women in the Chinese communist revolution: The question of political equality

EQUALS

361c EQUALS: Working with educators

Equity
see also Equality, Sex Equity

259m Equality or equity? - a European overview

262i Educational equity: Current and future needs

267f Equity for women at work: Models of change

320q Issues of educational equity in the 1980s: Multiple perspectives

351a Equity or equality: What shall it be?

352a Introduction: Barriers to equity - women, educational leadership, and social change

373e New technologies for food-related activities: An equity strategy

379c The planter's wife revisited: Women, equity law, and the Chancery Court in seventeenth-century Maryland

385j Women farmers and inequities in agricultural services

388a Development with equity for women

427e Gender inequities in childhood social life and adult work life

435d Pay equity: Beyond equal pay for equal work

ERA
see Equal Rights Amendment

Erectile

277e The assessment of sleep erections for diagnosis of erectile disorders

285l Differential diagnosis and treatment for organogenic and psychogenic erectile dysfunction

Erikson, Erik

51l Erik Erikson and Doris Lessing: Psychological theory and the female novel of development

Eros

102p Afterword: Toward the mobilization of Eros

109l Place and eros in Radcliffe, Lewis, and Brontë

127b Thanatos and Eros: Kate Chopin's *The Awakening*

285b Eros and thanatos: Lingering taboos in doctor-patient communication

313l Alienation and eros in three stories by Beatriz Guido, Marta Lynch and Amalia Jamilis

Erotic

7o Sadomasochism: Eroticized violence, eroticized powerlessness

31h Pornography and the erotics of domination

48m Gender, gender-role identification, and response to erotica

132d The bonds of love: Rational violence and erotic domination

224d Looking at pornography: Erotica and the socialist morality

225w   The forbidden: Eroticism and taboo

230d   Arousal, affect, and the aggression-moderating effect of erotica

231p   Master and slave: The fantasy of erotic domination

238f   The erotic South: Civilization and sexuality in American abolitionism

247f   From repressive tolerance to erotic liberation: *Maedchen in Uniform*

278d   Victorian erotica

278h   Erotic poetry in English

280l   Erotized repetitive hangings

460e   Physiological aspects of female sexual development: Gestation, lactation, menopause, and erotic physiology

Escape

40x   Escape from Trublem: The fiction of Gayl Jones

Eskimo

473l   The economic role of women in Alaskan Eskimo society

Espirit

130aa   The view from Spain: Rocco *finesse* and *espirit* versus plebian manners

Essay

14w   On the novels written by selected black women: A bibliographical essay

56a   Having a baby: A story essay

74h   A woman and her poems (essay)

74i   The word, that milk cow (essay)

74j   The arc of paradox (essay)

176o   Black lesbians before 1970: A bibliographical essay

193q   From schoolgirls' essays

223t   An essay on "Paederasty"

256g   One hand tied behind us: A review essay

308k   Family involvement, notification, and responsibility: A personal essay

Estradiol

372s   Exercise-induced changes in estradiol metabolism and their possible physiological meaning

Estrangement

105k   Marriage, estrangement, sobriety and recidivism: Some crucial process variables in the case of alcoholic men and their wives

Estrogen

28m   Estrogens and central nervous system function: Electroencephalography, cognition, and depression

51w   Aging, menopause, and estrogens: The clinician's dilemma

51x   Sociological observations on ethical issues implicated in estrogen replacement therapy at menopause

53p   Estrogens and endometrial cancer

Etcheverts, Sara de

408l   Sara de Etcheverts: The contradictions of literary feminism

Eternal

32a   The eternal feminine is leading us on

Ethacridine

252i   Extra-amniotic ethacridine (Rivanol)-catheter technique for midtrimester abortion

Ethic

3a   Social science and ethical issues: The policy implications of poll data on abortion

4k   Ethical issues of adolescent pregnancy

36c   Ethical problems in government-funded contraceptive research

36i   Depo-provera: Some ethical questions about a controversial contraceptive

36o   Drugs, birth, and ethics

36q   Ethical issues in childbirth technology

36u   Ethical issues relating to childbirth as experienced by the birthing woman and midwife

36bb   The ethicist in policymaking

51x   Sociological observations on ethical issues implicated in estrogen replacement therapy at menopause

79l   The politics of prenatal diagnosis: A feminist ethical analysis

79dd   Ethics and reproductive technology

140y   Sexual misconduct by psychiatrists: The ethical and clinical dilemma of confidentiality

168b   From feminism to a new conception of ethics

189o   Dirty fingers, grime and slag heaps: Purity and the scientific ethic

195o   Toward an ethic of nurturance: Luce Irigaray on mothering and power

223c   The ethics of having love affairs

229oo   Ethics and justice in goddess religion

273j   Ethics and public policy: Should sex choice be discouraged?

275u   A note on the ethics of theories of truth

276f   Ethics and ethical dilemmas in the treatment of sex offenders

281h   Ethical and legal aspects of sexual issues

297d   'It's great to have someone to talk to': The ethics and politics of interviewing women

308g   Ethical and legal issues in teenage pregnancies

310ee   Feminist ethics, ecology and vision

432o   The ethics of gender discrimination: A response to Ann Diller and Barbara Houston's "Women's Physical Education"

Ethnic

see also Minority, Race, specific ethnic groups

10c   Alcohol use and abuse in ethnic minority women

16t   The ethnic minority woman

73a   Ethnic women and the media

73f   The role of learning in the lives of Finnish and other ethnic women and a proposal for self-education

73g   Changing needs of ethnic women in higher education

73k   Achieving the dreams beyond tradition: Counseling white ethnic American girls

94b   Ethnicity, multiculturalism and neo-conservatism

199o   On the shop floor: Multi-ethnic unity against the conglomerate

213d   Sexual divisions and ethnic adaptation: The case of Greek-Cypriot women

265b   Ethnic differences in sex stereotyping by mothers: Implications for health care

269f   Being Cuna and female: Ethnicity mediating change in sex roles

296g   Racial-ethnic women and work: Towards an analysis of race and gender stratification

300c   The Minangkabau woman: Cultural centre or ethnic symbol?

344w   Race and ethnicity in the lives of minority women

385a   Women, work, and ethnicity: The Sierra Leone case

428k   The formation of an ethnic group: Colombian female workers in Venezuela

452h   In search of the black female self: African-American women's autobiographies and ethnicity

473d   Dioula women in town: A view of intra-ethnic variation (Ivory Coast)

Ethnography

192i   Se me acabó la canción: An ethnography of non-consenting sterilizations among Mexican women in Los Angeles

246d   "Women never hunt": The portrayal of women in Melanesian ethnography

Ethnohistory

269a   Rama men and women: An ethnohistorical analysis of change

Ethnology

379j   The ethnological mirror: American evangelical women and their heathen sisters, 1870-1910

Ethnopsychiatry

327e   Ethnopsychiatric dimensions in family violence

Ethopia

350h   The impact of land reform on women: The case of Ethopia

Etiology

28s   Premenstrual tension: Etiology

53o   Etiologic factors for invasive and noninvasive cervical abnormalities

78b   The etiology of female crime: A review of the literature

236a   Aetiology of premenstrual syndrome

295n   Substance abuse in women: Etiology and prevention

304f   Women and agoraphobia: A case for the etiological significance of the feminine sex-role stereotype

392b   The etiology of female crime: A review of the literature

Etiquette

402k   Etiquette among women in Karnataka: Forms of address in the village and the family

Etruscan

132l   For the Etruscans: Sexual difference and artistic production - the debate over a female aesthetic

419j   The women of Etruria

Eugenics

390e   Evolution, eugenics and women: The impact of scientific theories on attitudes towards women, 1870-1920

Euripides

419h   The menace of Dionysus: Sex roles and reversals in Euripides' *Bacchae*

Europe

see also individual countries

33e Learned women in the Europe of the sixteenth century

50d Women's work and the family in nineteenth-century Europe

52k Economic and family roles of men and women in Northern Europe: A historical cross-national comparison

73e The status of East European women in the family: Tradition and change

73e The status of East European women in the family: Tradition and change

89d Women's work and the family in nineteenth-century Europe

138k Gender, class and education: A teaching bibliography of European studies

145r An English-language bibliography on European and American women's history

153g Development and underdevelopment of household-based production in Europe

160j Memsahibs in colonial Malaya: A study of European wives in a British colony and protectorate, 1900-1940

179i Nuclear Europe

184e Illegitimacy, sexual revolution, and social change in modern Europe

184l Women's work and European fertility patterns

184o Age at menarche in Europe since the eighteenth century

228k Eastern Europe

229b Women and culture in goddess-oriented old Europe

246i European women in the Solomon Islands, 1900-1942: Accommodation and change on the Pacific frontier

252c Legal aspects of pregnancy termination in Europe

259m Equality or equity? - a European overview

291f Sexual abuse of children: An examination of European criminal law

331f The woman's song in Middle English and its European backgrounds

334f The European legal context of the Welsh law of matrimonial property

393d Worlds apart? A comparative study of European and African traditional family life as depicted in the novels of Laurie Lee and Camara Laye

405n Some demographic, particularly fertility, correlates of female status in eastern Europe and the republics of the Soviet Union

European Economic Community (EEC)

209e Government policies on new information technologies and their implications for employment: An overview of EEC countries, with particular reference to women

Evaluate

63a The sexually integrated prison: A legal and policy evaluation

65d Some problems with contemporary job evaluation systems

65e Effect of choice of factors and factor weights in job evaluation

66b Job evaluation and pay setting: Concepts and practices

67b Job evaluation and pay setting: Concepts and practices

146m Evaluation of child-sexual-abuse programs

169h Evaluating programs for working adults

266d Evaluation issues in women's studies

276c Prediction of recidivism and the evaluation of treatment programs for sex offenders

320l Undergraduates and their teachers: An analysis of student evaluations of male and female instructors

378l Candidate evaluations by men and women

404j The woman in treatment: Evaluation and diagnostic implications

447k Evaluation and control of embryofetotoxic substances

Evangelical

379j The ethnological mirror: American evangelical women and their heathen sisters, 1870-1910

412l "A new impulse": Progress in lay leadership and service by women of the United Brethren in Christ and the Evangelical Association, 1870-1910

412p Evangelical domesticity: The woman's temperance crusade of 1873-1874

Evans, Mari

40q The art of Mari Evans

40r Affirmation in the works of Mari Evans

Evans, Mary Ann

196e On exile and fiction: The Leweses and the Shelleys

Eve

117f Eve and Mary: Conflicting images of medieval woman

180c Eve's orphans: Mothers and daughters in medieval English literature

The Evening and the Morning

445q The Mormon novel: Virginia Sorensen's *The Evening and the Morning*

Event

354i Medicine and patriarchal violence: The social construction of a "private" event

411b Life events and the boundaries of midlife for women

Everything

381h Taking care of everything

Everything that Rises Must Converge

451i Introduction to *Everything That Rises Must Converge*

Evil

152d Overcoming the structured evil of male domination and heterosexism

Evolve

34a Have only men evolved?

84d Have only men evolved?

84e Evolution and patriarchal myths of scarcity and competition

88f The female oedipus complex: Its antecedents and evolution

185h The evolution of sex roles: The transformation of masculine and feminine values

254b The evolution of the woman scientist

340a The female chimpanzee as a human evolutionary prototype

353dd On the evolution of women's medical societies

390e Evolution, eugenics and women: The impact of scientific theories on attitudes towards women, 1870-1920

Examine

193n Sex differences in science examinations

222c High noon: Surviving the comprehensive exams

250h Sex differences in performance in science examinations

256h Examining family history

267d A psychological examination of sexual harassment

274c Subject image, examinations and teaching materials

291k The child psychiatric examination of the sexually abused child

447g Special needs of women in health examinations

Exampla

408c Sexual humor in misogynist medieval exampla

Example

130w The edifying examples

Excellence

122h In search of excellence in academic libraries, or, challenging the henhouse model

Exchange

82k Land tenure and cooperatives: Origin, development and persistence of Navajo matrifocality in subsistence, production, exchange and tenure

364c The exchange of women and property: Marriage in post-revolutionary China

Exclude

86k Keeping women in their place: Exclusionary policies and reproduction

117k Art history and its exclusions: The example of Dutch art

160a Incorporation and exclusion: Oxford academics' wives

457i Women excluded? Masking and masquerading in West Africa

Executive

288a The executive man and woman: The issue of sexuality

Exercise

29i Health maintenance: Exercise and nutrition

147d The ladies' department of the *American Farmer*, 1825-1830: A locus for the advocacy of family health and exercise

147e American women, 1880-1860 (sic): Recreational pursuits and exercise

169l Games and other exercises

214f The view from the bench: The exercise of power

372k Physiological and metabolic responses of female athletes during laboratory and field exercises

372s Exercise-induced changes in estradiol metabolism and their possible physiological meaning

372x Comparison of exercise between females and males

372y Pituitary response to physical exercise: Sex differences

374d Thesis: On the full exercise of women's equality

Exhibitionism

280f Genital exhibitionism in men and women

Exile

30j Exiles

120a Memoirs of an ontological exile: The methodological rebellions of feminist research

196e On exile and fiction: The Leweses and the Shelleys

445s Tradition of the exile: Judith Wright's Australian "West"

Exiles

409e Bertha's role in *Exiles*

Expectation

79o Perfectibility and the neonate: The burden of expectations on mothers and their health providers

105b Modern and traditional elements in the expectations of young married couples regarding their marital life

105c Marital expectations of wives in contemporary Poland

259c The hidden curriculum: Academic consequences of teacher expectations

Expenditure

283p Public expenditure and budgetary policy

Expense

108p Women and autobiography at author's expense

Experience

51z The Interdisciplinary Society for Menstrual Cycle Research: Creating knowledge from our experience

96e The experience of abortion

115j Called to priesthood: Interpreting women's experience

118d The dynamics of female experience: Process models and human values

190i Variations in the experience of menarche as a function of preparedness

190k Menstrual beliefs and experiences of mother-daughter dyads

249k The failure of affirmative action for women: One university's experience

307u New jobs in new technologies: Experienced only need apply

367e The religious experience of Southern women

461b The sexual experience of Afro-American women: A middle-income sample

Experiential

312k Experiential analysis: A contribution to feminist research

Experiment

5h Developing women's cooperatives: An experiment in rural Nigeria

132o Separation and survival: Mothers, daughters, sisters: - The women's experimental theater

174l Califia: An experiment in feminist education Califia community

209cc Experimental approaches towards telecommunications in France

292h The she-she-she camps: An experiment in living and learning, 1934-1937

387d Sex discrimination and employment practices: An experiment with unconventional job inquires

Expert

119a Inverts and experts: Radclyffe Hall and the lesbian identity

216k Experts and amateurs: Some unintended consequences of parent education

Exploit

55c Typology of sex rings exploiting children

55l Appendix A: Legal resources on sexual exploitation of children

139b Patriarchal exploitation and the rise of English capitalism

206c The patriarchal thread - A history of exploitation

288g The other side of the coin: Women who exploit their sexuality for gain

Export Processing Zone

424t Female employment and the family: A case study of the Bataan Export Processing Zone

Exposure

53j Environmental exposures and spontaneous abortion

230e Effects of massive exposure to pornography

447m The control of hazardous exposures in the workplace

Express

48n Future influences on the interaction of gender and human sexual expression

158h Psychology measures femininity and masculinity, 2: From "13 Gay Men" to the instrumental-expressive distinction

171h Men, inexpressiveness, and power

287g Varieties of sexual expression

387n The inexpressive male: Tragedy or sexual politics?

Expressionism

117o Gender or genius? The women artists of German expressionism

Extension

337j Women and cooperative home economics extension

Exterior

371d Essential objects and the sacred: Interior and exterior space in an urban Greek locality

Extra-Amniotic

252i Extra-amniotic ethacridine (Rivanol)-catheter technique for midtrimester abortion

Extramarital

461t Discussion: Extramarital sex: A multifaceted experience

Extraordinary

30q Ordinary. Extraordinary.

Extremism

433e Bengal politics of the first decade of the present century: A defence of extremism

Eye

84l The mind's eye

174w Black-eyed blues connections: From the inside out

Fable

206a Nimble fingers and other fables

Fabricate

244j Synthetic smiles and fabricated faces

Fabulation

197c Autonomy and fabulation in the fiction of Muriel Spark

Face

244j Synthetic smiles and fabricated faces

371g Place and face: Of women in Doshman Ziari, Iran

399kk The second face of the idol: Women in melodrama

401e The many faces of Cui Yingying

Facility

63e A study of a coeducational correctional facility

73c Developing a neighborhood-based health facility

78y Doing time with the boys: An analysis of women correctional officers in all-male facilities

191a Who uses mental health facilities?

Factory

see also Business, Company, Corporation, Industry, Management

73h The economic struggles of female factory workers: A comparison of French, Polish, and Portuguese immigrants

139c Not so much a factory, more a form of patriarchy: Gender and class during industrialisation

144f The family life-cycle: A study of factory workers in nineteenth century Württemberg

183e Women factory workers and the law

183f Hysteria among factory workers

206h A woman's home is her factory

207i The subordination of women and the internationalisation of factory production

208c The subordination of women and the internationalisation of factory production

215n The women who wire up the weapons: Workers in armament factories

310g Designer genes: A view from the factory

373k Women's work in multinational electronics factories

424e Towards meeting the needs of urban female factory workers in peninsular Malaysia

424i Women's work: Factory, family and social class in an industrializing order

424j Making the bread and bringing it home: Female factory workers and the family economy

428c Capitalism, imperialism, and patriarchy: The dilemma of Third-World women workers in multinational factories

428d Women, production, and reproduction in industrial capitalism: A comparison of Brazilian and U.S. factory workers

Faculty

see also Education

261g Faculty grievance procedure

337m Socio-economic profile of faculty women at Madison

394b   History of the Association of Faculty Women at Madison

416g   Responsibilities of women faculty in engineering schools

Failure

40ee   The quest for self: Triumph and failure in the works of Toni Morrison

41g   Invited presentation: The black professional woman — career success and interpersonal failure

43g   If all else fails, I'm still a mother

Fair

46i   Incremental change in social security needed to result in equal and fair treatment of men and women

288h   Responses of fair employment practice agencies to sexual harassment complaints: A report and recommendations

303i   Fair Harvard and the fairer sex

432f   Employment for women in athletics: What is fair play?

Fairy Tales

332j   Through the looking glass: When women tell fairy tales

Faith

189c   Methodocracy, misogyny and bad faith: The response of philosophy

Fallacy

51s   The fallacy of bodily reductionism

136j   The development of sex differences in nonverbal signals: Fallacies, facts, and fantasies

Fallen

17j   Stephen Crane and the fallen women

117m   Lost and *Found*: Once more the fallen woman

126i   The fallen woman in fiction

155h   The fate of the fallen woman in *Maggie* and *Sister Carrie*

286d   The fallen woman's sexuality: Childbirth and censure

286l   Fallen women, lost children: Wilde and the theatre in the nineties

Fame

147u   Women in the sports halls of fame

Family

see also Brother, Couple, Daughter, Father, Household, Husband, Marriage, Mother, Parent, Partner, Sister, Sibling, Son, Spouse, Wife

3c   Reflections on abortion, values, and the family

3e   A family perspective on abortion

6d   Women in the changing African family

8l   Depression in women: Epidemiology, explanations, and impact on the family

8r   Conflict and psychological development: Women in the family

10j   Female alcohol abuse: Its effects on the family

18d   Rural family size and economic change: A Middle Eastern case

18e   Population policy, family size, and the reproduction of the labor force in India: The case of Bombay

23n   A *Theory of Justice* and love: Rawls on the family

26g   Family trouble clinic: Family service of Detroit and Wayne County

29g   Marriage and the family: An unconscious male bias in behavioral treatment?

31a   Private rights and public virtues: Women, the family, and democracy

37a   Conceptualizations of black families

37b   Interpreting the African heritage in Afro-American family organization

37d   African-American family life: An instrument of culture

37e   Perspectives on black family empirical research: 1965-1978

37f   A demographic picture of black families

37g   Economics and mobility: A theoretical rationale for urban black family well-being

37i   Patterns of upward mobility in black families

37l   Women's values regarding marriage and the family

37n   Parenting in black families with young children: A historical perspective

37p   Support systems of significant others in black families

37q   Group identity development within black families

37r   Multiple public benefits and poor black families

37s   Policies affecting the status of black children and families

37t   An advocacy agenda for black families and children

38d   The black woman and family roles

38h   Black mothers and the extended family support network

39b   Female employment and family organization in West Africa

39v   Household and family in the Caribbean: Some definitions and concepts

39z   Female status, the family and male dominance in a West Indian community

45h   Family roles in a twenty-year perspective

47f   The family

50a   The butcher, the baker, the candlestick-maker: The shop and the family in the Industrial Revolution

50b   The home turned upside down? The working-class family in cotton textiles 1780-1850

50d   Women's work and the family in nineteenth-century Europe

50e   The 'family wage'

50k   The unnatural family

50n   From disregard to disrepute: The position of women in family law

51e   Attitudes of families toward menopause

52b   The changing roles of Canadian women in family and work: An overview

52f   The position of Austrian women in the family: Some data, many questions, and a few interpretations

52h   Changing sex roles in the Greek family and society

52j   The changing role of Swedish women in family and society

52k   Economic and family roles of men and women in Northern Europe: A historical cross-national comparison

52l   Soviet women in family and society

52m   Women and the family in Poland

52p   Women's roles and conjugal family systems in Ghana

52s   Egalitarianism in marriage? Graduate education and the sexual division of labour in the Canadian family

53c   The effect of employment, family and job stress on coronary heart disease patterns in women

54g   Structural family therapy: The Sanchez family

55f   Impact of child pornography and sex rings on child victims and their families

57c   Work, the family, and children's sexual learning

58h   Family planning and population policies

60f   The twenties' backlash: Compulsory heterosexuality, the consumer family, and the waning of feminism

60h   Feminism, the family, and the New Right

60l   Black family life-styles: A lesson in survival

60v   The challenge of profamily politics: A feminist defense of sexual freedom

69j   Separation: A family developmental process of midlife

73e   The status of East European women in the family: Tradition and change

73j   Family roles and identities of Scandinavian and German women

76e   'The policing of families'

80c   Changing aspects of the family: A psychoanalytic perspective on early intervention

80m   Families, children, and child care

81b   The economics of middle-income family life: Working women during the Great Depression

81c   Chicanas and Mexican immigrant families 1920-1940: Women's subordination and family exploitation

82t   The female family business: A Guatemalan example

87a   Three generations of dual-career family research

87d   Young marrieds: Wives' employment and family role structure

87i   The balancing act: Coping strategies for emerging family lifestyles

89d   Women's work and the family in nineteenth-century Europe

89e   Economic perspectives on the family

89f   Class struggle and the persistence of the working-class family

89g   Family investments in human capital: Earnings of women

89q   Wives' labor force behavior and family consumption patterns

89r   The employment of wives and the inequality of family income

93q   Social policies and the family: Their effect on women's paid employment in Great Britain

93r   Integration of family policy and labor market policy in Sweden

94k   Religion, law and family disputes in a Lebanese Muslim community in Sydney

96d   Mothers and their children: A study of low-income families

101a Introduction: The extended family as metaphor and the expansion of women's realm

101j The All-Pakistan Women's Association and the 1961 Muslim family laws ordinance

103a Contemporary American families: Decline or transformation?

103b The state, the patriarchal family, and working mothers

103g Fiscal policy and family structure

103p Women in a revolutionary society: The state and family policy in China

103q Family responsibilities as a labor market issue: A Scandinavian perspective

103s The family impact statement: Ideology and feasibility

103u "Sisters" or "comrades"? The politics of friends and families

103v Afterword: Feminism and families in a liberal policy

104b Cash crop production and family labour: Tobacco growers in Corrientes, Argentina

104d Co-operation on and between eastern Finnish family farms

104f A note on the custom of 'paying off' on family farms in Poland

105a Changing family and changing society

105f The family, the child, and social change

105g Social structure, family socialization, and children's achievement goals: A comparative analysis

105h Developing family invulnerability to stress: Coping patterns and strategies wives employ in managing family separations

105l Physical violence in a nationally representative sample of American families

106a Introduction: Toward a theory of the family and politics

106b Philosopher queens and private wives: Plato on women and the family

106g Hegel's conception of the family

106i Oedipus as hero: Family and family metaphors in Nietzsche

106j The working-class family: A Marxist perspective

106k The family in contemporary feminist thought: A critical review

106l Contemporary critical theory and the family: Private world and public crisis

106m Kafka and Laing on the trapped consciousness: The family as political life

111d Family violence: Women as offenders or victims

119e The family in socialist-feminist politics

126j Redefining the family and women's status within the family: The case of southern Appalachia

130e Women and family

134e Family fortunes

140q Families at risk for father-daughter incest

140t A feminist approach to family therapy

140u Men's new family roles: Some implications for therapists

141c Statistical model for the study of familial breast cancer

141d Pathologic aspects of familial carcinoma of breast

144a The German family: A critical survey of the current state of historical research

144c Family and 'modernisation': The peasant family and social change in nineteenth-century Bavaria

144d Family and household: Social structures in a German village between the two World Wars

144e Women, family and death: Excess mortality of women in child-bearing age in four communities in nineteenth-century Germany

144f The family life-cycle: A study of factory workers in nineteenth century Württemberg

144g Overcrowding and family life: Working-class families and the housing crisis in late nineteenth-century Duisburg

144h Women's work and the family: Women garment workers in Berlin and Hamburg before the First World War

144i Politics and the family: Social democracy and the working-class family in theory and practice before 1914

145n Social insurance and the family work of Oberlausitz home weavers in the late nineteenth century

145o The woman's role in the German working-class family in the 1890s from the perspective of women's autobiographies

146i Family treatment

147d The ladies' department of the *American Farmer*, 1825-1830: A locus for the advocacy of family health and exercise

149f Domestic labour and the reproduction of labour power: Towards an analysis of women, the family, and class

158e Not quite new worlds: Psychologists' conceptions of the ideal family in the twenties

158f "Give me a dozen healthy infants": John B. Watson's popular advice on childrearing, women, and the family

162a Interest and emotion in family and kinship studies: A critique of social history and anthropology

162f Tensions, dissensions, and ruptures inside the family in seventeenth- and eighteenth-century Haute Provence

162h 'A brother is a creative thing': Change and conflict in a Melpa family (Papua New Guinea)

162i The Aragonese royal family around 1300

162l Kinship and class consciousness: Family values and work experience among hospital workers in an American southern town

162m Linen was their life: Family survival strategies and parent-child relations in nineteenth-century France

162o Family fun in Starve Harbor: Custom, history and confrontation in village Newfoundland

167k Organising a mass lobby of Parliament: Families against the bomb

178p Families revisited

182e Housing the family

185b Social forces and the changing family

185c Marriage and the family: Styles and forms

185j Moral concepts in the year 2020: The individual, the family, and society

185k The work/family connection in the year 2020

185l Physical settings for families in 2020: In space, on earth

185m Family options, governments, and the social milieu: Viewed from the 21st century

185n Beyond the melting pot: Nationalism, militarism and the family

199a Generations of working-class families

199c Sacrifice, satisfaction, and social change: Employment and the family

203j Swedish women in single-family housing

203u Housing for single-parent families: A women's design

204a Parental behavior and child development in nontraditional families: An introduction

204b The two-provider family: Problems and potentials

204f Shared-caregiving families: An Australian study

204j Social development and parent-child interaction in father-custody and stepmother families

204k Comparative socialization practices in traditional and alternative families

210k Family relationships of older women: A women's issue

211b The Jewish family: Looking for a usable past

214q The work — family problem: Overloading the system

214r Dual-career families: Intimacy or productivity?

216e The black family: An adaptive perspective

216h The Asian-American family

216i The Puerto Rican family: Its role in cultural transition

216j Implications for national policy decisions: The black family perspective

220i Women, families and the state

221a The family as an influence on career development

221b Effects of maternal employment on children: Implications for the family therapist

221d Understanding dual career families

221e Voluntary mid-life career change: Family effects

221f Family effects of dislocation, unemployment, and discouragement

221g Burnout and job dissatisfaction: Impact on the family

222i The impossible dream: The Ph.D., marriage, and family

224f Happy families? Paedophilia examined

227g Women and the family

231e Family, sexual morality, and popular movements in turn-of-the-century America

243d The old world, new rights, and the limited rebellion: Challenges to traditional authority in immigrant families

243f Black families and childrearing support networks

243h Family, work, and individual development in dual-career marriages: Issues for research

243i Work experience and family relations among working-class and lower-middle-class

243l Unemployment and family stress

243m   Husbands' paid work and family roles: Current research issues

244d   Occupation-family-linkages as perceived by men in the early stages of professional and managerial careers

244e   The roles of men and women in French families: Change or stability in the patterns and practices?

244g   The nurture of adults by children in family settings

245a   Feminist rethinking of the family: An overview

245b   Is there a family? New anthropological views

245c   Why nineteenth-century feminists did not support "birth control" and twentieth-century feminists do: Feminism, reproduction, and the family

245j   Family and class in contemporary America: Notes toward an understanding of ideology

245k   The place of the family in the origins of the welfare state

245l   The family: The view from a room of her own

255c   Purdah and the Hindu family in central India

256h   Examining family history

258d   Social security and the family

263c   Symmetrical families? Changing gender role expectations and the breadwinner role in the contemporary United States

270a   Duofocal family structure and an alternative model of husband-wife relationship

270b   The significance of family and kinship in urban Turkey

270g   Female labor power relations in the urban Turkish family

270i   Economic change and the Gecekondu family

270l   Psychopathology and the Turkish family: A family systems theory analysis

270m   Social change and family crisis: The nature of Turkish divorce

281a   Human sexuality in the life cycle of the family system

281c   Sexual disorders and the family therapist

291b   Psychosexual development within the family

291m   Incest and dysfunctional family system

308b   The family's role in adolescent sexual behavior

308c   Implicating the family: Teenage parenthood and kinship involvement

308d   Government policies related to teenage family formation and functioning: An inventory

308f   Adolescent parent programs and family involvement

308i   The impact of adolescent pregnancy on Hispanic adolescents and their families

308j   Bringing in the family: Kinship support and contraceptive behavior

308k   Family involvement, notification, and responsibility: A personal essay

309a   Teenage family formation in postwar America

309r   Family support: Helping teenage mothers to cope

310l   Women as targets in India's family planning policy

313i   The fiction of family: Ideology and narrative in Elsa Morante

316f   Knots in the family tie

317e   Intergenerational relations in later life: A family system approach

317f   The widowed family member

319a   Family planning practices of Mexican Americans

319k   Social networks and survival strategies: An exploratory study of Mexican American, black and Anglo family female heads in San Jose, California

320o   Family formation and educational attainment

325g   Hindu women's family and household rites in a north Indian village

327a   A sociological perspective on the causes of family violence

327b   Discussion: Violence in the family

327c   Television viewing, family style and aggressive behavior in preschool children

327d   Discussion: Television violence and the family

327e   Ethnopsychiatric dimensions in family violence

327f   Discussion: Violence and the family in perspective

327g   Functions of the police and the justice system in family violence

335a   'The most important thing of all' - Rethinking the family: An overview

335b   'Smash the family?' Recalling the 1960s

335c   From utopian to scientific feminism? Early feminist critiques of the family

335d   Production rules OK? Waged work and the family

335f   Sex - A family affair

335g   Home thoughts from not so far away: A personal look at family

335i   No turning back - Thatcherism, the family and the future

339j   One family's decision: A leave of absence

344f   The origin of the family

345e   The family

349x   Reform school families

358b   Watching the family

359q   A starving family: An interactional view of anorexia nervosa

359z   Attitudes toward parenting in dual-career families

359aa Female-headed families: Trends and implications

359bb Lesbian families: Cultural and clinical issues

359tt A feminist approach to family therapy

365g   Marital and family conflicts

368n   Family planning in post-revolutionary Iran

370c   Sexual demography: The impact of the slave trade on family structure

374g   Appendix B: The family code

379r   The effects of the Chinese Revolution on women and their families

380g   Bringing down the rear: The decline in the economic position of single-mother families

380l   Women's work and the family wage in Canada

380r   Research on women's work and the family at the urban institute

387h   The work-family role system

387p   Dilemmas and contradictions of status: The case of the dual-career family

388c   Singapore women: Work and the family

390a   Women and the family in Australian history

393d   Worlds apart? A comparative study of European and African traditional family life as depicted in the novels of Laurie Lee and Camara Laye

393e   The stable African family: Traditional and modern family structures in two African societies (Basa and Manding)

395f   Perceptions of a family planning campaign in rural Mexico

395h   Family planning in rural China

396a   Male hegemony in family planning

400c   Women's income earning activities and family welfare in Bangladesh

402e   Family status and female work participation

402k   Etiquette among women in Karnataka: Forms of address in the village and the family

404u   The role of the family in teenage pregnancy: Support or sabotage

406b   Woman's place: The absent family of film noir

413h   Women, work and family: 1880-1926

418a   Work and the family: Who gets 'the best of both worlds'?

418c   The history of the family

418e   Left critiques of the family

421a   Cultural determinants of power for women within the family: A neglected aspect of family research

421c   A causal interpretation of the effect of mother's education and employment status on parental decision-making role patterns in the Korean family

421t   Fertility and family economy in the Iranian rural communities

421y   Variations in women's roles and family life under the socialist regime in China

423d   Women's work and family roles

424i   Women's work: Factory, family and social class in an industrializing order

424j   Making the bread and bringing it home: Female factory workers and the family economy

424r   Women, work and the family in a developing society: Taiwan

424t   Female employment and the family: A case study of the Bataan Export Processing Zone

426c   The apprenticeship model of organizational careers: A response to changes in the relation between work and family

427a   Introduction: Government response to working women and their families: Values, the policy-making process, and research utilization

427d   Child care options and decisions: Facts and figurings for families

427f   Men, women, work, and family

427i Conceptions of kinship and the family reproduction cycle

429b Small church — big family

440c Redistribution to children and to mothers: A history of child endowment and family allowances

440h Population policies and family policies: State construction of domestic life

446a Women, work, and family: New Soviet perspectives

446j Women's work and the family

446k Changing family roles and marital instability

446l Changes in the status of women and the demographic development of the family

446n Women with large families: A sociodemographic analysis

454c Widowhood in eighteenth-century Massachusetts: A problem in the history of the family

454k Family limitation, sexual control, and domestic feminism in Victorian America

454m Women and their families on the Overland Trail, 1842-1867

459e Family structure and women's reproductive and productive roles: Some conceptual and methodological issues

465c Who still cares for the family? Recent developments in income maintenance, taxation and family law

467c Managing work and family life: A comparative policy overview

467f The impact of work on the family

469e Transactional family patterns: A preliminary exploration of Puerto Rican female adolescents

469k Family roles of Hispanic women: Stereotypes, empirical findings, and implications for research

472c Social class and the older family member

Family Ties

332o *Family Ties*: Female development in Clarice Lispector

Famine

341f Feast and famine: Gifts of the goddess

Fandango

440j The women's movement's fandango with the state: The movement's role in public policy since 1972

Fantasia

313d Foucault's fantasia for feminists: The woman reading

Fantasy

7n The politics of sado-masochistic fantasies

33a The education of women in the Middle Ages in theory, fact, and fantasy

133i Gay fantasies in gay publications

134f Dance and social fantasy

136j The development of sex differences in nonverbal signals: Fallacies, facts, and fantasies

212c 'On the other side of the billboard...': Pornography, male fantasies and the objectification of women

225p Fat and the fantasy of perfection

231p Master and slave: The fantasy of erotic domination

245d The fantasy of the perfect mother

448g A wilderness of one's own: Feminist fantasy novels of the twenties: Rebecca West and Sylvia Townsend Warner

Far from the Madding Crowd

286g Bathsheba's lovers: Male sexuality in *Far from the Madding Crowd*

Farah

192m Women at Farah: An unfinished story

201k Women at Farah: An unfinished story

Farewell

30m Farewell to the farm

Farm

see also Agriculture, Farmer

30m Farewell to the farm

86f Following the harvest: The health hazards of migrant and seasonal farmworking women

104d Co-operation on and between eastern Finnish family farms

104e The estimation of work in a northern Finnish farming community

104f A note on the custom of 'paying off' on family farms in Poland

263f The sexual division of labor on American farms: 1750-1850

263g "Mom, it's a losing proposition": The decline of women's subsistence production on Iowa farms

310e Egg farming and women's future

341l Farming out the home: Women and agribusiness

Farm Security Administration

81g Photographing women: The Farm Security Administration work of Marion Post Wolcott

Farmer

see also Agriculture, Farm

373m The plight of the invisible farmer: The effect of national agriculture policy on women in Africa

385j Women farmers and inequities in agricultural services

466g Housewives and farmers: Malay women in the Muda Irrigation Scheme

Farris, Evlyn

157h Evlyn Farris and the University Women's Club

Fascism

95h Communist women and the fascist experience

102d Religion and the fearful father: Vision of liberation or American-style fascism?

405i The anti-fascist front of women and the Communist Party in Croatia: Conflicts within the resistance

Fashion

353t The rise and fall of Battey's operation: A fashion in surgery

442j Women and fashion

453i Women and fashion

Fast Track

339i Does becoming a parent mean falling off the fast track?

Fat

190a Fatness, menarche, and fertility

225p Fat and the fantasy of perfection

341b Thin fat people

341h Pregnancy: Is motherhood fattening?

Father

see also Family

37o Involvement of fathers in the socialization of black children

40p My father's passage

40z In the name of the father: The poetry of Audre Lord

56c Taking care of the little woman: Father-physician relations during pregnancy and childbirth

86j Mother, father, worker: Men and women and the reproduction risks of work

102a A society without fathers: Cooperative commonwealth or harmonious ant-heap?

102d Religion and the fearful father: Vision of liberation or American-style fascism?

102e Toward psychoanalytic feminism: The mother in dream-stealing, the father in dreams

102f Why the fathers cannot solve the problems: Some possible clues

103m Daddy's right: Incestuous assault

116n The obligations of mothers and fathers

140p Father-daughter incest

140q Families at risk for father-daughter incest

158b Freud's heritage: Fathers and daughters in German literature (1750-1850)

178j Fathers' support to mothers and children

190g Menarche: Its effects on mother-daughter and father-daughter interactions

195a The obligations of mothers and fathers

204g Primary caregiving and role-sharing fathers

204j Social development and parent-child interaction in father-custody and stepmother families

212k Fatherhood: Bringing it all back home

245f Mothering, fathering, and mental illness

284j Father-daughter incest

284l Humanistic treatment of father-daughter incest

309m Teenage mothers and teenage fathers: The impact of early childbearing on the parents' personal and professional lives

328d Fathers in general: The patriarchy in Virginia Woolf's fiction

352n Working and parenting: The male and father role

359oo Incest between fathers and daughters

369k Mothers, fathers, and children: From private to public patriarchy

427c Fathers, mothers, and childcare in the 1980s: Family influences on child development

460o Daughters and lovers: Reflections on the life cycle of father-daughter relationships

460p Role of the father

Fatigue

233i Occupational fatigue and preterm birth

Fatimeh

368e Fatimeh as a role model in the works of Ali Shariati

Faulkner, William

17o William Faulkner: A feminist consideration

Fauntleroy, Little Lord
17p Hemingway and Fauntleroy: An androgynous pursuit

Faust
448n Sister to Faust: The city's "hungry" woman as heroine

Faust
32c *Faust*: The tragedy reexamined

Favorite
313f Mis brujas favoritas

Fawcett, Millicent Garrett
125k Millicent Garrett Fawcett: Duty and determination

FCI
see Federal Corrections Institution

Fear
see also Emotion
29m Anxiety-related disorders, fears, and phobias
165a One hundred years of fear: Rape and the medical profession
271j Beyond the fear of success: Observations on women's fears
352l How real is fear of success?
463p The transportation implications of women's fear of assault

Fear of Flying
127j *Fear of Flying*: Developing the feminist novel

Feast
194e An Italian religious feast: The *Fujenti* rites of the Madonna dell'Arco, Naples
341a Introduction: Beauty and the feast
341f Feast and famine: Gifts of the goddess

Federal
23h Women and women's issues in the 1980 federal elections
65l A review of federal court decisions under Title VII of the Civil Rights Act of 1964
65n Comparable worth under various federal and state laws
70k American Indian women: Their relationship to the federal government
80o The politics of federal day care regulation
93d The effectiveness of federal laws prohibiting sex discrimination in employment in the United States
111q Sex-role concepts among federal female offenders
288l A federal response to sexual harassment: Policy-making at Johnson Space Center, NASA

Federal Corrections Institute (FCI)
63c Co-corrections-FCI Forth Worth after three years

Federation
211k Women and power in the Federation

Feeling
40t Nikki Giovanni: Taking a chance on feeling
271p Feeling states and the menstrual cycle
285f Sexual feelings in the terminally ill patient

Fefu and her Friends
399ww *Fefu and Her Friends*

Felix Holt
142l The unity of *Felix Holt*
143f Law, religion and the unity of *Felix Holt*

Fellow
394p An E.B. Fred Fellow

Felon
376a The certain wages of sin: Sentence and punishment of female felons in colonial Massachusetts, 1673-1774
376g Women before the law: Females as felons and prey in fourteenth-century England

Fem
225q The fem question

Female-Headed
359aa Female-headed families: Trends and implications

Femenina
363c Women and revolution: The brigadas femeninas and the Mexican Cristero Rebellion, 1926-1929

Femicide
310p Technology and prenatal femicide

Feminine
11b Femininity by the bottle
22a "Glory is like a circle in the water"...Thoughts and suggestions towards a definition of feminine historical research
27e George Sand and the myth of femininity
32a The eternal feminine is leading us on
63f Styles of doing time in a coed prison: Masculine and feminine alternatives
69a Feminine development: Changes in psychoanalytic theory
69b Changing views of the relationship between femininity and reproduction
74a "Feminine" testimony in the works of Teresa de la Parra, María Luisa Bombal, and Victoria Ocampo
102b Breaking free of symbolic bondage: From feminine submission to a vision of equality
109e The reconstruction of the gothic feminine ideal in Emily Brontë's *Wuthering Heights*
109m The Radcliffean gothic model: A form for feminine sexuality
116a The feminine as a universal
116d Freud: Masculinity, femininity, and reproduction
116e "Femininity," resistance and sabotage
116f The political epistemology of "masculine" and "feminine"
131l Charles Bronson, Samurai, and other feminine images: A transactive response to *The Left Hand of Darkness*
134b Femininity and adolescence
135d Masculine and feminine personae in the love poetry of Christine dePisan
154e Christine de Pizan's *Livre des Trois Vertus*: Feminine ideal or practical advice?
158g "Rather worse than folly?" psychology measures femininity and masculinity, 1: From Terman and Miles to the Guilfords
158h Psychology measures femininity and masculinity, 2: From "13 Gay Men" to the instrumental-expressive distinction
164i *Mansfield Park*: The revolt of the 'feminine' woman

185h The evolution of sex roles: The transformation of masculine and feminine values
187i Feminine lay piety in the High Middle Ages: The Beguines
211t Steps toward feminine imagery of deity in Jewish theology
211u Bride, spouse, daughter: Images of the feminine in classical Jewish sources
212b Femininity, masculinity and sexuality
214d Rhetoric and organizational change: New applications of feminine style
214h Styles of leadership: Power and feminine values
220d Poverty: The feminine complaint
242e Writing (from) the feminine: George Sand and the novel of female pastoral
265a Parents' sex role attitudes and children's concepts of femininity and masculinity
265e Language and attitudes toward masculine and feminine sex role
304f Women and agoraphobia: A case for the etiological significance of the feminine sex-role stereotype
304h Women's assertion and the feminine sex-role stereotype
356o The "feminine" language of Marianne Moore
387g Industrialization and femininity: A case study of nineteenth-century New England
442d Gertrude Stein: The complex force of her femininity
442f Shapes of the feminine experience in art
460i Femininity
466k The feminization of the teaching profession in Singapore

Feminism
see also Feminist, Feminist Critique, Women's Liberation, Women's Movement
7g Feminism and sadomasochism: Self-critical notes
7s Sadism, masochism, and lesbian-feminism
13l Feminism: An early tradition amongst western Australian labor women
14d Selected bibliography on black feminism
17a Charles Brockden Brown: Feminism in fiction
23a Political science, women and feminism
23d Women, feminism and the political process
32o Verena Stefan's *Häutungen*: Homoeroticism and feminism
35g Explaining "male chauvinism" and "feminism": Cultural differences in male and female reproductive strategies
43c Fundamental feminism: Process and perspective
50i Feminism and science
60b Male vice and female virtue: Feminism and the politics of prostitution in nineteenth-century Britain
60f The twenties' backlash: Compulsory heterosexuality, the consumer family, and the waning of feminism
60g Antifeminism and the New Right
60h Feminism, the family, and the New Right
76d Feminism and psychoanalysis
78z Marxist feminism: Implications for criminal justice

81j International feminism between the wars: The National Woman's Party versus the League of Women Voters

81m Socialist feminism between the two World Wars: Insights from oral history

91e Theological issues raised by feminism

91g Challenge of feminism to the church: A Bishop's perspective

94f Women on the move: Migration and feminism

95c When radical and socialist feminism were joined: The extraordinary failure of Madeleine Pelletier

95f Feminism: The essential ingredient in Federica Montseny's anarchist theory

95i Humanism versus feminism in the socialist movement: The life of Angelica Balabanoff

102e Toward psychoanalytic feminism: The mother in dream-stealing, the father in dreams

103v Afterword: Feminism and families in a liberal policy

114f Holding fast to feminism and moving beyond: Suzy McKee Charnas's *The Vampire Tapestry*

114h Sex, satire, and feminism in the science fiction of Suzette Haden Elgin

117a Introduction: Feminism and art history

118b Feminism and process thought: A two-way relationship

119b Feminism and the definition of cultural politics

120b Feminism and the critique of scientific method

120e Feminism and the writing and teaching of history

120h The personal is political: Feminism and the helping professions

120k Feminist praxis: Feminism and revolution; feminist theory and feminist practice

129a The roots of individualist feminism in 19th-century America

132h Introduction: Psychoanalysis and feminism in France

132q Black women and feminism

135m The laughter of maidens, the crackle of matriarchs: Notes on the collision between comedy and feminism

150ii Black macho and black feminism

168b From feminism to a new conception of ethics

174a If the mortarboard fits...radical feminism in academia

174z Charlotte Bunch and Betty Powell talk about feminism, blacks, and education as politics

181g Toward an ecological feminism and a feminist ecology

182a Women, architects and feminism

189d Women lost and found: The impact of feminism on history

189e Some of the boys won't play any more: The impact of feminism on sociology

189f Toward the emasculation of political science: The impact of feminism

189h Psychology and feminism - if you can't beat them, join them

189i The oldest, the most established, the most quantitative of the social sciences - and most dominated by men; The impact of feminism on economics

189j The impact of feminism on media studies - just another commercial break?

189k Education: The patriarchal paradigm and the response to feminism

189l Before and after: The impact of feminism on the academic discipline of law

189m Medicine as 'old husbands' tales': The impact of feminism

189n The emperor doesn't wear any clothes: The impact of feminism on biology

193s Feminism and science teaching: Some classroom observations

195q Feminism, pronatalism, and motherhood

223b Love and feminism

223s Pornography, feminism, and censorship

225v Search for tomorrow: On feminism and the reconstruction of teen romance

229kk Metaphysical feminism

229tt The Christian right's "Holy War" against feminism

231f Feminism, men, and modern love: Greenwich Village, 1900-1925

231y What we're rollin around in bed with: Sexual silences in feminism

231cc Male vice and female virtue: Feminism and the politics of prostitution in nineteenth-century Britain

231dd The new feminism of yin and yang

231ee Feminism, moralism, and pornography

231hh The fear that feminism will free men first

245c Why nineteenth-century feminists did not support "birth control" and twentieth-century feminists do: Feminism, reproduction, and the family

255h From purdah to politics: The social feminism of the all-India women's organizations

256f "The men are as bad as their masters...": Socialism, feminism and sexual antagonism in the London tailoring trade in the 1830s

275e Linguistics and feminism

307ff Feminism: A catalyst for the future

311d Feminism: A last chance for the humanities?

312f Feminism: A last chance for the humanities?

316j The lost cause: The aging woman in American feminism

319n Feminism: The Chicana and the Anglo versions, a historical analysis

335c From utopian to scientific feminism? Early feminist critiques of the family

335e 'The serious burdens of love?' Some questions on child-care, feminism and socialism

336h Sisterhood under siege: Feminism and anti-semitism in Germany, 1904-1938

344gg Keep us on the pedestal: Women against feminism in twentieth century America

352f Feminism and the woman school administrator

353bb Professionalism, feminism, and gender roles: A comparative study of nineteenth-century medical therapeutics

356c Textual feminism

356j Women's speech: The voice of feminism

359d The conflict between nurturance and autonomy in mother-daughter relationships and within feminism

359pp Psychotherapy with women clients: The impact of feminism

369b The unhappy marriage of Marxism and feminism: Towards a more progressive union

369d Socialism, feminism, and gay/lesbian liberation

369e The incompatible menage á trois: Marxism, feminism, and racism

369f The unhappy marriage of Marxism and feminism: Can it be saved?

369h Capitalism is an advanced stage of patriarchy: But Marxism is not feminism

369i Marxism and feminism: Unhappy marriage, trial separation or something else?

378g Unity is strength? Feminism and the labor movement

379n Feminism, professionalism, and germs: A study of the thought of Mary Putnam Jacobi and Elizabeth Blackwell

383b Method in her madness: Feminism in the crazy utopian vision of Tiptree's Courier

384c A study of feminism as a motif in "A journey to Pike's Peak and New Mexico" by Julia Archibald Holmes

384i The western roots of feminism in Agnes Smedley's *Daughter of Earth*

384k Hamlin Garland's feminism

388k Social feminism in France: A case study

405a Marxism, feminism, and sex equality

405d Socialism and feminism: The first stages of women's organizations in the eastern part of the Austrian empire

406h Klute 2: Feminism and Klute

408l Sara de Etcheverts: The contradictions of literary feminism

419k The role of women in Roman elegy: Counter-cultural feminism

439b Sex and power: Sexual bases of radical feminism

441h Feminist pedagogy and technology: Reflections on the Goddard feminism and ecology summer program

442o Reflections on feminism: Implications for today

443c The convergence of psychoanalysis and feminism: Gender identity and autonomy

444f Communist feminism: Its synthesis and demise

449d Feminism and literary technique in Ting Ling's early short stories

454k Family limitation, sexual control, and domestic feminism in Victorian America

457b Theosophy and feminism: Some explorations in nineteenth century biography

462d Making the world live: Feminism and the domination of nature

Feminist

see also Feminism, Feminist Critique

3o Abortion and the culture: Toward a feminist perspective

7w Sadomasochism: A contra-feminist activity

14b A black feminist's search for sisterhood

14c A black feminist statement

15j   Publishers on libraries: The library as motherlode: A feminist view

16f   The feminist Women's Health Center

17c   Thwarted nature: Nathaniel Hawthorne as feminist

17h   The *Bostonians*: Feminists and the new world

17o   William Faulkner: A feminist consideration

23l   Psychoanalysis and feminist social theory of gender

31d   A different reality: Feminist ontology

31n   A feminist analysis of the Universal Declaration of Human Rights

31q   Contemporary feminist perspectives on women and higher education

32f   A German writer and feminist in nineteenth century America: An archival study of Mathilde Franziska Anneke

32n   The question of a feminist aesthetic and Karin Struck's *Klassenliebe*

36g   Woman-controlled birth control: A feminist analysis of natural birth control

43d   Beyond either/or: Feminist options

43p   Do feminists need Marxism?

43w   The feminist workplace

43x   Building feminist organizations

46h   The housewife and social security reform: A feminist perspective

50x   Making science feminist

59a   Feminist theology and spirituality

59b   Emerging issues in feminist biblical interpretation

59c   The feminist redemption of Christ

60a   Notes toward a feminist dialectic

60c   The feminist theology of the black Baptist church, 1880-1900

60v   The challenge of profamily politics: A feminist defense of sexual freedom

79l   The politics of prenatal diagnosis: A feminist ethical analysis

79s   Living with an impaired neonate and child: A feminist issue

81l   Discontented black feminists: Prelude and postscript to the passage of the nineteenth amendment

84f   Charlotte Perkins Gilman: Forerunner of a feminist social science

84o   The feminist standpoint: Developing the ground for a specifically feminist historical materialism

91c   Feminist liberation theology: Its past and future

91d   The feminist viewpoint

91i   Through the feminist looking glass: Images of women

91m   Moral theology from a feminist perspective

95a   Anna Kuliscioff: Russian revolutionist, Italian feminist

95d   Sylvia Pankhurst: Suffragist, feminist, or socialist?

101e   Catalysts or helpers? British feminists, Indian women's rights, and Indian independence

103t   Reproductive freedom and the right to privacy: A paradox for feminists

118a   Androgynous life: A feminist appropriation of process thought

118c   Openness and mutuality in process thought and feminist action

119e   The family in socialist-feminist politics

120a   Memoirs of an ontological exile: The methodological rebellions of feminist research

120c   Gynocentric values and feminist psychology

120k   Feminist praxis: Feminism and revolution; feminist theory and feminist practice

122c   Seeking feminist transformation of the sciences and the teaching of science

124c   Notes on technique in feminist drama: *Apple Pie* and *Signs of Life*

124d   Widening the dialogue on feminist science fiction

124i   Feminist research methodology groups: Origins, forms, functions

124k   Split brain research and its implications for feminist education

125e   Margaret Fuller: Feminist writer and revolutionary

125j   Alice Paul: The quintessential feminist

125s   Vera Brittain: Feminist in a new age

125u   Simone de Beauvoir: Dilemmas of a feminist radical

125v   Modern feminist theorists: Reinventing rebellion

126a   The genesis of feminist visions for transforming the liberal arts curriculum

126f   A feminist challenge to Darwinism: Antoinette L. B. Blackwell on the relations of the sexes in nature and society

127j   *Fear of Flying*: Developing the feminist novel

129t   Are feminist businesses capitalistic?

131e   Coming Home: Four feminist utopias and patriarchal experience

131f   Recent feminist utopias

132g   To be or not to be ... a feminist speaker

133t   Lesbianfeminist rhetoric as a social movement

135g   Olive Schreiner - A note on sexist language and the feminist writer

140l   Cinderella's stepsisters: A feminist perspective on anorexia nervosa and bulimia

140t   A feminist approach to family therapy

150jj   Black lesbian/feminist organizing: A conversation

155b   French feminist theater and the subject of prostitution, 1870-1914

168d   What has the feminist perspective done for Canadian history?

168g   Production et communication du savior dans une perspective féministe: Enjuex et défis pour les femmes

168h   Creating and communicating knowledge from a feminist perspective: Risks and challenges for women

174g   Teaching the feminist minority

174l   Califia: An experiment in feminist education Califia community

174m   Feminist art and education at Califia: My personal experience

174o   Feminist education at the feminist studio workshop

174r   A feminist chautauqua for a rural state

174v   Feminist values: Guidelines for a teaching methodology in women's studies

174y   What are rights without means? Educating feminists for the future

174aa   Friends and critics: The feminist academy

176h   Lesbian literature: A Third World feminist perspective

176j   Teaching the psychology of women: A lesbian feminist perspective

181l   What if...science and technology in feminist utopias

187d   Benedictine life for women in central France, 850-1100: A feminist revival

195j   On conceiving motherhood and sexuality: A feminist materialist approach

206q   We are what we wear - The dilemma of the feminist consumer

211i   A feminist path to Judaism

211p   History, fiction, and the tradition: Creating a Jewish feminist poetic

211v   Feminist Judaism: Restoration of the moon

212d   Towards a revolutionary feminist analysis of rape

212m   Male feminists and divided women

212r   What can one do with a son? Feminist politics and male children

220f   Feminist counselling: Approach or technique?

224i   Lesbianism: A socialist feminist perspective

225b   Seeking ecstasy on the battlefield: Danger and pleasure in nineteenth-century feminist sexual thought

225c   The taming of the id: Feminist sexual politics, 1968-83

229u   Feminist witchcraft: Controlling our own inner space

229v   Contemporary feminist rituals

229cc   Feeding the feminist psyche through ritual theater

229jj   The politics of feminist spirituality

229mm   Feminist spirituality: The politics of the psyche

229qq   On common ground: Native American and feminist spirituality approaches in the struggle to save mother earth

229rr   Spiritual dimensions of feminist anti-nuclear activism

229yy   Afterword: Feminist politics and the nature of mind

240m   A feminist perspective on women and health

245a   Feminist rethinking of the family: An overview

245c   Why nineteenth-century feminists did not support "birth control" and twentieth-century feminists do: Feminism, reproduction, and the family

246a   Introduction: Feminist perceptions in anthropology

254a   Seeing our way clear: Feminist re-vision of the academy

254j   The problem: Idealism and accommodation in the feminist transformation of the academy

257g   Is a feminist heterosexuality possible?

257i From where I stand: A case for feminist bisexuality

257k Duty and desire: Creating a feminist morality

275i Feminist linguistics in philosophy

283d Feminists - The degenerates of the social?

283e Reply: Feminists - The degenerates of the social?

294k From delicacy to dilemma: A feminist perspective

305f Once more with feeling: Heterosexuality and feminist consciousness

305h Providing services the feminist way

305k Getting organized...in the feminist unions

305x Working with words: Feminist publishing in Canada

305z But is it feminist art?

306i Feminist pedagogy: Lost voices of American women

307h Women and appropriate technology: A feminist assessment

310aa Who is going to rock the petri dish? For feminists who have considered parthenogenesis when the movement is not enough

310ee Feminist ethics, ecology and vision

311e How to do what we want to do: Thoughts about feminist methodology

312g How to do what we want to do: Thoughts about feminist methodology

312h Passionate scholarship: Notes on values, knowing and method in feminist social science

312i Towards a methodology for feminist research

312j The value of quantitative methodology for feminist research

312k Experiential analysis: A contribution to feminist research

312l 'Back into the personal' or: Our attempt to construct 'feminist research'

313d Foucault's fantasia for feminists: The woman reading

313m A feminist reading of "Los ojos verdes"

313r Hacia un análisis feminista de *Tres tristes tigres*

315d Feminist counseling

329k *The Years*: A feminist novel

341e Women in the kitchen: The feminist boiling point

344dd The first feminists

344ff Feminist consciousness and black women

349k The victim in a forcible rape case: A feminist view

353g Voluntary motherhood: The beginnings of feminist birth control ideas in the United States

353q The perils of feminist history

353aa Feminist showplace

356a Linguistics and the feminist challenge

359r Cinderella's stepsisters: A feminist perspective on anorexia nervosa and bulimia

359ss A feminist works with nontraditional clients

359tt A feminist approach to family therapy

359xx A decade of feminist influence on psychotherapy

369j Cultural Marxism: Nonsynchrony and feminist practice

379e Was she a good mother? Some thoughts on a new issue for feminist biography

381b But will men like it? Or living as a feminist writer without committing murder

383c Utopia at the end of a male chauvinist dystopian world: Suzy McKee Charnas's feminist science fiction

383g *The Left Hand of Darkness*: Androgyny and the feminist utopia

387u Unresolved questions: Three feminist perspectives

396e Seizing the means of reproduction: An illegal feminist abortion collective — how and why it worked

398f 'They shared a laboratory together': Feminist collaboration in the academy

398h Beyond defensiveness: A feminist research strategies

399u Looking to women: Rachel Crothers and the feminist heroine

399qq Feminist theatre: A rhetorical phenomenon

399ss The Washington area feminist theatre

399tt New York feminist theater troupe

408i Gertrude the Great: Avellaneda, nineteenth-century feminist

413k Pioneer into feminist: Jane Mander's heroines

416n Class, race, sex, scientific objects of knowledge: A socialist-feminist perspective on the social construction of productive nature and some political consequences

417f Frances Wright: Utopian feminist

417q Twin Oaks: A feminist looks at indigenous socialism in the United States

417w Motherhood in feminist utopias

417aa Of time and revolution: Theories of social change in contemporary feminist science fiction

417ff Future visions: Today's politics: Feminist utopias in review

418k Feminist thought and reproductive control: The state and 'the right to choose'

419i Plato: Misogynist, phaedophile, and feminist

421k Feminist egalitarianism, social action orientation and occupational roles: A cross-national study

434n Toward a feminist model for planning for and with women

435i Antiobscenity: A comparison of the legal and feminist perspectives

443d Feminist psychoanalysis: Theory and practice

443l A feminist approach to math-anxiety reduction

443m Some feminist concerns in an age of networking

448g A wilderness of one's own: Feminist fantasy novels of the twenties: Rebecca West and Sylvia Townsend Warner

452m Towards a theory of form in feminist autobiography: Kate Millett's *Flying* and *Sita*; Maxine Hong Kingston's *The Woman Warrior*

453p Feminist theology

453s Feminist women's health centers

462j A black response to feminist theology

462o Feminist liberation theology and Yahweh as holy warrior: An analysis of symbol

462y A feminist approach to alternative enterprises

462v Claiming the center: A critical feminist theology of liberation

464a Power as ideology: A feminist analysis

472j Now for the feminist menopause that refreshes

Feminist Critique
see also Critique, Feminism, Feminist

7q Is sadomasochism feminist? A critique of the Samois position

14p Toward a black feminist criticism

85h The gatekeepers: A feminist critique of academic publishing

106k The family in contemporary feminist thought: A critical review

121a Introduction: Feminist critics read Emily Dickinson

122e The best feminist criticism is a new criticism

122q Marital metaphors in the Judeo-Christian tradition: A feminist critique

123b New directions for feminist criticism in theatre and the related arts

123c The feminist critique in religious studies

126h Against the grain: A working feminist art criticism

135s Feminist criticism reviewed

136i A feminist critique of androgyny: Toward the elimination of gender attributions for learned behavior

168c Hindsight is 20/20: The development, achievements and dilemmas of feminist literary criticism

176u Is feminist criticism really feminist?

189b Dancing through the minefield: Some observations on the theory, practice and politics of a feminist literary criticism

203m Architecture: Toward a feminist critique

223a Love: A feminist critique

247a Feminist film criticism: An introduction

247b Developments in feminist film criticism

247c The woman at the keyhole: Women's cinema and feminist criticism

313a Crítica feminista: Apuntes sobre definiciones y problemas

342g Feminist analysis of gender: A critique

406a Klute 1: A contemporary film noir and feminist criticism

464e Prologue to a feminist critique of war and politics

464g Consequences of seizing the reins in the household: A Marxist-feminist critique of Marx and Engels

Feminist Movement
see also Movement, Women's Movement

81i All pink sisters: The War Department and the feminist movement in the 1920s

147j Women's participation in sporting activities as an indicator of a feminist movement in Canada between 1867-1914

198f Early feminist movements in Turkey and Egypt

462g "Las Marías" of the feminist movement

Feminist Scholarship

174h   Feminist scholarship: The extent of the revolution

296j   Women and power within the historical dynamic of feminist scholarship

Feminist Theory

see also Theory

13j   Some problems and developments in Marxist feminist theory

31b   Human biology in feminist theory: Sexual equality reconsidered

31l   Feminist theory: The private and the public

120k   Feminist praxis: Feminism and revolution; feminist theory and feminist practice

125v   Modern feminist theorists: Reinventing rebellion

126c   Women knowing: Feminist theory and perspectives on pedagogy

174u   Not by degrees: Feminist theory and education

256i   The doubled vision of feminist theory

383j   Beyond defensiveness: Feminist research strategies

450l   Rita Mae Brown: Feminist theorist and southern novelist

Feminist Therapy

16c   Issues in feminist therapy: The work of a woman's study group

54f   Feminist therapy with female alcoholics

136m   Nonverbal processes in feminist therapy

150kk Reflections on black feminist therapy

360n   Feminist therapy: Implications for practitioners

365j   Feminist therapy

443a   Authenticity in feminist therapy

443i   Feminist therapy with minority clients

453r   Feminist therapy

Feminization

49f   The feminization of the labor force: Research for industrial/organizational psychology

139i   Feminisation and unionisation: A case study from banking

Femmage

117q   Miriam Schapiro and "femmage": Reflections on the conflict between decoration and abstraction in twentieth-century art

Ferguson, Miriam Amanda

175q   Pardon me, Governor Ferguson

Ferrara

33b   Women, learning, and power: Eleonora of Aragon and the Court of Ferrara

Ferré, Rosario

74g   From a woman's perspective: The short stories of Rosario Ferré and Ana Lydia Vega

Fertility

see also Reproduce

34e   No fertile women need apply: Employment discrimination and reproductive hazards in the workplace

38c   Black fertility: Recent demographic and sociological influences

79gg   The case against in vitro fertilization and implantation

79hh   In defense of in vitro fertilization

79ii   In vitro fertilization and embryo transfer: The process of making public policy

98h   Personal account of the role of a supervisor in the Bangladesh fertility survey

140k   Roles and role conflict of women in infertile couples

184l   Women's work and European fertility patterns

190a   Fatness, menarche, and fertility

240e   Infertility and alternative parenting

270f   Sex roles, value of children and fertility in Turkey

273b   Measuring sex preferences and their effects on fertility

273d   Timing of fertilization and the sex ratio of offspring

281b   The sexual self and fertility

308a   Teenage women in the United States: Sex, contraception, pregnancy, fertility, and maternal and infant health

309j   Some speculations on the future of marriage and fertility

309o   Early childbearing and subsequent fertility

309x   Teenagers: Fertility control behavior and attitudes before and after abortion, childbearing or negative pregnancy test

385l   Fertility and employment: An assessment of role incompatibility among African urban women

387l   The future of American fertility

393f   Plural marriage, fertility and the problem of multiple causation

393g   Education and fertility among Cameroonian working women

393h   The relationship between education and fertility

405n   Some demographic, particularly fertility, correlates of female status in eastern Europe and the republics of the Soviet Union

413d   Fertility, sexuality and social control in New Zealand

421s   Labor force participation and fertility, contraceptive knowledge, attitude and practice of the women of Barbados

421t   Fertility and family economy in the Iranian rural communities

424q   Effect of female labour force participation on fertility: The case of construction workers in Chiang Mai City

447l   Fetotoxicity and fertile female employees

456l   Infertility

457f   Women, fertility and the worship of gods in a Hindu village

459b   The allocation of women's time and its relation to fertility

459g   The interrelationship between the division of labour in the household, women's roles and their impact on fertility

Festival of Women

316p   Status report on the women's movement as indexed by a "Festival of Women" in West Virginia, Fall 1978

Fetal Alcoholism Syndrome

79k   Policy decisions in prenatal diagnosis: The example of fetal alcoholism syndrome

Fetotoxicity

447l   Fetotoxicity and fertile female employees

Fetus

see also Reproduce

2d   The juridical status of the fetus: A proposal for legal protection of the unborn

9p   The effects of alcohol on the fetus and offspring

9q   The effects of opiates, sedative-hypnotics, amphetamines, cannabis, and other psychoactive drugs on the fetus and newborn

11h   Fetal alcohol syndrome and drinking during pregnancy

36n   The electronic fetal monitor in perinatology

36p   Benefits and risks of electronic fetal monitoring

173b   The juridical status of the fetus: A proposal for legal protection of the unborn

233b   The effect of work on placental function and fetal growth

252n   Termination of pregnancy after intrauterine foetal death

345c   The foetal alcohol syndrome

Fever

40g   The field of the fever, the time of the tall-walkers

Fiction

see also Literature, individual types of fiction, e.g, Short Story

17a   Charles Brockden Brown: Feminism in fiction

17r   Papa Dick and Sister-Woman: Reflections on women in the fiction of Richard Wright

27k   A *Passage to India* as "marriage fiction": Forster's sexual politics

27m   Women and madness in the fiction of Joyce Carol Oates

38f   She who is black and mother: In sociology and fiction, 1940-1970

40x   Escape from Trublem: The fiction of Gayl Jones

40bb   The closing of the circle: Movement from division to wholeness in Paule Marshall's fiction

79kk   The biology of utopia: Science fiction perspectives on ectogenesis

126i   The fallen woman in fiction

130l   The novelists and their fictions

131o   Where's all the fiction in science fiction?

135i   May Sarton and fictions of old age

150q   Cultural legacy denied and discovered: Black lesbians in fiction by women

155e   The romantization of the prostitute in Dostoevsky's fiction

155f   The prostitute in Arab and North African fiction

180j   Mothers and daughters in the fiction of the New Republic

180t   A psychological journey: Mothers and daughters in English-Canadian fiction

190q   "Oh dear me! Why weren't we all boys, then there wouldn't be any bother": Menarche and popular American fiction

196e   On exile and fiction: The Leweses and the Shelleys

197c   Autonomy and fabulation in the fiction of Muriel Spark

211p History, fiction, and the tradition: Creating a Jewish feminist poetic

229ee Images of spiritual power in women's fiction

232e A note on the nobility of women in popular Tamil fiction

242a Fictional consensus and female casualties

242b The birth of the artist as heroine: (Re)production, the *Künslerroman* tradition, and the fiction of Katherine Mansfield

278e Sexual fiction in America, 1955-80

301j My Aunt Isadora (fiction)

301n Ole black Emelda (fiction)

301bb Paralyzed (fiction)

301ff Spilled salt (fiction)

301ii Delta (fiction)

301nn The lonesomes ain't no spring picnic (fiction)

313i The fiction of family: Ideology and narrative in Elsa Morante

315c Still crazy after all these years: The uses of madness in women's fiction

318a Passionate portrayal of things to come: Doris Lessing's recent fiction

318b The wages of intellectuality . . . and the fictional wagers of Iris Murdoch

318d Women victimised by fiction: Living and loving in the novels of Barbara Pym

318e Cold enclosures: The fiction of Susan Hill

328d Fathers in general: The patriarchy in Virginia Woolf's fiction

329n Virginia Woolf and the classics: Every Englishman's prerogative transmuted into fictional art

330g The form of fact and fiction: *Jacob's Room* as paradigm

384b Marie Louise Ritter: The pioneer woman in fact and fiction

384e Women in western American fiction: Images or real women?

384g Miscegenation in popular western history and fiction

384p The young girl in the West: Disenchantment in Jean Stafford's short fiction

408n The changing face of woman in Latin American fiction

417x Realities and fictions: Lesbian visions of utopia

417aa Of time and revolution: Theories of social change in contemporary feminist science fiction

419m Theodora and Antonina in the *Historia Arcana*: History and/or fiction?

433m The image of Bengal in the emerging literature of Bangladesh: The fiction of Hasan Azizul Huq

445d American dream, nightmare underside: Diaries, letters and fiction of women on the American frontier

445p Folk narrative in Caroline Gordon's frontier fiction

445r "On the *other* side of the mountains": The westering experiences in the fiction of Ethel Wilson

449b Images of women in Ping Hsin's fiction

449c Portraits by a lady: The fictional world of Ling Shuhua

450a The fiction of Anne Tyler

450d Eating the moment absolutely up: The fiction of Beverly Lowry

450i Mermaids, angels and free women: The heroines of Elizabeth Spencer's fiction

450n The miracle of realism: The bid for self-knowledge in the fiction of Ellen Gilchrist

451g The world of love: The fiction of Eudora Welty

457g Women in Judaism: The fact and the fiction

Fictive

371f Sexual prohibitions, shared space and fictive marriages in Shíite Iran

Fidái

368f An analysis of Fidái and Mujahidin positions on women's rights

Field

40g The field of the fever, the time of the tall-walkers

98b Research on women in Bangladesh: Notes on experiences from the field

98g Field research on women in the Comilla District, Bangladesh

147mm American women: Their debut in international track and field

169m Labor history through field trips

Fieldwork

see also Anthropology

85c Reminiscences of fieldwork among the Sikhs

98d Becoming an 'insider': Women's privileges in village field work

177f Doing fieldwork

198k Lessons from fieldwork in the Sudan

297c Researching spoonbending: Concepts and practice of participatory fieldwork

Fifteenth Century

33g Gender and genre: Women as historical writers, 1400-1820

112a Christine de Pisan: First professional woman of letters (French, 1364- 1430?)

112b Caterina Corner, Queen of Cyprus (Venetian, 1454?-1510)

112c Marguerite de Navarre and her circle (French, 1492-1549)

187j The nun as anchoress: England, 1100-1500

234j 'Woman-ing" the landscape: East Anglia 1300-1500: A discussion on sources and methodology

379d Aristocratic widows in fifteenth-century England

Fight

55o Appendix D: Fighting adult entertainment centers at the grassroots level

120m Fighting the good fight: Separation or integration?

179l Freedom fighters

205u Cheap at half the price: The history of the fight for equal pay in BC

209dd Women and the fight around office automation

235k The fight for equality

241a Social sciences and the state: Fighting like a woman

305b Claim no easy victories: The fight for reproductive rights

336n Comrade - woman - mother - resistance fighter

399o Mary Shaw: A fighting champion

File

249b To file of not to file

Film

68j Ancient song, new melody in Latin America: Women and film

98l Towards the making of a documentary film on rural women in Bangladesh

247a Feminist film criticism: An introduction

247b Developments in feminist film criticism

247d The "woman's film": Possession and address

254e Images of women in film

265s Changing sex roles reflected in the films of François Truffaut

453h Women's images in film

Film Noir

406a Klute 1: A contemporary film noir and feminist criticism

406b Woman's place: The absent family of film noir

406c Women in film noir

Filter

24f Process, filter and stage theories of attraction

Finance

153j Household economy and financial capital: The case of passbook savings in Brazil

Finch, Nancy

450h Doris Bett's Nancy Finch: A heroine for the 1980s

Findhorn, Scotland

417p Findhorn, Scotland: The people who talk to plants

Finesse

130aa The view from Spain: Rocco *finesse* and *espirit* versus plebian manners

Finger

206a Nimble fingers and other fables

Finland

73f The role of learning in the lives of Finnish and other ethnic women and a proposal for self-education

104d Co-operation on and between eastern Finnish family farms

104e The estimation of work in a northern Finnish farming community

159c Female criminality in Finland - What do the statistics show?

228j Finland

382c Finland

471h Women at work in Finland

Finnegan's Wake

409h The genuine Christine: Psychodynamics of Issy

409i Anna Livia Plurabelle: The dream woman

Fire

150g If I could write this in fire, I would write this in fire

280j Fire setting (pyromania) and its relationship to sexuality

Fiscal

103g   Fiscal policy and family structure

Fish

362f   "Big women" and politics in a Philippine fishing town

Fisher, Vardis

445l   Westering and woman: A thematic study of Kesey's *One Flew Over the Cuckoo's Nest* and Fisher's *Mountain Man*

Fitzgerald, F. Scott

17n   Fitzgerald's women: Beyond winter dreams

Flanders, Moll

384n   Marian Forrester and Moll Flanders: Fortunes and misfortunes

Flapper

454p   Prosperity's child: Some thoughts on the flapper

Flaubert, Gustave

135p   Emma Bovary's masculinization: Convention of clothes and morality of conventions

332b   The novel of awakening (five novels)

Flores, Señora de Andrade

192v   Señora Flores de Andrade

Florida

303j   Racial myths and attitudes among white female students at the University of Florida

469j   The emerging Cuban women of Florida's Dade County

Flush

329p   Combining 'the advantages of act and fiction': Virginia Woolf's biographies of Vita Sackville-West, Flush, and Roger Fry

Flying

452m   Towards a theory of form in feminist autobiography: Kate Millett's *Flying* and *Sita*; Maxine Hong Kingston's *The Woman Warrior*

Folk

319e   "La vieja Inés," a Mexican folk game: A research note

399v   Apropos of women and the folk play

445p   Folk narrative in Caroline Gordon's frontier fiction

Folklore

175x   Woman as victim in modern folklore

205s   Last back: Folklore and the telephone operators in the 1919 Vancouver general strike

Foltz, Clara Shortridge

375k   Clara Shortridge Foltz: Pioneer in the law

Fontevrault

187g   Male/female cooperation: The example of fontevrault

Food

92f   Indonesia: Socio-economic aspects of food consumption in rural Java

241f   'It's a pleasure to cook for him': Food, mealtimes and gender in some South Wales households

341i   Soul, black women and food

373e   New technologies for food-related activities: An equity strategy

395d   Women, food and health in Tanzania: A crisis of the 1980s

400f   Life cycle, food behaviour and nutrition of women in Bangladesh

402f   Women in Bangladesh: Food-for-work and socioeconomic change

Foodworld

341d   Barbara's foodworld: A case history

Fool

20j   *Lady Oracle*: The narrative of a fool-heroine

Foot

372dd   Foot disorders of female marathon runners before and after a marathon race

Footbinding

401k   The influence of western women on the anti-footbinding movement 1840-1911

for colored girls who have considered suicide

448l   "A laying on of hands": Transcending the city in Ntozake Shange's *for colored girls who have considered suicide/when the rainbow is enuf*

Force

36z   Forces impacting on the policymaker

49c   The age mix of the labor force in 1990: Implications for labor market research

49e   Implications of the increasing participation of women in the work force in the 1990's

49f   The feminization of the labor force: Research for industrial/organizational psychology

78m   Forcible rape: Institutionalized sexism in the criminal justice system

89a   Labor force participation of married women: A study of labor supply

89q   Wives' labor force behavior and family consumption patterns

185b   Social forces and the changing family

324d   Attitudes toward women working: Changes over time and implications for the labor-force behaviors of husbands and wives

349k   The victim in a forcible rape case: A feminist view

361b   Labor force participation of women baccalaureates in science

Ford Broadmeadows

94h   A new Australian working class leadership: The case of Ford Broadmeadows

Foreign

66e   A foreign perspective

67e   A foreign perspective

102m   Women in the U.S. Foreign Service: A quiet revolution

435l   The foreign policy beliefs of women in leadership positions

Foremother

301b   Legacy: Memories of our foremothers

Forest

82i   Agriculture, forestry, conservation and women

300m   The Thai forest tradition: Local and international manifestations

Form

107s   Measures of body size and form of elite female basketball players

186o   A note on May Sarton's use of form

306q   New forms for new research

Formula

300e   The infant formula controversy in Southeast Asia: Advocacy confrontation or applied anthropology?

Formulate

436c   Women's role in the formulation of public policies in Brazil

Fornes, Maria Irene

399ww   *Fefu and Her Friends*

Forrester, Marian

384n   Marian Forrester and Moll Flanders: Fortunes and misfortunes

Fort Worth, TX

63c   Co-corrections-FCI Forth Worth after three years

Fortune

108e   To restore honor and fortune: *The Autobiography of Lenor López de Córdobä*

134e   Family fortunes

Forum **Magazine**

290d   Theory into practice: Sexual liberation or social control? (*Forum* magazine 1968-1981)

Fossil

279d   The fossil record of sex

Foster

70g   American Indian children: Foster care and adoptions

355j   Domestic labor as work discipline: The struggle over housework in foster homes

Forster, E. M.

27k   A *Passage to India* as "marriage fiction": Forster's sexual politics

Foucault, Michel

313d   Foucault's fantasia for feminists: The woman reading

439t   *The History of Sexuality. Vol. 1: An Introduction* by Michel Foucault

Found

117m   Lost and *Found*: Once more the fallen woman

Foundation

40dd   Rootedness: The ancestor as foundation

169t   How foundations view funding proposals on working women

407h   Foundation support for administrative advancement: A mixed record

The Four-Gated City

448i   Reading the city as palimpsest: The experiential perception of the city in Doris Lessing's *The Four-Gated City*

Fourteenth Century

112a   Christine de Pisan: First professional woman of letters (French, 1364-1430?)

117g   Taking a second look: Observations on the iconography of a French queen, Jeanne de Bourbon (1338-1378)

162i   The Aragonese royal family around 1300

187j   The nun as anchoress: England, 1100-1500

234j   'Woman-ing' the landscape: East Anglia 1300-1500: A discussion on sources and methodology

376g Women before the law: Females as felons and prey in fourteenth-century England

Fourth Century
187a Muffled voices: The lives of consecrated women in the fourth century

Framework
66g The legal framework
67g The legal framework

France
52e Female marital behaviour in French society
93c Equal pay and equal opportunity law in France
112a Christine de Pisan: First professional woman of letters (French, 1364-1430?)
112c Marguerite de Navarre and her circle (French, 1492-1549)
112g Madame de Sévigné: Chronicler of an age (French, 1626-1696)
117z Taking a second look: Observations on the iconography of a French queen, Jeanne de Bourbon (1338-1378)
117l Happy mothers and other new ideas in eighteenth-century French art
130c Women, democracy, and revolution in Paris, 1789-1794
130u The death of an ideal: Female suicides in the eighteenth-century French novel
132e Language and revolution: The Franco-American Dis-connection
132h Introduction: Psychoanalysis and feminism in France
132j Psychoanalysis in France
155b French feminist theater and the subject of prostitution, 1870-1914
162f Tensions, dissensions, and ruptures inside the family in seventeenth- and eighteenth-century Haute Provence
162m Linen was their life: Family survival strategies and parent-child relations in nineteenth-century France
184m Parisian infants and Norman wet nurses in the early nineteenth century: A statistical study
186f A French view of May Sarton
187d Benedictine life for women in central France, 850-1100: A feminist revival
188c The French courtly poet: Marie de France
188d The French scholar-lover: Heloise
188i The French heretic Bequine: Marguerite Porete
188o The Franco-Italian professional writer: Christine de Pizan
200b Women and the dialectics of nature in eighteenth-century French thought
209cc Experimental approaches towards telecommunications in France
228e France
244e The roles of men and women in French families: Change or stability in the patterns and practices?
263k Industrial social workers in France, 1917-1939: A study in the sex/gender division of labor
356q Women's autobiography in France: For a dialectics of identification
378n Women in positions of political leadership in Britain, France and West Germany

379q Responses to the political activism of Women of the People in revolutionary Paris, 1789-1793
382d France
388k Social feminism in France: A case study
437b France
438e The wild cat (France and Italy)
442h Publishing in Paris
444a Women of the popular classes in revolutionary Paris, 1789-1795
444e Old wine in new bottles: The institutional changes for women of the people during the French revolution
444i Revolution and retreat: Upper-class French women after 1789

Franco, Francisco
408o The censored sex: Woman as author and character in Franco's Spain

Francophone
322e Francophone literature in north Africa

Frankenstein
27c Frankenstein's daughter: Mary Shelley and Mary Wollstonecraft
109j "A forced solitude": Mary Shelley and the creation of Frankenstein's monster

Frankish
188a The Frankish mother: Dhuoda

Fraser Valley
205c Rainbow women of the Fraser Valley: Lifesongs through the generations

Fraternity
31p Sex preselection: From here to fraternity

Fred, E.B.
394p An E.B. Fred Fellow

Free
231hh The fear that feminism will free men first
370j Slave wives, free sisters: Bakongo women and slavery c.1700-1850
474g On being female, black, and free

Freedom
see also Emancipate, Liberate, Women's Liberation
50h Typing our way to freedom: Is it true that new office technology can liberate women?
60v The challenge of profamily politics: A feminist defense of sexual freedom
114g Marion Zimmer Bradley's ethic of freedom
129s Some problems of social freedom
179l Freedom fighters
315f Women, reproductive freedom, and the law: A selected annotated bibliography
316h Toward freedom and self-determination: New directions in mental health services
372a Women and sport: A question of freedom
439e Reproductive freedom: Beyond "A woman's right to choose"
454o The American woman's pre-World War I freedom in manners and morals

Freelance
323p Organizing freelancers in the arts

Freeman, Mary Wilkins
301 "She is the one you call sister": Discovering Mary Wilkins Freeman

Freethought
129aa The economic tendency of freethought

French
73h The economic struggles of female factory workers: A comparison of French, Polish, and Portuguese immigrants

French America
367c Women in colonial French America

French Canadian
421l English-Canadian and French-Canadian attitudes towards women: Results of the Canadian Gallup polls

Freud, Sigmund
116d Freud: Masculinity, femininity, and the philosophy of mind
158b Freud's heritage: Fathers and daughters in German literature (1750-1850)
256b Freud's Dora, Dora's hysteria
286j On the enrichment of poor monkeys by myth and dream; or how Dickens Rousseauisticized and pre-Freudianized Victorian views of childhood
359a Women: From Freud to the present

Freya
384m Beret as the Norse mythological goddess Freya/Gurthr

Friend
103u "Sisters" or "comrades"? The politics of friends and families
174aa Friends and critics: The feminist academy
186j Patterns of love and friendship: Five novels by May Sarton
196c "Under the dominion of *some* woman": The friendship of Samuel Johnson and Hester Thrale
214m Women, work and friendship: Personal confirmation and support
265j Cross-sex friendship in the elementary school
397e The older lesbian: Love relationships and friendship patterns
399c Friendship and ritual in the WTUL
432j Competition, friendship, and human nature

Frisch, Max
32k "Eine frau, aber mehr als das, eine Personlichkeit, aber mehr als das: eine frau": The structural analysis of the female characters in the novels of Max Frisch

Front
213e In the front line
381a Right out in front

Frontier
246i European women in the Solomon Islands, 1900-1942: Accommodation and change on the Pacific frontier
353w Mary Breckinridge, the frontier nursing service, and the introduction of nurse-midwifery in the United States
356m Honing a habitable languagescape: Women's images for the new world frontiers
384r Where the West begins: Constance Rourke's images of her own frontierland
412g Ministry through marriage: Methodist clergy wives on the trans-Mississippi frontier

428j *Maquiladoras*: A new face of international capitalism on Mexico's northern frontier

445b Women's literature and the American frontier: A new perspective on the frontier myth

445d American dream, nightmare underside: Diaries, letters and fiction of women on the American frontier

445o Dorothy Scarborough's critique of the frontier experience in *The Wind*

445p Folk narrative in Caroline Gordon's frontier fiction

Fruit

143i Fruit and seed: The finale to *Middlemarch*

Fry, Roger

329p Combining 'the advantages of act and fiction': Virginia Woolf's biographies of Vita Sackville-West, Flush, and Roger Fry

Fuck

231ff My mother liked to fuck

Fuel

215i Fuel for the nuclear arms race: Nuclear power and nuclear weapons

Fujenti

194e An Italian religious feast: The *Fujenti* rites of the Madonna dell'Arco, Naples

Fuji Kita

167i At the foot of the mountain: The Shibokusa women of Kita Fuji

Fuller, Margaret

125e Margaret Fuller: Feminist writer and revolutionary

389e Margaret Fuller (1810-1850): Her work as an art critic

Fun

197b Fun and games with life-stories

Function

8i The organic-functional controversy

51v Endocrine functions in the woman's second half of life

132s Lesbianism and the social function of taboo

137n Gender and sexual functioning

Functionary

128b Women in the party bureaucracy: Subservient functionaries

Fund

36c Ethical problems in government-funded contraceptive research

169t How foundations view funding proposals on working women

169u Funding worker education through tuition refund plans

173c The abortion-funding cases and population control: An imaginary lawsuit and some reflections on the uncertain limits of reproductive privacy

314q A view from the funding agencies

Fundamental

43c Fundamental feminism: Process and perspective

133x Religious fundamentalism and the democratic process

Future

45j The past and future of the undergraduate woman

49l We can influence the future!

79v Futuristic implications of sex preselection

131p The future females: A selected checklist through 1979

174y What are rights without means? Educating feminists for the future

181k Reproductive technology: The future for women?

181m Afterward: Machina ex dea and future research

193f Biological inevitabilities or political choices? The future for girls in science

215s Contemplating a nuclear future: Nuclear war, politics and the individual

307bb Female futures in women's science fiction

309j Some speculations on the future of marriage and fertility

335i No turning back - Thatcherism, the family and the future

387l The future of American fertility

388m The future for women and development

417ff Future visions: Today's politics: Feminist utopias in review

423f Future research and policy questions

436m Future perspectives

441f Technology and the future of women: Haven't we met somewhere before?

462x Envisioning our hopes: Some models of the future

467g The future prospect

Futurism

229uu The voice of women's spirituality in futurism

GABe

307i The GABe self-cleaning house

Gaelic

338b The female principle in Gaelic poetry

Gage, Matilda Joslyn

125h Matilda Joslyn Gage: Active intellectual

Galdos, Benito Pérez

313n "Folly and a woman": Galdos' rhetoric of irony in *Tristana*

Gallup Poll

421l English-Canadian and French-Canadian attitudes towards women: Results of the Canadian Gallup polls

Gambia

5g Gambian women: Unequal partners in rice development projects?

385n Women's cooperative thrift and credit societies: An element of women's programs in the Gambia

Game

23c Losing the numbers game: Women, tokenism and power

48d The courtship game: Power in the sexual encounter

147a Ball game participation of North American Indian women

147g Generalizations on women and sport, games and play in the United States from settlement to 1860

147q Canadian women at the Olympic games

147r Canadian women at the Commonwealth games

169l Games and other exercises

197b Fun and games with life-stories

319e "La vieja Inés," a Mexican folk game: A research note

Gamp, Sarah

248c From Sarah Gamp to Florence Nightingale: A critical study of hospital nursing systems from 1840 to 1897

Gandhi, Indira

21k Indira Gandhi as head of government

García Lorca, Federico

408m The greatest punishment: Female and male in Lorca's tragedies

Garden

202b Woolf's 'Magical garden of women'

231o Garden paths, descents

Garífuna

269b Structural continuity in the division of men's and women's work among black Carib (Garífuna)

Garland, Hamlin

384k Hamlin Garland's feminism

445h Hamlin Garland and the cult of true womanhood

Garment

see also Cloth, Textile

144h Women's work and the family: Women garment workers in Berlin and Hamburg before the First World War

192l Los Angeles garment district sews a cloak of shame

201f The uprising in Chicago: The men's garment workers strike, 1910-1911

201l A stitch in our time: New York's Hispanic garment workers in the 1980s

Gaskell, Elizabeth

180i Mothers and daughters in *Wives and Daughters*: A study of Elizabeth Gaskell's last novel

Gatekeeper

85h The gatekeepers: A feminist critique of academic publishing

Gathering

457d Gender and religion in a Turkish town: A comparison of two types of formal women's gatherings

Gauthiers-Villars, Henri

196h The magic spinning wheel: Straw to gold - Colette, Willy and Sido

Gay

see also Homosexual, Lesbian

48k The intimate relationships of lesbians and gay men

133c Lesbians, gay men, and their "languages"

133h Gay masculinity in the gay disco

133i Gay fantasies in gay publications

133m Images of the gay male in contemporary drama

133o Media reaction to the 1979 gay march on Washington

133p Educational responsibilities to gay male and lesbian students

133q Consciousness-raising among gay males

133r From "commies" and "queers" to "gay is good"

133s Troy Perry: Gay advocate

133u Gay civil rights and the roots of oppression

133v Referendum campaigns vs. gay rights

133w Ideologies in two gay rights controversies

136l Nonverbal behavior and lesbian/gay orientation

152a Reflections of a gay Catholic

152g Gay men and women and the vowed life

158h Psychology measures femininity and masculinity, 2: From "13 Gay Men" to the instrumental-expressive distinction

212o 'Male needs': The problems and problems of working with gay men

223h Gay marriage

224c Lesbians and gay men: Hetero sexualities, common cause

224e Old and gay

224j Toward a scientific analysis of the gay question

224k Some thoughts on gay/lesbian oppression

224l Towards a Marxist theory of gay liberation

224n Lesbian and gay oppression in the '80s: Androgyny, men and power

231c Marching to a different drummer: Lesbian and gay GIs in World War II

231d Capitalism and gay identity

323j Lesbians and gays in the union movement

369d Socialism, feminism, and gay/lesbian liberation

Gayspeak

133d Gayspeak

133e "Gayspeak": A response

Gaze

231t Is the gaze male?

Gecekondu

270i Economic change and the Gecekondu family

Gender

see also Androgyny, Role, Sex, Sex Role

8p Research on gender and psychotherapy

13b Capitalism, gender and the labour process: Two case studies

23l Psychoanalysis and feminist social theory of gender

31c Is gender a variable in conceptions of rationality? A survey of issues

33g Gender and genre: Women as historical writers, 1400-1820

34b Boys will be boys will be boys: The language of sex and gender

35a Introduction: Biopolitics and gender

35b Biology, gender, and politics: An assessment and critique

35d The biopolitics of sex: Gender, genetics, and epigenetics

48n Future influences on the interaction of gender and human sexual expression

49g Commentary on studies of gender-mix in labor market research

50r Developmental aspects of gender

83c Gender, race and class in the United States: Lessons from Third World women

84k Gender and science

84p Why has the sex/gender system become visible only now?

88a On the origins of gender identity

90h Jobs and gender: A history of the structuring of educational employment by sex

90q The influence of gender on the verbal interactions among principals and staff members: An exploratory study

90r The gender of principals and principal/teacher relations in elementary schools

103j Gender and child-custody determinations: Exploding the myths

103l Teenage sexuality and public policy: An agenda for gender education

103o Work, gender, and technological innovation

117e Social status and gender in Roman art: The case of the saleswoman

117o Gender or genius? The women artists of German expressionism

122g Bem's gender schema theory

123g Anthropology and the study of gender

124f Transvestitism and the ideology of gender: Southeast Asia and beyond

132b Gender, relation, and difference in psychoanalytic perspective

136b Gender patterns in touching behavior

136g Gender gestures: Sex, sex-role, and nonverbal communication

136h Gender, androgyny, and conversational assertiveness

136i A feminist critique of androgyny: Toward the elimination of gender attributions for learned behavior

137a Gender and psychopathology in perspective

137b Gender as a model for mental health

137c Gender and child psychopathology

137d Gender and adult psychopathology

137f Gender and depression

137g Gender and schizophrenia

137h Gender and phobia

137i Gender, drinking, and alcohol abuse

137j Gender and drug use and abuse

137k Gender and crime

137l Gender, genes, and psychopathology

137m Gender, hormones, and psychopathology

137n Gender and sexual functioning

137o Gender, psychophysiological disorders, and mortality

137p Gender and obesity

138a Gender, class and education: A personal view

138b Intersections of gender and class: Accommodation and resistance by working-class and affluent females to contradictory sex-role ideologies

138c Gender, resistance and power

138e A cloud over co-education: An analysis of the forms of transmission of class and gender relations

138g Gender, patriarchy and class in the popular education of women

138k Gender, class and education: A teaching bibliography of European studies

138l Gender, class and education: A teaching bibliography of Australian and New Zealand studies

138m Gender, class and education: A teaching bibliography of American studies

139c Not so much a factory, more a form of patriarchy: Gender and class during industrialisation

139g Women, gender relations and wage labour

140v Teaching value clarification: The example of gender and psychotherapy

148d Male/female task differentiation among the Hidatsa: Toward the development of an archeological approach to the study of gender

148g The political economy of gender: A 19th century Plains Indian case study

153m Gender division within the U.S. working class: Households in the Philadelphia area, 1870-1945

171a Language, gender and society: Opening a second decade of research

195h Is male gender identity the cause of male domination?

200a Nature, culture and gender: A critique

200d The power of signs: Gender, culture and the wild in the Bolivian Andes

200f Gender, sexuality and marriage: A Kaulong model of nature and culture

207a Gender and economics: The sexual division of labour and the subordination of women

208b Gender and economics: The sexual division of labour and the subordination of women

217i Gender as forms of value

231w Gender systems, ideology, and sex research

241f 'It's a pleasure to cook for him': Food, mealtimes and gender in some South Wales households

241k Interviewing men: 'Taking gender seriously'

243b Gender and interaction in the workplace

250a Introduction: Women, work and schooling: The relevance of gender

250c The importance of being Ernest ... Emma ... Tom ... Jane. The perception and categorization of gender conformity and gender deviation in primary schools

253a Genes and gender update

253f Genes and gender in the workplace

256a Class and gender in Victorian England

258b Sex, gender and society

259g 'Telling how it is': Language and gender in the classroom

263j Professionalism, division of labor by gender, and the control of nursing practice

263k Industrial social workers in France, 1917-1939: A study in the sex/gender division of labor

268c Gender ideology and phobias in women

280e Gender dysphoria and dyssocial behavior

282b The gender revolution and the transition from bisexual horde to patrilocal band: The origins of gender hierarchy

282d Transforming "natural" woman: Female ritual leaders and gender ideology among Bimin-Kuskusmin

282e Self-interest and the social good: Some implications of Hagen gender imagery

282f Sexuality and gender in Samoa: Conceptions and missed conceptions

282i Politics and gender in simple societies

282k Gender and sexuality in hierarchical societies: The case of Polynesia and some comparative implications

289e Gender identity: A life-span view of sex-role development

295l The relation of stressful life events to gender

296g Racial-ethnic women and work: Towards an analysis of race and gender stratification

297i The personable and the powerful: Gender and status in sociological research

307c Gender and industry on Mexico's new frontier

314d The social sciences: Establishing gender as a category

314u Women, gender, and the curriculum

315b Attitudes toward gender in two cultures: Puerto Rico and the United States

321b Gender and dependency

321d Natural resources: Health, reproduction and the gender order

342g Feminist analysis of gender: A critique

344d Sexual harassment: The link between gender stratification, sexuality, and women's economic status

351d Biology: Its role in gender-related educational experiences

359l The influence of gender on diagnosis and psychopathology

362e Gender, politics and modernization: The Indian case

364a Introduction: Property, power and gender relations

365a Gender and psychotherapeutic outcome

365c Gender and the process of therapy

378a Male and female: Job versus gender models in the sociology of work

378m Gender, levels of political thinking and political action

387e Male and female: Job versus gender models in the sociology of work

414i The gender liberation: Black women as elected officials in Oklahoma

419c Workers and drones: Labor, idleness and gender definition in Hesiod's beehive

427e Gender inequities in childhood social life and adult work life

432a Justice and gender in school sports

432c Athletics, gender, and justice

432n Women's physical education: A gender-sensitive perspective

432o The ethics of gender discrimination: A response to Ann Diller and Barbara Houston's "Women's Physical Education"

439j Biological influences on human sex and gender

443c The convergence of psychoanalysis and feminism: Gender identity and autonomy

457d Gender and religion in a Turkish town: A comparison of two types of formal women's gatherings

462b Class, gender, and religion: A theoretical overview and some political implications

463g Analysis of activity schedules along the dimension of gender

463o Perceived safety and security in transportation systems as determined by the gender of the traveler

Gender Difference
see also Difference, Sex Difference

139h 'Getting on'. Gender differences in career development: A case study in the hairdressing industry

226e Women in political parties: Gender differences in motives among California party activists

349f Gender differences in delinquency: Quantity and quality

349w Gender differences in prisoner subcultures

463q Gender differences in reactions to vehicle environments

Gender Equality
see also Sex Equality

60p Women's role in economic development: Practical and theoretical implications of class and gender inequalities

417e The Shakers: Gender equality in hierarchy

Gender Neutral

275j Gender-neutral terms

Gender Role
see also Role, Sex Role

48a The intimate relationship between gender roles and sexuality

48b Sexual socialization and gender roles in childhood

48e Sexual response and gender roles

48g Sexuality and gender roles in the second half of life

48i Gender roles and sexuality in the world of work

48l Gender roles and sexual violence

48m Gender, gender-role identification, and response to erotica

244h Sexual customs and gender roles in Sweden and America: An analysis and interpretation

263c Symmetrical families? Changing gender role expectations and the breadwinner role in the contemporary United States

353bb Professionalism, feminism, and gender roles: A comparative study of nineteenth-century medical therapeutics

359f The prevalence of gender-role bias in mental health services

359jj Wife battering and the maintenance of gender roles: A sociopsychological perspective

427j Gender roles and the state

463t Gender-role identification in the methodology of transportation planning

Gene

137l Gender, genes, and psychopathology

253a Genes and gender update

253f Genes and gender in the workplace

310g Designer genes: A view from the factory

Generalist

209q The decline of the " secretary as generalist"

Generation

94j Generations and class: Sicilian-Australians in Melbourne

164j Muted discord: Generational conflict in Jane Austen

177m Contemporary generations

199a Generations of working-class families

199b Southern textile women: Generations of survival and struggle

205c Rainbow women of the Fraser Valley: Lifesongs through the generations

213c The second generation: West Indian female school-leavers

367d New England women: Ideology and experience in first-generation Puritanism (1630-1650)

450b Alice Walker's celebration of self in southern generations

Generativity

214t Dream vs. drift in women's careers: The question of generativity

289o Beyond generativity: Toward a sensuality of later life

Generic

275h The hidden joke: Generic uses of masculine terminology

Genesis

126a The genesis of feminist visions for transforming the liberal arts curriculum

Genetics

35d The biopolitics of sex: Gender, genetics, and epigenetics

83i Racism and sexism: They ain't genetic you know!

141a Introduction to breast cancer genetics

141b Genetic control of breast cancer susceptibility in animals

141f Genetic heterogeneity and breast cancer: Variable tumor spectra

141g Hormones, genetics, and breast cancer

141i Genetic counseling, patient and family management: Familial breast cancer

233m Animal and human studies in genetic toxicology

253b Update on genetics

Genital

88d The inner-genital phase - prephallic and preoedipal

88e A suggested developmental sequence for a preoedipal genital phase

280f Genital exhibitionism in men and women

Genius

40l The literary genius of Alice Childress

117o Gender or genius? The women artists of German expressionism

Genocide

395a Genocide can be bloodless

Genre

33g Gender and genre: Women as historical writers, 1400-1820

Gentileschi, Artemisia

108f Artemisia Gentileschi: The artist's autograph in letters and paintings

117i Artemisia and Susanna

Gentlewomen

205i The gentlewomen of Queen Mary's coronation hostel

Geography

274j Geography

302l Geographic mobility and career advancement of male and female librarians

Georgia

226c Conceptions of the "Political": White activists in Atlanta

399cc Women open Augusta's first theatre

Georgia, USSR

371h The sexual division of domestic space among two Soviet minorities: The Georgians and the Tadjiks

Germ

379n Feminism, professionalism, and germs: A study of the thought of Mary Putnam Jacobi and Elizabeth Blackwell

German

144a The German family: A critical survey of the current state of historical research

German American Woman

73j Family roles and identities of Scandinavian and German women

Germany

32f A German writer and feminist in nineteenth century America: An archival study of Mathilde Franziska Anneke

32g German women writers in the nineteenth century: Where are they?

60d Crisis, reaction, and resistance: Women in Germany in the 1920's and 1930's

93b Collective bargaining as a strategy for achieving equal opportunity and equal pay: Sweden and West Germany

93o Equal employment opportunity for women in West Germany today

93v Work analysis as a means to achieve equal pay for working women: The Federal Republic of Germany

113b Germany and the World Wars

117o Gender or genius? The women artists of German expressionism

130y The view from Germany

144c Family and 'modernisation': The peasant family and social change in nineteenth-century Bavaria

144d Family and household: Social structures in a German village between the two World Wars

144e Women, family and death: Excess mortality of women in child-bearing age in four communities in nineteenth-century Germany

144f The family life-cycle: A study of factory workers in nineteenth century Württemberg

144g Overcrowding and family life: Working-class families and the housing crisis in late nineteenth-century Duisburg

144h Women's work and the family: Women garment workers in Berlin and Hamburg before the First World War

145a Current research on German women's history in the nineteenth century

145b Enlightened reforms and Bavarian girls' education: Tradition through innovation

145g Female political opposition in pre-1848 Germany: The role of Kathinka Zitz-Halein

145h German women writers and the Revolution of 1848

145i Self-conscious histories: Biographies of German women in the nineteenth century

145l The impact of agrarian change on women's work and child care in early-nineteenth-century Prussia

145o The woman's role in the German working-class family in the 1890s from the perspective of women's autobiographies

145p The civilizing tendency of hygiene: Working-class women under medical control in Imperial Germany

145q The female victim: Homicide and women in Imperial Germany

158b Freud's heritage: Fathers and daughters in German literature (1750-1850)

159f Changing patterns of female criminality in Germany

162g Young bees in an empty hive: Relations between brothers-in-law in a south German village around 1800

162n Village spinning bees: Sexual culture and free time among rural youths in early modern Germany

162p Mothers, sons, and the sale of symbols and goods: The 'German Mother's Day' 1923-33

167a Starting a movement: Frauen für frieden (Women for Peace, West Germany)

184f Bastardy and socioeconomic structure of south Germany

184g Bastardy in south Germany: A comment

184h Bastardy in south Germany: A reply

188e The German visionary: Hildegard of Bingen

188g The German mystic: Mechthild of Magdeburg

209ff Collective bargaining strategies on new technology: The experience of West German trade unions

228g West Germany

231g The new woman and the rationalization of sexuality in Weimar Germany

260a Women in the labour market and equal opportunity policy in Sweden, United Kingdom, United States and West Germany

260b A look at the male female unemployment differentials in the Federal Republic of Germany, Sweden, United Kingdom, and the United States of America

260h Equal opportunity policies for women in the Federal Republic of Germany

260j Labour market policy in four countries: Are women adequately represented?

260k Estimating the impact of labor market policies on women: A discussion of the four-country studies on the employment of women

331c The woman's song in medieval German poetry

332p Shadowing/surfacing/shedding: Contemporary German writers in search of a female *Bildungsroman*

336a Introduction: Women in Weimar and Nazi Germany

336d The Bremen morality scandal

336f Mother's day in the Weimar Republic

336h Sisterhood under siege: Feminism and anti-semitism in Germany, 1904-1938

336k Racism and sexism in Nazi Germany: Motherhood, compulsory sterilization, and the state

336l Women and the holocaust: The case of German and German-Jewish women

372h The influence of women doctors on the origins of women's sports in Germany

378n Women in positions of political leadership in Britain, France and West Germany

380o Economic aspects of female labor force participation in the Federal Republic of Germany

382b Federal Republic of Germany

423e Women in the German Democratic Republic: Impact of culture and social policy

437a Federal Republic of Germany

444b "I don't call that *Volksgemeinschaft*": Women, class, and war in Nazi Germany

471c Women at work in the Federal Republic of Germany

Gertrude

343k A heart cleft in twain: The dilemma of Shakespeare's Gertrude

Gertrude the Great

408i Gertrude the Great: Avellaneda, nineteenth-century feminist

Gestation

460e Physiological aspects of female sexual development: Gestation, lactation, menopause, and erotic physiology

Gesture

136g Gender gestures: Sex, sex-role, and nonverbal communication

Ghana

52p Women's roles and conjugal family systems in Ghana

364h 'Fear woman': Property and modes of production in urban Ghana

370l Post-proclamation slavery in Accra: A female affair?

385k Women's employment and development: A conceptual framework applied to Ghana

Ghetto

323d Out of the ghettos: Affirmative action and unions

404f The sparse ghetto: Service delivery in a rural area

404ff Federal support: Understanding and utilizing the federal dollar

Ghost

27l Violet Hunt's *Tales of the Unneasy*: Ghost stories of a worldly woman

135k Edith Wharton and the ghost story

175f The ghost of Chipita: The crying woman of San Patricio

GI

see also Armed Forces, Army, Combatant

231c Marching to a different drummer: Lesbian and gay GIs in World War II

Giants in the Earth

384m Beret as the Norse mythological goddess Freya/Gurthr

445j Madness and personification in *Giants in the Earth*

Gifted

351c Career and life satisfactions among Terman's gifted women

377i An accelerative intervention program for mathematically gifted girls

Gilbertine

187h All ages, every condition, and both sexes: The emergence of a Gilbertine identity

Gilbreth, Lillian Moller

181b Lillian Moller Gilbreth and the founding of modern industrial engineering

Gilchrist, Ellen

450n The miracle of realism: The bid for self-knowledge in the fiction of Ellen Gilchrist

Gilda

406f Resistance through charisma: Rita Hayworth and Gilda

Gilman, Charlotte Perkins

84f Charlotte Perkins Gilman: Forerunner of a feminist social science

109n The gothic prism: Charlotte Perkins Gilman's gothic stories and her autobiography

125l Charlotte Perkins Gilman: The personal is political

131e Coming Home: Four feminist utopias and patriarchal experience

Gimi

200g Images of nature in Gimi thought

Giovanni, Nikki

40t Nikki Giovanni: Taking a chance on feeling

40u Sweet soft essence of possibility: The poetry of Nikki Giovanni

Girl

see also Child

8f The adolescent girl in a group home

8g Juvenile delinquency in girls

8h Childhood and adolescent suicidal behavior, with an emphasis on girls

70b Current educational status of American Indian girls

72g Guidance and counseling of Spanish-background girls

73k Achieving the dreams beyond tradition: Counseling white ethnic American girls

88c Considerations about the development of the girl during the separation-individuation process

106n "Thank heaven for little girls": The dialectics of development

107k Influence of athletic training on the maturity process of girls

134a Youth service provision, social order and the question of girls

145b Enlightened reforms and Bavarian girls' education: Tradition through innovation

157b To Columbia on the Tynemouth: The emigration of single women and girls in 1862

175s Glamor girl called Electra

190l Beliefs and attitudes of young girls regarding menstruation

193a Girls and science education: Is there a problem?

193f Biological inevitabilities or political choices? The future for girls in science

193g Factors differentially affecting the science subject preferences, choices and attitudes of girls and boys

193h Science options in a girls' grammar school

193j Who says girls can't be engineers?

193l Girls studying science in the sixth form

193m Differential treatment of boy and girl pupils during science lessons

193o Girls' science: Boys' science revisited

193r Girls, physics and sexism

225m No more nice girls

231bb A story of a girl and her dog

250d Studying girls at school: The implications of confusion

250f Education and the individual: Schooling for girls, or mixed schooling - a mixed blessing?

259b Boys and girls entering school

265h Sex typing in occupational preferences of high school boys and girls

265t Mental health in boys and girls: Awareness of attitudes for positive sex roles

291p The co-therapy relationship in group treatment of sexually mistreated adolescent girls

316k Education, girls, and power

343f As we like it: How a girl can be smart and still popular

351f Girls, women, and mathematics

352j Socialization and education of young black girls in school

356k Directive-response speech sequences in girls' and boys' task activities

379l City mothers, city daughters, and the dance hall girls: The limits of female political power in San Francisco, 1913

432i Equality and competition: Can sports make a women of a girl?

454d The lady and the mill girl: Changes in the status of women in the Age of Jackson

460a "Role, Jenny Jenkins, Roll": Little girls and maidens in American folksongs - an analysis of sexual attitudes

Girl Guides

205o Domesticity and discipline: The Girl Guides in British Columbia 1910-1943

Gisolo, Margaret

147nn Sexual discrimination in youth sport: The case of Margaret Gisolo

Glamor

175s Glamor girl called Electra

Gland

51i Potential role of the pineal gland in the human menstrual cycle

Glasgow, Ellen

180l Ellen Glasgow: Daughter as justified

Glaspell, Susan

399mm The women's world of Glaspell's *Trifles*

Glass

135b The looking-glass through Alice

332j Through the looking glass: When women tell fairy tales

Global

59h Re-membering: A global perspective on women

373a Foreword: Seeing our global economy whole

428r Global industries and Malay peasants in peninsular Malaysia

Goal

21d Female elite goals and national development: Some data from the Philippines

38i Marital interaction goals of black women: Strengths and effects

45l Sex differences in the educational and occupational goals of black college students: Continued inquiry into the black matriarchy theory

79n Neonatology: Directions and goals

God

see also Religion

42h Daughters of God

156e The god's wife of Amun in the 18th dynasty in Egypt

412q For god and home and native land: The W.C.T.U.'s image of woman in the late nineteenth century

457f Women, fertility and the worship of gods in a Hindu village

462n Why women need the war god

Goddard College

441h Feminist pedagogy and technology: Reflections on the Goddard feminism and ecology summer program

Goddess

117c The great goddess and the palace architecture of Crete

156o Goddesses, women and Jezebel

194h The goddess Kannagi: A dominant symbol of south Indian Tamil society

194j The goddess Chandi as an agent of change

194k Pox and the terror of childlessness: Images and ideas of the smallpox goddess in a north Indian village

194n The Great Goddess today in Burma and Thailand: An exploration of her symbolic relevance to monastic and female roles

194o Mother Earth: The great goddess of West Africa

229a The great goddess: Who was she?

229b Women and culture in goddess-oriented old Europe

229c Prepatriarchal female/goddess images

229d The origins of music: Women's goddess worship

229e Witchcraft as goddess religion

229f From the house of Yemanja: The goddess heritage of black women

229g The three faces of goddess spirituality

229h Why women need the goddess: Phenomenological, psychological, and political reflections

229oo Ethics and justice in goddess religion

338e The new woman and the old goddess: The shaping of Shaw's mythology

341f Feast and famine: Gifts of the goddess

384m Beret as the Norse mythological goddess Freya/Gurthr

433a Goddesses or rebels: The women revolutionaries of Bengal

453f Goddess imagery in ritual

453q Goddess worship in Wicce

Godwin, Gail

450c Gail Godwin and the ideal of southern womanhood

Godzilla

307w Bambi meets Godzilla: Life in the corporate jungle

Goethe, Johann Wolfgang von

32b A critical appraisal of Goethe's *Iphigenie*

32c *Faust*: The tragedy reexamined

Golden

408f Women against wedlock: The reluctant brides of Golden Age drama

Golden Rule

223m Abortion and the golden rule

Goldman, Emma

125m Emma Goldman: Anarchist Queen

Goldstein, Vida

125o Vida Goldstein: The women's candidate

Golf

147ll The development of women's organized sport in the 1920's: A study of the Canadian Ladies Golf Union

Gonadal

239c Gonadal hormones and cognitive functioning

271o Mood and behaviour changes in menopausal women receiving gonadal hormones or placebo

Good

27i Rebellions of good women

120m Fighting the good fight: Separation or integration?

429g Bearing the good news

Goods

153k The contribution of public goods to household reproduction: Case study from Brazil

162b Putting kin and kinship to good use: The circulation of goods, labour, and names on Karpathos (Greece)

162p Mothers, sons, and the sale of symbols and goods: The 'German Mother's Day' 1923-33

Gordon, Caroline

445p Folk narrative in Caroline Gordon's frontier fiction

Gorilla, My Love

450m Youth in Toni Cade Bambara's *Gorilla, My Love*

Gospel

see also Religion

42l Gospel principles and women

42p Women in the light of the Gospel

412j The social gospel according to Phoebe: Methodist deaconesses in the metropolis, 1885-1918

Gothic

109a Somebody's trying to kill me and I think it's my husband: The modern gothic

109b "But why do they read those things?" The female audience and the gothic novel

109c Victoria Holt's gothic romances: A structuralist inquiry

109d Had-I-but-known: The marriage of gothic terror and detection

109e The reconstruction of the gothic feminine ideal in Emily Brontë's *Wuthering Heights*

109f Domestic gothic: The imagery of anger in Christina Stead's *The Man Who Loved Children*

109g Monsters and madwomen: Changing female gothic

109h Gothic transformations: Isak Dinesen and the gothic

109i The mirror and the cameo: Margaret Atwood's comic/gothic novel, *Lady Oracle*

109k Terror-gothic: Nightmare and dream in Ann Radcliffe and Charlotte Brontë

109m The Radcliffean gothic model: A form for feminine sexuality

109n The gothic prism: Charlotte Perkins Gilman's gothic stories and her autobiography

109o The maternal legacy: The grotesque tradition in Flannery O'Connor's female gothic

Gothic Tales

155d The magic circle: The role of the prostitute in Isak Dinesen's *Gothic Tales*

Government

see also Politics, Power

21k Indira Gandhi as head of government

36c Ethical problems in government-funded contraceptive research

39c Asante queen mothers in government and politics in the nineteenth century

103f Women and housing: The impact of government housing policy

129f Government is women's enemy

185m Family options, governments, and the social milieu: Viewed from the 21st century

209e Government policies on new information technologies and their implications for employment: An overview of EEC countries, with particular reference to women

226a Women in local government: An overview

308d Government policies related to teenage family formation and functioning: An inventory

309g The effect of government policies on out-of-wedlock sex and pregnancy

337l Women and student government

427a Introduction: Government response to working women and their families: Values, the policy-making process, and research utilization

436e Women in government as policy-makers and bureaucrats: The Turkish case

470c Contemporary clerical work: A case study of local government

Governor Ferguson

175q Pardon me, Governor Ferguson

Graduate

see also Education

45k Changing sex roles: College graduates of the 1960's and 1970's

52s Egalitarianism in marriage? Graduate education and the sexual division of labour in the Canadian family

85g The expert's view? The sociological analysis of graduates' occupational and domestic roles

250m The experiences of women graduates in the labour market

320n Career commitment of female college graduates: Conceptualization and measurement issues

394e Graduate women assess the campus

398d Survival in the 'master's house': The role of graduate teaching assistants in effecting curriculum change

421aa Career constraints among women graduate students in a developing society: West Pakistan. A study in the changing status of women

425f Socialization experiences of women and men graduate students in male sex-typed career fields

Grammar

171c Prescriptive grammar and the pronoun problem

Grammar School

see also Education

193h Science options in a girls' grammar school

Grandmatology

108b Ceremonies of the alphabet: Female grandmatologies and the female autograph

Grandmother

473k The life of Sarah Penfield, rural Ohio grandmother: Tradition maintained, tradition threatened

474e My grandmother who painted

Grant, Maria

157g Maria Grant, 1854-1937: The life and times of an early twentieth century Christian

Grassroot

55o Appendix D: Fighting adult entertainment centers at the grassroots level

61g Women and radical reform in antebellum upstate New York: A profile of grassroots female abolitionists

73i Irish, Italian, and Jewish women at the grassroots level: A historical and sociological perspective

86n From grassroots activism to political power: Women organizing against environmental hazards

167b Organising at the grassroots: Vrouwen voor vrede (Women for peace, the Netherlands)

226d Filling the party vacuum: Women at the grassroots level in local politics

Grau, Shirley Ann

450e Shirley Ann Grau and the short story

Great Britain

see England

Great Depression

see also Depression (Historical)

81b The economics of middle-income family life: Working women during the Great Depression

390v Women and economic crises: The Great Depression and the present crises

Greece

52h Changing sex roles in the Greek family and society

94i Migrant communities and class politics: The Greek community in Australia

113h Greece: Reluctant presence

117c The great goddess and the palace architecture of Crete

117d Mourners on Greek vases: Remarks on the social history of women

156a Women: Model for possession by Greek daemons

156b Exit Atossa: Images of women in Greek historiography on Persia

156f Women and housing in classical Greece: The archaeological evidence

156g Women on Athenian vases: Problems of interpretation

156h Bound to bleed: Artemis and Greek women

156m Infanticide in Hellenistic Greece

156q The role of Jewish women in the religion, ritual and cult of Graeco-Roman Palestine

162b Putting kin and kinship to good use: The circulation of goods, labour, and names on Karpathos (Greece)

213d Sexual divisions and ethnic adaptation: The case of Greek-Cypriot women

244f The roles of Greek husbands and wives: Definitions and fulfillment

325e Ecstasy and possession: Women of ancient Greece and the cult of Dionysus

371d Essential objects and the sacred: Interior and exterior space in an urban Greek locality

372c Women and sport in ancient Greece

380m A statistical analysis of female participation in work and the effects on the population and socioeconomic development: A case study of Greece

419a Early Greece: The origins of the western attitude toward women

419e The maenad in early Greek art

419f Classical Greek attitudes to sexual behavior

471f Women at work in Greece: The sociological and legal perspectives

Greek Orthodox

see also Religion

457c Doves and magpies: Village women in the Greek Orthodox Church

Green

350b Women workers and the green revolution

Green, Anna Katharine

1f Anna Katharine Green

Greenham Common

167h On common ground: The women's peace camp at Greenham Common

215h A voice from the peace camps: Greenham Common and Upper Heyford

Greenwich Village

231f Feminism, men, and modern love: Greenwich Village, 1900-1925

Grief

344o Women and widowhood: The suffering beyond grief

Grievance

169o Grievance handling for women stewards

261g Faculty grievance procedure

261c Grievances and their redress in the eighties

Grimké, Angelina Weld

14x Black women playwrights from Grimké to Shange: Selected synopses of their works

150m "Under the days": The buried life and poetry of Angelina Weld Grmiké

Grotesque

109o The maternal legacy: The grotesque tradition in Flannery O'Connor's female gothic

Ground

371a Ground rules and social maps for women: An introduction

381g Covering the ground

Group

8f The adolescent girl in a group home

16c Issues in feminist therapy: The work of a woman's study group

16d Therapeutic aspects of consciousness-raising groups

26c Group treatment of children in shelters for battered women

36aa C/SEC: A special-interest interpersonal group brings about change

37q Group identity development within black families

38t The self/group actualization of black women

111i The Hillcrest School of Oregon: Guided group interaction in a juvenile institution

140e Some effects of proportions on group life: Skewed sex ratios and responses to token women

146e Group therapy with female adolescent incest victims

146g Individual and group treatment of mothers of incest victims

167c Working as a group

180w Mothers and daughters: Another minority group

209p Strengthening group solidarity of clericals: A case study

243c The role and status of women scientific research workers in research groups

285s Establishing a women's group for disabled clients

291o Group psychotherapy with sexually abused children

291p The co-therapy relationship in group treatment of sexually mistreated adolescent girls

326g Group work with preadolescent sexual assault victims

359s Group process for women with orgasmic difficulties

359hh Group work with widows

359uu The consciousness-raising group as a model for therapy with women

359vv The psychotherapeutic impact of women's consciousness-raising groups

367g Women in sectarian and utopian groups

428k The formation of an ethnic group: Colombian female workers in Venezuela

435a Representing women: The transition from social movement to interest group

447h Sex discrimination in group pensions

461c Discussion: Further thoughts on a group discussion by black women about sexuality

467e The stance of Britain's major parties and interest groups

Grow

68f Chinese women: The relative influences of ideological revolution, economic growth, and cultural change

69d The black woman growing up

93p Women's stake in a high-growth economy in the United States

104b Cash crop production and family labour: Tobacco growers in Corrientes, Argentina

107p Differences in males and females in joint movement range during growth

120f To grow a daughter: Cultural liberation and the dynamics of oppression in Jamaica

145j Growing up female in the nineteenth century

152b Growing up lesbian and Catholic

178d Growing up: The impact of loss and change

185f Growing up slowly: Another century of childhood

233b The effect of work on placental function and fetal growth

279k Normal and abnormal sexual dimorphic patterns of growth and development

301h Growing up southern & sexy

307x A spermdonor baby grows up

Guadalupe

68m La chicana: Guadalupe or malinche

Guadalupe, Mexico

194a The Virgin of Guadalupe and the female self-image: A Mexican case history

Guatemala

82m Participation by women in Guatemalan cooperatives

82t The female family business: A Guatemalan example

421b Female-headed households and domestic organization in San Isidro, Guatemala: A test of Hammel and Laslett's comparative typology

Guaymí

269e New roles for males in Guaymí society

Guess

309t Guessing and misinformation about pregnancy risk among urban mothers

Guidance

72g Guidance and counseling of Spanish-background girls

259h Guidance and pastoral care

Guido, Beatriz

313l Alienation and eros in three stories by Beatriz Guido, Marta Lynch and Amalia Jamilis

Guild of Empire

390l The Australian women's Guild of Empire

Guilford, J. P.
158g "Rather worse than folly?" psychology measures femininity and masculinity, 1: From Terman and Miles to the Guilfords

Guilford, Ruth B.
158g "Rather worse than folly?" psychology measures femininity and masculinity, 1: From Terman and Miles to the Guilfords

Guilt
78d Guilty by reason of sex: Young women and the juvenile justice system

Guinea-Bissau
39f The role of women in the revolution in Guinea-Bissau
370p A Nhara of the Guinea-Bissau region: Mãe Aurélia Correia

Guinea-Conakry
370q Women slavers of Guinea-Conakry

Gulma, Upper Volta
385h International development and the evolution of women's economic roles: A case study from northern Gulma, Upper Volta

Gun
129p If you liked gun control, you'll love the antiabortion amendment

Gurthr
384m Beret as the Norse mythological goddess Freya/Gurthr

Guru
325c Mother Guru: Jnanananda of Madras, India

Guthrie JR., A. B.
384j Pioneer women in the works of two Montana authors: Interviews with Dorothy M. Johnson and A. B. Guthrie, Jr.

Gutteridge, Helena
157j Helena Gutteridge: Votes for women and trade unions

Gutzkow, Karl
32e *Wally, die Zweiflerin* and *Madonna*: A discussion of sex-socialization in the nineteenth century

Gymnastics
107q Somatic and motor characteristics of female gymnasts
147x Adele Parot: Pathfinder for the Dioclesian Lewis school of gymnastic expression in the American west

Gyn/Ecology
229t Gyn/ecology: Spinning new time/space

Gynecologist
237a The gynecologist's approach (premenstrual tension)

Gynecology
240g Psychological aspects of gynaecological cancer
240i Psychological preparation for gynaecological surgery
253h Sexism in gynecologic practices
285m Sexual rehabilitation after gynecologic cancer
460t Self-help in gynecological practice

Gynecorps Project
16g The Gynecorps Project

Gynocentric
120c Gynocentric values and feminist psychology

Gynogram
27d Ambivalence in the Gynogram: Sade's utopian woman

Habitable
356m Honing a habitable languagescape: Women's images for the new world frontiers

Hadewijch
188h The Brabant mystic: Hadewijch

Hadith
368c Women in Shíi Fiqh: Images through the Hadith

Hage, Uta
399r Uta Hagen and Eva Le Gallienne

Hagen
200h No nature, no culture: The Hagen case
282e Self-interest and the social good: Some implications of Hagen gender imagery

Hagiography
187e Anglo-Saxon nuns in Anglo-Norman hagiography: Humility and power

Hairdressing
139h 'Getting on'. Gender differences in career development: A case study in the hairdressing industry

Haiti
39bb The black woman in Haitian society and literature

Hakka
177e Hakka women

Halakhah
211a The Jew who wasn't there: *Halakhah* and the Jewish woman

Hall
203q Women at city hall

Hall, Hazel
135h When silence has its way with you: Hazel Hall

Hall, Radclyffe
119a Inverts and experts: Radclyffe Hall and the lesbian identity

Hamburg, Germany
144h Women's work and the family: Women garment workers in Berlin and Hamburg before the First World War

Hammel, E.A.
421b Female-headed households and domestic organization in San Isidro, Guatemala: A test of Hammel and Laslett's comparative typology

Hand
108c The female hand in Heian Japan: A first reading
256g One hand tied behind us: A review essay
417s The craft of their hands

Handicap
see also Disability
79p Decisions about handicapped newborns: Values and procedures
79r Rights of a handicapped neonate: What every parent and professional should know

Handkerchief
7u New expanded-type version lesbian handkerchief code

Hanging
280l Erotized repetitive hangings

Hangover
84c The unit of political analysis: Our Aristotelian hangover

Happy
see also Emotion
42j Happily ever after
224m Revolution in the pursuit of happiness: Love and community-building on the left

Harassment
see also Sexual Harassment
176e Harassment in rural America
323i Coercion or male culture: A new look at co-worker harassment

Hardy, Thomas
286f "Swinburne planteth, Hardy watereth": Victorian views of pain and pleasure in human sexuality
286g Bathsheba's lovers: Male sexuality in *Far from the Madding Crowd*

Harem
68g Up from the harem? The effects of class and sex on political life in northern India

Harkness, Georgia
412f Georgia Harkness: Social activist and/or mystic

Harlem Renaissance
442i Poets and versifiers, singers and signifiers: Women of the Harlem Renaissance

Harleth, Gwendolen
142c A Meredithian glance at Gwendolen Harleth
143j Gwendolen Harleth and "The girl of the period"

Harlot
238h Harlot or heroine? Changing views of prostitution, 1870-1920
399j Enter the harlot

Harman, Moses
129o The persecutiion of Moses Harman

Harriet Martineau's Autobiography
452d *Harriet Martineau's Autobiography*: The making of a female philosopher

Harvard University
303i Fair Harvard and the fairer sex

Harvest
86f Following the harvest: The health hazards of migrant and seasonal farmworking women

Haunt
20b Atwood's haunted sequences: *The Circle Game, The Journals of Susanna Moodie,* and *Power Politics*

Hausa
350d Resource allocation and the sexual division of labor: A case study of a Moslem Hausa village in northern Nigeria
385c Dependence and autonomy: The economic activities of secluded Hausa women in Kano, Nigeria

473c Women's role in a Muslim Hausa town (Mirria, Republic of Niger)

Haute Provence

162f Tensions, dissensions, and ruptures inside the family in seventeenth- and eighteenth-century Haute Provence

Häutungen

32o Verena Stefan's Häutungen: Homoeroticism and feminism

Hawaii

190c Age at menarche and year of birth in relation to adult height and weight among Caucasian, Japanese, and Chinese women living in Hawaii

412r Korean women in Hawaii, 1903-1945: The role of Methodism in their liberation and in their participation in the Korean independence movement

420p Female Asian immigrants in Honolulu: Adaptation and success

Hawthorne, Nathaniel

17c Thwarted nature: Nathaniel Hawthorne as feminist

Hayworth, Rita

406f Resistance through charisma: Rita Hayworth and Gilda

Hazard

34e No fertile women need apply: Employment discrimination and reproductive hazards in the workplace

53h Health hazards associated with oral contraceptives

86b The risks of healing: The hazards of the nursing profession

86c The health hazards of office work

86f Following the harvest: The health hazards of migrant and seasonal farmworking women

86m The home is the workplace: Hazards, stress, and pollutants in the household

86n From grassroots activism to political power: Women organizing against environmental hazards

96c Passion as a mental health hazard

96f Women and employment: Some emotional hazards

183g Hazards faced by women at work

209x Health hazards in the computerized office

209z A union perspective on health hazards of VDTs

233c The hazards of work in pregnancy

233d Women workers at higher risk of reproductive hazards

233e Reproductive hazards of the American life style

233g The epidemiological identification of reproductive hazards

233l What evidence is required to identify a chemical as a reproductive hazard?

233p Legal considerations of reproductive hazards in industry in the United Kingdom

233q Legal considerations of reproductive hazards in industry in the United States

253g Reproductive hazards in the workplace: A course curriculum guide

305p Is your job hazardous to your health?

424h Occupational health hazards of female industrial workers in Malaysia

447i A legal perspective on workplace reproductive hazards

447m The control of hazardous exposures in the workplace

He/Man

171b Beyond the he/man approach: The case for nonsexist language

Head

21k Indira Gandhi as head of government

421b Female-headed households and domestic organization in San Isidro, Guatemala: A test of Hammel and Laslett's comparative typology

Heal

53d Health effects of becoming widowed

86b The risks of healing: The hazards of the nursing profession

229aa The healing powers of women

248h Old wives' tales? Women healers in English history

353z Ministries of healing: Mary Baker Eddy, Ellen G. White, and the religion of health

362g The politics of healing in Malaysia

466c Healing as women's work in Bali

Health

see also Health Care, Medicine

7t Smokers protest healthism

14l Black women's health: Notes for a course

29i Health maintenance: Exercise and nutrition

34j Black women's health: Notes for a course

34m Bibliography: Women, science, and health

53h Health hazards associated with oral contraceptives

53v Implications of epidemiologic data for developing health policy for women

55h The role of community health centers

70f Health problems facing American Indian women

71c Mental health issues among Asian-American women

71e Asian women in professional health schools, with emphasis on nursing

73c Developing a neighborhood-based health facility

79o Perfectibility and the neonate: The burden of expectations on mothers and their health providers

82g Nutrition and health

86c The health hazards of office work

86f Following the harvest: The health hazards of migrant and seasonal farmworking women

86g Sexual harassment and women's health

86h Minority women, work, and health

147d The ladies' department of the *American Farmer*, 1825-1830: A locus for the advocacy of family health and exercise

169p Occupational health and safety for women workers: Some teaching models

178o Physical health issues

183h Women's health

190aa Implications for women's health and well-being

209u Occupational health and the design of work

209v An issue of respect: Women workers demand healthy and safe offices

209x Health hazards in the computerized office

209y The health impacts of low-level radiation on VDT operators

209z A union perspective on health hazards of VDTs

210c Out of the *Mikvah* into the sauna: A study of women's health clubs

210l Concerns about parental health

233n A trade union view of reproductive health

233o A management view of reproductive health

233s The contribution of the occupational health services

240m A feminist perspective on women and health

253k The health of older women in our society

253l Sexism and racism in health policy

265o Strategies of healthy sex role development in modernized India

265p Effectiveness of self-persuasion in producing healthy attitudes towards polygyny

285a The impact of sexuality, professional authoritarianism, and health crises on rehabilitation

285e Physical disability, life-threatening illness, and enhancement of sexual health

295i Women's health issues

297e Incidence or incidents: Political and methodological underpinnings of a health research process in a small Italian town

304a Introduction: Warning! Sex-role stereotypes may be hazardous to your health

304i Women, weight, and health

305p Is your job hazardous to your health?

308a Teenage women in the United States: Sex, contraception, pregnancy, fertility, and maternal and infant health

309k The health and social consequences of teenage childbearing

317c Physical activity as it relates to the health of the aged

319l Health and illness perceptions of the Chicana

321d Natural resources: Health, reproduction and the gender order

324e Economic consequences of poor health in mature women

333m Women in the health role

344e Women, health, and medicine

353x Making women modern: Middle-class women and health reform in nineteenth-century America

353y Mary Gove Nichols, prophetess of health

353z Ministries of healing: Mary Baker Eddy, Ellen G. White, and the religion of health

354e Women workers in the health service industry

354f Employment and women's health: An analysis of causal relationships

395b Women as promoters of health in the developing world

395d Women, food and health in Tanzania: A crisis of the 1980s

395e Water and sanitation-related health constraints on women's contribution to the economic development of communities

395j Health beliefs and behaviors of middle class urban women in Lahore, Pakistan

396f Well woman clinics: A positive approach to women's health

423b Women and health: The social dimensions of biomedical data

424h Occupational health hazards of female industrial workers in Malaysia

440m In sickness and in health: Social policy and the control of women

465e Women and health policy

447b Overview: The health of working women

447f Employee health services for women workers

447g Special needs of women in health examinations

453s Feminist women's health centers

455j Women and the mental health system

456a Why women's health?

456p Health education

469h The utilization of pediatric health services by Hispanic mothers

Health Care

see also Care

16e Women and health care

80v Health care services for children in day care programs

265b Ethnic differences in sex stereotyping by mothers: Implications for health care

307aa Juggling health care technology and women's needs

354a Women and health care: A comparison of theories

354d Sexism and racism in the American health care industry: A comparative analysis

390y Sexism and health care

395c Women and health care personnel planning

397m Lesbians and contemporary health care systems: Oppression and opportunity

411m Health care and midlife women

455i Women and the health care system: Implications for social work practice

Heart

53c The effect of employment, family and job stress on coronary heart disease patterns in women

53r Epidemiology of coronary heart disease in women

231v Hearts of darkness

268e Sex roles and psychophysiological disorders: Coronary heart disease

Heathen

379j The ethnological mirror: American evangelical women and their heathen sisters, 1870-1910

Heaven

383e The heavenly utopia of Elizabeth Stuart Phelps

Hegel, Georg Wilhelm Friedrich

106g Hegel's conception of the family

Hegemony

120i Ideological hegemony in political discourse: Women's specificity and equality

396a Male hegemony in family planning

Heian

108c The female hand in Heian Japan: A first reading

Height

190c Age at menarche and year of birth in relation to adult height and weight among Caucasian, Japanese, and Chinese women living in Hawaii

Helen

419d Sappho and Helen

Hell

17k Brother Theodore, hell on women

Hellenistic

156m Infanticide in Hellenistic Greece

Hellman, Lillian

399z Lillian Hellman's memorial drama

452j Lillian Hellman and the strategy of the "other"

452k The metaphysics of matrilinearism in women's autobiography: Studies of Mead's *Blackberry Winter*, Hellman's *Pentimento*, Angelou's *I Know Why the Caged Bird Sings*, and Kingston's *The Woman Warrior*

Heloise

188d The French scholar-lover: Heloise

Help

111 Women helping women: Opening the door to treatment

96l The role and function of women's consciousness raising: Self-help, psychotherapy, or political activation?

120h The personal is political: Feminism and the helping professions

301m It seems to help me bear it better when she knows about it

365k Consciousness-raising and self-help

425e Trying hurts women, helps men: The meaning of effort

460s Self-help for sex

460t Self-help in gynecological practice

472i Widow-to-widow: The elderly widow and mutual help

Helpless

404b Learned helplessness

404c Learned helplessness, depression, and alcohol problems of women

Hemingway, Ernest

17p Hemingway and Fauntleroy: An androgynous pursuit

Henry Street Settlement

417k A utopian female support network: The case of the Henry Street Settlement

Hensel, Fanny Mendelssohn

108j Fanny Mendelssohn Hensel: Musician in her brother's shadow

Herb

395i Women's understanding about reproductive physiology and their choice of herbal medicines in Cali, Colombia

Heretic

188i The French heretic Beguine: Marguerite Porete

Heritage

37b Interpreting the African heritage in Afro-American family organization

42d Our heritage

76c The dual heritage

180x Heritages: Dimensions of mother-daughter relationships in women's autobiographies

229f From the house of Yemanja: The goddess heritage of black women

229o Our heritage is our power

287a Our sexual heritage

333c A certain heritage: Women and their children in north Australia

Hero

106i Oedipus as hero: Family and family metaphors in Nietzsche

143h The hero as dilettante: *Middlemarch* and *Nostromo*

254c The artist as hero in Maxine Hong Kingston's *The Woman Warrior*

254d *Song of Solomon*: The hero with a woman's face

332n Plain, black, and decently wild: The heroic possibilities of *Maud Martha*

445m Heroes vs women: Conflict and duplicity in Stegner

Heroin

392h Women, heroin, and property crime

Heroine

17b Fenimore Cooper's Heroines

20j *Lady Oracle*: The narrative of a fool-heroine

27g "Old maids have friends": The unmarried heroine of Trollope's Barsetshire novels

182b Homes fit for heroines: Housing in the twenties

238h Harlot or heroine? Changing views of prostitution, 1870-1920

242b The birth of the artist as heroine: (Re)production, the *Künslerroman* tradition, and the fiction of Katherine Mansfield

254k Know your heroines

338f 'Two words for women': A reassessment of O'Casey's heroines

399u Looking to women: Rachel Crothers and the feminist heroine

409f Gerty MacDowell: Joyce's sentimental heroine

413k Pioneer into feminist: Jane Mander's heroines

448n Sister to Faust: The city's "hungry" woman as heroine

450h Doris Bett's Nancy Finch: A heroine for the 1980s

450i Mermaids, angels and free women: The heroines of Elizabeth Spencer's fiction

Herstory

see also Women's History

455b A herstory of women in social work

Hesiod

419c Workers and drones: Labor, idleness and gender definition in Hesiod's beehive

Heterogeneity

141f Genetic heterogeneity and breast cancer: Variable tumor spectra

Heterosexual

24a Physical attractiveness, sex roles and heterosexual attraction

60e The social enforcement of heterosexuality and lesbian resistance in the 1920's

60f The twenties' backlash: Compulsory heterosexuality, the consumer family, and the waning of feminism

152d Overcoming the structured evil of male domination and heterosexism

212a Heterosexuality, couples and parenthood: A 'natural' cycle?

212p The 'perks' of male power: Heterosexuality and the oppression of women

231h Compulsory heterosexuality and lesbian existence

257g Is a feminist heterosexuality possible?

257h Heterosexual sex: Power and desire for the other

305f Once more with feeling: Heterosexuality and feminist consciousness

397i Compulsory heterosexuality and lesbian existence

397j Lesbians and the law: Where sexism and heterosexism meet

439d Compulsory heterosexuality and lesbian existence

Heywood, Charlotte

164k In between - Anne Elliot marries a sailor and Charlotte Heywood goes to the seaside

Hidatsa

148d Male/female task differentiation among the Hidatsa: Toward the development of an archeological approach to the study of gender

Hide

452g Selves in hiding

Hierarchy

115l Snakes and ladders: Reflections on hierarchy and the fall

229ww Spiritual hierarchies: The empress' new clothes?

282b The gender revolution and the transition from bisexual horde to patrilocal band: The origins of gender hierarchy

282k Gender and sexuality in hierarchical societies: The case of Polynesia and some comparative implications

387s The impact of hierarchical structures on the work behavior of women and men

417e The Shakers: Gender equality in hierarchy

Higgins, Henry

410d Recruitment of women to suburban city councils: Higgins vs. Chevalier

Higgins, Jennie

128e The "Jennie Higginses" of the "New South in the West": A regional survey of socialist activists, agitators, and organizers, 1901-1917

High School

see also Education

147ee Major influences on the development of high school girls' sports in Ontario

265h Sex typing in occupational preferences of high school boys and girls

309y Adolescent pregnancy prevention services in high school clinics

High Tech

see also Technology

36s Community alternatives to high technology birth

209bb Building new partnerships in a high-tech economy

307v Paths to power in high technology organizations

339c Women managers: Moving up in a high tech society

424c Trends in female labour force participation in Taiwan: The transition toward higher technology activities

Higher Education

see also Education

14m Three's a crowd: The dilemma of the black woman in higher education

31q Contemporary feminist perspectives on women and higher education

70c The status of American Indian women in higher education

72e Puerto Rican women in higher education in the United States

73g Changing needs of ethnic women in higher education

250k Women in higher education: A case study of the open university

302j Women in academic-library, higher-education, and corporate management: A research review

303c Mary Munford and higher education for women in Virginia

320b Culture, service, and work: Changing ideals of higher education for women

320c Recent trends in the higher education of women

320e Sex bias in aptitude and achievement tests used in higher education

344l Women and higher education: Sex differentials in the status of students and scholars

351i The participation of minority women in higher education

351j Women, space, and power in higher education

394c A history of the Wisconsin Coordinating Council of Women in Higher Education

Hildegard of Bingen

188e The German visionary: Hildegard of Bingen

Hill, Susan

318e Cold enclosures: The fiction of Susan Hill

Hillcrest School of Oregon

111i The Hillcrest School of Oregon: Guided group interaction in a juvenile institution

Hindsight

168c Hindsight is 20/20: The development, achievements and dilemmas of feminist literary criticism

Hindu

255b Purdah revisited: A comparison of Hindu and Muslim interpretations of the cultural meaning of purdah in South Asia

255c Purdah and the Hindu family in central India

255d The domestic realm in the lives of Hindu women in Calcutta

325f Golden handprints and red-painted feet: Hindu childbirth rituals in central India

325g Hindu women's family and household rites in a north Indian village

457f Women, fertility and the worship of gods in a Hindu village

Hire

394l We have hired couples for years

Hispanic

see also Ethnic, Minority

150i Something Latino was up with us

201l A stitch in our time: New York's Hispanic garment workers in the 1980s

216f Parenting for multiculturalism: A Mexican-American model

308i The impact of adolescent pregnancy on Hispanic adolescents and their families

319a Family planning practices of Mexican Americans

319c Mexican, Mexican American, and Chicana childbirth

319h "All the good and bad in this world": Women, traditional medicine, and Mexican American culture

Hispanic American Woman

72k Social issues confronting Hispanic-American women

Hispanic Woman

16v Social services and the Hispanic woman

36k Sterilization abuse and Hispanic women

54b The unidentified problem of alcoholism among Hispanic women

54c New approaches for prevention and education of alcoholism among Hispanic women

54d Program planning for Hispanic women: One ideal model

60m Laid bare by the system: Work and survival for black and Hispanic women

68m La chicana: Guadalupe or malinche

72a The lack of political involvement of Hispanic women as it relates to their educational background and occupational opportunities

72d Latinas in educational leadership: Chicago, Illinois

72f Impediments to Hispanic women organizing

72h Hispanic women move forward - Out of a marginal status

72j La Chicana: An overview

72l Chicana identity: Interaction of culture and sex roles

72m The need for an anthropological and cognitive approach to the education of Hispanic women

81c Chicanas and Mexican immigrant families 1920-1940: Women's subordination and family exploitation

192b Mexican women in organization

192c Lives of Chicana activists: The Chicano student movement (a case study)

192d Women in the Chicano movement

192i Se me acabó la canción: An ethnography of non-consenting sterilizations among Mexican women in Los Angeles

192w Appendix: Profile of the Chicana: A statistical fact sheet

225i Cultural and historical influences on sexuality in Hispanic/Latin women: Implications for psychotherapy

319b Chicana use of abortion: The case of Alcala

319c Mexican, Mexican American, and Chicana childbirth

319f Symbolic strategies for change: A discussion of the Chicana women's movement

319g Mexican American women as innovators

319k Social networks and survival strategies: An exploratory study of Mexican American, black and Anglo family female heads in San Jose, California

319l Health and illness perceptions of the Chicana

319n Feminism: The Chicana and the Anglo versions, a historical analysis

319m The status of Hispanic women in nursing

319p To be aged, Hispanic, and female: The triple risk

320i Educational and career progress of Chicana and Native-American college women

408g The convent as catalyst for autonomy: Two Hispanic nuns of the seventeenth century

408p Sexual politics and the theme of sexuality in Chicana poetry

412h Hispanic clergy wives: Their contribution to United Methodism in the southwest, later nineteenth century to the present

434h The Chicana in transition

469a Introduction: Latina women in transition

469d Hispanic women in suburbia

469h The utilization of pediatric health services by Hispanic mothers

469k Family roles of Hispanic women: Stereotypes, empirical findings, and implications for research

Hispanoamericana

313k Narradoras hispanoamericanas: Vieja y nueva problemática en renovadas laboraciones

Historie d'O

225u *Histoire d'O*: The construction of a female subject

Historia Arcana

419m Theodora and Antonina in the *Historia Arcana*: History and/or fiction?

Historian

112j Mercy Otis Warren: Playwright, poet, and historian of the American revolution (American, 1728-1814)

325m Empress Wu and the historians: A tyrant and saint of classical China

389f Lady Dilke (1840-1904): The six lives of an art historian

412b The last fifteen years: Historians' changing views of American women in religion and society

460c Discussion: A historian's approach

Historiography

156b Exit Atossa: Images of women in Greek historiography on Persia

History

see also Herstory, Social History, Women's History

7e On the history of cultural sadism

22a "Glory is like a circle in the water"...Thoughts and suggestions towards a definition of feminine historical research

22b Wills, deeds, and charters as sources for the history of medieval women

22c Iconography as a means of research on the history of the status of women

33g Gender and genre: Women as historical writers, 1400-1820

36b Historical styles of contraceptive advocacy

37n Parenting in black families with young children: A historical perspective

38a The black woman: A historical overview

39m Racism and tradition: Black womanhood in historical perspective

52k Economic and family roles of men and women in Northern Europe: A historical cross-national comparison

61c National Archives resources for research in the history of American women

61o Photographs as historical documents (American women through the camera's eye)

73i Irish, Italian, and Jewish women at the grassroots level: A historical and sociological perspective

81m Socialist feminism between the two World Wars: Insights from oral history

84o The feminist standpoint: Developing the ground for a specifically feminist historical materialism

90h Jobs and gender: A history of the structuring of educational employment by sex

96a Introduction: An historical view of psychotherapy and women's rights

100b Teaching and 'women's work': A comparative historical and ideological analysis

100c The Indian and African presence in the Americas: Some aspects of historical distortion

103d The transformation of patriarchy: The historic role of the state

104h Domestic work in rural Iceland: An historical overview

116l Women's work: Views from the history of philosophy

117a Introduction: Feminism and art history

117k Art history and its exclusions: The example of Dutch art

120e Feminism and the writing and teaching of history

123d What the women's movement has done to American history

126n Does equality mean sameness? A historical perspective on the college curriculum for women with reflections on the current situation

127i Eruptions of funk: Historicizing Toni Morrison

132p Visibility and difference: Black women in history and literature - pieces of a paper and some ruminations

144a The German family: A critical survey of the current state of historical research

145i Self-conscious histories: Biographies of German women in the nineteenth century

147v The eastern legacy - the early history of physical education for women

147z History and structure of the department of physical education at the University of California with special reference to women's sports

147gg The contributions of women to the history of competitive tennis in the United States in the twentieth century

147pp A historical perspective of women's membership in selected national sports organizations

157a Writing women into British Columbia's history

158a The power of the past: History and the psychology of women

162o Family fun in Starve Harbor: Custom, history and confrontation in village Newfoundland

166d The search for women in Indonesian history

168d What has the feminist perspective done for Canadian history?

169a Labor education and women workers: An historical perspective

169k Using oral history in the classroom

169m Labor history through field trips

176p Resources for lesbian history

176q Who hid lesbian history?

177a The life history method

177b Historical background on Chinese women

180h "The mother's history" in George Eliot's life, literature and political ideology

181a Women hold up two-thirds of the sky: Notes for a revised history of technology

184a Medieval marriage characteristics: A neglected factor in the history of medieval serfdom

187f Why English nunneries had no history: A study of the problems of the English nunneries founded after the conquest

189d Women lost and found: The impact of feminism on history

190o Menarche and teenage pregnancy: A misuse of historical data

194a The Virgin of Guadalupe and the female self-image: A Mexican case history

200c Natural facts: A historical perspective on science and sexuality

205b When you don't know the language, listen to the silence: An historical overview of native Indian women in BC

205r Sinners or sinned against?: Historical aspects of female juvenile delinquency in British Columbia

205u Cheap at half the price: The history of the fight for equal pay in BC

206c The patriarchal thread - A history of exploitation

211p History, fiction, and the tradition: Creating a Jewish feminist poetic

215t The women's peace crusade: The history of a forgotten campaign

225i Cultural and historical influences on sexuality in Hispanic/Latin women: Implications for psychotherapy

225s The historical repression of women's sexuality

227a The history of the housewife

231b "Charity girls" and city pleasures: Historical notes on working-class sexuality, 1880-1920

231k The Afro-American female: The historical context of the construction of sexual identity

234i Women and the concept of change in history

248a Introduction: The contemporary challenge in nursing history

248f Asylum nursing before 1914: A chapter in the history of labour

248g 'The history of the present' - contradiction and struggle in nursing

248h Old wives' tales? Women healers in English history

248i Archives and the history of nursing

256h Examining family history

264a Women's history and the revision of southern history

264f Historians construct the southern woman

268b A historical perspective

274i History

284a The sexual abuse of children and minors: A short history of legal control efforts

289b The cross-cultural and historical context

291a Definition and recognition of sexual child abuse: Historical and cultural perspectives

301g Corn shuckings, fiddle contests, square dances: Oral history with Lily May Ledford

302a Revision versus reality: Women in the history of the public library movement, 1876-1920

303p The historical perspective: A bibliographical essay

306o Oral history as a resource in teaching women's studies

315a The emergence of women in twentieth-century Chilean history and literature

318c Olivia Manning: Witness to history

319n Feminism: The Chicana and the Anglo versions, a historical analysis

320p Life after college: Historical links between women's education and women's work

329c Virginia Woolf and Julia Stephen: The distaff side of history

330l Nature and history in *The Years*

333g The recent history of the Borroloola aboriginal people and their struggle for land rights

333l Historical factors which have affected aboriginal lifestyles since colonisation

333s Recording our history

338i Rewriting history: Anna Parnell's The tale of a great *sham*

344cc The historical background

348b Hidden from history: Women victims of crime

351b The impacts of irrelevance: Women in the history of American education

352e Historical perspectives on women in educational leadership

352h Coeducation and the development of leadership skills in women: Historical perspectives from Cornell University, 1868-1900

353f "Imagine my surprise": Women's relationships in historical perspective

353n Chlorotic girls, 1870-1920: A historical perspective on female adolescence

368a Women in pre-revolutionary Iran: A historical overview

368m The institution of Mut'a marriage in Iran: A formal and historical perspective

370m Appendix: A note on Anlo (Ewe) slavery and the history of a slave

372b An historical overview

375h Historical background of "protective" labor legislation: *Muller v. Oregon*

384f Sacajawea of myth and history

384g Miscegenation in popular western history and fiction

390a Women and the family in Australian history

390p The unwritten history of Adela Pankhurst Walsh

394b History of the Association of Faculty Women at Madison

394c A history of the Wisconsin Coordinating Council of Women in Higher Education

412a Women's history/everyone's history

416l Women engineers in history: Profiles in holism and persistence

418c The history of the family

419m Theodora and Antonina in the *Historia Arcana*: History and/or fiction?

430e A historical background to the women's movement in Iran

434g Asian-American women: A historical and cultural perspective

440c Redistribution to children and to mothers: A history of child endowment and family allowances

445n Willa Cather and the sense of history

449a Introduction: A historical perspective

454c Widowhood in eighteenth-century Massachusetts: A problem in the history of the family

454q Cookbooks and law books: The hidden history of career women in twentieth-century America

458b Midlife work history and retirement income

459c Class and historical analysis for the study of women and economic change

460b The history of female sexuality in the United States

462f A historical addendum

469i A preliminary historical analysis of women and work in Puerto Rico: 1899-1975

History of Sexuality

439t *The History of Sexuality. Vol. 1: An Introduction* by Michel Foucault

Hittite

156i Hittite birth rituals

Holism

416l Women engineers in history: Profiles in holism and persistence

Holistic

82e The development process: A holistic approach

229dd see for yourself: Women's spirituality in holistic art

236c Premenstrual syndrome - a holistic approach

404i Holistic approaches for women

Holland

471d Women at work in Holland

Hollingworth, Leta

158d Leta Hollingworth: Toward a sexless intelligence

Holmes, Julia Archibald

384c A study of feminism as a motif in "A journey to Pike's Peak and New Mexico" by Julia Archibald Holmes

Holocaust

336l Women and the holocaust: The case of German and German-Jewish women

Holt, Victoria

109c Victoria Holt's gothic romances: A structuralist inquiry

Holy

22g Structural patterns in the legends of the holy women of Christianity

379g The holy woman and the urban community in sixteenth-century Avila

462o Feminist liberation theology and Yahweh as holy warrior: An analysis of symbol

Holy War

229tt The Christian right's "Holy War" against feminism

Homans, Miss

147y The influential Miss Homans

Home

8f The adolescent girl in a group home

50b The home turned upside down? The working-class family in cotton textiles 1780-1850

50o Technology and changes in the division of labour in the American home

86m The home is the workplace: Hazards, stress, and pollutants in the household

138f The conservative school? Sex roles at home, at work and at school

145n Social insurance and the family work of Oberlausitz home weavers in the late nineteenth century

150l Home

174s Creative teaching spaces: Home movies

182b Homes fit for heroines: Housing in the twenties

182h House and home

186e House, home and solitude: Memoirs and journals of May Sarton

203b The home: A critical problem for changing sex roles

205a "Sundays always make me think of home": Time and place in Canadian women's history

205j Six saucepans to one: Domestic science vs. the home in British Columbia 1900-1930

205bb From home to house: Women in the BC legislature

206h A woman's home is her factory

210g Labor markets and old ladies' homes

212f The sexual abuse of children in the home

212k Fatherhood: Bringing it all back home

216o The parent as educator: A home-school model of socialization

216p The relationship between home and school: A commentary on the current scene

227b The home: Its work and influence

235a At home

245i Home production for use in a market economy

305d Home sweet home?

305i The home: A contested terrain

335g Home thoughts from not so far away: A personal look at family

337j Women and cooperative home economics extension

341l Farming out the home: Women and agribusiness

355j Domestic labor as work discipline: The struggle over housework in foster homes

387f Home work and market work: Systematic segregation

390g Homes are divine workshops

392d Female delinquency and broken homes: A reassessment

412q For god and home and native land: The W.C.T.U.'s image of woman in the late nineteenth century

421v Some comments on the home roles of businesswomen in India, Australia and Canada

445e Homestead Home

Home Economics

274l Home economics

355f The new home economics: An agenda for sociological research

Homeland

213f Living in between: Turkish women in their homeland and in the Netherlands

Homeless

345h Single homeless women and alcohol

Homemaker

see also Domestic, Housewife, Housework

16s The displaced homemaker

46b Supplemental OASI benefits to homemakers through current spouse benefits, a homemaker credit, and child-care dropout years

344n The internalization of powerlessness: A case study of the displaced homemaker

355d Social status of the homemaker

458e Working women versus homemakers: Retirement resources and correlates of well-being

Homeopathy

353cc Homeopathy and sexual equality: The controversy over coeducation at Cincinnati's Pulte Medical College, 1873-1879

Homestead

445e Homestead Home

Homicide

145q The female victim: Homicide and women in Imperial Germany

270n Social psychological patterns of homicide in Turkey: A comparison of male and female convicted murders

280k Sexual dynamics in homicide and assault

Homoeroticism

32o Verena Stefan's Häutungen: Homoeroticism and feminism

Homophobia

133j Male homophobia

133l Androgyny, sex-role rigidity, and homophobia

150z Failure to transform: Homophobia in the black community

176i Homophobia in the classroom

254h Broaching the issue: Homophobia

434j Homophobia and social work practice with lesbians

Homosexual

see also Gay, Lesbian

111j Prison homosexuality: Re-examining conventional wisdom

133a Homosexual labeling and the male role

133n Views of homosexuality among social scientists

152c New sociological theory on homosexuality

152e Homosexuality, celibacy, religious life and ordination

152h Moral theology and homosexuality

152i Shifting attitudes toward homosexuality

223u The morality of homosexuality

223v Curing homosexuality

239f Homosexual orientation in women and men: A hormonal basis?

278g Homosexuality and literature

281e Homosexual and bisexual issues

282c The bow and the burden strap: A new look at institutionalized homosexuality in native North America

287h Homosexuality

418i Sexuality and homosexuality

Homosexuality in Perspective

439q *Homosexuality in Perspective* by William H. Masters and Virginia E. Johnson

Honduras

172h It all depends on the teacher (Honduras)

Honeymoon

369a New left women and men: The honeymoon is over

Hong Kong

177i Wage earners in Hong Kong

Honky Tonk

175w Honky Tonk Angels

Honolulu, HI

420p Female Asian immigrants in Honolulu: Adaptation and success

Honor

108e To restore honor and fortune: *The Autobiography of Lenor López de Córdoba*

205l Postscript: Women in whose honour BC schools have been named

229w Honor and ceremony in women's rituals

Hope

220l Change, hope and celebration

462x Envisioning our hopes: Some models of the future

Hopi

see also American Indian

417a Rethinking matriliny among the Hopi

Horizon

21g Expanding women's horizons in Indonesia: Toward maximum equality with minimum conflict

389b Widening horizons (1890-1930)

Hormone

34c From sin to sickness: Hormonal theories of lesbianism

53b The relationship of the sex hormone/prostaglandin interaction to female and male longevity

137m Gender, hormones, and psychopathology

141g Hormones, genetics, and breast cancer

239c Gonadal hormones and cognitive functioning

239d Human sex-hormone abnormalities viewed from an androgynous perspective: A reconsideration of the work of John Money

239f Homosexual orientation in women and men: A hormonal basis?

239j Adult life cycles: Changing roles and changing hormones

253c What's new in endocrinology? Target: Sex hormones

271n Hormones and behaviour: Introduction

271o Mood and behaviour changes in menopausal women receiving gonadal hormones or placebo

277b Hormones and sexual arousal

Horseback

102o Public nurturance and the man on horseback

Hosken Report: Genital and Sexual Mutiliation of Females

439r *The Hosken Report: Genital and Sexual Mutilation of Females* by Fran P. Hosken

Hosken, Fran P.

439r *The Hosken Report: Genital and Sexual Mutilation of Females* by Fran P. Hosken

Hospital

36t Contrasts in the birthing place: Hospital and birth center

162l Kinship and class consciousness: Family values and work experience among hospital workers in an American southern town

199j Computers, ward secretaries, and a walk-out in a Southern hospital

248b Nurse recruitment to four provincial hospitals 1881-1921

248c From Sarah Gamp to Florence Nightingale: A critical study of hospital nursing systems from 1840 to 1897

284r Courtroom use of hospital records in sexual assault cases

353gg "Little world of our own": The Pennsylvania Hospital Training School for Nurses, 1895-1907

396b Midwives, medical men and 'poor women labouring of child': Lying-in hospitals in eighteenth-century London

Hostel

205i The gentlewomen of Queen Mary's coronation hostel

Hostile

280c Nymphomania, hostile sex, and superego development

House

7y Hunger and thirst in the house of distorted mirrors

23i 'A woman's place is in the House and in the Senate': Women and the 1983 elections

103f Women and housing: The impact of government housing policy

144g Overcrowding and family life: Working-class families and the housing crisis in late nineteenth-century Duisburg

151a Housing ideals, structural constraints and the emancipation of women

156f Women and housing in classical Greece: The archaeological evidence

182b Homes fit for heroines: Housing in the twenties

182d House design and women's roles

182e Housing the family

182h House and home

186e House, home and solitude: Memoirs and journals of May Sarton

203d The appropriation of the house: Changes in house design and concepts of domesticity

203j Swedish women in single-family housing

203u Housing for single-parent families: A women's design

205bb From home to house: Women in the BC legislature

282h Pigs, women, and the men's house in Amazonia: An analysis of six Mundurucú myths

307i The GABe self-cleaning house

371c Women's space in a men's house: The British House of Commons

435f Women and housing: The limitations of liberal reform

House of Commons

371c Women's space in a men's house: The British House of Commons

The House of Mirth

27h Beauty in distress: *Daniel Deronda* and *The House of Mirth*

127c "The temptation to be a beautiful object": Double standard and double bind in *The House of Mirth*

House of Representatives

173g The politics of abortion in the House of Representatives in 1976

Household
see also Family

32q Literary emasculation: Household imagery in Christa Reinig's *Entmannung*

39v Household and family in the Caribbean: Some definitions and concepts

82s Household structure in Africa

86m The home is the workplace: Hazards, stress, and pollutants in the household

104a Aspects of non-capitalist social relations in rural Egypt: The small peasant household in an Egyptian delta village

104c Interhousehold co-operation in Peru's southern Andes: A case of multiple sibling-group marriage

144d Family and household: Social structures in a German village between the two World Wars

149a Domestic labour and the working-class household

149b Capital, the state and the origins of the working-class household

150nn Women's spirituality: A household act

153a Household structures and labor-force formation in the capitalist world-economy

153c Households as income-pooling units

153d The limits of using the household as a unit of analysis

153f Households, modes of living, and production systems

153g Development and underdevelopment of household-based production in Europe

153i Beyond the peasant to proletarian debate: African household formation in South Africa

153j Household economy and financial capital: The case of passbook savings in Brazil

153k The contribution of public goods to household reproduction: Case study from Brazil

153l State, collective, and household: The process of accumulation in China, 1949-65

153m Gender division within the U.S. working class: Households in the Philadelphia area, 1870-1945

153o Wages, consumption, and survival: Working class households in Puerto Rico in the 1930's

153q Conflicts inside and outside the household: A West African case study

203c The household as workplace: Wives, husbands, and children

207d Households as natural units

207e Work, consumption and authority within the household: A Moroccan case

208g Work, consumption and authority within the household: A Moroccan case

208h Households as natural units

241f 'It's a pleasure to cook for him': Food, mealtimes and gender in some South Wales households

307j Household technologies: Burden or blessing?

321j The distribution of income within households

325g Hindu women's family and household rites in a north Indian village

355a Prologue: Reflections on the study of household labor

355b An enlarged human existence? Technology and household work in nineteenth-century America

355c Housework technology and household work

355h Household time: A cross-cultural example

355i Contributions to household labor: Comparing wives' and husbands' reports

355l Household work, wage work, and sexual equality

388d Household economic strategies in Kingston, Jamaica

400h Energy needs of poor households: An abstract

421b Female-headed households and domestic organization in San Isidro, Guatemala: A test of Hammel and Laslett's comparative typology

424s The impact of female employment on household management

428e Household, community, national, and multinational industrial development

446p How working women combine work and household duties

458n Responsibility for household tasks: Comparing dual-earner and dual-retired marriages

459g The interrelationship between the division of labour in the household, women's roles and their impact on fertility

463b Intra-household implications of the involvement of women in the paid labor force

463d Influence of employment and children on intra-household travel behavior

463f The impact of women's employment on household travel patterns: A Swedish example

464g Consequences of seizing the reins in the household: A Marxist-feminist critique of Marx and Engels

468h Love and power: The division of household labour

Housekeeper

23e Labor women: Political housekeepers or politicians?

Housekeeping

129n Body housekeeping

Housewife
see also Domestic, Homemaker, Housework

46h The housewife and social security reform: A feminist perspective

58d Housewives

81h Two washes in the morning and a bridge party at night: The American housewife between the wars

153h The proletarian is dead: Long live the housewife?

227a The history of the housewife

227f The housewife

227o 'The housewife and her labour under capitalism' - a critique

307p Mother calls herself a housewife, but she buys bulls

336g "Professional" housewives: Stepsisters of the women's movement

386a Housewives

400d Impact of male migration on rural housewives

466g Housewives and farmers: Malay women in the Muda Irrigation Scheme

470g Standing on the edge: Working class housewives and the world of work

Housework
see also Domestic, Homemaker, Housewife

52u The industrialization of housework

89c Time spent in housework

103h Housework: Rethinking the costs and benefits

170e Single careers: Employment, housework and caring

181e Technology, housework, and women's liberation: A theoretical analysis

199d Housework and domestic labor: Racial and technological change

227e The politics of housework

227q Wages against housework

227r Wages for housework - political and theoretical considerations

263b Housework as a comparative advantage: The neoclassical theory of the sexual division of labor

355c Housework technology and household work

355e Satisfaction with housework: The social context

355j Domestic labor as work discipline: The struggle over housework in foster homes

417h Housework and utopia: Women and the Owenite socialist communities

Houston, Barbara

432o The ethics of gender discrimination: A response to Ann Diller and Barbara Houston's "Women's Physical Education"

Houston, TX

319d Breast-feeding and social class mobility: The case of Mexican migrant mothers in Houston, Texas

Howells, W.D. (William Dean)

17g W.D. Howells: The ever-womanly

Hrotsvit of Gandersheim

188b The Saxon canoness: Hrotsvit of Gandersheim

Hsin, Ping

449b Images of women in Ping Hsin's fiction

Huch, Ricarda

32j Ricarda Huch: Myth and reality

Hug, Fazlul

433f Bengal election, 1937: Fazlul Huq and M. A. Jinnah: A study in leadership stress in Bengal politics

Hull House

399dd Art theatre in Hull-House

Human

2g A human life statute

2m Abortion, privacy, and personhood: From *Roe v Wade* to the human life statute

3m Beneath the surface of the abortion dispute: Are women fully human?

23m 'Law reform and human reproduction': Implications for women

24d Perceptual and cognitive mechanisms in human sexual attraction

24e Social skill and human sexual attraction

24g Human sexuality in cross-cultural perspective

31b Human biology in feminist theory: Sexual equality reconsidered

48n Future influences on the interaction of gender and human sexual expression

49h Human resource planning and the intuitive manager: Models for the 1990's

51i Potential role of the pineal gland in the human menstrual cycle

57i Human sexuality: Messages in public environments

59g Human sexuality and mutuality

89g Family investments in human capital: Earnings of women

118d The dynamics of female experience: Process models and human values

118e Becoming human: A contextual approach to decisions about pregnancy and abortion

126p Human sexuality: New insights from women's history

158l Metatheoretical influences on conceptions of human development

178g The human cost of discrimination

185e Transformations in human reproduction

223j Sex, birth control, and human life

233m Animal and human studies in genetic toxicology

239d Human sex-hormone abnormalities viewed from an androgynous perspective: A reconsideration of the work of John Money

239e Biochemical and neurophysiological influences on human sexual behavior

239g A social psychological model of human sexuality

267e Career concepts and human resource management: The case of the dual-career couple

279b Sexual dimorphism in nonhuman primates

279l Human proportionality and sexual dimorphism

281a Human sexuality in the life cycle of the family system

298e Human sciences research on Algerian women

340a The female chimpanzee as a human evolutionary prototype

340b Women as shapers of the human adaptation

432j Competition, friendship, and human nature

439j Biological influences on human sex and gender

Human Rights

see also Right

31n A feminist analysis of the Universal Declaration of Human Rights

129b Human rights not founded on sex

Humanae Vitae

223i Humanae vitae

Humanism

33c Book-lined cells: Women and humanism in the early Italian Renaissance

33d Learned women of early modern Italy: Humanists and university scholars

95i Humanism versus feminism in the socialist movement: The life of Angelica Balabanoff

142g The choir invisible: The poetics of humanist piety

Humanistic

284l Humanistic treatment of father-daughter incest

Humanities

311d Feminism: A last chance for the humanities?

312f Feminism: A last chance for the humanities?

314c The humanities: Redefining the canon

Humanity

70a Insignificance of humanity, "Man is tampering with the moon and the stars": The employment status of American Indian women

142d *Middlemarch* and the new humanity

Humanize

343d Comic structure and the humanizing of Kate in *The Taming of the Shrew*

Humor

147n An analysis of humour pertaining to sportswomen in Canadian newspapers from 1910-1920

408c Sexual humor in misogynist medieval exampla

453e Humor in California underground women's comix

Hungary

159h Crimes against life committed by women in Hungary

Hunger

7y Hunger and thirst in the house of distorted mirrors

30t I had been hungry all the years

180s The hungry Jewish mother

211c The hungry Jewish mother

Hunt

157o Postscript: Huntresses

222k The job hunt

340c Woman the hunter: The Agta

Hunt, Violet

27l Violet Hunt's *Tales of the Unneasy*: Ghost stories of a worldly woman

Huq, Hasan Azizul

433m The image of Bengal in the emerging literature of Bangladesh: The fiction of Hasan Azizul Huq

Hurston, Zora Neale

14q "This infinity of conscious pain": Zora Neale Hurston and the black female literary tradition

17q Zora Neale Hurston: Changing her own words

30y Looking for Zora

Hurt

254g The hurt that lasts forever

425e Trying hurts women, helps men: The meaning of effort

Husband

see also Family

109a Somebody's trying to kill me and I think it's my husband: The modern gothic

203c The household as workplace: Wives, husbands, and children

243m Husbands' paid work and family roles: Current research issues

244f The roles of Greek husbands and wives: Definitions and fulfillment

270a Duofocal family structure and an alternative model of husband-wife relationship

301f Tribute to my husband

324d Attitudes toward women working: Changes over time and implications for the labor-force behaviors of husbands and wives

355i Contributions to household labor: Comparing wives' and husbands' reports

375g The law of husband and wife in nineteenth-century America: Changing views of divorce

Hutchinson, Anne

19b Mrs. Hutchinson's behavior in terms of menopausal symptoms

19f The case against Anne Hutchinson

19k   Anne Hutchinson and the Puritan attitude toward women

19m   Footsteps of Anne Hutchinson

454b   The case of the American Jezebels: Anne Hutchinson and female agitation during the years of the Antinomian turmoil, 1636-1640

Hygiene

145p   The civilizing tendency of hygiene: Working-class women under medical control in Imperial Germany

Hypatia

441b   Women and technology in ancient Alexandria: Maria and Hypatia

Hyperbole

108q   My memory's hyperbole

Hyperprolactinemia

190u   Steroidal contraceptive use and subsequent development of hyperprolactinemia

Hypertension

53s   Hypertension in women - a review

Hypertonic

252h   Intra-amniotic hypertonic saline instillation in the second trimester

Hypnotic

9q   The effects of opiates, sedative-hypnotics, amphetamines, cannabis, and other psychoactive drugs on the fetus and newborn

Hypothalamus

28d   Hypothalamic peptides and sexual behavior

Hypothesis

243j   Overtime over the life cycle: A test of the life cycle squeeze hypothesis

Hysterectomy

240h   Psychological aspects of hysterectomy

Hysteria

see also Emotion

183f   Hysteria among factory workers

253e   The myth of assembly-line hysteria

256b   Freud's Dora, Dora's hysteria

268d   Hysteria

359n   The hysterical personality: A "woman's disease"

365e   Anxieties: Agoraphobia and hysteria

454n   The hysterical woman: Sex roles and role conflict in nineteenth century America

I

64o   The anamnesis of a female "I": In the margins of self-portrayal (Colette)

455e   Ain't I a woman

I Know Why the Caged Bird Sings

452k   The metaphysics of matrilinearism in women's autobiography: Studies of Mead's *Blackberry Winter*, Hellman's *Pentimento*, Angelou's *I Know Why the Caged Bird Sings*, and Kingston's *The Woman Warrior*

Iatrogenic

354c   Vaginal cancer: An iatrogenic disease?

Ibsen, Henrik

122p   Ibsen's *A Doll's House*: A directorial perspective on performing Nora

Iceland

104h   Domestic work in rural Iceland: An historical overview

Iconography

22c   Iconography as a means of research on the history of the status of women

117g   Taking a second look: Observations on the iconography of a French queen, Jeanne de Bourbon (1338-1378)

Id

225c   The taming of the id: Feminist sexual politics, 1968-83

Ida

127e   *Ida*, A great American novel

Idea

125b   Mary Astell: Inspired by ideas

174j   The ideas and the realities: Sagaris, Session I

383a   A new anarchism: Social and political ideas in some recent feminist eutopias

Ideal

109e   The reconstruction of the gothic feminine ideal in Emily Brontë's *Wuthering Heights*

130u   The death of an ideal: Female suicides in the eighteenth-century French novel

154b   The crowned dame, dame opinion, and dame philosophy: The female characteristics of three ideals in Christine de Pizan's *L'Avision Christine*

154d   Virginity as an ideal in Christine de Pizan's *Cité des Dames*

154e   Christine de Pizan's *Livre des Trois Vertus*: Feminine ideal or practical advice?

154f   The ideal of the lady of the manor as reflected in Christine de Pizan's *Livre des Trois Vertus*

158e   Not quite new worlds: Psychologists' conceptions of the ideal family in the twenties

198a   Introduction: The ideal and contextual realities of Muslim women

254j   The problem: Idealism and accommodation in the feminist transformation of the academy

320b   Culture, service, and work: Changing ideals of higher education for women

401b   Taoism and the androgynous ideal

442b   Willa Cather: A problematic ideal

Identify

48m   Gender, gender-role identification, and response to erotica

211g   Women-identified women in male-identified Judaism

326k   Marital and sexual dysfunction following rape: Identification and treatment

378k   The party identifications of women: Parkin put to the test

407e   Toward a new era of leadership: The national identification program

434l   Dilemmas in role identification for low-income women

463t   Gender-role identification in the methodology of transportation planning

Identity

37q   Group identity development within black families

72l   Chicana identity: Interaction of culture and sex roles

73j   Family roles and identities of Scandinavian and German women

88a   On the origins of gender identity

103r   Antigone's daughters: Reflections on female identity and the state

114e   Toward new sexual identities: James Tiptree, Jr.

119a   Inverts and experts: Radclyffe Hall and the lesbian identity

124h   How psychology constructed masculinity: The theory of male sex role identity

158i   The theory of male sex role identity: Its rise and fall, 1936 to the present

187h   All ages, every condition, and both sexes: The emergence of a Gilbertine identity

195h   Is male gender identity the cause of male domination?

231d   Capitalism and gay identity

231k   The Afro-American female: The historical context of the construction of sexual identity

289e   Gender identity: A life-span view of sex-role development

342e   Indian women: Tribal identity as status quo

397b   Developing a lesbian identity

439c   Sexuality as the mainstay of identity: Psychoanalytic perspectives

443c   The convergence of psychoanalysis and feminism: Gender identity and autonomy

Ideology

2c   *Roe v Wade*: A study in male ideology

6f   Women in religion and in secular ideology

18b   The ideology of population control

18i   Neo-Malthusian ideology and colonial capitalism: Population dynamics in southwestern Puerto Rico

35c   Political ideology, sociobiology, and the U.S. women's rights movement

50u   Competing ideologies of reproduction: Medical and maternal perspectives on pregnancy

68f   Chinese women: The relative influences of ideological revolution, economic growth, and cultural change

79ll   Ectogenesis and ideology

94d   Migrantness, culture, and ideology

100b   Teaching and 'women's work': A comparative historical and ideological analysis

103s   The family impact statement: Ideology and feasibility

120i   Ideological hegemony in political discourse: Women's specificity and equality

124f   Transvestitism and the ideology of gender: Southeast Asia and beyond

133w   Ideologies in two gay rights controversies

138b   Intersections of gender and class: Accommodation and resistance by working-class and affluent females to contradictory sex-role ideologies

159l   Venezuelan female criminality: The ideology of diversity and marginality

180h   "The mother's history" in George Eliot's life, literature and political ideology

225f   Everything they always wanted you to know: The ideology of popular sex literature

231w   Gender systems, ideology, and sex research

238b Passionlessness: An interpretation of Victorian sexual ideology, 1790-1850

241i Purification or social control? Ideologies of reproduction and the churching of women after childbirth

245j Family and class in contemporary America: Notes toward an understanding of ideology

268c Gender ideology and phobias in women

271f Sex-role ideology and sex bias in judgments of occupational suitability

282d Transforming "natural" woman: Female ritual leaders and gender ideology among Bimin-Kuskusmin

282g Like wounded stags: Male sexual ideology in an Andalusian town

313g Ideology and *The Mysteries of Udolpho*

313i The fiction of family: Ideology and narrative in Elsa Morante

342h Ideologies of male dominance as divide and rule politics: An anthropologist's view

349a Criminological theory: Its ideology and implications concerning women

353d Passionlessness: An interpretation of Victorian sexual ideology, 1790-1850

367d New England women: Ideology and experience in first-generation Puritanism (1630-1650)

368k Women in the ideology of the Islamic Republic

368l State ideology and village women

369l The marriage of capitalist and patriarchal ideologies: Meanings of male bonding and male ranking in U.S. culture

370h The Songhay-Zarma female slave: Relations of production and ideological status

376k Criminological theory: Its ideology and implications concerning women

396c Competing ideologies of reproduction: Medical and maternal perspectives on pregnancy

408j Notes toward a definition of Gabriela Mistral's ideology

421j Attitudes and ideology: Correlates of liberal attitudes towards the role of women

464a Power as ideology: A feminist analysis

Idleness

419c Workers and drones: Labor, idleness and gender definition in Hesiod's beehive

Idol

399kk The second face of the idol: Women in melodrama

Idyll

448e Every woman is an island: Vita Sackville-West, the image of the city and the pastoral idyll

Ignorance

129z Cardinal Gibbons's ignorance

ILGWU

see International Lady Garment Workers Union

Illegal

see Legal

Illegitimacy

see Legitimacy

Illinois

72d Latinas in educational leadership: Chicago, Illinois

201f The uprising in Chicago: The men's garment workers strike, 1910-1911

448k Willa Cather's lost Chicago sisters

Illness

see also Disease, Sickness

8j The painful woman: Complaints, symptoms, and illness

12f 'Sickness is a woman's business?': Reflections on the attribution of illness

140n Victims of violence and psychiatric illness

285e Physical disability, life-threatening illness, and enhancement of sexual health

285f Sexual feelings in the terminally ill patient

285k Sexual dysfunction in the chronically ill male

319l Health and illness perceptions of the Chicana

354l Chlorosis and chronic disease in 19th-century Britain: The social constitution of somatic illness in a capitalist society

Illusion

43e The illusion of androgyny

64k Colette and Ravel: The enchantress and the illusionist

64n Polymorphemic perversity: Colette's illusory "real"

215e The illusion of protection: Civil defence

430a Islam's appeal to women in Iran: Illusions and reality

Iloilo, Philippines

206e Iloilo

431f Women and men in Iloilo, Philippines: 1903-1970

Image

see also Perception, Self Image, Self Perception

19e The image of Adam and the image of Christ

32q Literary emasculation: Household imagery in Christa Reinig's *Entmannung*

39u Images of black women in Afro-American poetry

39ee Images of the woman of color in Brazilian literature: O Cortico, Clara Dos Anjos, Gabriela Cravo E Canela, and O Quinze

40c Reconstruction of the composite self: New images of black women in Maya Angelou's continuing autobiography

40hh Imagery in the women poems: The art of Carolyn Rodgers

64j Image structure, codes, and recoding in *The Pure and the Impure*

86a The clean, light image of the electronics industry: Miracle or mirage?

91h Woman's image of herself

91i Through the feminist looking glass: Images of women

109f Domestic gothic: The imagery of anger in Christina Stead's *The Man Who Loved Children*

117f Eve and Mary: Conflicting images of medieval woman

131l Charles Bronson, Samurai, and other feminine images: A transactive response to *The Left Hand of Darkness*

133m Images of the gay male in contemporary drama

155i The uncommon prostitute: The contemporary image in an American age of pornography

156b Exit Atossa: Images of women in Greek historiography on Persia

161c Applauding servility - Images of women in advertisements

161g A fallen image - Women in India

176t Lesbian images in women's literature anthologies

193p The image of science

194k Pox and the terror of childlessness: Images and ideas of the smallpox goddess in a north Indian village

200g Images of nature in Gimi thought

211t Steps toward feminine imagery of deity in Jewish theology

211u Bride, spouse, daughter: Images of the feminine in classical Jewish sources

229c Prepatriarchal female/goddess images

229x Images and models - in process

229ee Images of spiritual power in women's fiction

254e Images of women in film

265n Sex role images in Lebanese text books

274c Subject image, examinations and teaching materials

282e Self-interest and the social good: Some implications of Hagen gender imagery

315h Two in one, one in two: An exploration of a birth experience and images of the sacred

341c A woman's body in a man's world: A review of findings on body image and weight control

356m Honing a habitable languagescape: Women's images for the new world frontiers

368c Women in Shíi Fiqh: Images through the Hadith

384e Women in western American fiction: Images or real women?

384r Where the West begins: Constance Rourke's images of her own frontierland

385g Reinventing the past and circumscribing the future: *Authenticité* and the negative image of women's work in Zaire

402h Women and religion: The status and image of women in some major religious traditions

412q For god and home and native land: The W.C.T.U.'s image of woman in the late nineteenth century

433m The image of Bengal in the emerging literature of Bangladesh: The fiction of Hasan Azizul Huq

448e Every woman is an island: Vita Sackville-West, the image of the city and the pastoral idyll

449b Images of women in Ping Hsin's fiction

453a Women's culture: Themes and images

453c Women's imagery/women's art

453f Goddess imagery in ritual

453h Women's images in film

453m Mirror images

Imagine
186h The country of the imagination
384s Pioneering the imagination: Eudora Welty's *The Robber Bridegroom*
330b Hunting the moth: Virginia Woolf and the creative imagination
417t Imagining a different world of talk

IMF
see Internatinal Monetary Fund

Immanence
462w Immanence: Uniting the spiritual and political

Immigrate
see also Migrate
58a Immigration to Southeast Asia
68o The schooling of Vietnamese immigrants: Internal colonialism and its impact on women
71h Immigration of Asian women and the status of recent Asian women immigrants
73h The economic struggles of female factory workers: A comparison of French, Polish, and Portuguese immigrants
81c Chicanas and Mexican immigrant families 1920-1940: Women's subordination and family exploitation
94a Immigration and class: The Australian experience
192n The election day immigration raids at Lilli Diamond Originals and the response of the ILGWU
205e The response of the WMS to the immigration of Asian women, 1888-1942
243d The old world, new rights, and the limited rebellion: Challenges to traditional authority in immigrant families
305v Immigrant women: The silent partners of the women's movement
323n Triple oppression: Immigrant women in the labour force
366c The leadership of nuns in immigrant Catholicism
420p Female Asian immigrants in Honolulu: Adaptation and success

Immoral
223d Is adultery immoral?
223q Sexual immorality delineated

Impact
103s The family impact statement: Ideology and feasibility

Impair
79s Living with an impaired neonate and child: A feminist issue

Impasse
283m The impasse facing CND

Impediment
71d Impediments to Asian-Pacific-American women organizing

Imperialism
428c Capitalism, imperialism, and patriarchy: The dilemma of Third-World women workers in multinational factories

Implantation
79gg The case against in vitro fertilization and implantation

Imposter
443b The therapist as imposter
443f Treatment of the imposter phenomenon in high-achieving women

Impotence
277h Evaluation and treatment of impotence: The urologist's viewpoint

Imprison
164b Jane Austen and romantic imprisonment
349v Imprisoned women and their children
368o Women imprisoned in the kingdom of the Mullahs
448d George Eliot and the city: The imprisonment of culture

In Vitro
79gg The case against in vitro fertilization and implantation
79hh In defense of in vitro fertilization
79ii In vitro fertilization and embryo transfer: The process of making public policy

In Utero
79c Assessment of risks from DES: An analysis of research on those exposed during pregnancy or in utero

Incarcerate
see also Crime
39s The incarcerated black female: The case of social double jeopardy
111m Beyond incarceration: A women's alternative
376i The incarceration of women: A search for answers
392o Mothers behind bars: A look at the parental rights of incarcerated women

Incest
8e Incest
78q Incest: Whose reality, whose theory?
103m Daddy's right: Incestuous assault
140p Father-daughter incest
140q Families at risk for father-daughter incest
146e Group therapy with female adolescent incest victims
146f Sibling incest
146g Individual and group treatment of mothers of incest victims
146h The incest offender
180m Mothers, daughters, and incest in the late novels of Edith Wharton
219b Incest and sexual abuse of children
281f Incest and sexual violence
284i Incest - an introduction
284j Father-daughter incest
284k Children not severely damaged by incest with a parent
284l Humanistic treatment of father-daughter incest
284m Incest policy recommendations
291h The nature of incest: A review of contributing factors
291i Incest: Intake and investigation
291m Incest and dysfunctional family system
326e Network aspects of treatment for incestuously abused children
359nn Identification and treatment of incest victims

359oo Incest between fathers and daughters
461j The cradle of sexual politics: Incest
461k Beyond belief: The reluctant discovery of incest

Incite
55m Appendix B: Review of legal cases regarding US Code, Section 1461 (mailing obscene or crime-inciting matter)

Income
see also Pay
81b The economics of middle-income family life: Working women during the Great Depression
82h Income-generating projects
89r The employment of wives and the inequality of family income
96d Mothers and their children: A study of low-income families
153c Households as income-pooling units
295g Enhancing childrearing skills in lower income women
321h Income inequality
321j The distribution of income within households
333r Income and employment for women in remote communities: Examples from the Northern Territory
360g Inequality and mental health: Low income and minority women
380j Poverty, work, and mental health: The experience of low-income mothers
400c Women's income earning activities and family welfare in Bangladesh
434l Dilemmas in role identification for low-income women
455k Women and income maintenance programs
458b Midlife work history and retirement income
461b The sexual experience of Afro-American women: A middle-income sample
465c Who still cares for the family? Recent developments in income maintenance, taxation and family law

Incongruity
40e From baptism to resurrection: Toni Cade Bambara and the incongruity of language

Incorporation
160a Incorporation and exclusion: Oxford academics' wives

Incorrect
225h Politically correct? Politically incorrect?

Increase
361h Increasing the participation of college women in mathematics-related fields

Indemnity
406g Double indemnity

Independence
101e Catalysts or helpers? British feminists, Indian women's rights, and Indian independence
180b Kriemhild and Clytemnestra - Sisters in crime or independent women?
344x What price independence? Social reactions to lesbians, spinsters, widows, and nuns

Index

176v   The lesbian periodicals index

176w   Note on "Reading A Subject" in periodical indexes

India

18e   Population policy, family size, and the reproduction of the labor force in India: The case of Bombay

68g   Up from the harem? The effects of class and sex on political life in northern India

75d   Career counselling for poor rural and urban women of South India

75e   Working women in India

91s   Religious women in North India

101b   Social reform and women's participation in political culture: Andhra and Madras

101c   The Indian women's movement: A struggle for women's rights or national liberation?

101d   Sisterhood or separation? The All-India Muslim Ladies' Conference and the Nationalist Movement

101e   Catalysts or helpers? British feminists, Indian women's rights, and Indian independence

101f   Kinship, women, and politics in twentieth-century Punjab

101g   Nationalism, universalization, and the extended female space in Bombay City

101h   The Indian women's movement and national development: An overview

101i   Two faces of protest: Alternative forms of women's mobilization in West Bengal and Maharashtra

101k   Towards equality? Cause and consequence of the political prominence of women in India

159m   Criminality amongst women in India: A study of female offenders and female convicts

161a   Movement against the portrayal of women in India

161e   Women and Bengali literature

161g   A fallen image - Women in India

161h   Women and mass media in Kerala

194h   The goddess Kannagi: A dominant symbol of south Indian Tamil society

194i   The village Mother in Bengal

194k   Pox and the terror of childlessness: Images and ideas of the smallpox goddess in a north Indian village

205f   A note on Asian Indian women in British Columbia, 1900-1935

206d   The case of India

218b   *Sati* or *Shakti*: Women, culture and politics in India

232a   On the meaning of sakti to women in Tamil Nadu

232c   Marriage in Tamil culture: The problem of conflicting "models"

232e   A note on the nobility of women in popular Tamil fiction

232f   The paradoxical powers of Tamil women

255c   Purdah and the Hindu family in central India

255d   The domestic realm in the lives of Hindu women in Calcutta

255e   Purdah among the Oswals of Mewar

255h   From purdah to politics: The social feminism of the all-India women's organizations

255i   Purdah politics: The role of Muslim women in Indian nationalism, 1911-1924

265o   Strategies of healthy sex role development in modernized India

299a   Socio-economic status of Indian women

310l   Women as targets in India's family planning policy

310r   Abortion of a special kind: Male sex selection in India

322i   Interview with Nabaneeta Deb-Sen (India)

325c   Mother Guru: Jnanananda of Madras, India

325f   Golden handprints and red-painted feet: Hindu childbirth rituals in central India

325g   Hindu women's family and household rites in a north Indian village

325h   The ladies of Lord Krishna: Rituals of middle-aged women in eastern India

325n   The case of the vanishing nuns: The fruits of ambivalence in ancient Indian Buddhism

325o   Accomplished women in tantric Buddhism of medieval India and Tibet

362e   Gender, politics and modernization: The Indian case

364d   Dowry in North India: Its consequences for women

388j   Women's organizations and social change: The age-of-marriage issue in India

402a   Women in India and South Asia: An introduction

402i   Muslim women in Uttar Pradesh: Social mobility and directions of change

402k   Etiquette among women in Karnataka: Forms of address in the village and the family

402m   The aging woman in India: Self-perceptions and changing roles

403f   Ritual status of Muslim women in rural India

420e   Rural-to-urban migration of women in India: Patterns and implications

421i   Attitudes of women towards certain selected cultural practices in Kerala state, India

421v   Some comments on the home roles of businesswomen in India, Australia and Canada

422a   Women in the labour force of India: A macro-level statistical profile

422b   Women workers of India: A case of market segmentation

422c   Women in the labour force in India

433a   Goddesses or rebels: The women revolutionaries of Bengal

433c   Madness as entropy: A Bengali view

433d   British tradesmen of Calcutta, 1830-1900: A preliminary study of their economic and political roles

433e   Bengal politics of the first decade of the present century: A defence of extremism

433f   Bengal election, 1937: Fazlul Huq and M. A. Jinnah: A study in leadership stress in Bengal politics

433g   Inequality and radical land reform: Some notes from west Bengal

433h   Forms of the Indian notion of sexuality and an interpretation of the Mymensing ballad of Kajalrekha

433i   British response to Bengali literature in the nineteenth century

433k   Radindranath Tagore: Cultural ambassador of India to the United States

438b   Opportunities for women scientists in India

438l   Autobiography of an unknown woman (India)

457e   Essence and existence: Women and religion in ancient Indian texts

459h   Women's work and their status: Rural Indian evidence of labour market and environment effects on sex differences in childhood mortality

459j   Sex discrimination in the urban labour markets: Some propositions based on Indian evidence

Indian

see also American Indian

100c   The Indian and African presence in the Americas: Some aspects of historical distortion

205b   When you don't know the language, listen to the silence: An historical overview of native Indian women in BC

395l   Anger sickness: Social stress and native diagnosis among Ecuadorian Indians

Indian Nationalist Movement

21h   Political change: Muslim women in conflict with Parda: Their role in the Indian Nationalist Movement

Indian Woman

402l   Asian women in Britain: Strategies of adjustment of Indian and Pakistani migrants

Indigenous

39i   Women in indigenous African cults and churches

417q   Twin Oaks: A feminist looks at indigenous socialism in the United States

Individual

96b   The mental health problems of women: Social roles and the individual

146g   Individual and group treatment of mothers of incest victims

185j   Moral concepts in the year 2020: The individual, the family, and society

215s   Contemplating a nuclear future: Nuclear war, politics and the individual

230b   Aggression against women: Cultural and individual causes

243h   Family, work, and individual development in dual-career marriages: issues for research

250f   Education and the individual: Schooling for girls, or mixed schooling-a mixed blessing?

407c   Preparing the individual for institutional leadership: The summer institute

Individualism

84m   Individualism and the objects of psychology

129a   The roots of individualist feminism in 19th-century America

Individuation

88c   Considerations about the development of the girl during the separation-individuation process

313b   The "I" in Adrienne Rich: Individuation and the androgyne archetype

Indonesia

21f   Women in Indonesian politics: The myth of functional interest

21g   Expanding women's horizons in Indonesia: Toward maximum equality with minimum conflict

92e   Indonesia: Married women's work pattern in rural Java

92f   Indonesia: Socio-economic aspects of food consumption in rural Java

92g   The advantages of functional education and credit facilities for Javanese rural women

166d   The search for women in Indonesian history

166e   Rights and responsibility, power and privilege: Women's roles in contemporary Indonesia

234d   Some perceptions of Indonesian women under Islam

373h   Java, Indonesia: The introduction of rice processing technology

424d   Employment patterns of educated women in Indonesian cities

466f   Women and work in an Indonesian mining town

466h   Indonesian women in development: State theory and urban kampung practice

466i   Separate but equal: Indonesian Muslim perceptions of the roles of women

Induce

see also Reproduce

354b   Convenience and the occurrence of births: Induction and labor in the United States and Canada

Industrial

see also Capitalism

49f   The feminization of the labor force: Research for industrial/organizational psychology

50a   The butcher, the baker, the candlestickmaker: The shop and the family in the Industrial Revolution

52u   The industrialization of housework

89i   Determinants of the structure of industrial type labor markets

99b   From the woman's view: Pre-industrial England, 1500-1750

139c   Not so much a factory, more a form of patriarchy: Gender and class during industrialisation

181b   Lillian Moller Gilbreth and the founding of modern industrial engineering

234a   Theoretical perspectives on pre-industrial women

251b   Women and technology in the industrialized countries

263d   "Blessed be the tie that binds": YWCA extension work among industrial women, Minneapolis, 1900-1910

263k   Industrial social workers in France, 1917-1939: A study in the sex/gender division of labor

283q   Industrial strategy and trade union politics

292c   Citizens for Democracy: The industrial programs of the YWCA

350g   From rural subsistence to an industrial peripheral work force: An examination of female Malaysian migrants and capital accumulation in Singapore

373f   Impact of selected industrial technologies on women in Mexico

378b   Industrial radicalism and the domestic division of labor

387g   Industrialization and femininity: A case study of nineteenth-century New England

412s   Shaping a new society: Methodist women and industrial reform in the south, 1880-1940

424f   Constraints on the organization of women industrial workers

424g   Islamic attitudes to female employment in industrializing economies: Some notes from Malaysia

424h   Occupational health hazards of female industrial workers in Malaysia

424i   Women's work: Factory, family and social class in an industrializing order

428d   Women, production, and reproduction in industrial capitalism: A comparison of Brazilian and U.S. factory workers

428e   Household, community, national, and multinational industrial development

428h   Labor migration and the new industrial division of labor

428i   Mexican border industrialization, female labor force participation, and migration

428o   The impact of industrialization on women: A Caribbean case

446e   The educational and occupational skill level of industrial workers

Industry

see also Business, Company, Corporation, Factory, Management

13h   Women working in heavy industry in World War II

86a   The clean, light image of the electronics industry: Miracle or mirage?

139h   'Getting on'. Gender differences in career development: A case study in the hairdressing industry

145m   Domestic industry: Work options and women's choices

183d   Women workers in the manufacturing industries

192j   Capital's flight: The apparel industry moves south

233p   Legal considerations of reproductive hazards in industry in the United Kingdom

233q   Legal considerations of reproductive hazards in industry in the United States

284s   The child sex industry - an introduction

307c   Gender and industry on Mexico's new frontier

310h   Inside the surrogate industry

354d   Sexism and racism in the American health care industry: A comparative analysis

354e   Women workers in the health service industry

428b   The new international division of labor and the U.S. work force: The case of the electronics industry

428l   Silicon Valley's women workers: A theoretical analysis of sex-segregation in the electronics industry labor market

428p   The emergence of small-scale industry in a Taiwanese rural community

428r   Global industries and Malay peasants in peninsular Malaysia

470a   Sex and skill in the organisation of the clothing industry

Inequality

see Equality

Inequity

see Equity

Infant

see also Child

80b   Infant day care: Relationships between theory and practice

80e   Developmental consequences of out-of-home care for infants in a low-income population

80k   The problem of infant day care

80l   A methodological comment on "The problem of infant day care"

158f   "Give me a dozen healthy infants": John B. Watson's popular advice on childrearing, women, and the family

184m   Parisian infants and Norman wet nurses in the early nineteenth century: A statistical study

204e   Varying degrees of paternal involvement in infant care: Attitudinal and behavioral correlates

233j   The effect of the mother's work on the infant

300e   The infant formula controversy in Southeast Asia: Advocacy confrontation or applied anthropology?

308a   Teenage women in the United States: Sex, contraception, pregnancy, fertility, and maternal and infant health

446m   Maternal care of infants

Infanticide

156m   Infanticide in Hellenistic Greece

162c   Infanticide in rural Bavaria in the nineteenth century

401j   Female infanticide in China

Inferiority

172e   Our national inferiority complex: A cause for violence? (El Salvador)

Infertility

see Fertility

Inflammatory

53i   Pelvic inflammatory disease: Causes and consequences

Influence

49l   We can influence the future!

57d   Television as a sphere of influence on the child's learning about sexuality

90q   The influence of gender on the verbal interactions among principals and staff members: An exploratory study

156d   Influential women

221a   The family as an influence on career development

296a   Introduction: An interdisciplinary perspective on women's power and influence

296c Women in intergenerational patterns of power and influence

296d Women's self-perceptions of power and influence across adult life

325p Women of influence and prestige among the Native American Iroquois

349p The underside of married life: Power, influence, and violence

Inform

309z Misinforming pregnant teenagers

Information

80s The prospects and dilemmas of child care information and referral

199i Women's work in the library/information sector

209c Bargaining over the social costs of information technology

209e Government policies on new information technologies and their implications for employment: An overview of EEC countries, with particular reference to women

309t Guessing and misinformation about pregnancy risk among urban mothers

310bb Taking the initiative: Information versus technology in pregnancy

460r A sex-information switchboard

Infrastructure

270o Civil violence in Turkey: Its infrastructural, social and cultural foundations

Inheritance

9f Sex differences in the inheritance of alcoholism

162e 'Avoir sa part': Sibling relations in partible inheritance Brittany

Injury

230l Bases of liability for injuries produced by media portrayals of violent pornography

285r Sexuality and the spinal cord injured woman: An interview

Injustice

see Justice

Inmate

see also Crime

63h The development of a scale to assess inmate and staff attitudes toward co-corrections

Innocence

17i Cool Diana and the Blood-red muse: Edith Wharton on innocence and art

Innovate

203t Emergency shelter: The development of an innovative women's environment

244i Traditional sex norms and the innovative function of afternoon dancing

319g Mexican American women as innovators

Inquiry

387d Sex discrimination and employment practices: An experiment with unconventional job inquires

Inseminate

see also Reproduce

310x Children by donor insemination: A new choice for lesbians

310y Doing it ourselves: Self insemination

Inside

301v It's something inside you

381i Insider

Instability

446k Changing family roles and marital instability

Instinct

158k "To pet, coddle, and 'Do For'": Caretaking and the concept of maternal instinct

Institution

60r Women on welfare: Public policy and institutional racism

63b Characteristics of co-correctional institutions

63l Two losers don't make a winner: The case against the co-correctional institution

78m Forcible rape: Institutionalized sexism in the criminal justice system

91r New wine in new skins: Women in secular institutes

102i Beyond consciousness raising: Changing sexist institutions

111i The Hillcrest School of Oregon: Guided group interaction in a juvenile institution

203l Introduction: Women in environmental decisionmaking: Institutional constraints

205n They also served: The British Columbia women's institutes in two World Wars

218h Women in development planning: Advocacy, institutionalization and implementation

222e Surviving in a predominantly white male institution

234c Shamanism as institutionalised ego defense and elite formation associated with transvestism in a Borneo society

261e Progress and pitfalls: Reports from participating institutions

282c The bow and the burden strap: A new look at institutionalized homosexuality in native North America

285n Sex in institutions

289h Long-term care institutions

289m Institutional life: The Canadian experience

317k Institutionalization of the aged

326h Sexual assault in correctional institutions: Prevention and intervention

352b Prophets, chiefs, commissioners, and queens: The moral and institutional context of leadership

353ee Doctors or ladies? Women physicians in psychiatric institutions, 1872-1900

368m The institution of Mutà marriage in Iran: A formal and historical perspective

376e Sex-based discrimination in the mental institutionalization of women

404r Breaking cycles of victimization: The shelter as an affirmative institution

407c Preparing the individual for institutional leadership: The summer institute

444e Old wine in new bottles: The institutional changes for women of the people during the French revolution

453t Institutions of women's culture

472f Institutionalized women: Some classic types, some common problems, and some partial solutions

Instructor

see also Education

320k Undergraduates and their teachers: An analysis of student evaluations of male and female instructors

Instrument

252g Instrumental abortion in the second trimester: An overview

266g Instruments and measures in a changing, diverse society

Instrumental-Expressive

158h Psychology measures femininity and masculinity, 2: From "13 Gay Men" to the instrumental-expressive distinction

Insult

171g Small insults: A study of interruptions in cross-sex conversations between unacquainted persons

Insurance

46f Disability insurance under proposed reforms

145n Social insurance and the family work of Oberlausitz home weavers in the late nineteenth century

Insurgency

113e Vietnam: War of insurgency

Intake

291i Incest: Intake and investigation

Integrated Rural Development Program (IRDP)

400e Population planning and rural women's cooperative in IRDP women's programme: Some critical issues

Integrate

63a The sexually integrated prison: A legal and policy evaluation

93r Integration of family policy and labor market policy in Sweden

120m Fighting the good fight: Separation or integration?

172i Integrating women into rural cooperatives: Pluses and minuses (Bolivia)

214u Conclusion: Integrating love and power

254n The whole thing: In search of relevance and integration made dynamic by creativity

266j Methods for integrative reviews

272l Job integration strategies: Today's programs and tomorrow's needs

312a Introduction: Theories of women's studies and the autonomy/integration debate

314a Where does integration fit: The development of women's studies

314j Appropriate teaching methods for integrating women

314l Moving beyond the curriculum: The 'political' value of an integration strategy

350a The dynamics of the sexual division of labor and integration of rural women into the world market

353ii Mabel K. Staupers and the integration of black nurses into the armed forces

373c Integration into what? Reflections on development planning for women

410f Women judges and public policy in sex integration

421d Social and economic integration of South Asian women in Montreal, Canada

Intellectual

87c   Intellectual development of women

125h   Matilda Joslyn Gage: Active intellectual

329a   Virginia Woolf and the intellectual origins of Bloomsbury

336e   Helene Stöcker: Left-wing intellectual and sex reformer

Intelligence

158d   Leta Hollingworth: Toward a sexless intelligence

Interaction

38i   Marital interaction goals of black women: Strengths and effects

48n   Future influences on the interaction of gender and human sexual expression

90q   The influence of gender on the verbal interactions among principals and staff members: An exploratory study

111i   The Hillcrest School of Oregon: Guided group interaction in a juvenile institution

171f   Interaction: The work women do

219d   The social uses of sexuality: Symbolic interaction, power and rape

274b   Classroom interaction

387o   Interaction: The work women do

410g   Organizational role orientations on female-dominant commissions: Focus on staff-commissioner interaction

Intercollegiate

see also Athlete, Collegiate, Interscholastic, Sport

147aa The first intercollegiate contest for women: Basketball, April 4, 1896

147dd The history of women's intercollegiate athletics in Ohio, 1945-1972

Intercourse

289a   Introduction: Beyond intercourse and orgasm

309h   The risk of adolescent pregnancy in the first months of intercourse

Interdisciplinary

296a   Introduction: An interdisciplinary perspective on women's power and influence

404dd Establishing interdisciplinary treatment networks

Interdisciplinary Society for Menstrual Cycle Research

51z   The Interdisciplinary Society for Menstrual Cycle Research: Creating knowledge from our experience

Interest

21f   Women in Indonesian politics: The myth of functional interest

162a   Interest and emotion in family and kinship studies: A critique of social history and anthropology

435a   Representing women: The transition from social movement to interest group

467e   The stance of Britain's major parties and interest groups

Interface

209n   The role of common sense in the process of interface design

Intergeneration

296c   Women in intergenerational patterns of power and influence

317e   Intergenerational relations in later life: A family system approach

Interior

371d   Essential objects and the sacred: Interior and exterior space in an urban Greek locality

International

18f   Cross-national labor migrants: Actors in the international division of labor

81j   International feminism between the wars: The National Woman's Party versus the League of Women Voters

82p   Views of women in international development

83d   Woman and the international division of labor

147mm American women: Their debut in international track and field

159a   International concern in light of the American experience

163a   International politics of female sexual slavery

169v   Labor education and women workers: An international comparison

207i   The subordination of women and the internationalisation of factory production

208c   The subordination of women and the internationalisation of factory production

270h   The effect of international labor migration on women's roles: The Turkish case

310m   Calling the shots? The international politics of depo-provera

428a   The impact of the changing international division of labor on different sectors of the labor force

428b   The new international division of labor and the U.S. work force: The case of the elctronics industry

428j   *Maquiladoras*: A new face of international capitalism on Mexico's northern frontier

428m   Fast forward: The internationalization of Silicon Valley

International Ladies Garment Workers Union (ILGWU)

192n   The election day immigration raids at Lilli Diamond Originals and the response of the ILGWU

192r   La costura en Los Angeles 1933-1939: The ILGWU and the politics of domination

292b   From soul to strawberries: The International Ladies' Garment Workers' Union and workers' education, 1914-1950

301o   Women in the Texas ILGWU, 1933-50

International Monetary Fund (IMF)

428f   Kitchens hit by priorities: Employed working-class Jamaican women confront the IMF

International Woodworkers of America (IWA)

205t   A union man's wife: The ladies' auxiliary movement in the IWA, the Lake Cowichan experience

Interparental

26h   Children's observations of interparental violence

Interpersonal

29f   Interpersonal effectiveness in assertive situations

36aa   C/SEC: A special-interest interpersonal group brings about change

41g   Invited presentation: The black professional woman — career success and interpersonal failure

344y   The sexual politics of interpersonal behavior

415f   Effective interpersonal communication for women of the corporation: Think like a man, talk like a lady

Interpretation

52f   The position of Austrian women in the family: Some data, many questions, and a few interpretations

124n   The ERA campaign: Reflections on interpretation and practice

156g   Women on Athenian vases: Problems of interpretation

353d   Passionlessness: An interpretation of Victorian sexual ideology, 1790-1850

381e   Interpretations

Interruption

171g   Small insults: A study of interruptions in cross-sex conversations between unacquainted persons

Interscholastic

see also Athlete, Collegiate, Intercollegiate, Sport

147bb Interscholastic basketball: Bane of collegiate physical educators

Intersection

138b   Intersections of gender and class: Accommodation and resistance by working-class and affluent females to contradictory sex-role ideologies

Interstice

225d   Interstices: A small drama of words

398b   Work in the interstices: Woman in academeme

Intervention

26a   Emergency room intervention: Detection, assessment, and treatment

26d   Crisis intervention with battered women

26e   Intervention with the abusive partner

26f   Police intervention

29d   Dissemination of behavioral interventions with women: Needed - a technology

80c   Changing aspects of the family: A psychoanalytic perspective on early intervention

146h   How to start a child-sexual-abuse intervention program

219g   Crisis intervention with victims of forcible rape: A police perspective

326b   Working for and with rape victims: Crisis intervention and advocacy

326f   Clinical intervention with boy victims of sexual abuse

326h   Sexual assault in correctional institutions: Prevention and intervention

359ll Development of a medical center rape crisis intervention program

361e   A short-term intervention program: Math-science conferences

404n   Plenary session: Intervention/service delivery systems

404o   Plenary session: Intervention/service delivery systems

404cc Postintervention and support systems

Interview

7f Interview with Audre Lorde

47i Middle age: Loss or gain? (interview)

85b Interviewing women: A contradiction in terms

186t "Sister of the mirage and echo": An interview with May Sarton

186u To be reborn: An interview with May Sarton

186v A further interview with May Sarton

186w "I live alone in a very beautiful place": An interview with May Sarton

205p "Especially when no one agrees": An interview with May Campbell

206p Using sex and satan to bust the union (an interviw with Corky Jennings)

241k Interviewing men: 'Taking gender seriously'

283h Interview with Frances Morrell

283i Interview with Jo Richardson

284o Interviewing child victims of sex offenders

285r Sexuality and the spinal cord injured woman: An interview

287o An interview with a sex surrogate

294h 'Working': An interview with Betty N.

297d 'It's great to have someone to talk to': The ethics and politics of interviewing women

307y Surrogate motherhood - an interview

310i An interview with Mirtha Quintanales, from the Third World women's archives

322b Interview with Miriam Tlali (South Africa)

322f Interview with Etel Adnan (Lebanon)

322i Interview with Nabaneeta Deb-Sen (India)

322k Interview with Astrid Roemer (Surinam)

322m Interview with Cristina Peri Rossi (Uruguay)

349q An interview with Sara Smith - One woman's experience with the cycle of violence

384j Pioneer women in the works of two Montana authors: Interviews with Dorothy M. Johnson and A. B. Guthrie, Jr.

Intimate

48a The intimate relationship between gender roles and sexuality

48k The intimate relationships of lesbians and gay men

140m Emotional intimacy among men

185i The transition from sex to sexuality and intimacy

214r Dual-career families: Intimacy or productivity?

214s One woman's perspective: intimacy and productivity

287c Female sexuality: Singlehood and the problems of intimacy

289g Intimacy and adaptation

343g Counsels of gall and grace: Intimate conversations between women in Shakespeare's plays

360k Sexual intimacy between psychotherapists and clients: Policy implications for the future

Intonation

171e Intonation in a man's world

Intra-Amniotic

252h Intra-amniotic hypertonic saline instillation in the second trimester

Intrauterine

252n Termination of pregnancy after intrauterine foetal death

Intuitive

49h Human resource planning and the intuitive manager: Models for the 1990's

Invalid

170h Natural selection: Perspectives on entitlement to the invalid care allowance

Invasive

53o Etiologic factors for invasive and noninvasive cervical abnormalities

Invent

307g From Africa to America: Black women inventors

Invert

119a Inverts and experts: Radclyffe Hall and the lesbian identity

Investigate

55b Scope of the problem: Investigation and prosecution

98i Working through local female investigators: Experiences in a broad survey

291i Incest: Intake and investigation

Investment

89g Family investments in human capital: Earnings of women

Invisible

30v Invisible mending

142g The choir invisible: The poetics of humanist piety

387k Invisible work: Unacknowledged contributions

Involvement

204h Antecedents and consequences of various degrees of paternal involvement in child rearing: The Israeli project

302k Mobility and professional involvement in librarianship: A study of the "Class of '55"

Iowa

11c Women and men problem drinkers: Sex differences in patients served by Iowa's community alcoholism centers

147kk The story: Six-player girls' basketball in Iowa

263g "Mom, it's a losing proposition": The decline of women's subsistence production on Iowa farms

226f Women as legislative candidates in six states

Iphigenie

32b A critical appraisal of Goethe's *Iphigenie*

Iran

244c Sex segregation and the women's roles in the economic system: The case of Iran

325j The controversial vows of urban Muslim women in Iran

325k Islam and tribal women in a village in Iran

368a Women in pre-revolutionary Iran: A historical overview

368i Poor women and social consciousness in revolutionary Iran

368m The institution of Mutà marriage in Iran: A formal and historical perspective

368n Family planning in post-revolutionary Iran

371f Sexual prohibitions, shared space and fictive marriages in Shíite Iran

371i Place and face: Of women in Doshman Ziari, Iran

403g Women, law, and social change in Iran

420n New models and traditional networks: Migrant women in Tehran

421t Fertiltiy and family economy in the Iranian rural communities

430a Islam's appeal to women in Iran: Illusions and reality

430b The economic base for the revival of Islam in Iran

430c Sexuality and women's oppression in Iran

430d The attitude of the Iranian left to the women's question

430e A historical background to the women's movement in Iran

430f The post-revolutionary women's movement in Iran

438f The achievement of Iranian women in science

Iraq

362d The mobilization of Iraqi women into the wage labor force

IRDP

see Integrated Rural Development Program

Ireland

194d The cult of Brigid: A study of pagan-Christian syncretism in Ireland

297h Bringing it all back home: An anthropologist in Belfast

318i Edna O'Brien: A kind of Irish childhood

331e Woman's songs in Irish, 800-1500

334a The normal paradigms of a woman's life in the Irish and Welsh texts

338a Irish women in legend, literature and life

382f Ireland

409b *Dubliners*: Women in Irish society

471b Women at work in Ireland

Irigaray, Luce

195o Toward an ethic of nurturance: Luce Irigaray on mothering and power

Irish American Woman

73i Irish, Italian, and Jewish women at the grassroots level: A historical and sociological perspective

Iron

372bb Iron deficiency in female athletes

Irony

313n "Folly and a woman": Galdos' rhetoric of irony in *Tristana*

450f Lisa Alther: The irony of return?

451e Irony with a center: Katherine Anne Porter

Iroquois

see also American Indian

325p Women of influence and prestige among the Native American Iroquois

Irrelevance

129h Irrelevancies

351b The impacts of irrelevance: Women in the history of American education

Isis

328f Isis unveiled: Virginia Woolf's use of Egyptian myth

441a Daughters of Isis, daughters of Demeter: When women sowed and reaped

Islam

see also Moslem, Muslim, Religion

198b The status of women in early Islam

198c The Islamic revolution and women: Quest for the Quranic model

198d Roles in transition: The evolving position of women in Arab-Islamic countries

198g A traditional ceremony in an Islamic milieu in Malaysia

198h Islam and the legal status of women in Tunisia

234d Some perceptions of Indonesian women under Islam

255k The status of women in Islam: A modernist interpretation

300o Islamic law in Christian Southeast Asia: The politics of establishing Shari'a courts in the Philippines

325k Islam and tribal women in a village in Iran

364b Cognatic descent, Islamic law and women's property on the East African coast

368k Women in the ideology of the Islamic Republic

379a Glimpses of Muslim urban women in classical Islam

403b Traditional affirmations concerning the role of women as found in contemporary Arab Islamic literature

403e Access to property and the states of women in Islam

424g Islamic attitudes to female employment in industrializing economies: Some notes from Malaysia

430a Islam's appeal to women in Iran: Illusions and reality

430b The economic base for the revival of Islam in Iran

Islandia

383f Wright's *Islandia*: Utopia with problems

Isoimmunization

252p Prevention of Rhesus (D) isoimmunization after abortion

Israel

104i The organization of labour in an Israeli kibbutz

113g Israel: The longest war

179k The Israeli example

204h Antecedents and consequences of various degrees of paternal involvement in child rearing: The Israeli project

211f Israeli women: Three myths

265m Sex role stereotyping and mental health standards in Israel: A cross-cultural comparison

421x Occupational choice among female academicians - The Israeli case

462p Women responding to the Arab-Israeli conflict

Issue

40d   Salvation is the issue

82q   Issues and alternatives in planning projects for women

231n Issues and answers

307ee Tomorrow is a woman's issue

314p From issue to action

Issy

409h The genuine Christine: Psychodynamics of Issy

Italian American

73d   The Museo Italo Americano: My involvement with the Italian American community in San Francisco

Italian American Woman

73i   Irish, Italian, and Jewish women at the grassroots level: A historical and sociological perspective

Italy

33b   Women, learning, and power: Eleonora of Aragon and the Court of Ferrara

33c   Book-lined cells: Women and humanism in the early Italian Renaissance

33d   Learned women of early modern Italy: Humanists and university scholars

33f   Womens's roles in early modern Venice: An exceptional case

52g   The changing role of women: The case of Italy

95a   Anna Kuliscioff: Russian revolutionist, Italian feminist

107h Machover test applied to 130 Italian female top athletes

184c Dowries and kinsmen in early Renaissance Venice

187b Byzantine asceticism and women's monasteries in early medieval Italy

188o The Franco-Italian professional writer: Christine de Pizan

194e An Italian religious feast: The *Fujenti* rites of the Madonna dell'Arco, Naples

228h Italy

297e Incidence or incidents: Political and methodological underpinnings of a health research process in a small Italian town

379p "If eight hours seems few to you...": Women workers' strikes in Italian rice fields, 1901-1906

382g Italy

438e The wild cat (France and Italy)

438g Reflections on a scientific adventure (Italy and United States)

444j Patriot mothers in the post-risorgimento: Women after the Italian revolution

471e Women at work in Italy: Legislation - evolution and prospects

Ivory Coast

347i Women and men, cloth and colonization: The transformation of production-distribution relations among the Baule (Ivory Coast)

473d Dioula women in town: A view of intra-ethnic variation (Ivory Coast)

IWA

see International Woodworkers of America

Jacob's Room

202e *Jacob's Room* as comedy: Woolf's parodic *Bildungsroman*

330g The form of fact and fiction: *Jacob's Room* as paradigm

Jacobi, Mary Putnam

379n Feminism, professionalism, and germs: A study of the thought of Mary Putnam Jacobi and Elizabeth Blackwell

Jaffna

232d Hidden powers: Cultural and socio-economic accounts of Jaffna women

Jail

see also Crime

165k Female patients and the medical profession in jails and prisons: A case of quintuple jeopardy

Jamaica

83e   Working class Jamaican women: Trade unions and political activity

120f To grow a daughter: Cultural liberation and the dynamics of oppression in Jamaica

388d Household economic strategies in Kingston, Jamaica

428f Kitchens hit by priorities: Employed working-class Jamaican women confront the IMF

James, Henry

17h   *The Bostonians*: Feminists and the new world

James, P.D.

1d   P. D. James

318f The clinical world of P.D. James

Jameson, Anna

389d Anna Jameson (1794-1860): Sacred art and social vision

Jamilis, Amalia

155j Women writing about prostitutes: Amalia Jamilis and Luisa Valenzuela

313l Alienation and eros in three stories by Beatriz Guido, Marta Lynch and Amalia Jamilis

Jane Eyre

30n   "Charlotte's Web": Reading *Jane Eyre* over time

109p Dreaming of children: Literalization in *Jane Eyre* and *Wuthering Heights*

332c "Fairy-born and human-bred": Jane Eyre's education in romance

332f The sisterhood of Jane Eyre and Antoinette Cosway

Janus

20k   Janus through the looking glass: Atwood's first three novels

Japan

21b   The Japanese woman: Evolving views of life and role

52i   The changing status and role of women in Japan

75a   Women's employment in Japan

108c The female hand in Heian Japan: A first reading

113i Japan: Cautious utilization

159n Emancipation of women and crime in Japan

190c Age at menarche and year of birth in relation to adult height and weight among Caucasian, Japanese, and Chinese women living in Hawaii

228m Japan

230g Pornography in Japan: Cross-cultural and theoretical considerations

325l No women's liberation: The heritage of a woman prophet in modern Japan

372g An outline of the history of women and western sport in Japan

382h Japan

387j Dilemmas of Japanese professional women

438d Becoming an anthropologist (Japan)

Java

92e Indonesia: Married women's work pattern in rural Java

92f Indonesia: Socio-economic aspects of food consumption in rural Java

92g The advantages of functional education and credit facilities for Javanese rural women

300d The psychology of politeness among the Javanese

373h Java, Indonesia: The introduction of rice processing technology

431e Women in Java's rural middle class: Progress or regress

466b The Peranankan Chinese woman at a crossroad

466e Rich woman, poor woman: Occupation differences in a textile producing village in Central Java

Jazz

40f Music as theme: The jazz mode in the works of Toni Cade Bambara

Jeanne de Bourbon

117g Taking a second look: Observations on the iconography of a French queen, Jeanne de Bourbon (1338-1378)

Jeans

206m Blue jeans blues

Jennings, Corky

206p Using sex and satan to bust the union (an interviw with Corky Jennings)

Jeopardy

39s The incarcerated black female: The case of social double jeopardy

165k Female patients and the medical profession in jails and prisons: A case of quintuple jeopardy

267c Double jeopardy: Resistance to affirmative action from potential beneficiaries

Jesuit

347a Montagnais women and the Jesuit program for colonization

Jesus

115f Jesus the Jew and women

Jew

see also Judaism, Yiddish

115f Jesus the Jew and women

156q The role of Jewish women in the religion, ritual and cult of Graeco-Roman Palestine

176k Teaching about Jewish lesbians in literature: From *Zeit* and *Richel* to *The Tree of Begats*

180s The hungry Jewish mother

211a The Jew who wasn't there: *Halakhah* and the Jewish woman

211b The Jewish family: Looking for a usable past

211c The hungry Jewish mother

211e Marriages made in heaven? Battered Jewish wives

211m Scenes from the life of a Jewish lesbian

211p History, fiction, and the tradition: Creating a Jewish feminist poetic

336l Women and the holocaust: The case of German and German-Jewish women

366d The Jewish woman's encounter with American culture

379o Jewish involvement in the New York City woman suffrage movement

Jewett, Sarah Orne

451a The art of Jewett's *Pointed Firs*

Jewish American Woman

73i Irish, Italian, and Jewish women at the grassroots level: A historical and sociological perspective

Jezebel

19g Jezebel before the judges

19l The case of the American Jezebels

156o Goddesses, women and Jezebel

454b The case of the American Jezebels: Anne Hutchinson and female agitation during the years of the Antinomian turmoil, 1636-1640

Jigalong, Australia

333d The social and economic importance of the women in Jigalong

Jinnah, M. A.

433f Bengal election, 1937: Fazlul Huq and M. A. Jinnah: A study in leadership stress in Bengal politics

Jnanananda

325c Mother Guru: Jnanananda of Madras, India

Job

see also Employment

11f Women employees and job-based alcoholism programs

53c The effect of employment, family and job stress on coronary heart disease patterns in women

65b Socioeconomic explanations of job segregation

65c Some psychological factors affecting job segregation and wages

65d Some problems with contemporary job evaluation systems

65e Effect of choice of factors and factor weights in job evaluation

66b Job evaluation and pay setting: Concepts and practices

67b Job evaluation and pay setting: Concepts and practices

87l Salary and job performance differences in dual-career couples

87m Going shopping: The professional couple in the job market

90h Jobs and gender: A history of the structuring of educational employment by sex

93m Improving job opportunities for women from a U.S. corporate perspective

209i Assessing the myths of the job market

210e Beyond the sweatshop: Older women in blue-collar jobs

221g Burnout and job dissatisfaction: Impact on the family

222k The job hunt

272c Job changing and occupational sex segregation: Sex and race comparisons

272h Work experience, job segregation, and wages

272k Commentary: The need to study the transformation of job structures

272l Job integration strategies: Today's programs and tomorrow's needs

288f The impact of sexual harassment on the job: A profile of the experiences of 92 women

305p Is your job hazardous to your health?

307u New jobs in new technologies: Experienced only need apply

337a Vocational aspirations and job realities

354g Do men and women have different jobs because of their biological differences?

378a Male and female: Job versus gender models in the sociology of work

380h Job creation and unemployment for Canadian women

387d Sex discrimination and employment practices: An experiment with unconventional job inquires

387e Male and female: Job versus gender models in the sociology of work

387r Job opportunities of black and white working-class women

425h Causal determinants of job satisfaction in dual career couples

425i Job evaluation and discrimination: Legal, economic, and measurement perspectives on comparable worth and women's pay

426e Moving forward, standing still: Women in white collar jobs

426f Women and nontraditional blue collar jobs in the 1980s: An overview

426g Corporate experiences in improving women's job opportunities

444c The job he left behind: American women in the shipyards during World War II

447d Moving women into outside craft jobs

Johnson Space Center

288l A federal response to sexual harassment: Policy-making at Johnson Space Center, NASA

Johnson, Dorothy M.

384f Pioneer women in the works of two Montana authors: Interviews with Dorothy M. Johnson and A. B. Guthrie, Jr.

Johnson, Esther

196b The secrets of Swift and Stella

Johnson, Samuel

196c "Under the dominion of *some* woman": The friendship of Samuel Johnson and Hester Thrale

Johnson, Virginia E.

439q *Homosexuality in Perspective* by William H. Masters and Virginia E. Johnson

Johnston, Jennifer

318j The masculine world of Jennifer Johnston

Joint

107p Differences in males and females in joint movement range during growth

Joke

275h The hidden joke: Generic uses of masculine terminology

Jones, Gayl

40w Singing a deep song: Language as evidence in the novels of Gayl Jones

40x Escape from Trublem: The fiction of Gayl Jones

Jong, Erica

127j *Fear of Flying*: Developing the feminist novel

Joplin, Janis

175u Janis and the Austin scene

Journal

161d Portrayal of women in women's journals

186e House, home and solitude: Memoirs and journals of May Sarton

301hh swing through the south journal, fall 1981

The Journal of Susanna Moodie

20b Atwood's haunted sequences: *The Circle Game, The Journals of Susanna Moodie,* and *Power Politics*

20d Meridians of perception: A reading of *The Journals of Susanna Moodie*

Journey

20i *Surfacing* and the rebirth journey

176l Journey into otherness: Teaching *The Well of Loneliness*

180t A psychological journey: Mothers and daughters in English-Canadian fiction

Journey to Pike's Peak and New Mexico

384c A study of feminism as a motif in "A journey to Pike's Peak and New Mexico" by Julia Archibald Holmes

Joyce, James

409a The woman hidden in James Joyce's *Chamber Music*

409b *Dubliners*: Women in Irish society

409f Gerty MacDowell: Joyce's sentimental heroine

409h The genuine Christine: Psychodynamics of Issy

409i Anna Livia Plurabelle: The dream woman

Juana Ines de la Cruz, Sor

112h Sor Juana Inés de la Cruz: Mexico's tenth muse (Mexican, 1651-1695)

Judaism

see also Jew, Yiddish, Religion

211g Women-identified women in male-identified Judaism

211i A feminist path to Judaism

211t Steps toward feminine imagery of deity in Jewish theology

211u Bride, spouse, daughter: Images of the feminine in classical Jewish sources

211v Feminist Judaism: Restoration of the moon

457g Women in Judaism: The fact and the fiction

457h Between law and custom: Women's experience of Judaism

Judeo-Christian

122q Marital metaphors in the Judeo-Christian tradition: A feminist critique

Judge

see also Law

19g Jezebel before the judges

394t From undergraduate to judge at sixty

410b Political culture and selection of women judges in trial courts

410f Women judges and public policy in sex integration

436l Will women judges make a difference in women's legal rights? A prediction from attitudes and simulated behaviour

Judgment

45c Do changes in women's rights change women's moral judgements?

271f Sex-role ideology and sex bias in judgments of occupational suitability

Judiciary

see also Law

219f The role of the judiciary in the failure of the Sexual Offences (Amendment) Act to improve the treatment of the rape victim

349s Judicial paternalism and the female status offender: Training women to know their place

Julia

325b Julia: An east African diviner

Julian of Norwich

188l The English mystic: Julian of Norwich

Julie

106f Julie and "La Maison Paternelle": Another look at Rousseau's *La Nouvelle Héloïse*

Juridical

2d The juridical status of the fetus: A proposal for legal protection of the unborn

173b The juridical status of the fetus: A proposal for legal protection of the unborn

Jurisprudence

90d The concept of sex equity in jurisprudence

Jury

249j A jury of one's peers

Just

116q Sex equality and education in Plato's Just State

Justice

see also Law

78d Guilty by reason of sex: Young women and the juvenile justice system

78g Sex role stereotypes and justice for women

78m Forcible rape: Institutionalized sexism in the criminal justice system

78z Marxist feminism: Implications for criminal justice

111k The treatment of convicted female offenders in the criminal justice system

111u Problems of policy development in criminal justice

150oo Only justice can stop a curse

165b Would you believe this woman? Prosecutorial screening for "credible" witnesses and a problem of justice

165m Women as criminal justice professionals: A challenge to change tradition

165n Sex-role operations: Strategies for women working in the criminal justice system

165o Women in the criminal justice profession: An analysis of status conflict

186l Rage for justice: Political, social and moral consciousness in selected novels of May Sarton

192s I'm talking for justice

229oo Ethics and justice in goddess religion

284n The victim and justice system - an introduction

284p The protection of the child victim of a sexual offense in the criminal justice system

321a Schooling and injustice for girls

321l The women's movement and social justice

321n Can there be justice for women under capitalism?: Questions about 'patriarchy'

321o Can there be justice for women under capitalism?: Social justice for whom?

327g Functions of the police and the justice system in family violence

347g "The universe has turned inside out...There is no justice for us here": Andean women under Spanish rule

349u Sex-role stereotypes and justice for women

392l Chivalry and paternalism: Disparities of treatment in the criminal justice system

404t In the pursuit of justice in sentencing and prison

404x Young female offenders in Massachusetts: Toward leaving the juvenile justice system successfully

432a Justice and gender in school sports

432c Athletics, gender, and justice

435k Women's crime, women's justice

462a Women, poverty, and economic justice

Juvenile

8g Juvenile delinquency in girls

78d Guilty by reason of sex: Young women and the juvenile justice system

78p Concurrent and consecutive abuse: The juvenile prostitute

111f The female juvenile offender

111g Juvenile prostitution

111h Contingency management in a juvenile treatment setting

111i The Hillcrest School of Oregon: Guided group interaction in a juvenile institution

205r Sinners or sinned against?: Historical aspects of female juvenile delinquency in British Columbia

348f The processing of juveniles in Victoria

376c The crime of precocious sexuality: Female juvenile delinquency and the progressive era

392m Unequal protection of males and females in the juvenile court

404x Young female offenders in Massachusetts: Toward leaving the juvenile justice system successfully

Kaddish

211n Kaddish from the "wrong" side of the *Mehitzah*

Kafka, Franz
106m Kafka and Laing on the trapped consciousness: The family as politcial life

Kajalrekha
433h Forms of the Indian notion of sexuality and an interpretation of the Mymensing ballad of Kajalrekha

Kampung
166b Women in a yogyakarta kampung
466h Indonesian women in development: State theory and urban kampung practice

Kannagi
194h The goddess Kannagi: A dominant symbol of south Indian Tamil society

Kano, Nigeria
385c Dependence and autonomy: The economic activities of secluded Hausa women in Kano, Nigeria

Karnataka, India
402k Etiquette among women in Karnataka: Forms of address in the village and the family

Karpathos, Greece
162b Putting kin and kinship to good use: The circulation of goods, labour, and names on Karpathos (Greece)

Kartini
166a Kartini - her life, work and influence

Kate
343d Comic structure and the humanizing of Kate in *The Taming of the Shrew*

Katie's Place
243g Katie's place: Women's work, professional work, and social reform

Kaulong
200f Gender, sexuality and marriage: A Kaulong model of nature and culture

Kelley, Peggy Clark
399gg Peggy Clark Kelley: Reminiscences of a "designing" woman

Kempe, Margery
108d Autobiography of a new 'creatur': Female spirituality, selfhood and authorship in *The Book of Margery Kempe*
188m The English religious enthusiast: Margery Kempe

Kennedy, Joan
205cc Joan Kennedy and the British Columbia Women's Service Corps

Kentucky
18j Country roads take me home: The political economy of wage-labor migration in an eastern Kentucky community

Kenya
68e Issues confronting professional African women: Illustrations from Kenya
347h Daughters of the lakes and rivers: Colonization and the land rights of Luo women
362b An examination of education, social change, and national development policy: The case of Kenyan women
370g Slavery and reproductive labor in Mombasa

Kerala, India
161h Women and mass media in Kerala
421i Attitudes of women towards certain selected cultural practices in Kerala state, India

Kesey, Ken
445l Westering and woman: A thematic study of Kesey's *One Flew Over the Cuckoo's Nest* and Fisher's *Mountain Man*

Key
42c Keys for a woman's progression

Kibbutz
see also Israel
104i The organization of labour in an Israeli kibbutz

Kill
2i Killing and letting die
109a Somebody's trying to kill me and I think it's my husband: The modern gothic

Kin
71i The effects of Asian-American kinship systems on women's educational and occupational attainment
101f Kinship, women, and politics in twentieth-century Punjab
162a Interest and emotion in family and kinship studies: A critique of social history and anthropology
162b Putting kin and kinship to good use: The circulation of goods, labour, and names on Karpathos (Greece)
162j Afro-American kinship before and after emancipation in North America
162l Kinship and class consciousness: Family values and work experience among hospital workers in an American southern town
184c Dowries and kinsmen in early Renaissance Venice
207g Women, kinship and capitalist development
208j Women, kinship and capitalist development
270b The significance of family and kinship in urban Turkey
308c Implicating the family: Teenage parenthood and kinship involvement
308j Bringing in the family: Kinship support and contraceptive behavior
334c Shame and reparation: Women's place in the kin
364j Men and women, kinship and property: Some general issues
379b Piety and kin: The limits of antebellum Southern women's reform
401g Women in the kinship system of the Southern Song upper class
427i Conceptions of kinship and the family reproduction cycle

Kinanthropometric
107i Proportionality and body composition in male and female Olympic athletes: A kinanthropometric overview

Kinder
336b Beyond *Kinder, Küche, Kirche*: Weimar women in politics and work

Kinflicks
135l New directions in the contemporary bildungsroman: Lisa Alther's *Kinflicks*

King Carnival
17f Mark Twain's capers: A chameleon in King Carnival's court

King, Charles William
142f Antique gems from *Romola* to *Daniel Deronda*

King, Georgiana Goddard
389h Georgiana Goddard King (1871-1939): Educator and pioneer in medieval Spanish art

Kingdom
234f The status of women in old and early middle kingdom Egypt?
368o Women imprisoned in the kingdom of the Mullahs

Kingston, Jamaica
388d Household economic strategies in Kingston, Jamaica

Kingston, Maxine Hong
124b Naming, magic and documentary: The subversion of the narrative in *Song of Solomon, Ceremony*, and *China Men*
254c The artist as hero in Maxine Hong Kingston's *The Woman Warrior*
452k The metaphysics of matrilinearism in women's autobiography: Studies of Mead's *Blackberry Winter*, Hellman's *Pentimento*, Angelou's *I Know Why the Caged Bird Sings*, and Kingston's *The Woman Warrior*
452m Towards a theory of form in feminist autobiography: Kate Millett's *Flying* and *Sita*; Maxine Hong Kingston's *The Woman Warrior*

Kinsey, Alfred C.
238j The scientist as sex crusader: Alfred C. Kinsey and American culture
290c Sexology and the universalization of male sexuality (from Ellis to Kinsey, and Masters and Johnson)

Kirche
336b Beyond *Kinder, Küche, Kirche*: Weimar women in politics and work

Kiriwina, Papua New Guinea
347k Stability in banana leaves: Colonization and women in Kiriwina, Trobriand Islands

Kisaeng Tour
163d Why I oppose Kisaeng tours

Kit
43q The reform tool kit

Kitchen
182g Private kitchens, public cooking
203p From kitchen to storefront: Women in the tenant movement
341e Women in the kitchen: The feminist boiling point
428f Kitchens hit by priorities: Employed working-class Jamaican women confront the IMF

Kiuk
333k Women and land rights: Kiuk and Wagaidj women in the Darwin area

Klassenliebe
32n The question of a feminist aesthetic and Karin Struck's *Klassenliebe*

Klein
460h   The early stages of female psychosexual development: A Kleinian view

Kleist, Heinrich Von
32d   Kleist's nation of amazons

Kleptomania
280g   The kleptomanias and female criminality

Klute
406a   Klute 1: A contemporary film noir and feminist criticism
406h   Klute 2: Feminism and Klute

Know
61a   What we wish we knew about women: A dialog
126b   Women as knowers
126c   Women knowing: Feminist theory and perspectives on pedagogy
249a   The most important thing for you to know
254k   Know your heroines

Knowledge
51z   The Interdisciplinary Society for Menstrual Cycle Research: Creating knowledge from our experience
168h   Creating and communicating knowledge from a feminist perspective: Risks and challenges for women
309s   Contraception, abortion and venereal disease: Teenagers' knowledge and the effect of education
309u   Sexual and contraceptive knowledge, attitudes and behavior of male adolescents
416n   Class, race, sex, scientific objects of knowledge: A socialist-feminist perspective on the social construction of productive nature and some political consequences
421s   Labor force participation and fertility, contraceptive knowledge, attitude and practice of the women of Barbados
450n   The miracle of realism: The bid for self-knowledge in the fiction of Ellen Gilchrist
455g   New knowledge and the drinking woman

Kollontai, Alexandra
95e   Alexandra Kollontai and the Russian Revolution

Korea
75b   Employment of Korean women
75c   Working women in Korea
325d   Possession sickness and women shamans in Korea
412r   Korean women in Hawaii, 1903-1945: The role of Methodism in their liberation and in their participation in the Korean independence movement
420j   Urban migrant women in the Republic of Korea
421c   A causal interpretation of the effect of mother's education and employment status on parental decision-making role patterns in the Korean family
424b   Trends in female labour force participation and occupational shifts in urban Korea

Korean Independence Movement
412r   Korean women in Hawaii, 1903-1945: The role of Methodism in their liberation and in their participation in the Korean independence movement

Krause, Alvina
399ff   Alvina Krause: A great teacher of acting

Kriemhild
180b   Kriemhild and Clytemnestra - Sisters in crime or independent women?

Krishna
325h   The ladies of Lord Krishna: Rituals of middle-aged women in eastern India

Küche
336b   Beyond *Kinder, Küche, Kirche*: Weimar women in politics and work

Künslerroman
242b   The birth of the artist as heroine: (Re)production, the *Künslerroman* tradition, and the fiction of Katherine Mansfield

Kuliscioff, Anna
95a   Anna Kuliscioff: Russian revolutionist, Italian feminist

Kynywedi
334b   Nau Kynywedi Teithiauc

L'Avision Christine
154b   The crowned dame, dame opinion, and dame philosophy: The female characteristics of three ideals in Christine de Pizan's *L'Avision Christine*

La Chasse et le de Part d'Amours
331h   Poems by "The Lady" in La Chasse et le de *part d'amours* (1509)

Lab
342f   The scientific mystique: Can a white lab coat guarantee purity in the search for knowledge about the nature of women?

Label
133a   Homosexual labeling and the male role

Labor
see also Division of Labor, Employment
5d   An analysis of the impact of labour migration on the lives of women in Lesotho
13b   Capitalism, gender and the labour process: Two case studies
13l   Feminism: An early tradition amongst western Australian labor women
18g   Population dynamics and migrant labor in South Africa
18j   Country roads take me home: The political economy of wage-labor migration in an eastern Kentucky community
23e   Labor women: Political housekeepers or politicians?
49i   The setting and the reality for labor relations in the 90's
50f   The need for women's labour in the First World War
50g   Women as a reserve army of labour: A note on recent British experience
65m   The role of labor
86i   Protection for women: Trade unions and labor laws
104b   Cash crop production and family labour: Tobacco growers in Corrientes, Argentina
104i   The organization of labour in an Israeli kibbutz
110a   Estimating labor supply functions for married women
110b   Married women's labor supply: A comparison of alternative estimation procedures

110c   Hours and weeks in the theory of labor supply
110d   Assets and labor supply
110f   A multivariate model of labor supply: Methodology and estimation
119c   'Mothers, vote labour!' The state, the labour movement and working-class mothers, 1900-1918
129w   Protective labor legislation
139g   Women, gender relations and wage labour
149a   Domestic labour and the working-class household
149c   Domestic labour: A methodological discussion
149e   The expanded reproduction cycle of labour power in twentieth-century capitalism
149f   Domestic labour and the reproduction of labour power: Towards an analysis of women, the family, and class
151b   Domestic labour and Soviet society
153e   Nonwage labor and subsistence
162b   Putting kin and kinship to good use: The circulation of goods, labour, and names on Karpathos (Greece)
169a   Labor education and women workers: An historical perspective
169m   Labor history through field trips
169v   Labor education and women workers: An international comparison
199d   Housework and domestic labor: Racial and technological change
201h   The uprising of the 20,000: The making of a labor legend
207c   Women's labours: The naturalisation of social inequality and women's subordination
208i   Women's labours: The naturalisation of social inequality and women's subordination
209t   Labor legislation in Norway: Its application to the introduction of new technology
209gg   Taking the initiative on new technology: Canadian labor approaches
227o   'The housewife and her labour under capitalism' - a critique
227p   Women's domestic labour
248f   Asylum nursing before 1914: A chapter in the history of labour
270g   Female labor power relations in the urban Turkish family
270h   The effect of international labor migration on women's roles: The Turkish case
323c   No proper deal: Women workers and the Canadian labour movement, 1870-1940
323q   Women's challenge to organized labour
323y   Building links: Labour and the women's movement
344r   "Union is power": Sketches from women's labor history
354b   Convenience and the occurrence of births: Induction and labor in the United States and Canada
355a   Prologue: Reflections on the study of household labor
355i   Contributions to household labor: Comparing wives' and husbands' reports
355j   Domestic labor as work discipline: The struggle over housework in foster homes

370g Slavery and reproductive labor in Mombasa

375h Historical background of "protective" labor legislation: *Muller v. Oregon*

378g Unity is strength? Feminism and the labor movement

385b Control of land, labor, and capital in rural southern Sierra Leone

390c Women and labour, 1880-1900

418b A commentary on theories of female wage labour

419c Workers and drones: Labor, idleness and gender definition in Hesiod's beehive

446b Current problems of female labor in the USSR

446g The utilization of female labor in agriculture

446h The twenty-fifth congress of the CPSU and current problems of employment of female labor in the republics of central Asia

446i Protection of female labor

470e Contemporary clothing 'sweatshops', Asian female labour and collective organisation

470f Migrant women and wage labour: The case of West Indian women in Britain

Labor Force
see also Employment

5a Conceptualizing the labor force: The underestimation of women's economic activities

18e Population policy, family size, and the reproduction of the labor force in India: The case of Bombay

49c The age mix of the labor force in 1990: Implications for labor market research

49f The feminization of the labor force: Research for industrial/organizational psychology

61l Women in the civilian labor force

89a Labor force participation of married women: A study of labor supply

89q Wives' labor force behavior and family consumption patterns

153a Household structures and labor-force formation in the capitalist world-economy

321f Women in the Australian labour force

323n Triple oppression: Immigrant women in the labour force

324d Attitudes toward women working: Changes over time and implications for the labor-force behaviors of husbands and wives

344p Women in the labor force: An overview

361b Labor force participation of women baccalaureates in science

362d The mobilization of Iraqi women into the wage labor force

380d The relationship between the labor force employment of women and the changing social organization in Canada

380k Microeconomic effects of women entering the labor force

380n Labor force participation and earnings of women in Andalusia

380o Economic aspects of female labor force participation in the Federal Republic of Germany

402d Trends and structure of female labour force participation in rural and urban Pakistan

421p Changes in Canadian female labour force participation and some possible implications for conjugal power

421s Labor force participation and fertility, contraceptive knowledge, attitude and practice of the women of Barbados

422a Women in the labour force of India: A macro-level statistical profile

422c Women in the labour force in India

424b Trends in female labour force participation and occupational shifts in urban Korea

424c Trends in female labour force participation in Taiwan: The transition toward higher technology activities

424q Effect of female labour force participation on fertility: The case of construction workers in Chiang Mai City

426a Increased labor force participation of women and affirmative action

428a The impact of the changing international division of labor on different sectors of the labor force

428i Mexican border industrialization, female labor force participation, and migration

433b Conditions influencing rural and town women's participation in the labor force

436d Women's education and participation in the labour force: The case of Nigeria

463b Intra-household implications of the involvement of women in the paid labor force

463c The movement of women into the labor force

Labor Market
see also Employment, Market

23k The employment of women in the commonwealth public service: The creation and reproduction of a dual labour market

49c The age of the labor force in 1990: Implications for labor market research

49g Commentary on studies of gender-mix in labor market research

89i Determinants of the structure of industrial type labor markets

89j A theory of labor market segmentation

89k Structured labour markets, worker organization and low pay

89m Sexual discrimination in the labour market

93h Equality between men and women in the labor market: The Swedish National Labor Market Board

93i Vocational training, the labor market, and the unions

93r Integration of family policy and labor market policy in Sweden

93u The contribution of labor market data in combating employment discrimination

103q Family responsibilities as a labor market issue: A Scandinavian perspective

110g Labor supply with costs of labor market entry

210g Labor markets and old ladies' homes

250j Young women in the labour market: Stability and change

250m The experiences of women graduates in the labour market

258f The labour market

260a Women in the labour market and equal opportunity policy in Sweden, United Kingdom, United States and West Germany

260c Patterns of occupational segregation by sex in the labor market

260f The effects of statutory employment policies on women in the United Kingdom labour market

260j Labour market policy in four countries: Are women adequately represented?

260k Estimating the impact of labor market policies on women: A discussion of the four-country studies on the employment of women

260l The political economy of labor market discrimination: A theoretical and comparative analysis of sex discrimination

272e Occupational segregation and labor market discrimination

315j Analyzing discrimination against women in the labor market - A few lessons from John Stuart Mill

324a Problems of labor-market reentry

357c The structure of labour markets and low pay for women

404y The unique employment problems of female offenders returning to the community and labor market

428l Silicon Valley's women workers: A theoretical analysis of sex-segregation in the electronics industry labor market

459h Women's work and their status: Rural Indian evidence of labour market and environment effects on sex differences in childhood mortality

459i Women and the urban labour market

459j Sex discrimination in the urban labour markets: Some propositions based on Indian evidence

465f Women's employment, legislation and the labour-market

468b Working hours and segmentation in the Norwegian labour market

468d Women's attempts to break down sex barriers in the labour market

Laboratory
176y Toward a laboratory of one's own: Lesbians in science

Laborer
386b Agricultural laborers

Labour Party
283g Women's organisation in the Labour Party

283k A left strategy for Labour

283l Does Labour always fail?

Lactate
372q Short time, maximal muscular performance: Relation to muscle lactate and fiber type in females

460e Physiological aspects of female sexual development: Gestation, lactation, menopause, and erotic physiology

Lady
175g The capitol's lady

175l Elisabet Ney: Texas' first lady of sculpture

205t   A union man's wife: The ladies' auxiliary movement in the IWA, the Lake Cowichan experience

323w   From ladies' auxiliaries to wives' committees

331h   Poems by "The Lady" in La Chasse et le de *part d'amours* (1509)

353ee Doctors or ladies? Women physicians in psychiatric institutions, 1872-1900

399ii The lady is a critic

415f   Effective interpersonal communication for women of the corporation: Think like a man, talk like a lady

445k   Conrad Richter's southwestern ladies

449c   Portraits by a lady: The fictional world of Ling Shuhua

452n   The lady's not for spurning: Kate Millett and the critics

454d   The lady and the mill girl: Changes in the status of women in the Age of Jackson

454e   Ladies bountiful: Organized women's benevolence in early nineteenth-century America

Lady in Blue

175a   María de Agreda: The lady in blue

Lady Macbeth

343m   Lady Macbeth: "Infirm of purpose"

Lady Oracle

20j   *Lady Oracle*: The narrative of a fool-heroine

109i   The mirror and the cameo: Margaret Atwood's comic/gothic novel, *Lady Oracle*

Lagos

385m   The child-care dilemma of working mothers in African cities: The case of Lagos, Nigeria

393c   Women and work: A study of female and male attitudes in the modern sector of an African metropolis (Lagos)

Lahore, Pakistan

395j   Health beliefs and behaviors of middle class urban women in Lahore, Pakistan

Laing, Ronald David

106m   Kafka and Laing on the trapped consciousness: The family as political life

Laity

see also Religion

412k   Laity rights and leadership: Winning them for women in the Methodist Protestant church, 1860-1900

412n   The laity rights movement, 1906-1918: Women's suffrage in the Methodist Episcopal Church, South

Lake Cowichan

205t   A union man's wife: The ladies' auxiliary movement in the IWA, the Lake Cowichan experience

Lakoff, Robin

275f   Lakoff on language and women

Lakota, Sioux

see also American Indian

148i   Male and female in traditional Lakota culture

Lamb, Myrna

124c   Notes on technique in feminist drama: *Apple Pie* and *Signs of Life*

Land

82k   Land tenure and cooperatives: Origin, development and persistence of Navajo matrifocality in subsistence, production, exchange and tenure

333f   Women and land rights: The Pitjantjatjara land claims

333g   The recent history of the Borroloola aboriginal people and their struggle for land rights

333h   Borroloola community and land rights

333j   Women and land rights: A review

333k   Women and land rights: Kiuk and Wagaidj women in the Darwin area

350h   The impact of land reform on women: The case of Ethiopia

385b   Control of land, labor, and capital in rural southern Sierra Leone

388f   Women and law: Land tenure in Africa

412q   For god and home and native land: The W.C.T.U.'s image of woman in the late nineteenth century

433g   Inequality and radical land reform: Some notes from west Bengal

466d   Land ownership in Negri Sembilan, 1900-1977

The Land of Little Rain

384t   The moral in Austin's *The Land of Little Rain*

Landscape

215o   Anger in a black landscape

234j   'Woman-ing" the landscape: East Anglia 1300-1500: A discussion on sources and methodology

306b   The "rooted" landscape and the woman writer

Lane, Mary Bradley

131e   Coming Home: Four feminist utopias and patriarchal experience

Lang, Fritz

406e   The place of women in Fritz Lang's The Blue Gardenia

Language

19j   The Antinomian language controversy

32p   Our language, our selves: Verena Stefan's critique of patriarchal language

34b   Boys will be boys will be boys: The language of sex and gender

40e   From baptism to resurrection: Toni Cade Bambara and the incongruity of language

40m   A simple language

40w   Singing a deep song: Language as evidence in the novels of Gayl Jones

64m   Writing, language, and the body

84h   How can language be sexist?

115d   'The faltering words of men': Exclusive language in the liturgy

121h   How "Low feet" stagger: Disruptions of language in Dickinson's poetry

121i   "Ransom in a voice": Language as defense in Dickinson's poetry

132e   Language and revolution: The Franco-American Dis-connection

132m   Difference and language: A linguist's perspective

133c   Lesbians, gay men, and their "languages"

135c   Wariness and women's language: Two modest verbal studies

135g   Olive Schreiner - A note on sexist language and the feminist writer

142b   George Eliot's language of the sense

171a   Language, gender and society: Opening a second decade of research

171b   Beyond the he/man approach: The case for nonsexist language

171k   Sex similarities and differences in language, speech, and nonverbal communication: An annotated bibliography

189a   A thief in the house: Women and language

259g   'Telling how it is': Language and gender in the classroom

265e   Language and attitudes toward masculine and feminine sex role

274e   Modern languages

275b   Sexist language and sexism

275f   Lakoff on language and women

304d   Sex roles and language use: Implications for mental health

344z   Sexism and the English language: The linguistic implications of being a woman

356d   Proprieters of language

356g   "Women's language" or "powerless language"?

356o   The "feminine" language of Marianne Moore

356t   Reading reading: Echo's abduction of language

448b   Marguerite Duras: Women's language in men's cities

453d   A female form language

Language and Woman's Place

275d   *Language and Woman's Place* (excerpts)

275f   Lakoff on language and women

Languagescape

356m   Honing a habitable languagescape: Women's images for the new world frontiers

Laslett, P.

421b   Female-headed households and domestic organization in San Isidro, Guatemala: A test of Hammel and Laslett's comparative typology

The Last of Chéri

64l   The theatre as literary model: Role-playing in *Chéri* and *The Last of Chéri*

Latency

88g   The latency period

Later Life

289o   Beyond generativity: Toward a sensuality of later life

Lathen, Emma

1i   Emma Lathen

Latin

22e   Women in Latin Medieval literature in Denmark e.g. annals and chronicles

225i   Cultural and historical influences on sexuality in Hispanic/Latin women: Implications for psychotherapy

331a   Woman's song in medieval Latin

Latin America

see also individual countries

68j Ancient song, new melody in Latin America: Women and film

74b Success and the Latin American writer

83f Working women in Latin America

218c Legitimizing political women: Expanding options for female political elites in Latin America

322l Women and literature in Latin America

363e Social policy and women in Latin America: The need for a new model

363f Research on women in Latin America: Problems of networking and comparative analysis in the last decade

408n The changing face of woman in Latin American fiction

Latina
see Hispanic

Laugh

135m The laughter of maidens, the crackle of matriarchs: Notes on the collision between comedy and feminism

303m She who laughs first

Laundry

13d Besides our size it's because we are women: The strike by the laundry workers union 15 January - 5 February 1982

Laurence, Margaret

448j Quest for the peaceable kingdom: Urban/rural codes in Roy, Laurence, and Atwood

Lavender

305g Shades of lavender: Lesbian sex and sexuality

Lavender Cellar

399uu The Lavender Cellar theatre

Law
see also Court, Crime, Judge, Judiciary, Justice, Lawyer, Legal, Litigation, Trial, case names

2l Abortion, slavery, and the law: A study in moral character

23m 'Law reform and human reproduction': Implications for women

50n From disregard to disrepute: The position of women in family law

65k Canada's equal pay for work of equal value law

65n Comparable worth under various federal and state laws

78a The criminal law and women

78c Females under the law: 'Protected' but unequal

78j Women prisoners and the law: Which way will the pendulum swing?

78aa Postscript: The future of women and the criminal law

86i Protection for women: Trade unions and labor laws

87k Equal opportunity laws and dual-career couples

93c Equal pay and equal opportunity law in France

93d The effectiveness of federal laws prohibiting sex discrimination in employment in the United States

93g The enforcement of laws against sex discrimination in England: Problems of institutional design

94k Religion, law and family disputes in a Lebanese Muslim community in Sydney

101j The All-Pakistan Women's Association and the 1961 Muslim family laws ordinance

108k Women as law clerks: Catherine G. Waugh

129bb A right to make laws?

130a Women and the law

143f Law, religion and the unity of *Felix Holt*

146k Law enforcement and child sexual abuse

173d *Roe v. Wade* and the lesson of the pre-*Roe* case law

183e Women factory workers and the law

189l Before and after: The impact of feminism on the academic discipline of law

235e Parliament and the law

245g Shifting perspectives on marital property law

260e Equal opportunity and the law in the United States

262g Laws prohibiting sex discrimination in schools

276e Sexual aggression and the law - implications for the future

283f Sexist bias and the law

291e Sexual child abuse: The legislation and the law in the United States

291f Sexual abuse of children: An examination of European criminal law

294g Prostitution and the law: The question of decriminalization

300o Islamic law in Christian Southeast Asia: The politics of establishing Shari'a courts in the Philippines

309bb Teenagers and pregnancy: The law in 1979

315e Women, reproductive freedom, and the law: A selected annotated bibliography

334d Property interests in the classical Welsh law of women

334f The European legal context of the Welsh law of matrimonial property

337g Women and the law school

344u Women, law, and public policy

346e Salient laws on women and children: A selected bibliography

348a Sexism in criminal law

363a In defense of motherhood: Divorce law in Cuba during the early republic

364b Cognatic descent, Islamic law and women's property on the East African coast

374f Appendix A: Maternity law for working women

375b Widows' rights in Anglo-Saxon law

375e Rape in thirteenth-century England: A study of the common-law courts

375f Under great temptations here: Women and divorce law in puritan Massachusetts

375g The law of husband and wife in nineteenth-century America: Changing views of divorce

375k Clara Shortridge Foltz: Pioneer in the law

375l Women's entry into corporate law firms

376g Women before the law: Females as felons and prey in fourteenth-century England

379c The planter's wife revisited: Women, equity law, and the Chancery Court in seventeenth-century Maryland

386j Women in law and administration

388f Women and law: Land tenure in Africa

397j Lesbians and the law: Where sexism and heterosexism meet

402g Women and the law: Constitutional rights and continuing inequalities

403g Women, law, and social change in Iran

415e Women in organizations: The impact of law

454q Cookbooks and law books: The hidden history of career women in twentieth-century America

457h Between law and custom: Women's experience of Judaism

465c Who still cares for the family? Recent developments in income maintenance, taxation and family law

Law Enforcement Assistance Administration (L.E.A.A.)

349j Women as victims: An examination of the results of L.E.A.A.'s National Crime Survey Program

Lawsuit

173c The abortion-funding cases and population control: An imaginary lawsuit and some reflections on the uncertain limits of reproductive privacy

Lawyer

78u Women in a male-dominated profession: The women lawyers

249e Not by lawyers alone: Ten practical lessons for academic litigants

Lay
see also Religion

187i Feminine lay piety in the High Middle Ages: The Beguines

366f Lay women in the Protestant tradition

412l "A new impulse": Progress in lay leadership and service by women of the United Brethren in Christ and the Evangelical Association, 1870-1910

Laye, Camara

393d Worlds apart? A comparative study of European and African traditional family life as depicted in the novels of Laurie Lee and Camara Laye

Laywomen

431c Laywomen in Theravada Buddhism

Le Ditié de Jehanne D'Arc

22i Un écrit militant de Christine de Pizan: *Le Ditié de Jehanne d'Arc*

Le Gallienne, Eva

399r Uta Hagen and Eva Le Gallienne

Le Guin, Ursula K.

131k You, U.K. Le Guin

131l Charles Bronson, Samurai, and other feminine images: A transactive response to *The Left Hand of Darkness*

383g *The Left Hand of Darkness*: Androgyny and the feminist utopia

Lead

20f One woman leads to another

Leader

38m Dilemmas of black females in leadership

43t Female leaders: Who was Rembrandt's mother?

45d Emerging patterns of female leadership in formal organizations, or must the female leader go formal?

49j Leadership and management in the 1990's

72d Latinas in educational leadership: Chicago, Illinois

93j Leadership training for union women in the United States: Route to equal opportunity

94h A new Australian working class leadership: The case of Ford Broadmeadows

136c Women and nonverbal leadership cues: When seeing is not believing

169e Training rank and file leaders: A case study

214h Styles of leadership: Power and feminine values

259d Staffing for sexism: Educational leadership and role models

282d Transforming "natural" woman: Female ritual leaders and gender ideology among Bimin-Kuskusmin

352a Introduction: Barriers to equity - women, educational leadership, and social change

352b Prophets, chiefs, commissioners, and queens: The moral and institutional context of leadership

352c The psychology of leadership: Implications for women

352d Power and opportunity in the principalship: The case of two women leaders in education

352e Historical perspectives on women in educational leadership

352g Single-sex education and leadership: The early years of Simmons College

352h Coeducation and the development of leadership skills in women: Historical perspectives from Cornell University, 1868-1900

352p Leadership training for increased effectiveness among women educational administrators: Two local models

366c The leadership of nuns in immigrant Catholicism

378n Women in positions of political leadership in Britain, France and West Germany

378o Beyond leadership

386i Women and political leadership

404ee Self-power and leadership

407c Preparing the individual for institutional leadership: The summer institute

407e Toward a new era of leadership: The national identification program

412c Women of the word: Selected leadership roles of women in Mr. Wesley's Methodism

412k Laity rights and leadership: Winning them for women in the Methodist Protestant church, 1860-1900

412l "A new impulse": Progress in lay leadership and service by women of the United Brethren in Christ and the Evangelical Association, 1870-1910

433f Bengal election, 1937: Fazlul Huq and M. A. Jinnah: A study in leadership stress in Bengal politics

435l The foreign policy beliefs of women in leadership positions

League of Women Voters

81j International feminism between the wars: The National Woman's Party versus the League of Women Voters

Learn

see also Education

30i New combinations: Learning from Virginia Woolf

33b Women, learning, and power: Eleonora of Aragon and the Court of Ferrara

33d Learned women of early modern Italy: Humanists and university scholars

33e Learned women in the Europe of the sixteenth century

57a Dimensions of sexual learning in childhood

57b Toward an understanding of sexual learning and communication: An examination of social learning theory and nonschool learning environments

57c Work, the family, and children's sexual learning

57d Television as a sphere of influence on the child's learning about sexuality

57e Sexual learning in the elementary school

57g Social services and sexual learning

57h Religion and sexual learning of children

73f The role of learning in the lives of Finnish and other ethnic women and a proposal for self-education

98e Learning from poor women: A method of village study

122d The learning climate and the non-traditional student

136i A feminist critique of androgyny: Toward the elimination of gender attributions for learned behavior

172d Learning to take hold of one's own destiny (Bolivia)

174p Unlearning complicity, remembering resistance: White women's anti-racism education

176m Learning through teaching: A lesbianism course in 1972

211o Learning to chant the Torah: A first step

268f Depression in relation to sex roles: Differences in learned susceptibility and precipitating factors

292h The she-she-she camps: An experiment in living and learning, 1934-1937

301rr There's not a child that can't learn

311b Learning women's studies

312e Learning women's studies

441g Teaching and learning about women and technology

460q Sex education versus sexual learning

473m Comparisons and implications: What have we learned?

Learned Helplessness

404b Learned helplessness

404c Learned helplessness, depression, and alcohol problems of women

Leave

213c The second generation: West Indian female school-leavers

339j One family's decision: A leave of absence

447n A legal perspective on pregnancy leave and benefits

467d Statutory maternity leave in the United Kingdom: A case study

Lebanon

75g Current status of employment of women in Lebanon

94k Religion, law and family disputes in a Lebanese Muslim community in Sydney

265n Sex role images in Lebanese text books

322f Interview with Etel Adnan (Lebanon)

421f Birth order and alienation among college women in Lebanon

Leben und Abenteuer der Trobadora Beatriz

32r Irmtraud Morgner's *Leben und Abenteuer der Trobadora Beatriz*

Lebensraum

336i The competition for women's *lebensraum*, 1928-1934

Ledford, Lily May

301g Corn shuckings, fiddle contests, square dances: Oral history with Lily May Ledford

Lee, Jaren

108i Neither auction block nor pedestal: *The Life and Religious Experience of Jaren Lee, A Coloured Lady*

Lee, Laurie

393d Worlds apart? A comparative study of European and African traditional family life as depicted in the novels of Laurie Lee and Camara Laye

Left

224m Revolution in the pursuit of happiness: Love and community-building on the left

283j Race, left strategies and the state

283k A left strategy for Labour

283o The socialist economic review project: Progress in the economics of the left

369a New left women and men: The honeymoon is over

336e Helene Stöcker: Left-wing intellectual and sex reformer

412t Winifred L. Chappell: Everybody on the left knew her

418e Left critiques of the family

430d The attitude of the Iranian left to the women's question

The Left Hand of Darkness

131l Charles Bronson, Samurai, and other feminine images: A transactive response to *The Left Hand of Darkness*

383g *The Left Hand of Darkness*: Androgyny and the feminist utopia

Legacy

2b The legacy of *Roe v Wade*

109o The maternal legacy: The grotesque tradition in Flannery O'Connor's female gothic

130bb Conclusion: The legacy of the eighteenth century: A look at the future

131h An ambiguous legacy: The role and position of women in the English Eutopia

147v The eastern legacy - the early history of physical education for women

150q Cultural legacy denied and discovered: Black lesbians in fiction by women

189g Anthropology - a discipline with a legacy

196k Emerson and the angel of midnight: The Legacy of Mary Moody Emerson

229j The Amazon legacy

301b Legacy: Memories of our foremothers

376f Nineteenth-century women's prison reform and its legacy

Legal

see also Law

2d The juridical status of the fetus: A proposal for legal protection of the unborn

4j Legal aspects of adolescent pregnancy

55l Appendix A: Legal resources on sexual exploitation of children

55m Appendix B: Review of legal cases regarding US Code, Section 1461 (mailing obscene or crime-inciting matter)

63a The sexually integrated prison: A legal and policy evaluation

65j Economic models as a means of calculating legal compensation claims

66g The legal framework

67g The legal framework

79d The legal aspects of the DES case: What can be done

129k Legal disabilities of women

173b The juridical status of the fetus: A proposal for legal protection of the unborn

198h Islam and the legal status of women in Tunisia

199h Brave new office: The changing world of the legal secretary

230k Using psychological research on violent pornography to inform legal change

233p Legal considerations of reproductive hazards in industry in the United Kingdom

233q Legal considerations of reproductive hazards in industry in the United States

252c Legal aspects of pregnancy termination in Europe

273h Legal aspects of prenatal sex selection

281h Ethical and legal aspects of sexual issues

308g Ethical and legal issues in teenage pregnancies

319o The nonconsenting sterilization of Mexican women in Los Angeles: Issues of psychocultural rupture and legal redress in paternalistic behavior

339e Coping with illegal sex discrimination

364f The legal and social transformation of rural women in Aegean Turkey

375j Barred from the bar: Women and legal education in the United States, 1870-1890

376d The weaker vessel: Legal versus social reality in mental commitments in nineteenth-century New York

392n Women in prison: Discriminatory practices and some legal solutions

396e Seizing the means of reproduction: An illegal feminist abortion collective — how and why it worked

425i Job evaluation and discrimination: Legal, economic, and measurement perspectives on comparable worth and women's pay

435i Antiobscenity: A comparison of the legal and feminist perspectives

436l Will women judges make a difference in women's legal rights? A prediction from attitudes and simulated behaviour

444d "Life, liberty, and dower": The legal status of women after the American Revolution

447i A legal perspective on workplace reproductive hazards

447n A legal perspective on pregnancy leave and benefits

461x Discussion: Legal victim or social victim?

471f Women at work in Greece: The sociological and legal perspectives

472e Legal issues affecting older women

Legend

22g Structural patterns in the legends of the holy women of Christianity

175o Aunt Dicy: Legendary black lady

175v Legends in their own time: The Dallas Cowboy cheerleaders

201h The uprising of the 20,000: The making of a labor legend

229l Growing up with legends of the Chinese swordswomen

338a Irish women in legend, literature and life

Legislate

93f Administering anti-discrimination legislation in Great Britain

93l Implementing equal pay and equal opportunity legislation in Great Britain

129w Protective labor legislation

147t The effect of current sports legislation on women in Canada and the U.S.A. - Title IX

209t Labor legislation in Norway: Its application to the introduction of new technology

209hh Legislative and research options for the U.S. Congress

291e Sexual child abuse: The legislation and the law in the United States

357b Relative female earnings in Great Britain and the impact of legislation

375h Historical background of "protective" labor legislation: *Muller v. Oregon*

436k The impact of the women's movement and legislative activity of women MPs on social development

440k Legislating for the right to be equal

465b Members and survivors: Women and retirement-pensions legislation

465f Women's employment, legislation and the labour-market

471e Women at work in Italy: Legislation - evolution and prospects

Legislature

205bb From home to house: Women in the BC legislature

226f Women as legislative candidates in six states

226g Women's organizational strategies in state legislatures

Legitimacy

184e Illegitimacy, sexual revolution, and social change in modern Europe

184i Female sexual attitudes and the rise of illegitimacy: A case study

205v The search for legitimacy: Nurses' registration in British Columbia 1913-1935

256c Servants, sexual relations and the risks of illegitimacy in London, 1801-1900

309b Teenage illegitimacy: An exchange

309c The legitimacy status of first births to U.S. women aged 15-24, 1939-1978

316a Legitimate theatre is illegitimate

Leisure

107c Women and sport: A leisure studies perspective

151k Reading as a leisure pursuit in the USSR

164h Jane Austen and the problem of leisure

271e Perspectives from women on sport and leisure

Lemos, Ramon M.

432d Reply to Moulton and Lemos

Leroy

150v LeRoy's birthday

Lesbian

see also Gay, Homosexual

7l Racism and sadomasochism: A conversation with two black lesbians

7s Sadism, masochism, and lesbian-feminism

7u New expanded-type version lesbian handkerchief code

7v Lesbian S & M: The politics of dis-illusion

11j Alcoholism and the lesbian community

12e From zero to infinity: Scientific views of lesbians

16k Alcoholism and the lesbian community

34c From sin to sickness: Hormonal theories of lesbianism

43f Not for lesbians only

48k The intimate relationships of lesbians and gay men

60e The social enforcement of heterosexuality and lesbian resistance in the 1920's

64h The test of love and nature: Colette and lesbians

119a Inverts and experts: Radclyffe Hall and the lesbian identity

132s Lesbianism and the social function of taboo

133c Lesbians, gay men, and their "languages"

133f Recognition among lesbians in straight settings

133g Communication patterns in established lesbian relationships

133p Educational responsibilities to gay male and lesbian students

133t Lesbianfeminist rhetoric as a social movement

136l Nonverbal behavior and lesbian/gay orientation

140s Issues in the psychotherapy of lesbians

150n Black lesbian in American literature: An overview

150q Cultural legacy denied and discovered: Black lesbians in fiction by women

150jj Black lesbian/feminist organizing: A conversation

152b Growing up lesbian and Catholic

176b Black lesbians in academia: Visible invisibility

176g "Kissing/Against the Light": A look at lesbian poetry

176h Lesbian literature: A Third World feminist perspective

176j Teaching the psychology of women: A lesbian feminist perspective

176k Teaching about Jewish lesbians in literature: From *Zeitl* and *Richel* to *The Tree of Begats*

176m Learning through teaching: A lesbianism course in 1972

176o Black lesbians before 1970: A bibliographical essay

176p Resources for lesbian history

176q Who hid lesbian history?

176r Lesbian biography, biography of lesbians

176s One out of thirty: Lesbianism in women's studies textbooks

176t Lesbian images in women's literature anthologies

176v The lesbian periodicals index

176x Older lesbians

176y Toward a laboratory of one's own: Lesbians in science

176z Lesbians in physical education and sport

176bb A lesbian perspective on women's studies

211m Scenes from the life of a Jewish lesbian

224c Lesbians and gay men: Hetero sexualities, common cause

224i Lesbianism: A socialist feminist perspective

224k Some thoughts on gay/lesbian oppression

224n Lesbian and gay oppression in the '80s: Androgyny, men and power

231c Marching to a different drummer: Lesbian and gay GIs in World War II

231h Compulsory heterosexuality and lesbian existence

257e The daughter is mother of the child: Cycles of lesbian sexuality

257l I'll climb the stairway to heaven: Lesbianism in the seventies

305g Shades of lavender: Lesbian sex and sexuality

310x Children by donor insemination: A new choice for lesbians

323j Lesbians and gays in the union movement

332l Exiting from patriarchy: The lesbian novel of development

344x What price independence? Social reactions to lesbians, spinsters, widows, and nuns

359bb Lesbian families: Cultural and clinical issues

360h Lesbian women and mental health policy

369d Socialism, feminism, and gay/lesbian liberation

397a Changing theories of lesbianism: Challenging the stereotypes

397b Developing a lesbian identity

397c The coming-out process: Violence against lesbians

397d Lesbian relationships: A struggle toward partner equality

397e The older lesbian: Love relationships and friendship patterns

397f Beloved women: The lesbian in American Indian culture

397g Reclamation: A lesbian Indian story

397h The Puerto Rican lesbian in the United States

397i Compulsory heterosexuality and lesbian existence

397j Lesbians and the law: Where sexism and heterosexism meet

397k Lesbianism and motherhood: Implications for child custody

397l Lesbian childbirth and woman-controlled conception

397m Lesbians and contemporary health care systems: Oppression and opportunity

397n Peril and promise: Lesbians' workplace participation

397o From accommodation to rebellion: The politicization of lesbianism

397p Culture-making: Lesbian classics in the year 2000

397q The black lesbian in American literature: An overview

397r Without approval: The lesbian poetry tradition

397s Lesbians and women's music

398i Is 'Chloe liked Olivia' a lesbian plot?

417x Realities and fictions: Lesbian visions of utopia

434j Homophobia and social work practice with lesbians

434k Social work with lesbian couples

439d Compulsory heterosexuality and lesbian existence

439u "I am not contented": Female masochism and lesbianism in early twentieth-century New England

455h Some mothers are lesbians

460m Finding self in the lesbian community

"Lesson I Bleed"

399h "Lesson I Bleed"

Lesotho

5d An analysis of the impact of labour migration on the lives of women in Lesotho

Lessing, Doris

51l Erik Erikson and Doris Lessing: Psychological theory and the female novel of development

180q The nightmare repetition: The mother-daughter conflict in Doris Lessing's *Children of Violence*

318a Passionate portrayal of things to come: Doris Lessing's recent fiction

332i Doris Lessing and the parables of growth

383h Truth and art in women's worlds: Doris Lessing's *Marriages Between Zones Three, Four, and Five*

383i Opposing necessity and truth: The argument against politics in Doris Lessing's utopian vision

417bb Change and art in women's worlds: Doris Lessing's *Canopus in Argos: Archives*

448i Reading the city as palimpsest: The experiential perception of the city in Doris Lessing's *The Four-Gated City*

Letter

7b Letter from a former masochist

7z A letter of the times, or should this sado-masochism be saved?

30f On "Clearing the Air": My letter to Simone de Beauvoir

43j An open letter to the academy

108f Artemisia Gentileschi: The artist's autograph in letters and paintings

108g Giving weight to words: Madame de Sévigné's letters to her daughter

108l The female sociograph: The theater of Virginia Woolf's letters

112a Christine de Pisan: First professional woman of letters (French, 1364-1430?)

193t From teachers' letters

301jj Speaking in tongues: A letter to Third World women writers

306e Tell me all you know: Reading letters and diaries of rural women

306n Letters and diaries: Demystifying archival research for undergraduates

445d American dream, nightmare underside: Diaries, letters and fiction of women on the American frontier

Lewes, George Henry

196e On exile and fiction: The Leweses and the Shelleys

Lewis, Dioclesian

147x Adele Parot: Pathfinder for the Dioclesian Lewis school of gymnastic expression in the American west

Lewis, Lena Morrow

128d Lena Morrow Lewis: Her rise and fall

Lewis, Matthew G.

109l Place and eros in Radcliffe, Lewis, and Brontë

Leyster, Judith

117j Judith Leyster's *Proposition* - Between virtue and vice

Liability

230l Bases of liability for injuries produced by media portrayals of violent pornography

Liberal

7h Sadomasochism and the liberal tradition

103v Afterword: Feminism and families in a liberal policy

106h Patriarchal liberalism and beyond: From John Stuart Mill to Harriet Taylor

126a The genesis of feminist visions for transforming the liberal arts curriculum

315k Women's studies and the re-vision of liberal education: "What is a nice girl/boy like you doing here?"

421j Attitudes and ideology: Correlates of liberal attitudes towards the role of women

435f Women and housing: The limitations of liberal reform

Liberal Party

157l The B.C. Liberal Party and women's reforms, 1916-1928

Liberate

see also Emancipate, Freedom, Women's Liberation

6j Women in contemporary national liberation movements

7i Why I'm against S/M liberation

31f Sexism, religion, and the social and spiritual liberation of women today

31g Liberating philosophy: An end to the dichotomy of matter and spirit

50h Typing our way to freedom: Is it true that new office technology can liberate women?

59f Liberating work

68n The black woman: Liberated or oppressed?

101c The Indian women's movement: A struggle for women's rights or national liberation?

102d Religion and the fearful father: Vision of liberation or American-style fascism?

120f To grow a daughter: Cultural liberation and the dynamics of oppression in Jamaica

131a Science fiction women before liberation

197h The liberated instant: Muriel Spark and the short story

224l Towards a Marxist theory of gay liberation

247f From repressive tolerance to erotic liberation: *Maedchen in Uniform*

290d Theory into practice: Sexual liberation or social control? (*Forum* magazine 1968-1981)

358c The 'liberated woman' in television drama

369d Socialism, feminism, and gay/lesbian liberation

412r Korean women in Hawaii, 1903-1945: The role of Methodism in their liberation and in their participation in the Korean independence movement

414i The gender liberation: Black women as elected officials in Oklahoma

Liberation Theology

91c Feminist liberation theology: Its past and future

462o Feminist liberation theology and Yahweh as holy warrior: An analysis of symbol

462v Claiming the center: A critical feminist theology of liberation

Liberty

129d Give me liberty

129dd Patriotism: A menace to liberty

242c Liberty, sorority, misogyny

Librarian

302b Sex-typing in education for librarianship: 1870-1920

302c The recruitment of men into librarianship, following World War II

302g Profiles of the careers of selected black female librarians

302l Geographic mobility and career advancement of male and female librarians

389n Dorothy Eugenia Miner (1904-1973): The varied career of a medievalist: Scholar and keeper of manuscripts, librarian and editor at the Walters Art Gallery

Library

15a Libraries and alternatives

15g Publishers on libraries: Walking through walls

15h Publishers on libraries: Stake your claim

15i Publishers on libraries: Small presses and the library

15j Publishers on libraries: The library as motherlode: A feminist view

15k Alternative and small publishers view libraries: An empirical study

15l Collections of contemporary alternative materials in libraries: A directory

122h In search of excellence in academic libraries, or, challenging the henhouse model

199i Women's work in the library/information sector

302a Revision versus reality: Women in the history of the public library movement, 1876-1920

302d Undergraduate women as potential recruits to the library profession

302e Assertiveness training for library-school students

302f Biographical research on women librarians: Its paucity, perils, and pleasures

302h The woman academic-library administrator: A career profile

302i Salary and position levels of females and males in academic libraries

302j Women in academic-library, higher-education, and corporate management: A research review

302k Mobility and professional involvement in librarianship: A study of the "Class of '55"

302m An analysis of the study, "Career paths of male and female librarians in Canada"

302n The reentry professional librarian

314m Library resources on women

337c Women's contributions to the library school

Lieh-Nü

401d The Chinese Lieh-nü tradition

Life

2g A human life statute

2m Abortion, privacy, and personhood: From *Roe v Wade* to the human life statute

3b Abortion and the meaning of life

21b The Japanese woman: Evolving views of life and role

30a Living our life

30x May Sarton: A metaphor for my life, my work, and my art

41c Sources of life satisfaction: The different worlds of black women and white women

47e Married life

48g Sexuality and gender roles in the second half of life

51u Predicting the close of menstrual life

51v Endocrine functions in the woman's second half of life

68g Up from the harem? The effects of class and sex on political life in northern India

140e Some effects of proportions on group life: Skewed sex ratios and responses to token women

149d Women's double work day: Twentieth-century changes in the reproduction of daily life

159h Crimes against life committed by women in Hungary

177a The life history method

180h "The mother's history" in George Eliot's life, literature and political ideology

187d Benedictine life for women in central France, 850-1100: A feminist revival

197b Fun and games with life-stories

210a Changing appearance for women in the middle years of life: Trauma?

223j Sex, birth control, and human life

231i Russian working women: Sexuality in bonding patterns and the politics of daily life

264e Southern literary women as chroniclers of southern life

289o Beyond generativity: Toward a sensuality of later life

295l The relation of stressful life events to gender

296b Differential power of women over the life course: A case study of age-roles as an indicator of power

296d Women's self-perceptions of power and influence across adult life

317b Life satisfaction research in aging: Implications for policy development

317e Intergenerational relations in later life: A family system approach

317g The clinical psychology of later life: Developmental paradigms

320p Life after college: Historical links between women's education and women's work

338a Irish women in legend, literature and life

379k "My spirit eye": Some functions of spiritual and visionary experience in the lives of five black women preachers, 1810-1880

403a The religious lives of Muslim women

411b Life events and the boundaries of midlife for women

427e Gender inequities in childhood social life and adult work life

435e Alternative work patterns and the double life

458c Life satisfaction among aging women: A causal model

468e Women's work strategies: An analysis of the organisation of everyday life in an urban neighbourhood

The Life and Religious Experience of Jaren Lee, a Coloured Lady

108i Neither auction block nor pedestal: *The Life and Religious Experience of Jaren Lee, A Coloured Lady*

Life Before Man

20l Prospects and retrospects in *Life Before Man*

Life Cycle

92b Bangladesh: Beliefs and customs observed by Muslim rural women during their life cycle

144f The family life-cycle: A study of factory workers in nineteenth century Württemberg

190b Endocrine aspects of menarche and menopause - milestones in the woman's life cycle

239j Adult life cycles: Changing roles and changing hormones

243j Overtime over the life cycle: A test of the life cycle squeeze hypothesis

355g Women's life-cycle time allocation: An econometric analysis

400f Life cycle, food behaviour and nutrition of women in Bangladesh

460o Daughters and lovers: Reflections on the life cycle of father-daughter relationships

Life Itself

330c Virginia Woolf's narrators and the art of "life itself"

Life Span

289e Gender identity: A life-span view of sex-role development

411c Methods for a life-span developmental approach to women in the middle years

Lifesong

205c Rainbow women of the Fraser Valley: Lifesongs through the generations

Lifestyle

48j Sink or swing? The lifestyles of single adults

59e American women and life-style change

60l Black family life-styles: A lesson in survival

87i The balancing act: Coping strategies for emerging family lifestyles

233e Reproductive hazards of the American life style

333l Historical factors which have affected aboriginal lifestyles since colonisation

Light

40a Shades and slashes of light

Lilith

111a Re-discovering Lilith: Misogyny and the "new" female criminal

211d The Lilith question

Lilli Diamond Originals

192n The election day immigration raids at Lilli Diamond Originals and the response of the ILGWU

Limb

107m Asymmetry of limb circumferences in female athletes

Liminal

238c Davey Crockett as trickster: Pornography, liminality and symbolic inversion in Victorian America

Line

134d Drawing the line

213e In the front line

Ling, Ting

449d Feminism and literary technique in Ting Ling's early short stories

Linguist

112f Bathsua Makin: Educator and linguist (English, 1608?-1675?)

132m Difference and language: A linguist's perspective

Linguistics

171d Linguistic options and choices for black women in the rural South

275e Linguistics and feminism

275i Feminist linguistics in philosophy

344z Sexism and the English language: The linguistic implications of being a woman

356a Linguistics and the feminist challenge

356p The construction of ambiguity in *The Awakening*: A linguistic analysis

417u The linguistic transformation of womanhood

Linnaeus, Carolus

379f Linnaeus's daughters: Women and British botany

Lispector, Clarice

332o *Family Ties*: Female development in Clarice Lispector

Literacy

265g Making literacy equally accessible to females and males

Literal

109p Dreaming of children: Literalization in *Jane Eyre* and *Wuthering Heights*

Literary

14i Studying slavery: Some literary and pedagogical considerations on the black female slave

14q "This infinity of conscious pain": Zora Neale Hurston and the black female literary tradition

14r Researching Alice Dunbar-Nelson: A personal and literary perspective

30g Alice Dunbar-Nelson: A personal and literary perspective

32q Literary emasculation: Household imagery in Christa Reinig's *Entmannung*

40l The literary genius of Alice Childress

51b Bad maps for an unknown region: Menopause from a literary perspective

64l The theatre as literary model: Role-playing in *Chéri* and *The Last of Chéri*

77d Creative women in artistic and literary change

168c Hindsight is 20/20: The development, achievements and dilemmas of feminist literary criticism

189b Dancing through the minefield: Some observations on the theory, practice and politics of a feminist literary criticism

198e The literary treatment of women in North Africa

264e Southern literary women as chroniclers of southern life

306d On the literary uses of private documents

408l Sara de Etcheverts: The contradictions of literary feminism

442a Colette's literary reputation

449d Feminism and literary technique in Ting Ling's early short stories

Literata

313o "La loca, la tonta, la literata": Women's destiny in Clarín's *La Regenta*

Literature

see also Author, Writer, individual authors and genres

6g Women in African literature

22e Women in Latin Medieval literature in Denmark e.g. annals and chronicles

39bb The black woman in Haitian society and literature

39ee Images of the woman of color in Brazilian literature: O Cortico, Clara Dos Anjos, Gabriela Cravo E Canela, and O Quinze

96g From renunciation to rebellion: The female in literature

132p Visibility and difference: Black women in history and literature - pieces of a paper and some ruminations

150n Black lesbian in American literature: An overview

151e Socialisation in the literature lesson

155g Courtesans and prostitutes in South Asian literature

158b Freud's heritage: Fathers and daughters in German literature (1750-1850)

161e Women and Bengali literature

165f Murdered women and women who murder: A critique of the literature

176h Lesbian literature: A Third World feminist perspective

176k Teaching about Jewish lesbians in literature: From *Zeitl* and *Richel* to *The Tree of Begats*

176t Lesbian images in women's literature anthologies

180a Mothers and daughters in ancient Near Eastern literature

180c Eve's orphans: Mothers and daughters in medieval English literature

180h "The mother's history" in George Eliot's life, literature and political ideology

180u "Don't never forget the bridge that you crossed over on": The literature of matrilineage

180v Spider woman's web: Mothers and daughters in Southwestern Native American literature

180y Mothers and daughters in literature: A preliminary bibliography

225f Everything they always wanted you to know: The ideology of popular sex literature

265d Review of the literature of non-sexist curriculum and a critique of the underlying assumptions and rationale

278a Sex and classical literature

278b 'Last Night's Rambles': Restoration literature and the war between the sexes

278c The secret nexus: Sex and literature in eighteenth-century Britain

278g Homosexuality and literature

278i Literature and pornography

306a The whole truth: Frameworks for the study of women's noncanonical literature

306l Southern women's literature and culture: Course development and the pedagogical process

314o Reconstructing American literature: A strategy for change

315a The emergence of women in twentieth-century Chilean history and literature

316l Challenging curricular assumptions: Teaching and studying women's literature from a regional perspective

322a Women and literature in Africa

322c Women and literature in the Arab world

322d Arab literature in north Africa

322e Francophone literature in north Africa

322g Women and literature in Asia: South Asia

322h Women and literature in Asia: South-east Asia

322j Women and literature in the Caribbean

322l Women and literature in Latin America

331g The "other" voice: Woman's song, its satire and its transcendence in late medieval British literature

338a Irish women in legend, literature and life

384a The civilizers: Women's organizations and western American literature

392b The etiology of female crime: A review of the literature

397q The black lesbian in American literature: An overview

403b Traditional affirmations concerning the role of women as found in contemporary Arab Islamic literature

408b Echoes of the Amazon myth in medieval Spanish literature

408k Female archetypes in Mexican literature

411d Middle-aged women in literature

414a Women in literature of the West

433i British response to Bengali literature in the nineteenth century

433m The image of Bengal in the emerging literature of Bangladesh: The fiction of Hasan Azizul Huq

445b Women's literature and the American frontier: A new perspective on the frontier myth

448o Literature and the city: A checklist of relevant secondary works

462k Women as makers of literature

Litigation
see also Law

249e Not by lawyers alone: Ten practical lessons for academic litigants

261a Litigation: Strategy of the last resort

Little Women

332e Female stories of experience: Alcott's *Little Women* in light of *Work*

442c Louisa May Alcott: The influence of *Little Women*

Liturgy
see also Religion

115d 'The faltering words of men': Exclusive language in the liturgy

429e Women and liturgy

Live

5d An analysis of the impact of labour migration on the lives of women in Lesotho

42e Blueprints for living

47j Conclusion: Living through

79s Living with an impaired neonate and child: A feminist issue

122l Finding one's way through the labyrinth: A symposium on women's lives: Introduction

122m Finding one's way through the labyrinth: A symposium on women's lives: Methodology

122n Finding one's way through the labyrinth: A symposium on women's lives: Life stories

122o Finding one's way through the labyrinth: A symposium on women's lives: Meals — chaos or community

153f Households, modes of living, and production systems

178c Daily lives

178e Work: Its meaning for women's lives

187a Muffled voices: The lives of consecrated women in the fourth century

217j Theoretical ambiguities - A reflection of women's lives?

257c Really being in love means wanting to live in a different world

307m Living better vicariously?

309m Teenage mothers and teenage fathers: The impact of early childbearing on the parents' personal and professional lives

325a Patterns in women's religious lives

Livelihood

201a Needlework as art, craft, and livelihood before 1900

Livestock

82j Livestock and range management

Livre des Trois Vertus

154e Christine de Pizan's *Livre des Trois Vertus*: Feminine ideal or practical advice?

154f The ideal of the lady of the manor as reflected in Christine de Pizan's *Livre des Trois Vertus*

La Llorona

175d The weeping woman: La Llorona

Lobby

167k Organising a mass lobby of Parliament: Families against the bomb

La Loca

313o "La loca, la tonta, la literata": Women's destiny in Clarin's *La Regent*

Local
see also City

226a Women in local government: An overview

226d Filling the party vacuum: Women at the grassroots level in local politics

226l State and local policies on motherhood

226m Resources and constraints on women in the policymaking process: States and local arenas

410c The effects of sex on recruitment: Connecticut local offices

410h Perceptions of women's roles on local councils in Connecticut

410i Commissions on the status of women and building a local policy agenda

435b Representing women at the state and local levels: Commissions on the status of women

Locke, John

196a "My idea in your mind": John Locke and Damaris Cudworth Masham

Logic

275v A note on logical truth and non-sexist semantics

London, England

50c Women's work in nineteenth-century London: A study of the years 1820-1850

153n Working or helping? London working-class children in the domestic economy

160e The suitable wife: Preparation for marriage in London and Rhodesia/Zimbabwe

250e Black girls in a London comprehensive school

256c Servants, sexual relations and the risks of illegitimacy in London, 1801-1900

256f "The men are as bad as their masters...": Socialism, feminism and sexual antagonism in the London tailoring trade in the 1830s

379i The London biblewomen and nurses mission, 1857-1880: Class relations/women's relations

396b Midwives, medical men and 'poor women labouring of child': Lying-in hospitals in eighteenth-century London

448h "A gigantic mother": Katherine Mansfield's London

Long Beach, CA

174f The new right challenges women's studies: The Long Beach women's studies program

Long Term Care

289h Long-term care institutions

Longevity

53b The relationship of the sex hormone/prostaglandin interaction to female and male longevity

Longitudinal

9e Longitudinal studies of alcohol and drug problems: Sex differences

98m Methodological issues in longitudinal and comparative research in Bangladesh

387t Sex stratification, technology and organization change: A longitudinal case study of AT&T

423g Longitudinal and cross-sectional data sources on women in the middle years

Look

247e When the woman looks

Looking Glass

20k Janus through the looking glass: Atwood's first three novels

91i Through the feminist looking glass: Images of women

135b The looking-glass through Alice

332j Through the looking glass: When women tell fairy tales

Loomis

353l The Loomis trial: Social mores and obstetrics in the mid-nineteenth century

Lorca
see Garcia Lorca, Frederico

Lord

412i Preparing women for the Lord's work: The story of three Methodist training schools, 1880-1940

Lorde, Audre

7f Interview with Audre Lorde

40z In the name of the father: The poetry of Audre Lord

40aa The unicorn is black: Audre Lorde in retrospect

Lore

301e Magnolias grow in dirt: The bawdy lore of southern women

Los Angeles, CA

192i Se me acabó la canción: An ethnography of non-consenting sterilizations among Mexican women in Los Angeles

192l Los Angeles garment district sews a cloak of shame

192r La costura en Los Angeles 1933-1939: The ILGWU and the politics of domination

203s The Los Angeles woman's building: A public center for woman's culture

319o The nonconsenting sterilization of Mexican women in Los Angeles: Issues of psychocultural rupture and legal redress in paternalistic behavior

Los Ojos Verdes

313m A feminist reading of "Los ojos verdes"

Loss

178d Growing up: The impact of loss and change

219h   Loss and mourning in victims of rape and sexual assault

244k   Role loss and manic depression

Lost Lady

384n   Marian Forrester and Moll Flanders: Fortunes and misfortunes

Love

see also Emotion

23n   A *Theory of Justice* and love: Rawls on the family

48f   What do women and men want from love and sex?

64h   The test of love and nature: Colette and lesbians

121f   "The love of thee-a prism be": Men and women in the love poetry of Emily Dickinson

121g   "Oh, vision of language!": Dickinson's poems of love and death

129m   Love, marriage and divorce

132d   The bonds of love: Rational violence and erotic domination

135d   Masculine and feminine personae in the love poetry of Christine de Pisan

163e   The woman, the love, and the power

170a   Caring: A labour of love

176aa Love between women in prison

186j   Patterns of love and friendship: Five novels by May Sarton

188n   The Spanish love poet: Florencia Pinar

195n   Preservative love and military destruction: Some reflections on mothering and peace

202j   The politics of city space in *The Years*: Street, love, pillar boxes and bridges

214u   Conclusion: Integrating love and power

217h   Love and power in marriage

220j   Romantic love and reproductive rights

223a   Love: A feminist critique

223b   Love and feminism

223c   The ethics of having love affairs

223g   Marriage, love, and procreation

224m   Revolution in the pursuit of happiness: Love and community-building on the left

231f   Feminism, men, and modern love: Greenwich Village, 1900-1925

242f   *Persuasion* and the promises of love

257c   Really being in love means wanting to live in a different world

257m   Psychoanalysis and women loving women

285g   Is there love before dying?

330j   *Orlando* and its genesis: Venturing and experimenting in art, love, and sex

353e   The female world of love and ritual: Relations between women in nineteenth-century America

397e   The older lesbian: Love relationships and friendship patterns

445i   Gertrude Atherton's California woman: From love story to psychological drama

454l   The female world of love and ritual: Relations between women in nineteenth-century America

468h   Love and power: The division of household labour

Lover

188d   The French scholar-lover: Heloise

286g   Bathsheba's lovers: Male sexuality in *Far from the Madding Crowd*

305t   Mothers, sisters, lovers, listen

460o   Daughters and lovers: Reflections on the life cycle of father-daughter relationships

Low Pay

see also Pay

89k   Structured labour markets, worker organization and low pay

357a   Low pay amongst women - the facts

357c   The structure of labour markets and low pay for women

357d   Low pay and female employment in Canada with selected references to the USA

357e   Shortcomings and problems in analyses of women and low pay

Lower Class

see also Class

184b   Childbearing among the lower classes of late medieval England

421r   Some aspirations of lower class black mothers

Lower Middle Class

see also Class

243i   Work experience and family relations among working-class and lower-middle-class

Lowry, Beverly

450d   Eating the moment absolutely up: The fiction of Beverly Lowry

Loyalty

344t   Trust, loyalty, and the place of women in the informal organization of work

Luck

325q   Rosinta, rats, and the river: Bad luck is banished in Andean Bolivia

Luo

347h   Daughters of the lakes and rivers: Colonization and the land rights of Luo women

Lusaka, Zambia

385e   Marginal lives: Conflict and contradiction in the position of female traders in Lusaka, Zambia

Lusi

246e   Revenge suicide by Lusi women: An expression of power

Luxury

132k   Poetry is not a luxury

Lying In

12h   Technology in the lying-in room

396b   Midwives, medical men and 'poor women labouring of child': Lying-in hospitals in eighteenth-century London

Lynch, Marta

313l   Alienation and eros in three stories by Beatriz Guido, Marta Lynch and Amalia Jamilis

Lyrique

22h   La lyrique portugaise primitive de "Cantigas de Amigo"

MacDowell, Gerty

409f   Gerty MacDowell: Joyce's sentimental heroine

Machina ex Dea

181m   Afterward: Machina ex dea and future research

Machine

201b   "If I didn't have my sewing machine...": Women and sewing-machine technology

206i   The sewing machine

441c   The machine in utopia: Shaker women and technology

441e   The culture of engineering: Woman, workplace and machine

Machismo

390u   Revolution and machismo: Women in the New South Wales Builders Labourers' Federation, 1961-75

Macho

150ii Black macho and black feminism

Machover Test

107h   Machover test applied to 130 Italian female top athletes

MacInnis, Grace

205z   The peacock and the guinea hen: Political profiles of Dorothy Gretchen Steeves and Grace MacInnis

Madam

175p   El Paso madams

Madam Bovary

132n   For a restricted thematics: Writing, speech, and difference in *Madame Bovary*

135p   Emma Bovary's masculinization: Convention of clothes and morality of conventions

332b   The novel of awakening (five novels)

Madison, WI

337m   Socio-economic profile of faculty women at Madison

394b   History of the Association of Faculty Women at Madison

394j   Women's athletics at Madison and Title IX

Madness

20g   Minuets and madness: Margaret Atwood's *Dancing Girls*

27m   Women and madness in the fiction of Joyce Carol Oates

196i   Virginia Woolf and her violin: Mothering, madness, and music

315c   Still crazy after all these years: The uses of madness in women's fiction

329b   Virginia Woolf and her violin: Mothering, madness and music

359o   Madness in women

383b   Method in her madness: Feminism in the crazy utopian vision of Tiptree's Courier

433c   Madness as entropy: A Bengali view

445j   Madness and personification in *Giants in the Earth*

Madonna

32e   *Wally, die Zweiflerin* and *Madonna*: A discussion of sex-socialization in the nineteenth century

135n   Mistresses and madonnas in the novels of Margaret Dabble

329e   The anti-madonna in the work and thought of Virginia Woolf

Madonna Dell'Arco

194e An Italian religious feast: The *Fujenti* rites of the Madonna dell'Arco, Naples

Madras, India

101b Social reform and women's participation in political culture: Andhra and Madras

325c Mother Guru: Jnanananda of Madras, India

Madrid, Spain

112d María de Zayas y Sotomayor: Sibyl of Madrid (Spanish, 1590?-1661?)

Madwomen

109g Monsters and madwomen: Changing female gothic

Maedchen in Uniform

247f From repressive tolerance to erotic liberation: *Maedchen in Uniform*

Maenad

419e The maenad in early Greek art

Mafia

349g Aw! Your mother's in the mafia: Women criminals in progressive New York

Magazine

136k The seven ages of woman: A view from American magazine advertisements

391e Changing Canadian and US magazine portrayals of women and work: Growing opportunities for choice

Maggie: A Girl of the Streets

155h The fate of the fallen woman in *Maggie* and *Sister Carrie*

Magic

202b Woolf's 'Magical garden of women'

229q Consciousness, politics, and magic

473e Spirit magic in the social relations between men and women (Saõ Paulo, Brazil)

Magpie

457c Doves and magpies: Village women in the Greek Orthodox Church

Maharashtra, India

101i Two faces of protest: Alternative forms of women's mobilization in West Bengal and Maharashtra

Maid

299b Maid servants

417n Women in the Children of God: "Revolutionary women" or "Mountin' maids"?

Maiden

135m The laughter of maidens, the crackle of matriarchs: Notes on the collision between comedy and feminism

238e From maidenhood to menopause: Sex education for women in Victorian America

460a "Role, Jenny Jenkins, Roll": Little girls and maidens in American folksongs - an analysis of sexual attitudes

Maidenhood

68l Native American women: Twilight of a long maidenhood

Mail

55m Appendix B: Review of legal cases regarding US Code, Section 1461 (mailing obscene or crime-inciting matter)

Maintenance

29i Health maintenance: Exercise and nutrition

455k Women and income maintenance programs

465c Who still cares for the family? Recent developments in income maintenance, taxation and family law

La Maison Paternelle

106f Julie and "La Maison Paternelle": Another look at Rousseau's *La Nouvelle Héloïse*

Majority

344v Women and politics: The real majority

Make

20e The making of *Selected Poems*, the process of surfacing

346c Making women visible

380a Women as world makers

436e Women in government as policy-makers and bureaucrats: The Turkish case

462k Women as makers of literature

Makin, Bathsua

112f Bathsua Makin: Educator and linguist (English, 1608?-1675?)

Malaya

160j Memsahibs in colonial Malaya: A study of European wives in a British colony and protectorate, 1900-1940

Malaysia

21e Some changing socioeconomic roles of village women in Malaysia

82u NEMOW: A project that stumbled and why

183a Rural women in development

198g A traditional ceremony in an Islamic milieu in Malaysia

350g From rural subsistence to an industrial peripheral work force: An examination of female Malaysian migrants and capital accumulation in Singapore

362g The politics of healing in Malaysia

420g Female rural-to-urban migration in peninsular Malaysia

420k Migration of women workers in peninsular Malaysia: Impact and implications

424e Towards meeting the needs of urban female factory workers in peninsular Malaysia

424g Islamic attitudes to female employment in industrializing economies: Some notes from Malaysia

424h Occupational health hazards of female industrial workers in Malaysia

428r Global industries and Malay peasants in peninsular Malaysia

431d Putting Malay women in their place

466d Land ownership in Negri Sembilan, 1900-1977

466g Housewives and farmers: Malay women in the Muda Irrigation Scheme

466j Four paces behind: Women's work in peninsular Malaysia

Male

see also Boy, Man, Masculine

2c *Roe v Wade*: A study in male ideology

9j Sex differences in mortality: A comparison of male and female alcoholics

10i Alcohol use and marital violence: Female and male differences in reactions to alcohol

28u Women in a male-dominated profession: The women lawyers

29g Marriage and the family: An unconscious male bias in behavioral treatment?

34i Displaced - the midwife by the male physician

35g Explaining "male chauvinism" and "feminism": Cultural differences in male and female reproductive strategies

39z Female status, the family and male dominance in a West Indian community

51y Male and female menopause: A cultural put-on

53b The relationship of the sex hormone/prostaglandin interaction to female and male longevity

60b Male vice and female virtue: Feminism and the politics of prostitution in nineteenth-century Britain

78y Doing time with the boys: An analysis of women correctional officers in all-male facilities

89n The female-male differential in unemployment rates

90k Male and female career paths in school administration

107i Proportionality and body composition in male and female Olympic athletes: A kinanthropometric overview

107p Differences in males and females in joint movement range during growth

115e The ordination of women and the 'maleness' of the Christ

124h How psychology constructed masculinity: The theory of male sex role identity

128g Women socialists and their male comrades: The Reading experience, 1927-1936

133a Homosexual labeling and the male role

133j Male homophobia

133m Images of the gay male in contemporary drama

133p Educational responsibilities to gay male and lesbian students

133q Consciousness-raising among gay males

148d Male/female task differentiation among the Hidatsa: Toward the development of an archeological approach to the study of gender

148i Male and female in traditional Lakota culture

152d Overcoming the structured evil of male domination and heterosexism

158i The theory of male sex role identity: Its rise and fall, 1936 to the present

187g Male/female cooperation: The example of fontevrault

195h Is male gender identity the cause of male domination?

199m Contrasting sexual harassment in female- and male-dominated occupations

211g Women-identified women in male-identified Judaism

212c 'On the other side of the billboard...': Pornography, male fantasies and the objectification of women

212e Rape and marital violence in the maintenance of male power

212l Female performers on a male stage: The
first women's liberation movement and the
authority of men

212m Male feminists and divided women

212o 'Male needs': The problems and problems
of working with gay men

212p The 'perks' of male power:
Heterosexuality and the oppression of
women

212r What can one do with a son? Feminist politics and male children

214o Ageism vs. sexism: Male models as a
source of support

222e Surviving in a predominantly white male
institution

231t Is the gaze male?

231cc Male vice and female virtue: Feminism
and the politics of prostitution in nineteenth-century Britain

241c Blowing the cover of the protective male:
A community study of violence to women

246c Complementarity: The relationship
between female and male in the East Sepik
village of Bun, Papua New Guinea

260b A look at the male female unemployment
differentials in the Federal Republic of
Germany, Sweden, United Kingdom, and
the United States of America

265f Does sex stereotyping lead to a higher incidence of male dyslexia?

265g Making literacy equally accessible to
females and males

269d New economic roles for Cuna males and
females: An examination of socioeconomic
change in a San Blas community

269e New roles for males in Guaymí society

269g Watch that pot or the *waksuk* will eat you
up: An analysis of male and female roles in
Rama Indian myth

270n Social psychological patterns of homicide
in Turkey: A comparison of male and
female convicted murders

275a Male chauvinism: A conceptual analysis

277c Physiology of male sexual arousal

277k Study of sexual dysfunction among male
diabetics

282g Like wounded stags: Male sexual ideology
in an Andalusian town

285k Sexual dysfunction in the chronically ill
male

286g Bathsheba's lovers: Male sexuality in *Far
from the Madding Crowd*

287b Male sexuality: Socio-sexual change and
the single status

290b Sexology and the social construction of
male sexuality (Havelock Ellis)

290c Sexology and the universalization of male
sexuality (from Ellis to Kinsey, and
Masters and Johnson)

302i Salary and position levels of females and
males in academic libraries

302l Geographic mobility and career advancement of male and female librarians

302m An analysis of the study, "Career paths of
male and female librarians in Canada"

309u Sexual and contraceptive knowledge, attitudes and behavior of male adolescents

310r Abortion of a special kind: Male sex selection in India

320k Undergraduates and their teachers: An
analysis of student evaluations of male and
female instructors

323i Coercion or male culture: A new look at
co-worker harassment

342h Ideologies of male dominance as divide
and rule politics: An anthropologist's view

351e Sex segregation and male preeminence in
elementary classrooms

352n Working and parenting: The male and
father role

369l The marriage of capitalist and patriarchal
ideologies: Meanings of male bonding and
male ranking in U.S. culture

372l Is the significance of muscle fibre types to
muscle metabolism different in females
than in males?

372m Fundamental performance characteristics
in females and males

372x Comparison of exercise between females
and males

378a Male and female: Job versus gender models in the sociology of work

380e Power and political behaviors in organizations: A new frontier for research on
male/female differences

383c Utopia at the end of a male chauvinist
dystopian world: Suzy McKee Charnas's
feminist science fiction

387e Male and female: Job versus gender models in the sociology of work

387n The inexpressive male: Tragedy or sexual
politics?

391g The influence of female and male communication styles on conflict strategies:
Problem areas

392m Unequal protection of males and females
in the juvenile court

393c Women and work: A study of female and
male attitudes in the modern sector of an
African metropolis (Lagos)

396a Male hegemony in family planning

396h Sex predetermination, artificial insemination and the maintenance of male-dominated culture

399k Women in male roles: Charlotte Cushman
and others

400d Impact of male migration on rural housewives

408m The greatest punishment: Female and
male in Lorca's tragedies

413j Mummy's boys: Pakeha men and male culture in New Zealand

452a Introduction: Women's autobiography and
the male tradition

Malignant

53n Risk factors for benign and malignant
breast disease

Malinche

68m La chicana: Guadalupe or malinche

408e Marina/Malinche: Masks and shadows

Malnutrition

279j Size sexual dimorphism and secular trend:
Indicators of subclinical malnutrition?

Malthus, Thomas Robert

18i Neo-Malthusian ideology and colonial
capitalism: Population dynamics in southwestern Puerto Rico

Mammal

79cc Biological manipulations for producing
and nurturing mammalian embryos

Man

see also Boy, Male, Masculine

9l Dependence on psychotropic drugs and
analgesics in men and women

11c Women and men problem drinkers: Sex
differences in patients served by Iowa's
community alcoholism centers

29a Women's behavior in a man's world: Sex
differences in competence

34a Have only men evolved?

34h Taking the men out of menopause

36m Man-midwifery and the rise of technology:
The problem and proposals for resolution

37k Black men in America: The quest for
"manhood"

46i Incremental change in social security
needed to result in equal and fair treatment of men and women

48f What do women and men want from love
and sex?

48k The intimate relationships of lesbians and
gay men

52a The changing positions of women and men
in comparative perspective

52k Economic and family roles of men and
women in Northern Europe: A historical
cross-national comparison

78f Trends in female crime: It's still a man's
world

84d Have only men evolved?

84j The man of professional wisdom

85d Men, masculinity and the process of sociological enquiry

86j Mother, father, worker: Men and women
and the reproduction risks of work

91n Is partnership possible? Ordained men
and unordained women in ministry

93h Equality between men and women in the
labor market: The Swedish National Labor
Market Board

99c 'Helpmeet for man': Women in mid-nineteenth century western Australia

102o Public nurturance and the man on horseback

105k Marriage, estrangement, sobriety and
recidivism: Some crucial process variables
in the case of alcoholic men and their
wives

107n Some differences between men and
women in various factors which determine
swimming performance

115d 'The faltering words of men': Exclusive
language in the liturgy

120d The problem of studying "economic man"

121f "The love of thee-a prism be": Men and
women in the love poetry of Emily
Dickinson

122k How women and men write about themselves (less differently than you might
expect)

123h Changing conceptions of men and women:
A psychologist's perspective

133c Lesbians, gay men, and their "languages"

136d Visual behavior and dominance in women and men

139d Women, men and social class

140f Men's power with women, other men, and society: A men's movement analysis

140m Emotional intimacy among men

140u Men's new family roles: Some implications for therapists

152g Gay men and women and the vowed life

158h Psychology measures femininity and masculinity, 2: From "13 Gay Men" to the instrumental-expressive distinction

171b Beyond the he/man approach: The case for nonsexist language

171e Intonation in a man's world

171h Men, inexpressiveness, and power

171j Men's speech to young children

172a Squatter settlement decision-making: For men only? (Peru)

172f Only you men have your needs satisfied (Ecuador)

176n But what about men...?

189i The oldest, the most established, the most quantitative of the social sciences - and most dominated by men; The impact of feminism on economics

191b Patterns of diagnoses received by men and women

195b Why men don't rear children: A power analysis

195c When women and men mother

201f The uprising in Chicago: The men's garment workers strike, 1910-1911

205t A union man's wife: The ladies' auxiliary movement in the IWA, the Lake Cowichan experience

212h Transsexualism: Can men turn men into women?

212l Female performers on a male stage: The first women's liberation movement and the authority of men

212o 'Male needs': The problems and problems of working with gay men

214i Women, men, and professional writing: Signature of power?

224c Lesbians and gay men: Hetero sexualities, common cause

224n Lesbian and gay oppression in the '80s: Androgyny, men and power

230i Sexually aggressive men: Empirical findings and theoretical implications

231f Feminism, men, and modern love: Greenwich Village, 1900-1925

231hh The fear that feminism will free men first

233k Mechanisms of teratogenesis: The extrapolation of the results of animal studies to man

239f Homosexual orientation in women and men: A hormonal basis?

241d Men and war: Status, class and the social reproduction of masculinity

241k Interviewing men: 'Taking gender seriously'

243k Weak links in men's worker-earner roles: A descriptive model

244d Occupation-family-linkages as perceived by men in the early stages of professional and managerial careers

244e The roles of men and women in French families: Change or stability in the patterns and practices?

245h Why men resist

256f "The men are as bad as their masters...": Socialism, feminism and sexual antagonism in the London tailoring trade in the 1830s

263l Men servants and women bosses: The domestic service institution in colonial Zambia

269a Rama men and women: An ethnohistorical analysis of change

269b Structural continuity in the division of men's and women's work among black Carib (Garífuna)

275g The myth of the neutral "man"

280f Genital exhibitionism in men and women

282h Pigs, women, and the men's house in Amazonia: An analysis of six Mundurucú myths

283a When women and men mother

288a The executive man and woman: The issue of sexuality

288b Worklife problems for both women and men

294f 'Black Velvet': Aboriginal women and their relations with white men in the Northern Territory, 1910-1940

302c The recruitment of men into librarianship, following World War II

313q Vipers, victims, and virgins: Women and their relationships with men in the poetry of Nicanor Parra

315i Can a man teach women's studies?

320d Mapping the road to academe: A review of research on women, men, and the college-selection process

326i Rape of men in the community

333i Borroloola women speak. Man and woman: Dance

339b Women and men at work: Jockeying for position

341c A woman's body in a man's world: A review of findings on body image and weight control

343l Women and men in *Othello*: "What should such a fool/Do with so good a woman?"

347d Contending with colonization: Tlingit men and women in change

347i Women and men, cloth and colonization: The transformation of production-distribution relations among the Baule (Ivory Coast)

353u "Safe delivered," but by whom? Midwives and men-midwives in early America

354g Do men and women have different jobs because of their biological differences?

364j Men and women, kinship and property: Some general issues

369a New left women and men: The honeymoon is over

371c Women's space in a men's house: The British House of Commons

378f Unions: the men's affair?

378l Candidate evaluations by men and women

378p The politics of private woman and public man

381b But will men like it? Or living as a feminist writer without committing murder

387s The impact of hierarchical structures on the work behavior of women and men

398j Women's studies and men's careers: How the 'social problem' of women in education maintained the academic status of men in the 1970s

413j Mummy's boys: Pakeha men and male culture in New Zealand

415f Effective interpersonal communication for women of the corporation: Think like a man, talk like a lady

416f Academic career mobility for women and men psychologists

416m Should professional women be like professional men?

417v Women in men's utopias

425e Trying hurts women, helps men: The meaning of effort

425f Socialization experiences of women and men graduate students in male sex-typed career fields

426b The MBA: Same passport to success for women and men?

427f Men, women, work, and family

431f Women and men in Iloilo, Philippines: 1903-1970

435n Women, men, and military service: Is protection necessarily a racket?

448b Marguerite Duras: Women's language in men's cities

457a Mediums, controls and eminent men

457j Men, women and misfortune in Bunyole

458g Retirement expectations and plans: A comparison of professional men and women

458j The process of retirement: Comparing women and men

464h The man question

473e Spirit magic in the social relations between men and women (Saõ Paulo, Brazil)

The Man Who Loved Children

109f Domestic gothic: The imagery of anger in Christina Stead's *The Man Who Loved Children*

Manage

49h Human resource planning and the intuitive manager: Models for the 1990's

111n Managing the female offender: Some observations

111o Managing the female offender: Crisis and change in the California Institution for Women

209g The issue of employment and office technology from a managerial perspective

244d Occupation-family-linkages as perceived by men in the early stages of professional and managerial careers

339c Women managers: Moving up in a high tech society

339d Being a manager in a multicultural world

426d Sex differences in factors affecting managerial career advancement

467c Managing work and family life: A comparative policy overview

Management

see also Business, Company, Corporation, Factory, Industry

5c   Mobilizing village women: Some organizational and management considerations

49j   Leadership and management in the 1990's

51c   Biochemical findings and medical management of the menopause

82j   Livestock and range management

87h   Time management and the dual-career couple

90g   The sex dimension of careers in educational management: Overview and synthesis

111h Contingency management in a juvenile treatment setting

146c An approach to case management

209k Automation and the quality of work life at the Swedish telephone company: A management view

214b Socialization and self-esteem: Women in management

233o A management view of reproductive health

233t Educating workers, management and the general public

267e Career concepts and human resource management: The case of the dual-career couple

268o Sex roles, psychological assessment, and patient management

288j Action plans for management and unions

302j Women in academic-library, higher-education, and corporate management: A research review

352q Changing women's representation in school management: A systems perspective

391f Career management and women

424s The impact of female employment on household management

425a An overview of the research on women in management: A typology and a prospectus

Mandate

387i Commitment and cultural mandate: Women in medicine

Mander, Jane

413k Pioneer into feminist: Jane Mander's heroines

Manding

393e The stable African family: Traditional and modern family structures in two African societies (Basa and Manding)

Mangala Kavya

433l Say it with structure: Tagore and *Mangala Kavya*

Mangbetu

370i Women in slavery among the Mangbetu c. 1800-1910

Manhood

37k   Black men in America: The quest for "manhood"

Manic

244k Role loss and manic depression

Manifesto

229p A consciousness manifesto

Manipulate

79cc Biological manipulations for producing and nurturing mammalian embryos

79ff Manipulative reproductive technologies discussion: Part I

79jj Manipulative reproductive technologies discussion: Part II

79mm Manipulative reproductive technologies discussion: Part III

Manner

130aa The view from Spain: Rocco *finesse* and *espirit* versus plebian manners

454o The American woman's pre-World War I freedom in manners and morals

Manning, Olivia

318c Olivia Manning: Witness to history

Manor

154f The ideal of the lady of the manor as reflected in Christine de Pizan's *Livre des Trois Vertus*

Mansfield Park

27b   The art of *Mansfield Park*

164i *Mansfield Park*: The revolt of the 'feminine' woman

Mansfield, Katherine

242b The birth of the artist as heroine: (Re)production, the *Künslerroman* tradition, and the fiction of Katherine Mansfield

328h An uneasy sisterhood: Virginia Woolf and Katherine Mansfield

448h "A gigantic mother": Katherine Mansfield's London

Manufacture

183d Women workers in the manufacturing industries

Manuscript

143a A new George Eliot manuscript

306m The editor and the writer: An approach to archival manuscripts

389n Dorothy Eugenia Miner (1904-1973): The varied career of a medievalist: Scholar and keeper of manuscripts, librarian and editor at the Walters Art Gallery

Maori

413b The role and status of Maori women

Map

51b   Bad maps for an unknown region: Menopause from a literary perspective

266a New maps of development: New visions of maturity

371a Ground rules and social maps for women: An introduction

407b Career mapping and the professional development process

Maquiladora

199n Maquiladoras: The view from the inside

428j Maquiladoras: A new face of international capitalism on Mexico's northern frontier

Marathon

372dd Foot disorders of female marathon runners before and after a marathon race

March

133o Media reaction to the 1979 gay march on Washington

Marholm, Laura

32h   Laura Marholm and the question of female nature

Maria, The Jewess

441b Women and technology in ancient Alexandria: Maria and Hypatia

Marías

462g "Las Marías" of the feminist movement

Marie, de France

188c The French courtly poet: Marie de France

Marina

408e Marina/Malinche: Masks and shadows

Marital

see also Marriage

10i   Alcohol use and marital violence: Female and male differences in reactions to alcohol

11k   Marital therapy of women alcoholics

37j   Race and marital status: An overview

38i   Marital interaction goals of black women: Strengths and effects

38j   On marital relations: Perceptions of black women

52e   Female marital behaviour in French society

52r   Economic recession and Swiss women's attitudes towards marital role segregation

105b Modern and traditional elements in the expectations of young married couples regarding their marital life

105c Marital expectations of wives in contemporary Poland

105e Toward a theory of extramarital sexual relationships

105j Some correlates of marital trust

106d Political and marital despotism: Montesquieu's *Persian Letters*

122q Marital metaphors in the Judeo-Christian tradition: A feminist critique

184q Premarital pregnancy in America, 1640-1971: An overview and interpretation

212e Rape and marital violence in the maintenance of male power

229y Martial art meditations

245g Shifting perspectives on marital property law

309f Contraceptive patterns and premarital pregnancy among women aged 15-19 in 1976

309n Marriage, remarriage, marital disruption and age at first birth

324f Economic consequences of midlife change in marital status

326k Marital and sexual dysfunction following rape: Identification and treatment

344h Marital relationships and mental health: The psychic costs of inequality

365g Marital and family conflicts

365o Women in marital transition

421m Comparative attitudes about marital sex among Negro women in the United States, Great Britain and Trinidad

421o Wife-employment and the emergence of egalitarian marital role prescriptions: 1900-1974

421q Sex role attitudes, female employment, and marital satisfaction

446k Changing family roles and marital instability

Maritime

388e Women's work and worth in an Acadian maritime village

Market

see also Labor market

66c The market system

67c The market system

87m Going shopping: The professional couple in the job market

187k Stixwould in the market place

209i Assessing the myths of the job market

241b Public and private: Marking the boundaries

245i Home production for use in a market economy

347j Desert politics: Choices in the "marriage market"

350a The dynamics of the sexual division of labor and integration of rural women into the world market

387f Home work and market work: Systematic segregation

422b Women workers of India: A case of market segmentation

Maroon

39x Black women and survival: A Maroon case

Marriage

see also Family, Marital, Marry, Matrimony

27k A *Passage to India* as "marriage fiction": Forster's sexual politics

29g Marriage and the family: An unconscious male bias in behavioral treatment?

37l Women's values regarding marriage and the family

45e Ground rules for marriage: Perspectives on the pattern of an era

50l Monogamy, marriage and economic dependence

52s Egalitarianism in marriage? Graduate education and the sexual division of labour in the Canadian family

69i Marriage and midlife: The impact of social change

87e Dual-career marriages: Benefits and costs

87g Parenthood, marriage, and careers: Situational constraints and role strain

104c Interhousehold co-operation in Peru's southern Andes: A case of multiple sibling-group marriage

105k Marriage, estrangement, sobriety and recidivism: Some crucial process variables in the case of alcoholic men and their wives

106e Marriage contract and social contract in seventeenth-century English political thought

109d Had-I-but-known: The marriage of gothic terror and detection

129j Marriage contract

129m Love, marriage and divorce

160e The suitable wife: Preparation for marriage in London and Rhodesia/Zimbabwe

165c The dark side of marriage: Battered wives and the domination of women

184a Medieval marriage characteristics: A neglected factor in the history of medieval serfdom

184p Toward a theory of remarriage: A case study of Newburyport at the beginning of the nineteenth century

185c Marriage and the family: Styles and forms

196f Gertrice/Altrude: Stein, Toklas, and the paradox of the happy marriage

200f Gender, sexuality and marriage: A Kaulong model of nature and culture

202g Where the spear plants grew: The Ramsays' marriage in *To the Lighthouse*

211e Marriages made in heaven? Battered Jewish wives

217h Love and power in marriage

221c Working mothers: Effects on the marriage and the mother

222i The impossible dream: The Ph.D., marriage, and family

223f The consolation of marriage

223g Marriage, love, and procreation

223h Gay marriage

232c Marriage in Tamil culture: The problem of conflicting "models"

243h Family, work, and individual development in dual-career marriages: Issues for research

281d Sexuality in divorce and remarriage

287d Marriage

297b Negotiating the problem: The DHSS and research on violence in marriage

309j Some speculations on the future of marriage and fertility

309n Marriage, remarriage, marital disruption and age at first birth

334e The status of women and the practice of marriage in late-medieval Wales

347j Desert politics: Choices in the "marriage market"

359p Phobias after marriage: Women's declaration of dependence

364c The exchange of women and property: Marriage in post-revolutionary China

368m The institution of Mut'a marriage in Iran: A formal and historical perspective

369b The unhappy marriage of Marxism and feminism: Towards a more progressive union

369c Beyond the unhappy marriage: A critique of the dual systems theory

369f The unhappy marriage of Marxism and feminism: Can it be saved?

369i Marxism and feminism: Unhappy marriage, trial separation or something else?

369m The unhappy marriage of patriarchy and capitalism

371f Sexual prohibitions, shared space and fictive marriages in Shiite Iran

388j Women's organizations and social change: The age-of-marriage issue in India

393f Plural marriage, fertility and the problem of multiple causation

394k Merging two careers and marriage

401h Widows and remarriage in Ming and early Qing China

412g Ministry through marriage: Methodist clergy wives on the trans-Mississippi frontier

421w The demands of work and the human quality of marriage: An exploratory study of professionals in two socialist societies

423c Adult development and women's development: Arrangements for a marriage

429k Colleagues in marriage and ministry

458n Responsibility for household tasks: Comparing dual-earner and dual-retired marriages

464c The shame of the marriage contract

Marriages Between Zones Three, Four, and Five

383h Truth and art in women's worlds: Doris Lessing's *Marriages Between Zones Three, Four, and Five*

Marry

see also Marriage

47e Married life

69f To marry or not to marry

87d Young marrieds: Wives' employment and family role structure

89a Labor force participation of married women: A study of labor supply

92e Indonesia: Married women's work pattern in rural Java

105b Modern and traditional elements in the expectations of young married couples regarding their marital life

110a Estimating labor supply functions for married women

110b Married women's labor supply: A comparison of alternative estimation procedures

164k In between - Anne Elliot marries a sailor and Charlotte Heywood goes to the seaside

232b The auspicious married woman

289f Old and alone: The unmarried in later life

309d Sexual and contraceptive experience of young unmarried women in the United States, 1976 and 1971

349p The underside of married life: Power, influence, and violence

375d The married women's property acts, 1839-1865: Reform, reaction or revolution?

390s Right-wing union officials versus married women workers

458h Attitudes toward retirement: A comparison of professional and nonprofessional married women

463j Residential location and transportation analyses: Married women workers

Marsh, Ngaio

1c Ngaio Marsh

Marshall, Paule

40bb The closing of the circle: Movement from division to wholeness in Paule Marshall's fiction

40cc And called every generation blessed: Theme, setting, and ritual in the works of Paule Marshall

196g I sign my mother's name: Alice Walker, Dorothy West and Paule Marshall

Martial D'Auvergne

135r On the birth of death: An *Arrest d'Amour* of Martial d'Auvergne

Martineau, Harriet

125d Harriet Martineau: A reassessment

180g Unmothered daughter and the radical reformer: Harriet Martineau's career

452d Harriet Martineau's *Autobiography*: The making of a female philosopher

Marx, Karl

464g Consequences of seizing the reins in the household: A Marxist-feminist critique of Marx and Engels

Marxism

13j Some problems and developments in Marxist feminist theory

43p Do feminists need Marxism?

78z Marxist feminism: Implications for criminal justice

106j The working-class family: A Marxist perspective

224h Why Marxism?

224l Towards a Marxist theory of gay liberation

369b The unhappy marriage of Marxism and feminism: Towards a more progressive union

369e The incompatible menage á trois: Marxism, feminism, and racism

369f The unhappy marriage of Marxism and feminism: Can it be saved?

369h Capitalism is an advanced stage of patriarchy: But Marxism is not feminism

369i Marxism and feminism: Unhappy marriage, trial separation or something else?

369j Cultural Marxism: Nonsynchrony and feminist practice

405a Marxism, feminism, and sex equality

405g Marxism and women's oppression: Bolshevik theory and practice in the 1920's

464g Consequences of seizing the reins in the household: A Marxist-feminist critique of Marx and Engels

Mary

115h Mary: My sister

117f Eve and Mary: Conflicting images of medieval woman

194g Postindustrial Marian pilgrimage

301i Three maxims in the life of Mary

Mary Catherine

301aa Dear Mary Catherine

Maryland

379c The planter's wife revisited: Women, equity law, and the Chancery Court in seventeenth-century Maryland

Masculine

see also Boy, Male, Man

12k The masculine face of science

13a Deconstructing the masculine universe: The case of women's work

27j Virginia Woolf's Miss Latrobe: The artist's last struggle against masculine values

50v Rape and the masculine mystique

63f Styles of doing time in a coed prison: Masculine and feminine alternatives

85d Men, masculinity and the process of sociological enquiry

116d Freud: Masculinity, femininity, and the philosophy of mind

116f The political epistemology of "masculine" and "feminine"

116p Women and "masculine" sports: Androgyny qualified

121e "Oh, Susie, it is dangerous": Emily Dickinson and the archetype of the masculine

124h How psychology constructed masculinity: The theory of male sex role identity

133h Gay masculinity in the gay disco

135d Masculine and feminine personae in the love poetry of Christine dePisan

135p Emma Bovary's masculinization: Convention of clothes and morality of conventions

158g "Rather worse than folly?" psychology measures femininity and masculinity, 1: From Terman and Miles to the Guilfords

158h Psychology measures femininity and masculinity, 2: From "13 Gay Men" to the instrumental-expressive distinction

185h The evolution of sex roles: The transformation of masculine and feminine values

212b Femininity, masculinity and sexuality

241d Men and war: Status, class and the social reproduction of masculinity

265a Parents' sex role attitudes and children's concepts of femininity and masculinity

265e Language and attitudes toward masculine and feminine sex role

275h The hidden joke: Generic uses of masculine terminology

318j The masculine world of Jennifer Johnston

356e The psychology of the generic masculine

Masham, Damaris Cudworth

196a "My idea in your mind": John Locke and Damaris Cudworth Masham

Mask

135f Symbol, mask, and meter in the poetry of Louise Bogan

408e Marina/Malinche: Masks and shadows

457i Women excluded? Masking and masquerading in West Africa

Masochism

7b Letter from a former masochist

7s Sadism, masochism, and lesbian-feminism

140j Female masochism and the enforced restriction of choice

439u "I am not contented": Female masochism and lesbianism in early twentieth-century New England

Mason, Bobbie Ann

450q Stopping places: Bobbie Ann Mason's short stories

Masquerade

457i Women excluded? Masking and masquerading in West Africa

Mass Media

15b The alternative press and the mass media: Two case studies

161h Women and mass media in Kerala

Massachusetts

353ff "Neither for the drawing room nor for the kitchen": Private duty nursing in Boston, 1873-1914

375f Under great temptations here: Women and divorce law in puritan Massachusetts

376a The certain wages of sin: Sentence and punishment of female felons in colonial Massachusetts, 1673-1774

404x Young female offenders in Massachusetts: Toward leaving the juvenile justice system successfully

454c Widowhood in eighteenth-century Massachusetts: A problem in the history of the family

Masseuse

424l The Bangkok masseuses: Origins, status and prospects

Massey, Sadie O.

7r The saga of Sadie O. Massey

Mastectomy

359gg Postmastectomy counseling

Master

231p Master and slave: The fantasy of erotic domination

Master of Business Administration (MBA)

426b The MBA: Same passport to success for women and men?

Masters and Johnson

290c Sexology and the universalization of male sexuality (from Ellis to Kinsey, and Masters and Johnson)

Masters, William H.

439q *Homosexuality in Perspective* by William H. Masters and Virginia E. Johnson

Mastery

296f Mastery and pleasure: A two-factor model of well-being of women in the middle years

Masturbation

460j Masturbation in women

Mate

185d "Mate" selection in the year 2020

Material

14z A listing of non-print materials on black women

15c The acquisition of alternative materials

15l Collections of contemporary alternative materials in libraries: A directory

90f The problem of sex bias in curriculum materials

169r How to choose and use materials in education for women workers

169s Subjects and materials: How to handle controversy

274c Subject image, examinations and teaching materials

369g What is the real material base of patriarchy and capital?

Materialism

84o The feminist standpoint: Developing the ground for a specifically feminist historical materialism

195j On conceiving motherhood and sexuality: A feminist materialist approach

418o Subjectivity, materialism and patriarchy

Maternal Instinct (1972)

195k The maternal instinct (1972) & Afterword (1982)

Maternity

see also Mother, Reproduce

50u Competing ideologies of reproduction: Medical and maternal perspectives on pregnancy

56g Alternative maternity care: Resistance and change

69g Maternal work and children

109o The maternal legacy: The grotesque tradition in Flannery O'Connor's female gothic

132i Rethinking the maternal

158k "To pet, coddle, and 'Do For'": Caretaking and the concept of maternal instinct

162d Possession and dispossession: Maternity and mortality in Morocco

195m Maternal thinking

204c Maternal employment and child development: A review

205x Reducing maternal mortality in British Columbia: An educational process

221b Effects of maternal employment on children: Implications for the family therapist

239i Sources of maternal stress in the postpartum period: A review of the literature and an alternative view

245e Maternal thinking

308a Teenage women in the United States: Sex, contraception, pregnancy, fertility, and maternal and infant health

374f Appendix A: Maternity law for working women

396c Competing ideologies of reproduction: Medical and maternal perspectives on pregnancy

439m Maternal sexuality and asexual motherhood

446m Maternal care of infants

467d Statutory maternity leave in the United Kingdom: A case study

Mathematician

377a Female mathematicians: A contemporary appraisal

377b The creative woman mathematician

Mathematics

96n Math anxiety and female mental health: Some unexpected links

181c Mathematization of engineering: Limits on women and the field

250g Sex differences in mathematical performance: A review of research and possible action

254i Increasing female participation in the mathematics classroom

259k Success in mathematics

274f Mathematics and science - Introduction

274g Mathematics

351f Girls, women, and mathematics

361a Leverage for equal opportunity through mastery of mathematics

361d Improving minority preparation for math-based disciplines

361e A short-term intervention program: Math-science conferences

361h Increasing the participation of college women in mathematics-related fields

377c Is mathematics a sexist discipline?

377d The mathematics filter and the education of women and minorities

377e Sex-related differences in mathematics achievement: Where and why

377f Sex differences in the development of precocious mathematical talent

377g An experiment in mathematics education at the college level

377h Factors affecting female participation in advanced placement programs in mathematics, chemistry, and physics

377i An accelerative intervention program for mathematically gifted girls

377k Conclusions: What do we know and where should we go?

416k Early socialization: Causes and cures of mathematics anxiety

443l A feminist approach to math-anxiety reduction

Matriarch

135m The laughter of maidens, the crackle of matriarchs: Notes on the collision between comedy and feminism

399hh Matriarchs of the regional theatre

Matriarchy

39q The myth of the black matriarchy

42f Patriarchy and matriarchy

45l Sex differences in the educational and occupational goals of black college students: Continued inquiry into the black matriarchy theory

195p The answer is matriarchy

202d Some female versions of pastoral: *The Voyage Out* and matriarchal mythologies

229m Meanings of matriarchy

229xx Myths and matriarchies

256d Free black women and the question of matriarchy

Matrifocal

82k Land tenure and cooperatives: Origin, development and persistence of Navajo matrifocality in subsistence, production, exchange and tenure

Matrilineage

117b Matrilineal reinterpretation of some Egyptian sacred cows

180u "Don't never forget the bridge that you crossed over on": The literature of matrilineage

306j "Full of memories": Teaching matrilineage

417a Rethinking matriliny among the Hopi

452k The metaphysics of matrilinearism in women's autobiography: Studies of Mead's *Blackberry Winter*, Hellman's *Pentimento*, Angelou's *I Know Why the Caged Bird Sings*, and Kingston's *The Woman Warrior*

Matrimony

see also Marriage

334f The European legal context of the Welsh law of matrimonial property

Matter

31g Liberating philosophy: An end to the dichotomy of matter and spirit

470b 'If it's only women it doesn't matter so much'

Maturity

107k Influence of athletic training on the maturity process of girls

266a New maps of development: New visions of maturity

458d Employment status and social support: The experience of the mature woman

461m Does motherhood mean maturity?

Maud Martha

332n Plain, black, and decently wild: The heroic possibilities of *Maud Martha*

Maugham, Somerset

155a The prostitute as scapegoat: Mildred Rogers in Somerset Maugham's *Of Human Bondage*

Maya

356h How and why are women more polite: Some evidence from a Mayan community

373j Changing role of Maya mothers and daughters

Mazeppa

399l Adah Isaacs Menken in *Mazeppa*

MBA

see Master of Business Administration

Mbuti

340e Mbuti womanhood

McWhirter, Martha White

175n Martha White McWhirter and the Belton Sanctificationists

Mead, Margaret

452k The metaphysics of matrilinearism in women's autobiography: Studies of Mead's *Blackberry Winter*, Hellman's *Pentimento*, Angelou's *I Know Why the Caged Bird Sings*, and Kingston's *The Woman Warrior*

Meal

122o Finding one's way through the labyrinth: A symposium on women's lives: Meals — chaos or community

139f Participation in local union organisation. School meals staff: A case study

241f 'It's a pleasure to cook for him': Food, mealtimes and gender in some South Wales households

462aa Reflections on the creation of a ritual meal

Measure

66f Statistical biases in the measurement of employment discrimination

67f Statistical biases in the measurement of employment discrimination

158g "Rather worse than folly?" psychology measures femininity and masculinity, 1: From Terman and Miles to the Guilfords

158h Psychology measures femininity and masculinity, 2: From "13 Gay Men" to the instrumental-expressive distinction

266g Instruments and measures in a changing, diverse society

271m Assertiveness: Sex differences in relationships between self-report and behavioural measures

273b Measuring sex preferences and their effects on fertility

320n Career commitment of female college graduates: Conceptualization and measurement issues

Mechanism

24d Perceptual and cognitive mechanisms in human sexual attraction

51h Neuroendocrine mechanisms of reproductive aging in women and female rats

Mechthild of Magdeburg

188g The German mystic: Mechthild of Magdeburg

Media

15f Alternative roads to alternative media

60u Women, media, and the dialectics of resistance

73a Ethnic women and the media

133o Media reaction to the 1979 gay march on Washington

189j The impact of feminism on media studies - just another commercial break?

230l Bases of liability for injuries produced by media portrayals of violent pornography

230m Afterword: Sex, violence, and the media: Where do we stand now?

235j The media

360o Media psychology and public policy

386k Women in media

432g Sports, sex-equality, and the media

Mediation

229y Martial art meditations

Medicine

see also Health, Patient, names of practitioners, types of medicine and specific illnesses

44e Medicine

50u Competing ideologies of reproduction: Medical and maternal perspectives on pregnancy

51c Biochemical findings and medical management of the menopause

56d The deliverers: A woman doctor's reflections on medical socialization

58g Women in medicine

77c Creative women in scientific-technological and medical change

129y Women and the rise of the American medical profession

140b Editorial: Morality in medicine

145p The civilizing tendency of hygiene: Working-class women under medical control in Imperial Germany

165a One hundred years of fear: Rape and the medical profession

165k Female patients and the medical profession in jails and prisons: A case of quintuple jeopardy

189m Medicine as 'old husbands' tales': The impact of feminism

235i The medical profession

268p Sex roles in medicine

291j Medical assessment of child sexual abuse

316e Women in medicine

319h "All the good and bad in this world": Women, traditional medicine, and Mexican American culture

337f Women in the medical school

344e Women, health, and medicine

353a The female animal: Medical and biological views of woman and her role in nineteenth-century America

353b Women, menstruation, and nineteenth-century medicine

353o Prostitution, venereal disease, and American medicine

353bb Professionalism, feminism, and gender roles: A comparative study of nineteenth-century medical therapeutics

353dd On the evolution of women's medical societies

354i Medicine and patriarchal violence: The social construction of a "private" event

359ll Development of a medical center rape crisis intervention program

361k Strategies to increase participation of minorities in medicine

386e Women in medicine

387i Commitment and cultural mandate: Women in medicine

395i Women's understanding about reproductive physiology and their choice of herbal medicines in Cali, Colombia

395k Obstetrical complications associated with traditional medical practices at Nsukka

396b Midwives, medical men and 'poor women labouring of child': Lying-in hospitals in eighteenth-century London

396c Competing ideologies of reproduction: Medical and maternal perspectives on pregnancy

396g A woman in medicine: Reflections from the inside

447o Non-medical issues presented by the pregnant worker

Medieval

22b Wills, deeds, and charters as sources for the history of medieval women

22d Le rôle et la place de la femme provenant de la classe sociale inférieure dans la vie quotidienne du Moyen-Age

22e Women in Latin Medieval literature in Denmark e.g. annals and chronicles

22f Une contribution au débat concernant le status de la femme dans les villes du Danemark au Moyen-Age

43u The Beguines: A medieval women's community

99a Brides of Christ and poor mortals: Women in medieval society

117f Eve and Mary: Conflicting images of medieval woman

180c Eve's orphans: Mothers and daughters in medieval English literature

184a Medieval marriage characteristics: A neglected factor in the history of medieval serfdom

184b Childbearing among the lower classes of late medieval England

187b Byzantine asceticism and women's monasteries in early medieval Italy

187c Strict active enclosure and its effects on the female monastic experience (500-1100)

187l Medieval Cistercian nunneries and English Bishops

331a Woman's song in medieval Latin

331c The woman's song in medieval German poetry

331e Woman's songs in Irish, 800-1500

331g The "other" voice: Woman's song, its satire and its transcendence in late medieval British literature

334e The status of women and the practice of marriage in late-medieval Wales

375c *Merchet* and women's property rights in medieval England

408b Echoes of the Amazon myth in medieval Spanish literature

408c Sexual humor in misogynist medieval exampla

Meditation

229bb Expanding personal power through meditation

278f Phallic worship: Some personal meditations on a sacred theme

431b Women meditation teachers in Thailand

Mediterranean

371e The problem of privacy in Mediterranean anthropology

Medium

454g The spiritualist medium: A study of female professionalization in Victorian America

457a Mediums, controls and eminent men

473f Spirit mediums in Umbanda Evangelizada of Porto Alegre, Brazil: Dimensions of power and authority

Medusa

180p The muse as Medusa

Mehitzah

211n Kaddish from the "wrong" side of the *Mehitzah*

Meinhof, Ulrike

95j Ulrike Meinhof: An emancipated terrorist?

Melanesia

246d "Women never hunt": The portrayal of women in Melanesian ethnography

Melbourne, Australia

94j Generations and class: Sicilian-Australians in Melbourne

390t Women's struggle to become tram drivers in Melbourne, 1956-75

Melodrama

399kk The second face of the idol: Women in melodrama

Melody

68j Ancient song, new melody in Latin America: Women and film

Melting Pot

185n Beyond the melting pot: Nationalism, militarism and the family

Melville, Herman

17e On Herman Melville

Member

465b Members and survivors: Women and retirement-pensions legislation

Memoir

108h *My Childhood Years*: A memoir by the czarist cavalry officer, Nadezhda Durova

108n *Difficult Journey - Mountainous Journey*, The memoirs of Fadwa Tuqan

120a Memoirs of an ontological exile: The methodological rebellions of feminist research

186d May Sarton's memoirs

186e House, home and solitude: Memoirs and journals of May Sarton

390m The memoirs of 'Cleopatra Sweatfigure'

Memoria

474d De memoria

Memorialist

130m The memorialists

Memory

108q My memory's hyperbole

Memories

292j Memories of a movement: A conversation

301b Legacy: Memories of our foremothers

40kk Sonia Sanchez: The bringer of memories

Memsahib

160j Memsahibs in colonial Malaya: A study of European wives in a British colony and protectorate, 1900-1940

Men's Movement

see also Movement

140f Men's power with women, other men, and society: A men's movement analysis

212n Now what are they up to? Men in the 'Men's movement'

Menance

129dd Patriotism: A menace to liberty

Menarche

184o Age at menarche in Europe since the eighteenth century

190a Fatness, menarche, and fertility

190b Endocrine aspects of menarche and menopause - milestones in the woman's life cycle

190c Age at menarche and year of birth in relation to adult height and weight among Caucasian, Japanese, and Chinese women living in Hawaii

190d Menarche: Meaning of measures and measuring meaning

190e Through the looking glass of menarche: What the adolescent girl sees

190f Recollections of menarche, current menstrual attitudes, and perimenstrual symptoms

190g Menarche: Its effects on mother-daughter and father-daughter interactions

190i Variations in the experience of menarche as a function of preparedness

190n Age at menarche and sexual conduct in adolescence and young adulthood

190o Menarche and teenage pregnancy: A misuse of historical data

190p Menarche and adolescent pregnancy

190q "Oh dear me! Why weren't we all boys, then there wouldn't be any bother": Menarche and popular American fiction

190r Clinical aspects of menarche: Normal variations and common disorders

190v Menarche: A psychoanalytic perspective

190w The psychological concomitants of menarche in psychiatric patients

359w A study of attitudes toward menarche in white middle-class American adolescent girls

Mending

30v Invisible mending

Menken, Adah Issacs

175k Adah Isaacs Menken: From Texas to Paris

399l Adah Isaacs Menken in *Mazeppa*

Menopause

12d The tyrannical womb: Menstruation and menopause

19b Mrs. Hutchinson's behavior in terms of menopausal symptoms

34h Taking the men out of menopause

47b The menopause: Physiological, pathological, and psychological aspects

47c Questions women want to ask about the menopause

51a Toward a biosocial paradigm for menopause research: Lessons and contributions from the behavioral sciences

51b Bad maps for an unknown region: Menopause from a literary perspective

51c Biochemical findings and medical management of the menopause

51e Attitudes of families toward menopause

51f Perceptions of menopause by Papago women

51g Variation in Navajo menopause: Toward an explanation

51j Menopausal hot flash

51k Smoking, alcohol, and body mass relationships to early menopause: Implications for risk of cardiovascular disease

51p Menopausal distress: A model for epidemiologic investigation

51q Psychosocial aspects of the menopause

51r Cultural models for coping with menopause

51t A critique of menopause research

51w Aging, menopause, and estrogens: The clinician's dilemma

51x Sociological observations on ethical issues implicated in estrogen replacement therapy at menopause

51y Male and female menopause: A cultural put-on

69h Midlife concerns of women: Implications of menopause

190b Endocrine aspects of menarche and menopause - milestones in the woman's life cycle

210n Physical changes after menopause

210b The crossroads of menopause: A chance and a risk for the aging process of women

238e From maidenhood to menopause: Sex education for women in Victorian America

271o Mood and behaviour changes in menopausal women receiving gonadal hormones or placebo

316i The menopause in changing times

359cc Midlife concerns of women: Implications of the menopause

411n Reproductive issues, including menopause

439n Toward a biology of menopause

456d Menopause

460e Physiological aspects of female sexual development: Gestation, lactation, menopause, and erotic physiology

472j Now for the feminist menopause that refreshes

Menstruation

see also Premenstrual

12d The tyrannical womb: Menstruation and menopause

28a The physiology of the menstrual cycle

28b The neuroendocrinologic control of the menstrual cycle

28e The psychology of the menstrual cycle: Biological and physiological perspectives

28f Cognitive behavior and the menstrual cycle

28g Epidemiological patterns of sexual behavior in the menstrual cycle

28h Sexual behavior and the menstrual cycle

28i A developmental analysis of menstrual distress in adolescence

28n The menstrual cycle in anorexia nervosa

28o Psychopathology and the menstrual cycle

28q Oral contraceptives and the menstrual cycle

34g Changing minds: Women, biology, and the menstrual cycle

51i Potential role of the pineal gland in the human menstrual cycle

51o Expectations regarding menstrual symptoms: Effects on evaluation and behavior of women

51u Predicting the close of menstrual life

91b Religion and menstruation

190f Recollections of menarche, current menstrual attitudes, and perimenstrual symptoms

190h Physical attractiveness and physical stigma: Menstruation and the common cold

190j Menstrual education: Past, present, and future

190k Menstrual beliefs and experiences of mother-daughter dyads

190l Beliefs and attitudes of young girls regarding menstruation

239k Research on menstrual-related psychological changes: Alternative perspectives

239l A social psychological perspective on the menstrual cycle

239m Body time and social time: Mood patterns by menstrual cycle phase and day of week

240k Psychological aspects of the menstruum and premenstruum

271p Feeling states and the menstrual cycle

271q Theoretical/conceptual implications of study design and statistical analysis: Research on the menstrual cycle

325r Menstruation and childbirth as ritual and religious experience among native Australians

353b Women, menstruation, and nineteenth-century medicine

372aa Menstrual effects of athletic training

439f Menstruation and reproduction: An Oglala case

439k Behavior and the menstrual cycle

456b Menstrual problems

Mental

376d The weaker vessel: Legal versus social reality in mental commitments in nineteenth-century New York

376e Sex-based discrimination in the mental institutionalization of women

Mental Health

16a Women and mental health: The problem of depression

71c Mental health issues among Asian-American women

96b The mental health problems of women: Social roles and the individual

96c Passion as a mental health hazard

96n Math anxiety and female mental health: Some unexpected links

137b Gender as a model for mental health

140c Inequality and women's mental health: An overview

178n Mental health problems and their treatment

191a Who uses mental health facilities?

191f Stress and the mental health of women: A discussion of research and issues

191g Tailoring evaluation to measure the accountability of mental health services to women

253i The effects of childbearing on women's mental health: A critical review of the literature

253j Women's mental health

265m Sex role stereotyping and mental health standards in Israel: A cross-cultural comparison

265t Mental health in boys and girls: Awareness of attitudes for positive sex roles

284b Sexual victimization of children: An urban mental health center survey

295o Older women and mental health

304b Sex-role stereotypes and mental health: Conceptual models in the 1970s and issues for the 1980s

304d Sex roles and language use: Implications for mental health

316h Toward freedom and self-determination: New directions in mental health services

344h Marital relationships and mental health: The psychic costs of inequality

359f The prevalence of gender-role bias in mental health services

359g Sex-role stereotypes and clinical judgements of mental health

360a Women in the mental health delivery system: Implications for research and public policy

360e Women, spirituality, and mental health

360g Inequality and mental health: Low income and minority women

360h Lesbian women and mental health policy

360i Women's mental health in times of transition

360j Violence against women: Implications for mental health policy

360l Women and work: Implications for mental health

360p Professional psychology's response to women's mental health needs

380j Poverty, work, and mental health: The experience of low-income mothers

400g Some aspects of mental health of women in Bangladesh

418f Mental illness, mental health: Changing norms and expectations

434a Redefining concepts of mental health

447e Changing roles and mental health in women

455j Women and the mental health system

469b Mental health needs of Puerto Rican women in the United States

Mental Illness

53k An epidemioligic perspective of mental illness and childbirth

191c Community surveys: Sex differences in mental illness

245f Mothering, fathering, and mental illness

418f Mental illness, mental health: Changing norms and expectations

469f Cultural attitudes toward mental illness among Puerto Rican migrant women

Mentally Retarded

29r Mentally retarded mothers

Mentor

261b Building mentorship frameworks as part of an effective equal opportunity ecology

261f "Go find yourself a mentor"

Merchet

375c *Merchet* and women's property rights in medieval England

Meredith, George

142c A Meredithian glance at Gwendolen Harleth

Meridian

20d Meridians of perception: A reading of *The Journals of Susanna Moodie*

Merry, Anne Brunton

399i Anne Brunton Merry: First star

Message

57i Human sexuality: Messages in public environments

Metabolism

345b The physical effects and metabolism of alcohol

372k Physiological and metabolic responses of female athletes during laboratory and field exercises

372l Is the significance of muscle fibre types to muscle metabolism different in females than in males?

372s Exercise-induced changes in estradiol metabolism and their possible physiological meaning

372v Anaerobic energy metabolism of women

Metamorphoses

419l Rape and rape victims in the *Metamorphoses*

Metamorphosis

408q From mistress to murderess: The metamorphosis of Buñuel's *Tristana*

Metaphor

30x May Sarton: A metaphor for my life, my work, and my art

101a Introduction: The extended family as metaphor and the expansion of women's realm

106i Oedipus as hero: Family and family metaphors in Nietzsche

122q Marital metaphors in the Judeo-Christian tradition: A feminist critique

186q Metaphor in five garden poems by May Sarton

229r The metaphors of power

275n How words hurt: Attitudes, metaphor and oppression

429c Preaching through metaphor

Metaphysics

84n Political philosophy and the patriarchal unconscious: A psychoanalytic perspective on epistemology and metaphysics

229kk Metaphysical feminism

452k The metaphysics of matrilinearism in women's autobiography: Studies of Mead's *Blackberry Winter*, Hellman's *Pentimento*,

Angelou's *I Know Why the Caged Bird Sings*, and Kingston's *The Woman Warrior*

Metatheoretical

158l Metatheoretical influences on conceptions of human development

Meter

135f Symbol, mask, and meter in the poetry of Louise Bogan

Methodism

see also Religion

412c Women of the word: Selected leadership roles of women in Mr. Wesley's Methodism

412g Ministry through marriage: Methodist clergy wives on the trans-Mississippi frontier

412h Hispanic clergy wives: Their contribution to United Methodism in the southwest, later nineteenth century to the present

412i Preparing women for the Lord's work: The story of three Methodist training schools, 1880-1940

412j The social gospel according to Phoebe: Methodist deaconesses in the metropolis, 1885-1918

412k Laity rights and leadership: Winning them for women in the Methodist Protestant church, 1860-1900

412m Creating a sphere for women: The Methodist Episcopal church, 1869-1906

412n The laity rights movement, 1906-1918: Women's suffrage in the Methodist Episcopal Church, South

412r Korean women in Hawaii, 1903-1945: The role of Methodism in their liberation and in their participation in the Korean independence movement

412s Shaping a new society: Methodist women and industrial reform in the south, 1880-1940

Methodocracy

189c Methodocracy, misogyny and bad faith: The response of philosophy

Method

56f Studying childbirth: The experience and methods of a woman anthropologist

84i A paradigm of philosophy: The adversary method

98e Learning from poor women: A method of village study

98m Methodological issues in longitudinal and comparative research in Bangladesh

98n Methodological interventions in programme assessment and evaluation research

110f A multivariate model of labor supply: Methodology and estimation

120a Memoirs of an ontological exile: The methodological rebellions of feminist research

120b Feminism and the critique of scientific method

122m Finding one's way through the labyrinth: A symposium on women's lives: Methodology

124i Feminist research methodology groups: Origins, forms, functions

169i Discussion method

174v Feminist values: Guidelines for a teaching methodology in women's studies

177a The life history method

177j The Chinese biographical method: A moral and didactic tradition

178a Research methods and sample characteristics

234j 'Woman-ing' the landscape: East Anglia 1300-1500: A discussion on sources and methodology

241j Do her answers fit his questions? Women and the survey method

266b Social science inquiries into female achievement: Recurrent methodological problems

266c Overview of research methods

266e Methodological issues in the study of sex-related differences

266j Methods for integrative reviews

266k The impact of societal biases on research methods

291r The effects of child sexual abuse: Methodological considerations

297e Incidence or incidents: Political and methodological underpinnings of a health research process in a small Italian town

311e How to do what we want to do: Thoughts about feminist methodology

312g How to do what we want to do: Thoughts about feminist methodology

312h Passionate scholarship: Notes on values, knowing and method in feminist social science

312i Towards a methodology for feminist research

312j The value of quantitative methodology for feminist research

314j Appropriate teaching methods for integrating women

402c The study of women in South Asia: Some current methodological and research issues

463s Can current transportation planning methods analyze women's travel issues?

463t Gender-role identification in the methodology of transportation planning

Metropolis
see also City

393c Women and work: A study of female and male attitudes in the modern sector of an African metropolis (Lagos)

420l Female migrants in Bangkok metropolis

428g The domestic clothing workers in the Mexican metropolis and their relation to dependent capitalism

Mewar
255e Purdah among the Oswals of Mewar

Mexican
81c Chicanas and Mexican immigrant families 1920-1940: Women's subordination and family exploitation

Mexican American
see Hispanic

Mexican American Woman
see Hispanic Woman

Mexican Woman
319d Breast-feeding and social class mobility: The case of Mexican migrant mothers in Houston, Texas

319i Selective acculturation of female Mexican migrants

319o The nonconsenting sterilization of Mexican women in Los Angeles: Issues of psychocultural rupture and legal redress in paternalistic behavior

Mexicana
192a Sex, nationality, and class: La obrera Mexicana

Mexico
111p Prison treatment of female offenders in Mexico

112h Sor Juana Inés de la Cruz: Mexico's tenth muse (Mexican, 1651-1695)

192o Working-class women in nineteenth century Mexico

194a The Virgin of Guadalupe and the female self-image: A Mexican case history

194b The Tonantsi cult of the Eastern Nahua

251d The impact of science and technology and the role of women in science in Mexico

307c Gender and industry on Mexico's new frontier

319c Mexican, Mexican American, and Chicana childbirth

319e "La vieja Inés," a Mexican folk game: A research note

347f Aztec women: The transition from status to class in empire and colony

350f The creation of a relative surplus population: A case study from Mexico

363c Women and revolution: The brigadas femeninas and the Mexican Cristero Rebellion, 1926-1929

373f Impact of selected industrial technologies on women in Mexico

395f Perceptions of a family planning campaign in rural Mexico

408k Female archetypes in Mexican literature

428g The domestic clothing workers in the Mexican metropolis and their relation to dependent capitalism

428i Mexican border industrialization, female labor force participation, and migration

428j *Maquiladoras*: A new face of international capitalism on Mexico's northern frontier

473i Women in Yucatán

Michigan
26g Family trouble clinic: Family service of Detroit and Wayne County

Microeconomic
380k Microeconomic effects of women entering the labor force

Microelectronic
441d Women and microelectronics: The case of word processors

Microtechnology
323f Under attack: Women, unions and microtechnology

Middle
474j The middle period

Middle Age
see also Age

30c A portrait of the *Puttana* as a middle-aged Woolf scholar

47i Middle age: Loss or gain? (interview)

210a Changing appearance for women in the middle years of life: Trauma?

296f Mastery and pleasure: A two-factor model of well-being of women in the middle years

317h Economic status of late middle-aged widows

325h The ladies of Lord Krishna: Rituals of middle-aged women in eastern India

411c Methods for a life-span developmental approach to women in the middle years

411d Middle-aged women in literature

411e The middle years: Changes and variations in social-role commitments

411g The psychological well-being of women in the middle years

411j Motherhood in the middle years: Women and their adult children

411k Black women in the middle years

411l Problems of American middle-class women in their middle years: A comparative approach

411r Sexuality and the middle-aged woman

423g Longitudinal and cross-sectional data sources on women in the middle years

Middle Ages (History)
22d Le rôle et la place de la femme provenant de la classe sociale inférieure dans la vie quotidienne du Moyen-Age

22f Une contribution au débat concernant le status de la femme dans les villes du Danemark au Moyen-Age

33a The education of women in the Middle Ages in theory, fact, and fantasy

156j Celtic women in the early middle ages

187i Feminine lay piety in the High Middle Ages: The Beguines

Middle Atlantic
347b Sunksquaws, shamans, and tradeswomen: Middle Atlantic coastal Algonkian women during the 17th and 18th centuries

Middle Class
see also Class

243i Work experience and family relations among working-class and lower-middle-class

353x Making women modern: Middle-class women and health reform in nineteenth-century America

359w A study of attitudes toward menarche in white middle-class American adolescent girls

395j Health beliefs and behaviors of middle class urban women in Lahore, Pakistan

404g Reaching the middle class female

404h Reaching the middle class alcoholic

411l Problems of American middle-class women in their middle years: A comparative approach

431e Women in Java's rural middle class: Progress or regress

Middle East
see also Arab, Islam, Muslim, individual countries

18d Rural family size and economic change: A Middle Eastern case

279f Sexual dimorphism and settlement pattern in Middle Eastern skeletal populations

362c Muslim Middle Eastern women's participation in violent political conflict: Causes and characteristics

421h The effect of religious affiliation on woman's role in Middle Eastern Arab Society

Middle English

331f The woman's song in Middle English and its European backgrounds

Middlemarch

142d *Middlemarch* and the new humanity

142e 'Stealthy convergence' in *Middlemarch*

142m 'This petty medium': In the middle of *Middlemarch*

143g Origins, *Middlemarch*, endings: George Eliot's crisis of the antecedent

143h The hero as dilettante: *Middlemarch* and *Nostromo*

143i Fruit and seed: The finale to *Middlemarch*

332b The novel of awakening (five novels)

Middleton, Clara

242d "Herself against herself": The clarification of Clara Middleton

Midlife

see also Age

69h Midlife concerns of women: Implications of menopause

69i Marriage and midlife: The impact of social change

69j Separation: A family developmental process of midlife

96h Toward choice and differentiation in the midlife crises of women

221e Voluntary mid-life career change: Family effects

324f Economic consequences of midlife change in marital status

359cc Midlife concerns of women: Implications of the menopause

411a Introduction: The study of women in midlife

411b Life events and the boundaries of midlife for women

411f Multiple roles of midlife women: A case for new directions in theory, research, and policy

411m Health care and midlife women

411o Midlife woman as student

458b Midlife work history and retirement income

461f Sex and sexuality: Women at midlife

461g Discussion: Midlife women: Lessons for sex therapy

Midstream

16r Women in midstream

Midtrimester

252a Midtrimester abortion: A global view

Midwife

see also Medicine, Reproduce

34i Displaced - the midwife by the male physician

36m Man-midwifery and the rise of technology: The problem and proposals for resolution

36u Ethical issues relating to childbirth as experienced by the birthing woman and midwife

36v Midwives in many settings

353u "Safe delivered," but by whom? Midwives and men-midwives in early America

353v The American midwife controversy: A crisis of professionalization

353w Mary Breckinridge, the frontier nursing service, and the introduction of nurse-midwifery in the United States

396b Midwives, medical men and 'poor women labouring of child': Lying-in hospitals in eighteenth-century London

Migraine

456o Migraine

Migrant

18f Cross-national labor migrants: Actors in the international division of labor

18g Population dynamics and migrant labor in South Africa

86f Following the harvest: The health hazards of migrant and seasonal farmworking women

94d Migrantness, culture and ideology

94i Migrant communities and class politics: The Greek community in Australia

270j The plight of urban migrants: Dynamics of service procurement in a squatter area

299g Tribal migrants

319d Breast-feeding and social class mobility: The case of Mexican migrant mothers in Houston, Texas

319i Selective acculturation of female Mexican migrants

350g From rural subsistence to an industrial peripheral work force: An examination of female Malaysian migrants and capital accumulation in Singapore

420f The female migrant in Pakistan

420j Urban migrant women in the Republic of Korea

420l Female migrants in Bangkok metropolis

420n New models and traditional networks: Migrant women in Tehran

420o Migrant women at work in Asia

420r Adaptation of Polynesian female migrants in New Zealand

424o Employment structure of female migrants to the cities in the Philippines

424p Women migrants in Bangkok: An economic analysis of their employment and earnings

469f Cultural attitudes toward mental illness among Puerto Rican migrant women

470f Migrant women and wage labour: The case of West Indian women in Britain

Migrate

see also Immigrate

5d An analysis of the impact of labour migration on the lives of women in Lesotho

18j Country roads take me home: The political economy of wage-labor migration in an eastern Kentucky community

94f Women on the move: Migration and feminism

213a Women in migration: Beyond the reductionist outlook

270h The effect of international labor migration on women's roles: The Turkish case

300h Rural-urban linkages and migration: A Philippines case study

400d Impact of male migration on rural housewives

420a Urbanization, migration and the status of women

420b The migration of women to cities: A comparative perspective

420c Female migration: A conceptual framework

420e Rural-to-urban migration of women in India: Patterns and implications

420g Female rural-to-urban migration in peninsular Malaysia

420h Female migration in Thailand

420i The migration of women in the Philippines

420k Migration of women workers in peninsular Malaysia: Impact and implications

420m The migration of rural women to Taipei

424n Urbanward migration and employment of women in Southeast and East Asian cities: Patterns and policy issues

428h Labor migration and the new industrial division of labor

428i Mexican border industrialization, female labor force participation, and migration

Mikvah

210c Out of the *Mikvah* into the sauna: A study of women's health clubs

Miles, Catherine Cox

158g "Rather worse than folly?" psychology measures femininity and masculinity, 1: From Terman and Miles to the Guilfords

Milieu

185m Family options, governments, and the social milieu: Viewed from the 21st century

198g A traditional ceremony in an Islamic milieu in Malaysia

Militant

323r Working, mothering and militancy: Women in the CNTU

378d Militancy and acquiescence among women workers

Militarism

185n Beyond the melting pot: Nationalism, militarism and the family

218f Women textile workers in the militarization of Southeast Asia

428q Women textile workers in the militarization of Southeast Asia

Military

see also Armed Forces, Army

61k Women in the military service

179a Militarization/civilianization

179d The military model

195n Preservative love and military destruction: Some reflections on mothering and peace

300n Church-military relations in the Philippines

435n Women, men, and military service: Is protection necessarily a racket?

Milk

194l The milk overflowing ceremony in Sri Lanka

Mill
301q Hard times cotton mill girls
454d The lady and the mill girl: Changes in the status of women in the Age of Jackson

Mill on the Floss
142k The ambivalence of *The Mill on the Floss*
143c *The Mill on the Floss* and the unreliable narrator

Mill, John Stuart
106h Patriarchal liberalism and beyond: From John Stuart Mill to Harriet Taylor
315j Analyzing discrimination against women in the labor market - A few lessons from John Stuart Mill

Millar, Margaret
1h Margaret Millar

Millett, Kate
452m Towards a theory of form in feminist autobiography: Kate Millett's *Flying* and *Sita*; Maxine Hong Kingston's *The Woman Warrior*
452n The lady's not for spurning: Kate Millett and the critics

Milwaukee, WI
394d Committee on the Status of Women at Milwaukee
394g The women's studies program at Milwaukee

Mime
399s Women mimes in America

Minangkabau
300c The Minangkabau woman: Cultural centre or ethnic symbol?

Mind
34g Changing minds: Women, biology, and the menstrual cycle
40oo Alice Walker's women: In search of some peace of mind
84l The mind's eye
116d Freud: Masculinity, femininity, and the philosophy of mind
229yy Afterword: Feminist politics and the nature of mind

Miner, Dorothy Eugenia
389n Dorothy Eugenia Miner (1904-1973): The varied career of a medievalist: Scholar and keeper of manuscripts, librarian and editor at the Walters Art Gallery

Ming
401h Widows and remarriage in Ming and early Qing China

Mining
83g Class consciousness and world view of a Bolivian mining woman
181f Mining the earth's womb
390f Women in mining communities
466f Women and work in an Indonesian mining town

Minister (Clergy)
see also Religion
59d Women and ministry: Problem or possibility?
91k Women in ministries
91l Preacher and priest: Typologies of ministry and ordination of women

91n Is partnership possible? Ordained men and unordained women in ministry
115a Women and the ministry: A case for theological seriousness
353z Ministries of healing: Mary Baker Eddy, Ellen G. White, and the religion of health
412d Minister as prophet? or as mother?: Two nineteenth-century models
412g Ministry through marriage: Methodist clergy wives on the trans-Mississippi frontier
429a Growing toward effective ministry
429f A ministry of presence
429k Colleagues in marriage and ministry

Minneapolis, MN
263d "Blessed be the tie that binds": YWCA extension work among industrial women, Minneapolis, 1900-1910
263e "For love and money both": Women's work-related decisions in twentieth century Minneapolis

Minnesota
263d "Blessed be the tie that binds": YWCA extension work among industrial women, Minneapolis, 1900-1910
263e "For love and money both": Women's work-related decisions in twentieth century Minneapolis

Minority
see also Ethnic, Race, names of individual minority groups
10c Alcohol use and abuse in ethnic minority women
16t The ethnic minority woman
68k Introduction: Minority women in the United States
86h Minority women, work, and health
174g Teaching the feminist minority
180w Mothers and daughters: Another minority group
216n The early education of minority children
344w Race and ethnicity in the lives of minority women
351i The participation of minority women in higher education
360g Inequality and mental health: Low income and minority women
361d Improving minority preparation for math-based disciplines
361k Strategies to increase participation of minorities in medicine
365l Minority women: Social-cultural issues
371h The sexual division of domestic space among two Soviet minorities: The Georgians and the Tadjiks
377d The mathematics filter and the education of women and minorities
404e The double bind: Minority women
407f Lifting as we climb: Networks for minority women
421bb Minority within a minority: On being South Asian and female in Canada
443i Feminist therapy with minority clients

Minuet
20g Minuets and madness: Margaret Atwood's *Dancing Girls*

Miranda
343p The miranda trap: Sexism and racism in Shakespeare's *Tempest*

Mirria, Niger
473c Women's role in a Muslim Hausa town (Mirria, Republic of Niger)

Mirror
7y Hunger and thirst in the house of distorted mirrors
109i The mirror and the cameo: Margaret Atwood's comic/gothic novel, *Lady Oracle*

Miscarriage
8k Emotional reactions to miscarriage

Miscegenation
384g Miscegenation in popular western history and fiction

Misfortune
457j Men, women and misfortune in Bunyole

Misogyny
111a Re-discovering Lilith: Misogyny and the "new" female criminal
117n Degas's "Misogyny"
189c Methodocracy, misogyny and bad faith: The response of philosophy
242c Liberty, sorority, misogyny
408c Sexual humor in misogynist medieval exampla
409d Stephen Dedalus and women: A portrait of the artist as a young misogynist
419g The dynamics of misogyny: Myth and mythmaking in the *Oresteia*
419i Plato: Misogynist, phaedophile, and feminist

Miss
193v Retrieving the missing half

Miss California
399e Crowning Miss California, again

Miss Esther's Land
150y Miss Esther's land

Miss Latrobe
27j Virginia Woolf's Miss Latrobe: The artist's last struggle against masculine values

Missile
167g Children need smiles not missiles: Planning a walk Oxford mothers for nuclear disarmament

Mission
379i The London biblewomen and nurses mission, 1857-1880: Class relations/women's relations

Missionary
414d Patient and useful servants: Women missionaries in Indian territory

Mississippi
303h Academic women in Mississippi: Oktoberfest 1980
412g Ministry through marriage: Methodist clergy wives on the trans-Mississippi frontier

Missouri
226f Women as legislative candidates in six states

Mistral, Gabriela

408j Notes toward a definition of Gabriela Mistral's ideology

Mistreat

291p The co-therapy relationship in group treatment of sexually mistreated adolescent girls

Mistress

135n Mistresses and madonnas in the novels of Margaret Dabble

408q From mistress to murderess: The metamorphosis of Buñuel's Tristana

Misuse

see also Abuse

284e The sexually misused child

Mobility

see also Social Mobility

37g Economics and mobility: A theoretical rationale for urban black family well-being

37i Patterns of upward mobility in black families

85f Occupational mobility and the use of the comparative method

302k Mobility and professional involvement in librarianship: A study of the "Class of '55"

302l Geographic mobility and career advancement of male and female librarians

319d Breast-feeding and social class mobility: The case of Mexican migrant mothers in Houston, Texas

371i Spatial domains and women's mobility in Yorubaland, Nigeria

416f Academic career mobility for women and men psychologists

Mobilize

5c Mobilizing village women: Some organizational and management considerations

101i Two faces of protest: Alternative forms of women's mobilization in West Bengal and Maharashtra

214n Mobilizing resources: Creating a support system

362d The mobilization of Iraqi women into the wage labor force

403h The political mobilization of women in the Arab world

436b Women and citizenship: Mobilisation, participation, representation

Model

see also Role Model

49h Human resource planning and the intuitive manager: Models for the 1990's

51p Menopausal distress: A model for epidemiologic investigation

51r Cultural models for coping with menopause

54a A systems model for planning culturally specific programs

54d Program planning for Hispanic women: One ideal model

63i Co-correctional models

64l The theatre as literary model: Role-playing in *Chéri* and *The Last of Chéri*

65j Economic models as a means of calculating legal compensation claims

92c Pakistan: *Mor* and *Tor*: Binary and opposing models of Pukhtun womanhood

109m The Radcliffean gothic model: A form for feminine sexuality

110f A multivariate model of labor supply: Methodology and estimation

118d The dynamics of female experience: Process models and human values

122h In search of excellence in academic libraries, or, challenging the henhouse model

136f Sex-role influences in dyadic interaction: A theoretical model

137b Gender as a model for mental health

141c Statistical model for the study of familial breast cancer

169d Conferences: The one-day model

169p Occupational health and safety for women workers: Some teaching models

179d The military model

198c The Islamic revolution and women: Quest for the Quranic model

209ee Alternative models of worker participation

214o Ageism vs. sexism: Male models as a source of support

216f Parenting for multiculturalism: A Mexican-American model

216o The parent as educator: A home-school model of socialization

229x Images and models - in process

229ii Politics, spirituality, and models of change

232c Marriage in Tamil culture: The problem of conflicting "models"

239g A social psychological model of human sexuality

266l Causal models: Their import and their triviality

296f Mastery and pleasure: A two-factor model of well-being of women in the middle years

352p Leadership training for increased effectiveness among women educational administrators: Two local models

359uu The consciousness-raising group as a model for therapy with women

363e Social policy and women in Latin America: The need for a new model

378a Male and female: Job versus gender models in the sociology of work

387e Male and female: Job versus gender models in the sociology of work

463v An alternative approach to travel demand modeling: Constraints-oriented theories and societal roles

Modern

105b Modern and traditional elements in the expectations of young married couples regarding their marital life

175x Woman as victim in modern folklore

353x Making women modern: Middle-class women and health reform in nineteenth-century America

Modernize

144c Family and 'modernisation': The peasant family and social change in nineteenth-century Bavaria

300a Modernization, changing roles of women and expectations for development in Southeast Asia

300f Changes in women's status associated with modernization in northern Thailand

362e Gender, politics and modernization: The Indian case

Modest

135c Wariness and women's language: Two modest verbal studies

Molar

252j Fact and fancy in the termination of molar pregnancy with particular reference to uterine stimulants

Molest

see also Abuse

284c Sexual molestation of children: The last frontier of child abuse

Moll

392j The molls

Mombasa, Kenya

370g Slavery and reproductive labor in Mombasa

Monastery

187b Byzantine asceticism and women's monasteries in early medieval Italy

Monastic

187c Strict active enclosure and its effects on the female monastic experience (500-1100)

194n The Great Goddess today in Burma and Thailand: An exploration of her symbolic relevance to monastic and female roles

401a The Chinese Buddhist monastic order for women: The first two centuries

Money

43r Put your money where your movement is

172m Saving money with bio-gas (Colombia)

217c Women's right to money

440g Sex and money in the welfare state

Money, John

239d Human sex-hormone abnormalities viewed from an androgynous perspective: A reconsideration of the work of John Money

Mongan, Agnes

389o Agnes Mongan (b. 1905): Connoisseur of old master drawings

Monitor

36n The electronic fetal monitor in perinatology

36p Benefits and risks of electronic fetal monitoring

Monogamy

50l Monogamy, marriage and economic dependence

212i The politics of monogamy

223e Monogamy: A critique

Monster

102c Tiamat and her children: An inquiry into the persistence of mythic archetypes of woman as monster/villainess/victim

109g Monsters and madwomen: Changing female gothic

109j "A forced solitude": Mary Shelley and the creation of Frankenstein's monster

Montagnais

347a Montagnais women and the Jesuit program for colonization

Montana

384j Pioneer women in the works of two Montana authors: Interviews with Dorothy M. Johnson and A. B. Guthrie, Jr.

Montana State University

314h Project on women in the curriculum: Montana State University

Montesquieu, Charles de Second

106d Political and marital despotism: Montesquieu's *Persian Letters*

130q Montesquieu and women

Month

309h The risk of adolescent pregnancy in the first months of intercourse

Montreal, Canada

421d Social and economic integration of South Asian women in Montreal, Canada

Montseny, Frederica

95f Feminism: The essential ingredient in Federica Montseny's anarchist theory

Mood

see also Emotion

239m Body time and social time: Mood patterns by menstrual cycle phase and day of week

271o Mood and behaviour changes in menopausal women receiving gonadal hormones or placebo

Moody, Mary

205g "Roughing it in the bush" in British Columbia: Mary Moody's pioneer life in New Westminister 1859-1863

Moon

211v Feminist Judaism: Restoration of the moon

Moore, Catherine L.

114b C. L. Moore's classic science fiction

Moore, Marianne

356o The "feminine" language of Marianne Moore

Mor

92c Pakistan: *Mor* and *Tor*: Binary and opposing models of Pukhtun womanhood

Moral

2l Abortion, slavery, and the law: A study in moral character

45c Do changes in women's rights change women's moral judgements?

47h Moral choice

91m Moral theology from a feminist perspective

132t In a different voice: Women's conceptions of self and of morality

135p Emma Bovary's masculinization: Convention of clothes and morality of conventions

138i Sex, education and social policy: A new moral economy?

140a Presidential address: Conceptual ambiguity and morality in modern psychiatry

140b Editorial: Morality in medicine

147l The effect of changing attitudes toward sexual morality upon the promotion of physical education for women in nineteenth century America

152h Moral theology and homosexuality

185j Moral concepts in the year 2020: The individual, the family, and society

186l Rage for justice: Political, social and moral consciousness in selected novels of May Sarton

223u The morality of homosexuality

224d Looking at pornography: Erotica and the socialist morality

231e Family, sexual morality, and popular movements in turn-of-the-century America

231ee Feminism, moralism, and pornography

257k Duty and desire: Creating a feminist morality

273i Toward a moral policy for sex choice

275t Moral redescription and political self-deception

286a Lewis Carroll and Victorian morality

313p Women as moral and political alternatives in Conrad's early novels

336d The Bremen morality scandal

352b Prophets, chiefs, commissioners, and queens: The moral and institutional context of leadership

384t The moral in Austin's *The Land of Little Rain*

450g Ellen Douglas: Moralist and realist

454o The American woman's pre-World War I freedom in manners and morals

465h The new right, sex, education and social policy: Towards a new moral economy in Britain and the USA

Morante, Elsa

313i The fiction of family: Ideology and narrative in Elsa Morante

Morbidity

9i Sex differences in morbidity of alcoholics

More

353l The Loomis trial: Social mores and obstetrics in the mid-nineteenth century

Morgan, Berry

450k The androgynous, bi-racial vision of Berry Morgan

Morgan, Emily

175c Emily Morgan: Yellow rose of Texas

Morgner, Irmtraud

32r Irmtraud Morgner's *Leben und Abenteuer der Trobadora Beatriz*

Mormon

see also Religion

42n The traditional role of the Mormon woman

238g The awesome power of sex: The polemical campaign against Mormon polygamy

445q The Mormon novel: Virginia Sorensen's *The Evening and the Morning*

Morocco

162d Possession and dispossession: Maternity and mortality in Morocco

207e Work, consumption and authority within the household: A Moroccan case

208g Work, consumption and authority within the household: A Moroccan case

298d Research in the social sciences on women in Morocco

403c The determinants of social position among rural Moroccan women

Morrell, Frances

283h Interview with Frances Morrell

Morris, Wright

384o Wright Morris, women, and American culture

Morrison, Toni

40ee The quest for self: Triumph and failure in the works of Toni Morrison

40ff Theme, characterization, and style in the works of Toni Morrison

124b Naming, magic and documentary: The subversion of the narrative in *Song of Solomon*, *Ceremony*, and *China Men*

127i Eruptions of funk: Historicizing Toni Morrison

254d *Song of Solomon*: The hero with a woman's face

Mortal

9j Sex differences in mortality: A comparison of male and female alcoholics

53m Time trends of cancer incidence and mortality among women

99a Brides of Christ and poor mortals: Women in medieval society

137o Gender, psychophysiological disorders, and mortality

144e Women, family and death: Excess mortality of women in child-bearing age in four communities in nineteenth-century Germany

162d Possession and dispossession: Maternity and mortality in Morocco

205x Reducing maternal mortality in British Columbia: An educational process

Moslem

see also Islam, Muslim

350d Resource allocation and the sexual division of labor: A case study of a Moslem Hausa village in northern Nigeria

Mother

see also Family, Maternity

17l Mothers, daughters, and the "art necessity": Willa Cather and the creative process

27a Artists and mothers: A false alliance

29h Parenting: Training mothers as behavior therapists for their children

29r Mentally retarded mothers

38f She who is black and mother: In sociology and fiction, 1940-1970

38h Black mothers and the extended family support network

39c Asante queen mothers in government and politics in the nineteenth century

41f Stress and support networks of working single black mothers

43g If all else fails, I'm still a mother

43t Female leaders: Who was Rembrandt's mother?

69e The early mother-child relationship: A developmental view of woman as mother

78i You can't be a mother and be in prison...can you? Impacts of the mother-child separation

79o Perfectability and the neonate: The burden of expectations on mothers and their health providers

86j Mother, father, worker: Men and women and the reproduction risks of work

96d   Mothers and their children: A study of low-income families

102e Toward psychoanalytic feminism: The mother in dream-stealing, the father in dreams

103b The state, the patriarchal family, and working mothers

116n The obligations of mothers and fathers

117l Happy mothers and other new ideas in eighteenth-century French art

119c 'Mothers, vote labour!' The state, the labour movement and working-class mothers, 1900-1918

124g Psychology views mothers and mothering: 1897-1980

132c Mother-daughter relationships: Psychodynamics, politics, and philosophy

132o Separation and survival: Mothers, daughters, sisters: - The women's experimental theater

146g Individual and group treatment of mothers of incest victims

158j Mother: Social sculptor and trustee of the faith

158m The study of employed mothers over half a century

162p Mothers, sons, and the sale of symbols and goods: The 'German Mother's Day' 1923-33

167g Children need smiles not missiles: Planning a walk Oxford mothers for nuclear disarmament

178j Fathers' support to mothers and children

178l The quality of mother-child relationships

180a Mothers and daughters in ancient Near Eastern literature

180c Eve's orphans: Mothers and daughters in medieval English literature

180d The new mother of the English renaissance: Her writings on motherhood

180e The great unwritten story: Mothers and daughters in Shakespeare

180f Jane Austen and the tradition of the absent mother

180g Unmothered daughter and the radical reformer: Harriet Martineau's career

180h "The mother's history" in George Eliot's life, literature and political ideology

180i Mothers and daughters in *Wives and Daughters*: A study of Elizabeth Gaskell's last novel

180j Mothers and daughters in the fiction of the New Republic

180m Mothers, daughters, and incest in the late novels of Edith Wharton

180n Reentering paradise: Cather, Colette, Woolf and their mothers

180q The nightmare repetition: The mother-daughter conflict in Doris Lessing's *Children of Violence*

180r A subtle psychic bond: The mother figure in Sylvia Plath's poetry

180s The hungry Jewish mother

180t A psychological journey: Mothers and daughters in English-Canadian fiction

180v Spider woman's web: Mothers and daughters in Southwestern Native American literature

180w Mothers and daughters: Another minority group

180x Heritages: Dimensions of mother-daughter relationships in women's autobiographies

180y Mothers and daughters in literature: A preliminary bibliography

188a The Frankish mother: Dhuoda

190g Menarche: Its effects on mother-daughter and father-daughter interactions

190k Menstrual beliefs and experiences of mother-daughter dyads

192t Lucy Duran - Wife, mother, and organizer

194i The village Mother in Bengal

194p Conclusion: New perspectives on mother worship

195a The obligations of mothers and fathers

195c When women and men mother

195e If all else fails, I'm still a mother

195f Reproduction, mothering, and the origins of patriarchy

195n Preservative love and military destruction: Some reflections on mothering and peace

195o Toward an ethic of nurturance: Luce Irigaray on mothering and power

196i Virginia Woolf and her violin: Mothering, madness, and music

202a Thinking back through our mothers

205q "Services rendered, rearing children for the state": Mothers' pensions in British Columbia 1919-1931

211c The hungry Jewish mother

212j Coping: Or how mothers are seen and not heard

213b Motherhood and waged work: West Indian, Asian and white mothers compared

221c Working mothers: Effects on the marriage and the mother

231ff My mother liked to fuck

233j The effect of the mother's work on the infant

243e Mothers as social agents: Structuring the community activities of school aged children

244b White mothers in the American civil rights movements

245d The fantasy of the perfect mother

245f Mothering, fathering, and mental illness

257e The daughter is mother of the child: Cycles of lesbian sexuality

265b Ethnic differences in sex stereotyping by mothers: Implications for health care

265q Overemphasis of mother role and inflexibility of roles

283a When women and men mother

295c Mothering and the young child

305t Mothers, sisters, lovers, listen

307p Mother calls herself a housewife, but she buys bulls

309m Teenage mothers and teenage fathers: The impact of early childbearing on the parents' personal and professional lives

309r Family support: Helping teenage mothers to cope

309t Guessing and misinformation about pregnancy risk among urban mothers

319d Breast-feeding and social class mobility: The case of Mexican migrant mothers in Houston, Texas

323r Working, mothering and militancy: Women in the CNTU

325c Mother Guru: Jnanananda of Madras, India

329b Virginia Woolf and her violin: Mothering, madness and music

336f Mother's day in the Weimar Republic

336n Comrade - woman - mother - resistance fighter

347c The mothers of the nation: Seneca resistance to Quaker intervention

349g Aw! Your mother's in the mafia: Women criminals in progressive New York

359d The conflict between nurturance and autonomy in mother-daughter relationships and within feminism

369k Mothers, fathers, and children: From private to public patriarchy

373j Changing role of Maya mothers and daughters

379e Was she a good mother? Some thoughts on a new issue for feminist biography

379l City mothers, city daughters, and the dance hall girls: The limits of female political power in San Francisco, 1913

380g Bringing down the rear: The decline in the economic position of single-mother families

380j Poverty, work, and mental health: The experience of low-income mothers

380q The attitude of Danish mothers to child care, 1975 to 1979

385m The child-care dilemma of working mothers in African cities: The case of Lagos, Nigeria

391c Children's impressions of television mothers

392o Mothers behind bars: A look at the parental rights of incarcerated women

393a Wage earner and mother: Compatibility of roles on a Cameroon plantation

399g *The Story of a Mother* (play)

412d Minister as prophet? or as mother?: Two nineteenth-century models

421c A causal interpretation of the effect of mother's education and employment status on parental decision-making role patterns in the Korean family

421r Some aspirations of lower class black mothers

427c Fathers, mothers, and childcare in the 1980s: Family influences on child development

434m Work requirements for AFDC mothers

440c Redistribution to children and to mothers: A history of child endowment and family allowances

444j Patriot mothers in the post-risorgimento: Women after the Italian revolution

455h Some mothers are lesbians

461n Discussion: Some developmental aspects of adolescent mothers

469h The utilization of pediatric health services by Hispanic mothers

Mother Earth

194f The worship of Mother Earth in Russian culture

194o Mother Earth: The great goddess of West Africa

Mother's Day
162p Mothers, sons, and the sale of symbols and goods: The 'German Mother's Day' 1923-33

Motherhood
50p Anger and tenderness: The experience of motherhood
76a The women's movement and motherhood
180d The new mother of the English renaissance: Her writings on motherhood
195j On conceiving motherhood and sexuality: A feminist materialist approach
195q Feminism, pronatalism, and motherhood
195r Motherhood: The annihilation of women
213b Motherhood and waged work: West Indian, Asian and white mothers compared
220c The power politics of motherhood
226l State and local policies on motherhood
257a Purity, motherhood, pleasure or threat? Definitions of female sexuality 1900-1970s
307y Surrogate motherhood - an interview
309v Early motherhood: Ignorance or bliss?
336k Racism and sexism in Nazi Germany: Motherhood, compulsory sterilization, and the state
341h Pregnancy: Is motherhood fattening?
344i Motherhood: Contemporary conflict for women
353g Voluntary motherhood: The beginnings of feminist birth control ideas in the United States
363a In defense of motherhood: Divorce law in Cuba during the early republic
364e Female power and the inequality of wealth and motherhood in north-western Portugal
397k Lesbianism and motherhood: Implications for child custody
411j Motherhood in the middle years: Women and their adult children
417w Motherhood in feminist utopias
418d Motherhood and mothering
439m Maternal sexuality and asexual motherhood
461l Effects of teenage motherhood
461m Does motherhood mean maturity?

Motherlode
15j Publishers on libraries: The library as motherlode: A feminist view

Motif
384c A study of feminism as a motif in "A journey to Pike's Peak and New Mexico" by Julia Archibald Holmes

Motivation
296e A three-generational analysis of change in women's achievement motivation and power
404q Motivation and the alcoholic woman

Motor
107q Somatic and motor characteristics of female gymnasts

Moulton, Janice
432d Reply to Moulton and Lemos

Mountain
167i At the foot of the mountain: The Shibokusa women of Kita Fuji

The Mountain Lion
332g Revolutionary turnings: *The Mountain Lion* reread

Mountain Man
445l Westering and woman: A thematic study of Kesey's *One Flew Over the Cuckoo's Nest* and Fisher's *Mountain Man*

Mountin' Maids
417n Women in the Children of God: "Revolutionary women" or "Mountin' maids"?

Mourn
117d Mourners on Greek vases: Remarks on the social history of women
219h Loss and mourning in victims of rape and sexual assault

Move
339f The single woman: Moving up by moving around

Movement
see also Feminist Movement, Men's Movement, Social Movement, Women's Liberation, Women's Movement
6j Women in contemporary national liberation movements
43r Put your money where your movement is
87b Catalytic movements: Civil rights and women
95i Humanism versus feminism in the socialist movement: The life of Angelica Balabanoff
101d Sisterhood or separation? The All-India Muslim Ladies' Conference and the Nationalist Movement
107p Differences in males and females in joint movement range during growth
119c 'Mothers, vote labour!' The state, the labour movement and working-class mothers, 1900-1918
122j A comparison of the movements toward equality in Yugoslavia and England
136e Sex differences in body movements and positions
167a Starting a movement: Frauen für frieden (Women for Peace, West Germany)
184n The origins of the birth control movement in England in the early nineteenth century
192c Lives of Chicana activists: The Chicano student movement (a case study)
192d Women in the Chicano movement
203p From kitchen to storefront: Women in the tenant movement
205t A union man's wife: The ladies' auxiliary movement in the IWA, the Lake Cowichan experience
227l The carrot, the stick and the movement
231e Family, sexual morality, and popular movements in turn-of-the-century America
244b White mothers in the American civil rights movements
292j Memories of a movement: A conversation
310aa Who is going to rock the petri dish? For feminists who have considered parthenogenesis when the movement is not enough
444k "The mother half of humanity": American women in the peace and preparedness movements in World War I

Movie
81e The projection of a new womanhood: The movie moderns in the 1920's
174s Creative teaching spaces: Home movies
231r Movie

Mrs. Dalloway
202f *Mrs Dalloway*: The communion of saints
328i Clarissa Dalloway's respectable suicide
329g 'The prime minister': A key to *Mrs. Dalloway*
329h Private and public consciousness in *Mrs. Dalloway* and *To the Lighthouse*
332h Narrative structure(s) and female development: The case of *Mrs.Dalloway*
330h *Mrs. Dalloway*: The unguarded moment

Ms.
275o Vs. Ms.
275p Against "Vs. Ms."
275q Beyond the miserable vision of "Vs. Ms."

Much
470b 'If it's only women it doesn't matter so much'

Much Ado About Nothing
343e Those "soft and delicate desires": *Much Ado* and the distrust of women

Muda, Malaysia
466g Housewives and farmers: Malay women in the Muda Irrigation Scheme

Mujahidin
368f An analysis of Fida'i and Mujahidin positions on women's rights

Mujer
192p A la mujer (to women)

Mujeres Libres
417l *Mujeres Libres* and the role of women in anarchist revolution

Mulatto
399oo Who put the "Tragic" in the Tragic Mulatto?

Mullah
368o Women imprisoned in the kingdom of the Mullahs

Muller v. Oregon
375h Historical background of "protective" labor legislation: *Muller v. Oregon*

Multicultural
94b Ethnicity, multiculturalism and neo-conservatism
94e Multiculturalism and education policy
216f Parenting for multiculturalism: A Mexican-American model
339d Being a manager in a multicultural world

Multidisciplinary
146l Multidisciplinary team review of child-sexual-abuse cases
277g The multidisciplinary approach to the diagnosis and treatment of male sexual dysfunction

Multinational
373k Women's work in multinational electronics factories
428c Capitalism, imperialism, and patriarchy: The dilemma of Third-World women workers in multinational factories

428e   Household, community, national, and multinational industrial development

Multiple Sclerosis
285q   Sexuality and multiple sclerosis - must they be mutually exclusive?

Multivariate
110f   A multivariate model of labor supply: Methodology and estimation
173e   Abortion and the presidential election of 1976: A multivariate analysis of voting behavior

Mundt, Theodor
32e   *Wally, die Zweiflerin* and *Madonna*: A discussion of sex-socialization in the nineteenth century

Mundurucú
282h   Pigs, women, and the men's house in Amazonia: An analysis of six Mundurucú myths

Munford, Mary
303c   Mary Munford and higher education for women in Virginia

Murder
165f   Murdered women and women who murder: A critique of the literature
172j   Where are our campesino brothers? Let the murderers answer! (Nicaragua)
270n   Social psychological patterns of homicide in Turkey: A comparison of male and female convicted murders
408q   From mistress to murderess: The metamorphosis of Buñuel's Tristana

Murdoch, Iris
318b   The wages of intellectuality . . . and the fictional wagers of Iris Murdoch

Murshida
399f   Murshida Ivy O. Duce

Muscle
372l   Is the significance of muscle fibre types to muscle metabolism different in females than in males?
372q   Short time, maximal muscular performance: Relation to muscle lactate and fiber type in females
372z   Effect of increased intensity of training on maximum oxygen uptake and muscular performance of young female cross-country skiers

Muse
17i   Cool Diana and the Blood-red muse: Edith Wharton on innocence and art
112h   Sor Juana Inés de la Cruz: Mexico's tenth muse (Mexican, 1651-1695)
130h   Women as muse
180p   The muse as Medusa
399y   The comic muse of Mary Chase
453l   Madonna or witch: Women's muse in contemporary American poetry

Museo Italo Americano
73d   The Museo Italo Americano: My involvement with the Italian American community in San Francisco

Museum
389j   Gisela Marie Augusta Richter (1882-1972): Scholar of classical art and museum archaeologist

417ee   A women's museum of art

Music
see also Composer, Song
30e   Music into words
39t   Black women and music: A survey from Africa to the new world
40f   Music as theme: The jazz mode in the works of Toni Cade Bambara
40qq   Music as theme: The blues mode in the works of Margaret Walker
130j   Women and music: Ornament of the profession?
196i   Virginia Woolf and her violin: Mothering, madness, and music
229d   The origins of music: Women's goddess worship
329b   Virginia Woolf and her violin: Mothering, madness and music
337h   Women in the school of music
397s   Lesbians and women's music
453j   Women's music

Musician
108j   Fanny Mendelssohn Hensel: Musician in her brother's shadow

Muslim
see also Moslem, Islam
21h   Political change: Muslim women in conflict with Parda: Their role in the Indian Nationalist Movement
21i   The modern Pakistani woman in a Muslim society
92b   Bangladesh: Beliefs and customs observed by Muslim rural women during their life cycle
94k   Religion, law and family disputes in a Lebanese Muslim community in Sydney
101d   Sisterhood or separation? The All-India Muslim Ladies' Conference and the Nationalist Movement
101j   The All-Pakistan Women's Association and the 1961 Muslim family laws ordinance
198a   Introduction: The ideal and contextual realities of Muslim women
255b   Purdah revisited: A comparison of Hindu and Muslim interpretations of the cultural meaning of purdah in South Asia
255i   Purdah politics: The role of Muslim women in Indian nationalism, 1911-1924
325j   The controversial vows of urban Muslim women in Iran
362c   Muslim Middle Eastern women's participation in violent political conflict: Causes and characteristics
379a   Glimpses of Muslim urban women in classical Islam
402i   Muslim women in Uttar Pradesh: Social mobility and directions of change
403a   The religious lives of Muslim women
403f   Ritual status of Muslim women in rural India
421g   Education of Muslim women: Tradition versus modernity
466i   Separate but equal: Indonesian Muslim perceptions of the roles of women
473c   Women's role in a Muslim Hausa town (Mirria, Republic of Niger)

Mutilation
285t   How to stubbornly refuse to disturb oneself emotionally about anything - even about death, dying and sexual mutilation

Mutuality
59g   Human sexuality and mutuality
118c   Openness and mutuality in process thought and feminist action

Muta'
368m   The institution of Muta' marriage in Iran: A formal and historical perspective

My Antonia
127d   The forgotten reaping-hook: Sex in *My Antonia*
384l   The Virginian and Antonia Shimerda: Different sides of the western coin

My Childhood Years
108h   *My Childhood Years*: A memoir by the czarist cavalry officer, Nadezhda Durova

My Mortal Enemy
332b   The novel of awakening (five novels)

Mymensing
433h   Forms of the Indian notion of sexuality and an interpretation of the Mymensing ballad of Kajalrekha

Myofascial
8m   The myofascial pain dysfunction syndrome: An unheeded neuromuscular disorder

Myself
30b   In quest of Ding Ling (In quest of myself)

Mysteries of Udolpho
313g   Ideology and *The Mysteries of Udolpho*

Mystic
188g   The German mystic: Mechthild of Magdeburg
188h   The Brabant mystic: Hadewijch
188l   The English mystic: Julian of Norwich
412f   Georgia Harkness: Social activist and/or mystic

Mystique
50v   Rape and the masculine mystique
342f   The scientific mystique: Can a white lab coat guarantee purity in the search for knowledge about the nature of women?

Myth
21f   Women in Indonesian politics: The myth of functional interest
27e   George Sand and the myth of femininity
32j   Ricarda Huch: Myth and reality
39q   The myth of the black matriarchy
40pp   Fields watered with blood: Myth and ritual in the poetry of Margaret Walker
78e   The new female offender: Reality or myth?
84e   Evolution and patriarchal myths of scarcity and competition
102c   Tiamat and her children: An inquiry into the persistence of mythic archetypes of woman as monster/villainess/victim
103j   Gender and child-custody determinations: Exploding the myths
107a   Women's sports - the unlikely myth of equality
143e   *Romola* and the myth of apocalypse

176c "Out" at the university: Myth and reality

181h Women, science, and popular mythology

186p The sculptor and the rock: Some uses of myth in the poetry of May Sarton

202d Some female versions of pastoral: *The Voyage Out* and matriarchal mythologies

209i Assessing the myths of the job market

225j The myth of the perfect body

229n Drawing from mythology in women's quest for selfhood

229xx Myths and matriarchies

252e The trimester threshold for pregnancy termination: Myth or truth?

253e The myth of assembly-line hysteria

263a Women and welfare work: Demystifying the myth of disembeddedness

269g Watch that pot or the *waksuk* will eat you up: An analysis of male and female roles in Rama Indian myth

275g The myth of the neutral "man"

282h Pigs, women, and the men's house in Amazonia: An analysis of six Mundurucú myths

286j On the enrichment of poor monkeys by myth and dream; or how Dickens Rousseauisticized and pre-Freudianized Victorian views of childhood

303j Racial myths and attitudes among white female students at the University of Florida

328f Isis unveiled: Virginia Woolf's use of Egyptian myth

332k The female novel of development and the myth of psyche

333a Mythical women, past and present

338e The new woman and the old goddess: The shaping of Shaw's mythology

342a Social effects of some contemporary myths about women

348g The myth of rising female crime

384f Sacajawea of myth and history

384m Beret as the Norse mythological goddess Freya/Gurthr

384q Toward a new paradigm: Mari Sandoz's study of red and white myth in *Cheyenne Autumn*

404s The mythology of rape

408b Echoes of the Amazon myth in medieval Spanish literature

416j You've come a long way baby: The myth and the reality

419g The dynamics of misogyny: Myth and mythmaking in the *Oresteia*

445b Women's literature and the American frontier: A new perspective on the frontier myth

461e Discussion: Myths in the midst of missing data

Mythinterpretation

348d The mythinterpretation of female crime

Mytilène

448c Return to Mytilène: Renée Vivien and the city of women

Naditu

156p The Naditu women of Sippar

Nadu

232a On the meaning of sakti to women in Tamil Nadu

Nagovisi

246f Women, work, and change in Nagovisi

Nahua, Mexico

194b The Tonantsi cult of the Eastern Nahua

Name

356l Anger and the politics of naming

162b Putting kin and kinship to good use: The circulation of goods, labour, and names on Karpathos (Greece)

Nana

155c Zola's view of prostitution in *Nana*

Naples, Italy

194e An Italian religious feast: The *Fujenti* rites of the Madonna dell'Arco, Naples

Narcissistic

88h Narcissistic development

Narradora

313k Narradoras hispanoamericanas: Vieja y nueva problemática en renovadas elaboraciones

Narrative

20j *Lady Oracle*: The narrative of a fool-heroine

124b Naming, magic and documentary: The subversion of the narrative in *Song of Solomon*, *Ceremony*, and *China Men*

135e The Wife of Bath: Narrator as victim

143c *The Mill on the Floss* and the unreliable narrator

313i The fiction of family: Ideology and narrative in Elsa Morante

330c Virginia Woolf's narrators and the art of "life itself"

332h Narrative structure(s) and female development: The case of *Mrs. Dalloway*

445p Folk narrative in Caroline Gordon's frontier fiction

449e The shaping of life: Structure and narrative process in Eileen Chang's *The Rouge of the North*

NASA

see National Aeronautic and Space Administration

Nation

see also Country, State, individual nations

32d Kleist's nation of amazons

39e Tanzanian women in nation building

113j Denmark: The small NATO nation

113k Sweden: The neutral nation

347c The mothers of the nation: Seneca resistance to Quaker intervention

National

6j Women in contemporary national liberation movements

21d Female elite goals and national development: Some data from the Philippines

65i Assessing pay discrimination using national data

68c African women and national development

101c The Indian women's movement: A struggle for women's rights or national liberation?

101h The Indian women's movement and national development: An overview

167d A national campaign: Women's party for survival

172e Our national inferiority complex: A cause for violence? (El Salvador)

198j The struggle of women in the national development of Pakistan

363b Working class Afro-Surinamese women and national politics: Traditions and changes in an independent state

373m The plight of the invisible farmer: The effect of national agriculture policy on women in Africa

428e Household, community, national, and multinational industrial development

435g In search of a national child-care policy: Background and prospects

National Academy of Sciences

67h An analysis of the National Academy of Sciences' comparable worth study

National Action Committee on the Status of Women

93k The role of the National Action Committee on the Status of Women in facilitating equal pay policy in Canada

National Aeronautic and Space Administration (NASA)

288l A federal response to sexual harassment: Policy-making at Johnson Space Center, NASA

National Archives

61c National Archives resources for research in the history of American women

National Crime Survey Program

349j Women as victims: An examination of the results of L.E.A.A.'s National Crime Survey Program

National Institute for Occupational Safety and Health (NIOSH)

209w An overview of NIOSH research on clerical workers

National Labor Market Board

93h Equality between men and women in the labor market: The Swedish National Labor Market Board

National Woman's Party

81j International feminism between the wars: The National Woman's Party versus the League of Women Voters

National Women's Advisory Council

23j The politics of the National Women's Advisory Council

National Youth Administration

61i Mary McLeod Bethune and the National Youth Administration

Nationalism

101g Nationalism, universalization, and the extended female space in Bombay City

185n Beyond the melting pot: Nationalism, militarism and the family

255i Purdah politics: The role of Muslim women in Indian nationalism, 1911-1924

Nationalist Movement

101d Sisterhood or separation? The All-India Muslim Ladies' Conference and the Nationalist Movement

Nationality

192a Sex, nationality, and class: La obrera Mexicana

Native

282c The bow and the burden strap: A new look at institutionalized homosexuality in native North America

325r Menstruation and childbirth as ritual and religious experience among native Australians

Native American

see American Indian

Native American Woman

205b When you don't know the language, listen to the silence: An historical overview of native Indian women in BC

Native Woman

220e Native women and the state

NATO

see North Atlantic Treaty Organization

Natural

36g Woman-controlled birth control: A feminist analysis of natural birth control

56b Natural childbirth and the reluctant physician

170h Natural selection: Perspectives on entitlement to the invalid care allowance

252k Natural prostaglandins alone or in combination for termination of pregnancy

314e The natural sciences: Casting a critical eye on 'objectivity'

321d Natural resources: Health, reproduction and the gender order

378h Politics an unnatural practice: Political science looks at female participation

418l 'If it's natural, we can't change it'

Naturalize

207c Women's labours: The naturalisation of social inequality and women's subordination

208i Women's labours: The naturalisation of social inequality and women's subordination

Naturalness

94c The 'naturalness' of inequality

Nature

9h Nature and development of alcoholism in women

17c Thwarted nature: Nathaniel Hawthorne as feminist

29b Unraveling the nature of sex roles

32h Laura Marholm and the question of female nature

46j The changing nature of social security

50z Oppressive dichotomies: The nature/culture debate

64h The test of love and nature: Colette and lesbians

116b Sex roles: The argument from nature

126f A feminist challenge to Darwinsim: Antoinette L. B. Blackwell on the relations of the sexes in nature and society

131d Woman as nature in science fiction

191d Depressions among women: Their nature and causes

200a Nature, culture and gender: A critique

200b Women and the dialectics of nature in eighteenth-century French thought

200c Natural facts: A historical perspective on science and sexuality

200f Gender, sexuality and marriage: A Kaulong model of nature and culture

200g Images of nature in Gimi thought

200h No nature, no culture: The Hagen case

307d Women, nature and domination

330k Nature and community: A study of cyclical reality in *The Waves*

330l Nature and history in *The Years*

338d Synge and the nature of woman

342b Women's nature and scientific objectivity

342f The scientific mystique: Can a white lab coat guarantee purity in the search for knowledge about the nature of women?

392a The extent and nature of female crime

416n Class, race, sex, scientific objects of knowledge: A socialist-feminist perspective on the social construction of productive nature and some political consequences

418m Oppressive dichotomies: The nature/culture debate

432j Competition, friendship, and human nature

462d Making the world live: Feminism and the domination of nature

Nature-Nurture

31e Concepts of woman in psychoanalytic theory: The nature-nurture controversy revisited

Nau

334b Nau Kynwedi Teithiauc

Navajo

see also American Indian

51g Variation in Navajo menopause: Toward an explanation

82k Land tenure and cooperatives: Origin, development and persistence of Navajo matrifocality in subsistence, production, exchange and tenure

Navarre, Marguerite de

112c Marguerite de Navarre and her circle (French, 1492-1549)

Nazi

336a Introduction: Women in Weimar and Nazi Germany

336k Racism and sexism in Nazi Germany: Motherhood, compulsory sterilization, and the state

444b "I don't call that *Volksgemeinschaft*": Women, class, and war in Nazi Germany

Near East

180a Mothers and daughters in ancient Near Eastern literature

Nebel, Ruth

336m The story of Ruth

Nebraska

226f Women as legislative candidates in six states

Necrophilia

280m Necrophilia and anti-social acts

Need

295m Differential needs and treatment approaches for women in psychotherapy

341j The nutritional needs of women

417r Utopia in question: Programming women's needs into the technology of tomorrow

447g Special needs of women in health examinations

Needlework

see also Art

201a Needlework as art, craft, and livelihood before 1900

Negation

160g The negation of structure: A note on British council wives

Neglect

16p Women as single parents: Alternative services for a neglected population

Negri Sembilan

466d Land ownership in Negri Sembilan, 1900-1977

Negro

see also African American, Minority, Race

421m Comparative attitudes about marital sex among Negro women in the United States, Great Britain and Trinidad

Neighborhood

73b Organizing neighborhood women for political and social action

73c Developing a neighborhood-based health facility

174d College for neighborhood women: Innovation and growth

203k Toward supportive neighborhoods: Women's role in changing the segregated city

468e Women's work strategies: An analysis of the organisation of everyday life in an urban neighbourhood

Nelken, Margarita

95g Margarita Nelken: Women and the crisis of Spanish politics

NEMOW

82u NEMOW: A project that stumbled and why

Neonate

see also Reproduce

79o Perfectability and the neonate: The burden of expectations on mothers and their health providers

79r Rights of a handicapped neonate: What every parent and professional should know

79s Living with an impaired neonate and child: A feminist issue

Neonatology

79n Neonatology: Directions and goals

Nepal

124e The founding of the first Sherpa nunnery, and the problem of "women" as an analytic category

Nersessian, Sirarpie der

389l Sirarpie Der Nersessian (b. 1896): Educator and scholar in Byzantine and Armenian art

Nervous

28m Estrogens and central nervous system function: Electroencephalography, cognition, and depression

Netherlands

52d The position of women in the Netherlands: Marginal change

112e Anna Maria van Schurman: The star of Utrecht (Dutch, 1607-1678)

117k Art history and its exclusions: The example of Dutch art

159b Female criminality in the Netherlands

167b Organising at the grassroots: Vrouwen voor vrede (Women for peace, the Netherlands)

213f Living in between: Turkish women in their homeland and in the Netherlands

380q The attitude of Danish mothers to child care, 1975 to 1979

Network

26i Coping with wife abuse: Personal and social networks

38h Black mothers and the extended family support network

41f Stress and support networks of working single black mothers

163b The network defines its issues: Theory, evidence and analysis of female sexual slavery

163c Network strategies and organizing against female sexual slavery

243f Black families and childrearing support networks

249l A network of one's own

256e The power of women's networks

314s Resource networks

319k Social networks and survival strategies: An exploratory study of Mexican American, black and Anglo family female heads in San Jose, California

326e Network aspects of treatment for incestuously abused children

363f Research on women in Latin America: Problems of networking and comparative analysis in the last decade

404dd Establishing interdisciplinary treatment networks

407f Lifting as we climb: Networks for minority women

415g Breakthrough: Making it happen with women's networks

417k A utopian female support network: The case of the Henry Street Settlement

420d Women in rural-urban circulation networks: Implications for social structural change

420n New models and traditional networks: Migrant women in Tehran

436j Women's employment networks: Strategies for development

443m Some feminist concerns in an age of networking

473h Adaptive strategies and social networks of women in St. Kitts

Neuroendocrine

28b The neuroendocrinologic control of the menstrual cycle

28c Neuroendocrine regulation of sexual behavior

51h Neuroendocrine mechanisms of reproductive aging in women and female rats

Neuromuscular

8m The myofascial pain dysfunction syndrome: An unheeded neuromuscular disorder

Neurophysiology

239e Biochemical and neurophysiological influences on human sexual behavior

Neutral

275g The myth of the neutral "man"

275j Gender-neutral terms

Nevada

349i Prostitution in Nevada

New

124a Rediscovering the "New Woman" of the 1890's: The stories of "George Egerton"

New Britain

246e Revenge suicide by Lusi women: An expression of power

New Deal

81k "The forgotten woman": Working women, the New Deal, and women's organizations

New Democratic Party (NDP)

323x Trade union women and the NDP

New England

367d New England women: Ideology and experience in first-generation Puritanism (1630-1650)

387g Industrialization and femininity: A case study of nineteenth-century New England

439u "I am not contented": Female masochism and lesbianism in early twentieth-century New England

New Guinea

364i Subject or object? Women and the circulation of valuables in highlands New Guinea

New Left Review

283n The silences of *New Left Review*

New Mexico

226f Women as legislative candidates in six states

New Republic

180j Mothers and daughters in the fiction of the New Republic

New Right

60g Antifeminism and the New Right

60h Feminism, the family, and the New Right

60i The New Right and the abortion issue

174f The new right challenges women's studies: The Long Beach women's studies program

465h The new right, sex, education and social policy: Towards a new moral economy in Britain and the USA

New South Wales

294e The making of a prostitute proletariat in early twentieth-century New South Wales

New South Wales Builders Labourers' Federation

390u Revolution and machismo: Women in the New South Wales Builders Labourers' Federation, 1961-75

New Westminister

205g "Roughing it in the bush" in British Columbia: Mary Moody's pioneer life in New Westminister 1859-1863

New York (City)

201l A stitch in our time: New York's Hispanic garment workers in the 1980s

231f Feminism, men, and modern love: Greenwich Village, 1900-1925

349g Aw! Your mother's in the mafia: Women criminals in progressive New York

376d The weaker vessel: Legal versus social reality in mental commitments in nineteenth-century New York

379o Jewish involvement in the New York City woman suffrage movement

399tt New York feminist theater troupe

New York (State)

61g Women and radical reform in antebellum upstate New York: A profile of grassroots female abolitionists

128f The politics of mutual frustration: Socialists and suffragists in New York and Wisconsin

165j Hard times: Custodial prisons for women and the example of the New York State Prison for Women at Auburn, 1893-1933

201e The great uprising in Rochester

New York State Prison for Women

165j Hard times: Custodial prisons for women and the example of the New York State Prison for Women at Auburn, 1893-1933

New Zealand

138l Gender, class and education: A teaching bibliography of Australian and New Zealand studies

413a Women in the political life of New Zealand

413c The origins of the women's movement in New Zealand: The Women's Christian Temperance Union 1885-1895

413d Fertility, sexuality and social control in New Zealand

413f Women and the professions in New Zealand

413i Women artists in New Zealand

413j Mummy's boys: Pakeha men and male culture in New Zealand

420r Adaptation of Polynesian female migrants in New Zealand

Newborn

see also Reproduce

9q The effects of opiates, sedative-hypnotics, amphetamines, cannabis, and other psychoactive drugs on the fetus and newborn

79p Decisions about handicapped newborns: Values and procedures

Newburyport, MA

184p Toward a theory of remarriage: A case study of Newburyport at the beginning of the nineteenth century

Newfoundland, Canada

162o Family fun in Starve Harbor: Custom, history and confrontation in village Newfoundland

241g 'Women and old boats': The sexual division of labour in a Newfoundland outport

News

429g Bearing the good news

Newspaper
147n An analysis of humour pertaining to sportswomen in Canadian newspapers from 1910-1920
286m "Morbid depression alternating with excitement": Sex in Victorian newspapers

Nexus
278c The secret nexus: Sex and literature in eighteenth-century Britain
286c Cash and the sex nexus

Ney, Elisabet
175l Elisabet Ney: Texas' first lady of sculpture

NGO
see Nongovernment Organization

Nhara
370p A Nhara of the Guinea-Bissau region: Mãe Aurélia Correia

Nicaragua
172j Where are our campesino brothers? Let the murderers answer! (Nicaragua)
269g Watch that pot or the *waksuk* will eat you up: An analysis of male and female roles in Rama Indian myth

Nice
225m No more nice girls

Nichols, Anne
399w Anne Nichols: $1,000,000.00 playwright

Nichols, Mary Gove
353y Mary Gove Nichols, prophetess of health

Nietzsche, Friedrich
106i Oedipus as hero: Family and family metaphors in Nietzsche

Niger
473c Women's role in a Muslim Hausa town (Mirria, Republic of Niger)

Nigeria
5h Developing women's cooperatives: An experiment in rural Nigeria
39d Women's political participation Nigeria
159i A preliminary study of female criminality in Nigeria
350d Resource allocation and the sexual division of labor: A case study of a Moslem Hausa village in northern Nigeria
371i Spatial domains and women's mobility in Yorubaland, Nigeria
385c Dependence and autonomy: The economic activities of secluded Hausa women in Kano, Nigeria
385m The child-care dilemma of working mothers in African cities: The case of Lagos, Nigeria
393b Education and socio-demographic change in Nigeria
393c Women and work: A study of female and male attitudes in the modern sector of an African metropolis (Lagos)
395k Obstetrical complications associated with traditional medical practices at Nsukka
436d Women's education and participation in the labour force: The case of Nigeria

Night
474n *Opening nights*: The opening days

Night and Day
330f Enchanted organs, magic bells: *Night and Day* as comic opera
448f Tradition and revision: The classic city novel and Virginia Woolf's *Night and Day*

Nightingale, Florence
248c From Sarah Gamp to Florence Nightingale: A critical study of hospital nursing systems from 1840 to 1897

Nightmare
109k Terror-gothic: Nightmare and dream in Ann Radcliffe and Charlotte Brontë

Nimble
206a Nimble fingers and other fables

Nin, Anaïs
452l Anaïs Nin's *Diary* in context

Nineteenth Amendment
81l Discontented black feminists: Prelude and postscript to the passage of the nineteenth amendment

Nineteenth Century
see also Victorian
9b Temperance and women in 19th-century United States
14u Afro-American women 1800-1910: A selected bibliography
14v Afro-American women poets of the nineteenth century: A guide to research and bio-bibliographies of the poets
17d Four novels of Harriet Beecher Stowe: A study in nineteenth-century androgyny
32e *Wally, die Zweiflerin* and *Madonna*: A discussion of sex-socialization in the nineteenth century
32f A German writer and feminist in nineteenth century America: An archival study of Mathilde Franziska Anneke
32g German women writers in the nineteenth century: Where are they?
39c Asante queen mothers in government and politics in the nineteenth century
39o Discrimination against Afro-American women in the woman's movement, 1830-1920
50b The home turned upside down? The working-class family in cotton textiles 1780-1850
50c Women's work in nineteenth-century London: A study of the years 1820-1850
50d Women's work and the family in nineteenth-century Europe
60b Male vice and female virtue: Feminism and the politics of prostitution in nineteenth-century Britain
60c The feminist theology of the black Baptist church, 1880-1900
81f Culture and radical politics: Yiddish women writers in America, 1890-1940
89d Women's work and the family in nineteenth-century Europe
99c 'Helpmeet for man': Women in mid-nineteenth century western Australia
99e 'As good a bloody woman as any other woman...': Prostitutes in western Australia, 1895-1939
112j Mercy Otis Warren: Playwright, poet, and historian of the American revolution (American, 1728-1814)

124a Rediscovering the "New Woman" of the 1890's: The stories of "George Egerton"
124g Psychology views mothers and mothering: 1897-1980
129a The roots of individualist feminism in 19th-century America
144b Family and role-division: The polarisation of sexual stereotypes in the nineteenth century - an aspect of the dissociation of work and family
144c Family and 'modernisation': The peasant family and social change in nineteenth-century Bavaria
144e Women, family and death: Excess mortality of women in child-bearing age in four communities in nineteenth-century Germany
144f The family life-cycle: A study of factory workers in nineteenth century Württemberg
144g Overcrowding and family life: Working-class families and the housing crisis in late nineteenth-century Duisburg
145a Current research on German women's history in the nineteenth century
145e The reading habits of women in the *Vormärz*
145g Female political opposition in pre-1848 Germany: The role of Kathinka Zitz-Halein
145h German women writers and the Revolution of 1848
145i Self-conscious histories: Biographies of German women in the nineteenth century
145j Growing up female in the nineteenth century
145l The impact of agrarian change on women's work and child care in early-nineteenth-century Prussia
145n Social insurance and the family work of Oberlausitz home weavers in the late nineteenth century
145o The woman's role in the German working-class family in the 1890s from the perspective of women's autobiographies
147c The rise and development of women's concern for the physical education of American women, 1776-1885: From independence to the foundation of the American Association for the Advancement of Physical Education
147d The ladies' department of the *American Farmer*, 1825-1830: A locus for the advocacy of family health and exercise
147e American women, 1880-1860 (sic): Recreational pursuits and exercise
147f Woman's place in nineteenth century Canadian sport
147g Generalizations on women and sport, games and play in the United States from settlement to 1860
147i The realm of sports and the athletic woman, 1850-1900
147j Women's participation in sporting activities as an indicator of a feminist movement in Canada between 1867-1914
147l The effect of changing attitudes toward sexual morality upon the promotion of physical education for women in nineteenth century America

147aa The first intercollegiate contest for women: Basketball, April 4, 1896

148b Beasts of burden and menial slaves: Nineteenth century observations of Northern Plains Indian women

148g The political economy of gender: A 19th century Plains Indian case study

153m Gender division within the U.S. working class: Households in the Philadelphia area, 1870-1945

155b French feminist theater and the subject of prostitution, 1870-1914

157b To Columbia on the Tynemouth: The emigration of single women and girls in 1862

157e Public and political: Documents of the woman's suffrage campaign in British Columbia, 1871-1917: The view from Victoria

158b Freud's heritage: Fathers and daughters in German literature (1750-1850)

160b Ambivalence and dedication: Academic wives in Cambridge University, 1870-1970

162c Infanticide in rural Bavaria in the nineteenth century

162g Young bees in an empty hive: Relations between brothers-in-law in a south German village around 1800

162m Linen was their life: Family survival strategies and parent-child relations in nineteenth-century France

165j Hard times: Custodial prisons for women and the example of the New York State Prison for Women at Auburn, 1893-1933

184m Parisian infants and Norman wet nurses in the early nineteenth century: A statistical study

184n The origins of the birth control movement in England in the early nineteenth century

184p Toward a theory of remarriage: A case study of Newburyport at the beginning of the nineteenth century

184q Premarital pregnancy in America, 1640-1971: An overview and interpretation

192o Working-class women in nineteenth century Mexico

201a Needlework as art, craft, and livelihood before 1900

201c "A paradise of fashion": A. T. Stewart's department store, 1862-1875

205d A preliminary sketch of Chinese women and work in British Columbia, 1858-1950

205e The response of the WMS to the immigration of Asian women, 1888-1942

205g "Roughing it in the bush" in British Columbia: Mary Moody's pioneer life in New Westminister 1859-1863

205w Vivian Dowding: Birth control activist 1892-

225b seeking ecstasy on the battlefield: Danger and pleasure in nineteenth-century feminist sexual thought

231b "Charity girls" and city pleasures: Historical notes on working-class sexuality, 1880-1920

231cc Male vice and female virtue: Feminism and the politics of prostitution in nineteenth-century Britain

238b Passionlessness: An interpretation of Victorian sexual ideology, 1790-1850

238d The spermatic economy: A nineteenth-century view of sexuality

238h Harlot or heroine? Changing views of prostitution, 1870-1920

238i Ideas of the early sex education movement in America, 1890-1920

245c Why nineteenth-century feminists did not support "birth control" and twentieth-century feminists do: Feminism, reproduction, and the family

248b Nurse recruitment to four provincial hospitals 1881-1921

248c From Sarah Gamp to Florence Nightingale: A critical study of hospital nursing systems from 1840 to 1897

248d The administration of poverty and the development of nursing practice in nineteenth-century England

256c Servants, sexual relations and the risks of illegitimacy in London, 1801-1900

256f "The men are as bad as their masters...": Socialism, feminism and sexual antagonism in the London tailoring trade in the 1830s

263f The sexual division of labor on American farms: 1750-1850

263h Creating a place for women: American book publishing in the nineteenth century

264b Sisters under their skins: Southern working women, 1880-1950

264d Black women in a southern city: Washington, D.C., 1890-1920

279i Sexual dimorphism for size in seven nineteenth-century Northwest coast populations

286h *The Bachelor's Pocket Book for 1851*

286l Fallen women, lost children: Wilde and the theatre in the nineties

290a 'Free from all uninvited touch of man': Women's campaigns around sexuality, 1880-1914

294b 'More sinned against than sinning'?: Prostitution in South Australia, 1836-1914

294d Dealing with the 'social evil': Prostitution and the police in Perth and on the eastern goldfields, 1895-1924

302a Revision versus reality: Women in the history of the public library movement, 1876-1920

313e El ángel del hogar: The cult of domesticity in nineteenth century Spain

323c No proper deal: Women workers and the Canadian labour movement, 1870-1940

349e The economics of female criminality: An analysis of police blotters, 1890-1976

352h Coeducation and the development of leadership skills in women: Historical perspectives from Cornell University, 1868-1900

353a The female animal: Medical and biological views of woman and her role in nineteenth-century America

353b Women, menstruation, and nineteenth-century medicine

353c What ought to be and what was: Women's sexuality in the nineteenth century

353d Passionlessness: An interpretation of Victorian sexual ideology, 1790-1850

353e The female world of love and ritual: Relations between women in nineteenth-century America

353h Patterns of abortion and the response of American physicians, 1790-1930

353i Doctors, birth control, and social values, 1830-1970

353j "On the importance of the obstetrick art": Changing customs of childbirth in America, 1760 to 1825

353l The Loomis trial: Social mores and obstetrics in the mid-nineteenth century

353n Chlorotic girls, 1870-1920: A historical perspective on female adolescence

353p "The fashionable diseases": Women's complaints and their treatment in nineteenth-century America

353x Making women modern: Middle-class women and health reform in nineteenth-century America

353bb Professionalism, feminism, and gender roles: A comparative study of nineteenth-century medical therapeutics

353cc Homeopathy and sexual equality: The controversy over coeducation at Cincinnati's Pulte Medical College, 1873-1879

353ee Doctors or ladies? Women physicians in psychiatric institutions, 1872-1900

353ff "Neither for the drawing room nor for the kitchen": Private duty nursing in Boston, 1873-1914

353gg "Little world of our own": The Pennsylvania Hospital Training School for Nurses, 1895-1907

354j Chlorosis and chronic disease in 19th-century Britain: The social constitution of somatic illness in a capitalist society

355b An enlarged human existence? Technology and household work in nineteenth-century America

370i Women in slavery among the Mangbetu c. 1800-1910

370j Slave wives, free sisters: Bakongo women and slavery c.1700-1850

370k The story of Swema: Female vulnerability in nineteenth century East Africa

370n Bwanikwa: Consciousness and protest among slave women in Central Africa, 1886-1911

375d The married women's property acts, 1839-1865: Reform, reaction or revolution?

375g The law of husband and wife in nineteenth-century America: Changing views of divorce

375j Barred from the bar: Women and legal education in the United States, 1870-1890

376d The weaker vessel: Legal versus social reality in mental commitments in nineteenth-century New York

376f Nineteenth-century women's prison reform and its legacy

379i The London biblewomen and nurses mission, 1857-1880: Class relations/women's relations

379k "My spirit eye": Some functions of spiritual and visionary experience in the lives of five black women preachers, 1810-1880

379m The limitations of sisterhood: Elizabeth Cady Stanton and division in the American suffrage movement, 1875-1902

387g Industrialization and femininity: A case study of nineteenth-century New England

389a Precursors and pioneers (1820-1890)

389b Widening horizons (1890-1930)

389d Anna Jameson (1794-1860): Sacred art and social vision

389e Margaret Fuller (1810-1850): Her work as an art critic

389f Lady Dilke (1840-1904): The six lives of an art historian

389g Mariana Griswold Van Rensselaer (1851-1934): America's first professional woman art critic

389h Georgiana Goddard King (1871-1939): Educator and pioneer in medieval Spanish art

389i Margarete Bieber (1879-1978): An archaeologist in two worlds

389j Gisela Marie Augusta Richter (1882-1972): Scholar of classical art and museum archaeologist

389k Erica Tietze-Conrat (1883-1958): Productive scholar in renaissance and baroque art

390b 'Feeding the poor and sapping their strength': The public role of ruling-class women in eastern Australia, 1788-1850

390c Women and labour, 1880-1900

390d Educated and white-collar women in the 1880s

390e Evolution, eugenics and women: The impact of scientific theories on attitudes towards women, 1870-1920

401k The influence of western women on the anti-footbinding movement 1840-1911

405b The women's liberation issue in nineteenth century Russia

408i Gertrude the Great: Avellaneda, nineteenth-century feminist

412d Minister as prophet? or as mother?: Two nineteenth-century models

412h Hispanic clergy wives: Their contribution to United Methodism in the Southwest, later nineteenth century to the present

412i Preparing women for the Lord's work: The story of three Methodist training schools, 1880-1940

412j The social gospel according to Phoebe: Methodist deaconesses in the metropolis, 1885-1918

412k Laity rights and leadership: Winning them for women in the Methodist Protestant church, 1860-1900

412l "A new impulse": Progress in lay leadership and service by women of the United Brethren in Christ and the Evangelical Association, 1870-1910

412m Creating a sphere for women: The Methodist Episcopal church, 1869-1906

412o Nineteenth-century A.M.E. preaching women: Cutting edge of women's inclusion in church polity

412p Evangelical domesticity: The woman's temperance crusade of 1873-1874

412q For god and home and native land: The W.C.T.U.'s image of woman in the late nineteenth century

412s Shaping a new society: Methodist women and industrial reform in the south, 1880-1940

413c The origins of the women's movement in New Zealand: The Women's Christian Temperance Union 1885-1895

413h Women, work and family: 1880-1926

414c Women of the Osage: A century of change, 1874-1982

414h Woman's suffrage, Oklahoma style, 1890-1918

417j The Woman's Commonwealth: Utopia in nineteenth-century Texas

433d British tradesmen of Calcutta, 1830-1900: A preliminary study of their economic and political roles

433l British response to Bengali literature in the nineteenth century

454d The lady and the mill girl: Changes in the status of women in the Age of Jackson

454e Ladies bountiful: Organized women's benevolence in early nineteenth-century America

454h Cultural hybrid in the slums: The college woman and the Settlement House, 1889-1894

454i The cult of true womanhood: 1820-1860

454l The female world of love and ritual: Relations between women in nineteenth-century America

454m Women and their families on the Overland Trail, 1842-1867

454n The hysterical woman: Sex roles and role conflict in nineteenth century America

457b Theosophy and feminism: Some explorations in nineteenth century biography

465a Dealing with dependency: State practices and social realities, 1870-1945

466a Women as cultural intermediaries in nineteenth-century Batavia

Ninth Century

187d Benedictine life for women in central France, 850-1100: A feminist revival

NIOSH

see National Institute for Occupational Safety and Health

Noah

211l The Noah syndrome

Nobility

232e A note on the nobility of women in popular Tamil fiction

Nonconsent

see Consent

Nongovernment Organization (NGO)

346b Child workers in the informal sector role of the NGOs: Some reflections

Nonhuman

see Human

Nonprint

14z A listing of non-print materials on black women

Nonschool

see School

Nonsexist

see Sexist

Nontraditional

see Tradition

Nonverbal

see Verbal

Nonviolent

see Violence

Nora

122p Ibsen's *A Doll's House*: A directorial perspective on performing Nora

Norm

244i Traditional sex norms and the innovative function of afternoon dancing

Normal

279k Normal and abnormal sexual dimorphic patterns of growth and development

Norman

184m Parisian infants and Norman wet nurses in the early nineteenth century: A statistical study

187e Anglo-Saxon nuns in Anglo-Norman hagiography: Humility and power

Norse

384m Beret as the Norse mythological goddess Freya/Gurthr

North America

282c The bow and the burden strap: A new look at institutionalized homosexuality in native North America

North Atlantic Treaty Organization (NATO)

113j Denmark: The small NATO nation

179j NATO: The lesson machine

179h NATO: What is it and why should women care?

North Carolina

81d Flawed victories: The experiences of black and white women workers in Durham during the 1930s

Northern Sung, China

401f Power and prestige: Palace women in the Northern Sung (960-1126)

Northern Territory, Australia

333r Income and employment for women in remote communities: Examples from the Northern Territory

Northwest

279i Sexual dimorphism for size in seven nineteenth-century Northwest coast populations

445g Women poets and the "Northwest School"

Norton, Andre

114c Andre Norton: Humanity amid the hardware

Norway

159d Norwegian women in court

209t Labor legislation in Norway: Its application to the introduction of new technology

382i Norway

468b Working hours and segmentation in the Norwegian labour market

468c Trade union participation of women in Norway: Structural changes, dilemmas and challenges

468g Conceptualising domestic work: Comments on definitions of "work" in some Norwegian studies

Nostromo

143h The hero as dilettante: *Middlemarch* and *Nostromo*

Note

20m Bashful but bold: Notes on Margaret Atwood as critic

60a Notes toward a feminist dialectic

Notification

308k Family involvement, notification, and responsibility: A personal essay

Notion

84g The trivialization of the notion of equality

Nouveau

64j Colette and art nouveau

La Nouvelle Héloïse

106f Julie and "La Maison Paternelle": Another look at Rousseau's *La Nouvelle Héloïse*

Novel

see also Literature

14w On the novels written by selected black women: A bibliographical essay

17d Four novels of Harriet Beecher Stowe: A study in nineteenth-century androgyny

20k Janus through the looking glass: Atwood's first three novels

27g "Old maids have friends": The unmarried heroine of Trollope's Barsetshire novels

32k "Eine frau, aber mehr als das, eine Persönlichkeit, aber mehr als das: eine frau": The structural analysis of the female characters in the novels of Max Frisch

40w Singing a deep song: Language as evidence in the novels of Gayl Jones

41b The concept of class in the novels of black women

51l Erik Erikson and Doris Lessing: Psychological theory and the female novel of development

64e Colette and the epistolary novel

64g A typology of women in Colette's novels

109b "But why do they read those things?" The female audience and the gothic novel

109i The mirror and the cameo: Margaret Atwood's comic/gothic novel, *Lady Oracle*

127e *Ida*, A great American novel

127j *Fear of Flying*: Developing the feminist novel

130u The death of an ideal: Female suicides in the eighteenth-century French novel

131j In and out of time: The form of Marge Piercy's novels

135j The woman at the window: Ann Radcliffe in the novels of Mary Wollstonecraft and Jane Austen

135n Mistresses and madonnas in the novels of Margaret Dabble

164c The influence of place: Jane Austen and the novel of social consciousness

164e Sex and social life in Jane Austen's novels

180i Mothers and daughters in *Wives and Daughters*: A study of Elizabeth Gaskell's last novel

180m Mothers, daughters, and incest in the late novels of Edith Wharton

186i Living rooms: Amity in the novels of May Sarton

186j Patterns of love and friendship: Five novels by May Sarton

186l Rage for justice: Political, social and moral consciousness in selected novels of May Sarton

186n Redefinitions of traditional Christian emblems and outlooks in May Sarton's novels of 1970-1975

242e Writing (from) the feminine: George Sand and the novel of female pastoral

286k Passion between women in the Victorian novel

313p Women as moral and political alternatives in Conrad's early novels

318d Women victimised by fiction: Living and loving in the novels of Barbara Pym

318g Women and children first: The novels of Margaret Drabble

329k *The Years*: A feminist novel

330a Introduction: Virginia Woolf, the novel, and a chorus of voices

332b The novel of awakening (five novels)

332k The female novel of development and the myth of psyche

332l Exiting from patriarchy: The lesbian novel of development

383d World views in utopian novels by women

393d Worlds apart? A comparative study of European and African traditional family life as depicted in the novels of Laurie Lee and Camara Laye

439i The front line: Notes on sex in novels by women, 1969-1979

445q The Mormon novel: Virginia Sorensen's *The Evening and the Morning*

448f Tradition and revision: The classic city novel and Virginia Woolf's *Night and Day*

448g A wilderness of one's own: Feminist fantasy novels of the twenties: Rebecca West and Sylvia Townsend Warner

453n The use of story in women's novels of the seventies

Novelist

see also Writer

130l The novelists and their fictions

164a Introduction: Jane Austen as a social novelist

197e Muriel Spark: Critic into Novelist

316c Playwrights, poets, and novelists: Sisters under the skin

318h Muriel Spark: The novelist as dandy

450l Rita Mae Brown: Feminist theorist and southern novelist

Nsukka, Nigeria

395k Obstetrical complications associated with traditional medical practices at Nsukka

Nuclear

167g Children need smiles not missiles: Planning a walk Oxford mothers for nuclear disarmament

179i Nuclear Europe

215b How I learnt to start worrying and hate the bomb: The effects of a nuclear bombardment

215i Fuel for the nuclear arms race: Nuclear power and nuclear weapons

215j Letter to my neighbour: Nuclear war and the countryside

215k Take the toys from the boys: Competition and the nuclear arms race

215l Alternative defence: The search for non-nuclear alternatives

215s Contemplating a nuclear future: Nuclear war, politics and the individual

215u Womanpower and nuclear politics: Women and the peace movement

215v Interesting times: A chronology of the nuclear age

229rr Spiritual dimensions of feminist anti-nuclear activism

Null

340f The null case: The Chipewyan

Nun

see also Sister (Catholic), Religion

121b The wayward nun beneath the hill: Emily Dickinson and the mysteries of womanhood

124e The founding of the first Sherpa nunnery, and the problem of "women" as an analytic category

187e Anglo-Saxon nuns in Anglo-Norman hagiography: Humility and power

187j The nun as anchoress: England, 1100-1500

187n Epilogue: Does St Bernard have a specific message for nuns?

325n The case of the vanishing nuns: The fruits of ambivalence in ancient Indian Buddhism

344x What price independence? Social reactions to lesbians, spinsters, widows, and nuns

366c The leadership of nuns in immigrant Catholicism

408g The convent as catalyst for autonomy: Two Hispanic nuns of the seventeenth century

Nunnery

187f Why English nunneries had no history: A study of the problems of the English nunneries founded after the conquest

187l Medieval Cistercian nunneries and English Bishops

Nurse

see also Medicine

5e Perspectives in development: The problem of nurses and nursing in Zambia

184m Parisian infants and Norman wet nurses in the early nineteenth century: A statistical study

205v The search for legitimacy: Nurses' registration in British Columbia 1913-1935

248b Nurse recruitment to four provincial hospitals 1881-1921

248e A constant casualty: Nurse education in Britain and the USA to 1939

353gg "Little world of our own": The Pennsylvania Hospital Training School for Nurses, 1895-1907

353ii Mabel K. Staupers and the integration of black nurses into the armed forces

379i The London biblewomen and nurses mission, 1857-1880: Class relations/women's relations

454f The war within a war: Women nurses in the Union Army

Nursery Rhyme

121c Emily Dickinson's nursery rhymes

Nursing

see also Medicine

44f Nursing

65f Dilemmas of implementation: The case of nursing

71e Asian women in professional health schools, with emphasis on nursing

86b   The risks of healing: The hazards of the nursing profession

248a   Introduction: The contemporary challenge in nursing history

248c   From Sarah Gamp to Florence Nightingale: A critical study of hospital nursing systems from 1840 to 1897

248d   The administration of poverty and the development of nursing practice in nineteenth-century England

248f   Asylum nursing before 1914: A chapter in the history of labour

248g   'The history of the present' - contradiction and struggle in nursing

248i   Archives and the history of nursing

263j   Professionalism, division of labor by gender, and the control of nursing practice

297g   A postscript to nursing

319m   The status of Hispanic women in nursing

337e   Nursing in the UW system

353w   Mary Breckinridge, the frontier nursing service, and the introduction of nurse-midwifery in the United States

353ff   "Neither for the drawing room nor for the kitchen": Private duty nursing in Boston, 1873-1914

353hh   More than "the physician's hand": Skill and authority in twentieth-century nursing

Nurturance

31e   Concepts of woman in psychoanalytic theory: The nature-nurture controversy revisited

102o   Public nurturance and the man on horseback

116c   Nurture theories: A critique

195o   Toward an ethic of nurturance: Luce Irigaray on mothering and power

244g   The nurture of adults by children in family settings

359d   The conflict between nurturance and autonomy in mother-daughter relationships and within feminism

Nutrient

279n   Sexual dimorphism and nutrient reserves

Nutrition

29i   Health maintenance: Exercise and nutrition

82g   Nutrition and health

237d   The nutritionist's approach (premenstrual tension)

341j   The nutritional needs of women

400f   Life cycle, food behaviour and nutrition of women in Bangladesh

Nuzi

156l   Bridewealth and dowry in Nuzi

Nymph

112i   Elizabeth Elstob: The Saxon nymph (English, 1683-1765)

Nymphomania

280c   Nymphomania, hostile sex, and superego development

O'Brien, Edna

318i   Edna O'Brien: A kind of Irish childhood

O'Casey, Sean

338f   'Two words for women': A reassessment of O'Casey's heroines

O'Connor, Flannery

109o   The maternal legacy: The grotesque tradition in Flannery O'Connor's female gothic

127g   The visionary art of Flannery O'Connor

451i   Introduction to *Everything That Rises Must Converge*

451j   Flannery O'Connor, a realist of distances

451l   The visionary art of Flannery O'Connor

O'Hara, Scarlett

175i   Sophia Porter: Texas' own Scarlett O'Hara

Oakland, CA

310z   Equal opportunity for babies? Not in Oakland!

OASI

see Old Age and Survivors Insurance

Oates, Joyce Carol

27m   Women and madness in the fiction of Joyce Carol Oates

135a   Is there a female voice? Joyce Carol Oates replies

Oberlausitz, Germany

145n   Social insurance and the family work of Oberlausitz home weavers in the late nineteenth century

Obesity

137p   Gender and obesity

365f   Eating disorders: Obesity and anorexia

Object

148f   The role of Sioux women in the production of ceremonial objects: The case of the star quilt

212c   'On the other side of the billboard...': Pornography, male fantasies and the objectification of women

364i   Subject or object? Women and the circulation of valuables in highlands New Guinea

371d   Essential objects and the sacred: Interior and exterior space in an urban Greek locality

Objectivity

120g   On the oppression of women in philosophy — or, Whatever happened to objectivity?

314e   The natural sciences: Casting a critical eye on 'objectivity'

342b   Women's nature and scientific objectivity

Obligation

116n   The obligations of mothers and fathers

195a   The obligations of mothers and fathers

Obscenity

55m   Appendix B: Review of legal cases regarding US Code, Section 1461 (mailing obscene or crime-inciting matter)

55n   Appendix C: Cases related to obscenity issues

Observer

280b   Pornography: Its consequences on the observer

Obstetrics

36x   An obstetrician's perspective

353j   "On the importance of the obstetrick art": Changing customs of childbirth in America, 1760 to 1825

353l   The Loomis trial: Social mores and obstetrics in the mid-nineteenth century

395k   Obstetrical complications associated with traditional medical practices at Nsukka

Ocampo, Victoria

74a   "Feminine" testimony in the works of Teresa de la Parra, María Luisa Bombal, and Victoria Ocampo

Occupation

see also Employment

13e   Bearers of burdens: Occupational safety without discrimination

41e   Shifts in the occupational and employment status of black women: Current trends and future implications

45l   Sex differences in the educational and occupational goals of black college students: Continued inquiry into the black matriarchy theory

46g   Occupational pension plans and spouse benefits

58c   Bazaar and service occupations

58f   Women in modern occupations

71i   The effects of Asian-American kinship systems on women's educational and occupational attainment

72a   The lack of political involvement of Hispanic women as it relates to their educational background and occupational opportunities

72b   Puerto Rican women in education and potential impact on occupational patterns

85f   Occupational mobility and the use of the comparative method

85g   The expert's view? The sociological analysis of graduates' occupational and domestic roles

89l   Occupational segregation, wages and profits when employers discriminate by race and sex

169p   Occupational health and safety for women workers: Some teaching models

199m   Contrasting sexual harassment in female- and male-dominated occupations

209u   Occupational health and the design of work

233f   Birth defects and parental occupation

233i   Occupational fatigue and preterm birth

233s   The contribution of the occupational health services

244d   Occupation-family-linkages as perceived by men in the early stages of professional and managerial careers

255g   Purdah in Pakistan: Seclusion and modern occupations for women

260c   Patterns of occupational segregation by sex in the labor market

265h   Sex typing in occupational preferences of high school boys and girls

271f   Sex-role ideology and sex bias in judgments of occupational suitability

272a   Trends in occupational segregation by sex and race, 1960-1981

272c   Job changing and occupational sex segregation: Sex and race comparisons

272d   Occupational sex segregation: Prospects for the 1980s

272e   Occupational segregation and labor market discrimination

272f   Toward a general theory of occupational sex segregation: The case of public school teaching

272g   Commentary: Strober's theory of occupational sex segregation

272i   Sex typing in occupational socialization

272m   Occupational desegregation in CETA programs

296h   Powerless by definition: Occupational and pay patterns of women in the workplace

320l   Sex differences in the implications of the links between major departments and the occupational structure

324c   Occupational atypicality: Changes, causes, and consequences

344q   Clerical work: The female occupation

387c   Women in the occupational world: Social disruption and conflict

405l   Women in contemporary Poland: Their social and occupational position and attitudes toward work

421k   Feminist egalitarianism, social action orientation and occupational roles: A cross-national study

421x   Occupational choice among female academicians - The Israeli case

424b   Trends in female labour force participation and occupational shifts in urban Korea

424h   Occupational health hazards of female industrial workers in Malaysia

446e   The educational and occupational skill level of industrial workers

466e   Rich woman, poor woman: Occupation differences in a textile producing village in Central Java

468a   The making of a female occupation: A case study of cleaning work

Oceania

246h   "Sing to the Lord a New Song": Women in the churches of Oceania

Odyssey

419b   "Reverse similes" and sex roles in the *Odyssey*

Oedipus

88d   The inner-genital phase - prephallic and preoedipal

88e   A suggested developmental sequence for a preoedipal genital phase

88f   The female oedipus complex: Its antecedents and evolution

106i   Oedipus as hero: Family and family metaphors in Nietzsche

Of Human Bondage

155a   The prostitute as scapegoat: Mildred Rogers in Somerset Maugham's *Of Human Bondage*

Offender

see also Crime

78e   The new female offender: Reality or myth?

111d   Family violence: Women as offenders or victims

111f   The female juvenile offender

111k   The treatment of convicted female offenders in the criminal justice system

111l   Women in court: Assisting the female offender

111n   Managing the female offender: Some observations

111o   Managing the female offender: Crisis and change in the California Institution for Women

111p   Prison treatment of female offenders in Mexico

111q   Sex-role concepts among federal female offenders

146h   The incest offender

159m   Criminality amongst women in India: A study of female offenders and female convicts

165g   Delinquency causation in female offenders

276b   The relationship between treatment for sex offenders and the court

276c   Prediction of recidivism and the evaluation of treatment programs for sex offenders

276f   Ethics and ethical dilemmas in the treatment of sex offenders

276g   Sentencing the sexual offender

284o   Interviewing child victims of sex offenders

291g   Sexual deviance: The adult offender

349s   Judicial paternalism and the female status offender: Training women to know their place

349t   Police processing of female offenders

392k   Discriminatory sentencing of women offenders: The argument for ERA in a nutshell

404x   Young female offenders in Massachusetts: Toward leaving the juvenile justice system successfully

404y   The unique employment problems of female offenders returning to the community and labor market

Offense

183j   Sexual offences

219a   The victim's contribution to sexual offences

284p   The protection of the child victim of a sexual offense in the criminal justice system

Office

50h   Typing our way to freedom: Is it true that new office technology can liberate women?

86c   The health hazards of office work

86e   Closed office-building syndrome

181d   Technology and work degradation: Effects of office automation on women clerical workers

199h   Brave new office: The changing world of the legal secretary

209a   Choices in the development of office automation

209b   Office automation: Jekyll or Hyde?

209g   The issue of employment and office technology from a managerial perspective

209o   Staff participation in office systems' design: Two case studies at the World Bank

209s   Office computerization: Research then and now

209v   An issue of respect: Women workers demand healthy and safe offices

209x   Health hazards in the computerized office

209dd   Women and the fight around office automation

209ii   Public policy and the employment impacts of office computerization

292g   Education in working-class solidarity: The summer school for office workers

307r   Women's work in the office of the future

307dd   The next move: Organizing women in the office

410c   The effects of sex on recruitment: Connecticut local offices

470d   New technology and women's office work

Officeholder

410e   Sex differences in role behavior and policy orientations of suburban officeholders: The effect of women's employment

Officer

78w   Female patrol officers: A review of the physical capability issue

78y   Doing time with the boys: An analysis of women correctional officers in all-male facilities

108h   *My Childhood Years*: A memoir by the czarist cavalry officer, Nadezhda Durova

219e   Police officer or doctor? Police surgeons' attitudes and opinions about rape

Official

390s   Right-wing union officials versus married women workers

414i   The gender liberation: Black women as elected officials in Oklahoma

Offspring

9p   The effects of alcohol on the fetus and offspring

Oglala

see also American Indian

439f   Menstruation and reproduction: An Oglala case

Ohio

147dd   The history of women's intercollegiate athletics in Ohio, 1945-1972

201g   The great uprising in Cleveland: When sisterhood failed

353cc   Homeopathy and sexual equality: The controversy over coeducation at Cincinnati's Pulte Medical College, 1873-1879

473k   The life of Sarah Penfield, rural Ohio grandmother: Tradition maintained, tradition threatened

Oklahoma

226f   Women as legislative candidates in six states

414f   Women in Oklahoma education

414g   College life in Oklahoma territory

414h   Woman's suffrage, Oklahoma style, 1890-1918

414i   The gender liberation: Black women as elected officials in Oklahoma

Oktoberfest

303h   Academic women in Mississippi: Oktoberfest 1980

Old Age and Survivors Insurance (OASI)

46b   Supplemental OASI benefits to homemakers through current spouse benefits, a homemaker credit, and child-care dropout years

Old Dominion University

303e   New women at Old Dominion

Older

see also Age

49b   When is old?

135i   May Sarton and fictions of old age

137e   Psychopathology and sex differences in the aged

170f   Care for elderly people: A conflict between women and the state

224e   Old and gay

268n   Senescence, sex roles, and stress: Shepherding resources into old age

285o   Sexual attitudes and activities in old age

287e   Sexuality verboten: Young and old

455d   Aging and old age: The last sexist rip-off

472c   Social class and the older family member

Older Woman

see also Age

16q   The older woman

71m   Elderly Pacific Island and Asian-American women: A framework for understanding

176x   Older lesbians

210d   The sexuality of older women

210e   Beyond the sweatshop: Older women in blue-collar jobs

210f   Beyond the hearth: Older women and retirement

210g   Labor markets and old ladies' homes

210i   Suburban older women

210j   The ever-single elderly woman

210k   Family relationships of older women: A women's issue

210o   Cardiovascular risk factors in the elderly woman

222j   Grandma! What big plans you've got!: The older woman's Ph.D. experience

253k   The health of older women in our society

289l   Continuity of self-actualization: Womanhood in climacterium and old age

295o   Older women and mental health

316j   The lost cause: The aging woman in American feminism

317c   Physical activity as it relates to the health of the aged

317d   The competent older woman

317e   Intergenerational relations in later life: A family system approach

317g   The clinical psychology of later life: Developmental paradigms

317j   Environmental change: The older person as initiator and responder

317k   Institutionalization of the aged

319p   To be aged, Hispanic, and female: The triple risk

324e   Economic consequences of poor health in mature women

326j   Sexual assault of the older woman

328m   Virginia Woolf in her fifties

397e   The older lesbian: Love relationships and friendship patterns

402m   The aging woman in India: Self-perceptions and changing roles

434e   Older women as victims of violence

461h   In praise of older women

472a   Double stigmata: Female and old

472b   The psychosocial problems of older women

472d   The abused older woman: A discussion of abuses and rape

472e   Legal issues affecting older women

472g   The "babushka" or older woman in Soviet society

472i   Widow to widow: The elderly widow and mutual help

472k   Policy directions and program design: Issues and implications in services for the older woman

Olympic

107i   Proportionality and body composition in male and female Olympic athletes: A kinanthropometric overview

107t   Body build of female Olympic rowers

147q   Canadian women at the Olympic games

One Flew Over the Cuckoo's Nest

445l   Westering and woman: A thematic study of Kesey's *One Flew Over the Cuckoo's Nest* and Fisher's *Mountain Man*

Oneself

474f   Creating oneself from scratch

Ontario Federation of Labor (OFL)

323u   Free universal day care: The OFL takes a stand

Ontario, Canada

147ee   Major influences on the development of high school girls' sports in Ontario

Ontology

31d   A different reality: Feminist ontology

120a   Memoirs of an ontological exile: The methodological rebellions of feminist research

Open

43j   An open letter to the academy

118c   Openness and mutuality in process thought and feminist action

474n   *Opening nights:* The opening days

Operation

165n   Sex-role operations: Strategies for women working in the criminal justice system

231q   Outside the operating room of the sex-change doctor

353t   The rise and fall of Battey's operation: A fashion in surgery

Operator

209y   The health impacts of low-level radiation on VDT operators

Opiate

9m   Opiate dependence in women

9q   The effects of opiates, sedative-hypnotics, amphetamines, cannabis, and other psychoactive drugs on the fetus and newborn

Opinion

2a   *Roe v Wade:* Majority opinion and Rehnquist dissent

154b   The crowned dame, dame opinion, and dame philosophy: The female characteristics of three ideals in Christine de Pizan's *L'Avision Christine*

219e   Police officer or doctor? Police surgeons' attitudes and opinions about rape

Opportunity

72a   The lack of political involvement of Hispanic women as it relates to their educational background and occupational opportunities

90i   Ambitions and the opportunity for professionals in the elementary school

93m   Improving job opportunities for women from a U.S. corporate perspective

258e   Educational opportunity and achievement

352d   Power and opportunity in the principalship: The case of two women leaders in education

387r   Job opportunities of black and white working-class women

397m   Lesbians and contemporary health care systems: Oppression and opportunity

426g   Corporate experiences in improving women's job opportunities

436f   Creating employment opportunities for rural women: Some issues affecting attitudes and policy

438a   Opportunities for women in science

438b   Opportunities for women scientists in India

Opposition

51aa   Beyond oppositional analysis: Concluding remarks

83h   The church, the unions, women and the opposition in Brazil

Oppress

50z   Oppressive dichotomies: The nature/culture debate

68n   The black woman: Liberated or oppressed?

91f   The role of the church in the oppression of women

95b   Clara Zetkin: A Socialist approach to the problem of women's oppression

120f   To grow a daughter: Cultural liberation and the dynamics of oppression in Jamaica

120g   On the oppression of women in philosophy — or, Whatever happened to objectivity?

133u   Gay civil rights and the roots of oppression

212p   The 'perks' of male power: Heterosexuality and the oppression of women

224k   Some thoughts on gay/lesbian oppression

224n   Lesbian and gay oppression in the '80s: Androgyny, men and power

227n   Oppressed politics

275n   How words hurt: Attitudes, metaphor and oppression

310j   Teenage oppression and reproductive rights

323n   Triple oppression: Immigrant women in the labour force

371j   Where women must dominate: Response to oppression in a South African urban community

397m   Lesbians and contemporary health care systems: Oppression and opportunity

405g   Marxism and women's oppression: Bolshevik theory and practice in the 1920's

418m   Oppressive dichotomies: The nature/culture debate

430c   Sexuality and women's oppression in Iran

462l   Political oppression and creative survival

Option

43d   Beyond either/or: Feminist options

Oral

81m Socialist feminism between the two World Wars: Insights from oral history

169k Using oral history in the classroom

301g Corn shuckings, fiddle contests, square dances: Oral history with Lily May Ledford

306o Oral history as a resource in teaching women's studies

Ordain

see also Religion

91l Preacher and priest: Typologies of ministry and ordination of women

91n Is partnership possible? Ordained men and unordained women in ministry

115b The ordination of women in the Roman Catholic Church

115e The ordination of women and the 'maleness' of the Christ

152e Homosexuality, celibacy, religious life and ordination

Order

134a Youth service provision, social order and the question of girls

160c Police wives: A reflection of police concepts of order and control

421f Birth order and alienation among college women in Lebanon

Order of the Rose

154c Christine de Pizan and Order of the Rose

Ordinance

101j The All-Pakistan Women's Association and the 1961 Muslim family laws ordinance

Ordinary

30q Ordinary. Extraordinary.

Oregon

90e Clues to sex bias in the selection of school administrators: A report from the Oregon network

111i The Hillcrest School of Oregon: Guided group interaction in a juvenile institution

Oresteia

419g The dynamics of misogyny: Myth and mythmaking in the *Oresteia*

Organ

460l The misnamed female sex organ

Organic-Functional

8i The organic-functional controversy

Organize

see also individual organizations

5c Mobilizing village women: Some organizational and management considerations

39b Female employment and family organization in West Africa

43x Building feminist organizations

45d Emerging patterns of female leadership in formal organizations, or must the female leader go formal?

49f The feminization of the labor force: Research for industrial/organizational psychology

70d Organizing American Indian women

71d Impediments to Asian-Pacific-American women organizing

72f Impediments to Hispanic women organizing

73b Organizing neighborhood women for political and social action

81k "The forgotten woman": Working women, the New Deal, and women's organizations

82v How your organization can participate

86n From grassroots activism to political power: Women organizing against environmental hazards

89k Structured labour markets, worker organization and low pay

90l Administrative careers in public school organizations

90m The sex dimension of school organization: Overview and synthesis

90o The impact of organizational structures on issues of sex equity

93n The impact of organizational structure: Models and methods for change

104i The organization of labour in an Israeli kibbutz

124j The Women's Trade Union League school for women organizers

128e The "Jennie Higginses" of the "New South in the West": A regional survey of socialist activists, agitators, and organizers, 1901-1917

139f Participation in local union organisation. School meals staff: A case study

150jj Black lesbian/feminist organizing: A conversation

163c Network strategies and organizing against female sexual slavery

167j A women's day for disarmament: Notes on organising a decentralised action

192b Mexican women in organization

214a The inside and the outsider: Women in organizations

214d Rhetoric and organizational change: New applications of feminine style

214e Structuring the inside: The impact of organizations on sex differences

217e The organizational woman and the trojan-horse effect

226g Women's organizational strategies in state legislatures

255h From purdah to politics: The social feminism of the all-India women's organizations

272b A woman's place is with other women: Sex segregation within organizations

288c Coping with Cupid: The formation, impact, and management of romantic relationships in organizations

295j Social support and efficacy in advocacy roles: A case study of two women's organizations

305k Getting organized...in the feminist unions

305l Getting organized...in the Confederation of Canadian Unions

305m Getting organized...in the Canadian Labour Congress

305n Getting organized...in Saskatchewan Working Women

307v Paths to power in high technology organizations

307dd The next move: Organizing women in the office

323m Why are so many women unorganized?

323p Organizing freelancers in the arts

323q Women's challenge to organized labour

380e Power and political behaviors in organizations: A new frontier for research on male/female differences

384a The civilizers: Women's organizations and western American literature

387t Sex stratification, technology and organization change: A longitudinal case study of AT&T

388j Women's organizations and social change: The age-of-marriage issue in India

392g Searching for women in organized crime

405d Socialism and feminism: The first stages of women's organizations in the eastern part of the Austrian empire

410g Organizational role orientations on female-dominant commissions: Focus on staff-commissioner interaction

415a Trust and power in the organization: An overview

415c Sexual harassment in the organization

415e Women in organizations: The impact of law

421b Female-headed households and domestic organization in San Isidro, Guatemala: A test of Hammel and Laslett's comparative typology

424f Constraints on the organization of women industrial workers

425g Estimating benefits and costs of antisexist training programs in organizations

434o Toward androgyny in community and organizational practice

454e Ladies bountiful: Organized women's benevolence in early nineteenth-century America

470a Sex and skill in the organisation of the clothing industry

470e Contemporary clothing 'sweatshops', Asian female labour and collective organisation

Organizer

192t Lucy Duran - Wife, mother, and organizer

Organogenic

285l Differential diagnosis and treatment for organogenic and psychogenic erectile dysfunction

Orgasm

12g The obsessive orgasm: Science, sex and female sexuality

289a Introduction: Beyond intercourse and orgasm

359s Group process for women with orgasmic difficulties

Orientation

38k Role transition in early adulthood: Orientations of young black women

45f Psychological orientations to the work role: 1957-1976

239f Homosexual orientation in women and men: A hormonal basis?

315e A dialogue critical issues in women's studies: Race, class, and sexual orientation

Origin

88a On the origins of gender identity

149b Capital, the state and the origins of the working-class household

195f Reproduction, mothering, and the origins of patriarchy

245k The place of the family in the origins of the welfare state

271d Women of South Asian and Anglo-Saxon origins in the Canadian context

289k Dysfunction: Origins and therapeutic approaches

342i Origins of the sexual division of labor

Orlando
202h Why is *Orlando* difficult?

330j *Orlando* and its genesis: Venturing and experimenting in art, love, and sex

Ornament
130j Women and music: Ornament of the profession?

Orthodox
211h Memories of an Orthodox youth

Osage Indians
see also American Indian
414c Women of the Osage: A century of change, 1874-1982

Osteoporosis
53u Epidemiology of osteoporosis

Oswal
255e Purdah among the Oswals of Mewar

Othello
343l Women and men in *Othello*: "What should such a fool/Do with so good a woman?"

Other
452j Lillian Hellman and the strategy of the "other"

Out
176c "Out" at the university: Myth and reality

Out of Home Care
80e Developmental consequences of out-of-home care for infants in a low-income population

Out of Wedlock
309g The effect of government policies on out-of-wedlock sex and pregnancy

Outpatient
252f Aspirotomy for outpatient termination of pregnancy in the second trimester

Outsider
30r Sister/outsider: Some thoughts on Simone Weil

Ovary
53q Risk factors for ovarian cancer

Overland Trail
454m Women and their families on the Overland Trail, 1842-1867

Overweight
29n Weight disorders: Overweight and anorexia

Ovid
419l Rape and rape victims in the *Metamorphoses*

Owen, Robert
417h Housework and utopia: Women and the Owenite socialist communities

Owner
370o Slaves, slave owners, and slave dealers: Sherbro coast and hinterland

466d Land ownership in Negri Sembilan, 1900-1977

Oxford
160a Incorporation and exclusion: Oxford academics' wives

167g Children need smiles not missiles: Planning a walk Oxford mothers for nuclear disarmament

Oxygen
372o Specificity of swim training on maximal oxygen uptake: An inter-sex comparison

372z Effect of increased intensity of training on maximum oxygen uptake and muscular performance of young female cross-country skiers

Pacific
246i European women in the Solomon Islands, 1900-1942: Accommodation and change on the Pacific frontier

Pacific Island
71m Elderly Pacific Island and Asian-American women: A framework for understanding

Package
212g The packaging of women: Science and our sexuality

Paederasty
223t An essay on "Paederasty"

Pagan
194d The cult of Brigid: A study of pagan-Christian syncretism in Ireland

Paid
355k Everyone needs three hands: Doing unpaid and paid work

427g Paid and unpaid work: Contradictions in American women's lives today

Pain
8j The painful woman: Complaints, symptoms, and illness

8m The myofascial pain dysfunction syndrome: An unheeded neuromuscular disorder

240f Chronic pelvic pain

286f "Swinburne planteth, Hardy watereth": Victorian views of pain and pleasure in human sexuality

Painting
see also Art
108f Artemisia Gentileschi: The artist's autograph in letters and paintings

117p Virility and domination in early twentieth-century vanguard painting

474e My grandmother who painted

Pakeha
413j Mummy's boys: Pakeha men and male culture in New Zealand

Pakistan
21i The modern Pakistani woman in a Muslim society

75f Career and employment of women in Pakistan

92c Pakistan: *Mor* and *Tor*: Binary and opposing models of Pukhtun womanhood

92d Pakistan: The role of women in reciprocal relationships in a Punjab village

101j The All-Pakistan Women's Association and the 1961 Muslim family laws ordinance

198j The struggle of women in the national development of Pakistan

255g Purdah in Pakistan: Seclusion and modern occupations for women

395j Health beliefs and behaviors of middle class urban women in Lahore, Pakistan

402d Trends and structure of female labour force participation in rural and urban Pakistan

420f The female migrant in Pakistan

421aa Career constraints among women graduate students in a developing society: West Pakistan. A study in the changing status of women

Pakistani Woman
402l Asian women in Britain: Strategies of adjustment of Indian and Pakistani migrants

Palace
117c The great goddess and the palace architecture of Crete

370r Servitude and worldly success in the palace of Dahomey

401f Power and prestige: Palace women in the Northern Sung (960-1126)

Palestine, Ancient
156q The role of Jewish women in the religion, ritual and cult of Graeco-Roman Palestine

Palimpsest
448i Reading the city as palimpsest: The experiential perception of the city in Doris Lessing's *The Four-Gated City*

Panama
269d New economic roles for Cuna males and females: An examination of socioeconomic change in a San Blas community

269e New roles for males in Guaymí society

269f Being Cuna and female: Ethnicity mediating change in sex roles

Pankhurst, Christabel
125p Christabel Pankhurst: Reclaiming her power

Pankhurst, Sylvia
95d Sylvia Pankhurst: Suffragist, feminist, or socialist?

Panshin, Alexei
131b Alexei Panshin's almost non-sexist *Rite of Passage*

Papa Dick
17r Papa Dick and Sister-Woman: Reflections on women in the fiction of Richard Wright

Papago
see also American Indian
51f Perceptions of menopause by Papago women

Pappenheim, Bertha
30p Anna O./Bertha Pappenheim and me

Papua New Guinea
83b Women, art and community in Papua New Guinea

162h 'A brother is a creative thing': Change and conflict in a Melpa family (Papua New Guinea)

200f Gender, sexuality and marriage: A Kaulong model of nature and culture

200g Images of nature in Gimi thought

200h No nature, no culture: The Hagen case

246c Complementarity: The relationship between female and male in the East Sepik village of Bun, Papua New Guinea

246f Women, work, and change in Nagovisi

246g Pigs, pearlshells, and 'women's work': Collective response to change in highland Papua New Guinea

282d Transforming "natural" woman: Female ritual leaders and gender ideology among Bimin-Kuskusmin

282e Self-interest and the social good: Some implications of Hagen gender imagery

347k Stability in banana leaves: Colonization and women in Kiriwina, Trobriand Islands

Parable

332i Doris Lessing and the parables of growth

474c The parable of the cave or: In praise of watercolors

Paradigm

51a Toward a biosocial paradigm for menopause research: Lessons and contributions from the behavioral sciences

84i A paradigm of philosophy: The adversary method

123i Women in sociological analysis: New scholarship versus old paradigms

126l Of paradigm and paradox: The case of Mary Boykin Chesnut

189k Education: The patriarchal paradigm and the response to feminism

317g The clinical psychology of later life: Developmental paradigms

330g The form of fact and fiction: *Jacob's Room* as paradigm

332a Spiritual *Bildung*: The beautiful soul as paradigm

334a The normal paradigms of a woman's life in the Irish and Welsh texts

343i "I wooed thee with my sword": Shakespeare's tragic paradigms

384q Toward a new paradigm: Mari Sandoz's study of red and white myth in *Cheyenne Autumn*

394h Sedition in a sexist society: The Platteville paradigm

439a Who is Sylvia? On the loss of sexual paradigms

Paradise

192k Silicon Valley: Paradise or paradox?

Paradox

74e The paradoxes of Silvina Bullrich

126l Of paradigm and paradox: The case of Mary Boykin Chesnut

147h Sport and the Cult of True Womanhood: A paradox at the turn of the century

186r The singing wound: Intensifying paradoxes in May Sarton's " A Divorce of Lovers"

192k Silicon Valley: Paradise or paradox?

196f Gertrice/Altrude: Stein, Toklas, and the paradox of the happy marriage

232f The paradoxical powers of Tamil women

Paragraph 218

336c Abortion and economic crisis: The 1931 campaign against paragraph 218

Parda

21h Political change: Muslim women in conflict with Parda: Their role in the Indian Nationalist Movement

Parent

see also Family

4i Parenting education

16p Women as single parents: Alternative services for a neglected population

29h Parenting: Training mothers as behavior therapists for their children

37n Parenting in black families with young children: A historical perspective

79h A look at prenatal diagnosis within the context of changing parental and reproductive norms

79r Rights of a handicapped neonate: What every parent and professional should know

80h Parents and day care workers: A failed partnership?

86l Walking a tightrope: Pregnancy, parenting, and work

87g Parenthood, marriage, and careers: Situational constraints and role strain

97d Parents, children and the state

129q Relations between parents and children

162k Parental strategies: Calculation or sentiment?: Fostering practices among West Africans

162m Linen was their life: Family survival strategies and parent-child relations in nineteenth-century France

178k Parenting philosophies and practices

185g Personal and social attitudes toward parenting

195d Against "parenting"

195l Parenting and property

203u Housing for single-parent families: A women's design

204a Parental behavior and child development in nontraditional families: An introduction

204i Effects of divorce on parents and children

204j Social development and parent-child interaction in father-custody and stepmother families

210l Concerns about parental health

212a Heterosexuality, couples and parenthood: A 'natural' cycle?

216a Introduction: Parenting in contemporary society

216b Significant sociocultural factors in effective parenting

216c A cross-cultural perspective on parenting

216d Developmental universals and their implications for parental competence

216f Parenting for multiculturalism: A Mexican-American model

216g Parenting in the Native-American community

216k Experts and amateurs: Some unintended consequences of parent education

216l What can "research experts" tell parents about effective socialization?

216o The parent as educator: A home-school model of socialization

216q An alternative perspective on parental support: Child-care information and referral service

216r Organizing delivery of parent education

216s Toward new methods in parent education

216t Parenting in a pluralistic society: Toward a policy of options and choices

233f Birth defects and parental occupation

240e Infertility and alternative parenting

265a Parents' sex role attitudes and children's concepts of femininity and masculinity

271c Parents and the sex-role development of the preschool child

273g Parental sex preferences and sex selection

283b Children and parents: Who chooses?

284k Children not severely damaged by incest with a parent

291c A psychoanalyst's view of sexual abuse by parents

307z Engineered conception: The new parenthood

308c Implicating the family: Teenage parenthood and kinship involvement

308f Adolescent parent programs and family involvement

309l The social consequences of teenage parenthood

309q The children of teenage parents

339i Does becoming a parent mean falling off the fast track?

352n Working and parenting: The male and father role

352o The transition from parenting to working and parenting

359z Attitudes toward parenting in dual-career families

359rr Adaptive and pathogenic aspects of sex-role stereotypes: Implications for parenting and psychotherapy

392o Mothers behind bars: A look at the parental rights of incarcerated women

411i The daughter of aging parents

421c A causal interpretation of the effect of mother's education and employment status on parental decision-making role patterns in the Korean family

427h Sexual inequality: The high cost of leaving parenting to women

467a Parents at work

Paris, France

130c Women, democracy, and revolution in Paris, 1789-1794

175k Adah Isaacs Menken: From Texas to Paris

184m Parisian infants and Norman wet nurses in the early nineteenth century: A statistical study

379q Responses to the political activism of Women of the People in revolutionary Paris, 1789-1793

442h Publishing in Paris

444a Women of the popular classes in revolutionary Paris, 1789-1795

Parker, Bonnie

175r "Tell them I don't smoke cigars": The story of Bonnie Parker

Parkin, Frank

378k The party identifications of women: Parkin put to the test

Parliament

23f The Parliamentary wife: Participant in the 'two-person single career'

167k Organising a mass lobby of Parliament: Families against the bomb

235e Parliament and the law

436k The impact of the women's movement and legislative activity of women MPs on social development

Parnell, Anna

338i Rewriting history: Anna Parnell's The tale of a great *sham*

Parody

202e *Jacob's Room* as comedy: Woolf's parodic *Bildungsroman*

Parole

see also Crime

111s Issues in the application of parole guidelines to females

111t Recent development in probation and parole in British Columbia

165h Are females treated differently? A review of the theories and evidence on sentencing and parole decisions

Parot, Adele

147x Adele Parot: Pathfinder for the Dioclesian Lewis school of gymnastic expression in the American west

Parra, Nicanor

313q Vipers, victims, and virgins: Women and their relationships with men in the poetry of Nicanor Parra

Part-Time

249c Paying your dues, part-time

323g Part-time work and unions

446q Part-time employment of women

Parthenogenesis

310aa Who is going to rock the petri dish? For feminists who have considered parthenogenesis when the movement is not enough

Participant

349h The woman participant in Washington's riots

Participate

39d Women's political participation Nigeria

49e Implications of the increasing participation of women in the work force in the 1990's

82c Participation through Title XII, consortia, and the project process in AID

82m Participation by women in Guatemalan cooperatives

82v How your organization can participate

82w Practicalities of participation

107d The influence of the traditional sex roles on women's participation and engagement in sport

139f Participation in local union organisation. School meals staff: A case study

147a Ball game participation of North American Indian women

147j Women's participation in sporting activities as an indicator of a feminist movement in Canada between 1867-1914

209o Staff participation in office systems' design: Two case studies at the World Bank

209ee Alternative models of worker participation

255j Purdah and participation: Women in the politics of Bangladesh

258g Political participation

297c Researching spoonbending: Concepts and practice of participatory fieldwork

316o Women's right to full participation in shaping society's course: An evolving constitutional precept

351i The participation of minority women in higher education

362c Muslim Middle Eastern women's participation in violent political conflict: Causes and characteristics

378h Politics an unnatural practice: Political science looks at female participation

402e Family status and female work participation

421p Changes in Canadian female labour force participation and some possible implications for conjugal power

436b Women and citizenship: Mobilisation, participation, representation

436d Women's education and participation in the labour force: The case of Nigeria

Particular

418n Universals and particulars in the position of women

Patrilocal

282b The gender revolution and the transition from bisexual horde to patrilocal band: The origins of gender hierarchy

Partner

see also Family

5g Gambian women: Unequal partners in rice development projects?

26e Intervention with the abusive partner

287n Surrogate partners and their use in sex therapy

292f Partners in progress: The affiliated schools for women workers, 1928-1939

397d Lesbian relationships: A struggle toward partner equality

Partnership

80h Parents and day care workers: A failed partnership?

209bb Building new partnerships in a high-tech economy

314k Black studies and women's studies: An overdue partnership

Party

81h Two washes in the morning and a bridge party at night: The American housewife between the wars

128b Women in the party bureaucracy: Subservient functionaries

128c May Wood Simons: Party theorist

167d A national campaign: Women's party for survival

205aa Tilly Jean Rolston: She knew how to throw a party

226d Filling the party vacuum: Women at the grassroots level in local politics

226e Women in political parties: Gender differences in motives among California party activists

244a Colombian women in party politics: A token role

378k The party identifications of women: Parkin put to the test

410a The invisible hands: Sex roles and the division of labor in two local political parties

467e The stance of Britain's major parties and interest groups

Passage

40p My father's passage

A *Passage to India*

27k *A Passage to India* as "marriage fiction": Forster's sexual politics

Passion

96c Passion as a mental health hazard

238b Passionlessness: An interpretation of Victorian sexual ideology, 1790-1850

286k Passion between women in the Victorian novel

353d Passionlessness: An interpretation of Victorian sexual ideology, 1790-1850

Passive

332m "Why are you afraid to have me at your side?": From passivity to power in *Salt of the Earth*

Past

45j The past and future of the undergraduate woman

462u Reclaiming our past

Pastoral

242e Writing (from) the feminine: George Sand and the novel of female pastoral

259h Guidance and pastoral care

448e Every woman is an island: Vita Sackville-West, the image of the city and the pastoral idyll

Pater-Patria

440i Pater-patria: Child-rearing and the state

Paternal

see also Father, Reproduce

204e Varying degrees of paternal involvement in infant care: Attitudinal and behavioral correlates

204h Antecedents and consequences of various degrees of paternal involvement in child rearing: The Israeli project

319o The nonconsenting sterilization of Mexican women in Los Angeles: Issues of psychocultural rupture and legal redress in paternalistic behavior

349s Judicial paternalism and the female status offender: Training women to know their place

376b Dealing with dependence: Paternalism and tax evasion in eighteenth-century Rhode Island

392l Chivalry and paternalism: Disparities of treatment in the criminal justice system

Path

231o Garden paths, descents

Pathogenic

133k The pathogenic secret

359rr Adaptive and pathogenic aspects of sex-role stereotypes: Implications for parenting and psychotherapy

Pathology

47b The menopause: Physiological, pathological, and psychological aspects

141d Pathologic aspects of familial carcinoma of breast

280a Prostitution: Profession and pathology

Patient
see also Medicine

11c Women and men problem drinkers: Sex differences in patients served by Iowa's community alcoholism centers

79j Antenatal diagnosis: The physician-patient relationship

140x Psychiatry's problem with no name: Therapist-patient sex

141i Genetic counseling, patient and family management: Familial breast cancer

165k Female patients and the medical profession in jails and prisons: A case of quintuple jeopardy

190w The psychological concomitants of menarche in psychiatric patients

190y Premenstrual affective syndrome in adolescent and adult psychiatric patients

268o Sex roles, psychological assessment, and patient management

284h Sexual assault center emergency room protocol: Child/adolescent patients

285b Eros and thanatos: Lingering taboos in doctor-patient communication

285f Sexual feelings in the terminally ill patient

285j Potency and its effects on patients

359i The psychiatrist-woman patient relationship

359k Psychiatry's problem with no name: Therapist-patient sex

359qq Women patients and women therapists: Some issues that come up in psychotherapy

Patriarchy

32p Our language, our selves: Verena Stefan's critique of patriarchal language

42f Patriarchy and matriarchy

43o Patriarchy and capitalism

79nn Reflections: Uncovering patriarchal agendas and exploring woman-oriented values

84e Evolution and patriarchal myths of scarcity and competition

84n Political philosophy and the patriarchal unconscious: A psychoanalytic perspective on epistemology and metaphysics

103b The state, the patriarchal family, and working mothers

103d The transformation of patriarchy: The historic role of the state

106h Patriarchal liberalism and beyond: From John Stuart Mill to Harriet Taylor

126g The contest between androgyny and patriarchy in early western tradition

131e Coming Home: Four feminist utopias and patriarchal experience

138g Gender, patriarchy and class in the popular education of women

139b Patriarchal exploitation and the rise of English capitalism

139c Not so much a factory, more a form of patriarchy: Gender and class during industrialisation

139j Patriarchal structures: The case of unemployment

179b Patriarchy - A working definition

189k Education: The patriarchal paradigm and the response to feminism

193d Socialisation in patriarchal society

195f Reproduction, mothering, and the origins of patriarchy

206c The patriarchal thread - A history of exploitation

229c Prepatriarchial female/goddess images

229pp WITCH: Spooking the patriarchy during the late sixties

254l Communication or collusion?: Maneuvering through the maze of patriarchal theology

282j Women, warriors, and patriarchs

321n Can there be justice for women under capitalism?: Questions about 'patriarchy'

328d Fathers in general: The patriarchy in Virginia Woolf's fiction

332l Exiting from patriarchy: The lesbian novel of development

354i Medicine and patriarchal violence: The social construction of a "private" event

369g What is the real material base of patriarchy and capital?

369h Capitalism is an advanced stage of patriarchy: But Marxism is not feminism

369k Mothers, fathers, and children: From private to public patriarchy

369l The marriage of capitalist and patriarchal ideologies: Meanings of male bonding and male ranking in U.S. culture

369m The unhappy marriage of patriarchy and capitalism

418o Subjectivity, materialism and patriarchy

428c Capitalism, imperialism, and patriarchy: The dilemma of Third-World women workers in multinational factories

440e Capitalism, patriarchy and the city

462m Patriarchy and death

464f Despotism and civil society: The limits of patriarchal citizenship

Patriotism

129dd Patriotism: A menace to liberty

444j Patriot mothers in the post-risorgimento: Women after the Italian revolution

Patrol

78w Female patrol officers: A review of the physical capability issue

Patron

363d Patrons, politics, and schools: An arena for Brazilian women

Patronage

270k Changing patterns of patronage: A study in structural change

Pattern

45d Emerging patterns of female leadership in formal organizations, or must the female leader go formal?

45e Ground rules for marriage: Perspectives on the pattern of an era

53c The effect of employment, family and job stress on coronary heart disease patterns in women

53e Changing patterns of smoking and risk of disease

136b Gender patterns in touching behavior

159f Changing patterns of female criminality in Germany

165d Exploring female crime patterns: Problems and prospects

186j Patterns of love and friendship: Five novels by May Sarton

191b Patterns of diagnoses received by men and women

203h Women's travel patterns in a suburban development

231i Russian working women: Sexuality in bonding patterns and the politics of daily life

260c Patterns of occupational segregation by sex in the labor market

296c Women in intergenerational patterns of power and influence

300g Patterns of urbanization in the Philippines

309f Contraceptive patterns and premarital pregnancy among women aged 15-19 in 1976

435e Alternative work patterns and the double life

Paul, Alice

125q Alice Paul: The quintessential feminist

Pauper

400b Rural pauperization: Its impact on the economic role and status of rural women in Bangladesh

Pay
see also Comparable Worth, Earn, Equal Pay, Income, Low Pay, Salary, Wage

65i Assessing pay discrimination using national data

66b Job evaluation and pay setting: Concepts and practices

67b Job evaluation and pay setting: Concepts and practices

243m Husbands' paid work and family roles: Current research issues

296h Powerless by definition: Occupational and pay patterns of women in the workplace

425i Job evaluation and discrimination: Legal, economic, and measurement perspectives on comparable worth and women's pay

440b Public policies and the paid work of women

463b Intra-household implications of the involvement of women in the paid labor force

Peace

40oo Alice Walker's women: In search of some peace of mind

124l Women and peace

167h On common ground: The women's peace camp at Greenham Common

179m The peaceful sex

195n Preservative love and military destruction: Some reflections on mothering and peace

205k Women on campus in British Columbia: Strategies for survival, years of war and peace, 1906-1920

215d The balance of terror: Deterrence and peace-keeping

215h A voice from the peace camps: Greenham Common and Upper Heyford

215m Alternative defence: Nonviolent struggle and peace building

215t The women's peace crusade: The history of a forgotten campaign

215u Womanpower and nuclear politics: Women and the peace movement

390i The Women's Peace Army

444k "The mother half of humanity": American women in the peace and preparedness movements in World War I

Peasant

104a Aspects of non-capitalist social relations in rural Egypt: The small peasant household in an Egyptian delta village

144c Family and 'modernisation': The peasant family and social change in nineteenth-century Bavaria

153i Beyond the peasant to proletarian debate: African household formation in South Africa

350c Peasant production, proletarianization, and the sexual division of labor in the Andes

428r Global industries and Malay peasants in peninsular Malaysia

Pedagogy

14i Studying slavery: Some literary and pedagogical considerations on the black female slave

126c Women knowing: Feminist theory and perspectives on pedagogy

306i Feminist pedagogy: Lost voices of American women

306l Southern women's literature and culture: Course development and the pedagogical process

441h Feminist pedagogy and technology: Reflections on the Goddard feminism and ecology summer program

Pederast

284v The pederasts

Pedestal

108i Neither auction block nor pedestal: *The Life and Religious Experience of Jaren Lee, A Coloured Lady*

344gg Keep us on the pedestal: Women against feminism in twentieth century America

Pediatric

469h The utilization of pediatric health services by Hispanic mothers

Pedophilia

224f Happy families? Paedophilia examined

224g Childhood sexuality and paedophilia

419i Plato: Misogynist, phaedophile, and feminist

Peer

57f Peer communication and sexuality

249j A jury of one's peers

Pelletier, Madeline

95c When radical and socialist feminism were joined: The extraordinary failure of Madeleine Pelletier

Pelvic

16h A pelvic teaching program

53i Pelvic inflammatory disease: Causes and consequences

240f Chronic pelvic pain

Penfield, Sarah

473k The life of Sarah Penfield, rural Ohio grandmother: Tradition maintained, tradition threatened

Pennsylvania

153m Gender division within the U.S. working class: Households in the Philadelphia area, 1870-1945

353gg "Little world of our own": The Pennsylvania Hospital Training School for Nurses, 1895-1907

Pennyroyal

301c Pipsissewa, Calamus, and Pennyroyal

Pension

46g Occupational pension plans and spouse benefits

205q "Services rendered, rearing children for the state": Mothers' pensions in British Columbia 1919-1931

447h Sex discrimination in group pensions

465b Members and survivors: Women and retirement-pensions legislation

Pentimento

452k The metaphysics of matrilinearism in women's autobiography: Studies of Mead's *Blackberry Winter*, Hellman's *Pentimento*, Angelou's *I Know Why the Caged Bird Sings*, and Kingston's *The Woman Warrior*

People

74f Elena Poniatowska: Witness for the people

142h How George Eliot's people think

170f Care for elderly people: A conflict between women and the state

310t Born and unborn: The implications of reproductive technologies for people with disabilities

341b Thin fat people

417p Findhorn, Scotland: The people who talk to plants

444e Old wine in new bottles: The institutional changes for women of the people during the French revolution

Peptide

28d Hypothalamic peptides and sexual behavior

Peranankan

466b The Peranankan Chinese woman at a crossroad

Perception

see also Image, Self Image, Self Perception

20d Meridians of perception: A reading of *The Journals of Susanna Moodie*

24d Perceptual and cognitive mechanisms in human sexual attraction

38j On marital relations: Perceptions of black women

401c Thunder over the lake: The five classics and the perception of woman in early China

410h Perceptions of women's roles on local councils in Connecticut

Perdita

343o A penchant for Perdita on the eighteenth-century stage

Perfect

79o Perfectability and the neonate: The burden of expectations on mothers and their health providers

225j The myth of the perfect body

225p Fat and the fantasy of perfection

Perform

107n Some differences between men and women in various factors which determine swimming performance

122p Ibsen's *A Doll's House*: A directorial perspective on performing Nora

212l Female performers on a male stage: The first women's liberation movement and the authority of men

372m Fundamental performance characteristics in females and males

372q Short time, maximal muscular performance: Relation to muscle lactate and fiber type in females

Perinatology

36n The electronic fetal monitor in perinatology

Period

474j The middle period

Periodicals

176v The lesbian periodicals index

176w Note on "Reading A Subject" in periodical indexes

Perk

212p The 'perks' of male power: Heterosexuality and the oppression of women

Permissive

119g 'An immense verbosity': Permissive sexual advice in the 1970s

280d Sexual permissiveness and its consequences

Perón, Eva

108m Of sparrows and condors: The autobiography of Eva Perón

Perpetual

129cc Perpetual vassalage

Perry, Troy

133s Troy Perry: Gay advocate

Persecution

129o The persecution of Moses Harman

Persia

156b Exit Atossa: Images of women in Greek historiography on Persia

Persian Letters

106d Political and marital despotism: Montesquieu's *Persian Letters*

Person

223n "Pricks" and "Chicks": A plea for persons

231gg Abortion: Is a woman a person?

275l "Pricks" and "chicks": A plea for "persons"

Personae

135d Masculine and feminine personae in the love poetry of Christine dePisan

Personal

14r Researching Alice Dunbar-Nelson: A personal and literary perspective

26i Coping with wife abuse: Personal and social networks

30g Alice Dunbar-Nelson: A personal and literary perspective

43n Race and class: Beyond personal politics

45i Assessing personal and social change in two generations

98h Personal account of the role of a supervisor in the Bangladesh fertility survey

120h The personal is political: Feminism and the helping professions

125l Charlotte Perkins Gilman: The personal is political

185g Personal and social attitudes toward parenting

214m Women, work and friendship: Personal confirmation and support

229bb Expanding personal power through meditation

229gg The personal is political

305a The last ten years: A personal/political view

309m Teenage mothers and teenage fathers: The impact of early childbearing on the parents' personal and professional lives

339k Personal choices

458m Personal problems and adjustment to retirement

Personality

107e Personality research: Implications for women in sport

359n The hysterical personality: A "woman's disease"

Personhood

2e Personhood and the abortion debate

2m Abortion, privacy, and personhood: From *Roe v Wade* to the human life statute

3g Children, personhood, and a pluralistic society

Personification

445j Madness and personification in *Giants in the Earth*

Personnel

395c Women and health care personnel planning

Perspective

67e A foreign perspective

194p Conclusion: New perspectives on mother worship

Persuasion

265p Effectiveness of self-persuasion in producing healthy attitudes towards polygyny

Persuasion

164k In between - Anne Elliot marries a sailor and Charlotte Heywood goes to the seaside

242f *Persuasion* and the promises of love

Perth, Australia

294d Dealing with the 'social evil': Prostitution and the police in Perth and on the eastern goldfields, 1895-1924

Peru

104c Interhousehold co-operation in Peru's southern Andes: A case of multiple sibling-group marriage

172a Squatter settlement decision-making: For men only? (Peru)

172c The only way (Peru)

172l The broken wing (Peru)

347g "The universe has turned inside out...There is no justice for us here": Andean women under Spanish rule

350c Peasant production, proletarianization, and the sexual division of labor in the Andes

388i Rural women and development planning in Peru

Perversion

64n Polymorphemic perversity: Colette's illusory "real"

223o Sexual perversion

Les Petites Filles Modèles

313h La poupée perdue: Ordre et désordre dans *Les Petites Filles Modèles* de la Comtesse de Ségur

PH.D.

222f New brains for old bodies: The impact of emotional and physical stress during the Ph.D. process

222i The impossible dream: The Ph.D., marriage, and family

222j Grandma! What big plans you've got!: The older woman's Ph.D. experience

222l Is the Ph.D. experience worth it?: A discussion

Phallic

88d The inner-genital phase - prephallic and preoedipal

278f Phallic worship: Some personal meditations on a sacred theme

Phase

88b The anal phase

88d The inner-genital phase - prephallic and preoedipal

88e A suggested developmental sequence for a preoedipal genital phase

Phelps, Elizabeth Stuart

383e The heavenly utopia of Elizabeth Stuart Phelps

Phenomenology

229h Why women need the goddess: Phenomenological, psychological, and political reflections

Philadelphia, PA

153m Gender division within the U.S. working class: Households in the Philadelphia area, 1870-1945

Philippines

21d Female elite goals and national development: Some data from the Philippines

300g Patterns of urbanization in the Philippines

300h Rural-urban linkages and migration: A Philippines case study

300n Church-military relations in the Philippines

300o Islamic law in Christian Southeast Asia: The politics of establishing Sharía courts in the Philippines

362f "Big women" and politics in a Philippine fishing town

420i The migration of women in the Philippines

420q Philippine urbanism and the status of women

424k Female domestic servants in Cagayan de Oro, Philippines: Social and economic implications of employment in a 'premodern' occupational role

424m Growth of the bazaar economy and its significance for women's employment: Trends of the 1970s in Davao City, Philippines

424o Employment structure of female migrants to the cities in the Philippines

431f Women and men in Iloilo, Philippines: 1903-1970

431g Sex roles in the Philippines: The ambiguous Cebuana

Philosophy

31g Liberating philosophy: An end to the dichotomy of matter and spirit

84i A paradigm of philosophy: The adversary method

84n Political philosophy and the patriarchal unconscious: A psychoanalytic perspective on epistemology and metaphysics

106b Philosopher queens and private wives: Plato on women and the family

116d Freud: Masculinity, femininity, and the philosophy of mind

116l Women's work: Views from the history of philosophy

120g On the oppression of women in philosophy — or, Whatever happened to objectivity?

132c Mother-daughter relationships: Psychodynamics, politics, and philosophy

154b The crowned dame, dame opinion, and dame philosophy: The female characteristics of three ideals in Christine de Pizan's *L'Avision Christine*

178k Parenting philosophies and practices

189c Methodocracy, misogyny and bad faith: The response of philosophy

275i Feminist linguistics in philosophy

432k The overemphasis on winning: A philosophical look

432l Philosophy of education, physical education, and the sexes

452d Harriet Martineau's *Autobiography*: The making of a female philosopher

Phobia

see also Emotion

29m Anxiety-related disorders, fears, and phobias

137h Gender and phobia

268c Gender ideology and phobias in women

359p Phobias after marriage: Women's declaration of dependence

Phoebe

412j The social gospel according to Phoebe: Methodist deaconesses in the metropolis, 1885-1918

Photo Essay

13c Photo essay: Women and work

Photography

see also Art

30h This is who she is to me: On photographing women

61o Photographs as historical documents (American women through the camera's eye)

81g   Photographing women: The farm security administration work of Marion Post Wolcott

414e   Pioneer women: A photographic perspective

Physical

24a   Physical attractiveness, sex roles and heterosexual attraction

29j   Physical aggression: Treating the victims

78w   Female patrol officers: A review of the physical capability issue

147w   School physical activity programs for the antebellum southern females

178o   Physical health issues

190h   Physical attractiveness and physical stigma: Menstruation and the common cold

210n   Physical changes after menopause

222f   New brains for old bodies: The impact of emotional and physical stress during the Ph.D. process

285e   Physical disability, life-threatening illness, and enhancement of sexual health

317c   Physical activity as it relates to the health of the aged

345b   The physical effects and metabolism of alcohol

Physical Education

see also Education

147c   The rise and development of women's concern for the physical education of American women, 1776-1885: From independence to the foundation of the American Association for the Advancement of Physical Education

147k   Women in sport and physical education in the United States 1900-1914

147l   The effect of changing attitudes toward sexual morality upon the promotion of physical education for women in nineteenth century America

147v   The eastern legacy - the early history of physical education for women

147z   History and structure of the department of physical education at the University of California with special reference to women's sports

147bb   Interscholastic basketball: Bane of collegiate physical educators

176z   Lesbians in physical education and sport

274r   Physical education

432l   Philosophy of education, physical education, and the sexes

432n   Women's physical education: A gender-sensitive perspective

432o   The ethics of gender discrimination: A response to Ann Diller and Barbara Houston's "Women's Physical Education"

Physician

see also Doctor, Medicine

34i   Displaced - the midwife by the male physician

56b   Natural childbirth and the reluctant physician

56c   Taking care of the little woman: Father-physician relations during pregnancy and childbirth

79j   Antenatal diagnosis: The physician-patient relationship

353h   Patterns of abortion and the response of American physicians, 1790-1930

353ee   Doctors or ladies? Women physicians in psychiatric institutions, 1872-1900

353hh   More than "the physician's hand": Skill and authority in twentieth-century nursing

Physics

193r   Girls, physics and sexism

361g   Career paths for women in physics

377h   Factors affecting female participation in advanced placement programs in mathematics, chemistry, and physics

Physiology

28a   The physiology of the menstrual cycle

28e   The psychology of the menstrual cycle: Biological and physiological perspectives

29l   Physiological and reproductive disorders

47b   The menopause: Physiological, pathological, and psychological aspects

277c   Physiology of male sexual arousal

289c   The physiological perspective

372k   Physiological and metabolic responses of female athletes during laboratory and field exercises

372n   Women and sport: An introduction to the physiological aspects

372r   Reproducibility of aerobic power and related physiological variables in women

372s   Exercise-induced changes in estradiol metabolism and their possible physiological meaning

395i   Women's understanding about reproductive physiology and their choice of herbal medicines in Cali, Colombia

460d   Physiological aspects of female sexual development: Conception through puberty

460e   Physiological aspects of female sexual development: Gestation, lactation, menopause, and erotic physiology

460f   Psychological and physiological concepts in female sexuality: A discussion of physiological aspects of female sexual development

Physiotherapy

44g   Physiotherapy

Physique

107l   Physique of female athletes - anthropological and proportional analysis

107r   Physique of college women athletes in five sports

Pie

43i   Who wants a piece of the pie?

Pierce, Mildred

406d   Duplicity in Mildred Pierce

Piercy, Marge

131j   In and out of time: The form of Marge Piercy's novels

Piety

142g   The choir invisible: The poetics of humanist piety

187i   Feminine lay piety in the High Middle Ages: The Beguines

379b   Piety and kin: The limits of antebellum Southern women's reform

Pig

282h   Pigs, women, and the men's house in Amazonia: An analysis of six Mundurucú myths

Pilgrimage

194g   Postindustrial Marian pilgrimage

Pillar

202j   The politics of city space in *The Years*: Street, love, pillar boxes and bridges

Pinar, Florencia

188n   The Spanish love poet: Florencia Pinar

Pineal

51i   Potential role of the pineal gland in the human menstrual cycle

Pink

81i   All pink sisters: The War Department and the feminist movement in the 1920s

Pioneer

147p   Eleonora Randolph Sears, pioneer in women's sports

205g   "Roughing it in the bush" in British Columbia: Mary Moody's pioneer life in New Westminister 1859-1863

306g   "Aunt Amelia's diary": The record of a reluctant pioneer

375k   Clara Shortridge Foltz: Pioneer in the law

384b   Marie Louise Ritter: The pioneer woman in fact and fiction

384d   Reluctant pioneers

384j   Pioneer women in the works of two Montana authors: Interviews with Dorothy M. Johnson and A. B. Guthrie, Jr.

384s   Pioneering the imagination: Eudora Welty's *The Robber Bridegroom*

389a   Precursors and pioneers (1820-1890)

389h   Georgiana Goddard King (1871-1939): Educator and pioneer in medieval Spanish art

413k   Pioneer into feminist: Jane Mander's heroines

414e   Pioneer women: A photographic perspective

Pipsissewa

301c   Pipsissewa, Calamus, and Pennyroyal

Pirate

401i   One woman's rise to power: Cheng I's wife and the pirates

Pisan, Christine de

see Christine, De Pisan

Pitfall

261e   Progress and pitfalls: Reports from participating institutions

Pitjantjatjara, Australia

333f   Women and land rights: The Pitjantjatjara land claims

Pituitary

53l   Epidemiology of pituitary adenomas

372y   Pituitary response to physical exercise: Sex differences

Pizan, Christine de

see Christine, De Pisan

Place

109l   Place and eros in Radcliffe, Lewis, and Brontë

164c The influence of place: Jane Austen and the novel of social consciousness

203g Women's place in the new suburbia

205a "Sundays always make me think of home": Time and place in Canadian women's history

205y Mary Ellen Smith: The right woman in the right place at the right time

317i Growing old "inside": Aging and attachment to place in an Appalachian community

349s Judicial paternalism and the female status offender: Training women to know their place

371g Place and face: Of women in Doshman Ziari, Iran

371k Private parts in public places: The case of actresses

470i A woman's place is her union

Placebo

237e The effect of placebos (premenstrual tension)

271o Mood and behaviour changes in menopausal women receiving gonadal hormones or placebo

Placement

387m Stay home, little Sheba: On placement, displacement, and social change

Placenta

233b The effect of work on placental function and fetal growth

Plains Indian

see also American Indian

148a Introduction: New perspectives on Plains Indian women

148b Beasts of burden and menial slaves: Nineteenth century observations of Northern Plains Indian women

148e Women's work: An examination of women's roles in Plains Indian arts and crafts

148j "Warrior women" - Sex role alternatives for Plains Indian women

148g The political economy of gender: A 19th century Plains Indian case study

Plan

49h Human resource planning and the intuitive manager: Models for the 1990's

54a A systems model for planning culturally specific programs

54d Program planning for Hispanic women: One ideal model

58h Family planning and population policies

82q Issues and alternatives in planning projects for women

174t The women's school of planning and architecture

203n Women in planning: There's more to affirmative action than gaining access

218h Women in development planning: Advocacy, institutionalization and implementation

310l Women as targets in India's family planning policy

319a Family planning practices of Mexican Americans

368n Family planning in post-revolutionary Iran

373c Integration into what? Reflections on development planning for women

388i Rural women and development planning in Peru

395f Perceptions of a family planning campaign in rural Mexico

395h Family planning in rural China

396a Male hegemony in family planning

421e Planning for women in the new towns: New concepts and dated roles

434n Toward a feminist model for planning for and with women

458g Retirement expectations and plans: A comparison of professional men and women

458i Retirement plans and retirement adjustment

462z Guidelines for planners of ritual

463s Can current transportation planning methods analyze women's travel issues?

463u The transportation planning process

Plant

417p Findhorn, Scotland: The people who talk to plants

Plantation

18h The effects of plantation economy on a Polynesian population

393a Wage earner and mother: Compatibility of roles on a Cameroon plantation

Planter

379c The planter's wife revisited: Women, equity law, and the Chancery Court in seventeenth-century Maryland

Plath, Sylvia

127h "A ritual for being born twice": Sylvia Plath's *The Bell Jar*

180r A subtle psychic bond: The mother figure in Sylvia Plath's poetry

399aa Sylvia Plath, a dramatic poet

Plato

106b Philosopher queens and private wives: Plato on women and the family

116q Sex equality and education in Plato's Just State

419i Plato: Misogynist, phaedophile, and feminist

Platteville, WI

394h Sedition in a sexist society: The Platteville paradigm

Play

147g Generalizations on women and sport, games and play in the United States from settlement to 1860

399v Apropos of women and the folk play

432f Employment for women in athletics: What is fair play?

Play (Drama)

see also Drama, Theater, individual playwrights

64l The theatre as literary model: Role-playing in *Chéri* and *The Last of Chéri*

301mm Mock trial (play)

338c Women in the plays of W.B. Yeats

343a The woman's part: Female sexuality as power in Shakespeare's plays

343g Counsels of gall and grace: Intimate conversations between women in Shakespeare's plays

399g *The Story of a Mother* (play)

399ll Women in Pulitzer Prize plays, 1918-1949

399nn Black women in plays by black playwrights

Player

107s Measures of body size and form of elite female basketball players

Playground

284u Preying on playgrounds

Playgroup

241h Dividing the rough and the respectable: Working-class women and pre-school playgroups

Playwright

see also Drama, Theater, individual playwrights

14x Black women playwrights from Grimké to Shange: Selected synopses of their works

112j Mercy Otis Warren: Playwright, poet, and historian of the American revolution (American, 1728-1814)

316c Playwrights, poets, and novelists: Sisters under the skin

399w Anne Nichols: $1,000,000.00 playwright

399nn Black women in plays by black playwrights

Pleasure

225n No progress in pleasure

257a Purity, motherhood, pleasure or threat? Definitions of female sexuality 1900-1970s

286f "Swinburne planteth, Hardy watereth": Victorian views of pain and pleasure in human sexuality

296f Mastery and pleasure: A two-factor model of well-being of women in the middle years

Plebeian

130aa The view from Spain: Rocco *finesse* and *espirit* versus plebeian manners

Plight

270j The plight of urban migrants: Dynamics of service procurement in a squatter area

Plot

398g Is 'Chloe liked Olivia' a lesbian plot?

Plurabelle, Anna Livia

409i Anna Livia Plurabelle: The dream woman

Pluralistic

216t Parenting in a pluralistic society: Toward a policy of options and choices

Poem

see also Literature

40hh Imagery in the women poems: The art of Carolyn Rodgers

72i Chicana evolution (poem)

121g "Oh, vision of language!": Dickinson's poems of love and death

150a Poem

150b For a Godchild, Regina, on the occasion of her first love (poem)

150c The damned (poem)

150d Hester's Song (poem)

150f Debra (poem)

150j "I used to think" (poem)

150k The black back-ups (poem)

150u Before I dress and soar again (poem)

150x   Maria de las Rosas (poem)

150aa   What will you be? (poem)

150bb   Among the things that use to be (poem)

150cc   From sea to shining sea (poem)

150ee   Tired poem: Last letter from a typical unemployed black professional woman (poem)

150gg   Billy de Lye (poem)

150ll   For strong women (poem)

150mm   Black goddess (poem)

186q   Metaphor in five garden poems by May Sarton

186r   The singing wound: Intensifying paradoxes in May Sarton's " A Divorce of Lovers"

211w   The secret Jew: An oral tradition of women (poem)

211x   Spring cleaning ritual on the eve of full moon Nisan (poem)

212s   Poems on my sons

215c   Three poems

215g   Two poems

215r   Poem

231aa   Bestiary (poem)

231z   In the morning (poem)

301a   Celebrate Emma (poem)

301d   Genealogy (poem)

301k   The rape of Dona (poem)

301ll   Mill village (poem)

301y   Tessa (poem)

301cc   My grandmother's gift (poem)

301ee   Two poems for Minnie's boy

301gg   The prodigal child's homecoming: California to Georgia (poem)

301ll   The challenge (poem)

301pp   Listen! (poem)

303b   IWY: Breaking the silence: a fantasy (poem)

303n   To Delois and Willie (poem)

310q   If you would be the mother of a son (poem)

331h   Poems by "The Lady" in *La Chasse et le depart d'amours (1509)*

417d   Al dente (poem)

417g   A song of Sojourner Truth (poem)

417i   What's that smell in the kitchen? (poem)

417m   A litany for survival (poem)

417o   Tulsa (poem)

417z   The land of ordinary people: For John Lennon (poem)

417dd   Outcome of the matter: The sun (poem)

433j   Some poems from *Citra* by Radindranath Tagore

445a   The old one and the wind (poem)

Poet

see also individual poets

14v   Afro-American women poets of the nineteenth century: A guide to research and bio-bibliographies of the poets

40h   Gwendolyn Brooks: Poet of the whirlwind

74d   Affirmation and resistance: Women poets from the Caribbean

112j   Mercy Otis Warren: Playwright, poet, and historian of the American revolution (American, 1728-1814)

188c   The French courtly poet: Marie de France

188n   The Spanish love poet: Florencia Pinar

316c   Playwrights, poets, and novelists: Sisters under the skin

399aa   Sylvia Plath, a dramatic poet

442i   Poets and versifiers, singers and signifiers: Women of the Harlem Renaissance

445g   Women poets and the "Northwest School"

474o   The education of a poet

Poetics

20c   Margaret Atwood and the poetics of duplicity

40i   Gwendolyn Brooks' poetic realism: A developmental survey

142g   The choir invisible: The poetics of humanist piety

211p   History, fiction, and the tradition: Creating a Jewish feminist poetic

Poetry

see also Literature

39u   Images of black women in Afro-American poetry

40o   Lucille Clifton: Warm water, greased legs, and dangerous poetry

40u   Sweet soft essence of possibility: The poetry of Nikki Giovanni

40z   In the name of the father: The poetry of Audre Lord

40ii   Running wild in her soul: The poetry of Carolyn Rodgers

40ll   The poetry of Sonia Sanchez

40pp   Fields watered with blood: Myth and ritual in the poetry of Margaret Walker

121f   "The love of thee-a prism be": Men and women in the love poetry of Emily Dickinson

121h   How "Low feet" stagger: Disruptions of language in Dickinson's poetry

121i   "Ransom in a voice": Language as defense in Dickinson's poetry

132k   Poetry is not a luxury

135d   Masculine and feminine personae in the love poetry of Christine de Pisan

135f   Symbol, mask, and meter in the poetry of Louise Bogan

150m   "Under the days": The buried life and poetry of Angelina Weld Grmiké

176g   "Kissing/Against the Light": A look at lesbian poetry

180r   A subtle psychic bond: The mother figure in Sylvia Plath's poetry

186p   The sculptor and the rock: Some uses of myth in the poetry of May Sarton

186s   "The risk is very great": The poetry of May Sarton

278h   Erotic poetry in English

313q   Vipers, victims, and virgins: Women and their relationships with men in the poetry of Nicanor Parra

331c   The woman's song in medieval German poetry

338b   The female principle in Gaelic poetry

384u   A laddered, rain-bearing rug: Paula Gunn Allen's poetry

397r   Without approval: The lesbian poetry tradition

408p   Sexual politics and the theme of sexuality in Chicana poetry

449f   A woman's voice: The poetry of Yungtzu

453l   Madonna or witch: Women's muse in contemporary American poetry

Poland

52m   Women and the family in Poland

104f   A note on the custom of 'paying off' on family farms in Poland

105c   Marital expectations of wives in contemporary Poland

111c   Women's criminality in Poland

159g   The criminality of women in Poland

243a   Urban and rural working women in Poland today: Between social change and social conflict

405l   Women in contemporary Poland: Their social and occupational position and attitudes toward work

405m   Procreation and new definitions in the role of women in a Soviet bloc country: The case of Poland

Polarity

49k   Reflections on polarities and bias

Polarization

144b   Family and role-division: The polarisation of sexual stereotypes in the nineteenth century - an aspect of the dissociation of work and family

Police

26f   Police intervention

76e   'The policing of families'

78v   A century of women in policing

160c   Police wives: A reflection of police concepts of order and control

219e   Police officer or doctor? Police surgeons' attitudes and opinions about rape

219g   Crisis intervention with victims of forcible rape: A police perspective

235f   The police and the courts

294d   Dealing with the 'social evil': Prostitution and the police in Perth and on the eastern goldfields, 1895-1924

327g   Functions of the police and the justice system in family violence

349e   The economics of female criminality: An analysis of police blotters, 1890-1976

349t   Police processing of female offenders

Policy

see also Social Policy, Public Policy

3a   Social science and ethical issues: The policy implications of poll data on abortion

18e   Population policy, family size, and the reproduction of the labor force in India: The case of Bombay

37s   Policies affecting the status of black children and families

53v   Implications of epidemiologic data for developing health policy for women

58h   Family planning and population policies

63a   The sexually integrated prison: A legal and policy evaluation

65h   A policy-capturing application in a union setting

79k   Policy decisions in prenatal diagnosis: The example of fetal alcoholism syndrome

86k   Keeping women in their place: Exclusionary policies and reproduction

93a   The policy and problem: Overview of seven countries

103f   Women and housing: The impact of government housing policy

103g   Fiscal policy and family structure

103v   Afterword: Feminism and families in a liberal policy

111u   Problems of policy development in criminal justice

173f   Public support for pro-choice abortion policies in the nation and states: Changes and stability after the *Roe* and *Doe* decisions

209d   Women, technological change and employment levels: The role of trade unions policies

209e   Government policies on new information technologies and their implications for employment: An overview of EEC countries, with particular reference to women

216j   Implications for national policy decisions: The black family perspective

226k   Women's collaborative activities and city life: Politics and policy

226l   State and local policies on motherhood

260i   Policies and implementation of anti-discrimination strategies

263m   The new economic readjustment policies: Implications for Chinese urban working women

273i   Toward a moral policy for sex choice

283p   Public expenditure and budgetary policy

284m   Incest policy recommendations

284w   Policy recommendations on child pornography control

288k   Policy statement and definition of sexual harassment

288l   A federal response to sexual harassment: Policy-making at Johnson Space Center, NASA

288m   Policy on sexual harassment

308d   Government policies related to teenage family formation and functioning: An inventory

308e   Sex education and the prevention of teenage pregnancy: An overview of policies and programs in the United States

309g   The effect of government policies on out-of-wedlock sex and pregnancy

317b   Life satisfaction research in aging: Implications for policy development

360k   Sexual intimacy between psychotherapists and clients: Policy implications for the future

360m   New sex therapies: Policy and practice

368g   To veil or not to veil: A matter of protest or policy

373m   The plight of the invisible farmer: The effect of national agriculture policy on women in Africa

373p   Applying policy analysis to women and technology: A framework for consideration

385i   Women's work in a communal setting: The Tanzanian policy of *Ujamaa*

395g   The political economy of population policy in South Africa

410e   Sex differences in role behavior and policy orientations of suburban officeholders: The effect of women's employment

410i   Commissions on the status of women and building a local policy agenda

411f   Multiple roles of midlife women: A case for new directions in theory, research, and policy

420s   Women in Asian cites: Policies, public services, and research

423f   Future research and policy questions

435h   The womb factor: Pregnancy policies and employment of women

435l   The foreign policy beliefs of women in leadership positions

436e   Women in government as policy-makers and bureaucrats: The Turkish case

436f   Creating employment opportunities for rural women: Some issues affecting attitudes and policy

446r   The position of women and demographic policy

447p   Challenges to corporate policy

463a   Women's travel issues: The research and policy environment

467c   Managing work and family life: A comparative policy overview

472k   Policy directions and program design: Issues and implications in services for the older woman

Policymaking

36y   Policymaking and projections overview

36z   Forces impacting on the policymaker

36bb   The ethicist in policymaking

226m   Resources and constraints on women in the policymaking process: States and local arenas

360b   Female psychologists in policymaking positions

427a   Introduction: Government response to working women and their families: Values, the policy-making process, and research utilization

Polish

73h   The economic struggles of female factory workers: A comparison of French, Polish, and Portuguese immigrants

Polite

300d   The psychology of politeness among the Javanese

356h   How and why are women more polite: Some evidence from a Mayan community

Political Science

23a   Political science, women and feminism

189f   Toward the emasculation of political science: The impact of feminism

378h   Politics an unnatural practice: Political science looks at female participation

Politician

23e   Labor women: Political housekeepers or politicians?

Politics

see also Government, Power

6i   African women in politics

7n   The politics of sado-masochistic fantasies

7v   Lesbian S & M: The politics of dis-illusion

13k   Conditions of entry: Women and politics in Australia

14a   Introduction: The politics of black women's studies

18a   Introduction: Population theory and the political economy of population processes

18j   Country roads take me home: The political economy of wage-labor migration in an eastern Kentucky community

19h   The political trial

21a   Women in Asian cities, their political and economic roles: Research problems and strategies

21f   Women in Indonesian politics: The myth of functional interest

21h   Political change: Muslim women in conflict with Parda: Their role in the Indian Nationalist Movement

21j   Women in politics: A case study of Bangladesh

23d   Women, feminism and the political process

23e   Labor women: Political housekeepers or politicians?

23j   The politics of the National Women's Advisory Council

27k   *A Passage to India* as "marriage fiction": Forster's sexual politics

31k   The political nature of relations between the sexes

35b   Biology, gender, and politics: An assessment and critique

35c   Political ideology, sociobiology, and the U.S. women's rights movement

35e   Sex, endocrines, and political behavior

38o   Political behavior of American black women: An overview

39c   Asante queen mothers in government and politics in the nineteenth century

39d   Women's political participation Nigeria

41d   Black women and the political process in the United States

43a   Political change: Two perspectives on power

43n   Race and class: Beyond personal politics

60b   Male vice and female virtue: Feminism and the politics of prostitution in nineteenth-century Britain

60v   The challenge of profamily politics: A feminist defense of sexual freedom

62c   The politics of single-sex schools

65p   Technical possibilities and political realities: Concluding remarks

68g   Up from the harem? The effects of class and sex on political life in northern India

72a   The lack of political involvement of Hispanic women as it relates to their educational background and occupational opportunities

73b   Organizing neighborhood women for political and social action

77a   Creative women in political change

79l   The politics of prenatal diagnosis: A feminist ethical analysis

80o   The politics of federal day care regulation

81f   Culture and radical politics: Yiddish women writers in America, 1890-1940

83e   Working class Jamaican women: Trade unions and political activity

84b   Aristotle and the politicization of the soul

84c   The unit of political analysis: Our Aristotelian hangover

84n   Political philosophy and the patriarchal unconscious: A psychoanalytic perspective on epistemology and metaphysics

86n   From grassroots activism to political power: Women organizing against environmental hazards

94i   Migrant communities and class politics: The Greek community in Australia

95g   Margarita Nelken: Women and the crisis of Spanish politics

96l   The role and function of women's consciousness raising: Self-help, psychotherapy, or political activation?

97c   The political economy of text publishing

101b   Social reform and women's participation in political culture: Andhra and Madras

101f   Kinship, women, and politics in twentieth-century Punjab

101k   Towards equality? Cause and consequence of the political prominence of women in India

102l   A political diary of an assertive woman

103c   Battered women's shelters and the political economy of sexual violence

103n   The politics of wife abuse

103u   "Sisters" or "comrades"? The politics of friends and families

106a   Introduction: Toward a theory of the family and politics

106d   Political and marital despotism: Montesquieu's *Persian Letters*

106e   Marriage contract and social contract in seventeenth-century English political thought

106m   Kafka and Laing on the trapped consciousness: The family as political life

116f   The political epistemology of "masculine" and "feminine"

119b   Feminism and the definition of cultural politics

119d   'What kind of woman is she?' Women and Communist Party politics, 1941-1955

119e   The family in socialist-feminist politics

119f   Invisible struggles: The politics of ageing

119h   Sexual politics and psychoanalysis: Some notes on their relation

120h   The personal is political: Feminism and the helping professions

120i   Ideological hegemony in political discourse: Women's specificity and quality

123e   Speaking from silence: Women and the science of politics

125l   Charlotte Perkins Gilman: The personal is political

128f   The politics of mutual frustration: Socialists and suffragists in New York and Wisconsin

130b   Women and politics

132c   Mother-daughter relationships: Psychodynamics, politics, and philosophy

132u   Women in power and politics

144i   Politics and the family: Social democracy and the working-class family in theory and practice before 1914

145g   Female political opposition in pre-1848 Germany: The role of Kathinka Zitz-Halein

148g   The political economy of gender: A 19th century Plains Indian case study

150pp Coalition politics: Turning the century

157e   Public and political: Documents of the woman's suffrage campaign in British

Columbia, 1871-1917: The view from Victoria

163a   International politics of female sexual slavery

163h   The torture of women political prisoners: A case study in female sexual slavery

169n   Training women for political action

173g   The politics of abortion in the House of Representatives in 1976

174b   The politics of black women's studies

174z   Charlotte Bunch and Betty Powell talk about feminism, blacks, and education as politics

178h   The politics of the poor

180h   "The mother's history" in George Eliot's life, literature and political ideology

186l   Rage for justice: Political, social and moral consciousness in selected novels of May Sarton

189b   Dancing through the minefield: Some observations on the theory, practice and politics of a feminist literary criticism

192r   La costura en Los Angeles 1933-1939: The ILGWU and the politics of domination

193f   Biological inevitabilities or political choices? The future for girls in science

202j   The politics of city space in *The Years*: Street, love, pillar boxes and bridges

202k   What is to console us?: The politics of deception in Woolf's short stories

205z   The peacock and the guinea hen: Political profiles of Dorothy Gretchen Steeves and Grace MacInnis

207f   'I'm hungry, mum': The politics of domestic budgeting

208f   'I'm hungry, mum': The politics of domestic budgeting

212i   The politics of monogamy

212r   What can one do with a son? Feminist politics and male children

215s   Contemplating a nuclear future: Nuclear war, politics and the individual

215u   Womanpower and nuclear politics: Women and the peace movement

218b   *Sati* or *Shakti*: Women, culture and politics in India

218c   Legitimizing political women: Expanding options for female political elites in Latin America

218e   Riot and rebellion among African women: Three examples of women's political clout

220c   The power politics of motherhood

224a   Culture and politics

225a   Pleasure and danger: Toward a politics of sexuality

225c   The taming of the id: Feminist sexual politics, 1968-83

225g   Above and beyond politics: The sexual socialization of children

225h   Politically correct? Politically incorrect?

225k   The body politic: The defense of sexual restriction by anti-abortion activists

225o   Beyond politics? Children and sexuality

225t   Thinking sex: Notes for a radical theory of the politics of sexuality

226b   Women and state politics: An assessment

226c   Conceptions of the "Political": White activists in Atlanta

226d   Filling the party vacuum: Women at the grassroots level in local politics

226e   Women in political parties: Gender differences in motives among California party activists

226k   Women's collaborative activities and city life: Politics and policy

227e   The politics of housework

227h   The political economy of women's liberation

227n   Oppressed politics

227r   Wages for housework - political and theoretical considerations

229h   Why women need the goddess: Phenomenological, psychological, and political reflections

229q   Consciousness, politics, and magic

229gg The personal is political

229ii Politics, spirituality, and models of change

229jj The politics of feminist spirituality

229ll The politics of women's spirituality

229mm Feminist spirituality: The politics of the psyche

229nn The unnatural divorce of spirituality and politics

229yy Afterword: Feminist politics and the nature of mind

231i   Russian working women: Sexuality in bonding patterns and the politics of daily life

231cc Male vice and female virtue: Feminism and the politics of prostitution in nineteenth-century Britain

234b   Women, politics and the formation of the Chinese state

244a   Colombian women in party politics: A token role

249i   Career politics and the practice of women's studies

255h   From purdah to politics: The social feminism of the all-India women's organizations

255i   Purdah politics: The role of Muslim women in Indian nationalism, 1911-1924

255j   Purdah and participation: Women in the politics of Bangladesh

258g   Political participation

260l   The political economy of labor market discrimination: A theoretical and comparative analysis of sex discrimination

262h   Context of change: The women's movement as a political process

275t   Moral redescription and political self-deception

282i   Politics and gender in simple societies

283q   Industrial strategy and trade union politics

297d   'It's great to have someone to talk to': The ethics and politics of interviewing women

297e   Incidence or incidents: Political and methodological underpinnings of a health research process in a small Italian town

300o   Islamic law in Christian Southeast Asia: The politics of establishing Sharía courts in the Philippines

305a   The last ten years: A personal/political view

310k   Refusing to take women seriously: 'Side effects' and the politics of contraception

310m Calling the shots? The international politics of depo-provera

313p Women as moral and political alternatives in Conrad's early novels

314l Moving beyond the curriculum: The 'political' value of an integration strategy

336b Beyond *Kinder, Küche, Kirche*: Weimar women in politics and work

342h Ideologies of male dominance as divide and rule politics: An anthropologist's view

344v Women and politics: The real majority

344y The sexual politics of interpersonal behavior

354h The politics of birth control, 1920-1940: The impact of professionals

356l Anger and the politics of naming

362a Women's politics in Africa

362c Muslim Middle Eastern women's participation in violent political conflict: Causes and characteristics

362e Gender, politics and modernization: The Indian case

362f "Big women" and politics in a Philippine fishing town

362g The politics of healing in Malaysia

363b Working class Afro-Surinamese women and national politics: Traditions and changes in an independent state

363d Patrons, politics, and schools: An arena for Brazilian women

378h Politics an unnatural practice: Political science looks at female participation

378m Gender, levels of political thinking and political action

378n Women in positions of political leadership in Britain, France and West Germany

378p The politics of private woman and public man

379l City mothers, city daughters, and the dance hall girls: The limits of female political power in San Francisco, 1913

379q Responses to the political activism of Women of the People in revolutionary Paris, 1789-1793

380c Elected women: Skewers of the political system

380e Power and political behaviors in organizations: A new frontier for research on male/female differences

383a A new anarchism: Social and political ideas in some recent feminist eutopias

383i Opposing necessity and truth: The argument against politics in Doris Lessing's utopian vision

386i Women and political leadership

387n The inexpressive male: Tragedy or sexual politics?

390q Sally Bowen: Political and social experiences of a working-class woman

390x Crime and sexual politics

395g The political economy of population policy in South Africa

396d Depo-provera: The extent of the problem: A case study in the politics of birth control

397o From accommodation to rebellion: The politicization of lesbianism

403d The social and political roles of Arab women: A study of conflict

403h The political mobilization of women in the Arab world

405c Women revolutionaries: The personal and the political

405j Have women's chances for political recruitment in the USSR really improved?

405k The social composition of women deputies in Soviet elective politics: A preliminary analysis of official biographies

408p Sexual politics and the theme of sexuality in Chicana poetry

410a The invisible hands: Sex roles and the division of labor in two local political parties

410b Political culture and selection of women judges in trial courts

413a Women in the political life of New Zealand

416n Class, race, sex, scientific objects of knowledge: A socialist-feminist perspective on the social construction of productive nature and some political consequences

417ff Future visions: Today's politics: Feminist utopias in review

431h Sexual status in Southeast Asia: Comparative perspectives on women, agriculture and political organization

433d British tradesmen of Calcutta, 1830-1900: A preliminary study of their economic and political roles

433e Bengal politics of the first decade of the present century: A defence of extremism

433f Bengal election, 1937: Fazlul Huq and M. A. Jinnah: A study in leadership stress in Bengal politics

436a Women, power and political systems

436g Demography, political reform and women's issues in Czechoslovakia

439h The politics of prostitution

442n Women and politics: The obscured dimension

444g Women in the Chinese communist revolution: The question of political equality

461j The cradle of sexual politics: Incest

462b Class, gender, and religion: A theoretical overview and some political implications

462l Political oppression and creative survival

462s A political perspective

462w Immanence: Uniting the spiritual and political

464b Overcoming the barriers: An approach to the study of how women's issues are kept from the political agenda

464e Prologue to a feminist critique of war and politics

Polity
412o Nineteenth-century A.M.E. preaching women: Cutting edge of women's inclusion in church polity

Poll
421l English-Canadian and French-Canadian attitudes towards women: Results of the Canadian Gallup polls

Pollute
86m The home is the workplace: Hazards, stress, and pollutants in the household

Polygamy
238g The awesome power of sex: The polemical campaign against Mormon polygamy

Polygyny
265p Effectiveness of self-persuasion in producing healthy attitudes towards polygyny

Polymorphemic
64n Polymorphemic perversity: Colette's illusory "real"

Polynesia
18h The effects of plantation economy on a Polynesian population

282k Gender and sexuality in hierarchical societies: The case of Polynesia and some comparative implications

420r Adaptation of Polynesian female migrants in New Zealand

Pom-Pom
432p Putting away the pom-poms: An educational psychologist's view of females and sports

Poniatowska, Elena
74f Elena Poniatowska: Witness for the people

Poor
see also Poverty

37r Multiple public benefits and poor black families

39dd The spread of capitalism in rural Colombia: Effects on poor women

75d Career counselling for poor rural and urban women of South India

98e Learning from poor women: A method of village study

145f Prelude to consciousness: Amalie Sieveking and the Female Association for the Care of the Poor and the Sick

178h The politics of the poor

346d Technologies for poor women

368i Poor women and social consciousness in revolutionary Iran

390b 'Feeding the poor and sapping their strength': The public role of ruling-class women in eastern Australia, 1788-1850

400h Energy needs of poor households: An abstract

466e Rich woman, poor woman: Occupation differences in a textile producing village in Central Java

Popular
138g Gender, patriarchy and class in the popular education of women

158f "Give me a dozen healthy infants": John B. Watson's popular advice on childrearing, women, and the family

181h Women, science, and popular mythology

225f Everything they always wanted you to know: The ideology of popular sex literature

231e Family, sexual morality, and popular movements in turn-of-the-century America

343f As we like it: How a girl can be smart and still popular

Population
see also Demography, Fertility

16p Women as single parents: Alternative services for a neglected population

18a Introduction: Population theory and the political economy of population processes

18b The ideology of population control

18e   Population policy, family size, and the reproduction of the labor force in India: The case of Bombay

18g   Population dynamics and migrant labor in South Africa

18h   The effects of plantation economy on a Polynesian population

18i   Neo-Malthusian ideology and colonial capitalism: Population dynamics in south-western Puerto Rico

58h   Family planning and population policies

80e   Developmental consequences of out-of-home care for infants in a low-income population

173c   The abortion-funding cases and population control: An imaginary lawsuit and some reflections on the uncertain limits of reproductive privacy

279f   Sexual dimorphism and settlement pattern in Middle Eastern skeletal populations

279g   Studies in modern populations: Unit of analysis

279i   Sexual dimorphism for size in seven nineteenth-century Northwest coast populations

350f   The creation of a relative surplus population: A case study from Mexico

380m   A statistical analysis of female participation in work and the effects on the population and socioeconomic development: A case study of Greece

395g   The political economy of population policy in South Africa

400e   Population planning and rural women's co-operative in IRDP women's programme: Some critical issues

440h   Population policies and family policies: State construction of domestic life

Porete, Marguerite

188i   The French heretic Bequine: Marguerite Porete

Pornography

7c   Pornography and the sexual revolution: The backlash of sadomasochism

31h   Pornography and the erotics of domination

55a   Child pornography in the 1970s

55f   Impact of child pornography and sex rings on child victims and their families

55j   Treatment issues with children involved in pornography and sex rings

55k   Combating child pornography and prostitution: One county's approach

78r   Pornography and repression: A reconsideration

155i   The uncommon prostitute: The contemporary image in an American age of pornography

212c   'On the other side of the billboard...': Pornography, male fantasies and the objectification of women

223r   Pornography and respect for women

223s   Pornography, feminism, and censorship

224d   Looking at pornography: Erotica and the socialist morality

230a   Introduction: Pornography and sex research

230c   Pornography: Its effect on violence against women

230e   Effects of massive exposure to pornography

230g   Pornography in Japan: Cross-cultural and theoretical considerations

230h   Sexual stratification, pornography, and rape in the United States

230k   Using psychological research on violent pornography to inform legal change

230l   Bases of liability for injuries produced by media portrayals of violent pornography

231m   Mass market romance: Pornography for women is different

231ee Feminism, moralism, and pornography

238c   Davey Crockett as trickster: Pornography, liminality and symbolic inversion in Victorian America

278i   Literature and pornography

280b   Pornography: Its consequences on the observer

284t   The last porno show

284w   Policy recommendations on child pornography control

305c   Whose body? Whose self? Beyond pornography

439g   Pornography and repression: A reconsideration

Porter, Katherine Anne

127f   Winning: Katherine Anne Porter's women

451e   Irony with a center: Katherine Anne Porter

Porter, Sophia

175i   Sophia Porter: Texas' own Scarlett O'Hara

Porto Alegre, Brazil

473f   Spirit mediums in Umbanda Evangelizada of Porto Alegre, Brazil: Dimensions of power and authority

Portrait

30c   A portrait of the *Puttana* as a middle-aged Woolf scholar

449c   Portraits by a lady: The fictional world of Ling Shuhua

A Portrait of an Artist as a Young Misogynist

409d   Stephen Dedalus and women: A portrait of the artist as a young misogynist

Portray

64o   The anamnesis of a female "I": In the margins of self-portrayal (Colette)

161a   Movement against the portrayal of women in India

161d   Portrayal of women in women's journals

246d   "Women never hunt": The portrayal of women in Melanesian ethnography

391e   Changing Canadian and US magazine portrayals of women and work: Growing opportunities for choice

Portugal

22h   La lyrique portugaise primitive de "Cantigas de Amigo"

364e   Female power and the inequality of wealth and motherhood in north-western Portugal

471i   Women at work in Portugal

Portuguese

73h   The economic struggles of female factory workers: A comparison of French, Polish, and Portuguese immigrants

Position

52a   The changing positions of women and men in comparative perspective

52d   The position of women in the Netherlands: Marginal change

52q   The changing position of black women in South Africa

129u   The economic position of women

131h   An ambiguous legacy: The role and position of women in the English Eutopia

136e   Sex differences in body movements and positions

164g   Jane Austen and the position of women

302i   Salary and position levels of females and males in academic libraries

339b   Women and men at work: Jockeying for position

368f   An analysis of Fida'i and Mujahidin positions on women's rights

403c   The determinants of social position among rural Moroccan women

Possession

162d   Possession and dispossession: Maternity and mortality in Morocco

325d   Possession sickness and women shamans in Korea

325e   Ecstasy and possession: Women of ancient Greece and the cult of Dionysus

Possibility

40u   Sweet soft essence of possibility: The poetry of Nikki Giovanni

Postindustrial

194g   Postindustrial Marian pilgrimage

Postpartum

see also Reproduce

239i   Sources of maternal stress in the postpartum period: A review of the literature and an alternative view

295k   Depression in women: The postpartum experience

359y   Psychological reactions of postpartum women

Postscript

49d   Postscripts and prospects

Potency

285i   Castration and sexual potency

285j   Potency and its effects on patients

Potential

72b   Puerto Rican women in education and potential impact on occupational patterns

Poverty

see also Poor

220d   Poverty: The feminine complaint

248d   The administration of poverty and the development of nursing practice in nineteenth-century England

344aa Poverty is a woman's problem

380i   Poverty viewed as a woman's problem - The U.S. case

380j   Poverty, work, and mental health: The experience of low-income mothers

440f   Women as welfare recipients: Women, poverty and the state

462a   Women, poverty, and economic justice

Powell, Betty

174z Charlotte Bunch and Betty Powell talk about feminism, blacks, and education as politics

Power

see also Government, Politics

23c Losing the numbers game: Women, tokenism and power

33b Women, learning, and power: Eleonora of Aragon and the Court of Ferrara

35f Power structures and perceptions of power holders in same-sex groups of young children

43a Political change: Two perspectives on power

43l Class realities: Create a new power base

48d The courtship game: Power in the sexual encounter

52o Change in the system of social power: Conditions for the social equality of women in Yugoslavia

74c Rosario Castellanos and the structures of power

86n From grassroots activism to political power: Women organizing against environmental hazards

97e Public education and the discourse of crisis, power and vision

120j Thoughts on women and power

122i Levels of female criminal activity as a correlate of female societal power

132f The powers of difference

132u Women in power and politics

132v Women and the uses of power

135q Power or sexuality: The bind of Corneille's *Pulcherie*

138c Gender, resistance and power

140f Men's power with women, other men, and society: A men's movement analysis

149e The expanded reproduction cycle of labour power in twentieth-century capitalism

163e The woman, the love, and the power

166e Rights and responsibility, power and privilege: Women's roles in contemporary Indonesia

171h Men, inexpressiveness, and power

186m Perimeters of power: An examination of *As We Are Now*

195b Why men don't rear children: A power analysis

195o Toward an ethic of nurturance: Luce Irigaray on mothering and power

211k Women and power in the Federation

212e Rape and marital violence in the maintenance of male power

212p The 'perks' of male power: Heterosexuality and the oppression of women

214f The view from the bench: The exercise of power

214g An administrator's viewpoint: The interaction of sex and power

214h Styles of leadership: Power and feminine values

214i Women, men, and professional writing: Signature of power?

214j The battle of the sexes: Power and sexual aggressiveness

214u Conclusion: Integrating love and power

215i Fuel for the nuclear arms race: Nuclear power and nuclear weapons

217h Love and power in marriage

218a An overview of women and power in Africa

218d Tea and power: The anatomy of a conflict

219d The social uses of sexuality: Symbolic interaction, power and rape

220c The power politics of motherhood

224n Lesbian and gay oppression in the '80s: Androgyny, men and power

227k The power of women and the subversion of the community

229o Our heritage is our power

229r The metaphors of power

229aa The healing powers of women

229bb Expanding personal power through meditation

229ee Images of spiritual power in women's fiction

232d Hidden powers: Cultural and socio-economic accounts of Jaffna women

232f The paradoxical powers of Tamil women

246e Revenge suicide by Lusi women: An expression of power

251e The power of persistence: Consciousness raising at international fora - the case of UNCSTD

256e The power of women's networks

257h Heterosexual sex: Power and desire for the other

270g Female labor power relations in the urban Turkish family

296a Introduction: An interdisciplinary perspective on women's power and influence

296b Differential power of women over the life course: A case study of age-roles as an indicator of power

296c Women in intergenerational patterns of power and influence

296d Women's self-perceptions of power and influence across adult life

296e A three-generational analysis of change in women's achievement motivation and power

296i Women's power in the workplace

296j Women and power within the historical dynamic of feminist scholarship

296k Sources and effects of women's power

307v Paths to power in high technology organizations

316k Education, girls, and power

332m "Why are you afraid to have me at your side?": From passivity to power in *Salt of the Earth*

343a The woman's part: Female sexuality as power in Shakespeare's plays

344g Power in dating relationships

344r "Union is power": Sketches from women's labor history

349l Rape: Power, anger, and sexuality

349n Sex roles, power, and woman battering

349p The underside of married life: Power, influence, and violence

351j Women, space, and power in higher education

352d Power and opportunity in the principalship: The case of two women leaders in education

364a Introduction: Property, power and gender relations

364e Female power and the inequality of wealth and motherhood in north-western Portugal

372p Measurement of maximal short-term (anaerobic) power output during cycling

372r Reproducibility of aerobic power and related physiological variables in women

379l City mothers, city daughters, and the dance hall girls: The limits of female political power in San Francisco, 1913

380e Power and political behaviors in organizations: A new frontier for research on male/female differences

398a Power and empowerment

401f Power and prestige: Palace women in the Northern Sung (960-1126)

401i One woman's rise to power: Cheng I's wife and the pirates

404ee Self-power and leadership

415a Trust and power in the organization: An overview

421a Cultural determinants of power for women within the family: A neglected aspect of family research

421p Changes in Canadian female labour force participation and some possible implications for conjugal power

434p Issues of power in social work practice

436a Women, power and political systems

439b Sex and power: Sexual bases of radical feminism

459d Female power, autonomy and demographic change in the Third World

464a Power as ideology: A feminist analysis

468h Love and power: The division of household labour

473f Spirit mediums in Umbanda Evangelizada of Porto Alegre, Brazil: Dimensions of power and authority

Power Politics

20b Atwood's haunted sequences: *The Circle Game, The Journals of Susanna Moodie,* and *Power Politics*

Powerless

7o Sadomasochism: Eroticized violence, eroticized powerlessness

85a Women and their doctors: Power and powerlessness in the research process

296h Powerless by definition: Occupational and pay patterns of women in the workplace

344n The internalization of powerlessness: A case study of the displaced homemaker

356g "Women's language" or "powerless language"?

Pox

194k Pox and the terror of childlessness: Images and ideas of the smallpox goddess in a north Indian village

Practice

60j Difference and domination in the women's movement: The dialectic of theory and practice

80b Infant day care: Relationships between theory and practice

120k Feminist praxis: Feminism and revolution; feminist theory and feminist practice

124n The ERA campaign: Reflections on interpretation and practice

178k Parenting philosophies and practices

189b Dancing through the minefield: Some observations on the theory, practice and politics of a feminist literary criticism

252d A review of abortion practices and their safety

257n Sexual theory and practice: Another double standard

288h Responses of fair employment practice agencies to sexual harassment complaints: A report and recommendations

351h Women's education and career choice: Disparities between theory and practice

360m New sex therapies: Policy and practice

421s Labor force participation and fertility, contraceptive knowledge, attitude and practice of the women of Barbados

434o Toward androgyny in community and organizational practice

443d Feminist psychoanalysis: Theory and practice

Practitioner

360n Feminist therapy: Implications for practitioners

Prairie

175j Elise Waerenskjold: A modern on the prairie

Praxis

120k Feminist praxis: Feminism and revolution; feminist theory and feminist practice

Preach

see also Religion

911 Preacher and priest: Typologies of ministry and ordination of women

366e The struggle for the right to preach

379k "My spirit eye": Some functions of spiritual and visionary experience in the lives of five black women preachers, 1810-1880

412o Nineteenth-century A.M.E. preaching women: Cutting edge of women's inclusion in church polity

429c Preaching through metaphor

429d Preaching in the black tradition

Precipitate

268f Depression in relation to sex roles: Differences in learned susceptibility and precipitating factors

Precocious

376c The crime of precocious sexuality: Female juvenile delinquency and the progressive era

Precursor

389a Precursors and pioneers (1820-1890)

Predetermination

396h Sex predetermination, artificial insemination and the maintenance of male-dominated culture

Predict

51u Predicting the close of menstrual life

276c Prediction of recidivism and the evaluation of treatment programs for sex offenders

Preeminent

351e Sex segregation and male preeminence in elementary classrooms

Preference

193g Factors differentially affecting the science subject preferences, choices and attitudes of girls and boys

273b Measuring sex preferences and their effects on fertility

273f The economics of sex preference and sex selection

273g Parental sex preferences and sex selection

Pregnancy

see also Reproduce

4c Psychiatric aspects of adolescent pregnancy

4d Adolescent sexuality, pregnancy, and childbearing

4h Issues surrounding adolescent pregnancy terminations

4j Legal aspects of adolescent pregnancy

4k Ethical issues of adolescent pregnancy

11h Fetal alcohol syndrome and drinking during pregnancy

31o Rights-conflict, pregnancy, and abortion

50u Competing ideologies of reproduction: Medical and maternal perspectives on pregnancy

56c Taking care of the little woman: Father-physician relations during pregnancy and childbirth

79c Assessment of risks from DES: An analysis of research on those exposed during pregnancy or in utero

79e DES and drugs in pregnancy: A consumer reaction

86l Walking a tightrope: Pregnancy, parenting, and work

118e Becoming human: A contextual approach to decisions about pregnancy and abortion

184q Premarital pregnancy in America, 1640-1971: An overview and interpretation

190o Menarche and teenage pregnancy: A misuse of historical data

190p Menarche and adolescent pregnancy

231l I just came out pregnant

233a Women at work in pregnancy

233c The hazards of work in pregnancy

233h The effects of work in pregnancy: Short- and long-term associations

233u Future research on work in pregnancy

240d Termination of pregnancy

252c Legal aspects of pregnancy termination in Europe

252e The trimester threshold for pregnancy termination: Myth or truth?

252f Aspirotomy for outpatient termination of pregnancy in the second trimester

252j Fact and fancy in the termination of molar pregnancy with particular reference to uterine stimulants

252k Natural prostaglandins alone or in combination for termination of pregnancy

252l Termination of second trimester pregnancy with prostaglandin analogues

252n Termination of pregnancy after intrauterine foetal death

252s Somatic sequelae and future reproduction after pregnancy termination

252t Some considerations on the psychosocial aspects of pregnancy termination

295e The antecedents and prevention of unwanted pregnancy

308a Teenage women in the United States: Sex, contraception, pregnancy, fertility, and maternal and infant health

308e Sex education and the prevention of teenage pregnancy: An overview of policies and programs in the United States

308g Ethical and legal issues in teenage pregnancies

308h Adolescent sexuality and teenage pregnancy from a black perspective

308i The impact of adolescent pregnancy on Hispanic adolescents and their families

309e First pregnancies to women aged 15-19: 1976 and 1971

309f Contraceptive patterns and premarital pregnancy among women aged 15-19 in 1976

309g The effect of government policies on out-of-wedlock sex and pregnancy

309h The risk of adolescent pregnancy in the first months of intercourse

309i Teenage pregnancies: Looking ahead to 1984

309t Guessing and misinformation about pregnancy risk among urban mothers

309w Psychological vulnerability to unwanted pregnancy

309x Teenagers: Fertility control behavior and attitudes before and after abortion, childbearing or negative pregnancy test

309y Adolescent pregnancy prevention services in high school clinics

309z Misinforming pregnant teenagers

309bb Teenagers and pregnancy: The law in 1979

310bb Taking the initiative: Information versus technology in pregnancy

341h Pregnancy: Is motherhood fattening?

359x Teenage pregnancy: A research review

396c Competing ideologies of reproduction: Medical and maternal perspectives on pregnancy

404u The role of the family in teenage pregnancy: Support or sabotage

404v Pregnancy and drinking

435h The womb factor: Pregnancy policies and employment of women

439l Pregnancy

447n A legal perspective on pregnancy leave and benefits

447o Non-medical issues presented by the pregnant worker

456h Unwanted pregnancy and abortion

461o Female sexuality and pregnancy

461p Discussion: The developmental crisis of pregnancy

Prejudice

50t Alleged psychogenic disorders in women - a possible manifestation of sexual prejudice

Premenstrual

see also Menstruation

28k Premenstrual tension: An overview

28l Classification of premenstrual syndromes

28p Premenstrual tension in borderline and related disorders

28r Recent trends in the treatment of premenstrual syndrome: A critical review

28s Premenstrual tension: Etiology

190y Premenstrual affective syndrome in adolescent and adult psychiatric patients

236a Aetiology of premenstrual syndrome

236b The premenstrual syndrome - an epidemiological and statistical exercise

236c Premenstrual syndrome - a holistic approach

236d An appraisal of the role of progesterone in the therapy of premenstrual syndrome

236e An explorative study into the clinical effects of dydrogesterone in the treatment of premenstrual syndrome

237a The gynecologist's approach (premenstrual tension)

237b The endocrinologist's approach (premenstrual tension)

237c The psychiatrist's approach (premenstrual tension)

237d The nutritionist's approach (premenstrual tension)

237e The effect of placebos (premenstrual tension)

456c Premenstrual tension

Prenatal

see also Reproduce

79h A look at prenatal diagnosis within the context of changing parental and reproductive norms

79i Prenatal diagnosis

79k Policy decisions in prenatal diagnosis: The example of fetal alcoholism syndrome

79l The politics of prenatal diagnosis: A feminist ethical analysis

79m Prenatal diagnosis discussion

273h Legal aspects of prenatal sex selection

310p Technology and prenatal femicide

Preoccupation

10a "When angels fall": Women's drinking as cultural preoccupation and as reality

Preparation

82r Curriculum: Preparation for involvement

361d Improving minority preparation for math-based disciplines

Preschool

see also Education

80a Social-emotional consequences of day care for preschool children

241h Dividing the rough and the respectable: Working-class women and pre-school playgroups

271c Parents and the sex-role development of the preschool child

327c Television viewing, family style and aggressive behavior in preschool children

333p The Yuendumu aboriginal cultural preschool

Prescription

171c Prescriptive grammar and the pronoun problem

421o Wife-employment and the emergence of egalitarian marital role prescriptions: 1900-1974

President

173e Abortion and the presidential election of 1976: A multivariate analysis of voting behavior

394m The president's wife: A changing role — observations of a chancellor's wife

Press

15b The alternative press and the mass media: Two case studies

161b Press coverage of women and women's concerns

Prestige

325p Women of influence and prestige among the Native American Iroquois

401f Power and prestige: Palace women in the Northern Sung (960-1126)

Prevent

10n Prevention of alcohol problems in women

54c New approaches for prevention and education of alcoholism among Hispanic women

252p Prevention of Rhesus (D) isoimmunization after abortion

287j Sources and prevention of dysfunction

295e The antecedents and prevention of unwanted pregnancy

295n Substance abuse in women: Etiology and prevention

308e Sex education and the prevention of teenage pregnancy: An overview of policies and programs in the United States

309y Adolescent pregnancy prevention services in high school clinics

326h Sexual assault in correctional institutions: Prevention and intervention

434b Depression in women: Explanations and prevention

Prey

376g Women before the law: Females as felons and prey in fourteenth-century England

Prick

223n "Pricks" and "Chicks": A plea for persons

275l "Pricks" and "chicks": A plea for "persons"

Priest

see also Religion

91j From chauvinism and clericalism to priesthood: The long march

91l Preacher and priest: Typologies of ministry and ordination of women

115g Crumbs from the table: Towards a whole priesthood

115j Called to priesthood: Interpreting women's experience

Primate

279b Sexual dimorphism in nonhuman primates

Prince

134g Some day my prince will come

Princess

229k Tales of a reincarnated Amazon princess: The invincible wonder woman?

Principal

see also Education

90q The influence of gender on the verbal interactions among principals and staff members: An exploratory study

90r The gender of principals and principal/teacher relations in elementary schools

352d Power and opportunity in the principalship: The case of two women leaders in education

Principle

42l Gospel principles and women

Prism

109n The gothic prism: Charlotte Perkins Gilman's gothic stories and her autobiography

Prison

see also Crime

63a The sexually integrated prison: A legal and policy evaluation

63d A coed prison

63f Styles of doing time in a coed prison: Masculine and feminine alternatives

63m The ERA and coed prisons

78i You can't be a mother and be in prison...can you? Impacts of the mother-child separation

78j Women prisoners and the law: Which way will the pendulum swing?

111j Prison homosexuality: Re-examining conventional wisdom

111p Prison treatment of female offenders in Mexico

163h The torture of women political prisoners: A case study in female sexual slavery

165j Hard times: Custodial prisons for women and the example of the New York State Prison for Women at Auburn, 1893-1933

165k Female patients and the medical profession in jails and prisons: A case of quintuple jeopardy

165l "The government's unique experiment in salvaging women criminals": Cooperation and conflict in the administration of a women's prison - The case of the Federal Industrial Institution for Women at Alderson

174c Teaching writing in prison

176aa Love between women in prison

235g In prison

313c Prisoner in utopia

348i Prisons, prisoners and the community

349w Gender differences in prisoner subcultures

376f Nineteenth-century women's prison reform and its legacy

392n Women in prison: Discriminatory practices and some legal solutions

404t In the pursuit of justice in sentencing and prison

Private

2h Constitutional privacy, religious disestablishment, and the abortion decisions

2m Abortion, privacy, and personhood: From *Roe v Wade* to the human life statute

31a Private rights and public virtues: Women, the family, and democracy

31l Feminist theory: The private and the public

31m Women and their privacy: What is at stake?

103t Reproductive freedom and the right to privacy: A paradox for feminists

106c Aristotle, the public-private split, and the case of the suffragists

173c The abortion-funding cases and population control: An imaginary lawsuit and some reflections on the uncertain limits of reproductive privacy

182g Private kitchens, public cooking

202i Private brother, public world

209j Productivity and service quality in the private sector

217b Women and the welfare state: The transition from private to public dependence

225e Public silence, private terror

241b Public and private: Marking the boundaries

306d On the literary uses of private documents

321e Production and consumption: Public versus private

329h Private and public consciousness in *Mrs. Dalloway* and *To the Lighthouse*

353ff "Neither for the drawing room nor for the kitchen": Private duty nursing in Boston, 1873-1914

354i Medicine and patriarchal violence: The social construction of a "private" event

369k Mothers, fathers, and children: From private to public patriarchy

371e The problem of privacy in Mediterranean anthropology

371k Private parts in public places: The case of actresses

378p The politics of private woman and public man

Private Benjamin

179c The Private Benjamin syndrome

Privilege

98d Becoming an 'insider': Women's privileges in village field work

166e Rights and responsibility, power and privilege: Women's roles in contemporary Indonesia

Prize

399ll Women in Pulitzer Prize plays, 1918-1949

Pro-Choice

see also Choice

173f Public support for pro-choice abortion policies in the nation and states: Changes and stability after the *Roe* and *Doe* decisions

Probation

111t Recent development in probation and parole in British Columbia

Problem

113l The problem

Process

24f Process, filter and stage theories of attraction

82e The development process: A holistic approach

118a Androgynous life: A feminist appropriation of process thought

118b Feminism and process thought: A two-way relationship

118c Openness and mutuality in process thought and feminist action

118d The dynamics of female experience: Process models and human values

174k Women and process: The Sagaris split, Session II

222a A professional socialization process

316g Continuing education: A vital process for women

348f The processing of juveniles in Victoria

Processor

441d Women and microelectronics: The case of word processors

Proclamation

370l Post-proclamation slavery in Accra: A female affair?

Procreation

see also Reproduce

37m Attitudes toward procreation among black adults

207h Sexuality and the control of procreation

208k Sexuality and control of procreation

223g Marriage, love, and procreation

405m Procreation and new definitions in the role of women in a Soviet bloc country: The case of Poland

Production

82k Land tenure and cooperatives: Origin, development and persistence of Navajo matrifocality in subsistence, production, exchange and tenure

94g Non English-speaking women: Production and social reproduction

132l For the Etruscans: Sexual difference and artistic production - the debate over a female aesthetic

148h Sioux women in transition: A study of their changing status in a domestic and capitalist sector of production

153f Households, modes of living, and production systems

153g Development and underdevelopment of household-based production in Europe

207b Subsistence production and extended reproduction

207i The subordination of women and the internationalisation of factory production

208c The subordination of women and the internationalisation of factory production

208d Subsistence production and extended reproduction

213g Transnational production and women workers

245i Home production for use in a market economy

321e Production and consumption: Public versus private

335d Production rules OK? Waged work and the family

342c Black women as producers and reproducers for profit

347i Women and men, cloth and colonization: The transformation of production-distribution relations among the Baule (Ivory Coast)

364h 'Fear woman': Property and modes of production in urban Ghana

370h The Songhay-Zarma female slave: Relations of production and ideological status

428d Women, production, and reproduction in industrial capitalism: A comparison of Brazilian and U.S. factory workers

Productive

459e Family structure and women's reproductive and productive roles: Some conceptual and methodological issues

Productivity

209j Productivity and service quality in the private sector

214r Dual-career families: Intimacy or productivity?

214s One woman's perspective: intimacy and productivity

Profamily

60v The challenge of profamily politics: A feminist defense of sexual freedom

Profession

see also Employment, individual professions

78u Women in a male-dominated profession: The women lawyers

86b The risks of healing: The hazards of the nursing profession

90n The sources and dynamics of sexual inequality in the profession of education

120h The personal is political: Feminism and the helping professions

129y Women and the rise of the American medical profession

130j Women and music: Ornament of the profession?

138h Women and teaching: A semi-detached sociology of a semi-profession

165a One hundred years of fear: Rape and the medical profession

165k Female patients and the medical profession in jails and prisons: A case of quintuple jeopardy

165o Women in the criminal justice profession: An analysis of status conflict

235i The medical profession

262d Differentiation by sex in educational professions

262e Why sex inequities exist in the profession of education

263i "Teacher, teacher": Teachers and educators in a stratified "female" profession

280a Prostitution: Profession and pathology

302d Undergraduate women as potential recruits to the library profession

413f Women and the professions in New Zealand

416a Central issues facing women in the science-based professions

416e Planning strategies for women in scientific professions

434r Issues for women in a 'woman's' profession

455f The social work profession encounters the battered woman

466k The feminization of the teaching profession in Singapore

Professional

38l Black female professionals: Dilemmas and contradictions of status

41g   Invited presentation: The black professional woman — career success and interpersonal failure

43m   Class attitudes and professionalism

68e   Issues confronting professional African women: Illustrations from Kenya

79r   Rights of a handicapped neonate: What every parent and professional should know

84j   The man of professional wisdom

87m   Going shopping: The professional couple in the job market

90i   Ambitions and the opportunity for professionals in the elementary school

112a   Christine de Pisan: First professional woman of letters (French, 1364- 1430?)

165m   Women as criminal justice professionals: A challenge to change tradition

188o   The Franco-Italian professional writer: Christine de Pizan

214i   Women, men, and professional writing: Signature of power?

214p   An attempt at collectivity: Professional confirmation and support

222a   A professional socialization process

243g   Katie's place: Women's work, professional work, and social reform

244d   Occupation-family-linkages as perceived by men in the early stages of professional and managerial careers

263j   Professionalism, division of labor by gender, and the control of nursing practice

302k   Mobility and professional involvement in librarianship: A study of the "Class of '55"

302n   The reentry professional librarian

309m   Teenage mothers and teenage fathers: The impact of early childbearing on the parents' personal and professional lives

344s   Professional women: How real are the recent gains?

353v   The American midwife controversy: A crisis of professionalization

353bb   Professionalism, feminism, and gender roles: A comparative study of nineteenth-century medical therapeutics

354h   The politics of birth control, 1920-1940: The impact of professionals

360p   Professional psychology's response to women's mental health needs

379n   Feminism, professionalism, and germs: A study of the thought of Mary Putnam Jacobi and Elizabeth Blackwell

387j   Dilemmas of Japanese professional women

389g   Mariana Griswold Van Rensselaer (1851-1934): America's first professional woman art critic

407b   Career mapping and the professional development process

416b   Professional women in developing nations: The United States and the Third World compared

416c   Professional women in transition

416m   Should professional women be like professional men?

416o   Evolving views of women's professional roles

421w   The demands of work and the human quality of marriage: An exploratory study of professionals in two socialist societies

454g   The spiritualist medium: A study of female professionalization in Victorian America

458g   Retirement expectations and plans: A comparison of professional men and women

458h   Attitudes toward retirement: A comparison of professional and nonprofessional married women

458k   After retirement: An exploratory study of the professional woman

458l   Professional women: Work pattern as a correlate of retirement satisfaction

Professor
see also Education

398c   Black woman professor — white university

Profile

16j   The first two years: A profile of women entering Women, Inc.

205z   The peacock and the guinea hen: Political profiles of Dorothy Gretchen Steeves and Grace MacInnis

Profit

89l   Occupational segregation, wages and profits when employers discriminate by race and sex

342c   Black women as producers and reproducers for profit

Progesterone

236d   An appraisal of the role of progesterone in the therapy of premenstrual syndrome

Program

4f   Programs for sexually active teens

11f   Women employees and job-based alcoholism programs

16f   The feminist Women's Health Center

16g   The Gynecorps Project

16h   A pelvic teaching program

16j   The first two years: A profile of women entering Women, Inc.

16l   CASPAR: A women's alcoholism program

50j   The state and training programmes for women

54a   A systems model for planning culturally specific programs

54d   Program planning for Hispanic women: One ideal model

78h   National study of women's correctional programs

80i   The Yale Child Welfare Research Program: Description and results

80o   Women's roles and culturally sensitive programs

98n   Methodological interventions in programme assessment and evaluation research

146m   Evaluation of child-sexual-abuse programs

146n   How to start a child-sexual-abuse intervention program

147w   School physical activity programs for the antebellum southern females

169f   Credit programs for working women

169h   Evaluating programs for working adults

291n   A comprehensive child sexual abuse treatment program

308e   Sex education and the prevention of teenage pregnancy: An overview of policies and programs in the United States

308f   Adolescent parent programs and family involvement

361e   A short-term intervention program: Math-science conferences

361f   Affirmative action programs that work

361l   An evaluation of programs for reentry women scientists

373n   The differential impact of programs and policies on women in development

400e   Population planning and rural women's co-operative in IRDP women's programme: Some critical issues

404p   Innovative alcoholism programs for women

407d   The administrative skills program: What have we learned?

417r   Utopia in question: Programming women's needs into the technology of tomorrow

435m   Bureaucratic resistance to women's programs: The case of women in development

441h   Feminist pedagogy and technology: Reflections on the Goddard feminism and ecology summer program

455k   Women and income maintenance programs

472k   Policy directions and program design: Issues and implications in services for the older woman

Progress

42c   Keys for a woman's progression

225n   No progress in pleasure

261e   Progress and pitfalls: Reports from participating institutions

425d   Career progress of women: Getting in and staying in

Progressive

349g   Aw! Your mother's in the mafia: Women criminals in progressive New York

Progressive Era

376c   The crime of precocious sexuality: Female juvenile delinquency and the progressive era

Prohibition

93d   The effectiveness of federal laws prohibiting sex discrimination in employment in the United States

371f   Sexual prohibitions, shared space and fictive marriages in Shíite Iran

Project

82c   Participation through Title XII, consortia, and the project process in AID

82h   Income-generating projects

82q   Issues and alternatives in planning projects for women

82u   NEMOW: A project that stumbled and why

441k   Women and technology project, Missoula, Montana

Proletarian

153h   The proletarian is dead: Long live the housewife?

153i   Beyond the peasant to proletarian debate: African household formation in South Africa

294e   The making of a prostitute proletariat in early twentieth-century New South Wales

336j   The creation of a female assembly-line proletariat

350c Peasant production, proletarianization, and the sexual division of labor in the Andes

387q Degraded and deskilled: The proletarianization of clerical work

Promise

127a The sentimentalists: Promise and betrayal in the home

271b Androgyny: A dead end or a promise

Promote

169b Promoting and recruiting: Reaching the target audience

Pronatalism

195q Feminism, pronatalism, and motherhood

Pronoun

171c Prescriptive grammar and the pronoun problem

Property

195l Parenting and property

245g Shifting perspectives on marital property law

334d Property interests in the classical Welsh law of women

334f The European legal context of the Welsh law of matrimonial property

349c Crime and the contemporary woman: An analysis of changing levels of female property crime, 1960-1975

349d Patterns of female property crime, 1960-1978: A postscript

364a Introduction: Property, power and gender relations

364b Cognatic descent, Islamic law and women's property on the East African coast

364c The exchange of women and property: Marriage in post-revolutionary China

364h 'Fear woman': Property and modes of production in urban Ghana

364j Men and women, kinship and property: Some general issues

375a Women as property in the early Roman empire

375c *Merchet* and women's property rights in medieval England

375d The married women's property acts, 1839-1865: Reform, reaction or revolution?

392h Women, heroin, and property crime

403e Access to property and the states of women in Islam

Prophet

325l No women's liberation: The heritage of a woman prophet in modern Japan

353y Mary Gove Nichols, prophetess of health

412d Minister as prophet? or as mother?: Two nineteenth-century models

Prophetic

448m Another view of the "City upon a Hill": The prophetic vision of Adrienne Rich

Prophylaxis

461z Discussion: Prophylaxis of sexually transmitted diseases: An overview

Proportion

107i Proportionality and body composition in male and female Olympic athletes: A kinanthropometric overview

107l Physique of female athletes - anthropological and proportional analysis

279l Human proportionality and sexual dimorphism

Proposal

169t How foundations view funding proposals on working women

Proposition

117j Judith Leyster's *Proposition* - Between virtue and vice

Proprietary

80t Considering proprietary child care

Proprieter

356d Proprieters of language

Prose

see also Literature

130v The problem of sexual equality in Sadean prose

Prosecution

55b Scope of the problem: Investigation and prosecution

165b Would you believe this woman? Prosecutorial screening for "credible" witnesses and a problem of justice

Prospect

20l Prospects and retrospects in *Life Before Man*

49d Postscripts and prospects

467g The future prospect

Prosperity

454p Prosperity's child: Some thoughts on the flapper

Prostaglandin

53b The relationship of the sex hormone/prostaglandin interaction to female and male longevity

190s Prostaglandins in primary dysmenorrhea: Basis for the new therapy

252k Natural prostaglandins alone or in combination for termination of pregnancy

252l Termination of second trimester pregnancy with prostaglandin analogues

252m Prostaglandin therapy for second trimester abortion: An overview of current status and recent trends

Prostitution

55g Youth prostitution

55k Combating child pornography and prostitution: One county's approach

58b Prostitution

60b Male vice and female virtue: Feminism and the politics of prostitution in nineteenth-century Britain

78o The prostitute as victim

78p Concurrent and consecutive abuse: The juvenile prostitute

99c 'As good a bloody woman as any other woman...': Prostitutes in western Australia, 1895-1939

111g Juvenile prostitution

129i Prostitution

155a The prostitute as scapegoat: Mildred Rogers in Somerset Maugham's *Of Human Bondage*

155b French feminist theater and the subject of prostitution, 1870-1914

155c Zola's view of prostitution in *Nana*

155d The magic circle: The role of the prostitute in Isak Dinesen's *Gothic Tales*

155e The romantization of the prostitute in Dostoevsky's fiction

155f The prostitute in Arab and North African fiction

155g Courtesans and prostitutes in South Asian literature

155i The uncommon prostitute: The contemporary image in an American age of pornography

155j Women writing about prostitutes: Amalia Jamilis and Luisa Valenzuela

157k The 'social evil': Prostitution in Vancouver, 1900-1920

165e Work and the addicted prostitute

219c Aspects of violence in prostitution

231cc Male vice and female virtue: Feminism and the politics of prostitution in nineteenth-century Britain

238h Harlot or heroine? Changing views of prostitution, 1870-1920

280a Prostitution: Profession and pathology

294a Prostitution in Tasmania during the transition from penal settlement to 'civilized' society

294b 'More sinned against than sinning'?: Prostitution in South Australia, 1836-1914

294c 'Soiled doves': Prostitution in colonial Queensland

294d Dealing with the 'social evil': Prostitution and the police in Perth and on the eastern goldfields, 1895-1924

294e The making of a prostitute proletariat in early twentieth-century New South Wales

294g Prostitution and the law: The question of decriminalization

294j Prostitution: One experience

301w Prostitution I: Trying to make a living

301x Prostitution II: Not no easy business

326n Treatment of prostitute victims of sexual assault

349i Prostitution in Nevada

353o Prostitution, venereal disease, and American medicine

392i The economics of prostitution

404w Prostitution and sexual violence

439h The politics of prostitution

461w The prostitute as victim

Protect

2d The juridical status of the fetus: A proposal for legal protection of the unborn

78c Females under the law: 'Protected' but unequal

86i Protection for women: Trade unions and labor laws

173b The juridical status of the fetus: A proposal for legal protection of the unborn

215e The illusion of protection: Civil defence

241c Blowing the cover of the protective male: A community study of violence to women

392m Unequal protection of males and females in the juvenile court

435n Women, men, and military service: Is protection necessarily a racket?

446i Protection of female labor

Protectorate

160j Memsahibs in colonial Malaya: A study of European wives in a British colony and protectorate, 1900-1940

Protest

101i Two faces of protest: Alternative forms of women's mobilization in West Bengal and Maharashtra

368g To veil or not to veil: A matter of protest or policy

370n Bwanikwa: Consciousness and protest among slave women in Central Africa, 1886-1911

Protestant

see also Religion

91q Women ... Where are you? Women in the Protestant churches

366f Lay women in the Protestant tradition

412k Laity rights and leadership: Winning them for women in the Methodist Protestant church, 1860-1900

Protestant Orphan's Home

157c Notes on the British Columbia Protestant Orphan's Home

Proto-Social

200e Proto-social to adult: A Sherbro transformation

Provençal

188f The provençal *Trobairitz*: Castelloza

Provide

102g The good-provider role: Its rise and fall

204b The two-provider family: Problems and potentials

220g Women as providers and consumers

Prussia

145l The impact of agrarian change on women's work and child care in early-nineteenth-century Prussia

Psyche

229cc Feeding the feminist psyche through ritual theater

229mm Feminist spirituality: The politics of the psyche

332k The female novel of development and the myth of psyche

Psychiatry

4c Psychiatric aspects of adolescent pregnancy

140a Presidential address: Conceptual ambiguity and morality in modern psychiatry

140n Victims of violence and psychiatric illness

140x Psychiatry's problem with no name: Therapist-patient sex

140y Sexual misconduct by psychiatrists: The ethical and clinical dilemma of confidentiality

190w The psychological concomitants of menarche in psychiatric patients

190y Premenstrual affective syndrome in adolescent and adult psychiatric patients

237c The psychiatrist's approach (premenstrual tension)

291k The child psychiatric examination of the sexually abused child

353ee Doctors or ladies? Women physicians in psychiatric institutions, 1872-1900

359i The psychiatrist-woman patient relationship

359k Psychiatry's problem with no name: Therapist-patient sex

Psychic

158c The Victorians, the psychologists, and psychic birth control

344h Marital relationships and mental health: The psychic costs of inequality

Psychoactive

9d Sex differences in psychoactive drug use: Recent epidemiology

9o Sex differences in the effects of alcohol and other psychoactive drugs on endocrine function: Clinical and experimental evidence

9q The effects of opiates, sedative-hypnotics, amphetamines, cannabis, and other psychoactive drugs on the fetus and newborn

Psychoanalysis

see also Psychotherapy, Therapy

8o The therapeutic alliance in psychoanalytic treatment

23l Psychoanalysis and feminist social theory of gender

31e Concepts of woman in psychoanalytic theory: The nature-nurture controversy revisited

69a Feminine development: Changes in psychoanalytic theory

76d Feminism and psychoanalysis

80c Changing aspects of the family: A psychoanalytic perspective on early intervention

84n Political philosophy and the patriarchal unconscious: A psychoanalytic perspective on epistemology and metaphysics

96i From traditional psychoanalysis to alternatives to psychotherapy

96j A new look at the psychoanalytic view of the female

102e Toward psychoanalytic feminism: The mother in dream-stealing, the father in dreams

119h Sexual politics and psychoanalysis: Some notes on their relation

132b Gender, relation, and difference in psychoanalytic perspective

132h Introduction: Psychoanalysis and feminism in France

132j Psychoanalysis in France

190v Menarche: A psychoanalytic perspective

257m Psychoanalysis and women loving women

291c A psychoanalyst's view of sexual abuse by parents

439c Sexuality as the mainstay of identity: Psychoanalytic perspectives

443c The convergence of psychoanalysis and feminism: Gender identity and autonomy

443d Feminist psychoanalysis: Theory and practice

461v Discussion: Psychoanalytic reflections on the "beaten wife syndrome"

Psychocultural

see also Culture

319o The nonconsenting sterilization of Mexican women in Los Angeles: Issues of psychocultural rupture and legal redress in paternalistic behavior

Psychodynamics

132c Mother-daughter relationships: Psychodynamics, politics, and philosophy

326a Psychodynamics of sexual assault experiences

359mm The rape victim: Psychodynamic considerations

365h Psychodynamic perspectives

409h The genuine Christine: Psychodynamics of Issy

Psychogenic

50t Alleged psychogenic disorders in women - a possible manifestation of sexual prejudice

285l Differential diagnosis and treatment for organogenic and psychogenic erectile dysfunction

Psychology

see also Behavior, Social Psychology

8r Conflict and psychological development: Women in the family

12b Psychological sex differences

28e The psychology of the menstrual cycle: Biological and physiological perspectives

45f Psychological orientations to the work role: 1957-1976

47b The menopause: Physiological, pathological, and psychological aspects

49f The feminization of the labor force: Research for industrial/organizational psychology

51l Erik Erikson and Doris Lessing: Psychological theory and the female novel of development

65c Some psychological factors affecting job segregation and wages

84m Individualism and the objects of psychology

91a A new outlook on women: Psychological and biological

123h Changing conceptions of men and women: A psychologist's perspective

124g Psychology views mothers and mothering: 1897-1980

124h How psychology constructed masculinity: The theory of male sex role identity

132r Androgyny and the psychology of sex differences

140d The effects of inequality on psychology

158a The power of the past: History and the psychology of women

158c The Victorians, the psychologists, and psychic birth control

158e Not quite new worlds: Psychologists' conceptions of the ideal family in the twenties

158g "Rather worse than folly?" psychology measures femininity and masculinity, 1: From Terman and Miles to the Guilfords

158h Psychology measures femininity and masculinity, 2: From "13 Gay Men" to the instrumental-expressive distinction

176j Teaching the psychology of women: A lesbian feminist perspective

180t A psychological journey: Mothers and daughters in English-Canadian fiction

189h Psychology and feminism - if you can't beat them, join them

190w The psychological concomitants of menarche in psychiatric patients

229h Why women need the goddess: Phenomenological, psychological, and political reflections

230k Using psychological research on violent pornography to inform legal change

239k Research on menstrual-related psychological changes: Alternative perspectives

240g Psychological aspects of gynaecological cancer

240h Psychological aspects of hysterectomy

240i Psychological preparation for gynaecological surgery

240k Psychological aspects of the menstruum and premenstruum

267d A psychological examination of sexual harassment

268o Sex roles, psychological assessment, and patient management

276a The classification of sexual aggressives and their associated demographic, social, developmental and psychological features

277a Psychological causes of lack of arousal

287m Psychological aspects of sexual dysfunction

300d The psychology of politeness among the Javanese

309w Psychological vulnerability to unwanted pregnancy

317g The clinical psychology of later life: Developmental paradigms

345d Psychological aspects of women and alcohol

352c The psychology of leadership: Implications for women

356e The psychology of the generic masculine

359c Psychological consequences of sexual inequality

359e Psychology of women: Perspectives on theory and research for the eighties

359y Psychological reactions of postpartum women

360b Female psychologists in policymaking positions

360f Reproductive advancements: Theory, research applications, and psychological issues

360o Media psychology and public policy

360p Professional psychology's response to women's mental health needs

411g The psychological well-being of women in the middle years

416f Academic career mobility for women and men psychologists

425c Women and the psychology of achievement: Implications for personal and social change

432p Putting away the pom-poms: An educational psychologist's view of females and sports

445i Gertrude Atherton's California woman: From love story to psychological drama

460f Psychological and physiological concepts in female sexuality: A discussion of physiological aspects of female sexual development

Psychopathology

28o Psychopathology and the menstrual cycle

137a Gender and psychopathology in perspective

137c Gender and child psychopathology

137d Gender and adult psychopathology

137e Psychopathology and sex differences in the aged

137l Gender, genes, and psychopathology

137m Gender, hormones, and psychopathology

268a Sex roles and psychopathology

268i Sex roles, criminality, and psychopathology

268l Sex-related differences in the epidemiology of child psychopathology

270l Psychopathology and the Turkish family: A family systems theory analysis

359l The influence of gender on diagnosis and psychopathology

Psychophysiology

137o Gender, psychophysiological disorders, and mortality

268e Sex roles and psychophysiological disorders: Coronary heart disease

277f Psychophysiologic measurement of sexual arousal in females

Psychosexual

4a Adolescent psychosexual development

239a Psychosexual neutrality: Is anatomy destiny?

240j Psychosexual problems

291b Psychosexual development within the family

460h The early stages of female psychosexual development: A Kleinian view

Psychosocial

51q Psychosocial aspects of the menopause

240c Psychosocial aspects of contraception

240l A psychosocial study of the climacteric

252t Some considerations on the psychosocial aspects of pregnancy termination

359ii Psychosocial aspects of wife battering

472b The psychosocial problems of older women

Psychotherapy
see also Psychoanalysis, Therapy

8a Social change and psychotherapeutic implications

8p Research on gender and psychotherapy

8q Special issues for women in psychotherapy

96a Introduction: An historical view of psychotherapy and women's rights

96i From traditional psychoanalysis to alternatives to psychotherapy

96l The role and function of women's consciousness raising: Self-help, psychotherapy, or political activation?

96m The treatment of depressed women: The efficacy of psychotherapy

140r Special issues for women in psychotherapy

140s Issues in the psychotherapy of lesbians

140v Teaching value clarification: The example of gender and psychotherapy

225i Cultural and historical influences on sexuality in Hispanic/Latin women: Implications for psychotherapy

291o Group psychotherapy with sexually abused children

295m Differential needs and treatment approaches for women in psychotherapy

359h Report of the task force on sex bias and sex-role stereotyping in psychotherapeutic practice

359pp Psychotherapy with women clients: The impact of feminism

359qq Women patients and women therapists: Some issues that come up in psychotherapy

359rr Adaptive and pathogenic aspects of sex-role stereotypes: Implications for parenting and psychotherapy

359vv The psychotherapeutic impact of women's consciousness-raising groups

359xx A decade of feminist influence on psychotherapy

360c Women and psychotherapy research

360k Sexual intimacy between psychotherapists and clients: Policy implications for the future

365a Gender and psychotherapeutic outcome

365p Psychotherapy and women: Priorities for research

443h Psychotherapy with black women and the dual effects of racism and sexism

Psychotropic

9l Dependence on psychotropic drugs and analgesics in men and women

359j A review of women's psychotropic drug use

Puberty

190m Virginity rituals and chastity control during puberty: Cross-cultural patterns

372u VO2 max and anaerobic threshold in pre- and post-pubescent girls

460d Physiological aspects of female sexual development: Conception through puberty

Public

13f Queensland public service women

23k The employment of women in the commonwealth public service: The creation and reproduction of a dual labour market

31a Private rights and public virtues: Women, the family, and democracy

31l Feminist theory: The private and the public

37r Multiple public benefits and poor black families

57i Human sexuality: Messages in public environments

76b Domestic and public

97e Public education and the discourse of crisis, power and vision

102o Public nurturance and the man on horseback

106c Aristotle, the public-private split, and the case of the suffragists

153k The contribution of public goods to household reproduction: Case study from Brazil

157e Public and political: Documents of the woman's suffrage campaign in British Columbia, 1871-1917: The view from Victoria

173f Public support for pro-choice abortion policies in the nation and states: Changes and stability after the *Roe* and *Doe* decisions

178f The public welfare system: Regulation and dehumanization

182c Women and public space

182g Private kitchens, public cooking

202i Private brother, public world

203s The Los Angeles woman's building: A public center for woman's culture

217b Women and the welfare state: The transition from private to public dependence

225e Public silence, private terror

233t Educating workers, management and the general public

241b Public and private: Marking the boundaries

264c The public role of southern women

283p Public expenditure and budgetary policy

300i The public bureaucracy and social change in Singapore

321e Production and consumption: Public versus private

329h Private and public consciousness in *Mrs. Dalloway* and *To the Lighthouse*

369k Mothers, fathers, and children: From private to public patriarchy

371k Private parts in public places: The case of actresses

378p The politics of private woman and public man

388h Public day care in Britain and Sweden: A sociological perspective

401m In the public eye: Women in early twentieth-century China

402j Purdah and public space

420s Women in Asian cites: Policies, public services, and research

Public Policy

see also Policy

60r Women on welfare: Public policy and institutional racism

79ii In vitro fertilization and embryo transfer: The process of making public policy

80p Beyond the stalemate in child care public policy

103l Teenage sexuality and public policy: An agenda for gender education

209ii Public policy and the employment impacts of office computerization

273j Ethics and public policy: Should sex choice be discouraged?

344u Women, law, and public policy

360a Women in the mental health delivery system: Implications for research and public policy

360d The relational self in women: Developmental theory and public policy

360o Media psychology and public policy

388g Women in Communist countries: Comparative public policy

410f Women judges and public policy in sex integration

435c Women and public policy: An overview

435j Battered women and public policy

436c Women's role in the formulation of public policies in Brazil

440b Public policies and the paid work of women

440j The women's movement's fandango with the state: The movement's role in public policy since 1972

Public School

see also Education

90j "If they can, I can": Women aspirants to administrative positions in public schools

90l Administrative careers in public school organizations

272f Toward a general theory of occupational sex segregation: The case of public school teaching

Publication

15e Reference service for alternative publications

133i Gay fantasies in gay publications

Publish

15g Publishers on libraries: Walking through walls

15h Publishers on libraries: Stake your claim

15i Publishers on libraries: Small presses and the library

15j Publishers on libraries: The library as motherlode: A feminist view

15k Alternative and small publishers view libraries: An empirical study

85h The gatekeepers: A feminist critique of academic publishing

97c The political economy of text publishing

263h Creating a place for women: American book publishing in the nineteenth century

305x Working with words: Feminist publishing in Canada

442h Publishing in Paris

Puerto Rican Woman

72b Puerto Rican women in education and potential impact on occupational patterns

72e Puerto Rican women in higher education in the United States

Puerto Rico

18i Neo-Malthusian ideology and colonial capitalism: Population dynamics in southwestern Puerto Rico

60n Issues of race and class in women's studies: A Puerto Rican woman's thoughts

153o Wages, consumption, and survival: Working class households in Puerto Rico in the 1930's

216i The Puerto Rican family: Its role in cultural transition

315b Attitudes toward gender in two cultures: Puerto Rico and the United States

397h The Puerto Rican lesbian in the United States

469b Mental health needs of Puerto Rican women in the United States

469c The self-perception of Puerto Rican women toward their societal roles

469e Transactional family patterns: A preliminary exploration of Puerto Rican female adolescents

469f Cultural attitudes toward mental illness among Puerto Rican migrant women

469g "La operacion": An analysis of sterilization in a Puerto Rican community in Connecticut

469i A preliminary historical analysis of women and work in Puerto Rico: 1899-1975

Pukhtun

92c Pakistan: *Mor* and *Tor*: Binary and opposing models of Pukhtun womanhood

Pulcherie

135q Power or sexuality: The bind of Corneille's *Pulcherie*

Pulitzer

399ll Women in Pulitzer Prize plays, 1918-1949

Pulte Medical College

353cc Homeopathy and sexual equality: The controversy over coeducation at Cincinnati's Pulte Medical College, 1873-1879

Punishment

348c Women, crime and punishment

376a The certain wages of sin: Sentence and punishment of female felons in colonial Massachusetts, 1673-1774

Punjab, India

92d Pakistan: The role of women in reciprocal relationships in a Punjab village

101f Kinship, women, and politics in twentieth-century Punjab

Pupil

see Student

Purdah

255a Purdah: Separate worlds and symbolic shelter

255b Purdah revisited: A comparison of Hindu and Muslim interpretations of the cultural meaning of purdah in South Asia

255c Purdah and the Hindu family in central India

255e Purdah among the Oswals of Mewar

255f Gradations of purdah and the creation of social boundaries on a Baluchistan oasis

255g Purdah in Pakistan: Seclusion and modern occupations for women

255h From purdah to politics: The social feminism of the all-India women's organizations

255i Purdah politics: The role of Muslim women in Indian nationalism, 1911-1924

255j Purdah and participation: Women in the politics of Bangladesh

402j Purdah and public space

The Pure and the Impure

64p Image structure, codes, and recoding in *The Pure and the Impure*

Purify

241i Purification or social control? Ideologies of reproduction and the churching of women after childbirth

Puritan

see also Religion

19i Wayward Puritans

19k Anne Hutchinson and the Puritan attitude toward women

184d Elizabethan birth control and Puritan attitudes

238a The Puritans and sex

375f Under great temptations here: Women and divorce law in puritan Massachusetts

367d New England women: Ideology and experience in first-generation Puritanism (1630-1650)

367h Women and revivalism: The Puritan and Wesleyan traditions

452c Quest for community: Spiritual autobiographies of eighteenth-century Quaker and Puritan women in America

Purity

189o Dirty fingers, grime and slag heaps: Purity and the scientific ethic

257a Purity, motherhood, pleasure or threat? Definitions of female sexuality 1900-1970s

342f The scientific mystique: Can a white lab coat guarantee purity in the search for knowledge about the nature of women?

Puttana

30c A portrait of the *Puttana* as a middle-aged Woolf scholar

Pym, Barbara

318d Women victimised by fiction: Living and loving in the novels of Barbara Pym

Pyromania

280j Fire setting (pyromania) and its relationship to sexuality

Qing

401h Widows and remarriage in Ming and early Qing China

Quaker

see also Religion

347c The mothers of the nation: Seneca resistance to Quaker intervention

452c Quest for community: Spiritual autobiographies of eighteenth-century Quaker and Puritan women in America

Qualify

78t A sexist selection process keeps qualified women off the bench

116p Women and "masculine" sports: Androgyny qualified

Quality

80d Janus faces day care: Perspectives on quality and cost

421w The demands of work and the human quality of marriage: An exploratory study of professionals in two socialist societies

446o The quantity and quality of work: A round table

Quantity

189i The oldest, the most established, the most quantitative of the social sciences - and most dominated by men; The impact of feminism on economics

446o The quantity and quality of work: A round table

Quebec, Canada

27o Quebec women writers

323e "Action Positive" in the Quebec trade union movement

323s Women's committees: The Quebec experience

Queen

39c Asante queen mothers in government and politics in the nineteenth century

301oo Queen of the road

338g The look of a queen

Queensland, Australia

13f Queensland public service women

294c 'Soiled doves': Prostitution in colonial Queensland

Queer

133r From "commies" and "queers" to "gay is good"

Quest

30b In quest of Ding Ling (In quest of myself)

40ee The quest for self: Triumph and failure in the works of Toni Morrison

198c The Islamic revolution and women: Quest for the Quranic model

229n Drawing from mythology in women's quest for selfhood

Question

17m The question of Gertrude Stein

32h Laura Marholm and the question of female nature

40s An answer to some questions on how I write: In three parts

47c Questions women want to ask about the menopause

211j Notes toward finding the right question

211s The right question is theological

224j Toward a scientific analysis of the gay question

225q The fem question

241j Do her answers fit his questions? Women and the survey method

387u Unresolved questions: Three feminist perspectives

423a Women in adulthood: Unanswered questions

430d The attitude of the Iranian left to the women's question

464h The man question

Quilt

see also Art

117r Quilts: The great American art

148f The role of Sioux women in the production of ceremonial objects: The case of the star quilt

301dd Quilting women

315g The art of quilting: Thoughts from a contemporary quilter

Quintanales, Mirtha

310i An interview with Mirtha Quintanales, from the Third World women's archives

Quirl

34k The quirls of a woman's brain

Quixote

303l Tilting at windmills in the Quixotic South

Quran

see also Islam

198c The Islamic revolution and women: Quest for the Quranic model

368b Status of women in the Qur'an

Rabbi

see also Religion

211r Reactions to a woman Rabbi

Race

see also Ethnic, Minority, names of individual races

37j Race and marital status: An overview

39p Black women and racial "uplift" prior to emancipation

43n Race and class: Beyond personal politics

60k "On the hem of life": Race, class, and the prospects for sisterhood

60n Issues of race and class in women's studies: A Puerto Rican woman's thoughts

68h Caribbean women: The impact of race, sex, and class

83c Gender, race and class in the United States: Lessons from Third World women

89l Occupational segregation, wages and profits when employers discriminate by race and sex

199d Housework and domestic labor: Racial and technological change

215i Fuel for the nuclear arms race: Nuclear power and nuclear weapons

215k Take the toys from the boys: Competition and the nuclear arms race

231u "The mind that burns in each body": Women, rape, and racial violence

253l Sexism and racism in health policy

272a Trends in occupational segregation by sex and race, 1960-1981

272c Job changing and occupational sex segregation: Sex and race comparisons

283j Race, left strategies and the state

296g Racial-ethnic women and work: Towards an analysis of race and gender stratification

303j Racial myths and attitudes among white female students at the University of Florida

315e A dialogue critical issues in women's studies: Race, class, and sexual orientation

344w Race and ethnicity in the lives of minority women

372dd Foot disorders of female marathon runners before and after a marathon race

416n Class, race, sex, scientific objects of knowledge: A socialist-feminist perspective on the social construction of productive nature and some political consequences

450k The androgynous, bi-racial vision of Berry Morgan

Racism

7l Racism and sadomasochism: A conversation with two black lesbians

14f Racism - a white issue

14g Racism and women's studies

14h Face-to-face, day-to-day - racism CR

39m Racism and tradition: Black womanhood in historical perspective

60r Women on welfare: Public policy and institutional racism

60s From slavery to social welfare: Racism and the control of black women

83i Racism and sexism: They ain't genetic you know!

89h The statistical theory of racism and sexism

126k Sexism and racism: Obstacles to the development of black women in South Africa

174p Unlearning complicity, remembering resistance: White women's anti-racism education

206k Racism at work

206l Working on racism: Centro Obrero

275r Sexism and racism: Some conceptual differences

275w Reference and truth: The case of sexist and racist utterances

336k Racism and sexism in Nazi Germany: Motherhood, compulsory sterilization, and the state

343p The miranda trap: Sexism and racism in Shakespeare's *Tempest*

354d Sexism and racism in the American health care industry: A comparative analysis

369e The incompatible menage à trois: Marxism, feminism, and racism

443h Psychotherapy with black women and the dual effects of racism and sexism

462e Racism and the bonding of women

462h Anti-semitism: The unacknowledged racism

462i White women and racism

Radcliffe, Ann

109k Terror-gothic: Nightmare and dream in Ann Radcliffe and Charlotte Brontë

109l Place and eros in Radcliffe, Lewis, and Brontë

109m The Radcliffean gothic model: A form for feminine sexuality

135j The woman at the window: Ann Radcliffe in the novels of Mary Wollstonecraft and Jane Austen

313g Ideology and *The Mysteries of Udolpho*

Radiation

209y The health impacts of low-level radiation on VDT operators

Radical

95c When radical and socialist feminism were joined: The extraordinary failure of Madeleine Pelletier

125g Lucy Stone: Radical beginnings

125u Simone de Beauvoir: Dilemmas of a feminist radical

145k The radicalization of Lily Braun

174a If the mortarboard fits...radical feminism in academia

180g Unmothered daughter and the radical reformer: Harriet Martineau's career

225t Thinking sex: Notes for a radical theory of the politics of sexuality

305y More radical with age: Women and education

378b Industrial radicalism and the domestic division of labor

439b Sex and power: Sexual bases of radical feminism

Radio

358j He admits...but she confesses

Rahel Varnhagen

145c Hannah Arendt's *Rahel Varnhagen*

Raid

192n The election day immigration raids at Lilli Diamond Originals and the response of the ILGWU

Railway

385d Women and agricultural change in the railway region of Zambia: Dispossession and counterstrategies, 1930-1970

Rain-Moon

64f The relationship between meaning and structure in Colette's *Rain-moon*

Rainbow

205c Rainbow women of the Fraser Valley: Lifesongs through the generations

399xx A rainbow of voices

Rama Indians

269a Rama men and women: An ethnohistorical analysis of change

269g Watch that pot or the *waksuk* will eat you up: An analysis of male and female roles in Rama Indian myth

Ramirez, Sara Estela

192q Sara Estela Ramirez: Una rosa roja en el movimiento

Ramsays

202g Where the spear plants grew: The Ramsays' marriage in *To the Lighthouse*

Rangda the Witch

194m Rangda the witch

Range

82j Livestock and range management

Rape

16o Rape victims

50v Rape and the masculine mystique

78l Rape: The all-American crime

78m Forcible rape: Institutionalized sexism in the criminal justice system

165a One hundred years of fear: Rape and the medical profession

212d Towards a revolutionary feminist analysis of rape

212e Rape and marital violence in the maintenance of male power

219d The social uses of sexuality: Symbolic interaction, power and rape

219e Police officer or doctor? Police surgeons' attitudes and opinions about rape

219f The role of the judiciary in the failure of the Sexual Offences (Amendment) Act to improve the treatment of the rape victim

219g Crisis intervention with victims of forcible rape: A police perspective

219h Loss and mourning in victims of rape and sexual assault

230h Sexual stratification, pornography, and rape in the United States

231u "The mind that burns in each body": Women, rape, and racial violence

305e Breaking the hold: Women against rape

326b Working for and with rape victims: Crisis intervention and advocacy

326c Rape trauma syndrome: Developmental variations

326i Rape of men in the community

326k Marital and sexual dysfunction following rape: Identification and treatment

326m Rape and the college student: Multiple crises in late adolescence

333n Study into the needs of aboriginal women who have been raped or sexually assaulted

343c Shakespeare and the soil of rape

344b The rape culture

349k The victim in a forcible rape case: A feminist view

349l Rape: Power, anger, and sexuality

349r Barriers to becoming a "successful" rape victim

359kk Rape: Sexual disruption and recovery

359ll Development of a medical center rape crisis intervention program

359mm The rape victim: Psychodynamic considerations

375e Rape in thirteenth-century England: A study of the common-law courts

404s The mythology of rape

419l Rape and rape victims in the *Metamorphoses*

434d Rape crisis theory revisited

472d The abused older woman: A discussion of abuses and rape

Rat

51h Neuroendocrine mechanisms of reproductive aging in women and female rats

Ratio

140e Some effects of proportions on group life: Skewed sex ratios and responses to token women

273d Timing of fertilization and the sex ratio of offspring

Rational

31c Is gender a variable in conceptions of rationality? A survey of issues

84a Women is not a rational animal: On Aristotle's biology of reproduction

132d The bonds of love: Rational violence and erotic domination

231g The new woman and the rationalization of sexuality in Weimar Germany

Rationale

265d Review of the literature of non-sexist curriculum and a critique of the underlying assumptions and rationale

Ravel, Maurice

64k Colette and Ravel: The enchantress and the illusionist

Rawls, John

23n *A Theory of Justice* and love: Rawls on the family

Re-Vision

254a seeing our way clear: Feminist re-vision of the academy

Reaction

60d Crisis, reaction, and resistance: Women in Germany in the 1920's and 1930's

Read

see also Book, Textbook

30n "Charlotte's Web": Reading *Jane Eyre* over time

109b "But why do they read those things?" The female audience and the gothic novel

145e The reading habits of women in the *Vormärz*

151k Reading as a leisure pursuit in the USSR

356t Reading reading: Echo's abduction of language

452f The autobiographer and her readers: From apology to affirmation

Reagan, Ronald

103e Women and the Reagan revolution: Thermidor for the social welfare economy

Real

64n Polymorphemic perversity: Colette's illusory "real"

Realism

32i Gabriele Reuter: Romantic and realist

40i Gwendolyn Brooks' poetic realism: A developmental survey

450n The miracle of realism: The bid for self-knowledge in the fiction of Ellen Gilchrist

450g Ellen Douglas: Moralist and realist

Reality

10a "When angels fall": Women's drinking as cultural preoccupation and as reality

31d A different reality: Feminist ontology

32j Ricarda Huch: Myth and reality

43l Class realities: Create a new power base

49i The setting and the reality for labor relations in the 90's

62e The realities of mixed schooling

65p Technical possibilities and political realities: Concluding remarks

68p Third World women and social reality: A conclusion

78q Incest: Whose reality, whose theory?

174j The ideas and the realities: Sagaris, Session I

176c "Out" at the university: Myth and reality

198a Introduction: The ideal and contextual realities of Muslim women

330k Nature and community: A study of cyclical reality in *The Waves*

416j You've come a long way baby: The myth and the reality

417x Realities and fictions: Lesbian visions of utopia

430a Islam's appeal to women in Iran: Illusions and reality

465a Dealing with dependency: State practices and social realities, 1870-1945

Reap

172k Some sow, others reap (Colombia)

Rear

38e The black woman and child rearing

38g "The means to put my children through": Child-rearing goals and strategies among black female domestic servants

204h Antecedents and consequences of various degrees of paternal involvement in child rearing: The Israeli project

440i Pater-patria: Child-rearing and the state

Reason

2f Understanding Blackmun's argument: The reasoning of *Roe v Wade*

Rebeccah (Theater)

399vv *Rebeccah*: Rehearsal notes

Rebel

99d Victorian spinsters: Dutiful daughters, desperate rebels and the transition to the new women

433a Goddesses or rebels: The women revolutionaries of Bengal

Rebellion

27i Rebellions of good women

96g From renunciation to rebellion: The female in literature

120a Memoirs of an ontological exile: The methodological rebellions of feminist research

125v Modern feminist theorists: Reinventing rebellion

218e Riot and rebellion among African women: Three examples of women's political clout

243d The old world, new rights, and the limited rebellion: Challenges to traditional authority in immigrant families

397o From accommodation to rebellion: The politicization of lesbianism

Rebirth

20i *Surfacing* and the rebirth journey

Recession

52r Economic recession and Swiss women's attitudes towards marital role segregation

89p The 1974-1975 recession and the employment of women

Recidivism

105k Marriage, estrangement, sobriety and recidivism: Some crucial process variables in the case of alcoholic men and their wives

276c Prediction of recidivism and the evaluation of treatment programs for sex offenders

Recipient

440f Women as welfare recipients: Women, poverty and the state

Recode

64p Image structure, codes, and recoding in *The Pure and the Impure*

Recognition

31i From domination to recognition

291a Definition and recognition of sexual child abuse: Historical and cultural perspectives

291d Recognition of child sexual abuse in the United Kingdom

345f Response and recognition

Recommend

126d Research on women's communication: Critical assessment and recommendations

407i Getting the best: Conclusions, recommendations, and selected resources

Reconsider

135o Snow beneath snow: A reconsideration of the virgin of *Villette*

Reconstruct

40c Reconstruction of the composite self: New images of black women in Maya Angelou's continuing autobiography

109e The reconstruction of the gothic feminine ideal in Emily Brontë's *Wuthering Heights*

225v Search for tomorrow: On feminism and the reconstruction of teen romance

314o Reconstructing American literature: A strategy for change

Record

279d The fossil record of sex

Recovery

404aa Stereotypes and stigma: Barriers to recovery

Recreation

147b Recreational activities of women in colonial America

147e American women, 1880-1860 (sic): Recreational pursuits and exercise

151i Achievements and problems in Soviet recreational planning

Recruit

169b Promoting and recruiting: Reaching the target audience

179g The recruitment of women

248b Nurse recruitment to four provincial hospitals 1881-1921

302c The recruitment of men into librarianship, following World War II

302d Undergraduate women as potential recruits to the library profession

410c The effects of sex on recruitment: Connecticut local offices

410d Recruitment of women to suburban city councils: Higgins vs. Chevalier

405j Have women's chances for political recruitment in the USSR really improved?

416d Changing patterns of recruitment and employment

Redefine

126j Redefining the family and women's status within the family: The case of southern Appalachia

Redemption

59c The feminist redemption of Christ

Redescribe

275t Moral redescription and political self-deception

Rediscover

124a Rediscovering the "New Woman" of the 1890's: The stories of "George Egerton"

Redress

214l The probability of redress: Seeking external support

261c Grievances and their redress in the eighties

Reductionism

51s The fallacy of bodily reductionism

213a Women in migration: Beyond the reductionist outlook

Reentry

302n The reentry professional librarian

324a Problems of labor-market reentry

394r Meeting the needs of re-entering students

361l An evaluation of programs for reentry women scientists

Reference

15e Reference service for alternative publications

275m Sex and reference

275w Reference and truth: The case of sexist and racist utterances

Referendum

133v Referendum campaigns vs. gay rights

Referral

80s The prospects and dilemmas of child care information and referral

Reflection

40jj Ruminations/Reflections

124n The ERA campaign: Reflections on interpretation and practice

Reform

see also Social Reform

23m 'Law reform and human reproduction': Implications for women

43q The reform tool kit

46c Earnings sharing: Incremental and fundamental reform

46f   Disability insurance under proposed reforms

46h   The housewife and social security reform: A feminist perspective

56e   Awake and aware, or false consciousness: The cooption of childbirth reform in America

61g   Women and radical reform in antebellum upstate New York: A profile of grassroots female abolitionists

97a   Women, educational reform and the process of change

157l   The B.C. Liberal Party and women's reforms, 1916-1928

157n   Women and reform in British Columbia: Some preliminary suggestions

180g   Unmothered daughter and the radical reformer: Harriet Martineau's career

336e   Helene Stöcker: Left-wing intellectual and sex reformer

349x   Reform school families

350h   The impact of land reform on women: The case of Ethiopia

369n   Reform and/or revolution: Towards a unified women's movement

376f   Nineteenth-century women's prison reform and its legacy

379b   Piety and kin: The limits of antebellum Southern women's reform

412s   Shaping a new society: Methodist women and industrial reform in the south, 1880-1940

435f   Women and housing: The limitations of liberal reform

436g   Demography, political reform and women's issues in Czechoslovakia

La Regenta

313o   "La loca, la tonta, la literata": Women's destiny in Clarín's *La Regenta*

Regime

464d   Women and authoritarian regimes

Region

51b   Bad maps for an unknown region: Menopause from a literary perspective

Regional

316l   Challenging curricular assumptions: Teaching and studying women's literature from a regional perspective

Regulate

28c   Neuroendocrine regulation of sexual behavior

50y   'Guardians of the race' or 'vampires upon the nation's health'? Female sexuality and its regulation in early twentieth century Britain

79b   The DES controversy: Discovery, distribution and regulation

80o   The politics of federal day care regulation

178f   The public welfare system: Regulation and dehumanization

Rehabilitate

285a   The impact of sexuality, professional authoritarianism, and health crises on rehabilitation

285m   Sexual rehabilitation after gynecologic cancer

404z   Vocational rehabilitation: Options for women

Rehearsal

399vv   *Rebeccah*: Rehearsal notes

Rehnquist, William

2a   *Roe v Wade*: Majority opinion and Rehnquist dissent

Richel

176k   Teaching about Jewish lesbians in literature: From *Zeitl* and *Richel* to *The Tree of Begats*

Reincarnate

229k   Tales of a reincarnated Amazon princess: The invincible wonder woman?

Reinig, Christa

32q   Literary emasculation: Household imagery in Christa Reinig's *Entmannung*

Relation

24h   The dramaturgy of sexual relations

31k   The political nature of relations between the sexes

38j   On marital relations: Perceptions of black women

56c   Taking care of the little woman: Father-physician relations during pregnancy and childbirth

132b   Gender, relation, and difference in psychoanalytic perspective

138e   A cloud over co-education: An analysis of the forms of transmission of class and gender relations

Relationship

38p   Dialectics of black male-female relationships

48a   The intimate relationship between gender roles and sexuality

48k   The intimate relationships of lesbians and gay men

51k   Smoking, alcohol, and body mass relationships to early menopause: Implications for risk of cardiovascular disease

79j   Antenatal diagnosis: The physician-patient relationship

105e   Toward a theory of extramarital sexual relationships

178l   The quality of mother-child relationships

180x   Heritages: Dimensions of mother-daughter relationships in women's autobiographies

210k   Family relationships of older women: A women's issue

222h   In and out of relationships: A serious game for the woman doctoral student

230j   Sexual signaling and sexual aggression in adolescent relationships

271m   Assertiveness: Sex differences in relationships between self-report and behavioural measures

353f   "Imagine my surprise": Women's relationships in historical perspective

Relevant

254n   The whole thing: In search of relevance and integration made dynamic by creativity

Religion

see also Bible, Church, Deity, God, Laity, Liturgy, Preach, Theology, individual denominations and practitioners, e.g. Rabbi

2h   Constitutional privacy, religious disestablishment, and the abortion decisions

6f   Women in religion and in secular ideology

31f   Sexism, religion, and the social and spiritual liberation of women today

37c   Old-time religion: Benches can't say "Amen"

57h   Religion and sexual learning of children

60t   Religion as an instrument of social control

91b   Religion and menstruation

91s   Religious women in North India

91t   Women religious and the new society

94k   Religion, law and family disputes in a Lebanese Muslim community in Sydney

102d   Religion and the fearful father: Vision of liberation or American-style fascism?

123c   The feminist critique in religious studies

133x   Religious fundamentalism and the democratic process

143f   Law, religion and the unity of *Felix Holt*

152e   Homosexuality, celibacy, religious life and ordination

156q   The role of Jewish women in the religion, ritual and cult of Graeco-Roman Palestine

188m   The English religious enthusiast: Margery Kempe

194e   An Italian religious feast: The *Fujenti* rites of the Madonna dell'Arco, Naples

229e   Witchcraft as goddess religion

229oo   Ethics and justice in goddess religion

325a   Patterns in women's religious lives

325r   Menstruation and childbirth as ritual and religious experience among native Australians

353z   Ministries of healing: Mary Baker Eddy, Ellen G. White, and the religion of health

367a   American Indian women and religion

367b   Women and religion in Spanish America

367e   The religious experience of Southern women

367f   Black women and religion in the colonial period

367i   Women, civil religion, and the American Revolution

368j   Aliabad women: Revolution as religious activity

402h   Women and religion: The status and image of women in some major religious traditions

403a   The religious lives of Muslim women

412b   The last fifteen years: Historians' changing views of American women in religion and society

412e   Mary McLeod Bethune as religionist

421h   The effect of religious affiliation on woman's role in Middle Eastern Arab Society

457c   Gender and religion in a Turkish town: A comparison of two types of formal women's gatherings

457e   Essence and existence: Women and religion in ancient Indian texts

462b   Class, gender, and religion: A theoretical overview and some political implications

462r   A religious perspective

Rembrandt

43t   Female leaders: Who was Rembrandt's mother?

Remedial

274s Remedial education

Remember

59h Re-membering: A global perspective on women

Reminiscence

85c Reminiscences of fieldwork among the Sikhs

399gg Peggy Clark Kelley: Reminiscences of a "designing" woman

Renaissance

33c Book-lined cells: Women and humanism in the early Italian Renaissance

168a The renaissance of women

180d The new mother of the English renaissance: Her writings on motherhood

184c Dowries and kinsmen in early Renaissance Venice

372d Women and sport during the Renaissance

389k Erica Tietze-Conrat (1883-1958): Productive scholar in renaissance and baroque art

442i Poets and versifiers, singers and signifiers: Women of the Harlem Renaissance

Rendell, Ruth

1e Ruth Rendell

Rensselaer, Mariana Griswold Van

389g Mariana Griswold Van Rensselaer (1851-1934): America's first professional woman art critic

Renunciation

96g From renunciation to rebellion: The female in literature

Reparation

334c Shame and reparation: Women's place in the kin

Repetitive

280l Erotized repetitive hangings

Replacement

51x Sociological observations on ethical issues implicated in estrogen replacement therapy at menopause

Reply

338j Appendix: A reply to the toast to Canada

Report

271m Assertiveness: Sex differences in relationships between self-report and behavioural measures

306p Public presentation reports

316p Status report on the women's movement as indexed by a "Festival of Women" in West Virginia, Fall 1978

Represent

260j Labour market policy in four countries: Are women adequately represented?

352q Changing women's representation in school management: A systems perspective

435a Representing women: The transition from social movement to interest group

435b Representing women at the state and local levels: Commissions on the status of women

436b Women and citizenship: Mobilisation, participation, representation

Repress

78r Pornography and repression: A reconsideration

225s The historical repression of women's sexuality

247f From repressive tolerance to erotic liberation: *Maedchen in Uniform*

439g Pornography and repression: A reconsideration

Reproduce

see also Birth, Birth Control, Conception, Contraception, Fertility, Inseminate, Maternity, Midwife, Neonate, Newborn, Paternal, Postpartum, Pregnancy, Procreation, Sterilize

10f Alcohol use and reproduction

12j Reproductive engineering: The final solution?

18c "Reproductive choice" in the contemporary United States: A social analysis of female sterilization

23m 'Law reform and human reproduction': Implications for women

29l Physiological and reproductive disorders

34e No fertile women need apply: Employment discrimination and reproductive hazards in the workplace

35g Explaining "male chauvinism" and "feminism": Cultural differences in male and female reproductive strategies

36a Reproductive technologies: The birth of a women-centered analysis

48h Reproduction, roles, and responsibilities

50u Competing ideologies of reproduction: Medical and maternal perspectives on pregnancy

51h Neuroendocrine mechanisms of reproductive aging in women and female rats

60o Reproduction and class divisions among women

69b Changing views of the relationship between femininity and reproduction

79a Reproductive technologies: The birth of a women-centered analysis

79h A look at prenatal diagnosis within the context of changing parental and reproductive norms

79dd Ethics and reproductive technology

79ff Manipulative reproductive technologies discussion: Part I

79jj Manipulative reproductive technologies discussion: Part II

79mm Manipulative reproductive technologies discussion: Part III

84a Women is not a rational animal: On Aristotle's biology of reproduction

86j Mother, father, worker: Men and women and the reproduction risks of work

86k Keeping women in their place: Exclusionary policies and reproduction

94g Non English-speaking women: Production and social reproduction

103t Reproductive freedom and the right to privacy: A paradox for feminists

149e The expanded reproduction cycle of labour power in twentieth-century capitalism

153b Subsistence reproduction: A framework for analysis

153k The contribution of public goods to household reproduction: Case study from Brazil

173c The abortion-funding cases and population control: An imaginary lawsuit and some reflections on the uncertain limits of reproductive privacy

181k Reproductive technology: The future for women?

185e Transformations in human reproduction

195f Reproduction, mothering, and the origins of patriarchy

207b Subsistence production and extended reproduction

208d Subsistence production and extended reproduction

220j Romantic love and reproductive rights

233d Women workers at higher risk of reproductive hazards

233e Reproductive hazards of the American life style

233g The epidemiological identification of reproductive hazards

233l What evidence is required to identify a chemical as a reproductive hazard?

233n A trade union view of reproductive health

233o A management view of reproductive health

233p Legal considerations of reproductive hazards in industry in the United Kingdom

233q Legal considerations of reproductive hazards in industry in the United States

241d Men and war: Status, class and the social reproduction of masculinity

241i Purification or social control? Ideologies of reproduction and the churching of women after childbirth

242b The birth of the artist as heroine: (Re)production, the *Künslerroman* tradition, and the fiction of Katherine Mansfield

245c Why nineteenth-century feminists did not support "birth control" and twentieth-century feminists do: Feminism, reproduction, and the family

252s Somatic sequelae and future reproduction after pregnancy termination

253g Reproductive hazards in the workplace: A course curriculum guide

265r Sex without reproduction: Voluntary childlessness as a response to contemporary sex roles

305b Claim no easy victories: The fight for reproductive rights

310b The meanings of choice in reproductive technology

310j Teenage oppression and reproductive rights

310n Subtle forms of sterilization abuse: A reproductive rights analysis

310s Claiming all of our bodies: Reproductive rights and disabilities

310t Born and unborn: The implications of reproductive technologies for people with disabilities

310w Reproductive technologies: The final solution to the woman question?

315f Women, reproductive freedom, and the law: A selected annotated bibliography

321d Natural resources: Health, reproduction and the gender order

342c Black women as producers and reproducers for profit

360f Reproductive advancements: Theory, research applications, and psychological issues

365m Reproductive crises

370g Slavery and reproductive labor in Mombasa

372cc Sport and reproduction in women

395i Women's understanding about reproductive physiology and their choice of herbal medicines in Cali, Colombia

396c Competing ideologies of reproduction: Medical and maternal perspectives on pregnancy

396e Seizing the means of reproduction: An illegal feminist abortion collective — how and why it worked

411n Reproductive issues, including menopause

418k Feminist thought and reproductive control: The state and 'the right to choose'

427i Conceptions of kinship and the family reproduction cycle

428d Women, production, and reproduction in industrial capitalism: A comparison of Brazilian and U.S. factory workers

436h A hard day's night: Women, reproduction and service society

439e Reproductive freedom: Beyond "A woman's right to choose"

439f Menstruation and reproduction: An Oglala case

447i A legal perspective on workplace reproductive hazards

447j The biology of toxic effects on reproductive outcomes

459e Family structure and women's reproductive and productive roles: Some conceptual and methodological issues

468i Perspectives on work and reproduction with special reference to women's opportunities and adaptation

The Reproduction of Mothering

195i Review of Chodorow's *The Reproduction of Mothering*

Republic

336f Mother's day in the Weimar Republic

368k Women in the ideology of the Islamic Republic

Reputation

442a Colette's literary reputation

Research

21a Women in Asian cities, their political and economic roles: Research problems and strategies

22a "Glory is like a circle in the water"...Thoughts and suggestions towards a definition of feminine historical research

22c Iconography as a means of research on the history of the status of women

36f Women-controlled research

37e Perspectives on black family empirical research: 1965-1978

51a Toward a biosocial paradigm for menopause research: Lessons and contributions from the behavioral sciences

61c National Archives resources for research in the history of American women

63g Problems with research in co-corrections

79c Assessment of risks from DES: An analysis of research on those exposed during pregnancy or in utero

87a Three generations of dual-career family research

90b Women in educational administration: A descriptive analysis of dissertation research and paradigm for future research

107e Personality research: Implications for women in sport

120a Memoirs of an ontological exile: The methodological rebellions of feminist research

124i Feminist research methodology groups: Origins, forms, functions

124k Split brain research and its implications for feminist education

144a The German family: A critical survey of the current state of historical research

145a Current research on German women's history in the nineteenth century

171a Language, gender and society: Opening a second decade of research

178a Research methods and sample characteristics

181m Afterward: Machina ex dea and future research

190z Future directions for research

243c The role and status of women scientific research workers in research groups

243h Family, work, and individual development in dual-career marriages: Issues for research

266c Overview of research methods

266f Sampling: Issues and problems in sex role and social change research

266k The impact of societal biases on research methods

289j Research: Status, gaps, and design

298g The conditions required for women to conduct research on women in the Arab region

302f Biographical research on women librarians: Its paucity, perils, and pleasures

302j Women in academic-library, higher-education, and corporate management: A research review

306h Dusting the mirror: Researching women's history

306q New forms for new research

310f From mice to men? Implications of progress in cloning research

312k Experiential analysis: A contribution to feminist research

312l 'Back into the personal' or: Our attempt to construct 'feminist research'

351k Studying women's studies: A guide to archival research

363f Research on women in Latin America: Problems of networking and comparative analysis in the last decade

383j Beyond defensiveness: Feminist research strategies

398h Beyond defensiveness: A feminist research strategies

402c The study of women in South Asia: Some current methodological and research issues

421a Cultural determinants of power for women within the family: A neglected aspect of family research

423f Future research and policy questions

443j Hidden assumptions in theory and research on women

463a Women's travel issues: The research and policy environment

Researcher

98f Anthropological approach to study of rural women in Bangladesh: Experience of a female researcher

Reservation

70j Transition from the reservation to an urban setting and the changing roles of American Indian women

Reserve

279n Sexual dimorphism and nutrient reserves

Residential

169g Residential schools

463j Residential location and transportation analyses: Married women workers

Resist

39n Female slave resistance: The economics of sex

56g Alternative maternity care: Resistance and change

60d Crisis, reaction, and resistance: Women in Germany in the 1920's and 1930's

60e The social enforcement of heterosexuality and lesbian resistance in the 1920's

60u Women, media, and the dialectics of resistance

74d Affirmation and resistance: Women poets from the Caribbean

113d Yugoslavia: War of resistance

116e "Femininity," resistance and sabotage

138b Intersections of gender and class: Accommodation and resistance by working-class and affluent females to contradictory sex-role ideologies

138c Gender, resistance and power

199k Resistance strategies: The routine struggle for bread and roses

206n Resistance, strikes and strategies

245h Why men resist

267c Double jeopardy: Resistance to affirmative action from potential beneficiaries

316n Resistance to the women's movement in the United States: The ERA controversy as prototype

336n Comrade - woman - mother - resistance fighter

435m Bureaucratic resistance to women's programs: The case of women in development

Resolution

271h Assertiveness training for improved conflict resolution style

Resource

49h Human resource planning and the intuitive manager: Models for the 1990's

226m Resources and constraints on women in the policymaking process: States and local arenas

268n Senescence, sex roles, and stress: Shepherding resources into old age

314m Library resources on women

314r   In-house resources

314s   Resource networks

321d   Natural resources: Health, reproduction and the gender order

323aa   Trade union resources on women

350d   Resource allocation and the sexual division of labor: A case study of a Moslem Hausa village in northern Nigeria

373b   Overview: Women and technology — resources for our future

Respect

223r   Pornography and respect for women

Response

42m   A response, and more questions

48e   Sexual response and gender roles

80g   Day care and children's responsiveness to adults

116k   On curing conceptual confusion: Response to Mary Anne Warren

131n   A personal response to Whetmore's "A female captain's enterprise"

226j   Community responses to violence against women: The case of a battered women's shelter

345f   Response and recognition

461a   Women's sexual response

Responsibility

48h   Reproduction, roles, and responsibilities

166e   Rights and responsibility, power and privilege: Women's roles in contemporary Indonesia

223w   Taking responsibility for sexuality

308k   Family involvement, notification, and responsiblility: A personal essay

411p   The anxiety of the unknown - choice, risk, responsibility: Therapeutic issues for today's adult women

458n   Responsibility for household tasks: Comparing dual-earner and dual-retired marriages

Restoration

278b   'Last Night's Rambles': Restoration literature and the war between the sexes

Restrict

140j   Female masochism and the enforced restriction of choice

225k   The body politic: The defense of sexual restriction by anti-abortion activists

Restructure

123f   How the study of women has restructured the discipline of economics

206b   Restructuring: The cutting edge

Resurrection

40e   From baptism to resurrection: Toni Cade Bambara and the incongruity of language

Retail

199f   Women in retail sales work: The continuing dilemma of service

Rethink

122a   Rethinking the ways we teach

132i   Rethinking the maternal

Retire

210f   Beyond the hearth: Older women and retirement

221h   The process of retirement: Implications for late-life counseling

458a   Introduction: Research on women's retirement

458b   Midlife work history and retirement income

458e   Working women versus homemakers: Retirement resources and correlates of well-being

458f   Preretirement preparation: Sex differences in access, sources, and use

458g   Retirement expectations and plans: A comparison of professional men and women

458h   Attitudes toward retirement: A comparison of professional and nonprofessional married women

458i   Retirement plans and retirement adjustment

458j   The process of retirement: Comparing women and men

458k   After retirement: An exploratory study of the professional woman

458l   Professional women: Work pattern as a correlate of retirement satisfaction

458m   Personal problems and adjustment to retirement

458n   Responsibility for household tasks: Comparing dual-earner and dual-retired marriages

458o   Conclusion: Service needs of women retirees

465b   Members and survivors: Women and retirement-pensions legislation

Retrieve

193v   Retrieving the missing half

Retrospect

20l   Prospects and retrospects in *Life Before Man*

Reuter, Gabriele

32i   Gabriele Reuter: Romantic and realist

Review

135s   Feminist criticism reviewed

146l   Multidisciplinary team review of child-sexual-abuse cases

165h   Are females treated differently? A review of the theories and evidence on sentencing and parole decisions

253i   The effects of childbearing on women's mental health: A critical review of the literature

256g   One hand tied behind us: A review essay

265d   Review of the literature of non-sexist curriculum and a critique of the underlying assumptions and rationale

266j   Methods for integrative reviews

271k   Female superiority in sex difference competence comparisons: A review of the literature

341c   A woman's body in a man's world: A review of findings on body image and weight control

392b   The etiology of female crime: A review of the literature

417ff   Future visions: Today's politics: Feminist utopias in review

Revision

264a   Women's history and the revision of southern history

314b   Interactive phases of curricular re-vision

448f   Tradition and revision: The classic city novel and Virginia Woolf's *Night and Day*

Revisit

30s   Carrington revisited

31e   Concepts of woman in psychoanalytic theory: The nature-nurture controversy revisited

45b   The challenge of sex equality: Old values revisited or a new culture?

178p   Families revisited

193o   Girls' science: Boys' science revisited

253d   Sex and temperament revisited

255b   Purdah revisited: A comparison of Hindu and Muslim interpretations of the cultural meaning of purdah in South Asia

329o   The whole contention between Mr. Bennett and Mrs. Woolf, revisited

379c   The planter's wife revisited: Women, equity law, and the Chancery Court in seventeenth-century Maryland

434d   Rape crisis theory revisited

Revitalization

368h   Revitalization: Some reflections on the work of Saffar-Zadeh

Revivalism

187d   Benedictine life for women in central France, 850-1100: A feminist revival

366a   Women and revivalism

367h   Women and revivalism: The Puritan and Wesleyan traditions

Revolution

see also War

7c   Pornography and the sexual revolution: The backlash of sadomasochism

39f   The role of women in the revolution in Guinea-Bissau

50a   The butcher, the baker, the candlestick-maker: The shop and the family in the Industrial Revolution

61e   Women in the American revolution: Vignettes or profiles?

68f   Chinese women: The relative influences of ideological revolution, economic growth, and cultural change

68i   Women in Cuba: The revolution within the revolution

95a   Anna Kuliscioff: Russian revolutionist, Italian feminist

95e   Alexandra Kollontai and the Russian Revolution

102m   Women in the U.S. Foreign Service: A quiet revolution

103e   Women and the Reagan revolution: Thermidor for the social welfare economy

105d   Recent data reflecting upon the sexual revolution in America

112j   Mercy Otis Warren: Playwright, poet, and historian of the American revolution (American, 1728-1814)

113c   Russia: Revolution and war

120k   Feminist praxis: Feminism and revolution; feminist theory and feminist practice

125e   Margaret Fuller: Feminist writer and revolutionary

130c Women, democracy, and revolution in Paris, 1789-1794

132e Language and revolution: The Franco-American Dis-connection

174h Feminist scholarship: The extent of the revolution

177k Yenan women in revolution

198c The Islamic revolution and women: Quest for the Quranic model

212d Towards a revolutionary feminist analysis of rape

224b Cosmetics as an act of revolution

224m Revolution in the pursuit of happiness: Love and community-building on the left

282b The gender revolution and the transition from bisexual horde to patrilocal band: The origins of gender hierarchy

350b Women workers and the green revolution

363c Women and revolution: The brigadas femeninas and the Mexican Cristero Rebellion, 1926-1929

364c The exchange of women and property: Marriage in post-revolutionary China

367i Women, civil religion, and the American Revolution

368a Women in pre-revolutionary Iran: A historical overview

368i Poor women and social consciousness in revolutionary Iran

368j Aliabad women: Revolution as religious activity

368n Family planning in post-revolutionary Iran

369n Reform and/or revolution: Towards a unified women's movement

374b The revolution within the Revolution

379q Responses to the political activism of Women of the People in revolutionary Paris, 1789-1793

379r The effects of the Chinese Revolution on women and their families

390u Revolution and machismo: Women in the New South Wales Builders Labourers' Federation, 1961-75

399t Mercy Warren, satirist of the revolution

417l *Mujeres Libres* and the role of women in anarchist revolution

417n Women in the Children of God: "Revolutionary women" or "Mountin' maids"?

417aa Of time and revolution: Theories of social change in contemporary feminist science fiction

430f The post-revolutionary women's movement in Iran

444a Women of the popular classes in revolutionary Paris, 1789-1795

444d "Life, liberty, and dower": The legal status of women after the American Revolution

444e Old wine in new bottles: The institutional changes for women of the people during the French revolution

444g Women in the Chinese communist revolution: The question of political equality

444h Revolution and *conciencia*: Women in Cuba

444i Revolution and retreat: Upper-class French women after 1789

444j Patriot mothers in the post-risorgimento: Women after the Italian revolution

460u Young women and the sexual revolution

Revolution of 1848

145h German women writers and the Revolution of 1848

Revolutionary

103p Women in a revolutionary society: The state and family policy in China

405c Women revolutionaries: The personal and the political

433a Goddesses or rebels: The women revolutionaries of Bengal

Rewrite

338i Rewriting history: Anna Parnell's *The tale of a great sham*

Rhesus(D)

252p Prevention of Rhesus(D) isoimmunization after abortion

Rhetoric

133t Lesbianfeminist rhetoric as a social movement

214d Rhetoric and organizational change: New applications of feminine style

313n "Folly and a woman": Galdos' rhetoric of irony in *Tristana*

Rhode Island

376b Dealing with dependence: Paternalism and tax evasion in eighteenth-century Rhode Island

Rhodesia

160e The suitable wife: Preparation for marriage in London and Rhodesia/Zimbabwe

160h Settler wives in southern Rhodesia: A case study

Rhyme

121c Emily Dickinson's nursery rhymes

Rhys, Jean

332f The sisterhood of Jane Eyre and Antoinette Cosway

Rice

5g Gambian women: Unequal partners in rice development projects?

373h Java, Indonesia: The introduction of rice processing technology

379p "If eight hours seems few to you...": Women workers' strikes in Italian rice fields, 1901-1906

Rich

466e Rich woman, poor woman: Occupation differences in a textile producing village in Central Java

Rich, Adrienne

313b The "I" in Adrienne Rich: Individuation and the androgyne archetype

448m Another view of the "City upon a Hill": The prophetic vision of Adrienne Rich

Richard III

343b "Neither mother, wife, nor England's queen": The roles of women in *Richard III*

Richardson, Dorothy

328g Political aesthetics: Virginia Woolf and Dorothy Richardson

Richardson, Jo

283i Interview with Jo Richardson

Richter, Conrad

445k Conrad Richter's southwestern ladies

Richter, Gisela Marie Augusta

389j Gisela Marie Augusta Richter (1882-1972): Scholar of classical art and museum archaeologist

Riddick, Elsie

301z Miss Elsie Riddick

Right

see also Civil Rights, Equal Rights Amendment, Equality, Human Rights, Women's Rights

31a Private rights and public virtues: Women, the family, and democracy

31o Rights-conflict, pregnancy, and abortion

60g Antifeminism and the New Right

60h Feminism, the family, and the New Right

60i The New Right and the abortion issue

79r Rights of a handicapped neonate: What every parent and professional should know

91o Bondage: Denial or fundamental rights to women

103t Reproductive freedom and the right to privacy: A paradox for feminists

129bb A right to make laws?

133v Referendum campaigns vs. gay rights

133w Ideologies in two gay rights controversies

151c 'A woman's right to choose' in the Soviet Union

166e Rights and responsibility, power and privilege: Women's roles in contemporary Indonesia

174f The new right challenges women's studies: The Long Beach women's studies program

174y What are rights without means? Educating feminists for the future

211j Notes toward finding the right question

217c Women's right to money

220j Romantic love and reproductive rights

223l Abortion and a woman's right to decide

229tt The Christian right's "Holy War" against feminism

243d The old world, new rights, and the limited rebellion: Challenges to traditional authority in immigrant families

305b Claim no easy victories: The fight for reproductive rights

310j Teenage oppression and reproductive rights

310n Subtle forms of sterilization abuse: A reproductive rights analysis

310s Claiming all of our bodies: Reproductive rights and disabilities

323k The right to strike

333f Women and land rights: The Pitjantjatjara land claims

333g The recent history of the Borroloola aboriginal people and their struggle for land rights

333h Borroloola community and land rights

333j Women and land rights: A review

333k Women and land rights: Kiuk and Wagaidj women in the Darwin area

347h Daughters of the lakes and rivers: Colonization and the land rights of Luo women

366e The struggle for the right to preach

375b Widows' rights in Anglo-Saxon law

375c *Merchet* and women's property rights in medieval England

379h   Right-wing female activists in Buenos
       Aires, 1900-1932

390s   Right-wing union officials versus married
       women workers

392o   Mothers behind bars: A look at the
       parental rights of incarcerated women

399d   Rites and rights

402g   Women and the law: Constitutional rights
       and continuing inequalities

412k   Laity rights and leadership: Winning them
       for women in the Methodist Protestant
       church, 1860-1900

412n   The laity rights movement, 1906-1918:
       Women's suffrage in the Methodist
       Episcopal Church, South

418k   Feminist thought and reproductive con-
       trol: The state and 'the right to choose'

436l   Will women judges make a difference in
       women's legal rights? A prediction from
       attitudes and simulated behaviour

439e   Reproductive freedom: Beyond "A
       woman's right to choose"

440k   Legislating for the right to be equal

465h   The new right, sex, education and social
       policy: Towards a new moral economy in
       Britain and the USA

Rigidity

133l   Androgyny, sex-role rigidity, and homo-
       phobia

Rinehart, Mary Roberts

1g   Mary Roberts Rinehart

Riot

218e   Riot and rebellion among African women:
       Three examples of women's political clout

349h   The woman participant in Washington's
       riots

Rise

401i   One woman's rise to power: Cheng I's wife
       and the pirates

Risk

36p   Benefits and risks of electronic fetal moni-
       toring

51k   Smoking, alcohol, and body mass relation-
       ships to early menopause: Implications for
       risk of cardiovascular disease

53a   Sex differences in disease risk

53e   Changing patterns of smoking and risk of
       disease

53g   Women, alcohol, and the risk of disease

53n   Risk factors for benign and malignant
       breast disease

53q   Risk factors for ovarian cancer

86b   The risks of healing: The hazards of the
       nursing profession

86j   Mother, father, worker: Men and women
       and the reproduction risks of work

140q   Families at risk for father-daughter incest

191e   Risk factors for depression: What do we
       learn from them?

210o   Cardiovascular risk factors in the elderly
       woman

233d   Women workers at higher risk of repro-
       ductive hazards

309h   The risk of adolescent pregnancy in the
       first months of intercourse

309t   Guessing and misinformation about preg-
       nancy risk among urban mothers

411p   The anxiety of the unknown - choice, risk,
       responsibility: Therapeutic issues for
       today's adult women

Rite

194e   An Italian religious feast: The *Fujenti* rites
       of the Madonna dell'Arco, Naples

325g   Hindu women's family and household rites
       in a north Indian village

325i   Black Carib women and rites of death

399d   Rites and rights

Rite of Passage

131b   Alexei Panshin's almost non-sexist *Rite of
       Passage*

Ritter, Marie Louise

384b   Marie Louise Ritter: The pioneer woman
       in fact and fiction

Ritual

40cc   And called every generation blessed:
       Theme, setting, and ritual in the works of
       Paule Marshall

40pp   Fields watered with blood: Myth and ritual
       in the poetry of Margaret Walker

156i   Hittite birth rituals

156q   The role of Jewish women in the religion,
       ritual and cult of Graeco-Roman Palestine

190m   Virginity rituals and chastity control during
       puberty: Cross-cultural patterns

229v   Contemporary feminist rituals

229w   Honor and ceremony in women's rituals

229cc Feeding the feminist psyche through ritual
       theater

282d   Transforming "natural" woman: Female
       ritual leaders and gender ideology among
       Bimin-Kuskusmin

325f   Golden handprints and red-painted feet:
       Hindu childbirth rituals in central India

325h   The ladies of Lord Krishna: Rituals of
       middle-aged women in eastern India

325r   Menstruation and childbirth as ritual and
       religious experience among native
       Australians

353e   The female world of love and ritual:
       Relations between women in nineteenth-
       century America

399c   Friendship and ritual in the WTUL

403f   Ritual status of Muslim women in rural
       India

453f   Goddess imagery in ritual

454l   The female world of love and ritual:
       Relations between women in nineteenth-
       century America

462z   Guidelines for planners of ritual

462aa Reflections on the creation of a ritual meal

Rivanol

252i   Extra-amniotic ethacridine (Rivanol)-
       catheter technique for midtrimester abor-
       tion

Rølvaag, Ole E.

384m   Beret as the Norse mythological goddess
       Freya/Gurthr

445j   Madness and personification in *Giants in
       the Earth*

Road

265k   Sex differences in children's road accidents

301oo Queen of the road

The Robber Bridegroom

384s   Pioneering the imagination: Eudora
       Welty's *The Robber Bridegroom*

Roberts, Joan

249d   Joan Roberts and the university

Rocco

130aa The view from Spain: Rocco *finesse* and
       espirit versus plebian manners

Rochester, NY

201e   The great uprising in Rochester

Rodeo

147ff From sidesaddle to rodeo

Rodgers, Carolyn

40hh   Imagery in the women poems: The art of
       Carolyn Rodgers

40ii   Running wild in her soul: The poetry of
       Carolyn Rodgers

Rodriguez, Chipita

175f   The ghost of Chipita: The crying woman of
       San Patricio

Roe v Wade

see also Abortion

2a   *Roe v Wade*: Majority opinion and
       Rehnquist dissent

2b   The legacy of *Roe v Wade*

2c   *Roe v Wade*: A study in male ideology

2f   Understanding Blackmun's argument: The
       reasoning of *Roe v Wade*

2m   Abortion, privacy, and personhood: From
       Roe v Wade to the human life statute

173a   Rewriting *Roe v. Wade*

173d   *Roe v. Wade* and the lesson of the pre-*Roe*
       case law

173f   Public support for pro-choice abortion
       policies in the nation and states: Changes
       and stability after the *Roe* and *Doe* deci-
       sions

Roeg, Nicholas

247h   Now and nowhere: Roeg's *Bad Timing*

Roemer, Astrid

322k   Interview with Astrid Roemer (Surinam)

Rogers, Mildred

155a   The prostitute as scapegoat: Mildred
       Rogers in Somerset Maugham's *Of Human
       Bondage*

Role

see also Gender Role, Role Model, Sex Role,
Social Role

16n   Counselor's roles

21a   Women in Asian cities, their political and
       economic roles: Research problems and
       strategies

21b   The Japanese woman: Evolving views of
       life and role

21e   Some changing socioeconomic roles of vil-
       lage women in Malaysia

22d   Le rôle et la place de la femme provenant
       de la classe sociale inférieure dans la vie
       quotidienne du Moyen-Age

33f   Women's roles in early modern Venice: An
       exceptional case

38d   The black woman and family roles

38k   Role transition in early adulthood:
       Orientations of young black women

39f The role of women in the revolution in Guinea-Bissau

39g The African woman as entrepreneur: Problem and perspectives on their roles

39l The role of women in the struggle against *apartheid* in South Africa

39w Women's role in West Indian society

39aa Economic role and cultural tradition

42k A woman's role and destiny

42n The traditional role of the Mormon woman

45f Psychological orientations to the work role: 1957-1976

45h Family roles in a twenty-year perspective

48h Reproduction, roles, and responsibilities

52b The changing roles of Canadian women in family and work: An overview

52g The changing role of women: The case of Italy

52i The changing status and role of women in Japan

52j The changing role of Swedish women in family and society

52k Economic and family roles of men and women in Northern Europe: A historical cross-national comparison

52p Women's roles and conjugal family systems in Ghana

52r Economic recession and Swiss women's attitudes towards marital role segregation

55h The role of community health centers

60p Women's role in economic development: Practical and theoretical implications of class and gender inequalities

65m The role of labor

68d Women in Zaire: Disparate status and roles

70j Transition from the reservation to an urban setting and the changing roles of American Indian women

73j Family roles and identities of Scandinavian and German women

82l Tenure and the role of the female

82o Women's roles and culturally sensitive programs

85g The expert's view? The sociological analysis of graduates' occupational and domestic roles

87d Young marrieds: Wives' employment and family role structure

87f Spouses' contributions to each other's roles

87g Parenthood, marriage, and careers: Situational constraints and role strain

92a An action-oriented study of the role of women in rural development

92d Pakistan: The role of women in reciprocal relationships in a Punjab village

92h Rural women and their multiple roles

96l The role and function of women's consciousness raising: Self-help, psychotherapy, or political activation?

98h Personal account of the role of a supervisor in the Bangladesh fertility survey

102g The good-provider role: Its rise and fall

103d The transformation of patriarchy: The historic role of the state

131h An ambiguous legacy: The role and position of women in the English Eutopia

133a Homosexual labeling and the male role

140k Roles and role conflict of women in infertile couples

140u Men's new family roles: Some implications for therapists

144b Family and role-division: The polarisation of sexual stereotypes in the nineteenth century - an aspect of the dissociation of work and family

145d Henriette Schleiermacher: A woman in a traditional role

145o The woman's role in the German working-class family in the 1890s from the perspective of women's autobiographies

148e Women's work: An examination of women's roles in Plains Indian arts and crafts

148f The role of Sioux women in the production of ceremonial objects: The case of the star quilt

148j "Warrior women" - Sex role alternatives for Plains Indian women

155d The magic circle: The role of the prostitute in Isak Dinesen's *Gothic Tales*

156q The role of Jewish women in the religion, ritual and cult of Graeco-Roman Palestine

166e Rights and responsibility, power and privilege: Women's roles in contemporary Indonesia

182d House design and women's roles

194n The Great Goddess today in Burma and Thailand: An exploration of her symbolic relevance to monastic and female roles

198d Roles in transition: The evolving position of women in Arab-Islamic countries

203k Toward supportive neighborhoods: Women's role in changing the segregated city

204g Primary caregiving and role-sharing fathers

205h From pastels to chisel: The changing role of BC women artists

209d Women, technological change and employment levels: The role of trade unions policies

209n The role of common sense in the process of interface design

219f The role of the judiciary in the failure of the Sexual Offences (Amendment) Act to improve the treatment of the rape victim

236d An appraisal of the role of progesterone in the therapy of premenstrual syndrome

239j Adult life cycles: Changing roles and changing hormones

243c The role and status of women scientific research workers in research groups

243k Weak links in men's worker-earner roles: A descriptive model

243m Husbands' paid work and family roles: Current research issues

244a Colombian women in party politics: A token role

244c Sex segregation and the women's roles in the economic system: The case of Iran

244e The roles of men and women in French families: Change or stability in the patterns and practices?

244f The roles of Greek husbands and wives: Definitions and fulfillment

244k Role loss and manic depression

251d The impact of science and technology and the role of women in science in Mexico

255i Purdah politics: The role of Muslim women in Indian nationalism, 1911-1924

263c Symmetrical families? Changing gender role expectations and the breadwinner role in the contemporary United States

264c The public role of southern women

265q Overemphasis of mother role and inflexibility of roles

269d New economic roles for Cuna males and females: An examination of socioeconomic change in a San Blas community

269e New roles for males in Guaymí society

269g Watch that pot or the *waksuk* will eat you up: An analysis of male and female roles in Rama Indian myth

269h Symbolic aspects of Bribri roles on the occasions of birth and death

270c Urban change and women's roles in Turkey: An overview and evaluation

270h The effect of international labor migration on women's roles: The Turkish case

295j Social support and efficacy in advocacy roles: A case study of two women's organizations

296b Differential power of women over the life course: A case study of age-roles as an indicator of power

300a Modernization, changing roles of women and expectations for development in Southeast Asia

308b The family's role in adolescent sexual behavior

333e The conflicting role of aboriginal women in today's society

333m Women in the health role

333o Aboriginal women's role today in early childhood school education

343b "Neither mother, wife, nor England's queen": The roles of women in *Richard III*

346b Child workers in the informal sector role of the NGOs: Some reflections

351d Biology: Its role in gender-related educational experiences

352n Working and parenting: The male and father role

353a The female animal: Medical and biological views of woman and her role in nineteenth-century America

368d Social and economic change in the role of women, 1956-1978

373j Changing role of Maya mothers and daughters

373o Roles of women: UNCSTD background discussion paper

385h International development and the evolution of women's economic roles: A case study from northern Gulma, Upper Volta

385l Fertility and employment: An assessment of role incompatibility among African urban women

387h The work-family role system

390b 'Feeding the poor and sapping their strength': The public role of ruling-class women in eastern Australia, 1788-1850

393a   Wage earner and mother: Compatibility of roles on a Cameroon plantation

394m   The president's wife: A changing role — observations of a chancellor's wife

398d   Survival in the 'master's house': The role of graduate teaching assistants in effecting curriculum change

399k   Women in male roles: Charlotte Cushman and others

400b   Rural pauperization: Its impact on the economic role and status of rural women in Bangladesh

402m   The aging woman in India: Self-perceptions and changing roles

403b   Traditional affirmations concerning the role of women as found in contemporary Arab Islamic literature

404u   The role of the family in teenage pregnancy: Support or sabotage

405m   Procreation and new definitions in the role of women in a Soviet bloc country: The case of Poland

410e   Sex differences in role behavior and policy orientations of suburban officeholders: The effect of women's employment

410g   Organizational role orientations on female-dominant commissions: Focus on staff-commissioner interaction

410h   Perceptions of women's roles on local councils in Connecticut

411f   Multiple roles of midlife women: A case for new directions in theory, research, and policy

411h   Social change and equality: The roles of women and economics

412c   Women of the word: Selected leadership roles of women in Mr. Wesley's Methodism

413b   The role and status of Maori women

416o   Evolving views of women's professional roles

417l   *Mujeres Libres* and the role of women in anarchist revolution

419k   The role of women in Roman elegy: Counter-cultural feminism

421c   A causal interpretation of the effect of mother's education and employment status on parental decision-making role patterns in the Korean family

421e   Planning for women in the new towns: New concepts and dated roles

421h   The effect of religious affiliation on woman's role in Middle Eastern Arab Society

421j   Attitudes and ideology: Correlates of liberal attitudes towards the role of women

421k   Feminist egalitarianism, social action orientation and occupational roles: A cross-national study

421o   Wife-employment and the emergence of egalitarian marital role prescriptions: 1900-1974

421v   Some comments on the home roles of businesswomen in India, Australia and Canada

421y   Variations in women's roles and family life under the socialist regime in China

423d   Women's work and family roles

434l   Dilemmas in role identification for low-income women

436c   Women's role in the formulation of public policies in Brazil

440j   The women's movement's fandango with the state: The movement's role in public policy since 1972

443e   Female role socialization: The analyst and the analysis

446k   Changing family roles and marital instability

447e   Changing roles and mental health in women

459a   Demographic change and the role of women: A research programme in developing countries

459e   Family structure and women's reproductive and productive roles: Some conceptual and methodological issues

459f   A social anthropological approach to women's roles and status in developing countries: The domestic cycle

459g   The interrelationship between the division of labour in the household, women's roles and their impact on fertility

460p   Role of the father

463k   Role influence in transportation decision making

463v   An alternative approach to travel demand modeling: Constraints-oriented theories and societal roles

466i   Separate but equal: Indonesian Muslim perceptions of the roles of women

469c   The self-perception of Puerto Rican women toward their societal roles

469k   Family roles of Hispanic women: Stereotypes, empirical findings, and implications for research

473c   Women's role in a Muslim Hausa town (Mirria, Republic of Niger)

473j   The uses of traditional concepts in the development of new urban roles: Cuban women in the United States

473l   The economic role of women in Alaskan Eskimo society

Role Model
259d   Staffing for sexism: Educational leadership and role models

352m   The need for female role models in education

368e   Fatimeh as a role model in the works of Ali Shari'ati

Role Play
64l   The theatre as literary model: Role-playing in *Chéri* and *The Last of Chéri*

Role, Jenny Jenkins, Roll
460a   "Role, Jenny Jenkins, Roll": Little girls and maidens in American folksongs - an analysis of sexual attitudes

Rolston, Tilly Jean
205aa Tilly Jean Rolston: She knew how to throw a party

Roman Catholic
see Catholicism

Romance
20h   The dark voyage: *The Edible Woman* as romance

109c   Victoria Holt's gothic romances: A structuralist inquiry

225v   Search for tomorrow: On feminism and the reconstruction of teen romance

231m   Mass market romance: Pornography for women is different

332c   "Fairy-born and human-bred": Jane Eyre's education in romance

343q   "O sacred, shadowy, cold, and constant queen": Shakespeare's imperiled and chastening daughters of romance

Romantic
32i   Gabriele Reuter: Romantic and realist

155e   The romantization of the prostitute in Dostoevsky's fiction

164b   Jane Austen and romantic imprisonment

220j   Romantic love and reproductive rights

288c   Coping with Cupid: The formation, impact, and management of romantic relationships in organizations

Rome
117e   Social status and gender in Roman art: The case of the saleswoman

156q   The role of Jewish women in the religion, ritual and cult of Graeco-Roman Palestine

375a   Women as property in the early Roman empire

419k   The role of women in Roman elegy: Counter-cultural feminism

Romola
142f   Antique gems from *Romola* to *Daniel Deronda*

143e   *Romola* and the myth of apocalypse

Roosevelt, Eleanor
61n   Eleanor Roosevelt's role in women's history

Rootedness
40dd   Rootedness: The ancestor as foundation

Rose
175c   Emily Morgan: Yellow rose of Texas

Rosie the Riveter
305r   Rosie the Riveter meets the sexual division of labour

Rossetti, Dante Gabriel
117m   Lost and *Found*: Once more the fallen woman

Rossi, Cristina Peri
322m   Interview with Cristina Peri Rossi (Uruguay)

Rotate
107u   Body segment contributions of female athletes to translational and rotational requirements of non-twisting springboard dive takeoffs

The Rouge of the North
449e   The shaping of life: Structure and narrative process in Eileen Chang's *The Rouge of the North*

Rourke, Constance
384r   Where the West begins: Constance Rourke's images of her own frontierland

Rousseau, Jean Jacques
106f   Julie and "La Maison Paternelle": Another look at Rousseau's *La Nouvelle Héloïse*

130t   Rousseau's "antifeminism" reconsidered

286j On the enrichment of poor monkeys by myth and dream; or how Dickens Rousseauisticized and pre-Freudianized Victorian views of childhood

Rower

107t Body build of female Olympic rowers

Roy, Gabrielle

448j Quest for the peaceable kingdom: Urban/rural codes in Roy, Laurence, and Atwood

Royal Australian Nursing Federation

390h 'I have never liked trade unionism': The development of the Royal Australian Nursing Federation, Queensland Branch, 1904-1945

Ruiz, Juan

408d Women in the *Book of Good Love*

Rule

45e Ground rules for marriage: Perspectives on the pattern of an era

335d Production rules OK? Waged work and the family

371a Ground rules and social maps for women: An introduction

Ruling Class

390b 'Feeding the poor and sapping their strength': The public role of ruling-class women in eastern Australia, 1788-1850

Ruminate

40jj Ruminations/Reflections

Runaway

201j Dorothy Jacobs Bellanca: Women clothing workers and the runaway shops

Rural

see also City

5h Developing women's cooperatives: An experiment in rural Nigeria

6a Women in the rural economy: Past, present and future

6b Women in the rural economy: Contemporary variations

18d Rural family size and economic change: A Middle Eastern case

39dd The spread of capitalism in rural Colombia: Effects on poor women

75d Career counselling for poor rural and urban women of South India

92a An action-oriented study of the role of women in rural development

92b Bangladesh: Beliefs and customs observed by Muslim rural women during their life cycle

92e Indonesia: Married women's work pattern in rural Java

92f Indonesia: Socio-economic aspects of food consumption in rural Java

92g The advantages of functional education and credit facilities for Javanese rural women

92h Rural women and their multiple roles

98a Getting to know a rural community in Bangladesh

98j Survey research with rural women in Bangladesh

98k Action research with rural women in Bangladesh: Some observations and experiences

98l Towards the making of a documentary film on rural women in Bangladesh

104a Aspects of non-capitalist social relations in rural Egypt: The small peasant household in an Egyptian delta village

104g Women's work in rural south-west England

104h Domestic work in rural Iceland: An historical overview

162c Infanticide in rural Bavaria in the nineteenth century

162n Village spinning bees: Sexual culture and free time among rural youths in early modern Germany

171d Linguistic options and choices for black women in the rural South

172b Research experiences with rural women (Costa Rica)

172i Integrating women into rural cooperatives: Pluses and minuses (Bolivia)

174r A feminist chautauqua for a rural state

176e Harassment in rural America

183a Rural women in development

183c Status of rural women

243a Urban and rural working women in Poland today: Between social change and social conflict

270e Women's education in rural Turkey

300h Rural-urban linkages and migration: A Philippines case study

306e Tell me all you know: Reading letters and diaries of rural women

350a The dynamics of the sexual division of labor and integration of rural women into the world market

350g From rural subsistence to an industrial peripheral work force: An examination of female Malaysian migrants and capital accumulation in Singapore

350i The sexual division of labor in rural China

364f The legal and social transformation of rural women in Aegean Turkey

385b Control of land, labor, and capital in rural southern Sierra Leone

388b Rural women in development

388i Rural women and development planning in Peru

395f Perceptions of a family planning campaign in rural Mexico

395h Family planning in rural China

400b Rural pauperization: Its impact on the economic role and status of rural women in Bangladesh

400d Impact of male migration on rural housewives

400e Population planning and rural women's co-operative in IRDP women's programme: Some critical issues

402d Trends and structure of female labour force participation in rural and urban Pakistan

403c The determinants of social position among rural Moroccan women

403f Ritual status of Muslim women in rural India

404f The sparse ghetto: Service delivery in a rural area

404ff Federal support: Understanding and utilizing the federal dollar

420d Women in rural-urban circulation networks: Implications for social structural change

420e Rural-to-urban migration of women in India: Patterns and implications

420g Female rural-to-urban migration in peninsular Malaysia

420m The migration of rural women to Taipei

421t Fertility and family economy in the Iranian rural communities

428p The emergence of small-scale industry in a Taiwanese rural community

431e Women in Java's rural middle class: Progress or regress

433b Conditions influencing rural and town women's participation in the labor force

436f Creating employment opportunities for rural women: Some issues affecting attitudes and policy

448j Quest for the peaceable kingdom: Urban/rural codes in Roy, Laurence, and Atwood

459h Women's work and their status: Rural Indian evidence of labour market and environment effects on sex differences in childhood mortality

473k The life of Sarah Penfield, rural Ohio grandmother: Tradition maintained, tradition threatened

Russ, Joanna

131g A footnote to Russ's "Recent feminist utopias"

Russia

52l Soviet women in family and society

95a Anna Kuliscioff: Russian revolutionist, Italian feminist

95e Alexandra Kollontai and the Russian Revolution

113c Russia: Revolution and war

130z The view from Russia

142i George Eliot and the Russians

151b Domestic labour and Soviet society

151c 'A woman's right to choose' in the Soviet Union

151f Soviet boarding education: Its rise and progress

151g Soviet child care: Its organisation at local level

151h Backward children in the USSR: An unfamiliar approach to a familiar problem

151i Achievements and problems in Soviet recreational planning

151j Sport in Soviet society: Fetish or free play?

151k Reading as a leisure pursuit in the USSR

194f The worship of Mother Earth in Russian culture

215p Building on the positives: The USSR

228l USSR

231i Russian working women: Sexuality in bonding patterns and the politics of daily life

371h The sexual division of domestic space among two Soviet minorities: The Georgians and the Tadjiks

405b The women's liberation issue in nineteenth century Russia

405h Soviet women in combat in World War II: The ground/air defense forces

405j   Have women's chances for political recruitment in the USSR really improved?

405k   The social composition of women deputies in Soviet elective politics: A preliminary analysis of official biographies

405m   Procreation and new definitions in the role of women in a Soviet bloc country: The case of Poland

405n   Some demographic, particularly fertility, correlates of female status in eastern Europe and the republics of the Soviet Union

438i   A little about myself, and more about a more important matter - the brain (USSR)

446a   Women, work, and family: New Soviet perspectives

446b   Current problems of female labor in the USSR

446h   The twenty-fifth congress of the CPSU and current problems of employment of female labor in the republics of central Asia

471k   Women at work in the USSR

472g   The "babushka" or older woman in Soviet society

Sabotage
116e   "Femininity," resistance and sabotage

Sacajawea
384f   Sacajawea of myth and history

Sackville-West, Vita
329p   Combining 'the advantages of act and fiction': Virginia Woolf's biographies of Vita Sackville-West, Flush, and Roger Fry

448e   Every woman is an island: Vita Sackville-West, the image of the city and the pastoral idyll

Sacred
278f   Phallic worship: Some personal meditations on a sacred theme

315h   Two in one, one in two: An exploration of a birth experience and images of the sacred

371d   Essential objects and the sacred: Interior and exterior space in an urban Greek locality

Sacrifice
199c   Sacrifice, satisfaction, and social change: Employment and the family

Sade, Marquis de
27d   Ambivalence in the Gynogram: Sade's utopian woman

130v   The problem of sexual equality in Sadean prose

Sadism
7e   On the history of cultural sadism

7s   Sadism, masochism, and lesbian-feminism

Sadomasochism
7a   Introduction: Against sadomasochism

7c   Pornography and the sexual revolution: The backlash of sadomasochism

7d   Sadomasochism and the social construction of desire

7g   Feminism and sadomasochism: Self-critical notes

7h   Sadomasochism and the liberal tradition

7i   Why I'm against S/M liberation

7j   Sadomasochism: A personal experience

7l   Racism and sadomasochism: A conversation with two black lesbians

7m   An opinionated piece on sadomasochism

7n   The politics of sado-masochistic fantasies

7o   Sadomasochism: Eroticized violence, eroticized powerlessness

7q   Is sadomasochism feminist? A critique of the Samois position

7v   Lesbian S & M: The politics of dis-illusion

7w   Sadomasochism: A contra-feminist activity

7x   Sadomasochism and the erosion of self: A critical reading of *Story of O*

7z   A letter of the times, or should this sado-masochism be saved?

280n   Bondage and sadomasochism

Safe
13e   Bearers of burdens: Occupational safety without discrimination

169p   Occupational health and safety for women workers: Some teaching models

206j   The safety catch

209v   An issue of respect: Women workers demand healthy and safe offices

252d   A review of abortion practices and their safety

463o   Perceived safety and security in transportation systems as determined by the gender of the traveler

Saffar-Zadeh
368h   Revitalization: Some reflections on the work of Saffar-Zadeh

Sagaris
174i   A note on Sagaris

174j   The ideas and the realities: Sagaris, Session I

174k   Women and process: The Sagaris split, Session II

Sahara
5b   Women and agriculture in sub-Saharan Africa: Implications for development

Sailor
164k   In between - Anne Elliot marries a sailor and Charlotte Heywood goes to the seaside

Saint
19n   Saints and sisters

325m   Empress Wu and the historians: A tyrant and saint of classical China

St. Bernard
187n   Epilogue: Does St Bernard have a specific message for nuns?

Saint Bridget
188j   The Swedish visionary: Saint Bridget

Saint Catherine of Siena
188k   The Tuscan visionary: Saint Catherine of Siena

St. Kilda
294i   Introduction: St. Kilda voices

St. Kitts
473h   Adaptive strategies and social networks of women in St. Kitts

St. Vincent
473g   Sex and status: Women in St. Vincent

Sakti
232a   On the meaning of sakti to women in Tamil Nadu

Salary
see also Pay

87l   Salary and job performance differences in dual-career couples

302i   Salary and position levels of females and males in academic libraries

Sale
162p   Mothers, sons, and the sale of symbols and goods: The 'German Mother's Day' 1923-33

Saleswoman
117e   Social status and gender in Roman art: The case of the saleswoman

Saline
252h   Intra-amniotic hypertonic saline instillation in the second trimester

Salon
442g   Salonists and chroniclers

The Salt Eaters
150r   What it is I think she's doing anyhow: A reading of Toni Cade Bambara's *The Salt Eaters*

Salt of the Earth (Film)
332m   "Why are you afraid to have me at your side?": From passivity to power in *Salt of the Earth*

Salvation
40d   Salvation is the issue

Samaritanism
2k   Abortion and the claims of samaritanism

Same-Sex
35f   Power structures and perceptions of power holders in same-sex groups of young children

Sammelan
91v   Sammelan of the spirit

Samoa
282f   Sexuality and gender in Samoa: Conceptions and missed conceptions

Samois
7k   A response to Samois

7q   Is sadomasochism feminist? A critique of the Samois position

Sample
110e   Sample selection bias as a specification error

178a   Research methods and sample characteristics

266f   Sampling: Issues and problems in sex role and social change research

Samurai
131l   Charles Bronson, Samurai, and other feminine images: A transactive response to *The Left Hand of Darkness*

San Blas
269d   New economic roles for Cuna males and females: An examination of socioeconomic change in a San Blas community

San Francisco, CA
73d   The Museo Italo Americano: My involvement with the Italian American community in San Francisco

379l City mothers, city daughters, and the dance hall girls: The limits of female political power in San Francisco, 1913

San Isidro, Guatemala

421b Female-headed households and domestic organization in San Isidro, Guatemala: A test of Hammel and Laslett's comparative typology

San Jose, CA

319k Social networks and survival strategies: An exploratory study of Mexican American, black and Anglo family female heads in San Jose, California

San Patricio

175f The ghost of Chipita: The crying woman of San Patricio

Sanchez Family

54g Structural family therapy: The Sanchez family

Sanchez, Sonia

40kk Sonia Sanchez: The bringer of memories

40ll The poetry of Sonia Sanchez

Sanctificationist

175n Martha White McWhirter and the Belton Sanctificationists

Sand, George

27e George Sand and the myth of femininity

242e Writing (from) the feminine: George Sand and the novel of female pastoral

Sandition

164k In between - Anne Elliot marries a sailor and Charlotte Heywood goes to the seaside

Sandoz, Mari

384q Toward a new paradigm: Mari Sandoz's study of red and white myth in *Cheyenne Autumn*

445f Mari Sandoz and western biography

Sands, Diana

150p I've been thinking of Diana Sands

Sanitary

299c Sanitary workers

Sanitation

395e Water and sanitation-related health constraints on women's contribution to the economic development of communities

Saõ Paulo, Brazil

473e Spirit magic in the social relations between men and women (Saõ Paulo, Brazil)

Sapphire

14j Debunking Sapphire: Toward a non-racist and non-sexist social science

Sappho

419d Sappho and Helen

Sarton, May

27n A conversation with May Sarton

30x May Sarton: A metaphor for my life, my work, and my art

135i May Sarton and fictions of old age

186a May Sarton: Reaching the lighthouse

186c May Sarton: Approaches to autobiography

186d May Sarton's memoirs

186e House, home and solitude: Memoirs and journals of May Sarton

186f A French view of May Sarton

186g "The Action of the beautiful": The concept of balance in the writings of May Sarton

186i Living rooms: Amity in the novels of May Sarton

186j Patterns of love and friendship: Five novels by May Sarton

186k May Sarton's *The Small Room*: A comparison and an analysis

186l Rage for justice: Political, social and moral consciousness in selected novels of May Sarton

186m Perimeters of power: An examination of *As We Are Now*

186n Redefinitions of traditional Christian emblems and outlooks in May Sarton's novels of 1970-1975

186o A note on May Sarton's use of form

186p The sculptor and the rock: Some uses of myth in the poetry of May Sarton

186q Metaphor in five garden poems by May Sarton

186r The singing wound: Intensifying paradoxes in May Sarton's " A Divorce of Lovers"

186s "The risk is very great": The poetry of May Sarton

186t "Sister of the mirage and echo": An interview with May Sarton

186u To be reborn: An interview with May Sarton

186v A further interview with May Sarton

186w "I live alone in a very beautiful place": An interview with May Sarton

186x A shining in the dark: May Sarton's accomplishment

Saskatchewan Working Women

305n Getting organized...in Saskatchewan Working Women

Satan

206p Using sex and satan to bust the union (an interview with Corky Jennings)

Sati

218b *Sati* or *Shakti*: Women, culture and politics in India

Satire

114h Sex, satire, and feminism in the science fiction of Suzette Haden Elgin

197f Muriel Spark and satire

331g The "other" voice: Woman's song, its satire and its transcendence in late medieval British literature

399t Mercy Warren, satirist of the revolution

Satisfaction

41c Sources of life satisfaction: The different worlds of black women and white women

199c Sacrifice, satisfaction, and social change: Employment and the family

221g Burnout and job dissatisfaction: Impact on the family

317b Life satisfaction research in aging: Implications for policy development

351c Career and life satisfactions among Terman's gifted women

355e Satisfaction with housework: The social context

421q Sex role attitudes, female employment, and marital satisfaction

425h Causal determinants of job satisfaction in dual career couples

458c Life satisfaction among aging women: A causal model

458l Professional women: Work pattern as a correlate of retirement satisfaction

Saudi

473a The contemporary Saudi woman

Sauna

210c Out of the *Mikvah* into the sauna: A study of women's health clubs

Save

153j Household economy and financial capital: The case of passbook savings in Brazil

172m Saving money with bio-gas (Colombia)

Saxon

112i Elizabeth Elstob: The Saxon nymph (English, 1683-1765)

188b The Saxon canoness: Hrotsvit of Gandersheim

Sayers, Dorothy

1a Dorothy Sayers

Scale

63h The development of a scale to assess inmate and staff attitudes toward co-corrections

Scandal

125a Aphra Behn: A scandal to modesty

336d The Bremen morality scandal

Scandinavia

103q Family responsibilities as a labor market issue: A Scandinavian perspective

218g Women and social policy: Lessons from Scandinavia

Scandinavian American Woman

73j Family roles and identities of Scandinavian and German women

Scapegoat

155a The prostitute as scapegoat: Mildred Rogers in Somerset Maugham's *Of Human Bondage*

Scarborough, Dorothy

445o Dorothy Scarborough's critique of the frontier experience in *The Wind*

Scarcity

84e Evolution and patriarchal myths of scarcity and competition

Schapiro, Miriam

117q Miriam Schapiro and "femmage": Reflections on the conflict between decoration and abstraction in twentieth-century art

Schema

122g Bem's gender schema theory

Schizophrenia

137g Gender and schizophrenia

268h Schizophrenia

Schleiermacher, Henriette

145d Henriette Schleiermacher: A woman in a traditional role

Scholar

30c A portrait of the *Puttana* as a middle-aged Woolf scholar

33d   Learned women of early modern Italy: Humanists and university scholars

188d   The French scholar-lover: Heloise

344l   Women and higher education: Sex differentials in the status of students and scholars

389j   Gisela Marie Augusta Richter (1882-1972): Scholar of classical art and museum archaeologist

389k   Erica Tietze-Conrat (1883-1958): Productive scholar in renaissance and baroque art

389l   Sirarpie Der Nersessian (b. 1896): Educator and scholar in Byzantine and Armenian art

389n   Dorothy Eugenia Miner (1904-1973): The varied career of a medievalist: Scholar and keeper of manuscripts, librarian and editor at the Walters Art Gallery

Scholarship

123i   Women in sociological analysis: New scholarship versus old paradigms

174h   Feminist scholarship: The extent of the revolution

296j   Women and power within the historical dynamic of feminist scholarship

312h   Passionate scholarship: Notes on values, knowing and method in feminist social science

School

see also Education, various levels and types of schools

49n   Whom should the schools serve, When...?

57b   Toward an understanding of sexual learning and communication: An examination of social learning theory and nonschool learning environments

62c   The politics of single-sex schools

62e   The realities of mixed schooling

68o   The schooling of Vietnamese immigrants: Internal colonialism and its impact on women

70e   The interaction of culture and sex roles in the schools

70h   Indian boarding schools and Indian women: Blessing or curse?

71e   Asian women in professional health schools, with emphasis on nursing

90e   Clues to sex bias in the selection of school administrators: A report from the Oregon network

90k   Male and female career paths in school administration

90m   The sex dimension of school organization: Overview and synthesis

97b   In/Forming schooling: Space/time/textuality in compulsory state provided "mass" schooling systems

124j   The Women's Trade Union League school for women organizers

138f   The conservative school? Sex roles at home, at work and at school

139f   Participation in local union organisation. School meals staff: A case study

147w   School physical activity programs for the antebellum southern females

147x   Adele Parot: Pathfinder for the Dioclesian Lewis school of gymnastic expression in the American west

169g   Residential schools

174t   The women's school of planning and architecture

193u   Sex typing in schools

205l   Postscript: Women in whose honour BC schools have been named

213c   The second generation: West Indian female school-leavers

216o   The parent as educator: A home-school model of socialization

216p   The relationship between home and school: A commentary on the current scene

235b   At school

250a   Introduction: Women, work and schooling: The relevance of gender

250c   The importance of being Ernest ... Emma ... Tom ... Jane. The perception and categorization of gender conformity and gender deviation in primary schools

250d   Studying girls at school: The implications of confusion

250e   Black girls in a London comprehensive school

250f   Education and the individual: Schooling for girls, or mixed schooling - a mixed blessing?

250n   Women, school and work: Some conclusions

259a   School as a sexist amplifier

259b   Boys and girls entering school

262g   Laws prohibiting sex discrimination in schools

265c   The role of schools in developing sex role attitudes

274a   School life - Organization and control

292a   The Women's Trade Union League training school for women organizers, 1914-1926

292d   Blue collars and bluestockings: The Bryn Mawr summer school for women workers, 1921-1938

292e   Recognizing regional differences: The southern summer school for women workers

292f   Partners in progress: The affiliated schools for women workers, 1928-1939

292g   Education in working-class solidarity: The summer school for office workers

302e   Assertiveness training for library-school students

321a   Schooling and injustice for girls

333o   Aboriginal women's role today in early childhood school education

337c   Women's contributions to the library school

337f   Women in the medical school

337g   Women and the law school

337h   Women in the school of music

349x   Reform school families

352f   Feminism and the woman school administrator

352i   Sex bias in school administration

352j   Socialization and education of young black girls in school

352q   Changing women's representation in school management: A systems perspective

353gg   "Little world of our own": The Pennsylvania Hospital Training School for Nurses, 1895-1907

363d   Patrons, politics, and schools: An arena for Brazilian women

408h   A school for wives: Women in eighteenth-century Spanish theater

412i   Preparing women for the Lord's work: The story of three Methodist training schools, 1880-1940

416g   Responsibilities of women faculty in engineering schools

432a   Justice and gender in school sports

445g   Women poets and the "Northwest School"

School-Age

see also Child

80w   School-age child care

Schoolgirl

193q   From schoolgirls' essays

Schreiner, Olive

125n   Olive Schreiner: New women, free women, all women

135g   Olive Schreiner - A note on sexist language and the feminist writer

Schurman, Anna Maria van

112e   Anna Maria van Schurman: The star of Utrecht (Dutch, 1607-1678)

Science

12a   Science education: Did she drop out or was she pushed?

12e   From zero to infinity: Scientific views of lesbians

12g   The obsessive orgasm: Science, sex and female sexuality

12k   The masculine face of science

34l   Adventures of a woman in science

34m   Bibliography: Women, science, and health

50i   Feminism and science

50x   Making science feminist

51a   Toward a biosocial paradigm for menopause research: Lessons and contributions from the behavioral sciences

77c   Creative women in scientific-technological and medical change

83a   Science and the status quo

84k   Gender and science

120b   Feminism and the critique of scientific method

122c   seeking feminist transformation of the sciences and the teaching of science

122f   The social determination of science: Some implications for women's studies

123e   Speaking from silence: Women and the science of politics

129x   State aid to science

130k   Women in science

176y   Toward a laboratory of one's own: Lesbians in science

181h   Women, science, and popular mythology

181l   What if...science and technology in feminist utopias

189o   Dirty fingers, grime and slag heaps: Purity and the scientific ethic

192g   Toward a science of women's liberation

193a   Girls and science education: Is there a problem?

193b Sex differences in science achievement: Some results and hypotheses

193c A biological basis for the sex differences in achievement in science?

193e Science achievement as an aspect of sex roles

193f Biological inevitabilities or political choices? The future for girls in science

193g Factors differentially affecting the science subject preferences, choices and attitudes of girls and boys

193h Science options in a girls' grammar school

193k Predicting specialisation in science

193l Girls studying science in the sixth form

193m Differential treatment of boy and girl pupils during science lessons

193n Sex differences in science examinations

193o Girls' science: Boys' science revisited

193p The image of science

193s Feminism and science teaching: Some classroom observations

200c Natural facts: A historical perspective on science and sexuality

212g The packaging of women: Science and our sexuality

214c Different is not lesser: Women in science

224j Toward a scientific analysis of the gay question

243c The role and status of women scientific research workers in research groups

250h Sex differences in performance in science examinations

251d The impact of science and technology and the role of women in science in Mexico

251f Some reflections on women in science and technology after UNCSTD

274f Mathematics and science - Introduction

274h Science

298e Human sciences research on Algerian women

307b Sex differences, science, and society

314e The natural sciences: Casting a critical eye on 'objectivity'

335c From utopian to scientific feminism? Early feminist critiques of the family

337b Women in science

342b Women's nature and scientific objectivity

342f The scientific mystique: Can a white lab coat guarantee purity in the search for knowledge about the nature of women?

361b Labor force participation of women baccalaureates in science

361e A short-term intervention program: Math-science conferences

361j Effectiveness of science career conferences

390e Evolution, eugenics and women: The impact of scientific theories on attitudes towards women, 1870-1920

416a Central issues facing women in the science-based professions

416e Planning strategies for women in scientific professions

416h Alternative development of a scientific career

416i Scientific sexism: The world of chemistry

416n Class, race, sex, scientific objects of knowledge: A socialist-feminist perspective on

the social construction of productive nature and some political consequences

438a Opportunities for women in science

438f The achievement of Iranian women in science

438g Reflections on a scientific adventure (Italy and United States)

438k The progress of science in Africa

Science Fiction

43v Reflections on science fiction

79kk The biology of utopia: Science fiction perspectives on ectogenesis

114b C. L. Moore's classic science fiction

114h Sex, satire, and feminism in the science fiction of Suzette Haden Elgin

114i From alienation to personal triumph: The science fiction of Joan D. Vinge

124d Widening the dialogue on feminist science fiction

131a Science fiction women before liberation

131d Woman as nature in science fiction

131o Where's all the fiction in science fiction?

307bb Female futures in women's science fiction

383c Utopia at the end of a male chauvinist dystopian world: Suzy McKee Charnas's feminist science fiction

417aa Of time and revolution: Theories of social change in contemporary feminist science fiction

Scientist

238j The scientist as sex crusader: Alfred C. Kinsey and American culture

254b The evolution of the woman scientist

361l An evaluation of programs for reentry women scientists

380b The education and employment of women scientists and engineers in the United States

438b Opportunities for women scientists in India

438h Women scientists in Sweden

Scotland

197g Spark and Scotland

417p Findhorn, Scotland: The people who talk to plants

Scratch

303o Scratching at the compound

474f Creating oneself from scratch

Scripture
see also Bible

115c Women and authority in the scriptures

Sculpture
see also Art

175l Elisabet Ney: Texas' first lady of sculpture

Search

287i In search of a vagina

400o Alice Walker's women: In search of some peace of mind

Sears, Eleonora Randolph

147p Eleonora Randolph Sears, pioneer in women's sports

Seaside

164k In between - Anne Elliot marries a sailor and Charlotte Heywood goes to the seaside

Season

86f Following the harvest: The health hazards of migrant and seasonal farmworking women

Seclusion

255g Purdah in Pakistan: Seclusion and modern occupations for women

Secondary Education
see also Education

151d Secondary education for all in a forward-looking society

Secondary School
see also Education

351g Women's studies at the secondary school level

Secret

133k The pathogenic secret

196b The secrets of Swift and Stella

Secretary

199h Brave new office: The changing world of the legal secretary

199j Computers, ward secretaries, and a walk-out in a Southern hospital

209q The decline of the " secretary as generalist"

209r Turning secretaries into word processors: Some fiction and a fact or two

305q When all the secretaries demand what they are worth

Sectarian

367g Women in sectarian and utopian groups

Section 1461

55m Appendix B: Review of legal cases regarding US Code, Section 1461 (mailing obscene or crime-inciting matter)

Sector

209j Productivity and service quality in the private sector

Secular

6f Women in religion and in secular ideology

91r New wine in new skins: Women in secular institutes

Security
see also Social Security

215f Defend us against our defenders: Democracy and security

463o Perceived safety and security in transportation systems as determined by the gender of the traveler

Sedative

9q The effects of opiates, sedative-hypnotics, amphetamines, cannabis, and other psychoactive drugs on the fetus and newborn

Seed

143i Fruit and seed: The finale to *Middlemarch*

Seek

252b Second trimester abortion as a social problem: Delay in abortion seeking behaviour and its causes

Segmentation

89j A theory of labor market segmentation

Segregate
see also Discriminate

52r   Economic recession and Swiss women's attitudes towards marital role segregation

65b   Socioeconomic explanations of job segregation

65c   Some psychological factors affecting job segregation and wages

89l   Occupational segregation, wages and profits when employers discriminate by race and sex

203k Toward supportive neighborhoods: Women's role in changing the segregated city

244c Sex segregation and the women's roles in the economic system: The case of Iran

260c Patterns of occupational segregation by sex in the labor market

272a Trends in occupational segregation by sex and race, 1960-1981

272b A woman's place is with other women: Sex segregation within organizations

272c Job changing and occupational sex segregation: Sex and race comparisons

272d Occupational sex segregation: Prospects for the 1980s

272e Occupational segregation and labor market discrimination

272f Toward a general theory of occupational sex segregation: The case of public school teaching

272g Commentary: Strober's theory of occupational sex segregation

272h Work experience, job segregation, and wages

272j Institutional factors contributing to sex segregation in the workplace

351e Sex segregation and male preeminence in elementary classrooms

387f Home work and market work: Systematic segregation

428l Silicon Valley's women workers: A theoretical analysis of sex-segregation in the electronics industry labor market

Ségur, Comtesse de

313h La poupée perdue: Ordre et désordre dans *Les Petites Filles Modéles* de la Comtesse de Ségur

Selected Poems (Margaret Atwood)

20e   The making of *Selected Poems*, the process of surfacing

Selection

31p   Sex preselection: From here to fraternity

78t   A sexist selection process keeps qualified women off the bench

79u   Technical aspects of sex preselection

79v   Futuristic implications of sex preselection

79w   Unnatural selection: On choosing children's sex

79aa Sex preselection: Discussion moderator's remarks

79bb Sex preselection discussion

110e Sample selection bias as a specification error

185d "Mate" selection in the year 2020

273a Sex selection of children: An overview

273c Sex selection through amniocentesis and selective abortion

273e Decision making and sex selection with biased technologies

273f The economics of sex preference and sex selection

273g Parental sex preferences and sex selection

273h Legal aspects of prenatal sex selection

287l Selecting a qualified therapist

320d Mapping the road to academe: A review of research on women, men, and the college-selection process

Self

2j   Abortion and self-defense

7x   Sadomasochism and the erosion of self: A critical reading of *Story of O*

38t   The self/group actualization of black women

40c   Reconstruction of the composite self: New images of black women in Maya Angelou's continuing autobiography

40ee The quest for self: Triumph and failure in the works of Toni Morrison

64o   The anamnesis of a female "I": In the margins of self-portrayal (Colette)

73f   The role of learning in the lives of Finnish and other ethnic women and a proposal for self-education

96l   The role and function of women's consciousness raising: Self-help, psychotherapy, or political activation?

132t In a different voice: Women's conceptions of self and of morality

145i Self-conscious histories: Biographies of German women in the nineteenth century

154a Self-consciousness and self concepts in the work of Christine de Pizan

174x Self-disclosure and the commitment to social change

265p Effectiveness of self-persuasion in producing healthy attitudes towards polygyny

271m Assertiveness: Sex differences in relationships between self-report and behavioural measures

275t Moral redescription and political self-deception

281b The sexual self and fertility

289l Continuity of self-actualization: Womanhood in climacterium and old age

305c Whose body? Whose self? Beyond pornography

307i The GABe self-cleaning house

310y Doing it ourselves: Self insemination

316h Toward freedom and self-determination: New directions in mental health services

360d The relational self in women: Developmental theory and public policy

365k Consciousness-raising and self-help

398e Self-disclosure and the commitment to social change

404ee Self-power and leadership

450b Alice Walker's celebration of self in southern generations

450n The miracle of realism: The bid for self-knowledge in the fiction of Ellen Gilchrist

452g Selves in hiding

452h In search of the black female self: African-American women's autobiographies and ethnicity

460m Finding self in the lesbian community

460s Self-help for sex

460t Self-help in gynecological practice

Self Esteem

214b Socialization and self-esteem: Women in management

Self Image

see also Image, Perception

194a The Virgin of Guadalupe and the female self-image: A Mexican case history

Self Perception

see also Image, Perception

296d Women's self-perceptions of power and influence across adult life

402m The aging woman in India: Self-perceptions and changing roles

469c The self-perception of Puerto Rican women toward their societal roles

Selfhood

108d Autobiography of a new 'creatur': Female spirituality, selfhood, and authorship in *The Book of Margery Kempe*

229n Drawing from mythology in women's quest for selfhood

Semantic

275v A note on logical truth and non-sexist semantics

Semitism

see also Jew, Judaism

336h Sisterhood under siege: Feminism and anti-semitism in Germany, 1904-1938

462h Anti-semitism: The unacknowledged racism

Senate

23i   'A woman's place is in the House and in the Senate': Women and the 1983 elections

Senator

226h Female state senators as cue givers: ERA roll-call voting, 1972-1979

Seneca

347c The mothers of the nation: Seneca resistance to Quaker intervention

Senescence

268n Senescence, sex roles, and stress: Shepherding resources into old age

Sense

142b George Eliot's language of the sense

164d Disregarded designs: Jane Austen's sense of the volume

Sensitive

432n Women's physical education: A gender-sensitive perspective

Sensual

257b Sensual uncertainty, or why the clitoris is not enough

289o Beyond generativity: Toward a sensuality of later life

Sentence

see also Crime

165h Are females treated differently? A review of the theories and evidence on sentencing and parole decisions

276g Sentencing the sexual offender

376a The certain wages of sin: Sentence and punishment of female felons in colonial Massachusetts, 1673-1774

Sentiment

392k Discriminatory sentencing of women offenders: The argument for ERA in a nutshell

404t In the pursuit of justice in sentencing and prison

Sentiment

127a The sentimentalists: Promise and betrayal in the home

162k Parental strategies: Calculation or sentiment?: Fostering practices among West Africans

286n "Here a captive heart busted": From Victorian sentimentality to modern sexuality

409f Gerty MacDowell: Joyce's sentimental heroine

Separate

43b The future of female separatism

69j Separation: A family developmental process of midlife

78i You can't be a mother and be in prison...can you? Impacts of the mother-child separation

88c Considerations about the development of the girl during the separation-individuation process

105h Developing family invulnerability to stress: Coping patterns and strategies wives employ in managing family separations

120m Fighting the good fight: Separation or integration?

132o Separation and survival: Mothers, daughters, sisters: - The women's experimental theater

259l Should the sexes be separated?

295f Sex differences in separation and divorce: A longitudinal perspective

466i Separate but equal: Indonesian Muslim perceptions of the roles of women

Sequelae

252s Somatic sequelae and future reproduction after pregnancy termination

Serfdom

184a Medieval marriage characteristics: A neglected factor in the history of medieval serfdom

Servant

38g "The means to put my children through": Child-rearing goals and strategies among black female domestic servants

256c Servants, sexual relations and the risks of illegitimacy in London, 1801-1900

263l Men servants and women bosses: The domestic service institution in colonial Zambia

299b Maid servants

414d Patient and useful servants: Women missionaries in Indian territory

424k Female domestic servants in Cagayan de Oro, Philippines: Social and economic implications of employment in a 'premodern' occupational role

Serve

49n Whom should the schools serve, When...?

Service

see also Social Service

13f Queensland public service women

23k The employment of women in the commonwealth public service: The creation and reproduction of a dual labour market

26g Family trouble clinic: Family service of Detroit and Wayne County

58c Bazaar and service occupations

102m Women in the U.S. Foreign Service: A quiet revolution

134a Youth service provision, social order and the question of girls

191g Tailoring evaluation to measure the accountability of mental health services to women

199f Women in retail sales work: The continuing dilemma of service

209j Productivity and service quality in the private sector

270j The plight of urban migrants: Dynamics of service procurement in a squatter area

305h Providing services the feminist way

309aa Contraceptive services for adolescents: An overview

320b Culture, service, and work: Changing ideals of higher education for women

404f The sparse ghetto: Service delivery in a rural area

404n Plenary session: Intervention/service delivery systems

404o Plenary session: Intervention/service delivery systems

404ff Federal support: Understanding and utilizing the federal dollar

436h A hard day's night: Women, reproduction and service society

447f Employee health services for women workers

458o Conclusion: Service needs of women retirees

472k Policy directions and program design: Issues and implications in services for the older woman

Serviceman

71n Asian wives of U.S. servicemen: Women in triple jeopardy

Servitude

370r Servitude and worldly success in the palace of Dahomey

Setting

40cc And called every generation blessed: Theme, setting, and ritual in the works of Paule Marshall

62f Single-sex setting

67b Job evaluation and pay setting: Concepts and practices

Settle, Mary Lee

450j Mary Lee Settle's connections: Class and clothes in the Beulah quintet

Settlement

147g Generalizations on women and sport, games and play in the United States from settlement to 1860

172a Squatter settlement decision-making: For men only? (Peru)

279f Sexual dimorphism and settlement pattern in Middle Eastern skeletal populations

417k A utopian female support network: The case of the Henry Street Settlement

Settlement House

454h Cultural hybrid in the slums: The college woman and the Settlement House, 1889-1894

Settler

160h Settler wives in southern Rhodesia: A case study

Sévigné, Madame de

108g Giving weight to words: Madame de Sévigné's letters to her daughter

112g Madame de Sévigné: Chronicler of an age (French, 1626-1696)

Seventeenth Century

33g Gender and genre: Women as historical writers, 1400-1820

99b From the woman's view: Pre-industrial England, 1500-1750

106e Marriage contract and social contract in seventeenth-century English political thought

112d María de Zayas y Sotomayor: Sibyl of Madrid (Spanish, 1590?-1661?)

112e Anna Maria van Schurman: The star of Utrecht (Dutch, 1607-1678)

112f Bathsua Makin: Educator and linguist (English, 1608?-1675?)

112g Madame de Sévigné: Chronicler of an age (French, 1626-1696)

112h Sor Juana Inés de la Cruz: Mexico's tenth muse (Mexican, 1651-1695)

112i Elizabeth Elstob: The Saxon nymph (English, 1683-1765)

162f Tensions, dissensions, and ruptures inside the family in seventeenth-and eighteenth-century Haute Provence

184d Elizabethan birth control and Puritan attitudes

184q Premarital pregnancy in America, 1640-1971: An overview and interpretation

347b Sunksquaws, shamans, and tradeswomen: Middle Atlantic coastal Algonkian women during the 17th and 18th centuries

367d New England women: Ideology and experience in first-generation Puritanism (1630-1650)

376a The certain wages of sin: Sentence and punishment of female felons in colonial Massachusetts, 1673-1774

379c The planter's wife revisited: Women, equity law, and the Chancery Court in seventeenth-century Maryland

408g The convent as catalyst for autonomy: Two Hispanic nuns of the seventeenth century

454b The case of the American Jezebels: Anne Hutchinson and female agitation during the years of the Antinomian turmoil, 1636-1640

Sewing

201b "If I didn't have my sewing machine...": Women and sewing-machine technology

206i The sewing machine

Sex

see also Gender

12g The obsessive orgasm: Science, sex and female sexuality

34b Boys will be boys will be boys: The language of sex and gender

35d The biopolitics of sex: Gender, genetics, and epigenetics

35e Sex, endocrines, and political behavior

35f Power structures and perceptions of power holders in same-sex groups of young children

39h The second sex in town

39n Female slave resistance: The economics of sex

47d Sex

48f What do women and men want from love and sex?

53b The relationship of the sex hormone/prostaglandin interaction to female and male longevity

68g Up from the harem? The effects of class and sex on political life in northern India

68h Caribbean women: The impact of race, sex, and class

78d Guilty by reason of sex: Young women and the juvenile justice system

84p Why has the sex/gender system become visible only now?

90a The sex dimension - An overview

90g The sex dimension of careers in educational management: Overview and synthesis

90h Jobs and gender: A history of the structuring of educational employment by sex

90m The sex dimension of school organization: Overview and synthesis

114h Sex, satire, and feminism in the science fiction of Suzette Haden Elgin

127d The forgotten reaping-hook: Sex in *My Antonia*

129b Human rights not founded on sex

134c Groping towards sexism: Boys' sex talk

138i Sex, education and social policy: A new moral economy?

140e Some effects of proportions on group life: Skewed sex ratios and responses to token women

140x Psychiatry's problem with no name: Therapist-patient sex

158d Leta Hollingworth: Toward a sexless intelligence

164e Sex and social life in Jane Austen's novels

171g Small insults: A study of interruptions in cross-sex conversations between unacquainted persons

179m The peaceful sex

185i The transition from sex to sexuality and intimacy

192a Sex, nationality, and class: La obrera Mexicana

206p Using sex and satan to bust the union (an interview with Corky Jennings)

214g An administrator's viewpoint: The interaction of sex and power

223j Sex, birth control, and human life

223p Better sex

223x Adult-child sex

225f Everything they always wanted you to know: The ideology of popular sex literature

225t Thinking sex: Notes for a radical theory of the politics of sexuality

227j The dialectic of sex

230a Introduction: Pornography and sex research

230f Sex and violence: A ripple effect

230m Afterword: Sex, violence, and the media: Where do we stand now?

231a Sex and society: A research note from social history and anthropology

231w Gender systems, ideology, and sex research

238a The Puritans and sex

238g The awesome power of sex: The polemical campaign against Mormon polygamy

238j The scientist as sex crusader: Alfred C. Kinsey and American culture

239d Human sex-hormone abnormalities viewed from an androgynous perspective: A reconsideration of the work of John Money

244i Traditional sex norms and the innovative function of afternoon dancing

251a Technology, economic development, and the division of labour by sex

253c What's new in endocrinology? Target: Sex hormones

253d Sex and temperament revisited

257f Sex and childbirth

257h Heterosexual sex: Power and desire for the other

258b Sex, gender and society

260c Patterns of occupational segregation by sex in the labor market

262d Differentiation by sex in educational professions

263k Industrial social workers in France, 1917-1939: A study in the sex/gender division of labor

265j Cross-sex friendship in the elementary school

265r Sex without reproduction: Voluntary childlessness as a response to contemporary sex roles

266e Methodological issues in the study of sex-related differences

272a Trends in occupational segregation by sex and race, 1960-1981

273d Timing of fertilization and the sex ratio of offspring

275m Sex and reference

278a Sex and classical literature

278c The secret nexus: Sex and literature in eighteenth-century Britain

279d The fossil record of sex

280c Nymphomania, hostile sex, and superego development

284s The child sex industry - an introduction

285c The social relation of sex and death

285n Sex in institutions

285p Sex and disability - sociosexual education presentation format

286c Cash and the sex nexus

286m "Morbid depression alternating with excitement": Sex in Victorian newspapers

287o An interview with a sex surrogate

288d A proposal: We need taboos on sex at work

303i Fair Harvard and the fairer sex

305g Shades of lavender: Lesbian sex and sexuality

308a Teenage women in the United States: Sex, contraception, pregnancy, fertility, and maternal and infant health

309g The effect of government policies on out-of-wedlock sex and pregnancy

330j *Orlando* and its genesis: Venturing and experimenting in art, love, and sex

335f Sex - A family affair

336e Helene Stöcker: Left-wing intellectual and sex reformer

351e Sex segregation and male preeminence in elementary classrooms

352g Single-sex education and leadership: The early years of Simmons College

372o Specificity of swim training on maximal oxygen uptake: An inter-sex comparison

387t Sex stratification, technology and organization change: A longitudinal case study of AT&T

396h Sex predetermination, artificial insemination and the maintenance of male-dominated culture

408o The censored sex: Woman as author and character in Franco's Spain

410c The effects of sex on recruitment: Connecticut local offices

410f Women judges and public policy in sex integration

416n Class, race, sex, scientific objects of knowledge: A socialist-feminist perspective on the social construction of productive nature and some political consequences

421m Comparative attitudes about marital sex among Negro women in the United States, Great Britain and Trinidad

432l Philosophy of education, physical education, and the sexes

439b Sex and power: Sexual bases of radical feminism

439i The front line: Notes on sex in novels by women, 1969-1979

439j Biological influences on human sex and gender

440g Sex and money in the welfare state

460l The misnamed female sex organ

460r A sex-information switchboard

460s Self-help for sex

461f Sex and sexuality: Women at midlife

461t Discussion: Extramarital sex: A multifaceted experience

465h The new right, sex, education and social policy: Towards a new moral economy in Britain and the USA

468d Women's attempts to break down sex barriers in the labour market

470a Sex and skill in the organisation of the clothing industry

473g Sex and status: Women in St. Vincent

Sex Bias
see also Discriminate

10m Treatment outcome of alcoholic women: The state of the art in relation to sex bias and expectancy effects

90e Clues to sex bias in the selection of school administrators: A report from the Oregon network

90f The problem of sex bias in curriculum materials

260f Sex-role ideology and sex bias in judgments of occupational suitability

266h All things being equal, a behavior is superior to an attitude: Studies of sex-typed and sex-biased attitudes and behaviors

320e Sex bias in aptitude and achievement tests used in higher education

352i Sex bias in school administration

359h Report of the task force on sex bias and sex-role stereotyping in psychotherapeutic practice

402b The data base for studies on women: Sex biases in national data systems

Sex Change

231q Outside the operating room of the sex-change doctor

Sex Choice

273i Toward a moral policy for sex choice

273j Ethics and public policy: Should sex choice be discouraged?

Sex Difference

see also Difference

9a Sex differences in alcohol and drug problems - some highlights

9c Sex differences in the prevalence of problem drinking

9d Sex differences in psychoactive drug use: Recent epidemiology

9e Longitudinal studies of alcohol and drug problems: Sex differences

9f Sex differences in the inheritance of alcoholism

9i Sex differences in morbidity of alcoholics

9j Sex differences in mortality: A comparison of male and female alcoholics

9o Sex differences in the effects of alcohol and other psychoactive drugs on endocrine function: Clinical and experimental evidence

11c Women and men problem drinkers: Sex differences in patients served by Iowa's community alcoholism centers

12b Psychological sex differences

29a Women's behavior in a man's world: Sex differences in competence

45l Sex differences in the educational and occupational goals of black college students: Continued inquiry into the black matriarchy theory

50q Biological sex differences and sex stereotyping

53a Sex differences in disease risk

53t Sex differences in diabetes mellitus

126o Sex differences in the brain: Implications for curriculum change

132l For the Etruscans: Sexual difference and artistic production - the debate over a female aesthetic

132r Androgyny and the psychology of sex differences

136e Sex differences in body movements and positions

136j The development of sex differences in nonverbal signals: Fallacies, facts, and fantasies

137e Psychopathology and sex differences in the aged

191c Community surveys: Sex differences in mental illness

193b Sex differences in science achievement: Some results and hypotheses

193c A biological basis for the sex differences in achievement in science?

193i Sex differences in science examinations

214e Structuring the inside: The impact of organizations on sex differences

239b Biopsychosocial processes in the development of sex-related differences

250g Sex differences in mathematical performance: A review of research and possible action

250h Sex differences in performance in science examinations

258a Sex differences and this book

258i Sex differences in Britain

259f Sex differences in achievement orientations: Consequences for academic choices and attainments

259i Sex differentiation and careers

260l The political economy of labor market discrimination: A theoretical and comparative analysis of sex discrimination

265k Sex differences in children's road accidents

266e Methodological issues in the study of sex-related differences

268l Sex-related differences in the epidemiology of child psychopathology

271k Female superiority in sex difference competence comparisons: A review of the literature

271l Sex differences in assertiveness: Implications for research and treatment

271m Assertiveness: Sex differences in relationships between self-report and behavioural measures

279c Sex differences: The female as baseline for species description

279m Absolute and relative sex differences in body composition

295f Sex differences in separation and divorce: A longitudinal perspective

307b Sex differences, science, and society

320f Sex differences in the significance of economic resources for choosing and attending a college

320j Sex differences in the impact of college environments on black students

320l Sex differences in the implications of the links between major departments and the occupational structure

344l Women and higher education: Sex differentials in the status of students and scholars

359m Sex differences and the epidemiology of depression

372y Pituitary response to physical exercise: Sex differences

376j Sex differences in the processing of criminal defendants

377e Sex-related differences in mathematics achievement: Where and why

377f Sex differences in the development of precocious mathematical talent

385f Colonialism, education, and work: Sex differentiation in colonial Zaire

410e Sex differences in role behavior and policy orientations of suburban officeholders: The effect of women's employment

426d Sex differences in factors affecting managerial career advancement

458f Preretirement preparation: Sex differences in access, sources, and use

459h Women's work and their status: Rural Indian evidence of labour market and environment effects on sex differences in childhood mortality

463m Sex differences in travel preferences and decision making

Sex Discrimination

see also Discriminate

89l Occupational segregation, wages and profits when employers discriminate by race and sex

89m Sexual discrimination in the labour market

93d The effectiveness of federal laws prohibiting sex discrimination in employment in the United States

93g The enforcement of laws against sex discrimination in England: Problems of institutional design

147nn Sexual discrimination in youth sport: The case of Margaret Gisolo

260l The political economy of labor market discrimination: A theoretical and comparative analysis of sex discrimination

261d Strategies for eliminating sex discrimination: Times that try men's souls

262g Laws prohibiting sex discrimination in schools

316m De jure sex discrimination

339e Coping with illegal sex discrimination

376e Sex-based discrimination in the mental institutionalization of women

387d Sex discrimination and employment practices: An experiment with unconventional job inquires

447h Sex discrimination in group pensions

459j Sex discrimination in the urban labour markets: Some propositions based on Indian evidence

Sex Education

see also Education

4l Sex education

238e From maidenhood to menopause: Sex education for women in Victorian merica

238i Ideas of the early sex education movement in America, 1890-1920

274q Sex education

308e Sex education and the prevention of teenage pregnancy: An overview of policies and programs in the United States

460q Sex education versus sexual learning

Sex Equality

see also Equality, Gender Equality

31b Human biology in feminist theory: Sexual equality reconsidered

45b The challenge of sex equality: Old values revisited or a new culture?

90n The sources and dynamics of sexual inequality in the profession of education

116o Sex equality in sports

116q Sex equality and education in Plato's Just State

130v The problem of sexual equality in Sadean prose

353cc Homeopathy and sexual equality: The controversy over coeducation at Cincinnati's Pulte Medical College, 1873-1879

355l Household work, wage work, and sexual equality

359c Psychological consequences of sexual inequality

405a Marxism, feminism, and sex equality

427h Sexual inequality: The high cost of leaving parenting to women

432g Sports, sex-equality, and the media

465d Sex equality and social security

Sex Equity

see also Equity

90c Sex equity in educational policies and practices

90d The concept of sex equity in jurisprudence

90o The impact of organizational structures on issues of sex equity

262b Sex inequities in the experience of students

262c Why sex inequities exist for students

262e Why sex inequities exist in the profession of education

Sex Offender

276b The relationship between treatment for sex offenders and the court

276c Prediction of recidivism and the evaluation of treatment programs for sex offenders

276d The assessment and treatment of sexual offenders

276f Ethics and ethical dilemmas in the treatment of sex offenders

276g Sentencing the sexual offender

284o Interviewing child victims of sex offenders

Sex Preference

273b Measuring sex preferences and their effects on fertility

273f The economics of sex preference and sex selection

273g Parental sex preferences and sex selection

Sex Ring

55c Typology of sex rings exploiting children

55f Impact of child pornography and sex rings on child victims and their families

55j Treatment issues with children involved in pornography and sex rings

Sex Role

see also Androgyny, Gender, Role

11a Sex-role adjustment in women alcoholics

24a Physical attractiveness, sex roles and heterosexual attraction

29b Unraveling the nature of sex roles

31j Women's work and sex roles

39r Sex roles and survival strategies in the urban black community

45k Changing sex roles: College graduates of the 1960's and 1970's

52h Changing sex roles in the Greek family and society

52t Wife and/or worker: Sex role concepts of Canadian female students

63j Sex-role differentiation in a co-correctional setting

70e The interaction of culture and sex roles in the schools

72l Chicana identity: Interaction of culture and sex roles

78g Sex role stereotypes and justice for women

91p Sex roles defined: As others see us

107d The influence of the traditional sex roles on women's participation and engagement in sport

111q Sex-role concepts among federal female offenders

114d C. J. Cherryh and tomorrow's new sex roles

116b Sex roles: The argument from nature

116g Sex and social roles: How to deal with the data

116m Sex roles and the sexual division of labor

124h How psychology constructed masculinity: The theory of male sex role identity

133l Androgyny, sex-role rigidity, and homophobia

136a Nonverbal behavior: Barrier or agent for sex role change?

136f Sex-role influences in dyadic interaction: A theoretical model

136g Gender gestures: Sex, sex-role, and nonverbal communication

138b Intersections of gender and class: Accommodation and resistance by working-class and affluent females to contradictory sex-role ideologies

138f The conservative school? Sex roles at home, at work and at school

140g Women in positions of authority: A case study of changing sex roles

140h Early origins of envy and devaluation of women: Implications for sex-role stereotypes

140w Toward an analysis of sex-role-related issues in the therapeutic relationship

148j "Warrior women" - Sex role alternatives for Plains Indian women

158i The theory of male sex role identity: Its rise and fall, 1936 to the present

165n Sex-role operations: Strategies for women working in the criminal justice system

185h The evolution of sex roles: The transformation of masculine and feminine values

193e Science achievement as an aspect of sex roles

203b The home: A critical problem for changing sex roles

262a Sex roles in education

265a Parents' sex role attitudes and children's concepts of femininity and masculinity

265c The role of schools in developing sex role attitudes

265e Language and attitudes toward masculine and feminine sex role

265i Aspirations and sex roles - Are they in conflict?

265l Cultural differences in children's sex role stereotypes

265m Sex role stereotyping and mental health standards in Israel: A cross-cultural comparison

265n Sex role images in Lebanese text books

265o Strategies of healthy sex role development in modernized India

265r Sex without reproduction: Voluntary childlessness as a response to contemporary sex roles

265s Changing sex roles reflected in the films of François Truffaut

265t Mental health in boys and girls: Awareness of attitudes for positive sex roles

266f Sampling: Issues and problems in sex role and social change research

266i Statistical analysis in sex roles and social change

268a Sex roles and psychopathology

268e Sex roles and psychophysiological disorders: Coronary heart disease

268f Depression in relation to sex roles: Differences in learned susceptibility and precipitating factors

268i Sex roles, criminality, and psychopathology

268j A sex-roles perspective on drug and alcohol use by women

268k Sex roles and sexual dysfunction

268m Sex-role stereotypes and the development of eating disorders

268n Senescence, sex roles, and stress: Shepherding resources into old age

268o Sex roles, psychological assessment, and patient management

268p Sex roles in medicine

269c Sex roles and subsistence: A comparative analysis of three Central American communities

269f Being Cuna and female: Ethnicity mediating change in sex roles

270f Sex roles, value of children and fertility in Turkey

271c Parents and the sex-role development of the preschool child

271f Sex-role ideology and sex bias in judgments of occupational suitability

289e Gender identity: A life-span view of sex-role development

304a Introduction: Warning! Sex-role stereotypes may be hazardous to your health

304b Sex-role stereotypes and mental health: Conceptual models in the 1970s and issues for the 1980s

304c The development of sex-role stereotypes in children: Crushing realities

304d Sex roles and language use: Implications for mental health

304e Sex-role stereotypes and depression in women

304f Women and agoraphobia: A case for the etiological significance of the feminine sex-role stereotype

304g Sex-role stereotypes and female sexual dysfunction

304h Women's assertion and the feminine sex-role stereotype

304k Sex-role stereotypes and violence against women

319j Cultural styles and adolescent sex role perceptions: An exploration of responses to a value picture projective test

344k Sex-role socialization: A focus on women

349n Sex roles, power, and woman battering

349u Sex-role stereotypes and justice for women

359b Early origins of envy and devaluation of women: Implications for sex-role stereotypes

359g Sex-role stereotypes and clinical judgements of mental health

359h Report of the task force on sex bias and sex-role stereotyping in psychotherapeutic practice

359rr Adaptive and pathogenic aspects of sex-role stereotypes: Implications for parenting and psychotherapy

365b Therapist attitudes and sex-role stereotyping

380f Sex-role stereotypes and personal attributes within a developmental framework

392c Female deviance and the female sex role: A preliminary investigation

399a Sex roles and shamans

399pp Creative drama: Sex role stereotyping?

410a The invisible hands: Sex roles and the division of labor in two local political parties

419b "Reverse similes" and sex roles in the *Odyssey*

419h The menace of Dionysus: Sex roles and reversals in Euripides' *Bacchae*

421q Sex role attitudes, female employment, and marital satisfaction

431a Buddhism, sex-roles and the Thai economy

431g Sex roles in the Philippines: The ambiguous Cebuana

443g Strategies for dealing with sex-role stereotypes

454n The hysterical woman: Sex roles and role conflict in nineteenth century America

455a Sex roles and sexism

Sex Segregation
see also Segregate

244c Sex segregation and the women's roles in the economic system: The case of Iran

272b A woman's place is with other women: Sex segregation within organizations

272c Job changing and occupational sex segregation: Sex and race comparisons

272d Occupational sex segregation: Prospects for the 1980s

272f Toward a general theory of occupational sex segregation: The case of public school teaching

272g Commentary: Strober's theory of occupational sex segregation

272j Institutional factors contributing to sex segregation in the workplace

428l Silicon Valley's women workers: A theoretical analysis of sex-segregation in the electronics industry labor market

Sex Selection

31p Sex preselection: From here to fraternity

79u Technical aspects of sex preselection

79v Futuristic implications of sex preselection

79w Unnatural selection: On choosing children's sex

79aa Sex preselection: Discussion moderator's remarks

79bb Sex preselection discussion

273a Sex selection of children: An overview

273c Sex selection through amniocentesis and selective abortion

273e Decision making and sex selection with biased technologies

273f The economics of sex preference and sex selection

273g Parental sex preferences and sex selection

273h Legal aspects of prenatal sex selection

310r Abortion of a special kind: Male sex selection in India

Sex Socialization

32e *Wally, die Zweiflerin* and *Madonna*: A discussion of sex-socialization in the nineteenth century

Sex Stereotype
see also Stereotype

50q Biological sex differences and sex stereotyping

69c Changing sex stereotypes

116i Is androgyny the answer to sexual stereotyping?

144b Family and role-division: The polarisation of sexual stereotypes in the nineteenth century - an aspect of the dissociation of work and family

265b Ethnic differences in sex stereotyping by mothers: Implications for health care

265f Does sex stereotyping lead to a higher incidence of male dyslexia?

Sex Therapy
see also Therapy

277j Current approaches in sex therapy

287n Surrogate partners and their use in sex therapy

359k Psychiatry's problem with no name: Therapist-patient sex

360m New sex therapies: Policy and practice

461g Discussion: Midlife women: Lessons for sex therapy

Sex Typing

193u Sex typing in schools

265h Sex typing in occupational preferences of high school boys and girls

266h All things being equal, a behavior is superior to an attitude: Studies of sex-typed and sex-biased attitudes and behaviors

272i Sex typing in occupational socialization

302b Sex-typing in education for librarianship: 1870-1920

Sexes

31k The political nature of relations between the sexes

115i Stereotyping the sexes in society and in the Church

126f A feminist challenge to Darwinism: Antoinette L. B. Blackwell on the relations of the sexes in nature and society

187h All ages, every condition, and both sexes: The emergence of a Gilbertine identity

214j The battle of the sexes: Power and sexual aggressiveness

259l Should the sexes be separated?

278b 'Last Night's Rambles': Restoration literature and the war between the sexes

Sexism
see also Discriminate

31f Sexism, religion, and the social and spiritual liberation of women today

78m Forcible rape: Institutionalized sexism in the criminal justice system

83i Racism and sexism: They ain't genetic you know!

89h The statistical theory of racism and sexism

126e Darwin and sexism: Victorian causes, contemporary effects

126k Sexism and racism: Obstacles to the development of black women in South Africa

134c Groping towards sexism: Boys' sex talk

157i Sexism in British Columbia trade unions, 1900-1920

193r Girls, physics and sexism

214o Ageism vs. sexism: Male models as a source of support

253h Sexism in gynecologic practices

253l Sexism and racism in health policy

259d Staffing for sexism: Educational leadership and role models

275b Sexist language and sexism

275r Sexism and racism: Some conceptual differences

275s Thomas on sexism

307e Doubletalk: Sexism in tech talk

336k Racism and sexism in Nazi Germany: Motherhood, compulsory sterilization, and the state

343p The miranda trap: Sexism and racism in Shakespeare's *Tempest*

344z Sexism and the English language: The linguistic implications of being a woman

348a Sexism in criminal law

354d Sexism and racism in the American health care industry: A comparative analysis

390y Sexism and health care

397j Lesbians and the law: Where sexism and heterosexism meet

404k Sexism in treatment

404l Sexism in drug abuse treatment programs

416i Scientific sexism: The world of chemistry

443h Psychotherapy with black women and the dual effects of racism and sexism

455a Sex roles and sexism

Sexist

14j Debunking Sapphire: Toward a non-racist and non-sexist social science

78t A sexist selection process keeps qualified women off the bench

84h How can language be sexist?

102i Beyond consciousness raising: Changing sexist institutions

131b Alexei Panshin's almost non-sexist *Rite of Passage*

135g Olive Schreiner - A note on sexist language and the feminist writer

171b Beyond the he/man approach: The case for nonsexist language

259a School as a sexist amplifier

265d Review of the literature of non-sexist curriculum and a critique of the underlying assumptions and rationale

275b Sexist language and sexism

275c Sexist speech: Two basic questions

275v A note on logical truth and non-sexist semantics

275w Reference and truth: The case of sexist and racist utterances

283f   Sexist bias and the law

377c   Is mathematics a sexist discipline?

394h   Sedition in a sexist society: The Platteville paradigm

425g   Estimating benefits and costs of antisexist training programs in organizations

455d   Aging and old age: The last sexist rip-off

Sexology

290b   Sexology and the social construction of male sexuality (Havelock Ellis)

290c   Sexology and the universalization of male sexuality (from Ellis to Kinsey, and Masters and Johnson

Sexual

4f   Programs for sexually active teens

4m   Sexual counseling for adolescents

24c   The influence of special sexual desires

24h   The dramaturgy of sexual relations

39y   Social inequality and sexual status in Barbados

48b   Sexual socialization and gender roles in childhood

48c   Becoming sexual in adolescence

48d   The courtship game: Power in the sexual encounter

48e   Sexual response and gender roles

48n   Future influences on the interaction of gender and human sexual expression

50t   Alleged psychogenic disorders in women - a possible manifestation of sexual prejudice

52s   Egalitarianism in marriage? Graduate education and the sexual division of labour in the Canadian family

55l   Appendix A: Legal resources on sexual exploitation of children

60v   The challenge of profamily politics: A feminist defense of sexual freedom

63a   The sexually integrated prison: A legal and policy evaluation

105e   Toward a theory of extramarital sexual relationships

114e   Toward new sexual identities: James Tiptree, Jr.

116m   Sex roles and the sexual division of labor

119g   'An immense verbosity': Permissive sexual advice in the 1970s

137n   Gender and sexual functioning

140y   Sexual misconduct by psychiatrists: The ethical and clinical dilemma of confidentiality

147l   The effect of changing attitudes toward sexual morality upon the promotion of physical education for women in nineteenth century America

153p   Towards a theory of the sexual division of labor

162n   Village spinning bees: Sexual culture and free time among rural youths in early modern Germany

176f   Sexual energy in the classroom

179e   Sexual division of labour

184i   Female sexual attitudes and the rise of illegitimacy: A case study

190n   Age at menarche and sexual conduct in adolescence and young adulthood

207a   Gender and economics: The sexual division of labour and the subordination of women

208b   Gender and economics: The sexual division of labour and the subordination of women

212q   Sexual assumptions in the women's movement

213d   Sexual divisions and ethnic adaptation: The case of Greek-Cypriot women

214j   The battle of the sexes: Power and sexual aggressiveness

223o   Sexual perversion

223q   Sexual immorality delineated

225b   seeking ecstasy on the battlefield: Danger and pleasure in nineteenth-century feminist sexual thought

225g   Above and beyond politics: The sexual socialization of children

225k   The body politic: The defense of sexual restriction by anti-abortion activists

225r   The misunderstanding: Toward a more precise sexual vocabulary

230h   Sexual stratification, pornography, and rape in the United States

230i   Sexually aggressive men: Empirical findings and theoretical implications

230j   Sexual signaling and sexual aggression in adolescent relationships

231e   Family, sexual morality, and popular movements in turn-of-the-century America

231k   The Afro-American female: The historical context of the construction of sexual identity

231y   What we're rollin around in bed with: Sexual silences in feminism

238b   Passionlessness: An interpretation of Victorian sexual ideology, 1790-1850

241g   'Women and old boats': The sexual division of labour in a Newfoundland outport

244h   Sexual customs and gender roles in Sweden and America: An analysis and interpretation

256c   Servants, sexual relations and the risks of illegitimacy in London, 1801-1900

256f   "The men are as bad as their masters...": Socialism, feminism and sexual antagonism in the London tailoring trade in the 1830s

257n   Sexual theory and practice: Another double standard

263b   Housework as a comparative advantage: The neoclassical theory of the sexual division of labor

263f   The sexual division of labor on American farms: 1750-1850

276a   The classification of sexual aggressives and their associated demographic, social, developmental and psychological features

276e   Sexual aggression and the law - implications for the future

277b   Hormones and sexual arousal

277c   Physiology of male sexual arousal

277d   Mechanisms of sexual arousal in females

277f   Psychophysiologic measurement of sexual arousal in females

277l   Sexual arousal responses and disability

277m   Effects of aging on sexual arousal

277n   Effect of drugs on sexual arousal

278e   Sexual fiction in America, 1955-80

280d   Sexual permissiveness and its consequences

280i   Burglaries with sexual dynamics

280k   Sexual dynamics in homicide and assault

281c   Sexual disorders and the family therapist

281b   The sexual self and fertility

281h   Ethical and legal aspects of sexual issues

282a   Introduction: Accounting for sexual meanings

282g   Like wounded stags: Male sexual ideology in an Andalusian town

284b   Sexual victimization of children: An urban mental health center survey

284c   Sexual molestation of children: The last frontier of child abuse

284e   The sexually misused child

284f   Observations after sexual traumata suffered in childhood

284g   Sexual trauma of children and adolescents

284x   Sexual emancipation - an introduction

284y   The age of sexual consent: Fault, friction, freedom

285e   Physical disability, life-threatening illness, and enhancement of sexual health

285f   Sexual feelings in the terminally ill patient

285i   Castration and sexual potency

285m   Sexual rehabilitation after gynecologic cancer

285o   Sexual attitudes and activities in old age

285t   How to stubbornly refuse to disturb oneself emotionally about anything - even about death, dying and sexual mutilation

287a   Our sexual heritage

287g   Varieties of sexual expression

290d   Theory into practice: Sexual liberation or social control? (*Forum* magazine 1968-1981)

291g   Sexual deviance: The adult offender

291p   The co-therapy relationship in group treatment of sexually mistreated adolescent girls

305r   Rosie the Riveter meets the sexual division of labour

309d   Sexual and contraceptive experience of young unmarried women in the United States, 1976 and 1971

309u   Sexual and contraceptive knowledge, attitudes and behavior of male adolescents

342i   Origins of the sexual division of labor

344a   Sexual terrorism

349m   Sexual aggression: A second look at the offended female

350a   The dynamics of the sexual division of labor and integration of rural women into the world market

350c   Peasant production, proletarianization, and the sexual division of labor in the Andes

350d   Resource allocation and the sexual division of labor: A case study of a Moslem Hausa village in northern Nigeria

350i   The sexual division of labor in rural China

353d   Passionlessness: An interpretation of Victorian sexual ideology, 1790-1850

359kk Rape: Sexual disruption and recovery

360k Sexual intimacy between psychotherapists and clients: Policy implications for the future

370c Sexual demography: The impact of the slave trade on family structure

371f Sexual prohibitions, shared space and fictive marriages in Shi'ite Iran

371h The sexual division of domestic space among two Soviet minorities: The Georgians and the Tadjiks

408c Sexual humor in misogynist medieval exampla

431h Sexual status in Southeast Asia: Comparative perspectives on women, agriculture and political organization

439a Who is Sylvia? On the loss of sexual paradigms

439b Sex and power: Sexual bases of radical feminism

454k Family limitation, sexual control, and domestic feminism in Victorian America

456k Sexual problems

460a "Role, Jenny Jenkins, Roll": Little girls and maidens in American folksongs - an analysis of sexual attitudes

460d Physiological aspects of female sexual development: Conception through puberty

460e Physiological aspects of female sexual development: Gestation, lactation, menopause, and erotic physiology

461a Women's sexual response

461b The sexual experience of Afro-American women: A middle-income sample

461d Sexual consequences of acculturation of American Indian women

461z Discussion: Prophylaxis of sexually transmitted diseases: An overview

Sexual Abuse

see also Abuse

146a A conceptual framework for child sexual abuse

146b Validation of child sexual abuse

146d Treatment of the sexually abused child

146j Arts therapy with sexually abused children

146k Law enforcement and child sexual abuse

146l Multidisciplinary team review of child-sexual-abuse cases

146m Evaluation of child-sexual-abuse programs

146n How to start a child-sexual-abuse intervention program

212f The sexual abuse of children in the home

219b Incest and sexual abuse of children

229ss Spiritual techniques for re-powering survivors of sexual assault

284a The sexual abuse of children and minors: A short history of legal control efforts

291a Definition and recognition of sexual child abuse: Historical and cultural perspectives

291c A psychoanalyst's view of sexual abuse by parents

291d Recognition of child sexual abuse in the United Kingdom

291e Sexual child abuse: The legislation and the law in the United States

291f Sexual abuse of children: An examination of European criminal law

291j Medical assessment of child sexual abuse

291k The child psychiatric examination of the sexually abused child

291l Special problems in the treatment of child sexual abuse

291n A comprehensive child sexual abuse treatment program

291o Group psychotherapy with sexually abused children

291q Long-term effects of sexual abuse in childhood

291r The effects of child sexual abuse: Methodological considerations

326d Treatment of sexually abused children

326f Clinical intervention with boy victims of sexual abuse

Sexual Assault

see also Abuse

219h Loss and mourning in victims of rape and sexual assault

280h The dynamics of sexual assault

284h Sexual assault center emergency room protocol: Child/adolescent patients

284r Courtroom use of hospital records in sexual assault cases

326a Psychodynamics of sexual assault experiences

326g Group work with preadolescent sexual assault victims

326h Sexual assault in correctional institutions: Prevention and intervention

326j Sexual assault of the older woman

326l Behavioral treatment of sexual dysfunction in sexual assault survivors

326n Treatment of prostitute victims of sexual assault

333n Study into the needs of aboriginal women who have been raped or sexually assaulted

Sexual Attraction

24b Social background, attitudes and sexual attraction

24d Perceptual and cognitive mechanisms in human sexual attraction

24e Social skill and human sexual attraction

24i Sexual attraction in animals

Sexual Behavior

28c Neuroendocrine regulation of sexual behavior

28d Hypothalamic peptides and sexual behavior

28g Epidemiological patterns of sexual behavior in the menstrual cycle

28h Sexual behavior and the menstrual cycle

239e Biochemical and neurophysiological influences on human sexual behavior

308b The family's role in adolescent sexual behavior

419f Classical Greek attitudes to sexual behavior

Sexual Dimorphism

279b Sexual dimorphism in nonhuman primates

279e Sexual dimorphism in skeletal samples

279f Sexual dimorphism and settlement pattern in Middle Eastern skeletal populations

279h A cross-cultural investigation into the sexual dimorphism of stature

279i Sexual dimorphism for size in seven nineteenth-century Northwest coast populations

279j Size sexual dimorphism and secular trend: Indicators of subclinical malnutrition?

279k Normal and abnormal sexual dimorphic patterns of growth and development

279l Human proportionality and sexual dimorphism

279n Sexual dimorphism and nutrient reserves

Sexual Dysfunction

10g Drinking, sexuality, and sexual dysfunction in women

268k Sex roles and sexual dysfunction

277g The multidisciplinary approach to the diagnosis and treatment of male sexual dysfunction

277k Study of sexual dysfunction among male diabetics

285k Sexual dysfunction in the chronically ill male

287m Psychological aspects of sexual dysfunction

304g Sex-role stereotypes and female sexual dysfunction

326k Marital and sexual dysfunction following rape: Identification and treatment

326l Behavioral treatment of sexual dysfunction in sexual assault survivors

Sexual Excitement

439s *Sexual Excitement* by Robert J. Stoller

Sexual Harassment

see also Harassment

43h Sexual harassment, working women's dilemma

60q Defining and combating sexual harassment

78s Sexual harassment: The experience

86g Sexual harassment and women's health

199m Contrasting sexual harassment in female- and male-dominated occupations

267d A psychological examination of sexual harassment

288f The impact of sexual harassment on the job: A profile of the experiences of 92 women

288h Responses of fair employment practice agencies to sexual harassment complaints: A report and recommendations

288i Sexual harassment in the workplace — What should the employer do?

288k Policy statement and definition of sexual harassment

288l A federal response to sexual harassment: Policy-making at Johnson Space Center, NASA

288m Policy on sexual harassment

288n Sexual harassment cases

288o Sexual harassment and Title VII: The foundation for the elimination of sexual cooperation as an employment condition

288p Sexual harassment: Finding a cause of action under Title VII

305o Sexual harassment as a form of social control

323h Sexual harassment: An issue for unions

344d Sexual harassment: The link between gender stratification, sexuality, and women's economic status

415c Sexual harassment in the organization

Sexual Learning

57a Dimensions of sexual learning in childhood

57b Toward an understanding of sexual learning and communication: An examination of social learning theory and nonschool learning environments

57c Work, the family, and children's sexual learning

57e Sexual learning in the elementary school

57g Social services and sexual learning

57h Religion and sexual learning of children

460q Sex education versus sexual learning

Sexual Offences Act

219f The role of the judiciary in the failure of the Sexual Offences (Amendment) Act to improve the treatment of the rape victim

Sexual Offenses

183j Sexual offences

219a The victim's contribution to sexual offences

284p The protection of the child victim of a sexual offense in the criminal justice system

Sexual Orientation

315e A dialogue critical issues in women's studies: Race, class, and sexual orientation

Sexual Politics

27k *A Passage to India* as "marriage fiction": Forster's sexual politics

119h Sexual politics and psychoanalysis: Some notes on their relation

225c The taming of the id: Feminist sexual politics, 1968-83

344y The sexual politics of interpersonal behavior

387n The inexpressive male: Tragedy or sexual politics?

390x Crime and sexual politics

408p Sexual politics and the theme of sexuality in Chicana poetry

461j The cradle of sexual politics: Incest

Sexual Revolution

7c Pornography and the sexual revolution: The backlash of sadomasochism

105d Recent data reflecting upon the sexual revolution in America

184e Illegitimacy, sexual revolution, and social change in modern Europe

460u Young women and the sexual revolution

Sexual Slavery

163a International politics of female sexual slavery

163b The network defines its issues: Theory, evidence and analysis of female sexual slavery

163c Network strategies and organizing against female sexual slavery

163h The torture of women political prisoners: A case study in female sexual slavery

Sexual Violence

see also Abuse

48l Gender roles and sexual violence

103c Battered women's shelters and the political economy of sexual violence

281f Incest and sexual violence

404w Prostitution and sexual violence

Sexuality

4d Adolescent sexuality, pregnancy, and childbearing

10g Drinking, sexuality, and sexual dysfunction in women

12g The obsessive orgasm: Science, sex and female sexuality

24g Human sexuality in cross-cultural perspective

29e Sexuality

48a The intimate relationship between gender roles and sexuality

48g Sexuality and gender roles in the second half of life

48i Gender roles and sexuality in the world of work

50s Female sexuality

50y 'Guardians of the race' or 'vampires upon the nation's health'? Female sexuality and its regulation in early twentieth century Britain

57d Television as a sphere of influence on the child's learning about sexuality

57f Peer communication and sexuality

57i Human sexuality: Messages in public environments

57j Sexuality and social policy: The unwritten curriculum

59g Human sexuality and mutuality

103l Teenage sexuality and public policy: An agenda for gender education

109m The Radcliffean gothic model: A form for feminine sexuality

116j Are androgyny and sexuality compatible?

125c Mary Wollstonecraft: Sexuality and women's rights

126p Human sexuality: New insights from women's history

135q Power or sexuality: The bind of Corneille's *Pulcherie*

185i The transition from sex to sexuality and intimacy

195j On conceiving motherhood and sexuality: A feminist materialist approach

200c Natural facts: A historical perspective on science and sexuality

200f Gender, sexuality and marriage: A Kaulong model of nature and culture

207h Sexuality and the control of procreation

208k Sexuality and control of procreation

210d The sexuality of older women

212b Femininity, masculinity and sexuality

212g The packaging of women: Science and our sexuality

219d The social uses of sexuality: Symbolic interaction, power and rape

223w Taking responsibility for sexuality

224c Lesbians and gay men: Hetero sexualities, common cause

224g Childhood sexuality and paedophilia

225a Pleasure and danger: Toward a politics of sexuality

225i Cultural and historical influences on sexuality in Hispanic/Latin women: Implications for psychotherapy

225o Beyond politics? Children and sexuality

225s The historical repression of women's sexuality

225t Thinking sex: Notes for a radical theory of the politics of sexuality

231b "Charity girls" and city pleasures: Historical notes on working-class sexuality, 1880-1920

231g The new woman and the rationalization of sexuality in Weimar Germany

231i Russian working women: Sexuality in bonding patterns and the politics of daily life

238d The spermatic economy: A nineteenth-century view of sexuality

238f The erotic South: Civilization and sexuality in American abolitionism

239g A social psychological model of human sexuality

257a Purity, motherhood, pleasure or threat? Definitions of female sexuality 1900-1970s

257e The daughter is mother of the child: Cycles of lesbian sexuality

277o Sexuality with cardiac disease

279a Introduction: Consequences of sexuality

280j Fire setting (pyromania) and its relationship to sexuality

281a Human sexuality in the life cycle of the family system

281d Sexuality in divorce and remarriage

281g Sexuality and disability

282f Sexuality and gender in Samoa: Conceptions and missed conceptions

282k Gender and sexuality in hierarchical societies: The case of Polynesia and some comparative implications

285a The impact of sexuality, professional authoritarianism, and health crises on rehabilitation

285d Death and sexuality

285h Sexuality and cancer

285q Sexuality and multiple sclerosis - must they be mutually exclusive?

285r Sexuality and the spinal cord injured woman: An interview

286d The fallen woman's sexuality: Childbirth and censure

286f "Swinburne planteth, Hardy watereth": Victorian views of pain and pleasure in human sexuality

286g Bathsheba's lovers: Male sexuality in *Far from the Madding Crowd*

286i Sexuality and the Victorian artist: Dickens and Swinburne

286n "Here a captive heart busted": From Victorian sentimentality to modern sexuality

286o The worlds of Victorian sexuality: Work in progress

287b Male sexuality: Socio-sexual change and the single status

287c Female sexuality: Singlehood and the problems of intimacy

287e Sexuality verboten: Young and old

287f Black sexuality

287k Communicating sexuality

287p Creative sexuality: Androgyny

288a The executive man and woman: The issue of sexuality

288g The other side of the coin: Women who exploit their sexuality for gain

290a 'Free from all uninvited touch of man': Women's campaigns around sexuality, 1880-1914

290b Sexology and the social construction of male sexuality (Havelock Ellis)

290c Sexology and the universalization of male sexuality (from Ellis to Kinsey, and Masters and Johnson)

305g Shades of lavender: Lesbian sex and sexuality

308h Adolescent sexuality and teenage pregnancy from a black perspective

343a The woman's part: Female sexuality as power in Shakespeare's plays

349l Rape: Power, anger, and sexuality

344d Sexual harassment: The link between gender stratification, sexuality, and women's economic status

353c What ought to be and what was: Women's sexuality in the nineteenth century

376c The crime of precocious sexuality: Female juvenile delinquency and the progressive era

411r Sexuality and the middle-aged woman

413d Fertility, sexuality and social control in New Zealand

418i Sexuality and homosexuality

430c Sexuality and women's oppression in Iran

433h Forms of the Indian notion of sexuality and an interpretation of the Mymensing ballad of Kajalrekha

439c Sexuality as the mainstay of identity: Psychoanalytic perspectives

439m Maternal sexuality and asexual motherhood

439o Social and behavioral constructions of female sexuality

439v Female sexuality and the Catholic confessional

460b The history of female sexuality in the United States

460f Discussion: Psychological and physiological concepts in female sexuality: A discussion of physiological aspects of female sexual development

461c Discussion: Further thoughts on a group discussion by black women about sexuality

461f Sex and sexuality: Women at midlife

461i Discussion: Aging and female sexuality

461o Female sexuality and pregnancy

Sexy
301h Growing up southern & sexy

Shade
40a Shades and slashes of light

Shadow
108j Fanny Mendelssohn Hensel: Musician in her brother's shadow

332p Shadowing/surfacing/shedding: Contemporary German writers in search of a female *Bildungsroman*

408e Marina/Malinche: Masks and shadows

Shakers
417e The Shakers: Gender equality in hierarchy

441c The machine in utopia: Shaker women and technology

Shakespeare, William
180e The great unwritten story: Mothers and daughters in Shakespeare

202c Shakespeare's *other* sister

343a The woman's part: Female sexuality as power in Shakespeare's plays

343b "Neither mother, wife, nor England's queen": The roles of women in *Richard III*

343c Shakespeare and the soil of rape

343d Comic structure and the humanizing of Kate in *The Taming of the Shrew*

343e Those "soft and delicate desires": *Much Ado* and the distrust of women

343f As we like it: How a girl can be smart and still popular

343g Counsels of gall and grace: Intimate conversations between women in Shakespeare's plays

343h Shakespeare's Cressida: "A kind of self"

343i "I wooed thee with my sword": Shakespeare's tragic paradigms

343j Coming of age in Verona

343k A heart cleft in twain: The dilemma of Shakespeare's Gertrude

343l Women and men in *Othello*: "What should such a fool/Do with so good a woman?"

343m Lady Macbeth: "Infirm of purpose"

343n Shakespeare's female characters as actors and audience

343o A penchant for Perdita on the eighteenth-century stage

343p The miranda trap: Sexism and racism in Shakespeare's *Tempest*

343q "O sacred, shadowy, cold, and constant queen": Shakespeare's imperiled and chastening daughters of romance

343r Women and men in Shakespeare: A selective bibliography

Shakespearean
399n Henrietta Vinton Davis: Shakespearean actress

Shakti
218b *Sati* or *Shakti*: Women, culture and politics in India

Shaman
234c Shamanism as institutionalised ego defense and elite formation associated with transvestism in a Borneo society

325d Possession sickness and women shamans in Korea

347b Sunksquaws, shamans, and tradeswomen: Middle Atlantic coastal Algonkian women during the 17th and 18th centuries

399a Sex roles and shamans

Shame
334c Shame and reparation: Women's place in the kin

Shange, Ntozake
14x Black women playwrights from Grimké to Shange: Selected synopses of their works

448l "A laying on of hands": Transcending the city in Ntozake Shange's *for colored girls who have considered suicide/when the rainbow is enuf*

Shape
340b Women as shapers of the human adaptation

442f Shapes of the feminine experience in art

Share
46c Earnings sharing: Incremental and fundamental reform

204g Primary caregiving and role-sharing fathers

Shari'a
300o Islamic law in Christian Southeast Asia: The politics of establishing Shari'a courts in the Philippines

Shari'ati, Ali
368e Fatimeh as a role model in the works of Ali Shari'ati

Shaw, George Bernard
338e The new woman and the old goddess: The shaping of Shaw's mythology

Shaw, Mary
399o Mary Shaw: A fighting champion

Shed
332p Shadowing/surfacing/shedding: Contemporary German writers in search of a female *Bildungsroman*

Shelley, Mary
27c Frankenstein's daughter: Mary Shelley and Mary Wollstonecraft

109j "A forced solitude": Mary Shelley and the creation of Frankenstein's monster

196e On exile and fiction: The Leweses and the Shelleys

Shelley, Percy
196e On exile and fiction: The Leweses and the Shelleys

Shelter
26c Group treatment of children in shelters for battered women

103c Battered women's shelters and the political economy of sexual violence

203t Emergency shelter: The development of an innovative women's environment

226j Community responses to violence against women: The case of a battered women's shelter

404r Breaking cycles of victimization: The shelter as an affirmative institution

Shenkar, Joan
124c Notes on technique in feminist drama: *Apple Pie* and *Signs of Life*

Sherbro, Sierra Leone
200e Proto-social to adult: A Sherbro transformation

370o Slaves, slave owners, and slave dealers: Sherbro coast and hinterland

Sherpa
124e The founding of the first Sherpa nunnery, and the problem of "women" as an analytic category

Shi'ite
371f Sexual prohibitions, shared space and fictive marriages in Shi'ite Iran

Shibokusa
167i At the foot of the mountain: The Shibokusa women of Kita Fuji

Shimerda, Antonia
384l The Virginian and Antonia Shimerda: Different sides of the western coin

Shipyard
444c The job he left behind: American women in the shipyards during World War II

Shi'i Fiqh
368c Women in Shi'i Fiqh: Images through the Hadith

Shoe
150ff Shoes are made for walking

Shop
50a The butcher, the baker, the candlestick-maker: The shop and the family in the Industrial Revolution
199o On the shop floor: Multi-ethnic unity against the conglomerate
201j Dorothy Jacobs Bellanca: Women clothing workers and the runaway shops

Shopping
463e Shopping trips: Who makes them and when?

Shopping-Bag
210h Shopping-bag women: Aging deviants in the city

Short Story
see also Literature
74g From a woman's perspective: The short stories of Rosario Ferré and Ana Lydia Vega
197h The liberated instant: Muriel Spark and the short story
202k What is to console us?: The politics of deception in Woolf's short stories
330d Forms of the Woolfian short story
449d Feminism and literary technique in Ting Ling's early short stories
450e Shirley Ann Grau and the short story
450q Stopping places: Bobbie Ann Mason's short stories
451b Introduction to *The Collected Short Stories of Edith Wharton*

Shoulder
301p Should to shoulder

Showplace
353aa Feminist showplace

Shuhua, Ling
449c Portraits by a lady: The fictional world of Ling Shuhua

Sibling
see also Family
104c Interhousehold co-operation in Peru's southern Andes: A case of multiple sibling-group marriage
146f Sibling incest
162e 'Avoir sa part': Sibling relations in partible inheritance Brittany

Sibyl
112d María de Zayas y Sotomayor: Sibyl of Madrid (Spanish, 1590?-1661?)

Sicily
94j Generations and class: Sicilian-Australians in Melbourne

Sickness
see also Disease, Illness
12f 'Sickness is a woman's business?': Reflections on the attribution of illness

34c From sin to sickness: Hormonal theories of lesbianism
145f Prelude to consciousness: Amalie Sieveking and the Female Association for the Care of the Poor and the Sick
325d Possession sickness and women shamans in Korea
395l Anger sickness: Social stress and native diagnosis among Ecuadorian Indians
440m In sickness and in health: Social policy and the control of women

Sidesaddle
147ff From sidesaddle to rodeo

Sidney, Philip
329m 'What right have I, a woman?': Virginia Woolf's reading notes on Sidney and Spenser

Sido
196h The magic spinning wheel: Straw to gold - Colette, Willy and Sido

Sierra Leone
200e Proto-social to adult: A Sherbro transformation
370o Slaves, slave owners, and slave dealers: Sherbro coast and hinterland
385a Women, work, and ethnicity: The Sierra Leone case
385b Control of land, labor, and capital in rural southern Sierra Leone

Sieveking, Amalie
145f Prelude to consciousness: Amalie Sieveking and the Female Association for the Care of the Poor and the Sick

Sign
64q Colette and signs: A partial reading of a writer "Born *not* to Write"
200d The power of signs: Gender, culture and the wild in the Bolivian Andes

Signal
136j The development of sex differences in nonverbal signals: Fallacies, facts, and fantasies
230j Sexual signaling and sexual aggression in adolescent relationships

Significant Other
37p Support systems of significant others in black families

Signify
442i Poets and versifiers, singers and signifiers: Women of the Harlem Renaissance

Signs of Life
124c Notes on technique in feminist drama: *Apple Pie* and *Signs of Life*

Sikh
85c Reminiscences of fieldwork among the Sikhs

Silence
30o Silence: Access and aspiration
225e Public silence, private terror
231y What we're rollin around in bed with: Sexual silences in feminism
356n The silence is broken

Silicon Valley
192k Silicon Valley: Paradise or paradox?

199l Women and work in Silicon Valley: Options and futures
428l Silicon Valley's women workers: A theoretical analysis of sex-segregation in the electronics industry labor market
428m Fast forward: The internationalization of Silicon Valley

Silko, Leslie
124b Naming, magic and documentary: The subversion of the narrative in *Song of Solomon, Ceremony,* and *China Men*

Simile
419b "Reverse similes" and sex roles in the *Odyssey*

Simmons College
352g Single-sex education and leadership: The early years of Simmons College

Simons, May Wood
128c May Wood Simons: Party theorist

Simple
40m A simple language

Sin
34c From sin to sickness: Hormonal theories of lesbianism

Singapore
300i The public bureaucracy and social change in Singapore
300j The CHIT fund in Singapore: Failure of a large-scale rotating credit fund
350g From rural subsistence to an industrial peripheral work force: An examination of female Malaysian migrants and capital accumulation in Singapore
388c Singapore women: Work and the family
466k The feminization of the teaching profession in Singapore

Singer
442i Poets and versifiers, singers and signifiers: Women of the Harlem Renaissance

Single
16p Women as single parents: Alternative services for a neglected population
23f The Parliamentary wife: Participant in the 'two-person single career'
41f Stress and support networks of working single black mothers
48j Sink or swing? The lifestyles of single adults
157b To Columbia on the Tynemouth: The emigration of single women and girls in 1862
170e Single careers: Employment, housework and caring
203j Swedish women in single-family housing
203u Housing for single-parent families: A women's design
210j The ever-single elderly woman
287b Male sexuality: Socio-sexual change and the single status
287c Female sexuality: Singlehood and the problems of intimacy
304j The resocialization of single-again women
339f The single woman: Moving up by moving around
380g Bringing down the rear: The decline in the economic position of single-mother families

Single Sex

62c The politics of single-sex schools

62f Single-sex setting

Sioux Indians

see also American Indian

148f The role of Sioux women in the production of ceremonial objects: The case of the star quilt

148h Sioux women in transition: A study of their changing status in a domestic and capitalist sector of production

148i Male and female in traditional Lakota culture

Sippar, Babylonia

156p The Nadiu women of Sippar

Sister

see also Family

19n Saints and sisters

30l "She is the one you call sister": Discovering Mary Wilkins Freeman

30r Sister/outsider: Some thoughts on Simone Weil

42a Our sisters in the church

81i All pink sisters: The War Department and the feminist movement in the 1920s

103u "Sisters" or "comrades"? The politics of friends and families

115h Mary: My sister

132o Separation and survival: Mothers, daughters, sisters: - The women's experimental theater

150e The sisters

180b Kriemhild and Clytemnestra - Sisters in crime or independent women?

202c Shakespeare's *other* sister

305t Mothers, sisters, lovers, listen

310gg The courage of sisters

347l Putting down sisters and wives: Tongan women and colonization

370j Slave wives, free sisters: Bakongo women and slavery c.1700-1850

379j The ethnological mirror: American evangelical women and their heathen sisters, 1870-1910

448k Willa Cather's lost Chicago sisters

448n Sister to Faust: The city's "hungry" woman as heroine

Sister (Catholic)

see also Nun, Religion

401l Catholic sisters in China: An effort to raise the status of women

Sister Carrie

155h The fate of the fallen woman in *Maggie* and *Sister Carrie*

Sister-Woman

17r Papa Dick and Sister-Woman: Reflections on women in the fiction of Richard Wright

Sisterhood

14b A black feminist's search for sisterhood

23b Black sisterhood: The situation of urban aboriginal women and their relationship to the white women's movement

60k "On the hem of life": Race, class, and the prospects for sisterhood

101d Sisterhood or separation? The All-India Muslim Ladies' Conference and the Nationalist Movement

177c Spinster sisterhoods

201g The great uprising in Cleveland: When sisterhood failed

229ff Sisterhood as cosmic covenant

336h Sisterhood under siege: Feminism and anti-semitism in Germany, 1904-1938

379m The limitations of sisterhood: Elizabeth Cady Stanton and division in the American suffrage movement, 1875-1902

Sita

452m Towards a theory of form in feminist autobiography: Kate Millett's *Flying* and *Sita*; Maxine Hong Kingston's *The Woman Warrior*

Sixshooter

175h Two sixshooters and a sunbonnet: The story of Sally Skull

Sixteenth Century

33e Learned women in the Europe of the sixteenth century

33g Gender and genre: Women as historical writers, 1400-1820

99b From the woman's view: Pre-industrial England, 1500-1750

112b Caterina Corner, Queen of Cyprus (Venetian, 1454?-1510)

112c Marguerite de Navarre and her circle (French, 1492-1549)

112d María de Zayas y Sotomayor: Sibyl of Madrid (Spanish, 1590?-1661?)

184d Elizabethan birth control and Puritan attitudes

187j The nun as anchoress: England, 1100-1500

234j 'Woman-ing" the landscape: East Anglia 1300-1500: A discussion on sources and methodology

331h Poems by "The Lady" in *La Chasse et le depart d'amours (1509)*

379g The holy woman and the urban community in sixteenth-century Avila

Size

107s Measures of body size and form of elite female basketball players

279i Sexual dimorphism for size in seven nineteenth-century Northwest coast populations

279j Size sexual dimorphism and secular trend: Indicators of subclinical malnutrition?

Skate

372w Energy cost of ice skating with figure skates for women

Skeletal

279e Sexual dimorphism in skeletal samples

279f Sexual dimorphism and settlement pattern in Middle Eastern skeletal populations

Skid Row

11g Women on skid row

Skier

372z Effect of increased intensity of training on maximum oxygen uptake and muscular performance of young female cross-country skiers

Skill

241e Women and caring: Skills, tasks and taboos

353hh More than "the physician's hand": Skill and authority in twentieth-century nursing

387q Degraded and deskilled: The proletarianization of clerical work

407d The administrative skills program: What have we learned?

434s Social work values and skills to empower women

446f Raising the skill level of women workers

470a Sex and skill in the organisation of the clothing industry

Skull, Sally

175h Two sixshooters and a sunbonnet: The story of Sally Skull

Slash

40a Shades and slashes of light

Slave

2l Abortion, slavery, and the law: A study in moral character

14i Studying slavery: Some literary and pedagogical considerations on the black female slave

14n Slave codes and liner notes

39n Female slave resistance: The economics of sex

60s From slavery to social welfare: Racism and the control of black women

148b Beasts of burden and menial slaves: Nineteenth century observations of Northern Plains Indian women

163a International politics of female sexual slavery

163b The network defines its issues: Theory, evidence and analysis of female sexual slavery

163c Network strategies and organizing against female sexual slavery

163h The torture of women political prisoners: A case study in female sexual slavery

231p Master and slave: The fantasy of erotic domination

370a Women's importance in African slave systems

370b African women in the Atlantic slave trade

370c Sexual demography: The impact of the slave trade on family structure

370d Female slavery

370e Women in slavery in the western Sudan

370g Slavery and reproductive labor in Mombasa

370h The Songhay-Zarma female slave: Relations of production and ideological status

370i Women in slavery among the Mangbetu c. 1800-1910

370j Slave wives, free sisters: Bakongo women and slavery c.1700-1850

370l Post-proclamation slavery in Accra: A female affair?

370m Appendix: A note on Anlo (Ewe) slavery and the history of a slave

370n Bwanikwa: Consciousness and protest among slave women in Central Africa, 1886-1911

370o Slaves, slave owners, and slave dealers: Sherbro coast and hinterland

370q Women slavers of Guinea-Conakry

Sleep

121d Notes on sleeping with Emily Dickinson

277e The assessment of sleep erections for diagnosis of erectile disorders

Slum
454h Cultural hybrid in the slums: The college woman and the Settlement House, 1889-1894

Small Press
15i Publishers on libraries: Small presses and the library

The Small Room
186k May Sarton's *The Small Room*: A comparison and an analysis

Smallpox
194k Pox and the terror of childlessness: Images and ideas of the smallpox goddess in a north Indian village

Smart
343f As we like it: How a girl can be smart and still popular

Smedley, Agnes
332b The novel of awakening (five novels)
384i The western roots of feminism in Agnes Smedley's *Daughter of Earth*

Smile
244j Synthetic smiles and fabricated faces

Smith College
314f Project on women and social change: Smith College

Smith, Lee
450o The world of Lee Smith

Smith, Mary Ellen
205y Mary Ellen Smith: The right woman in the right place at the right time

Smith, Sara
349q An interview with Sara Smith - One woman's experience with the cycle of violence

Smoking
7t Smokers protest healthism
51k Smoking, alcohol, and body mass relationships to early menopause: Implications for risk of cardiovascular disease
53e Changing patterns of smoking and risk of disease

Snatcher
310c Egg snatchers

Snow
135o Snow beneath snow: A reconsideration of the virgin of *Villette*

Sobriety
105k Marriage, estrangement, sobriety and recidivism: Some crucial process variables in the case of alcoholic men and their wives

Social
see also Culture, Socialize, Society
4e Social implications of teenage childbearing
7d Sadomasochism and the social construction of desire
18c "Reproductive choice" in the contemporary United States: A social analysis of female sterilization
24e Social skill and human sexual attraction
26i Coping with wife abuse: Personal and social networks

31f Sexism, religion, and the social and spiritual liberation of women today
34d Social bodies: The interaction of culture and women's biology
39s The incarcerated black female: The case of social double jeopardy
52o Change in the system of social power: Conditions for the social equality of women in Yugoslavia
57b Toward an understanding of sexual learning and communication: An examination of social learning theory and nonschool learning environments
68p Third World women and social reality: A conclusion
72k Social issues confronting Hispanic-American women
106e Marriage contract and social contract in seventeenth-century English political thought
117e Social status and gender in Roman art: The case of the saleswoman
122f The social determination of science: Some implications for women's studies
129s Some problems of social freedom
132s Lesbianism and the social function of taboo
134a Youth service provision, social order and the question of girls
134f Dance and social fantasy
144i Politics and the family: Social democracy and the working-class family in theory and practice before 1914
145n Social insurance and the family work of Oberlausitz home weavers in the late nineteenth century
147ii The Edmonton Grads: The team and its social significance from 1915-1940
164a Introduction: Jane Austen as a social novelist
164e Sex and social life in Jane Austen's novels
178i Social ties and social support
185b Social forces and the changing family
185g Personal and social attitudes toward parenting
185m Family options, governments, and the social milieu: Viewed from the 21st century
186l Rage for justice: Political, social and moral consciousness in selected novels of May Sarton
200e Proto-social to adult: A Sherbro transformation
204j Social development and parent-child interaction in father-custody and stepmother families
209c Bargaining over the social costs of information technology
219d The social uses of sexuality: Symbolic interaction, power and rape
239m Body time and social time: Mood patterns by menstrual cycle phase and day of week
241d Men and war: Status, class and the social reproduction of masculinity
243e Mothers as social agents: Structuring the community activities of school aged children
255f Gradations of purdah and the creation of social boundaries on a Baluchistan oasis

255h From purdah to politics: The social feminism of the all-India women's organizations
270o Civil violence in Turkey: Its infrastructural, social and cultural foundations
274k Social studies
276a The classification of sexual aggressives and their associated demographic, social, developmental and psychological features
280m Necrophilia and anti-social acts
282e Self-interest and the social good: Some implications of Hagen gender imagery
283c The genesis of the social
283d Feminists - The degenerates of the social?
283e Reply: Feminists - The degenerates of the social?
290b Sexology and the social construction of male sexuality (Havelock Ellis)
295j Social support and efficacy in advocacy roles: A case study of two women's organizations
309k The health and social consequences of teenage childbearing
309l The social consequences of teenage parenthood
319k Social networks and survival strategies: An exploratory study of Mexican American, black and Anglo family female heads in San Jose, California
321l The women's movement and social justice
321o Can there be justice for women under capitalism?: Social justice for whom?
333d The social and economic importance of the women in Jigalong
342a Social effects of some contemporary myths about women
344x What price independence? Social reactions to lesbians, spinsters, widows, and nuns
353i Doctors, birth control, and social values, 1830-1970
353l The Loomis trial: Social mores and obstetrics in the mid-nineteenth century
354i Medicine and patriarchal violence: The social construction of a "private" event
354j Chlorosis and chronic disease in 19th-century Britain: The social constitution of somatic illness in a capitalist society
355d Social status of the homemaker
355e Satisfaction with housework: The social context
356b Anthropology: Social and cultural perspectives
364f The legal and social transformation of rural women in Aegean Turkey
365l Minority women: Social-cultural issues
371a Ground rules and social maps for women: An introduction
376d The weaker vessel: Legal versus social reality in mental commitments in nineteenth-century New York
380d The relationship between the labor force employment of women and the changing social organization in Canada
383a A new anarchism: Social and political ideas in some recent feminist eutopias
387c Women in the occupational world: Social disruption and conflict
388k Social feminism in France: A case study

390q Sally Bowen: Political and social experiences of a working-class woman

395l Anger sickness: Social stress and native diagnosis among Ecuadorian Indians

403c The determinants of social position among rural Moroccan women

405k The social composition of women deputies in Soviet elective politics: A preliminary analysis of official biographies

405l Women in contemporary Poland: Their social and occupational position and attitudes toward work

412f Georgia Harkness: Social activist and/or mystic

412j The social gospel according to Phoebe: Methodist deaconesses in the metropolis, 1885-1918

416n Class, race, sex, scientific objects of knowledge: A socialist-feminist perspective on the social construction of productive nature and some political consequences

421d Social and economic integration of South Asian women in Montreal, Canada

423b Women and health: The social dimensions of biomedical data

424k Female domestic servants in Cagayan de Oro, Philippines: Social and economic implications of employment in a 'premodern' occupational role

427e Gender inequities in childhood social life and adult work life

436k The impact of the women's movement and legislative activity of women MPs on social development

439o Social and behavioral constructions of female sexuality

458d Employment status and social support: The experience of the mature woman

459f A social anthropological approach to women's roles and status in developing countries: The domestic cycle

461x Discussion: Legal victim or social victim?

465a Dealing with dependency: State practices and social realities, 1870-1945

473h Adaptive strategies and social networks of women in St. Kitts

Social Action

73b Organizing neighborhood women for political and social action

421k Feminist egalitarianism, social action orientation and occupational roles: A cross-national study

Social Change

8a Social change and psychotherapeutic implications

45i Assessing personal and social change in two generations

69i Marriage and midlife: The impact of social change

77b Creative women in economic and social change

82n Dynamics of social and cultural change

100a The dialectic of education: An alternative approach to education and social change in developing countries

105f The family, the child, and social change

144c Family and 'modernisation': The peasant family and social change in nineteenth-century Bavaria

174x Self-disclosure and the commitment to social change

184e Illegitimacy, sexual revolution, and social change in modern Europe

199c Sacrifice, satisfaction, and social change: Employment and the family

243a Urban and rural working women in Poland today: Between social change and social conflict

266f Sampling: Issues and problems in sex role and social change research

266i Statistical analysis in sex roles and social change

270m Social change and family crisis: The nature of Turkish divorce

300i The public bureaucracy and social change in Singapore

300k Buddhist attitudes toward social change in Burma and Thailand

314f Project on women and social change: Smith College

352a Introduction: Barriers to equity - women, educational leadership, and social change

362b An examination of education, social change, and national development policy: The case of Kenyan women

368d Social and economic change in the role of women, 1956-1978

387m Stay home, little Sheba: On placement, displacement, and social change

388j Women's organizations and social change: The age-of-marriage issue in India

398e Self-disclosure and the commitment to social change

403g Women, law, and social change in Iran

411h Social change and equality: The roles of women and economics

417aa Of time and revolution: Theories of social change in contemporary feminist science fiction

425c Women and the psychology of achievement: Implications for personal and social change

448a The city as catalyst for Flora Tristan's vision of social change

Social Class
see also Class

22d Le rôle et la place de la femme provenant de la classe sociale inférieure dans la vie quotidienne du Moyen-Age

139d Women, men and social class

319d Breast-feeding and social class mobility: The case of Mexican migrant mothers in Houston, Texas

424i Women's work: Factory, family and social class in an industrializing order

472c Social class and the older family member

Social Consciousness
see also Consciousness

164c The influence of place: Jane Austen and the novel of social consciousness

186l Rage for justice: Political, social and moral consciousness in selected novels of May Sarton

368i Poor women and social consciousness in revolutionary Iran

378e Women as employees: Social consciousness and collective action

Social Control
see also Control

60t Religion as an instrument of social control

241i Purification or social control? Ideologies of reproduction and the churching of women after childbirth

290d Theory into practice: Sexual liberation or social control? (*Forum* magazine 1968-1981)

305o Sexual harassment as a form of social control

413d Fertility, sexuality and social control in New Zealand

436i Technology, 'Women's work' and the social control of women

Social History
see also History

117d Mourners on Greek vases: Remarks on the social history of women

162a Interest and emotion in family and kinship studies: A critique of social history and anthropology

164f 'Real solemn history' and social history

231a Sex and society: A research note from social history and anthropology

234g Social history and women's history

Social Inequality
see also Equality

39y Social inequality and sexual status in Barbados

207c Women's labours: The naturalisation of social inequality and women's subordination

208i Women's labours: The naturalisation of social inequality and women's subordination

Social Mobility
see also Mobility

71l Social mobility of Asian women in America: A critical review

139e Trends in female social mobility

402i Muslim women in Uttar Pradesh: Social mobility and directions of change

Social Movement
see also Movement

133t Lesbianfeminist rhetoric as a social movement

435a Representing women: The transition from social movement to interest group

Social Policy
see also Policy

57j Sexuality and social policy: The unwritten curriculum

93q Social policies and the family: Their effect on women's paid employment in Great Britain

138i Sex, education and social policy: A new moral economy?

218g Women and social policy: Lessons from Scandinavia

363e Social policy and women in Latin America: The need for a new model

423e Women in the German Democratic Republic: Impact of culture and social policy

440l Social policy, education and women

440m   In sickness and in health: Social policy and the control of women

465h   The new right, sex, education and social policy: Towards a new moral economy in Britain and the USA

Social Problem

128i   Appendix: Woman and the social problem

252b   Second trimester abortion as a social problem: Delay in abortion seeking behaviour and its causes

398j   Women's studies and men's careers: How the 'social problem' of women in education maintained the academic status of men in the 1970s

Social Psychology
see also Psychology

111e   Social-psychological research and relevant speculation on the issue of domestic violence

239g   A social psychological model of human sexuality

239l   A social psychological perspective on the menstrual cycle

262f   A social-psychological analysis of the context for change

270n   Social psychological patterns of homicide in Turkey: A comparison of male and female convicted murders

320h   Social psychology looks at but does not see the undergraduate woman

359jj   Wife battering and the maintenance of gender roles: A sociopsychological perspective

Social Reform
see also Reform

101b   Social reform and women's participation in political culture: Andhra and Madras

157p   Appendix: Votes for women: Profiles of prominent British Columbia suffragists and social reformers

243g   Katie's place: Women's work, professional work, and social reform

366g   Women in social reform movements

Social Relation

104a   Aspects of non-capitalist social relations in rural Egypt: The small peasant household in an Egyptian delta village

138j   Social theory, social relations and education

285c   The social relation of sex and death

473e   Spirit magic in the social relations between men and women (Saõ Paulo, Brazil)

Social Role
see also Role

96b   The mental health problems of women: Social roles and the individual

116g   Sex and social roles: How to deal with the data

403d   The social and political roles of Arab women: A study of conflict

411e   The middle years: Changes and variations in social-role commitments

Social Science

3a   Social science and ethical issues: The policy implications of poll data on abortion

14j   Debunking Sapphire: Toward a non-racist and non-sexist social science

84f   Charlotte Perkins Gilman: Forerunner of a feminist social science

133n   Views of homosexuality among social scientists

189i   The oldest, the most established, the most quantitative of the social sciences - and most dominated by men; The impact of feminism on economics

241a   Social sciences and the state: Fighting like a woman

266b   Social science inquiries into female achievement: Recurrent methodological problems

298a   Arab women: The status of research in the social sciences and the status of women

298c   Research in the social sciences on North African women: Problems, trends, and needs

298d   Research in the social sciences on women in Morocco

298i   A survey of trends in social sciences research on women in the Arab region, 1960-1980

312h   Passionate scholarship: Notes on values, knowing and method in feminist social science

314d   The social sciences: Establishing gender as a category

Social Science Research Council (SRRC)

297a   The SSRC: Restructured and defended

Social Security
see also Security

46a   Concepts underlying the current controversy about women's social security benefits

46d   Women and a two-tier social security system

46e   The double-decker alternative for eliminating dependency under social security

46h   The housewife and social security reform: A feminist perspective

46i   Incremental change in social security needed to result in equal and fair treatment of men and women

46j   The changing nature of social security

146a   Concepts underlying the current controversy about women's social security benefits

258d   Social security and the family

375i   Adult derivative benefits in social security: A women's issue

465d   Sex equality and social security

Social Service
see also Service

16u   Alternative social services and the black woman

16v   Social services and the Hispanic woman

57g   Social services and sexual learning

Social Structure
see also Structure

105g   Social structure, family socialization, and children's achievement goals: A comparative analysis

144d   Family and household: Social structures in a German village between the two World Wars

Social Theory
see also Theory

23l   Psychoanalysis and feminist social theory of gender

138j   Social theory, social relations and education

152c   New sociological theory on homosexuality

217a   Women's research and social theory

Social Welfare
see also Welfare

60s   From slavery to social welfare: Racism and the control of black women

103e   Women and the Reagan revolution: Thermidor for the social welfare economy

Social Work

263k   Industrial social workers in France, 1917-1939: A study in the sex/gender division of labor

434i   Observations on social work with American Indian women

434j   Homophobia and social work practice with lesbians

434k   Social work with lesbian couples

434p   Issues of power in social work practice

434s   Social work values and skills to empower women

455b   A herstory of women in social work

455f   The social work profession encounters the battered woman

455i   Women and the health care system: Implications for social work practice

455l   Women administrators in social work

Social-Emotional

80a   Social-emotional consequences of day care for preschool children

Socialism

81m   Socialist feminism between the two World Wars: Insights from oral history

95b   Clara Zetkin: A Socialist approach to the problem of women's oppression

95c   When radical and socialist feminism were joined: The extraordinary failure of Madeleine Pelletier

95d   Sylvia Pankhurst: Suffragist, feminist, or socialist?

95i   Humanism versus feminism in the socialist movement: The life of Angelica Balabanoff

119e   The family in socialist-feminist politics

128e   The "Jennie Higginses" of the "New South in the West": A regional survey of socialist activists, agitators, and organizers, 1901-1917

128f   The politics of mutual frustration: Socialists and suffragists in New York and Wisconsin

128g   Women socialists and their male comrades: The Reading experience, 1927-1936

207j   Women in socialist societies: Problems of theory and practice

208e   Women in socialist societies: Problems of theory and practice

224d   Looking at pornography: Erotica and the socialist morality

224i   Lesbianism: A socialist feminist perspective

256f   "The men are as bad as their masters...": Socialism, feminism and sexual ntagonism in the London tailoring trade in the 1830s

283o The socialist economic review project: Progress in the economics of the left

335e 'The serious burdens of love?' Some questions on child-care, feminism and socialism

369d Socialism, feminism, and gay/lesbian liberation

405d Socialism and feminism: The first stages of women's organizations in the eastern part of the Austrian empire

416n Class, race, sex, scientific objects of knowledge: A socialist-feminist perspective on the social construction of productive nature and some political consequences

417h Housework and utopia: Women and the Owenite socialist communities

417q Twin Oaks: A feminist looks at indigenous socialism in the United States

421w The demands of work and the human quality of marriage: An exploratory study of professionals in two socialist societies

421y Variations in women's roles and family life under the socialist regime in China

Socialize

see also Culture, Social, Society

32e *Wally, die Zweiflerin* and *Madonna*: A discussion of sex-socialization in the nineteenth century

37o Involvement of fathers in the socialization of black children

48b Sexual socialization and gender roles in childhood

56d The deliverers: A woman doctor's reflections on medical socialization

71j The early socialization of Asian-American female children

105g Social structure, family socialization, and children's achievement goals: A comparative analysis

151e Socialisation in the literature lesson

193d Socialisation in patriarchal society

204k Comparative socialization practices in traditional and alternative families

214b Socialization and self-esteem: Women in management

216l What can "research experts" tell parents about effective socialization?

216o The parent as educator: A home-school model of socialization

222a A professional socialization process

225g Above and beyond politics: The sexual socialization of children

272i Sex typing in occupational socialization

304j The resocialization of single-again women

344k Sex-role socialization: A focus on women

352j Socialization and education of young black girls in school

416k Early socialization: Causes and cures of mathematics anxiety

425f Socialization experiences of women and men graduate students in male sex-typed career fields

443e Female role socialization: The analyst and the analysis

Society

see also Culture, Social, Socialize

3g Children, personhood, and a pluralistic society

21i The modern Pakistani woman in a Muslim society

39w Women's role in West Indian society

39bb The black woman in Haitian society and literature

52h Changing sex roles in the Greek family and society

52j The changing role of Swedish women in family and society

52l Soviet women in family and society

78n Battered women: Society's problem

91t Women religious and the new society

99a Brides of Christ and poor mortals: Women in medieval society

102a A society without fathers: Cooperative commonwealth or harmonious ant-heap?

103p Women in a revolutionary society: The state and family policy in China

115i Stereotyping the sexes in society and in the Church

122i Levels of female criminal activity as a correlate of female societal power

126f A feminist challenge to Darwinsim: Antoinette L. B. Blackwell on the relations of the sexes in nature and society

140f Men's power with women, other men, and society: A men's movement analysis

151b Domestic labour and Soviet society

151d Secondary education for all in a forward-looking society

151j Sport in Soviet society: Fetish or free play?

171a Language, gender and society: Opening a second decade of research

185j Moral concepts in the year 2020: The individual, the family, and society

193d Socialisation in patriarchal society

207j Women in socialist societies: Problems of theory and practice

208e Women in socialist societies: Problems of theory and practice

216a Introduction: Parenting in contemporary society

216t Parenting in a pluralistic society: Toward a policy of options and choices

231a Sex and society: A research note from social history and anthropology

234c Shamanism as institutionalised ego defense and elite formation associated with transvestism in a Borneo society

253k The health of older women in our society

258b Sex, gender and society

266g Instruments and measures in a changing, diverse society

266k The impact of societal biases on research methods

269e New roles for males in Guaymí society

282i Politics and gender in simple societies

282k Gender and sexuality in hierarchical societies: The case of Polynesia and some comparative implications

295d Black women in American society: A resource development perspective

300b Women, society and change: Perspectives on the division of labour

307b Sex differences, science, and society

316o Women's right to full participation in shaping society's course: An evolving constitutional precept

333e The conflicting role of aboriginal women in today's society

353dd On the evolution of women's medical societies

354j Chlorosis and chronic disease in 19th-century Britain: The social constitution of somatic illness in a capitalist society

385n Women's cooperative thrift and credit societies: An element of women's programs in the Gambia

393e The stable African family: Traditional and modern family structures in two African societies (Basa and Manding)

394h Sedition in a sexist society: The Platteville paradigm

409b *Dubliners*: Women in Irish society

412b The last fifteen years: Historians' changing views of American women in religion and society

412s Shaping a new society: Methodist women and industrial reform in the south, 1880-1940

421h The effect of religious affiliation on woman's role in Middle Eastern Arab Society

421w The demands of work and the human quality of marriage: An exploratory study of professionals in two socialist societies

421aa Career constraints among women graduate students in a developing society: West Pakistan. A study in the changing status of women

424r Women, work and the family in a developing society: Taiwan

436h A hard day's night: Women, reproduction and service society

461s Women in swinging: America's Amazon society?

463v An alternative approach to travel demand modeling: Constraints-oriented theories and societal roles

464f Despotism and civil society: The limits of patriarchal citizenship

469c The self-perception of Puerto Rican women toward their societal roles

472g The "babushka" or older woman in Soviet society

473l The economic role of women in Alaskan Eskimo society

Sociobiology

12c Sociobiology: So what?

35c Political ideology, sociobiology, and the U.S. women's rights movement

354k Sociobiology: Another biological determinism

Sociocultural

51n A sociocultural approach

216b Significant sociocultural factors in effective parenting

250b Socio-cultural reproduction and women's education

Sociodemographic

393b Education and socio-demographic change in Nigeria

446n Women with large families: A sociodemographic analysis

Socioeconomic

21e Some changing socioeconomic roles of village women in Malaysia

65b   Socioeconomic explanations of job segregation

92f   Indonesia: Socio-economic aspects of food consumption in rural Java

184f   Bastardy and socioeconomic structure of south Germany

232d   Hidden powers: Cultural and socio-economic accounts of Jaffna women

269d   New economic roles for Cuna males and females: An examination of socioeconomic change in a San Blas community

299a   Socio-economic status of Indian women

337m   Socio-economic profile of faculty women at Madison

373i   Baseline study for socio-economic evaluation of Tangaye solar site

380m   A statistical analysis of female participation in work and the effects on the population and socioeconomic development: A case study of Greece

402f   Women in Bangladesh: Food-for-work and socioeconomic change

446c   Socioeconomic problems of female employment

Sociography

108l   The female sociograph: The theater of Virigina Woolf's letters

Sociology

14k   Two representative issues in contemporary sociological work on black women

32l   Sociological implications of Gabriele Wohmann's critical reception

38c   Black fertility: Recent demographic and sociological influences

38f   She who is black and mother: In sociology and fiction, 1940-1970

51x   Sociological observations on ethical issues implicated in estrogen replacement therapy at menopause

73i   Irish, Italian, and Jewish women at the grassroots level: A historical and sociological perspective

85d   Men, masculinity and the process of sociological enquiry

85g   The expert's view? The sociological analysis of graduates' occupational and domestic roles

107b   Attitudes to women in sport: Preface towards a sociological theory

123i   Women in sociological analysis: New scholarship versus old paradigms

138h   Women and teaching: A semi-detached sociology of a semi-profession

152c   New sociological theory on homosexuality

168e   Conceptualizing "women" in anthropology and sociology

189e   Some of the boys won't play any more: The impact of feminism on sociology

289d   The sociological perspective

297i   The personable and the powerful: Gender and status in sociological research

327a   A sociological perspective on the causes of family violence

355f   The new home economics: An agenda for sociological research

378a   Male and female: Job versus gender models in the sociology of work

387e   Male and female: Job versus gender models in the sociology of work

388h   Public day care in Britain and Sweden: A sociological perspective

398k   On the bottom rung: A discussion of women's work in sociology

471f   Women at work in Greece: The sociological and legal perspectives

Sociosexual

285p   Sex and disability - sociosexual education presentation format

287b   Male sexuality: Socio-sexual change and the single status

461u   Wife beating: A product of sociosexual development

Sociotechnology

387b   Toward a sociotechnological theory of the women's movement

Softball

147hh   The establishment of softball for American women, 1900-1940

Solar

373i   Baseline study for socio-economic evaluation of Tangaye solar site

Solder

307s   Cold solder on a hot stove

Soleilmont

187m   Ten centuries of growth: The Cistercian Abbey of Soleilmont

Solidarity

209p   Strengthening group solidarity of clericals: A case study

292g   Education in working-class solidarity: The summer school for office workers

305u   A message of solidarity

Solitude

186e   House, home and solitude: Memoirs and journals of May Sarton

Solomon Islands

246i   European women in the Solomon Islands, 1900-1942: Accommodation and change on the Pacific frontier

Solution

392n   Women in prison: Discriminatory practices and some legal solutions

Solve

102f   Why the fathers cannot solve the problems: Some possible clues

Somatic

107q   Somatic and motor characteristics of female gymnasts

252s   Somatic sequelae and future reproduction after pregnancy termination

354j   Chlorosis and chronic disease in 19th-century Britain: The social constitution of somatic illness in a capitalist society

Somatotype

107j   Somatotypes of female athletes

107o   Body composition and somatotype characteristics of sportswomen

Something

301v   It's something inside you

Son

see also Family

62d   How shall we educate our sons?

162p   Mothers, sons, and the sale of symbols and goods: The 'German Mother's Day' 1923-33

212r   What can one do with a son? Feminist politics and male children

Song

see also Music

40w   Singing a deep song: Language as evidence in the novels of Gayl Jones

68j   Ancient song, new melody in Latin America: Women and film

301s   What she aims to be (song)

331a   Woman's song in medieval Latin

331c   The woman's song in medieval German poetry

331d   The woman's songs of Hartmann von Aue

331e   Woman's songs in Irish, 800-1500

331f   The woman's song in Middle English and its European backgrounds

331g   The "other" voice: Woman's song, its satire and its transcendence in late medieval British literature

401g   Women in the kinship system of the Southern Song upper class

Song of Solomon

124b   Naming, magic and documentary: The subversion of the narrative in *Song of Solomon*, *Ceremony*, and *China Men*

254d   *Song of Solomon*: The hero with a woman's face

Songhay-Zarma

370h   The Songhay-Zarma female slave: Relations of production and ideological status

Sonnets from the Portuguese

27f   *Sonnets from the Portuguese*: A negative and a positive context

Sorensen, Virginia

445q   The Mormon novel: Virginia Sorensen's *The Evening and the Morning*

Sorority

242c   Liberty, sorority, misogyny

Soul

40ii   Running wild in her soul: The poetry of Carolyn Rodgers

84b   Aristotle and the politicization of the soul

332a   Spiritual *Bildung*: The beautiful soul as paradigm

341i   Soul, black women and food

Source

22b   Wills, deeds, and charters as sources for the history of medieval women

61b   An abundance of riches: The women's history sources survey

178b   Sources of stress: Events or conditions?

211u   Bride, spouse, daughter: Images of the feminine in classical Jewish sources

287j   Sources and prevention of dysfunction

296k   Sources and effects of women's power

423g   Longitudinal and cross-sectional data sources on women in the middle years

South (United States)

147w   School physical activity programs for the antebellum southern females

171d   Linguistic options and choices for black women in the rural South

199j Computers, ward secretaries, and a walk-out in a Southern hospital

238f The erotic South: Civilization and sexuality in American abolitionism

264a Women's history and the revision of southern history

264b Sisters under their skins: Southern working women, 1880-1950

264c The public role of southern women

264d Black women in a southern city: Washington, D.C., 1890-1920

264e Southern literary women as chroniclers of southern life

264f Historians construct the southern woman

301e Magnolias grow in dirt: The bawdy lore of southern women

301h Growing up southern & sexy

301hh swing through the south journal, fall 1981

301kk Women's consciousness and the southern black

303l Tilting at windmills in the Quixotic South

306l Southern women's literature and culture: Course development and the pedagogical process

367e The religious experience of Southern women

379b Piety and kin: The limits of antebellum Southern women's reform

412s Shaping a new society: Methodist women and industrial reform in the south, 1880-1940

450b Alice Walker's celebration of self in southern generations

450c Gail Godwin and the ideal of southern womanhood

450l Rita Mae Brown: Feminist theorist and southern novelist

450r Why there are no southern writers

South Africa

18g Population dynamics and migrant labor in South Africa

39k The black woman in South Africa: An Azanian profile

39l The role of women in the struggle against *apartheid* in South Africa

52q The changing position of black women in South Africa

126k Sexism and racism: Obstacles to the development of black women in South Africa

153i Beyond the peasant to proletarian debate: African household formation in South Africa

322b Interview with Miriam Tlali (South Africa)

364g Divorce and the disadvantaged: African women in urban South Africa

371j Where women must dominate: Response to oppression in a South African urban community

395g The political economy of population policy in South Africa

South Wales, Australia

241f 'It's a pleasure to cook for him': Food, mealtimes and gender in some South Wales households

Southern Song

401g Women in the kinship system of the Southern Song upper class

Southwest (United States)

180v Spider woman's web: Mothers and daughters in Southwestern Native American literature

412h Hispanic clergy wives: Their contribution to United Methodism in the Southwest, later nineteenth century to the present

Soviet

see Russia

Sow

172k Some sow, others reap (Colombia)

Space

97b In/Forming schooling: Space/time/textuality in compulsory state provided "mass" schooling systems

101g Nationalism, universalization, and the extended female space in Bombay City

174s Creative teaching spaces: Home movies

182c Women and public space

185l Physical settings for families in 2020: In space, on earth

202j The politics of city space in *The Years*: Street, love, pillar boxes and bridges

229t Gyn/ecology: Spinning new time/space

229u Feminist witchcraft: Controlling our own inner space

351j Women, space, and power in higher education

371b Andean women and the concept of space/time

371c Women's space in a men's house: The British House of Commons

371d Essential objects and the sacred: Interior and exterior space in an urban Greek locality

371f Sexual prohibitions, shared space and fictive marriages in Shi'ite Iran

371h The sexual division of domestic space among two Soviet minorities: The Georgians and the Tadjiks

371i Spatial domains and women's mobility in Yorubaland, Nigeria

402j Purdah and public space

463i Individual spatial behavior

Spain

95g Margarita Nelken: Women and the crisis of Spanish politics

112d María de Zayas y Sotomayor: Sibyl of Madrid (Spanish, 1590?-1661?)

130aa The view from Spain: Rocco *finesse* and *espirit* versus plebian manners

188n The Spanish love poet: Florencia Pinar

228f Spain

282g Like wounded stags: Male sexual ideology in an Andalusian town

313e El ángel del hogar: The cult of domesticity in nineteenth century Spain

379g The holy woman and the urban community in sixteenth-century Avila

389h Georgiana Goddard King (1871-1939): Educator and pioneer in medieval Spanish art

408a Spain's first women writers

408b Echoes of the Amazon myth in medieval Spanish literature

408h A school for wives: Women in eighteenth-century Spanish theater

408o The censored sex: Woman as author and character in Franco's Spain

Spanish

72g Guidance and counseling of Spanish-background girls

347g "The universe has turned inside out...There is no justice for us here": Andean women under Spanish rule

Spanish America

367b Women and religion in Spanish America

Spark, Muriel

197c Autonomy and fabulation in the fiction of Muriel Spark

197d Calvinism and Catholicism in Muriel Spark

197e Muriel Spark: Critic into Novelist

197f Muriel Spark and satire

197g Spark and Scotland

197h The liberated instant: Muriel Spark and the short story

197i Mrs. Spark's verse

318h Muriel Spark: The novelist as dandy

Sparrow

108m Of sparrows and condors: The autobiography of Eva Perón

Spatiality

313j The off-center spatiality of womens' discourse

Speak

23g 'Women candidates speak'

132g To be or not to be ... a feminist speaker

Specialize

193k Predicting specialisation in science

Species

279c Sex differences: The female as baseline for species description

Specificity

120i Ideological hegemony in political discourse: Women's specificity and equality

Speculum

310dd Through the speculum

Speech

71a Keynote address

71g Chairperson's report

129r The Speech of Polly Baker

132n For a restricted thematics: Writing, speech, and difference in *Madame Bovary*

171j Men's speech to young children

171k Sex similarities and differences in language, speech, and nonverbal communication: An annotated bibliography

275c Sexist speech: Two basic questions

329i Speech acts in *To the Lighthouse*

356i Women in their speech communities

356j Women's speech: The voice of feminism

356k Directive-response speech sequences in girls' and boys' task activities

463w Speech

463x Speech

463y Speech

463z Speech

463aa Speech

463bb Speech

463cc Speech

Spencer, Elizabeth
450i   Mermaids, angels and free women: The heroines of Elizabeth Spencer's fiction

Spenser, Edmund
329m   'What right have I, a woman?': Virginia Woolf's reading notes on Sidney and Spenser

Sperm
238d   The spermatic economy: A nineteenth-century view of sexuality

Spermdonor
307x   A spermdonor baby grows up

Spice
107f   Sugar and spice and everything nice: Is that what female athletes behave like?

Spider Woman
180v   Spider woman's web: Mothers and daughters in Southwestern Native American literature

Spin
222g   The diary of a web spinner

Spinal
285r   Sexuality and the spinal cord injured woman: An interview

Spinifex
390j   'Spinifex fairies': Aboriginal workers in the Northern territory, 1911-39

Spinster
99d   Victorian spinsters: Dutiful daughters, desperate rebels and the transition to the new women
177c   Spinster sisterhoods
344x   What price independence? Social reactions to lesbians, spinsters, widows, and nuns

Spirit
31g   Liberating philosophy: An end to the dichotomy of matter and spirit
91v   Sammelan of the spirit
229vv   Women's collective spirit: Exemplified and envisioned
473e   Spirit magic in the social relations between men and women (Saõ Paulo, Brazil)
473f   Spirit mediums in Umbanda Evangelizada of Porto Alegre, Brazil: Dimensions of power and authority

Spiritual
31f   Sexism, religion, and the social and spiritual liberation of women today
229ee   Images of spiritual power in women's fiction
229rr   Spiritual dimensions of feminist anti-nuclear activism
229ss   Spiritual techniques for re-powering survivors of sexual assault
229ww   Spiritual hierarchies: The empress' new clothes?
332a   Spiritual *Bildung*: The beautiful soul as paradigm
379k   "My spirit eye": Some functions of spiritual and visionary experience in the lives of five black women preachers, 1810-1880
452c   Quest for community: Spiritual autobiographies of eighteenth-century Quaker and Puritan women in America

462w   Immanence: Uniting the spiritual and political

Spiritualist
454g   The spiritualist medium: A study of female professionalization in Victorian America

Spirituality
59a   Feminist theology and spirituality
108d   Autobiography of a new 'creatur': Female spirituality, selfhood, and authorship in *The Book of Margery Kempe*
150nn   Women's spirituality: A household act
229g   The three faces of goddess spirituality
229dd   See for yourself: Women's spirituality in holistic art
229hh   Dimensions of spirituality
229ii   Politics, spirituality, and models of change
229jj   The politics of feminist spirituality
229ll   The politics of women's spirituality
229mm   Feminist spirituality: The politics of the psyche
229nn   The unnatural divorce of spirituality and politics
229qq   On common ground: Native American and feminist spirituality approaches in the struggle to save mother earth
229uu   The voice of women's spirituality in futurism
360e   Women, spirituality, and mental health

Split
174k   Women and process: The Sagaris split, Session II

Spontaneous
53j   Environmental exposures and spontaneous abortion

Sport
see also Athlete, Collegiate, Intercollegiate, Title IX, names of individual sports
107a   Women's sports - the unlikely myth of equality
107b   Attitudes to women in sport: Preface towards a sociological theory
107c   Women and sport: A leisure studies perspective
107d   The influence of the traditional sex roles on women's participation and engagement in sport
107e   Personality research: Implications for women in sport
107r   Physique of college women athletes in five sports
116o   Sex equality in sports
116p   Women and "masculine" sports: Androgyny qualified
147f   Woman's place in nineteenth century Canadian sport
147g   Generalizations on women and sport, games and play in the United States from settlement to 1860
147h   Sport and the Cult of True Womanhood: A paradox at the turn of the century
147i   The realm of sports and the athletic woman, 1850-1900
147j   Women's participation in sporting activities as an indicator of a feminist movement in Canada between 1867-1914
147k   Women in sport and physical education in the United States 1900-1914

147o   Women's sport: A trial of equality
147p   Eleonora Randolph Sears, pioneer in women's sports
147s   Women in sport in the United States, 1945 to 1978
147t   The effect of current sports legislation on women in Canada and the U.S.A. - Title IX
147u   Women in the sports halls of fame
147z   History and structure of the department of physical education at the University of California with special reference to women's sports
147cc   The controlled development of collegiate sport for women, 1923-1936
147ee   Major influences on the development of high school girls' sports in Ontario
147ll   The development of women's organized sport in the 1920's: A study of the Canadian Ladies Golf Union
147nn   Sexual discrimination in youth sport: The case of Margaret Gisolo
147pp   A historical perspective of women's membership in selected national sports organizations
151j   Sport in Soviet society: Fetish or free play?
176z   Lesbians in physical education and sport
271e   Perspectives from women on sport and leisure
372a   Women and sport: A question of freedom
372b   An historical overview
372c   Women and sport in ancient Greece
372d   Women and sport during the Renaissance
372e   Development of women's sport in the 20th century
372f   Women and sports in Egypt: History and problems
372g   An outline of the history of women and western sport in Japan
372h   The influence of women doctors on the origins of women's sports in Germany
372i   The "sporty" Australians
372n   Women and sport: An introduction to the physiological aspects
372cc   Sport and reproduction in women
372ee   Traumatological aspects of sports of high achievements for women
432a   Justice and gender in school sports
432b   Education and sports: A reply to "Justice and gender in school sports"
432g   Sports, sex-equality, and the media
432h   Cooperative competition in sport
432i   Equality and competition: Can sports make a women of a girl?
432p   Putting away the pom-poms: An educational psychologist's view of females and sports

Sportswoman
107o   Body composition and somatotype characteristics of sportswomen
147m   The American sportswoman from 1900 to 1920
147n   An analysis of humour pertaining to sportswomen in Canadian newspapers from 1910-1920

Spouse
see also Family

46b Supplemental OASI benefits to homemakers through current spouse benefits, a homemaker credit, and child-care dropout years

46g Occupational pension plans and spouse benefits

87f Spouses' contributions to each other's roles

211u Bride, spouse, daughter: Images of the feminine in classical Jewish sources

349o Secondary battering and alternatives of female victims to spouse abuse

Springboard

107u Body segment contributions of female athletes to translational and rotational requirements of non-twisting springboard dive takeoffs

Spurn

452n The lady's not for spurning: Kate Millett and the critics

Squatter

172a Squatter settlement decision-making: For men only? (Peru)

270j The plight of urban migrants: Dynamics of service procurement in a squatter area

Squeeze

102n "No more squeezing into one"

Sri Lanka

194l The milk overflowing ceremony in Sri Lanka

232c Marriage in Tamil culture: The problem of conflicting "models"

232e A note on the nobility of women in popular Tamil fiction

232f The paradoxical powers of Tamil women

431c Laywomen in Theravada Buddhism

SSRC

see Social Science Research Council

Stability

250j Young women in the labour market: Stability and change

Staff

63h The development of a scale to assess inmate and staff attitudes toward co-corrections

90q The influence of gender on the verbal interactions among principals and staff members: An exploratory study

209o Staff participation in office systems' design: Two case studies at the World Bank

259d Staffing for sexism: Educational leadership and role models

337k Women on the academic staff

410g Organizational role orientations on female-dominant commissions: Focus on staff-commissioner interaction

Stafford, Jean

332g Revolutionary turnings: *The Mountain Lion* reread

384p The young girl in the West: Disenchantment in Jean Stafford's short fiction

Stage

24f Process, filter and stage theories of attraction

212l Female performers on a male stage: The first women's liberation movement and the authority of men

343o A penchant for Perdita on the eighteenth-century stage

Stagnation

199e Economic stagnation and discrimination

Stake

31m Women and their privacy: What is at stake?

Standard

257n Sexual theory and practice: Another double standard

344m The double standard: Age

Stanley, Aileen

399p Aileen Stanley, Her life and times

Stanton, Elizabeth Cady

379m The limitations of sisterhood: Elizabeth Cady Stanton and division in the American suffrage movement, 1875-1902

452e The paradox and success of Elizabeth Cady Stanton

Stanton, Mary

131e Coming Home: Four feminist utopias and patriarchal experience

Star

399i Anne Brunton Merry: First star

Star Trek

131m A female captain's enterprise: The implications of *Star Trek's* "Turnabout Intruder"

Starr, Belle

175e Belle Starr: The Bandit Queen of Dallas

Starve Harbor, Newfoundland

162o Family fun in Starve Harbor: Custom, history and confrontation in village Newfoundland

State

see also Country, Nation

50j The state and training programmes for women

65n Comparable worth under various federal and state laws

65o Developments in selected states

97b In/Forming schooling: Space/time/textuality in compulsory state provided "mass" schooling systems

97d Parents, children and the state

103b The state, the patriarchal family, and working mothers

103d The transformation of patriarchy: The historic role of the state

103p Women in a revolutionary society: The state and family policy in China

103r Antigone's daughters: Reflections on female identity and the state

116q Sex equality and education in Plato's Just State

119c 'Mothers, vote labour!' The state, the labour movement and working-class mothers, 1900-1918

129x State aid to science

149b Capital, the state and the origins of the working-class household

153l State, collective, and household: The process of accumulation in China, 1949-65

170f Care for elderly people: A conflict between women and the state

174r A feminist chautauqua for a rural state

217b Women and the welfare state: The transition from private to public dependence

217d Caring as women's work in the welfare state

220e Native women and the state

220i Women, families and the state

226b Women and state politics: An assessment

226g Women's organizational strategies in state legislatures

226h Female state senators as cue givers: ERA roll-call voting, 1972-1979

226i Women on the state bench: Correlates of access

226l State and local policies on motherhood

226m Resources and constraints on women in the policymaking process: States and local arenas

234b Women, politics and the formation of the Chinese state

241a Social sciences and the state: Fighting like a woman

245k The place of the family in the origins of the welfare state

271p Feeling states and the menstrual cycle

283j Race, left strategies and the state

335h The state, welfare and women's dependence

336k Racism and sexism in Nazi Germany: Motherhood, compulsory sterilization, and the state

368l State ideology and village women

418k Feminist thought and reproductive control: The state and 'the right to choose'

427j Gender roles and the state

435b Representing women at the state and local levels: Commissions on the status of women

440f Women as welfare recipients: Women, poverty and the state

440g Sex and money in the welfare state

440h Population policies and family policies: State construction of domestic life

440i Pater-patria: Child-rearing and the state

440j The women's movement's fandango with the state: The movement's role in public policy since 1972

465a Dealing with dependency: State practices and social realities, 1870-1945

466h Indonesian women in development: State theory and urban kampung practice

Statement

14c A black feminist statement

40b Maya Angelou and the autobiographical statement

150hh Combahee River collective statement

Statistics

6l Appendix: Some selected statistics on African women

50w Women in official statistics

66f Statistical biases in the measurement of employment discrimination

67f Statistical biases in the measurement of employment discrimination

89h The statistical theory of racism and sexism

141c Statistical model for the study of familial breast cancer

159c Female criminality in Finland - What do the statistics show?

159k Argentine statistics on female criminality

184j A case of naivete' in the use of statistics

192w Appendix: Profile of the Chicana: A statistical fact sheet

236b The premenstrual syndrome - an epidemiological and statistical exercise

258c Vital statistics

266i Statistical analysis in sex roles and social change

271q Theoretical/Conceptual implications of study design and statistical analysis: Research on the menstrual cycle

323b Women and unions in Canada: A statistical overview

422a Women in the labour force of India: A macro-level statistical profile

Stature

279h A cross-cultural investigation into the sexual dimorphism of stature

Status

11e Prevention of alcohol problems in women: Current status

22c Iconography as a means of research on the history of the status of women

22f Une contribution au débat concernant le status de la femme dans les villes du Danemark au Moyen-Age

36e Status of contraceptive technology development

38l Black female professionals: Dilemmas and contradictions of status

39y Social inequality and sexual status in Barbados

39z Female status, the family and male dominance in a West Indian community

41e Shifts in the occupational and employment status of black women: Current trends and future implications

52i The changing status and role of women in Japan

61j Darkness before the dawn: The status of women in the Depression years

68d Women in Zaire: Disparate status and roles

70a Insignificance of humanity, "Man is tampering with the moon and the stars": The employment status of American Indian women

70b Current educational status of American Indian girls

71h Immigration of Asian women and the status of recent Asian women immigrants

72h Hispanic women move forward - Out of a marginal status

73e The status of East European women in the family: Tradition and change

117e Social status and gender in Roman art: The case of the saleswoman

126j Redefining the family and women's status within the family: The case of southern Appalachia

148h Sioux women in transition: A study of their changing status in a domestic and capitalist sector of production

165o Women in the criminal justice profession: An analysis of status conflict

183c Status of rural women

198b The status of women in early Islam

198h Islam and the legal status of women in Tunisia

234f The status of women in old and early middle kingdom Egypt?

234k Summing up: Beyond the 'status of women'

241d Men and war: Status, class and the social reproduction of masculinity

243c The role and status of women scientific research workers in research groups

255k The status of women in Islam: A modernist interpretation

287b Male sexuality: Socio-sexual change and the single status

297i The personable and the powerful: Gender and status in sociological research

298a Arab women: The status of research in the social sciences and the status of women

299a Socio-economic status of Indian women

300f Changes in women's status associated with modernization in northern Thailand

317h Economic status of late middle-aged widows

334e The status of women and the practice of marriage in late-medieval Wales

347f Aztec women: The transition from status to class in empire and colony

349s Judicial paternalism and the female status offender: Training women to know their place

355d Social status of the homemaker

368b Status of women in the Qur'an

370h The Songhay-Zarma female slave: Relations of production and ideological status

398j Women's studies and men's careers: How the 'social problem' of women in education maintained the academic status of men in the 1970s

400b Rural pauperization: Its impact on the economic role and status of rural women in Bangladesh

401l Catholic sisters in China: An effort to raise the status of women

403f Ritual status of Muslim women in rural India

405n Some demographic, particularly fertility, correlates of female status in eastern Europe and the republics of the Soviet Union

410i Commissions on the status of women and building a local policy agenda

413b The role and status of Maori women

420a Urbanization, migration and the status of women

420q Philippine urbanism and the status of women

421aa Career constraints among women graduate students in a developing society: West Pakistan. A study in the changing status of women

431h Sexual status in Southeast Asia: Comparative perspectives on women, agriculture and political organization

435b Representing women at the state and local levels: Commissions on the status of women

444d "Life, liberty, and dower": The legal status of women after the American Revolution

446l Changes in the status of women and the demographic development of the family

458d Employment status and social support: The experience of the mature woman

459f A social anthropological approach to women's roles and status in developing countries: The domestic cycle

459h Women's work and their status: Rural Indian evidence of labour market and environment effects on sex differences in childhood mortality

473g Sex and status: Women in St. Vincent

Status Quo

83a Science and the status quo

Statute

2g A human life statute

2m Abortion, privacy, and personhood: From *Roe v Wade* to the human life statute

Statutory

260f The effects of statutory employment policies on women in the United Kingdom labour market

467d Statutory maternity leave in the United Kingdom: A case study

Staupers, Mabel K.

353ii Mabel K. Staupers and the integration of black nurses into the armed forces

Stead, Christina

109f Domestic gothic: The imagery of anger in Christina Stead's *The Man Who Loved Children*

Steeves, Dorothy Gretchen

205z The peacock and the guinea hen: Political profiles of Dorothy Gretchen Steeves and Grace MacInnis

Stefan, Verena

32o Verena Stefan's Häutungen: Homoeroticism and feminism

32p Our language, our selves: Verena Stefan's critique of patriarchal language

Stegner, Wallace

445m Heroes vs women: Conflict and duplicity in Stegner

Stein, Gertrude

17m The question of Gertrude Stein

127e *Ida*, A great American novel

196f Gertrice/Altrude: Stein, Toklas, and the paradox of the happy marriage

442d Gertrude Stein: The complex force of her femininity

452i Gertrude Stein and the problems of autobiography

Stella

196b The secrets of Swift and Stella

Stephen Hero

409c Emma Clery in *Stephen Hero*: A young woman walking proudly through the decayed city

Stephen, Caroline

328b The niece of a nun: Virginia Woolf, Caroline Stephen, and the cloistered imagination

Stephen, Julia

329c Virginia Woolf and Julia Stephen: The distaff side of history

Stepmother

204j Social development and parent-child interaction in father-custody and stepmother families

Stepsister

336g "Professional" housewives: Stepsisters of the women's movement

Stereotype

see also Sex Stereotype

32m The left-handed compliment: Perspectives and stereotypes in criticism

78g Sex role stereotypes and justice for women

115i Stereotyping the sexes in society and in the Church

140h Early origins of envy and devaluation of women: Implications for sex-role stereotypes

265l Cultural differences in children's sex role stereotypes

268m Sex-role stereotypes and the development of eating disorders

304a Introduction: Warning! Sex-role stereotypes may be hazardous to your health

304b Sex-role stereotypes and mental health: Conceptual models in the 1970s and issues for the 1980s

304c The development of sex-role stereotypes in children: Crushing realities

304e Sex-role stereotypes and depression in women

304f Women and agoraphobia: A case for the etiological significance of the feminine sex-role stereotype

304g Sex-role stereotypes and female sexual dysfunction

304h Women's assertion and the feminine sex-role stereotype

304k Sex-role stereotypes and violence against women

349u Sex-role stereotypes and justice for women

359b Early origins of envy and devaluation of women: Implications for sex-role stereotypes

359g Sex-role stereotypes and clinical judgements of mental health

359h Report of the task force on sex bias and sex-role stereotyping in psychotherapeutic practice

359rr Adaptive and pathogenic aspects of sex-role stereotypes: Implications for parenting and psychotherapy

365b Therapist attitudes and sex-role stereotyping

380f Sex-role stereotypes and personal attributes within a developmental framework

397a Changing theories of lesbianism: Challenging the stereotypes

399pp Creative drama: Sex role stereotyping?

404aa Stereotypes and stigma: Barriers to recovery

443g Strategies for dealing with sex-role stereotypes

469k Family roles of Hispanic women: Stereotypes, empirical findings, and implications for research

Sterilize

see also Reproduce

18c "Reproductive choice" in the contemporary United States: A social analysis of female sterilization

34f Sterilization abuse

36h Depo-provera and sterilization abuse overview

36k Sterilization abuse and Hispanic women

36l Depo-provera and sterilization abuse discussion

192h Sterilization: An overview

192i Se me acabó la canción: An ethnography of non-consenting sterilizations among Mexican women in Los Angeles

240a Sterilization

240b Regret and reversal of sterilization

252r Sterilization combined with midtrimester abortion

310n Subtle forms of sterilization abuse: A reproductive rights analysis

336k Racism and sexism in Nazi Germany: Motherhood, compulsory sterilization, and the state

319o The nonconsenting sterilization of Mexican women in Los Angeles: Issues of psychocultural rupture and legal redress in paternalistic behavior

461r Discussion: Voluntary sterilization in childless women

469g "La operacion": An analysis of sterilization in a Puerto Rican community in Connecticut

Steroid

190u Steroidal contraceptive use and subsequent development of hyperprolactinemia

Steward

42o The stewardship of talents

169o Grievance handling for women stewards

Stewart, A.T.

201c "A paradise of fashion": A. T. Stewart's department store, 1862-1875

Stick

227l The carrot, the stick and the movement

Stigma

190h Physical attractiveness and physical stigma: Menstruation and the common cold

404d The stigmatized woman

404aa Stereotypes and stigma: Barriers to recovery

472a Double stigmata: Female and old

Stimulant

252j Fact and fancy in the termination of molar pregnancy with particular reference to uterine stimulants

Stixwould

187k Stixwould in the market place

Stöcker, Helene

336e Helene Stöcker: Left-wing intellectual and sex reformer

Stoker, Bram

286b "Dual life": The status of women in Stoker's *Dracula*

Stoller, Robert J.

439s *Sexual Excitement* by Robert J. Stoller

Stone, Lucy

125g Lucy Stone: Radical beginnings

Store

201c "A paradise of fashion": A. T. Stewart's department store, 1862-1875

Storefront

203p From kitchen to storefront: Women in the tenant movement

Story

see also Literature

27l Violet Hunt's *Tales of the Uneasy*: Ghost stories of a worldly woman

56a Having a baby: A story essay

109n The gothic prism: Charlotte Perkins Gilman's gothic stories and her autobiography

122n Finding one's way through the labyrinth: A symposium on women's lives: Life stories

124a Rediscovering the "New Woman" of the 1890's: The stories of "George Egerton"

135k Edith Wharton and the ghost story

180e The great unwritten story: Mothers and daughters in Shakespeare

197b Fun and games with life-stories

231s Street dream #1 (story)

297f Surveying through stories

310u XYLO: A true story

332e Female stories of experience: Alcott's *Little Women* in light of *Work*

370k The story of Swema: Female vulnerability in nineteenth century East Africa

417cc Therrillium (story)

445i Gertrude Atherton's California woman: From love story to psychological drama

451f The eye of the story

453n The use of story in women's novels of the seventies

Story of O

7x Sadomasochism and the erosion of self: A critical reading of *Story of O*

The Story of a Mother

399g *The Story of a Mother* (play)

Stove

307s Cold solder on a hot stove

Stowe, Harriet Beecher

17d Four novels of Harriet Beecher Stowe: A study in nineteenth-century androgyny

Straight

133f Recognition among lesbians in straight settings

Strap

282c The bow and the burden strap: A new look at institutionalized homosexuality in native North America

Strategy

35g Explaining "male chauvinism" and "feminism": Cultural differences in male and female reproductive strategies

39r Sex roles and survival strategies in the urban black community

87i   The balancing act: Coping strategies for emerging family lifestyles

93e   Strategies for improving the economic situation of women in the United States: Systemic thinking, systemic discrimination, and systemic enforcement

105h Developing family invulnerability to stress: Coping patterns and strategies wives employ in managing family separations

163c Network strategies and organizing against female sexual slavery

199k Resistance strategies: The routine struggle for bread and roses

206n Resistance, strikes and strategies

220k Strategies for the eighties

226g Women's organizational strategies in state legislatures

260i Policies and implementation of anti-discrimination strategies

261a Litigation: Strategy of the last resort

272l Job integration strategies: Today's programs and tomorrow's needs

283j Race, left strategies and the state

283k A left strategy for Labour

283q Industrial strategy and trade union politics

361k Strategies to increase participation of minorities in medicine

391g The influence of female and male communication styles on conflict strategies: Problem areas

436j Women's employment networks: Strategies for development

Stratification

85e   Women in stratification studies

230h Sexual stratification, pornography, and rape in the United States

296g Racial-ethnic women and work: Towards an analysis of race and gender stratification

387t Sex stratification, technology and organization change: A longitudinal case study of AT&T

Street

7p   Swastikas: The street and the university

202j The politics of city space in *The Years*: Street, love, pillar boxes and bridges

235d On the streets

Strength

378g Unity is strength? Feminism and the labor movement

447c The state of the art of strength testing

Stress

41f   Stress and support networks of working single black mothers

53c   The effect of employment, family and job stress on coronary heart disease patterns in women

86m   The home is the workplace: Hazards, stress, and pollutants in the household

105h Developing family invulnerability to stress: Coping patterns and strategies wives employ in managing family separations

178b Sources of stress: Events or conditions?

191f Stress and the mental health of women: A discussion of research and issues

222f New brains for old bodies: The impact of emotional and physical stress during the Ph.D. process

239i Sources of maternal stress in the postpartum period: A review of the literature and an alternative view

243l Unemployment and family stress

268n Senescence, sex roles, and stress: Shepherding resources into old age

295l The relation of stressful life events to gender

395l Anger sickness: Social stress and native diagnosis among Ecuadorian Indians

433f Bengal election, 1937: Fazlul Huq and M. A. Jinnah: A study in leadership stress in Bengal politics

443k Working women and stress

Strike

13d   Besides our size it's because we are women: The strike by the laundry workers union 15 January - 5 February 1982

201f The uprising in Chicago: The men's garment workers strike, 1910-1911

205s Last back: Folklore and the telephone operators in the 1919 Vancouver general strike

206n Resistance, strikes and strategies

323k The right to strike

323v Wives supporting the strike

379p "If eight hours seems few to you...": Women workers' strikes in Italian rice fields, 1901-1906

Strober, Myra

272g Commentary: Strober's theory of occupational sex segregation

Struck, Karin

32n   The question of a feminist aesthetic and Karin Struck's *Klassenliebe*

Structuralism

109c Victoria Holt's gothic romances: A structuralist inquiry

Structure

see also Social Structure

32k   "Eine frau, aber mehr als das, eine Persönlichkeit, aber mehr als das: eine frau": The structural analysis of the female characters in the novels of Max Frisch

35f   Power structures and perceptions of power holders in same-sex groups of young children

40k   Alice Childress's dramatic structure

54g   Structural family therapy: The Sanchez family

64f   The relationship between meaning and structure in Colette's *Rain-moon*

64p   Image structure, codes, and recoding in *The Pure and the Impure*

82s   Household structure in Africa

90o   The impact of organizational structures on issues of sex equity

93n   The impact of organizational structure: Models and methods for change

151a Housing ideals, structural constraints and the emancipation of women

160g The negation of structure: A note on British council wives

214e Structuring the inside: The impact of organizations on sex differences

270a Duofocal family structure and an alternative model of husband-wife relationship

270k Changing patterns of patronage: A study in structural change

272k Commentary: The need to study the transformation of job structures

332h Narrative structure(s) and female development: The case of *Mrs. Dalloway*

343d Comic structure and the humanizing of Kate in *The Taming of the Shrew*

387s The impact of hierarchical structures on the work behavior of women and men

420d Women in rural-urban circulation networks: Implications for social structural change

449e The shaping of life: Structure and narrative process in Eileen Chang's *The Rouge of the North*

459e Family structure and women's reproductive and productive roles: Some conceptual and methodological issues

Struggle

39l   The role of women in the struggle against *apartheid* in South Africa

76f   Women's struggles in the Third World

101c The Indian women's movement: A struggle for women's rights or national liberation?

119f Invisible struggles: The politics of ageing

198j The struggle of women in the national development of Pakistan

199b Southern textile women: Generations of survival and struggle

199k Resistance strategies: The routine struggle for bread and roses

257d Struggling to change, changing with struggle

366e The struggle for the right to preach

374c The struggle for women's equality

Student

see also Education

45l   Sex differences in the educational and occupational goals of black college students: Continued inquiry into the black matriarchy theory

49m   College student values and the world of work

52t   Wife and/or worker: Sex role concepts of Canadian female students

122d The learning climate and the non-traditional student

133p Educational responsibilities to gay male and lesbian students

192c Lives of Chicana activists: The Chicano student movement (a case study)

193m Differential treatment of boy and girl pupils during science lessons

222h In and out of relationships: A serious game for the woman doctoral student

262b Sex inequities in the experience of students

262c Why sex inequities exist for students

302e Assertiveness training for library-school students

303j Racial myths and attitudes among white female students at the University of Florida

320j Sex differences in the impact of college environments on black students

320k Undergraduates and their teachers: An analysis of student evaluations of male and female instructors

326m Rape and the college student: Multiple crises in late adolescence

337l Women and student government

344l Women and higher education: Sex differentials in the status of students and scholars

394r Meeting the needs of re-entering students

411o Midlife woman as student

421aa Career constraints among women graduate students in a developing society: West Pakistan. A study in the changing status of women

425f Socialization experiences of women and men graduate students in male sex-typed career fields

Studio

174o Feminist education at the feminist studio workshop

Study

14t Teaching *Black-eyed Susans*: An approach to the study of black women writers

16c Issues in feminist therapy: The work of a woman's study group

56f Studying childbirth: The experience and methods of a woman anthropologist

120d The problem of studying "economic man"

148d Male/female task differentiation among the Hidatsa: Toward the development of an archeological approach to the study of gender

193l Girls studying science in the sixth form

266e Methodological issues in the study of sex-related differences

271q Theoretical/Conceptual implications of study design and statistical analysis: Research on the menstrual cycle

302m An analysis of the study, "Career paths of male and female librarians in Canada"

316l Challenging curricular assumptions: Teaching and studying women's literature from a regional perspective

351k Studying women's studies: A guide to archival research

441i A preview of AAUW's biennial study/action topic 'Taking hold of technology'

Style

40ff Theme, characterization, and style in the works of Toni Morrison

171i Consciousness as style: Style as aesthetic

214d Rhetoric and organizational change: New applications of feminine style

214h Styles of leadership: Power and feminine values

271h Assertiveness training for improved conflict resolution style

Subclinical

279j Size sexual dimorphism and secular trend: Indicators of subclinical malnutrition?

Subculture

349w Gender differences in prisoner subcultures

Subject

30w Biographer and subject: A critical connection

169s Subjects and materials: How to handle controversy

225u *Histoire d'O*: The construction of a female subject

364i Subject or object? Women and the circulation of valuables in highlands New Guinea

Subjectivity

418o Subjectivity, materialism and patriarchy

Submission

102b Breaking free of symbolic bondage: From feminine submission to a vision of equality

Subordination

207a Gender and economics: The sexual division of labour and the subordination of women

207c Women's labours: The naturalisation of social inequality and women's subordination

207i The subordination of women and the internationalisation of factory production

208a Introduction: The continuing subordination of women in the development process

208b Gender and economics: The sexual division of labour and the subordination of women

208c The subordination of women and the internationalisation of factory production

208i Women's labours: The naturalisation of social inequality and women's subordination

Subsistence

82k Land tenure and cooperatives: Origin, development and persistence of Navajo matrifocality in subsistence, production, exchange and tenure

153b Subsistence reproduction: A framework for analysis

153e Nonwage labor and subsistence

207b Subsistence production and extended reproduction

208d Subsistence production and extended reproduction

263g "Mom, it's a losing proposition": The decline of women's subsistence production on Iowa farms

269c Sex roles and subsistence: A comparative analysis of three Central American communities

350g From rural subsistence to an industrial peripheral work force: An examination of female Malaysian migrants and capital accumulation in Singapore

Substance

10d Multiple substance abuse among women with alcohol-related problems

295n Substance abuse in women: Etiology and prevention

404m Women and substance abuse: Treatment issues

447k Evaluation and control of embryofetotoxic substances

Suburb

see also City

165i Female delinquents in a suburban court

203g Women's place in the new suburbia

203h Women's travel patterns in a suburban development

203i Women in the suburban environment: A U.S.-Sweden comparison

210i Suburban older women

410d Recruitment of women to suburban city councils: Higgins vs. Chevalier

410e Sex differences in role behavior and policy orientations of suburban officeholders: The effect of women's employment

469d Hispanic women in suburbia

Subversion

227k The power of women and the subversion of the community

Success

see also Achieve

41g Invited presentation: The black professional woman — career success and interpersonal failure

74b Success and the Latin American writer

259k Success in mathematics

271j Beyond the fear of success: Observations on women's fears

352l How real is fear of success?

Sudan

198k Lessons from fieldwork in the Sudan

298f The history, development, organization and position of women's studies in the Sudan

370e Women in slavery in the western Sudan

Suffer

344o Women and widowhood: The suffering beyond grief

Suffrage

see also Vote, Woman's Suffrage

95d Sylvia Pankhurst: Suffragist, feminist, or socialist?

106c Aristotle, the public-private split, and the case of the suffragists

128f The politics of mutual frustration: Socialists and suffragists in New York and Wisconsin

157p Appendix: Votes for women: Profiles of prominent British Columbia suffragists and social reformers

Sugar

107f Sugar and spice and everything nice: Is that what female athletes behave like?

Suicide

8h Childhood and adolescent suicidal behavior, with an emphasis on girls

38r Black female suicides: Is the excitement justified?

130u The death of an ideal: Female suicides in the eighteenth-century French novel

246e Revenge suicide by Lusi women: An expression of power

268g Suicide

328i Clarissa Dalloway's respectable suicide

Suitability

271f Sex-role ideology and sex bias in judgments of occupational suitability

Sumer

417c Women in transition: Crete and Sumer

Summer

150dd Women of summer

292e Recognizing regional differences: The southern summer school for women workers

441h Feminist pedagogy and technology: Reflections on the Goddard feminism and ecology summer program

Summing

44i Summing Up

Sunbonnet

175h Two sixshooters and a sunbonnet: The story of Sally Skull

Sung

401f Power and prestige: Palace women in the Northern Sung (960-1126)

Sunksquaws

347b Sunksquaws, shamans, and tradeswomen: Middle Atlantic coastal Algonkian women during the 17th and 18th centuries

Superego

280c Nymphomania, hostile sex, and superego development

Superintend

90p Hormones and harems: Are the activities of superintending different for a woman?

Superiority

271k Female superiority in sex difference competence comparisons: A review of the literature

Supervisor

98h Personal account of the role of a supervisor in the Bangladesh fertility survey

Supply

110a Estimating labor supply functions for married women

110b Married women's labor supply: A comparison of alternative estimation procedures

110c Hours and weeks in the theory of labor supply

110d Assets and labor supply

110f A multivariate model of labor supply: Methodology and estimation

110g Labor supply with costs of labor market entry

Support

37p Support systems of significant others in black families

38h Black mothers and the extended family support network

41f Stress and support networks of working single black mothers

103k Women and child support

173f Public support for pro-choice abortion policies in the nation and states: Changes and stability after the *Roe* and *Doe* decisions

178i Social ties and social support

178j Fathers' support to mothers and children

214k The minutiae of discrimination: The need for support

214l The probability of redress: Seeking external support

214m Women, work and friendship: Personal confirmation and support

214n Mobilizing resources: Creating a support system

214o Ageism vs. sexism: Male models as a source of support

214p An attempt at collectivity: Professional confirmation and support

216q An alternative perspective on parental support: Child-care information and referral service

243f Black families and childrearing support networks

295j Social support and efficacy in advocacy roles: A case study of two women's organizations

323v Wives supporting the strike

404cc Postintervention and support systems

417k A utopian female support network: The case of the Henry Street Settlement

458d Employment status and social support: The experience of the mature woman

Surface

20e The making of *Selected Poems*, the process of surfacing

332p Shadowing/surfacing/shedding: Contemporary German writers in search of a female *Bildungsroman*

Surfacing

20i *Surfacing* and the rebirth journey

Surgeon

219e Police officer or doctor? Police surgeons' attitudes and opinions about rape

Surgery

240i Psychological preparation for gynaecological surgery

353t The rise and fall of Battey's operation: A fashion in surgery

Surinam

322k Interview with Astrid Roemer (Surinam)

363b Working class Afro-Surinamese women and national politics: Traditions and changes in an independent state

Surrogate

287n Surrogate partners and their use in sex therapy

287o An interview with a sex surrogate

307y Surrogate motherhood - an interview

310h Inside the surrogate industry

Survey

31c Is gender a variable in conceptions of rationality? A survey of issues

61b An abundance of riches: The women's history sources survey

98i Working through local female investigators: Experiences in a broad survey

98j Survey research with rural women in Bangladesh

191c Community surveys: Sex differences in mental illness

241j Do her answers fit his questions? Women and the survey method

297f Surveying through stories

298b Survey of research on women in the Arab gulf region

463r A comparative survey of women car buyers

Survive

39r Sex roles and survival strategies in the urban black community

39x Black women and survival: A Maroon case

60l Black family life-styles: A lesson in survival

60m Laid bare by the system: Work and survival for black and Hispanic women

64d Colette and the art of survival

132o Separation and survival: Mothers, daughters, sisters: - The women's experimental theater

153o Wages, consumption, and survival: Working class households in Puerto Rico in the 1930's

162m Linen was their life: Family survival strategies and parent-child relations in nineteenth-century France

167d A national campaign: Women's party for survival

199b Southern textile women: Generations of survival and struggle

205k Women on campus in British Columbia: Strategies for survival, years of war and peace, 1906-1920

229ss Spiritual techniques for re-powering survivors of sexual assault

326l Behavioral treatment of sexual dysfunction in sexual assault survivors

398d Survival in the 'master's house': The role of graduate teaching assistants in effecting curriculum change

462l Political oppression and creative survival

465b Members and survivors: Women and retirement-pensions legislation

Susanna and the Elders

117i Artemisia and Susanna

Susceptible

268f Depression in relation to sex roles: Differences in learned susceptibility and precipitating factors

Swastika

7p Swastikas: The street and the university

Sweatshop

210e Beyond the sweatshop: Older women in blue-collar jobs

220h The electronic sweatshop

470e Contemporary clothing 'sweatshops', Asian female labour and collective organisation

Sweden

52j The changing role of Swedish women in family and society

93b Collective bargaining as a strategy for achieving equal opportunity and equal pay: Sweden and West Germany

93h Equality between men and women in the labor market: The Swedish National Labor Market Board

93r Integration of family policy and labor market policy in Sweden

113k Sweden: The neutral nation

188j The Swedish visionary: Saint Bridget

203i Women in the suburban environment: A U.S. - Sweden comparison

203j Swedish women in single-family housing

209k Automation and the quality of work life at the Swedish telephone company: A management view

209l Automation and the quality of work life at the Swedish telephone company: A union view

228i Sweden

244h Sexual customs and gender roles in Sweden and America: An analysis and interpretation

260a Women in the labour market and equal opportunity policy in Sweden, United Kingdom, United States and West Germany

260b A look at the male female unemployment differentials in the Federal Republic of Germany, Sweden, United Kingdom, and the United States of America

260g Equal opportunity policies in Sweden

260j Labour market policy in four countries: Are women adequately represented?

260k Estimating the impact of labor market policies on women: A discussion of the four-country studies on the employment of women

289n A view from Sweden

382j Sweden

388h Public day care in Britain and Sweden: A sociological perspective

437c Sweden

438h Women scientists in Sweden

463f The impact of women's employment on household travel patterns: A Swedish example

471g Women at work in Sweden

Sweeper

386c Sweepers

Swema

370k The story of Swema: Female vulnerability in nineteenth century East Africa

Swift, Jonathan

196b The secrets of Swift and Stella

Swim

107n Some differences between men and women in various factors which determine swimming performance

372o Specificity of swim training on maximal oxygen uptake: An inter-sex comparison

Swinburne, Algernon Charles

196j Closer than a brother: Swinburne and Watts-Dunton

286f "Swinburne planteth, Hardy watereth": Victorian views of pain and pleasure in human sexuality

286i Sexuality and the Victorian artist: Dickens and Swinburne

Switzerland

52r Economic recession and Swiss women's attitudes towards marital role segregation

Swordswomen

229l Growing up with legends of the Chinese swordswomen

Sydney, Australia

94k Religion, law and family disputes in a Lebanese Muslim community in Sydney

Symbol

135f Symbol, mask, and meter in the poetry of Louise Bogan

162p Mothers, sons, and the sale of symbols and goods: The 'German Mother's Day' 1923-33

194h The goddess Kannagi: A dominant symbol of south Indian Tamil society

194n The Great Goddess today in Burma and Thailand: An exploration of her symbolic relevance to monastic and female roles

219d The social uses of sexuality: Symbolic interaction, power and rape

238c Davey Crockett as trickster: Pornography, liminality and symbolic inversion in Victorian America

255a Purdah: Separate worlds and symbolic shelter

269h Symbolic aspects of Bribri roles on the occasions of birth and death

300c The Minangkabau woman: Cultural centre or ethnic symbol?

319f Symbolic strategies for change: A discussion of the Chicana women's movement

462o Feminist liberation theology and Yahweh as holy warrior: An analysis of symbol

Symptom

8j The painful woman: Complaints, symptoms, and illness

51o Expectations regarding menstrual symptoms: Effects on evaluation and behavior of women

Syncretism

194d The cult of Brigid: A study of pagan-Christian syncretism in Ireland

Syndrome

8m The myofascial pain dysfunction syndrome: An unheeded neuromuscular disorder

11h Fetal alcohol syndrome and drinking during pregnancy

28l Classification of premenstrual syndromes

28r Recent trends in the treatment of premenstrual syndrome: A critical review

86e Closed office-building syndrome

179c The Private Benjamin syndrome

190y Premenstrual affective syndrome in adolescent and adult psychiatric patients

236a Aetiology of premenstrual syndrome

236b The premenstrual syndrome - an epidemiological and statistical exercise

236c Premenstrual syndrome - a holistic approach

236d An appraisal of the role of progesterone in the therapy of premenstrual syndrome

236e An explorative study into the clinical effects of dydrogesterone in the treatment of premenstrual syndrome

345c The foetal alcohol syndrome

461v Discussion: Psychoanalytic reflections on the "beaten wife syndrome"

Synge, J.M.

338d Synge and the nature of woman

Synthetic

244j Synthetic smiles and fabricated faces

Syria

156r Women in early Syrian Christianity

System

37p Support systems of significant others in black families

54a A systems model for planning culturally specific programs

60m Laid bare by the system: Work and survival for black and Hispanic women

66c The market system

67c The market system

93e Strategies for improving the economic situation of women in the United States: Systemic thinking, systemic discrimination, and systemic enforcement

369c Beyond the unhappy marriage: A critique of the dual systems theory

370a Women's importance in African slave systems

370f Sustaining the system: Trading towns along the middle Zaire

387f Home work and market work: Systematic segregation

404n Plenary session: Intervention/service delivery systems

404o Plenary session: Intervention/service delivery systems

436a Women, power and political systems

Taboo

132s Lesbianism and the social function of taboo

225w The forbidden: Eroticism and taboo

241e Women and caring: Skills, tasks and taboos

285b Eros and thanatos: Lingering taboos in doctor-patient communication

288d A proposal: We need taboos on sex at work

Tadzhikistan, USSR

371h The sexual division of domestic space among two Soviet minorities: The Georgians and the Tadjiks

Tagore, Radindranath

433j Some poems from *Citra* by Radindranath Tagore

433k Radindranath Tagore: Cultural ambassador of India to the United States

433l Say it with structure: Tagore and *Mangala Kavya*

Tailor

256f "The men are as bad as their masters...": Socialism, feminism and sexual antagonism in the London tailoring trade in the 1830s

Taipei

420m The migration of rural women to Taipei

Taiwan

177g Taiwan garment workers

177h Taiwan electronics workers

424c Trends in female labour force participation in Taiwan: The transition toward higher technology activities

424r Women, work and the family in a developing society: Taiwan

428p The emergence of small-scale industry in a Taiwanese rural community

Take

381h Taking care of everything

Tale

45m Change and constancy: A hundred years' tale

310a A yenga tale

332j Through the looking glass: When women tell fairy tales

The Tale of a Great Sham

338i Rewriting history: Anna Parnell's *The Tale of a Great Sham*

Talent
42o The stewardship of talents

Tales of the Uneasy
27l Violet Hunt's *Tales of the Uneasy*: Ghost stories of a worldly woman

Talk
134c Groping towards sexism: Boys' sex talk
417t Imagining a different world of talk

Tall-Walker
40g The field of the fever, the time of the tall-walkers

Tamil
194h The goddess Kannagi: A dominant symbol of south Indian Tamil society
232a On the meaning of sakti to women in Tamil Nadu
232c Marriage in Tamil culture: The problem of conflicting "models"
232e A note on the nobility of women in popular Tamil fiction
232f The paradoxical powers of Tamil women

The Taming of the Shrew
343d Comic structure and the humanizing of Kate in *The Taming of the Shrew*

Tangaye
373i Baseline study for socio-economic evaluation of Tangaye solar site

Tantric
325o Accomplished women in tantric Buddhism of medieval India and Tibet

Tanzania
5f Development policies in Tanzania - some implications for women
39e Tanzanian women in nation building
385i Women's work in a communal setting: The Tanzanian policy of Ujamaaunder
395d Women, food and health in Tanzania: A crisis of the 1980s

Taoism
401b Taoism and the androgynous ideal

Tar Beach
150s Tar beach

Target
169b Promoting and recruiting: Reaching the target audience

Task
148d Male/female task differentiation among the Hidatsa: Toward the development of an archeological approach to the study of gender
241e Women and caring: Skills, tasks and taboos
429j The task of enabling

Tasmania
294a Prostitution in Tasmania during the transition from penal settlement to 'civilized' society

Tax
465c Who still cares for the family? Recent developments in income maintenance, taxation and family law
376b Dealing with dependence: Paternalism and tax evasion in eighteenth-century Rhode Island

Taylor, Harriet
106h Patriarchal liberalism and beyond: From John Stuart Mill to Harriet Taylor

Taylor, Juliet
399jj "Casting by Juliet Taylor" (Interview)

Tea
218d Tea and power: The anatomy of a conflict

Teacher
see also Education
19a Thine eyes shall see thy teachers
90r The gender of principals and principal/teacher relations in elementary schools
172h It all depends on the teacher (Honduras)
193t From teachers' letters
231x The teacher
259c The hidden curriculum: Academic consequences of teacher expectations
263i "Teacher, teacher": Teachers and educators in a stratified "female" profession
320k Undergraduates and their teachers: An analysis of student evaluations of male and female instructors
399ff Alvina Krause: A great teacher of acting
431b Women meditation teachers in Thailand

Teach
see also Education
14s Black-eyed blues connections: Teaching black women
14t Teaching *Black-eyed Susans*: An approach to the study of black women writers
16h A pelvic teaching program
44h Teaching
100b Teaching and 'women's work': A comparative historical and ideological analysis
120e Feminism and the writing and teaching of history
122a Rethinking the ways we teach
122c Seeking feminist transformation of the sciences and the teaching of science
138d Work, class and teaching
138h Women and teaching: A semi-detached sociology of a semi-profession
140v Teaching value clarification: The example of gender and psychotherapy
169p Occupational health and safety for women workers: Some teaching models
174c Teaching writing in prison
174g Teaching the feminist minority
174s Creative teaching spaces: Home movies
174v Feminist values: Guidelines for a teaching methodology in women's studies
176j Teaching the psychology of women: A lesbian feminist perspective
176k Teaching about Jewish lesbians in literature: From *Zeitl* and *Richel* to *The Tree of Begats*
176l Journey into otherness: Teaching *The Well of Loneliness*
176m Learning through teaching: A lesbianism course in 1972
193s Feminism and science teaching: Some classroom observations
272f Toward a general theory of occupational sex segregation: The case of public school teaching

274c Subject image, examinations and teaching materials
303g Teaching women's studies at the University of Arkansas
306j "Full of memories": Teaching matrilineage
306o Oral history as a resource in teaching women's studies
314j Appropriate teaching methods for integrating women
315i Can a man teach women's studies?
316l Challenging curricular assumptions: Teaching and studying women's literature from a regional perspective
398d Survival in the 'master's house': The role of graduate teaching assistants in effecting curriculum change
441g Teaching and learning about women and technology
441j Teaching women and technology at the University of Washington
466k The feminization of the teaching profession in Singapore

Team
147ii The Edmonton Grads: The team and its social significance from 1915-1940

Technical
65p Technical possibilities and political realities: Concluding remarks
79u Technical aspects of sex preselection

Technique
449d Feminism and literary technique in Ting Ling's early short stories

Technology
see also High Tech
12h Technology in the lying-in room
12i Contraception: The growth of a technology
29d Dissemination of behavioral interventions with women: Needed - a technology
36a Reproductive technologies: The birth of a women-centered analysis
36e Status of contraceptive technology development
36m Man-midwifery and the rise of technology: The problem and proposals for resolution
36q Ethical issues in childbirth technology
50h Typing our way to freedom: Is it true that new office technology can liberate women?
50o Technology and changes in the division of labour in the American home
77c Creative women in scientific-technological and medical change
79a Reproductive technologies: The birth of a women-centered analysis
79dd Ethics and reproductive technology
79ff Manipulative reproductive technologies discussion: Part I
79jj Manipulative reproductive technologies discussion: Part II
79mm Manipulative reproductive technologies discussion: Part III
82f Appropriate technology
103o Work, gender, and technological innovation
168f Will women change technology or will technology change women?

181a Women hold up two-thirds of the sky: Notes for a revised history of technology

181d Technology and work degradation: Effects of office automation on women clerical workers

181e Technology, housework, and women's liberation: A theoretical analysis

181i Women and the assessment of technology: To think, to be, to unthink, to free

181j An end to technology: A modest proposal

181k Reproductive technology: The future for women?

181l What if...science and technology in feminist utopias

199d Housework and domestic labor: Racial and technological change

201b "If I didn't have my sewing machine...": Women and sewing-machine technology

209c Bargaining over the social costs of information technology

209d Women, technological change and employment levels: The role of trade unions policies

209e Government policies on new information technologies and their implications for employment: An overview of EEC countries, with particular reference to women

209g The issue of employment and office technology from a managerial perspective

209h The implications of technology for U.S. employment

209m New technology and its implications in U.S. clerical work

209t Labor legislation in Norway: Its application to the introduction of new technology

209aa Let the technology adapt!

209ff Collective bargaining strategies on new technology: The experience of West German trade unions

209gg Taking the initiative on new technology: Canadian labor approaches

251a Technology, economic development, and the division of labour by sex

251b Women and technology in the industrialized countries

251c Women and technology in peripheral countries: An overview

251d The impact of science and technology and the role of women in science in Mexico

251f Some reflections on women in science and technology after UNCSTD

273e Decision making and sex selection with biased technologies

274m Craft, design, and technology

307a Introduction: New technology, old values

307e Doubletalk: Sexism in tech talk

307h Women and appropriate technology: A feminist assessment

307j Household technologies: Burden or blessing?

307o Abortion: A domestic technology

307u New jobs in new technologies: Experienced only need apply

307aa Juggling health care technology and women's needs

307cc EQUALS in computer technology

310b The meanings of choice in reproductive technology

310p Technology and prenatal femicide

310t Born and unborn: The implications of reproductive technologies for people with disabilities

310w Reproductive technologies: The final solution to the woman question?

310bb Taking the initiative: Information versus technology in pregnancy

346d Technologies for poor women

355b An enlarged human existence? Technology and household work in nineteenth-century America

355c Housework technology and household work

373b Overview: Women and technology — resources for our future

373d Women, technology and the development process

373e New technologies for food-related activities: An equity strategy

373f Impact of selected industrial technologies on women in Mexico

373h Java, Indonesia: The introduction of rice processing technology

373l Technologies appropriate for women: Theory, practice and policy

373p Applying policy analysis to women and technology: A framework for consideration

387t Sex stratification, technology and organization change: A longitudinal case study of AT&T

390w Women, work and technological change

417r Utopia in question: Programming women's needs into the technology of tomorrow

424c Trends in female labour force participation in Taiwan: The transition toward higher technology activities

436i Technology, 'Women's work' and the social control of women

441b Women and technology in ancient Alexandria: Maria and Hypatia

441c The machine in utopia: Shaker women and technology

441f Technology and the future of women: Haven't we met somewhere before?

441g Teaching and learning about women and technology

441h Feminist pedagogy and technology: Reflections on the Goddard feminism and ecology summer program

441i A preview of AAUW's biennial study/action topic 'Taking hold of technology'

441j Teaching women and technology at the University of Washington

441k Women and technology project, Missoula, Montana

470d New technology and women's office work

Teenage
see Adolescent

Tehran, Iran
420n New models and traditional networks: Migrant women in Tehran

Teithiauc
334b Nau Kynywedi Teithiauc

Telecommunication
209cc Experimental approaches towards telecommunications in France

Telephone
205s Last back: Folklore and the telephone operators in the 1919 Vancouver general strike

209k Automation and the quality of work life at the Swedish telephone company: A management view

209l Automation and the quality of work life at the Swedish telephone company: A union view

Television
57d Television as a sphere of influence on the child's learning about sexuality

161f Television and women

327c Television viewing, family style and aggressive behavior in preschool children

327d Discussion: Television violence and the family

358c The 'liberated woman' in television drama

391c Children's impressions of television mothers

391d Time, television, and women's career perspectives

Temperament
253d Sex and temperament revisited

Temperance
9b Temperance and women in 19th-century United States

412p Evangelical domesticity: The woman's temperance crusade of 1873-1874

413c The origins of the women's movement in New Zealand: The Women's Christian Temperance Union 1885-1895

Tempest
343p The miranda trap: Sexism and racism in Shakespeare's *Tempest*

Tenant
203p From kitchen to storefront: Women in the tenant movement

Tendency
129aa The economic tendency of freethought

Tender
50p Anger and tenderness: The experience of motherhood

Tennis
147gg The contributions of women to the history of competitive tennis in the United States in the twentieth century

Tension
28k Premenstrual tension: An overview

28p Premenstrual tension in borderline and related disorders

28s Premenstrual tension: Etiology

162f Tensions, dissensions, and ruptures inside the family in seventeenth- and eighteenth-century Haute Provence

456c Premenstrual tension

Tenth Century
187d Benedictine life for women in central France, 850-1100: A feminist revival

401f Power and prestige: Palace women in the Northern Sung (960-1126)

Tenure
82k Land tenure and cooperatives: Origin, development and persistence of Navajo matrifocality in subsistence, production, exchange and tenure

82l   Tenure and the role of the female
249h Fighting for tenure: A bittersweet victory
388f Women and law: Land tenure in Africa

Teratogenesis
233k Mechanisms of teratogenesis: The extrapolation of the results of animal studies to man

Term
275j Gender-neutral terms

Terman, Lewis M.
158g "Rather worse than folly?" psychology measures femininity and masculinity, 1: From Terman and Miles to the Guilfords
351c Career and life satisfactions among Terman's gifted women

Terminal
86d   The particular problems of video display terminals
285f Sexual feelings in the terminally ill patient

Terminate
240d Termination of pregnancy
252c Legal aspects of pregnancy termination in Europe
252e The trimester threshold for pregnancy termination: Myth or truth?
252f Aspirotomy for outpatient termination of pregnancy in the second trimester
252j Fact and fancy in the termination of molar pregnancy with particular reference to uterine stimulants
252k Natural prostaglandins alone or in combination for termination of pregnancy
252l Termination of second trimester pregnancy with prostaglandin analogues
252n Termination of pregnancy after intrauterine foetal death
252s Somatic sequelae and future reproduction after pregnancy termination
252t Some considerations on the psychosocial aspects of pregnancy termination

Terminology
275h The hidden joke: Generic uses of masculine terminology

Territory
414d Patient and useful servants: Women missionaries in Indian territory
414g College life in Oklahoma territory

Terror
95j   Ulrike Meinhof: An emancipated terrorist?
109d Had-I-but-known: The marriage of gothic terror and detection
109k Terror-gothic: Nightmare and dream in Ann Radcliffe and Charlotte Brontë
111b Female terrorists: Competing perspectives
215d The balance of terror: Deterrence and peace-keeping
225e Public silence, private terror
344a Sexual terrorism

Terry, Megan
399rr Megan Terry (Interview)

Test
243j Overtime over the life cycle: A test of the life cycle squeeze hypothesis

309x Teenagers: Fertility control behavior and attitudes before and after abortion, childbearing or negative pregnancy test
320e Sex bias in aptitude and achievement tests used in higher education
447c The state of the art of strength testing

Testimony
74a   "Feminine" testimony in the works of Teresa de la Parra, María Luisa Bombal, and Victoria Ocampo

Texas
63c   Co-corrections-FCI Forth Worth after three years
175c Emily Morgan: Yellow rose of Texas
175e Belle Starr: The Bandit Queen of Dallas
175i Sophia Porter: Texas' own Scarlett O'Hara
175k Adah Isaacs Menken: From Texas to Paris
175l Elisabet Ney: Texas' first lady of sculpture
175n Martha White McWhirter and the Belton Sanctificationists
175p El Paso madams
175u Janis and the Austin scene
175v Legends in their own time: The Dallas Cowboy cheerleaders
192u Personal chronicle of Crystal City
301o Women in the Texas ILGWU, 1933-50
319d Breast-feeding and social class mobility: The case of Mexican migrant mothers in Houston, Texas
417j The Woman's Commonwealth: Utopia in nineteenth-century Texas

Text
97c   The political economy of text publishing
334a The normal paradigms of a woman's life in the Irish and Welsh texts
457e Essence and existence: Women and religion in ancient Indian texts

Textbook
see also Book, Read
176s One out of thirty: Lesbianism in women's studies textbooks
265n Sex role images in Lebanese text books

Textile
see also Cloth, Garment
50b   The home turned upside down? The working-class family in cotton textiles 1780-1850
199b Southern textile women: Generations of survival and struggle
218f Women textile workers in the militarization of Southeast Asia
428q Women textile workers in the militarization of Southeast Asia
466e Rich woman, poor woman: Occupation differences in a textile producing village in Central Java

Textual
356c Textual feminism

Textuality
97b   In/Forming schooling: Space/time/textuality in compulsory state provided "mass" schooling systems

Tey, Josephine
1b   Josephine Tey

Thailand
194n The Great Goddess today in Burma and Thailand: An exploration of her symbolic relevance to monastic and female roles
300f Changes in women's status associated with modernization in northern Thailand
300k Buddhist attitudes toward social change in Burma and Thailand
300m The Thai forest tradition: Local and international manifestations
420h Female migration in Thailand
420l Female migrants in Bangkok metropolis
424l The Bangkok masseuses: Origins, status and prospects
424p Women migrants in Bangkok: An economic analysis of their employment and earnings
431a Buddhism, sex-roles and the Thai economy
431b Women meditation teachers in Thailand

Thanatos
127b Thanatos and Eros: Kate Chopin's *The Awakening*
285b Eros and thanatos: Lingering taboos in doctor-patient communication

Thatcher, Margaret
335i No turning back - Thatcherism, the family and the future

Theater
see also Drama, Play (Drama), names of individual playwrights
64l   The theatre as literary model: Role-playing in *Chéri* and *The Last of Chéri*
108l The female sociograph: The theater of Virginia Woolf's letters
123b New directions for feminist criticism in theatre and the related arts
130i Women and the theatre arts
132o Separation and survival: Mothers, daughters, sisters: - The women's experimental theater
155b French feminist theater and the subject of prostitution, 1870-1914
229cc Feeding the feminist psyche through ritual theater
286l Fallen women, lost children: Wilde and the theatre in the nineties
316b Better than a shriveled husk: New forms for the theatre
399cc Women open Augusta's first theatre
399dd Art theatre in Hull-House
399hh Matriarchs of the regional theatre
399qq Feminist theatre: A rhetorical phenomenon
399ss The Washington area feminist theatre
399tt New York feminist theater troupe
399uu The Lavender Cellar theatre
408h A school for wives: Women in eighteenth-century Spanish theater
442k Suppressed desires: Women in the theater
453g Women's theatre: Creating the dream now

Thematic
132n For a restricted thematics: Writing, speech, and difference in *Madame Bovary*

Theme
40f   Music as theme: The jazz mode in the works of Toni Cade Bambara

40cc And called every generation blessed: Theme, setting, and ritual in the works of Paule Marshall

40ff Theme, characterization, and style in the works of Toni Morrison

40qq Music as theme: The blues mode in the works of Margaret Walker

278f Phallic worship: Some personal meditations on a sacred theme

408p Sexual politics and the theme of sexuality in Chicana poetry

453a Women's culture: Themes and images

Theodora

419m Theodora and Antonina in the *Historia Arcana*: History and/or fiction?

Theology
see also Religion

19d The theological dimension

59a Feminist theology and spirituality

60c The feminist theology of the black Baptist church, 1880-1900

91c Feminist liberation theology: Its past and future

91e Theological issues raised by feminism

91m Moral theology from a feminist perspective

115a Women and the ministry: A case for theological seriousness

152h Moral theology and homosexuality

211s The right question is theological

211t Steps toward feminine imagery of deity in Jewish theology

254l Communication or collusion?: Maneuvering through the maze of patriarchal theology

453p Feminist theology

462j A black response to feminist theology

462o Feminist liberation theology and Yahweh as holy warrior: An analysis of symbol

462v Claiming the center: A critical feminist theology of liberation

Theorist

450l Rita Mae Brown: Feminist theorist and southern novelist

Theory
see also Feminist Theory, Social Theory

18a Introduction: Population theory and the political economy of population processes

24f Process, filter and stage theories of attraction

30u Daughters writing: Toward a theory of women's biography

31e Concepts of woman in psychoanalytic theory: The nature-nurture controversy revisited

33a The education of women in the Middle Ages in theory, fact, and fantasy

34c From sin to sickness: Hormonal theories of lesbianism

37g Economics and mobility: A theoretical rationale for urban black family well-being

45l Sex differences in the educational and occupational goals of black college students: Continued inquiry into the black matriarchy theory

51l Erik Erikson and Doris Lessing: Psychological theory and the female novel of development

57b Toward an understanding of sexual learning and communication: An examination of social learning theory and nonschool learning environments

60j Difference and domination in the women's movement: The dialectic of theory and practice

60p Women's role in economic development: Practical and theoretical implications of class and gender inequalities

69a Feminine development: Changes in psychoanalytic theory

80b Infant day care: Relationships between theory and practice

89b A theory of the allocation of time

89h The statistical theory of racism and sexism

89j A theory of labor market segmentation

95f Feminism: The essential ingredient in Federica Montseny's anarchist theory

105e Toward a theory of extramarital sexual relationships

106a Introduction: Toward a theory of the family and politics

106l Contemporary critical theory and the family: Private world and public crisis

107b Attitudes to women in sport: Preface towards a sociological theory

110c Hours and weeks in the theory of labor supply

116c Nurture theories: A critique

122g Bem's gender schema theory

124h How psychology constructed masculinity: The theory of male sex role identity

125i Josephine Butler: From sympathy to theory

125j Hedwig Dohm: Passionate theorist

128c May Wood Simons: Party theorist

136f Sex-role influences in dyadic interaction: A theoretical model

144i Politics and the family: Social democracy and the working-class family in theory and practice before 1914

153p Towards a theory of the sexual division of labor

158i The theory of male sex role identity: Its rise and fall, 1936 to the present

163b The network defines its issues: Theory, evidence and analysis of female sexual slavery

165h Are females treated differently? A review of the theories and evidence on sentencing and parole decisions

181e Technology, housework, and women's liberation: A theoretical analysis

184p Toward a theory of remarriage: A case study of Newburyport at the beginning of the nineteenth century

189b Dancing through the minefield: Some observations on the theory, practice and politics of a feminist literary criticism

227r Wages for housework - political and theoretical considerations

234a Theoretical perspectives on pre-industrial women

257n Sexual theory and practice: Another double standard

263b Housework as a comparative advantage: The neoclassical theory of the sexual division of labor

270l Psychopathology and the Turkish family: A family systems theory analysis

272f Toward a general theory of occupational sex segregation: The case of public school teaching

272g Commentary: Strober's theory of occupational sex segregation

275u A note on the ethics of theories of truth

298h Toward a theoretical framework for the study of women in the Arab world

311f Selected annotated bibliography of articles on theories of women's studies

312b Theorising about theorising

312n In praise of theory: The case for women's studies

348e Theorizing about female crime

349a Criminological theory: Its ideology and implications concerning women

351h Women's education and career choice: Disparities between theory and practice

354a Women and health care: A comparison of theories

369c Beyond the unhappy marriage: A critique of the dual systems theory

387b Toward a sociotechnological theory of the women's movement

417aa Of time and revolution: Theories of social change in contemporary feminist science fiction

428l Silicon Valley's women workers: A theoretical analysis of sex-segregation in the electronics industry labor market

440n Volunteer work as work: Some theoretical considerations

443d Feminist psychoanalysis: Theory and practice

443j Hidden assumptions in theory and research on women

452m Towards a theory of form in feminist autobiography: Kate Millett's *Flying* and *Sita*; Maxine Hong Kingston's *The Woman Warrior*

463h Women's work trips: An empirical and theoretical overview

463v An alternative approach to travel demand modeling: Constraints-oriented theories and societal roles

A Theory of Justice

23n *A Theory of Justice* and love: Rawls on the family

Theosophy

457b Theosophy and feminism: Some explorations in nineteenth century biography

Therapist

29h Parenting: Training mothers as behavior therapists for their children

140u Men's new family roles: Some implications for therapists

140x Psychiatry's problem with no name: Therapist-patient sex

221b Effects of maternal employment on children: Implications for the family therapist

281c Sexual disorders and the family therapist

287l Selecting a qualified therapist

359k Psychiatry's problem with no name: Therapist-patient sex

359qq Women patients and women therapists: Some issues that come up in psychotherapy

365b   Therapist attitudes and sex-role stereotyping

443b   The therapist as imposter

Therapy

see also Psychoanalysis, Psychotherapy, Treatment, specific types of therapy

8o   The therapeutic alliance in psychoanalytic treatment

10l   Therapeutic issues in the treatment of alcoholic women

11k   Marital therapy of women alcoholics

16d   Therapeutic aspects of consciousness-raising groups

26b   Conjoint therapy for the treatment of domestic violence

51x   Sociological observations on ethical issues implicated in estrogen replacement therapy at menopause

54g   Structural family therapy: The Sanchez family

55i   Victim advocacy as therapy

140t   A feminist approach to family therapy

140w   Toward an analysis of sex-role-related issues in the therapeutic relationship

146e   Group therapy with female adolescent incest victims

190s   Prostaglandins in primary dysmenorrhea: Basis for the new therapy

236d   An appraisal of the role of progesterone in the therapy of premenstrual syndrome

252m   Prostaglandin therapy for second trimester abortion: An overview of current status and recent trends

289k   Dysfunction: Origins and therapeutic approaches

291p   The co-therapy relationship in group treatment of sexually mistreated adolescent girls

353bb   Professionalism, feminism, and gender roles: A comparative study of nineteenth-century medical therapeutics

359tt   A feminist approach to family therapy

359uu   The consciousness-raising group as a model for therapy with women

365c   Gender and the process of therapy

365i   Behavior therapies

411p   The anxiety of the unknown - choice, risk, responsibility: Therapeutic issues for today's adult women

411q   Reflections and perspectives on 'therapeutic issues for today's adult women'

434c   Therapy with battered women

Theravada

431c   Laywomen in Theravada Buddhism

Thin

341b   Thin fat people

Thing

30d   Trying to make things real

Think

30k   Hannah Arendt: Thinking as we are

93e   Strategies for improving the economic situation of women in the United States: Systemic thinking, systemic discrimination, and systemic enforcement

142h   How George Eliot's people think

150p   I've been thinking of Diana Sands

195m   Maternal thinking

202a   Thinking back through our mothers

245e   Maternal thinking

335h   'The most important thing of all' - Rethinking the family: An overview

378m   Gender, levels of political thinking and political action

474k   What it is I think I'm doing anyhow

Third World

see also Developing Country, Development (Economic), individual countries

68a   Perspectives of Third World women: An introduction

68p   Third World women and social reality: A conclusion

76f   Women's struggles in the Third World

83c   Gender, race and class in the United States: Lessons from Third World women

176h   Lesbian literature: A Third World feminist perspective

301jj   Speaking in tongues: A letter to Third World women writers

310i   An interview with Mirtha Quintanales, from the Third World women's archives

416b   Professional women in developing nations: The United States and the Third World compared

428c   Capitalism, imperialism, and patriarchy: The dilemma of Third-World women workers in multinational factories

459d   Female power, autonomy and demographic change in the Third World

Thirst

7y   Hunger and thirst in the house of distorted mirrors

Thirteenth Century

187j   The nun as anchoress: England, 1100-1500

375e   Rape in thirteenth-century England: A study of the common-law courts

Thomas, Laurence

275s   Thomas on sexism

Thompson, Dorothy Burr

389m   Dorothy Burr Thompson (b. 1900): Classical archaeologist

Thompson, Lydia

399m   Lydia Thompson and the "British Blondes"

Thought

30r   Sister/outsider: Some thoughts on Simone Weil

106k   The family in contemporary feminist thought: A critical review

118a   Androgynous life: A feminist appropriation of process thought

118b   Feminism and process thought: A two-way relationship

118c   Openness and mutuality in process thought and feminist action

120j   Thoughts on women and power

225b   Seeking ecstasy on the battlefield: Danger and pleasure in nineteenth-century feminist sexual thought

311e   How to do what we want to do: Thoughts about feminist methodology

329e   The anti-madonna in the work and thought of Virginia Woolf

335g   Home thoughts from not so far away: A personal look at family

379e   Was she a good mother? Some thoughts on a new issue for feminist biography

418k   Feminist thought and reproductive control: The state and 'the right to choose'

Thrale, Hester

196c   "Under the dominion of *some* woman": The friendship of Samuel Johnson and Hester Thrale

Thread

206c   The patriarchal thread - A history of exploitation

Threat

257a   Purity, motherhood, pleasure or threat? Definitions of female sexuality 1900-1970s

Three Guineas

328n   *Three Guineas* before and after: Further answers to correspondents

Tiamat

102c   Tiamat and her children: An inquiry into the persistence of mythic archetypes of woman as monster/villainess/victim

Tibet

325o   Accomplished women in tantric Buddhism of medieval India and Tibet

Tietze-Conrat, Erica

389k   Erica Tietze-Conrat (1883-1958): Productive scholar in renaissance and baroque art

Tightrope

86l   Walking a tightrope: Pregnancy, parenting, and work

Tilt

303l   Tilting at windmills in the Quixotic South

Time

30n   "Charlotte's Web": Reading *Jane Eyre* over time

47a   A time of change

87h   Time management and the dual-career couple

89b   A theory of the allocation of time

89c   Time spent in housework

97b   In/Forming schooling: Space/time/textuality in compulsory state provided "mass" schooling systems

115k   The right time

131j   In and out of time: The form of Marge Piercy's novels

162n   Village spinning bees: Sexual culture and free time among rural youths in early modern Germany

205a   "Sundays always make me think of home": Time and place in Canadian women's history

205y   Mary Ellen Smith: The right woman in the right place at the right time

220a   There comes a time

229t   Gyn/ecology: Spinning new time/space

239m   Body time and social time: Mood patterns by menstrual cycle phase and day of week

249c   Paying your dues, part-time

273d   Timing of fertilization and the sex ratio of offspring

307k   The lonely squandering of urban time

323g   Part-time work and unions

355g   Women's life-cycle time allocation: An econometric analysis

355h Household time: A cross-cultural example

371b Andean women and the concept of space/time

391d Time, television, and women's career perspectives

417aa Of time and revolution: Theories of social change in contemporary feminist science fiction

459b The allocation of women's time and its relation to fertility

Tiptree, James

114e Toward new sexual identities: James Tiptree, Jr.

383b Method in her madness: Feminism in the crazy utopian vision of Tiptree's Courier

Title VII

see also Discriminate

65l A review of federal court decisions under Title VII of the Civil Rights Act of 1964

288o Sexual harassment and Title VII: The foundation for the elimination of sexual cooperation as an employment condition

288p Sexual harassment: Finding a cause of action under Title VII

Title IX

see also Discriminate

147t The effect of current sports legislation on women in Canada and the U.S.A. - Title IX

394j Women's athletics at Madison and Title IX

Title XII

82c Participation through Title XII, consortia, and the project process in AID

Tlali, Miriam

322b Interview with Miriam Tlali (South Africa)

Tlingit

see also American Indian

347d Contending with colonization: Tlingit men and women in change

To the Lighthouse

180o How light a *Lighthouse* for today's women?

202g Where the spear plants grew: The Ramsays' marriage in *To the Lighthouse*

329h Private and public consciousness in *Mrs. Dalloway* and *To the Lighthouse*

329i Speech acts in *To the Lighthouse*

330i *To the Lighthouse*: Virginia Woolf's Winter's Tale

356u Unmaking and making in *To the Lighthouse*

Toast to Canada

338j Appendix: A reply to the toast to Canada

Tobacco

9n Problems related to the use of tobacco by women

104b Cash crop production and family labour: Tobacco growers in Corrientes, Argentina

Together

399bb Woman alone, women together

Token

23c Losing the numbers game: Women, tokenism and power

140e Some effects of proportions on group life: Skewed sex ratios and responses to token women

Toklas, Alice B.

196f Gertrice/Altrude: Stein, Toklas, and the paradox of the happy marriage

Tomorrow

307ee Tomorrow is a woman's issue

Tonantsi

194b The Tonantsi cult of the Eastern Nahua

Tonga

347l Putting down sisters and wives: Tongan women and colonization

Tonopah, CA

445c The Tonopah ladies

Tonta

313o "La loca, la tonta, la literata": Women's destiny in Clarin's *La Regenta*

Tool

43q The reform tool kit

Top

102j Women at the top

Tor

92c Pakistan: *Mor* and *Tor*: Binary and opposing models of Pukhtun womanhood

Torah

211o Learning to chant the Torah: A first step

Torture

163h The torture of women political prisoners: A case study in female sexual slavery

Touch

136b Gender patterns in touching behavior

Tour

163d Why I oppose Kisaeng tours

Town

see also City

39h The second sex in town

162l Kinship and class consciousness: Family values and work experience among hospital workers in an American southern town

362f "Big women" and politics in a Philippine fishing town

370f Sustaining the system: Trading towns along the middle Zaire

421e Planning for women in the new towns: New concepts and dated roles

433b Conditions influencing rural and town women's participation in the labor force

457d Gender and religion in a Turkish town: A comparison of two types of formal women's gatherings

466f Women and work in an Indonesian mining town

473c Women's role in a Muslim Hausa town (Mirria, Republic of Niger)

473d Dioula women in town: A view of intra-ethnic variation (Ivory Coast)

Toxic

447j The biology of toxic effects on reproductive outcomes

Toxicology

233m Animal and human studies in genetic toxicology

Track

147mm American women: Their debut in international track and field

339i Does becoming a parent mean falling off the fast track?

Trade

256f "The men are as bad as their masters...": Socialism, feminism and sexual antagonism in the London tailoring trade in the 1830s

305s Women in trades in British Columbia

370b African women in the Atlantic slave trade

370c Sexual demography: The impact of the slave trade on family structure

370f Sustaining the system: Trading towns along the middle Zaire

Trade Union

see also Employment, Union

83e Working class Jamaican women: Trade unions and political activity

86i Protection for women: Trade unions and labor laws

124j The Women's Trade Union League school for women organizers

129v Trade unionism and women's work

157i Sexism in British Columbia trade unions, 1900-1920

157j Helena Gutteridge: Votes for women and trade unions

209d Women, technological change and employment levels: The role of trade unions policies

209ff Collective bargaining strategies on new technology: The experience of West German trade unions

233n A trade union view of reproductive health

283q Industrial strategy and trade union politics

323e "Action Positive" in the Quebec trade union movement

323x Trade union women and the NDP

323aa Trade union resources on women

378c Workers side by side: Women and the trade union movement

390h 'I have never liked trade unionism': The development of the Royal Australian Nursing Federation, Queensland Branch, 1904-1945

468c Trade union participation of women in Norway: Structural changes, dilemmas and challenges

Trademark

353s The woman behind the trademark

Trader

299f Petty traders

385e Marginal lives: Conflict and contradiction in the position of female traders in Lusaka, Zambia

Tradesmen

433d British tradesmen of Calcutta, 1830-1900: A preliminary study of their economic and political roles

Tradeswoman

347b Sunksquaws, shamans, and tradeswomen: Middle Atlantic coastal Algonkian women during the 17th and 18th centuries

Tradition

7h Sadomasochism and the liberal tradition

20a The where of here: Margaret Atwood and a Canadian tradition

39m   Racism and tradition: Black womanhood in historical perspective

39aa Economic role and cultural tradition

42n   The traditional role of the Mormon woman

73e   The status of East European women in the family: Tradition and change

73k   Achieving the dreams beyond tradition: Counseling white ethnic American girls

96i   From traditional psychoanalysis to alternatives to psychotherapy

105b Modern and traditional elements in the expectations of young married couples regarding their marital life

107d The influence of the traditional sex roles on women's participation and engagement in sport

109o The maternal legacy: The grotesque tradition in Flannery O'Connor's female gothic

122d The learning climate and the non-traditional student

122q Marital metaphors in the Judeo-Christian tradition: A feminist critique

126g The contest between androgyny and patriarchy in early western tradition

129c Anarchism and American traditions

145b Enlightened reforms and Bavarian girls' education: Tradition through innovation

145d Henriette Schleiermacher: A woman in a traditional role

148c The shackles of tradition

148i Male and female in traditional Lakota culture

165m Women as criminal justice professionals: A challenge to change tradition

177j The Chinese biographical method: A moral and didactic tradition

180f Jane Austen and the tradition of the absent mother

186n Redefinitions of traditional Christian emblems and outlooks in May Sarton's novels of 1970-1975

198g A traditional ceremony in an Islamic milieu in Malaysia

204a Parental behavior and child development in nontraditional families: An introduction

204k Comparative socialization practices in traditional and alternative families

211p History, fiction, and the tradition: Creating a Jewish feminist poetic

242b The birth of the artist as heroine: (Re)production, the *Künslerroman* tradition, and the fiction of Katherine Mansfield

243d The old world, new rights, and the limited rebellion: Challenges to traditional authority in immigrant families

300m The Thai forest tradition: Local and international manifestations

319h "All the good and bad in this world": Women, traditional medicine, and Mexican American culture

337n Traditional and non-traditional choices of disciplines by women

363b Working class Afro-Surinamese women and national politics: Traditions and changes in an independent state

366f Lay women in the Protestant tradition

367h Women and revivalism: The Puritan and Wesleyan traditions

389c The tradition continues (1930-1979)

401d The Chinese Lieh-nü tradition

402h Women and religion: The status and image of women in some major religious traditions

403b Traditional affirmations concerning the role of women as found in contemporary Arab Islamic literature

421g Education of Muslim women: Tradition versus modernity

448f Tradition and revision: The classic city novel and Virginia Woolf's *Night and Day*

452a Introduction: Women's autobiography and the male tradition

462t Affirming diversity and Biblical tradition

Traffic

163g Traffic of children

Tragedy

32c   *Faust*: The tragedy reexamined

387n The inexpressive male: Tragedy or sexual politics?

408m The greatest punishment: Female and male in Lorca's tragedies

Tragic

343i "I wooed thee with my sword": Shakespeare's tragic paradigms

399oo Who put the "Tragic" in the Tragic Mulatto?

Train

29h   Parenting: Training mothers as behavior therapists for their children

50j   The state and training programmes for women

93i   Vocational training, the labor market, and the unions

93j   Leadership training for union women in the United States: Route to equal opportunity

96k   Assertion training for women

107k Influence of athletic training on the maturity process of girls

169e Training rank and file leaders: A case study

169n Training women for political action

209f Training: The magic cure for all ills?

271h Assertiveness training for improved conflict resolution style

271i Beyond a cognitive/behavioural approach: Congruent assertion training

292a The Women's Trade Union League training school for women organizers, 1914-1926

302e Assertiveness training for library-school students

349s Judicial paternalism and the female status offender: Training women to know their place

353gg "Little world of our own": The Pennsylvania Hospital Training School for Nurses, 1895-1907

372o Specificity of swim training on maximal oxygen uptake: An inter-sex comparison

372t Effects of training intensity on cardiac output in young women

372z Effect of increased intensity of training on maximum oxygen uptake and muscular performance of young female cross-country skiers

372aa Menstrual effects of athletic training

425g Estimating benefits and costs of antisexist training programs in organizations

Tram

390t Women's struggle to become tram drivers in Melbourne, 1956-75

Trample

399b Trampling out the vintage

Trans-Mississippi

412g Ministry through marriage: Methodist clergy wives on the trans-Mississippi frontier

Transcendence

331g The "other" voice: Woman's song, its satire and its transcendence in late medieval British literature

Transsexual

212h Transsexualism: Can men turn men into women?

Transform

109h Gothic transformations: Isak Dinesen and the gothic

122c Seeking feminist transformation of the sciences and the teaching of science

126a The genesis of feminist visions for transforming the liberal arts curriculum

364f The legal and social transformation of rural women in Aegean Turkey

417u The linguistic transformation of womanhood

Transition

38k   Role transition in early adulthood: Orientations of young black women

148h Sioux women in transition: A study of their changing status in a domestic and capitalist sector of production

198d Roles in transition: The evolving position of women in Arab-Islamic countries

282b The gender revolution and the transition from bisexual horde to patrilocal band: The origins of gender hierarchy

360i Women's mental health in times of transition

365o Women in marital transition

417c Women in transition: Crete and Sumer

Translation

107u Body segment contributions of female athletes to translational and rotational requirements of non-twisting springboard dive takeoffs

Transmit

461z Discussion: Prophylaxis of sexually transmitted diseases: An overview

Transnational

213g Transnational production and women workers

Transportation

307l Getting there: Women and transportation

463j Residential location and transportation analyses: Married women workers

463k Role influence in transportation decision making

463o Perceived safety and security in transportation systems as determined by the gender of the traveler

463p The transportation implications of women's fear of assault

463s Can current transportation planning methods analyze women's travel issues?

463t Gender-role identification in the methodology of transportation planning

463u The transportation planning process

Transvestism

124f Transvestism and the ideology of gender: Southeast Asia and beyond

234c Shamanism as institutionalised ego defense and elite formation associated with transvestism in a Borneo society

Trap

179f Equal opportunity trap

415d Lady you're trapped: Breaking out of conflict cycles

Trauma

284f Observations after sexual traumata suffered in childhood

284g Sexual trauma of children and adolescents

326c Rape trauma syndrome: Developmental variations

372ee Traumatological aspects of sports of high achievements for women

Travel

203h Women's travel patterns in a suburban development

463a Women's travel issues: The research and policy environment

463d Influence of employment and children on intra-household travel behavior

463f The impact of women's employment on household travel patterns: A Swedish example

463l Women's travel behavior and attitudes: An empirical analysis

463m Sex differences in travel preferences and decision making

463n Travel patterns and behavior of women in urban areas

463o Perceived safety and security in transportation systems as determined by the gender of the traveler

463s Can current transportation planning methods analyze women's travel issues?

463v An alternative approach to travel demand modeling: Constraints-orientedtheories and societal roles

Treadwell, Sophie

399x Sophie Treadwell: Agent for change

Treatment

see also Therapy

8o The therapeutic alliance in psychoanalytic treatment

9k Alcoholism in women: Treatment modalities and outcomes

10k Patterns of women's use of alcohol treatment agencies

10l Therapeutic issues in the treatment of alcoholic women

10m Treatment outcome of alcoholic women: The state of the art in relation to sex bias and expectancy effects

11i Diagnosis, casefinding, and treatment of alcohol problems in women

11l Women helping women: Opening the door to treatment

16b Cognitive-behavioral strategies for the treatment of depression in women

26a Emergency room intervention: Detection, assessment, and treatment

26b Conjoint therapy for the treatment of domestic violence

26c Group treatment of children in shelters for battered women

28r Recent trends in the treatment of premenstrual syndrome: A critical review

29g Marriage and the family: An unconscious male bias in behavioral treatment?

46i Incremental change in social security needed to result in equal and fair treatment of men and women

55j Treatment issues with children involved in pornography and sex rings

96m The treatment of depressed women: The efficacy of psychotherapy

111h Contingency management in a juvenile treatment setting

111k The treatment of convicted female offenders in the criminal justice system

111p Prison treatment of female offenders in Mexico

146d Treatment of the sexually abused child

146g Individual and group treatment of mothers of incest victims

146i Family treatment

178n Mental health problems and their treatment

193m Differential treatment of boy and girl pupils during science lessons

198e The literary treatment of women in North Africa

219f The role of the judiciary in the failure of the Sexual Offences (Amendment) Act to improve the treatment of the rape victim

236e An explorative study into the clinical effects of dydrogesterone in the treatment of premenstrual syndrome

276b The relationship between treatment for sex offenders and the court

276c Prediction of recidivism and the evaluation of treatment programs for sex offenders

276d The assessment and treatment of sexual offenders

276f Ethics and ethical dilemmas in the treatment of sex offenders

277g The multidisciplinary approach to the diagnosis and treatment of male sexual dysfunction

277h Evaluation and treatment of impotence: The urologist's viewpoint

284l Diagnosis and treatment - an introduction

284l Humanistic treatment of father-daughter incest

285l Differential diagnosis and treatment for organogenic and psychogenic erectile dysfunction

291l Special problems in the treatment of child sexual abuse

291n A comprehensive child sexual abuse treatment program

291p The co-therapy relationship in group treatment of sexually mistreated adolescent girls

295m Differential needs and treatment approaches for women in psychotherapy

326d Treatment of sexually abused children

326e Network aspects of treatment for incestuously abused children

326k Marital and sexual dysfunction following rape: Identification and treatment

326l Behavioral treatment of sexual dysfunction in sexual assault survivors

326n Treatment of prostitute victims of sexual assault

338h The dramatic treatment of Robert Emmet and Sarah Curran

353p "The fashionable diseases": Women's complaints and their treatment in nineteenth-century America

359t Issues in the treatment of female addiction: A review and critique of the literature

359v Women's treatment needs

359nn Identification and treatment of incest victims

392l Chivalry and paternalism: Disparities of treatment in the criminal justice system

404j The woman in treatment: Evaluation and diagnostic implications

404k Sexism in treatment

404l Sexism in drug abuse treatment programs

404m Women and substance abuse: Treatment issues

404dd Establishing interdisciplinary treatment networks

443f Treatment of the imposter phenomenon in high-achieving women

The Tree of Begats

176k Teaching about Jewish lesbians in literature: From *Zeitl* and *Richel* to *The Tree of Begats*

Tres Tristes Tigres

313r Hacia un análisis feminista de *Tres tristes tigres*

Trial

see also Law

19h The political trial

147o Women's sport: A trial of equality

353l The Loomis trial: Social mores and obstetrics in the mid-nineteenth century

410b Political culture and selection of women judges in trial courts

Tribe

70i Relevancy of tribal interests and tribal diversity in determining the educational needs of American Indians

299g Tribal migrants

325k Islam and tribal women in a village in Iran

342e Indian women: Tribal identity as status quo

Tribute

301f Tribute to my husband

Trick

381c Box of tricks

474l Blood and guts: The tricky problem of being a woman writer in the late twentieth century

Trickster

238c Davey Crockett as trickster: Pornography, liminality and symbolic inversion in Victorian America

Trifles
399mm The women's world of Glaspell's *Trifles*

Trimester
252e The trimester threshold for pregnancy termination: Myth or truth?
252f Aspirotomy for outpatient termination of pregnancy in the second trimester
252g Instrumental abortion in the second trimester: An overview
252h Intra-amniotic hypertonic saline instillation in the second trimester
252i Extra-amniotic ethacridine (Rivanol)-catheter technique for midtrimester abortion
252l Termination of second trimester pregnancy with prostaglandin analogues
252m Prostaglandin therapy for second trimester abortion: An overview of current status and recent trends
252o Complications of second trimester abortion
252q Contraception following second trimester abortion
252r Sterilization combined with midtrimester abortion

Trinidad
421m Comparative attitudes about marital sex among Negro women in the United States, Great Britain and Trinidad

Trip
169m Labor history through field trips
463e Shopping trips: Who makes them and when?
463h Women's work trips: An empirical and theoretical overview

Tristan, Flora
448a The city as catalyst for Flora Tristan's vision of social change

Tristana
313n "Folly and a woman": Galdos' rhetoric of irony in *Tristana*
408q From mistress to murderess: The metamorphosis of Buñuel's *Tristana*

Triumph
40ee The quest for self: Triumph and failure in the works of Toni Morrison

Trivia
84g The trivialization of the notion of equality

Trobairitz
188f The provençal *Trobairitz*: Castelloza

Trobriand Islands, Papua New Guinea
347k Stability in banana leaves: Colonization and women in Kiriwina, Trobriand Islands

Trojan Horse
217e The organizational woman and the trojan-horse effect

Trollope, Anthony
27g "Old maids have friends": The unmarried heroine of Trollope's Barsetshire novels

Trouble
26g Family trouble clinic: Family service of Detroit and Wayne County

Trublem
40x Escape from Trublem: The fiction of Gayl Jones

True
310u XYLO: A true story

Truffaut, François
265s Changing sex roles reflected in the films of François Truffaut

Trumpet
455c No drums, no trumpets: Working-class women

Trust
105j Some correlates of marital trust
310cc Regaining trust
344t Trust, loyalty, and the place of women in the informal organization of work
415a Trust and power in the organization: An overview

Truth
252e The trimester threshold for pregnancy termination: Myth or truth?
275u A note on the ethics of theories of truth
275v A note on logical truth and non-sexist semantics
275w Reference and truth: The case of sexist and racist utterances
383h Truth and art in women's worlds: Doris Lessing's *Marriages Between Zones Three, Four, and Five*
383i Opposing necessity and truth: The argument against politics in Doris Lessing's utopian vision

Try
425e Trying hurts women, helps men: The meaning of effort

Tuath
417b Women of the Celtic Tuath

Tuition
169u Funding worker education through tuition refund plans

Tumor
141f Genetic heterogeneity and breast cancer: Variable tumor spectra

Tunisia
198h Islam and the legal status of women in Tunisia

Tuqan, Fadwa
108n *Difficult Journey - Mountainous Journey*, The memoirs of Fadwa Tuqan

Turkey
198f Early feminist movements in Turkey and Egypt
213f Living in between: Turkish women in their homeland and in the Netherlands
270b The significance of family and kinship in urban Turkey
270c Urban change and women's roles in Turkey: An overview and evaluation
270d Dualism in values toward education of Turkish women
270e Women's education in rural Turkey
270f Sex roles, value of children and fertility in Turkey
270g Female labor power relations in the urban Turkish family
270h The effect of international labor migration on women's roles: The Turkish case
270l Psychopathology and the Turkish family: A family systems theory analysis

270m Social change and family crisis: The nature of Turkish divorce
270n Social psychological patterns of homicide in Turkey: A comparison of male and female convicted murders
270o Civil violence in Turkey: Its infrastructural, social and cultural foundations
364f The legal and social transformation of rural women in Aegean Turkey
436e Women in government as policy-makers and bureaucrats: The Turkish case
457g Gender and religion in a Turkish town: A comparison of two types of formal women's gatherings

Turkish Women
213f Living in between: Turkish women in their homeland and in the Netherlands

Tuscan
188k The Tuscan visionary: Saint Catherine of Siena

Twain, Mark (Pseud)
17f Mark Twain's capers: A chameleon in King Carnival's court

Twelfth Century
187d Benedictine life for women in central France, 850-1100: A feminist revival
187j The nun as anchoress: England, 1100-1500
401f Power and prestige: Palace women in the Northern Sung (960-1126)

Twentieth Century
13d Besides our size it's because we are women: The strike by the laundry workers union 15 January - 5 February 1982
14u Afro-American women 1800-1910: A selected bibliography
22j New trends in the Danish women's movement, 1970-1978
23h Women and women's issues in the 1980 federal elections
23i 'A woman's place is in the House and in the Senate': Women and the 1983 elections
37e Perspectives on black family empirical research: 1965-1978
38b Some demographic characteristics of the black woman: 1940 to 1975
38f She who is black and mother: In sociology and fiction, 1940-1970
39o Discrimination against Afro-American women in the woman's movement, 1830-1920
45f Psychological orientations to the work role: 1957-1976
45k Changing sex roles: College graduates of the 1960's and 1970's
49c The age mix of the labor force in 1990: Implications for labor market research
49e Implications of the increasing participation of women in the work force in the 1990's
49h Human resource planning and the intuitive manager: Models for the 1990's
49i The setting and the reality for labor relations in the 90's
49j Leadership and management in the 1990's
50y 'Guardians of the race' or 'vampires upon the nation's health'? Female sexuality and its regulation in early twentieth century Britain
55a Child pornography in the 1970s

60d Crisis, reaction, and resistance: Women in Germany in the 1920's and 1930's

60e The social enforcement of heterosexuality and lesbian resistance in the 1920's

60f The twenties' backlash: Compulsory heterosexuality, the consumer family, and the waning of feminism

62b Co-education: Perspectives and debates in the early twentieth century

65l A review of federal court decisions under Title VII of the Civil Rights Act of 1964

81a The new woman: Changing views of women in the 1920s

81c Chicanas and Mexican immigrant families 1920-1940: Women's subordination and family exploitation

81d Flawed victories: The experiences of black and white women workers in Durham during the 1930s

81e The projection of a new womanhood: The movie moderns in the 1920's

81f Culture and radical politics: Yiddish women writers in America, 1890-1940

81h Two washes in the morning and a bridge party at night: The American housewife between the wars

81i All pink sisters: The War Department and the feminist movement in the 1920s

81j International feminism between the wars: The National Woman's Party versus the League of Women Voters

81k "The forgotten woman": Working women, the New Deal, and women's organizations

89p The 1974-1975 recession and the employment of women

99e 'As good a bloody woman as any other woman...': Prostitutes in western Australia, 1895-1939

101f Kinship, women, and politics in twentieth-century Punjab

101j The All-Pakistan Women's Association and the 1961 Muslim family laws ordinance

117p Virility and domination in early twentieth-century vanguard painting

117q Miriam Schapiro and "femmage": Reflections on the conflict between decoration and abstraction in twentieth-century art

119c 'Mothers, vote labour!' The state, the labour movement and working-class mothers, 1900-1918

119g 'An immense verbosity': Permissive sexual advice in the 1970s

124g Psychology views mothers and mothering: 1897-1980

128e The "Jennie Higginses" of the "New South in the West": A regional survey of socialist activists, agitators, and organizers, 1901-1917

128g Women socialists and their male comrades: The Reading experience, 1927-1936

133o Media reaction to the 1979 gay march on Washington

144d Family and household: Social structures in a German village between the two World Wars

144h Women's work and the family: Women garment workers in Berlin and Hamburg before the First World War

144i Politics and the family: Social democracy and the working-class family in theory and practice before 1914

147j Women's participation in sporting activities as an indicator of a feminist movement in Canada between 1867-1914

147k Women in sport and physical education in the United States 1900-1914

147m The American sportswoman from 1900 to 1920

147n An analysis of humour pertaining to sportswomen in Canadian newspapers from 1910-1920

147s Women in sport in the United States, 1945 to 1978

147cc The controlled development of collegiate sport for women, 1923-1936

147dd The history of women's intercollegiate athletics in Ohio, 1945-1972

147gg The contributions of women to the history of competitive tennis in the United States in the twentieth century

147hh The establishment of softball for American women, 1900-1940

147ii The Edmonton Grads: The team and its social significance from 1915-1940

147jj The 1930 U.B.C. women's basketball team: Those other world champions

147ll The development of women's organized sport in the 1920's: A study of the Canadian Ladies Golf Union

147oo The All-American Girls' Baseball League, 1943-1954

149d Women's double work day: Twentieth-century changes in the reproduction of daily life

149e The expanded reproduction cycle of labour power in twentieth-century capitalism

153l State, collective, and household: The process of accumulation in China, 1949-65

153m Gender division within the U.S. working class: Households in the Philadelphia area, 1870-1945

153o Wages, consumption, and survival: Working class households in Puerto Rico in the 1930's

155b French feminist theater and the subject of prostitution, 1870-1914

157g Maria Grant, 1854-1937: The life and times of an early twentieth century Christian

157i Sexism in British Columbia trade unions, 1900-1920

157k The 'social evil': Prostitution in Vancouver, 1900-1920

157l The B.C. Liberal Party and women's reforms, 1916-1928

158e Not quite new worlds: Psychologists' conceptions of the ideal family in the twenties

158i The theory of male sex role identity: Its rise and fall, 1936 to the present

160b Ambivalence and dedication: Academic wives in Cambridge University, 1870-1970

160j Memsahibs in colonial Malaya: A study of European wives in a British colony and protectorate, 1900-1940

162p Mothers, sons, and the sale of symbols and goods: The 'German Mother's Day' 1923-33

165j Hard times: Custodial prisons for women and the example of the New York State Prison for Women at Auburn, 1893-1933

173e Abortion and the presidential election of 1976: A multivariate analysis of voting behavior

173g The politics of abortion in the House of Representatives in 1976

176m Learning through teaching: A lesbianism course in 1972

176o Black lesbians before 1970: A bibliographical essay

184q Premarital pregnancy in America, 1640-1971: An overview and interpretation

186n Redefinitions of traditional Christian emblems and outlooks in May Sarton's novels of 1970-1975

192r La costura en Los Angeles 1933-1939: The ILGWU and the politics of domination

201d The great uprisings: 1900-1920

201f The uprising in Chicago: The men's garment workers strike, 1910-1911

201i Inside and outside the unions: 1920-1980

201l A stitch in our time: New York's Hispanic garment workers in the 1980s

205d A preliminary sketch of Chinese women and work in British Columbia, 1858-1950

205e The response of the WMS to the immigration of Asian women, 1888-1942

205f A note on Asian Indian women in British Columbia, 1900-1935

205j Six saucepans to one: Domestic science vs. the home in British Columbia 1900-1930

205k Women on campus in British Columbia: Strategies for survival, years of war and peace, 1906-1920

205m The brightest women of our land: Vancouver clubwomen 1919-1928

205o Domesticity and discipline: The Girl Guides in British Columbia 1910-1943

205q "Services rendered, rearing children for the state": Mothers' pensions in British Columbia 1919-1931

205s Last back: Folklore and the telephone operators in the 1919 Vancouver general strike

205v The search for legitimacy: Nurses' registration in British Columbia 1913-1935

205w Vivian Dowding: Birth control activist 1892-

220b Perspectives on women in the 1980s: The Baird Poskanzer Memorial Lecture

220k Strategies for the eighties

224n Lesbian and gay oppression in the '80s: Androgyny, men and power

225c The taming of the id: Feminist sexual politics, 1968-83

226h Female state senators as cue givers: ERA roll-call voting, 1972-1979

229pp WITCH: Spooking the patriarchy during the late sixties

231b "Charity girls" and city pleasures: Historical notes on working-class sexuality, 1880-1920

231f Feminism, men, and modern love: Greenwich Village, 1900-1925

238h Harlot or heroine? Changing views of prostitution, 1870-1920

238i Ideas of the early sex education movement in America, 1890-1920

245c Why nineteenth-century feminists did not support "birth control" and twentieth-century feminists do: Feminism, reproduction, and the family

246i European women in the Solomon Islands, 1900-1942: Accommodation and change on the Pacific frontier

248b Nurse recruitment to four provincial hospitals 1881-1921

248e A constant casualty: Nurse education in Britain and the USA to 1939

248f Asylum nursing before 1914: A chapter in the history of labour

250l How many women academics 1912-76?

255i Purdah politics: The role of Muslim women in Indian nationalism, 1911-1924

257a Purity, motherhood, pleasure or threat? Definitions of female sexuality 1900-1970s

257l I'll climb the stairway to heaven: Lesbianism in the seventies

261c Grievances and their redress in the eighties

263d "Blessed be the tie that binds": YWCA extension work among industrial women, Minneapolis, 1900-1910

263e "For love and money both": Women's work-related decisions in twentieth century Minneapolis

263k Industrial social workers in France, 1917-1939: A study in the sex/gender division of labor

264b Sisters under their skins: Southern working women, 1880-1950

264d Black women in a southern city: Washington, D.C., 1890-1920

272a Trends in occupational segregation by sex and race, 1960-1981

272d Occupational sex segregation: Prospects for the 1980s

278e Sexual fiction in America, 1955-80

290a 'Free from all uninvited touch of man': Women's campaigns around sexuality, 1880-1914

290d Theory into practice: Sexual liberation or social control? (*Forum* magazine 1968-1981)

292a The Women's Trade Union League training school for women organizers, 1914-1926

292b From soul to strawberries: The International Ladies' Garment Workers' Union and workers' education, 1914-1950

292d Blue collars and bluestockings: The Bryn Mawr summer school for women workers, 1921-1938

292f Partners in progress: The affiliated schools for women workers, 1928-1939

292h The she-she-she camps: An experiment in living and learning, 1934-1937

294b 'More sinned against than sinning'?: Prostitution in South Australia, 1836-1914

294d Dealing with the 'social evil': Prostitution and the police in Perth and on the eastern goldfields, 1895-1924

294e The making of a prostitute proletariat in early twentieth-century New South Wales

294f 'Black Velvet': Aboriginal women and their relations with white men in the Northern Territory, 1910-1940

295p New directions for women: Moving beyond the 1980s

298i A survey of trends in social sciences research on women in the Arab region, 1960-1980

301o Women in the Texas ILGWU, 1933-50

301hh swing through the south journal, fall 1981

302a Revision versus reality: Women in the history of the public library movement, 1876-1920

303d Women's studies at Vanderbilt: Toward a strategy for the eighties

303h Academic women in Mississippi: Oktoberfest 1980

304b Sex-role stereotypes and mental health: Conceptual models in the 1970s and issues for the 1980s

309a Teenage family formation in postwar America

309c The legitimacy status of first births to U.S. women aged 15-24, 1939-1978

309d Sexual and contraceptive experience of young unmarried women in the United States, 1976 and 1971

309e First pregnancies to women aged 15-19: 1976 and 1971

309f Contraceptive patterns and premarital pregnancy among women aged 15-19 in 1976

309i Teenage pregnancies: Looking ahead to 1984

309bb Teenagers and pregnancy: The law in 1979

310v Personal courage is not enough: Some hazards of childbearing in the 1980s

315a The emergence of women in twentieth-century Chilean history and literature

320q Issues of educational equity in the 1980s: Multiple perspectives

335b 'Smash the family?' Recalling the 1960s

336c Abortion and economic crisis: The 1931 campaign against paragraph 218

336h Sisterhood under siege: Feminism and anti-semitism in Germany, 1904-1938

336i The competition for women's *lebensraum*, 1928-1934

344gg Keep us on the pedestal: Women against feminism in twentieth century America

349c Crime and the contemporary woman: An analysis of changing levels of female property crime, 1960-1975

349d Patterns of female property crime, 1960-1978: A postscript

349e The economics of female criminality: An analysis of police blotters, 1890-1976

353h Patterns of abortion and the response of American physicians, 1790-1930

353i Doctors, birth control, and social values, 1830-1970

353n Chlorotic girls, 1870-1920: A historical perspective on female adolescence

353ff "Neither for the drawing room nor for the kitchen": Private duty nursing in Boston, 1873-1914

353gg "Little world of our own": The Pennsylvania Hospital Training School for Nurses, 1895-1907

353hh More than "the physician's hand": Skill and authority in twentieth-century nursing

354h The politics of birth control, 1920-1940: The impact of professionals

359e Psychology of women: Perspectives on theory and research for the eighties

363c Women and revolution: The brigadas femeninas and the Mexican Cristero Rebellion, 1926-1929

368d Social and economic change in the role of women, 1956-1978

370i Women in slavery among the Mangbetu c. 1800-1910

370n Bwanikwa: Consciousness and protest among slave women in Central Africa, 1886-1911

372e Development of women's sport in the 20th century

379h Right-wing female activists in Buenos Aires, 1900-1932

379l City mothers, city daughters, and the dance hall girls: The limits of female political power in San Francisco, 1913

379m The limitations of sisterhood: Elizabeth Cady Stanton and division in the American suffrage movement, 1875-1902

379p "If eight hours seems few to you...": Women workers' strikes in Italian rice fields, 1901-1906

380q The attitude of Danish mothers to child care, 1975 to 1979

385d Women and agricultural change in the railway region of Zambia: Dispossession and counterstrategies, 1930-1970

389b Widening horizons (1890-1930)

389c The tradition continues (1930-1979)

389f Lady Dilke (1840-1904): The six lives of an art historian

389g Mariana Griswold Van Rensselaer (1851-1934): America's first professional woman art critic

389h Georgiana Goddard King (1871-1939): Educator and pioneer in medieval Spanish art

389i Margarete Bieber (1879-1978): An archaeologist in two worlds

389j Gisela Marie Augusta Richter (1882-1972): Scholar of classical art and museum archaeologist

389k Erica Tietze-Conrat (1883-1958): Productive scholar in renaissance and baroque art

389l Sirarpie Der Nersessian (b. 1896): Educator and scholar in Byzantine and Armenian art

389m Dorothy Burr Thompson (b. 1900): Classical archaeologist

389n Dorothy Eugenia Miner (1904-1973): The varied career of a medievalist: Scholar and keeper of manuscripts, librarian and editor at the Walters Art Gallery

390e Evolution, eugenics and women: The impact of scientific theories on attitudes towards women, 1870-1920

390h 'I have never liked trade unionism': The development of the Royal Australian Nursing Federation, Queensland Branch, 1904-1945

390j 'Spinifex fairies': Aboriginal workers in the Northern territory, 1911-39

390n Rooms of their own: The domestic situation of Australian women writers between the wars

390o From balaclavas to bayonets: Women's voluntary war work, 1939-41

390r Equal pay case, 1951

390t Women's struggle to become tram drivers in Melbourne, 1956-75

390u Revolution and machismo: Women in the New South Wales Builders Labourers' Federation, 1961-75

395d Women, food and health in Tanzania: A crisis of the 1980s

397p Culture-making: Lesbian classics in the year 2000

398j Women's studies and men's careers: How the 'social problem' of women in education maintained the academic status of men in the 1970s

398l Academic women, affirmative action, and mid-America in the eighties

399ll Women in Pulitzer Prize plays, 1918-1949

401k The influence of western women on the anti-footbinding movement 1840-1911

401m In the public eye: Women in early twentieth-century China

405g Marxism and women's oppression: Bolshevik theory and practice in the 1920's

412i Preparing women for the Lord's work: The story of three Methodist training schools, 1880-1940

412j The social gospel according to Phoebe: Methodist deaconesses in the metropolis, 1885-1918

412l "A new impulse": Progress in lay leadership and service by women of the United Brethren in Christ and the Evangelical Association, 1870-1910

412m Creating a sphere for women: The Methodist Episcopal church, 1869-1906

412n The laity rights movement, 1906-1918: Women's suffrage in the Methodist Episcopal Church, South

412r Korean women in Hawaii, 1903-1945: The role of Methodism in their liberation and in their participation in the Korean independence movement

412s Shaping a new society: Methodist women and industrial reform in the south, 1880-1940

413h Women, work and family: 1880-1926

414c Women of the Osage: A century of change, 1874-1982

414h Woman's suffrage, Oklahoma style, 1890-1918

418g Domestic violence: Battered women in Britain in the 1970s

421o Wife-employment and the emergence of egalitarian marital role prescriptions: 1900-1974

421z Women in the Cuban bureaucracies: 1968-1974

424m Growth of the bazaar economy and its significance for women's employment: Trends of the 1970s in Davao City, Philippines

426f Women and nontraditional blue collar jobs in the 1980s: An overview

427c Fathers, mothers, and childcare in the 1980s: Family influences on child development

431f Women and men in Iloilo, Philippines: 1903-1970

433f Bengal election, 1937: Fazlul Huq and M. A. Jinnah: A study in leadership stress in Bengal politics

439i The front line: Notes on sex in novels by women, 1969-1979

439p "The love crisis": Couples advice books of the late 1970s

439u "I am not contented": Female masochism and lesbianism in early twentieth-century New England

440a The end is where we start from: Women and welfare since 1901

440j The women's movement's fandango with the state: The movement's role in public policy since 1972

448g A wilderness of one's own: Feminist fantasy novels of the twenties: Rebecca West and Sylvia Townsend Warner

450h Doris Bett's Nancy Finch: A heroine for the 1980s

453n The use of story in women's novels of the seventies

454q Cookbooks and law books: The hidden history of career women in twentieth-century America

465a Dealing with dependency: State practices and social realities, 1870-1945

466d Land ownership in Negri Sembilan, 1900-1977

469i A preliminary historical analysis of women and work in Puerto Rico: 1899-1975

474l Blood and guts: The tricky problem of being a woman writer in the late twentieth century

Twenty First Century

185a Looking toward the year 2020

185d "Mate" selection in the year 2020

185j Moral concepts in the year 2020: The individual, the family, and society

185k The work/family connection in the year 2020

185l Physical settings for families in 2020: In space, on earth

185m Family options, governments, and the social milieu: Viewed from the 21st century

185o 2020 and beyond

Twin Oaks, VA

417q Twin Oaks: A feminist looks at indigenous socialism in the United States

Twist

107u Body segment contributions of female athletes to translational and rotational requirements of non-twisting springboard dive takeoffs

Tyler, Anne

450a The fiction of Anne Tyler

Tynemouth (Ship)

157b To Columbia on the Tynemouth: The emigration of single women and girls in 1862

Type

50h Typing our way to freedom: Is it true that new office technology can liberate women?

Typescript

328k A track of our own: Typescript drafts of *The Years*

Typology

55c Typology of sex rings exploiting children

55e Typology of collectors

64g A typology of women in Colette's novels

421b Female-headed households and domestic organization in San Isidro, Guatemala: A test of Hammel and Laslett's comparative typology

425a An overview of the research on women in management: A typology and a prospectus

Tyrant

325m Empress Wu and the historians: A tyrant and saint of classical China

U.B.C.

see University of British Columbia

Uganda

457j Men, women and misfortune in Bunyole

Ujamaa

385i Women's work in a communal setting: The Tanzanian policy of *Ujamaa*

Ulysses

409f Gerty MacDowell: Joyce's sentimental heroine

409g The conventional Molly Bloom

Umbanda Evangelizada

473f Spirit mediums in Umbanda Evangelizada of Porto Alegre, Brazil: Dimensions of power and authority

Unborn

2d The juridical status of the fetus: A proposal for legal protection of the unborn

173b The juridical status of the fetus: A proposal for legal protection of the unborn

Unconscious

29g Marriage and the family: An unconscious male bias in behavioral treatment?

84n Political philosophy and the patriarchal unconscious: A psychoanalytic perspective on epistemology and metaphysics

203o No academic matter: Unconscious discrimination in environmental design education

UNCSTD

see United Nations Conference on Science and Technology Development

Undergraduate

see also Education

45j The past and future of the undergraduate woman

302d Undergraduate women as potential recruits to the library profession

306n Letters and diaries: Demystifying archival research for undergraduates

320a The undergraduate woman: Theme and variations

320g Epistemology and agency in the development of undergraduate women

320h Social psychology looks at but does not see the undergraduate woman

320k Undergraduates and their teachers: An analysis of student evaluations of male and female instructors

394t From undergraduate to judge at sixty

Underground

453e Humor in California underground women's comix

Understand

470h The 'understanding' employer

Unemployment

see also Employment

89n   The female-male differential in unemployment rates

89o   Curing high unemployment rates among blacks and women

139j   Patriarchal structures: The case of unemployment

221f   Family effects of dislocation, unemployment, and discouragement

243l   Unemployment and family stress

260b   A look at the male female unemployment differentials in the Federal Republic of Germany, Sweden, United Kingdom, and the United States of America

380h   Job creation and unemployment for Canadian women

Unicorn

40aa   The unicorn is black: Audre Lorde in retrospect

Union

see also Trade Union, Employment

13d   Besides our size it's because we are women: The strike by the laundry workers union 15 January - 5 February 1982

13i   Women and unions in Australia

65h   A policy-capturing application in a union setting

83h   The church, the unions, women and the opposition in Brazil

93i   Vocational training, the labor market, and the unions

93j   Leadership training for union women in the United States: Route to equal opportunity

139f   Participation in local union organisation. School meals staff: A case study

139i   Feminisation and unionisation: A case study from banking

169q   Education for affirmative action: Two union approaches

201i   Inside and outside the unions: 1920-1980

205t   A union man's wife: The ladies' auxiliary movement in the IWA, the Lake Cowichan experience

206o   Can the union make us strong

206p   Using sex and satan to bust the union (an interview with Corky Jennings)

209l   Automation and the quality of work life at the Swedish telephone company: A union view

209z   A union perspective on health hazards of VDTs

288j   Action plans for management and unions

305k   Getting organized...in the feminist unions

323b   Women and unions in Canada: A statistical overview

323d   Out of the ghettos: Affirmative action and unions

323f   Under attack: Women, unions and microtechnology

323g   Part-time work and unions

323h   Sexual harassment: An issue for unions

323j   Lesbians and gays in the union movement

323z   Women, work and unions: A cineography

323bb   Women and unions: A selected bibliography

344r   "Union is power": Sketches from women's labor history

378f   Unions: the men's affair?

390s   Right-wing union officials versus married women workers

470i   A woman's place is her union

Union Army

454f   The war within a war: Women nurses in the Union Army

United Brethren in Christ

see also Religion

412l   "A new impulse": Progress in lay leadership and service by women of the United Brethren in Christ and the Evangelical Association, 1870-1910

United Nations Conference on Science and Technology Development (UNCSTD)

251e   The power of persistence: Consciousness raising at international fora - the case of UNCSTD

251f   Some reflections on women in science and technology after UNCSTD

373o   Roles of women: UNCSTD background discussion paper

United States

9b   Temperance and women in 19th-century United States

18c   "Reproductive choice" in the contemporary United States: A social analysis of female sterilization

19l   The case of the American Jezebels

32f   A German writer and feminist in nineteenth century America: An archival study of Mathilde Franziska Anneke

35c   Political ideology, sociobiology, and the U.S. women's rights movement

41a   Working women in the United States: A look at the facts

42b   The American woman's movement

45a   American demographic directions

45g   The American divorce rate: What does it mean? What should we worry about?

50o   Technology and changes in the division of labour in the American home

52c   A comparative view on the changing position of women in the United States

56e   Awake and aware, or false consciousness: The cooption of childbirth reform in America

59e   American women and life-style change

61c   National Archives resources for research in the history of American women

61e   Women in the American revolution: Vignettes or profiles?

61o   Photographs as historical documents (American women through the camera's eye)

68k   Introduction: Minority women in the United States

71n   Asian wives of U.S. servicemen: Women in triple jeopardy

73k   Achieving the dreams beyond tradition: Counseling white ethnic American girls

78l   Rape: The all-American crime

80q   The battle for day care in America: A view from the trenches

81f   Culture and radical politics: Yiddish women writers in America, 1890-1940

81h   Two washes in the morning and a bridge party at night: The American housewife between the wars

83c   Gender, race and class in the United States: Lessons from Third World women

93d   The effectiveness of federal laws prohibiting sex discrimination in employment in the United States

93e   Strategies for improving the economic situation of women in the United States: Systemic thinking, systemic discrimination, and systemic enforcement

93j   Leadership training for union women in the United States: Route to equal opportunity

93m   Improving job opportunities for women from a U.S. corporate perspective

93p   Women's stake in a high-growth economy in the United States

102d   Religion and the fearful father: Vision of liberation or American-style fascism?

102m   Women in the U.S. Foreign Service: A quiet revolution

103a   Contemporary American families: Decline or transformation?

103i   Why the United States has no child-care policy

105d   Recent data reflecting upon the sexual revolution in America

105l   Physical violence in a nationally representative sample of American families

112j   Mercy Otis Warren: Playwright, poet, and historian of the American revolution (American, 1728-1814)

117r   Quilts: The great American art

123d   What the women's movement has done to American history

127e   *Ida*, A great American novel

128e   The "Jennie Higginses" of the "New South in the West": A regional survey of socialist activists, agitators, and organizers, 1901-1917

129a   The roots of individualist feminism in 19th-century America

129c   Anarchism and American traditions

129y   Women and the rise of the American medical profession

132e   Language and revolution: The Franco-American Dis-connection

136k   The seven ages of woman: A view from American magazine advertisements

138m   Gender, class and education: A teaching bibliography of American studies

145r   An English-language bibliography on European and American women's history

147b   Recreational activities of women in colonial America

147c   The rise and development of women's concern for the physical education of American women, 1776-1885: From independence to the foundation of the American Association for the Advancement of Physical Education

147e   American women, 1880-1860 (sic): Recreational pursuits and exercise

147g   Generalizations on women and sport, games and play in the United States from settlement to 1860

147k   Women in sport and physical education in the United States 1900-1914

147l   The effect of changing attitudes toward sexual morality upon the promotion of physical education for women in nineteenth century America

147m The American sportswoman from 1900 to 1920

147s Women in sport in the United States, 1945 to 1978

147t The effect of current sports legislation on women in Canada and the U.S.A. - Title IX

147x Adele Parot: Pathfinder for the Dioclesian Lewis school of gymnastic expression in the American west

147gg The contributions of women to the history of competitive tennis in the United States in the twentieth century

147hh The establishment of softball for American women, 1900-1940

147mm American women: Their debut in international track and field

147oo The All-American Girls' Baseball League, 1943-1954

153m Gender division within the U.S. working class: Households in the Philadelphia area, 1870-1945

155i The uncommon prostitute: The contemporary image in an American age of pornography

162l Kinship and class consciousness: Family values and work experience among hospital workers in an American southern town

176e Harassment in rural America

180j Mothers and daughters in the fiction of the New Republic

184q Premarital pregnancy in America, 1640-1971: An overview and interpretation

190q "Oh dear me! Why weren't we all boys, then there wouldn't be any bother": Menarche and popular American fiction

192e Toward a democratic women's movement in the United States

203i Women in the suburban environment: A U.S.-Sweden comparison

209h The implications of technology for U.S. employment

209m New technology and its implications in U.S. clerical work

209hh Legislative and research options for the U.S. Congress

215q Building on the positives: The USA

228b USA

230h Sexual stratification, pornography, and rape in the United States

231e Family, sexual morality, and popular movements in turn-of-the-century America

233e Reproductive hazards of the American life style

233q Legal considerations of reproductive hazards in industry in the United States

238c Davey Crockett as trickster: Pornography, liminality and symbolic inversion in Victorian America

238e From maidenhood to menopause: Sex education for women in Victorian America

238f The erotic South: Civilization and sexuality in American abolitionism

238i Ideas of the early sex education movement in America, 1890-1920

238j The scientist as sex crusader: Alfred C. Kinsey and American culture

239h American birth practices: A critical review

244b White mothers in the American civil rights movements

244h Sexual customs and gender roles in Sweden and America: An analysis and interpretation

245j Family and class in contemporary America: Notes toward an understanding of ideology

248e A constant casualty: Nurse education in Britain and the USA to 1939

254m American female dramatists: Show but no go?

260a Women in the labour market and equal opportunity policy in Sweden, United Kingdom, United States and West Germany

260b A look at the male female unemployment differentials in the Federal Republic of Germany, Sweden, United Kingdom, and the United States of America

260e Equal opportunity and the law in the United States

260j Labour market policy in four countries: Are women adequately represented?

260k Estimating the impact of labor market policies on women: A discussion of the four-country studies on the employment of women

263c Symmetrical families? Changing gender role expectations and the breadwinner role in the contemporary United States

263f The sexual division of labor on American farms: 1750-1850

263h Creating a place for women: American book publishing in the nineteenth century

278e Sexual fiction in America, 1955-80

291e Sexual child abuse: The legislation and the law in the United States

306i Feminist pedagogy: Lost voices of American women

308a Teenage women in the United States: Sex, contraception, pregnancy, fertility, and maternal and infant health

308e Sex education and the prevention of teenage pregnancy: An overview of policies and programs in the United States

309a Teenage family formation in postwar America

309c The legitimacy status of first births to U.S. women aged 15-24, 1939-1978

309d Sexual and contraceptive experience of young unmarried women in the United States, 1976 and 1971

314o Reconstructing American literature: A strategy for change

315b Attitudes toward gender in two cultures: Puerto Rico and the United States

316j The lost cause: The aging woman in American feminism

316n Resistance to the women's movement in the United States: The ERA controversy as prototype

344gg Keep us on the pedestal: Women against feminism in twentieth century America

349b American women and crime

351b The impacts of irrelevance: Women in the history of American education

353a The female animal: Medical and biological views of woman and her role in nineteenth-century America

353e The female world of love and ritual: Relations between women in nineteenth-century America

353g Voluntary motherhood: The beginnings of feminist birth control ideas in the United States

353h Patterns of abortion and the response of American physicians, 1790-1930

353j "On the importance of the obstetrick art": Changing customs of childbirth in America, 1760 to 1825

353k "Down to death door's": Women's perceptions of childbirth in America

353o Prostitution, venereal disease, and American medicine

353p "The fashionable diseases": Women's complaints and their treatment in nineteenth-century America

353u "Safe delivered," but by whom? Midwives and men-midwives in early America

353v The American midwife controversy: A crisis of professionalization

353w Mary Breckinridge, the frontier nursing service, and the introduction of nurse-midwifery in the United States

353x Making women modern: Middle-class women and health reform in nineteenth-century America

354b Convenience and the occurrence of births: Induction and labor in the United States and Canada

354d Sexism and racism in the American health care industry: A comparative analysis

355b An enlarged human existence? Technology and household work in nineteenth-century America

357d Low pay and female employment in Canada with selected references to the USA

358a Women in broadcasting (U.S.) *de jure, de facto*

359w A study of attitudes toward menarche in white middle-class American adolescent girls

366d The Jewish woman's encounter with American culture

367d New England women: Ideology and experience in first-generation Puritanism (1630-1650)

367i Women, civil religion, and the American Revolution

369l The marriage of capitalist and patriarchal ideologies: Meanings of male bonding and male ranking in U.S. culture

375g The law of husband and wife in nineteenth-century America: Changing views of divorce

375j Barred from the bar: Women and legal education in the United States, 1870-1890

379j The ethnological mirror: American evangelical women and their heathen sisters, 1870-1910

379m The limitations of sisterhood: Elizabeth Cady Stanton and division in the American suffrage movement, 1875-1902

380b The education and employment of women scientists and engineers in the United States

380i Poverty viewed as a woman's problem - The U.S. case

380p Child care use and constraints in the United States

382k The United States of America

384a The civilizers: Women's organizations and western American literature

384e Women in western American fiction: Images or real women?

384o Wright Morris, women, and American culture

387l The future of American fertility

388l The contemporary American women's movement

389g Mariana Griswold Van Rensselaer (1851-1934): America's first professional woman art critic

391e Changing Canadian and US magazine portrayals of women and work: Growing opportunities for choice

398l Academic women, affirmative action, and mid-America in the eighties

399s Women mimes in America

411l Problems of American middle-class women in their middle years: A comparative approach

412b The last fifteen years: Historians' changing views of American women in religion and society

416b Professional women in developing nations: The United States and the Third World compared

417q Twin Oaks: A feminist looks at indigenous socialism in the United States

421n Working wives in the United States and Venezuela: A cross-national study of decision making

427g Paid and unpaid work: Contradictions in American women's lives today

428b The new international division of labor and the U.S. work force: The case of the electronics industry

428d Women, production, and reproduction in industrial capitalism: A comparison of Brazilian and U.S. factory workers

433k Radindranath Tagore: Cultural ambassador of India to the United States

437e United States

438c It takes more than luck (United States)

438g Reflections on a scientific adventure (Italy and United States)

444c The job he left behind: American women in the shipyards during World War II

444d "Life, liberty, and dower": The legal status of women after the American Revolution

444k "The mother half of humanity": American women in the peace and preparedness movements in World War I

445b Women's literature and the American frontier: A new perspective on the frontier myth

445d American dream, nightmare underside: Diaries, letters and fiction of women on the American frontier

452c Quest for community: Spiritual autobiographies of eighteenth-century Quaker and Puritan women in America

453l Madonna or witch: Women's muse in contemporary American poetry

454a American women and domestic culture: An approach to women's history

454e Ladies bountiful: Organized women's benevolence in early nineteenth-century America

454g The spiritualist medium: A study of female professionalization in Victorian America

454j Catharine Beecher and the education of American women

454k Family limitation, sexual control, and domestic feminism in Victorian America

454l The female world of love and ritual: Relations between women in nineteenth-century America

454n The hysterical woman: Sex roles and role conflict in nineteenth century America

454o The American woman's pre-World War I freedom in manners and morals

454q Cookbooks and law books: The hidden history of career women in twentieth-century America

460a "Role, Jenny Jenkins, Roll": Little girls and maidens in American folksongs - an analysis of sexual attitudes

460b The history of female sexuality in the United States

461s Women in swinging: America's Amazon society?

465g Equal opportunity policies: Some implications for women of contrasts between enforcement bodies in Britain and the USA

465h The new right, sex, education and social policy: Towards a new moral economy in Britain and the USA

469b Mental health needs of Puerto Rican women in the United States

471j Women at work in the USA

473j The uses of traditional concepts in the development of new urban roles: Cuban women in the United States

United States Code

55m Appendix B: Review of legal cases regarding US Code, Section 1461 (mailing obscene or crime-inciting matter)

Unity

199o On the shop floor: Multi-ethnic unity against the conglomerate

378g Unity is strength? Feminism and the labor movement

Universal

116a The feminine as a universal

323u Free universal day care: The OFL takes a stand

418n Universals and particulars in the position of women

Universal Declaration of Human Rights

31n A feminist analysis of the Universal Declaration of Human Rights

Universalization

101g Nationalism, universalization, and the extended female space in Bombay City

Universe

13a Deconstructing the masculine universe: The case of women's work

University

see also Education, names of individual institutions

7p Swastikas: The street and the university

33d Learned women of early modern Italy: Humanists and university scholars

176c "Out" at the university: Myth and reality

250k Women in higher education: A case study of the open university

394a The women's movement and the university

394n Child care and the university

398c Black woman professor — white university

407a Careers in college and university administration: How are women affected?

University of Arkansas

303g Teaching women's studies at the University of Arkansas

University of British Columbia

147jj The 1930 U.B.C. women's basketball team: Those other world champions

University of California

147z History and structure of the department of physical education at the University of California with special reference to women's sports

University of Florida

303j Racial myths and attitudes among white female students at the University of Florida

University of Montana

441k Women and technology project, Missoula, Montana

University of Pennsylvania

261g Faculty grievance procedure

University of Washington

441j Teaching women and technology at the University of Washington

University of Wisconsin

249d Joan Roberts and the university

337e Nursing in the UW system

394b History of the Association of Faculty Women at Madison

394c A history of the Wisconsin Coordinating Council of Women in Higher Education

394d Committee on the Status of Women at Milwaukee

394f A women's studies plan for Wisconsin

394g The women's studies program at Milwaukee

394h Sedition in a sexist society: The Platteville paradigm

394j Women's athletics at Madison and Title IX

394q Continuing education services in the UW system

University Women's Club

157h Evlyn Farris and the University Women's Club

Unmarried

27g "Old maids have friends": The unmarried heroine of Trollope's Barsetshire novels

Unnatural

50k The unnatural family

79w Unnatural selection: On choosing children's sex

Up

381f Up to now

Upper Class

see also Class

401g Women in the kinship system of the Southern Song upper class

444i Revolution and retreat: Upper-class French women after 1789

Upper Heyford, England

215h A voice from the peace camps: Greenham Common and Upper Heyford

Upper Volta

385h International development and the evolution of women's economic roles: A case study from northern Gulma, Upper Volta

Uprising

201d The great uprisings: 1900-1920

201e The great uprising in Rochester

201f The uprising in Chicago: The men's garment workers strike, 1910-1911

201g The great uprising in Cleveland: When sisterhood failed

201h The uprising of the 20,000: The making of a labor legend

Urban

see also City

6c Women in the urban economy

23b Black sisterhood: The situation of urban aboriginal women and their relationship to the white women's movement

37g Economics and mobility: A theoretical rationale for urban black family well-being

39r Sex roles and survival strategies in the urban black community

70j Transition from the reservation to an urban setting and the changing roles of American Indian women

75d Career counselling for poor rural and urban women of South India

203f Introduction: Urban design: The price women pay

243a Urban and rural working women in Poland today: Between social change and social conflict

263m The new economic readjustment policies: Implications for Chinese urban working women

270b The significance of family and kinship in urban Turkey

270c Urban change and women's roles in Turkey: An overview and evaluation

270g Female labor power relations in the urban Turkish family

270j The plight of urban migrants: Dynamics of service procurement in a squatter area

284b Sexual victimization of children: An urban mental health center survey

295h The impact of crime on urban women

300g Patterns of urbanization in the Philippines

300h Rural-urban linkages and migration: A Philippines case study

307k The lonely squandering of urban time

309t Guessing and misinformation about pregnancy risk among urban mothers

325j The controversial vows of urban Muslim women in Iran

364g Divorce and the disadvantaged: African women in urban South Africa

364h 'Fear woman': Property and modes of production in urban Ghana

371d Essential objects and the sacred: Interior and exterior space in an urban Greek locality

371j Where women must dominate: Response to oppression in a South African urban community

379a Glimpses of Muslim urban women in classical Islam

379g The holy woman and the urban community in sixteenth-century Avila

385l Fertility and employment: An assessment of role incompatibility among African urban women

395j Health beliefs and behaviors of middle class urban women in Lahore, Pakistan

402d Trends and structure of female labour force participation in rural and urban Pakistan

420a Urbanization, migration and the status of women

420d Women in rural-urban circulation networks: Implications for social structural change

420e Rural-to-urban migration of women in India: Patterns and implications

420g Female rural-to-urban migration in peninsular Malaysia

420j Urban migrant women in the Republic of Korea

420q Philippine urbanism and the status of women

424b Trends in female labour force participation and occupational shifts in urban Korea

424e Towards meeting the needs of urban female factory workers in peninsular Malaysia

448j Quest for the peaceable kingdom: Urban/rural codes in Roy, Laurence, and Atwood

459i Women and the urban labour market

459j Sex discrimination in the urban labour markets: Some propositions based on Indian evidence

463n Travel patterns and behavior of women in urban areas

466h Indonesian women in development: State theory and urban kampung practice

468e Women's work strategies: An analysis of the organisation of everyday life in an urban neighbourhood

473j The uses of traditional concepts in the development of new urban roles: Cuban women in the United States

Urologist

277h Evaluation and treatment of impotence: The urologist's viewpoint

Uruguay

322m Interview with Cristina Peri Rossi (Uruguay)

U.S.

see United States

U.S.S.R.

see Russia

Usurer

321k The bureaucrat as usurer

Uterine

252j Fact and fancy in the termination of molar pregnancy with particular reference to uterine stimulants

Utero

79c Assessment of risks from DES: An analysis of research on those exposed during pregnancy or in utero

Utilization

427a Introduction: Government response to working women and their families: Values, the policy-making process, and research utilization

446g The utilization of female labor in agriculture

Utopia

27d Ambivalence in the Gynogram: Sade's utopian woman

79kk The biology of utopia: Science fiction perspectives on ectogenesis

131e Coming Home: Four feminist utopias and patriarchal experience

131f Recent feminist utopias

131g A footnote to Russ's "Recent feminist utopias"

131h An ambiguous legacy: The role and position of women in the English Eutopia

181l What if...science and technology in feminist utopias

313c Prisoner in utopia

329j *The Waves*: A utopia of androgyny?

335c From utopian to scientific feminism? Early feminist critiques of the family

366b Women in utopian movements

367g Women in sectarian and utopian groups

383a A new anarchism: Social and political ideas in some recent feminist eutopias

383b Method in her madness: Feminism in the crazy utopian vision of Tiptree's Courier

383c Utopia at the end of a male chauvinist dystopian world: Suzy McKee Charnas's feminist science fiction

383d World views in utopian novels by women

383e The heavenly utopia of Elizabeth Stuart Phelps

383f Wright's *Islandia*: Utopia with problems

383g *The Left Hand of Darkness*: Androgyny and the feminist utopia

383i Opposing necessity and truth: The argument against politics in Doris Lessing's utopian vision

417f Frances Wright: Utopian feminist

417h Housework and utopia: Women and the Owenite socialist communities

417j The Woman's Commonwealth: Utopia in nineteenth-century Texas

417k A utopian female support network: The case of the Henry Street Settlement

417r Utopia in question: Programming women's needs into the technology of tomorrow

417v Women in men's utopias

417w Motherhood in feminist utopias

417x Realities and fictions: Lesbian visions of utopia

417ff Future visions: Today's politics: Feminist utopias in review

441c The machine in utopia: Shaker women and technology

Utrecht

112e Anna Maria van Schurman: The star of Utrecht (Dutch, 1607-1678)

Uttar Pradesh, India

402i Muslim women in Uttar Pradesh: Social mobility and directions of change

Utterance

275w   Reference and truth: The case of sexist and racist utterances

The Vagabond

64i   *The Vagabond*: A vision of androgyny

Vagina

287i   In search of a vagina

354c   Vaginal cancer: An iatrogenic disease?

456m   Vaginal discharge

Valenzuela, Luisa

155j   Women writing about prostitutes: Amalia Jamilis and Luisa Valenzuela

Valuable

364i   Subject or object? Women and the circulation of valuables in highlands New Guinea

Value

3c   Reflections on abortion, values, and the family

3s   Value choices in abortion

27j   Virginia Woolf's Miss Latrobe: The artist's last struggle against masculine values

36d   Value conflicts in biomedical research into future contraceptives

37l   Women's values regarding marriage and the family

49m   College student values and the world of work

65k   Canada's equal pay for work of equal value law

71b   Some effects of childrearing practices on the value systems of Asian-American women

79p   Decisions about handicapped newborns: Values and procedures

79nn   Reflections: Uncovering patriarchal agendas and exploring women-oriented values

118d   The dynamics of female experience: Process models and human values

120c   Gynocentric values and feminist psychology

140v   Teaching value clarification: The example of gender and psychotherapy

162l   Kinship and class consciousness: Family values and work experience among hospital workers in an American southern town

174v   Feminist values: Guidelines for a teaching methodology in women's studies

185h   The evolution of sex roles: The transformation of masculine and feminine values

214h   Styles of leadership: Power and feminine values

217i   Gender as forms of value

270d   Dualism in values toward education of Turkish women

307a   Introduction: New technology, old values

312h   Passionate scholarship: Notes on values, knowing and method in feminist social science

312j   The value of quantitative methodology for feminist research

353i   Doctors, birth control, and social values, 1830-1970

427a   Introduction: Government response to working women and their families: Values, the policy-making process, and research utilization

Vampire

280o   Vampirism and autovampirism

The Vampire Tapestry

114f   Holding fast to feminism and moving beyond: Suzy McKee Charnas's *The Vampire Tapestry*

Vancouver, British Columbia

157k   The 'social evil': Prostitution in Vancouver, 1900-1920

157m   A response to the depression: The local Council of Women of Vancouver

205m   The brightest women of our land: Vancouver clubwomen 1919-1928

205s   Last back: Folklore and the telephone operators in the 1919 Vancouver general strike

Vanderbilt University

303d   Women's studies at Vanderbilt: Toward a strategy for the eighties

Variety

225l   Variety: The pleasure in looking

Vase

117d   Mourners on Greek vases: Remarks on the social history of women

156g   Women on Athenian vases: Problems of interpretation

Vassalage

129cc   Perpetual vassalage

VDT

see Video Display Terminal

Vega, Ana Lydia

74g   From a woman's perspective: The short stories of Rosario Ferré and Ana Lydia Vega

Vehicle

463q   Gender differences in reactions to vehicle environments

Veil

368g   To veil or not to veil: A matter of protest or policy

Vendor

386g   Street vendors

Venereal Disease

4g   Venereal disease and the adolescent

309s   Contraception, abortion and venereal disease: Teenagers' knowledge and the effect of education

353o   Prostitution, venereal disease, and American medicine

461y   Women - victims of the VD rip-off

Venezuela

159l   Venezuelan female criminality: The ideology of diversity and marginality

421n   Working wives in the United States and Venezuela: A cross-national study of decision making

428k   The formation of an ethnic group: Colombian female workers in Venezuela

Venice

33f   Women's roles in early modern Venice: An exceptional case

112b   Caterina Corner, Queen of Cyprus (Venetian, 1454?-1510)

Venice, Italy

184c   Dowries and kinsmen in early Renaissance Venice

Venus

341g   Venus as endomorph

Verbal

90q   The influence of gender on the verbal interactions among principals and staff members: An exploratory study

135c   Wariness and women's language: Two modest verbal studies

136a   Nonverbal behavior: Barrier or agent for sex role change?

136c   Women and nonverbal leadership cues: When seeing is not believing

136g   Gender gestures: Sex, sex-role, and nonverbal communication

136j   The development of sex differences in nonverbal signals: Fallacies, facts, and fantasies

136l   Nonverbal behavior and lesbian/gay orientation

136m   Nonverbal processes in feminist therapy

171k   Sex similarities and differences in language, speech, and nonverbal communication: An annotated bibliography

Verboten

287e   Sexuality verboten: Young and old

Verona

343j   Coming of age in Verona

Verse

197i   Mrs. Spark's verse

442i   Poets and versifiers, singers and signifiers: Women of the Harlem Renaissance

Vice

60b   Male vice and female virtue: Feminism and the politics of prostitution in nineteenth-century Britain

117j   Judith Leyster's *Proposition* - Between virtue and vice

231cc   Male vice and female virtue: Feminism and the politics of prostitution in nineteenth-century Britain

Victim

see also Crime

16o   Rape victims

29j   Physical aggression: Treating the victims

53f   Women as victims of crime

55f   Impact of child pornography and sex rings on child victims and their families

55i   Victim advocacy as therapy

78o   The prostitute as victim

102c   Tiamat and her children: An inquiry into the persistence of mythic archetypes of woman as monster/villainess/victim

111d   Family violence: Women as offenders or victims

135e   The Wife of Bath: Narrator as victim

140n   Victims of violence and psychiatric illness

145q   The female victim: Homicide and women in Imperial Germany

146e   Group therapy with female adolescent incest victims

146g   Individual and group treatment of mothers of incest victims

160i   Colonial wives: Villains or victims?

175x Woman as victim in modern folklore

219a The victim's contribution to sexual offences

219f The role of the judiciary in the failure of the Sexual Offences (Amendment) Act to improve the treatment of the rape victim

219g Crisis intervention with victims of forcible rape: A police perspective

219h Loss and mourning in victims of rape and sexual assault

284b Sexual victimization of children: An urban mental health center survey

284n The victim and justice system - an introduction

284o Interviewing child victims of sex offenders

284p The protection of the child victim of a sexual offense in the criminal justice system

326b Working for and with rape victims: Crisis intervention and advocacy

326f Clinical intervention with boy victims of sexual abuse

326g Group work with preadolescent sexual assault victims

326n Treatment of prostitute victims of sexual assault

348b Hidden from history: Women victims of crime

349j Women as victims: An examination of the results of L.E.A.A.'s National Crime Survey Program

349k The victim in a forcible rape case: A feminist view

349o Secondary battering and alternatives of female victims to spouse abuse

349r Barriers to becoming a "successful" rape victim

359mm The rape victim: Psychodynamic considerations

359nn Identification and treatment of incest victims

404r Breaking cycles of victimization: The shelter as an affirmative institution

419l Rape and rape victims in the *Metamorphoses*

434e Older women as victims of violence

434f Black women: The resilient victims

461w The prostitute as victim

461x Discussion: Legal victim or social victim?

461y Women - victims of the VD rip-off

Victoria, Australia

348f The processing of juveniles in Victoria

Victoria, British Columbia

157e Public and political: Documents of the woman's suffrage campaign in British Columbia, 1871-1917: The view from Victoria

Victorian

see also Nineteenth Century

99d Victorian spinsters: Dutiful daughters, desperate rebels and the transition to the new women

126e Darwin and sexism: Victorian causes, contemporary effects

158c The Victorians, the psychologists, and psychic birth control

238b Passionlessness: An interpretation of Victorian sexual ideology, 1790-1850

238c Davey Crockett as trickster: Pornography, liminality and symbolic inversion in Victorian America

238e From maidenhood to menopause: Sex education for women in Victorian America

256a Class and gender in Victorian England

278d Victorian erotica

286a Lewis Carroll and Victorian morality

286f "Swinburne planteth, Hardy watereth": Victorian views of pain and pleasure in human sexuality

286i Sexuality and the Victorian artist: Dickens and Swinburne

286j On the enrichment of poor monkeys by myth and dream; or how Dickens Rousseauisticized and pre-Freudianized Victorian views of childhood

286k Passion between women in the Victorian novel

286m "Morbid depression alternating with excitement": Sex in Victorian newspapers

286n "Here a captive heart busted": From Victorian sentimentality to modern sexuality

286o The worlds of Victorian sexuality: Work in progress

353d Passionlessness: An interpretation of Victorian sexual ideology, 1790-1850

454g The spiritualist medium: A study of female professionalization in Victorian America

454k Family limitation, sexual control, and domestic feminism in Victorian America

Video Display Terminal

86d The particular problems of video display terminals

209y The health impacts of low-level radiation on VDT operators

209z A union perspective on health hazards of VDTs

Vietnam

68o The schooling of Vietnamese immigrants: Internal colonialism and its impact on women

113e Vietnam: War of insurgency

View

81a The new woman: Changing views of women in the 1920s

116l Women's work: Views from the history of philosophy

Village

see also City

5c Mobilizing village women: Some organizational and management considerations

21e Some changing socioeconomic roles of village women in Malaysia

92d Pakistan: The role of women in reciprocal relationships in a Punjab village

98c Access to village women: Experiences in breaking barriers

98d Becoming an 'insider': Women's privileges in village field work

98e Learning from poor women: A method of village study

104a Aspects of non-capitalist social relations in rural Egypt: The small peasant household in an Egyptian delta village

144d Family and household: Social structures in a German village between the two World Wars

162g Young bees in an empty hive: Relations between brothers-in-law in a south German village around 1800

162o Family fun in Starve Harbor: Custom, history and confrontation in village Newfoundland

177d Village wives

194i The village Mother in Bengal

194k Pox and the terror of childlessness: Images and ideas of the smallpox oddess in a north Indian village

246c Complementarity: The relationship between female and male in the East Sepik village of Bun, Papua New Guinea

325g Hindu women's family and household rites in a north Indian village

325k Islam and tribal women in a village in Iran

350d Resource allocation and the sexual division of labor: A case study of a Moslem Hausa village in northern Nigeria

368l State ideology and village women

388e Women's work and worth in an Acadian maritime village

402k Etiquette among women in Karnataka: Forms of address in the village and the family

457c Doves and magpies: Village women in the Greek Orthodox Church

457f Women, fertility and the worship of gods in a Hindu village

466e Rich woman, poor woman: Occupation differences in a textile producing village in Central Java

Villain

102c Tiamat and her children: An inquiry into the persistence of mythic archetypes of woman as monster/villainess/victim

160i Colonial wives: Villains or victims?

Ville

22f Une contribution au débat concernant le status de la femme dans les villes du Danemark au Moyen-Age

Villette

135o Snow beneath snow: A reconsideration of the virgin of *Villette*

332d The reflecting reader in *Villette*

Vinge, Joan D.

114i From alienation to personal triumph: The science fiction of Joan D. Vinge

Vintage

399b Trampling out the vintage

Violence

see also Abuse

7o Sadomasochism: Eroticized violence, eroticized powerlessness

8c Women and violence

10i Alcohol use and marital violence: Female and male differences in reactions to alcohol

26b Conjoint therapy for the treatment of domestic violence

26h Children's observations of interparental violence

48l Gender roles and sexual violence

50m   The violent event

78k   Violence against women: Some considerations regarding its causes and eliminations

103c   Battered women's shelters and the political economy of sexual violence

105l   Physical violence in a nationally representative sample of American families

111d   Family violence: Women as offenders or victims

111e   Social-psychological research and relevant speculation on the issue of domestic violence

132d   The bonds of love: Rational violence and erotic domination

140n   Victims of violence and psychiatric illness

172e   Our national inferiority complex: A cause for violence? (El Salvador)

212e   Rape and marital violence in the maintenance of male power

215m   Alternative defence: Nonviolent struggle and peace building

219c   Aspects of violence in prostitution

226j   Community responses to violence against women: The case of a battered women's shelter

230c   Pornography: Its effect on violence against women

230f   Sex and violence: A ripple effect

230k   Using psychological research on violent pornography to inform legal change

230l   Bases of liability for injuries produced by media portrayals of violent pornography

230m   Afterword: Sex, violence, and the media: Where do we stand now?

231u   "The mind that burns in each body": Women, rape, and racial violence

241c   Blowing the cover of the protective male: A community study of violence to women

270o   Civil violence in Turkey: Its infrastructural, social and cultural foundations

281f   Incest and sexual violence

297b   Negotiating the problem: The DHSS and research on violence in marriage

304k   Sex-role stereotypes and violence against women

327a   A sociological perspective on the causes of family violence

327b   Discussion: Violence in the family

327d   Discussion: Television violence and the family

327e   Ethnopsychiatric dimensions in family violence

327f   Discussion: Violence and the family in perspective

327g   Functions of the police and the justice system in family violence

349p   The underside of married life: Power, influence, and violence

349q   An interview with Sara Smith - One woman's experience with the cycle of violence

354i   Medicine and patriarchal violence: The social construction of a "private" event

360j   Violence against women: Implications for mental health policy

362c   Muslim Middle Eastern women's participation in violent political conflict: Causes and characteristics

392f   Crimes of violence by women

397c   The coming-out process: Violence against lesbians

404w   Prostitution and sexual violence

418g   Domestic violence: Battered women in Britain in the 1970s

434e   Older women as victims of violence

Virgin

72c   The cult of virginity

135o   Snow beneath snow: A reconsideration of the virgin of *Villette*

154d   Virginity as an ideal in Christine de Pizan's *Cité des Dames*

190m   Virginity rituals and chastity control during puberty: Cross-cultural patterns

194c   In quest of the Black Virgin: She is black because she is black

Virgin of Guadalupe

194a   The Virgin of Guadalupe and the female self-image: A Mexican case history

Virginia

303c   Mary Munford and higher education for women in Virginia

417q   Twin Oaks: A feminist looks at indigenous socialism in the United States

The Virginian

384l   The Virginian and Antonia Shimerda: Different sides of the western coin

Virility

117p   Virility and domination in early twentieth-century vanguard painting

Virtue

31a   Private rights and public virtues: Women, the family, and democracy

60b   Male vice and female virtue: Feminism and the politics of prostitution in nineteenth-century Britain

117j   Judith Leyster's *Proposition* - Between virtue and vice

231cc Male vice and female virtue: Feminism and the politics of prostitution in nineteenth-century Britain

Visibility

84p   Why has the sex/gender system become visible only now?

132p   Visibility and difference: Black women in history and literature - pieces of a paper and some ruminations

176b   Black lesbians in academia: Visible invisibility

346c   Making women visible

Vision

97e   Public education and the discourse of crisis, power and vision

126a   The genesis of feminist visions for transforming the liberal arts curriculum

256i   The doubled vision of feminist theory

266a   New maps of development: New visions of maturity

310ee Feminist ethics, ecology and vision

312m   Women's studies as a strategy for change: Between criticism and vision

383b   Method in her madness: Feminism in the crazy utopian vision of Tiptree's Courier

383i   Opposing necessity and truth: The argument against politics in Doris Lessing's utopian vision

389d   Anna Jameson (1794-1860): Sacred art and social vision

417x   Realities and fictions: Lesbian visions of utopia

417ff Future visions: Today's politics: Feminist utopias in review

448a   The city as catalyst for Flora Tristan's vision of social change

448m   Another view of the "City upon a Hill": The prophetic vision of Adrienne Rich

Visionary

188e   The German visionary: Hildegard of Bingen

188j   The Swedish visionary: Saint Bridget

188k   The Tuscan visionary: Saint Catherine of Siena

379k   "My spirit eye": Some functions of spiritual and visionary experience in the lives of five black women preachers, 1810-1880

Visual

130o   Women and the visual arts

136d   Visual behavior and dominance in women and men

Vital Statistics

258c   Vital statistics

Vivien, Renée

448c   Return to Mytilène: Renée Vivien and the city of women

Vocabulary

225r   The misunderstanding: Toward a more precise sexual vocabulary

Vocation

see also Employment

64a   A womanly vocation (Colette)

93i   Vocational training, the labor market, and the unions

337a   Vocational aspirations and job realities

404z   Vocational rehabilitation: Options for women

Voice

132t   In a different voice: Women's conceptions of self and of morality

135a   Is there a female voice? Joyce Carol Oates replies

187a   Muffled voices: The lives of consecrated women in the fourth century

247g   Dis-embodying the female voice

294i   Introduction: St. Kilda voices

306r   Authentic voices

331b   Voice and audience: The emotional world of the *cantigas de amigo*

356j   Women's speech: The voice of feminism

399xx A rainbow of voices

442m   Women's voices

449f   A woman's voice: The poetry of Yungtzu

462q   My voice...and many others

Voltaire

130r   Voltaire and women

Volume

164d   Disregarded designs: Jane Austen's sense of the volume

Voluntary

6e   Women's voluntary associations

461q   Voluntary childlessness

461r Discussion: Voluntary sterilization in childless women

Volunteer

390o From balaclavas to bayonets: Women's voluntary war work, 1939-41

440n Volunteer work as work: Some theoretical considerations

Vormärz

145e The reading habits of women in the *Vormärz*

Vote

see also Suffrage, Women's Suffrage

119c 'Mothers, vote labour!' The state, the labour movement and working-class mothers, 1900-1918

157j Helena Gutteridge: Votes for women and trade unions

173e Abortion and the presidential election of 1976: A multivariate analysis of voting behavior

226h Female state senators as cue givers: ERA roll-call voting, 1972-1979

378j Women and voting in Britain

Vow

152g Gay men and women and the vowed life

325j The controversial vows of urban Muslim women in Iran

Voyage

20h The dark voyage: *The Edible Woman* as romance

The Voyage Out

202d Some female versions of pastoral: *The Voyage Out* and matriarchal mythologies

330e "Surely order did prevail": Virginia Woolf and *The Voyage Out*

Vs. Ms.

275o Vs. Ms.

275p Against "Vs. Ms."

275q Beyond the miserable vision of "Vs. Ms."

Vulnerability

10e Vulnerability to the biomedical consequences of alcoholism and alcohol-related problems among women

370k The story of Swema: Female vulnerability in nineteenth century East Africa

W.C.T.U.

see Women's Christian Temperance Union

Waerenskjold, Elise

175j Elise Waerenskjold: A modern on the prairie

Wage

see also Pay

18j Country roads take me home: The political economy of wage-labor migration in an eastern Kentucky community

50e The 'family wage'

65a "A want of harmony": Perspectives on wage discrimination and comparable worth

65c Some psychological factors affecting job segregation and wages

66d Wage setting and collective bargaining

67d Wage setting and collective bargaining

89l Occupational segregation, wages and profits when employers discriminate by race and sex

139g Women, gender relations and wage labour

153e Nonwage labor and subsistence

153o Wages, consumption, and survival: Working class households in Puerto Rico in the 1930's

177i Wage earners in Hong Kong

213b Motherhood and waged work: West Indian, Asian and white mothers compared

227m When is a wage not a wage?

227q Wages against housework

227r Wages for housework - political and theoretical considerations

272h Work experience, job segregation, and wages

335d Production rules OK? Waged work and the family

355l Household work, wage work, and sexual equality

362d The mobilization of Iraqi women into the wage labor force

380l Women's work and the family wage in Canada

393a Wage earner and mother: Compatibility of roles on a Cameroon plantation

418b A commentary on theories of female wage labour

470f Migrant women and wage labour: The case of West Indian women in Britain

Waggoner, Electra

175s Glamor girl called Electra

Wagiadj

333k Women and land rights: Kiuk and Wagaidj women in the Darwin area

Waksuk

269g Watch that pot or the *waksuk* will eat you up: An analysis of male and female roles in Rama Indian myth

Wales

159e Female crime in England and Wales

334a The normal paradigms of a woman's life in the Irish and Welsh texts

334d Property interests in the classical Welsh law of women

334e The status of women and the practice of marriage in late-medieval Wales

334f The European legal context of the Welsh law of matrimonial property

Walk

150ff Shoes are made for walking

409c Emma Clery in *Stephen Hero*: A young woman walking proudly through the decayed city

Walker, Alice

40mm Writing *The Color Purple*

40nn Alice Walker: The black woman artist as wayward

40oo Alice Walker's women: In search of some peace of mind

196g I sign my mother's name: Alice Walker, Dorothy West and Paule Marshall

450b Alice Walker's celebration of self in southern generations

Walker, Margaret

40pp Fields watered with blood: Myth and ritual in the poetry of Margaret Walker

40qq Music as theme: The blues mode in the works of Margaret Walker

Walkout

199j Computers, ward secretaries, and a walkout in a Southern hospital

Wally, die Zweiflerin

32e *Wally, die Zweiflerin* and *Madonna*: A discussion of sex-socialization in the nineteenth century

Walsh, Adela Pankhurst

390p The unwritten history of Adela Pankhurst Walsh

Walters Art Gallery

389n Dorothy Eugenia Miner (1904-1973): The varied career of a medievalist: Scholar and keeper of manuscripts, librarian and editor at the Walters Art Gallery

War

see also Armed Forces, Army, Combatant, names of wars

113c Russia: Revolution and war

113d Yugoslavia: War of resistance

113e Vietnam: War of insurgency

113f Algeria: Anticolonial war

113g Israel: The longest war

205k Women on campus in British Columbia: Strategies for survival, years of war and peace, 1906-1920

215j Letter to my neighbour: Nuclear war and the countryside

215s Contemplating a nuclear future: Nuclear war, politics and the individual

241d Men and war: Status, class and the social reproduction of masculinity

278b 'Last Night's Rambles': Restoration literature and the war between the sexes

444b "I don't call that *Volksgemeinschaft*": Women, class, and war in Nazi Germany

454f The war within a war: Women nurses in the Union Army

462n Why women need the war god

464e Prologue to a feminist critique of war and politics

War Department

81i All pink sisters: The War Department and the feminist movement in the 1920s

Warner, Sylvia Townsend

448g A wilderness of one's own: Feminist fantasy novels of the twenties: Rebecca West and Sylvia Townsend Warner

Warren, Mercy Otis

112j Mercy Otis Warren: Playwright, poet, and historian of the American revolution (American, 1728-1814)

399t Mercy Warren, satirist of the revolution

Warrior

148j "Warrior women" - Sex role alternatives for Plains Indian women

282j Women, warriors, and patriarchs

462o Feminist liberation theology and Yahweh as holy warrior: An analysis of symbol

Wary

135c Wariness and women's language: Two modest verbal studies

Wash
81h   Two washes in the morning and a bridge party at night: The American housewife between the wars

Washington, D.C.
133o   Media reaction to the 1979 gay march on Washington
264d   Black women in a southern city: Washington, D.C., 1890-1920
349h   The woman participant in Washington's riots
399ss   The Washington area feminist theatre

Washington (State)
93s   Beyond equal pay for equal work: Comparable worth in the state of Washington

Wasteland
215a   Beyond the wasteland

Water
353r   "All hail to pure cold water!"
395e   Water and sanitation-related health constraints on women's contribution to the economic development of communities

Watercolor
474c   The parable of the cave or: In praise of watercolors

Watson, John B.
158f   "Give me a dozen healthy infants": John B. Watson's popular advice on childrearing, women, and the family

Watts, Walter Theodore
196j   Closer than a brother: Swinburne and Watts-Dunton

Waugh, Catherine G.
108k   Women as law clerks: Catherine G. Waugh

The Waves
329j   *The Waves*: A utopia of androgyny?
330k   Nature and community: A study of cyclical reality in *The Waves*

Wayne County, MI
26g   Family trouble clinic: Family service of Detroit and Wayne County

Wealth
156n   Women and wealth
364e   Female power and the inequality of wealth and motherhood in north-western Portugal

Weapon
36j   The depo-provera weapon
215i   Fuel for the nuclear arms race: Nuclear power and nuclear weapons
215n   The women who wire up the weapons: Workers in armament factories

A Weave of Women
417y   Neither Arcadia nor Elysium: E.M. Broner's *A Weave of Women*

Weaver
145n   Social insurance and the family work of Oberlausitz home weavers in the late nineteenth century

Web
222g   The diary of a web spinner

Wedding
see also Bride, Dowry, Marriage
150w   Wedding

Wedlock
309g   The effect of government policies on out-of-wedlock sex and pregnancy
408f   Women against wedlock: The reluctant brides of Golden Age drama

Weep
175d   The weeping woman: La Llorona

Weight
29n   Weight disorders: Overweight and anorexia
65e   Effect of choice of factors and factor weights in job evaluation
190c   Age at menarche and year of birth in relation to adult height and weight among Caucasian, Japanese, and Chinese women living in Hawaii
304i   Women, weight, and health
341c   A woman's body in a man's world: A review of findings on body image and weight control

Weil, Simone
30r   Sister/outsider: Some thoughts on Simone Weil

Weimar
see also Germany
231g   The new woman and the rationalization of sexuality in Weimar Germany
336a   Introduction: Women in Weimar and Nazi Germany
336b   Beyond *Kinder, Küche, Kirche*: Weimar women in politics and work
336f   Mother's day in the Weimar Republic

Welfare
see also Social Welfare
60r   Women on welfare: Public policy and institutional racism
178f   The public welfare system: Regulation and dehumanization
217b   Women and the welfare state: The transition from private to public dependence
217d   Caring as women's work in the welfare state
245k   The place of the family in the origins of the welfare state
263a   Women and welfare work: Demystifying the myth of disembeddedness
335h   The state, welfare and women's dependence
344bb   Farewell to alms: Women's fare under welfare
400c   Women's income earning activities and family welfare in Bangladesh
440a   The end is where we start from: Women and welfare since 1901
440f   Women as welfare recipients: Women, poverty and the state
440g   Sex and money in the welfare state

Well
396f   Well woman clinics: A positive approach to women's health

Well Being
190aa   Implications for women's health and well-being
296f   Mastery and pleasure: A two-factor model of well-being of women in the middle years
411g   The psychological well-being of women in the middle years

458e   Working women versus homemakers: Retirement resources and correlates of well-being

The Well of Loneliness
176l   Journey into otherness: Teaching *The Well of Loneliness*

Welty, Eudora
384s   Pioneering the imagination: Eudora Welty's *The Robber Bridegroom*
451g   The world of love: The fiction of Eudora Welty
451h   Love and separateness in Eudora Welty

Wesley, John
412c   Women of the word: Selected leadership roles of women in Mr. Wesley's Methodism

Wesleyan
367h   Women and revivalism: The Puritan and Wesleyan traditions

West (United States)
384p   The young girl in the West: Disenchantment in Jean Stafford's short fiction
384r   Where the West begins: Constance Rourke's images of her own frontierland West
414a   Women in literature of the West

West Bengal, India
101i   Two faces of protest: Alternative forms of women's mobilization in West Bengal and Maharashtra

West Germany
see Germany

West Indian Woman
213b   Motherhood and waged work: West Indian, Asian and white mothers compared
213c   The second generation: West Indian female school-leavers
470f   Migrant women and wage labour: The case of West Indian women in Britain

West Indies
39w   Women's role in West Indian society
39z   Female status, the family and male dominance in a West Indian community
39cc   West Indian characteristics of the black Carib
473h   Adaptive strategies and social networks of women in St. Kitts

West Sumatra
300c   The Minangkabau woman: Cultural centre or ethnic symbol?

West Virginia
316p   Status report on the women's movement as indexed by a "Festival of Women" in West Virginia, Fall 1978

West, Dorothy
196g   I sign my mother's name: Alice Walker, Dorothy West and Paule Marshall

West, Rebecca
448g   A wilderness of one's own: Feminist fantasy novels of the twenties: Rebecca West and Sylvia Townsend Warner

Western
401k   The influence of western women on the anti-footbinding movement 1840-1911

445f Mari Sandoz and western biography

445k Conrad Richter's southwestern ladies

445l Westering and woman: A thematic study of Kesey's *One Flew Over the Cuckoo's Nest* and Fisher's *Mountain Man*

445r "On the *other* side of the mountains": The westering experiences in the fiction of Ethel Wilson

445s Tradition of the exile: Judith Wright's Australian "West"

Wet Nurse

184m Parisian infants and Norman wet nurses in the early nineteenth century: A statistical study

Wharton, Edith

17i Cool Diana and the Blood-red muse: Edith Wharton on innocence and art

27h Beauty in distress: *Daniel Deronda* and *The House of Mirth*

127c "The temptation to be a beautiful object": Double standard and double bind in *The House of Mirth*

135k Edith Wharton and the ghost story

180m Mothers, daughters, and incest in the late novels of Edith Wharton

451b Introduction to *The Collected Short Stories of Edith Wharton*

What

474k What it is I think I'm doing anyhow

Wheaton College

314g Toward a balanced curriculum: Wheaton College

314t Wheaton's assessment process: A case study and its lessons

Where

359ww Where do we go from here?

Whetmore, Edward

131n A personal response to Whetmore's "A female captain's enterprise"

Whirlwind

40h Gwendolyn Brooks: Poet of the whirlwind

White

see also Caucasian, Ethnic, Race

14f Racism - a white issue

23b Black sisterhood: The situation of urban aboriginal women and their relationship to the white women's movement

41c Sources of life satisfaction: The different worlds of black women and white women

43s Confrontation: Black/white

73k Achieving the dreams beyond tradition: Counseling white ethnic American girls

81d Flawed victories: The experiences of black and white women workers in Durham during the 1930s

174p Unlearning complicity, remembering resistance: White women's anti-racism education

213b Motherhood and waged work: West Indian, Asian and white mothers compared

222e Surviving in a predominantly white male institution

226c Conceptions of the "Political": White activists in Atlanta

244b White mothers in the American civil rights movements

303j Racial myths and attitudes among white female students at the University of Florida

359w A study of attitudes toward menarche in white middle-class American adolescent girls

387r Job opportunities of black and white working-class women

398c Black woman professor — white university

462i White women and racism

White Collar

see also Employment

390d Educated and white-collar women in the 1880s

426e Moving forward, standing still: Women in white collar jobs

White, Ellen G.

353z Ministries of healing: Mary Baker Eddy, Ellen G. White, and the religion of health

Wholeness

40bb The closing of the circle: Movement from division to wholeness in Paule Marshall's fiction

Why

271a Why?

Wicce

453q Goddess worship in Wicce

Wide Sargasso Sea

332f The sisterhood of Jane Eyre and Antoinette Cosway

Widow

see also Family, Wife

53d Health effects of becoming widowed

317f The widowed family member

317h Economic status of late middle-aged widows

344o Women and widowhood: The suffering beyond grief

344x What price independence? Social reactions to lesbians, spinsters, widows, and nuns

359hh Group work with widows

375b Widows' rights in Anglo-Saxon law

379d Aristocratic widows in fifteenth-century England

401h Widows and remarriage in Ming and early Qing China

454c Widowhood in eighteenth-century Massachusetts: A problem in the history of the family

472h Widowhood: The last stage in wifedom

472i Widow-to-widow: The elderly widow and mutual help

Wife

see also Family

8d Wife abuse: Culture as destiny

23f The Parliamentary wife: Participant in the 'two-person single career'

26i Coping with wife abuse: Personal and social networks

52t Wife and/or worker: Sex role concepts of Canadian female students

71n Asian wives of U.S. servicemen: Women in triple jeopardy

87d Young marrieds: Wives' employment and family role structure

89q Wives' labor force behavior and family consumption patterns

89r The employment of wives and the inequality of family income

103n The politics of wife abuse

105c Marital expectations of wives in contemporary Poland

105h Developing family invulnerability to stress: Coping patterns and strategies wives employ in managing family separations

105k Marriage, estrangement, sobriety and recidivism: Some crucial process variables in the case of alcoholic men and their wives

106b Philosopher queens and private wives: Plato on women and the family

140o Overview: The "wife-beater's wife" reconsidered

156e The god's wife of Amun in the 18th dynasty in Egypt

160a Incorporation and exclusion: Oxford academics' wives

160b Ambivalence and dedication: Academic wives in Cambridge University, 1870-1970

160c Police wives: A reflection of police concepts of order and control

160d Camp followers: A note on wives of the armed services

160e The suitable wife: Preparation for marriage in London and Rhodesia/Zimbabwe

160f Shell wives in limbo

160g The negation of structure: A note on British council wives

160h Settler wives in southern Rhodesia: A case study

160i Colonial wives: Villains or victims?

160j Memsahibs in colonial Malaya: A study of European wives in a British colony and protectorate, 1900-1940

165c The dark side of marriage: Battered wives and the domination of women

170d The caring wife

177d Village wives

192t Lucy Duran - Wife, mother, and organizer

203c The household as workplace: Wives, husbands, and children

205t A union man's wife: The ladies' auxiliary movement in the IWA, the Lake Cowichan experience

211e Marriages made in heaven? Battered Jewish wives

227d Working-class wives

244f The roles of Greek husbands and wives: Definitions and fulfillment

270a Duofocal family structure and an alternative model of husband-wife relationship

323v Wives supporting the strike

323w From ladies' auxiliaries to wives' committees

324d Attitudes toward women working: Changes over time and implications for the labor-force behaviors of husbands and wives

347l Putting down sisters and wives: Tongan women and colonization

355i Contributions to household labor: Comparing wives' and husbands' reports

359ii Psychosocial aspects of wife battering

359jj Wife battering and the maintenance of gender roles: A sociopsychological perspective

370j Slave wives, free sisters: Bakongo women and slavery c.1700-1850

375g The law of husband and wife in nineteenth-century America: Changing views of divorce

379c The planter's wife revisited: Women, equity law, and the Chancery Court in seventeenth-century Maryland

394m The president's wife: A changing role — observations of a chancellor's wife

401i One woman's rise to power: Cheng I's wife and the pirates

408h A school for wives: Women in eighteenth-century Spanish theater

412g Ministry through marriage: Methodist clergy wives on the trans-Mississippi frontier

412h Hispanic clergy wives: Their contribution to United Methodism in the southwest, later nineteenth century to the present

421n Working wives in the United States and Venezuela: A cross-national study of decision making

421o Wife-employment and the emergence of egalitarian marital role prescriptions: 1900-1974

461u Wife beating: A product of sociosexual development

461v Discussion: Psychoanalytic reflections on the "beaten wife syndrome"

472h Widowhood: The last stage in wifedom

Wife of Bath
135e The Wife of Bath: Narrator as victim

Wilde, Oscar
286l Fallen women, lost children: Wilde and the theatre in the nineties

Williams, Joan
450p The career of Joan Williams: Problems in assessment

Wills
22b Wills, deeds, and charters as sources for the history of medieval women

Willy
196h The magic spinning wheel: Straw to gold - Colette, Willy and Sido

Wilson, Edith Bolling
61m Edith Bolling Wilson: A documentary view

Wilson, Ethel
445r "On the *other* side of the mountains": The westering experiences in the fiction of Ethel Wilson

Win
432k The overemphasis on winning: A philosophical look

Wind
40j A candle in a gale wind

The Wind
445o Dorothy Scarborough's critique of the frontier experience in *The Wind*

Windmill
303l Tilting at windmills in the Quixotic South

Windward Islands
473g Sex and status: Women in St. Vincent

Winter's Tale
330i *To the Lighthouse*: Virginia Woolf's Winter's Tale

Wisconsin
128f The politics of mutual frustration: Socialists and suffragists in New York and Wisconsin

Wisdom
84j The man of professional wisdom

Wister, Owen
384l The Virginian and Antonia Shimerda: Different sides of the western coin

Witch
194m Rangda the witch

229pp WITCH: Spooking the patriarchy during the late sixties

Witchcraft
156c Women and witchcraft in ancient Assyria

229e Witchcraft as goddess religion

229u Feminist witchcraft: Controlling our own inner space

Witness
74f Elena Poniatowska: Witness for the people

165b Would you believe this woman? Prosecutorial screening for "credible" witnesses and a problem of justice

284q Special techniques for child witnesses

318c Olivia Manning: Witness to history

Wives and Daughters
180i Mothers and daughters in *Wives and Daughters*: A study of Elizabeth Gaskell's last novel

WMS
see Women's Missionary Society

Wohmann, Gabriele
321 Sociological implications of Gabriele Wohmann's critical reception

Wolcott, Marion Post
81g Photographing women: The farm security administration work of Marion Post Wolcott

Wolfe, Thomas
448n Sister to Faust: The city's "hungry" woman as heroine

Wollstonecraft, Mary
27c Frankenstein's daughter: Mary Shelley and Mary Wollstonecraft

125c Mary Wollstonecraft: Sexuality and women's rights

135j The woman at the window: Ann Radcliffe in the novels of Mary Wollstonecraft and Jane Austen

The Woman Warrior
254c The artist as hero in Maxine Hong Kingston's *The Woman Warrior*

452k The metaphysics of matrilinearism in women's autobiography: Studies of Mead's *Blackberry Winter*, Hellman's *Pentimento*, Angelou's *I Know Why the Caged Bird Sings*, and Kingston's *The Woman Warrior*

452m Towards a theory of form in feminist autobiography: Kate Millett's *Flying* and *Sita*; Maxine Hong Kingston's *The Woman Warrior*

The Woman's Commonwealth
417j The Woman's Commonwealth: Utopia in nineteenth-century Texas

Woman's Land Army
61h The Woman's Land Army, World War I

Woman's Suffrage
see also Suffrage, Vote
157e Public and political: Documents of the woman's suffrage campaign in British Columbia, 1871-1917: The view from Victoria

379m The limitations of sisterhood: Elizabeth Cady Stanton and division in the American suffrage movement, 1875-1902

379o Jewish involvement in the New York City woman suffrage movement

412n The laity rights movement, 1906-1918: Women's suffrage in the Methodist Episcopal Church, South

414h Woman's suffrage, Oklahoma style, 1890-1918

Womanhood
81e The projection of a new womanhood: The movie moderns in the 1920's

121b The wayward nun beneath the hill: Emily Dickinson and the mysteries of womanhood

229i Ancient mirrors of womanhood

289l Continuity of self-actualization: Womanhood in climacterium and old age

340e Mbuti womanhood

417u The linguistic transformation of womanhood

445h Hamlin Garland and the cult of true womanhood

450c Gail Godwin and the ideal of southern womanhood

454i The cult of true womanhood: 1820-1860

Womanpower
229s Womanpower: Energy re-sourcement

Womb
12d The tyrannical womb: Menstruation and menopause

195g Womb envy: An explanatory concept

310ff A womb of one's own

435h The womb factor: Pregnancy policies and employment of women

Women Centered
79a Reproductive technologies: The birth of a women-centered analysis

Women for Peace
167a Starting a movement: Frauen für frieden (Women for Peace, West Germany)

167b Organising at the grassroots: Vrouwen voor vrede (Women for Peace, the Netherlands)

Women Inc.
16j The first two years: A profile of women entering Women, Inc.

Women of Color
39ee Images of the woman of color in Brazilian literature: O Cortico, Clara Dos Anjos, Gabriela Cravo E Canela, and O Quinze

174n Women of color Califia

Women of the People
379q Responses to the political activism of Women of the People in revolutionary Paris, 1789-1793

Women's Christian Temperance Union
412q For god and home and native land: The W.C.T.U.'s image of woman in the late nineteenth century
413c The origins of the women's movement in New Zealand: The Women's Christian Temperance Union 1885-1895

Women's Community Health Center
16h A pelvic teaching program

Women's Health Center
16f The feminist Women's Health Center

Women's History
see also Herstory, History
61b An abundance of riches: The women's history sources survey
117d Mourners on Greek vases: Remarks on the social history of women
126p Human sexuality: New insights from women's history
145a Current research on German women's history in the nineteenth century
145r An English-language bibliography on European and American women's history
147dd The history of women's intercollegiate athletics in Ohio, 1945-1972
205a "Sundays always make me think of home": Time and place in Canadian women's history
205j Six saucepans to one: Domestic science vs. the home in British Columbia 1900-1930
205bb From home to house: Women in the BC legislature
206h A woman's home is her factory
210g Labor markets and old ladies' homes
234g Social history and women's history
234h The limitations of demography for women's history
264a Women's history and the revision of southern history
306h Dusting the mirror: Researching women's history
344r "Union is power": Sketches from women's labor history
353q The perils of feminist history
412a Women's history/everyone's history
454a American women and domestic culture: An approach to women's history

Women's Issues
307ee Tomorrow is a woman's issue
464b Overcoming the barriers: An approach to the study of how women's issues are kept from the political agenda

Women's Liberation
see also Emancipate, Liberate, Feminism
38s The women's liberation movement: Understanding black women's attitudes
174e All-women classes and the struggle for women's liberation
181e Technology, housework, and women's liberation: A theoretical analysis
192f The rise and demise of women's liberation: A class analysis
192g Toward a science of women's liberation

212l Female performers on a male stage: The first women's liberation movement and the authority of men
227h The political economy of women's liberation
325l No women's liberation: The heritage of a woman prophet in modern Japan
344ee The women's liberation movement: Its origins, structure, activities, and ideas
405b The women's liberation issue in nineteenth century Russia

Women's Missionary Society
205e The response of the WMS to the immigration of Asian women, 1888-1942

Women's Movement
see also Movement
22j New trends in the Danish women's movement, 1970-1978
23b Black sisterhood: The situation of urban aboriginal women and their relationship to the white women's movement
35c Political ideology, sociobiology, and the U.S. women's rights movement
39o Discrimination against Afro-American women in the woman's movement, 1830-1920
42b The American woman's movement
60j Difference and domination in the women's movement: The dialectic of theory and practice
76a The women's movement and motherhood
101c The Indian women's movement: A struggle for women's rights or national liberation?
101h The Indian women's movement and national development: An overview
123d What the women's movement has done to American history
192e Toward a democratic women's movement in the United States
212q Sexual assumptions in the women's movement
262h Context of change: The women's movement as a political process
305v Immigrant women: The silent partners of the women's movement
305w Beyond barriers: Native women and the women's movement
316n Resistance to the women's movement in the United States: The ERA controversy as prototype
316p Status report on the women's movement as indexed by a "Festival of Women" in West Virginia, Fall 1978
319f Symbolic strategies for change: A discussion of the Chicana women's movement
321l The women's movement and social justice
323y Building links: Labour and the women's movement
328j Virginia Woolf and the women's movement
336g "Professional" housewives: Stepsisters of the women's movement
369n Reform and/or revolution: Towards a unified women's movement
387b Toward a sociotechnological theory of the women's movement
388l The contemporary American women's movement

394a The women's movement and the university
413c The origins of the women's movement in New Zealand: The Women's Christian Temperance Union 1885-1895
413e The road ahead for the women's movement - out of the womb and into the world
430e A historical background to the women's movement in Iran
430f The post-revolutionary women's movement in Iran
436k The impact of the women's movement and legislative activity of women MPs on social development
440j The women's movement's fandango with the state: The movement's role in public policy since 1972

Women's Peace Army
390i The Women's Peace Army

Women's Pentagon Action USA
167e All is connectedness: Scenes from the Women's Pentagon Action USA

Women's Question
430d The attitude of the Iranian left to the women's question

Women's Rights
see also Right
35c Political ideology, sociobiology, and the U.S. women's rights movement
45c Do changes in women's rights change women's moral judgements?
96a Introduction: An historical view of psychotherapy and women's rights
101c The Indian women's movement: A struggle for women's rights or national liberation?
101e Catalysts or helpers? British feminists, Indian women's rights, and Indian independence
125c Mary Wollstonecraft: Sexuality and women's rights
223l Abortion and a woman's right to decide
316o Women's right to full participation in shaping society's course: An evolving constitutional precept
368f An analysis of Fida'i and Mujahidin positions on women's rights

Women's Service Corps
205cc Joan Kennedy and the British Columbia Women's Service Corps

Women's Studies
14a Introduction: The politics of black women's studies
14g Racism and women's studies
60n Issues of race and class in women's studies: A Puerto Rican woman's thoughts
122b Black studies/women's studies: Points of convergence
122f The social determination of science: Some implications for women's studies
174b The politics of black women's studies
174f The new right challenges women's studies: The Long Beach women's studies program
174v Feminist values: Guidelines for a teaching methodology in women's studies
176s One out of thirty: Lesbianism in women's studies textbooks
176bb A lesbian perspective on women's studies

249i Career politics and the practice of women's studies

266d Evaluation issues in women's studies

298f The history, development, organization and position of women's studies in the Sudan

303d Women's studies at Vanderbilt: Toward a strategy for the eighties

303g Teaching women's studies at the University of Arkansas

306o Oral history as a resource in teaching women's studies

311a Is women's studies an academic discipline?

311b Learning women's studies

311c Women's studies as an academic discipline: Why and how to do it

311f Selected annotated bibliography of articles on theories of women's studies

312a Introduction: Theories of women's studies and the autonomy/integration debate

312c Is women's studies an academic discipline?

312d Women's studies as an academic discipline: Why and how to do it

312e Learning women's studies

312m Women's studies as a strategy for change: Between criticism and vision

312n In praise of theory: The case for women's studies

312o Selected annotated bibliography of articles on theories of women's studies

314a Where does integration fit: The development of women's studies

314i The women's studies program: Yale University

314k Black studies and women's studies: An overdue partnership

314n Resources in black women's studies

315e A dialogue critical issues in women's studies: Race, class, and sexual orientation

315i Can a man teach women's studies?

315k Women's studies and the re-vision of liberal education: "What is a nice girl/boy like you doing here?"

351g Women's studies at the secondary school level

351k Studying women's studies: A guide to archival research

351l Women's studies: A discipline takes shape

394f A women's studies plan for Wisconsin

394g The women's studies program at Milwaukee

398j Women's studies and men's careers: How the 'social problem' of women in education maintained the academic status of men in the 1970s

Women's Trade Union League (WTUL)

124j The Women's Trade Union League school for women organizers

292a The Women's Trade Union League training school for women organizers, 1914-1926

399c Friendship and ritual in the WTUL

Wonderland

134h Alice in the consumer wonderland

Woolf, Virginia

27j Virginia Woolf's Miss Latrobe: The artist's last struggle against masculine values

30c A portrait of the *Puttana* as a middle-aged Woolf scholar

30i New combinations: Learning from Virginia Woolf

108l The female sociograph: The theater of Virigina Woolf's letters

125r Virginia Woolf: The life of natural happiness

180n Reentering paradise: Cather, Colette, Woolf and their mothers

180o How light a *Lighthouse* for today's women?

196i Virginia Woolf and her violin: Mothering, madness, and music

202b Woolf's 'Magical garden of women'

202d Some female versions of pastoral: *The Voyage Out* and matriarchal mythologies

202e *Jacob's Room* as comedy: Woolf's parodic *Bildungsroman*

202f *Mrs Dalloway*: The communion of saints

202g Where the spear plants grew: The Ramsays' marriage in *To the Lighthouse*

202h Why is *Orlando* difficult?

202j The politics of city space in *The Years*: Street, love, pillar boxes and bridges

202k What is to console us?: The politics of deception in Woolf's short stories

202l Virginia Woolf's last words on words: *Between the Acts* and 'Anon'

328a Introduction: Virginia Woolf aslant

328b The niece of a nun: Virginia Woolf, Caroline Stephen, and the cloistered imagination

328c Virginia liked Elizabeth

328d Fathers in general: The patriarchy in Virginia Woolf's fiction

328e 1897: Virginia Woolf at fifteen

328f Isis unveiled: Virginia Woolf's use of Egyptian myth

328g Political aesthetics: Virginia Woolf and Dorothy Richardson

328h An uneasy sisterhood: Virginia Woolf and Katherine Mansfield

328i Clarissa Dalloway's respectable suicide

328j Virginia Woolf and the women's movement

328k A track of our own: Typescript drafts of *The Years*

328l Theater of war: Virginia Woolf's *Between the Acts*

328m Virginia Woolf in her fifties

329a Virginia Woolf and the intellectual origins of Bloomsbury

329b Virginia Woolf and her violin: Mothering, madness and music

329c Virginia Woolf and Julia Stephen: The distaff side of history

329d The squirrel's heart beat and the death of a moth

329e The anti-madonna in the work and thought of Virginia Woolf

329f Virginia Woolf and the problem of the body

329g 'The prime minister': A key to *Mrs. Dalloway*

329h Private and public consciousness in *Mrs. Dalloway* and *To the Lighthouse*

329i Speech acts in *To the Lighthouse*

329j *The Waves*: A utopia of androgyny?

329k *The Years*: A feminist novel

329l A common sitting room: Virginia Woolf's critique of women writers

329m 'What right have I, a woman?': Virginia Woolf's reading notes on Sidney and Spenser

329n Virginia Woolf and the classics: Every Englishman's prerogative transmuted into fictional art

329o The whole contention between Mr. Bennett and Mrs. Woolf, revisited

329p Combining 'the advantages of act and fiction': Virginia Woolf's biographies of Vita Sackville-West, Flush, and Roger Fry

330a Introduction: Virginia Woolf, the novel, and a chorus of voices

330b Hunting the moth: Virginia Woolf and the creative imagination

330c Virginia Woolf's narrators and the art of "life itself"

330d Forms of the Woolfian short story

330e "Surely order did prevail": Virgina Woolf and *The Voyage Out*

330f Enchanted organs, magic bells: *Night and Day* as comic opera

330g The form of fact and fiction: *Jacob's Room* as paradigm

330h *Mrs. Dalloway*: The unguarded moment

330i *To the Lighthouse*: Virginia Woolf's Winter's Tale

330j *Orlando* and its genesis: Venturing and experimenting in art, love, and sex

330k Nature and community: A study of cyclical reality in *The Waves*

330l Nature and history in *The Years*

330m Woolf's peculiar comic world: *Between the Acts*

332h Narrative structure(s) and female development: The case of *Mrs. Dalloway*

356u Unmaking and making in *To the Lighthouse*

448f Tradition and revision: The classic city novel and Virginia Woolf's *Night and Day*

Word

17q Zora Neale Hurston: Changing her own words

30e Music into words

40y My words will be there

108g Giving weight to words: Madame de Sévigné's letters to her daughter

202l Virginia Woolf's last words on words: *Between the Acts* and 'Anon'

275n How words hurt: Attitudes, metaphor and oppression

412c Women of the word: Selected leadership roles of women in Mr. Wesley's Methodism

442e City of words

Word Processing

199g Word processing: Forward for business, backward for women

209r Turning secretaries into word processors: Some fiction and a fact or two

307q Word processing: "This is not a final draft"

441d Women and microelectronics: The case of word processors

Wordsworth, Dorothy

196l "A spirit, yet a woman too!": Dorothy and William Wordsworth

Wordsworth, William

196l "A spirit, yet a woman too!": Dorothy and William Wordsworth

Work

see also Employment

13a Deconstructing the masculine universe: The case of women's work

13c Photo essay: Women and work

13h Women working in heavy industry in World War II

31j Women's work and sex roles

38n "Holding back the ocean with a broom": Black women and community work

41a Working women in the United States: A look at the facts

41f Stress and support networks of working single black mothers

43h Sexual harassment, working women's dilemma

45f Psychological orientations to the work role: 1957-1976

47g Work

48i Gender roles and sexuality in the world of work

49m College student values and the world of work

50c Women's work in nineteenth-century London: A study of the years 1820-1850

50d Women's work and the family in nineteenth-century Europe

52b The changing roles of Canadian women in family and work: An overview

57c Work, the family, and children's sexual learning

59f Liberating work

60m Laid bare by the system: Work and survival for black and Hispanic women

65k Canada's equal pay for work of equal value law

69g Maternal work and children

75c Working women in Korea

75e Working women in India

81b The economics of middle-income family life: Working women during the Great Depression

81g Photographing women: The farm security administration work of Marion Post Wolcott

81k "The forgotten woman": Working women, the New Deal, and women's organizations

83f Working women in Latin America

86c The health hazards of office work

86h Minority women, work, and health

86j Mother, father, worker: Men and women and the reproduction risks of work

86l Walking a tightrope: Pregnancy, parenting, and work

89d Women's work and the family in nineteenth-century Europe

92e Indonesia: Married women's work pattern in rural Java

93s Beyond equal pay for equal work: Comparable worth in the state of Washington

93v Work analysis as a means to achieve equal pay for working women: The Federal Republic of Germany

98d Becoming an 'insider': Women's privileges in village field work

98i Working through local female investigators: Experiences in a broad survey

100b Teaching and 'women's work': A comparative historical and ideological analysis

103o Work, gender, and technological innovation

104e The estimation of work in a northern Finnish farming community

104g Women's work in rural south-west England

104h Domestic work in rural Iceland: An historical overview

116l Women's work: Views from the history of philosophy

129v Trade unionism and women's work

130f Women and work

138d Work, class and teaching

138f The conservative school? Sex roles at home, at work and at school

139a Introduction: Class and work: Bringing women back in

144b Family and role-division: The polarisation of sexual stereotypes in the nineteenth century - an aspect of the dissociation of work and family

145l The impact of agrarian change on women's work and child care in early-nineteenth-century Prussia

145m Domestic industry: Work options and women's choices

145n Social insurance and the family work of Oberlausitz home weavers in the late nineteenth century

148e Women's work: An examination of women's roles in Plains Indian arts and crafts

149d Women's double work day: Twentieth-century changes in the reproduction of daily life

153n Working or helping? London working-class children in the domestic economy

162l Kinship and class consciousness: Family values and work experience among hospital workers in an American southern town

165e Work and the addicted prostitute

167c Working as a group

169f Credit programs for working women

169h Evaluating programs for working adults

169t How foundations view funding proposals on working women

170g The economics of work and caring

171f Interaction: The work women do

178e Work: Its meaning for women's lives

181d Technology and work degradation: Effects of office automation on women clerical workers

182f Working with women

183g Hazards faced by women at work

184l Women's work and European fertility patterns

185k The work/family connection in the year 2020

199f Women in retail sales work: The continuing dilemma of service

199i Women's work in the library/information sector

199l Women and work in Silicon Valley: Options and futures

205d A preliminary sketch of Chinese women and work in British Columbia, 1858-1950

206f Woman worker/working woman

206k Racism at work

206l Working on racism: Centro Obrero

207e Work, consumption and authority within the household: A Moroccan case

208g Work, consumption and authority within the household: A Moroccan case

209k Automation and the quality of work life at the Swedish telephone company: A management view

209l Automation and the quality of work life at the Swedish telephone company: A union view

209m New technology and its implications in U.S. clerical work

209u Occupational health and the design of work

212o 'Male needs': The problems and problems of working with gay men

213b Motherhood and waged work: West Indian, Asian and white mothers compared

214m Women, work and friendship: Personal confirmation and support

214q The work — family problem: Overloading the system

217d Caring as women's work in the welfare state

217f The female working class

221c Working mothers: Effects on the marriage and the mother

227b The home: Its work and influence

227i Women's work in never done

231i Russian working women: Sexuality in bonding patterns and the politics of daily life

233a Women at work in pregnancy

233b The effect of work on placental function and fetal growth

233c The hazards of work in pregnancy

233h The effects of work in pregnancy: Short- and long-term associations

233j The effect of the mother's work on the infant

233u Future research on work in pregnancy

233v Adverse influences of the working environment

235c At work

243a Urban and rural working women in Poland today: Between social change and social conflict

243g Katie's place: Women's work, professional work, and social reform

243h Family, work, and individual development in dual-career marriages: Issues for research

243i Work experience and family relations among working-class and lower-middle-class

243m Husbands' paid work and family roles: Current research issues

246f Women, work, and change in Nagovisi

246g Pigs, pearlshells, and 'women's work': Collective response to change in highland Papua New Guinea

250a Introduction: Women, work and schooling: The relevance of gender

250i Into work: Continuity and change

250n Women, school and work: Some conclusions

263a Women and welfare work: Demystifying the myth of disembeddedness

263d "Blessed be the tie that binds": YWCA extension work among industrial women, Minneapolis, 1900-1910

263e "For love and money both": Women's work-related decisions in twentieth century Minneapolis

263m The new economic readjustment policies: Implications for Chinese urban working women

264b Sisters under their skins: Southern working women, 1880-1950

267f Equity for women at work: Models of change

269b Structural continuity in the division of men's and women's work among black Carib (Garífuna)

272h Work experience, job segregation, and wages

288d A proposal: We need taboos on sex at work

288e Women's work

294h 'Working': An interview with Betty N.

296g Racial-ethnic women and work: Towards an analysis of race and gender stratification

307r Women's work in the office of the future

320b Culture, service, and work: Changing ideals of higher education for women

320p Life after college: Historical links between women's education and women's work

323a Women at work in Canada

323g Part-time work and unions

323r Working, mothering and militancy: Women in the CNTU

323z Women, work and unions: A cineography

324d Attitudes toward women working: Changes over time and implications for the labor-force behaviors of husbands and wives

326b Working for and with rape victims: Crisis intervention and advocacy

326g Group work with preadolescent sexual assault victims

335d Production rules OK? Waged work and the family

336b Beyond *Kinder, Küche, Kirche*: Weimar women in politics and work

339b Women and men at work: Jockeying for position

339h Working couples and child care

341k Working up an appetite

344q Clerical work: The female occupation

344t Trust, loyalty, and the place of women in the informal organization of work

350e Accounting for women's work

350g From rural subsistence to an industrial peripheral work force: An examination of female Malaysian migrants and capital accumulation in Singapore

352n Working and parenting: The male and father role

352o The transition from parenting to working and parenting

355b An enlarged human existence? Technology and household work in nineteenth-century America

355c Housework technology and household work

355j Domestic labor as work discipline: The struggle over housework in foster homes

355k Everyone needs three hands: Doing unpaid and paid work

355l Household work, wage work, and sexual equality

359ss A feminist works with nontraditional clients

360l Women and work: Implications for mental health

361c EQUALS: Working with educators

361f Affirmative action programs that work

373k Women's work in multinational electronics factories

374f Appendix A: Maternity law for working women

378a Male and female: Job versus gender models in the sociology of work

380j Poverty, work, and mental health: The experience of low-income mothers

380l Women's work and the family wage in Canada

380m A statistical analysis of female participation in work and the effects on the population and socioeconomic development: A case study of Greece

380r Research on women's work and the family at the urban institute

380s Women's work participation and the economic support of children

385a Women, work, and ethnicity: The Sierra Leone case

385f Colonialism, education, and work: Sex differentiation in colonial Zaire

385g Reinventing the past and circumscribing the future: *Authenticité* and the negative image of women's work in Zaire

385i Women's work in a communal setting: The Tanzanian policy of *Ujamaa*

385m The child-care dilemma of working mothers in African cities: The case of Lagos, Nigeria

387e Male and female: Job versus gender models in the sociology of work

387f Home work and market work: Systematic segregation

387h The work-family role system

387k Invisible work: Unacknowledged contributions

387o Interaction: The work women do

387q Degraded and deskilled: The proletarianization of clerical work

387s The impact of hierarchical structures on the work behavior of women and men

388c Singapore women: Work and the family

388e Women's work and worth in an Acadian maritime village

389e Margaret Fuller (1810-1850): Her work as an art critic

390o From balaclavas to bayonets: Women's voluntary war work, 1939-41

390w Women, work and technological change

391e Changing Canadian and US magazine portrayals of women and work: Growing opportunities for choice

393c Women and work: A study of female and male attitudes in the modern sector of an African metropolis (Lagos)

393g Education and fertility among Cameroonian working women

398b Work in the interstices: Woman in academe

398k On the bottom rung: A discussion of women's work in sociology

402e Family status and female work participation

402f Women in Bangladesh: Food-for-work and socioeconomic change

405l Women in contemporary Poland: Their social and occupational position and attitudes toward work

413h Women, work and family: 1880-1926

418a Work and the family: Who gets 'the best of both worlds'?

420o Migrant women at work in Asia

421n Working wives in the United States and Venezuela: A cross-national study of decision making

421w The demands of work and the human quality of marriage: An exploratory study of professionals in two socialist societies

423d Women's work and family roles

424i Women's work: Factory, family and social class in an industrializing order

424r Women, work and the family in a developing society: Taiwan

426c The apprenticeship model of organizational careers: A response to changes in the relation between work and family

427a Introduction: Government response to working women and their families: Values, the policy-making process, and research utilization

427e Gender inequities in childhood social life and adult work life

427f Men, women, work, and family

427g Paid and unpaid work: Contradictions in American women's lives today

428b The new international division of labor and the U.S. work force: The case of the electronics industry

434m Work requirements for AFDC mothers

435d Pay equity: Beyond equal pay for equal work

435e Alternative work patterns and the double life

436i Technology, 'Women's work' and the social control of women

440b Public policies and the paid work of women

440n Volunteer work as work: Some theoretical considerations

443k Working women and stress

446a Women, work, and family: New Soviet perspectives

446j Women's work and the family

446o The quantity and quality of work: A round table

446p How working women combine work and household duties

447b Overview: The health of working women

458b Midlife work history and retirement income

458e Working women versus homemakers: Retirement resources and correlates of well-being

458l Professional women: Work pattern as a correlate of retirement satisfaction

459h Women's work and their status: Rural Indian evidence of labour market and environment effects on sex differences in childhood mortality

463h Women's work trips: An empirical and theoretical overview

466c Healing as women's work in Bali

466f Women and work in an Indonesian mining town

466j Four paces behind: Women's work in peninsular Malaysia

467a Parents at work

467c Managing work and family life: A comparative policy overview

467f The impact of work on the family

468a The making of a female occupation: A case study of cleaning work

468b Working hours and segmentation in the Norwegian labour market

468e Women's work strategies: An analysis of the organisation of everyday life in an urban neighbourhood

468f On work, art and women: A discussion of the ambiguous position of women artists

468g Conceptualising domestic work: Comments on definitions of "work" in some Norwegian studies

468i Perspectives on work and reproduction with special reference to women's opportunities and adaptation

469i A preliminary historical analysis of women and work in Puerto Rico: 1899-1975

470c Contemporary clerical work: A case study of local government

470d New technology and women's office work

470g Standing on the edge: Working class housewives and the world of work

471a Women at work in Great Britain

471b Women at work in Ireland

471c Women at work in the Federal Republic of Germany

471d Women at work in Holland

471e Women at work in Italy: Legislation - evolution and prospects

471f Women at work in Greece: The sociological and legal perspectives

471g Women at work in Sweden

471h Women at work in Finland

471i Women at work in Portugal

471j Women at work in the USA

471k Women at work in the USSR

474i *One* child of one's own: A meaningful digression within the work(s)

Work (Literary)

14e One child of one's own: A meaningful digression within the work(s) - an excerpt

14x Black women playwrights from Grimké to Shange: Selected synopses of their works

30x May Sarton: A metaphor for my life, my work, and my art

40f Music as theme: The jazz mode in the works of Toni Cade Bambara

40n Tell the good news: A view of the works of Lucille Clifton

40r Affirmation in the works of Mari Evans

40v About my work

40cc And called every generation blessed: Theme, setting, and ritual in the works of Paule Marshall

40ee The quest for self: Triumph and failure in the works of Toni Morrison

40ff Theme, characterization, and style in the works of Toni Morrison

40qq Music as theme: The blues mode in the works of Margaret Walker

329e The anti-madonna in the work and thought of Virginia Woolf

Work: A Story of Experience

332e Female stories of experience: Alcott's *Little Women* in light of *Work*

Worker

see also Employee, Employment

13d Besides our size it's because we are women: The strike by the laundry workers union 15 January - 5 February 1982

52t Wife and/or worker: Sex role concepts of Canadian female students

73h The economic struggles of female factory workers: A comparison of French, Polish, and Portuguese immigrants

80h Parents and day care workers: A failed partnership?

81d Flawed victories: The experiences of black and white women workers in Durham during the 1930s

86j Mother, father, worker: Men and women and the reproduction risks of work

89k Structured labour markets, worker organization and low pay

91u Women community workers

103b The state, the patriarchal family, and working mothers

144f The family life-cycle: A study of factory workers in nineteenth century Württemberg

144h Women's work and the family: Women garment workers in Berlin and Hamburg before the First World War

162l Kinship and class consciousness: Family values and work experience among hospital workers in an American southern town

169a Labor education and women workers: An historical perspective

169p Occupational health and safety for women workers: Some teaching models

169r How to choose and use materials in education for women workers

169u Funding worker education through tuition refund plans

169v Labor education and women workers: An international comparison

177g Taiwan garment workers

177h Taiwan electronics workers

183d Women workers in the manufacturing industries

183e Women factory workers and the law

183f Hysteria among factory workers

201f The uprising in Chicago: The men's garment workers strike, 1910-1911

201j Dorothy Jacobs Bellanca: Women clothing workers and the runaway shops

201l A stitch in our time: New York's Hispanic garment workers in the 1980s

206f Woman worker/working woman

209v An issue of respect: Women workers demand healthy and safe offices

209w An overview of NIOSH research on clerical workers

209ee Alternative models of worker participation

213g Transnational production and women workers

215n The women who wire up the weapons: Workers in armament factories

218f Women textile workers in the militarization of Southeast Asia

227c Women as domestic workers

233d Women workers at higher risk of reproductive hazards

233t Educating workers, management and the general public

243c The role and status of women scientific research workers in research groups

243k Weak links in men's worker-earner roles: A descriptive model

263k Industrial social workers in France, 1917-1939: A study in the sex/gender division of labor

292b From soul to strawberries: The International Ladies' Garment Workers' Union and workers' education, 1914-1950

292d Blue collars and bluestockings: The Bryn Mawr summer school for women workers, 1921-1938

292e Recognizing regional differences: The southern summer school for women workers

292f Partners in progress: The affiliated schools for women workers, 1928-1939

292g Education in working-class solidarity: The summer school for office workers

292i To rekindle the spirit: Current education programs for women workers

299c Sanitary Workers

299d Beedi workers

299e Construction workers

323c No proper deal: Women workers and the Canadian labour movement, 1870-1940

323i Coercion or male culture: A new look at co-worker harassment

323o Domestic workers: The experience in B.C.

346b Child workers in the informal sector role of the NGOs: Some reflections

350b Women workers and the green revolution

354e Women workers in the health service industry

378c Workers side by side: Women and the trade union movement

378d Militancy and acquiescence among women workers

379p "If eight hours seems few to you...": Women workers' strikes in Italian rice fields, 1901-1906

386h Construction workers

390j 'Spinifex fairies': Aboriginal workers in the Northern territory, 1911-39

390s Right-wing union officials versus married women workers

419c Workers and drones: Labor, idleness and gender definition in Hesiod's beehive

420k Migration of women workers in peninsular Malaysia: Impact and implications

422b Women workers of India: A case of market segmentation

424e Towards meeting the needs of urban female factory workers in peninsular Malaysia

424f Constraints on the organization of women industrial workers

424h Occupational health hazards of female industrial workers in Malaysia

424j Making the bread and bringing it home: Female factory workers and the family economy

424q Effect of female labour force participation on fertility: The case of construction workers in Chiang Mai City

428c Capitalism, imperialism, and patriarchy: The dilemma of Third-World women workers in multinational factories

428d Women, production, and reproduction in industrial capitalism: A comparison of Brazilian and U.S. factory workers

428g The domestic clothing workers in the Mexican metropolis and their relation to dependent capitalism

428k The formation of an ethnic group: Colombian female workers in Venezuela

428l Silicon Valley's women workers: A theoretical analysis of sex-segregation in the electronics industry labor market

428q Women textile workers in the militarization of Southeast Asia

446e The educational and occupational skill level of industrial workers

446f Raising the skill level of women workers

447f Employee health services for women workers

447o Non-medical issues presented by the pregnant worker

463j Residential location and transportation analyses: Married women workers

Workforce

49e Implications of the increasing participation of women in the work force in the 1990's

166c Women in the workforce

Working Class

see also Class

50b The home turned upside down? The working-class family in cotton textiles 1780-1850

83e Working class Jamaican women: Trade unions and political activity

89f Class struggle and the persistence of the working-class family

94h A new Australian working class leadership: The case of Ford Broadmeadows

106j The working-class family: A Marxist perspective

119c 'Mothers, vote labour!' The state, the labour movement and working-class mothers, 1900-1918

138b Intersections of gender and class: Accommodation and resistance by working-class and affluent females to contradictory sex-role ideologies

144g Overcrowding and family life: Working-class families and the housing crisis in late nineteenth-century Duisburg

144i Politics and the family: Social democracy and the working-class family in theory and practice before 1914

145o The woman's role in the German working-class family in the 1890s from the perspective of women's autobiographies

145p The civilizing tendency of hygiene: Working-class women under medical control in Imperial Germany

149a Domestic labour and the working-class household

149b Capital, the state and the origins of the working-class household

153m Gender division within the U.S. working class: Households in the Philadelphia area, 1870-1945

153n Working or helping? London working-class children in the domestic economy

153o Wages, consumption, and survival: Working class households in Puerto Rico in the 1930's

192o Working-class women in nineteenth century Mexico

199a Generations of working-class families

217f The female working class

227d Working-class wives

231b "Charity girls" and city pleasures: Historical notes on working-class sexuality, 1880-1920

241h Dividing the rough and the respectable: Working-class women and pre-school playgroups

243i Work experience and family relations among working-class and lower-middle-class

292g Education in working-class solidarity: The summer school for office workers

363b Working class Afro-Surinamese women and national politics: Traditions and changes in an independent state

387r Job opportunities of black and white working-class women

390q Sally Bowen: Political and social experiences of a working-class woman

428f Kitchens hit by priorities: Employed working-class Jamaican women confront the IMF

455c No drums, no trumpets: Working-class women

470g Standing on the edge: Working class housewives and the world of work

Worklife

288b Worklife problems for both women and men

Workplace

34e No fertile women need apply: Employment discrimination and reproductive hazards in the workplace

43w The feminist workplace

86m The home is the workplace: Hazards, stress, and pollutants in the household

102h A primer on women and the democratization of the workplace

203a Introduction: The domestic workplace

203c The household as workplace: Wives, husbands, and children

203e Redesigning the domestic workplace

243b Gender and interaction in the workplace

253f Genes and gender in the workplace

253g Reproductive hazards in the workplace: A course curriculum guide

272j Institutional factors contributing to sex segregation in the workplace

288i Sexual harassment in the workplace — What should the employer do?

296h Powerless by definition: Occupational and pay patterns of women in the workplace

296i Women's power in the workplace

397n Peril and promise: Lesbians' workplace participation

441e The culture of engineering: Woman, workplace and machine

447i A legal perspective on workplace reproductive hazards

447m The control of hazardous exposures in the workplace

Works

448o Literature and the city: A checklist of relevant secondary works

Workshop

77e An eclectic workshop

174o Feminist education at the feminist studio workshop

390g Homes are divine workshops

World

153a Household structures and labor-force formation in the capitalist world-economy

171e Intonation in a man's world

202i Private brother, public world

257c Really being in love means wanting to live in a different world

318f The clinical world of P.D. James

339d Being a manager in a multicultural world

341c A woman's body in a man's world: A review of findings on body image and weight control

356m Honing a habitable languagescape: Women's images for the new world frontiers

380a Women as world makers

383c Utopia at the end of a male chauvinist dystopian world: Suzy McKee Charnas's feminist science fiction

383d World views in utopian novels by women

383h Truth and art in women's worlds: Doris Lessing's *Marriages Between Zones Three, Four, and Five*

World Bank

209o Staff participation in office systems' design: Two case studies at the World Bank

World War

81m Socialist feminism between the two World Wars: Insights from oral history

113a Great Britain and the World Wars

113b Germany and the World Wars

144d Family and household: Social structures in a German village between the two World Wars

205n They also served: The British Columbia women's institutes in two World Wars

World War I

50f The need for women's labour in the First World War

61h The Woman's Land Army, World War I

444k "The mother half of humanity": American women in the peace and preparedness movements in World War I

454o The American woman's pre-World War I freedom in manners and morals

World War II

13h Women working in heavy industry in World War II

205dd Women at Cominco during the second World War

231c Marching to a different drummer: Lesbian and gay GIs in World War II

302c The recruitment of men into librarianship, following World War II

390o From balaclavas to bayonets: Women's voluntary war work, 1939-41

405h Soviet women in combat in World War II: The ground/air defense forces

444c The job he left behind: American women in the shipyards during World War II

Worry

215b How I learnt to start worrying and hate the bomb: The effects of a nuclear bombardment

Worship

194f The worship of Mother Earth in Russian culture

194p Conclusion: New perspectives on mother worship

229d The origins of music: Women's goddess worship

278f Phallic worship: Some personal meditations on a sacred theme

457f Women, fertility and the worship of gods in a Hindu village

453q Goddess worship in Wicce

Worth

see also Comparable Worth

305q When all the secretaries demand what they are worth

388e Women's work and worth in an Acadian maritime village

Wright, Austin Tappan

383f Wright's *Islandia*: Utopia with problems

Wright, Frances

417f Frances Wright: Utopian feminist

Wright, Judith

445s Tradition of the exile: Judith Wright's Australian "West"

Wright, Richard

17r Papa Dick and Sister-Woman: Reflections on women in the fiction of Richard Wright

Write

see also Literature

20n A checklist of writings by and about Margaret Atwood

30u Daughters writing: Toward a theory of women's biography

40s An answer to some questions on how I write: In three parts

40mm Writing *The Color Purple*

64c Colette and the enterprise of writing: A reappraisal

64m Writing, language, and the body

120e Feminism and the writing and teaching of history

120l My body in writing

122k How women and men write about themselves (less differently than you might expect)

132n For a restricted thematics: Writing, speech, and difference in *Madame Bovary*

150g If I could write this in fire, I would write this in fire

155j Women writing about prostitutes: Amalia Jamilis and Luisa Valenzuela

173a Rewriting *Roe v. Wade*

174c Teaching writing in prison

180d The new mother of the English renaissance: Her writings on motherhood

186g "The Action of the beautiful": The concept of balance in the writings of May Sarton

214i Women, men, and professional writing: Signature of power?

222d Taking the giant step: Writing the dissertation

242e Writing (from) the feminine: George Sand and the novel of female pastoral

356s Writing like a woman

399ee The adventure of life: Writing for children

474a Still just writing

474b Why I write

474h Thoughts on writing: A diary

Writer

see also Author, Literature, Novelist, individual writers

14t Teaching *Black-eyed Susans*: An approach to the study of black women writers

27o Quebec women writers

32f A German writer and feminist in nineteenth century America: An archival study of Mathilde Franziska Anneke

32g German women writers in the nineteenth century: Where are they?

33g Gender and genre: Women as historical writers, 1400-1820

64b The first steps in a writer's career

64q Colette and signs: A partial reading of a writer "Born *not* to Write"

74b Success and the Latin American writer

81f Culture and radical politics: Yiddish women writers in America, 1890-1940

125e Margaret Fuller: Feminist writer and revolutionary

135g Olive Schreiner - A note on sexist language and the feminist writer

145h German women writers and the Revolution of 1848

174q The women's writer's center: An interview with the directors

188o The Franco-Italian professional writer: Christine de Pizan

301jj Speaking in tongues: A letter to Third World women writers

306b The "rooted" landscape and the woman writer

306m The editor and the writer: An approach to archival manuscripts

329l A common sitting room: Virginia Woolf's critique of women writers

332p Shadowing/surfacing/shedding: Contemporary German writers in search of a female *Bildungsroman*

381b But will men like it? Or living as a feminist writer without committing murder

390n Rooms of their own: The domestic situation of Australian women writers between the wars

408a Spain's first women writers

450r Why there are no southern writers

474l Blood and guts: The tricky problem of being a woman writer in the late twentieth century

474p Becoming a writer

WTLU

see Women's Trade Union League

Württemberg

144f The family life-cycle: A study of factory workers in nineteenth century Württemberg

Wuthering Heights

109e The reconstruction of the gothic feminine ideal in Emily Brontë's *Wuthering Heights*

109p Dreaming of children: Literalization in *Jane Eyre* and *Wuthering Heights*

Wyoming

226f Women as legislative candidates in six states

Xylo

310u XYLO: A true story

Yahweh

462o Feminist liberation theology and Yahweh as holy warrior: An analysis of symbol

Yale Child Welfare Research Program

80i The Yale Child Welfare Research Program: Description and results

80j A five-year follow-up of participants in the Yale Child Welfare Research Program

Yale University

314i The women's studies program: Yale University

Yang

231dd The new feminism of yin and yang

Year

30t I had been hungry all the years

374a The early years

The Years

202j The politics of city space in *The Years*: Street, love, pillar boxes and bridges

328k A track of our own: Typescript drafts of *The Years*

329k *The Years*: A feminist novel

330l Nature and history in *The Years*

Yeats, W.B.

338c Women in the plays of W.B. Yeats

Yellow

175c Emily Morgan: Yellow rose of Texas

Yemanja

229f From the house of Yemanja: The goddess heritage of black women

Yenan

177k Yenan women in revolution

Yenga

310a A yenga tale

Yiddish Women

see also Jew, Judiasm

81f Culture and radical politics: Yiddish women writers in America, 1890-1940

Yin

231dd The new feminism of yin and yang

Yogyakarta

166b Women in a yogyakarta kampung

Yoke

129l Cupid's yokes

Yorubaland, Nigeria

371i Spatial domains and women's mobility in Yorubaland, Nigeria

Young

see also Child, Adolescent

287e Sexuality verboten: Young and old

309c The legitimacy status of first births to U.S. women aged 15-24, 1939-1978

404x Young female offenders in Massachusetts: Toward leaving the juvenile justice system successfully

Young Women's Christian Association (YWCA)

263d "Blessed be the tie that binds": YWCA extension work among industrial women, Minneapolis, 1900-1910

292c Citizens for Democracy: The industrial programs of the YWCA

Youth

see Adolescent

Yucatán

473i Women in Yucatán

Yuendumu

333p The Yuendumu aboriginal cultural pre-school

Yugoslavia

52o Change in the system of social power: Conditions for the social equality of women in Yugoslavia

113d Yugoslavia: War of resistance

122j A comparison of the movements toward equality in Yugoslavia and England

Yungtzu

449f A woman's voice: The poetry of Yungtzu

YWCA

see Young Women's Christian Association

Zaire

68d Women in Zaire: Disparate status and roles

370f Sustaining the system: Trading towns along the middle Zaire

385f Colonialism, education, and work: Sex differentiation in colonial Zaire

385g Reinventing the past and circumscribing the future: *Authenticité* and the negative image of women's work in Zaire

Zambia

5e Perspectives in development: The problem of nurses and nursing in Zambia

263l Men servants and women bosses: The domestic service institution in colonial Zambia

385d Women and agricultural change in the railway region of Zambia: Dispossession and counterstrategies, 1930-1970

385e Marginal lives: Conflict and contradiction in the position of female traders in Lusaka, Zambia

Zayas y Sotomayor, María

112d María de Zayas y Sotomayor: Sibyl of Madrid (Spanish, 1590?-1661?)

Zeitl

176k Teaching about Jewish lesbians in literature: From *Zeitl* and *Richel* to *The Tree of Begats*

Zetkin, Clara

95b Clara Zetkin: A Socialist approach to the problem of women's oppression

Zhenotdel

405f The early decrees of Zhenotdel

Zimbabwe

160e The suitable wife: Preparation for marriage in London and Rhodesia/Zimbabwe

Zitz-Halein, Kathinka

145g Female political opposition in pre-1848 Germany: The role of Kathinka Zitz-Halein

Zola, Emile

155c Zola's view of prostitution in *Nana*